SELECTED
PROSE & POETRY
OF
RUDYARD KIPLING

Authorized Edition

GARDEN CITY PUBLISHING CO., INC.

Garden City   *New York*

1937
GARDEN CITY PUBLISHING CO., INC.

Preface

A COLLECTION of my earlier work, written before the United States had a Copyright Law, has recently been put upon the market, without my consent or supervision, under the misleading title of *The Works of Rudyard Kipling.*

I have therefore arranged with my publishers, Messrs. Doubleday, Doran & Company, Inc., to issue a duly authorized volume, which, in addition to all the material contained in the unauthorized one, includes three tales which have not before appeared in book form.

Rudyard Kipling.

CONTENTS

Volume I

BALLADS AND BARRACK-ROOM BALLADS

BALLADS

BARRACK-ROOM BALLADS

v

Volume II

Volume III

Volume IV

PLAIN TALES FROM THE HILLS

Volume IV—Continued

Volume V

Volume VI

Volume VI—Continued

Volume VII

Volume VIII

Volume IX

Volume X

WEE WILLIE WINKIE

Volume XI

THE STORY OF THE GADSBYS

Volume XII

DEPARTMENTAL DITTIES AND OTHER VERSES

DEPARTMENTAL DITTIES

Volume XII—Continued

DEPARTMENTAL VERSES AND OTHER DITTIES

VOLUME I

Ballads and Barrack-Room Ballads

The Ballad of East and West

Oh, East is East, and West is West, and never the twain shall meet,
Till Earth and Sky stand presently at God's great Judgment Seat;
But there is neither East nor West, Border, nor Breed, nor Birth,
When two strong men stand face to face, tho' they come from the
ends of the earth!

KAMAL is out with twenty men to raise
 the Border side,
And he has lifted the Colonel's mare
 that is the Colonel's pride:
He has lifted her out of the stable-door
 between the dawn and the day,
And turned the calkins upon her feet,
 and ridden her far away.
Then up and spoke the Colonel's son
 that led a troop of the Guides:
"Is there never a man of all my men
 can say where Kamal hides?"
Then up and spoke Mohammed Khan,
 the son of the Ressaldar,
"If ye know the track of the morning-
 mist, ye know where his pickets are.
"At dusk he harries the Abazai—at
 dawn he is into Bonair,
"But he must go by Fort Bukloh to his
 own place to fare,
"So if ye gallop to Fort Bukloh as fast
 as a bird can fly,
"By the favor of God ye may cut him
 off ere he win to the Tongue of
 Jagai,
"But if he be passed the Tongue of
 Jagai, right swiftly turn ye then,
"For the length and the breadth of that
 grisly plain is sown with Kamal's
 men.

"There is rock to the left, and rock to
 the right, and low lean thorn between,
"And ye may hear a breech-bolt snick
 where never a man is seen."
The Colonel's son has taken a horse,
 and a raw rough dun was he,
With the mouth of a bell and the heart
 of Hell, and the head of the gallows-
 tree.
The Colonel's son to the Fort has won,
 they bid him stay to eat—
Who rides at the tail of a Border thief,
 he sits not long at his meat.
He's up and away from Fort Bukloh as
 fast as he can fly,
Till he was aware of his father's mare
 in the gut of the Tongue of Jagai,
Till he was aware of his father's mare
 with Kamal upon her back,
And when he could spy the white of her
 eye, he made the pistol crack.
He has fired once, he has fired twice,
 but the whistling ball went wide.
"Ye shoot like a soldier," Kamal said.
 "Show now if ye can ride."
It's up and over the Tongue of Jagai,
 as blown dust-devils go,
The dun he fled like a stag of ten, but
 the mare like a barren doe.

The dun he leaned against the bit and slugged his head above,

But the red mare played with the snaffle-bars, as a maiden plays with a glove.

There was rock to the left and rock to the right and low and lean thorn between,

And thrice he heard a breech-bolt snick tho' never a man was seen.

They have ridden the low moon out of the sky, their hoofs drum up the dawn,

The dun he went like a wounded bull, but the mare like a new-roused fawn.

The dun he fell at a water-course—in a woful heap tell he,

And Kamal has turned the red mare back, and pulled the rider free.

He has knocked the pistol out of his hand—small room was there to strive,

" 'Twas only by favor of mine," quoth he, "ye rode so long alive:

"There was not a rock for twenty mile, there was not a clump of tree,

"But covered a man of my own men with his rifle cocked on his knee.

"If I had raised my bridle-hand, as I have held it low,

"The little jackals that flee so fast, were feasting all in a row:

"If I had bowed my head on my breast, as I have held it high,

"The kite that whistles above us now were gorged till she could not fly."

Lightly answered the Colonel's son: "Do good to bird and beast,

"But count who come for the broken meats before thou makest a feast.

"If there should follow a thousand swords to carry my bones away,

"Belike the price of a jackal's meal were more than a thief could pay.

"They will feed their horse on the standing crop, their men on the garnered grain,

"The thatch of the byres will serve their fires when all the cattle are slain.

"But if thou thinkest the price be fair, —thy brethren wait to sup,

"The hound is kin to the jackal-spawn, —howl, dog, and call them up!

"And if thou thinkest the price be high, in steer and gear and stack,

"Give me my father's mare again, and I'll fight my own way back!"

Kamal has gripped him by the hand and set him upon his feet.

"No talk shall be of dogs," said he, "when wolf and grey wolf meet.

"May I eat dirt if thou hast hurt of me in deed or breath;

"What dam of lances brought thee forth to jest at the dawn with Death?"

Lightly answered the Colonel's son: "I hold by the blood of my clan:

"Take up the mare for my father's gift —by God, she has carried a man!"

The red mare ran to the Colonel's son, and nuzzled against his breast,

"We be two strong men," said Kamal then, "but she loveth the younger best.

"So she shall go with a lifter's dower, my turquoise-studded rein,

"My broidered saddle and saddle-cloth, and silver stirrups twain."

The Colonel's son a pistol drew and held it muzzle-end,

"Ye have taken the one from a foe," said he; "will ye take the mate from a friend?"

"A gift for a gift," said Kamal straight;
  "a limb for the risk of a limb.
"Thy father has sent his son to me, I'll
  send my son to him!"
With that he whistled his only son,
  that dropped from a mountain-
  crest—
He trod the ling like a buck in spring,
  and he looked like a lance in rest.
"Now here is thy master," Kamal said,
  "who leads a troop of the Guides,
"And thou must ride at his left side as
  shield on shoulder rides.
"Till Death or I cut loose the tie, at
  camp and board and bed,
"Thy life is his—thy fate it is to guard
  him with thy head.
"So thou must eat the White Queen's
  meat, and all her foes are thine,
"And thou must harry thy father's hold
  for the peace of the Border-line,
"And thou must make a trooper tough
  and hack thy way to power—
"Belike they will raise thee to Ressaldar when I am hanged in Peshawur."
They have looked each other between
  the eyes, and there they found no
  fault,
They have taken the Oath of the Broth-
  er-in-Blood on leavened bread and
  salt:

They have taken the Oath of the Broth-
  er-in-Blood on fire and fresh-cut sod,
On the hilt and the haft of the Khyber
  knife, and the Wondrous Names
  of God.
The Colonel's son he rides the mare and
  Kamal's boy the dun,
And two have come back to Fort Bukloh
  where there went forth but one.
And when they drew to the Quarter-
  Guard, full twenty swords flew
  clear—
There was not a man but carried his
  feud with the blood of the mount-
  aineer.
"Ha' done! ha' done!" said the Colonel's son. "Put up the steel at your
  sides!
"Last night ye had struck at a Border
  thief—to-night 'tis a man of the
  Guides!"

*Oh, East is East, and West is West,
  and never the two shall meet,*
*Till Earth and Sky stand presently at
  God's great Judgment Seat;*
*But there is neither East nor West,
  Border, nor Breed, nor Birth,*
*When two strong men stand face to
  face, tho' they come from the ends
  of the earth.*

———•———

The Last Suttee

*Not many years ago a King died in
one of the Rajpoot States. His wives,
disregarding the orders of the English
against suttee, would have broken out
of the palace had not the gates been
barred. But one of them, disguised as
the King's favorite dancing-girl, passed
through the line of guards and reached
the pyre. There, her courage failing,
she prayed her cousin, a baron of the*

court, to kill her. This he did, not knowing who she was.

UDAI CHAND lay sick to death
  In his hold by Gungra hill.
All night we heard the death-gongs ring
For the soul of the dying Rajpoot King,
All night beat up from the women's
    wing
  A cry that we could not still.

All night the barons came and went,
  The lords of the outer guard:
All night the cressets glimmered pale
On Ulwar sabre and Tonk jezail,
Mewar headstall and Marwar mail,
  That clinked in the palace yard.

In the Golden room on the palace roof
  All night he fought for air:
And there was sobbing behind the
    screen,
Rustle and whisper of women unseen,
And the hungry eyes of the Boondi
    Queen
  On the death she might not share.

He passed at dawn—the death-fire
    leaped
  From ridge to river-head,
From the Malwa plains to the Abu
    scaurs:
And wail upon wail went up to the stars
Behind the grim zenana-bars,
  When they knew that the King
    was dead.

The dumb priest knelt to tie his mouth
  And robe him for the pyre.
The Boondi Queen beneath us cried:
"See, now, that we die as our mother's
    died
"In the bridal-bed by our master's side!
  "Out, women!—to the fire!"

We drove the great gates home apace:
  White hands were on the sill:
But ere the rush of the unseen feet
Had reached the turn to the open street,
The bars shot down, the guard-drum
    beat—
  We held the dove-cot still.

A face looked down in the gathering day,
  And laughing spoke from the wall:
"Ohé, they mourn here: let me by—
"Azizun, the Lucknow nautch-girl, I?
"When the house is rotten, the rats
    must fly,
  "And I seek another thrall.

"For I ruled the King as ne'er did
    Queen,—
  "To-night the Queens rule me!
"Guard them safely, but let me go,
"Or ever they pay the debt they owe
"In scourge and torture!" She leaped
    below,
  And the grim guard watched her flee.

They knew that the King had spent his
    soul
  On a North-bred dancing-girl:
That he prayed to a flat-nosed Lucknow
    god,
And kissed the ground where her feet
    had trod,
And doomed to death at her drunken
    nod
  And swore by her lightest curl.

We bore the King to his father's place,
  Where the tombs of the Sun-born
    stand:
Where the grey apes swing, and the
    peacocks preen
On fretted pillar and jeweled screen,
And the wild boar couch in the house of
    the Queen
  On the drift of the desert sand.

The herald read his titles forth,
  We set the logs aglow:
"Friend of the English, free from fear
"Baron of Luni to Jeysulmeer,
"Lord of the Desert of Bikaneer,
  "King of the Jungle,—go!"

All night the red flame stabbed the sky
  With wavering wind-tossed spears:
And out of a shattered temple crept
A woman who veiled her head and wept,
And called on the King—but the great
      King slept,
  And turned not for her tears.

Small thought had he to mark the
      strife—
  Cold fear with hot desire—
When thrice she leaped from the leap-
      ing flame,
And thrice she beat her breast for
      shame,
And thrice like a wounded dove she
      came
  And moaned about the fire.

One watched, a bow-shot from the blaze,
  The silent streets between,
Who had stood by the King in sport
      and fray,
To blade in ambush or boar at bay,
And he was a baron old and grey,
  And kin to the Boondi Queen.

He said: "O shameless, put aside
  "The veil upon thy brow!
"Who held the King and all his land
'To the wanton will of a harlot's hand!

'Will the white ash rise from the blist-
      ered brand?
  "Stoop down, and call him now!"

Then she: "By the faith of my tarn-
      ished soul,
  "All things I did not well
"I had hoped to clear ere the fire died,
"And lay me down by my master's side
"To rule in Heaven his only bride,
  "While the others howl in Hell.

"But I have felt the fire's breath,
  "And hard it is to die!
"Yet if I may pray a Rajpoot lord
"To sully the steel of a Thakur's sword
"With base-born blood of a trade ab-
      horred"—
  And the Thakur answered, "Ay."

He drew and struck: the straight blade
      drank
  The life beneath the breast.
"I had looked for the Queen to face the
      flame,
"But the harlot dies for the Rajpoot
      dame—
"Sister of mine, pass, free from shame.
  "Pass with thy King to rest!"

The black log crashed above the white:
  The little flames and lean,
Red as slaughter and blue as steel,
That whistled and fluttered from head
      to heel,
Leaped up anew, for they found their
      meal
  On the heart of—the Boondi Queen!

The Ballad of the King's Mercy

Abdhur Rahman, the Durani Chief,
of him is the story told.
His mercy fills the Khyber hills—
his grace is manifold;
He has taken toll of the North and
the South—his glory reacheth
far,
And they tell the tale of his charity
from Balkh to Kandahar.

Before the old Peshawur Gate, where
Kurd and Kaffir meet,
The Governor of Kabul dealt the Jus-
tice of the Street,
And that was strait as running noose
and swift as plunging knife,
Tho' he who held the longer purse might
hold the longer life.

There was a hound of Hindustan had
struck a Euzufzai,
Wherefore they spat upon his face and
led him out to die.
It chanced the King went forth that
hour when throat was bared to
knife;
The Kaffir groveled under-hoof and
clamored for his life.

Then said the King: "Have hope, O
friend! Yea, Death disgraced is
hard;
"Much honor shall be thine;" and called
the Captain of the Guard,
Yar Khan, a bastard of the Blood, so
city-babble saith,
And he was honored of the King—the
which is salt to Death;

And he was son of Daoud Shah the
Reiver of the Plains,
And blood of old Durani Lords ran fire
in his veins;
And 'twas to tame an Afghan pride nor
Hell nor Heaven could bind,
The King would make him butcher to a
yelping cur of Hind.
"Strike!" said the King. "King's blood
art thou—his death shall be his
pride!"
Then louder, that the crowd might
catch: "Fear not—his arms are tied!"
Yar Khan drew clear the Khyber knife,
and struck, and sheathed again.
"O man, thy will is done," quoth he;
"A King this dog hath slain."

Abdhur Rahman, the Durani Chief,
to the North and the South is
sold.
The North and the South shall open
their mouth to a Ghilzai flag un-
rolled,
When the big guns speak to the
Khyber peak, and his dog-Hera-
tis fly,
Ye have heard the song—How long?
How long? Wolves of the Ab-
azai!

That night before the watch was set,
when all the streets were clear,
The Governor of Kabul spoke: "My
King, hast thou no fear?
"Thou knowest—thou hast heard,"—
his speech died at his master's face.

And grimly said the Afghan King: "I
rule the Afghan race.
"My path is mine—see thou to thine—
to-night upon thy bed
"Think who there be in Kabul now that
clamor for thy head."

That night when all the gates were shut
to City and to Throne,
Within a little garden-house the King
lay down alone.
Before the sinking of the moon, which
is the Night of Night,
Yar Khan came softly to the King to
make his honor white.

The children of the town had mocked
beneath his horse's hoofs,
The harlots of the town had hailed him
"butcher!" from their roofs.
But as he groped against the wall, two
hands upon him fell,
The King behind his shoulder spoke:
"Dead man, thou dost not well!
" 'Tis ill to jest with Kings by day and
seek a boon by night;
"And that thou bearest in thy hand is
all too sharp to write.
"But three days hence, if God be good,
and if thy strength remain,
"Thou shalt demand one boon of me
and bless me in thy pain.
"For I am merciful to all, and most of
all to thee.
"My butcher of the shambles, rest—no
knife hast thou for me!"

Abdhur Rahman, the Durani Chief,
holds hard by the South and the
North;
But the Ghilzai knows, ere the melt-
ing snows, when the swollen
banks break forth,

When the red-coats crawl to the sun-
gar wall, and his Usbeg lances
fail.
Ye have heard the song—How long?
How long? Wolves of the Zuka
Kheyl!

They stoned him in the rubbish-field
when dawn was in the sky,
According to the written word, "See
that he do not die."

They stoned him till the stones were
piled above him on the plain,
And those the laboring limbs displaced
they tumbled back again.

One watched beside the dreary mound
that veiled the battered thing,
And him the King with laughter called
the Herald of the King.

It was upon the second night, the night
of Ramazan,
The watcher leaning earthward heard
the message of Yar Khan.

From shattered breast through shriveled
lips broke forth the rattling breath:
"Creature of God, deliver me from
agony of Death."

They sought the King among his girls,
and risked their lives thereby:
"Protector of the Pitiful, give orders
that he die!"

"Bid him endure until the day," a
lagging answer came;
"The night is short, and he can pray
and learn to bless my name."

Before the dawn three times he spoke,
And on the day once more:

"Creature of God deliver me and bless
the King therefor!"

They shot him at the morning prayer,
to ease him of his pain,
And when he heard the matchlocks
clink, he blessed the King again.

Which thing the singers made a song
for all the world to sing,
that the Outer Seas may know the
mercy of the King.

Abdhur Rahman, the Durani Chief,
of him is the story told.

He has opened his mouth to the
North and the South, they have
stuffed his mouth with gold.

Ye know the truth of his tender
ruth—and sweet his favors are.

Ye have heard the song—How long?
How long? from Balkh to Kan-
dahar.

The Ballad of the King's Jest

WHEN springtime flushes the desert
grass,
Our kafilas wind through the Khyber
Pass.
Lean are the camels but fat the frails,
Light are the purses but heavy the
bales,
As the snowbound trade of the North
comes down
To the market-square of Peshawur
town.

In a turquoise twilight, crisp and chill,
A kafila camped at the foot of the hill.
Then blue smoke-haze of the cooking
rose,
And tentpeg answered to hammer-nose;
And the picketed ponies shag and wild,
Strained at their ropes as the feed was
piled;
And the bubbling camels beside the load
Sprawled for a furlong adown the road;
And the Persian pussy-cats, brought for
sale,
Spat at the dogs from the camel-bale;

And the tribesmen bellowed to hasten
the food;
And the camp-fires twinkled by Fort
Jumrood;
And there fled on the wings of the
gathering dusk
A savor of camels and carpets and
musk,
A murmur of voices, a reek of smoke,
To tell us the trade of the Khyber woke.

The lid of the flesh-pot chattered high,
The knives were whetted and—then
came I
To Mahbub Ali, the muleteer,
Patching his bridles and counting his
gear,
Crammed with the gossip of half a year.
But Mahbub Ali the kindly said,
"Better is speech when the belly is fed."
So we plunged the hand to the mid-wrist
deep
In a cinnamon stew of the fat-tailed
sheep,
And he who never hath tasted the food,

By Allah! he knoweth not bad from
good.

We cleansed our beards of the mutton-
grease,
We lay on the mats and were filled with
peace,
And the talk slid north, and the talk
slid south,
With the sliding puffs from the hookah-
mouth.
Four things greater than all things
are,—
Women and Horses and Power and War.
We spake of them all, but the last the
most,
For I sought a word of a Russian post,
Of a shifty promise, an unsheathed sword
And a grey-coat guard on the Helmund
ford.
Then Mahbub Ali lowered his eyes
In the fashion of one who is weaving
lies.
Quoth he: "Of the Russians who can
say?
"When the night is gathering all is grey.
"But we look that the gloom of the
night shall die
"In the morning flush of a blood-red
sky.
"Friend of my heart, is it meet or wise
"To warn a King of his enemies?
"We know what Heaven or Hell may
bring,
"But no man knoweth the mind of the
King.
"That unsought counsel is cursed of
God
"Attesteth the story of Wali Dad.

"His sire was leaky of tongue and pen,
"His dam was a clucking Khuttuck hen;

"And the colt bred close to the vice of
each,
"For he carried the curse of an un-
staunched speech.
"Therewith madness—so that he sought
"The favor of kings at the Kabul court;
"And traveled, in hope of honor, far
"To the line where the grey-coat squad-
rons are.
"There have I journeyed too— but I
"Saw naught, said naught, and—did not
die!
"He hearked to rumor, and snatched at
a breath
"Of 'this one knoweth' and 'that one
saith,'—
"Legends that ran from mouth to mouth
"Of a grey-coat coming, and sack of the
South.
"These have I also heard—they pass
"With each new spring and the winter
grass.

"Hot-foot southward, forgotten of God,
"Back to the city ran Wali Dad,
"Even to Kabul—in full durbar
"The King held talk with his Chief in
War.
"Into the press of the crowd he broke,
"And what he heard of the coming
spoke.

"Then Gholam Hyder, the Red Chief,
smiled,
"As a mother might on a babbling
child;
"But those who would laugh restrained
their breath,
"When the face of the King showed
dark as death.
"Evil it is in full durbar
"To cry to a ruler of gathering war!
"Slowly he led to a peach-tree small,

"That grew by a cleft of the city wall.
"And he said to the boy: 'They shall praise thy zeal
" 'So long as the red spurt follows the steel.
" 'And the Russ is upon us even now?
" 'Great is thy prudence—await them, thou.
" 'Watch from the tree. Thou art young and strong,
" 'Surely thy vigil is not for long.
" 'The Russ is upon us, thy clamor ran?
" 'Surely an hour shall bring their van.
" 'Wait and watch. When the host is near,
" 'Shout aloud that my men may hear.'

"Friend of my heart, is it meet or wise
"To warn a King of his enemies?
"A guard was set that he might not flee—
"A score of bayonets ringed the tree.
"The peach-bloom fell in showers of snow,
"When he shook at his death as he looked below.
"By the power of God, who alone is great,

"Till the seventh day he fought with his fate.
"Then madness took him, and men de-clare
"He mowed in the branches as ape and bear,
"And last as a sloth, ere his body failed,
"And he hung as a bat in the forks, and wailed,
"And sleep the cord of his hands untied,
"And he fell, and was caught on the points and died.

"Heart of my heart, is it meet or wise
"To warn a King of his enemies?
"We know what Heaven or Hell may bring,
"But no man knoweth the mind of the King.
"Of the grey-coat coming who can say?
"When the night is gathering all is grey.
"Two things greater than all things are,
"The first is Love, and the second War.
"And since we know not how War may prove,
"Heart of my heart, let us talk of Love!"

———————•———————

The Ballad of Boh Da Thone

This is the ballad of Boh Da Thone,
Erst a Pretender to Theebaw's throne,
Who harried the district of Alalone:
How he met with his fate and the V.P.P.
At the hand of Harendra Mukerji,
Senior Gomashta, G.B.T.

BOH DA THONE was a warrior bold,
His sword and his Snider were bossed with gold,

And the Peacock Banner his henchmen bore
Was stiff with bullion but stiffer with gore.

He shot at the strong and he slashed at
the weak
From the Salween scrub to the Chindwin teak:

He crucified noble, he sacrificed mean,
He filled old women with kerosene:

While over the water the papers cried,
"The patriot fights for his countryside!"

But little they cared for the Native
Press,
The worn white soldiers in Khaki dress,

Who tramped through the jungle and
camped in the byre,
Who died in the swamp and were
tombed in the mire,

Who gave up their lives, at the Queen's
Command,
For the Pride of their Race and the
Peace of the Land.

Now· first of the foemen of Boh Da
Thone
Was Captain O'Neil of the "Black Ty-
rene,"

And his was a Company, seventy strong,
Who hustled that dissolute Chief along.

There were lads from Galway and Louth
and Meath
Who went to their death with a joke in
their teeth,

And worshipped with fluency, fervor
and zeal
The mud on the boot-heels of "Crook"
O'Neil.

But ever a blight on their labors lay,
And ever their quarry would vanish
away,

Till the sun-dried boys of the Black
Tyrone
Took a brotherly interest in Boh Da
Thone:

And, sooth, if pursuit in possession ends,
The Boh and his trackers were best of
friends.

The word of a scout—a march by
night—
A rush through the mist—a scattering
fight—

A volley from cover— a corpse in the
clearing—
The glimpse of a lion-cloth and heavy
jade earring—

The flare of a village—the tally of
slain—
And . . . the Boh was abroad "on
the raid" again!

They cursed their luck as the Irish will,
They gave him credit for cunning and
skill,

They buried their dead, they bolted
their beef,
And started anew on the track of the
thief

Till, in place of the "Kalends of
Greece," men said,
"When Crook and his darlings come
back with the head."

They had hunted the Boh from the Hills
to the plain—
He doubled and broke for the hills
again:

They had crippled his power for rapine
and raid,
They had routed him out of his pet
stockade,

And at last, they came, when the Day
Star tired
To a camp deserted—a village fired.

A black cross blistered the Morning-
gold,
And the body upon it was stark and
cold.

The wind of the dawn went merrily
past,
The high grass bowed her plumes to
the blast.

And out of the grass, on a sudden,
broke
A spirtle of fire, a whorl of smoke—

And Captain O'Neil of the Black Tyrone
Was blessed with a slug in the ulna-
bone—

The gift of his enemy Boh Da Thone.
(Now a slug that is hammered from
telegraph wire
Is a thorn in the flesh and a rankling
fire.)

*   *   *   *   *   *

The shot - wound festered—as shot -
wounds may
In a steaming barrack at Mandalay.

The left arm throbbed, and the Captain swore,
"I'd like to be after the Boh once
more!"

The fever held him—the Captain said,
"I'd give a hundred to look at his
head!"

The Hospital punkahs creaked and whir-
red,
But Babu Harendra (Gomashta) heard.

He thought of the cane-brake, green
and dank,
That girdled his home by the Dacca
tank.

He thought of his wife and his High
School son,
He thought—but abandoned the thought
—of a gun.

His sleep was broken by visions dread
Of a shining Boh with a silver head.

He kept his counsel and went his way,
And swindled the cartmen of half their
pay.

*   *   *   *   *   *

And the months went on, as the worst
must do,
And the Boh returned to the raid anew.

But the Captain had quitted the long-
drawn strife,
And in far Simoorie had taken a wife.

And she was a damsel of delicate mould,
With hair like the sunshine and heart
of gold,

And little she knew the arms that embraced
Had cloven a man from the brow to the
waist:

And little she knew that the loving
lips
Had ordered a quivering life's eclipse.

And the eye that lit at her lightest
breath
Had glared unawed in the Gates of
Death.

(For these be matters a man would
hide,
As a general rule, from an innocent
Bride.)

And little the Captain thought of the
past,
And, of all men, Babu Harendra last.
 *   *   *   *   *   *
But slow, in the sludge of the Kathun
road,
The Government Bullock Train toted
its load.

Speckless and spotless and shining with
ghee,
In the rearmost cart sat the Babu-jee.

And ever a phantom before him fled
Of a scowling Boh with a silver head.

Then the lead-cart stuck, though the
coolies slaved,
And the cartmen flogged and the escort
raved;

And out of the jungle, with yells and
squeals,
Pranced Boh Da Thone, and his gang
at his heels!

Then belching blunderbuss answered
back
The Snider's snarl and the carbine's
crack,

And the blithe revolver began to sing
To the blade that twanged on the lock-
ing-ring,

And the brown flesh blued where the
bay net kissed,
As the steel shot back with a wrench
and a twist.

And the great white bullocks with onyx
eyes
Watched the souls of the dead arise,

And over the smoke of the fusillade
The Peacock Banner staggered and
swayed.

Oh, gayest of scrimmages man may see
Is a well-worked rush on the G.B.T.!

The Babu shook at the horrible sight,
And girded his ponderous loins for
flight,

But Fate had ordained that the Boh
should start
On a lone-hand raid of the rearmost
cart,

And out of that cart, with a bellow of
woe,
The Babu fell—flat on the top of the
Boh!

For years had Harendra served the
State,
To the growth of his purse and the girth
of his *pêt*—

There were twenty stone as the tally-
man knows,
On the broad of the chest of this best
of Bohs.

And twenty stone from a height dis-
charged
Are bad for a Boh with a spleen enlarged.

Oh, short was the struggle—severe was
the shock—
He dropped like a bullock—he lay like
a block;

And the Babu above him, convulsed
with fear,
Heard the laboring life-breath hissed out
in his ear.

And thus in a fashion undignified
The princely pest of the Chindwin died.

* * * * * *

Turn now to Simoorie where, lapped in
his ease,
The Captain is petting the Bride on his
knees,

Where the *whit* of the bullet, the
wounded man's scream
Are mixed as the mist of some devilish
dream—

Forgotten, forgotten the sweat of the
shambles
Where the hill-daisy blooms and the
grey monkey gambols,

From the sword-belt set free and re-
leased from the steel,
The Peace of the Lord is with Captain
O'Neil.

Up the hill to Simoorie—most patient
of drudges—
The bags on his shoulder, the mail-
runner trudges.

"For Captain O'Neil, *Sahib*. One hundred and ten
Rupees to collect on delivery."

Then
(Their breakfast was stopped while the
screw-jack and hammer

Tore wax-cloth, split teak-wood, and
chipped out the dammer;)

Open-eyed, open-mouthed, on the nap-
ery's snow,
With a crash and a thud, rolled—the
Head of the Boh!

And gummed to the scalp was a letter
which ran:
"IN FIELDING FORCE SERVICE.
    "Encampment,
        "10th Jan.

"Dear Sir,—I have honor to send, *as
you said,*
"For final approval (see under) Boh's
Head;
"Was took by myself in most bloody
affair.
"By High Education brought pressure
to bear.

"Now violate Liberty, time being bad,
"To mail V.P.P. (rupees hundred)
Please add

"Whatever Your Honor can pass. Price
of Blood
"Much cheap at one hundred, and
children want food.

"So trusting Your Honor will somewhat retain
"True love and affection for Govt. Bullock Train,

"And show awful kindness to satisfy
me,
    "I am,
        "Graceful Master,
            "Your
                "H. Mukerji."
* * * * * *

As the rabbit is drawn to the rattle-
snake's power,
As the smoker's eye fills at the opium
hour,

As a horse reaches up to the manger
above,
As the waiting ear yearns for the
whisper of love,

From the arms of the Bride, iron-vis-
aged and slow,
The Captain bent down to the Head of
the Boh.

And e'en as he looked on the Thing
where It lay
'Twixt the winking new spoons and the
napkins' array,

The freed mind fled back to the long-
ago days—
The hand-to-hand scuffle—the smoke
and the blaze—

The forced march at night and the
quick rush at dawn—
The banjo at twilight, the burial ere
morn—

The stench of the marshes—the raw,
piercing smell
When the overhand stabbing-cut silenced the yell—

The oaths of his Irish that surged
when they stood
Where the black crosses hung o'er the
Kuttamow flood.

As a derelict ship drifts away with the
tide
The Captain went out on the Past from
his Bride,

Back, back, through the springs to the
chill of the year,
When he hunted the Boh from Maloon
to Tsaleer.

As the shape of a corpse dimmers up
through deep water,
In his eye lit the passionless passion of
slaughter,

And men who had fought with O'Neil
for the life
Had gazed on his face with less dread
than his wife.

For she who had held him so long
could not hold him—
Though a four-month Eternity should
have controlled him—

But watched the twin Terror—the head
turned to head—
The scowling, scarred Black, and the
flushed savage Red—

The spirit that changed from her knowing and flew to
Some grim hidden Past she had never
a clue to,

But it knew as It grinned, for he
touched it unfearing,
And muttered aloud, "So you kept that
jade earring!"

Then nodded, and kindly, as friend
nods to friend,
"Old man, you fought well, but you
lost in the end."

* * * * * *

The visions departed, and Shame followed Passion,
"He took what I said in this horrible
fashion,

"I'll write to Harendra!" With language unsainted
The Captain came back to the Bride
    . . . who had fainted.

*   *   *   *   *   *

And this is a fiction? No. Go to Simoorie
And look at their baby, a twelve-month old Houri,

A pert little, Irish-eyed Kathleen Mavournin—
She's always about on the Mall of a mornin'—

And you'll see, if her right shoulder-strap is displaced,
This: *Gules* upon *argent*, a Boh's Head, *erased!*

The Lament of the Border Cattle Thief

O woe is me for the merry life
I led beyond the Bar,
And a treble woe for my winsome wife
That weeps at Shalimar.

They have taken away my long jezail,
My shield and sabre fine,
And heaved me into the Central Jail
For lifting of the kine.

The steer may low within the byre,
The Jut may tend his grain,
But there'll be neither loot nor fire
Till I come back again.

And God have mercy on the Jut
When once my fetters fall,
And Heaven defend the farmer's hut
When I am loosed from thrall.

It's woe to bend the stubborn back
Above the grinching quern,
It's woe to hear the leg-bar clack
And jingle when I turn!

But for the sorrow and the shame,
The brand on me and mine,
I'll pay you back in leaping flame
And loss of the butchered kine.

For every cow I spared before
In charity set free,
If I may reach my hold once more
I'll reive an honest three!

For every time I raised the low
That scared the dusty plain,
By sword and cord, by torch and tow
I'll light the land with twain!

Ride hard, ride hard to Abazai,
Young *Sahib* with the yellow hair—
Lie close, lie close as khuttucks lie,
Fat herds below Bonair!

The one I'll shoot at twilight tide,
At dawn I'll drive the other;
The black shall mourn for hoof and hide,
The white man for his brother!

'Tis war, red war, I'll give you then,
War till my sinews fail,
For the wrong you have done to a chief of men
And a thief of the Zukka Kheyl.

And if I fail to your hand afresh
I give you leave for the sin,
That you cram my throat with the foul pig's flesh
And swing me in the skin!

The Rhyme of the Three Captains

This ballad appears to refer to one of the exploits of the notorious Paul Jones, the American Pirate. It is founded on fact.

. . . AT the close of a winter day,
Their anchors down, by London town, the Three Great Captains lay.
And one was Admiral of the North from Solway Firth to Skye,
And one was Lord of the Wessex coast and all the lands thereby,
And one was Master of the Thames from Limehouse to Blackwall,
And he was Captain of the Fleet—the bravest of them all.
Their good guns guarded their great grey sides that were thirty foot in the sheer,
When there came a certain trading-brig with news of a privateer.
Her rigging was rough with the clotted drift that drives in a Northern breeze,
Her sides were clogged with the lazy weed that spawns in the Eastern seas.
Light she rode in the rude tide-rip, to left and right she rolled,
And the skipper sat on the scuttle-butt and stared at an empty hold.
"I ha' paid Port dues for your Law," quoth he, "and where is the Law ye boast
"If I sail unscathed from a heathen port to be robbed on a Christian coast?

"Ye have smoked the hives of the Laccadives as we burn the lice in a bunk;
"We tack not now to a Gallang prow or a plunging Pei-ho junk;
"I had no fear but the seas were clear as far as a sail might fare
"Till I met with a lime-washed Yankee brig that rode off Finisterre.
"There were canvas blinds to his bow-gun ports to screen the weight he bore
"And the signals ran for a merchant-man from Sandy Hook to the Nore.
"He would not fly the Rover's flag—the bloody or the black,
"But now he floated the Gridiron and now he flaunted the Jack.
"He spoke of the Law as he crimped my crew—he swore it was only a loan;
"But when I would ask for my own again, he swore it was none of my own.
"He has taken my little parrakeets that nest beneath the Line,
"He has stripped my rails of the shad-dock-frails and the green unripened pine;
"He has taken my bale of dammer and spice I won beyond the seas,

"He has taken my grinning heathen
gods—and what should he want o'
these?

"My foremast would not mend his
boom, my deck-house patch his
boats

"He has whittled the two this Yank
Yahoo, to peddle for shoepeg-oats.

"I could not fight for the failing light
and a rough beam-sea beside,

"But I hulled him once for a clumsy
crimp and twice because he lied.

"Had I had guns (as I had goods) to
work my Christian harm,

"I had run him up from his quarter-
deck to trade with his own yard-
arm;

"I had nailed his ears to my capstan-
head, and ripped them off with a
saw,

"And soused them in the bilgewater,
and served them to him raw;

"I had flung him blind in a rudderless
boat to rot in the rocking dark

"I had towed him aft of his own craft,
a bait for his brother shark;

"I had lapped him round with cocoa
husk, and drenched him with the oil,

"And lashed him fast to his own mast
to blaze above my spoil;

"I had stripped his hide for my ham-
mock-side, and tasselled his beard i'
the mesh

"And spitted his crew on the live bamboo that grows through the gang-
rened flesh;

"I had hove him down by the man-
groves brown, where the mud-reef
sucks and draws,

"Moored by the heel to his own keel to
wait for the land-crab's claws!

"He is lazar within and lime without, ye
can nose him far enow,

"For he carries the taint of a musky
ship—the reek of the slaver's
dhow!"

The skipper looked at the tiering guns
and the bulwarks tall and cold,

And the Captains Three full courteously peered down at the gutted
hole,

And the Captains Three called courteously from deck to scuttle-butt:

"Good Sir, we ha' dealt with that
merchantman or ever your teeth
were cut.

"Your words be words of a lawless race,
and the Law it standeth thus:

"He comes of a race that have never a
Law, and he never has boarded us.

"We ha' sold him canvas and rope and
spar— we know that his price is
fair,

"And we know that he weeps for the
lack of a Law as he rides off Finisterre.

"And since he is damned for a gallows-
thief by you and better than you,

"We hold it meet that the English fleet
should know that we hold him
true."

The skipper called to the tall taffrail:
"And what is that to me?

"Did ever you hear of a privateer that
rifled a Seventy-three?

"Do I loom so large from your quarter-
deck that I lift like a ship o' the
Line?

"He has learned to run from a shotted
gun and harry such craft as mine.

"There is never a Law on the Cocos
Keys to hold a white man in,

"But we do not steal the nigger's meal,
for that is a nigger's sin.

"Must he have his Law as a quid to
chaw, or laid in brass on his wheel?

"Does he steal with tears when he buccaneers? 'Fore Gad, then, why does
he steal?"
The skipper bit on a deep-sea word, and
the word it was not sweet,
For he could see the Captains Three had
signalled to the Fleet.
But three and two, in white and blue,
the whimpering flags began:
"We have heard a tale of a foreign sail,
but he is a merchantman."
The skipper peered beneath his palm
and swore by the Great Horn Spoon,
" 'Fore Gad, the Chaplain of the Fleet
would bless my picaroon!"
By two and three the flags blew free to
lash the laughing air,
"We have sold our spars to the merchantman—we know that his price
is fair."
The skipper winked his Western eye,
and swore by a China storm:
"They ha' rigged him a Joseph's jury-
coat to keep his honor warm."
The halliards twanged against the tops,
the bunting bellied broad,
The skipper spat in the empty hold and
mourned for a wasted cord.
Masthead—masthead, the signal sped by
the line o' the British craft;
The skipper called to his Lascar crew,
and put her about and laughed:
"It's mainsail haul, my bully boys all—
we'll out to the seas again;

"Ere they set us to paint their pirate
saint, or scrub at his grapnel-chain
"It's fore-sheet free, with her head to
the sea, and the swing of the un-
bought brine—
"We'll make no sport in an English
court till we come as a ship o' the
Line,
"Till we come as a ship o' the Line, my
lads, of thirty foot in the sheer,
"Lifting again from the outer main with
news of a privateer;
"Flying his pluck at our mizzen-truck
for weft of Admiralty,
"Heaving his head for our dipsy-lead
in sign that we keep the sea.
"Then fore-sheet home as she lifts to
the foam—we stand on the outward
tack
"We are paid in the coin of the white
man's trade—the bezant is hard, ay,
and black.
"The frigate-bird shall carry my word
to the Kling and the Orang-Laut
"How a man may sail from a heathen
coast to be robbed in a Christian
port;
"How a man may be robbed in Christian port while Three Great Captains
there
"Shall dip their flag to a slaver's rag—
to show that his trade is fair!"

The Ballad of the "Clampherdown"

It was our war-ship "Clampherdown"
  Would sweep the Channel clean,
Wherefore she kept her hatches close
When the merry Channel chops arose,
  To save the bleached marine.

She had one bow-gun of a hundred ton,
  And a great stern-gun beside;
They dipped their noses deep in the sea,
They racked their stays and staunchions
    free
  In the wash of the wind-whipped tide.

It was our war-ship "Clampherdown,"
  Fell in with a cruiser light
That carried the dainty Hotchkiss gun
And a pair o' heels wherewith to run,
  From the grip of a close-fought fight.

She opened fire at seven miles—
  As ye shoot at a bobbing cork—
And once she fired and twice she fired,
Till the bow-gun drooped like a lily tired
  That lolls upon the stalk.

"Captain, the bow-gun melts apace,
  "The deck-beams break below,
"'Twere well to rest for an hour or
    twain,
"And botch the shattered plates again."
  And he answered, "Make it so."

She opened fire within the mile—
  As ye shoot at the flying duck—
And the great stern-gun shot fair and
    true,

With the heave of the ship, to the stain-
    less blue,
  And the great stern-turret stuck.

"Captain, the turret fills with steam,
  "The feed-pipes burst below—
"You can hear the hiss of helpless ram,
"You can hear the twisted runners jam."
  And he answered, "Turn and go!"

It was our war-ship "Clampherdown,"
  And grimly did she roll;
Swung round to take the cruiser's fire
As the White Whale faces the Thresher's
    ire,
  When they war by the frozen Pole.

"Captain, the shells are falling fast,
  "And faster still fall we;
"And it is not meet for English stock,
"To bide in the heart of an eight-day
    clock,
  "The death they cannot see."

"Lie down, lie down my bold A.B.,
  "We drift upon her beam;
"We dare not ram for she can run;
"And dare ye fire another gun,
  "And die in the peeling steam?"

It was our war-ship "Clampherdown"
  That carried an armor-belt;
But fifty feet at stern and bow,
Lay bare as the paunch of the purser's
    sow,
  To the hail of the Nordenfeldt.

"Captain, they lack us through and
through;
"The chilled steel bolts are swift!
"We have emptied the bunkers in open
sea,
"Their shrapnel bursts where our coal
should be."
And he answered, "Let her drift."

It was our war-ship "Clampherdown,"
Swung round upon the tide,
Her two dumb guns glared south and
north,
And the blood and the bubbling steam
ran forth,
And she ground the cruiser's side.

"Captain, they cry, the fight is done,
"They bid you send your sword."
And he answered, "Grapple her stern
and bow.
"They have asked for the steel. They
shall have it now;
"Out cutlasses and board!"

It was our war-ship "Clampherdown,"
Spewed up four hundred men;

And the scalded stokers yelped delight,
As they rolled in the waist and heard
the fight,
Stamp o'er their steel-walled pen.

They cleared the cruiser end to end,
From conning-tower to hold.
They fought as they fought in Nelson's
fleet;
They were stripped to the waist, they
were bare to the feet,
As it was in the days of old.

It was the sinking "Clampherdown"
Heaved up her battered side—
And carried a million pounds in steel,
To the cod and the corpse-fed conger-
eel,
And the scour of the Channel tide.

It was the crew of the "Clampherdown"
Stood out to sweep the sea,
On a cruiser won from an ancient foe,
As it was in the days of long-ago,
And as it still shall be.

The Ballad of the "Bolivar"

*Seven men from all the world, back
to Docks again,
Rolling down the Ratcliffe Road
drunk and raising Cain:
Give the girls another drink 'fore we
sign away—
We that took the "Bolivar" out across
the Bay!*

WE put out from Sunderland loaded
down with rails;
We put back to Sunderland 'cause our
cargo shifted;
We put out from Sunderland—met the
winter gales—
Seven days and seven nights to the
Start we drifted,

Racketing her rivets loose, smoke-
stack white as snow,
All the coals adrift a deck, half the
rails below
Leaking like a lobster-pot, steering
like a dray—
Out we took the "Bolivar," out
across the Bay!

One by one the Lights came up, winked
and let us by;
Mile by mile we waddled on, coal and
fo'c'sle short;
Met a blow that laid us down, heard a
bulkhead fly;
Left The Wolf behind us with a two
foot-list to port.

Trailing like a wounded duck,
working out her soul;
Clanging like a smithy-shop after
every roll;
Just a funnel and a mast lurching
through the spray—
So we threshed the "Bolivar" out
across the Bay!

Felt her hog and felt her sag, betted
when she'd break;
Wondered every time she raced if
she'd stand the shock;
Heard the seas like drunken men
pounding at her strake;
Hoped the Lord 'ud keep his thumb
on the plummer-block.

Banged against the iron decks,
bilges choked with coal;
Flayed and frozen foot and hand,
sick of heart and soul;
'Last we prayed she'd buck herself
into Judgment Day—
Hi! we cursed the "Bolivar" knocking round the Bay!

Oh! her nose flung up to sky, groaning
to be still—
Up and down and back we went,
never time for breath;
Then the money paid at Lloyd's caught
her by the heel,
And the stars ran round and round
dancin' at our death.

Aching for an hour's sleep, dozing
off between;
Heard the rotten rivets draw when
she took it green;
Watched the compass chase its tail
like a cat at play—
That was on the "Bolivar," south
across the Bay.

Once we saw between the squalls, lyin'
head to swell—
Mad with work and weariness, wishin'
they was we—
Some damned Liner's lights go by like a
grand hotel;
Cheered her from the "Bolivar,"
swampin' in the sea.

Then a greyback cleared us out,
then the skipper laughed;
"Boys, the wheel has gone to Hell
—rig the winches aft!
"Yoke the kicking rudder-head—get
her under way!"
So we steered her, pulley-haul, out
across the Bay!

Just a pack o' rotten plates puttied up
with tar,
In we came, an' time enough 'cross
Bilbao Bar.
Overloaded, undermanned, meant to
founder, we
Euchred God Almighty's storm,
bluffed the Eternal Sea!

Seven men from all the world, back to
town again,
Rollin' down the Ratcliffe Road drunk
and raising Cain:

Seven men from out of Hell. Ain't
the owners gay,
'Cause we took the "Bolivar" safe
across the Bay?

———•———

The English Flag

Above the portico a flagstaff, bearing
the Union Jack, remained fluttering in
the flames for some time, but ultimately
when it fell the crowds rent the air with
shouts, and seemed to see significance in
the incident.—DAILY PAPERS.

WINDS of the World, give answer?
They are whimpering to and fro—
And what should they know of England
who only England know?—
The poor little street-bred people that
vapor and fume and brag,
They are lifting their heads in the still-
ness to yelp at the English Flag!

Must we borrow a clout from the Boer
—to plaster anew with dirt?
An Irish liar's bandage, or an English
coward's shirt?
We may not speak of England; her
Flag's to sell or share.
What is the Flag of England? Winds
of the World, declare!

The North Wind blew: "From Bergen
my steel-shod vanguards go;
"I chase your lazy whalers home from
the Disko floe;
"By the great North Lights above me I
work the will of God,
"That the liner splits on the ice-field or
the Dogger fills with cod.

"I barred my gates with iron, I shuttered my doors with flame,
"Because to force my ramparts your
nutshell navies came;
"I took the sun from their presence, I
cut them down with my blast,
"And they died, but the Flag of England blew free ere the spirit passed.

"The lean white bear hath seen it in
the long, long Arctic night,
"The musk-ox knows the standard that
flouts the Northern Light:
"What is the Flag of England? Ye
have but my bergs to dare,
"Ye have but my drifts to conquer.
Go forth, for it is there!"

The South Wind sighed: "From The
Virgins my mid-sea course was ta'en
"Over a thousand islands lost in an idle
main,
"Where the sea-egg flames on the coral
and the long-backed breakers croon
"Their endless ocean legends to the lazy,
locked lagoon.

"Strayed amid lonely islets, mazed amid
outer keys,
"I waked the palms to laughter—I
tossed the scud in the breeze—

"Never was aisle so little, never was
  sea so lone,
"But over the scud and the palm-trees
  an English flag was flown.

"I have wrenched it free from the
  halliard to hang for a wisp on the
  Horn;
"I have chased it north to the Lizard—
  ribboned and rolled and torn;
"I have spread its fold o'er the dying,
  adrift in a hopeless sea;
"I have hurled it swift on the slaver,
  and seen the slave set free.

"My basking sunfish know it, and wheeling albatross,
"Where the lone wave fills with fire beneath the Southern Cross.
"What is the Flag of England? Ye have
  but my reefs to dare,
"Ye have but my seas to furrow. Go
  forth, for it is there!"

The East Wind roared: "From the
  Kuriles, the Bitter Seas, I come,
"And me men call the Home-Wind, for
  I bring the English home.
"Look—look well to your shipping! By
  the breath of my mad typhoon
"I swept your close-packed Praya and
  beached your best at Kowloon!

"The reeling junks behind me and the
  racing seas before,
"I raped your richest roadstead—I
  plundered Singapore!
"I set my hand on the Hoogli; as a
  hooded snake she rose,
"And I flung your stoutest steamers to
  roost with the startled crows.

"Never the lotos closes, never the wild
  fowl wake,
"But a soul goes out on the East Wind
  that died for England's sake—
"Man or woman or suckling, mother or
  bride or maid—
"Because on the bones of the English
  the English Flag is stayed.

"The desert-dust hath dimmed it, the
  flying wild-ass knows
"The scared white leopard winds it
  across the taintless snows.
"What is the Flag of England? Ye have
  but my sun to dare,
"Ye have but my sands to travel. Go
  forth, for it is there!"

The West Wind called: "In squadrons
  the thoughtless galleons fly
"That bear the wheat and cattle lest
  street-bred people die.
"They make my might their porter, they
  make my house their path,
"Till I loose my neck from their rudder
  and whelm them all in my wrath.

"I draw the gliding fog-bank as a snake
  is drawn from the hole;
"They bellow one to the other, the
  frighted ship-bells toll,
"For day is a drifting terror till I raise
  the shroud with my breath,
"And they see strange bows above them
  and the two go locked to death.

"But whether in calm or wrack-wreath,
  whether by dark or day,
"I heave them whole to the conger or
  rip their plates away,
"First of the scattered legions, under a
  shrieking sky,
"Dipping between the rollers, the English Flag goes by.

"The dead dumb fog hath wrapped it—
  the frozen dews have kissed—
"The naked stars have seen it, a fellow-
  star in the mist.

"What is the Flag of England? Ye
  have but my breath to dare,
"Ye have but my waves to conquer. Go
  forth, for it is there!"

———•———

"Cleared"

(IN MEMORY OF A COMMISSION)

HELP for a patriot distressed, a spotless
  spirit hurt,
Help for an honorable clan sore
  trampled in the dirt!
From Queenstown Bay to Donegal, O
  listen to my song,
The honorable gentlemen have suffered
  grievous wrong.

Their noble names were mentioned—O
  the burning black disgrace!—
By a brutal Saxon paper in an Irish
  shooting-case;
They sat upon it for a year, then steeled
  their heart to brave it,
And "coruscating innocence" the learned
  Judges gave it.

Bear witness, Heaven, of that grim
  crime beneath the surgeon's knife,
The honorable gentleman deplored the
  loss of life;
Bear witness of those chanting choirs
  that burk and shirk and snigger,
No man laid hand upon the knife or
  finger to the trigger!

Cleared in the face of all mankind beneath the winking skies,
Like phœnixes from Phœnix Park (and
  what lay there) they rise!

Go shout it to the emerald seas—give
  word to Erin now,
Her honorable gentlemen are cleared—
  and this is how:

They only paid the Moonlighter his
  cattle-hocking price,
They only helped the murderer with
  council's best advice,
But—sure it keeps their honor white—
  the learned Court believes
They never gave a piece of plate to
  murderers and thieves.

They never told the ramping crowd to
  card a woman's hide,
They never marked a man for death—
  what fault of theirs he died?—
They only said "intimidate," and talked
  and went away—
By God, the boys that did the work
  were braver men than they!

Their sin it was that fed the fire—small
  blame to them that heard—
The "bhoys" get drunk on rhetoric, and
  madden at the word—
They knew whom they were talking at,
  if they were Irish too,
The gentlemen that lied in Court, they
  knew and well they knew.

They only took the Judas-gold from
   Fenians out of jail,
They only fawned for dollars on the
   blood-dyed Clan-na-Gael.
If black is black or white is white, in
   black and white it's down,
They're only traitors to the Queen and
   rebels to the Crown.

"Cleared," honorable gentlemen. Be
   thankful it's no more:
The widow's curse is on your house, the
   dead are at your door.
On you the shame of open shame, on
   you from North to South
The hand of every honest man flat-
   heeled across your mouth.

"Less black than we were painted"?—
   Faith, no word of black was said;
The lightest touch was human blood,
   and that, ye know, runs red.
It's sticking to your fist to-day for all
   your sneer and scoff,
And by the Judge's well-weighed word
   you cannot wipe it off.

Hold up those hands of innocence—go,
   scare your sheep, together,
The blundering, tripping tups that bleat
   behind the old bell-weather;
And if they snuff the taint and break to
   find another pen,
Tell them it's tar that glistens so, and
   daub them yours again!

"The charge is old"?—As old as Cain—
   as fresh as yesterday;
Old as the Ten Commandments, have ye
   talked those laws away?
If words are words, or death is death, or
   powder sends the ball,
You spoke the words that sped the shot
   —the curse be on you all.

"Our friends believe"? Of course they
   do—as sheltered women may;
But have they seen the shrieking soul
   ripped from the quivering clay?
They!—If their own front door is shut,
   they'll swear the whole world's
   warm;
What do they know of dread of death
   or hanging fear of harm?

The secret half a county keeps, the
   whisper in the lane,
The shriek that tells the shot went home
   behind the broken pane,
The dry blood crisping in the sun that
   scares the honest bees,
And shows the "bhoys" have heard your
   talk—what do they know of these?

But you—you know—ay, ten times
   more; the secrets of the dead,
Black terror on the country-side by
   word and whisper bred,
The mangled stallion's scream at night,
   the tail-cropped heifer's low.
Who set the whisper going first? You
   know, and well you know!

My soul! I'd sooner lie in jail for
   murder plain and straight,
Pure crime I'd done with my own hand
   for money, lust, or hate,
Than take a seat in Parliament by fel-
   low-felons cheered,
While one of those "not provens"
   proved me cleared as you are cleared.

Cleared—you that "lost" the League accounts—go, guard our honor still,
Go, help to make our country's laws
   that broke God's law at will—
One hand stuck out behind the back, to
   signal "strike again";
The other on your dress-shirt front to
   show your heart is clane.

If black is black or white is white, in
black and white it's down,
You're only traitors to the Queen and
rebels to the Crown.

If print is print or words are words,
the learned Court perpends:
We are not ruled by murderers, but
only—by their friends.

—————•—————

An Imperial Rescript

Now this is the tale of the Council the
German Kaiser decreed,
To ease the strong of their burden, to
help the weak in their need
He sent a word to the peoples, who
struggle, and pant, and sweat,
That the straw might be counted fairly
and the tally of bricks be set.

The Lords of Their Hands assembled;
from the East and the West they
drew—
Baltimore, Lille, and Essen, Brumma-
gem, Clyde, and Crewe.
And some were black from the furnace,
and some were brown from the soil,
And some were blue from the dye-vat;
but all were wearied of toil.

And the young King said "I have found
it, the road to the rest ye seek
"The strong shall wait for the weary,
the hale shall halt for the weak;
"With the even tramp of an army
where no man breaks from the line,
"Ye shall march to peace and plenty in
the bond of brotherhood—sign!"

The paper lay on the table, the strong
heads bowed thereby,
And a wail went up from the peoples:
"Ay, sign—give rest, for we die!"

A hand was stretched to the goose-quill,
a fist was cramped to scrawl,
When—the laugh of a blue-eyed maiden
ran clear through the council-hall.

And each one heard Her laughing as
each one saw Her plain—
Saidie, Mimi, or Olga, Gretchen, or
Mary Jane.
And the Spirit of Man that is in Him
to the light of the vision woke;
And the men drew back from the paper,
as a Yankee delegate spoke:

"There's a girl in Jersey City who works
on the telephone;
"We're going to hitch our horses and dig
for a house of our own,
"With gas and water connections, and
steamheat through to the top;
"And, W. Hohenzollern, I guess I shall
work till I drop."

And an English delegate thundered:
"The weak an' the lame be blowed!
"I've a berth in the Sou'-West work-
shops, a home in the Wandsworth
Road;
"And till the 'sociation has footed my
buryin' bill,
"I work for the kids an' the missus.
Pull up! I'll be damned if I will!"

And over the German benches the bearded whisper ran:

"Lager, der girls und der dollars, dey makes or dey breaks a man.

"If Schmitt haf collared der dollars, he collars der girl deremit;

"But if Schmitt bust in der pizness, we collars der girl from Schmitt."

They passed one resolution: "Your subcommittee believe

"You can lighten the curse of Adam when you've lightened the curse of Eve.

"But till we are built like angels—with hammer and chisel and pen,

"We will work for ourself and a woman, forever and ever. Amen."

Now this is the tale of the Council the German Kaiser held—

The day that they razored the Grindstone, the day that the Cat was belled,

The day of the Figs from Thistles, the day of the Twisted Sands,

The day that the laugh of a maiden made light of the Lords of Their Hands.

———•———

Tomlinson

Now Tomlinson gave up the ghost in his house in Berkeley Square,

And a Spirit came to his bedside and gripped him by the hair—

A Spirit gripped him by the hair and carried him far away,

Till he heard as the roar of a rain-fed ford the roar of the Milky Way,

Till he heard the roar of the Milky Way die down and drone and cease,

And they came to the Gate within the Wall where Peter holds the keys.

"Stand up, stand up now, Tomlinson, and answer loud and high

"The good that ye did for the sake of men or ever ye came to die—

"The good that ye did for the sake of men in little earth so lone!"

And the naked soul of Tomlinson grew white as a rain-washed bone.

"Oh, I have a friend on earth," he said, "that was my priest and guide,

"And well would he answer all for me if he were by my side."

—"For that ye strove in neighbor-love it shall be written fair,

"But now ye wait at Heaven's Gate and not in Berkeley Square:

"Though we called your friend from his bed this night, he could not speak for you,

"For the race is run by one and one and never by two and two."

Then Tomlinson looked up and down, and little gain was there,

For the naked stars grinned overhead, and he saw that his soul was bare:

The Wind that blows between the worlds, it cut him like a knife,

And Tomlinson took up his tale and spoke of his good in life.

"This I have read in a book," he said,
"and that was told to me,
"And this I have thought that another
man thought of a Prince in Mus-
covy."
The good souls flocked like homing
doves and bade him clear the path,
And Peter twirled the jangling keys in
weariness and wrath.
"Ye have read, ye have heard, ye have
thought," he said, "and the tale is
yet to run:
"By the worth of the body that once ye
had, give answer—what ha' ye
done?"
Then Tomlinson looked back and forth,
and little good it bore,
For the Darkness stayed at his shoulder-
blade and Heaven's Gate before:
"Oh, this I have felt, and this I have
guessed, and this I have heard men
say,
"And this they wrote that another man
wrote of a carl in Norroway."
"Ye have read, ye have felt, ye have
guessed, good lack! Ye have hampered Heaven's Gate;
"There's little room between the stars in
idleness to prate!
"Oh, none may reach by hired speech
of neighbor, priest, and kin,
"Through borrowed deed to god's good
meed that lies so far within;
"Get hence, get hence to the Lord of
Wrong, for doom has yet to run,
"And . . . the faith that ye share
with Berkeley Square uphold you,
Tomlinson!"

*   *   *   *   *   *

The Spirit gripped him by the hair, and
sun by sun they fell
Till they came to the belt of Naughty
Stars that rim the mouth of Hell:

The first are red with pride and wrath,
the next are white with pain,
But the third are black with clinkered
sin that cannot burn again:
They may hold their path, they may
leave their path, with never a soul
to mark,
They may burn or freeze, but they must
not cease in the Scorn of the Outer
Dark.
The Wind that blows between the
worlds, it nipped him to the bone,
And he yearned to the flare of Hell-gate
there as the light of his own hearth-
stone.
The Devil he sat behind the bars, where
the desperate legions drew,
But he caught the hasting Tomlinson
and would not let him through.
"Wot ye the price of good pit-coal that
I must pay?" said he,
"That ye rank yoursel' so fit for Hell
and ask no leave of me?
"I am all o'er-sib to Adam's breed that
ye should give me scorn,
"For I strove with God for your First
Father the day that he was born.
"Sit down, sit down upon the slag, and
answer loud and high
"The harm that ye did to the Sons of
Men or ever you came to die."
And Tomlinson looked up and up, and
saw against the night
The belly of a tortured star blood-red
in Hell-Mouth light;
And Tomlinson looked down and down,
and saw beneath his feet
The frontlet of a tortured star milk-
white in Hell-Mouth heat.
"Oh, I had a love on earth," said he,
"that kissed me to my fall,
"And if ye would call my love to me I
know she would answer all."

—"All that ye did in love forbid it shall
be written fair,
"But now ye wait at Hell-Mouth Gate
and not in Berkeley Square:
"Though we whistled your love from
her bed to-night, I trow she would
not run,
"For the sin ye do by two and two ye
must pay for one by one!"
The Wind that blows between the
worlds, it cut him like a knife,
And Tomlinson took up the tale and
spoke of his sin in life:
"Once I ha' laughed at the power of
Love and twice at the grip of the
Grave,
"And thrice I ha' patted my God on the
head that men might call me brave."
The Devil he blew on a brandered soul
and set it aside to cool:
"Do ye think I would waste my good
pit-coal on the hide of a brain-sick
fool?
"I see no worth in the hobnailed mirth
or the jolt-head jest ye did
"That I should waken my gentlemen
that are sleeping three on a grid."
Then Tomlinson looked back and forth,
and there was little grace,
For Hell-Gate filled the houseless Soul
with the Fear of Naked Space.
"Nay, this I ha' heard," quo' Tomlinson, "and this was noised abroad,
"And this I ha' got from a Belgian book
on the word of a dead French lord."
—"Ye ha' heard, ye ha' read, ye ha' got,
good lack! And the tale begins a-
fresh—
"Have ye sinned one sin for the pride o'
the eye or the sinful lust of the
flesh?"
Then Tomlinson he gripped the bars
and yammered "Let me in—

"For I mind that I borrowed my neighbor's wife to sin the deadly sin."
The Devil he grinned behind the bars,
and banked the fires high:
"Did ye read of that sin in a book?"
said he, and Tomlinson said "Ay!"
The Devil he blew upon his nails, and
the little devils ran;
And he said, "Go husk this whimpering
thief that comes in the guise of a
man:
"Winnow him out 'twixt star and star,
and sieve his proper worth:
"There's sore decline in Adam's line if
this be spawn of earth."
Empusa's crew, so naked-new they may
not face the fire,
But weep that they bin too small to
sin to the height of their desire,
Over the coal they chased the Soul, and
racked it all abroad,
As children rifle a caddis-case or the
raven's foolish hoard.
And back they came with the tattered
Thing, as children after play,
And they said: "The soul that he got
from God he has bartered clean
away.
"We have threshed a stook of print and
book, and winnowed a chattering
wind
"And many a soul wherefrom he stole,
but his we cannot find:
"We have handled him, we have dandled
him, we have seared him to the bone,
"And sure if tooth and nail show truth
he has no soul of his own."
The Devil he bowed his head on his
breast and rumbled deep and low:
"I'm all o'er-sib to Adam's breed that I
should bid him go.
"Yet close we lie, and deep we lie, and
if I gave him place,

"My gentlemen that are so proud would flout me to my face;
"They'd call my house a common stews and me a careless host,
"And—I would not anger my gentlemen for the sake of a shiftless ghost."
The Devil he looked at the mangled Soul that prayed to feel the flame,
And he thought of Holy Charity, but he thought of his own good name:
"Now ye could haste my coal to waste, and sit ye down to fry:
"Did ye think of that theft for yourself?" said he; and Tomlinson said "Ay!"
The Devil he blew an outward breath, for his heart was free from care:
"Ye have scarce the soul of a louse," he said, "but the roots of sin are there,
"And for that sin should ye come in were I the lord alone.
"But sinful pride has rule inside—and mightier than my own.
"Honor and Wit, fore-damned they sit, to each his priest and whore:

"Nay, scarce I dare myself go there, and you they'd torture sore.
"Ye are neither spirit nor spirk," he said; "ye are neither book nor brute—
"Go, get ye back to the flesh again for the sake of Man's repute.
"I'm all o'er-sib to Adam's breed that I should mock your pain,
"But look that ye win to worthier sin ere ye come back again.
"Get hence, the hearse is at your door— the grim black stallions wait—
"They bear your clay to place to-day. Speed, lest ye come too late!
"Go back to Earth with a lip unsealed— go back with an open eye,
"And carry my word to the Sons of Men or ever ye come to die:
"That the sin they do by two and two they must pay for one by one—
"And . . . the God that you took from a printed book be with you, Tomlinson!"

———————•———————

Danny Deever

"WHAT are the bugles blowin' for?" said Files-on-Parade.
"To turn you out, to turn you out," the Color-Sergeant said.
"What makes you look so white, so white?" said Files-on-Parade.
"I'm dreadin' what I've got to watch," the Color-Sergeant said.

For they're hangin' Danny Deever, you can hear the Dead March play,
The regiment's in 'ollow square— they're hangin' him to-day;
They've taken of his buttons off an' cut his stripes away,
An' they're hangin' Danny Deever in the mornin'.

"What makes the rear-rank breathe so
'ard?" said Files-on-Parade.

"It's bitter cold, it's bitter cold," the
Color-Sergeant said.

"What makes that front-rank man fall
down?" says Files-on-Parade.

"A touch o' sun, a touch o' sun," the
Color-Sergeant said.

They are hangin' Danny Deever,
they are marchin' of 'im round,
They 'ave 'alted Danny Deever
by 'is coffin on the ground;
An' 'e'll swing in 'arf a minute
for a sneakin' shootin' hound—
O they're hangin' Danny Deever
in the mornin'!

" 'Is cot was right-'and cot to mine,"
said Files-on-Parade.

" 'E's sleepin' out an' far to-night," the
Color-Sergeant said.

"I've drunk 'is beer a score o' times,"
said Files-on-Parade.

" 'E's drinkin' bitter beer alone," the
Color-Sergeant said.

They are hangin' Danny Deever,
you must mark 'im to 'is place,
For 'e shot a comrade sleepin'—
you must look 'im in the face;
Nine 'undred of 'is county and
the regiment's disgrace,
While they're hanging Danny
Deever in the morning

"What's that so black agin the sun?"
said Files-on-Parade.

"It's Danny fightin' 'ard for life," the
Color-Sergeant said.

"What's that that whimpers over'ead?"
said Files-on-Parade.

"It's Danny's soul that's passin' now,"
the Color-Sergeant said.

For they're done with Danny
Deever, you can 'ear the quick-
step play,
The regiment's in column, an'
they're marchin' us away;
Ho! the young recruits are
shakin', an' they'll want their
beer to-day,
After hangin' Danny Deever in
the mornin'.

———— • ————

Tommy

I went into a public-'ouse to get a
pint o' beer,
The publican 'e up an' sez, "We serve
no red-coats here."
The girls be'ind the bar they laughed
an' giggled fit to die,
I outs into the street again an' to myself sez I:

O it's Tommy this, an' Tommy
that, an' "Tommy, go away";
But it's "Thank you, Mister Atkins," when the band begins to
play,
The band begins to play, my
boys, the band begins to play,

O it's "Thank you, Mister Atkins," when the band begins to play.

I went into a theatre as sober as could be,
They gave a drunk civilian room, but 'adn't none for me;
They sent me to the gallery or round the music-'alls,
But when it comes to fightin', Lord! they'll shove me in the stalls!

    For it's Tommy this, an' Tommy that, an' "Tommy, wait outside";
    But it's "Special train for Atkins" when the trooper's on the tide,
    The troopship's on the tide, my boys, the troopship's on the tide,
    O it's "Special train for Atkins" when the trooper's on the tide.

Yes, makin' mock o' uniforms that guard you while you sleep
Is cheaper than them uniforms, an' they're starvation cheap;
An' hustlin' drunken soldiers when they're goin' large a bit
Is five times better business than paradin' in full kit.

    Then it's Tommy this, an' Tommy that, an' "Tommy, 'ow's yer soul?"
    But it's "Thin red line of 'eroes" when the drums begin to roll,
    The drums begin to roll, my boys, the drums begin to roll,
    O it's "Thin red line of 'eroes" when the drums begin to roll.

We aren't no thin red 'eroes, nor we aren't no blackguards too,
But single men in barricks, most remai kable like you;
An' if sometimes our conduck isn't all your fancy paints:
Why, single men in barricks don't grow into plaster saints;

    While it's Tommy this, an' Tommy that, an' "Tommy, fall be'ind,"
    But it's "Please to walk in front, sir," when there's trouble in the wind,
    There's trouble in the wind, my boys, there's trouble in the wind,
    O it's "Please to walk in front, sir," when there's trouble in the wind.

You talk o' better food for us, an' schools, an' fires, an' all:
We'll wait for extry rations if you treat us rational.
Don't mess about the cook-room slops, but prove it to our face
The Widow's Uniform is not the soldier-man's disgrace.

    For it's. Tommy this, an' Tommy that, an' "Chuck him out, the brute!"
    But it's "Saviour of 'is country,' when the guns begin to shoot;
    Yes it's Tommy this, an' Tommy that, an' anything you please;
    But Tommy ain't a bloomin' fool —you bet that Tommy sees!

"Fuzzy-Wuzzy"

(SOUDAN EXPEDITIONARY FORCE)

WE'VE fought with many men acrost the
seas,
An' some of 'em was brave an' some
was not.
The Paythan an' the Zulu an' Burmese;
But the Fuzzy was the finest o' the
lot.
We never got a ha'porth's change of 'im:
'E squatted in the scrub an' 'ocked
our 'orses,
'E cut our sentries up at Sua*kim*,
An' 'e played the cat an' banjo with
our forces.
    So 'ere's *to* you, Fuzzy-Wuzzy, at
    your 'ome in the Soudan;
    You're a pore benighted 'eathen
    but a first-class fightin' man;
    We gives you your certificate, an'
    if you want it signed
    We'll come an' 'ave a romp with
    you whenever you're inclined.

We took our chanst among the Kyber
'ills,
The Boers knocked us silly at a mile,
The Burman give us Irriwaddy chills,
An' a Zulu *impi* dished us up in style:
But all we ever got from such as they
Was pop to what the Fuzzy made us
swaller;
We 'eld our bloomin' own, the papers
say,
But man for man the Fuzzy knocked
us 'oller.

Then 'ere's *to* you, Fuzzy-Wuzzy,
an' the missis and the kid;
Our orders was to break you, an'
of course we went an' did.
We sloshed you with Martinis,
an' it wasn't 'ardly fair;
But for all the odds agin' you,
Fuzzy-Wuz you broke the
square.

'E 'asn't got no papers of 'is own,
'E 'asn't got no medals nor rewards,
So we must certify the skill 'e's shown
In usin' of 'is long two-'anded swords:
When 'e's 'oppin' in an' out among the
bush
With 'is coffin-'eaded shield an'
shovel-spear,
An 'appy day with Fuzzy on the rush
Will last an 'ealthy Tommy for a
year.
    So 'ere's *to* you, Fuzzy-Wuzzy,
    an' your friends which are no
    more,
    If we 'adn't lost some messmates
    we would 'elp you to deplore;
    But give an' take's the gospel, an'
    we'll call the bargain fair,
    For if you 'ave lost more than
    us, you crumpled up the
    square!

'E rushes at the smoke when we let
drive,

An', before we know, 'e's 'ackin' at
  our 'ead;
'E's all 'ot sand an' ginger when alive,
  An' 'e's generally shammin' when 'e's
  dead.
'E's a daisy, 'e's a ducky, 'e's a lamb!
  'E's a injia-rubber idiot on the spree,
'E's the on'y thing that doesn't give a
  damn
  For a Regiment o' British Infantree!

So 'ere's *to* you, Fuzzy-Wuzzy
  at your 'ome in the Soudan;
You're a pore benighted 'eathen
  but a first-class fightin' man;
An' 'ere's *to* you, Fuzzy-Wuzzy,
  with your 'ayrick 'ead of 'air—
You big black boundin' beggar—
  for you broke a British square!

———— • ————

Soldier, Soldier

"SOLDIER, soldier, come from the wars,
Why don't you march with my true
  love?"
"We're fresh from off the ship an' 'e's
  maybe give the slip,
An' you'd best go look for a new love."

  New love! True love!
  Best go look for a new love,
  The dead they cannot rise, an'
    you'd better dry your eyes,
  An' you'd best go look for a new
    love.

"Soldier, soldier, come from the wars,
What did you see o' my true love?"
"I seed 'im serve the Queen in a suit
  o' rifle-green,
An' you'd best go look for a new love."

"Soldier, soldier, come from the wars,
Did ye see no more o' my true love?"
"I seed 'im runnin' by when the shots
  began to fly—
But you'd best go look for a new love."

"Soldier, soldier, come from the wars,
Did aught take 'arm to my true love?"
"I couldn't see the fight, for the smoke
  it lay so white—
An' you'd best go look for a new love."

"Soldier, soldier, come from the wars,
I'll up an' tend to my true love!"
"'E's lying on the dead with a bullet
  through 'is 'ead,
An' you'd best go look for a new love."

"Soldier, soldier, come from the wars,
I'll down an' die with my true love!"
"The pit we dug'll 'ide 'im an' the
  twenty men beside 'im—
An' you'd best go look for a new love."

"Soldier, soldier, come from the wars,
Do you bring no sign from my true
  love?"
"I bring a lock of 'air that 'e allus used
  to wear,
An' you'd best go look for a new love."

"Soldier, soldier, come from the wars,
O then I know it's true I've lost my
    true love!"
"An' I tell you the truth again—when
    you've lost the feel o' pain
You'd best take me for your true love."

True love! New love!
Best take 'im for a new love.
The dead they cannot rise, an'
    you'd better dry your eyes,
An' you'd best take 'im for your
    true love.

Screw-Guns

SMOKIN' my pipe on the mountings,
    sniffin' the mornin' cool,
I walks in my old brown gaiters along
    o' my old brown mule,
With seventy gunners be'ind me, an'
    never a beggar forgets
It's only the pick of the Army that
    handles the dear little pets—'Tss!
    'Tss!

For you all love the screw-guns,
    the screw-guns they all love
    you!
So when we call round with a few
    guns, o' course you will know
    what to do—hoo! hoo!
Jest send in your Chief an' sur-
    render—it's worse if you fights
    or you runs:
You can go where you please,
    you can skid up the trees, but
    you don't get away from the
    guns.

They sends us along where the roads are,
    but mostly we goes where they
    ain't:
We'd climb up the side of a sign-board
    an' trust to the stick o' the paint:

We've chivied the Naga an' Looshai,
    we've give the Afreedeeman fits,
For we fancies ourselves at two thou-
    sand, we guns that are built in two
    bits—'Tss! 'Tss!
    For you all love the screw-guns,
    etc.

If a man doesn't work, why, we drills
    'im an' teaches 'im 'ow to behave;
If a beggar can't march, why, we kills
    'im an' rattles 'im into 'is grave.
You've got to stand up to our business
    an' spring without snatchin' or fuss.
D'you say that you sweat with the field-
    guns? By God, you must lather
    with us—'Tss! 'Tss!
    For you all love the screw-guns,
    etc.

The eagles is screamin' around us, the
    river's a-moanin' below,
We're clear o' the pine an' the oak-scrub,
    we're out on the rocks an' the snow,
An' the wind is as thin as a whip-lash
    what carries away to the plains
The rattle an' stamp o' the lead-mules—
    the jinglety-jink o' the chains—
    'Tss! 'Tss!
    For you all love the screw-guns,
    etc.

There's a wheel on the Horns o' the
Mornin', an' a wheel on the edge o'
the Pit,
An' a drop into nothin' beneath you as
straight as a beggar can spit:
With the sweat runnin' out o' your shirt-
sleeves, an' the sun off the snow in
your face,
An' 'arf o' the men on the drag-ropes
to hold the old gun in 'er place—
'Tss! 'Tss!
For you all love the screw-guns,
etc.

Smokin' my pipe on the mountings,
sniffin' the mornin' cool,
I climbs in my old brown gaiters along
o' my old brown mule.

The monkey can say what our road was
—the wild-goat 'e knows where we
passed.
Stand easy, you long-eared old darlin's!
Out drag-ropes! With shrapnel!
Hold fast—'Tss! 'Tss!

For you all love the screw-guns—
the screw-guns they all love
you!
So when we take tea with a few
guns, o' course you will know
what to do—hoo! hoo!
Just send in your Chief and surrender—it's worse if you fights
or you runs:
You may hide in the caves,
they'll be only your graves, but
you can't get away from the
guns!

---·---

Gunga Din

You may talk o' gin and beer
When you're quartered safe out 'ere,
An' you're sent to penny-fights an' Al-
dershot it;
But when it comes to slaughter
You will do your work on water,
An' you'll lick the bloomin' boots of 'im
that's got it,
Now in Injia's sunny clime,
Where I used to spend my time
A-servin' of 'Er Majesty the Queen,
Of all them blackfaced crew
The finest man I knew
Was our regimental bhisti, Gunga Din.
He was "Din! Din! Din!

You limping lump o' brick-dust, Gunga
Din!
Hi! slippery hitherao!
Water! get it! Panee lao![1]
You squidgy-nosed old idol,
Gunga Din."

The uniform 'e wore
Was nothin' much before,
An' rather less than 'arf o' that be'ind,
For a piece o' twisty rag
An' a goatskin water-bag
Was all the field-equipment 'e could find.

[1] Bring water swiftly.

When the sweatin' troop-train lay
In a sidin' through the day,
Where the 'eat would make your
    bloomin' eyebrows crawl,
We shouted "Harry By!"[1]
Till our throats were brick-dry,
Then we wopped 'im cause 'e couldn't
    serve us all.
        It was "Din! Din! Din!
        You 'eathen, where the mischief
            'ave you been?
        You put some juldee[2] in it
        Or I'll marrow you this minute[3]
        If you don't fill up my helmet,
            Gunga Din!"

        'E would dot an' carry one
        Till the longest day was done;
    An' 'e didn't seem to know the use o'
        fear.
        If we charged or broke or cut,
        You could bet your bloomin' nut,
    'E'd be waitin' fifty paces right flank
        rear.
        With 'is mussick[4] on 'is back,
        'E would skip with our attack,
    An' watch us till the bugles made "Re-
        tire,"
        An' for all 'is dirty 'ide
        'E was white, clear white, inside
    When 'e went to tend the wounded un-
        der fire!
        It was "Din! Din! Din!"
    With the bullets kickin' dust-spots on
        the green
        When the cartridges ran out,
        You could hear the front-files
            shout,
    "Hi! ammunition-mules an' Gunga
        Din!"

        I shan't forgit the night
        When I dropped be'ind the fight
    With a bullet where my belt-plate
        should 'a' been.
        I was chokin' mad with thirst
        An' the man that spied me first
    Was our good old grinnin', gruntin'
        Gunga Din.
        'E lifted up my 'ead,
        An' he plugged me where I bled,
    An' 'e guv me 'arf-a-pint o' water-
        green:
        It was crawlin' and it stunk,
        But of all the drinks I've drunk,
    I'm gratefullest to one from Gunga Din.
        It was "Din! Din! Din!"
    'Ere's a beggar with a bullet though
        'is spleen,
        'E's chawin' up the ground,
        An' 'e's kickin' all around:
    For Gawd's sake git the water, Gunga
        Din!

        'E carried me away
        To where a dooli lay,
    An' a bullet come an' drilled the beggar
        clean.
        'E put me safe inside,
        An' just before 'e died:
    "I hope you liked your drink," sez
        Gunga Din.
        So I'll meet 'im later on
        At the place where 'e is gone—
    Where it's always double drill and no
        canteen;
        'E'll be squattin' on the coals,
        Givin' drink to poor damned
            souls,
    An' I'll get a swig in hell from Gunga
        Din!
        Yes, Din! Din! Din!

---

[1] Mr. Atkins' equivalent   [2] Be quick.
    for "O brother."
[3] Hit you.   [4] Water skin.

You Lazarushian-leather Gunga Din!
Though I've belted you and
flayed you,

By the living Gawd that made
you,
You're a better man than I am, Gunga
Din!

———•———

Oonts

(NORTHERN INDIA TRANSPORT TRAIN)

WOT makes the soldier's 'eart to penk,
wot makes him to perspire?
It isn't standin' up to charge nor lyin'
down to fire;
But it's everlastin' waitin' on a everlastin' road
For the commissariat camel an' 'is commissariat load.
O the oont,[1] O the oont, O the
commissariat oont!
With 'is silly neck a-bobbin' like
a basket full o' snakes;
We packs 'im like an idol, an' you
ought to 'ear 'im grunt,
An' when we gets 'im loaded up
'is blessed girth-rope breaks.

Wot makes the rear-guard swear so
'ard when night is drorin' in,
An' every native follower is shiverin' for
'is skin?
It ain't the chanst o' being rushed by
Paythans from the 'ills,
It's the commissariat camel puttin' on
'is bloomin' frills!
O the oont, O the oont, O the hairy
scary oont!

[1] Camel—*oo* is pronounced like *u* in "bull,"
but by Mr. Atkins to rhyme with "front."

A-trippin' over tent-ropes when
we've got the night alarm!
We socks 'im with a stretcher-pole
an' 'eads 'im off in front,
An' when we've saved 'is bloomin' life 'e chaws our bloomin'
arm.

The 'orse 'e knows above a bit, the
bullock's but a fool,
The elephant's a gentleman, the battery-
mule's a mule;
But the commissariat cam-u-el, when
all is said an' done,
'E's a devil an' a ostrich an' a orphan-
child in one.
O the oont, O the oont, O the
Gawd-forsaken oont!
The lumpy-'umpy 'ummin'-bird
a-singin' where 'e lies,
'E's blocked the whole division
from the rear-guard to the
front,
An' when we get him up again—
the beggar goes an' dies!

'E'll gall an' chafe an' lame an' fight—
'e smells most awful vile!
'E'll lose 'isself forever if you let 'im
stray a mile;

'E's game to graze the 'ole day long an'
　'owl the 'ole night through,
An' when 'e comes to greasy ground 'e
　splits 'isself in two.
　　　O the oont, O the oont, O the
　　　　floppin', droppin' oont!
　　　When 'is long legs give from un-
　　　　der an' 'is meltin' eye is dim,
　　　The tribes is up be'ind us, and the
　　　　tribes is out in front—
　　　　It ain't no jam for Tommy, but
　　　　　it's kites an' crows for 'im.

So when the cruel march is done, an'
　when the roads is blind,

An' when we sees the camp in front an'
　'ears the shots be'ind,
Ho then we strips 'is saddle off, and all
　'is woes is past:
'E thinks on us that used 'im so, and
　gets revenge at last.
　　　O the oont, O the oont, O the
　　　　floatin', bloatin' oont!
　　　The late lamented camel in the
　　　　water-cut 'e lies;
　　　We keeps a mile behind 'im an' we
　　　　keeps a mile in front,
　　　But 'e gets into the drinkin'-
　　　　casks, and then o' course we
　　　　dies.

Loot

If you've ever stole a pheasant-egg
　be'ind the keeper's back,
　If you've ever snigged the washin'
　　from the line,
If you've every crammed a gander in
　your bloomin' 'aversack,
　You will understand this little song
　　o' mine.
But the service rules are 'ard, and from
　such we are debarred,
　For the same with English morals
　　does not suit.
　　　(Cornet: Toot! toot!)
W'y, they call a man a robber if 'e
　stuffs 'is marchin' clobber
With the—

(Chorus.) Loo! loo! Lulu! lulu!
　　　Loo loo! Loot! loot! loot!
　　　　Ow the loot!
　　　　Bloomin' loot!

That's the thing to make the boys
　git up an' shoot!
　It's the same with dogs an' men,
　If you'd make 'em come again
Clap 'em forward with a Loo! loo!
　Lulu! Loot!
(ff) Whoopee! Tear 'im, puppy! Loo!
　loo!
　Lulu! Loot! loot! loot!
If you've knocked a nigger edgeways
　when 'e's thrustin' for your life,
　You must leave 'im very carefui
　　where 'e fell;
An' may thank your stars an' gaiters if
　you didn't feel 'is knife
　That you ain't told off to bury 'im
　　as well.
Then the sweatin' Tommies wonder as
　they spade the beggars under
　Why lootin' should be entered as a
　　crime;

So if my song you'll 'ear, I will learn
     you plain an' clear
  'Ow to pay yourself for fightin' over-
     time
     (*Chorus.*) With the loot, etc.
Now remember when you're 'acking
     round a gilded Burma god
  That 'is eyes is very often precious
     stones;
An' if you treat a nigger to a dose o'
     cleanin'-rod
  'Es like to show you everything 'e
     owns.
When 'e won't prodooce no more, pour
     some water on the floor
  Where you 'ear it answer 'ollow to the
     boot
     (*Cornet:* Toot! toot!)—
When the ground begins to sink, shove
     your baynick down the chink,
  An' you're sure to touch the—
(*Chorus.*) Loo! loo! Lulu! Loot!
     loot! loot!
          Ow the loot! etc.

When from 'ouse to 'ouse you're 'un-
     ting, you must always work in
     pairs—
  It 'alves the gain, but safer you will
     find—
For a single man gets bottle on them
     twisty-wisty stairs,
  An' a woman comes and clobs 'im
     from be'ind.
When you've turned 'em inside out, an'
     it seems beyond a doubt

As if there weren't enough to dust a
     flute
     (*Cornet:* Toot! toot!)—
Before you sling your 'ook, at the
     'ouse-tops take a look,
  For it's underneath the tiles they 'ide
     the loot.
     (*Chorus.*) Ow the loot, etc.

You can mostly square a Sergint an' a
     Quartermaster too,
  If you only take the proper way to
     go;
I could never keep my pickin's, but
     I've learned you all I knew—
  An' don't you never say I told you so.
An' now I'll bid good-bye, for I'm
     gettin' rather dry,
  An' I see another tunin' up to toot
     (*Cornet:* Toot! toot!)—
So 'ere's good-luck to those that wears
     the Widow's clo'es,
  An' the Devil send 'em all they want
     o' loot!
     (*Chorus.*) Yes, the loot,
               Bloomin' loot.
  In the tunic an' the mess-tin an' the
     boot!
     It's the same with dogs an' men,
     If you'd make 'em come again
  (*fff*) Whoop 'em forward with a Loo!
     loo! Lulu! Loot! loot! loot!
Heeya! Sick 'im, puppy! Loo! loo!
     Lulu! Loot! loot! loot!

"Snarleyow"

THIS 'appened in a battle to a batt'ry
of the corps
Which is first among the women an'
amazin' first in war;
An' what the bloomin' battle was I
don't remember now,
But Two's off-lead 'e answered to the
name o' *Snarleyow*.

Down in the Infantry, nobody
cares;
Down in the Cavalry, Colonel 'e
swears;
But down in the lead with the
wheel at the flog
Turns the bold Bombardier to a
little whipped dog!

They was movin' into action, they was
needed very sore,
To learn a little schoolin' to a native
army corps,
They 'ad nipped against an uphill, they
was tuckin' down the brow,
When a tricky, trundlin' round-shot give
the knock to *Snarleyow*.

They cut 'im loose an' left 'im—'e was
almost tore in two—
But he tried to follow after as a well-
trained 'orse should do;
'E went an' fouled the limber, an' the
Driver's Brother squeals:
"Pull up, pull up for *Snarleyow*—'is
'ead's between 'is 'eels!"

The Driver 'umped 'is shoulder, for the
wheels was goin' round,
An' there aren't no "Stop, conductor!"
when a batt'ry's changin' ground;
Sez 'e: "I broke the beggar in, an' very
sad I feels,
But I could't pull up, not for *you*—your
'ead between your 'eels!"

'E 'adn't 'ardly spoke the word, before
a droppin' shell
A little right the batt'ry an' between the
sections fell;
An' when the smoke 'ad cleared away,
before the limber wheels,
There lay the Driver's Brother with 'is
'ead between 'is 'eels.

Then sez the Driver's Brother, an' 'is
words was very plain,
"For Gawd's own sake get over me, an'
put me out o' pain."
They saw 'is wounds was mortial, an'
they judged that it was best,
So they took an' drove the limber
straight across 'is back an' chest.

The Driver 'e give nothin' 'cept a little
coughin' grunt,
But 'e swung 'is 'orses 'andsome when
it came to "Action front!"
An' if one wheel was juicy, you may
lay your Monday head
'Twas juicier for the niggers when the
case begun to spread.

The moril of this story, it is plainly to
be seen:
You 'avn't got no families when servin'
of the Queen—
You 'avn't got no brothers, fathers, sisters, wives, or sons—
If you want to win your battles take an'
work your bloomin' guns!

Down in the Infantry, nobody
cares;
Down in the Cavalry, Colonel 's
swears;
But down in the lead with the
wheel at the flog
Turns the bold Bombardier to a
little whipped dog!

The Widow At Windsor

'AVE you 'eard o' the Widow at
Windsor
With a hairy gold crown on 'er 'ead?
She 'as ships on the foam—she 'as
millions at 'ome,
An' she pays us poor beggars in red.
(Ow, poor beggars in red!)
There's 'er nick on the cavalry 'orses,
There's 'er mark on the medical
stores—
An' 'er troopers you'll find with a fair
wind be'ind
That takes us to various wars.
(Poor beggars!—barbarious wars!)

    Then 'ere's to the Widow at
    Windsor,
      An' 'ere's to the stores an' the
      guns,
    The men an' the 'orses what
    makes up the forces
    O' Missis Victorier's sons.
      (Poor beggars! Victorier's
      sons!)

Walk wide o' the Widow at Windsor,
For 'alf o' Creation she owns:

We 'ave bought 'er the same with the
sword an' the flame,
An' we've salted it down with our
bones.
(Poor beggars!—it's blue with our
bones!)
Hands off o' the sons of the Widow,
Hands off o' the goods in 'er shop,
For the Kings must come down an' the
Emperors frown
When the Widow at Windsor says
"Stop!"
(Poor beggars!—we're sent to say
"Stop!")

    Then 'ere's to the Lodge o' the
    Widow,
      From the Pole to the Tropics
      it runs—
    To the Lodge that we tile with
    the rank an' the file,
    An' open in form with the guns.
      (Poor beggars!—it's always
      they guns!)

We 'ave 'eard o' the Widow at Windsor,
It's safest to leave 'er alone:

For 'er sentries we stand by the sea an'
 the land
Wherever the bugles are blown.
 (Poor beggars!—an' don't we get
 blown!)
Take 'old o' the Wings o' the Mornin',
An' flop round the earth till you're
 dead;
But you won't get away from the tune
 that they play

To the bloomin' old Rag over'ead.
 (Poor beggars!—it's 'ot over'ead!)

Then 'ere's to the sons o' the
 Widow
Wherever, 'owever they roam.
'Ere's all they desire, an' if they
 require
A speedy return to their 'ome.
 (Poor beggars! — they'll
 never see 'ome!)

———•———

Belts

THERE was a row in Silver Street that's
 near to Dublin Quay,
Between an Irish regiment an' English
 cavalree;
It started at Revelly an' it lasted on
 till dark:
The first man dropped at Harrison's, the
 last fornist the Park.

 For it was "Belts, belts, belts, an'
  that's one for you!"
 An' it was "Belts, belts, belts, an'
  that's done for you!"
 O buckle an' tongue
 Was the song that we sung
 From Harrison's down to the Park!

There was a row in Silver Street—the
 regiments was out,
They called us "Delhi Rebels," an' we
 answered "Three about!"
That drew them like a hornet's nest—
 we met them good an' large,
The English at the double an' the Irish
 at the charge.
  Then it was: Belts—

There was a row in Silver Street—an' 1
 was in it too;
We passed the time o' day, an' then the
 belts went whirraru!
I misremember what occurred, but subsequint the storm
A *Freeman's Journal Supplemint* was
 all my uniform.
  O it was: Belts—

There was a row in Silver Street—they
 sent the Polis there,
The English were too drunk to know,
 the Irish didn't care;
But when they grew impertinint we
 simultaneous rose,
Till half o' them was Liffey mud an'
 half was tatthered clo'es.
  For it was: Belts—

There was a row in Silver Street—it
 might ha' raged till now,
But some one drew his side-arm clear,
 an' nobody knew how;
'Twas Hogan took the point an'
 dropped; we saw the red blood run:

An' so we all was murderers that started
    cut in fun.
            While it was: Belts—

There was a row in Silver Street—but
    that put down the shine,
Wid each man whisperin' to his next:
    " 'Twas never work o' mine!"
We went away like beaten dogs, an'
    down the street we bore him,
The poor dumb corpse that coudn't tell
    the bhoys were sorry for him.
            When it was: Belts—

There was a row in Silver Street—it
    isn't over yet,
For half of us are under guard wid
    punishments to get;
'Tis all a miracle to me as in the Clink
    I lie:
There was a row in Silver Street—be-
    god, I wonder why!
        But it was "Belts, belts, belts, an'
            that's one for you!"
        An' it was "Belts, belts, belts, an'
            that's done for you!"
        O buckle and tongue
        Was the song that we sung
        From Harrison's down to the Park!

———— • ————

The Young British Soldier

WHEN the 'arf-made recruity goes out
    to the East
'E acts like a babe an' 'e drinks like a
    beast,
An' 'e wonders because 'e is frequent
    deceased
        Ere 'e's fit for to serve as a soldier,
        Serve, serve, serve as a soldier,
        Serve, serve, serve as a soldier,
        Serve, serve, serve as a soldier,
        So-oldier of the Queen!

Now all you recruities what's drafted
    to-day,
You shut up your rag-box an' 'ark to
    my lay,
An' I'll sing you a soldier as far as I
    may:
        A soldier what's fit for a soldier.
        Fit, fit, fit for a soldier.

First mind you steer clear o' the grog-
    sellers' huts,
For they sell you Fixed Bay'nets that
    rots out your guts—
Ay, drink that 'ud eat the live steel from
    your butts—
        An' it's bad for the young British
            soldier.
        Bad, bad, bad for the soldier.

When the cholera comes—as it will past
    a doubt—
Keep out of the wet and don't go on
    the shout,
For the sickness gets in as the liquor
    dies out,
        An' it crumples the young British
            soldier.
        Crum-, crum-, crumples the sol-
            dier. . . .

But the worst o' your foes is the sun
over'ead:
You *must* wear your 'elmet for all that
is said:
If 'e finds you uncovered 'e'll knock you
down dead,
    An' you'll die like a fool of a sol-
    dier.
      Fool, fool, fool of a soldier. . . .
If you're cast for fatigue by a sergeant
unkind,
Don't grouse like a woman nor crack on
nor blind;
Be handy and civil and then you will
find
    That it's beer for the young British
    soldier.
      Beer, beer, beer for the sol-
      dier. . . .
Now, if you must marry, take care she
is old—
A troop-sergeant's widow's the nicest
I'm told—
For beauty won't help if your rations
is cold,
    Not love ain't enough for a soldier.
      'Nough, 'nough, 'nough for a
      soldier. . . .
If the wife should go wrong with a com-
rade, be loth
To shoot when you catch 'em—you'll
swing, on my oath!—
Make 'im take 'er and keep 'er: that's
Hell for them both.
    An' you're shut o' the curse of a
    soldier.
      Curse, curse, curse o' a soldier . . .
When first under fire an' you're wishful
to duck,
Don't look nor take 'eed at the man that
is struck,
Be thankful you're livin', and trust to
your luck

And march to your front like a
soldier.
    Front, front, front like a sol-
    dier. . . .
When 'arf of your bullets fly wide in
the ditch,
Don't call your Martini a cross-eyed
old bitch;
She's human as you are—you treat her
as sich,
    An' she'll fight for the young
    British soldier.
      Fight, fight, fight for the
      soldier. . . .
When shakin' their bustles like ladies so
fine,
The guns o' the enemy wheel into line;
Shoot low at the limbers an' don't mind
the shine,
    For noise never startles the soldier.
      Start-, start-, startles the sol-
      dier. . . .
If your officer's dead and the sergeants
look white,
Remember it's ruin to run from a fight:
So take open order, lie down, and sit
tight,
    And wait for supports like a sol-
    dier.
      Wait, wait, wait like a sol-
      dier. . .
When you're wounded and left on
Afghanistan's plains,
And the women come out to cut up
what remains,
Jest roll to your rifle and blow out your
brains
    An' go to your Gawd like a soldier.
      Go, go, go like a soldier,
      Go, go, go like a soldier,
      Go, go, go like a soldier,
        So-oldier *of* the Queen!

Mandalay

By the old Moulmein Pagoda, lookin'
eastward to the sea,
There's a Burma girl a-settin', and I
know she thinks o' me;
For the wind is in the palm-trees, and
the temple-bells they say:
"Come you back, you British soldier;
come you back to Mandalay!"

Come you back to Mandalay,
Where the old Flotilla lay:
Can't you 'ear their paddles chun-
kin' from Rangoon to Mandalay?
On the road to Mandalay,
Where the flyin'-fishes play,
An' the dawn comes up like thun-
der outer China 'crost the Bay!

'Er petticoat was yeller an' 'er little cap
was green,
An' 'er name was Supi-yaw-lat—jes' the
same as Theebaw's Queen,
An' I seed her first a-smokin' of a
whackin' white cheroot,
An' a-wastin' Christian kisses on an
'eathen idol's foot:
Bloomin' idol made o' mud—
What they called the Great Gawd
Budd—
Plucky lot she cared for idols when
I kissed 'er where she stud!
On the road to Mandalay, etc.

When the mist was on the rice-fields an'
the sun was droppin' slow,
She'd get 'er little banjo an' she'd sing
"Kulla-lo-lo!"

With 'er arm upon my shoulder an' er
cheek agin my cheek
We useter watch the steamers an' the
hathis pilin' teak.

Elephints a-pilin' teak
In the sludgy, squdgy creek,
Where the silence 'ung that 'eavy
you was 'arf afraid to speak!
On the road to Mandalay, etc.

But that's all shove be'ind me—long ago
an' fur away,
An' there ain't no 'busses runnin' from
the Bank to Mandalay;
An' I'm learnin' 'ere in London what
the ten-year soldier tells:
"If you've 'eard the East a-callin', you
won't never 'eed naught else."

No! you won't 'eed nothin' else
But them spicy garlic smells,
An' the sunshine an' the palm-trees
an' the tinky temple-bells;
On the road to Mandalay, etc.

I am sick o' wastin' leather on these
gritty pavin'-stones,
An' the blasted Henglish drizzle wakes
the fever in my bones;
Tho' I walks with fifty 'ousemaids outer
Chelsea to the Strand,
An' they talks a lot o' lovin', but wot
do they understand?

Beefy face an' grubby 'and—
Law! wot do they understand?
I've a neater, sweeter maiden in a
cleaner, greener land!
On the road to Mandalay, etc.

Ship me somewhere east of Suez, where
the best is like the worst,
Where there aren't no Ten Commandments an' a man can raise a thirst;
For the temple-bells are callin', and it's
there that I would be—

By the old Moulmein Pagoda, looking
lazy at the sea;
   On the road to Mandalay,
   Where the old Flotilla lay,
   With our sick beneath the awnings
      when we went to Mandalay!
   On the road to Mandalay,
   Where the flyin'-fishes play,
   An' the dawn comes up like thun-
      der outer China 'crost the Bay!

———•———

Troopin'

(OUR ARMY IN THE EAST)

TROOPIN', troopin', troopin' to the sea:
'Ere's September come again—the six-
year men are free.
O leave the dead be'ind us, for they
cannot come away
To where the ship's a-coalin' up that
takes us 'ome to-day.

   We're goin' 'ome, we're goin' 'ome,
   Our ship is *at* the shore,
   An' you must pack your 'aversack,
   For we won't come back no more.
   Ho, don't you grieve for me,
   My lovely Mary-Ann,
   For I'll marry you yit on a
      fourp'ny bit
   As a time-expired man!

The Malabar's in 'arbor with the Jumner
at 'er tail,
An' the time-expired's waitin' of 'is orders for to sail.

Ho! the weary waitin' when on Khyber
'ills we lay,
But the time-expired's waitin' of 'is orders 'ome to-day.

They'll turn us out at Portsmouth wharf
in cold an' wet an' rain,
All wearin' Injian cotton kit, but we will
not complain;
They'll kill us of pneumonia—for that's
their little way—
But damn the chills and fever, men,
we're goin' 'ome to day!

Troopin', troopin', winter's round again!
See the new draf's pourin' in for the old
campaign;
Ho, you poor recruities, but you've got
to earn your pay—
What's the last from Lunnon, lads?
We're goin' there to-day.

Troopin', troopin', give another cheer—
'Ere's to English women an' a quart of
   English beer;
The Colonel an' the regiment an' all
   who've got to stay,
Gawd's mercy strike 'em gentle—
   Whoop! we're goin' 'ome to day.

We're goin' 'ome, we're goin' 'ome,
Our ship is at the shore,
An' you must pack your 'aversack,
For we won't come back no more.
Ho, don't you grieve for me,
My lovely Mary- Ann,
For I'll marry you yit on a
   fourp'ny bit
As a time-expired man.

Ford O' Kabul River

KABUL town's by Kabul river—
  Blow the bugle, draw the sword—
There I lef' my mate forever,
  Wet an' drippin' by the ford.
    Ford, ford, ford o' Kabul river,
      Ford o' Kabul river in the dark!
    There's the river up and brimmin',
      an' there's 'arf a squadron
      swimmin'
      'Cross the ford o' Kabul river in
      the dark.

Kabul town's a blasted place—
  Blow the bugle, draw the sword—
'Strewth I shan't forget 'is face
  Wet an' drippin' by the ford!
    Ford, ford, ford o' Kabul river,
      Ford o' Kabul river in the dark!
    Keep the crossing-stakes beside you,
      an' they will surely guide you
      'Cross the ford of Kabul river in
      the dark.

Kabul town is sun and dust—
  Blow the bugle, draw the sword—
I'd ha' sooner drownded fust
  'Stead of 'im beside the ford.

Ford, ford, ford o' Kabul river,
  Ford o' Kabul river in the dark!
You can 'ear the 'orses threshin',
   you can 'ear the men
   a-splashin',
   'Cross the ford o' Kabul river in
   the dark.

Kabul town was ours to take—
  Blow the bugle, draw the sword—
I'd ha' left it for 'is sake—
  'Im that left me by the ford.
    Ford, ford, ford o' Kabul river,
      Ford o' Kabul river in the dark!
    It's none so bloomin' dry there;
      ain't you never comin' nigh
      there,
      'Cross the ford o' Kabul river in
      the dark?

Kabul town'll go to hell—
  Blow the bugle, draw the sword—
'For I see him 'live an' well—
  'Im the best beside the ford.
    Ford, ford, ford o' Kabul river,
      Ford o' Kabul river in the dark!

Gawd 'elp 'em if they blunder, for
     their boots'll pull 'em under,
By the ford o' Kabul river in the
     dark.

Turn your 'orse from Kabul town—
Blow the bugle, draw the sword—

'Im an' 'arf my troop is down,
     Down an' drownded by the ford.
     Ford, ford, ford o' Kabul river,
          Ford o' Kabul river in the dark!
     There's the river low an' fallin', but
          it ain't no use o' callin'
          'Cross the ford o' Kabul river in
          the dark.

————•————

Route-Marchin'

WE'RE marchin' on relief over Injia's
     sunny plains,
A little front o' Christmas time an' just
     be'ind the Rains,
Ho! get away, you bullock-man, you've
     'eard the bugle blowed,
There's a regiment a-comin' down the
     Grand Trunk Road;
     With its best foot first
     And the road a-sliding past,
     An' every bloomin' campin'-ground
          exactly like the last;
     While the Big Drum says,
     With 'is *"rowdy-dowdy-dow!"*—
     "Kiko kissywarsti don't you *kam-
     sher argy-jow?"*

Oh, there's them Injian temples to ad-
     mire when you see,
There's the peacock round the corner
     an' the monkey up the tree,
An' there's that rummy silver grass
     a-wavin' in the wind,
An' the old Grand Trunk a trailin' like
     a rifle-sling be'ind.
     While it's best foot first, etc.

At half-past five's Revelly, an' our
     tents they down must come,

Like a lot of button mushrooms when
     you pick 'em up at 'ome.
But it's over in a minute, an' at six
     the column starts,
While the women and the kiddies sit an'
     shiver in the carts.
     And it's best foot first, etc.

Oh, then it's open order, an' we lights
     our pipes an' sings,
An' we talks about our rations an' a lot
     of other things.
And we thinks o' friends in England, an'
     we wonders what they're at,
An' 'ow they would admire for to hear
     us sling the *bat*.[1]
     An' it's best foot first, etc.

It's none so bad o' Sunday, when you're
     lyin' at your ease,
To watch the kites a-wheelin' round
     them feather-'eaded trees,
For although there ain't no women yet
     there ain't no barrick-yards,
So the orficers goes shootin' an' the
     men they plays at cards.
     Till it's best foot first, etc.

[1] Thomas's first and firmest conviction is
that he is a profound Orientalist and a fluent
speaker of Hindustani. As a matter of fact,
he depends largely on the sign-language.

So 'ark an' 'eed you rookies, which is
    always grumblin' sore,
There's worser things than marchin'
    from Umballa to Cawnpore;
And if your 'eels are blistered an' they
    feels to 'urt like 'ell
You drop some tallow in your socks an'
    that will make 'em well.
      For it's best foot first, etc.

We're marchin' on relief over Injia's
    coral strand,
Eight 'undred fightin' Englishmen, the
    Colonel, *and* the Band.

Ho! get away, you bullock-man, you've
    'eard the bugle blowed,
There's a regiment a-comin' down the
    Grand Trunk Road.
    With its best foot first
    And the road a-sliding past,
    An' every bloomin' campin'-ground
      exactly like the last;
    While the Big Drum says,
    With 'is *"rowdy-dowdy-dow!"*—
    "Kiko kissywarsti don't you *ham\
    sher argy-jow?"*[1]

    [1] Why don't you get on?

VOLUME II

The Light That Failed

The Light That Failed

CHAPTER I

So we settled it all when the storm was done
As comf'y as comf'y could be;
And I was to wait in the barn, my dears,
Because I was only three,
And Teddy would run to the rainbow's foot,
Because he was five and a man;
And that's how it all began, my dears,
And that's how it all began.
                                                —*Big Barn Stories.*

"WHAT do you think she'd do if she caught us? We oughtn't to have it, you know," said Maisie.

"Beat me, and lock you up in your bedroom," Dick answered, without hesitation. "Have you got the cartridges?"

"Yes; they're in my pocket, but they are joggling horribly. Do pin-fire cartridges go off of their own accord?"

"Don't know. Take the revolver, if you are afraid, and let me carry them."

"I'm *not* afraid." Maisie strode forward swiftly, a hand in her pocket and her chin in the air. Dick followed with a small pin-fire revolver.

The children had discovered that their lives would be unendurable without pistol-practice. After much forethought and self-denial, Dick had saved seven shillings and sixpence, the price of a badly-constructed Belgian revolver. Maisie could only contribute half a crown to the syndicate for the purchase of a hundred cartridges. "You can save better than I can, Dick," she explained; "I like nice things to eat, and it doesn't

matter to you. Besides, boys ought to do these things."

Dick grumbled a little at the arrangement, but went out and made the purchases, which the children were then on their way to test. Revolvers did not lie in the scheme of their daily life as decreed for them by the guardian who was incorrectly supposed to stand in the place of a mother to these two orphans. Dick had been under her care for six years, during which time she had made her profit of the allowances supposed to be expended on his clothes, and, partly through thoughtlessness, partly through a natural desire to pain,—she was a widow of some years anxious to marry again,—had made his days burdensome on his young shoulders. Where he had looked for love, she gave him first aversion and then hate. Where he, growing older, had sought a little sympathy, she gave him ridicule. The many hours that she could spare from the ordering of her small house she devoted to what she called the home-training of Dick

Heldar. Her religion, manufactured in the main by her own intelligence and a keen study of the Scriptures, was an aid to her in this matter. At such times as she herself was not personally displeased with Dick, she left him to understand that he had a heavy account to settle with his Creator; wherefore Dick learned to loathe his God as intensely as he loathed Mrs. Jennett; and this is not a wholesome frame of mind for the young. Since she chose to regard him as a hopeless liar, when dread of pain drove him to his first untruth he naturally developed into a liar, but an economical and self-contained one, never throwing away the least unnecessary fib, and never hesitating at the blackest, were it only plausible, that might make his life a little easier. The treatment taught him at least the power of living alone,—a power that was of service to him when he went to a public school and the boys laughed at his clothes, which were poor in quality and much mended. In the holidays he returned to the teachings of Mrs. Jennett, and, that the chain of discipline might not be weakened by association with the world, was generally beaten, on one count or another, before he had been twelve hours under her roof.

The autumn of one year brought him a companion in bondage, a long-haired, grey-eyed little atom, as self-contained as himself, who moved about the house silently and for the first few weeks spoke only to the goat that was her chiefest friend on earth and lived in the back-garden. Mrs. Jennett objected to the goat on the grounds that he was un-Christian,—which he certainly was. "Then," said the atom, choosing her words very deliberately, "I shall write to my lawyer-peoples and tell them that you are a very bad woman. Amomma is mine, mine, mine!" Mrs. Jennett made a movement to the hall, where certain umbrellas and canes stood in a rack. The atom understood as clearly as Dick what this meant. "I have been beaten before," she said, still in the same passionless voice; "I have been beaten worse than you can ever beat me. If you beat me I shall write to my lawyer-peoples and tell them that you do not give me enough to eat. I am not afraid of you." Mrs. Jennett did not go into the hall, and the atom, after a pause to assure herself that all danger of war was past, went out, to weep bitterly on Amomma's neck.

Dick learned to know her as Maisie, and at first mistrusted her profoundly, for he feared that she might interfere with the small liberty of action left to him. She did not, however; and she volunteered no friendliness until Dick had taken the first steps. Long before the holidays were over, the stress of punishment shared in common drove the children together, if it were only to play into each other's hands as they prepared lies for Mrs. Jennett's use. When Dick returned to school, Maisie whispered, "Now I shall be all alone to take care of myself; but," and she nodded her head bravely, "I can do it. You promised to send Amomma a grass collar. Send it soon." A week later she asked for that collar by return of post, and was not pleased when she learned that it took time to make. When at last Dick forwarded the gift she forgot to thank him for it.

Many holidays had come and gone since that day, and Dick had grown into a lanky hobbledehoy more than ever conscious of his bad clothes. Not for a moment had Mrs. Jennett relaxed her tender care of him, but the average canings of a public school—Dick fell under punishment about three times a month—filled him with contempt for her powers. "She doesn't hurt," he explained to Maisie, who urged him to rebellion, "and she is kinder to you after she has whacked me." Dick shambled through the days unkept in body and savage in soul, as the smaller boys of the school learned to know, for when the spirit moved him he would hit them, cunningly and with science. The same spirit made him more than once try to tease Maisie, but the girl refused to be made unhappy. "We are both miserable as it is," said she. "What is the use of trying to make things worse? Let's find things to do, and forget things."

The pistol was the outcome of that search. It could only be used on the muddiest foreshore of the beach, far away from bathing-machines and pierheads, below the grassy slopes of Fort Keeling. The tide ran out nearly two miles on that coast and the many-colored mud-banks, touched by the sun, sent up a lamentable smell of dead weed. It was late in the afternoon when Dick and Maisie arrived on their ground, Amomma trotting patiently behind them.

"My!" said Maisie, sniffing the air. "I wonder what makes the sea so smelly. I don't like it."

"You never like anything that isn't made just for you," said Dick, bluntly. "Give me the cartridges, and I'll try first shot. How far does one of these little revolvers carry?"

"Oh, half a mile," said Maisie, promptly. "At least it makes an awful noise. Be careful with the cartridges; I don't like those jagged stick-up things on the rim. Dick, do be careful."

"All right. I know how to load. I'll fire at the breakwater out there."

He fired, and Amomma ran away bleating. The bullet threw up a spurt of mud to the right of the weed-wreathed piles.

"Throws high and to the right. You try, Maisie. Mind, it's loaded all round."

Maisie took the pistol and stepped delicately to the verge of the mud, her hand firmly closed on the butt, her mouth and left eye screwed up. Dick sat down on a tuft of bank and laughed. Amomma returned very cautiously. He was accustomed to strange experiences in his afternoon walks, and, finding the cartridge-box unguarded, made investigations with his nose. Maisie fired, but could not see where the bullet went.

"I think it hit the post," she said, shading her eyes and looking out across the sailless sea.

"I know it has gone out to the Marazion Bell Buoy," said Dick, with a chuckle. "Fire low and to the left; then perhaps you'll get it. Oh, look at Amomma!—he's eating the cartridges!"

Maisie turned, the revolver in her hand, just in time to see Amomma scampering away from the pebbles Dick threw after him. Nothing is sacred to a billy-goat. Being well fed and the adored of his mistress, Amomma had naturally swallowed two loaded pin-fire cartridges. Maisie hurried up to assure herself that Dick had not miscounted the tale.

"Yes, he's eaten two."

"Horrid little beast! Then they'll joggle about inside him and blow up, and serve him right. . . . Oh, Dick! have I killed you?"

Revolvers are tricky things for young hands to deal with. Maisie could not explain how it had happened, but a veil of reeking smoke separated her from Dick, and she was quite certain that the pistol had gone off in his face. Then she heard him sputter, and dropped on her knees beside him, crying, "Dick, you aren't hurt, are you? I didn't mean it."

"Of course you didn't," said Dick, coming out of the smoke and wiping his cheek. "But you nearly blinded me. That powder stuff stings awfully." A neat little splash of grey lead on a stone showed where the bullet had gone. Maisie began to whimper.

"Don't," said Dick, jumping to his feet and shaking himself. "I'm not a bit hurt."

"No, but I might have killed you," protested Maisie, the corners of her mouth drooping. "What should I have done then?"

"Gone home and told Mrs. Jennett." Dick grinned at the thought; then, softening, "Please don't worry about it. Beside, we are wasting time. We've got to get back to tea. I'll take the revolver for a bit."

Maisie would have wept on the least encouragement, but Dick's indifference, albeit his hand was shaking as he picked up the pistol, restrained her. She lay panting on the beach while Dick methodically bombarded the breakwater. "Got it at last!" he exclaimed, as a lock of weed flew from the wood.

"Let me try," said Maisie, imperiously. "I'm all right now."

They fired in turns till the rickety little revolver nearly shook itself to pieces, and Amomma the outcast—because he might blow up at any moment —browsed in the background and wondered why stones were thrown at him. Then they found a balk of timber floating in a pool which was commanded by the seaward slope of Fort Keeling, and they sat down together before this new target.

"Next holidays," said Dick, as the now thoroughly fouled revolver kicked wildly in his hand, "we'll get another pistol,—central fire,—that will carry farther."

"There won't be any next holidays for me," said Maisie. "I'm going away."

"Where to?"

"I don't know. My lawyers have written to Mrs. Jennett, and I've got to be educated somewhere,—in France, perhaps,—I don't know where; but I shall be glad to go away."

"I shan't like it a bit. I suppose I shall be left. Look here, Maisie, is it really true you're going? Then these holidays will be the last I shall see anything of you; and I go back to school next week. I wish"—

The young blood turned his cheeks scarlet. Maisie was picking grass-tufts and throwing them down the slope at a yellow sea-poppy nodding all by itself to the illimitable levels of the mud-flats and the milk-white sea beyond.

"I wish," she said, after a pause, "that I could see you again some time. You wish that too?"

"Yes, but it would have been better

if—if—you had—shot straight over there—down by the breakwater."

Maisie looked with large eyes for a moment. And this was the boy who only ten days before had decorated Amomma's horns with cut-paper ham-frills and turned him out, a bearded derision, among the public ways! Then she dropped her eyes: this was not the boy.

"Don't be stupid," she said, reprovingly, and with swift instinct attacked the side-issue. "How selfish you are! Just think what I should have felt if that horrid thing had killed you! I'm quite miserable enough already."

"Why? Because you're going away from Mrs. Jennett?"

"No."

"From me, then?"

No answer for a long time. Dick dared not look at her. He felt, though he did not know, all that the past four years had been to him, and this the more acutely since he had no knowledge to put his feelings in words.

"I don't know," she said. "I suppose it is."

"Maisie, you must know. *I'm* not supposing."

"Let's go home," said Maisie, weakly. But Dick was not minded to retreat. "I can't say things," he pleaded, "and I'm awfully sorry for teasing you about Amomma the other day. It's all different now, Maisie, can't you see? And you might have told me that you were going, instead of leaving me to find out."

"You didn't. I did tell. Oh, Dick, what's the use of worrying?"

"There isn't any; but we've been together years and years, and I didn't know how much I cared."

"I don't believe you ever did care."

"No, I didn't; but I do,—I care awfully now, Maisie," he gulped,—"Maisie, darling, say you care too, please."

"I do; indeed I do; but it won't be any use."

"Why?"

"Because I am going away."

"Yes, but if you promise before you go. Only say—will you?" A second "darling" came to his lips more easily than the first. There were few endearments in Dick's home or school life; he had to find them by instinct. Dick caught the little hand blackened with the escaped gas of the revolver.

"I promise," she said, solemnly; "but if I care there is no need for promising."

"And you do care?" For the first time in the last few minutes their eyes met and spoke for them who had no skill in speech. . . .

"Oh, Dick, don't! please don't! It was all right when we said good-morning; but now it's all different!" Amomma looked on from afar. He had seen his property quarrel frequently, but he had never seen kisses exchanged before. The yellow sea-poppy was wiser, and nodded its head approvingly. Considered as a kiss, that was a failure, but since it was the first, other than those demanded by duty, in all the world that either had ever given or taken, it opened to them new worlds, and every one of them glorious, so that they were lifted above the consideration of any worlds at all, especially those in which tea is necessary, and sat still, holding each other's hands and saying not a word.

"You can't forget now," said Dick at last. There was that on his cheek that **stung more than gunpowder.**

"I shouldn't have forgotten anyhow," said Maisie, and they looked at each other and saw that each was changed from the companion of an hour ago to a wonder and a mystery they could not understand. The sun began to set, and a night-wind thrashed along the bents of the foreshore.

"We shall be awfully late for tea," said Maisie. "Let's go home."

"Let's use the rest of the cartridges first," said Dick; and he helped Maisie down the slope of the fort to the sea,— a descent that she was quite capable of covering at full speed. Equally gravely Maisie took the grimy hand. Dick bent forward clumsily; Maisie drew the hand away, and Dick blushed.

"It's very pretty," he said.

"Pooh!" said Maisie, with a little laugh of gratified vanity. She stood close to Dick as he loaded the revolver for the last time and fired over the sea with a vague notion at the back of his head that he was protecting Maisie from all the evils in the world. A puddle far across the mud caught the last rays of the sun and turned into a wrathful red disc. The light held Dick's attention for a moment, and as he raised his revolver there fell upon him a renewed sense of the miraculous, in that he was standing by Maisie who had promised to care for him for an indefinite length of time till such date as— A gust of the growing wind drove the girl's long black hair across his face as she stood with her hand on his shoulder calling Amomma "a little beast," and for a moment he was in the dark,—a darkness that stung. The bullet went singing out to the empty sea.

"Spoiled my aim," said he, shaking his head. "There aren't any more car‹ tridges; we shall have to run home." But they did not run. They walked very slowly, arm in arm. And it was a matter of indifference to them whether the neglected Amomma with two pin-fire cartridges in his inside blew up or trotted beside them; for they had come into a golden heritage and were disposing of it with all the wisdom of all their years.

"And I shall be"— quoth Dick, valiantly. Then he checked himself: "I don't know what I shall be. I don't seem to be able to pass any exams., but I can make awful caricatures of the masters. Ho! ho!"

"Be an artist, then," said Maisie. "You're always laughing at my trying to draw; and it will do you good."

"I'll never laugh at anything you do," he answered. "I'll be an artist, and I'll do things."

"Artists always want money, don't they?"

"I've got a hundred and twenty pounds a year of my own. My guardians tell me I'm to have it when I come of age. That will be enough to begin with."

"Ah, I'm rich," said Maisie. "I've got three hundred a year all my own when I'm twenty-one. That's why Mrs. Jennett is kinder to me than she is to you. I wish, though, that I had somebody that belonged to me,—just a father or a mother."

"You belong to me," said Dick, "forever and ever."

"Yes, we belong—forever. It's very nice." She squeezed his arm. The kindly darkness hid them both, and, emboldened because he could only just see the profile of Maisie's cheek with the long lashes veiling the grey eyes, Dick at the front door delivered himself of the words he had been boggling over for the last two hours.

"And I—love you, Maisie," he said, in a whisper that seemed to him to ring across the world,—the world that he would to-morrow or next day set out to conquer.

There was a scene, not, for the sake of discipline, to be reported, when Mrs. Jennett would have fallen upon him, first for disgraceful unpunctuality, and secondly for nearly killing himself with a forbidden weapon.

"I was playing with it, and it went off by itself," said Dick, when the powder-pocked cheek could no longer be hidden, "but if you think you're going to lick me you're wrong. You are never going to touch me again. Sit down and give me my tea. You can't cheat us out of that, anyhow."

Mrs. Jennett gasped and became livid. Maisie said nothing, but encouraged Dick with her eyes, and he behaved abominably all that evening. Mrs. Jennett prophesied an immediate judgment of Providence and a descent into Tophet later, but Dick walked in Paradise and would not hear. Only when he was going to bed Mrs. Jennett recovered and asserted herself. He had bidden Maisie good-night with down-dropped eyes and from a distance.

"If you aren't a gentleman you might try to behave like one," said Mrs. Jennett, spitefully. "You've been quarreling with Maisie again."

This meant that the usual good-night kiss had been omitted. Maisie, white to the lips, thrust her cheek forward with a fine air of indifference, and was

duly pecked by Dick, who tramped out of the room red as fire. That night he dreamed a wild dream. He had won all the world and brought it to Maisie in a cartridge-box, but she turned it over with her foot, and, instead of saying, "Thank you," cried—"Where is the grass collar you promised for Amomma? Oh, how selfish you are!"

CHAPTER II

Then we brought the lances down, then the bugles blew,
When we went to Kandahar, ridin' two an' two,
Ridin', ridin', ridin,' two an' two,
Ta-ra-ra-ra-ra-ra-ra,
All the way to Kandahar, ridin' two an' two.
—*Barrack-Room Ballad.*

"I'm not angry with the British public, but I wish we had a few thousand of them scattered among these rocks. They wouldn't be in such a hurry to get at their morning papers then. Can't you imagine the regulation householder—Lover of Justice, Constant Reader, Paterfamilias, and all that lot—frizzling on hot gravel?"

"With a blue veil over his head, and his clothes in strips. Has any man here a needle? I've got a piece of sugar-sack."

"I'll lend you a packing-needle for six square inches of it then. Both my knees are worn through."

"Why not six square acres, while you're about it? But lend me the needle, and I'll see what I can do with the selvage. I don't think there's enough to protect my royal body from the cold blast as it is. What are you doing with that everlasting sketch-book of yours, Dick?"

"Study of our Special Correspondent repairing his wardrobe," said Dick, gravely, as the other man kicked off a pair of sorely-worn riding-breeches and began to fit a square of coarse canvas over the most obvious open space. He grunted disconsolately as the vastness of the void developed itself.

"Sugar-bags, indeed! Hi! you pilot-man there! lend me all the sails of that whale-boat."

A fez-crowned head bobbed up in the stern-sheets, divided itself into exact halves with one flashing grin, and bobbed down again. The man of the tattered breeches, clad only in a Norfolk jacket and a grey flannel shirt, went on with his clumsy sewing, while Dick chuckled over the sketch.

Some twenty whale-boats were nuzzling a sand-bank which was dotted with English soldiery of half a dozen corps, bathing or washing their clothes. A heap of boat-rollers, commissariat-boxes, sugar-bags, and flour- and small-arm-ammunition-cases showed where one of the whale-boats had been compelled to unload hastily; and a regimental carpenter was swearing aloud as he tried, on a wholly insufficient allowance of white lead, to plaster up the sun-parched gaping seams of the boat herself.

"First the bloomin' rudder snaps," said he to the world in general; "then the mast goes; an' then, s' 'elp me, when she can't do nothin' else, she opens 'erself out like a cock-eyed Chinese lotus."

"Exactly the case with my breeches, whoever you are," said the tailor, with-out looking up. "Dick, I wonder when I shall see a decent shop again."

There was no answer, save the incessant angry murmur of the Nile as it raced round a basalt-walled bend and foamed across a rock-ridge half a mile up-stream. It was as though the brown weight of the river would drive the white men back to their own country. The indescribable scent of Nile mud in the air told that the stream was falling and that the next few miles would be no light thing for the whale-boats to over-pass. The desert ran down almost to the banks, where, among grey, red, and black hillocks, a camel-corps was en-camped. No man dared even for a day lose touch of the slow-moving boats; there had been no fighting for weeks past, and throughout all that time the Nile had never spared them. Rapid had followed rapid, rock rock, and island-group island-group, till the rank and file had long since lost all count of di-rection and very nearly of time. They were moving somewhere, they did not know why, to do something, they did not know what. Before them lay the Nile, and at the other end of it was one Gordon, fighting for the dear life, in a town called Khartoum. There were columns of British troops in the desert, or in one of the many deserts; there were columns on the river; there were yet more columns waiting to embark on the river; there were fresh drafts wait-ing at Assioot and Assuan; there were lies and rumors running over the face of the hopeless land from Suakin to the Sixth Cataract, and men supposed gen-erally that there must be some one in authority to direct the general scheme of the many movements. The duty of that particular river-column was to keep the whale-boats afloat in the water, to avoid trampling on the villagers' crops when the gangs "tracked" the boats with lines thrown from midstream, to get as much sleep and food as was possible, and, above all, to press on without delay in the teeth of the churning Nile.

With the soldiers sweated and toiled the correspondents of the newspapers, and they were almost as ignorant as their companions. But it was above all things necessary that England at breakfast should be amused and thrilled and interested, whether Gordon lived or died, or half the British army went to pieces in the sands. The Soudan campaign was a picturesque one, and lent itself to vivid word-painting. Now and again a "Special" managed to get slain,—which was not altogether a disadvantage to the paper that employed him,—and more often the hand-to-hand nature of the fighting allowed of miraculous escapes which were worth telegraphing home at eighteenpence the word. There were many correspondents with many corps and columns,—from the veterans who had followed on the heels of the cavalry that occupied Cairo in '82, what time Arabi Pasha called himself king, who had seen the first miserable work round Suakin when the sentries were cut up nightly and the scrub swarmed with spears, to youngsters jerked into the business at the end of a telegraph-wire to take the place of their betters killed or invalided.

Among the seniors—those who knew every shift and change in the perplexing postal arrangements, the value of the seediest, weediest Egyptian garron offered for sale in Cairo or Alexandria, who could talk a telegraph clerk into amiability and soothe the ruffled vanity of a newly-appointed staff-officer when press regulations became burdensome— was the man in the flannel shirt, the black-browed Torpenhow. He represented the Central Southern Syndicate in the campaign, as he had represented it in the Egyptian war, and elsewhere. The syndicate did not concern itself greatly with criticisms of attack and the like. It supplied the masses, and all it demanded was picturesqueness and abundance of detail; for there is more joy in England over a soldier who insubordinately steps out of square to rescue a comrade than over twenty generals slaving even to baldness at the gross details of transport and commissariat.

He had met at Suakin a young man, sitting on the edge of a recently-abandoned redoubt about the size of a hat-box, sketching a clump of shell-torn bodies on the gravel plain.

"What are you for?" said Torpenhow. The greeting of the correspondent is that of the commercial traveler on the road.

"My own hand," said the young man, without looking up. "Have you any tobacco?"

Torpenhow waited till the sketch was finished, and when he had looked at it said, "What's your business here?"

"Nothing; there was a row, so I came. I'm supposed to be doing something down at the painting-slips among the boats, or else I'm in charge of the condenser on one of the water-ships. I've forgotten which."

"You've cheek enough to build a redoubt with," said Torpenhow, and took stock of the new acquaintance. "Do you always draw like that?"

The young man produced more sketches. "Row on a Chinese pig-boat," said he, sententiously, showing them one after another.—"Chief mate dirked by a comprador.—Junk ashore off Hakodate.—Somali muleteer being flogged.—Starshell bursting over camp at Berbera.—Slave-dhow being chased round Tajurrah Bay.—Soldier lying dead in the moonlight outside Suakin,—throat cut by Fuzzies."

"H'm!" said Torpenhow, "can't say I care for Verestchagin-and-water myself, but there's no accounting for tastes. Doing anything now, are you?"

"No. I'm amusing myself here."

Torpenhow looked at the aching desolation of the place. " 'Faith, you've queer notions of amusement. 'Got any money?"

"Enough to go on with. Look here: do you want me to do war-work?"

"*I* don't. My syndicate may, though. You can draw more than a little, and I don't suppose you care much what you get, do you?"

"Not this time. I want my chance first."

Torpenhow looked at the sketches again, and nodded. "Yes, you're right to take your first chance when you can get it."

He rode away swiftly through the Gate of the Two War-Ships, rattled across the causeway into the town, and wired to his syndicate, "Got man here, picture-work. Good and cheap. Shall I arrange? Will do letterpress with sketches."

The man on the redoubt sat swinging his legs and murmuring. "I knew the chance would come, sooner or later. By Gad, they'll have to sweat for it if I come through this business alive!"

In the evening Torpenhow was able to announce to his friend that the Central Southern Agency was willing to take him on trial, paying expenses for three months. "And, by the way, what's your name?" said Torpenhow.

"Heldar. Do they give me a free hand?"

"They've taken you on chance. You must justify the choice. You'd better stick to me. I'm going up-country with a column, and I'll do what I can for you. Give me some of your sketches taken here, and I'll send 'em along." To himself he said, "That's the best bargain the Central Southern has ever made; and they got me cheaply enough."

So it came to pass that, after some purchase of horse-flesh and arrangements financial and political, Dick was made free of the New and Honorable Fraternity of war correspondents, who all possess the inalienable right of doing as much work as they can and getting as much for it as Providence and their owners shall please. To these things are added in time, if the brother be worthy, the power of glib speech that neither man nor woman can resist when a meal or a bed is in question, the eye of a horse-coper, the skill of a cook, the constitution of a bullock, the digestion of an ostrich, and an infinite adaptability to all circumstances. But many die before they attain to this degree, and the past-masters in the craft appear for the most part in dress-clothes when they are in England, and thus their glory is hidden from the multitude.

Dick followed Torpenhow wherever

the latter's fancy chose to lead him, and between the two they managed to accomplish some work that almost satisfied themselves. It was not an easy life in any way, and under its influence the two were drawn very closely together, for they ate from the same dish, they shared the same water-bottle, and, most binding tie of all, their mails went off together. It was Dick who managed to make gloriously drunk a telegraph-clerk in a palm hut far beyond the Second Cataract, and, while the man lay in bliss on the floor, possessed himself of some laboriously acquired exclusive information, forwarded by a confiding correspondent of an opposition syndicate, made a careful duplicate of the matter, and brought the result to Torpenhow, who said that all was fair in love or war correspondence, and built an excellent descriptive article from his rival's riotous waste of words. It was Torpennow who—but the tale of their adventures, together and apart, from Philæ to the waste wilderness of Herawi and Muella, would fill many books. They had been penned into a square side by side, in deadly fear of being shot by over-excited soldiers; they had fought with baggage-camels in the chill dawn; they had jogged along in silence under blinding sun on indefatigable little Egyptian horses; and they had floundered on the shallows of the Nile when the whale-boat in which they had found a berth chose to hit a hidden rock and rip out half her bottom-planks.

Now they were sitting on the sand-bank, and the whale-boats were bringing up the remainder of the column.

"Yes," said Torpenhow, as he put the last rude stitches into his over-long-neglected gear, "it has been a beautiful business."

"The patch or the campaign?" said Dick. "Don't think much of either, myself."

"You want the Euryalus brought up above the Third Cataract, don't you? and eighty-one-ton guns at Jakdul? Now, *I'm* quite satisfied with my breeches." He turned round gravely to exhibit himself, after the manner of a clown.

"It's very pretty. Specially the lettering on the sack. G.B.T. Government Bullock Train. That's a sack from India."

"It's my initials,—Gilbert Belling Torpenhow. I stole the cloth on purpose. What the mischief are the camel-corps doing yonder?" Torpenhow shaded his eyes and looked across the scrub-strewn gravel.

A bugle blew furiously, and the men on the bank hurried to their arms and accoutrements.

" 'Pisan soldiery surprised while bathing,' " remarked Dick, calmly. "D'you remember the picture? It's by Michael Angelo; all beginners copy it. That scrub's alive with enemy."

The camel-corps on the bank yelled to the infantry to come to them, and a hoarse shouting down the river showed that the remainder of the column had wind of the trouble and was hastening to take share in it. As swiftly as a reach of still water is crisped by the wind, the rock-strewn ridges and scrub-topped hills were troubled and alive with armed men. Mercifully, it occurred to these to stand far off for a time, to shout and gesticulate joyously. One man even delivered himself of a long story. The camel-corps did not fire. They were only too glad of a little breathing-space, until some sort of square could be formed. The men on the sand-bank ran to their side; and the whale-boats, as they toiled up within shouting distance, were thrust into the nearest bank and emptied of all save the sick and a few men to guard them. The Arab orator ceased his outcries, and his friends howled.

"They look like the Mahdi's men," said Torpenhow, elbowing himself into the crush of the square; "but what thousands of 'em there are! The tribes hereabout aren't against us, I know."

"Then the Mahdi's taken another town," said Dick, "and set all these yelping devils free to chaw us up. Lend us your glass."

"Our scouts should have told us of this. We've been trapped," said a subaltern. "Aren't the camel-guns ever going to begin? Hurry up, you men!"

There was no need for any order. The men flung themselves panting against the sides of the square, for they had good reason to know that whoso was left outside when the fighting began would very probably die in an extremely unpleasant fashion. The little hundred-and-fifty-pound camel-guns posted at one corner of the square opened the ball as the square moved forward by its right to get possession of a knoll of rising ground. All had fought in this manner many times before, and there was no novelty in the entertainment: always the same hot and stifling formation, the smell of dust and leather, the same boltlike rush of the enemy, the same pressure on the weakest side of the square, the few minutes of desper-

ate hand-to-hand scuffle, and then the silence of the desert, broken only by the yells of those whom the handful of cavalry attempted to pursue. They had grown careless. The camel-guns spoke at intervals, and the square slouched forward amid the protests of the camels. Then came the attack of three thousand men who had not learned from books that it is impossible for troops in close order to attack against breech-loading fire. A few dropping shots heralded their approach, and a few horsemen led, but the bulk of the force was naked humanity mad with rage, and armed with the spear and the sword. The instinct of the desert, where there is always much war, told them that the right flank of the square was the weakest, for they swung clear of the front. The camel-guns shelled them as they passed, and opened for an instant lanes through their midst, most like those quick-closing vistas in a Kentish hop-garden seen when the train races by at full speed; and the infantry fire, held till the opportune moment, dropped them in close-packed hundreds. No civilized troops in the world could have endured the hell through which they came, the living leaping high to avoid the dying who clutched at their heels, the wounded cursing and staggering forward, till they fell—a torrent black as the sliding water above a mill-dam—full on the right flank of the square. Then the line of the dusty troops and the faint blue desert sky overhead went out in rolling smoke, and the little stones on the heated ground and the tinder-dry clumps of scrub became matters of surpassing interest, for men measured their agonized retreat and recovery by these things, counting mechanically and hewing their way back to chosen pebble and branch. There was no semblance of any concerted fighting. For aught the men knew, the enemy might be attempting all four sides of the square at once. Their business was to destroy what lay in front of them, to bayonet in the back those who passed over them, and, dying, to drag down the slayer till he could be knocked on the head by some avenging gun-butt. Dick waited quietly with Torpenhow and a young doctor till the stress became unendurable. There was no hope of attending to the wounded till the attack was repulsed, so the three moved forward gingerly toward the weakest side. There was a rush from without, the short *hough-hough* of the stabbing spears, and a man on a horse, followed by thirty or forty others, dashed through, yelling and hacking. The right flank of the square sucked in after them, and the other sides sent help. The wounded, who knew that they had but a few hours more to live, caught at the enemy's feet and brought them down, or, staggering to a discarded rifle, fired blindly into the scuffle that raged in the centre of the square. Dick was conscious that somebody had cut him violently across his helmet, that he had fired his revolver into a black, foam-flecked face which forthwith ceased to bear any resemblance to a face, and that Torpenhow had gone down under an Arab whom he had tried to "collar low," and was turning over and over with his captive, feeling for the man's eyes. The doctor was jabbing at a venture with a bayonet, and a helmetless soldier was firing over Dick's shoulder: the flying grains of powder stung his

cheek. It was to Torpenhow that Dick turned by instinct. The representative of the Central Southern Syndicate had shaken himself clear of his enemy, and rose, wiping his thumb on his trousers. The Arab, both hands to his forehead, screamed aloud, then snatched up his spear and rushed at Torpenhow, who was panting under shelter of Dick's revolver. Dick fired twice, and the man dropped limply. His upturned face lacked one eye. The musketry-fire redoubled, but cheers mingled with it. The rush had failed, and the enemy were flying. If the heart of the square were shambles, the ground beyond was a butcher's shop. Dick thrust his way forward between the maddened men. The remnant of the enemy were retiring, as the few—the very few—English cavalry rode down the laggards.

Beyond the lines of the dead, a broad blood-stained Arab spear cast aside in the retreat lay across a stump of scrub, and beyond this again the illimitable dark levels of the desert. The sun caught the steel and turned it into a savage red disc. Some one behind him was saying, "Ah, get away, you brute!" Dick raised his revolver and pointed toward the desert. His eye was held by the red splash in the distance, and the clamor about him seemed to die down to a very far-away whisper, like the whisper of a level sea. There was the revolver and the red light, . . . and the voice of some one scaring something away, exactly as had fallen somewhere before,—probably in a past life. Dick waited for what should happen afterward. Something seemed to crack inside his head, and for an instant he stood in the dark,—a darkness that stung. He fired at random, and the bullet went out across the desert as he muttered, "Spoiled my aim. There aren't any more cartridges. . We shall have to run home." He put his hand to his head and brought it away covered with blood.

"Old man, you're cut rather badly," said Torpenhow. "I owe you something for this business. Thanks. Stand up! I say, you can't be ill here."

Dick had fallen stiffly on Torpenhow's shoulder, and was muttering something about aiming low and to the left. Then he sank to the ground and was silent. Torpenhow dragged him off to a doctor and sat down to work out an account of what he was pleased to call "a sanguinary battle, in which our arms had acquitted themselves," etc.

All that night, when the troops were encamped by the whale-boats, a black figure danced in the strong moonlight on the sand-bar and shouted that Khartoum the accursed one was dead,—was dead,—was dead,—that two steamers were rock-staked on the Nile outside the city, and that of all their crews there remained not one; and Khartoum was dead,—was dead,—was dead!

But Torpenhow took no heed. He was watching Dick, who was calling aloud to the restless Nile for Maisie,—and again Maisie!

"Behold a phenomenon," said Torpenhow, rearranging the blanket. "Here is a man, presumably human, who mentions the name of one woman only. And I've seen a good deal of delirium, too.—Dick, here's some fizzy drink."

"Thank you, Maisie," said Dick.

CHAPTER III

So he thinks he shall take to the sea again
  For one more cruise with his buccaneers,
To singe the beard of the King of Spain,
And capture another Dean of Jaen
  And sell him in Algiers.
          —A Dutch Picture.

THE Soudan campaign and Dick's broken head had been some months ended and mended, and the Central Southern Syndicate had paid Dick a certain sum on account for work done, which work they were careful to assure him was not altogether up to their standard. Dick heaved the letter into the Nile at Cairo, cashed the draft in the same town, and bade a warm farewell to Torpenhow at the station.

"I am going to lie up for a while and rest," said Torpenhow. "I don't know where I shall live in London, but if God brings us to meet, we shall meet. Are you staying here on the off-chance of another row? There will be none till the Southern Soudan is reoccupied by our troops. Mark that. Good-bye; bless you; come back when your money's spent; and give me your address."

Dick loitered in Cairo, Alexandria, Ismaïlia, and Port Said,—especially Port Said. There is iniquity in many parts of the world, and vice in all, but the concentrated essence of all the iniquities and all the vices in all the continents finds itself at Port Said. And through the heart of that sand-bordered hell, where the mirage flickers day long above the Bitter Lakes, move, if you will only wait, most of the men and women you have known in this life. Dick established himself in quarters more riotous than respectable. He spent his evenings on the quay, and boarded many ships, and saw very many friends,—gracious Englishwomen with whom he had talked not too wisely in the veranda of Shepheards Hotel, hurrying war correspondents, skippers of the contract troopships employed in the campaign, army officers by the score, and others of less reputable trades. He had choice of all the races of the East and West for studies, and the advantage of seeing his subjects under the influence of strong excitement, at the gaming-tables, saloons, dancing-hells, and elsewhere. For recreation there was the straight vista of the Canal, the blazing sands, the procession of shipping, and the white hospitals where the English soldiers lay. He strove to set down in black and white and color all that Providence sent him, and when that supply was ended sought about for fresh material. It was a fascinating employment, but it ran away with his money, and he had drawn in advance the hundred and twenty pounds to which he was entitled yearly. "Now I shall have to work and starve!" thought he, and was addressing himself to this new fate when a mysterious telegram arrived from Torpenhow in England, which said, "Come back, quick: you have caught on. Come."

A large smile overspread his face. "So soon! that's good hearing," said he to himself. "There will be an orgie to-night. I'll stand or fall by my luck. 'Faith, it's time it came!" He deposited half of his funds in the hands of his well-known friends Monsieur and Madame Binat, and ordered himself a Zanzibar dance of the finest. Monsieur

Binat was shaking with drink, but Madame smiled sympathetically—

"Monsieur needs a chair, of course, and of course Monsieur will sketch: Monsieur amuses himself strangely."

Binat raised a blue-white face from a cot in the inner room. "I understand," he quavered. "We all know Monsieur. Monsieur is an artist, as I have been." Dick nodded. "In the end," said Binat, with gravity, "Monsieur will descend alive into hell, as I have descended." And he laughed.

"You must come to the dance, too," said Dick; "I shall want you."

"For my face? I knew it would be so. For my face? My God! and for my degradation so tremendous! I will not. Take him away. He is a devil. Or at least do thou, Céleste, demand of him more." The excellent Binat began to kick and scream.

"All things are for sale in Port Said," said Madame. "If my husband comes it will be so much more. Eh, 'ow you call—'alf a sovereign."

The money was paid, and the mad dance was held at night in a walled courtyard at the back of Madame Binat's house. The lady herself, in faded mauve silk always about to slide from her yellow shoulders, played the piano, and to the tin-pot music of a Western waltz the naked Zanzibari girls danced furiously by the light of kerosene lamps. Binat sat upon a chair and stared with eyes that saw nothing, till the whirl of the dance and the clang of the rattling piano stole into the drink that took the place of blood in his veins, and his face glistened. Dick took him by the chin brutally and turned that face to the light. Madame

Binat looked over her shoulder and smiled with many teeth. Dick leaned against the wall and sketched for an hour, till the kerosene lamps began to smell, and the girls threw themselves panting on the hard-beaten ground. Then he shut his book with a snap and moved away, Binat plucking feebly at his elbow. "Show me," he whimpered. "I too was once an artist, even I!" Dick showed him the rough sketch. "Am I that?" he screamed. "Will you take that away with you and show all the world that it is I,—Binat?" He moaned and wept.

"Monsieur has paid for all," said Madame "To the pleasure of seeing Monsieur again."

The courtyard gate shut, and Dick hurried up the sandy street to the nearest gambling hell, where he was well known. "If the luck holds, it's an omen; if I lose, I must stay here." He placed his money picturesquely about the board, hardly daring to look at what he did. The luck held. Three turns of the wheel left him richer by twenty pounds, and he went down to the shipping to make friends with the captain of a decayed cargo-steamer, who landed him in London with fewer pounds in his pocket than he cared to think about.

A thin grey fog hung over the city, and the streets were very cold; for summer was in England.

"It's a cheerful wilderness, and it hasn't the knack of altering much," Dick thought, as he tramped from the Docks westward. "Now, what must I do?"

The packed houses gave no answer. Dick looked down the long lightless streets and at the appalling rush of traffic. "Oh, you rabbit-hutches!" said he, addressing a row of highly-respectable semi-detached residences. "Do you know what you've got to do later on? You have to supply me with menservants and maidservants,"—here he smacked his lips,—"and the peculiar treasure of kings. Meantime I'll get clothes and boots, and presently I will return and trample on you." He stepped forward energetically; he saw that one of his shoes was burst at the side. As he stooped to make investigations, a man jostled him into the gutter. "All right," he said. "That's another nick in the score. I'll jostle you later on."

Good clothes and boots are not cheap, and Dick left his last shop with the certainty that he would be respectably arrayed for a time, but with only fifty shillings in his pocket. He returned to streets by the Docks, and lodged himself in one room, where the sheets on the bed were almost audibly marked in case of theft, and where nobody seemed to go to bed at all. When his clothes arrived he sought the Central Southern Syndicate for Torpenhow's address, and got it, with the intimation that there was still some money owing to him.

"How much?" said Dick, as one who habitually dealt in millions.

"Between thirty and forty pounds. If it would be any convenience to you, of course we could let you have it at once; but we usually settle accounts monthly."

"If I show that I want anything now, I'm lost," he said to himself. "All I need I'll take later on." Then, aloud, "It's hardly worth while; and I'm going into the country for a month, too. Wait till I come back, and I'll see about it."

"But we trust, Mr. Heldar, that you do not intend to sever your connection with us?"

Dick's business in life was the study of faces, and he watched the speaker keenly. "That man means something," he said. "I'll do no business till I've seen Torpenhow. There's a big deal coming." So he departed, making no promises, to his one little room by the Docks. And that day was the seventh of the month, and that month, he reckoned with awful distinctness, had thirty-one days in it!

It is not easy for a man of catholic tastes and healthy appetites to exist for twenty-four days on fifty shillings. Nor is it cheering to begin the experiment alone in all the loneliness of London. Dick paid seven shillings a week for his lodging, which left him rather less than a shilling a day for food and drink. Naturally, his first purchase was of the materials of his craft; he had been without them too long. Half a day's investigation and comparison brought him to the conclusion that sausages and mashed potatoes, two-pence a plate were the best food. Now, sausages once or twice a week for breakfast are not unpleasant. As lunch, even, with mashed potatoes, they become monotonous. As dinner they are impertinent. At the end of three days Dick loathed sausages, and, going forth, pawned his watch to revel on sheep's head, which is not as cheap as it looks, owing to the bones and the gravy. Then he returned to sausages and mashed potatoes. Then he confined himself entirely to mashed potatoes for a day, and was unhappy because of pain in his inside. Then he pawned his waistcoat and his tie, and thought regretfully of money thrown away in times past. There are few things more edifying unto Art than the actual belly-pinch of hunger, and Dick in his few walks abroad—he did not care for exercise; it raised desires that could not be satisfied—found himself dividing mankind into two classes,—those who looked as if they might give him something to eat, and those who looked otherwise. "I never knew what I had to learn about the human face before," he thought; and, as a reward for his humility, Providence caused a cab-driver at a sausage-shop where Dick fed that night to leave half-eaten a great chunk of bread. Dick took it,—would have fought all the world for its possession,—and it cheered him.

The month dragged through at last, and, nearly prancing with impatience, he went to draw his money. Then he hastened to Torpenhow's address and smelt the smell of cooking meats all along the corridors of the chambers. Torpenhow was on the top floor, and Dick burst into his room, to be received with a hug which nearly cracked his ribs, as Torpenhow dragged him to the light and spoke of twenty different things in the same breath.

"But you're looking tucked up," he concluded.

"Got anything to eat?" said Dick, his eye roaming round the room.

"I shall be having breakfast in a minute. What do you say to sausages?"

"No, anything but sausages! Torp, I've been starving on that accursed horse-flesh for thirty days and thirty nights."

"Now, what lunacy has been your latest?"

Dick spoke of the last few weeks with

unbridled speech. Then he opened his coat; there was no waistcoat below. "I ran it fine, awfully fine, but I've just scraped through."

"You haven't much sense, but you've got a backbone, anyhow. Eat, and talk afterward." Dick fell upon eggs and bacon and gorged till he could gorge no more. Torpenhow handed him a filled pipe, and he smoked as men smoke who for three weeks have been deprived of good tobacco.

"Ouf!" said he. "That's heavenly! Well?"

"Why in the world didn't you come to me?"

"Couldn't; I owe you too much already, old man. Beside, I had a sort of superstition that this temporary starvation—that's what it was, and it hurt—would bring me more luck later. It's over and done with now, and none of the syndicate know how hard up I was. Fire away. What's the exact state of affairs as regards myself?"

"You had my wire? You've caught on here. People like your work immensely. I don't know why, but they do. They say you have a fresh touch and a new way of drawing things. And, because they're chiefly home-bred English, they say you have insight. You're wanted by half a dozen papers; you're wanted to illustrate books."

Dick grunted scornfully.

"You're wanted to work up your smaller sketches and sell them to the dealers. They seem to think the money sunk in you is a good investment. Good Lord! who can account for the fathomless folly of the public?"

"They're a remarkably sensible people."

"They are subject to fits, if that's what you mean; and you happen to be the object of the latest fit among those who are interested in what they call Art. Just now you're a fashion, a phenomenon, or whatever you please. I appeared to be the only person who knew anything about you here, and I have been showing the most useful men a few of the sketches you gave me from time to time. Those coming after your work on the Central Southern Syndicate appear to have done your business. You're in luck."

"Huh! call it luck! Do call it luck, when a man has been kicking about the world like a dog, waiting for it to come! I'll luck 'em later on. I want a place to work in first."

"Come here," said Torpenhow, crossing the landing. "This place is a big box room really, but it will do for you. There's your skylight, or your north light, or whatever window you call it, and plenty of room to thrash about in, and a bedroom beyond. What more do you need?"

"Good enough," said Dick, looking round the large room that took up a third of a top story in the rickety chambers overlooking the Thames. A pale yellow sun shone through the skylight and showed the much dirt of the place. Three steps led from the door to the landing, and three more to Torpenhow's room. The well of the staircase disappeared into darkness, pricked by tiny gasjets, and there were sounds of men talking and doors slamming seven flights below, in the warm gloom.

"Do they give you a free hand here?" said Dick, cautiously. He was Ishmael enough to know the value of liberty.

"Anything you like: latch-keys and license unlimited. We are permanent tenants for the most part here. 'Tisn't a place I would recommend for a Young Men's Christian Association, but it will serve. I took these rooms for you when I wired."

"You're a great deal too kind, old man."

"You didn't suppose you were going away from me, did you?" Torpenhow put his hand on Dick's shoulder, and the two walked up and down the room, henceforward to be called the studio, in sweet and silent communion. They heard rapping at Torpenhow's door. "That's some ruffian come up for a drink," said Torpenhow; and he raised his voice cheerily. There entered no one more ruffianly than a portly middle-aged gentleman in a satin-faced frock-coat. His lips were parted and pale, and there were deep pouches under the eyes.

"Weak heart," said Dick to himself, and, as he shook hands, "very weak heart. His pulse is shaking his fingers."

The man introduced himself as the head of the Central Southern Syndicate and "one of the most ardent admirers of your work, Mr. Heldar. I assure you, in the name of the syndicate, that we are immensely indebted to you; and I trust, Mr. Heldar, you won't forget that we were largely instrumental in bringing you before the public." He panted because of the seven flights of stairs.

Dick glanced at Torpenhow, whose left eyelid lay for a moment dead on his cheek.

"I shan't forget," said Dick, every instinct of defence roused in him.

"You've paid me so well that I couldn't, you know. By the way, when I am settled in this place I should like to send and get my sketches. There must be nearly a hundred and fifty of them with you."

"That is er—is what I came to speak about. I fear we can't allow it exactly, Mr. Heldar. In the absence of any specified agreement, the sketches are our property, of course."

"Do you mean to say that you are going to keep them?"

"Yes; and we hope to have your help, on your own terms, Mr. Heldar, to assist us in arranging a little exhibition, which, backed by our name and the influence we naturally command among the press, should be of material service to you. Sketches such as yours"—

"Belong to me. You engaged me by wire, you paid me the lowest rates you dared. You can't mean to keep them! Good God alive, man, they're all I've got in the world!"

Torpenhow watched Dick's face and whistled.

Dick walked up and down, thinking. He saw the whole of his little stock in trade, the first weapon of his equipment, annexed at the outset of his campaign by an elderly gentleman whose name Dick had not caught aright, who said that he represented a syndicate, which was a thing for which Dick had not the least reverence. The injustice of the proceedings did not much move him; he had seen the strong hand prevail too often in other places to be squeamish over the moral aspects of right and wrong. But he ardently desired the blood of the gentleman in the frock-coat, and when he spoke again it was with a strained sweetness that Torpenhow knew well for the beginning of strife.

"Forgive me, sir, but you have no— no younger man who can arrange this business with me?"

"I speak for the syndicate. I see no reason for a third party to"—

"You will in a minute. Be good enough to give back my sketches."

The man stared blankly at Dick, and then at Torpenhow, who was leaning against the wall. He was not used to ex-employees who ordered him to be good enough to do things.

"Yes, it is rather a cold-blooded steal," said Torpenhow, critically; "but I'm afraid, I am very much afraid, you've struck the wrong man. Be careful, Dick: remember, this isn't the Soudan."

"Considering what services the syndicate have done you in putting your name before the world"—

This was not a fortunate remark; it reminded Dick of certain vagrant years lived out in loneliness and strife and unsatisfied desires. The memory did not contrast well with the prosperous gentleman who proposed to enjoy the fruit of those years.

"I don't know quite what to do with you," began Dick, meditatively. "Of course you're a thief, and you ought to be half killed, but in your case you'd probably die. I don't want you dead on this floor, and, besides, it's unlucky just as one's moving in. Don't hit, sir; you'll only excite yourself." He put one hand on the man's forearm and ran the other down the plump body beneath the coat. "My goodness!" said he to Torpenhow, "and this grey oaf dares to

be a thief! I have seen an Esneh camel-driver have the black hide taken off his body in strips for stealing half a pound of wet dates, and *he* was as tough as whipcord. This thing's soft all over— like a woman."

There are few things more poignantly humiliating than being handled by a man who does not intend to strike. The head of the syndicate began to breathe heavily. Dick walked round him, pawing him, as a cat paws a soft hearth-rug. Then he traced with his forefinger the leaden pouches underneath the eyes and shook his head. "You were going to steal my things,—mine, mine, mine! —you, who don't know when you may die. Write a note to your office,—you say you're the head of it,—and order them to give Torpenhow my sketches,— every one of them. Wait a minute: your hand's shaking. Now!" He thrust a pocketbook before him. The note was written. Torpenhow took it and departed without a word, while Dick walked round and round the spellbound captive, giving him such advice as he conceived best for the welfare of his soul. When Torpenhow returned with a gigantic portfolio, he heard Dick say, almost soothingly, "Now, I hope this will be a lesson to you; and if you worry me when I have settled down to work with any nonsense about actions for assault, believe me, I'll catch you and manhandle you, and you'll die. You haven't very long to live, anyhow. Go! *Imshi, Vootsak,*—get out!" The man departed, staggering and dazed. Dick drew a long breath: "Phew! what a lawless lot these people are! The first thing a poor orphan meets is gang robbery, organized burglary! Think of the cideous blackness of that man's mind! Are my sketches all right, Torp?"

"Yes; one hundred and forty-seven of them. Well, I *must* say, Dick, you've begun well."

"He was interfering with me. It only meant a few pounds to him, but it was everything to me. I don't think he'll bring an action. I gave him some medical advice gratis about the state of his body. It was cheap at the little flurry it cost him. Now, let's look at my things."

Two minutes later Dick had thrown himself down on the floor and was deep in the portfolio, chuckling lovingly as he turned the drawings over and thought of the price at which they had been bought.

The afternoon was well advanced when Torpenhow came to the door and saw Dick dancing a wild saraband under the skylight.

"I builded better than I knew, Torp," he said, without stopping the dance. "They're good! They're damned good! They'll go like flame! I shall have an exhibition of them on my own brazen hook. And that man would have cheated me out of it! Do you know that I'm sorry now that I didn't actually hit him?"

"Go out," said Torpenhow,—"go out and pray to be delivered from the sin of arrogance, which you never will be. Bring your things up from whatever place you're staying in, and we'll try to make this barn a little more shipshape."

"And then—oh, then," said Dick, still capering, "we will spoil the Egyptians!"

CHAPTER IV

The wolf-cub at even lay hid in the corn,
  When the smoke of the cooking hung grey:
He knew where the doe made a couch for her fawn,
And he looked to his strength for his prey.
But the moon swept the smoke-wreaths away.
And he turned from his meal in the villager's close,
And he bayed to the moon as she rose.
    —*In Seonee.*

"WELL, and how does success taste?" said Torpenhow, some three months later. He had just returned to chambers after a holiday in the country.

"Good," said Dick, as he sat licking his lips before the easel in the studio. "I want more,—heaps more. The lean years have passed, and I approve of these fat ones."

"Be careful, old man. That way lies bad work."

Torpenhow was sprawling in a long chair with a small fox-terrier asleep on his chest, while Dick was preparing a canvas. A dais, a background, and a lay-figure were the only fixed objects in the place. They rose from a wreck of oddments that began with felt-covered water-bottles, belts, and regimental badges, and ended with a small bale of second-hand uniforms and a stand of mixed arms. The mark of muddy feet on the dais showed that a military model had just gone away. The watery autumn sunlight was failing, and shadows sat in the corners of the studio.

"Yes," said Dick, deliberately, "I like the power; I like the fun; I like the fuss; and above all I like the money. I almost like the people who make the fuss and pay the money. Almost. But they're a queer gang,—an amazingly queer gang!"

"They have been good enough to you, at any rate. That tin-pot exhibition of your sketches must have paid. Did you see that the papers called it the 'Wild Work Show'?"

"Never mind. I sold every shred of canvas I wanted to; and, on my word, I believe it was because they believed I was a self-taught flagstone artist. I should have got better prices if I had worked my things on wool or scratched them on camel-bone instead of using mere black and white and color. Verily, they are a queer gang, these people. Limited isn't the word to describe 'em. I met a fellow the other day who told me that it was impossible that shadows on white sand should be blue,—ultramarine,—as they are. I found out, later, that that man had been as far as Brighton beach; but he knew all about Art, confound him. He gave me a lecture on it, and recommended me to go to school to learn technique. I wonder what old Kami would have said to that."

"When were you under Kami, man of extraordinary beginnings?"

"I studied with him for two years in Paris. He taught by personal magnetism. All he ever said was, '*Continuez, mes enfants,*' and you had to make the best you could of that. He had a divine touch, and he knew something about color. Kami used to dream color; I swear he could never have seen the genuine article; but he evolved it; and it was good."

"Recollect some of those views in the Soudan?" said Torpenhow, with a provoking drawl.

Dick squirmed in his place. "Don't! It makes me want to get out there again. What color that was! Opal and umber and amber and claret and brick-red and sulphur—cockatoo-crest sulphur—against brown, with a nigger-black rock sticking up in the middle of it all, and a decorative frieze of camels festooning in front of a pure pale turquoise sky." He began to walk up and down. "And yet, you know, if you try to give these people the thing as God gave it keyed down to their comprehension and according to the powers He has given you"—

"Modest man! Go on."

"Half a dozen epicene young pagans who haven't even been to Algiers will tell you, first, that your notion is borrowed, and, secondly, that it isn't Art."

"This comes of my leaving town for a month. Dickie, you've been promenading among the toy-shops and hearing people talk."

"I couldn't help it," said Dick, penitently. "You weren't here, and it was lonely these long evenings. A man can't work forever."

"A man might have gone to a pub, and got decently drunk."

"I wish I had; but I forgathered with some men of sorts. They said they were artists, and I knew some of them could draw,—but they wouldn't draw. They gave me tea,—tea at five in the afternoon!—and talked about Art and the state of their souls. As if their souls mattered. I've heard more about Art and seen less of her in the last six months than in the whole of my life. Do you remember Cassavetti, who worked for some continental syndicate, out with the desert column? He was a regular Christmas-tree of contraptions when he took the field in full fig, with his water-bottle, lanyard, revolver, writing-case, housewife, gig-lamps, and the Lord knows what all. He used to fiddle about with 'em and show us how they worked; but he never seemed to do much except fudge his reports from the Nilghai. See?"

"Dear old Nilghai! He's in town, fatter than ever. He ought to be up here this evening. I see the comparison perfectly. You should have kept clear of all that man-millinery. Serves you right; and I hope it will unsettle your mind."

"It won't. It has taught me what Art—holy sacred Art—means."

"You've learned something while I've been away. What is Art?"

"Give 'em what they know, and when you've done it once do it again." Dick dragged forward a canvas laid face to the wall. "Here's a sample of real Art. It's going to be a facsimile reproduction for a weekly. I called it 'His Last Shot.' It's worked up from the little water-color I made outside El Maghrib. Well, I lured my model, a beautiful rifleman, up here with drink; I drored him, and I redrored him, and I tredrored him, and I made him a flushed, disheveled, bedevilled scallawag, with his helmet at the back of his head, and the living fear of death in his eye, and the blood oozing out of a cut over his anklebone. He wasn't pretty. but he was all soldier and very much man."

"Once more, modest child!"

Dick laughed. "Well, it's only to you I'm talking. I did him just as well as I knew how, making allowance for the slickness of oils. Then the art-manager of that abandoned paper said that his subscribers wouldn't like it. It was brutal and coarse and violent,—man being naturally gentle when he's fighting for his life. They wanted something more restful, with a little more color. I could have said a good deal, but you might as well talk to a sheep as an art-manager. I took my 'Last Shot' back. Behold the result! I put him into a lovely red coat without a speck on it. That is Art. I polished his boots,—observe the high light on the toe. That is Art. I cleaned his rifle,—rifles are always clean on service—because that is Art. I pipeclayed his helmet,—pipeclay is always used on active service, and is indispensable to Art. I shaved his chin, I washed his hands, and gave him an air of fatted peace. Result, military tailor's pattern-plate. Price, thank Heaven, twice as much as for the first sketch, which was moderately decent."

"And do you suppose you're going to give that thing out as your work?"

"Why not? I did it. Alone I did it, in the interests of sacred, home-bred Art and *Dickenson's Weekly*."

Torpenhow smoked in silence for a while. Then came the verdict, delivered from rolling clouds: "If you were only a mass of blathering vanity, Dick, I wouldn't mind,—I'd let you go to the deuce on your own mahl-stick; but when I consider what you are to me, and when I find that to vanity you add the twopenny-halfpenny pique of a twelve-year-old girl, then I bestir myself in your behalf. Thus!"

The canvas ripped as Torpenhow's booted foot shot through it, and the terrier jumped down, thinking rats were about.

"If you have any bad language to use, use it. You have not. I continue. You are an idiot, because no man born of woman is strong enough to take liberties with his public, even though they be—which they ain't—all you say they are."

"But they don't know any better. What can you expect from creatures born and bred in this light?" Dick pointed to the yellow fog. "If they want furniture-polish, let them have furniture-polish, so long as they pay for it. They are only men and women. You talk as though they were gods."

"That sounds very fine, but it has nothing to do with the case. They are the people you have to work for, whether you like it or not. They are your masters. Don't be deceived, Dickie, you aren't strong enough to trifle with them, —or with yourself, which is more important. Moreover,—Come back, Binkie: that red daub isn't going anywhere, —unless you take precious good care, you will fall under the damnation of the check-book, and that's worse than death. You will get drunk—you're half drunk already — on easily-acquired money. For that money and your own infernal vanity you are willing to deliberately turn out bad work. You'll do quite enough bad work without knowing it. And, Dickie, as I love you and as I know you love me, I am not going to let you cut off your nose to spite your face for all the gold in England. That's settled. Now swear."

"Don't know," said Dick. "I've been trying to make myself angry, but I can't, you're so abominably reasonable. There will be a row on *Dickenson's Weekly*, I fancy."

"Why the Dickenson do you want to work on a weekly paper? It's slow bleeding of power."

"It brings in the very desirable dollars," said Dick, his hands in his pockets.

Torpenhow watched him with large contempt. "Why, I thought it was a man!" said he. "It's a child."

"No, it isn't," said Dick, wheeling quickly. "You've no notion what the certainty of cash means to a man who has always wanted it badly. Nothing will pay me for some of my life's joys; on that Chinese pig-boat, for instance, when we ate bread and jam for every meal, because Ho-Wang wouldn't allow us anything better, and it all tasted of pig,—Chinese pig. I've worked for this, I've sweated and I've starved for this, line on line and month after month. And now I've got it I am going to make the most of it while it lasts. Let them pay—they've no knowledge."

"What does Your Majesty please to want? You can't smoke more than you do; you won't drink; you're a gross feeder; and you dress in the dark, by the look of you. You wouldn't keep a horse the other day when I suggested, because, you said, it might fall lame, and whenever you cross the street you take a hansom. Even you are not foolish enough to suppose that theatres and all the live things you can buy thereabouts mean Life. What earthly need have you for money?"

"It's there, bless its golden heart," said Dick. "It's there all the time. Providence has sent me nuts while I have teeth to crack 'em with. I haven't yet found the nut I wish to crack, but I'm keeping my teeth filed. Perhaps some day you and I will go for a walk round the wide earth."

"With no work to do, nobody to worry us, and nobody to compete with? You would be unfit to speak to in a week. Besides, I shouldn't go. I don't care to profit by the price of a man's soul,—for that's what it would mean. Dick, it's no use arguing. You're a fool."

"Don't see it. When I was on that Chinese pig-boat, our captain got enormous credit for saving about twenty-five thousand very sea-sick little pigs, when our old tramp of a steamer fell foul of a timber-junk. Now, taking those pigs as a parallel"—

"Oh, confound your parallels! Whenever I try to improve your soul, you always drag in some irrelevant anecdote from your very shady past. Pigs aren't the British public; credit on the high seas isn't credit here; and self-respect is self-respect all the world over. Go out for a walk and try to catch some self-respect. And, I say, if the Nilghai comes up this evening can I show him your diggings?"

"Surely. You'll be asking whether you must knock at my door, next." And Dick departed, to take counsel with himself in the rapidly-gathering London fog.

Half an hour after he had left, the Nilghai labored up the staircase. He was the chiefest, as he was the hugest, of the war correspondents, and his experiences dated from the birth of the needle-gun. Saving only his ally, Keneu the Great War Eagle, there was no man mightier in the craft than he, and he always opened his conversation with the news that there would be trouble in the Balkans in the spring. Torpenhow laughed as he entered.

"Never mind the trouble in the Balkans. Those little states are always screeching. You've heard about Dick's luck?"

"Yes; he has been called up to notoriety, hasn't he? I hope you keep him properly humble. He wants suppressing from time to time."

"He does. He's beginning to take liberties with what he thinks is his reputation."

"Already! By Jove, he has cheek! I don't know about his reputation, but he'll come a cropper if he tries that sort of thing."

"So I told him. I don't think he believes it."

"They never do when they first start off. What's that wreck on the ground there?"

"Specimen of his latest impertinence." Torpenhow thrust the torn edges of the canvas together and showed the well-groomed picture to the Nilghai, who looked at it for a moment and whistled.

"It's a chromo," said he,—"a chromo-litholeomargarine fake! What possessed him to do it? And yet how thoroughly he has caught the note that catches a public who think with their boots and read with their elbows! The cold-blooded insolence of the work almost saves it; but he mustn't go on with this. Hasn't he been praised and cockered up too much? You know these people here have no sense of proportion. They'll call him a second Detaille and a third-hand Meissonier while his fashion lasts. It's windy diet for a colt."

"I don't think it affects Dick much. You might as well call a young wolf a lion and expect him to take the compliment in exchange for a shin-bone. Dick's soul is in the bank. He's working for cash."

"Now he has thrown up war work, I suppose he doesn't see that the obligations of the service are just the same, only the proprietors are changed."

"How should he know? He thinks he is his own master."

"Does he? I could undeceive him for his good, if there's any virtue in print. He wants the whip-lash."

"Lay it on with science, then. I'd flay him myself, but I like him too much."

"I've no scruples. He had the audacity to try to cut me out with a woman at Cairo once. I forgot that, but I remember now."

"Did he cut you out?"

"You'll see when I have dealt with him. But, after all, what's the good? Leave him alone and he'll come home, if he has any stuff in him, dragging or wagging his tail behind him. There's more in a week of life than in a lively weekly. None the less I'll slate him. I'll slate him ponderously in the *Cataclysm*."

"Good luck to you; but I fancy nothing short of a crowbar would make Dick wince. His soul seems to have been fired before we came across him. He's intensely suspicious and utterly lawless."

"Matter of temper," said the Nilghai. "It's the same with horses. Some you wallop and they work, some you wallop and they jib, and some you wallop and they go out for a walk with their hands in their pockets."

"That's exactly what Dick has done," said Torpenhow. "Wait till he comes back. In the meantime, you can begin your slating here. I'll show you some of his last and worst work in his studio."

Dick had instinctively sought running water for a comfort to his mood of mind. He was leaning over the Embankment wall, watching the rush of the Thames through the arches of Westminster Bridge. He began by thinking of Torpenhow's advice, but, as of custom, lost himself in the study of the faces flocking past. Some had death written on their features, and Dick marveled that they could laugh. Others, clumsy and coarse-built for the most part, were alight with love; others were merely drawn and lined with work; but there was something, Dick knew, to be made out of them all. The poor at least should suffer that he might learn, and the rich should pay for the output of his learning. Thus his credit in the world and his cash balance at the bank would be increased. So much the better for him. He had suffered. Now he would take toll of the ills of others.

The fog was driven apart for a moment, and the sun shone, a blood-red wafer, on the water. Dick watched the spot till he heard the voice of the tide between the piers die down like the wash of the sea at low tide. A girl hard pressed by her lover shouted shamelessly, "Ah, get away, you beast!" and a shift of the same wind that had opened the fog drove across Dick's face the black smoke of a river-steamer at her berth below the wall. He was blinded for the moment, then spun round and found himself face to face with—Maisie.

There was no mistaking. The years had turned the child to a woman, but they had not altered the dark-grey eyes, the thin scarlet lips, or the firmly modeled mouth and chin; and, that all should be as it was old, she wore a closely-fitting grey dress.

Since the human soul is finite and not in the least under its own command, Dick, advancing, said, "Halloo!" after the manner of schoolboys, and Maisie answered, "Oh, Dick, is that you?" Then against his will, and before the brain newly released from considerations of the cash balance had time to dictate to the nerves, every pulse of Dick's body throbbed furiously and his palate dried in his mouth. The fog shut down again, and Maisie's face was pearl-white through it. No word was spoken, but Dick fell into step at her side, and the two paced the Embankment together, keeping the step as perfectly as in their afternoon excursions to the mud-flats. Then Dick, a little hoarsely—

"What has happened to Amomma?"

"He died, Dick. Not cartridges; over-eating. He was always greedy. Isn't it funny?"

"Yes. No. Do you mean Amomma?"

"Ye—es. No. This. Where have you come from?"

"Over there." He pointed eastward through the fog. "And you?"

"Oh, I'm in the north,—the black north, across all the Park. I am very busy."

"What do you do?"

"I paint a great deal. That's all I have to do."

"Why, what's happened? You had three hundred a year."

"I have that still. I am painting; that's all."

"Are you alone, then?"

"There's a girl living with me. Don't walk so fast, Dick; you're out of step."

"Then you noticed it too?"

"Of course I did. You're always out of step."

"So I am. I'm sorry. You went on with the painting?"

"Of course. I said I should. I was at the Slade, then at Merton's in St. John's Wood, the big studio, then I pepper-potted,—I mean I went to the National,—and now I'm working under Kami."

"But Kami is in Paris surely?"

"No; he has his teaching studio at Vitry-sur-Marne. I work with him in the summer, and I live in London in the winter. I'm a householder."

"Do you sell much?"

"Now and again, but not often. There is my 'bus. I must take it or lose half an hour. Good-bye, Dick."

"Good-bye, Maisie. Won't you tell me where you live? I must see you again; and perhaps I could help you. I—I paint a little myself."

"I may be in the Park to-morrow, if there is no working light. I walk from the Marble Arch down and back again; that is my little excursion. But of course I shall see you again." She stepped into the omnibus and was swallowed up by the fog.

"Well—I—am—damned!" exclaimed Dick, and returned to the chambers.

Torpenhow and the Nilghai found him sitting on the steps to the studio door, repeating the phrase with an awful gravity.

"You'll be more damned when I've done with you," said the Nilghai, upheaving his bulk from behind Torpenhow's shoulder and waving a sheaf of half-dry manuscript. "Dick, it is of common report that you are suffering from swelled head."

"Halloo, Nilghai. Back again? How are the Balkans and all the little Balkans? One side of your face is out of drawing, as usual."

"Never mind that. I am commissioned to smite you in print. Torpenhow refuses from false delicacy. I've been overhauling the pot-boilers in your studio. They are simply disgraceful."

"Oho! that's it, is it? If you think you can slate me, you're wrong. You can only describe, and you need as much room to turn in, on paper, as a P. and O. cargo-boat. But continue, and be swift. I'm going to bed."

"H'm! h'm! h'm! The first part only deals with your pictures. Here's the peroration: 'For work done without conviction, for power wasted on trivialities, for labor expended with levity for the deliberate purpose of winning the easy applause of a fashion-driven public'"—

"That's 'His Last Shot,' second edition. Go on."

"——'public, there remains but one end,—the oblivion that is preceded by toleration and cenotaphed with contempt. From that fate Mr. Heldar has yet to prove himself out of danger.'"

"*Wow — wow — wow—wow—wow!*" said Dick, profanely. "It's a clumsy ending and vile journalese, but it's quite true. And yet,"—he sprang to his feet and snatched at the manuscript,—"you scarred, deboshed, battered old gladiator! you're sent out when a war begins, to minister to the blind, brutal, British public's bestial thirst for blood. They have no arenas now, but they must have

special correspondents. You're a fat gladiator who comes up through a trap-door and talks of what he's seen. You stand on precisely the same level as an energetic bishop, an affable actress, a devastating cyclone, or — mine own sweet self. And you presume to lecture me about my work! Nilghai, if it were worth while I'd caricature you in four papers!"

The Nilghai winced. He had not thought of this.

"As it is, I shall take this stuff and tear it small—so!" The manuscript fluttered in slips down the dark well of the staircase. "Go home, Nilghai," said Dick; "go home to your lonely little bed, and leave me in peace. I am about to turn in till to-morrow."

"Why, it isn't seven yet!" said Torpenhow, with amazement.

"It shall be two in the morning, if I choose," said Dick, backing to the studio door. "I go to grapple with a serious crisis, and I shan't want any dinner."

The door shut and was locked.

"What can you do with a man like that?" said the Nilghai.

"Leave him alone. He's as mad as a hatter."

At eleven there was kicking on the studio door. "Is the Nilghai with you still?" said a voice from within. "Then tell him he might have condensed the whole of his lumbering nonsense into an epigram: 'Only the free are bond, and only the bond are free.' Tell him he's an idiot, Torp, and tell him I'm another."

"All right. Come out and have supper. You're smoking on an empty stomach."

There was no answer.

CHAPTER V

"I have a thousand men," said he,
  "To wait upon my will,
And towers nine upon the Tyne,
  And three upon the Till."

"And what care I for your men," said
    she,
  "Or towers from Tyne to Till,
Sith you must go with me," she said,
  "To wait upon my will?"
        —*Sir Hoggie and the Fairies.*

NEXT morning Torpenhow found Dick sunk in deepest repose of tobacco.

"Well, madman, how d'you feel?"

"I don't know. I'm trying to find out."

"You had much better do some work."

"Maybe; but I'm in no hurry. I've made a discovery. Torp, there's too much Ego in my Cosmos."

"Not really! Is this revelation due to my lectures, or the Nilghai's?"

"It came to me suddenly, all on my own account. Much too much Ego; and now I'm going to work."

He turned over a few half-finished sketches, drummed on a new canvas, cleaned three brushes, set Binkie to bite the toes of the lay-figure, rattled through his collection of arms and accoutrements, and then went out abruptly, declaring that he had done enough for the day.

"This is positively indecent," said Torpenhow, "and the first time that Dick has ever broken up a light morning. Perhaps he has found out that he has a soul, or an artistic temperament, or something equally valuable. That comes of leaving him alone for a month. Perhaps he has been going out of evenings. I must look to this." He rang for the baldheaded old housekeeper, whom nothing could astonish or annoy.

"Beeton, did Mr. Heldar dine out at all while I was out of town?"

"Never laid 'is dress-clothes out once, sir, all the time. Mostly 'e dined in; but 'e brought some most remarkable fancy young gentlemen up 'ere after theatres once or twice. Remarkable fancy they was. You gentlemen on the top floor does very much as you likes, but it do seem to me, sir, droppin' a walkin'-stick down five flights o' stairs an' then goin' down four abreast to pick it up again at half-past two in the mornin' singin', 'Bring back the whiskey, Willie darlin','—not once, or twice, but scores o' times—isn't charity to the other tenants. What I say is, 'Do as you would be done by.' That's my motto."

"Of course! of course! I'm afraid the top floor isn't the quietest in the house."

"I make no complaints, sir. I have spoke to Mr. Heldar friendly, an' he laughed, an' did me a picture of the missis that is as good as a colored print. It 'asn't the 'igh shine of a photograph, but what I say is, 'Never look a gift-horse in the mouth.' Mr. Heldar's dress-clothes 'aven't been on him for weeks."

"Then it's all right," said Torpenhow to himself. "Orgies are healthy, and Dick has a head of his own, but when it comes to women making eyes I'm not so certain—Binkie, never you be a man, little dorglums. They're contrary brutes, and they do things without any reason."

Dick had turned northward across the Park, but he was walking in the spirit on the mud-flats with Maisie. He laughed aloud as he remembered the day when he had decked Amomma's horns with the ham-frills, and Maisie, white with rage, had cuffed him. How long those four years seemed in review, and how closely Maisie was connected with every hour of them! Storm across the sea, and Maisie in a grey dress on the beach, sweeping her drenched hair out of her eyes and laughing at the homeward race of the fishing-smacks; hot sunshine on the mud-flats, and Maisie sniffing scornfully, with her chin in the air; Maisie flying before the wind that threshed the foreshore and drove the sand like small shot about her ears; Maisie, very composed and independent, telling lies to Mrs. Jeonet while Dick supported her with coarser perjuries; Maisie picking her way delicately from stone to stone, a pistol in her hand and her teeth firm-set; and Maisie in a grey dress sitting on the grass between the mouth of a cannon and a nodding yellow sea-poppy. The pictures passed before him one by one, and the last stayed the longest. Dick was perfectly happy with a quiet peace that was as new to his mind as it was foreign to his experience. It never occurred to him that there might be other calls upon his time than loafing across the Park in the forenoon.

"There's a good working light now," he said, watching his shadow placidly. "Some poor devil ought to be grateful for this. And there's Maisie."

She was walking toward him from the Marble Arch, and he saw that no mannerism of her gait had been changed. It was good to find her still Maisie, and, so to speak, his next-door neighbor. No greeting passed between them, because there had been none in the old days.

"What are you doing out of your studio at this hour?" said Dick, as one who was entitled to ask.

"Idling. Just idling. I got angry with a chin and scraped it out. Then I left it in a little heap of paint-chips and came away."

"I know what palette-knifing means. What was the piccy?"

"A fancy head that wouldn't come right,—horrid thing!"

"I don't like working over scraped paint when I'm doing flesh. The grain comes up woolly as the paint dries."

"Not if you scrape properly." Maisie waved her hand to illustrate her methods. There was a dab of paint on the white cuff. Dick laughed.

"You're as untidy as ever."

"That comes well from you. Look at your own cuff."

"By Jove, yes! It's worse than yours. I don't think we've much altered in anything. Let's see, though." He looked at Maisie critically. The pale blue haze of an autumn day crept between the tree-trunks of the Park and made a background for the grey dress, the black velvet toque above the black hair, and the resolute profile.

"No, there's nothing changed. How good it is! D'you remember when I fastened your hair into the snap of a hand-bag?"

Maisie nodded, with a twinkle in her eyes, and turned her full face to Dick.

"Wait a minute," said he. "That mouth is down in the corners a little. Who's been worrying you, Maisie?"

"No one but myself. I never seem to get on with my work, and yet I try hard enough, and Kami says"—

" 'Continuez, mesdemoiselles. Con-

tinuez toujours, mes enfants.' Kami is depressing. I beg your pardon."

"Yes, that's what he says. He told me last summer that I was doing better and he'd let me exhibit this year."

"Not in this place, surely?"

"Of course not. The Salon."

"You fly high."

"I've been beating my wings long enough. Where do you exhibit, Dick?"

"I don't exhibit. I sell."

"What is your line, then?"

"Haven't you heard?" Dick's eyes opened. Was this thing possible? He cast about for some means of conviction. They were not far from the Marble Arch. "Come up Oxford Street a little and I'll show you."

A small knot of people stood round a printshop that Dick knew well. "Some reproduction of my work inside," he said, with suppressed triumph. Never before had success tasted so sweet upon the tongue. "You see the sort of things I paint. D'you like it?"

Maisie looked at the wild whirling rush of a field-battery going into action under fire. Two artillerymen stood behind her in the crowd.

"They've chucked the off lead-'orse," said one to the other. " 'E's tore up awful, but they're makin' good time with the others. That lead-driver drives better nor you, Tom. See 'ow cunnin' 'e's nursin' 'is 'orse."

"Number Three'll be off the limber, next jolt," was the answer.

"No, 'e won't. See 'ow 'is foot's braced against the iron? 'E's all right."

Dick watched Maisie's face and swelled with joy—fine, rank, vulgar triumph. She was more interested in the little crowd than in the picture.

That was something that she could understand.

"And I wanted it so! Oh, I did want it so!" she said at last, under her breath.

"Me,—all me!" said Dick, placidly. "Look at their faces. It hits 'em. They don't know what makes their eyes and mouths open; but I know. And I know my work's right."

"Yes. I see. Oh, what a thing to have come to one!"

"Come to one, indeed! I had to go out and look for it. What do you think?"

"I call it success. Tell me how you got it."

They returned to the Park, and Dick delivered himself of the saga of his own doings, with all the arrogance of a young man speaking to a woman. From the beginning he told the tale, the I—I—I's flashing through the records as telegraph-poles fly past the traveler. Maisie listened and nodded her head. The histories of strife and privation did not move her a hair's-breadth. At the end of each canto he would conclude, "And *that* gave me some notion of handling color," or light, or whatever it might be that he had set out to pursue and understand. He led her breathless across half the world, speaking as he had never spoken in his life before. And in the flood-tide of his exaltation there came upon him a great desire to pick up this maiden who nodded her head and said, "I understand. Go on,"—to pick her up and carry her away with him, because she was Maisie, and because she understood, and because she was his right, and a woman to be desired above all women.

Then he checked himself abruptly.

"And so I took all I wanted," he said, "and had to fight for it. Now you tell."

Maisie's tale was almost as grey as her dress. It covered years of patient toil backed by savage pride that would not be broken though dealers laughed, and fogs delayed work, and Kami was unkind and even sarcastic, and girls in other studios were painfully polite. It had a few bright spots, in pictures accepted at provincial exhibitions, but it wound up with the oft-repeated wail, "And so you see, Dick, I had no success, though I worked so hard."

Then pity filled Dick. Even thus had Maisie spoken when she could not hit the breakwater, half an hour before she had kissed him. And that had happened yesterday.

"Never mind," he said. "I'll tell you something, if you'll believe it." The words were shaping themselves of their own accord. "The whole thing, lock, stock, and barrel, isn't worth one big yellow sea-poppy below Fort Keeling."

Maisie flushed a little. "It's all very well for you to talk, but you've had the success and I haven't."

"Let me talk, then. I know you'll understand. Maisie, dear, it sounds a bit absurd, but those ten years never existed, and I've come back again. It really is just the same. Can't you see? You're alone now and I'm alone. What's the use of worrying? Come to me instead, darling."

Maisie poked the gravel with her parasol. They were sitting on a bench. "I understand," she said, slowly. "But I've got my work to do, and I must do it."

"Do it with me, then, dear. I won't interrupt."

"No, I couldn't. It's my work,—mine, —mine,—mine! I've been alone all my life in myself, and I'm not going to belong to anybody except myself. I remember things as well as you do, but that dosen't count. We were babies then, and we didn't know what was before us. Dick, don't be selfish. I think I see my way to a little success next year. Don't take it away from me."

"I beg your pardon, darling. It's my fault for speaking stupidly. I can't expect you to throw up all your life just because I'm back. I'll go to my own place and wait a little."

"But, Dick, I don't want you to—go —out of—my life, now you've just come back."

"I'm at your orders; forgive me." Dick devoured the troubled little face with his eyes. There was triumph in them, because he could not conceive that Maisie should refuse sooner or later to love him, since he loved her.

"It's wrong of me," said Maisie, more slowly than before; "It's wrong and selfish; but, oh, I've been so lonely! No, you misunderstand. Now I've seen you again,—it's absurd, but I want to keep you in my life."

"Naturally. We belong."

"We don't; but you always understood me, and there is so much in my work that you could help me in. You know things and the ways of doing things. You must."

"I do, I fancy, or else I don't know myself. Then I suppose you won't care to lose sight of me altogether, and you want me to help you in your work?"

"Yes; but remember, Dick, nothing will ever come of it. That's why I feel so selfish. Let things stay as they are. I do want your help."

"You shall have it. But let's consider. I must see your pics first, and overhaul your sketches, and find out about your tendencies. You should see what the papers say about my tendencies! Then I'll give you good advice, and you shall paint according. Isn't that it, Maisie?"

Again there was unholy triumph in Dick's eye.

"It's too good of you,—much too good. Because you are consoling yourself with what will never happen, and I know that, and yet I wish to keep you. Don't blame me later, please."

"I'm going into the matter with my eyes open. Moreover, the queen can do no wrong. It isn't your selfishness that impresses me. It's your audacity in proposing to make use of me."

"Pooh! You're only Dick,—and a print-shop."

"Very good: that's all I am. But, Maisie, you believe, don't you, that I love you? I don't want you to have any false notions about brothers and sisters."

Maisie looked up for a moment and dropped her eyes.

"It's absurd, but—I believe. I wish I could send you away before you get angry with me. But—but the girl that lives with me is red-haired, and an impressionist, and all our notions clash."

"So do ours, I think. Never mind. Three months from to-day we shall be laughing at this together."

Maisie shook her head mournfully. "I knew you wouldn't understand, and it will only hurt you more when you find out. Look at my face, Dick, and tell me what you see."

They stood up and faced each other for a moment. The fog was gathering, and it stifled the roar of the traffic of London beyond the railings. Dick brought all his painfully-acquired knowledge of faces to bear on the eyes, mouth, and chin underneath the black velvet toque.

"It's the same Maisie, and it's the same me," he said. "We've both nice little wills of our own, and one or other of us has to be broken. Now about the future. I must come and see your pictures some day,—I suppose when the red-haired girl is on the premises."

"Sundays are my best times. You must come on Sundays. There are such heaps of things I want to talk about and ask your advice about. Now I must get back to work."

"Try to find out before next Sunday what I am," said Dick. "Don't take my word for anything I've told you. Good-bye, darling, and bless you."

Maisie stole away like a little grey mouse. Dick watched her till she was out of sight, but he did not hear her say to herself, very soberly, "I'm a wretch, —a horrid, selfish wretch. But it's Dick, and Dick will understand."

No one has yet explained what actually happens when an irresistible force meets the immovable post, though many have thought deeply, even as Dick thought. He tried to assure himself that Maisie would be led in a few weeks by his mere presence and discourse to a better way of thinking. Then he remembered much too distinctly her face and all that was written on it.

"If I know anything of heads," he

said, "there's everything in that face but love. I shall have to put that in myself; and that chin and mouth won't be won for nothing. But she's right. She knows what she wants, and she's going to get it. What insolence! Me! Of all the people in the wide world, to use me! But then she's Maisie. There's no getting over that fact; and it's good to see her again. This business must have been simmering at the back of my head for years. . . . She'll use me as I used Binat at Port Said. She's quite right. It will hurt a little. I shall have to see her every Sunday,—like a young man courting a housemaid. She's sure to come round. and yet—that mouth isn't a yielding mouth. I shall be wanting to kiss her all the time, and I shall have to look at her pictures,—I don't even know what sort of work she does yet, and I shall have to talk about Art,—Woman's Art! Therefore, particularly and perpetually, damn all varieties of Art. It did me a good turn once, and now it's in my way. I'll go home and do some Art."

Half-way to the studio, Dick was smitten with a terrible thought. The figure of a solitary woman in the fog suggested it.

"She's all alone in London, with a red-haired impressonist girl, who probably has the digestion of an ostrich. Most red-haired people have. Maisie's a bilious little body. They'll eat like lone women,—meals at all hours, and tea with all meals. I remember how the students in Paris used to pig along. She may fall ill at any minute, and I shan't be able to help. Whew! this is ten times worse than owning a wife."

Torpenhow came into the studio at dusk, and looked at Dick with his eyes full of the austere love that springs up between men who have tugged at the same oar together and are yoked by custom and use and the intimacies of toil. This is a good love, and, since it allows, and even encourages, strife, recrimination, and the most brutal sincerity, does not die, but increases, and is proof against any absence and evil conduct.

Dick was silent after he handed Torpenhow the filled pipe of council. He thought of Maisie and her possible needs. It was a new thing to think of anybody but Torpenhow who could think for himself. Here at last was an outlet for that cash balance. He could adorn Maisie barbarically with jewelry,—a thick gold necklace round that little neck, bracelets upon the rounded arms, and rings of price upon her hands,—the cool, temperate, ringless hands that he had taken between his own. It was an absurd thought, for Maisie would not even allow him to put one ring on one finger, and she would laugh at golden trappings. It would be better to sit with her quietly in the dusk, his arm round her neck and her face on his shoulder, as befitted husband and wife. Torpenhow's boots creaked that night, and his strong voice jarred. Dick's brows contracted and he murmured an evil word because he had taken all his success as a right and part payment for past discomfort, and now he was checked in his stride by a woman who admitted all the success and did not instantly care for him.

"I say, old man," said Torpenhow, who had made one or two vain attempts at conversation, "I haven't put your back up by anything I've said lately, have I?"

"You! No. How could you?"

"Liver out of order?"

"The truly healthy man doesn't know he has a liver. I'm only a bit worried about things in general. I suppose it's my soul."

"The truly healthy man doesn't know he has a soul. What business have you with luxuries of that kind?"

"It came of itself. Who's the man that says that we're all islands shouting lies to each other across seas of misunderstanding?"

"He's right, whoever he is,—except about the misunderstanding. I don't think we could misunderstand each other."

The blue smoke curled back from the ceiling in clouds. Then Torpenhow, insinuatingly—

"Dick, is it a woman?"

"Be hanged if it's anything remotely resembling a woman; and if you begin to talk like that, I'll hire a red-brick studio with white paint trimmings, and begonias and petunias and blue Hungarias to play among three-and-sixpenny pot-palms, and I'll mount all my pics in aniline-dye plush plasters, and I'll invite every woman who yelps and maunders and moans over what her guide-books tell her is Art, and you shall receive 'em, Torp,—in a snuff-brown velvet coat with yellow trousers and an orange tie. You'll like that."

"Too thin, Dick. A better man than you denied with cursing and swearing on a memorable occasion. You've overdone it, just as he did. It's no business of mine, of course, but it's comforting to think that somewhere under the stars there's saving up for you a tremendous thrashing. Whether it'll come from heaven or earth, I don't know, but it's bound to come and break you up a little. You want hammering."

Dick shivered. "All right," said he. "When this island is disintegrated it will call for you."

"I shall come round the corner and help to disintegrate it some more. We're talking nonsense. Come along to a theatre."

CHAPTER VI

"And you may lead a thousand men,
  Nor ever draw the rein,
But ere ye lead the Faery Queen
  'Twill burst your heart in twain."

He has slipped his foot from the
    stirrup-bar,
  The bridle from his hand,
And he is bound by hand and foot
  To the Queen o' Faery-land.
        —*Sir Hoggie and the Fairies.*

SOME weeks later, on a very foggy Sunday, Dick was returning across the Park to his studio. "This," he said, "is evidently the thrashing that Torp meant. It hurts more than I expected; but the queen can do no wrong; and she certainly has some notion of drawing."

He had just finished a Sunday visit to Maisie,—always under the green eyes of the red-haired impressionist girl, whom he learned to hate at sight,—and was tingling with a keen sense of shame. Sunday after Sunday, putting on his best clothes, he had walked over to the untidy house north of the Park, first to see Maisie's pictures, and then to criticise and advise upon them as he realized that they were productions on which advice would not be wasted. Sunday after Sunday, and his love grew with each visit, he had been compelled to cram his heart back from between his lips when it prompted him to kiss Maisie several times and very much indeed. Sunday after Sunday, the head above the heart had warned him that Maisie was not yet attainable, and that it would be better to talk as connectedly as possible upon the mysteries of the craft that was all in all to her. Therefore it was his fate to endure weekly torture in the studio built out over the clammy back garden of a frail stuffy little villa where nothing was ever in its right place and nobody ever called,—to endure and to watch Maisie moving to and fro with the teacups. He abhorred tea, but, since it gave him a little longer time in her presence, he drank it devoutly, and the red-haired girl sat in an untidy heap and eyed him without speaking. She was always watching him. Once, and only once, when she had left the studio, Maisie showed him an album that held a few poor cuttings from provincial papers,—the briefest of hurried notes on some of her pictures sent to outlying exhibitions. Dick stooped and kissed the paint-smudged thumb on the open page. "Oh, my love, my love," he muttered, "do you value these things? Chuck 'em into the waste-paper basket!"

"Not till I get something better," said Maisie, shutting the book.

Then Dick, moved by no respect for his public and a very deep regard for the maiden, did deliberately propose, in order to secure more of these coveted cuttings, that he should paint a picture which Maisie should sign.

"That's childish," said Maisie, "and I didn't think it of you. It must be my work. Mine,—mine,—mine!"

"Go and design decorative medallions for rich brewers' houses. You are thoroughly good at that." Dick was sick and savage.

"Better things than medallions, Dick," was the answer, in tones that recalled a grey-eyed atom's fearless speech to Mrs. Jennett. Dick would have abased himself utterly, but that the other girl trailed in.

Next Sunday he laid at Maisie's feet small gifts of pencils that could almost draw of themselves and colors in whose permanence he believed, and he was ostentatiously attentive to the work in hand. It demanded, among other things, an exposition of the faith that was in him. Torpenhow's hair would have stood on end had he heard the fluency with which Dick preached his own gospel of Art.

A month before, Dick would have been equally astonished; but it was Maisie's will and pleasure, and he dragged his words together to make plain to her comprehension all that had been hidden to himself of the whys and wherefores of work. There is not the least difficulty in doing a thing if you only know how to do it; the trouble is to explain your method.

"I could put this right if I had a brush in my hand," said Dick despairingly, over the modeling of a chin that Maisie complained would not "look flesh,"—it was the same chin that she had scraped out with the palette-knife, —"but I find it almost impossible to teach you. There's a queer grim Dutch touch about your painting that I like; but I've a notion that you're weak in drawing. You foreshorten as though you never used the model, and you've caught Kami's pasty way of dealing with flesh in shadow. Then, again, though you don't know it yourself, you shirk hard work. Suppose you spend some of your time on line alone. Line doesn't allow of shirking. Oils do, and three square inches of flashy, tricky stuff in a corner of a pic sometimes carry a bad thing off,—as I know. That's immoral. Do line-work for a little while, and then I can tell more about your powers, as old Kami used to say."

Maisie protested: she did not care for the pure line.

"I know," said Dick. "You want to do your fancy heads with a bunch of flowers at the base of the neck to hide bad modeling." The red-haired girl laughed a little. "You want to do landscapes with cattle knee-deep in grass to hide bad drawing. You want to do a great deal more than you can do. You have sense of color, but you want form. Color's a gift,—put it aside and think no more about it,—but form you can be drilled into. Now, all your fancy heads—and some of them are very good —will keep you exactly where you are. With line you must go forward or backward, and it will show up all your weaknesses."

"But other people"—began Maisie.

"You mustn't mind what other people do. If their souls were your soul, it would be different. You stand and fall by your own work, remember, and it's waste of time to think of any one else in this battle."

Dick paused, and the longing that had been so resolutely put away came back into his eyes. He looked at Maisie, and the look asked as plainly as words, Was it not time to leave all this barren wilderness of canvas and counsel and join hands with Life and Love?

Maisie assented to the new programme of schooling so adorably that Dick could hardly restrain himself from picking her up then and there and carrying her off to the nearest registrar's office. It was the implicit obedience to the spoken word and the blank indifference to the unspoken desire that baffled and buffeted his soul. He held authority in that house,—authority limited, indeed, to one-half of one afternoon in seven, but very real while it lasted. Maisie had learned to appeal to him on many subjects, from the proper packing of pictures to the condition of a smoky chimney. The red-haired girl never consulted him about anything. On the other hand, she accepted his appearances without protest, and watched him always. He discovered that the meals of the establishment were irregular and fragmentary. They depended chiefly on tea, pickles, and biscuit, as he had suspected from the beginning. The girls were supposed to market week and week about, but they lived, with the help of a charwoman, as casually as the young Ravens. Maisie spent most of her income on models, and the other girl reveled in apparatus as refined as her work was rough. Armed with knowledge dear-bought from the Docks, Dick warned Maisie that the end of semi-starvation meant the crippling of power to work, which was considerably worse than death. Maisie took the warning, and gave more thought to what she ate and drank. When his trouble returned upon him, as it generally did in the long winter twilights, the remembrance of that little act of domestic authority and his coercion with a hearth-brush of the smoky drawing-room chimney stung Dick like a whip-lash.

He conceived that this memory would be the extreme of his sufferings, till one Sunday, the red-haired girl announced that she would make a study of Dick's head, and that he would be good enough to sit still, and—quite as an after-thought—look at Maisie. He sat, because he could not well refuse, and for the space of half an hour he reflected on all the people in the past whom he had laid open for the purposes of his own craft. He remembered Binat most distinctly,—that Binat who had once been an artist and talked about degradation.

It was the merest monochrome roughing in of a head, but it presented the dumb waiting, the longing, and, above all, the hopeless enslavement of the man, in a spirit of bitter mockery.

"I'll buy it," said Dick, promptly, "at your own price."

"My price is too high, but I dare say you'll be as grateful if"— The wet sketch fluttered from the girl's hand and fell into the ashes of the studio stove. When she picked it up it was hopelessly smudged.

"Oh, it's all spoiled!" said Maisie. "And I never saw it. Was it like?"

"Thank you," said Dick, under his breath to the red-haired girl, and he removed himself swiftly.

"How that man hates me!" said the girl. "And how he loves you, Maisie!"

"What nonsense! I know Dick's very fond of me, but he has his work to do, and I have mine."

"Yes, he is fond of you, and I think he knows there is something in impressionism, after all. Maisie, can't you see?"

"See? See what?"

"Nothing; only, I know that if I could get any man to look at me as that man looks at you, I'd—I don't know what I'd do. But he hates me. Oh, how he hates me!"

She was not altogether correct. Dick's hatred was tempered with gratitude for a few moments, and then he forgot the girl entirely. Only the sense of shame remained, and he was nursing it across the Park in the fog. "There'll be an explosion one of these days," he said, wrathfully. "But it isn't Maisie's fault; she's right, quite right, as far as she knows, and I can't blame her. This business has been going on for three months nearly. Three months!—and it cost me ten years' knocking about to get at the notion, the merest raw notion, of my work. That's true; but then I didn't have pins, drawing-pins and palette-knives, stuck into me every Sunday. Oh, my little darling, if ever I break you, somebody will have a very bad time of it. No, she won't. I'd be as big a fool about her as I am now. I'll poison that red-haired girl on my wedding-day,— she's unwholesome,—and now I'll pass on these present bad times to Torp."

Torpenhow had been moved to lecture Dick more than once lately on the sin of levity, and Dick had listened and replied not a word. In the weeks between the first few Sundays of his discipline he had flung himself savagely into his work, resolved that Maisie should at least know the full stretch of his powers. Then he had taught Maisie that she must not pay the least attention to any work outside her own, and Maisie had obeyed him all too well. She took his counsels, but was not interested in his pictures.

"Your things smell of tobacco and blood," she said once. "Can't you do anything except soldiers?"

"I could do a head of you that would startle you," thought Dick,—this was before the red-haired girl had brought him under the guillotine,—but he only said, "I am very sorry," and harrowed Torpenhow's soul that evening with blasphemies against Art. Later, insensibly and to a large extent against his own will, he ceased to interest himself in his own work. For Maisie's sake, and to soothe the self-respect that it seemed to him he lost each Sunday he would not consciously turn out bad stuff, but, since Maisie did not care even for his best, it were better not to do anything at all save wait and mark time between Sunday and Sunday. Torpenhow was disgusted as the weeks went by fruitless, and then attacked him one Sunday evening when Dick felt utterly exhausted after three hours' biting self-restraint in Maisie's presence. There was Language, and Torpenhow withdrew to consult the Nilghai, who had come in to talk continental politics.

"Bone-idle, is he? Careless, and touched in the temper?" said the Nilghai. "It isn't worth worrying over. Dick is probably playing the fool with a woman."

"Isn't that bad enough?"

"No. She may throw him out of gear and knock his work to pieces for a while. She may even turn up here some day and make a scene on the staircase: one never knows. But until Dick speaks of his own accord you had better not touch him. He is no easy-tempered man to handle."

"No; I wish he were. He is such an aggressive, cocksure, you-be-damned fellow."

"He'll get that knocked out of him in time. He must learn that he can't storm up and down the world with a box of moist tubes and a slick brush. You're fond of him?"

"I'd take any punishment that's in store for him if I could; but the worst of it is, no man can save his brother."

"No, and the worser of it is, there is no discharge in this war. Dick must learn his lesson like the rest of us. Talking of war, there'll be trouble in the Balkans in the spring."

"That trouble is long coming. I wonder if we could drag Dick out there when it comes off?"

Dick entered the room soon afterward, and the question was put to him "Not good enough," he said, shortly. "I'm too comf'y where I am."

"Surely you aren't taking all the stuff in the papers seriously?" said the Nilghai. "Your vogue will be ended in less than six months,—the public will know your touch and go on to something new,—and where will you be then?"

"Here in England."

"When you might be doing decent work among us out there? Nonsense! I shall go, the Keneu will be there, Torp will be there, Cassavetti will be there, and the whole lot of us will be there, and we shall have as much as ever we can do, with unlimited fighting and the chance for you of seeing things that would make the reputation of three Verestchagins."

"Um!" said Dick, pulling at his pipe.

"You prefer to stay here and imagine that all the world is gaping at your pictures? Just think how full an average man's life is of his own pursuits and pleasures. When twenty thousand of him find time to look up between mouthfuls and grunt something about something they aren't the least interested in, the net result is called fame, reputation, or notoriety, according to the taste and fancy of the speller my lord."

"I know that as well as you do. Give me credit for a little gumption."

"Be hanged if I do!"

"*Be* hanged, then; you probably will be,—for a spy, by excited Turks. Heigh-ho! I'm weary, dead weary, and virtue has gone out of me." Dick dropped into a chair, and was fast asleep in a minute.

"That's a bad sign," said the Nilghai, in an undertone.

Torpenhow picked the pipe from the waistcoat where it was beginning to burn, and put a pillow behind the head. "We can't help; we can't help," he said. "It's a good ugly sort of old cocoa-nut, and I'm fond of it. There's the scar of the wipe he got when he was cut over in the square."

"Shouldn't wonder if that has made him a trifle mad."

"I should. He's a most business-like madman."

Then Dick began to snore furiously.

"Oh, here, no affection can stand this sort of thing. Wake up, Dick, and go and sleep somewhere else if you intend to make a noise about it."

"When a cat has been out on the tiles all night," said the Nilghai in his beard, "I notice that she usually sleeps all day. This is natural history."

Dick staggered away rubbing his eyes and yawning. In the night-watches he was overtaken with an idea, so simple and so luminous that he wondered he had never conceived it before. It was full of craft. He would seek Maisie on a week-day,—would suggest an excursion, and would take her by train to Fort Keeling, over the very ground that they two had trodden together ten years ago.

"As a general rule," he explained to his chin-lathered reflection in the morning, "it isn't safe to cross an old trail twice. Things remind one of things, and a cold wind gets up, and you feel sad; but this is an exception to every rule that ever was. I'll go to Maisie at once."

Fortunately, the red-haired girl was out shopping when he arrived, and Maisie in a paint-spattered blouse was warring with her canvas. She was not pleased to see him; for week-day visits were a stretch of the bond; and it needed all his courage to explain his errand.

"I know you've been working too hard," he concluded, with an air of authority. "If you do that, you'll break down. You had much better come."

"Where?" said Maisie, wearily. She had been standing before her easel too long, and was very tired.

"Anywhere you please. We'll take a train tomorrow and see where it stops.

We'll have lunch somewhere, and I'll bring you back in the evening."

"If there's a good working light to-morrow I lose a day." Maisie balanced the heavy white chestnut palette irreso-lutely.

Dick bit back an oath that was hurry-ing to his lips. He had not yet learned patience with the maiden to whom her work was all in all.

"You'll lose ever so many more, dear, if you use every hour of working light. Overwork's only murderous idleness. Don't be unreasonable. I'll call for you to-morrow after breakfast early."

"But surely you are going to ask"—

"No, I am not. I want you and no-body else. Besides, she hates me as much as I hate her. She won't care to come. To-morrow, then; and pray that we get sunshine."

Dick went away delighted, and by consequence did no work whatever. He strangled a wild desire to order a special train, but bought a great grey kangaroo cloak lined with glossy black marten, and then retired into himself to con-sider things.

"I'm going out for the day to-mor-row with Dick," said Maisie to the red-haired girl when the latter returned, tired, from marketing in the Edgware Road.

"He deserves it. I shall have the studio floor thoroughly scrubbed while you're away. It's very dirty."

Maisie had enjoyed no sort of holiday for months, and looked forward to the little excitement, but not without mis-givings.

"There's nobody nicer than Dick when he talks sensibly," she thought, "but, I'm sure he'll be silly and worry me, and I'm sure I can't tell him any-thing he'd like to hear. If he'd only be sensible I should like him so much better."

Dick's eyes were full of joy when he made his appearance next morning and saw Maisie, grey-ulstered and black-velvet-hatted, standing in the hallway. Palaces of marble, and not sordid imi-tations of grained wood, were surely the fittest background for such a divinity. The red-haired girl drew her into the studio for a moment and kissed her hurriedly. Maisie's eyebrows climbed to the top of her forehead; she was alto-gether unused to these demonstrations. "Mind my hat," she said, hurrying away, and ran down the steps to Dick waiting by the hansom.

"Are you quite warm enough? Are you sure you wouldn't like some more breakfast? Put this cloak over your knees."

"I'm quite comf'y, thanks. Where are we going, Dick? Oh, do stop sing-ing like that. People will think we're mad."

"Let 'em think,—if the exertion doesn't kill them. They don't know who we are, and I'm sure I don't care who they are. My faith, Maisie, you're looking lovely!"

Maisie stared directly in front of her and did not reply. The wind of a keen clear winter morning had put color into her cheeks. Overhead, the creamy-yellow smoke-clouds were thinning away one by one against a pale-blue sky, and the improvident sparrows broke off from water-spout committees and cab-rank cabals to clamor of the coming of spring.

"It will be lovely weather in the country," said Dick.

"But where are we going?"

"Wait and see."

They stopped at Victoria, and Dick sought tickets. For less than half the fraction of an instant it occurred to Maisie, comfortably settled by the waiting-room fire, that it was much more pleasant to send a man to the booking-office than to elbow one's own way through the crowd. Dick put her into a Pullman,—solely on account of the warmth there; and she regarded the extravagance with grave scandalized eyes as the train moved out into the country.

"I wish I knew where we are going," she repeated for the twentieth time. The name of a well-remembered station flashed by, toward the end of the run, and Maisie was enlightened.

"Oh, Dick, you villain!"

"Well, I thought you might like to see the place again. You haven't been here since old times, have you?"

"No. I never cared to see Mrs. Jennett again; and she was all that was ever there."

"Not quite. Look out a minute. There's 'the windmill above the potato-fields; they haven't built villas there yet; d'you remember when I shut you up in it?"

"Yes. How she beat you for it! I never told it was you."

"She guessed. I jammed a stick under the door and told you that I was burying Amomma alive in the potatoes, and you believed me. You had a trusting nature in those days."

They laughed and leaned to look out, identifying ancient landmarks with many reminiscences. Dick fixed his weather eye on the curve of Maisie's cheek, very near his own, and watched the blood rise under the clear skin. He congratulated himself upon his cunning, and looked that the evening would bring him a great reward.

When the train stopped they went out to look at an old town with new eyes. First, but from a distance, they regarded the house of Mrs. Jennett.

"Suppose she should come out now, what would you do?" said Dick, with mock terror.

"I should make a face."

"Show, then," said Dick, dropping into the speech of childhood.

Maisie made that face in the direction of the mean little villa, and Dick laughed aloud.

" 'This is disgraceful,' " said Maisie, mimicking Mrs. Jennett's tone. " 'Maisie, you run in at once, and learn the collect, gospel, and epistle for the next three Sundays. After all I've taught you, too, and three helps every Sunday at dinner! Dick's always leading you into mischief. If you aren't a gentleman, Dick, you might at least' "—

The sentence ended abruptly. Maisie remembered when it had last been used.

" 'Try to behave like one,' " said Dick, promptly. "Quite right. Now we'll get some lunch and go on to Fort Keeling,—unless you'd rather drive there?"

"We must walk, out of respect to the place. How little changed it all is!"

They turned in the direction of the sea through unaltered streets, and the influence of old things lay upon them. Presently they passed a confectioner's shop much considered in the days when their joint pocket-money amounted to a shilling a week.

"Dick, have you any pennies?" said Maisie, half to herself.

"Only three; and if you think you're going to have two of 'em to buy peppermints with, you're wrong. She says peppermints aren't ladylike."

Again they laughed, and again the color came into Maisie's cheeks as the blood boiled through Dick's heart. After a large lunch they went down to the beach and to Fort Keeling across the waste, wind-bitten land that no builder had thought it worth his while to defile. The winter breeze came in from the sea and sang about their ears.

"Maisie," said Dick, "your nose is getting a crude Prussian blue at the tip. I'll race you as far as you please for as much as you please."

She looked round cautiously, and with a laugh set off, swiftly as the ulster allowed, till she was out of breath.

"We used to run miles," she panted. "It's absurd that we can't run now."

"Old age, dear. This it is to get fat and sleek in town. When I wished to pull your hair you generally ran for three miles, shrieking at the top of your voice. I ought to know, because those shrieks were meant to call up Mrs. Jennett with a cane and"—

"Dick, I never got you a beating on purpose in my life."

"No, of course you never did. Good heavens! look at the sea."

"Why, it's the same as ever!" said Maisie.

Torpenhow had gathered from Mr. Beeton that Dick, properly dressed and shaved, had left the house at half-past eight in the morning with a traveling-rug over his arm. The Nilghai rolled in at midday for chess and polite conversation.

"It's worse than anything I imagined," said Torpenhow.

"Oh, the everlasting Dick, I suppose! You fuss over him like a hen with one chick. Let him run riot if he think's it'll amuse him. You can whip a young pup off feather, but you can't whip a young man."

"It isn't a woman. It's one woman; and it's a girl."

"Where's your proof?"

"He got up and went out at eight this morning,—got up in the middle of the night, by Jove! a thing he never does except when he's on service. Even then, remember, we had to kick him out of his blankets before the fight began at El-Maghrib. It's disgusting."

"It looks odd; but maybe he's decided to buy a horse at last. He might get up for that, mightn't he?"

"Buy a blazing wheelbarrow! He'd have told us if there was a horse in the wind. It's a girl."

"Don't be certain. Perhaps it's only a married woman."

"Dick has some sense of humor, if you haven't. Who gets up in the grey dawn to call on another man's wife? It's a girl."

"Let it be a girl, then. She may teach him that there's somebody else in the world besides himself."

"She'll spoil his hand. She'll waste his time, and she'll marry him, and ruin his work forever. He'll be a respectable married man before we can stop him, and—he'll never go on the long trail again."

"All quite possible, but the earth won't spin the other way when it happens. . . . Ho! ho! I'd give something to see Dick 'go wooing with the boys.' Don't worry about it. These things be with Allah, and we can only look on. Get the chessmen."

The red-haired girl was lying down in her own room, staring at the ceiling. The footsteps of people on the pavement sounded, as they grew indistinct in the distance, like a many-times-repeated kiss that was all one long kiss. Her hands were by her side, and they opened and shut savagely from time to time.

The charwoman in charge of the scrubbing of the studio knocked at her door: "Beg y' pardon, miss, but in cleanin' of a floor there's two, not to say three, kind of soap, which is yaller, an' mottled, an' disinfectink. Now, jist before I took my pail into the passage I thought it would be pre'aps jest as well if I was to come up 'ere an ask you what sort of soap you was wishful that I should use on them boards. The yaller soap, miss"—

There was nothing in the speech to have caused the paroxysm of fury that drove the red-haired girl into the middle of the room, almost shouting—

"Do you suppose *I* care what you use? Any kind will do!—*any* kind!"

The woman fled, and the red-haired girl looked at her own reflection in the glass for an instant and covered her face with her hands. It was as though she had shouted some shameless secret aloud.

CHAPTER VII

Roses red and roses white
Plucked I for my love's delight.
She would none of all my posies,—
Bade me gather her blue roses.

Half the world I wandered through,
Seeking where such flowers grew;
Half the world unto my quest
Answered but with laugh and jest.

It may be beyond the grave
She shall find what she would have.
Oh, 'twas but an idle quest,—
Roses white and red are best!
            —*Blue Roses.*

INDEED the sea had not changed. Its waters were low on the mud-banks, and the Marazion bell-buoy clanked and swung in the tide-way. On the white beach-sand dried stumps of sea-poppy shivered and chatted together.

"I don't see the old breakwater," said Maisie under her breath.

"Let's be thankful that we have as much as we have. I don't believe they've mounted a single new gun on the fort since we were here. Come and look."

They came to the glacis of Fort Keeling, and sat down in a nook sheltered from the wind under the tarred throat of a forty-pounder cannon.

"Now, if Amomma were only here!" said Maisie.

For a long time both were silent. Then Dick took Maisie's hand and called her by her name.

She shook her head and looked out to sea.

"Maisie, darling, doesn't it make any difference?"

"No!" between clenched teeth. "I'd —I'd tell you if it did; but it doesn't. Oh, Dick, please be sensible."

"Don't you think that it ever will?"

"No, I'm sure it won't."

"Why?"

Maisie rested her chin on her hand, and, still regarding the sea, spoke hurriedly—

"I know what you want perfectly well, but I can't give it you, Dick. It isn't my fault; indeed it isn't. If I felt that I could care for any one—But I don't feel that I care. I simply don't understand what the feeling means."

"Is that true, dear?"

"You've been very good to me, Dickie; and the only way I can pay you back is by speaking the truth. I daren't tell a fib. I despise myself quite enough as it is."

"What in the world for?"

"Because—because I take everything that you give me and I give you nothing in return. It's mean and selfish of me, and whenever I think of it it worries me."

"Understand once for all, then, that I can manage my own affairs, and if I choose to do anything you aren't to blame. You haven't a single thing to reproach yourself with, darling."

"Yes, I have, and talking only makes it worse."

"Then don't talk about it."

"How can I help myself? If you find me alone for a minute you are always talking about it; and when you aren't you look it. You don't know how I despise myself sometimes."

"Great goodness!" said Dick, nearly jumping to his feet. "Speak the truth now, Maisie, if you never speak it again! Do I—does this worrying bore you?"

"No. It does not."

"You'd tell me if it did?"

"I should let you know, I think."

"Thank you. The other thing is fatal. But you must learn to forgive a man when he's in love. He's always a nuisance. You must have known that?"

Maisie did not consider the last question worth answering, and Dick was forced to repeat it.

"There were other men, of course. They always worried just when I was in the middle of my work, and wanted me to listen to them."

"Did you listen?"

"At first; and they couldn't understand why I didn't care. And they used to praise my pictures; and I thought they meant it. I used to be proud of the praise, and tell Kami, and—I shall never forget—once Kami laughed at me."

"You don't like being laughed at, Maisie, do you?"

"I hate it. I never laugh at other people unless—unless they do bad work. Dick, tell me honestly what you think of my pictures generally,—of everything of mine that you've seen."

" 'Honest, honest, and honest over!' " quoted Dick from a catchword of long ago. "Tell me what Kami always says."

Maisie hesitated. "He—he says that there is feeling in them."

"How dare you tell me a fib like that? Remember, I was under Kami for two years. I know exactly what he says."

"It isn't a fib."

"It's worse; it's a half truth. Kami says, when he puts his head on one side, —so,—'Il y a du sentiment, mais il n'y a pas de parti pris.' " He rolled the r threateningly, as Kami used to do.

"Yes, that is what he says; and I'm beginning to think that he is right."

"Certainly he is." Dick admitted that two people in the world could do and say no wrong. Kami was the man.

"And now you say the same thing. It's so disheartening."

"I'm sorry, but you asked me to speak the truth. Besides, I love you too much to pretend about your work. It's strong, it's patient sometimes,—not always,—and sometimes there's power in it, but there's no special reason why it should be done at all. At least that's how it strikes me."

"There's no special reason why anything in the world should ever be done. You know that as well as I do. I only want success."

"You're going the wrong way to get it, then. Hasn't Kami ever told you so?"

"Don't quote Kami to me. I want to know what you think. My work's bad, to begin with."

"I didn't say that, and I don't think it."

"It's amateurish, then."

"That it most certainly is not. You're a workwoman, darling, to your bootheels, and I respect you for that."

"You don't laugh at me behind my back?"

"No, dear. You see, you are more to me than any one else. Put this cloak thing round you, or you'll get chilled."

Maisie wrapped herself in the soft marten skins, turning the grey kangaroo fur to the outside.

"This is delicious," she said, rubbing her chin thoughtfully along the fur. "Well? Why am I wrong in trying to get a little success?"

"Just because you try. Don't you understand, darling? Good work has nothing to do with—doesn't belong to —the person who does it. It's put into him or her from outside."

"But how does that affect"—

"Wait a minute. All we can do is to learn how to do our work, to be masters of our materials instead of servants, and never to be afraid of anything."

"I understand that."

"Everything else comes from outside ourselves. Very good. If we sit down quietly to work out notions that are sent to us, we may or we may not do something that isn't bad. A great deal depends on being master of the bricks and mortar of the trade. But the instant we begin to think about success and the effect of our work—to play with one eye on the gallery—we lose power and touch and everything else. At least that's how I have found it. Instead of being quiet and giving every power you possess to your work, you're fretting over something which you can neither help nor hinder by a minute. See?"

"It's so easy for you to talk in that way. People like what you do. Don't you ever think about the gallery?"

"Much too often; but I'm always punished for it by loss of power. It's as simple as the Rule of Three. If we make light of our work by using it for our own ends, our work will make light of us, and, as we're the weaker, we shall suffer."

"I don't treat my work lightly. You know that it's everything to me."

"Of course; but, whether you realize it or not, you give two strokes for yourself to one for your work. It isn't your fault, darling. I do exactly the same thing, and know that I'm doing it. Most of the French schools, and all the schools here, drive the students to work for their own credit, and for the sake of their pride. I was told that all the world was interested in my work, and everybody at Kami's talked turpentine, and I honestly believed that the world needed elevating and influencing, and all manner of impertinences, by my brushes. By Jove, I actually believed that! When my little head was bursting with a notion that I couldn't handle because I hadn't sufficient knowledge of my craft, I used to run about wondering at my own magnificence and getting ready to astonish the world."

"But surely one can do that sometimes?"

"Very seldom with malice aforethought, darling. And when it's done it's such a tiny thing, and the world's so big, and all but a millionth part of it doesn't care. Maisie, come with me and I'll show you something of the size of the world. One can no more avoid working than eating,—that goes on by itself,—but try to see what you are working for. I know such little heavens that I could take you to,—islands tucked away under the Line. You sight them after weeks of crashing through water as black as black marble because it's so deep, and you sit in the forechains day after day and see the sun rise almost afraid because the sea's so lonely."

"Who is afraid?—you, or the sun?"

"The sun, of course. And there are noises under the sea, and sounds overhead in a clear sky. Then you find your island alive with hot, moist orchids that make mouths at you and can do everything except talk. There's a waterfall in it three hundred feet high, just like a sliver of green jade laced with silver; and millions of wild bees live up in the rocks; and you can hear the fat cocoanuts falling from the palms; and you order an ivory-white servant to sling you a long, yellow hammock with tassels on it like ripe maize, and you put up your feet and hear the bees hum and the water fall till you go to sleep."

"Can one work there?"

"Certainly. One must do something always. You hang your canvas up in a palm-tree and let the parrots criticise. When they scuffle you heave a ripe custard-apple at them, and it bursts in a lather of cream. There are hundreds of places. Come and see them.

"I don't quite like that place. It sounds lazy. Tell me another."

"What do you think of a big, red, dead city built of red sandstone, with raw green aloes growing between the stones, lying out neglected on honey-colored sands? There are forty dead kings there, Maisie, each in a gorgeous tomb finer than all the others. You look at the palaces and streets and shops and tanks, and think that men must live there, till you find a wee grey squirrel rubbing its nose all alone in the market-place, and a jeweled peacock struts out of a carved doorway and spreads its tail against a marble screen as fine pierced as point-lace. Then a monkey— a little black monkey—walks through the main square to get a drink from a tank forty feet deep. He slides down the creepers to the water's edge, and a friend holds him by the tail, in case he should fall in."

"Is all that true?"

"I have been there and seen. Then evening comes, and the lights change till it's just as though you stood in the heart of a king-opal. A little before sundown, as punctually as clockwork, a big bristly wild boar, with all his family following, trots through the city gate, churning the foam on his tusks. You climb on the shoulder of a blind black stone god and watch that pig choose himself a palace for the night and stump in wagging his tail. Then the night-wind gets up, and the sands move, and you hear the desert outside the city singing, 'Now I lay me down to sleep,' and everything is dark till the moon rises. Maisie darling, come with me and see what the world is really like. It's very lovely, and it's very horrible,—but I won't let you see anything horrid,—and it doesn't care your life or mine for pictures or anything else except doing its own work and making love. Come, and I'll show you how to brew sangaree, and sling a hammock, and—oh, thou-sands of things, and you'll see for your-self what color means, and we'll find out together what love means, and then, maybe, we shall be allowed to do some good work. Come away!"

"Why?" said Maisie.

"How can you do anything until you have seen everything, or as much as you can? And besides, darling, I love you. Come along with me. You have no business here; you don't belong to this place; you're half a gypsy,—your face tells that; and I—even the smell of open water makes me restless. Come across the sea and be happy!"

He had risen to his feet, and stood in the shadow of the gun, looking down at the girl. The very short winter after-noon had worn away, and, before they knew, the winter moon was walking the

untroubled sea. Long rule' lines of silver showed where a ripple of the rising tide was turning over the mud-banks. The wind had dropped, and in the intense stillness they could hear a donkey cropping the frosty grass many yards away. A faint beating like that of a muffled drum, came out of the moon-haze.

"What's that?" said Maisie, quickly. "It sounds like a heart beating. Where is it?"

Dick was so angry at this sudden wrench to his pleadings that he could not trust himself to speak, and in this silence caught the sound. Maisie from her seat under the gun watched him with a certain amount of fear. She wished so much that he would be sensi-ble and cease to worry her with over-sea emotion that she both could and could not understand. She was not pre-pared, however, for the change in his face as he listened.

"It's a steamer," he said,—"a twin-screw steamer, by the beat. I can't make her out, but she must be stand-ing very close in-shore. Ah!" as the red of a rocket streaked the haze, "she's standing in to signal before she clears the Channel."

"Is it a wreck?" said Maisie, to whom these words were as Greek.

Dick's eyes were turned to the sea. "Wreck! What nonsense! She's only reporting herself. Red rocket forward—there's a green light aft now, and two red rockets from the bridge."

"What does that mean?"

"It's the signal of the Cross Keys Line running to Australia. I wonder which steamer it is." The note of his voice had changed; he seemed to be talking to himself, and Maisie did not approve of it. The moonlight broke the haze for a moment, touching the black sides of a long steamer working down Channel. "Four masts and three funnels—she's in deep draught, too. That must be the *Barralong*, or the *Bhutia*. No, the *Bhutia* has a clipper bow. It's the *Barralong*, to Australia. She'll lift the Southern Cross in a week,—lucky old tub!—oh, lucky old tub!"

He stared intently, and moved up the slope of the fort to get a better view, but the mist on the sea thickened again, and the beating of the screws grew fainter. Maisie called to him a little angrily, and he returned, still keeping his eyes to seaward. "Have you ever seen the Southern Cross blazing right over your head?" he asked. "It's superb!"

"No," she said, shortly, "and I don't want to. If you think it's so lovely, why don't you go and see it yourself?"

She raised her face from the soft blackness of the marten skins about her throat, and her eyes shone like diamonds. The moonlight on the grey kangaroo fur turned it to frosted silver of the coldest.

"By Jove, Maisie, you look like a little heathen idol tucked up there." The eyes showed that they did not appreciate the compliment. "I'm sorry," he continued. "The Southern Cross isn't worth looking at unless some one helps you to see. That steamer's out of hearing."

"Dick," she said, quietly, "suppose I were to come to you now,—be quiet a minute,—just as I am, and caring for you just as much as I do."

"Not as a brother, though? You said you didn't—in the Park."

"I never had a brother. Suppose I said, 'Take me to those places, and in time, perhaps, I might really care for you,' what would you do?"

"Send you straight back to where you came from, in a cab. No, I wouldn't; I'd let you walk. But you couldn't do it, dear. And I wouldn't run the risk. You're worth waiting for till you can come without reservation."

"Do you honestly believe that?"

"I have a hazy sort of idea that I do. Has it never struck you in that light?"

"Ye—es. I feel so wicked about it."

"Wickeder than usual?"

"You don't know all I think. It's almost too awful to tell."

"Never mind. You promised to tell me the truth—at least."

"It's so ungrateful of me, but—but, though I know you care for me, and I like to have you with me, I'd—I'd even sacrifice you, if that would bring me what I want."

"My poor little darling! I know that state of mind. It doesn't lead to good work."

"You aren't angry? Remember, I do despise myself."

"I'm not exactly flattered,—I had guessed as much before,—but I'm not angry. I'm sorry for you. Surely you ought to have left a littleness like that behind you, years ago."

"You've no right to patronize me! I only want what I have worked for so long. It came to *you* without any trouble, and—and I don't think it's fair."

"What can I do? I'd give ten years of my life to get you what you want.

But I can't help you; even I can't help."

A murmur of dissent from Maisie. He went on—

"And I know by what you have just said that you're on the wrong road to success. It isn't got at by sacrificing other people,—I've had that much knocked into me; you must sacrifice yourself, and live under orders, and never think for yourself, and never have real satisfaction in your work except just at the beginning, when you're reaching out after a notion."

"How can you believe all that?"

"There's no question of belief or disbelief. That's the law, and you take it or refuse it as you please. I try to obey, but I can't, and then my work turns bad on my hands. Under any circumstances, remember, four-fifths of everybody's work must be bad. But the remnant is worth the trouble for its own sake."

"Isn't it nice to get credit even for bad work?"

"It's much too nice. But— May I tell you something? It isn't a pretty tale, but you're so like a man that I forget when I'm talking to you."

"Tell me."

"Once when I was out in the Soudan I went over some ground that we had been fighting on for three days. There were twelve hundred dead; and we hadn't time to bury them."

"How ghastly!"

"I had been at work on a big double-sheet sketch, and I was wondering what people would think of it at home. The sight of that field taught me a good deal. It looked just like a bed of horrible toadstools in all colors, and—I'd never seen men in bulk go back to their beginnings before. So I began to understand that men and women were only material to work with, and that what they said or did was of no consequence. See? Strictly speaking, you might just as well put your ear down to the palette to catch what your colors are saying."

"Dick, that's disgraceful!"

"Wait a minute. I said, strictly speaking. Unfortunately, everybody must be either a man or a woman."

"I'm glad you allow that much."

"In your case I don't. You aren't a woman. But ordinary people, Maisie, must behave and work as such. That's what makes me so savage." He hurled a pebble toward the sea as he spoke. "I know that it is outside my business to care what people say; I can see that it spoils my output if I listen to 'em; and yet, confound it all,"—another pebble flew seaward,—"I can't help purring when I'm rubbed the right way. Even when I can see on a man's forehead that he is lying his way through a clump of pretty speeches, those lies make me happy and play the mischief with my hand."

"And when he doesn't say pretty things?"

"Then, belovedest,"—Dick grinned,— "I forget that I am the steward of these gifts, and I want to make that man love and appreciate my work with a thick stick. It's too humiliating altogether; but I suppose even if one were an angel and painted humans altogether from outside, one would lose in touch what one gained in grip."

Maisie laughed at the idea of Dick as an angel.

"But you seem to think," she said, "that everything nice spoils your hand."

"I don't think It's the law,—just the same as it was at Mrs. Jennett's. Everything that is nice does spoil your hand. I'm glad you see so clearly."

"I don't like the view."

"Nor I. But—have got orders: what can do? Are you strong enough to face it alone?"

"I suppose I must."

"Let me help, darling. We can hold each other very tight and try to walk straight. We shall blunder horribly, but it will be better than stumbling apart. Maisie, can't you see reason?"

"I don't think we should get on together. We should be two of a trade, so we should never agree."

"How I should like to meet the man who made that proverb! He lived in a cave and ate raw bear, I fancy. I'd make him chew his own arrow-heads. Well?"

"I should be only half married to you. I should worry and fuss about my work, as I do now. Four days out of the seven I'm not fit to speak to."

"You talk as if no one else in the world had ever used a brush. D'you suppose that I don't know the feeling of worry and bother and can't-get-at-ness? You're lucky if you only have it four days out of the seven. What difference would that make?"

"A great deal—if you had it too."

"Yes, but I could respect it. Another man might not. He might laugh at you. But there's no use talking about it. If you can think in that way you can't care for me—yet."

The tide had nearly covered the mud-banks, and twenty little ripples broke on the beach before Maisie chose to speak.

"Dick," she said, slowly, "I believe very much that you are better than I am."

"This doesn't seem to bear on the argument—but in what way?"

"I don't quite know, but in what you said about work and things; and then you're so patient. Yes, you're better than I am."

Dick considered rapidly the murkiness of an average man's life. There was nothing in the review to fill him with a sense of virtue. He lifted the hem of the cloak to his lips.

"Why," said Maisie, making as though she had not noticed, "can you see things that I can't? I don't believe what you believe; but you're right, I believe."

"If I've seen anything, God knows I couldn't have seen it but for you, and I know that I couldn't have said it except to you. You seemed to make everything clear for a minute; but I don't practice what I preach. You would help me. . . . There are only us two in the world for all purposes, and —and you like to have me with you?"

"Of course I do. I wonder if you can realize how utterly lonely I am!"

"Darling, I think I can."

"Two years ago, when I first took the little house, I used to walk up and down the back-garden trying to cry. I never can cry. Can you?"

"It's some time since I tried. What was the trouble? Overwork?"

"I don't know; but I used to dream that I had broken down, and had no money, and was starving in London. I thought about it all day, and it frightened me—oh, how it frightened me!"

"I know that fear. It's the most

terrible of all. It wakes me up in the night sometimes. You oughtn't to know anything about it."

"How do *you* know?"

"Never mind. Is your three hundred a year safe?"

"It's in Consols."

"Very well. If any one comes to you and recommends a better investment,—even if I should come to you,—don't you listen. Never shift the money for a minute, and never lend a penny of it,—even to the red-haired girl."

"Don't scold me so! I'm not likely to be foolish."

"The earth is full of men who'd sell their souls for three hundred a year; and women come and talk, and borrow a five-pound note here and a ten-pound note there; and a woman has no conscience in a money debt. Stick to your money, Maisie; for there's nothing more ghastly in the world than poverty in London. It's scared me. By Jove, it put the fear into *me!* And one oughtn't to be afraid of anything."

To each man is appointed his particular dread,—the terror that, if he does not fight against it, must cow him even to the loss of his manhood. Dick's experience of the sordid misery of want had entered into the deeps of him, and, lest he might find virtue too easy, that memory stood behind him, tempting to shame, when dealers came to buy his wares. As the Nilghai quaked against his will at the still green water of a lake or mill-dam, as Torpenhow flinched before any white arm that could cut or stab and loathed himself for flinching, Dick feared the poverty he has once tasted half in jest. His burden was heavier than the burdens of his companions. Maisie watched the face working in the moonlight.

"You've plenty of pennies now," she said, soothingly.

"I shall never get enough," he began, with vicious emphasis. Then, laughing, "I shall always be threepence short in my accounts."

"Why threepence?"

"I carried a man's bag once from Liverpool Street Station to Blackfriars Bridge. It was a six-penny job,—you needn't laugh; indeed it was,—and I wanted the money desperately. He only gave me threepence; and he hadn't even the decency to pay in silver. Whatever money I make, I shall never get that odd threepence out of the world."

This was not language befitting the man who had preached of the sanctity of work. It jarred on Maisie, who preferred her payment in applause, which, since all men desire it, must be of the right. She hunted for her little purse and gravely took out a threepenny bit.

"There it is," she said. "I'll pay you, Dickie; and don't worry any more; it isn't worth while. Are you paid?"

"I am," said the very human apostle of fair craft, taking the coin. "I'm paid a thousand times, and we'll close that account. It shall live on my watchchain; and you're an angel, Maisie."

"I'm very cramped, and I'm feeling a little cold. Good gracious! the cloak is all white, and so is your moustache! I never knew it was so chilly."

A light frost lay white on the shoulder of Dick's ulster. He, too, had forgotten the state of the weather. They laughed together, and with that laugh ended all serious discourse.

They ran inland across the waste

to warm themselves, then turned to look at the glory of the full tide under the moonlight and the intense black shadows of the furze-bushes. It was an additional joy to Dick that Maisie could see color even as he saw it,—could see the blue in the white of the mist, the violet that is in grey palings, and all things else as they are,—not of one hue, but a thousand. And the moonlight came into Maisie's soul, so that she, usually reserved, chattered of herself and of the things she took interest in,—of Kami, wisest of teachers, and of the girls in the studio,—of the Poles, who will kill themselves with overwork if they are not checked; of the French, who talk at great length of much more than they will ever accomplish; of the slovenly English, who toil hopelessly and cannot understand that inclination does not imply power; of the Americans, whose rasping voices in the hush of a hot afternoon strain tense-drawn nerves to breaking-point, and whose suppers lead to indigestion; of tempestuous Russians, neither to hold nor to bind, who tell the girls ghost stories till the girls shriek; of stolid Germans, who come to learn one thing, and, having mastered that much, stolidly go away and copy pictures forevermore. Dick listened enraptured because it was Maisie who spoke. He knew the old life.

"It hasn't changed much," he said. "Do they still steal colors at lunchtime?"

"Not steal. Attract is the word. Of course they do. I'm good—I only attract ultramarine; but there are students who'd attract flake-white."

"I've done it myself. You can't help it when the palettes are hung up. Every color is common property once it runs down,—even though you do start it with a drop of oil. It teaches people not to waste their tubes."

"I should like to attract some of your colors, Dick. Perhaps I might catch your success with them."

"I mustn't say a bad word, but I should like to. What in the world, which you've just missed a lovely chance of seeing, does success or want of success, or a three-storied success, matter compared with—No, I won't open that question again. It's time to go back to town."

"I'm sorry, Dick, but"—

"You're much more interested in that than you are in me."

"I don't know. I don't think I am."

"What will you give me if I tell you a sure short-cut to everything you want,—the trouble and the fuss and the tangle and all the rest? Will you promise to obey me?"

"Of course."

"In the first place, you must never forget a meal because you happen to be at work. You forgot your lunch twice last week," said Dick, at a venture, for he knew with whom he was dealing.

"No, no,—only once, really."

"That's bad enough. And you mustn't take a cup of tea and a biscuit in place of a regular dinner, because dinner happens to be a trouble."

"You're making fun of me!"

"I never was more in earnest in my life. Oh, my love, my love, hasn't it dawned on you yet what you are to me? Here's the whole earth in a conspiracy to give you a chill, or run over you, or drench you to the skin, or cheat you out of your money, or let you die of overwork and under feeding, and I haven't the mere right to look after you. Why, I don't even know if you have sense enough to put on warm things when the weather's cold."

"Dick, you're the most awful boy to talk to—really! How do you suppose I managed when you were away?"

"I wasn't here, and I didn't know. But now I'm back I'd give everything I have for the right of telling you to come in out of the rain."

"Your success too?"

This time it cost Dick a severe struggle to refrain from bad words.

"As Mrs. Jennett used to say, you're a trial, Maisie! You've been cooped up in the schools too long, and you think every one is looking at you. There aren't twelve hundred people in the world who understand pictures. The others pretend and don't care. Remember, I've seen twelve hundred men dead in toadstool-beds. It's only the voice of the tiniest little fraction of people that makes success. The real world doesn't care a tinker's—doesn't care a bit. For aught you or I know, every man in the world may be arguing with a Maisie of his own."

"Poor Maisie!"

"Poor Dick, I think. Do you believe while he's fighting for what's dearer than his life he wants to look at a picture? And even if he did, and if all the world did, and a thousand million people rose up and shouted hymns to my honor and glory, would that make up to me for the knowledge that you were out shopping in the Edgware Road on a rainy day without an umbrella? Now we'll go to the station."

"But you said on the beach"—persisted Maisie, with a certain fear.

Dick groaned aloud: "Yes, I know what I said. My work is everything I have, or am, or hope to be, to me, and I believe I've learned the law that governs it; but I've some lingering sense of fun left,—though you've nearly knocked it out of me. I can just see that it isn't everything to all the world. Do what I say, and not what I do."

Maisie was careful not to reopen debatable matters, and they returned to London joyously. The terminus stopped Dick in the midst of an eloquent harangue on the beauties of exercise. He would buy Maisie a horse,—such a horse as never yet bowed head to bit,— would stable it, with a companion, some twenty miles from London, and Maisie, solely for her health's sake, should ride with him twice or thrice a week.

"That's absurd," said she. "It wouldn't be proper."

"Now, who in all London to-night would have sufficient interest or audacity to call us two to account for anything we chose to do?"

Maisie looked at the lamps, the fog, and the hideous turmoil. Dick was right; but horseflesh did not make for Art as she understood it.

"You're very nice sometimes, but you're very foolish more times. I'm not going to let you give me horses, or take you out of your way to-night. I'll go home by myself. Only I want you to promise me something. You won't think any more about that extra threepence, will you? Remember, you've been paid; and I won't allow you to be spiteful and do bad work for a little thing like that.

You can be so big that you mustn't be tiny."

This was turning the tables with a vengeance. There remained only to put Maisie into her hansom.

"Good-bye," she said, simply. "You'll come on Sunday. It has been a beautiful day, Dick. Why can't it be like this always?"

"Because love's like line-work: you must go forward or backward; you can't stand still. By the way, go on with your line-work. Good-night, and, for my—for any sake, take care of yourself."

He turned to walk home, meditating. The day had brought him nothing that he had hoped for, but—surely this was worth many days—it had brought him nearer to Maisie. The end was only a question of time now, and the prize well worth the waiting. By instinct, once more, he turned to the river.

"And she understood at once," he said, looking at the water. "She found out my pet besetting sin on the spot, and paid it off. My God, how she understood! And she said I was better than she was! Better than she was!" He laughed at the absurdity of the notion. "I wonder if girls guess at one-half a man's life. They can't, or—they wouldn't marry us." He took her gift out of his pocket, and considered it in the light of a miracle and a pledge of the comprehension that, one day, would lead to perfect happiness. Meantime, Maisie was alone in London, with none to save her from danger. And the packed wilderness was very full of danger.

Dick made his prayer to Fate disjointedly after the manner of the heathen as he threw the piece of silver into the river. If any evil were to befall, let him bear the burden and let Maisie go unscathed, since the three-penny piece was dearest to him of all his possessions. It was a small coin in itself, but Maisie had given it, and the Thames held it, and surely the Fates would be bribed for this once.

The drowning of the coin seemed to cut him free from thought of Maisie for the moment. He took himself off the bridge and went whistling to his chambers with a strong yearning for some man-talk and tobacco after his first experience of an entire day spent in the society of a woman. There was a stronger desire at his heart when there rose before him an unsolicited vision of the *Barralong* dipping deep and sailing free for the Southern Cross.

CHAPTER VIII

And these two, as I have told you,
Were the friends of Hiawatha,
Chibiabos, the musician,
And the very strong man, Kwasind.
                              —*Hiawatha.*

TORPENHOW was paging the last sheets of some manuscript, while the Nilghai, who had come for chess and remained to talk tactics, was reading through the first part, commenting scornfully the while.

"It's picturesque enough and it's sketchy," said he; "but as a serious consideration of affairs in Eastern Europe, it's not worth much."

"It's off my hands at any rate. . . . Thirty-seven, thirty-eight, thirty-nine slips altogether, aren't there? That should make between eleven and twelve pages of valuable misinformation. Heigho!" Torpenhow shuffled the writing together and hummed—

Young lambs to sell, young lambs to sell,
If I'd as much money as I could tell,
I never would cry, Young lambs to sell!

Dick entered, self-conscious and a little defiant, but in the best of tempers with all the world.

"Back at last?" said Torpenhow.

"More or less. What have you been doing?"

"Work. Dickie, you behave as though the Bank of England were behind you. Here's Sunday, Monday, and Tuesday gone and you haven't done a line. It's scandalous."

"The notions come and go, my children—they come and go like our 'baccy," he answered, filling his pipe. "Moreover," he stooped to thrust a spill into the grate, "Apollo does not always stretch his— Oh, confound your clumsy jests, Nilghai!"

"This is not the place to preach the theory of direct inspiration," said the Nilghai, returning Torpenhow's large and workmanlike bellows to their nail on the wall. "We believe in cobblers' wax. La!—where you sit down."

"If you weren't so big and fat," said Dick, looking round for a weapon, "I'd"—

"No skylarking in my rooms. You two smashed half my furniture last time you threw the cushions about. You might have the decency to say How d' you do? to Binkie. Look at him."

Binkie had jumped down from the sofa and was fawning round Dick's knee, and scratching at his boots.

"Dear man!" said Dickie, snatching him up, and kissing him on the black patch above his right eye. "Did ums was, Binks? Did that ugly Nilghai turn you off the sofa? Bite him, Mr. Binkle." He pitched him on the Nilghai's stomach, as the big man lay at ease, and Binkie pretended to destroy the Nilghai inch by inch, till a sofa cushion extinguished him, and panting he stuck out his tongue at the company.

"The Binkie-boy went for a walk this morning before you were up, Torp. I saw him making love to the butcher at the corner when the shutters were being taken down—just as if he hadn't enough to eat in his own proper house," said Dick.

"Binks, is that a true bill?" said Torpenhow severely. The little dog retreated under the sofa-cushion, and showed by the fat white back of him that he really had no further interest in the discussion.

"'Strikes me that another disreputable dog went for a walk, too," said the Nilghai. "What made you get up so early? Torp said you might be buying a horse?"

"He knows it would need three of us for a serious business like that. No, I felt lonesome and unhappy, so I went out to look at the sea, and watch the pretty ships go by."

"Where did you go?"

"Somewhere on the Channel. Progly or Snigly, or some one horse watering-place was its name; I've forgotten; but it was only two hours' run from London and the ships went by."

"Did you see anything you knew?"

"Only the *Barralong* outward to Australia, and an Odessa grain-boat loaded down by the head. It was a thick day, but the sea smelt good."

"Wherefore put on one's best trousers to see the *Barralong?*" said Torpenhow, pointing.

"Because I've nothing except these things and my painting duds. Besides, I wanted to do honor to the sea."

"Did she make you feel restless?" asked the Nilghai, keenly.

"Crazy. Don't speak of it. I'm sorry I went."

Torpenhow and the Nilghai exchanged a look as Dick, stooping, busied himself among the former's boots and trees. "These will do," he said at last; "I can't say I think much of your taste in slippers, but the fit's the thing." He slipped his feet into a pair of sock-like sambhur-skin foot coverings, found a long chair, and lay at length.

"They're my own pet pair," Torpenhow said. "I was just going to put them on myself."

" 'All your reprehensible selfishness. Just because you see me happy for a minute, you want to worry me and stir me up. Find another pair."

"Good for you that Dick can't wear your clothes, Torp. You two live communistically," said the Nilghai.

"Dick never has anything that I can wear. He's only useful to sponge upon."

"Confound you, have you been rummaging round among my caches, then?" said Dick. "I put a sovereign in the tobacco-jar yesterday. How do you expect a man to keep his accounts properly if you"—

Here the Nilghai began to laugh, and Torpenhow joined him.

"Hid a sovereign yesterday! You're no sort of a financier. You loaned me

a fiver about a month back. Do you remember?" Torpenhow said.

"Yes, of course."

"Do you remember that I paid it you ten days later, and you put it at the bottom of the tobacco?"

"By Jove, did I? I thought it was in one of my color-boxes."

"You thought! About a week ago I went into your studio to get some 'baccy and found it."

"What did you do with it?"

"Took the Nilghai to a theatre and fed him."

"You couldn't feed the Nilghai under twice the money—not though you gave him Army beef. Well, I suppose I should have found it out sooner or later. What is there to laugh at?"

"You're a most amazing cuckoo in many directions," said the Nilghai, still chuckling over the thought of the dinner. "Never mind. We had both been working very hard, and it was your unearned increment we spent, and as you're only a loafer it didn't matter."

"That's pleasant—from the man who is bursting with my meat, too. I'll get that dinner back one of these days. Suppose we go to a theatre now."

" 'Put our boots on,—and dress.— *and* wash?" The Nilghai spoke very lazily.

"I withdraw the motion."

"Suppose, just for a change—as a startling variety, you know—we, that is to say *we,* get our charcoal and our canvas and go on with our work." Torpenhow spoke pointedly, but Dick only wriggled his toes inside the soft leather moccasins.

"What a one-idea'd clucker it is! If I had any unfinished figures on hand, I haven't any model; if I had my model, I haven't any spray, and I never leave charcoal unfixed over night; and if I had my spray and twenty photographs of backgrounds, I couldn't do anything to-night. I don't feel that way."

"Binkie-dog, he's a lazy hog, isn't he?" said the Nilghai.

"Very good, I *will* do some work," said Dick, rising swiftly. "I'll fetch the Nungapunga Book, and we'll add another picture to the Nilghai Saga."

"Aren't you worrying him a little too much?" asked the Nilghai, when Dick had left the room.

"Perhaps, but I know what he can turn out if he likes. It makes me savage to hear him praised for past work when I know what he ought to do. You and I are arranged for"—

"By Kismet and our own powers, more's the pity. I have dreamed of a good deal."

"So have I, but we know our limitations now. I'm dashed if I know what Dick's may be when he gives himself to his work. That's what makes me so keen about him."

"And when all's said and done, you will be put aside—quite rightly—for a female girl."

"I wonder. . . . Where do you think he has been to-day?"

"To the sea. Didn't you see the look in his eyes when he talked about her? He's as restless as a swallow in autumn."

"Yes; but did he go alone?"

"I don't know, and I don't care, but he has the beginnings of the go-fever upon him. He wants to up-stakes and move out. There's no mistaking the signs. Whatever he may have said before, he has the call upon him now."

"It might be his salvation," Torpenhow said.

"Perhaps—if you care to take the responsibility of being a saviour: I'm averse to tampering with souls myself."

Dick returned with a great clasp sketch-book that the Nilghai knew well and did not love too much. In it Dick had drawn in his playtime all manner of moving incidents, experienced by himself or related to him by the others, of all the four corners of the earth. But the wider range of the Nilghai's body and life attracted him most. When truth failed here he fell back on fiction of the wildest, and represented incidents in the Nilghai's career that were unseemly,—his marriages with many African princesses, his shameless betrayal, for Arab wives, of army corps to the Mahdi, his tattooment by skilled operators in Burmah, his interview (and his fears) with the yellow headsman in the blood-stained execution-ground of Canton, and finally, the passings of his spirit into the bodies of whales, elephants, and toucans. Torpenhow from time to time had added rhymed descriptions, and the whole was a curious piece of art, because Dick decided, having regard to the name of the book which being interpreted means "naked," that it would be wrong to draw the Nilghai with any clothes on, under any circumstances. Consequently the last sketch, representing that much-enduring man calling on the War Office to press his claims to the Egyptian medal, was hardly delicate. He settled himself comfortably at Torpenhow's table and turned over the pages.

"What a fortune you would have been to Blake, Nilghai!" he said. "There's a succulent pinkness about some of these sketches that's more than lifelike. 'The Nilghai surrounded while bathing by the Madieh'—that was founded on fact, eh?"

"It was very nearly my last bath, you irreverent dauber. Has Binkie come into the Saga yet?"

"No; the Binkie-boy hasn't done anything except eat and kill cats. Let's see. Here you are as a stained-glass saint in a church. 'Deuced decorative lines about your anatomy; you ought to be grateful for being handed down to posterity in this way. Fifty years hence you'll exist in rare and curious facsimiles at ten guineas each. What shall I try this time? The domestic life of the Nilghai?"

"'Hasn't got any."

"The undomestic life of the Nilghai, then. Of course! Mass-meeting of his wives in Trafalgar Square. That's it. They came from the ends of the earth to attend Nilghai's wedding to an English bride. This shall be in sepia. It's a sweet material to work with."

"It's a scandalous waste of time," said Torpenhow.

"Don't worry; it keeps one's hand in—specially when you begin without the pencil." He set to work rapidly. "That's Nelson's Column. Presently the Nilghai will appear shinning up it."

"Give him some clothes this time."

"Certainly—a veil and an orange-wreath, because he's been married."

"Gad, that's clever enough!" said Torpenhow, over his shoulder, as Dick brought out of the paper with three twirls of the brush a very fat back and laboring shoulder pressed against the stone.

"Just imagine," Dick continued, "if we could publish a few of these dear little things every time the Nilghai subsidizes a man who can write, to give the public an honest opinion of my pictures."

"Well, you'll admit I always tell you when I have done anything of that kind. I know I can't hammer you as you ought to be hammered, so I give the job to another. Young Maclagan, for instance"—

"No-o—one half-minute, old man; stick your hand out against the dark of the wall-paper—you only burble and call me names. That left shoulder's out of drawing. I must literally throw a veil over that. Where's my pen-knife? Well, what about Maclagan?"

"I only gave him his riding-orders to—to lambast you on general principles for not producing work that will last."

"Whereupon that young fool,"—Dick threw back his head and shut one eye as he shifted the page under his hand,—"being left alone with an ink-pot and what he conceived were his own notions, went and spilled them both over me in the papers. You might have engaged a grown man for the business, Nilghai. How do you think the bridal veil looks now, Torp?"

"How the deuce do three dabs and two scratches make the stuff stand away from the body as it does?" said Torpenhow, to whom Dick's methods were always new.

"It just depends on where you put 'em. If Maclagan had known that much about his business he might have done better."

"Why don't you put the damned dabs into something that will stay, then?"

insisted the Nilghai, who had really taken considerable trouble in hiring for Dick's benefit the pen of a young gentleman who devoted most of his waking hours to an anxious consideration of the aims and ends of Art, which, he wrote, was one and indivisible.

"Wait a minute till I see how I am going to manage my procession of wives. You seem to have married extensively, and I must rough 'em in with the pencil —Medes, Parthians, Edomites. . . . Now, setting aside the weakness and the wickedness and—and the fat-headedness of deliberately trying to do work that will live, as they call it, I'm content with the knowledge that I've done my best up to date, and I shan't do anything like it again for some hours at least—probably years. Most probably never."

"What! any stuff you have in stock your best work?" said Torpenhow.

"Anything you've sold?" said the Nilghai.

"Oh no. It isn't here and it isn't sold. Better than that, it can't be sold, and I don't think any one knows where it is. I'm sure I don't. . . . And yet more and more wives, on the north side of the square. Observe the virtuous horror of the lions!"

"You may as well explain," said Torpenhow, and Dick lifted his head from the paper.

"The sea reminded me of it," he said, slowly. "I wish it hadn't. It weighs some few thousand tons—unless you cut it out with a cold chisel."

"Don't be an idiot. You can't pose with us here," said the Nilghai.

"There's no pose in the matter at all. It's a fact. I was loafing from Lima to Auckland in a big, old, condemned passenger-ship turned into a cargo-boat and owned by a second-hand Italian firm. She was a crazy basket. We were cut down to fifteen tons of coal a day, and we thought ourselves lucky when we kicked seven knots an hour out of her. Then we used to stop and let the bearings cool down, and wonder whether the crack in the shaft was spreading."

"Were you a steward or a stoker in those days?"

"I was flush for the time being, so I was a passenger, or else I should have been a steward, I think," said Dick, with perfect gravity, returning to the procession of angry wives. "I was the only other passenger from Lima, and the ship was half empty, and full of rats and cockroaches and scorpions."

"But what has this to do with the picture?"

"Wait a minute. She had been in the China passenger trade and her lower deck had bunks for two thousand pigtails. Those were all taken down, and she was empty up to her nose, and the lights came through the port-holes— most annoying lights to work in till you got used to them. I hadn't anything to do for weeks. The ship's charts were in pieces and our skipper daren't run south for fear of catching a storm. So he did his best to knock all the Society Islands out of the water one by one, and I went into the lower deck, and did my picture on the port side as far forward in her as I could go. There was some brown paint and some green paint that they used for the boats, and some black paint for ironwork, and that was all I had."

"The passengers must have thought you mad."

"There was only one, and it was a woman; but it gave me the notion of my picture."

"What was she like?" said Torpenhow.

"She was a sort of Negroid-Jewess-Cuban; with morals to match. She couldn't read or write, and she didn't want to, but she used to come down and watch me paint, and the skipper didn't like it, because he was paying her passage and had to be on the bridge occasionally."

"I see. That must have been cheerful."

"It was the best time I ever had. To begin with, we didn't know whether we should go up or go down any minute when there was a sea on; and when it was calm it was paradise; and the woman used to mix the paints and talk broken English, and the skipper used to steal down every few minutes to the lower deck, because he said he was afraid of fire. So, you see, we could never tell when we might be caught, and I had a splendid notion to work out in only three keys of color."

"What was the notion?"

"Two lines in Poe—

"Neither the angels in Heaven above nor
    the demons down under the sea,
Can ever dissever my soul from the soul
    of the beautiful Annabel Lee.

It came out of the sea—all by itself. I drew that fight, fought out in green water over the naked, choking soul, and the woman served as the model for the devils and the angels both—sea-devils and sea-angels, and the soul half drowned between them. It doesn't sound much, but when there was a good light on the lower deck it looked very fine and creepy. It was seven by fourteen feet, all done in shifting light for shifting light."

"Did the woman inspire you much?" said Torpenhow.

"She and the sea between them—immensely. There was a heap of bad drawing in that picture. I remember I went out of my way to foreshorten for sheer delight of doing it, and I foreshortened damnably, but for all that it's the best thing I've ever done; and now I suppose the ship's broken up or gone down. Whew! What a time that was!"

"What happened after all?"

"It all ended. They were loading her with wool when I left the ship, but even the stevedores kept the picture clear to the last. The eyes of the demons scared them, I honestly believe."

"And the woman?"

"She was scared too when it was finished. She used to cross herself before she went down to look at it. Just three colors and no chance of getting any more, and the sea outside and unlimited love-making inside, and the fear of death atop of everything else, O Lord!" He had ceased to look at the sketch, but was staring straight in front of him across the room.

"Why don't you try something of the same kind now?" said Nilghai.

"Because those things come not by fasting and prayer. When I find a cargo-boat and a Jewess-Cuban and another notion and the same old life, I may."

"You won't find them here," said the Nilghai.

"No, 1 shall not." Dick shut the sketch-book with a bang. "This room's as hot as an oven. Open the window, some one."

He leaned into the darkness, watching the greater darkness of London below him. The chambers stood much higher than the other houses, commanding a hundred chimneys—crooked cowls that looked like sitting cats as they swung round, and other uncouth brick and zinc mysteries supported by iron stanchions and clamped by S-pieces. Northward the lights of Piccadilly Circus and Leicester Square threw a copper-colored glare above the black roofs, and southward lay all the orderly lights of the Thames. A train rolled out across one of the railway bridges, and its thunder drowned for a minute the dull roar of the streets. The Nilghai looked at his watch and said shortly, "That's the Paris night-mail. You can book from here to St. Petersburg if you choose."

Dick crammed head and shoulders out of the window and looked across the river. Torpenhow came to his side, while the Nilghai passed over quietly to the piano and opened it. Binkie, making himself as large as possible, spread out upon the sofa with the air of one who is not to be lightly disturbed.

"Well," said the Nilghai to the two pairs of shoulders, "have you never seen this place before?"

A steam-tug on the river hooted as she towed her barges to wharf. Then the boom of the traffic came into the room. Torpenhow nudged Dick. "Good place to bank in—bad place to bunk in, Dickie, isn't it?"

Dick's chin was in his hand as he answered, in the words of a general not without fame, still looking out on the darkness—" 'My God, what a city to loot!' "

Binkie found the night air tickling his whiskers and sneezed plaintively.

"We shall give the Binkie-dog a cold," said Torpenhow. "Come in," and they withdrew their heads. "You'll be buried in Kensal Green, Dick, one of these days, if it isn't closed by the time you want to go there—buried within two feet of some one else, his wife and his family."

"Allah forbid! I shall get away before that time comes. Give a man room to stretch his legs, Mr. Binkle." Dick flung himself down on the sofa and tweaked Binkie's velvet ears, yawning heavily the while.

"You'll find that wardrobe-case very much out of tune," Torpenhow said to the Nilghai. "It's never touched except by you."

"A piece of gross extravagance," Dick grunted. "The Nilghai only comes when I'm out."

"That's because you're always out. Howl, Nilghai, and let him hear."

The life of the Nilghai is fraud and
    slaughter,
His writings are watered Dickens and
    water;
But the voice of the Nilghai raised on
    high
Makes even the Mahdieh glad to die!

Dick quoted from Torpenhow's letter-press in the Nungapunga Book. "How do they call moose in Canada, Nilghai?"

The man laughed. Singing was his one polite accomplishment, as many Press-tents in far-off lands had known.

"What shall I sing?" said he, turning in the chair.

"'Moll Roe in the Morning,'" said Torpenhow, at a venture.

"No," said Dick, sharply, and the Nilghai opened his eyes. The old chanty whereof he, among a very few, possessed all the words was not a pretty one, but Dick had heard it many times before without wincing. Without prelude he launched into that stately tune that calls together and troubles the hearts of the gipsies of the sea—

Farewell and adieu to you, Spanish ladies,
Farewell and adieu to you, ladies of Spain.

Dick turned uneasily on the sofa, for he could hear the bows of the *Barralong* crashing into the green seas on her way to the Southern Cross. Then came the chorus—

We'll rant and we'll roar like true British sailors,
We'll rant and we'll roar across the salt seas,
Until we take soundings in the Channel of Old England
From Ushant to Scilly 'tis forty-five leagues.

"Thirty-five—thirty-five," said Dick, petulantly. "Don't tamper with Holy Writ. Go on, Nilghai."

The first land we made it was called the Deadman,

and they sang to the end very vigorously.

"That would be a better song if her

head were turned the other way—to the Ushant light, for instance," said the Nilghai.

"Flinging its arms about like a mad windmill," said Torpenhow. "Give us something else, Nilghai. You're in fine fog-horn form to-night."

"Give us the 'Ganges Pilot': you sang that in the square the night before El-Maghrib. By the way, I wonder how many of the chorus are alive to-night," said Dick.

Torpenhow considered for a minute. "By Jove! I believe only you and I. Raynor, Vickery and Deenes— all dead; Vincent caught smallpox in Cairo, carried it here and died of it. Yes, only you and I and the Nilghai."

"Umph! And yet the men here who've done their work in a well-warmed studio all their lives, with a policeman at each corner, say that I charge too much for my pictures."

"They are buying your work, not your insurance policies, dear child," said the Nilghai.

"I gambled with one to get at the other. Don't preach. Go on with the 'Pilot.' Where in the world did you get that song?"

"On a tombstone," said the Nilghai. "On a tombstone in a distant land. I made it an accompaniment with heaps of bass chords."

"Oh, Vanity! Begin." And the Nilghai began—

"I have slipped my cable, messmates, I'm drifting down with the tide,
I have my sailing orders, while ye at anchor ride.
And never on fair June morning have I put out to sea
With clearer conscience or better hope, or a heart more light and free.

"Shoulder to shoulder, Joe, my boy, into
    the crowd like a wedge
Strike with the hangers, messmates, but
    do not cut with the edge.
Cries Charnock, 'Scatter the fagots,
    double that Brahmin in two,
The tall pale widow for me, Joe, the
    little brown girl for you!'

"Young Joe (you're nearing sixty), why
    is your hide so dark?
Katie has soft fair blue eyes, who black-
    ened yours?—Why, hark!"

They were all singing now, Dick with
the roar of the wind of the open sea
about his ears as the deep bass voice
let itself go.

"The morning gun—Ho, steady!—the
    arquebuses to me!
I ha' sounded the Dutch High Admiral's
    heart as my lead doth sound the sea.

"Sounding, sounding the Ganges, float-
    ing down with the tide,
Moor me close to Charnock, next to my
    nut-brown bride.
My blessing to Kate at Fairlight—Hol-
    well, my thanks to you;
Steady! We steer for Heaven, through
    sand-drifts cold and blue."

"Now what is there in that nonsense
to make a man restless?" said Dick,
hauling Binkie from his feet to his
chest.

"It depends on the man," said Torpenhow.

"The man who has been down to
look at the sea," said the Nilghai.

"I didn't know she was going to upset me in this fashion."

"That's what men say when they go
to say good-bye to a woman. It's more
easy though to get rid of three women
than a piece of one's life and surroundings."

"But a woman can be"—began Dick,
unguardedly.

"A piece of one's life," continued
Torpenhow. "No, she can't." His face
darkened for a moment. "She says
she wants to sympathize with you and
help you in your work, and everything
else that clearly a man must do for
himself. Then she sends round five
notes a day to ask why the dickens you
haven't been wasting your time with
her."

"Don't generalize," said the Nilghai.
"By the time you arrive at five notes a
day you must have gone through a
good deal and behaved accordingly.
'Shouldn't begin these things, my son."

"I shouldn't have gone down to the
sea," said Dick, just a little anxious to
change the conversation. "And you
shouldn't have sung."

"The sea isn't sending you five notes
a day," said the Nilghai.

"No, but I'm fatally compromised.
She's an enduring old hag, and I'm
sorry I ever met her. Why wasn't I
born and bred and dead in a three-pair
back?"

"Hear him blaspheming his first love!
Why in the world shouldn't you listen to
her?" said Torpenhow.

Before Dick could reply the Nilghai
lifted up his voice with a shout that
shook the windows, in "The Men of the
Sea," that begins, as all know, "The
sea is a wicked old woman," and after
racing through eight lines whose imagery is truthful, ends in a refrain, slow
as the clacking of a capstan when the
boat comes unwillingly up to the bars
where the men sweat and tramp in the
shingle.

" 'Ye that bore us, O restore us!
She is kinder than ye;
For the call is on our heart-strings!'
Said The Men of the Sea."

The Nilghai sang the verse twice,
with simple craft, intending that Dick
should hear. But Dick was waiting
for the farewell of the men to their
wives.

" 'Ye that love us, can ye move us?
She is dearer than ye;
And your sleep will be the sweeter,'
Said The Men of the Sea."

The rough words beat like the blows
of the waves on the bows of the rickety
boat from Lima in the days when Dick
was mixing paints, making love, drawing
devils and angels in the half dark, and
wondering whether the next minute would
place the Italian captain's knife between
his shoulder-blades. And the go-fever,
which is more real than many doctors'
diseases, waked and raged, urging him
who loved Maisie beyond anything in
the world, to go away and taste the
old hot, unregenerate life again,—to
scuffle, swear, gamble, and love light
loves with his fellows; to take ship and
know the sea once more, and by her be-
get pictures; to talk to Binat among the
sands of Port Said while Yellow 'Tina
mixed the drinks; to hear the crackle of
musketry, and see the smoke roll outward, thin and thicken again till the
shining black faces came through, and in
that hell every man was strictly responsible for his own head, and his own
alone, and struck with an unfettered
arm. It was impossible, utterly impossible, but—

" 'Oh, our fathers, in the churchyard,
She is older than ye,

And our graves will be the greener;
Said The Men of the Sea."

"What is there to hinder?" said Torpenhow, in the long hush that followed
the song.

"You said a little time since that you
wouldn't come for a walk round the
world, Torp."

"That was months ago, and I only
objected to your making money for
traveling expenses. You've shot your
bolt here and it has gone home. Go
away and do some work, and see some
things."

"Get some of the fat off you; you're
disgracefully out of condition," said the
Nilghai, making a plunge from the chair
and grasping a handful of Dick generally over the right ribs. "Soft as
putty—pure tallow born of over-feed-
ing. Train it off, Dickie."

"We're all equally gross, Nilghai.
Next time you have to take the field
you'll sit down, wink your eyes, gasp,
and die in a fit."

"Never mind. You go away on a
ship. Go to Lima again, or to Brazil.
There's always trouble in South America."

"Do you suppose I want to be told
where to go. Great Heavens, the only
difficulty is to know where I'm to stop.
But I shall stay here, as I told you
before."

"Then you'll be buried in Kensal
Green and turn into adipocere with the
others," said Torpenhow. "Are you
thinking of commissions in hand? Pay
forfeit and go. You've money enough
to travel as a king if you please."

"You've the grisliest notions of
amusement, Torp. I think I see myself
shipping first class on a six-thousand-

ton hotel, and asking the third engineer what makes the engines go round, and whether it isn't very warm in the stoke-hold. Ho! ho! I should ship as a loafer if ever I shipped at all, which I'm not going to do. I shall compromise, and go for a small trip to begin with."

"That's something at any rate. Where will you go?" said Torpenhow. "It would do you all the good in the world, old man."

The Nilghai saw the twinkle in Dick's eye and refrained from speech.

"I shall go in the first place to Rath-ray's stable, where I shall hire one horse, and take him very carefully as far as Richmond Hill. Then I shall walk him back again, in case he should accidentally burst into a lather and make Rathray angry. I shall do that to-mor-row, for the sake of air and exercise."

"Bah!" Dick had barely time to throw up his arm and ward off the cush-ion that the disgusted Torpenhow heav-ed at his head.

"Air and exercise indeed," said the Nilghai, sitting down heavily on Dick. "Let's give him a little of both. Get the bellows, Torp."

At this point the conference broke up in disorder, because Dick would not open his mouth till the Nilghai held his nose fast, and there was some trouble in forcing the nozzle of the bellows be-tween his teeth; and even when it was there he weakly tried to puff against the force of the blast, and his cheeks blew up with a great explosion; and the enemy becoming helpless with laughter he so beat them over the head with a soft sofa-cushion that that became un-sewn and distributed its feathers, and Binkie, interfering in Torpenhow's inter-ests, was bundled into the half-empty bag and advised to scratch his way out, which he did after a while, traveling rapidly up and down the floor in the shape of an agitated green haggis, and when he came out looking for satisfac-tion, the three pillars of his world were picking feathers out of their hair.

"A prophet has no honor in his own country," said Dick, ruefully, dusting his knees. "This filthy fluff will never brush off my bags."

"It was all for your good," said the Nilghai. " 'Nothing like air and exer-cise."

"All for your good," said Torpenhow, not in the least with reference to past clowning. "It would let you focus things at their proper worth and prevent your becoming slack in this hot-house of a town. Indeed it would, old man. I shouldn't have spoken if I hadn't thought so. Only, you make a joke of everything."

"Before God I do no such thing," said Dick, quickly and earnestly. "You don't know me if you think that."

"I don't think it," said the Nilghai.

"How can fellows like ourselves, who know what life and death really mean, dare to make a joke of anything? I know we pretend it, to save ourselves from breaking down or going to the other extreme. Can't I see, old man, how you're always anxious about me, and try to advise me to make my work better? Do you suppose I don't think about that myself? But you can't help me—you can't help me—not even you. I must play my own hand alone in my own way."

"Hear, hear," from the Nilghai.

"What's the one thing in the Nilghai

Saga that I've never drawn in the Nungapunga Book?" Dick continued to Torpenhow, who was a little astonished at the outburst.

Now there was one blank page in the book given over to the sketch that Dick had not drawn of the crowning exploit in the Nilghai's life; when that man, being young and forgetting that his body and bones belonged to the paper that employed him, had ridden over sunburned slippery grass in the rear of Bredow's brigade on the day that the troopers flung themselves at Canrobert's artillery, and for aught they knew twenty battalions in front, to save the battered 24th German Infantry, to give time to decide the fate of Vionville, and to learn ere their remnant came back to Flavigay that cavalry can attack and crumple and break unshaken infantry. Whenever he was inclined to think over a life that might have been better, an income that might have been larger, and a soul that might have been considerably cleaner, the Nilghai would comfort himself with the thought, "I rode with Bredow's brigade at Vionville," and take heart for any lesser battle the next day might bring.

"I know," he said, very gravely. "I was always glad that you left it out."

"I left it out because Nilghai taught me what the German army learned then, and what Schmidt taught their cavalry. I don't know German. What is it? 'Take care of the time and the dressing will take care of itself.' I must ride my own line to my own beat, old man."

"*Tempo ist richtung*. You've learned your lesson well," said the Nilghai. "He must go alone. He speaks truth, Torp."

"Maybe I'm as wrong as I can be—

hideously wrong. I must find that out for myself, as I have to think things out for myself, but I daren't turn my head to dress by the next man. It hurts me a great deal more than you know not to be able to go, but I cannot, that's all. I must do my own work and live my own life in my own way, because I'm responsible for both. Only don't think I frivol about it, Torp. I have my own matches and sulpher, and I'll make my own hell, thanks."

There was an uncomfortable pause. Then Torpenhow said blandly, "What did the Governor of North Carolina say to the Governor of South Carolina?"

"Excellent notion. It *is* a long time between drinks. There are the makings of a very fine prig in you, Dick," said the Nilghai.

"I've liberated my mind, estimable Binkie, with the feathers in his mouth." Dick picked up the still indignant one and shook him tenderly. "You're tied up in a sack and made to run about blind, Binkie-wee, without any reason, and it has hurt your little feelings. Never mind. *Sic volo, sic jubeo, stet pro ratione voluntas*, and don't sneeze in my eye, because I talk Latin. Goodnight."

He went out of the room.

"That's distinctly one for you," said the Nilghai. "I told you it was hopeless to meddle with him. He's not pleased."

"He'd swear at me if he weren't. I can't make it out. He has the go-fever upon him and he won't go. I only hope that he mayn't have to go some day when he doesn't want to," said Torpenhow.

* * * * * *

In his own room Dick was settling a

question with himself—and the question was whether all the world, and all that was therein, and a burning desire to exploit both, was worth one three-penny piece thrown into the Thames.

"It came of seeing the sea, and I'm a cur to think about it," he decided. "After all the honeymoon will be that tour—with reservations; only . . . only I didn't realize that the sea was so strong. I didn't feel it so much when I was with Maisie. These damnable songs did it. He's beginning again."

But it was only Herrick's Nightpiece to Julia that the Nilghai sang, and before it was ended Dick reappeared on the threshold, not altogether clothed indeed, but in his right mind, thirsty and at peace.

The mood had come and gone with the rising and the falling of the tide by Fort Keeling.

CHAPTER IX

"If I have taken the common clay
    And wrought it cunningly
In the shape of a god that was digged a
        clod,
    The greater honor to me."

"If thou hast taken the common clay,
    And thy hands be not free
From the taint of the soil, thou hast
        made thy spoil
    The greater shame to thee."
                    —*The Two Potters.*

He did no work of any kind for the rest of the week. Then came another Sunday. He dreaded and longed for the day always, but since the red-haired girl had sketched him there was rather more dread than desire in his mind.

He found that Maisie had entirely neglected his suggestions about line-work. She had gone off at score filled with some absurd notion for "fancy

head." It cost Dick something to command his temper.

"What's the good of suggesting anything?" he said, pointedly.

"Ah, but this will be a picture,—a real picture; and I know that Kami will let me send it to the Salon. You don't mind, do you?"

"I suppose not. But you won't have time for the Salon."

Maisie hesitated a little. She even felt uncomfortable.

"We're going over to France a month sooner because of it. I shall get the idea sketched out here and work it up at Kami's."

Dick's heart stood still, and he came very near to being disgusted with his queen who could do no wrong. "Just when I thought I had made some headway, she goes off chasing butterflies. It's too maddening!"

There was no possibility of arguing, for the red-haired girl was in the studio. Dick could only look unutterable reproach.

"I'm sorry," he said, "and I think you make a mistake. But what's the idea of your new picture?"

"I took it from a book."

"That's bad, to begin with. Books aren't the places for pictures. And"—

"It's this," said the red-haired girl behind him. "I was reading it to Maisie the other day from *The City of Dreadful Night*. D'you know the book?"

"A little. I am sorry I spoke. There are pictures in it. What has taken her fancy?"

"The description of the Melancolia—
"Her folded wings as of a mighty eagle,
But all too impotent to lift the regal
Robustness of her earth-born strength
            and pride.

And here again. (Maisie, get the tea, dear.)

"The forehead charged with baleful thoughts and dreams,
The household bunch of keys, the housewife's gown,
Voluminous indented, and yet rigid
As though a shell of burnished metal frigid,
Her feet thick-shod to tread all weakness down."

There was no attempt to conceal the scorn of the lazy voice. Dick winced.

"But that has been done already by an obscure artist of the name of Durer," said he. "How does the poem run?—

"Three centuries and threescore years ago,
With phantasies of his peculiar thought.

You might as well try to rewrite *Hamlet*. It will be waste of time."

"No, it won't," said Maisie, putting down the teacups with clatter to reassure herself. "And I mean to do it. Can't you see what a beautiful thing it would make?"

"How in perdition can one do work when one hasn't had the proper training? Any fool can get a notion. It needs training to drive the thing through,—training and conviction; not rushing after the first fancy." Dick spoke between his teeth.

"You don't understand," said Maisie. "I think I can do it."

Again the voice of the girl behind him—

"Baffled and beaten back, she works on still;
Weary and sick of soul, she works the more.

Sustained by her indomitable will,
The hands shall fashion, and the brain shall pore,
And all her sorrow shall be turned to labor—

I fancy Maisie means to embody herself in the picture."

"Sitting on a throne of rejected pictures? No, I shan't, dear. The notion in itself has fascinated me.—Of course you don't care for fancy heads, Dick. I don't think you could do them. You like blood and bones."

"That's a direct challenge. If you can do a Melancolia that isn't merely a sorrowful female head, I can do a better one; and I will, too. What d'you know about Melancolias?" Dick firmly believed that he was even then tasting three-quarters of all the sorrow in the world.

"She was a woman," said Maisie, "and she suffered a great deal,—till she could suffer no more. Then she began to laugh at it all, and then I painted her and sent her to the Salon."

The red-haired girl rose up and left the room, laughing.

Dick looked at Maisie humbly and hopelessly.

"Never mind about the picture," he said. "Are you really going back to Kami's a month before your time?"

"I must, if I want to get the picture done."

"And that's all you want?"

"Of course. Don't be stupid, Dick."

"You haven't the power. You have only the ideas—the ideas and the little cheap impulses. How you could have kept at your work for ten years steadily is a mystery to me. So you are really going,—a month before you need?"

"I must do my work."

"Your work—bah! . . . No, I didn't mean that. It's all right, dear. Of course you must do your work, and —I think I'll say good-bye for this week."

"Won't you even stay for tea?"

"No, thank you. Have I your leave to go, dear? There's nothing more you particularly want me to do, and the line-work doesn't matter."

"I wish you could stay, and then we could talk over my picture. If only one single picture's a success it draws attention to all the others. I know some of my work is good, if only people could see. And you needn't have been so rude about it."

"I'm sorry. We'll talk the Melancolia over some one of the other Sundays. There are four more—yes, one, two, three, four—before you go. Good-bye, Maisie."

Maisie stood by the studio window, thinking, till the red-haired girl returned, a little white at the corners of her lips.

"Dick's gone off," said Maisie. "Just when I wanted to talk about the picture. Isn't it selfish of him?"

Her companion opened her lips as if to speak, shut them again, and went on reading *The City of Dreadful Night*.

Dick was in the Park, walking round and round a tree that he had chosen as his confidante for many Sundays past. He was swearing audibly, and when he found that the infirmities of the English tongue hemmed in his rage, he sought consolation in Arabic, which is expressly designed for the use of the afflicted. He was not pleased with the reward of his patient service; nor was he pleased

with himself; and it was long before he arrived at the proposition that the queen could do no wrong.

"It's a losing game," he said. "I'm worth nothing when a whim of hers is in question. But in a losing game at Port Said we used to double the stakes and go on. She do a Melancolia! She hasn't the power, or the insight, or the training. Only the desire. She's cursed with the curse of Reuben. She won't do line-work, because it means real work; and yet she's stronger than I am. I'll make her understand that I can beat her on her own Melancolia. Even then she wouldn't care. She says I can only do blood and bones. I don't believe she has blood in her veins. All the same I love her; and I must go on loving her; and if I can humble her inordinate vanity I will. I'll do a Melancolia that shall be something like a Melancolia,— 'the Melancolia that transcends all wit.' I'll do it at once, con—bless her."

He discovered that the notion would not come to order, and that he could not free his mind for an hour from the thought of Maisie's departure. He took very small interest in her rough studies for the Melancolia when she showed them next week. The Sundays were racing past, and the time was at hand when all the church bells in London could not ring Maisie back to him. Once or twice he said something to Binkie about "hermaphroditic futilities," but the little dog received so many confidences both from Torpenhow and Dick that he did not trouble his tulip-ears to listen.

Dick was permitted to see the girls off. They were going by the Dover night-boat; and they hoped to return in August. It was then February, and Dick felt that he was being hardly used. Maisie was so busy stripping the small house across the Park, and packing her canvases, that she had no time for thought. Dick went down to Dover and wasted a day there fretting over a wonderful possibility. Would Maisie at the very last allow him one small kiss? He reflected that he might capture her by the strong arm, as he had seen women captured in the Southern Soudan, and lead her away; but Maisie would never be led. She would turn her grey eyes upon him and say, "Dick, how selfish you are!" Then his courage would fail him. It would be better, after all, to beg for that kiss.

Maisie looked more than usually kissable as she stepped from the night-mail on to the windy pier, in a grey waterproof and a little grey cloth traveling-cap. The red-haired girl was not so lovely. Her green eyes were hollow and her lips were dry. Dick saw the trunks aboard, and went to Maisie's side in the darkness under the bridge. The mail-bags were thundering into the forehold, and the red-haired girl was watching them.

"You'll have a rough passage to-night," said Dick. "It's blowing outside. I suppose I may come over and see you if I'm good?"

"You mustn't. I shall be busy. At least, if I want you I'll send for you. But I shall write from Vitry-sur-Marne. I shall have heaps of things to consult you about. Oh, Dick, you have been so good to me!—so good to me!"

"Thank you for that, dear. It hasn't made any difference, has it?"

"I can't tell a fib. It hasn't—in that way. But don't think I'm not grateful."

"Damn the gratitude!" said Dick, huskily, to the paddle-box.

"What's the use of worrying? You know I should ruin your life, and you'd ruin mine, as things are now. You remember what you said when you were so angry that day in the Park? One of us has to be broken. Can't you wait till that day comes?"

"No, love. I want you unbroken—all to myself."

Maisie shook her head. "My poor Dick, what can I say?"

"Don't say anything. Give me a kiss? Only one kiss, Maisie. I'll swear I won't take any more. You might as well, and then I can be sure you're grateful."

Maisie put her cheek forward, and Dick took his reward in the darkness. It was only one kiss, but, since there was no time-limit specified, it was a long one. Maisie wrenched herself free angrily, and Dick stood abashed and tingling from head to heel.

"Good-bye, darling. I didn't mean to scare you. I'm sorry. Only—keep well and do good work,—specially the Melancolia. I'm going to do one, too. Remember me to Kami, and be careful what you drink. Country drinking-water is bad everywhere, but it's worse in France. Write to me if you want anything, and good-bye. Say good-bye to the what-you-call-um girl, and—can't I have another kiss? No. You're quite right. Good-bye."

A shout told him that it was not seemly to charge up the mail-bag incline. He reached the pier as the steamer began to move off, and he followed her with his heart.

"And there's nothing—nothing in the wide world—to keep us apart except her obstinacy. These Calais night-boats are much too small. I'll get Torp to write to the papers about it. She's beginning to pitch already."

Maisie stood where Dick had left her till she heard a little gasping cough at her elbow. The red-haired girl's eyes were alight with cold flame.

"He kissed you!" she said. "How could you let him, when he wasn't anything to you? How dared you take a kiss from him! Oh, Maisie, let's go to the ladies' cabin. I'm sick,—deadly sick."

"We aren't into open water yet. Go down, dear, and I'll stay here. I don't like the smell of the engines. . . . Poor Dick! He deserved one,—only one. But I didn't think he'd frighten me so."

Dick returned to town next day just in time for lunch, for which he had telegraphed. To his disgust, there were only empty plates in the studio. He lifted up his voice like the bears in the fairy-tale, and Torpenhow entered, looking very guilty.

"H'sh!" said he. "Don't make such a noise. I took it. Come into my rooms, and I'll show you why."

Dick paused amazed at the threshold, for on Torpenhow's sofa lay a girl asleep and breathing heavily. The little cheap sailor-hat, the blue-and-white dress, fitter for June than for February, dabbled with mud at the skirts, the jacket trimmed with imitation Astrakhan and ripped at the shoulder-seams, the one-and-elevenpenny umbrella, and, above all, the disgraceful condition of the kid-topped boots, declared all things.

"Oh, I say, old man, this is too bad! You mustn't bring this sort up here. They steal things from the rooms."

"It looks bad, I admit, but I was coming in after lunch, and she staggered into the hall. I thought she was drunk at first, but it was collapse. I couldn't leave her as she was, so I brought her up here and gave her your lunch. She was fainting from want of food. She went fast asleep the minute she had finished."

"I know something of that complaint. She's been living on sausages, I suppose. Torp, you should have handed her over to a policeman for presuming to faint in a respectable house. Poor little wretch! Look at that face! There isn't an ounce of immorality in it. Only folly,—slack, fatuous, feeble, futile folly. It's a typical head. D'you notice how the skull begins to show through the flesh padding on the face and cheek-bone?"

"What a cold-blooded barbarian it is! Don't hit a woman when she's down. Can't we do anything? She was simply dropping with starvation. She almost fell into my arms, and when she got to the food she ate like a wild beast. It was horrible."

"I can give her money, which she would probably spend in drinks. Is she going to sleep forever?"

The girl opened her eyes and glared at the men between terror and effrontery.

"Feeling better?" said Torpenhow.

"Yes. Thank you. There aren't many gentlemen that are as kind as you are. Thank you."

"When did you leave service?" said

Dick, who had been watching the scarred and chapped hands.

"How did you know I was in service? I was. General servant. I didn't like it."

"And how do you like being your own mistress?"

"Do I look as if I liked it?"

"I suppose not. One moment. Would you be good enough to turn your face to the window?"

The girl obeyed, and Dick watched her face keenly,—so keenly that she made as if to hide behind Torpenhow.

"The eyes have it," said Dick, walking up and down. "They are superb eyes for my business. And, after all, every head depends on the eyes. This has been sent from heaven to make up for—what was taken away. Now the weekly strain's off my shoulders, I can get to work in earnest. Evidently sent from heaven. Yes. Raise your chin a little, please."

"Gently, old man, gently. You're scaring somebody out of her wits," said Torpenhow, who could see the girl trembling.

"Don't let him hit me! Oh, please don't let him hit me! I've been hit cruel to-day because I spoke to a man. Don't let him look at me like that! He's reg'lar wicked that one. Don't let him look at me like that, neither! Oh, I feel as if I hadn't nothing on when he looks at me like that!"

The overstrained nerves in the frail body gave way, and the girl wept like a little child and began to scream. Dick threw open the window, and Torpenhow flung the door back.

"There you are," said Dick, soothingly. "My friend here can call for a policeman, and you can run through that door. Nobody is going to hurt you."

The girl sobbed convulsively for a few minutes, and then tried to laugh.

"Nothing in the world to hurt you. Now listen to me for a minute. I'm what they call an artist by profession. You know what artists do?"

"They draw the things in red and black ink on the pop-shop labels."

"I dare say. I haven't risen to pop-shop labels yet. Those are done by the Academicians. I want to draw your head."

"What for?"

"Because it's pretty. That is why you will come to the room across the landing three times a week at eleven in the morning, and I'll give you three quid a week just for sitting still and being drawn. And there's a quid on account."

"For nothing? Oh, my!" The girl turned the sovereign in her hand, and with more foolish tears; "Ain't neither o' you two gentlemen afraid of my bilking you?"

"No. Only ugly girls do that. Try and remember this place. And, by the way, what's your name?"

"I'm Bessie,—Bessie— It's no use giving the rest. Bessie Broke,—Stone-broke if you like. What's your names? But there,—no one ever gives the real ones."

Dick consulted Torpenhow with his eyes.

"My name's Heldar, and my friend's called Torpenhow; and you must be sure to come here. Where do you live?"

"South-the-water, — one room,—five

and sixpence a week. Aren't you making fun of me about that three quid?"

"You'll see later on. And, Bessie, next time you come, remember, you needn't wear that paint. It's bad for the skin, and I have all the colors you'll be likely to need."

Bessie withdrew, scrubbing her cheek with a ragged pocket-handkerchief. The two men looked at each other.

"You're a man," said Torpenhow.

"I'm afraid I've been a fool. It isn't our business to run about the earth reforming Bessie Brokes. And a woman of any kind has no right on this landing."

"Perhaps she won't come back."

"She will if she thinks she can get food and warmth here. I know she will, worse luck. But remember, old man, she isn't a woman: she's my model; and be careful."

"The idea! She's a dissolute little scarecrow,—a gutter-snippet and nothing more."

"So you think. Wait till she has been fed a little and freed from fear. That fair type recovers itself very quickly. You won't know her in a week or two, when that abject fear has died out of her eyes. She'll be too happy and smiling for my purposes."

"But surely you're taking her out of charity?—to please me?"

"I am not in the habit of playing with hot coals to please anybody. She has been sent from heaven, as I may have remarked before, to help me with my Melancolia."

"Never heard a word about the lady before."

"What's the use of having a friend, if you must sling your notions at him in words? You ought to know what I'm thinking about. You've heard me grunt lately?"

"Even so; but grunts mean anything in your language, from bad 'baccy to wicked dealers. And I don't think I've been much in your confidence for some time."

"It was a high and soulful grunt. You ought to have understood that it meant the Melancolia." Dick walked Torpenhow up and down the room, keeping silence. Then he smote him in the ribs. "*Now* don't you see it? Bessie's abject futility, and the terror in her eyes, welded on to one or two details in the way of sorrow that have come under my experience lately. Likewise some orange and black,—two keys of each. But I can't explain on an empty stomach."

"It sounds mad enough. You'd better stick to your soldiers, Dick, instead of maundering about heads and eyes and experiences."

"Think so?" Dick began to dance on his heels, singing—

"They're as proud as a turkey when they hold the ready cash,
    You ought to 'ear the way they laugh an' joke;
They are tricky an' they're funny when they've got the ready money,—
    Ow! but see 'em when they're all stone-broke."

Then he sat down to pour out his heart to Maisie in a four-sheet letter of counsel and encouragement, and registered an oath that he would get to work with an undivided heart as soon as Bessie should reappear.

The girl kept her appointment unpainted and unadorned, afraid and overbold by turns. When she found that she was merely expected to sit still, she grew calmer, and criticised the appointments of the studio with freedom and some point. She liked the warmth and the comfort and the release from fear of physical pain. Dick made two or three studies of her head in monochrome, but the actual notion of the Melancolia would not arrive.

"What a mess you keep your things in!" said Bessie, some days later, when she felt herself thoroughly at home. "I s'pose your clothes are just as bad. Gentlemen never think what buttons and tape are made for."

"I buy things to wear, and wear 'em till they go to pieces. I don't know what Torpenhow does."

Bessie made diligent inquiry in the latter's room, and unearthed a bale of disreputable socks. "Some of these I'll mend now," she said, "and some I'll take home. D'you know, I sit all day long at home doing nothing, just like a lady, and no more noticing them other girls in the house than if they was so many flies? I don't have any unnecessary words, but I put 'em down quick, I can tell you, when they talk to me. No; it's quite nice these days. I lock my door, and they can only call me names through the keyhole, and I sit inside, just like a lady, mending socks. Mr. Torpenhow wears his socks out both ends at once."

"Three quid a week from me, and the delights of my society. No socks mended. Nothing from Torp except a nod on the landing now and again, and all his socks mended. Bessie is very much a woman," thought Dick; and he looked at her between half-shut eyes.

Food and rest had transformed the girl, as Dick knew they would.

"What are you looking at me like that for?" she said, quickly. "Don't. You look reg'lar bad when you look that way. You don't think much o' me, do you?"

"That depends on how you behave."

Bessie behaved beautifully. Only it was difficult at the end of a sitting to bid her go out into the grey streets. She very much preferred the studio and a big chair by the stove, with some socks in her lap as an excuse for delay. Then Torpenhow would come in, and Bessie would be moved to tell strange and wonderful stories of her past, and still stranger ones of her present improved circumstances. She would make them tea as though she had a right to make it; and once or twice on these occasions Dick caught Torpenhow's eyes fixed on the trim little figure, and because Bessie's flittings about the room made Dick ardently long for Maisie, he realized whither Torpenhow's thoughts were tending. And Bessie was exceedingly careful of the condition of Torpenhow's linen. She spoke very little to him, but sometimes they talked together on the landing.

"I was a great fool," Dick said to himself. "I know what red firelight looks like when a man's trampling through a strange town; and ours is a lonely, selfish sort of life at the best. I wonder Maisie doesn't feel that sometimes. But I can't order Bessie away. That's the worst of beginning things. One never knows where they stop."

One evening, after a sitting prolonged to the last limit of the light, Dick was roused from a nap by a broken voice in Torpenhow's room. He jumped to his feet. "Now what ought I to do? It looks foolish to go in.—Oh, bless you, Binkie!" The little terrier thrust Torpenhow's door open with his nose and came out to take possession of Dick's chair. The door swung wide unheeded, and Dick across the landing could see Bessie in the half-light making her little supplication to Torpenhow. She was kneeling by his side, and her hands were clasped across his knee.

"I know,—I know," she said, thickly. "'Tisn't right o' me to do this, but I can't help it; and you were so kind,—so kind; and you never took any notice o' me. And I've mended all your things so carefully,—I did. Oh, please, 'tisn't as if I was asking you to marry me. I wouldn't think of it. But cou—couldn't you take and live with me till Miss Right comes along? I'm only Miss Wrong, I know, but I'd work my hands to the bare bone for you. And I'm not ugly to look at. Say you will?"

Dick hardly recognized Torpenhow's voice in reply—

"But look here. It's no use. I'm liable to be ordered off anywhere at a minute's notice if a war breaks out. At a minute's notice—dear."

"What does that matter? Until you go, then. Until you go. 'Tisn't much I'm asking, and—you don't know how good I can cook." She had put an arm round his neck and was drawing his head down.

"Until—I—go, then."

"Torp," said Dick across the landing. He could hardly steady his voice. "Come here a minute, old man. I'm in trouble."—"Heaven send he'll listen to me!" There was something very like

an oath from Bessie's lips. She was afraid of Dick, and disappeared down the staircase in panic, but it seemed an age before Torpenhow entered the studio. He went to the mantelpiece, buried his head on his arms, and groaned like a wounded bull.

"What the devil right have you to interfere?" he said, at last.

"Who's interfering with which? Your own sense told you long ago you couldn't be such a fool. It was a tough rack, St. Anthony, but you're all right now."

"I oughtn't to have seen her moving about these rooms as if they belonged to her. That's what upset me. It gives a lonely man a sort of hankering, doesn't it?" said Torpenhow, piteously.

"Now you talk sense. It does. But, since you aren't in a condition to discuss the disadvantages of double housekeeping, do you know what you're going to do?"

"I don't. I wish I did."

"You're going away for a season on a brilliant tour to regain tone. You're going to Brighton, or Scarborough, or Prawle Point, to see the ships go by. And you're going at once. Isn't it odd? I'll take care of Binkie, but out you go immediately. Never resist the devil. He holds the bank. Fly from him. Pack your things and go."

"I believe you're right. Where shall I go?"

"And you call yourself a special correspondent! Pack first and inquire afterward."

An hour later Torpenhow was despatched into the night in a hansom. "You'll probably think of some place to go while you're moving," said Dick.

"Go to Euston, to begin with, and—oh yes—get drunk to-night."

He returned to the studio and lighted more candles, for he found the room very dark.

"Oh, you Jezebel! you futile little Jezebel! Won't you hate me to-morrow?—Binkie, come here."

Binkie turned over on his back on the hearth-rug, and Dick stirred him with a meditative foot.

"I said she was not immoral. I was wrong. She said she could cook. That showed premeditated sin. Oh, Binkie, if you are a man you will go to perdition; but if you are a woman, and say that you can cook, you will go to a much worse place."

CHAPTER X

What's you that follows at my side?—
  The foe that ye must fight, my lord,—
That hirples swift as I can ride?—
  The shadow of the night, my lord.—
Then wheel my horse against the foe!—
  He's down and overpast, my lord.
Ye war against the sunset glow:
  The darkness gathers fast, my lord.
  —*The Fight of Heriot's Fora.*

"THIS is a cheerful life," said Dick, some days later. "Torp's away; Bessie hates me; I can't get at the notion of the Melancolia; Maisie's letters are scrappy; and I believe I have indigestion. What gives a man pains across his head and spots before his eyes, Binkie? Shall us take some liver pills?"

Dick had just gone through a lively scene with Bessie. She had for the fiftieth time reproached him for sending Torpenhow away. She explained her enduring hatred for Dick, and made it clear to him that she only sat for the sake of his money. "And Mr. Torpenhow's ten times a better man than you," she concluded.

"He is. That's why he went away. I should have stayed and made love to you."

The girl sat with her chin on her hand, scowling. "To me! I'd like to catch you! If I wasn't afraid o' being hung I'd kill you. That's what I'd do. D'you believe me?"

Dick smiled wearily. It is not pleasant to live in the company of a notion that will not work out, a fox-terrier that cannot talk, and a woman who talks too much. He would have answered, but at that moment there unrolled itself from one corner of the studio a veil, as it were, of the filmiest gauze. He rubbed his eyes, but the grey haze would not go.

"This is disgraceful indigestion. Binkie, we will go to a medicine-man. We can't have our eyes interfered with, for by these we get our bread; also mutton-chop bones for little dogs."

The doctor was an affable local practitioner with white hair, and he said nothing till Dick began to describe the grey film in the studio.

"We all want a little patching and repairing from time to time," he chirped. "Like a ship, my dear sir,—exactly like a ship. Sometimes the hull is out of order, and we consult the surgeon; sometimes the rigging, and then I advise; sometimes the engines, and we go to the brain-specialist; sometimes the look-out on the bridge is tired, and then we see an oculist. I should recommend you to see an oculist. A little patching and repairing from time to time is all we want. An oculist, by all means."

Dick sought an oculist,—the best in London. He was certain that the local practitioner did not know anything about his trade, and more certain that Maisie would laugh at him if he were forced to wear spectacles.

"I've neglected the warnings of my lord the stomach too long. Hence these spots before the eyes, Binkie. I can see as well as I ever could."

As he entered the dark hall that led to the consulting-room a man cannoned against him. Dick saw the face as it hurried out into the street.

"That's the writer-type. He has the same modeling of the forehead as Torp. He looks very sick. Probably heard something he didn't like."

Even as he thought, a great fear came upon Dick, a fear that made him hold his breath as he walked into the oculist's waiting-room, with the heavy carved furniture, the dark-green paper, and the sober-hued prints on the wall. He recognized a reproduction of one of his own sketches.

Many people were waiting their turn before him. His eye was caught by a flaming red-and-gold Christmas-carol book. Little children came to that eye-doctor, and they needed large-type amusement.

"That's idolatrous bad Art," he said, drawing the book toward himself. "From the anatomy of the angels, it has been made in Germany." He opened it mechanically, and there leaped to his eyes a verse printed in red ink—

The next good joy that Mary had,
  It was the joy of three,
To see her good Son Jesus Christ
  Making the blind to see;

Making the blind to see, good Lord,
  And happy may we be.
Praise Father, Son, and Holy Ghost
  To all eternity!

Dick read and re-read the verse till his turn came, and the doctor was bending above him seated in an armchair. The blaze of a gas-microscope in his eyes made him wince. The doctor's hand touched the scar of the sword-cut on Dick's head, and Dick explained briefly how he had come by it. When the flame was removed, Dick saw the doctor's face, and the fear came upon him again. The doctor wrapped himself in a mist of words. Dick caught allusions to "scar," "frontal bone," "optic nerve," "extreme caution," and the "avoidance of mental anxiety."

"Verdict?" he said faintly. "My business is painting, and I daren't waste time. What do you make of it?"

Again the whirl of words, but this time they conveyed a meaning.

"Can you give me anything to drink?"

Many sentences were pronounced in that darkened room, and the prisoners often needed cheering. Dick found a glass of liquor brandy in his hand.

"As far as I can gather," he said, coughing above the spirit, "you call it decay of the optic nerve, or something, and therefore hopeless. What is my time-limit, avoiding all strain and worry?"

"Perhaps one year."

"My God! And if I don't take care of myself?"

"I really could not say. One cannot ascertain the exact amount of injury inflicted by the sword-cut. The scar is an old one, and—exposure to the strong light of the desert, did you say?—with excessive application to fine work? I really could not say."

"I beg your pardon, but it has come without any warning. If you will let me, I'll sit here for a minute, and then I'll go. You have been very good in telling me the truth. Without any warning; without any warning. Thanks."

Dick went into the street, and was rapturously received by Binkie. "We've got it very badly, little dog! Just as badly as we can get it. We'll go to the Park to think it out."

They headed for a certain tree that Dick knew well, and they sat down to think, because his legs were trembling under him and there was cold fear at the pit of his stomach.

"How could it have come without any warning? It's as sudden as being shot. It's the living death, Binkie. We're to be shut up in the dark in one year if we're careful, and we shan't see anybody, and we shall never have anything we want, not though we live to be a hundred." Binkie wagged his tail joyously. "Binkie, we must think. Let's see how it feels to be blind." Dick shut his eyes, and flaming commas and Catherine-wheels floated inside the lids. Yet when he looked across the Park the scope of his vision was not contracted. He could see perfectly, until a procession of slow-wheeling fire-works defiled across his eyeballs.

"Little dorglums, we aren't at all well. Let's go home. If only Torp were back, now!"

But Torpenhow was in the south of England, inspecting dockyards in the company of the Nilghai. His letters were brief and full of mystery.

Dick had never asked anybody to help him in his joys or his sorrows. He argued, in the loneliness of the studio, henceforward to be decorated with a film of grey gauze in one corner, that, if his fate were blindness, all the Torpenhows in the world could not save him. "I can't call him off his trip to sit down and sympathize with me. I must pull through the business alone," he said. He was lying on the sofa, eating his moustache and wondering what the darkness of the night would be like. Then came to his mind the memory of a quaint scene in the Soudan. A soldier had been nearly hacked in two by a broad-bladed Arab spear. For one instant the man felt no pain. Looking down, he saw that his life-blood was going from him. The stupid bewilderment on his face was so intensely comic that both Dick and Torpenhow, still panting and unstrung from a fight for life, had roared with laughter, in which the man seemed as if he would join, but, as his lips parted in a sheepish grin, the agony of death came upon him, and he pitched grunting at their feet. Dick laughed again, remembering the horror. It seemed so exactly like his own case. "But I have a little more time allowed me," he said. He paced up and down the room, quietly at first, but afterward with the hurried feet of fear. It was as though a black shadow stood at his elbow and urged him to go forward; and there were only weaving circles and floating pin-dots before his eyes.

"We must be calm, Binkie; we must be calm." He talked aloud for the sake of distraction. "This isn't nice at all. What shall we do? We must do something. Our time is short. I shouldn't have believed that this morning; but now things are different. Binkie, where was Moses when the light went out?"

Binkie smiled from ear to ear, as a well-bred terrier should, but made no suggestion.

" 'Were there but world enough and time, This coyness, Binkie, were no crime. . . . But at my back I always hear' "— He wiped his forehead, which was unpleasantly damp. "What can I do? What can I do? I haven't any notions left, and I can't think connectedly, but I must do something, or I shall go off my head."

The hurried walk recommenced, Dick stopping every now and again to drag forth long-neglected canvases and old notebooks; for he turned to his work by instinct, as a thing that could not fail. "You won't do, and you won't do," he said, at each inspection. "No more soldiers. I couldn't paint 'em. Sudden death comes home too nearly, and this is battle and murder both for me."

The day was failing, and Dick thought for a moment that the twilight of the blind had come upon him unawares. "Allah Almighty!" he cried, despairingly, "help me through the time of waiting, and I won't whine when my punishment comes. What can I do now, before the light goes?"

There was no answer. Dick waited till he could regain some sort of control over himself. His hands were shaking, and he prided himself on their steadiness; he could feel that his lips were quivering, and the sweat was running down his face. He was lashed by fear, driven forward by the desire to get to work at once and accomplish something, and maddened by the refusal of his brain to do more than repeat the news

that he was about to go blind. "It's a humiliating exhibition," he thought, "and I'm glad Torp isn't here to see. The doctor said I was to avoid mental worry. Come here and let me pet you, Binkie."

The little dog yelped because Dick nearly squeezed the bark out of him. Then he heard the man speaking in the twilight, and, doglike, understood that his trouble stood off from him—

"Allah is good, Binkie. Not quite so gentle as we could wish, but we'll discuss that later. I think I see my way to it now. All those studies of Bessie's head were nonsense, and they nearly brought your master into a scrape. I hold the notion now as clear as crystal, —'the Melancolia that transcends all wit.' There shall be Maisie in that head, because I shall never get Maisie; and Bess, of course, because she knows all about Melancolia, though she doesn't know she knows; and there shall be some drawing in it, and it shall all end up with a laugh. That's for myself. Shall she giggle or grin? No, she shall laugh right out of the canvas, and every man and woman that ever had a sorrow of their own shall—what is it the poem says?—

"Understand the speech and feel a stir
Of fellowship in all disastrous fight.

'In all disastrous fight'? That's better than painting the thing merely to pique Maisie. I can do it now because I have it inside me. Binkie, I'm going to hold you up by your tail. You're an omen. Come here."

Binkie swung head downward for a moment without speaking.

" 'Rather like holding a guinea-pig; but you're a brave little dog, and you don't yelp when you're hung up. It is an omen."

Binkie went to his own chair, and as often as he looked saw Dick walking up and down, rubbing his hands and chuckling. That night Dick wrote a letter to Maisie full of the tenderest regard for her health, but saying very little about his own, and dreamed of the Melancolia to be born. Not till morning did he remember that something might happen to him in the future.

He fell to work, whistling softly, and was swallowed up in the clean, clear joy of creation, which does not come to man too often, lest he should consider himself the equal of his God, and so refuse to die at the appointed time. He forgot Maisie, Torpenhow, and Binkie at his feet, but remembered to stir Bessie, who needed very little stirring, into a tremendous rage, that he might watch the smouldering lights in her eyes. He threw himself without reservation into his work, and did not think of the doom that was to overtake him, for he was possessed with his notion, and the things of this world had no power upon him.

"You're pleased to-day," said Bessie.

Dick waved his mahl-stick in mystic circles and went to the sideboard for a drink. In the evening, when the exaltation of the day had died down, he went to the sideboard again, and after some visits became convinced that the eye-doctor was a liar, since he still could see everything very clearly. He was of opinion that he would even make a home for Maisie, and that whether she liked it or not she should be his wife.

The mood passed next morning, but the sideboard and all upon it remained for his comfort. Again he set to work, and his eyes troubled him with spots and dashes and blurs till he had taken counsel with the sideboard, and the Melancolia both on the canvas and in his own mind appeared lovelier than ever. There was a delightful sense of irresponsibility upon him, such as they feel who walking among their fellow-men know that the death-sentence of disease is upon them, and, since fear is but waste of the little time left, are riotously happy. The days passed without event. Bessie arrived punctually always, and, though her voice seemed to Dick to come from a distance, her face was always very near, and the Melancolia began to flame on the canvas, in the likeness of a woman who had known all the sorrow in the world and was laughing at it. It was true that the corners of the studio draped themselves in grey film and retired into the darkness, that the spots in his eyes and the pains across his head were very troublesome, and that Maisie's letters were hard to read and harder still to answer. He could not tell her of his trouble, and he could not laugh at her accounts of her own Melancolia which was always going to be finished. But the furious days of toil and the nights of wild dreams made amends for all, and the sideboard was his best friend on earth. Bessie was singularly dull. She used to shriek with rage when Dick stared at her between half-closed eyes. Now she sulked, or watched him with disgust, saying very little.

Torpenhow had been absent for six weeks. An incoherent note heralded his return. "News! great news!" he wrote.

"The Nilghai knows, and so does the Keneu. We're all back on Thursday. Get lunch and clean your accountrements."

Dick showed Bessie the letter, and she abused him for that he had ever sent Torpenhow away and ruined her life.

"Well," said Dick, brutally, "you're better as you are, instead of making love to some drunken beast in the street." He felt that he had rescued Torpenhow from great temptation.

"I don't know if that's any worse than sitting to a drunken beast in a studio. *You* haven't been sober for three weeks. You've been soaking the whole time; and yet you pretend you're better than me!"

"What d'you mean?" said Dick.

"Mean! You'll see when Mr. Torpenhow comes back."

It was not long to wait. Torpenhow met Bessie on the staircase without a sign of feeling. He had news that was more to him than many Bessies, and the Keneu and the Nilghai were trampling behind him, calling for Dick.

"Drinking like a fish," Bessie whispered. "He's been at it for nearly a month." She followed the men stealthily to hear judgment done.

They came into the studio, rejoicing, to be welcomed over-effusively by a drawn, lined, shrunken, haggard wreck, —unshaven, blue-white about the nostrils, stooping in the shoulders, and peering under his eyebrows nervously. The drink had been at work as steadily as Dick.

"Is this you?" said Torpenhow.

"All that's left of me. Sit down. Binkie's quite well, and I've been doing some good work." He reeled where he stood.

"You've done some of the worst work you've ever done in your life. Man alive, you're"—

Torpenhow turned to his companions appealingly, and they left the room to find lunch elsewhere. Then he spoke; but, since the reproof of a friend is much too sacred and intimate a thing to be printed, and since Torpenhow used figures and metaphors which were unseemly, and contempt untranslatable, it will never be known what was actually said to Dick, who blinked and winked and picked at his hands. After a time the culprit began to feel the need of a little self-respect. He was quite sure that he had not in any way departed from virtue, and there were reasons, too, of which Torpenhow knew nothing. He would explain.

He rose, tried to straighten his shoulders, and spoke to the face he could hardly see.

"You are right," he said. "But I am right, too. After you went away I had some trouble with my eyes. So I went to an oculist, and he turned a gasogene —I mean a gas-engine—into my eye. That was very long ago. He said, 'Scar on the head,—sword-cut and optic nerve.' Make a note of that. So I am going blind. I have some work to do before I go blind, and I suppose that I must do it. I cannot see much now, but I can see best when I am drunk. I did not know I was drunk till I was told, but I must go on with my work. If you want to see it, there it is." He pointed to the all but finished Melancolia and looked for applause.

Torpenhow said nothing, and Dick

began to whimper feebly, for joy at seeing Torpenhow again, for grief at misdeeds—if indeed they were misdeeds —that made Torpenhow remote and unsympathetic and for childish vanity hurt, since Torpenhow had not given a word of praise to his wonderful picture.

Bessie looked through the keyhole after a long pause, and saw the two walking up and down as usual, Torpenhow's hand on Dick's shoulder. Hereat she said something so improper that it shocked even Binkie, who was dribbling patiently on the landing with the hope of seeing his master again.

CHAPTER XI

The lark will make her hymn to God,
  The partridge call her brood,
While I forget the heath I trod,
  The fields wherein I stood.
'Tis dule to know not night from morn,
  But deeper dule to know
I can but hear the hunter's horn
  That once I used to blow.
          —*The Only Son.*

It was the third day after Torpenhow's return, and his heart was heavy.

"Do you mean to tell me that you can't see to work without whiskey? It's generally the other way about."

"Can a drunkard swear on his honor?" said Dick.

"Yes, if he has been as good a man as you."

"Then I give you my word of honor," said Dick, speaking hurriedly through parched lips. "Old man, I can hardly see your face now. You've kept me sober for two days,—if I ever was drunk,—and I've done no work. Don't keep me back any more. I don't know

when my eyes may give out. The spots and dots and the pains and things are crowding worse than ever. I swear I can see all right when I'm—when I'm moderately screwed as you say. Give me three more sittings from Bessie and all the—stuff I want, and the picture will be done. I can't kill myself in three days. It only means a touch of D. T. at the worst."

"If I give you three days more will you promise me to stop work and—the other thing, whether the picture's finished or not?"

"I can't. You don't know what that picture means to me. But surely you could get the Nilghai to help you, and knock me down and tie me up. I shouldn't fight for the whiskey, but I should for the work."

"Go on, then. I give you three days; but you're nearly breaking my heart."

Dick returned to his work, toiling as one possessed; and the yellow devil of whiskey stood by him and chased away the spots in his eyes. The Melancolia was nearly finished, and was all or nearly all that he had hoped she would be. Dick jested with Bessie, who reminded him that he was "a drunken beast"; but the reproof did not move him.

"You can't understand, Bess. We are in sight of land now, and soon we shall lie back and think about what we've done. I'll give you three months' pay when the picture's finished, and next time I have any more work in hand— but that doesn't matter. Won't three months' pay make you hate me less?"

"No, it won't! I hate you, and I'll go on hating you. Mr. Torpenhow won't speak to me any more. He's always looking at map-things and red-backed books."

Bessie did not say that she had again laid siege to Torpenhow, or that he had at the end of her passionate pleading picked her up, given her a kiss, and put her outside the door with a recommendation not to be a little fool. He spent most of his time in the company of the Nilghai, and their talk was of war in the near future, the hiring of transports, and secret preparations among the dockyards. He did not care to see Dick till the picture was finished.

"He's doing first-class work," he said to the Nilghai, "and it's quite out of his regular line. But, for the matter of that, so's his infernal drinking."

"Never mind. Leave him alone. When he has come to his senses again we'll carry him off from this place and let him breathe clean air. Poor Dick! I don't envy you, Torp, when his eyes fail."

"Yes, it will be a case of 'God help the man who's chained to our Davie.' The worst is that we don't know when it will happen; and I believe the uncertainty and the waiting have sent Dick to the whiskey more than anything else."

"How the Arab who cut his head open would grin if he knew!"

"He's at perfect liberty to grin if he can. He's dead. That's poor consolation now."

In the afternoon of the third day Torpenhow heard Dick calling for him. "All finished!" he shouted. "I've done it! Come in! Isn't she a beauty? Isn't she a darling? I've been down to hell to get her; but isn't she worth it?"

Torpenhow looked at the head of a woman who laughed,—a full-lipped, hollow-eyed woman who laughed from out of the canvas as Dick had intended she should.

"Who taught you how to do it?" said Torpenhow. "The touch and notion have nothing to do with your regular work. What a face it is! What eyes, and what insolence!" Unconsciously he threw back his head and laughed with her. "She's seen the game played out,— I don't think she had a good time of it, —and now she doesn't care. Isn't that the idea?"

"Exactly."

"Where did you get the mouth and chin from? They don't belong to Bess."

"They're—some one else's. But isn't it good? Isn't it thundering good? Wasn't it worth the whiskey? I did it. Alone I did it, and it's the best I can do." He drew his breath sharply, and whispered, "Just God! what could I not do ten years hence, if I can do this now!—By the way, what do you think of it, Bess?"

The girl was biting her lips. She loathed Torpenhow because he had taken no notice of her.

"I think it's just the horridest, beastliest thing I ever saw," she answered, and turned away.

"More than you will be of that way of thinking, young woman.—Dick, there's a sort of murderous, viperine suggestion in the poise of the head that I don't understand," said Torpenhow.

"That's trick-work," said Dick, chuckling with delight of being completely understood. "I couldn't resist one little bit of sheer swagger. It's a French trick, and you wouldn't understand; but it's got at by slewing round the head a trifle, and a tiny, tiny fore-shortening of one side of the face from the angle of the chin to the top of the left ear. That, and deepening the shadow under the lobe of the ear. It was flagrant trick-work; but, having the notion fixed, I felt entitled to play with it.— Oh, you beauty!"

"Amen! She is a beauty. I can feel it."

"So will every man who has any sorrow of his own," said Dick, slapping his thigh. "He shall see his trouble there, and, by the Lord Harry, just when he's feeling properly sorry for himself he shall throw back his head and laugh,—as she is laughing. I've put the life of my heart and the light of my eyes into her, and I don't care what comes. . . . I'm tired,—awfully tired. I think I'll get to sleep. Take away the whiskey, it has served its turn,.and give Bessie thirty-six quid, and three over for luck. Cover the picture."

He dropped asleep in the long chair, his face white and haggard, almost before he had finished the sentence. Bessie tried to take Torpenhow's hand. "Aren't you never going to speak to me any more?" she said; but Torpenhow was looking at Dick.

"What a stock of vanity the man has! I'll take him in hand to-morrow and make much of him. He deserves it. —Eh! what was that, Bess?"

"Nothing. I'll put things tidy here a little, and then I'll go. You couldn't give me that three months' pay now, could you? He said you were to."

Torpenhow gave her a check and went to his own rooms. Bessie faithfully tidied up the studio, set the door ajar for flight, emptied half a bottle of turpentine on a duster, and began to scrub the face of the Melancolia viciously. The paint did not smudge quickly enough. She took a palette-knife and scraped, following each stroke with the wet duster. In five minutes the picture was a formless, scarred muddle of colors. She threw the paint-stained duster into the studio stove, stuck out her tongue at the sleeper, and whispered, "Bilked!" as she turned to run down the staircase. She would never see Torpenhow any more, but she had at least done harm to the man who had come between her and her desire and who used to make fun of her. Cashing the check was the very cream of the jest to Bessie. Then the little privateer sailed across the Thames, to be swallowed up in the grey wilderness of South-the-water.

Dick slept till late in the evening, when Torpenhow dragged him off to bed. His eyes were as bright as his voice was hoarse. "Let's have another look at the picture," he said, insistently as a child.

"You—go—to—bed," said Torpenhow. "You aren't at all well, though you mayn't know it. You're as jumpy as a cat."

"I reform to-morrow. Good-night."

As he repassed through the studio, Torpenhow lifted the cloth above the picture, and almost betrayed himself by outcries: "Wiped out!—scraped out and turped out! If Dick knows this to-night he'll go perfectly mad. He's on the verge of jumps as it is. That's Bess, —the little fiend! Only a woman could have done that!—with the ink not dry on the check, too! Dick will be raving mad to-morrow. It was all my fault for trying to help gutter-devils. Oh, my poor Dick, the Lord is hitting you very hard!"

Dick could not sleep that night, partly for pure joy, and partly because the well-known Catherine-wheels inside his eyes had given place to crackling volcanoes of many-colored fire. "Spout away," he said, aloud. "I've done my work, and now you can do what you please." He lay still, staring at the ceiling, the long-pent-up delirium of drink in his veins, his brain on fire with racing thoughts that would not stay to be considered, and his hands crisped and dry. He had just discovered that he was painting the face of the Melancolia on a revolving dome ribbed with millions of lights, and that all his wondrous thoughts stood embodied hundreds of feet below his tiny swinging plank, shouting together in his honor, when something cracked inside his temples like an overstrained bowstring, the glittering dome broke inward, and he was alone in the thick night.

"I'll go to sleep. The room's very dark. Let's light a lamp and see how the Melancolia looks. There ought to have been a moon."

It was then that Torpenhow heard his name called by a voice that he did not know,—in the rattling accents of deadly fear.

"He's looked at the picture," was his first thought, as he hurried into the bedroom and found Dick sitting up and beating the air with his hands. "Torp! Torp! Where are you? For pity's sake, come to me!"

"What's the matter?"

Dick clutched at his shoulder. "Mat-ter! I've been lying here for hours in the dark, and you never heard me. Torp, old man, don't go away. I'm all in the dark. In the dark, I tell you!"

Torpenhow held the candle within a foot of Dick's eyes, but there was no light in those eyes. He lit the gas, and Dick heard the flame catch. The grip of his fingers on Torpenhow's shoulder made Torpenhow wince.

"Don't leave me. You wouldn't leave me alone now, would you? I can't see. D'you understand? It's black,—quite black,—and I feel as if I was falling through it all."

"Steady, does it." Torpenhow put his arm round Dick and began to rock him gently to and fro.

"That's good. Now don't talk. If I keep very quiet for a while, this darkness will lift. It seems just on the point of breaking. H'sh!" Dick knit his brows and stared desperately in front of him. The night air was chilling Torpenhow's toes.

"Can you stay like that a minute?" he said. "I'll get my dressing-gown and some slippers."

Dick clutched the bed-head with both hands and waited for the darkness to clear away. "What a time you've been!" he cried, when Torpenhow returned. "It's as black as ever. What are you banging about in the doorway?"

"Long chair,—horse-blanket,—pillow. Going to sleep by you. Lie down now; you'll be better in the morning."

"I shan't!" The voice rose to a wail. "My God! I'm blind! I'm blind, and the darkness will never go away." He made as if to leap from the bed, but Torpenhow's arms were round him, and Torpenhow's chin was on his shoulder, and his breath was squeezed out of him. He could only gasp, "Blind!" and wriggle feebly.

"Steady, Dickie, steady!" said the deep voice in his ear, and the grip tightened. "Bite on the bullet, old man, and don't let them think you're afraid." The grip could draw no closer. Both men were breathing heavily. Dick threw his head from side to side and groaned. "Let me go," he panted. "You're cracking my ribs. We—we mustn't let them think we're afraid, must we,— all the powers of darkness and that lot?"

"Lie down. It's all over now."

"Yes," said Dick, obediently. "But would you mind letting me hold your hand? I feel as if I wanted something to hold on to. One drops through the dark so."

Torpenhow thrust out a large and hairy paw from the long chair. Dick clutched it tightly, and in half an hour had fallen asleep. Torpenhow withdrew his hand, and, stooping over Dick, kissed him lightly on the forehead, as men do sometimes kiss a wounded comrade in the hour of death, to ease his departure.

In the grey dawn Torpenhow heard Dick talking to himself. He was adrift on the shoreless tides of delirium, speaking very quickly—

"It's a pity,—a great pity; but it's helped, and it must be eaten, Master George. Sufficient unto the day is the blindness thereof, and, further, putting aside all Melancolias and false humors, it is of obvious notoriety—such as mine was—that the queen can do no wrong. Torp doesn't know that. I'll tell him when we're a little farther into the

desert. What a bungle those boatmen are making of the steamer-ropes! They'll have that four-inch hawser chafed through in a minute. I told you so—there she goes! White foam on green water, and the steamer slewing round. How good that looks! I'll sketch it. No, I can't. I'm afflicted with ophthalmia. That was one of the ten plagues of Egypt, and it extends up the Nile in the shape of cataract. Ha! That's a joke, Torp. Laugh, you graven image, and stand clear of the hawser. . . . It'll knock you into the water and make your dress all dirty, Maisie dear."

"Oh!" said Torpenhow. "This happened before. That night on the river."

"She'll be sure to say it's my fault if you get muddy, and you're quite near enough to the breakwater. Maisie, that's not fair. Ah! I knew you'd miss. Low and to the left, dear. But you've no conviction. Everything in the world except conviction. Don't be angry, darling. I'd cut my hand off if it would give you anything more than obstinacy. My right hand, if it would serve."

"Now we mustn't listen. Here's an island shouting across seas of misunderstanding with a vengeance. But it's shouting truth, I fancy," said Torpenhow.

The babble continued. It all bore upon Maisie. Sometimes Dick lectured at length on his craft, then he cursed himself for his folly in being enslaved. He pleaded to Maisie for a kiss—only one kiss—before she went away, and called to her to come back from Vitry-sur-Marne, if she would; but through all his ravings he bade heaven and earth witness that the queen could do no wrong.

Torpenhow listened attentively, and learned every detail of Dick's life that had been hidden from him. For three days Dick raved through his past, and then slept a natural sleep. "What a strain he has been running under, poor chap!" said Torpenhow. "Dick, of all men, handing himself over like a dog! And I was lecturing him on arrogance! I ought to have known that it was no use to judge a man. But I did it. What a demon that girl must be! Dick's give her his life,—confound him!—and she's given him one kiss apparently."

"Torp," said Dick from the bed, "go out for a walk. You've been here too long. I'll get up. Hi! This is annoying. I can't dress myself. Oh, it's too absurd!"

Torpenhow helped him into his clothes and led him to the big chair in the studio. He sat quietly waiting under strained nerves for the darkness to lift. It did not lift that day, nor the next. Dick adventured on a voyage round the walls. He hit his shins against the stove, and this suggested to him that it would be better to crawl on all-fours, one hand in front of him. Torpenhow found him on the floor.

"I'm trying to get the geography of my new possessions," said he. "D'you remember that nigger you gouged in the square? Pity you didn't keep the odd eye. It would have been useful. Any letters for me? Give me all the ones in fat grey envelopes with a sort of crown thing outside. They're of no importance."

Torpenhow gave him a letter with a black M. on the envelope flap. Dick put it into his pocket. There was nothing in it that Torpenhow might not have read, but it belonged to himself and to Maisie, who would never belong to him.

"When she finds that I don't write, she'll stop writing. It's better so. I couldn't be any use to her now," Dick argued, and the tempter suggested that he should make known his condition. Every nerve in him revolted. "I have fallen low enough already. I'm not going to beg for pity. Besides, it would be cruel to her." He strove to put Maisie out of his thoughts; but the blind have many opportunities for thinking, and as the tides of his strength came back to him in the long employless days of dead darkness, Dick's soul was troubled to the core. Another letter, and another, came from Maisie. Then there was silence, and Dick sat by the window, the pulse of summer in the air, and pictured her being won by another man, stronger than himself. His imagination, the keener for the dark background it worked against, spared him no single detail that might send him raging up and down the studio, to stumble over the stove that seemed to be in four places at once. Worst of all, tobacco would not taste in the darkness. The arrogance of the man had disappeared, and in its place were settled despair that Torpenhow knew, and blind passion that Dick confided to his pillow at night. The intervals between the paroxysms were filled with intolerable waiting and the weight of intolerable darkness.

"Come out into the Park," said Torpenhow. "You haven't stirred out since the beginning of things."

"What's the use? There's no movement in the dark; and, besides,"—he paused irresolutely at the head of the stairs,—"something will run over me."

"Not if I'm with you. Proceed gingerly."

The roar of the streets filled Dick with nervous terror, and he clung to Torpenhow's arm. "Fancy having to feel for a gutter with your foot!" he said, petulantly, as he turned into the Park. "Let's curse God and die."

"Sentries are forbidden to pay unauthorized compliments. By Jove, there are the Guards!"

Dick's figure straightened. "Let's get near 'em. Let's go in and look. Let's get on the grass and run. I can smell the trees."

"Mind the low railing. That's all right!" Torpenhow kicked out a tuft of grass with his heel. "Smell that," he said. "Isn't it good?" Dick snuffed luxuriously. "Now pick up your feet and run." They approached as near to the regiment as was possible. The clank of bayonets being unfixed made Dick's nostrils quiver.

"Let's get nearer. They're in column, aren't they?"

"Yes. How did you know?"

"Felt it. Oh, my men!—my beautiful men!" He edged forward as though he could see. "I could draw those chaps once. Who'll draw 'em now?"

"They'll move off in a minute. Don't jump when the band begins."

"Huh! I'm not a new charger. It's the silences that hurt. Nearer, Torp!—nearer! Oh, my God, what wouldn't I give to see 'em for a minute!—one half minute!"

He could hear the armed life almost within reach of him, could hear the slings tighten across the bandsman's chest as he heaved the big drum from the ground.

"Sticks crossed above his head," whispered Torpenhow.

"I know. *I* know! Who should know if I don't? H'sh!"

The drum-sticks fell with a boom, and the men swung forward to the crash of the band. Dick felt the wind of the massed movement in his face, heard the maddening tramp of feet and the friction of the pouches on the belts. The big drum pounded out the tune. It was a music-hall refrain that made a perfect quickstep—

He must be a man of decent height,
    He must be a man of weight,
He must come home on a Saturday night
    In a thoroughly sober state;

He must know how to love me,
    And he must know how to kiss;
And if he's enough to keep us both
    I can't refuse him bliss.

"What's the matter?" said Torpenhow, as he saw Dick's head fall when the last of the regiment had departed.

"Nothing. I feel a little bit out of the running,—that's all. Torp, take me back. Why did you bring me out?"

CHAPTER XII

There were three friends that buried the fourth,
    The mould in his mouth and the dust in his eyes;
And they went south and east, and north,—
    The strong man fights, but the sick man dies.

There were three friends that spoke of
    the dead,—
  The strong man fights, but the sick
    man dies.—
"And would he were here with us now,"
    they said,
  "The sun in our face and the wind in
    our eyes."
                  —Ballad.

THE Nilghai was angry with Torpenhow. Dick had been sent to bed,—
blind men are ever under the orders of
those who can see,—and since he had
returned from the Park had fluently
sworn at Torpenhow because he was
alive, and all the world because it was
alive and could see, while he, Dick, was
dead in the death of the blind, who, at
the best, are only burdens upon their
associates. Torpenhow had said something about a Mrs. Gummidge, and Dick
had retired in a black fury to handle
and rehandle three unopened letters
from Maisie.

The Nilghai, fat, burly, and aggressive, was in Torpenhow's rooms. Behind him sat the Keneu, the Great war
Eagle, and between them lay a large
map embellished with black and white-
headed pins.

"I was wrong about the Balkans,"
said the Nilghai. "But I'm not wrong
about this business. The whole of our
work in the Southern Soudan must be
done over again. The public doesn't
care, of course, but the government
does, and they are making their arrangements quietly. You know that as well
as I do."

"I remember how the people cursed
us when our troops withdrew from
Omdurman. It was bound to crop up
sooner or later. But I can't go," said
Torpenhow. He pointed through the
open door; it was a hot night. "Can
you blame me?"

The Keneu purred above his pipe
like a large and very happy cat—

"Don't blame you in the least. It's
uncommonly good of you, and all the
rest of it, but every man—even you,
Torp—must consider his work. I know
it sounds brutal, but Dick's out of the
race,—down,—*gastados,* expended, finished, done for. He has a little money
of his own. He won't starve, and you
can't pull out of your slide for his sake.
Think of your own reputation."

"Dick's was five times bigger than
mine and yours put together."

"That was because he signed his
name to everything he did. It's all
ended now. You must hold yourself in
readiness to move out. You can command your own prices, and you do better work than any three of us."

"Don't tell me how tempting it is.
I'll stay here to look after Dick for a
while. He's as cheerful as a bear with
a sore head, but I think he likes to
have me near him."

The Nilghai said something uncompli-
mentary about soft-headed fools who
throw away their careers for other
fools. Torpenhow flushed angrily. The
constant strain of attendance on Dick
had worn his nerves thin.

"There remains a third fate," said
the Keneu, thoughtfully. "Consider
this, and be not larger fools than is
necessary. Dick is—or rather was—an
able-bodied man of moderate attractions
and a certain amount of audacity."

"Oho!" said the Nilghai, who remembered an affair at Cairo. "I begin to see.
—Torp, I'm sorry."

Torpenhow nodded forgiveness: "You

were more sorry when he cut you out, though.—Go on Keneu."

"I've often thought, when I've seen men die out in the desert, that if the news could be sent through the world, and the means of transport were quick enough, there would be one woman at least at each man's bedside."

"There would be some mighty quaint revelations. Let us be grateful things are as they are," said the Nilghai.

"Let us rather reverently consider whether Torp's three-cornered ministrations are exactly what Dick needs just now.—What do you think yourself, Torp?"

"I know they aren't. But what can I do?"

"Lay the matter before the board. We are all Dick's friends here. You've been most in his life."

"But I picked it up when he was off his head."

"The greater chance of its being true. I thought we should arrive. Who is she?"

Then Torpenhow told a tale in plain words, as a special correspondent who knows how to make a verbal *précis* should tell it. The men listened without interruption.

"Is it possible that a man can come back across the years to his calf-love?" said the Keneu. "Is it possible?"

"I give the facts. He says nothing about it now, but he sits fumbling three letters from her when he thinks I'm not looking. What am I to do?"

"Speak to him," said the Nilghai.

"Oh yes! Write to her,—I don't know her full name, remember,—and ask her to accept him out of pity. I believe you once told Dick you were

sorry for him, Nilghai. You remember what happened, eh? Go into the bedroom and suggest full confession and an appeal to this Maisie girl, whoever she is. I honestly believe he'd try to kill you; and the blindness has made him rather muscular."

"Torpenhow's course is perfectly clear," said the Keneu. "He will go to Vitry-sur-Marne, which is on the Bézières-Landes Railway,—single track from Tourgas. The Prussians shelled it out in '70 because there was a poplar on the top of a hill eighteen hundred yards from the church spire. There's a squadron of cavalry quartered there,— or ought to be. Where this studio Torp spoke about may be I cannot tell. That is Torp's business. I have given him his route. He will dispassionately explain the situation to the girl, and she will come back to Dick,—the more especially because, to use Dick's words, 'there is nothing but her damned obstinacy to keep them apart.' "

"And they have four hundred and twenty pounds a year between 'em. Dick never lost his head for figures, even in his delirium. You haven't the shadow of an excuse for not going," said the Nilghai.

Torpenhow looked very uncomfortable. "But it's absurd and impossible. I can't drag her back by the hair."

"Our business—the business for which we draw our money—is to do absurd and impossible things,—generally with no reason whatever except to amuse the public. Here we have a reason. The rest doesn't matter. I shall share these rooms with the Nilghai till Torpenhow returns. There will be a batch of unbridled 'specials' coming to town in a little while, and these will serve as their headquarters. Another reason for sending Torpenhow away. Thus Providence helps those who help others, and"—here the Keneu dropped his measured speech—"we can't have you tied by the leg to Dick when the trouble begins. It's your only chance of getting away; and Dick will be grateful."

"He will,—worse luck! I can but go and try. I can't conceive a woman in her senses refusing Dick."

"Talk that out with the girl. I have seen you wheedle an angry Mahdieh woman into giving you dates. This won't be a tithe as difficult. You had better not be here to-morrow afternoon, because the Nilghai and I will be in possession. It is an order. Obey."

"Dick," said Torpenhow next morning, "can I do anything for you?"

"No! Leave me alone. How often must I remind you that I'm blind?"

"Nothing I could go for to fetch for to carry for to bring?"

"No. Take those infernal creaking boots of yours away."

"Poor chap!" said Torpenhow to himself. "I must have been sitting on his nerves lately. He wants a lighter step." Then, aloud, "Very well. Since you're so independent, I'm going off for four or five days. Say good-bye at least. The housekeeper will look after you, and Keneu has my rooms."

Dick's face fell. "You won't be longer than a week at the outside? I know I'm touched in the temper, but I can't get on without you."

"Can't you? You'll have to do without me in a little time, and you'll be glad I'm gone."

Dick felt his way back to the big chair, and wondered what these things might mean. He did not wish to be tended by the housekeeper, and yet Torpenhow's constant tendernesses jarred on him. He did not exactly know what he wanted. The darkness would not lift, and Maisie's unopened letters felt worn and old from much handling. He could never read them for himself as long as life endured; but Maisie might have sent him some fresh ones to play with. The Nilghai entered with a gift,—a piece of red modeling-wax. He fancied that Dick might find interest in using his hands. Dick poked and patted the stuff for a few minutes, and, "Is it like anything in the world?" he said, drearily. "Take it away. I may get the touch of the blind in fifty years. Do you know where Torpenhow has gone?"

The Nilghai knew nothing. "We're staying in his rooms till he comes back. Can we do anything for you?"

"I'd like to be left alone, please. Don't think I'm ungrateful; but I'm best alone."

The Nilghai chuckled, and Dick resumed his drowsy brooding and sullen rebellion against fate. He had long since ceased to think about the work he had done in the old days, and the desire to do more work had departed from him. He was exceedingly sorry for himself, and the completeness of his tender grief soothed him. But his soul and his body cried for Maisie,—Maisie who would understand. His mind pointed out that Maisie, having her own work to do, would not care. His experience had taught him that when money was exhausted women went away, and that when a man was knocked out of the race the others trampled on him. "Then at the least," said Dick, in reply, "she could use me as I used Binat,—for some sort of a study. I wouldn't ask more than to be near her again, even though I knew that another man was making love to her. Ugh! what a dog I am!"

A voice on the staircase began to sing joyfully—

When we go—go—go away from here,
  Our creditors will weep and they will wail,
Our absence much regretting when they find that we've been getting
Out of England by next Tuesday's Indian mail.

Following the trampling of feet, slamming of Torpenhow's door, and the sound of voices in strenuous debate, some one squeaked, "And see, you good fellows, I have found a new water-bottle,—firs'-class patent—eh, how you say? Open himself inside out."

Dick sprang to his feet. He knew the voice well. "That's Cassavetti, come back from the Continent. Now I know why Torp went away. There's a row somewhere, and—I'm out of it!"

The Nilghai commanded silence in vain. "That's for my sake," Dick said, bitterly. "The birds are getting ready to fly, and they wouldn't tell me. I can hear Morten-Sutherland and Mackaye. Half the War Correspondents in London are there;—and I'm out of it."

He stumbled across the landing and plunged into Torpenhow's room. He could feel that it was full of men. "Where's the trouble?" said he. "In the Balkans at last? Why didn't some one tell me?"

"We thought you wouldn't be interested," said the Nilghai, shamefacedly. 'It's in the Soudan, as usual."

"You lucky dogs! Let me sit here while you talk. I shan't be a skeleton at the feast.—Cassavetti, where are you? Your English is as bad as ever."

Dick was led into a chair. He heard the rustle of the maps, and the talk swept forward, carrying him with it. Everybody spoke at once, discussing press censorships, railway-routes, transport, water-supply, the capacities of generals,—these in language that would have horrified a trusting public,— ranting, asserting, denouncing, and laughing at the top of their voices. There was the glorious certainty of war in the Soudan at any moment. The Nilghai said so, and it was well to be in readiness. The Keneu had telegraphed to Cairo for horses; Cassavetti had stolen a perfectly inaccurate list of troops that would be ordered forward, and was reading it out amid profane interruptions, and the Keneu introduced to Dick some man unknown who would be employed as war artist by the Central Southern Syndicate. "It's his first outing," said the Keneu. "Give him some tips—about riding camels."

"Oh, those camels!" groaned Cassavetti. "I shall learn to ride him again, and now I am so much all soft! Listen, you good fellows. I know your military arrangement very well. There will go the Royal Argalshire Sutherlanders. So it was read to me upon best authority."

A roar of laughter interrupted him.

"Sit down," said the Nilghai. "The lists aren't even made out in the War Office."

"Will there be any force at Suakin?" said a voice.

Then the outcries redoubled, and grew mixed, thus: "How many Egyptian troops will they use?—God help the Fellaheen!—There's a railway in Plumstead marshes doing duty as a fives-court.—We shall have the Suakin-Berber line built at last.—Canadian voyagers are too careful. Give me a half-drunk Krooman in a whale-boat.—Who commands the Desert column?—No, they never blew up the big rock in the Ghineh bend. We shall have to be hauled up, as usual.—Somebody tell me if there's an Indian contingent, or I'll break everybody's head.—Don't tear the map in two.—It's a war of occupation, I tell you, to connect with the African companies in the South.—There's Guinea-worm in most of the wells on that route." Then the Nilghai, despairing of peace, bellowed like a fog-horn and beat upon the table with both hands.

"But what becomes of Torpenhow?" said Dick, in the silence that followed.

"Torp's in abeyance just now. He's off love-making somewhere, I suppose," said the Nilghai.

"He said he was going to stay at home," said the Keneu.

"Is he?" said Dick with an oath. "He won't. I'm not much good now, but if you and the Nilghai hold him down I'll engage to trample on him till he sees reason. He stay behind, indeed! He's the best of you all. There'll be some tough work by Omdurman. We shall come there to stay, this time. But I forgot. I wish I were going with you."

'So do we all, Dickie," said the Keneu.

"And I most of all," said the new artist of the Central Southern Syndicate. "Could you tell me"—

"I'll give you one piece of advice," Dick answered, moving toward the door. "If you happen to be cut over the head in a scrimmage, don't guard. Tell the man to go on cutting. You'll find it cheapest in the end. Thanks for letting me look in."

"There's grit in Dick," said the Nilghai, an hour later, when the room was emptied of all save the Keneu.

"It was the sacred call of the war-trumpet. Did you notice how he answered to it? Poor fellow! Let's look at him," said the Keneu.

The excitement of the talk had died away. Dick was sitting by the studio table, with his head on his arms, when the men came in. He did not change his position.

"It hurts," he moaned. "God forgive me, but it hurts cruelly; and yet, y'know, the world has a knack of spinning round all by itself. Shall I see Torp before he goes?"

"Oh yes. You'll see him," said the Nilghai.

CHAPTER XIII

The sun went down an hour ago,
　I wonder if I face toward home,
If I lost my way in the light of day
　How shall I find it now night is come?
　　　　　—*Old Song.*

"MAISE, come to bed."

"It's so hot I can't sleep. Don't worry."

Maisie put her elbows on the window-sill and looked at the moonlight on the straight, poplar-flanked road. Summer had come upon Vitry-sur-Marne and parched it to the bone. The grass was dry-burned in the meadows, the clay by the bank of the river was caked to brick, the roadside flowers were long since dead, and the roses in the garden hung withered on their stalks. The heat in the little low bedroom under the eaves was almost intolerable. The very moonlight on the wall of Kami's studio across the road seemed to make the night hotter, and the shadow of the big bell-handle by the closed gate cast a bar of inky black that caught Maisie's eye and annoyed her.

"Horrid thing! It should be all white," she murmured. "And the gate isn't in the middle of the wall, either. I never noticed that before."

Maisie was hard to please at that hour. First, the heat of the past few weeks had worn her down; secondly, her work, and particularly the study of a female head intended to represent the Melancolia and not finished in time for the Salon, was unsatisfactory; thirdly, Kami had said as much two days before; fourthly,—but so completely fourthly that it was hardly worth thinking about,—Dick, her property, had not written to her for more than six weeks. She was angry with the heat, with Kami, and with her work, but she was exceedingly angry with Dick.

She had written to him three times, —each time proposing a fresh treatment of her Melancolia. Dick had taken no notice of these communications. She had resolved to write no more. When she returned to England in the autumn —for her pride's sake she could not return earlier—she would speak to him. She missed the Sunday afternoon conferences more than she cared to admit. All that Kami said was, "*Continuez, mademoiselle, continuez toujours,*" and he had been repeating his wearisome counsel through the hot summer, exactly like a cicala,—an old grey cicala in a black alpaca coat, white trousers, and a huge felt hat. But Dick had tramped masterfully up and down her little studio north of the cool green London park, and had said things ten times worse than *continuez*, before he snatched the brush out of her hand and showed her where her error lay. His last letter, Maisie remembered, contained some trivial advice about not sketching in the sun or drinking water at wayside farmhouses; and he had said that not once, but three times,—as if he did not know that Maisie could take care of herself.

But what was he doing, that he could not trouble to write? A murmur of voices in the road made her lean from the window. A cavalryman of the little garrison in the town was talking to Kami's cook. The moonlight glittered on the scabbard of his sabre, which he was holding in his hand lest it should clank inopportunely. The cook's cap cast deep shadows on her face, which was close to the conscript's. He slid his arm round her waist, and there followed the sound of a kiss.

"Faugh!" said Maisie, stepping back.

"What's that?" said the red-haired girl, who was tossing uneasily outside her bed.

"Only a conscript kissing the cook," said Maisie. "They've gone away now."

She leaned out of the window again, and put a shawl over her nightgown to guard against chills. There was a very small night-breeze abroad, and a sun-baked rose below nodded its head as one who knew unutterable secrets. Was it possible that Dick should turn his thoughts from her work and his own and descend to the degradation of Suzanne and the conscript? He could not! The rose nodded its head and one leaf therewith. It looked like a naughty little devil scratching its ear. Dick could not, "because," thought Maisie, "he is mine,—mine,—mine. He said he was. I'm sure I don't care what he does. It will only spoil his work if he does; and it will spoil mine too."

The rose continued to nod in the futile way peculiar to flowers. There was no earthly reason why Dick should not disport himself as he chose, except that he was called by Providence, which was Maisie, to assist Maisie in her work. And her work was the preparation of pictures that went sometimes to English provincial exhibitions, as the notices in the scrapbook proved, and that were invariably rejected by the Salon when Kami was plagued into allowing her to send them up. Her work in the future, it seemed, would be the preparation of pictures on exactly similar lines which would be rejected in exactly the same way—

The red-haired girl threshed distressfully across the sheets. "It's too hot to sleep," she moaned; and the interruption jarred.

Exactly the same way. Then she would divide her years between the little studio in England and Kami's big studio at Vitry-sur-Marne. No, she would go to another master, who should force her into the success that was her right, if patient toil and desperate endeavor gave one a right to anything. Dick had told her that he had worked ten years to understand his craft. She had worked ten years, and ten years were nothing. Dick had said that ten years were nothing,—but that was in regard to herself only. He had said—this very man who could not find time to write—that he would wait ten years for her, and that she was bound to come back to him sooner or later. He had said this in the absurd letter about sunstroke and diphtheria; and then he had stopped writing. He was wandering up and down moonlit streets, kissing cooks. She would like to lecture him now,—not in her nightgown, of course, but properly dressed, severely and from a height. Yet if he was kissing other girls he certainly would not care whether she lectured him or not. He would laugh at her. Very good. She would go back to her studio and prepare pictures that went, etc., etc. The mill-wheel of thought swung round slowly, that no section of it might be slurred over, and the red-haired girl tossed and turned behind her.

Maisie put her chin in her hands and decided that there could be no doubt whatever of the villany of Dick. To justify herself, she began, unwomanly, to weigh the evidence. There was a boy, and he had said he loved her. And he kissed her,—kissed her on the cheek,—by a yellow sea-poppy that nodded its head exactly like the maddening dry rose in the garden. Then there was an interval, and men had told her that they loved her—just when she was busiest with her work. Then the boy came back, and at their very second meeting had told her that he loved her. Then he had— But there was no end to the things he had done. He had given her his time and his powers. He had spoken to her of Art, housekeeping, technique, teacups, the abuse of pickles as a stimulant,—that was rude,—sable hair-brushes,—he had given her the best in her stock,—she used them daily; he had given her advice that she profited by, and now and again—a look. Such a look! The look of a beaten hound waiting for the word to crawl to his mistress's feet. In return she had given him nothing whatever, except—here she brushed her mouth against the open-work sleeve of her nightgown—the privilege of kissing her once. And on the mouth, too. Disgraceful! Was that not enough, and more than enough? and if it was not, had he not cancelled the debt by not writing and—probably kissing other girls?

"Maisie, you'll catch a chill. Do go and lie down," said the wearied voice of her companion. "I can't sleep a wink with you at the window."

Maisie shrugged her shoulders and did not answer. She was reflecting on the meannesses of Dick, and on other meannesses with which he had nothing to do. The remorseless moonlight would not let her sleep. It lay on the skylight of the studio across the road in cold silver; she stared at it intently and her thoughts began to slide one into the other. The shadow of the big bell-handle in the wall grew short, lengthened again, and faded out as the moon went down behind the pasture and a hare came limping home across the

road. Then the dawn-wind washed through the upland grasses, and brought coolness with it, and the cattle lowed by the drought-shrunk river. Maisie's head fell forward on the window-sill, and the tangle of black hair covered her arms.

"Maisie, wake up. You'll catch a chill."

"Yes, dear; yes, dear." She staggered to her bed like a wearied child, and as she buried her face in the pillows she muttered, "I think—I think. . . . But he ought to have written."

Day brought the routine of the studio, the smell of paint and turpentine, and the monotonous wisdom of Kami, who was a leaden artist, but a golden teacher if the pupil were only in sympathy with him. Maisie was not in sympathy that day, and she waited impatiently for the end of the work. She knew when it was coming; for Kami would gather his black alpaca coat into a bunch behind him, and, with faded blue eyes that saw neither pupils nor canvas, look back into the past to recall the history of one Binat. "You have all done not so badly," he would say. "But you shall remember that it is not enough to have the method, and the art, and the power, nor even that which is touch, but you shall have also the conviction that nails the work to the wall. Of the so many I have taught,"—here the students would begin to unfix drawing-pins or get their tubes together,— "the very so many that I have taught, the best was Binat. All that comes of the study and the work and the knowledge was to him even when he came. After he left me he should have done all that could be done with the color, the form, and the knowledge. Only, he had not the conviction. So to-day I hear no more of Binat,—the best of my pupils,—and that is long ago. So to-day, too, you will be glad to hear no more of me. *Continuez, mesdemoiselles,* and, above all, with conviction."

He went into the garden to smoke and mourn over the lost Binat as the pupils dispersed to their several cottages or loitered in the studio to make plans for the cool of the afternoon.

Maisie looked at her very unhappy Melancolia, restrained a desire to grimace before it, and was hurrying across the road to write a letter to Dick, when she was aware of a large man on a white troop-horse. How Torpenhow had managed in the course of twenty-four hours to find his way to the hearts of the cavalry officers in quarters at Vitry-sur-Marne, to discuss with them the certainty of a glorious revenge for France, to reduce the colonel to tears of pure affability, and to borrow the best horse in the squadron for the journey to Kami's studio, is a mystery that only special correspondents can unravel.

"I beg your pardon," said he. "It seems an absurd question to ask, but the fact is that I don't know her by any other name: Is there any young lady here that is called Maisie?"

"I am Maisie," was the answer from the depths of a great sun-hat.

"I ought to introduce myself," he said, as the horse capered in the blinding white dust. "My name is Torpenhow. Dick Heldar is my best friend, and—and—the fact is that he has gone blind."

"Blind!" said Maisie, stupidly. "He can't be blind."

"He has been stone-blind for nearly two months."

Maisie lifted up her face, and it was pearly white. "No! No! Not blind! I wont have him blind!"

"Would you care to see for yourself?" said Torpenhow.

"Now,—at once?"

"Oh no! The Paris train doesn't go through this place till eight to-night. There will be ample time."

"Did Mr. Heldar send you to me?"

"Certainly not. Dick wouldn't do that sort of thing. He's sitting in his studio, turning over some letters that he can't read because he's blind."

There was a sound of choking from the sun-hat. Maisie bowed her head and went into the cottage, where the red-haired girl was on a sofa, complaining of a headache.

"Dick's blind!" said Maisie, taking her breath quickly as she steadied herself against a chairback. "My Dick's blind!"

"What?" The girl was on the sofa no longer.

"A man has come from England to tell me. He hasn't written to me for six weeks."

"Are you going to him?"

"I must think."

"Think! *I* should go back to London and see him, and I should kiss his eyes and kiss them and kiss them until they got well again! If you don't go I shall. Oh, what am I talking about? You wicked little idiot! Go to him at once. Go!"

Torpenhow's neck was blistering, but he preserved a smile of infinite patience as Maisie appeared bare-headed in the sunshine.

"I am coming," said she, her eyes on the ground.

"You will be at Vitry Station, then, at seven this evening." This was an order delivered by one who was used to being obeyed. Maisie said nothing, but she felt grateful that there was no chance of disputing with this big man who took everything for granted and managed a squealing horse with one hand. She returned to the red-haired girl, who was weeping bitterly, and between tears, kisses,—very few of those——menthol, packing, and an interview with Kami, the sultry afternoon wore away. Thought might come afterward. Her present duty was to go to Dick,—Dick who owned the wondrous friend and sat in the dark playing with her unopened letters.

"But what will you do?" she said to her companion.

"I? Oh, I shall stay here and—finish your Melancolia," she said, smiling pitifully. "Write to me afterward."

That night there ran a legend through Vitry-sur-Marne of a mad Englishman, doubtless suffering from sunstroke, who had drunk all the officers of the garrison under the table, had borrowed a horse from the lines, and had then and there eloped, after the English custom, with one of those more than mad English girls who drew pictures down there under the care of that good Monsieur Kami.

"They are very droll," said Suzanne to the conscript in the moonlight by the studio wall. "She walked always with those big eyes that saw nothing, and yet she kisses me on both cheeks as though she were my sister, and gives me—see—ten francs!"

The conscript levied a contribution on both gifts; for he prided himself on being a good soldier.

Torpenhow spoke very little to Maisie during the journey to Calais; but he was careful to attend to all her wants, to get her a compartment entirely to herself, and to leave her alone. He was amazed at the ease with which the matter had been accomplished.

"The safest thing would be to let her think things out. By Dick's showing,—when he was off his head,—she must have ordered him about very thoroughly. Wonder how she likes being under orders."

Maisie never told. She sat in the empty compartment often with her eyes shut, that she might realize the sensation of blindness. It was an order that she should return to London swiftly, and she found herself at last almost beginning to enjoy the situation. This was better than looking after luggage and a red-haired friend who never took any interest in her surroundings. But there appeared to be a feeling in the air that she, Maisie,—of all people,—was in disgrace. Therefore she justified her conduct to herself with great success, till Torpenhow came up to her on the steamer and without preface began to tell the story of Dick's blindness, suppressing a few details, but dwelling at length on the miseries of his delirium. He stopped before he reached the end, as though he had lost interest in the subject, and went forward to smoke. Maisie was furious with him and with herself.

She was hurried on from Dover to

London almost before she could ask for breakfast, and—she was past any feeling of indignation now—was bidden curtly to wait in a hall at the foot of some lead-covered stairs while Torpenhow went up to make inquiries. Again the knowledge that she was being treated like a naughty little girl made her pale cheeks flame. It was all Dick's fault for being so stupid as to go blind.

Torpenhow led her up to a shut door, which he opened very softly. Dick was sitting by the window, with his chin on his chest. There were three envelopes in his hand, and he turned them over and over. The big man who gave orders was no longer by her side, and the studio door snapped behind her.

Dick thrust the letters into his pocket as he heard the sound. "Hullo, Torp! Is that you? I've been so lonely."

His voice had taken the peculiar flatness of the blind. Maisie pressed herself up into a corner of the room. Her heart was beating furiously, and she put one hand on her breast to keep it quiet. Dick was staring directly at her, and she realized for the first time that he was blind. Shutting her eyes in a railway-carriage to open them when she pleased was child's play. This man was blind though his eyes were wide open.

"Torp, is that you? They said you were coming." Dick looked puzzled and a little irritated at the silence.

"No: it's only me," was the answer, in a strained little whisper. Maisie could hardly move her lips.

"H'm!" said Dick, composedly, without moving. "This is a new phenomenon. Darkness I'm getting used to; but I object to hearing voices."

Was he mad, then, as well as blind, that he talked to himself? Maisie's heart beat more wildly, and she breathed in gasps. Dick rose and began to feel his way across the room, touching each table and chair as he passed. Once he caught his foot on a rug, and swore, dropping on his knees to feel what the obstruction might be. Maisie remembered him walking in the Park as though all the earth belonged to him, tramping up and down her studio two months ago, and flying up the gangway of the Channel steamer. The beating of her heart was making her sick, and Dick was coming nearer, guided by the sound of her breathing. She put out a hand mechanically to ward him off or to draw him to herself, she did not know which. It touched his chest, and he stepped back as though he had been shot.

"It's Maisie!" said he, with a dry sob. "What are you doing here?"

"I came—I came—to see you, please."

Dick's lips closed firmly.

"Won't you sit down, then? You see, I've had some bother with my eyes, and"—

"I know. I know. Why didn't you tell me?"

"I couldn't write."

"You might have told Mr. Torpenhow."

"What has he to do with my affairs?"

"He—he brought me from Vitry-sur-Marne. He thought I ought to see you."

"Why, what has happened? Can I do anything for you? No, I can't. I forgot."

"Oh, Dick, I'm so sorry! I've come

to tell you, and— Let me take you back to your chair."

"Don't! I'm not a child. You only do that out of pity. I never meant to tell you anything about it. I'm no good now. I'm down and done for. Let me alone!"

He groped back to his chair, his chest laboring as he sat down.

Maisie watched him, and the fear went out of her heart, to be followed by a very bitter shame. He had spoken a truth that had been hidden from the girl through every step of the impetuous flight to London; for he was, indeed, down and done for— masterful no longer but rather a little abject; neither an artist stronger than she, nor a man to be looked up to— only some blind one that sat in a chair and seemed on the point of crying. She was immensely and unfeignedly sorry for him—more sorry than she had ever been for any one in her life, but not sorry enough to deny his words. So she stood still and felt ashamed and a little hurt, because she had honestly intended that her journey should end triumphantly; and now she was only filled with pity most startlingly distinct from love.

"Well?" said Dick, his face steadily turned away. "I never meant to worry you any more. What's the matter?"

He was conscious that Maisie was catching her breath, but was as unprepared as herself for the torrent of emotion that followed. People who cannot cry easily weep unrestrainedly when the fountains of the great deep are broken up. She had dropped into a chair and was sobbing with her face hidden in her hands.

"I can't—I can't!" she cried, desperately. "Indeed, I can't. It isn't my fault. I'm so sorry. Oh, Dickie, I'm so sorry."

Dick's shoulders straightened again, for the words lashed like a whip. Still the sobbing continued. It is not good to realize that you have failed in the hour of trial or flinched before the mere possibility of making sacrifices.

"I do despise myself—indeed I do. But I can't. Oh, Dickie, you wouldn't ask me—would you?" wailed Maisie.

She looked up for a minute, and by chance it happened that Dick's eyes fell on hers. The unshaven face was very white and set, and the lips were trying to force themselves into a smile. But it was the worn-out eyes that Maisie feared. Her Dick had gone blind and left in his place some one that she could hardly recognize till he spoke.

"Who is asking you to do anything, Maisie? I told you how it would be. What's the use of worrying? For pity's sake don't cry like that; it isn't worth it."

"You don't know how I hate myself. Oh, Dick, help me—help me!" The passion of tears had grown beyond her control and was beginning to alarm the man. He stumbled forward and put his arm around her, and her head fell on his shoulder.

"Hush, dear, hush! Don't cry. You're quite right, and you've nothing to reproach yourself with—you never had. You're only a little upset by the journey, and I don't suppose you've had any breakfast. What a brute Torp was to bring you over."

"I wanted to come. I did indeed," she protested.

"Very well. And now you've come and seen, and I'm—immensely grateful. When you're better you shall go away and get something to eat. What sort of a passage did you have coming over?"

Maisie was crying more subduedly, for the first time in her life glad that she had something to lean against. Dick patted her on the shoulder tenderly but clumsily, for he was not quite sure where her shoulder might be.

She drew herself out of his arms at last and waited, trembling and most unhappy. He had felt his way to the window to put the width of the room between them, and to quiet a little the tumult in his heart.

"Are you better now?" he said.

"Yes, but—don't you hate me?"

"I hate you? My God! I?"

"Isn't—isn't there anything I could do for you, then? I'll stay here in England to do it, if you like. Perhaps I could come and see you sometimes."

"I think not, dear. It would be kindest not to see me any more, please. I don't want to seem rude, but—don't you think—perhaps you had almost better go now."

He was conscious that he could not bear himself as a man if the strain continued much longer.

"I don't deserve anything else. I'll go, Dick. Oh, I'm so miserable."

"Nonsense. You've nothing to worry about; I'd tell you if you had. Wait a moment, dear. I've got something to give you first. I meant it for you ever since this little trouble began. It's my Melancolia; she was a beauty when I last saw her. You can keep her for me, and if ever you're poor you can sell her. She's worth a few hundreds at any state of the market." He groped among his canvases. "She's framed in black. Is this a black frame that I have my hand on? There she is. What do you think of her?"

He turned a scared formless muddle of paint toward Maisie, and the eyes strained as though they would catch her wonder and surprise. One thing and one thing only could she do for him.

"Well?"

The voice was fuller and more rounded, because the man knew he was speaking of his best work. Maisie looked at the blur, and a lunatic desire to laugh caught her by the throat. But for Dick's sake—whatever this mad blankness might mean—she must make no sign. Her voice choked with hard-held tears as she answered, still gazing on the wreck—

"Oh, Dick, it *is* good!"

He heard the little hysterical gulp and took it for tribute. "Won't you have it, then? I'll send it over to your house if you will."

"I? Oh yes—thank you. Ha! ha!" If she did not fly at once the laughter that was worse than tears would kill her. She turned and ran, choking and blinded, down the staircases that were empty of life to take refuge in a cab and go to her house across the Parks. There she sat down in the almost dismantled drawing-room and thought of Dick in his blindness, useless till the end of life, and of herself in her own eyes Behind the sorrow, the shame, and the humiliation, lay fear of the cold wrath of the red-haired girl when Maisie should return. Maisie had never feared her companion before. Not until she found herself saying, "Well, he never asked me," did she realize her scorn of herself.

And that is the end of Maisie.

For Dick was reserved more searching torment. He could not realize at first that Maisie, whom he had ordered to go, had left him without a word of farewell. He was savagely angry against Torpenhow, who had brought upon him this humiliation and troubled his miserable peace. Then his dark hour came and he was alone with himself and his desires to get what help he could from the darkness. The queen could do no wrong, but in following the right, so far as it served her work, she had wounded her one subject more than his own brain would let him know.

"It's all I had and I've lost it," he said, as soon as the misery permitted clear thinking. "And Torp will think that he has been so infernally clever that I shan't have the heart to tell him. I must think this out quietly."

"Hullo!" said Torpenhow, entering the studio after Dick had enjoyed two hours of thought. "I'm back. Are you feeling any better?"

"Torp, I don't know what to say. Come here." Dick coughed huskily, wondering, indeed, what he should say, and how to say it temperately.

"What's the need for saying anything? Get up and tramp." Torpenhow was perfectly satisfied.

They walked up and down as of custom, Torpenhow's hand on Dick's shoulder, and Dick buried in his own thoughts.

"How in the world did you find it all out?" said Dick at last.

"You shouldn't go off your head if you want to keep secrets, Dickie. It was absolutely impertinent on my part; but if you'd seen me rocketing about on a half-trained French troop-horse under a blazing sun you'd have laughed. There will be a charivari in my rooms to-night. Seven other devils"—

"I know—the row in the Southern Soudan. I surprised their councils the other day, and it made me unhappy. Have you fixed your flint to go? Who d'you work for?"

" 'Haven't signed any contracts yet. I wanted to see how your business would turn out."

"Would you have stayed with me, then, if—things had gone wrong?" He put his question cautiously.

"Don't ask me too much. I'm only a man."

"You've tried to be an angel very successfully."

"Oh ye—es! . . . Well, do you attend the function to-night? We shall be half screwed before the morning. All the men believe the war's a certainty."

"I don't think I will, old man, if it's all the same to you. I'll stay quiet here."

"And meditate? I don't blame you. You deserve a good time if ever a man did."

That night there was tumult on the stairs. The correspondents poured in from theatre, dinner, and music-hall to Torpenhow's room that they might discuss their plan of campaign in the event of military operations being a certainty. Torpenhow, the Keneu, and the Nilghai had bidden all the men they had worked with to the orgy; and Mr. Beeton, the housekeeper, declared that never before in his checkered experience had he seen quite such a fancy lot of gentlemen. They waked the chambers with shoutings and song; and the elder men were quite as bad as the younger. For the chances of war were in front of them, and all knew what those meant.

Sitting in his own room, a little perplexed by the noise across the landing, Dick suddenly began to laugh to himself. "When one comes to think of it the situation is intensely comic. Maisie's quite right—poor little thing. I didn't know she could cry like that before; but now I know what Torp thinks, I'm sure he'd be quite fool enough to stay at home and try to console me—if he knew. Besides, it isn't nice to own that you've been thrown over like a broken chair. I must carry this business through alone—as usual. If there isn't a war, and Torp finds out, I shall look foolish, that's all. If there is a war I mustn't interfere with another man's chances. Business is business, and I want to be alone—I want to be alone. What a row they're making!"

Somebody hammered at the studio door.

"Come out and frolic, Dickie," said the Nilghai.

"I should like to, but I can't. I'm not feeling frolicsome."

"Then I'll tell the boys and they'll draw you like a badger."

"Please not, old man. On my word, I'd sooner be left alone just now."

"Very good. Can we send anything in to you? Fizz, for instance. Cassavetti is beginning to sing songs of the Sunny South already."

For one minute Dick considered the proposition seriously.

"No, thanks. I've a headache already."

"Virtuous child. That's the effect of emotion on the young. All my congratulations, Dick. I also was concerned in the conspiracy for your welfare."

"Go to the devil and—oh, send Binkie in here."

The little dog entered on elastic feet, riotous from having been made much of all the evening. He had helped to sing the choruses; but scarcely inside the studio he realized that this was no place for tail-wagging, and settled himself on Dick's lap till it was bedtime. Then he went to bed with Dick, who counted every hour as it struck, and rose in the morning with a painfully clear head to receive Torpenhow's more formal congratulations and a particular account of the last night's revels.

"You aren't looking very happy for a newly-accepted man," said Torpenhow.

"Never mind that—it's my own affair, and I'm all right. Do you really go?"

"Yes. With the old Central Southern as usual. They wired and I accepted on better terms than before."

"When do you start?"

"The day after to-morrow—for Brindisi."

"Thank God." Dick spoke from the bottom of his heart.

"Well, that's not a pretty way of saying you're glad to get rid of me. But men in your condition are allowed to be selfish."

"I didn't mean that. Will you get a hundred pounds cashed for me before you leave?"

"That's a slender amount for house-keeping, isn't it?"

"Oh, it's only for—marriage expenses."

Torpenhow brought him the money, counted it out in fives and tens, and carefully put it away in the writing-table.

"Now I suppose I shall have to listen to his ravings about his girl until I go. Heaven send us patience with a man in love!" said he to himself.

But never a word did Dick say of Maisie or marriage. He hung in the doorway of Torpenhow's room when the latter was packing and asked innumerable questions about the coming campaign, till Torpenhow began to feel annoyed.

"You're a secretive animal, Dickie, and you consume your own smoke, don't you?" he said on the last evening.

"I—I suppose so. By the way, how long do you think this war will last?"

"Days, weeks, or months. One can never tell. It may go on for years."

"I wish I were going."

"Good heavens! You're the most unaccountable creature! Hasn't it occurred to you that you're going to be married—thanks to me?"

"Of course, yes. I'm going to be married—so I am. Going to be married. I'm awfully grateful to you. Haven't I told you that?"

"You might be going to be hanged by the look of you," said Torpenhow.

And the next day Torpenhow bade him good-bye, and left him to the loneliness he had so much desired.

CHAPTER XIV

Yet at the last, ere our spearmen had
  found him
Yet at the last, ere a sword-thrust
  could save,
Yet at the last, with his masters around
  him,
He of the Faith spoke as master to
  slave;
Yet at the last, tho' the Kafirs had
  maimed him,
Broken by bondage and wrecked by
  the reiver,—
Yet at the last, tho' the darkness had
  claimed him,
He called upon Allah and died a
  believer.
    —*Kizilbashi.*

"Beg your pardon, Mr. Heldar, but —but isn't nothin' going to happen?" said Mr. Beeton.

"No!" Dick had just waked to another morning of blank despair and his temper was of the shortest.

"'Tain't my regular business o' course, sir; and what I say is, 'Mind your own business and let other people mind theirs'; but just before Mr. Torpenhow went away he give me to understand, like, that you might be moving into a house of your own, so to speak— a sort of house with rooms upstairs and downstairs where you'd be better attended to, though I try to act just by all our tenants. Don't I?"

"Ah! That must have been a mad-house. I shan't trouble you to take me there yet. Get me my breakfast, please, and leave me alone."

"I hope I haven't done any thing wrong, sir, but you know I hope that as far as a man can I tries to do the proper thing by all the gentlemen in chambers—and more particular those whose lot is hard—such as you, for instance, Mr. Heldar. You likes soft-roe bloater, don't you? Soft-roe bloaters is scarcer than hard-roe, but what I says is, 'Never mind a little extra trouble so long as you gives satisfaction to the tenants.' "

Mr. Beeton withdrew and left Dick to himself. Torpenhow had been long away; there was no more rioting in the chambers, and Dick had settled down to his new life, which he was weak enough to consider nothing better than death.

It is hard to live alone in the dark, confusing the day and night; dropping to sleep through sheer weariness at midday, and rising restless in the chill of the dawn. At first Dick, on his awakenings, would grope along the corridors of the chambers till he heard some one snore. Then he would know that the day had not yet come, and return wearily to his bedroom. Later he learned not to stir till there was a noise and movement in the house and Mr. Beeton advised him to get up. Once dressed—and dressing, now that Torpenhow was away, was a lengthy business, because collars, ties, and the like, hid themselves in far corners of the room, and search meant head-beating against chairs and trunks—once dressed, there was nothing whatever to do except to sit still and brood till the three daily meals came. Centuries separated breakfast from lunch and lunch from dinner, and though a man prayed for hundreds of years that his mind might be taken from him, God would never hear. Rather the mind was quickened and the revolving thoughts ground against each other as millstones grind when there is no corn between; and yet the brain would not wear out and give him rest. It continued to think, at length, with imagery and all manner of reminiscences. It recalled Maisie and past success, reckless travels by land and sea, the glory of doing work and feeling that it was good, and suggested all that might have happened had the eyes only been faithful to their duty. When thinking ceased through sheer weariness, there poured into Dick's soul tide on tide of overwhelming, purposeless fear—dread of starvation always, terror lest the unseen ceiling should crush down upon him, fear of fire in the chambers and a louse's death in red flame, and agonies of fiercer horror that had nothing to do with any fear of death. Then Dick bowed his head, and clutching the arms of his chair fought with his sweating self till the tinkle of plates told him that something to eat was being set before him.

Mr. Beeton would bring the meal when he had time to spare, and Dick learned to hang upon his speech which dealt with badly-fitted gas-plugs, waste-pipes out of repair, little tricks for driving picture-nails into walls, and the sins of the char-woman or the housemaids. In the lack of better things the small gossip of a servant's hall becomes immensely interesting, and the screwing of a washer on a tap an event to be talked over for days.

Once or twice a week, too, Mr. Beeton would take Dick out with him when he went marketing in the morning to haggle with tradesmen over fish, lampwicks, mustard, tapioca, and so forth, while Dick rested his weight first on one foot and then on the other and played aimlessly with the tins and string-ball on the counter. Then they would perhaps meet one of Mr. Beeton's friends, and Dick, standing aside a little, would hold his peace till Mr. Beeton was willing to go on again.

The life did not increase his self-respect. He abandoned shaving as a dangerous exercise, and being shaved in a barber's shop meant exposure of his infirmity. He could not see that his clothes were properly brushed, and since he had never taken any care of his personal appearance he became every known variety of sloven. A blind man cannot eat with cleanliness till he has been some months used to the darkness. If he demand attendance and grow angry at the want of it, he must assert himself and stand upright. Then the meanest menial can see that he is blind and, therefore, of no consequence. A wise man will keep his eyes on the floor and sit still. For amusement he may pick coal lump by lump out of the scuttle with the tongs and pile it in a little heap in the fender, keeping count of the lumps, which must all be put back again, one by one and very carefully. He may set himself sums if he cares to work them out; he may talk to himself or to the cat if she chooses to visit him; and if his trade has been that of an artist, he may sketch in the air with his forefinger; but that is too much like drawing a pig with the eyes shut. He may go to his bookshelves and count his books, ranging them in order of their size; or to his wardrobe and count his shirts, laying them in piles of two or three on the bed, as they suffer from frayed cuffs or lost buttons. Even this entertainment wearies after

a time; and all the times are very, very long.

Dick was allowed to sort a tool-chest where Mr. Beeton kept hammers, taps and nuts, lengths of gas-pipes, oil-bottles and string.

"If I don't have everything just where I know where to look for it, why, then, I can't find anything when I do want it. You've no idea, sir, the amount of little things that these chambers uses up," said Mr. Beeton. Fumbling at the handle of the door as he went out: "It's hard on you, sir, I *do* think it's hard on you. Ain't you going to do anything, sir?"

"I'll pay my rent and messing. Isn't that enough?"

"I wasn't doubting for a moment that you couldn't pay your way, sir; but I'ave often said to my wife, 'It's 'ard on 'im because it isn't as if he was an old man, nor yet a middle-aged one, but quite a young gentleman. *That's* where it comes so 'ard.'"

"I suppose so," said Dick, absently. This particular nerve through a long battering had ceased to feel—much.

"I was thinking," continued Mr. Beeton, still making as if to go, " that you might like to hear my boy Alf read you the papers sometimes of an evening. He do read beautiful, seeing's he's only nine."

"I should be very grateful," said Dick. "Only let me make it worth his while."

"We wasn't thinking of *that*, sir, but of course it's in your own 'ands; but only to 'ear Alf sing 'A Boy's best Friend is 'is Mother!' Ah!"

"I'll hear him sing that too. Let him

come in this evening with the newspapers."

Alf was not a nice child, being puffed up with many school-board certificates for good conduct, and inordinately proud of his singing. Mr. Beeton remained, beaming, while the child wailed his way through a song of some eight eight-line verses in the usual whine of the young Cockney, and, after compliments, left him to read Dick the foreign telegrams. Ten minutes later Alf returned to his parents rather pale and scared.

" 'E said 'e couldn't stand it no more," he explained.

"He never said you read badly, Alf?" Mrs. Beeton spoke.

"No. 'E said I read beautiful. Said 'e never 'eard any one read like that, but 'e said 'e couldn't abide the stuff in the papers."

"P'raps he's lost some money in the Stocks. Were you readin' him about Stocks, Alf?"

"No; it was all about fightin' out there where the soldiers is gone—a great long piece with all the lines close together and very hard words in it. 'E give me 'arf a crown because I read so well. And 'e says the next time there's anything 'e wants read 'e'll send for me."

"That's good hearing, but I do think for all the half-crown—put it into the kicking-donkey money-box, Alf and let me see you do it—he might have kept you longer. Why, he couldn't have begun to understand how beautiful you read."

"He's best left to hisself—gentlemen always are when they're downhearted," said Mr. Beeton.

Alf's rigorously limited powers of comprehending Torpenhow's special correspondence had waked the devil of unrest in Dick. He could hear, through the boy's nasal chant, the camels grunting in the squares behind the soldiers outside Suakin; could hear the men swearing and chaffing across the cooking pots, and could smell the acrid wood-smoke as it drifted over the camp before the wind of the desert.

That night he prayed to God that his mind might be taken from him, offering for proof that he was worthy of this favor the fact that he had not shot himself long ago. That prayer was not answered, and indeed Dick knew in his heart of hearts that only a lingering sense of humor and no special virtue had kept him alive. Suicide, he had persuaded himself, would be a ludicrous insult to the gravity of the situation as well as a weak-kneed confession of fear.

"Just for the fun of the thing," he said to the cat, who had taken Binkie's place in his establishment, "I should like to know how long this is going to last. I can live for a year on the hundred pounds Torp cashed for me. I must have two or three thousand at least at the Bank—twenty or thirty years more provided for, that is to say. Then I fall back on my hundred and twenty a year which will be more by that time. Let's consider. Twenty-five — thirty-five — a man's in his prime then, they say — forty-five—a middle-aged man just entering politics—fifty-five — died at the comparatively early age of fifty-five,' according to the newspapers. Bah! How these Christians funk death! Sixty-five—we're only getting on in years. Seventy-five is just possible though.

Great Hell, cat O! fifty years more of solitary confinment in the dark! You'll die, and Beeton will die, and Torp will die, and Mai—everbody else will die, but I shall be alive and kicking with nothing to do. I'm very sorry for myself. I should like some one else to be sorry for me. Evidently I'm not going mad before I die, but the pain's just as bad as ever. Some day when you're vivisected, cat O! they'll tie you down on a little table and cut you open—but don't be afraid; they'll take precious good care that you don't die. You'll live, and you'll be very sorry then that you weren't sorry for me. Perhaps Torp will come back or . . . I wish I could go to Torp and the Nilghai, even though I were in their way."

Pussy left the room before the speech was ended, and Alf, as he entered, found Dick addressing the empty hearth-rug.

"There's a letter for you, sir," he said. "Perhaps you'd like me to read it."

"Lend it to me for a minute and I'll tell you."

The outstretched hand shook just a little and the voice was not over-steady. It was within the limits of human possibility that—that was no letter from Maisie. He knew the heft of three closed envelopes only too well. It was a foolish hope that the girl should write to him, for he did not realize that there is a wrong which admits of no reparation though the evildoer may with tears and the heart's best love strive to mend all. It is best to forget that wrong whether it be caused or endured, since it is as remediless as bad work once put forward.

"Read it, then," said Dick, and Alf began intoning according to the rules of the Board School—

"*I could have given you love, I could have given you loyalty, such as you never dreamed of. Do you suppose I cared what you were? But you choose to whistle everything down the wind for nothing. My only excuse for you is that you are so young.*"

"That's all," he said, returning the paper to be dropped into the fire.

"What was in the letter?" asked Mrs. Beeton when Alf returned.

"I don't know. I think it was a circular or a tract about not whistlin' at everything when you're young."

"I must have stepped on something when I was alive and walking about and it has bounced up and hit me. God help it, whatever it is—unless it was all a joke. But I don't know any one who'd take the trouble to play a joke on me. . . . Love and loyalty for nothing. It sounds tempting enough. I wonder whether I have lost anything really?"

Dick considered for a long time but could not remember when or how he had put himself in the way of winning these trifles at a woman's hands.

Still, the letter as touching on matters that he preferred not to think about stung him into a fit of frenzy that lasted for a day and night. When his heart was so full of despair that it would hold no more, body and soul together seemed to be dropping without check through the darkness. Then came fear of darkness and desperate attempts to reach the light again. But there was no light to be reached. When that agony had left him sweating and breathless, the downward flight would recommence till the gathering torture of it spurred him into another fight as hopeless as the first. Followed some few minutes of sleep in which he dreamed that he saw. Then the procession of events would repeat itself till he was utterly worn out and the brain took up its everlasting consideration of Maisie and might-have-beens.

At the end of everything Mr. Beeton came to his room and volunteered to take him out. "Not marketing this time, but we'll go into the Parks if you like."

"Be damned if I do," quoth Dick. "Keep to the streets and walk up and down. I like to hear the people round me."

This was not altogether true. The blind in the first stages of their infirmity dislike those who can move with a free stride and unlifted arms—but Dick had no earthly desire to go to the Parks. Once and only once since Maisie had shut the door he had gone there under Alf's charge. Alf forgot him and fished for minnows in the Serpentine with some companions. After half an hour's waiting Dick, almost weeping with rage and wrath, caught a passer-by who introduced him to a friendly policeman, who led him to a four-wheeler opposite the Albert Hall. He never told Mr. Beeton of Alf's forgetfulness, but . . . this was not the manner in which he was used to walk the Parks aforetime.

"What streets would you like to walk down, then?" said Mr. Beeton, sympathetically. His own ideas of a riotous holiday meant picnicing on the grass of the Green Park with his family, and half a dozen paper bags full of food.

"Keep to the river," said Dick, and they kept to the river, and the rush of it was in his ears till they came to Blackfriars Bridge and struck thence on to the Waterloo Road, Mr. Beeton explaining the beauties of the scenery as he went on.

"And walking on the other side of the pavement," said he, "unless I'm much mistaken, is the young woman that used to come to your rooms to be drawed. I never forgets a face and I never remembers a name, except paying tenants, o' course!"

"Stop her," said Dick. "It's Bessie Broke. Tell her I'd like to speak to her again. Quick, man!"

Mr. Beeton crossed the road under the noses of the omnibuses and arrested Bessie then on her way northward. She recognized him as the man in authority who used to glare at her when she passed up Dick's staircase, and her first impulse was to run.

"Wasn't you Mr. Heldar's model?" said Mr. Beeton, planting himself in front of her. "You was. He's on the other side of the road and he'd like to see you."

"Why?" said Bessie, faintly. She remembered—indeed had never for long forgotten—an affair connected with a newly-finished picture.

"Because he has asked me to do so, and because he's most particular blind."

"Drunk?"

"No. 'Orspital blind. He can't see. That's him over there."

Dick was leaning against the parapet of the bridge as Mr. Beeton pointed him out—a stub-bearded, bowed creature wearing a dirty magenta colored neckcloth outside an unbrushed coat. There was nothing to fear from such an one.

Even if he chased her, Bessie thought, he could not follow far. She crossed over and Dick's face lighted up. It was long since a woman of any kind had taken the trouble to speak to him.

"I hope you're well, Mr. Heldar?" said Bessie, a little puzzled. Mr. Beeton stood by with the air of an ambassador and breathed responsibly.

"I'm very well indeed, and, by Jove! I'm glad to see—hear you, I mean, Bess. You never thought it worth while to turn up and see us again after you got your money. I don't know why you should. Are you going anywhere in particular just now?"

"I was going for a walk," said Bessie.

"Not the old business?" Dick spoke under his breath.

"Lor, no! I paid my premium"—Bessie was very proud of that word—"for a barmaid, sleeping in, and I'm at the bar now quite respectable. Indeed I am."

Mr. Beeton had no special reason to believe in the loftiness of human nature. Therefore he dissolved himself like a mist and returned to his gas-plugs without a word of apology. Bessie watched the flight with a certain uneasiness; but so long as Dick appeared to be ignorant of the harm that had been done to him. . . .

"It's hard work pulling the beer-handles," she went on, "and they've got one of them penny-in-the-slot cash-machines, so if you get wrong by a penny at the end of the day—but then I don't believe the machinery is right. Do you?"

"I've only seen it work. Mr. Beeton."

"He's gone."

"I'm afraid I must ask you to help me home, then. I'll make it worth your while. You see." The sightless eyes turned toward her and Bessie saw.

"It isn't taking you out of your way?" he said, hesitatingly. "I can ask a policeman if it is."

"Not at all. I come on at seven and I'm off at four. That's easy hours."

"Good God!—but I'm on all the time. I wish I had some work to do too. Let's go home, Bess."

He turned and cannoned into a man on the sidewalk, recoiling with an oath. Bessie took his arm and said nothing—as she had said nothing when he had ordered her to turn her face a little more to the light. They walked for some time in silence, the girl steering him deftly through the crowd.

"And where's—where's Mr. Torpenhow?" she inquired at last.

"He has gone away to the desert."

"Where's that?"

Dick pointed to the right. "East—out of the mouth of the river," said he. "Then west, then south, and then east again, all along the under-side of Europe. Then south again, God knows how far." The explanation did not enlighten Bessie in the least, but she held her tongue and looked to Dick's path till they came to the chambers.

"We'll have tea and muffins," he said, joyously. "I can't tell you, Bessie, how glad I am to find you again. What made you go away so suddenly?"

"I didn't think you'd want me any more," she said, emboldened by his ignorance.

"I didn't as a matter of fact—but afterward— At any rate I'm glad you've come. You know the stairs."

So Bessie led him home to his own

place—there was no one to hinder—and shut the door of the studio.

"What a mess!" was her first word. "All these things haven't been looked after for months and months."

"No, only weeks, Bess. You can't expect them to care."

"I don't know what you expect them to do. They ought to know what you've paid them for. The dust's just awful. It's all over the easel."

"I don't use it much now."

"All over the pictures and the floor, and all over your coat. I'd like to speak to them housemaids."

"Ring for tea, then." Dick felt his way to the one chair he used by custom. Bessie saw the action and, as far as in her lay, was touched. But there remained always a keen sense of new-found superiority, and it was in her voice when she spoke.

"How long have you been like this?" she said, wrathfully, as though the blindness were some fault of the housemaids.

"How?"

"As you are."

"The day after you went away with the check, almost as soon as my picture was finished; I hardly saw her alive."

"Then they've been cheating you ever since, that's all. I know their nice little ways."

A woman may love one man and despise another, but on general feminine principles she will do her best to save the man she despises from being defrauded. Her loved one can look to himself, but the other man, being obviously an idiot, needs protection.

"I don't think Mr. Beeton cheats much," said Dick. Bessie was flouncing

up and down the room, and he was conscious of a keen sense of enjoyment as he heard the swish of her skirts and the light step between.

"Tea *and* muffins," she said, shortly, when the ring at the bell was answered; "two teaspoonfuls and one over for the pot. I don't want the old teapot that was here when I used to come. It don't draw. Get another."

The housemaid went away scandalized, and Dick chuckled. Then he began to cough as Bessie banged up and down the studio disturbing the dust.

"What are you trying to do?"

"Put things straight. This is like unfurnished lodgings. How could you let it go so?"

"How could I help it? Dust away."

She dusted furiously, and in the midst of all the pother entered Mrs. Beeton. Her husband on his return had explained the situation, winding up with the peculiarly felicitous proverb, "Do unto others as you would be done by." She had descended to put into her place the person who demanded muffins and an uncracked teapot as though she had a right to both.

"Muffins ready yet?" said Bess, still dusting. She was no longer a drab of the streets but a young lady who, thanks to Dick's check, had paid her premium and was entitled to pull beer-handles with the best. Being neatly dressed in black she did not hesitate to face Mrs. Beeton, and there passed between the two women certain regards that Dick would have appreciated. The situation adjusted itself by eye. Bessie had won, and Mrs. Beeton returned to cook muffins and make scathing remarks about models, hussies, trollops, and the like, to her husband.

"There's nothing to be got of interfering with him, Liza," he said. "Alf, you go along into the street to play. When he isn't crossed he's as kindly as kind, but when he's crossed he's the devil and all. We took too many little things out of his room since he was blind to be that particular about what he does. They ain't no objects to a blind man, of course, but if it was to come into court we'd get the sack. Yes, I did introduce him to that girl because I'm a feelin' man myself."

"Much too feelin'!" Mrs. Beeton slapped the muffins into the dish, and thought of comely housemaids long since dismissed on suspicion.

"I ain't ashamed of it, and it isn't for us to judge him hard so long as he pays quiet and regular as he do. I know how to manage young gentlemen, you know how to cook for them, and what I says is, let each stick to his own business and there won't be any trouble. Take them muffins down, Liza, and be sure you have no words with that young woman. His lot is cruel hard, and if he's crossed he do swear worse than any one I've ever served.

"That's a little better," said Bessie, sitting down to tea. "You needn't wait, thank you, Mrs. Beeton."

"I had no intention of doing such, I do assure you."

Bessie made no answer whatever. This, she knew, was the way in which real ladies routed their foes, and when one is a barmaid at a first-class public-house one may become a real lady at ten minutes' notice.

Her eyes fell on Dick opposite her

and she was both shocked and displeased. There were droppings of food all down the front of his coat; the mouth under the ragged ill-grown beard drooped sullenly; the forehead was lined and contracted; and on the lean temples the hair was a dusty indeterminate color that might or might not have been called grey. The utter misery and self-abandonment of the man appealed to her, and at the bottom of her heart lay the wicked feeling that he was humbled and brought low who had once humbled her.

"Oh! it *is* good to hear you moving about," said Dick, rubbing his hands. "Tell us all about your bar successes, Bessie, and the way you live now."

"Never mind that. I'm quite respectable, as you'd see by looking at me. *You* don't seem to live too well. What made you go blind that sudden? Why isn't there any one to look after you?"

Dick was too thankful for the sound of her voice to resent the tone of it.

"I was cut across the head a long time ago, and that ruined my eyes. I don't suppose anybody thinks it worth while to look after me any more. Why should they?—and Mr. Beeton really does everything I want."

"Don't you know any gentlemen and ladies, then, while you was—well?"

"A few, but I don't care to have them looking at me."

"I suppose that's why you've growed a beard. Take it off, it don't become you."

"Good gracious, child, do you imagine that I think of what becomes me these days?"

"You ought. Get that taken off before I come here again. I suppose I can come, can't I?"

"I'd be only too grateful if you did. I don't think I treated you very well in the old days. I used to make you angry."

"Very angry, you did."

"I'm sorry for it, then. Come and see me when you can and as often as you can. God knows, there isn't a soul in the world to take that trouble except you and Mr. Beeton."

"A lot of trouble *he's* taking and *she* too." This with a toss of the head. "They've let you do anyhow and they haven't done anything for you. I've only to look to see that much. I'll come, and I'll be glad to come, but you must go and be shaved, and you must get some other clothes—those ones aren't fit to be seen."

"I have heaps somewhere," he said, helplessly.

"I know you have. Tell Mr. Beeton to give you a new suit and I'll brush it and keep it clean. You may be as blind as a barn-door, Mr. Heldar, but it doesn't excuse you looking like a sweep."

"Do I look like a sweep, then?"

"Oh, I'm sorry for you. I'm that sorry for you!" she cried, impulsively, and took Dick's hands. Mechanically, he lowered his head as if to kiss—she was the only woman who had taken pity on him, and he was not too proud for a little pity now. She stood up to go.

"Nothing o' that kind till you look more like a gentleman. It's quite easy when you get shaved and some clothes."

He could hear her drawing on her gloves and rose to say good-bye. She passed behind him, kissed him auda-

ciously on the back of the neck, and ran away as swiftly as on the day when she had destroyed the Melancolia.

"To think of me kissing Mr. Heldar," she said to herself, "after all he's done to me and all! Well, I'm sorry for him, and if he was shaved he wouldn't be so bad to look at, but . . . Oh them Beetons, how shameful they've treated him! I know Beeton's wearing his shirts on his back to-day just as well as if I'd aired it. To-morrow, I'll see . . . I wonder if he has much of his own. It might be worth more than the bar—I wouldn't have to do any work—and just as respectable if no one knew."

Dick was not grateful to Bessie for her parting gift. He was acutely conscious of it in the nape of his neck throughout the night, but it seemed, among very many other things, to enforce the wisdom of getting shaved. He was shaved accordingly in the morning, and felt the better for it. A fresh suit of clothes, white linen, and the knowledge that some one in the world said that she took an interest in his personal appearance, made him carry himself almost upright; for the brain was relieved for a while from thinking of Maisie, who, under other circumstances, might have given that kiss and a million others.

"Let us consider," said he after lunch. "The girl can't care, and it's a toss-up whether she comes again or not, but if money can buy her to look after me she shall be bought. Nobody else in the world would take the trouble, and I can make it worth her while. She's a child of the gutter holding brevet rank as a barmaid; so she shall have every-thing she wants if she'll only come and talk and look after me." He rubbed his newly-shorn chin and began to perplex himself with the thought of her not coming. "I suppose I did look rather a sweep," he went on. "I had no reason to look otherwise. I knew things dropped on my clothes, but it didn't matter. It would be cruel if she didn't come. She must. Maisie came once, and that was enough for her. She was quite right. She had something to work for. This creature has only beer-handles to pull, unless she has deluded some young man into keeping company with her. Fancy being cheated for the sake of a counter-jumper! We're falling pretty low."

Something cried aloud within him:— This will hurt more than anything that has gone before. It will recall and remind and suggest and tantalize, and in the end drive you mad.

"I know it, I know it!" Dick cried, clenching his hands despairingly; "but, good heavens! is a poor blind beggar never to get anything out of his life except three meals a day and a greasy waistcoat? I wish she'd come."

Early in the afternoon time she came, because there was no young man in her life just then, and she thought of material advantages which would allow her to be idle for the rest of her days.

"I shouldn't have known you," she said, approvingly. "You look as you used to look—a gentleman that was proud of himself."

"Don't you think I deserve another kiss then?" said Dick, flushing a little.

"Maybe—but you won't get it yet. Sit down and let's see what I can do for you. I'm certain sure Mr. Beeton cheats you, now that you can't go

through the housekeeping books every month. Isn't that true?"

"You'd better come and housekeep for me then, Bessie."

"'Couldn't do it in these chambers—you know that as well as I do."

"I know, but we might go somewhere else, if you thought it worth your while."

"I'd try to look after you, anyhow; but I shouldn't care to have to work for both of us.' This was tentative.

Dick laughed.

"Do you remember where I used to keep my bank-book?" said he. "Torp took it to be balanced just before he went away. Look and see."

"It was generally under the tobacco-jar. Ah!"

"Well?"

"Oh! Four thousand two hundred and ten pounds nine shillings and a penny! Oh my!"

"You can have the penny. That's not bad for one year's work. Is that and a hundred and twenty pounds a year good enough?"

The idleness and the pretty clothes were almost within her reach now, but she must, by being housewifely, show that she deserved them.

"Yes; but you'd have to move, and if we took an inventory, I think we'd find that Mr. Beeton has been prigging little things out of the rooms here and there. They don't look as full as they used."

"Never mind, we'll let him have them. The only thing I'm particularly anxious to take away is that picture I used you for—when you used to swear at me. We'll pull out of this place, Bess, and get away as far as ever we can."

"Oh yes," she said, uneasily.

"I don't know where I can go to get away from myself, but I'll try, and you shall have all the pretty frocks that you care for. You'll like that. Give me that kiss now, Bess. Ye gods! it's good to put one's arms round a woman's waist again."

Then came the fulfilment of the prophecy within the brain. If his arm were thus round Maisie's waist and a kiss had just been given and taken between them,—why then. . . . He pressed the girl more closely to himself because the pain whipped him. She was wondering how to explain a little accident to the Melancolia. At any rate, if this man really desired the solace of her company—and certainly he would relapse into his original slough if she withdrew it—He would not be more than just a little vexed. It would be delightful at least to see what would happen, and by her teachings it was good for a man to stand in certain awe of his companion.

She laughed nervously, and slipped out of his reach.

"I shouldn't worrit about that picture if I was you," she began, in the hope of turning his attention.

"It's at the back of all my canvases somewhere. Find it, Bess; you know it as well as I do."

"I know—but"—

"But what? You've wit enough to manage the sale of it to a dealer. Women haggle much better than men. It might be a matter of eight or nine hundred pounds to—to us. I simply didn't like to think about it for a long time. It was mixed up with my life so.—But we'll cover up our tracks and get rid of everything, eh? Make a fresh start from the beginning, Bess. "

Then she began to repent very much indeed, because she knew the value of money. Still, it was probable that the blind man was overestimating the value of his work. Gentlemen, she knew, were absurdly particular about their things. She giggled as a nervous housemaid giggles when she tries to explain the breakage of a pipe.

"I'm very sorry, but you remember I was—I was angry with you before Mr. Torpenhow went away?"

"You were very angry, child; and on my word I think you had some right to be."

"Then I—but aren't you sure Mr. Torpenhow didn't tell you?"

"Tell me what? Good gracious, what are you making such a fuss about when you might just as well be giving me another kiss."

He was beginning to learn, not for the first time in his experience, that kissing is a cumulative poison. The more you get of it, the more you want. Bessie gave the kiss promptly, whispering, as she did so, "I was so angry I rubbed out that picture with the turpentine. You aren't angry, are you?"

"What? Say that again." The man's hand had closed on her wrist.

"I rubbed it out with turps and the knife," faltered Bessie. "I thought you'd only have to do it over again. You did do it over again, didn't you? Oh, let go of my wrist; you're hurting me."

"Isn't there anything left of the thing?"

"N'nothing that looks like anything. I'm sorry—I didn't know you'd take on about it; I only meant to do it in fun. You aren't going to hit me?"

"Hit you! No! Let's think."

He did not relax his hold upon her wrist but stood staring at the carpet. Then he shook his head as a young steer shakes it when the lash of the stock-whip across his nose warns him back to the path to the shambles that he would escape. For weeks he had forced himself not to think of the Melancolia, because she was a part of his dead life. With Bessie's return and certain new prospects that had developed themselves the Melancolia—lovelier in his imagination than she had ever been on canvas—reappeared. By her aid he might have procured more money wherewith to amuse Bess and to forget Maisie, as well as another taste of an almost forgotten success. Now, thanks to a vicious little housemaid's folly, there was nothing to look for—not even the hope that he might some day take an abiding interest in the housemaid. Worst of all, he had been made to appear ridiculous in Maisie's eyes. A woman will forgive the man who has ruined her life's work so long as he gives her love: a man may forgive those who ruin the love of his life, but he will never forgive the destruction of his work.

"Tck—tck—tck," said Dick between his teeth, and then laughed softly. It's an omen, Bessie, and—a good many things considered, it serves me right for doing what I have done. By Jove! that accounts for Maisie's running away. She must have thought me perfectly mad—small blame to her! The whole picture ruined, isn't it so? What made you do it?"

"Because I was that angry. I'm not angry now—I'm awful sorry."

"I wonder.—It doesn't matter any. how. I'm to blame for making the mistake."

"What mistake?"

"Something you wouldn't understand, dear. Great heavens! to think that a little piece of dirt like you could throw me out of my stride!" Dick was talking to himself as Bessie tried to shake off his grip on her wrist.

"I ain't a piece of dirt, and you shouldn't call me so! I did it 'cause I hated you, and I'm only sorry now 'cause you're—'cause you're"—

"Exactly—because I'm blind. There's nothing like tact in little things."

Bessie began to sob. She did not like being shackled against her will; she was afraid of the blind face and the look upon it, and was sorry too that her great revenge had only made Dick laugh.

"Don't cry," he said, and took her into his arms. "You only did what you thought right."

"I—I ain't a little piece of dirt, and if you say that I'll never come to you again."

"You don't know what you've done to me. I'm not angry—indeed, I'm not. Be quiet for a minute."

Bessie remained in his arms shrinking. Dick's first thought was connected with Maisie, and it hurt him as white-hot iron hurts an open sore.

Not for nothing is a man permitted to ally himself to the wrong woman. The first pang—the first sense of things lost is but the prelude to the play, for the very just Providence who delights in causing pain has decreed that the agony shall return, and that in the midst of keenest pleasure. They know this pain equally who have forsaken or been forsaken by the love of their life, and in their new wives' arms are compelled to realize it. It is better to remain alone and suffer only the misery of being alone, so long as it is possible to find distraction in daily work. When that resource goes the man is to be pitied and left alone.

These things and some others Dick considered while he was holding Bessie to his heart.

"Though you mayn't know it," he said, raising his head, "the Lord is a just and a terrible God, Bess; with a very strong sense of humor. It serves me right—how it serves me right! Torp could understand it if he were here; he must have suffered something at your hands, child, but only for a minute or so. I saved him. Set that to my credit, some one."

"Let me go," said Bess, her face darkening. "Let me go."

"All in good time. Did you ever attend Sunday-school?"

"Never. Let me go, I tell you; you're making fun of me."

"Indeed, I'm not. I'm making fun of myself. . . . Thus. 'He saved others, himself he cannot save.' It isn't exactly a school-board text." He released her wrist, but since he was between her and the door, she could not escape. "What an enormous amount of mischief one little woman can do!"

"I'm sorry; I'm awful sorry about the picture."

"I'm not. I'm grateful to you for spoiling it. . . . What were we talk-ing about before you mentioned the thing?"

"About getting away—and money. Me and you going away."

"Of course. We will get away—that is to say, I will."

"And me?"

"You shall have fifty whole pounds for spoiling a picture."

"Then you won't?"—

"I'm afraid not, dear. Think of fifty pounds for pretty things all to yourself."

"You said you couldn't do anything without me."

"That was true a little while ago. I'm better now, thank you. Get me my hat."

"S'pose I don't?"

"Beeton will, and you'll lose fifty pounds. That's all. Get it."

Bessie cursed under her breath. She had pitied the man sincerely, had kissed him with almost equal sincerity, for he was not unhandsome; it pleased her to be in a way and for a time his protector, and above all there were four thousand pounds to be handled by some one. Now through a slip of the tongue and a little feminine desire to give a little, not too much, pain she had lost the money, the blessed idleness and the pretty things, the companionship, and the chance of looking outwardly as respectable as a real lady.

"Now fill me a pipe. Tobacco doesn't taste, but it doesn't matter, and I'll think things out. What's the day of the week, Bess?"

"Tuesday."

"Then Thursday's mail-day. What a fool—what a blind fool I have been! Twenty-two pounds covers my passage home again. Allow ten for additional expenses. We must put up at Madame Binat's for old sake's sake. Thirty-two pounds altogether. Add a hundred for the cost of the last trip—Gad, won't Torp stare to see me!—a hundred and thirty-two leaves seventy-eight for *baksheesh*—I shall need it—and to play with. What are you crying for, Bess? It wasn't your fault, child; it was mine altogether. Oh, you funny little opossum, mop your eyes and take me out! I want the pass-book and the check-book. Stop a minute. Four thousand pounds at four per cent.—that's safe interest—means a hundred and sixty pounds a year; one hundred and twenty pounds a year—also safe—is two eighty, and two hundred and eighty pounds added to three hundred a year means gilded luxury tor a single woman. Bess, we'll go to the bank."

Richer by two hundred and ten pounds stored in his money belt, Dick caused Bessie, now thoroughly bewildered, to hurry from the bank to the P. and O. offices, where he explained things tersely.

"Port Said, single first; cabin as close to the baggage-hatch as possible. What ship's going?"

"The *Colgong*," said the clerk.

"She's a wet little hooker. Is it Tilbury and a tender, or Galleons and the docks?"

"Galleons. Twelve-forty, Thursday."

"Thanks. Change, please. I can't see very well—will you count it into my hand?"

"If they all took their passages like that instead of talking about their trunks, life would be worth something," said the clerk to his neighbor, who was trying to explain to a harassed mother of many that condensed milk is just as good for babes at sea as daily dairy. Being nineteen and unmarried, he spoke with conviction.

"We are now," quoth Dick, as they returned to the studio, patting the place where his money-belt covered ticket and money, "beyond the reach of man, or devil, or woman—which is much more important. I've three little affairs to carry through before Thursday, but I needn't ask you to help, Bess. Come here on Thursday morning at nine. We'll breakfast, and you shall take me down to Galleons Station."

"What are you going to do?"

"Going away of course.' What should I stay for?"

"But you can't look after yourself?"

"I can do anything. I didn't realize it before, but I can. I've done a great deal already. Resolution shall be treated to one kiss if Bessie doesn't object." Strangely enough, Bessie objected, and Dick laughed. "I suppose you're right. Well, come at nine the day after to-morrow and you'll get your money."

"Shall I sure?"

"I don't bilk, and you won't know whether I do or not unless you come. Oh, but it's long and long to wait! Good-bye, Bessie,—send Beeton here as you go out."

The housekeeper came.

"What are all the fittings of my rooms worth?" said Dick, imperiously.

"'Tisn't for me to say, sir. Some things is very pretty and some is wore out dreadful."

"I'm insured for two hundred and seventy."

"Insurance policies is no criterion, though I don't say"—

"Oh, damn your longwindedness! You've made your pickings out of me and the other tenants. Why, you talked of retiring and buying a public-house the other day. Give a straight answer to a straight question."

"Fifty," said Mr. Beeton, without a moment's hesitation.

"Double it; or I'll break up half my sticks and burn the rest."

He felt his way to a bookstand that supported a pile of sketch-books, and wrenched out one of the mahogany pillars.

"That's sinful, sir," said the housekeeper, alarmed.

"It's my own. One hundred or"—

"One hundred it is. It'll cost me three and six to get that there pilaster mended."

"I thought so. What an out and out swindler you must have been to spring that price at once!"

"I hope I've done nothing to dissatisfy any of the tenants, least of all you, sir."

"Never mind that. Get me the money tomorrow, and see that all my clothes are packed in the little brown bullock-trunk. I'm going."

"But the quarter's notice?"

"I'll pay forfeit. Look after the packing and leave me alone."

Mr. Beeton discussed this new departure with his wife, who decided that Bessie was at the bottom of it all. Her husband took a more charitable view.

"It's very sudden—but then he was always sudden in his ways. Listen to him now!"

There was a sound of chanting from Dick's room.

"We'll never come back any more, boys,
We'll never come back no more;
We'll go to the deuce on any excuse,
And never come back no more!
Oh say we're afloat or ashore, boys,
Oh say we're afloat or ashore;
But we'll never come back any more,
  boys,
We'll never come back no more!"

"Mr. Beeton! Mr. Beeton! Where the deuce is my pistol?"

"Quick, he's going to shoot himself— 'avin' gone mad!" said Mrs. Beeton.

Mr. Beeton addressed Dick soothingly, but it was some time before the latter, threshing up and down his bedroom, could realize the intention of the promises to "find everything to-morrow, sir."

"Oh, you copper-nosed old fool—you impotent Academician!" he shouted at last. "Do you suppose I want to shoot myself? Take the pistol in your silly shaking hand then. If you touch it, it will go off, because it's loaded. It's among my campaign-kit somewhere— in the parcel at the bottom of the trunk."

Long ago Dick had carefully possessed himself of a forty-pound weight field-equipment constructed by the knowledge of his own experience. It was this put-away treasure that he was trying to find and rehandle. Mr. Beeton whipped the revolver out of its place on the top of the package, and Dick drove his hand among the *khaki* coat and breeches, the blue cloth leg-bands, and the heavy flannel shirts doubled over a pair of swan-neck spurs. Under these and the water-bottle lay a sketch-book and a pigskin case of stationery.

"These we don't want; you can have them, Mr. Beeton. Everything else I'll keep. Pack 'em on the top right-hand side of my trunk. When you've done that come into the studio with your wife. I want you both. Wait a minute; get me a pen and a sheet of notepaper."

It is not an easy thing to write when you cannot see, and Dick had particular reasons for wishing that his work should be clear. So he began, following his right hand with his left: " 'The badness of this writing is because I am blind and cannot see my pen.' H'mph! —Even a lawyer can't mistake that. It must be signed, I suppose, but it needn't be witnessed. Now an inch lower—why did I never learn to use a typewriter?—'This is the last will and testament of me, Richard Heldar. I am in sound bodily and mental health, and there is no previous will to revoke.' —That's all right. Damn the pen! Whereabouts on the paper was I?—'I leave everything that I possess in the world, including four thousand pounds, and two thousand seven hundred and twenty-eight pounds held for me'— Oh, I can't get this straight." He tore off half the sheet and began again with the caution about the handwriting. Then: "I leave all the money I possess in the world to"—here followed Maisie's name, and the names of the two banks that held his money.

"It mayn't be quite regular, but no one has a shadow of a right to dispute it, and I've given Maisie's address. Come in, Mr. Beeton. This is my signature; you've seen it often enough to know it. I wan't you and your wife to witness it. Thanks. To-morrow you must take me to the landlord and I'll pay forfeit for leaving without notice, and I'll lodge this paper with him in case anything.happens when I'm away. Now we're going to light up the studio stove. Stay with me, and give me my papers as I want 'em."

No one knows until he has tried how fine a blaze a year's accumulation of bills, letters and dockets can make. Dick stuffed into the stove every document in the studio—saving only three unopened letters: destroyed sketch-books, rough note-books, new and half-finished canvases alike.

"What a lot of rubbish a tenant gets about him if he stays long enough in one place, to be sure," said Mr. Beeton at last.

"He does. Is there anything more left?" Dick felt round the walls.

"Not a thing, and the stove's nigh red-hot."

"Excellent, and you've lost about a thousand pounds' worth of sketches. Ho! ho! Quite a thousand pounds' worth, if I caఁ remember what I used to be."

"Yes, sir," politely. Mr. Beeton was quite sure that Dick had gone mad, otherwise he would have never parted with his excellent furniture for a song. The canvas things took up storage room and were much better out of the way.

There remained only to leave the little will in safe hands: that could not be accomplished till to-morrow. Dick groped about the floor picking up the last pieces of paper, assured himself again and again that there remained no written word or sign of his past life in drawer or desk, and sat down before the stove till the fire died out and the contracting iron cracked in the silence of the night.

CHAPTER XV

With a heart of furious fancies,
  Whereof I am commander;
With a burning spear and a horse of air,
  To the wilderness I wander.
With a knight of ghosts and shadows
  I summoned am to tourney—
Ten leagues beyond the wide world's
    end,
  Methinks it is no journey.
          —*Tom a' Bedlam's Song.*

"Good-bye, Bess; I promised you fifty. Here's a hundred—all that I got for my furniture from Beeton. That will keep you in pretty frocks for some time. You've been a good little girl, all things considered, but you've given me and Torpenhow a fair amount of trouble."

"Give Mr. Torpenhow my love if you see him, won't you?"

"Of course I will, dear. Now take me up the gang-plank and into the cabin. Once aboard the lugger and the maid is—and I am free, I mean."

"Who'll look after you on the ship?"

"The head-steward, if there's any use in money. The doctor when we come ~o Port Said, if I know anything of P. and O. doctors. After that, the Lord will provide, as He used to do."

Bess found Dick his cabin in the wild turmoil of a ship full of leave-takers and weeping relatives. Then he kissed her, and laid himself down in his bunk until the decks should be clear. He who had taken so long to move about his own darkened rooms well understood the geography of a ship, and the necessity of seeing to his own comforts was as wine to him. Before the screw began to thrash the ship along the Docks he had been introduced to the head-steward, had royally tipped him, secured a good place at table, opened out his baggage, and settled himself down with joy in the cabin. It was scarcely necessary to feel his way as he moved about, for he knew everything so well. Then God was very kind: a deep sleep of weariness came upon him just as he would have thought of Maisie, and he slept till the steamer had cleared the mouth of the Thames and was lifting to the pulse of the Channel.

The rattle of the engines, the reek of oil and paint, and a very familiar sound in the next cabin roused him to his new inheritance.

"Oh, it's good to be alive again!" He yawned, stretched himself vigorously, and went on deck to be told that they were almost abreast of the lights of Brighton. This is no more open water than Trafalgar Square is a common; the free levels begin at Ushant; but none the less Dick could feel the healing of the sea at work upon him already. A boisterous little cross-swell swung the steamer disrespectfully by the nose; and one wave breaking far aft spattered the quarterdeck and the pile of new deck chairs. He heard the foam fall with the clash of broken glass, was stung in the face by a cupful, and sniffing luxuriously, felt his way to the smoking-room by the wheel. There a strong breeze found him, blew his cap off and left him bare-headed in the doorway, and the smoking-room steward, understanding that he was a voyager of experience, said that the weather would be stiff in the chops off the Channel and more than half a gale in the Bay. These things fell as they were foretold, and Dick enjoyed himself to the utmost. It is allowable and even necessary at sea to lay firm hold upon tables, stanchions, and ropes in moving from place to place. On land the man who feels with his hands is patently blind. At sea even a blind man who is not seasick can jest with the doctor over the weakness of his fellows. Dick told the doctor many tales—and these are coin of more value than silver if properly handled—smoked with him till unholy hours of the night, and so won his shortlived regard that he promised Dick a few hours of his time when they came to Port Said.

And the sea roared or was still as the winds blew, and the engines sang their song day and night, and the sun grew stronger day by day, and Tom the Lascar barber shaved Dick of a morning under the opened hatch-grating where the cool winds blew, and the awnings were spread and the passengers made merry, and at last they came to Port Said.

"Take me," said Dick to the doctor, "to Madame Binat's—if you know where that is."

"Whew!" said the doctor, "I do. There's not much to choose between 'em; but I suppose you're aware that that's one of the worst houses in the place. They'll rob you to begin with, and knife you later."

"Not they." Take me there, and I can look after myself."

So he was brought to Madame Binat's and filled his nostrils with the well-remembered smell of the East,

that runs without a change from the Canal head to Hong-Kong, and his mouth with the villainous Lingua Franca of the Levant. The heat smote him between the shoulder-blades with the buffet of an old friend, his feet slipped on the sand, and his coat-sleeve was warm as new-baked bread when he lifted it to his nose.

Madame Binat smiled with the smile that knows no astonishment when Dick entered the drinking-shop which was one source of her gains. But for a little accident of complete darkness he could hardly realize that he had ever quitted the old life that hummed in his ears. Somebody opened a bottle of peculiarly strong Schiedam. The smell reminded Dick of Monsieur Binat, who, by the way, had spoken of art and degradation. Binat was dead; Madame said as much when the doctor departed, scandalized, so far as a ship's doctor can be, at the warmth of Dick's reception. Dick was delighted at it. "They remember me here after a year. They have forgotten me across the water by this time. Madame, I want a long talk with you when you're at liberty. It is good to be back again."

In the evening she set an iron-topped cafe-table out on the sands, and Dick and she sat by it, while the house behind them filled with riot, merriment, oaths, and threats. The stars came out and the lights of the shipping in the harbor twinkled by the head of the Canal.

"Yes. The war is good for trade, my friend; but what dost thou do here? We have not forgotten thee."

"I was over there in England and I went blind."

"But there was the glory first. We heard of it here, even here—I and Binat; and thou hast used the head of Yellow 'Tina—she is still alive—so often and so well that 'Tina laughed when the papers arrived by the mail-boats. It was always something that we here could recognize in the paintings. And then there was always the glory and the money for thee."

"I am not poor—I shall pay you well."

"Not to me. Thou hast paid for everything." Under her breath, "Mon Dieu, to be blind and so young! What horror!"

Dick could not see her face with the pity on it, or his own with the discolored hair at the temples. He did not feel the need of pity; he was too anxious to get to the front once more, and explained his desire.

"And where? The Canal is full of the English ships. Sometimes they fire as they used to do when the war was here—ten years ago. Beyond Cairo there is fighting, but how canst thou go there without a correspondent's passport? And in the desert there is always fighting, but that is impossible also," said she.

"I must go to Suakin." He knew, thanks to Alf's readings, that Torpenhow was at work with the column that was protecting the construction of the Suakin-Berber line. P. and O. steamers do not touch at that port, and, besides, Madame Binat knew everybody whose help or advice was worth anything. They were not respectable folk, but they could cause things to be accomplished, which is much more important when there is work toward.

"But at Suakin they are always fighting. That desert breeds men always—and always more men. And they are so bold! Why to Suakin?"

"My friend is there."

"Thy friend! Chtt! Thy friend is death, then."

Madame Binat dropped a fat arm on the table-top, filled Dick's glass anew, and looked at him closely under the stars. There was no need that he should bow his head in assent and say—

"No. He is a man, but—if it should arrive . . . blamest thou?"

"I blame?" she laughed, shrilly. "Who am I that I should blame any one—except those who try to cheat me over their consommations. But it is very terrible."

"I must go to Suakin. Think for me. A great deal has changed within the year, and the men I knew are not here. The Egyptian lighthouse steamer goes down the Canal to Suakin—and the post-boats— But even then"—

"Do not think any longer. *I* know, and it is for me to think. Thou shalt go—thou shalt go and see thy friend. Be wise. Sit here until the house is a little quiet—I must attend to my guests—and afterward go to bed. Thou shalt go, in truth, thou shalt go."

"To-morrow?"

"As soon as may be." She was talking as though he were a child.

He sat at the table listening to the voices in the harbor and the streets, and wondering how soon the end would come, till Madame Binat carried him off to bed and ordered him to sleep. The house shouted and sang and danced and reveled, Madame Binat moving through it with one eye on the liquor payments and the girls and the other on Dick's interests. To this latter end she smiled upon scowling and furtive Turkish officers of fellaheen regiments, was gracious to Cypriote commissariat underlings, and more than kind to camel agents of no nationality whatever.

In the early morning, being then appropriately dressed in a flaming red silk ball-dress, with a front of tarnished gold embroidery and a necklace of plate-glass diamonds, she made chocolate and carried it in to Dick.

"It is only I, and I am of discreet age, eh? Drink and eat the roll too. Thus in France mothers bring their sons, when those behave wisely, the morning chocolate." She sat down on the side of the bed whispering:

"It is all arranged. Thou wilt go by the light-house boat. That is a bribe of ten pounds English. The captain is never paid by the Government. The boat comes to Suakin in four days. There will go with thee George, a Greek muleteer. Another bribe of ten pounds. I will pay; they must not know of thy money. George will go with thee as far as he goes with his mules. Then he comes back to me, for his well-beloved is here, and if I do not receive a telegram from Suakin saying that thou art well, the girl answers for George."

"Thank you." He reached out sleepily for the cup. You are much too kind, Madame."

"If there were anything that I might do I would say, stay here and be wise; but I do not think that would be best for thee." She looked at her liquor-stained dress with a sad smile. "Nay,

thou shalt go, in truth, thou shalt go. It is best so. My boy, it is best so."

She stooped and kissed Dick between the eyes. "That is for good-morning," she said, going away. "When thou art dressed we will speak to George and make everything ready. But first we must open the little trunk. Give me the keys."

"The amount of kissing lately has been simply scandalous. I shall expect Torp to kiss me next. He is more likely to swear at me for getting in his way, though. Well, it won't last long—Ohé, Madame, help me to my toilette of the guillotine! There will be no chance of dressing properly out yonder."

He was rummaging among his new campaign kit, and roweling his hands with the spurs. There are two ways of wearing well-oiled ankle-jacks, spotless blue leg-bands, *khaki* coat and breeches, and a perfectly pipeclayed helmet. The right way is the way of the untired man, master of himself, setting out upon an expedition, well pleased.

"Everything must be very correct," Dick explained. "It will become dirty afterward, but now it is good to feel well dressed. Is everything as it should be?"

He patted the revolver neatly hidden under the fulness of the blouse on the right hip and fingered his collar.

"I can do no more," Madame said, between laughing and crying. "Look at thyself—but I forgot."

"I am very content." He stroked the creaseless spirals of his leggings. "Now let us go and see the captain and George and the lighthouse boat. Be quick, Madame."

"But thou canst not be seen by the harbor walking with me in the daylight. Figure to yourself if some English ladies"—

"There are no English ladies; and if there are, I have forgotten them. Take me there."

In spite of his burning impatience it was nearly evening ere the lighthouse boat began to move. Madame had said a great deal both to George and the captain touching the arrangements that were to be made for Dick's benefit. Very few men who had the honor of her acquaintance cared to disregard Madame's advice. That sort of contempt might end in being knifed by a stranger in a gambling hell upon surprisingly short provocation.

For six days—two of them were wasted in the crowded Canal—the little steamer worked her way to Suakin, where she was to pick up the superintendent of lighthouses; and Dick made it his business to propitiate George, who was distracted with fears for the safety of his light-of-love and half inclined to make Dick responsible for his own discomfort. When they arrived George took him under his wing, and together they entered the red-hot seaport, encumbered with the material and wastage of the Suakin-Berber line, from locomotives in disconsolate fragments to mounds of chairs and pot-sleepers.

"If you keep with me," said George, "nobody will ask for passports or what you do. They are all very busy."

"Yes; but I should like to hear some of the Englishmen talk. They might remember me. I was known here a long time ago—when I was some one indeed."

"A long time ago is a very long time ago here. The graveyards are full. Now listen. This new railway runs out so far as Tanai-el-Hassan—that is seven miles. Then there is a camp. They say that beyond Tanai-el-Hassan the English troops go forward, and everything that they require will be brought to them by this line."

"Ah! Base camp. I see. That's a better business than fighting Fuzzies in the open."

"For this reason even the mules go up in the iron-train."

"Iron what?"

"It is all covered with iron, because it is still being shot at."

"An armored train. Better and better! Go on, faithful George."

"And I go up with my mules tonight. Only those who particularly require to go to the camp go out with the train. They begin to shoot not far from the city."

"The dears—they always used to!" Dick snuffed the smell of parched dust, heated iron, and flaking paint with delight. Certainly the old life was welcoming him back most generously.

"When I have got my mules together I go up to-night, but you must first send a telegram to Port Said, declaring that I have done you no harm."

"Madame has you well in hand. Would you stick a knife into me if you had the chance?"

"I have no chance," said the Greek. "She is there with that woman."

"I see. It's a bad thing to be divided between love of woman and the chance of loot. I sympathize with you, George."

They went to the telegraph-office unquestioned, for all the world was desperately busy and had scarcely time to turn its head, and Suakin was the last place under sky that would be chosen for holiday-ground. On their return the voice of an English subaltern asked Dick what he was doing. The blue goggles were over his eyes and he walked with his hand on George's elbow as he replied—

"Egyptian Government—mules. My orders are to give them over to the A. C. G. at Tanai-el-Hassan. 'Any occasion to show my papers?"

"Oh, certainly not. I beg your pardon. I'd no right to ask, but not seeing your face before I"—

"I go out in the train to-night, I suppose," said Dick, boldly. "There will be no difficulty in loading up the mules, will there?"

"You can see the horse-platforms from here. You must have them loaded up early." The young man went away wondering what sort of broken down waif this might be who talked like a gentleman and consorted with Greek muleteers. Dick felt unhappy. To outface an English officer is no small thing, but the bluff loses relish when one plays it from the utter dark, and stumbles up and down rough ways, thinking and eternally thinking of what might have been if things had fallen out otherwise, and all had been as it was not.

George shared his meal with Dick and went off to the mule-lines. His charge sat alone in a shed with his face in his hands. Before his tight-shut eyes danced the face of Maisie, laughing, with parted lips. There was a great bustle and clamor about him. He grew afraid and almost called for George.

"I say, have you got your mules ready?" It was the voice of the subaltern over his shoulder.

"My man's looking after them. The —the fact is I've a touch of ophthalmia and I can't see very well."

"By Jove! that's bad. You ought to lie up in hospital for a whole. I've had a turn of it myself. It's as bad as being blind."

"So I find it. When does this armored train go?"

"At six o'clock. It takes an hour to cover the seven miles."

"Are the Fuzzies on the rampage—eh?"

"About three nights a week. 'Fact is I'm in acting command of the night-train. It generally runs back empty to Tanai for the night."

"Big camp at Tanai, I suppose?"

"Pretty big. It has to feed our desert-column somehow."

"Is that far off?"

"Between thirty and forty miles—in an infernal thirsty country."

"Is the country quiet between Tanai and our men?"

"More or less. I shouldn't care to cross it alone, or with a subaltern's command for the matter of that, but the scouts get through in some extraordinary fashion."

"They always did."

"Have you been here before, then?"

"I was through most of the trouble when it first broke out."

"In the service and cashiered," was the subaltern's first thought, so he refrained from putting any questions.

"There's your man coming up with the mules. It seems rather queer"—

"That I should be mule-leading?" said Dick.

"I didn't mean to say so but it is. Forgive me—it's beastly impertinence I know, but you speak like a man who has been at a public school. There's no mistaking the tone."

"I am a public school man."

"I thought so. I say, I don't want to hurt your feelings, but you're a little down on your luck, aren't you? I saw you sitting with your head in your hands, and that's why I spoke."

"Thanks. I am about as thoroughly and completely broke as a man need be."

"Suppose—I mean I'm a public school man myself. Couldn't I perhaps —take it as a loan y' know and"—

"You're much too good, but on my honor I've as much money as I want. . . . I tell you what you could do for me, though, and put me under an everlasting obligation. Let me come into the bogie truck of the train. There is a fore-truck, isn't there?"

"Yes. How d'you know?"

"I've been in an armored train before. Only let me see—hear some of the fun I mean, and I'll be grateful. I go at my own risk as a non-combatant."

The young man thought for a minute. "All right," he said. "We're supposed to be an empty train, and there's no one to blow me up at the other end."

George and a horde of yelling amateur assistants had loaded up the mules, and the narrow-gauge armored train, plated with three-eighths inch boiler-plate till it looked like one long coffin, stood ready to start.

Two bogie trucks running before the locomotive were completely covered in with plating, except that the leading one was pierced in front for the nozzle of a machine-gun, and the second at either side for lateral fire. The trucks together made one long iron-vaulted chamber in which a score of artillerymen were rioting.

"Whitechapel—last train! Ah, I see yer kissin' in the first class there!" somebody shouted, just as Dick was clambering into the forward truck.

"Lordy! 'Ere's a real live passenger for the Kew, Tanai, Acton, and Ealin' train. *Echo*, sir. Speshul edition! *Star*, sir."—"Shall I get you a foot-warmer?" said another.

"Thanks. I'll pay my footing," said Dick, and relations of the most amicable were established ere silence came with the arrival of the subaltern, and the train jolted out over the rough track.

"This is an immense improvement on shooting the unimpressionable Fuzzy in the open," said Dick, from his place in the corner.

"Oh, but he's still unimpressed. There he goes!" said the subaltern, as a bullet struck the outside of the truck. "We always have at least one demonstration against the night-train. Generally they attack the rear-truck where my junior commands. He gets all the fun of the fair."

"Not to-night though! Listen!" said Dick. A flight of heavy-handed bullets was succeeded by yelling and shouts. The children of the desert valued their nightly amusement, and the train was an excellent mark.

"Is it worth while giving them half a hopper full?" the subaltern asked of the engine which was driven by a Lieutenant of Sappers.

"I should just think so! This is my section of the line. They'll be playing old Harry with my permanent way if we don't stop 'em."

"Right O!"

"*Hrrmph!*" said the machine gun through all its five noses as the subaltern drew the lever home. The empty cartridges clashed on the floor and the smoke blew back through the truck. There was indiscriminate firing at the rear of the train, a return fire from the darkness without and unlimited howling. Dick stretched himself on the floor, wild with delight at the sounds and the smells.

"God is very good—I never thought I'd hear this again. Give 'em hell, men. Oh, give 'em hell!" he cried.

The train stopped for some obstruction on the line ahead and a party went out to reconnoitre, but came back cursing, for spades. The children of the desert had piled sand and gravel on the rails, and twenty minutes were lost in clearing it away. Then the slow progress recommenced, to be varied with more shots, more shoutings, the steady clack and kick of the machine guns, and a final difficulty with a half-lifted rail ere the train came under the protection of the roaring camp at Tanai-el-Hassan.

"Now, you see why it takes an hour and a half to fetch her through," said the subaltern, unshipping the cartridge-hopper above his pet gun.

"It was a lark, though. I only wish it had lasted twice as long. How superb it must have looked from outside!" said Dick, sighing regretfully.

"It palls after the first few nights. By the way, when you've settled about your mules, come and see what we can find to eat in my tent. I'm Bennil of the Gunners—in the artillery lines—and mind you don't fall over my tent-ropes in the dark."

But it was all dark to Dick. He could only smell the camels, the hay-bales, the cooking, the smoky fires, and the tanned canvas of the tents as he stood, where he had dropped from the train, shouting for George. There was a sound of light-hearted kicking on the iron skin of the rear trucks, with squealing and grunting. George was unloading the mules.

The engine was blowing off steam nearly in Dick's ear; a cold wind of the desert danced between his legs; he was hungry, and felt tired and dirty—so dirty that he tried to brush his coat with his hands. That was a hopeless job; he thrust his hands into his pockets and began to count over the many times that he had waietd in strange or remote places for trains or camels, mules or horses, to carry him to his business. In those days he could see—few men more clearly—and the spectacle of an armed camp at dinner under the stars was an ever fresh pleasure to the eye. There was color, light, and motion, without which no man has much pleasure in living. This night there remained for him only one more journey through the darkness that never lifts to tell a man how far he has traveled. Then he would grip Torpenhow's hand again—Torpenhow, who was alive and strong, and lived in the midst of the action that had once made the reputation of a man called Dick Heldar: not in the least to be confused with the blind, bewildered vagabond who seemed to answer to the same name. Yes, he would find Tor-

penhcw, and come as near to the old life
as might be. Afterward he would forget
everything: Bessie, who had wrecked
the Melancolia and so nearly wrecked
his life; Beeton, who lived in a strange
unreal city full of tin-tacks and gas-
plugs and matters that no men needed;
that irrational being who had offered
him love and loyalty for nothing, but
had not signed her name; and most of
all Maisie, who, from her own point of
view, was undeniably right in all she
did, but oh, at this distance, so tan-
talizingly fair.

George's hand on his arm pulled him
back to the situation.

"And what now?" said George.

"Oh yes, of course. What now? Take
me to the camel-men. Take me to where
the scouts sit when they come in from
the desert. They sit by their camels,
and the camels eat grain out of a black
blanket held up at the corners, and the
men eat by their side just like camels.
Take me there!"

The camp was rough and rutty, and
Dick stumbled many times over the
stumps of scrub. The scouts were sitting by their beasts, as Dick knew they
would. The light of the dung-fires flickered on their bearded faces, and the
camels bubbled and mumbled beside
them at rest. It was no part of Dick's
policy to go into the desert with a convoy of supplies. That would lead to
impertinent questions, and since a blind
non-combatant is not needed at the
front, he would probably be forced to
return to Suakin. He must go up alone,
and go immediately.

"Now for one last bluff—the biggest
of all," he said. "Peace be with you,
brethren!" The watchful George steered

him to the circle of the nearest fire. The
heads of the camel-sheiks bowed gravely,
and the camels, scenting a European,
looked sideways curiously like brooding
hens, half ready to get to their feet.

"A beast and a driver to go to the
fighting line to-night," said Dick.

"A Mulaid?" said a voice, scornfully
naming the best baggage-breed that he
knew.

"A Bisharin," returned Dick, with
perfect gravity. "A Bisharin without
saddle-galls. Therefore no charge of
thine shock-head."

Two or three minutes passed. Then—
"We be knee-haltered for the night.
There is no going out from the camp."

"Not for money?"

"H'm! Ah! English money?"

Another depressing interval of silence.

"How much?"

"Twenty-five pounds English paid
into the hand of the driver at my journey's end, and as much more into the
hand of the camel-sheik here, to be
paid when the driver returns."

This was royal payment, and the
sheik, who knew that he would get his
commission on the deposit, stirred in
Dick's behalf.

"For scarcely one night's journey—
fifty pounds. Land and wells and good
trees and wives to make a man content for the rest of his days. Who
speaks?" said Dick.

"I," said a voice. "I will go—but
there is no going from the camp."

"Fool! I know that a camel can
break his knee-halter, and the sentries
do not fire if one goes in chase. Twenty-
five pounds and another twenty-five
pounds. But the beast must be a good

Bisharin; I will take no baggage-camel."

Then the bargaining began, and at the end of half an hour the first deposit was paid over to the sheik, who talked in low tones to the driver. Dick heard the latter say: "A little way out only. Any baggage-beast will serve. Am I a fool to waste my cattle for a blind man?"

"And though I cannot see"—Dick lifted his voice a little—"yet I carry that which has six eyes, and the driver will sit before me. If we do not reach the English troops in the dawn he will be dead."

"But where, in God's name, are the troops?"

"Unless thou knowest let another man ride. *Dost* thou know? Remember it will be life or death to thee."

"I know," said the driver, sullenly. "Stand back from my beast. I am going to slip him."

"Not so swiftly. George, hold the camel's head a moment. I want to feel his cheek." The hands wandered over the hide till they found the branded half-circle that is the mark of the Bisharin, the light-built riding-camel. "That is well. Cut this one loose. Remember no blessing of God comes on those who try to cheat the blind."

The men chuckled by the fires at the camel-driver's discomfiture. He had intended to substitute a slow, saddle-galled baggage-colt.

"Stand back!" one shouted, lashing the Bisharin under the belly with a quirt. Dick obeyed as soon as he felt the nose-string tighten in his hand,—and a cry went up, "Illaha! Aho! He is loose."

With a roar and a grunt the Bisharin rose to his feet and plunged forward toward the desert, his driver following with shouts and lamentation. George caught Dick's arm and hurried him stumbling and tripping past a disgusted sentry who was used to stampeding camels.

"What's the row now?" he cried.

"Every stitch of my kit on that blasted dromedary," Dick answered, after the manner of a common soldier.

"Go on, and take care your throat's not cut outside—you and your dromedary's."

The outcries ceased when the camel had disappeared behind a hillock, and his driver had called him back and made him kneel down.

"Mount first," said Dick. Then climbing into the second seat and gently screwing the pistol muzzle into the small of his companion's back, "Go on in God's name, and swiftly. Good-bye, George. Remember me to Madame, and have a good time with your girl. Get forward, child of the Pit!"

A few minutes later he was shut up in a great silence, hardly broken by the creaking of the saddle and the soft pad of the tireless feet. Dick adjusted himself comfortably to the rock and pitch of the pace, girthed his belt tighter, and felt the darkness slide past. For an hour he was conscious only of the sense of rapid progress.

"A good camel," he said at last.

"He has never been underfed. He is my own and clean bred," the driver replied.

"Go on."

His head dropped on his chest and he tried to think, but the tenor of his thoughts was broken because he was very sleepy. In the half doze it seemed that he was learning a punishment hymn at Mrs. Jennett's. He had committed some crime as bad as Sabbath-breaking, and she had locked him up in his bedroom. But he could never repeat more than the first two lines of the hymn—

When Israel of the Lord beloved
Out of the land of bondage came.

He said them over and over thousands of times. The driver turned in the saddle to see if there were any chance of capturing the revolver and ending the ride. Dick roused, struck him over the head with the butt, and stormed himself wide awake. Somebody hidden in a clump of camel-thorn shouted as the camel toiled up rising ground. A shot was fired, and the silence shut down again, bringing the desire to sleep. Dick could think no longer. He was too tired and stiff and cramped to do more than nod uneasily from time to time, waking with a start and punching the driver with the pistol.

"Is there a moon?" he asked, drowsily.

"She is near her setting."

"I wish that I could see her. Halt the camel. At least let me hear the desert talk."

The man obeyed. Out of the utter stillness came one breath of wind. It rattled the dead leaves of a shrub some distance away and ceased. A handful of dry earth detached itself from the edge of a rain trench and crumbled softly to the bottom.

"Go on. The night is very cold."

Those who have watched till the morn-ing know how the last hour before the light lengthens itself into many eternities. It seemed to Dick that he had never since the begining of original darkness done anything at all save jolt through the air. Once in a thousand years he would finger the nail-heads on the saddle-front and count them all carefully. Centuries later he would shift his revolver from his right hand to his left and allow the eased arm to drop down at his side. From the safe distance of London he was watching himself thus employed,—watching critically. Yet whenever he put out his hand to the canvas that he might paint the tawny yellow desert under the glare of the sinking moon, the black shadow of the camel and the two bowed figures atop, that hand held a revolver and the arm was numbed from the wrist to collarbone. Moreover, he was in the dark, and could see no canvas of any kind whatever.

The driver grunted, and Dick was conscious of a change in the air.

"I smell the dawn," he whispered.

"It is here, and yonder are the troops. Have I done well?"

The camel streched out its neck and roared as there came down wind the pungent reek of camels in square.

"Go on. We must get there swiftly. Go on."

"They are moving in their camp. There is so much dust that I cannot see what they do."

"Am I in better case? Go forward."

They could hear the hum of voices ahead, the howling and the bubbling of the beasts and the hoarse cries of the soldiers girthing up for the day. Two or three shots were fired.

"Is that at us? Surely they can see that I am English," Dick spoke angrily.

"Nay, it is from the desert," the driver answered, cowering in his saddle. "Go forward, my child! Well it is that the dawn did not uncover us an hour ago."

The camel headed straight for the column and the shots behind multiplied. The children of the desert had arranged that most uncomfortable of surprises, a dawn attack for the English troops, and were getting their distance by snap-shots at the only moving object without the square.

"What luck! What stupendous and imperial luck!" said Dick. "It's 'just before the battle, mother.' Oh, God has been most good to me! Only"—the agony of the thought made him screw up his eyes for an instant—"Maisie. ."

"Allahu! We are in," said the man, as he drove into the rearguard and the camel knelt.

"Who the deuce are you? Despatches or what? What's the strength of the enemy behind that ridge? How did you get through?" asked a dozen voices. For all answer Dick took a long breath, unbuckled his belt, and shouted from the saddle at the top of a wearied and dusty voice, "Torpenhow! Ohé Torp! Cooee, Torpen-how."

A bearded man raking in the ashes of a fire for a light to his pipe moved very swiftly toward that cry, as the rearguard, facing about, began to fire at the puffs of smoke from the hillocks

around. Gradually the scattered white cloudlets drew out into long lines of banked white that hung heavily in the stillness of the dawn before they turned over wave-like and glided into the valleys. The soldiers in the square were coughing and swearing as their own smoke obstructed their view, and they edged forward to get beyond it. A wounded camel leaped to its feet and roared aloud, the cry ending in a bubbling grunt. Some one had cut its throat to prevent confusion. Then came the thick sob of a man receiving his death-wound from a bullet; then a yell of agony and redoubled firing.

There was no time to ask any questions.

"Get down, man! Get down behind the camel!"

"No. Put me, I pray, in the forefront of the battle." Dick turned his face to Torpenhow and raised his hand to set his helmet straight, but, miscalculating the distance, knocked it off. Torpenhow saw that his hair was gray on the temples, and that his face was the face of an old man.

"Come down, you damned fool! Dickie, come off!"

And Dick came obediently, but as a tree falls, pitching sideways from the Bisharin's saddle at Torpenhow's feet. His luck had held to the last, even to the crowning mercy of a kindly bullet through his head.

Torpenhow knelt under the lee of the camel, with Dick's body in his arms.

THE END

VOLUME III

City of Dreadful Night

City of Dreadful Night

CHAPTER I

A REAL LIVE CITY

WE are all backwoodsmen and barbarians together—we others dwelling beyond the Ditch, in the outer darkness of the Mofussil. There are no such things as commissioners and heads of departments in the world, and there is only one city in India. Bombay is too green, too pretty and too stragglesome; and Madras died ever so long ago. Let us take off our hats to Calcutta, the many-sided, the smoky, the magnificent, as we drive in over the Hugli Bridge in the dawn of a still February morning. We have left India behind us at Howrah Station, and now we enter foreign parts. No, not wholly foreign. Say rather too familiar.

All men of certain age know the feeling of caged irritation—an illustration in the *Graphic*, a bar of music of the light words of a friend from home may set it ablaze—that comes from the knowledge of our lost heritage of London. At home they, the other men, our equals, have at their disposal all that town can supply—the roar of the streets, the lights, the music, the pleasant places, the millions of their own kind, and a wilderness full of pretty, fresh-colored Englishwomen, theatres and restaurants. It is their right. They

accept it as such, and even affect to look upon it with contempt. And we, we have nothing except the few amusements that we painfully build up for ourselves—the dolorous dissipations of gymkhanas where every one knows everybody else, or the chastened intoxication of dances where all engagements are booked, in ink, ten days ahead, and where everybody's antecedents are as patent as his or her method of waltzing. We have been deprived of our inheritance. The men at home are enjoying it all, not knowing how fair and rich it is, and we at the most can only fly westward for a few months and gorge what, properly speaking, should take seven or eight or ten luxurious years. That is the lost heritage of London; and the knowledge of the forfeiture, wilful or forced, comes to most men at times and seasons, and they get cross.

Calcutta holds out false hopes of some return. The dense smoke hangs low, in the chill of the morning, over an ocean of roofs, and, as the city wakes, there goes up to the smoke a deep, full-throated boom of life and motion and humanity. For this reason does he who sees Calcutta for the first time hang joyously out of the *ticca-gharri* and sniff the smoke, and turn his face toward the tumult, saying: "This is, at last, some portion of my heritage

187

returned to me. This is a city. There is life here, and there should be all manner of pleasant things for the having, across the river and under the smoke." When Leland, he who wrote the Hans Breitmann Ballads, once desired to know the name of an austere, plug-hatted red-skin of repute, his answer, from the lips of a half-bred, was: "He Injun. He big Injun. He heap big Injun. He dam big heap Injun. He dam mighty great big heap Injun. He Jones!" The litany is an expressive one, and exactly describes the first emotions of a wandering savage adrift in Calcutta. The eye has lost its sense of proportion, the focus has contracted through overmuch residence in up-country stations—twenty minutes' canter from hospital to parade ground, you know—and the mind has shrunk with the eye. Both say together, as they take in the sweep of shipping above and below the Hugli Bridge: "Why, this is London! This is the docks. This is Imperial. This is worth coming across India to see!"

Then a distinctly wicked idea takes possession of the mind: "What a divine —what a heavenly place to *loot!*" This gives place to a much worse devil—that of Conservatism. It seems not only a wrong but a criminal thing to allow natives to have any voice in the control of such a city—adorned, docked, wharfed, fronted and reclaimed by Englishmen, existing only because England lives, and dependent for its life on England. All India knows of the Calcutta Municipality; but has any one thoroughly investigated the Big Calcutta Stink? There is only one. Benares is fouler in point of concentrated, pent-up muck, and there are local stenches in Pesha-

wur which are stronger than the B. C. S.; but, for diffused, soul-sickening expansiveness, the reek of Calcutta beats both Benares and Peshawur. Bombay cloaks her stenches with a veneer of assafœtida and *huga*-tobacco; Calcutta is above pretence. There is no tracing back the Calcutta plague to any one source. It is faint, it is sickly, and it is indescribable; but Americans at the Great Eastern Hotel say that it is something like the smell of the Chinese quarter in San Francisco. It is certainly not an Indian smell. It resembles the essence of corruption that has rotted for the second time—the clammy odor of blue slime. And there is no escape from it. It blows across the *maidan;* it comes in gusts into the corridors of the Great Eastern Hotel; what they are pleased to call the "Palaces of Chouringhi" carry it; it swirls round the Bengal Club; it pours out of by-streets with sickening intensity, and the breeze of the morning is laden with it. It is first found, in spite of the fume of the engines, in Howrah Station. It seems to be worst in the little lanes at the back of Lal Bazar where the drinking-shops are, but it is nearly as bad opposite Government House and in the Public offices. The thing is intermittent. Six moderately pure mouthfuls of air may be drawn without offence. Then comes the seventh wave and the queasiness of an uncultured stomach. If you live long enough in Calcutta you grow used to it. The regular residents admit the disgrace, but their answer is: "Wait till the wind blows off the Salt Lakes where all the sewage goes, and *then* you'll smell something." That is their defence! Small wonder that they consider Calcutta is a fit place for a permanent Viceroy. Englishmen who can calmly extenuate one shame by another are capable of asking for anything —and expecting to get it.

If an up-country station holding three thousand troops and twenty civilians owned such a possession as Calcutta does, the Deputy Commissioner or the Cantonment Magistrate would have all the natives off the board of management or decently shoveled into the background until the mess was abated. Then they might come on again and talk of "high-handed oppression" as much as they liked. That stink, to an unprejudiced nose, damns Calcutta as a City of Kings. And in spite of that stink, they allow, they even encourage, natives to look after the place! The damp, drainage-soaked soil is sick with the teeming life of a hundred years, and the Municipal Board list is choked with the names of natives—men of the breed born in and raised off this surfeited muck-heap! They own property, these amiable Aryans on the Municipal and the Bengal Legislative Council. Launch a proposal to tax them on that property, and they naturally howl. They also howl up-country, but there the halls for mass-meetings are few, and the vernacular papers fewer, and with a *zubbardusti* Secretary and a President whose favor is worth the having and whose wrath is undesirable, men are kept clean despite themselves, and may not poison their neighbors. Why, asks a savage, let them vote at all? They can put up with this filthiness. They *cannot* have any feelings worth caring a rush for. Let them live quietly and hide away their money under our protection, while we tax them till they know through their purses the measure of their neglect in the past, and when a little of the smell has been abolished, bring them back again to talk and take the credit of enlightenment. The better classes own their broughams and barouches; the worse can shoulder an Englishman into the kennel and talk to him as though he were a *khitmatgar*. They can refer to an English lady as an *aurat;* they are permitted a freedom—not to put it too coarsely—of speech, which, if used by an Englishman toward an Englishman, would end in serious trouble. They are fenced and protected and made inviolate. Surely they might be content with all those things without entering into matters which they cannot, by the nature of their birth, understand.

Now, whether all this genial diatribe be the outcome of an unbiased mind or the result first of sickness caused by that ferocious stench, and secondly of headache due to day-long smoking to drown the stench, is an open question. Anyway, Calcutta is a fearsome place for a man not educated up to it.

A word of advice to other barbarians. Do not bring a north-country servant into Calcutta. He is sure to get into trouble, because he does not understand the customs of the city. A Punjabi in this place for the first time esteems it his bounden duty to go to the *Ajaibghar*—the Museum. Such an one has gone and is even now returned very angry and troubler in the spirit.

"I went to the Museum," says he, "and no one gave me any *gali*. I went to the market to buy my food, and then I sat upon a seat. There came a *chaprissi* who said: 'Go away, I want to sit here.'

I said: 'I am here first.' He said: 'I am a *chaprissi! nikal jao!*' and he hit me. Now that sitting-place was open to all, so I hit him till he wept. He ran away for the Police, and I went away too, for the Police here are all *Sahibs.* Can I have leave from two o'clock to go and look for that *chaprissi* and hit him again?"

Behold the situation! An unknown city full of smell that makes one long for rest and retirement, and a champing *naukar*, not yet six hours in the stew, who has started a blood-feud with an unknown *chaprissi* and clamors to go forth to the fray. General orders that, whatever may be said or done to him, he must not say or do anything in return lead to an eloquent harangue on the quality of *izzat* and the nature of "face blackening." There is no *izzat* in Calcutta, and this Awful Smell blackens the face of any Englishman who sniffs it.

Alas! for the lost delusion of the heritage that was to be restored. Let us sleep, let us sleep, and pray that Calcutta may be better to-morrow.

At present it is remarkably like sleeping with a corpse.

CHAPTER II

THE REFLECTIONS OF A SAVAGE

MORNING brings counsel. *Does* Calcutta smell so pestiferously after all? Heavy rain has fallen in the night. She Is newly-washed, and the clear sunlight shows her at her best. Where, oh where, in all this wilderness of life shall a man go? Newman and Co. publish a three-rupee guide which produces first despair and then fear in the mind of the reader.

Let us drop Newman and Co. out of the topmost window of the Great Eastern, trusting to luck and the flight of the hours to evolve wonders and mysteries and amusements.

The Great Eastern hums with life through all its hundred rooms. Doors slam merrily, and all the nations of the earth run up and down the staircases. This alone is refreshing, because the passers bump you and ask you to stand aside. Fancy finding any place outside a Levée-room where Englishmen are crowded together to this extent! Fancy sitting down seventy strong to *table d' hôte* and with a deafening clatter of knives and forks! Fancy finding a real bar whence drinks may be obtained! and, joy of joys, fancy stepping out of the hotel into the arms of a live, white, helmeted, buttoned, truncheoned Bobby! A beautiful, burly Bobby—just the sort of man who, seven thousand miles away, staves off the stuttering witticism of the three-o'clock-in-the-morning reveler by the strong badged arm of authority. What would happen if one spoke to this Bobby? Would he be offended? He is not offended. He is affable. He has to patrol the pavement in front of the Great Eastern and to see that the crowding *ticca-gharris* do not jam. Toward a presumably respectable white he behaves as a man and a brother. There is no arrogance about him. And this is disappointing. Closer inspection shows that he is not a *real* Bobby after all. He is a Municipal Police something and his uniform is not correct; at least if they have not changed the dress of the men at home. But no matter. Later on we will inquire into the Calcutta Bobby, because he is a white man, and has to deal with some of the "toughest" folk that ever set out of malice aforethought to paint Job Charnock's city vermillion. You must not, you cannot cross Old Court House Street without looking carefully to see that you stand no chance of being run over. This is beautiful. There is a steady roar of traffic, cut every two minutes by the deeper roll of the trams. The driving is eccentric, not to say bad, but there is the traffic—more that unsophisticated eyes have beheld for a certain number of years. It means business, it means money-making, it means crowded and hurrying life, and it gets into the blood and makes it move. Here be big shops with plate-glass fronts —all displaying the well-known names of firms that we savages only correspond with through the V. P. P. and Parcels Post. They are all here, as large as life, ready to supply anything you need if you only care to sign. Great is the fascination of being able to obtain a thing on the spot without having to write for a week and wait for a month, and then get something quite different. No wonder pretty ladies, who live anywhere within a reasonable distance, come down to do their shopping personally.

"Look here. If you want to be respectable you mustn't smoke in the streets. Nobody does it." This is advice kindly tendered by a friend in a black coat. There is no Levée or Lieutenant-Governor in sight; but he wears the frock-coat because it is daylight, and he can be seen. He also refrains from smoking for the same reason. He admits that Providence built the open air to be smoked in, but he says that "it isn't the thing." This man has a brougham, a remarkably natty little pill-box with a curious wabble about the wheels. He steps into the brougham and puts on—a top-hat, a shiny black "plug."

There was a man up-country once who owned a top-hat. He leased it to amateur theatrical companies for some seasons until the nap wore off. Then he threw it into a tree and wild bees hived in it. Men were wont to come and look at the hat, in its palmy days, for the sake of feeling homesick. It interested all the station, and died with two seers of *babul* flower honey in its bosom. But top-hats are not intended to be worn in India. They are as sacred as home letters and old rosebuds. The friend cannot see this. He allows that if he stepped out of his brougham and walked about in the sunshine for ten minutes he would get a bad headache. In half-an-hour he would probably catch sunstroke. He allows all this, but he keeps to his hat and cannot see why a barbarian is moved to inextinguishable laughter at the sight. Every one who owns a brougham and many people who hire *ticca-gharris* keep top-hats and black frock-coats. The effect is curious, and at first fills the beholder with surprise.

And now, "let us see the handsome houses where the wealthy nobles dwell." Northerly lies the great human jungle of the native city, stretching from Burra Bazar to Chitpore. That can keep. Southerly is the *maidan* and Chouringhi. "If you get out into the centre of the *maidan* you will understand why Calcutta is called the City of Palaces." The traveled American said so at the Great Eastern. There is a short tower, falsely called a "memorial," standing in a waste of soft, sour green. That is as good a place to get to as any other. Near here the newly-landed waler is taught the whole duty of the trap-horse and careers madly in a brake. Near here young Calcutta gets upon a horse and is incontinently run away with. Near here hundreds of kine feed, close to the innumerable trams and the whirl of traffic along the face of Chouringhi Road. The size of the *maidan* takes the heart out of any one accustomed to the "gardens" of up-country, just as they say Newmarket Heath cows a horse accustomed to more shut-in course. The huge level is studded with brazen statutes of eminent gentlemen riding fretful horses on diabolically severe curbs. The expanse dwarfs the statues, dwarfs everything except the frontage of the far-away Chouringhi Road. It is big—it is impressive. There is no escaping the fact. They built houses in the old days when the rupee was two shillings and a penny. Those houses are three-storied, and ornamented with service-staircases like houses in the Hills. They are also very close together, and they own garden walls of *pukka*-masonry pierced with a single gate. In their shut-upness they are British. In their spaciousness they are Oriental, but those service-staircases do not look healthy. We will form an amateur sanitary commission and call upon Chouringhi.

A first introduction to the Calcutta *durwan* is not nice. If he is chewing *pan*, he does not take the trouble to get rid of his quid. If he is sitting on his *charpoy* chewing sugarcane, he does not think it worth his while to rise. He has to be taught those things, and he cannot understand why he should be reproved. Clearly he is a survival of a played-out system. Providence never intended that any native should be made a *concierge* more insolent than any of the French variety. The people of Calcutta put an Uria in a little lodge close to the gate of their house, in order that loafers may be turned away, and the houses protected from theft. The natural result is that the *durwan* treats everybody whom he does not know as a loafer, has an intimate and vendible knowledge of all the outgoings and incomings in that house, and controls, to a large extent, the nomination of the *naukar-log*. They say that one of the estimable class is now suing a bank for about three lakhs of rupees. Up-country, a Lieutenant-Governor's *chaprissi* has to work for thirty years before he can retire on seventy thousand rupees of savings. The Calcutta *durwan* is a great institution. The head and front of his offence is that he will insist upon trying to talk English. How he protects the houses Calcutta only knows. He can be frightened out of his wits by severe speech, and is generally asleep in calling hours. If a rough round of visits be any guide, three times out of seven he is fragrant of drink. So much for the *durwan*. Now for the houses he guards.

Very pleasant is the sensation of being ushered into a pestiferously stable-some drawing-room. "Does this always happen?" "No, not unless you shut up the room for some time; but if you open the *jhilmills* there are other smells. You see the stables and the servants' quarters are close too." People pay five hundred a month for half-a-dozen rooms filled with *attr* of this kind. They make no complaint. When they think the honor of the city is at stake they say defiantly: "Yes, but you must remember we're a metropolis. We are crowded here. We have no room. We aren't like your little stations." Chouringhi is a stately place full of sumptuous houses, but it is best to look at it hastily. Stop to consider for a moment what the cramped compounds, the black soaked soil, the netted intricacies, of the service-staircases, the packed stables, the seethment of human life round the *durwans'* lodges and the curious arrangement of little open drains means, and you will call it a whited sepulchre.

Men living in expensive tenements suffer from chronic sore-throat, and will tell you cheerily that "we've got typhoid in Calcutta now." Is the pest ever out of it? Everything seems to be built with a view to its comfort. It can lodge comfortably on roofs, climb along from the gutter-pipe to piazza, or rise from sink to veranda and thence to the topmost story. But Calcutta says that all is sound and produces figures to prove it; at the same time admitting that healthy cut flesh will not readily heal. Further evidence may be dispensed with.

Here come pouring down Park Street on the *maidan* a rush of broughams, neat buggies, the lightest of gigs, trim office brownberrys, shining victorias, and a sprinkling of veritable hansom cabs. In the broughams sit men in top-hats. In the other carts, young men, all very much alike, and all immaculately turned out. A fresh stream from Chouringhi joins the Park Street detachment, and the two together stream away across the *maidan* toward the business quarter of the city. This is Calcutta going to office—the civilians to the Government Buildings and the young men to their firms and their blocks and their wharves. Here one sees that Calcutta has the best turn-out in the Empire. Horses and traps alike are enviably perfect, and—mark the touchstone of civilization—*the lamps are in the sockets.* This is distinctly refreshing. Once more we will take off our hats to Calcutta, the well-appointed, the luxurious. The country-bred is a rare beast here; his place is taken by the waler, and the waler, though a ruffian at heart, can be made to look like a gentleman. It would be indecorous as well as insane to applaud the winking harness, the perfectly lacquered panels, and the liveried *saises*. They show well in the outwardly fair roads shadowed by the Palaces.

How many sections of the complex society of the place do the carts carry? *Imprimis*, the Bengal Civilian who goes to Writers' Buildings and sits in a perfect office and speaks flippantly of "sending things into India," meaning thereby the Supreme Government. He is a great person, and his mouth is full of promotion-and-appointment "shop." Generally he is referred to as a "rising man." Calcutta seems full of "rising men." *Secondly*, the Government of India man, who wears a familiar Simla face, rents a flat when he is not up in the Hills, and is rational on the subject of the drawbacks of Calcutta. *Thirdly*, the man of the "firms," the pure non-official who fights under the banner of one of the great houses of the City, or for his own hand in a neat office, or dashes about Clive Street in a brougham doing "share work" or something of the kind. He fears not "Bengal," nor regards he "India." He swears impartially at both when their actions interfere with his operations. His "shop" is quite unintelligible. He is like the English city man with the chill off, lives well and entertains hospitably. In the old days he was greater than he is now, but still he bulks large. He is rational in so far that he will help the abuse of the Municipality, but womanish in his insistence on the excellencies of Calcutta. Over and above these who are hurrying to work are the various brigades, squads and detachments of the other interests. But they are sets and not sections, and revolve round Belvedere, Government House, and Fort William. Simla and Darjeeling claim them in the hot weather. Let them go. They wear top-nats and frock-coats.

It is time to escape from Chouringhi Road and get among the long-shore folk, who have no prejudices against tobacco, and who all use pretty nearly the same sort of hat.

CHAPTER III

THE COUNCIL OF THE GODS

He set up conclusions to the number of nine thousand seven hundred and sixty four . . . he went afterward to the Sorbonne, where he maintained argument against the theologians for the space of six weeks, from four o'clock in the morning till six in the evening, except for an interval of two hours to refresh themselves and take their repasts, and at this were present the greatest part of the lords of the court the masters of request,

presidents, counsellors, those of the ac-compts, secretaries, advocates and others; as also the sheriffs of the said town.— *Pantagruel.*

"THE Bengal Legislative Council is sitting now. You will find it in an octagonal wing of Writers' Buildings: straight across the *maidan.* It's worth seeing." "What are they sitting on?" "Municipal business. No end of a debate." So much for trying to keep low company. The long-shore loafers must stand over. Without doubt this Council is going to hang some one for the state of the City, and Sir Steuart Bayley will be chief executioner. One does not come across Councils every day.

Writers' Buildings are large. You can trouble the busy workers of half-a-dozen departments before you stumble upon the black-stained staircase that leads to an upper chamber looking out over a populous street. Wild *chaprissis* block the way. The Councillor Sahibs are sitting, but any one can enter. "To the right of the Lât Sahib's chair, and go quietly." Ill-mannered minion! Does he expect the awe-stricken spectator to prance in with a jubilant war-whoop or turn Catherine-wheels round that sumptuous octagonal room with the blue-domed roof? There are gilt capitals to the half pillars and an Egyptian patterned lotus-stencil makes the walls decorously gay. A thick piled carpet covers all the floor, and must be delightful in the hot weather. On a black wooden throne, comfortably cushioned in green leather, sits Sir Steuart Bayley, Ruler of Bengal. The rest are all great men, or else they would not be there. Not to know them argues oneself unknown. There are a dozen of them, and sit six aside at two slightly curved lines of beautifully polished desks. Thus Sir Steuart Bayley occupies the frog of a badly made horseshoe split at the toe. In front of him, at a table covered with books and pamphlets and papers, toils a secretary. There is a seat for the Reporters, and that is all. The place enjoys a chastened gloom, and its very atmosphere fills one with awe. This is the heart of Bengal, and uncommonly well upholstered. If the work matches the first-class furniture, the inkpots, the carpet, and the resplendent ceiling, there will be something worth seeing. But where is the criminal who is to be hanged for the stench that runs up and down Writers' Buildings staircases, for the rubbish heaps in the Chitpore Road, for the sickly savor of Chouringhi, for the dirty little tanks at the back of Belvedere, for the street full of smallpox, for the reeking gharri-stand outside the Great Eastern, for the state of the stone and dirt pavements, for the condition of the gullies of Shampooker, and for a hundred other things?

"This, I submit, is an artificial scheme in supersession of Nature's unit, the individual." The speaker is a slight, spare native in a flat hat-turban, and a black alpaca frock-coat. He looks like a *vakil* to the boot-heels, and, with his unvarying smile and regulated gesticulation, recalls memories of up-country courts. He never hesitates, is never at a loss for a word, and never in one sentence repeats himself. He talks and talks and talks in a level voice, rising occasionally half an octave when a point has to be driven home. Some of his periods sound very familiar. This, for instance, might be a sentence from the

Mirror: "So much for the principle. Let us now examine how far it is supported by precedent." This sounds bad. When a fluent native is discoursing of "principles" and "precedents," the chances are that he will go on for some time. Moreover, where is the criminal, and what is all this talk about abstractions? They want shovels not sentiments, in this part of the world.

A friendly whisper brings enlightenment: "They are plowing through the Calcutta Municipal Bill—plurality of votes you know; here are the papers." And so it is! A mass of motions and amendments on matters relating to ward votes. Is *A* to be allowed to give two votes in one ward and one in another? Is section ten to be omitted, and is one man to be allowed one vote and no more? How many votes does three hundred rupees' worth of landed property carry? Is it better to kiss a post or throw it in the fire? Not a word about carbolic acid and gangs of *domes*. The little man in the black *choga* revels in his subject. He is great on principles and precedents, and the necessity of "popularizing our system." He fears that under certain circumstances "the status of the candidates will decline." He riots in "self-adjusting majorities," and the healthy influence of the educated middle classes.

For a practical answer to this, there steals across the council chamber just one faint whiff. It is as though some one laughed low and bitterly. But no man heeds. The Englishmen look supremely bored, the native members stare stolidly in front of them. Sir Steuart Bayley's face is as set as the face of the Sphinx. For these things he draws his pay, and his is a low wage for heavy labor. But the speaker, now adrift, is not altogether to be blamed. He is a Bengali, who has got before him just such a subject as his soul loveth—an elaborate piece of academical reform leading no-whither. Here is a quiet room full of pens and papers, and there are men who must listen to him. Apparently there is no time limit to the speeches. Can you wonder that he talks? He says "I submit" once every ninety seconds, varying the form with "I do submit." The popular element in the electoral body should have prominence. Quite so. He quotes one John Stuart Mill to prove it. There steals over the listener a numbering sense of nightmare. He has heard all this before somewhere —yea; even down to J. S. Mill and the references to the "true interests of the ratepayers." He sees what is coming next. Yes, there is the old Sabha Anjuman journalistic formula—"Western education is an exotic plant of recent importation." How on earth did this man drag Western education into this discussion? Who knows? Perhaps Sir Steuart Bayley does. He seems to be listening. The others are looking at their watches. The spell of the level voice sinks the listener yet deeper into a trance. He is haunted by the ghosts of all the cant of all the political platforms of Great Britain. He hears all the old, old vestry phrases, and once more he smells the smell. *That* is no dream. Western education is an exotic plant. It is the upas tree, and it is all our fault. We brought it out from England exactly as we brought out the ink bottles and the patterns for the chairs. We planted it and it grew—monstrous as a banian.

Now we are choked by the roots of it spreading so thickly in this fat soil of Bengal. The speaker continues. Bit by bit. We builded this dome, visible and invisible, the crown of Writers' Buildings, as we have built and peopled the buildings. Now we have gone too far to retreat, being "tied and bound with the chain of our own sins." The speech continues. We made that florid sentence. That torrent of verbiage is ours. We taught him what was constitutional and what was unconstitutional in the days when Calcutta smelt. Calcutta smells still, but we must listen to all that he has to say about the plurality of votes and the threshing of wind and the weaving of ropes of sand. It is our own fault absolutely.

The speech ends, and there rises a grey Englishman in a black frock-coat. He looks a strong man, and a worldly. Surely he will say: "Yes, Lala Sahib, all this may be true talk, but there's a *burra krab* smell in this place, and everything must be *safkaroed* in a week, or the Deputy Commissioner will not take any notice of you in *durbar*." He says nothing of the kind. This is a Legislative Council, where they call each other "Honorable So-and-So's." The Englishman in the frock-coat begs all to remember that "we are discussing principles, and no consideration of the details ought to influence the verdict on the principles." Is he then like the rest? How does this strange thing come about? Perhaps these so English office fittings are responsible for the warp. The Council Chamber might be a London Board-room. Perhaps after long years among the pens and papers its occupants grow to think that it really

is, and in this belief give *résumés* of
the history of Local Self-Government
in England.

The black frock-coat, emphasizing his
points with his spectacle-case, is telling
his friends how the parish was first the
unit of self-government. He then explains how burgesses were elected, and
in tones of deep fervor announces:
"Commissioners of Sewers are elected
in the same way." Whereunto all this
lecture? Is he trying to run a motion
through under cover of a cloud of words,
essaying the well-known "cuttle-fish
trick" of the West?

He abandons England for a while, and
now we get a glimpse of the cloven hoof
in a casual reference to Hindus and
Mahomedans. The Hindus will lose
nothing by the complete establishment
of plurality of votes. They will have
the control of their own wards as they
used to have. So there is race-feeling,
to be explained away, even among these
beautiful desks. Scratch the Council,
and you come to the old, old trouble.
The black frock-coat sits down, and a
keen-eyed, black-bearded Englishman
rises with one hand in his pocket to explain his views on an alteration of the
vote qualification. The idea of an
amendment seems to have just struck
him. He hints that he will bring it forward later on. He is academical like the
others, but not half so good a speaker.
All this is dreary beyond words. Why
do they talk and talk about owners
and occupiers and burgesses in England
and the growth of autonomous institutions when the city, the great city, is
here crying out to be cleansed? What
has England to do with Calcutta's evil,
and why should Englishmen be forced

to wander through mazes of unprofitable
argument against men who cannot understand the iniquity of dirt?

A pause follows the black-bearded
man's speech. Rises another native, a
heavily-built Babu, in a black gown and
a strange head-dress. A snowy white
strip of cloth is thrown *jharun*-wise over
his shoulders. His voice is high, and
not always under control. He begins:
"I will try to be as brief as possible."
This is ominous. By the way, in Council there seems to be no necessity for a
form of address. The orators plunge
in *medias res,* and only when they are
well launched throw an occasional "Sir"
toward Sir Steuart Bayley, who sits with
one leg doubled under him and a dry
pen in his hand. This speaker is no
good. He talks, but he says nothing,
and he only knows where he is drifting
to. He says: "We must remember that
we are legislating for the Metropolis of
India, and therefore we should borrow
our institutions from large English
towns, and not from parochial institutions." If you think for a minute, that
shows a large and healthy knowledge of
the history of Local Self-Government.
It also reveals the attitude of Calcutta.
If the city thought less about itself as
a metropolis and more as a midden, its
state would be better. The speaker
talks patronizingly of "my friend," al-
luding to the black frock-coat. Then
he flounders afresh, and his voice gallops
up the gamut as he declares, "and therefore that makes all the difference." He
hints vaguely at threats, something to do
with the Hindus and the Mahomedans,
but what he means it is difficult to discover. Here, however, is a sentence
taken *verbatim.* It is not likely to ap-

pear in this form in the Calcutta papers. The black frock-coat had said that if a wealthy native "had eight votes to his credit, his vanity would prompt him to go to the polling-booth, because he would feel better than half-a-dozen *gharri-wans* or petty traders." (Fancy allowing a *gharri-wan* to vote! He has yet to learn how to drive!) Hereon the gentleman with the white cloth: "Then the complaint is that influential voters will not take the trouble to vote. In my humble opinion, if that be so, adopt voting papers. *That* is the way to meet them. In the same way—The Calcutta T r a d e s ' Association—you abolish all plurality of votes: and that is the way to meet *them.*" Lucid, is it not? Up flies the irresponsible voice, and delivers this statement: "In the election for the House of Commons plurality are allowed for persons having interest in different districts." Then hopeless, hopeless fog. It is a great pity that India ever heard of anybody higher than the heads of the Civil Service. The country appeals from the *Chota* to the *Burra Sahib* all too readily as it is. Once more a whiff. The gentleman gives a defiant jerk of his shoulder-cloth, and sits down.

Then Sir Steuart Bayley: "The question before the Council is," etc. There is a ripple of "Ayes" and "Noes," and the "Noes" have it, whatever it may be. The black-bearded gentleman springs his amendment about the voting qualifications. A large senator in a white waistcoat, and with a most genial smile, rises and proceeds to smash up the amendment. Can't see the use of it. Calls it in effect rubbish. The black frock-coat rises to explain his friend's amendment

and incidentally makes a funny little slip. He is a knight, and his friend has been newly knighted. He refers to him as "Mister." The black *choga,* he who spoke first of all, speaks again, and talks of the *"sojorner* who comes here for a little time, and then leaves the land." Well it is for the black *choga* that the sojourner does come, or there would be no comfy places wherein to talk about the power that can be measured by wealth and the intellect "which, sir, I submit, cannot be so measured." The amendment is lost, and trebly and quadruply lost is the listener. In the name of sanity and to preserve the tattered shirt tails of a torn illusion, let us escape. This is the Calcutta Municipal Bill. They have been at it for several Saturdays. Last Saturday Sir Steuart Bayley pointed out that at their present rate they would be about two years in getting it through. Now they will sit till dusk, unless Sir Steuart Bayley, who wants to see Lord Connemara off, puts up the black frock-coat to move an adjournment. It is not good to see a Government close to. This leads to the formation of blatantly self-satisfied judgments, which may be quite as wrong as the cramping system with which we have encompassed ourselves. And in the streets outside Englishmen summarize the situation brutally, thus: "The whole thing is a farce. Time is money to us. We can't stick out those everlasting speeches in the municipality. The natives choke us off, but we know that if things get too bad the Government will step in and interfere, and so we worry along somehow." Meantime Calcutta continues to cry out for the bucket and the broom.

CHAPTER IV

ON THE BANKS OF THE HUGLI

THE clocks of the city have struck two. Where can a man get food? Calcutta is not rich in respect of dainty accommodation. You can stay your stomach at Peliti's or Bonsard's, but their shops are not to be found in Hasting Street, or in the places where brokers fly to and fro in office-jauns, sweating and growing visibly *rich.* There must be some sort of entertainment where sailors congregate. "Honest Bombay Jack" supplies nothing but Burma cheroots and whisky in liquor-glasses, but in Lal Bazar, not far from "The Sailors' Coffee-rooms," a board gives bold advertisement that "officers and seamen can find good quarters." In evidence a row of neat officers and seamen are sitting on a bench by the "hotel" door smoking. There is an almost military likeness in their clothes. Perhaps "Honest Bombay Jack" only keeps one kind of felt hat and one brand of suit. When Jack of the mercantile marine is sober, he is very sober. When he is drunk he is—but ask the river police what a lean, mad Yankee can do with his nails and teeth. These gentlemen smoking on the bench are impassive almost as Red Indians. Their attitudes are unrestrained, and they do not wear braces. Nor, it would appear from the bill of fare, are they particular as to what they eat when they attend *tâble d'hôte.* The fare is substantial and the regulation peg—every house has its own depth of peg if you will refrain from stopping Ganymede—something to wonder at. Three fingers and a trifle over seems to be the

use of the officers and seamen who are talking so quietly in the doorway. One says—he has evidently finished a long story—"and so he shipped for four pound ten with a first mate's certificate and all, and that was in a German barque." Another spits with conviction and says genially, without raising his voice: "That was a hell of a ship; who knows her?" No answer from the *panchayet,* but a Dane or a German wants to know whether the *Myra* is "up" yet. A dry, red-haired man gives her exact position in the river —(How in the world can he know?)— and the probable hour of her arrival. The grave debate drifts into a discussion of a recent river accident, whereby a big steamer was damaged, and had to put back and discharge cargo. A burly gentleman who is taking a constitutional down Lal Bazar strolls up and says: "I tell you she fouled her own chain with her own forefoot. Hev you seen the plates?" "No." Then how the —— can any —— like you —— say what it —— well was?" He passes on, having delivered his highly-flavored opinion without heat or passion. No one seems to resent the expletives.

Let us get down to the river and see this stamp of men more thoroughly. Clarke Russell has told us that their lives are hard enough in all conscience. What are their pleasures and diversions? The Port Office, where lives the gentlemen who make improvements in the Port of Calcutta, ought to supply information. It stands large and fair, and built in an orientalized manner after the Italians at the corner of Fairlie Place upon the great Strand Road, and a continual clamor of traffic by land

and by sea goes up throughout the day and far into the night against its windows. This is a place to enter more reverently than the Bengal Legislative Council, for it houses the direction of the uncertain Hugli down to the Sandheads, owns enormous wealth, and spends huge sums on the frontaging of river banks, the expansion of jetties, and the manufacture of docks costing two hundred lakhs of rupees. Two million tons of sea-going shippage yearly find their way up and down the river by the guidance of the Port Office, and the men of the Port Office know more than it is good for men to hold in their heads. They can without reference to telegraphic bulletins give the position of all the big steamers, coming up or going down, from the Hugli to the sea, day by day with their tonnage, the names of their captains and the nature of their cargo. Looking out from the veranda of their officer over a lancer-regiment of masts, they can declare truthfully the name of every ship within eye-scope, with the day and hour when she will depart.

In a room at the bottom of the building lounge big men, carefully dressed. Now there is a type of face which belongs almost exclusively to Bengal Cavalry officers—majors for choice. Everybody knows the bronzed, black-moustached, clear-speaking Native Cavalry officer. He exists unnaturally in novels, and naturally on the frontier. These men in the big room have its caste of face so strongly marked that one marvels what officers are doing by the river. "Have they come to book passengers for home?" "Those men! They're pilots. Some of them draw between two and three thousand rupees a month. They are responsible for half-a-million pounds' worth of cargo sometimes." They certainly are men, and they carry themselves as such. They confer together by twos and threes, and appeal frequently to shipping lists.

"*Isn't* a pilot a man who always wears a pea-jacket and shouts through a speaking-trumpet?" "Well, you can ask those gentlemen if you like. You've got your notions from home pilots. Ours aren't that kind exactly. They are a picked service, as carefully weeded as the Indian Civil. Some of 'em have brothers in it, and some belong to the old Indian army families." But they are not all equally well paid. The Calcutta papers sometimes echo the groans of the junior pilots who are not allowed the handling of ships over a certain tonnage. As it is yearly growing cheaper to build one big steamer that two little ones, these juniors are crowded out, and, while the seniors get their thousands, some of the youngsters make at the end of one month exactly thirty rupees. This is a grievance with them; and it seems well-founded.

In the flats above the pilots' room are hushed and chapel-like offices, all sumptuously fitted, where Englishmen write and telephone and telegraph, and deft Babus forever draw maps of the shifting Hugli. Any hope of understanding the work of the Port Commissioners is thoroughly dashed by being taken through the Port maps of a quarter of a century past. Men have played with the Hugli as children play with a gluttor-runnel, and, in return, the Hugli once rose and played with men and ships till the Strand Road was littered with the raffle and the carcasses of big ships. There are photos on the walls of the cyclone of '64, when the *Thunder* came inland and sat upon an American barque, obstructing all the traffic. Very curious are these photos, and almost impossible to believe. How can a big, strong steamer have her three masts razed to deck level? How can a heavy, country boat be pitched on to the poop of a high-walled liner? and how can the side be bodily torn out of a ship? The photos say that all these things are possible, and men aver that a cyclone may come again and scatter the craft like chaff. Outside the Port Office are the export and import sheds, buildings that can hold a ship's cargo a-piece, all standing on reclaimed ground. Here be several strong smells, a mass of railway lines, and a multitude of men. "Do you see where that trolly is standing, behind the big P. and O. berth? In that place as nearly as may be the Govindpur went down about twenty years ago, and began to shift out!" "But that is solid ground." "She sank there, and the next tide made a scour-hole on one side of her. The returning tide knocked her into it. Then the mud made up behind her. Next tide the business was repeated —Always the scour-hole in the mud and the filling up behind her. So she rolled and was pushed out and out until she got in the way of the shipping right out yonder, and we had to blow her up. When a ship sinks in mud or quicksand she regularly digs her own grave and wriggles herself into it deeper and deeper till she reaches moderately solid stuff. Then she sticks." Horrible idea, is it not, to go down and down with each tide into the foul Hugli mud?

Close to the Port Offices is the Shipping Office, where the captains engage their crews. The men must produce their discharges from their last ships in the presence of the shipping master, or as they call him—"The Deputy Shipping." He passes them as correct after having satisfied himself that they are not deserters from other ships, and they then sign articles for the voyage. This is the ceremony, beginning with the "dearly beloved" of the crew-hunting captain down to the "amazement" of the identified deserter. There is a dingy building, next door to the Sailors' Home, at whose gate stand the cast-ups of all the seas in all manner of raiment. There are Seedee boys, Bombay *serangs* and Madras fishermen of the salt villages, Malays who insist upon marrying native women grow jealous and run *amok:* Malay-Hindus, Hindu-Malay-whites, Burmese, Burma-whites, Burma-native-whites, Italians with gold earrings and a thirst for gambling, Yankees of all the States, with Mulattoes and pure buck-niggers, red and rough Danes, Cingalese, Cornish boys who seem fresh taken from the plough-tail "corn-stalks from colonial ships where they got four pound ten a month as seamen, tun-bellied Germans, Cockney mates keeping a little aloof from the crowd and talking in knots together, unmistakable "Tommies" who have tumbled into sea-faring life by some mistake, cockatoo-tufted Welshmen spitting and swearing like cats, broken-down loafers, grey-headed, penniless, and pitiful, swaggering boys, and very quiet men with gashes and cuts on their faces. It is an ethnological museum where all the specimens are playing comedies and tragedies. The head of it all is the "Deputy Shipping," and he sits, supported by an English policeman whose fists are knobby, in a great Chair of State. The "Deputy Shipping" knows all the iniquity of the riverside, all the ships, all the captains, and a fair amount of the men. He is fenced off from the crowd by a strong wooden railing, behind which are gathered those who "stand and wait," the unemployed of the mercantile marine. They have had their spree—poor devils—and now they will go to sea again on as low a wage as three pound ten a month, to fetch up at the end in some Shanghai stew or San Francisco hell. They have turned their backs on the seductions of the Howrah boarding-houses and the delights of Colootollah. If Fate will, "Nightingales" will know them no more for a season, and their successors may paint Collinga Bazar vermillion. But what captain will take some of these battered, shattered wrecks whose hands shake and whose eyes are red?

Enter suddenly a bearded captain, who has made his selection from the crowd on a previous day, and now wants to get his men passed. He is not fastidious in his choice. His eleven seem a tough lot for such a mild-eyed, civil-spoken man to manage. But the captain in the Shipping Office and the captain on the ship are two different things. He brings his crew up to the "Deputy Shipping's" bar, and hands in their greasy, tattered discharges. But the heart of the "Deputy Shipping" is hot within him, because, two days ago, a Howrah crimp stole a whole crew from a down-dropping ship, insomuch that the captain had to come back and whip up a new crew at one o'clock in the day. Evil will it be if the "Deputy Shipping" finds one of these bounty-jumpers in the chosen crew of the *Blenkindoon*, let us say.

"The Deputy Shipping" tells the story with heat. "I didn't know they did such things in Calcutta," says the captain. "Do such things! They'd steal the eye-teeth out of your head there, Captain." He picks up a discharge and calls for Michael Donelly, who is a loose-knit, vicious-looking Irish-American who chews. "Stand up, man, stand up!" Michael Donelly wants to lean against the desk, and the English policeman won't have it. "What was your last ship?" "*Fairy Queen.*" "When did you leave her?" " 'Bout 'leven days." "Captain's name?" "Flahy." "That'll do. Next man: Jules Anderson." Jules Anderson is a Dane. His statements tally with the discharge-certificate of the United States, as the Eagle attesteth. He is passed and falls back. Slivey, the Englishman, and David, a huge plum-colored negro who ships as cook are also passed. Then comes Bassompra, a little Italian, who speaks English. "What's your last ship?" "*Ferdinand.*" "No, after that?" "German barque." Bassompra does not look happy. "When did she sail?" "About three weeks ago." "What's her name?" "*Haidée.*" You deserted from her?" "Yes, but she's left port." The "Deputy Shipping" runs rapidly through a shipping-list, throws it down with a bang. " 'Twon't do. No German barque *Haidée* here for three months. How do I know you don't belong to the *Jackson's* crew? Cap'ain, I'm afraid you'll have to ship another man. He must stand over. Take the rest away and make 'em sign."

The bead-eyed Bassompra seems to have lost his chance of a voyage, and his case will be inquired into. The captain departs with his men and they sign articles for the voyage, while the "Deputy Shipping" tells strange tales of the sailorman's life. "They'll quit a good ship for the sake of a spree, and catch on again at three po·nd ten, and by Jove, they'll let their skippers pay 'em at ten rupees to the sovereign—poor beggars! As soon as the money's gone they'll ship, but not before. Every one under rank of captain engages here. The competition makes first mates ship sometimes for five pounds or as low as four ten a month." (The gentleman in the boarding-house was right, you see.) "A first mate's wages are seven ten or eight, and foreign captains ship for twelve pounds a month and bring their own small stores—everything, that is to say, except beef, peas, flour, coffee and molasses."

These things are not pleasant to listen to while the hungry-eyed men in the bad clothes lounge and scratch and loaf behind the railing. What comes to them in the end? They die, it seems, though that is not altogether strange. They die at sea in strange and horrible ways; they die, a few of them, in the Kintals, being lost and suffocated in the great sink of Calcutta; they die in strange places by the water-side, and the Hugli takes them away under the mooring chains and the buoys, and casts them up on the sands below, if the River Police have missed the capture. They sail the sea because they must live; and there is no end to their toil.

Very, very few find haven of any kind, and the earth, whose ways they do not understand, is cruel to them, when they walk upon it to drink and be merry after the manner of beasts. Jack ashore is a pretty thing when he is in a book or in the blue jacket of the Navy. Mercantile Jack is not so lovely. Later on, we will see where his "sprees" lead him.

CHAPTER V

WITH THE CALCUTTA POLICE

"The City was of Night—perchance of Death,
But certainly of Night."
—*The City of Dreadful Night.*

IN the beginning, the Police were responsible. They said in a patronizing way that, merely as a matter of convenience, they would prefer to take a wanderer round the great city themselves, sooner than let him contract a broken head on his own account in the slums. They said that there were places and places where a white man, unsupported by the arm of the law, would be robbed and mobbed; and that there were other places where drunken seamen would make it very unpleasant for him. There was a night fixed for the patrol, but apologies were offered beforehand for the comparative insignificance of the tour.

"Come up to the fire lookout in the first place, and then you'll be able to see the city." This was at No. 22, Lal Bazar, which is the headquarters of the Calcutta Police, the centre of the great web of telephone wires where Justice sits all day and all night looking after one million people and a floating population of one hundred thousand. But her work shall be dealt with later on. The fire lookout is a little sentry-box on the top of the three-storied police offices. Here a native watchman waits always, ready to give warning to the brigade below if the smoke rises by day or the flames by night in any ward of the city. From this eyrie, in the warm night, one hears the heart of Calcutta beating. Northward, the city stretches away three long miles, with three more miles of suburbs beyond, to Dum-Dum and Barrackpore. The lamplit dusk on this side is full of noises and shouts and smells. Close to the Police Office, jovial mariners at the sailors' coffee-shop are roaring hymns. Southerly, the city's confused lights give place to the orderly lamp-rows of the *maidan* and Chouringhi, where the respectabilities live and the Police have very little to do. From the east goes up to the sky the clamor of Sealdah, the rumble of the trams, and the voices of all Bow Bazar chaffering and making merry. Westward are the business quarters, hushed now, the lamps of the shipping on the river, and the twinkling lights on the Howrah side. It is a wonderful sight—this Pisgah view of a huge city resting after the labors of the day. "Does the noise of traffic go on all through the hot weather?" "Of course. The hot months are the busiest in the year and money's tightest. You should see the brokers cutting about at that season. Calcutta *can't* stop, my dear sir." "What happens then?" "Nothing happens; the death-rate goes up a little. That's all!" Even in February, the weather would, up-country, be called muggy and stifling, but Calcutta is convinced that it is

her cold season. The noises of the city grow perceptibly; it is the night side of Calcutta waking up and going abroad. Jack in the sailors' coffee-shop is singing joyously: "Shall we gather at the River —the beautiful, the beautiful, the River?" What an incongruity there is about his selections. However, that it amuses before it shocks the listeners, is not to be doubted. An Englishman, far from his native land is liable to become careless, and it would be remarkable if he did otherwise in ill-smelling Calcutta. There is a clatter of hoofs in the courtyard below. Some of the Mounted Police have come in from somewhere or other out of the great darkness. A clog-dance of iron hoof follows, and an Englishman's voice is heard soothing an agitated horse who seems to be standing on his hind legs. Some of the Mounted Police are going out into the great darkness. "What's on?" "Walk round at Government House. The Reserve men are being formed up below. They're calling the roll." The Reserve men are all English, and big English at that. They form up and tramp out of the courtyard to line Government Place, and see that Mrs. Lollipop's brougham does not get smashed up by Sirdar Chuckerbutty Bahadur's lumbering C-spring barouche with the two raw Walers. Very military men are the Calcutta European Police in their set-up, and he who knows their composition knows some startling stories of gentlemen-rankers and the like. They are, despite the wearing climate they work in and the wearing work they do, as fine five-score of Englishmen as you shall find east of Suez.

Listen for a moment from the fire

lookout to the voices of the night, and you will see why they must be so. Two thousand sailors of fifty nationalities are adrift in Calcutta every Sunday, and of these perhaps two hundred are distinctly the worse for liquor. There is a mild row going on, even now, somewhere at the back of Bow Bazar, which at nightfall fills with sailor-men who have a wonderful gift of falling foul of the native population. To keep the Queen's peace is of course only a small portion of Police duty, but it is trying. The burly president of the lock-up for European drunks — Calcutta central lock-up is worth seeing—rejoices in a sprained thumb just now, and has to do his work left-handed in consequence. But his left hand is a marvelously persuasive one, and when on duty his sleeves are turned up to the shoulder that the jovial mariner may see that there is no deception. The president's labors are handicapped in that the road of sin to the lock-up runs through a grimy little garden—the brick paths are worn deep with the tread of many drunken feet—where a man can give a great deal of trouble by sticking his toes into the ground and getting mixed up with the shrubs. "A straight run in" would be much more convenient both for the president and the drunk. Generally speaking—and here Police experience is pretty much the same all over the civilized world—a woman drunk is a good deal worse than a man drunk. She scratches and bites like a Chinaman and swears like several fiends. Strange people may be unearthed in the lock-ups. Here is a perfectly true story, not three weeks old. A visitor, an unofficial one, wandered into the native

side of the spacious accommodation provided for those who have gone or done wrong. A wild-eyed Babu rose from the fixed charpoy and said in the best of English: "Good-morning, sir." "*Good*-morning: who are you, and what are you in for?" Then the Babu, in one breath: "I would have you know that I do not go to prison as a criminal but as a reformer. You've read the *Vicar of Wakefield*?" "Ye-es." "Well, *I* am the Vicar of Bengal—at least that's what I call myself." The visitor collapsed. He had not nerve enough to continue the conversation. Then said the voice of the authority: "He's down in connection with a cheating case at Serampore. May be shamming. But he'll be looked to in time."

The best place to hear about the Police is the fire lookout. From that eyrie one can see how difficult must be the work of control over the great, growling beast of a city. By all means let us abuse the Police, but let us see what the poor wretches have to do with their three thousand natives and one hundred Englishmen. From Howrah and Bally and the other suburbs at least a hundred thousand people come in to Calcutta for the day and leave at night. Also Chandernagore is handy for the fugitive law-breaker, who can enter in the evening and get away before the noon of the next day, having marked his house and broken into it.

"But how can the prevalent offence be housebreaking in a place like this?" "Easily enough. When you've seen a little of the city you'll see. Natives sleep and lie about all over the place, and whole quarters are just so many rabbit-warrens. Wait till you see the

Machua Bazar. Well, besides the petty theft and burglary, we have heavy cases of forgery and fraud, that leaves us with our wits pitted against a Bengali's. When a Bengali criminal is working a fraud of the sort he loves, he is *about* the cleverest soul you could wish for. He gives us cases a year long to unravel. Then there are the murders in the low houses—very curious things they are. You'll see the house where Sheikh Babu was murdered presently, and you'll understand. The Burra Bazar and Jora Bagan sections are the two worst ones for heavy cases; but Colootollah is the most aggravating. There's Colootollah over yonder—that patch of darkness beyond the lights. That section is full of tuppenny-ha'penny petty cases, that keep the men up all night and make 'em swear. You'll see Colootollah, and then perhaps you'll understand. Bamun Bustee is the quietest of all, and Lal Bazar and Bow Bazar, as you can see for yourself, are the rowdiest. You've no notion what the natives come to the *thannahs* for. A *naukar* will come in and want a summons against his master for refusing him half-an-hour's *chuti*. I suppose it *does* seem rather revolutionary to an up-country man, but they try to do it here. Now wait a minute, before we go down into the city and see the Fire Brigade turned out. Business is slack with them just now, but you time 'em and see." An order is given, and a bell strikes softly thrice. There is an orderly rush of men, the click of a bolt, a red fire-engine, spitting and swearing with the sparks flying from the furnace, is dragged out of its shelter. A huge brake, which holds supplementary horses, men, and hatchets, follows, and a hose-cart is the third on the list. The men push the heavy things about as though they were pith toys. Five horses appear. Two are shot into the fire-engine, two—monsters these—into the brake, and the fifth, a powerful beast, warranted to trot fourteen miles an hour, backs into the hose-cart shafts. The men clamber up, some one says softly, "All ready there," and with an angry whistle the fire-engine, followed by the other two, flies out into Lal Bazar, the sparks trailing behind. Time—1 min. 40 secs. "They'll find out it's a false alarm, and come back again in five minutes." "Why?" "Because there will be no constables on the road to give 'em the direction of the fire, and because the driver wasn't told the ward of the outbreak when he went out!" "Do you mean to say that you can from this absurd pigeon-loft locate the wards in the night-time?" "Of course: what would be the good of a lookout if the man couldn't tell where the fire was?" "But it's all pitchy black, and the lights are so confusing."

"Ha! Ha! You'll be more confused in ten minutes. You'll have lost your way as you never lost it before. You're going to go round Bow Bazar section."

"And the Lord have mercy on my soul!" Calcutta, the darker portion of it, does not look an inviting place to dive into at night.

CHAPTER VI

THE CITY OF DREADFUL NIGHT

"And since they cannot spend or use
   aright
   The little time here given them in
      trust,
But lavish it in weary undelight
Of foolish toil, and trouble, strife and
      lust—
They naturally claimeth to inherit
The Everlasting Future—that their
      merit
May have full scope. . . . As
      surely is most just."
   —*The City of Dreadful Night.*

THE difficulty is to prevent this account from growing steadily unwholesome. But one cannot rake through a big city without encountering muck.

The Police kept their word. In five short minutes, as they had prophesied, their charge was lost as he had never been lost before. "Where are we now?" "Somewhere off the Chitpore Road, but you wouldn't understand if you were told. Follow now, and step pretty much where we step—there's a good deal of filth hereabouts."

The thick, greasy night shuts in everything. We have gone beyond the ancestral houses of the Ghoses of the Boses, beyond the lamps, the smells, and the crowd of Chitpore Road, and have come to a great wilderness of packed houses—just such mysterious, conspiring tenements as Dickens would have loved. There is no breath of breeze here, and the air is perceptibly warmer. There is little regularity in the drift, and the utmost niggardliness in the spacing of what, for want of a better name, we must call the streets. If Calcutta keeps such luxuries as Commissioners of Sewers and Paving, they die before they reach this place. The air is heavy with a faint, sour stench—the essence of long-neglected abominations—and it cannot escape from among the tall, three-storied houses. "This, my dear sir, is a *perfectly* respectable quarter as quarters go. That house at the head of the alley, with the elaborate stucco-work round the top of the door, was built long ago by a celebrated midwife. Great people used to live here once. Now it's the—Aha! Look out for that carriage." A big mail-phaeton crashes out of the darkness and, recklessly driven, disappears. The wonder is how is it ever got into this maze of narrow streets, where nobody seems to be moving, and where the dull throbbing of the city's life only comes faintly and by snatches. "Now it's the what?" "St. John's Wood of Calcutta —for the rich Babus. That 'fitton' belonged to one of them." "Well, it's not much of a place to look at?" "Don't judge by appearances. About here live the women who have beggared kings. We aren't going to let you down into unadulterated vice all at once. You must see it first with the gilding on— and mind that rotten board."

Stand at the bottom of a lift and look upward. Then you will get both the size and the design of the tiny courtyard round which one of these big dark houses is built. The central square may be perhaps ten feet every way, but the balconies that run inside it overhang, and seem to cut away half the available space. To reach the square a man must go round many corners, down a covered-in way, and up and down two or three baffling and confused steps. There are no lamps to guide, and the janitors of the establishment seem to be compelled to sleep in the passages. The central square, the *patio* or whatever it must be called, reeks with the faint, sour smell which finds its way impartially into every room. "Now you will understand," say the Police kindly, as their charge blunders, shin-first, into a well-dark winding staircase, "that these are not the sort of places to visit alone." "Who wants to? Of all the disgusting, inaccessible dens—Holy Cupid, what's this?"

A glare of light on the stair-head, a clink of innumerable bangles, a rustle of much fine gauze, and the Dainty Iniquity stands revealed, blazing—literally blazing—with jewelry from head to foot. Take one of the fairest miniatures that the Delhi painters draw, and multiply it by ten; throw in one of Angelica Kaufmann's best portraits, and add anything that you can think of from Beckford to Lalla Rookh, and you will still fall short of the merits of that perfect face. For an instant, even the grim, professional gravity of the Police is relaxed in the presence of the Dainty Iniquity with the gems, who so prettily invites every one to be seated, and proffers such refreshments as she conceives the palates of the barbarians would prefer. Her Abigails are only one degree less gorgeous than she. Half a lakh, or fifty thousand pounds' worth—it is easier to credit the latter statement than the former—are disposed upon her little body. Each hand carries five jeweled rings which are connected by golden chains to a great jeweled boss of gold in the centre of the back of the hand. Earrings weighted with emeralds and

pearls, diamond nose-rings, and how many other hundred articles make up the list of adornments. English furniture of a gorgeous and gimcrack kind, unlimited chandeliers and a collection of atrocious Continental prints — something, but not altogether, like the glazed plaques on *bon-bon* boxes—are scattered about the house, and on every landing—let us trust this is a mistake —lies, squats or loafs a Bengali who can talk English with unholy fluency. The recurrence suggests — only suggests, mind—a grim possibility of the affectation of excessive virtue by day, tempered with the sort of unwholesome enjoyment after dusk—this loafing and lobbying and chattering and smoking, and unless the bottles lie, tippling among the foul-tongued handmaidens of the Dainty Iniquity. How many men follow this double, deleterious sort of life? The Police are discreetly dumb.

"Now *don't* go talking about 'domiciliary visits' just because this one happens to be a pretty woman. We've *got* to know these creatures. They make the rich man and the poor spend their money; and when a man can't get money for 'em honestly, he comes under *our* notice. *Now* do you see? If there was any domiciliary 'visit' about it, the whole houseful would be hidden past our finding as soon as we turned up in the courtyard. We're friends— to a certain extent." And, indeed, it seemed no difficult thing to be friends to any extent with the Dainty Iniquity who was so surpassingly different from all that experience taught of the beauty of the East. Here was the face from which a man could write *Lalla Rookhs* by the dozen, and believe every work that he wrote. Hers was the beauty that Byron sang of when he wrote—

"Remember, if you come here alone, the chances are that you'll be clubbed, or stuck, or, anyhow, mobbed. You'll understand that this part of the world is shut to Europeans—absolutely. Mind the steps, and follow on." The vision dies out in the smells and gross darkness of the night, in evil, time-rotten brickwork, and another wilderness of shut-up houses, wherein it seems that people do continually and feebly strum stringed instruments of a plaintive and wailsome nature.

Follows, after another plunge into a passage of a courtyard, and up a staircase, the apparition of a Fat Vice, in whom is no sort of romance, nor beauty, but unlimited coarse humor. She too is studded with jewels, and her house is even finer than the house of the other, and more infested with the extraordinary men who speak such good English and are so deferential to the Police. The Fat Vice has been a great leader of fashion in her day, and stripped a zemindar Raja to his last acre—insomuch that he ended in the House of Correction for a theft committed for her sake. Native opinion has it that she is a "monstrous well-preserved woman." On this point, as on some others, the races will agree to differ.

The scene changes suddenly as a slide in a magic lantern. Dainty Iniquity and Fat Vice slide away on a roll of streets and alleys, each more squalid than its predecessor. We are "somewhere at the back of the Machua Bazar," well in the heart of the city. There are no houses here—nothing but acres and acres, it seems, of foul wat-tle-and-dab huts, any one of which would be a disgrace to a frontier village. The whole arrangement is a neatly contrived germ and fire trap, reflecting great credit upon the Calcutta Municipality.

"What happens when these pigsties catch fire?" "They're built up again," say the Police, as though this were the natural order of things. "Land is immensely valuable here." All the more reason, then, to turn several Hausmanns loose in the city, with instructions to make barracks for the population that cannot find room in the huts and sleeps in the open ways, cherishing dogs and worse, much worse, in its unwashen bosom. "Here is a licensed coffee-shop. This is where your *naukers* go for amusement and to see nautches." There is a huge *chappar* shed, ingeniously ornamented with insecure kerosene lamps, and crammed with *gharri-wans, khitmatgars,* small store-keepers and the like. Never a sign of a European. Why? "Because if an Englishman messed about here, he'd get into trouble. Men don't come here unless they're drunk or have lost their way." The *gharri-wans*—they have the privilege of voting, have they not?— look peaceful enough as they squat on tables or crowd by the doors to watch the nautch that is going forward. Five pitiful draggle-tails are huddled together on a bench under one of the lamps, while the sixth is squirming and shrieking before the impassive crowd. She sings of love as understood by the Oriental—the love that dries the heart and consumes the liver. In this place, the words that would look so well on paper, have an evil and ghastly significance.

The *gharri-wans* stare or sup tumblers and cups of a filthy decoction, and the *kunchenee* howls with renewed vigor in the presence of the Police. Where the Dainty Iniquity was hung with gold and gems, she is trapped with pewter and glass; and where there was heavy embroidery on the Fat Vice's dress, defaced, stamped tinsel faithfully reduplicates the pattern on the tawdry robes of the *kunchenee*. So you see, if one cares to moralize, they are sisters of the same class.

Two or three men, blessed with uneasy consciences, have quietly slipped out of the coffee-shop into the mazes of the huts beyond. The Police laugh, and those nearest in the crowd laugh applausively, as in duty bound. Perhaps the rabbits grin uneasily when the ferret lands at the bottom of the burrow and begins to clear the warren.

"The *chandoo*-shops shut up at six, so you'll have to see opium-smoking before dark some day. No, you won't, though." The detective nose sniffs, and the detective body makes for a half-opened door of a hut whence floats the fragrance of the black smoke. Those of the inhabitants who are able to stand promptly clear out—they have no love for the Police—and there remain only four men lying down and one standing up. This latter has a pet mongoose coiled round his neck. He speaks English fluently. Yes, he has no fear. It was a private smoking party and—"No business to-night—show how you smoke opium." "Aha! You want to see. Very good, I show. Hiya! you"—he kicks a man on the floor—"show how opium-smoking." The kickee grunts lazily and turns on his elbow. The mongoose, always keeping to the man's neck, erects every hair of its body like an angry cat, and chatters in its owner's ear. The lamp for the opium-pipe is the only one in the room, and lights a scene as wild as anything in the witches' revel; the mongoose acting as the familiar spirit. A voice from the ground says, in tones of infinite weariness: "You take *afim,* so"—a long, long pause, and another kick from the man possessed of the devil—the mongoose. "You take *afim?*" He takes a pellet of the black, treacly stuff on the end of a knitting-needle. "And light *afim.*" He plunges the pellet into the night-light, where it swells and fumes greasily. "And then you put it in your pipe." The smoking pellet is jammed into the tiny bowl of the thick, bamboo-stemmed pipe, and all speech ceases, except the unearthly noise of the mongoose. The man on the ground is sucking at his pipe, and when the smoking pellet has ceased to smoke will be half way to *Nibhan.* "Now you go," says the man with the mongoose. "I am going smoke." The hut door closes upon a red-lit view of huddled legs and bodies, and the man with the mongoose sinking, sinking onto his knees, his head bowed forward, and the little hairy devil chattering on the nape of his neck.

After this the fetid night air seems almost cool, for the hut is as hot as a furnace. "See the *pukka chandu* shops in full blast to-morrow. Now for Colootollah. Come through the huts. There is no decoration about *this* vice."

The huts now gave place to houses very tall and spacious and very dark. But for the narrowness of the streets we might have stumbled upon Chouringhi in the dark. An hour and a half has passed, and up to this time we have not crossed our trail once. "You might knock about the city for a night and never cross the same line. Recollect Calcutta isn't one of your poky up-country cities of a lakh and a half of people." "How long does it take to know it then?" "About a lifetime, and even then some of the streets puzzle you." "How much has the head of a ward to know?" "Every house in his ward if he can, who owns it, what sort of character the inhabitants are, who are their friends, who go out and in, who loaf about the place at night, and so on and so on." "And he knows all this by night as well as by day?" "Of course. Why shouldn't he?" "No reason in the world. Only it's pitchy black just now, and I'd like to see where this alley is going to end." "Round the corner beyond that dead wall. There's a lamp there. Then you'll be able to see." A shadow flits out of a gully and disappears. "Who's that?" "Sergeant of Police just to see we're going in case of accidents." Another shadow staggers into the darkness. "Who's *that?*" "Man from the fort or a sailor from the ships. I couldn't quite see." The Police open a shut door in a high wall, and stumble unceremoniously among a gang of women cooking their food. The floor is of beaten earth, the steps that lead into the upper stories are unspeakably grimy, and the heat is the heat of April. The women rise hastily, and the light of the bull's eye —for the Police have now lighted a lantern in regular "rounds of London" fashion—shows six bleared faces—one a half native half Chinese one, and the

others Bengali. "There are no men here!" they cry. "The house is empty." Then they grin and jabber and chew *pan* and spit, and hurry up the steps into the darkness. A range of three big rooms has been knocked into one here, and there is some sort of arrangement of mats. But an average country-bred is more sumptuously accommodated in an Englishman's stable. A home horse would snort at the accommodation.

"Nice sort of place, isn't it?" say the Police, genially. "This is where the sailors get robbed and drunk." "They must be blind drunk before they come." "Na—Na! Na sailor men ee—yah!" chorus the women, catching at the one word they understand. "Arl gone!" The Police take no notice, but tramp down the big room with the mat looseboxes. A woman is shivering in one of these. "What's the matter?" "Fever. Seek. Vary, *vary* seek." She huddles herself into a heap on the *charpoy* and groans.

A tiny, pitch-black closet opens out of the long room, and into this the Police plunge. "Hullo! What's here?" Down flashes the lantern, and a white hand with black nails comes out of the gloom. Somebody is asleep or drunk in the cot. The ring of lantern light travels slowly up and down the body. "A sailor from the ships. He's got his *dungarees* on. He'll be robbed before the morning most likely." The man is sleeping like a little child, both arms thrown over his head, and he is not unhandsome. He is shoeless, and there are huge holes in his stockings. He is a pure-blooded white, and carries the flush of innocent sleep on his cheeks.

The light is turned off, and the Police depart; while the woman in the loose-box shivers, and moans that she is "seek: vary, *vary* seek." It is not surprising.

CHAPTER VII

DEEPER AND DEEPER STILL

I built myself a lordly pleasure-house,
   Wherein at ease for aye to dwell;
I said: "O Soul, make merry and carouse.
   Dear Soul—for all is well."
                    —*The Palace of Art.*

"AND where next? I don't like Colootollah." The Police and their charge are standing in the interminable waste of houses under the starlight. "To the lowest sink of all," say the Police after the manner of Virgil when he took the Italian with the indigestion to look at the frozen sinners. "And where's that?" "Somewhere about here; but you wouldn't know if you were told." They lead and they lead and they lead, and they cease not from leading till they come to the last circle of the Inferno— a long, long, winding, quiet road. "There you are; you can see for yourself."

But there is nothing to be seen. On one side are houses—gaunt and dark, naked and devoid of furniture; on the other, low, mean stalls, lighted, and with shamelessly open doors, wherein women stand and lounge, and mutter and whisper one to another. There is a hush here, or at least the busy silence of an officer of counting-house in working hours. One look down the street is sufficient. Lead on, gentlemen of the Calcutta Police. Let us escape from the lines of open doors, the flaring lamps within, the glimpses of the tawdry toilet-tables adorned with little plaster dogs, glass balls from Christmas-trees, and—for religion must not be despised though women be fallen—pictures of the saints and statuettes of the Virgin. The street is a long one, and other streets, full of the same pitiful wares, branch off from it.

"Why are they so quiet? Why don't they make a row and sing and shout, and so on?" "Why should they, poor devils?" say the Police, and fall to telling tales of horror, of women decoyed into *palkis* and shot into this trap. Then other tales that shatter one's belief in all things and folk of good repute. "How can you Police have faith in humanity?"

"That's because you're seeing it all in a lump for the first time, and it's not nice that way. Makes a man jump rather, doesn't it? But, recollect, you've *asked* for the worst places, and you can't complain." "Who's complaining? Bring on your atrocities. Isn't that a European woman at that door?" "Yes. Mrs. D——, widow of a soldier, mother of seven children." "Nine, if you please, and good-evening to you," shrills Mrs. D——, leaning against the doorpost, her arms folded on her bosom. She is a rather pretty, slightly-made Eurasian, and whatever shame she may have owned she has long since cast behind her. A shapeless Burmo-native trot, with high cheek-bones and mouth like a shark, calls Mrs. D—— "Mem-Sahib." The word jars unspeakably. Her life is a matter between herself and her Maker, but in that she—the widow of a soldier of the Queen—has stooped to this common foulness in the face of the city, she has offended against the white race. The Police fail to fall in with this righteous indignation. More. They laugh at it out of the wealth of their unholy knowledge. "You're from up-country, and of course you don't understand. There are any amount of that lot in the city." Then the secret of the insolence of Calcutta is made plain. Small wonder the natives fail to respect the Sahib, seeing what they see and knowing what they know. In the good old days, the honorable the directors deported him or her who misbehaved grossly, and the white man preserved his *izzat*. He may have been a ruffian, but he was a ruffian on a large scale. He did not sink in the presence of the people. The natives are quite right to take the wall of the Sahib who has been at great pains to prove that he is of the same flesh and blood.

All this time Mrs. D—— stands on the threshold of her room and looks upon the men with unabashed eyes. If the spirit of that English soldier, who married her long ago by the forms of the English Church, be now flitting batwise above the roofs, how singularly pleased and proud it must be! Mrs. D—— is a lady with a story. She is not averse to telling it. "What was —ahem—the case in which you were —er—hmn—concerned, Mrs. D——?" "They said I'd poisoned my husband by putting something into his drinking water." This is interesting. How much modesty *has* this creature? Let us see. "And — ah — *did* y o u?" "Twasn't proved," says Mrs. D—— with a laugh, a pleasant, lady-like laugh that does infinite credit to her education and upbringing. Worthy Mrs. D——! It

would pay a novelist—a French one let us say—to pick you out of the stews and make you talk.

The Police move forward, into a region of Mrs. D——'s. This is horrible; but they are used to it, and evidently consider indignation affectation. Everywhere are the empty houses, and the babbling women in print gowns. The clocks in the city are close upon midnight, but the Police show no signs of stopping. They plunge hither and thither, like wreckers into the surf; and each plunge brings up a sample of misery, filth and woe.

"Sheikh Babu was murdered just here," they say, pulling up in one of the most troublesome houses in the ward. It would never do to appear ignorant of the murder of Sheikh Babu. "I only wonder that more aren't killed." The houses with their breakneck staircases, their hundred corners, low roofs, hidden courtyards and winding passages, seem specially built for crime of every kind. A woman—Eurasian—rises to a sitting position on a board-charpoy and blinks sleepily at the Police. Then she throws herself down with a grunt. "What's the matter with you?" "I live in Markiss Lane and"—this with intense gravity—"I'm *so* drunk." She has a rather striking gipsy-like face, but her language might be improved.

"Come along," say the Police, "we'll head back to Bentinck Street, and put you on the road to the Great Eastern." They walk long and steadily, and the talk falls on gambling hell. "You ought to see our men rush one of 'em. They like the work—natives of course. When we've marked a hell down, we post men at the entrances and carry it. Sometimes the Chinese bite, but as a rule they fight fair. It's a pity we hadn't a hell to show you. Let's go in here—there may be something forward." "Here" appears to be in the heart of a Chinese quarter, for the pigtails—do they ever go to bed?—are scuttling about the streets. "Never go into a Chinese place alone," say the Police, and swung open a postern gate in a strong, green door. Two Chinamen appear.

"What are we going to see?" "Japanese gir— No, we aren't, by Jove! Catch that Chinaman, *quick.*" The pigtail is trying to double back across a courtyard into an inner chamber; but a large hand on his shoulder spins him round and puts him in rear of the line of advancing Englishmen, who are, be it observed, making a fair amount of noise with their boots. A second door is thrown open, and the visitors advance into a large, square room blazing with gas. Here thirteen pigtails, deaf and blind to the outer world, are bending over a table. The captured Chinaman dodges uneasily in the rear of the procession. Five—ten—fifteen seconds pass, the Englishmen standing in the full light less than three paces from the absorbed gang who see nothing. Then burly Superintendent Lamb brings down his hand on his thigh with a crack like a pistol-shot and shouts: "How do, John?" Follows a frantic rush of scared Celestials, almost tumbling over each other in their anxiety to get clear. Gudgeon before the rush of the pike are nothing to John Chinaman detected in the act of gambling. One pigtail scoops up a pile of copper money, another a chinaware soup-bowl and only a little mound of accusing cowries remains on the white matting that covers the table. In less than half a minute two facts are forcibly brought home to the visitor. First, that a pigtail is largely composed of silk, and rasps the palm of the hand as it slides through; and secondly, that the forearm of a Chinaman is surprisingly muscular and well-developed. "What's going to be done?" "Nothing. They're only three of us, and all the ringleaders would get away. Look at the doors. We've got 'em safe any time we want to catch 'em, if this little visit doesn't make 'em shift their quarters. Hi! John. No pidgin to-night. Show how you makee play. That fat youngster there is our informer."

Half the pigtails have fled into the darkness, but the remainder, assured and trebly assured that the Police really mean "no pidgin," return to the table and stand round while the croupier proceeds to manipulate the cowries, the little curved slip of bamboo and the soup-bowl. They never gamble, these innocents. They only come to look on, and smoke opium in the next room. Yet as the game progresses their eyes light up, and one by one they lose in to deposit their price on odd or even—the number of the cowries that are covered and left uncovered by the little soup-bowl. *Mythan* is the name of the amusement and, whatever may be its demerits, it is *clean.* The Police look on while their charge plays and oots a parchment-skinned horror—one of Swift's Struldburgs, strayed from Laputa—of the enormous sum of two annas. The return of this wealth, doubled, sets the loser beating his forehead against the table from sheer gratitude.

"*Most* immortal game this. A man might drop five whole rupees, if he began playing at sun-down and kept it up all night. Don't *you* ever play whist occasionally?"

"Now, we didn't bring you round to make fun of this department. A man can lose as much as ever he likes and he can fight as well, and if he loses all his money he steals to get more. A Chinaman is insane about gambling, and half his crime comes from it. It *must* be kept down." "And the other business. Any sort of supervision there?" "No; so long as they keep outside the penal code. Ask Dr.—— about that. It's outside our department. Here we are in Bentinck Street and you can be driven to the Great Eastern in a few minutes. Joss houses? Oh, yes. If you want more horrors, Superintendent Lamb will take you round with him to-morrow afternoon at five. Report yourself at the Bow Bazar Thanna at five minutes to. Good-night."

The Police depart, and in a few minutes the silent, well-ordered respectability of Old Council House Street, with the grim Free Kirk at the end of it, is reached. All good Calcutta has gone to bed, the last tram has passed, and the peace of the night is upon the world. Would it be wise and rational to climb the spire of that kirk, and shout after the fashion of the great Lion-slayer of Tarescon: "O true believers! Decency is a fraud and a sham. There is nothing clean or pure or wholesome under the stars, and we are all going to perdition together. Amen!" On second thoughts it would not; for

the spire is slippery, the night is hot, and the Police have been specially careful to warn their charge that he must not be carried away by the sight of horrors that cannot be written or hinted at.

"Good morning," says the Policeman, tramping the pavement in front of the Great Eastern, and he nods his head pleasantly to show that he is the representative of Law and Peace and that the city of Calcutta is safe from itself for the present.

CHAPTER VIII

CONCERNING LUCIA

"Was a woman such a woman—cheeks so round and lips so red?
On the neck the small head buoyant like the bell flower in its bed."

TIME must be filled in somehow till five this afternoon, when Superintendent Lamb will reveal more horrors. Why not, the trams aiding, go to the Old Park Street Cemetery? It is presumption, of course, because none other than the great Sir W. W. Hunter once went there, and wove from his visit certain fascinating articles for the *Englishman;* the memory of which lingers even to this day, though they were written fully two years since.

But the Great Sir W. W. went in his Legislative Consular brougham and never in an unbridled tram-car which pulled up somewhere in the middle of Dhurrumtollah. "You want go Park Street? No trams going Park Street. You get out here." Calcutta tram conductors are not polite. Some day one of them will be hurt. The car shuffles unsympathetically down the street, and the evicted is stranded in Dhurrumtollah, which may be the Hammersmith Highway of Calcutta. Providence arranged this mistake, and paved the way to a Great Discovery now published for the first time. Dhurrumtollah is full of the People of India, walking in family parties and groups and confidential couples. And the people of India are neither Hindu nor Mussulman—Jew, Ethiop, Gueber nor expatriated British. They are the Eurasians, and there are hundreds and hundreds of them in Dhurrumtollah now. There is Papa with a shining black hat fit for a counsellor of the Queen, and Mamma, whose silken attire is tight upon her portly figure, and The Brood made up of straw-hatted, olive-cheeked, sharp-eyed little boys, and leggy maidens wearing white, open-work stockings calculated to show dust. There are the young men who smoke bad cigars and carry themselves lordily—such as have incomes. There are also the young women with the beautiful eyes and the wonderful dresses which always fit so badly across the shoulders. And they carry prayer-books or baskets, because they are either going to mass or the market. Without doubt, these are the people of India. They were born in it, bred in it, and will die in it. The Englishman only comes to the country, and the natives of course were there from the first, but these people have been made here, and no one has done anything for them except talk and write about them. Yet they belong, some of them, to old and honorable families, hold "houses, messuages, and tenements" in Sealdah, and are rich, a few of them. They all look prosperous and contented, and they chatter eternally in that curious dialect that no one has yet reduced to print. Beyond what little they please to reveal now and again in the newspapers, we know nothing about their life which touches so intimately the white on the one hand and the black on the other. It must be interesting—more interesting than the colorless Anglo-Indian article; but who has treated of it? There was one novel once in which the second heroine was an Eurasienne. She was a strictly subordinate character, and came to a sad end. The poet of the race, Henry Derozio—he of whom Mr. Thomas Edwards wrote a history—was bitten with Keats and Scott and Shelley, and overlooked in his search for material things that lay nearest to him. All this mass of humanity in Dhurrumtollah is unexploited and almost unknown. Wanted, therefore, a writer from among the Eurasians, who shall write so that men shall be pleased to read a story of Eurasian life; then outsiders will be interested in the People of India, and will admit that the race has possibilities.

A futile attempt to get to Park Street from Dhurrumtollah ends in the market—the Hogg Market men call it. Perhaps a knight of that name built it. It is not one-half as pretty as the Crawford Market, in Bombay but . . . it appears to be the trysting-place of Young Calcutta. The natural inclination of youth is to lie abed late, and to let the seniors do all the hard work. Why, therefore, should Pyramus who has to be ruling account forms at ten, and Thisbe, who *cannot* be interested in the price of second quality beef, wander. in studiously correct raiment, round and about the stalls before the sun is well clear of the earth? Pyramus carries a walking stick with imitation silver straps upon it, and there are cloth tops to his boots; but his collar has been two days worn. Thisbe crowns her dark head with a blue velvet Tam-o'-Shanter; but one of her boots lacks a button, and there is a tear in the left-hand glove. Mamma, who despises gloves, is rapidly filling a shallow basket, that the coolie-boy carries, with vegetables, potatoes, purple brinjals, and— Oh, Pryamus! Do you ever kiss Thisbe when Mamma is not near?—garlic— yea, *lusson* of the bazar. Mamma is generous in her views on garlic. Pyramus comes round the corner of the stall looking for nobody in particular— not he—and is elaborately polite to Mamma. Somehow, he and Thisbe drift off together, and Mamma, very portly and very voluble, is left to chaffer and sort and select alone. In the name of the Sacred Unities, do not, young people, retire to the meat-stalls to exchange confidences! Come up to this end, where the roses are arriving in great flat baskets, where the air is heavy with the fragrance of flowers, and the young buds and greenery are littering all the floor. They won't—they prefer talking by the dead, unromantic muttons, where there are not so many buyers. How they babble! There must have been a quarrel to make up. Thiebe shakes the blue velvet Tam-o'-Shanter and says: "O yess!" scornfully. Pyramus answers: "No-a, no-a. Do-ant say thatt." Mamma's basket is full and she picks up Thisbe hastily. Pyramus departs. *He* never came here to do any market-

ing. He came to meet Thisbe, who in ten years will own a figure very much like Mamma's. May their ways be smooth before them, and after honest service of the Government, may Pyramus retire on Rs. 250 per mensen, into a nice little house somewhere in Monghyr or Chunar.

From love by natural sequence to death. Where *is* the Park Street Cemetery? A hundred *gharri-wans* leap from their boxes and invade the market, and after a short struggle one of them uncarts his capture in a burial-ground— a ghastly new place, close to a tramway. This is not what is wanted. The living dead are here—the people whose names are not yet altogether perished and whose tombstones are tended. "Where are the *old* dead?" "Nobody goes there," says the *gharri-wan*. "It is up that road." He points up a long and utterly deserted thoroughfare, running between high walls. This is the place, and the entrance to it, with its *mallee* waiting with one brown, battered rose, its grilled door and its professional notices, bears a hideous likeness to the entrance of Simla churchyard. But, once inside, the sightseer stands in the heart of utter desolation—all the more forlorn for being swept up. Lower Park Street cuts a great graveyard in two. The guide-books will tell you when the place was opened and when it was closed. The eye is ready to swear that it is as old as Herculaneum and Pompeii. The tombs are small houses. It is as though we walked down the streets of a town, so tall are they and so closely do they stand—a town shriveled by fire, and scarred by frost and siege. They must have been afraid of their friends rising up before the due time that they weighted them with such cruel mounds of masonry. Strong man, weak woman, or somebody's "infant son aged fifteen months" —it is all the same. For each the squat obelisk, the defaced classic temple, the cellaret of chunam, or the candlestick of brickwork—the heavy slab, the rust-eaten railings, the whopper-jawed cherubs and the apoplectic angels. Men were rich in those days and could afford to put a hundred cubic feet of masonry into the grave of even so humble a person as "Jno. Clements, Captain of the Country Service, 1820." When the "dearly beloved" had held rank answering to that of Commissioner, the efforts are still more sumptuous and the verse ، . . Well, the following speaks for itself:

"Soft on thy tomb shall fond Remem-
        brance shed
    The warm yet unavailing tear,
And purple flowers that deck the hon-
        ored dead
    Shall strew the loved and honored
        bier."

Failure to comply with the contract does not, let us hope, entail to forfeiture of the earnest-money; or the honored dead might be grieved. The slab is out of his tomb, and leans foolishly against it; the railings are rotted, and there are no more lasting ornaments than blisters and stains, which are the work of the weather, and not the result of the "warm yet unavailing tear." The eyes that promised to shed them have been closed any time these seventy years.

Let us go about and moralize cheaply on the tombstones, trailing the robe of

pious reflection up and down the pathways of the grave. Here is a big and stately tomb sacred to "Lucia," who died in 1776 A. D., aged 23. Here also be verses which an irreverent thumb can bring to light. Thus they wrote, when their hearts were heavy in them, one hundred and sixteen years ago:

"What needs the emblem, what the plain-
        tive strain,
    What all the arts that sculpture e'er
        expressed,
To tell the treasure that these walls
        contain?
    Let those declare it most who knew
        her best.

"The tender pity she would oft display
    Shall be with interest at her shrine
        returned,
Connubial love, connubial tears repay,
    And Lucia loved shall still be Lucia
        mourned.

"Though closed the lips, though stopped
        the tuneful breath,
    The silent, clay-cold monitress shall
        teach—
In all the alarming eloquence of death
    With double pathos to the heart shall
        preach.

"Shall teach the virtuous maid, the faith-
        ful wife,
    If young and fair, that young and
        fair was she,
Then close the useful lesson of her life,
    And tell them what she is, they soon
        must be."

That goes well, even after all these years, does it not? and seems to bring Lucia very near, in spite of what the later generation is pleased to call the stiltedness of the old-time verse.

Who will declare the merits of Lucia —dead in her spring before there was even a *Hickey's Gazette* to chronicle the amusements of Calcutta, and publish, with scurrilous asterisks, the *liaisons* of heads of departments? What pot-bellied East Indiaman brought the "virtuous maid" up the river, and did Lucia "make her bargain," as the cant of those times went, on the first, second, or third day after her arrival? Or did she, with the others of the batch, give a spinsters' ball as a last trial—following the custom of the country? No. She was a fair Kentish maiden, sent out, at a cost of five hundred pounds, English money, under the captain's charge, to wed the man of her choice, and *he* knew Clive well, had had dealings with Omichand, and talked to men who had lived through the terrible night in the Black Hole. He was a rich man, Lucia's battered tomb proves it, and he gave Lucia all that her heart could wish. A green-painted boat to take the air in on the river of evenings. Coffree slave-boys who could play on the French horn, and even a very elegant, neat coach with a genteel rutlan roof ornamented with flowers very highly finished, ten best polished plate glasses, ornamented with a few elegant medallions enriched with mother-o'-pearl, that she might take her drive on the course as befitted a factor's wife. All these things he gave her. And when the convoys came up the river, and the guns thundered, and the servants of the Honorable the East India Company drank to the king's health, be sure that Lucia before all the other ladies in the fort had her choice of the new stuffs from England and was cordially hated in consequence. Tilly Kettle painted her picture a little before she died, and the hot-blooded young writers did duel with small swords in the fort

ditch for the honor of piloting her through a minuet at the Calcutta theatre or the Punch House. But Warren Hastings danced with her instead, and the writers were confounded—every man of them. She was a toast far up the river. And she walked in the evening on the bastions of Fort-William, and said: "La! I protest!" It was there that she exchanged congratulations with all her friends on the 20th of October, when those who were alive gathered together to felicitate themselves on having come through another hot season; and the men—even the sober factor saw no wrong here—got most royally and Britishly drunk on Madeira that had twice rounded the Cape. But Lucia fell sick, and the doctor—he who went home after seven years with five lakhs and a half, and a corner of this vast graveyard to his account—said that it was a pukka or putrid fever, and the system required strengthening. So they fed Lucia on hot curries, and mulled wine worked up with spirits and fortified with spices, for nearly a week; at the end of which time she closed her eyes on the weary, weary river and the fort forever, and a gallant, with a turn for *belles lettres,* wept openly as men did then and had no shame of it, and composed the verses above set, and thought himself a neat. hand at the pen—stap his vitals! But the factor was so grieved that he could write nothing at all—could only spend his money—and he counted his wealth by lakhs—on a sumptuous grave. A little later on he took comfort, and when the next batch came out—

But this has nothing whatever to do with the story of Lucia, the virtuous maid, the faithful wife. Her ghost went to Mrs. Westland's powder ball, and looked very beautiful.

PART SECOND

CHAPTER I

A RAILWAY SETTLEMENT

JAMALPUR is the headquarters of the E. I. Railway. This in itself is not a startling statement. The wonder begins with the exploration of Jamalpur, which is a station entirely made by, and devoted to, the use of those untiring servants of the public, the railway folk. They have towns of their own at Toondla and Assensole, a sun-dried sanitarium at Bandikui; and Howrah, Ajmir, Allahabad, Lahore and Pindi know their colonies. But Jamalpur is unadulteratedly "Railway," and he who has nothing to do with the E. I. Railway in some shape or another feels a stranger and an "interloper." Running always east and southerly, the train carries him from the torments of the northwest into the wet, woolly warmth of Bengal, where may be found the hot-house heat that has ruined the temper of the good people of Calcutta. Here the land is fat and greasy with good living, and the wealth of the bodies of innumerable dead things; and here—just above Mokameh —may be seen fields stretching, without stick, stone or bush to break the view, from the railway line to the horizon.

Up-country innocents must look at the map to learn that Jamalpur is near the top left-hand corner of the big loop that the E. I. R. throws out round Bhagalpur and part of the Bara-Banki districts.

Northward of Jamalpur, as near as may be, lies the Ganges and Tirhoot, and eastward an offshoot of the volcanic Rajmehal range blocks the view.

A station which has neither Judge, Commissioner, Deputy or 'Stunt, which is devoid of law courts, ticca-gharries, District Superintendents of Police, and many other evidences of an overcultured civilization, is a curiosity. "We administer ourselves," says Jamalpur, proudly, "or we did—till we had lokil sluff brought in—and now the racketmarker administers us." This is a solemn fact. The station, which had its beginnings thirty odd years ago, used, till comparatively recent times, to control its own roads, sewage, conservancy, and the like. But, with the introduction of local self-government, it was ordained that the "inestimable boon" should be extended to a place made by, and maintained for, Europeans, and a brand new municipality was created and nominated according to the many rules of the game. In the skirmish that ensued, the club racket-marker fought his way to the front, secured a place on a board largely composed of Babus, and since that day Jamalpur's views on "local sluff" have not been fit for publication. To understand the magnitude of the insult, one must study the city— for station, in the strict sense of the word, it is not. Crotons, palms, mangoes, *mellingtonias,* teak, and bamboos adorn it, and the *poinsetta* and *bougainvillea,* the railway creeper and the *bignoniavenusta* make it gay with many colors. It is laid out with military precision on the right-hand side of the line going down to Calcutta—to each house its just share of garden and green *jilmil,* its red *surki* path, its growth of trees, and its neat little wicket gate. Its general aspect, in spite of the Dutch formality, is that of an English village, such a thing as enterprising stage-managers put on the theatres at home. The hills have thrown a protecting arm round nearly three sides of it, and on the fourth it is bounded by what are locally known as the "shed;" in other words, the station, offices, and workshops of the company. The E. I. R. only exists for outsiders. Its servants speak of it reverently, angrily, despitefully, or enthusiastically as "The Company;" and they never omit the big, big C. Men must have treated the Honorable East India Company in something the same fashion ages ago. "The Company" in Jamalpur is Lord Dufferin, all the Members of Council, the Body-Guard, Sir Frederick Roberts, Mr. Westland, whose name is at the bottom of the currency notes, the Oriental Life Assurance Company, and the Bengal Government all rolled into one. At first, when a stranger enters this life, he is inclined to scoff and ask, in his ignorance: "*What* is this Company that you talk so much about?" Later on, he ceases to scoff, and his mouth opens slowly; for the Company is a "big" thing—almost big enough to satisfy an American.

Ere beginning to describe its doings, let it be written, and repeated several times hereafter, that the E. I. R. passenger carriages, and especially the second-class, are just now—horrid, being filthy and unwashen, dirty to look at, and dirty to live in. Having cast this small stone, we will examine Jamalpur. When it was laid out, in or before the Mutiny year, its designers allowed room for growth, and made the houses of one general design—some of brick, some of stone, some three, four, and six-roomed, some single men's barracks and some two-storied—all for the use of the *employees*. King's Road, Prince's Road, Queen's Road, and Victoria Road —Jamalpur is loyal—cut the breadth of the station; and Albert Road, Church Street, and Steam Road the length of it. Neither on these roads or on any of the cool-shaded smaller ones is anything unclean or unsightly to be found. There is a dreary *bustee* in the neighborhood which is said to make the most of any cholera that may be going, but Jamalpur itself is specklessly and spotlessly neat. From St. Mary's Church to the railway station, and from the buildings where they print daily about half a lakh of tickets to the ringing, roaring, rattling workshops, everything has the air of having been cleaned up at ten that very morning and put under a glass case. Also there is a holy calm about the roads—totally unlike anything in an English manufacturing town. Wheeled conveyances are few, because every man's bungalow is close to his work, and when the day has begun and the offices of the "Loco." and "Traffic" have soaked up their thousands of natives and hundreds of Europeans, you shall pass under the dappled shadows of the teak trees, hearing nothing louder than the croon of some bearer playing with a child in the veranda or the faint tinkle of a piano. This is pleasant, and produces an impression of Watteau-like refinement tempered with Arcadian simplicity. The dry, anguished howl of the "buzzer," the big steam-whistle, breaks the hush, and all Jamalpur is alive with the tramping of tiffin-seeking feet. The Company gives one hour for meals between eleven and twelve. On the stroke of noon there is another rush back to the works or the offices, and Jamalpur sleeps through the afternoon till four or half-past, and then rouses for tennis at the institute.

It is a quiet, restful place to live or die in, but not great for enterprise. Tropical or semi-tropical cities are never remarkable for excessive energy or activity. Nor do the inhabitants arrive at fortune made by the exertion of the persons possessing it. Fortunes are made in such places, but by the dull continuous labor of inferiors and natives for some supervisor or director usually foreign.

In the hot weather it splashes in the swimming bath, or reads, for it has a library of several thousand books. One of the most flourishing lodges in the Bengal jurisdiction—"St. George in the East"—lives at Jamalpur, and meets twice a month. Its members point out with justifiable pride that all the fittings were made by their own hands; and the lodge in its accoutrements and the energy of the craftsmen can compare with any in India. But the institute seems to be the central gathering place, and its half-dozen tennis-courts and neatly-laid-out grounds seem to be always full. Here, if a stranger could judge, the greater part of the flirtation of Jamalpur is carried out, and here the dashing apprentice—the apprentices are the liveliest of all—learns that there are problems harder than any he studies at the night school, and that the heart of a maiden is more inscrutable than the

mechanism of a locomotive. On Tuesdays and Fridays, as a printed notification witnesseth, the volunteers parade. A and B Companies, one hundred and fifty strong in all, of the E. I. R. Volunteers, are stationed here with the band. Their uniform, grey with red facings, is not lovely, but they know how to shoot and drill. They have to. The "Company" makes it a condition of service that a man must be a volunteer; and volunteer in something more than name he must be, or some one will ask the reason why. Seeing that there are no regulars between Howrah and Dinapore, the "Company" does well in exacting this toll. Some of the old soldiers are wearied of drill, some of the youngsters don't like it, but—the way they entrain and detrain is worth seeing. They are as mobile a corps as can be desired, and perhaps ten or twelve years hence the Government may possibly be led to take a real interest in them and spend a few thousand rupees in providing them with real soldiers' kits—not uniform and rifle merely. Their ranks include all sorts and conditions of men—heads of the "loco." and "traffic," the "Company" is no great respecter of rank—clerks in the "audit," boys from mercantile firms at home, fighting with the intricacies of time, fare and freight tables; guards who have grown grey in the service of the Company; mail and passenger drivers with nerves of cast iron, who can shoot through a long afternoon without losing temper or flurrying; light-built East Indians; Tyne-side men, slow of speech and uncommonly strong in the arm; lathy apprentices who have not yet "filled out;" fitters, turners, foremen, full assistant and sub-assistant station-masters, and a host of others. In the hands of the younger men the regulation Martini-Henri naturally goes off the line occasionally on a *shikar* expedition.

There is a twelve-hundred yards' range running down one side of the station, and the condition of the grass by the firing butts tells its own tale. Scattered in the ranks of the volunteers are a fair number of old soldiers, for the Company has a weakness for recruiting from the army for its guards who may, in time, become station-masters. A good man from the army, with his papers all correct and certificates from his commanding officer, may, after depositing twenty pounds to pay his home passage, in the event of his services being dispensed with, enter the Company's service on something less than one hundred rupees a month and rise in time to four hundred as a station-master. A railway bungalow—and they are as substantially built as the engines—cannot cost him more than one-ninth of the pay of his grade, and the Provident Fund provides for his latter end.

Think for a moment of the number of men that a line running from Howrah to Delhi must use, and you will realize what an enormous amount of patronage the Company holds in its hands. Naturally a father who has worked for the line expects the line to do something for the son; and the line is not backward in meeting his wishes where possible. The sons of old servants may be taken on at fifteen years of age, or thereabouts, as apprentices in the "shops," receiving twenty rupees in the first and fifty in the last year of the indentures.

Then they come on the books as full "men" on perhaps Rs. 65 a month, and the road is open to them in many ways. They may become foremen of departments on Rs. 500 a month, or drivers earning with overtime Rs. 370; or if they have been brought into the audit or the traffic, they may control innumerable Babus and draw several hundreds of rupees monthly; or, at eighteen or nineteen, they may be ticket-collectors, working up to the grade of guard, etc. Every rank of the huge, human hive has a desire to see its sons placed properly, and the native workmen, about three thousand, in the locomotive department only, are, said one man, "making a family affair of it altogether. You see all those men turning brass and looking after the machinery? They've all got relatives, and a lot of 'em own land out Monghyr-way close to us. They bring on their sons as soon as they are old enough to do anything, and the Company rather encourages it. You see the father is in a way responsible for his son, and he'll teach him all he knows, and in that way the Company has a hold on them all. You've no notion how sharp a native is when he's working on his own hook. All the district round here, right up to Monghyr, is more or less dependent on the railway."

The Babus in the traffic department, in the stores, issue department, in all the departments where men sit through the long, long Indian day among ledgers, and check and pencil and deal in figures and items and rupees, may be counted by hundreds. Imagine the struggle among them to locate their sons in comfortable cane-bottomed chairs, in front of a big pewter inkstand and stacks of paper! The Babus make beautiful accountants, and if we could only see it, a merciful Providence has made the Babu for figures and detail. Without him on the Bengal side, the dividends of any company would be eaten up by the expenses of English or country-bred clerks. The Babu is a great man, and, to respect him, you must see five score or so of him in a room a hundred yards long bending over ledgers, ledgers, and yet more ledgers—silent as the Sphinx and busy as a bee. He is the lubricant of the great machinery of the Company whose ways and works cannot be dealt with in a single scrawl.

CHAPTER II

THE MIGHTY SHOPS

A STUDY of this Republic of Jamalpur is not easy. The railway folk, like the army and civilian castes, have their own language and life, which an outsider cannot hope to understand. For instance, when Jamalpur refers to itself as being "on the long siding," a lengthy explanation is necessary before the visitor grasps the fact that the whole of the two hundred and thirty odd miles of the loop from Luckeeserai to Kanu-Junction via Bhagalpur is thus contemptuously treated. Jamalpur insists that it is out of the world, and makes this an excuse for being proud of itself and all its institutions. But in one thing it is badly, disgracefully provided. At a moderate estimate there must be about two hundred Europeans with their families in this place. They can, and do, get their small supplies from Calcutta, but they are dependent on the tender

mercies of the bazar for their meat, which seems to be hawked from door to door. Also, there is a Raja who owns or has an interest in the land on which the station stands, and he is averse to cow-killing. For these reasons, Jamalpur is not too well supplied with good meat, and what it wants is a decent meat-market with cleanly controlled slaughtering arrangements. The "Company," who gives grants to the schools and builds the institute and throws the shadow of its protection all over the place, might help this scheme forward.

The heart of Jamalpur is the "shops," and here a visitor will see more things in an hour than he can understand in a year. Steam Street very appropriately leads to the forty or fifty acres that the "shops" cover, and to the busy silence of the loco. superintendent's office, where a man must put down his name and his business on a slip of paper before he can penetrate into the Temple of Vulcan. About three thousand five hundred men are in the "shops," and, ten minutes after the day's work has begun, the assistant superintendent knows exactly how many are "in." The heads of departments—silent, heavy-handed men, captains of five hundred or more—have their names fairly printed on a board which is exactly like a pool-marker. They "star a life" when they come in, and their few names alone represent salaries to the extent of six thousand a month. They are men worth hearing deferentially. They hail from Manchester and the Clyde, and the great ironworks of the North, and pleasant as cold water in a thirsty land is it to hear again the full Northumbrian burr or the long-drawn Yorkshire "aye."

Under their great gravity of demeanor —a man who is in charge of a few lakhs' worth of plant cannot afford to be riotously mirthful—lurks melody and humor. They can sing like north-countrymen, and in their hours of ease go back to the speech of the iron countries they have left behind, when "Ab o' th' yate" and all "Ben Briarly's" shrewd wit shakes the warm air of Bengal with deep-chested laughter. Hear "Ruglan' Toon," with a chorus as true as the fall of trip-hammers, and fancy that you are back again in the smoky, rattling, ringing North.

But this is the "unofficial" side. Let us go forward through the gates under the mango trees, and set foot at once in sheds which have as little to do with mangoes as a locomotive with Lakshmi. The "buzzer" howls, for it is nearly tiffin time. There is a rush from every quarter of the shops, a cloud of flying natives, and a procession of more sedately pacing Englishmen, and in three short minutes you are left absolutely alone among arrested wheels and belts, pulleys, cranks, and cranes—in a silence only broken by the soft sigh of a far-away steam-valve or the cooing of pigeons. You are, by favor freely granted, at liberty to wander anywhere you please through the deserted works. Walk into a huge, brick-built, tin-roofed stable, capable of holding twenty-four locomotives under treatment, and see what must be done to the Iron Horse once in every three years if he is to do his work well. On reflection, Iron Horse is wrong. An engine is a she—as distinctly feminine as a ship or a mine. Here stands the *Echo*, her wheels off, resting on blocks, her underside machinery taken out, and her side scrawled with mysterious hieroglyphics in chalk. An enormous green-painted iron marness-rack bears her piston and eccentric rods, and a neatly-painted board shows that such and such Englishmen are the fitter, assistant and apprentice engaged in editing the *Echo*. An engine seen from the platform and an engine viewed from underneath are two very different things. The one is as unimpressive as a *ticca-gharri;* the other as imposing as a man-of-war in the yard.

In this manner is an engine treated for navicular, laminitis, backsinew, or whatever it is that engines most suffer from. No 607, we will say, goes wrong at Dinapore, Assensole, Buxar, or whatever it may be, after three years' work. The place she came from is stencilled on the boiler, and the foreman examines her. Then he fills in a hospital sheet, which bears one hundred and eighty printed heads under which an engine can come into the shops. No. 607 needs repair in only one hundred and eighteen particulars, ranging from mud-hole flanges and blower-cocks to lead-plugs, and platform brackets which have shaken loose. This certificate the foreman signs, and it is framed near the engine for the benefit of the three Europeans and the eight or nine natives who have to mend No. 607. To the ignorant the superhuman wisdom of the examiner seems only equalled by the audacity of the two men and the boy who are to undertake what is frivolously called the "job." No. 607 is in a sorely mangled condition, but 403 is much worse. She is reduced to a shell—is a very lean woman of an engine, bearing only her funnel, the iron frame and the saddle that supports the boiler. All the pretty little instruction primers say that an engine takes to pieces like a watch, but it is not good to see an engine so treated. Better had a man believe that "they light the fire under the water, y'know, and that makes the water steam, and that gets into those piston things, and that drives the train."

Four-and-twenty engines in every stage of decomposition stand in one huge shop. A traveling crane runs overhead, and the men have hauled up one end of a bright vermillion loco. The effect is the silence of a scornful stare— just such a look as a colonel's portly wife gives through her *pince-nez* at the audacious subaltern. Engines are the "liveliest" things that man ever made. They glare through their spectacle-plates, they tilt their noses contemptuously, and when their insides are gone they adorn themselves with red lead and leer like decayed beauties; and in the Jamalpur works there is no escape from them. The shops can hold fifty without pressure, and on occasion as many again. Everywhere there are engines, and everywhere brass domes lie about on the ground like huge helmets in a pantomime. The silence is the weirdest touch of all. Some sprightly soul—an apprentice be sure—has daubed in red lead on the end of an iron tool box a caricature of some friend who is evidently a riveter. The picture has all the interest of an Egyptian cartouche, for it shows that men have been here, and that the engines do not have it all their own way.

And so, out in the open, away from the three great sheds between and under

more engines, till we strike a wilderness of lines all converging to one turn-table. Here be elephant stalls ranged round a half-circle, and in each stall stands one engine, and each engine stares at the turn-table. A stolid and disconcerting company is this ring of eyed monsters; 324, 432, and 8 are shining like Bon Marche toys. They are ready for their turn of duty, and are as spruce as hansoms. Lacquered chocolate, picked out with black, red and white, is their dress, and delicate lemon graces the ceilings of the cabs. The driver should be a gentleman in evening dress with white kid gloves, and there should be gold-headed champagne bottles in the spick and span tenders. Huckleberry Finn says of a timber raft: "It amounted to something being captain of that raft." Thrice enviable is the man who, drawing Rs. 226 a month, is allowed to make Rs. 150 overtime out of locos. Nos. 324, 432 or 8. Fifty yards beyond this gorgeous trinity are ten to twelve engines who have put in to Jamalpur to bait. They are alive, their fires are lighted, and they are swearing and purring and growling one at another as they stand alone—all alone. Here is evidently one of the newest type—No. 25, a giant who has just brought the mail in and waits to be cleaned up preparatory to going out afresh.

The tiffin hour has ended. The buzzer blows, and with a roar, a rattle and a clang the shops take up their toil. The hubbub that followed on the prince's kiss to the sleeping beauty was not so loud or sudden. Experience, with a footrule in his pocket, authority in his port, and a merry twinkle in his eye, comes up and catches Ignorance walking gingerly round No. 25. "That's one of the best we have," says Experience, "a four-wheeled coupled bogie they call her. She's by Dobbs. She's done her hundred and fifty miles to-day; and she'll run in to Rampore Haut this afternoon; then she'll rest a day and be cleaned up. Roughly, she does her three hundred miles in the four-and-twenty hours. She's a beauty. She's out from home, but we can build our engines—all except the wheels. We're building ten locos. now, and we've got a dozen boilers ready if you care to look at them. How long does a loco. last? That's just as may be. She will do as much as her driver lets her. Some men play the mischief with a loco. and some handle 'em properly. Our drivers prefer Hawthorne's old four-wheel coupled engines because they give the least bother. There is one in that shed, and it's a good 'un to travel. But 80,000 miles generally sees the gloss off an engine, and she goes into the shops to be overhauled and re-fitted and re-planed, and a lot of things that you wouldn't understand if I told you about them. No. 1, the first loco. on the line, is running still, but very little of the original engine must be left by this time. That one there, called the *Fawn*, came out in the Mutiny year. She's by Slaughter and Grunning, and she's built for speed in front of a light load. French-looking sort of thing, isn't she? That's because her cylinders are on a tilt. We used her for the mail once, but the mail has grown heavier and heavier, and now we use six-wheel coupled eighteen inch, inside cylinder, 45-ton locos. to shift thousand-ton trains. *No!* All locos. aren't alike. It

isn't merely pulling a lever. The company likes its drivers to know their locos., and a man will keep his Hawthorne for two or three years. The more mileage he gets out of her before she has to be overhauled the better man he is. It pays to let a man have his fancy engine. The Company knows that. Other lines don't. There's the ——. They run the life out of the men and the locos. together. They'll run an engine into the cleaning shed wherever it may be, and then another driver jumps on and runs her back again, and so on till they've run the inside out of her. The drivers don't care. 'Tisn't *their* engine? The other man always said to have damaged her, and so the —— get their stock into a sweet state. 'Come in with a slide bar about red hot, and everything else to match. A man must take an interest in his loco., and that means she must belong to him. Some locos. won't do anything, even if you coax and humor them. I don't *think* there are any unlucky ones now, but some years ago No. 31 wasn't popular. The drivers went sick or took leave when they were told off for her. She killed her driver on the Jubbulpore line, she left the rails at Kajra, she did something or other at Rampur Haunt, and Lord knows what she didn't do or try to do in other places! All the drivers fought shy of her, and in the end she disappeared. They said she was condemned, but I shouldn't wonder if the Company changed her number quietly, and changed the luck at the same time. You see, the Government Inspector comes and looks at our stock now and again, and when an engine's condemned he puts his dhobi mark on her, and she's broken up. Well, No. 31 was condemned, but there was a whisper that they only shifted her number, and ran her out again. When the drivers didn't know there were no accidents. I don't think we've got an unlucky one running now. Some are different from others, but there are no man-eaters. Yes, a driver of the mail *is* somebody. He can make Rs. 370 a month if he's a covenanted man. We get a lot of our drivers in the country, and we don't import from England as much as we did. Stands to reason that, now there's more competition both among lines and in the labor market, the Company can't afford to be as generous as it used to be. It doesn't trap a man though. It's this way with the drivers. A native driver gets about Rs. 20 a month, and in his way he's supposed to be good enough for branch work and shunting and such. Well, an English driver'll get from Rs. 80 to Rs. 220, and overtime. The English driver knows what the native gets, and in time they tell the driver that the native'll improve. The driver has that to think of. You see? That's competition! A driver, one day with another, does his hundred miles a day. Say a man leaves Buxar at 2 p. m. he gets to Allahabad at 7 p. m. That's 163 miles. He rests at Allahabad till 8:20 next morning, when he goes back to Buxar, and rests till about 2 p. m. the next day. Then goes to Mokameh, reaches Mokameh at 7 p. m., stays till 4 next morning, and gets back to Buxar at 9:20 a. m. Then it all begins over again. He has got about three thousand pounds' worth of the Company's property to look after under his own hand, and the Lord knows how much value in the train

behind him. Oh, he's got quite enough to think of when he's on his engine."

Experience returns to the engine-sheds, now full of clamor, and enlarges on the beauties of sick locomotives. The fitters and the assistants and the apprentices are hammering and punching and gauging, and otherwise technically disporting themselves round their enormous patients, and their language, as caught in snatches, is beautifully unintelligible.

But one flying sentence goes straight to the heart. It is the cry of humanity over the task of life, done into unrefined English. An apprentice, grimed to his eyebrows, his cloth cap well on the back of his curly head and his hands deep in his pockets, is sitting on the edge of a tool-box ruefully regarding the very much disorganized engine whose slave is he. A handsome boy, this apprentice, and well made. He whistles softly between his teeth and his brow puckers. Then he addresses the engine, saying, half in expostulation and half in despair: "Oh, you condemned old female dog!" He puts the sentence more crisply—much more crisply—and ignorance chuckles sympathetically.

Ignorance also is puzzled over these engines.

CHAPTER III

AT VULCAN'S FORGE

IN the wilderness of the railway shops—and machinery that planes and shaves, and bevels and stamps, and punches and hoists and nips—the first idea that occurs to an outsider, when he has seen the men who people the place, is that it must be the birthplace of inventions—a pasture-ground of fat patents. If a writing-man, who plays with shadows and dresses dolls that others may laugh at their antics, draws help and comfort and new methods of working old ideas from the stored shelves of a library, how, in the name of Commonsense, his god, can a doing-man, whose mind is set upon things that snatch a few moments from flying Time or put power into weak hands, refrain from going forward and adding new inventions to the hundreds among which he daily moves?

Appealed to on this subject, Experience, who had served the E. I. R. loyally for many years, held his peace. "We don't go in much for patents; but," he added, with a praiseworthy attempt to turn the conversation, "we can build you any mortal thing you like. We've got the *Bradford Leslie* for the Sahibgunge ferry. Come and see the brass-work for her bows. It's in the casting-shed."

It would have been cruel to have pressed Experience further, and Ignorance to foredate matters a little, went about to discover why Experience shied off this question, and why the men of Jamalpur had not each and all invented and patented something. He won his information in the end, but did not come from Jamalpur. *That* must be clearly understood. It was found anywhere you please between Howrah and Hoti Mardan; and here it is that all the world may admire a prudent and far-sighted Board of Directors. Once upon a time, as every one in the profession knows, two men invented the D. and O. sleeper—cast iron, of five pieces,

very serviceable. The men were in the Company's employ and their masters said: "Your brains are ours. Hand us over those sleepers." Being of pay and position, D. and O. made some sort of resistance and got a royalty or a bonus. At any rate, the Company had to pay for its sleepers. But thereafter, and the condition exists to this day, they caused it to be written in each servant's covenant, that if by chance he invented aught, his invention was to belong to the Company. Providence has mercifully arranged that no man or syndicate of men can buy the "holy spirit of man" outright without suffering in some way or another just as much as the purchase. America fully, and Germany in part, recognizes this law. The E. I. Railway's breach of it is thoroughly English. They say, or it is said of them, that they say: "We are afraid of our men, who belong to us waking and sleeping, wasting their time on trying to invent."

It is wholly impossible, then, for men of mechanical experience and large sympathies to check the mere patent-hunter and bring forward the man with an idea? Is there no supervision in the "shops," or have the men who play tennis and billiards at the institute not a minute which they can rightly call their very own? Would it ruin the richest Company in India to lend their model shop and their lathes to half-a-dozen, or, for the matter of that, half-a-hundred, abortive experiments? A Massachusetts organ factory, a Racine buggy shop, an Oregon lumber yard would laugh at the notion. An American toymaker might swindle an *employee* after the invention, but he would in his own interests help the man to "see what comes of the thing." Surely a wealthy, a powerful and, as all Jamalpur bears witness, a considerate Company might cut that clause out of the covenant and await the issue. There would be quite enough jealousy between man and man, grade and grade, to keep down all the keenest souls; and with due respect to the steam-hammer and the rolling-mill, we have not yet made machinery perfect. The "shops" are not likely to spawn unmanageable Stephensons or grasping Brunels; but in the minor turns of mechanical thought that find concrete expressions in links, axle-boxes, joint-packings, valves and spring-stirrups something might—something would—be done were the practical prohibition removed. Will a North countryman give you anything but warm hospitality for nothing? Or if you claim from him overtime service as a right, will he fall to work zealously? "Onything but t'brass," is his motto, and his ideas are his "brass."

Gentlemen in authority, if this should meet your august eyes, spare it a minute's thought, and, clearing away the floridity, get to the heart of the mistake and see if it cannot be rationally put right. Above all, remember that Jamalpur supplied no information. It was as mute as an oyster. There is no one within your jurisdiction to—ahem —"drop upon."

Let us, after this excursion into the offices, return to the shops and only ask Experience such questions as he can without disloyalty answer.

"We used once," says he, leading to the foundry, "to sell our old rails and import new ones. Even when we used

'em for roof beams and so on, we had more than we knew what to do with. Now we have got rolling-mills, and we use the rails to make tie-bars for the D. and O. sleepers and all sorts of things. We turn out five hundred D. and O. sleepers a day. Altogether, we use about seventy-five tons of our own iron a month here. Iron in Calcutta costs about five-eight a hundredweight; ours cost between three-four and three-eight, and on that item alone we save three thousand a month. Don't ask me how many miles of rails we own. There are fifteen hundred miles of line, and you can make your own calculation. All those things like babies' graves, down in that shed, are the moulds of the D. and O. sleepers. We test them by dropping three hundredweight and three hundred quarters of iron on top of them from a height of seven feet, or eleven sometimes. They don't often smash. We have a notion here that our iron is as good as the home stuff."

A sleek, white and brindled pariah thrusts himself into the conversation, His home appears to be on the warm ashes of the bolt-maker. This is a horrible machine, which chews red-hot iron bars and spits them out perfect bolts. Its manners are disgusting, and it gobbles over its food.

"Hi, Jack!" says Experience, stroking the interloper, "you've been trying to break your leg again. That's the dog of the works. At least he makes believe that the works belong to him. He'll follow any one of us about the shops as far as the gate, but never a step further. You can see he's first-class condition. The boys give him his ticket, and, one of these days, he'll try to get on to the Company's books as a regular worker. He's too clever to live." Jack heads the procession as far as the walls of the rolling-shed and then returns to his machinery room. He waddles with fatness and despises strangers. "How would you like to be hot-potted there?" says Experience, who has read and who is enthusiastic over *She*, as he points to the great furnaces whence the slag is being dragged out by hooks. "Here is the old material going into the furnace in that big iron bucket. Look at the scraps of iron. There's an old D. and O. sleeper, there's a lot of clips from a cylinder, there's a lot of snipped-up rails, there's a driving-wheel block, there's an old hook, and a sprinkling of boiler-plates and rivets." The bucket is tipped into the furnace with a thunderous roar and the slag below pours forth more quickly. "An engine," says Experience, reflectively, "can run over herself so to say. After she's broken up she is made into sleepers for the line. You'll see how she's broken up later." A few paces further on, semi-nude demons are capering over strips of glowing hot iron which are put into a mill as rails and emerge as thin, shapely tie-bars. The natives wear rough sandals and some pretence of aprons, but the greater part of them is "all face." "As I said before," says Experience, "a native's cuteness when he's working on ticket is something startling. Beyond occasionally hanging on to a red-hot bar too long and so letting their pincers be drawn through the mills, these men take precious good care not to go wrong. Our machinery is fenced and guard-railed as much as possible, and these men don't get caught up by the belting. In the first place, they're careful—the father warns the son and so on—and in the second, there's nothing about 'em for the belting to catch on unless the man shoves his hand in. Oh, a native's no fool! He knows that it doesn't do to be foolish when he's dealing with a crane or a driving-wheel. You're looking at all those chopped rails? We make our iron as they blend baccy. We mix up all sorts to get the required quality. Those rails have just been chopped by this tobacco-cutter thing." Experience bends down and sets a vicious-looking, parrot-headed beam to work. There is a quiver—a snap—and a dull smash and a heavy 76-pound rail is nipped in two like a stick of barley-sugar.

Elsewhere, a bull-nosed hydraulic cutter is rail cutting as if it enjoyed the fun. In another shed stand the steam-hammers; the unemployed ones murmuring and muttering to themselves, as is the uncanny custom of all steam-souled machinery. Experience, with his hand on a long lever, makes one of the monsters perform: and though Ignorance knows that a man designed and men do continually build steam hammers, the effect is as though Experience were maddening a chained beast. The massive block slides down the guides, only to pause hungrily an inch above the anvil, or restlessly throb through a foot and a half of space, each motion being controlled by an almost imperceptible handling of the levers. "When these things are newly overhauled, you can regulate your blow to within an eighth of an inch," says Experience. "We had a foreman here once who could work 'em beautifully. He had the touch. One day a visitor, no end of a swell in a tall, white hat, came round the works, and our foreman borrowed the hat and brought the hammer down just enough to press the knap and no more. 'How wonderful!' said the visitor, putting his hand carelessly upon this lever rod here." Experience suits the action to the word and the hammer thunders on the anvil. "Well you can guess for yourself. Next minute there wasn't enough left of that tall, white hat to make a postage-stamp of. Steam-hammers aren't things to play with. Now we'll go over to the stores and see what happens to the old stock."

Experience leads the way to the Golgotha of Jamalpur. A great tripod, whence depends a pulley, chain, and hook, hangs over a circular fence, strong as an elephant stockade. Inside the stockade is a pit some ten feet deep and twelve or fourteen in diameter. The logs that shore its sides are scarred and bruised and dented and splinted in horrible fashion: even the timbers of the stockade bear the marks of manglement, and at the bottom of the pit lie two enormous iron balls, each nearly a ton's weight, and each bearing a handle. One look at the tripod and chain above and a rent cylinder below explains everything. A row of hopelessly decayed engines and tenders are the "subjects" of this grim dissecting-room. "You see," says Experience, "they hook on one of these balls to that chain, and haul it up by the winch in that fenced shed. Then they drop it on whatever is to be broken up, and—well, they dropped it upon that cylinder, and you can see for yourself what happened. Now, it has often struck me that Rider

Haggard might use this place for a sort of variety entertainment, you know. No need to put a man in the pit. Just keep him inside the stockade when the ball fell, and let him dodge the splinters. A shell would be a joke to it. We break up old cannons here. There's the breach of one of them, but some are so curious I've saved them and mounted 'em yonder. They look neat on the red gravel by that fountain—don't they?"

Whatever apparent disorder there might have been in the works, the store department is as clean as a new pin, and stupefying in its naval order. Copper plates, bar, angle, and rod iron, duplicate cranks and slide bars, the piston rods of the *Bradford Leslie* steamer, engine grease, files and hammer-heads—every conceivable article, from leather laces of beltings to head-lamps, necessary for the due and proper working of a long line, is stocked, stacked, piled, and put away in appropriate compartments. In the midst of it all, neck deep in ledgers and indent forms, stands the many-handed Babu, the steam of the engine whose power extends from Howrah to Ghaziabad.

One small set of pigeon-holes contains the bulk of the daily correspondence. It is noticeable that "Sir Bradford Leslie" has a pigeon-hole all to himself. A surreptitious grab at one paper shows that a sergeant-instructor of volunteers, four hundred miles away, has had something done to his kitchen table. And this department knows all about it? *Wah! Wah!* one can only gape vacantly. The E. I. R. is a great chief. When it cracks its whip, we stand on our hind legs, and walk round the ring backward. Jamalpur does not say this, but that is the feeling in the air.

The Company does everything, and *knows everything*. The gallant apprentice may be a wild youth with an earnest desire to go occasionally "upon the bend." But three times a week, between 7 and 8 p. m., he must attend the night-school and sit at the feet of M. Bonnaud, who teaches him mechanics and statistics so thoroughly that even the awful Government Inspector is pleased. And when there is no night-school the Company will by no means wash its hands of its men out of working-hours. No man can be violently restrained from going to the bad if he insists upon it, but in the service of the Company a man has every warning; his escapades are known, and a judiciously-arranged transfer sometimes keeps a good fellow clear of the downgrade. No one can flatter himself that in the multitude he is overlooked, or believe that between 4 p. m. and 9 a. m. he is at liberty to misdemean himself. Sooner or later, but generally sooner, his goings-on are known, and he is reminded that "Britons never shall be slaves"—to things that destroy good work as well as souls. Maybe the Company acts only in its own interest, but the result is good.

Best and prettiest of the many good and pretty things in Jamalpur is the institute of a Saturday when the Volunteer Band is playing and the tennis courts are full and the babydom of Jamalpur—fat, sturdy children—frolic round the band-stand. The people dance—but big as the institute is, it is getting too small for their dances— they act, they play billiards, they study

their newspapers, they play cards and everything else, and they flirt in a sumptuous building, and in the hot weather the gallant apprentice ducks his friend in the big swimming-bath. Decidedly the railway folk make their lives pleasant.

Let us go down southward to the big Giridih collieries and see the coal that feeds the furnace that smelts the iron that makes the sleeper that bears the loco. that pulls the carriage that holds the freight that comes from the country that is made richer by the Great Company Bahadur, the East Indian Railway.

PART THIRD

CHAPTER I

ON THE SURFACE

SOUTHWARD, always southward and easterly, runs the Calcutta Mail from Luckeeserai, till she reaches Madapur in the Sonthal Parganas. From Madapur a train, largely made up of coal-trucks, heads westward into the Hazaribah district and toward Giridih. A week would not have exhausted "Jamalpur and its environs," as the guide-books say. But since time drives and man must e'en be driven, the weird, echoing bund in the hills above Jamalpur, where the owls hoot at night and hyenas come down to laugh over the grave of "Qullem Roberts, who died from the effects of an encounter with a tiger near this place, A. D. 1864," goes undescribed. Nor is it possible to deal with Monghyr, the headquarters of the district, where one sees for the first time the age of ald Bengal in the sleepy, creepy station, built in a time-eaten fort, which runs out into the Ganges, and is full of quaint houses, with fat-legged balustrades on the roofs. Pensioners certainly, and probably a score of ghosts, live in Monghyr. All the country seems haunted. Is there not at Pir Bahar a lonely house on a bluff, the grave of a young lady, who, thirty years ago, rode her horse down the *khud* and perished? Has not Monghyr a haunted house in which tradition say skeptics have seen much more than they could account for? And is it not notorious throughout the countryside that the seven miles of road between Jamalpur and Monghyr are nightly paraded by tramping battalions of spectres, phantoms of an old-time army massacred, who but Sir W. W. Hunter knows how long ago? The common voice attests all these things, and an eerie cemetery packed with blackened, lichened, candle-extinguished tombstones persuades the listener to believe all that he hears. Bengal is second—or third is it?—in order of seniority among the Provinces, and like an old nurse, she tells many witch-tales.

But ghosts have nothing to do with collieries, and that ever-present "Company," the E. I. R., has more or less made Giridih—principally more. "Before the E. I. R. came," say the people, "we had one meal a day. Now we have two." Stomachs do not tell fibs, whatever mouths may say. That "Company," in the course of business, throws about five lakhs a year into the Hazari-bah district in the form of wages alone, and Giridih Bazar has to supply the wants of twelve thousand men, women and children. But we have now the authority of a number of high-souled and intelligent native prints that the Sahib of all grades spends his time in "sucking the blood out of the country," and "flying to England to spend his ill-gotten gains." It is curious to watch a Sahib engaged in this operation. He—but no matter. His way shall be dealt with later on.

Giridih is perfectly mad—quite insane! Geologically, the big, thick books show that the country is in the metamorphic higher grounds that rise out of the alluvial flats of Lower Bengal between the Osri and the Barakar rivers. Translated, this sentence means that you can twist your ankle on pieces of pure white, pinky and yellowish granite, slip over weather-worn sandstone, grievously cut your boots over flakes of trap, and throw hornblende pebbles at the dogs. Never was such a place for stone-throwing as Giridih. The general aspect of the country is falsely park-like, because it swells and sings in a score of grass-covered undulations, and is adorned with plantation-like *sal* jungle. There are low hills on every side, and twelve miles away bearing south the blue bulk of the holy hills of Parasnath, greatest of the Jain Tirthankars, overlooks the world. In Bengal they consider four thousand five hundred feet good enough for a Dagshai or Kasauli, and once upon a time tried to put troops on Parasnath. There was a scarcity of water, and Thomas of those days found the silence and seclusion prey upon his spirits. Since twenty years, therefore, Parasnath has been abandoned by Her Majesty's Army.

As to Giridih itself, the last few miles of train bring up the reek of the

"Black Country." Memory depends on smell. A noseless man is devoid of sentiment, just as a noseless woman, in this country, must be devoid of honor. That first breath of the coal should be the breath of the murky, clouded tract between Yeadon and Dale—or Barnsley, rough and hospitable Barnsley—or Dewsbury and Batley and the Derby Canal, on a Sunday afternoon when the wheels are still and the young men and maidens walk stolidly in pairs. Unfortunately, it is nothing more than Giridh —seven thousand miles away from home and blessed with a warm and genial sunshine, soon to turn into something very much worse. The insanity of the place is visible at the station door. A. G. B. T. cart once married a bathing-machine, and they called the child *tum-tum*. You who in flannel and Cawnpore harness drive bamboo-carts about up-country roads, remember that a Giridih *tum-tum* is painfully pushed by four men, and must be entered crawling on all-fours, head first. So strange are the ways of Bengal.

"They drive mad horses in Giridih— animals that become hysterical as soon as the dusk falls and the countryside blazes with the fires of the great coke ovens. If you expostulate tearfully, they produce another horse, a raw, red fiend whose ear has to be screwed round and round, and round and round, in a twitch before she will by any manner of means, consent to start. Also, the roads carry neat little eighteen inch trenches at their sides, admirably adapted to hold the flying wheel. Skirling about this savage land in the dark, the white population beguile the time by raptuously recounting past accidents, insisting throughout on the super-equine "steadiness" of their cattle. Deep and broad and wide is their jovial hospitality; but somebody —the Tirhoot planters for choice— ought to start a mission to teach the men of Giridih what to drive. They know how, or they would be severally and separately and many times dead, but they do not, they do not indeed, know that animals who stand on one hind leg and beckon with all the rest, or try to pikstick in harness, are not trap-horses worthy of endearing names, but things to be pole-axed. Their feelings are hurt when you say this. "Sit tight," say the men of Giridih; "we're insured! We can't be hurt."

And now with grey hairs, dry mouth, and chattering teeth to the colliers. The E. I. R. estate, bought or leased in perpetuity from the Serampore Raja, may be about four miles long and between one and two miles across. It is in two pieces, the Serampore field being separated from Karharbari (or Kurhurballi or Kabarbari) field by the property of the Bengal Coal Company. The Raneegunge Coal Association lies to the east of all other workings. So we have three companies at work on about eleven square miles of land.

There is no such thing as getting a full view of the whole place. A short walk over a grassy down gives on to an outcrop of very dirty sandstone, which in the excessive innocence of their hearts most visitors will naturally take to be the coal lying neatly on the surface. Up to this sandstone the path seems to be made of crushed sugar, so white and shiny is the quartz. Over the brow of the down comes in sight the old familiar pit-head wheel, spinning for the dear life, and the eye loses itself in a maze of pumping sheds, red-tiled, mud-walled miners' huts, dotted all over the landscape and railway lines that seem to run on every kind of gradient. There are lines that dip into valleys and disappear round the shoulders of slopes, and lines that career on the tops of rises and disappear over the brow of the slopes. Along these lines whistle and pant metre-gauge engines, some with trucks at their tail and others rattling back to the pit-bank with the absurd air of a boy late for school that an unemployed engine always assumes. There are six engines in all, and as it is easiest to walk along the lines one sees a good deal of them. They bear not altogether unfamiliar names. Here, for instance, passes the "Cockburn" whistling down a grade with thirty tons of coal at her heels; while the "Whitly" and the "Olpherts" are waiting for their complements of trucks. Now a Mr. T. F. Cockburn was superintendent of these mines nearly thirty years ago, in the days before the chord lines from Kanu to Luckeeserai was built, and all the coal was carted to the latter place: and surely Mr. Olpherts was an engineer who helped to think out a new sleeper. What may these things mean?

"Apotheosis of the manager," is the reply. "Christen the engines after the managers. You'll find Cockburn, Dunn, Whitly, Abbott, Olpherts and Saise knocking about the place. Sounds funny, doesn't it? Doesn't sound so funny, when one of these idiots does his best to derail Saise, though, by putting a line down anyhow. Look at that line! Laid out in knots—by Jove!" To the unprofessional eye the rails seem all cor-

rect; but there must be something wrong, because "one of those idiots" is asked why in the name of all he considers sacred he does not ram the ballast properly.

"What would happen if you threw an engine off the line?" "Can't say that I know exactly. You see, our business is to keep them *on*, and we do that. Here's rather a curiosity. You see that pointsman! They say he's an old mutineer, and when he relaxes he boasts of the Sahibs he has killed. He's glad enough to eat the Company's salt now." Such a withered old face was the face of the pointsman at No. 11 point! The information suggested a host of questions, and the answers were these: "You won't be able to understand till you've been down into a mine. We work our men in two ways: some by direct payment—*sirkari*—under our own hand, and some by contractors. The contractor undertakes to deliver us the coal, supplying his own men, tools and props. He's responsible for the safety of his men, and of course the Company knows and sees his work. Just fancy, among these five thousand people, what sort of effect the *khuber* of an accident would produce! It would go all through the Sonthal Parganas. We have any amount of Sonthal besides Mahomedans and Hindus of every possible caste, down to those Musahers who eat pig. They don't require much administering in the civilian sense of the word. On Sundays, as a rule, if any man has had his daughter eloped with, or anything of that kind, he generally comes up to the manager's bungalow to get the matter put straight. If a man is disabled through accident he knows that as long as he's in the hospital he gets full wages, and the Company pays for the food of any of his women-folk who come to look after him. One of course: not the whole clan. That makes our service popular with the people—poor beggars. Don't you believe that a native is a fool. You can train him to everything except responsibility. There's a rule in the workings that if there is any dangerous work, no—we haven't choke damps, I will show you when we get down—no gang must work without an Englishman to look after them. A native wouldn't be wise enough to understand what the danger was, or where it came in. Even if he did, he'd shirk the responsibility. We can't afford to risk a single life. All our output is just as much as the Company want—about a thousand tons per working day. Three hundred thousand in the year. We could turn out more? Yes —a little. Well, yes, twice as much. I won't go on, because you wouldn't believe me. There's the coal under us, and we work it at any depth from following up an outcrop down to six hundred feet. That is our deepest shaft. We have no necessity to go deeper. At home the mines are sometimes fifteen hundred feet down. Well, the thickness of this coal here varies from anything you please to anything you please. There's enough of it to last your time and one or two hundred years longer. Perhaps even longer than that. Look at that stuff. That's big coal from the pit."

It was aristocratic-looking coal, just like the picked lumps that are stacked in baskets of coal agencies at home with the printed legend atop "only 23s a ton." But there was no picking in this case. The great piled banks were all "equal to samples," and beyond them lay piles of small, broken, "smithy" coal. "The Company doesn't sell to the public. This small, broken coal is an exception. That is sold, but the big stuff is for the engines and the shops. It doesn't cost much to get out, as you say; but our men can earn as much as twelve rupees a month. Very often when they've earned enough to go on with they retire from the concern till they've spent their money and then come on again. It's piecework and they are improvident. If some of them only lived like other natives they would have enough to buy land and cows with. When there's a press of work they make a good deal by overtime, but they don't seem to keep it. You should see Giridih Bazar on a Sunday if you want to know where the money goes. About ten thousand rupees change hands once a week there. If you want to get at the number of people who are indirectly dependent or profit by the E. I. R. you'll have to conduct a census of your own. After Sunday is over the men generally lie off on Monday and take it easy on Tuesday. Then they work hard for the next four days and make it up. Of course there's nothing in the wide world to prevent a man from resigning and going away to wherever he came from—behind those hills if he's a Sonthal. He loses his employment, that's all. And they have their own point of honor. A man hates to be told by his friends that he has been guilty of *nimakharami*. And now we'll go to breakfast. You shall be 'pitted' tomorrow to any depth you like."

CHAPTER II

IN THE DEPTHS

"PITTED to any extent you please." The only difficulty was for Joseph to choose his pit. Giridih was full of them. There was an arch in the side of a little hill, a blackened brick arch leading into thick night.. A stationary engine was hauling a procession of coal-laden trucks—"tubs" is the technical word—out of its depths. The tubs were neither pretty nor clean. "We are going down in those when they are emptied. Put on your helmet, and *keep* it on and keep your head down." The trucks were unloaded into the wagons of the metre-gauge colliery line in this wise. Drawn out by the engine along the line, they were pulled on to a platform of smooth iron, dexterously swung round by black demons in attendance, and slid on to what is technically termed a "tippler." This is a most crafty arrangement, partaking of the nature of a drop and a safety-stirrup. The tub goes forward until it is brought up by the curved ends of the metals it travels on, and sticks in a sort of gigantic stirrup. Then, gravely and solemnly, it overbalances itself, turns through half a circle, and shoots its load into the big truck below. Some of the "tipplers" are fixed on traveling platforms and can be moved down the whole length of a waiting coal-train. The Ratel—is it not?—is the eccentric beast in the Zoo who runs' round his cage and turns head-over-heels at a given place. These absurd tubs are Ratels, and the gravity of their self-arranged somersaults is very comic. But there is nothing mirth-provoking in going down a coal-mine—even though it be only a shallow incline running to one hundred and forty feet vertical below the earth. "Get into the tub and lie down. Hang it, no! This is not a railway carriage: you can't see the country out of the windows. *Lie down* in the dust and don't lift your head. Let her go!"

The tubs strain on the wire rope and slide down fourteen hundred feet of incline, at first through a chastened gloom, and then through darkness. An absurd sentence from a trial report rings in the head: "About this time prisoner expressed a desire for the consolations of religion." A hand with a reeking flare-lamp hangs over the edge of the tub, and there is a glimpse of a blackened *solah topee* near it, for those accustomed to the pits have a merry trick of going down sitting or crouching on the coupling of the rear tub. The noise is deafening, and the roof is very close indeed. The tubs bump, and the occupant crouches lovingly in the coal dust. What would happen if the train went off the line? The desire for the "consolations of religion" grows keener and keener as the air grows closer and closer. The tubs stop in darkness spangled, not lifted, by the light of the flare-lamps which many black devils carry. Underneath and on both sides there is the greasy blackness of the coal, and, above, a roof of grey sandstone, smooth as the flow of a river at evening. "Now, remember that if you don't keep your *topee* on, you'll get your head broken, because you will forget to stoop. If you hear any tubs coming up behind you step off to one side. There's a tramway under your feet, and be careful not to trip over it."

The miner has a gait as peculiarly his own as Tommy's measured paces or the blue jacket's roll. Big men who slouch in the light of day become almost things of beauty underground. Their foot is on their native heather; and the slouch is a very necessary act of homage to the great earth, which if a man observe not, he shall without doubt have his *solah topee*—bless the man who invented pith hats!—grievously cut and dented, and himself dowered with an aching head.

The road turns and winds and the roof becomes lower, but those accursed tubs still rattle by on the tramways. The roof throws back their noises, and when all the place is full of a grumbling and a growling, how under earth is one to know whence danger will turn up next? Also, the air is choking, and brings about, to the unacclimatized, a singing in the ears, a hotness of the eyeballs, and a jumping of the heart. "That's because the pressure here is different from the pressure up above. It'll wear off in a minute. *We* don't notice it. Wait till you get down a four-hundred-foot pit. *Then* your ears will begin to sing, if you like." Most people know the One Night of each hot weather—that still, clouded night just before the rain breaks, when there seems to be no more breathable air under the bowl of the pitiless skies, and all the weight of the silent, dark house lies on the chest of the sleep-hunter. This is the feeling in a coal-mine—only more so—much more so, for the darkness is the "gross darkness of the inner sepulchre." It is hard to see which is the black coal and

which the passage driven through it. From far away, down the side galleries, come the regular beat of the pick—thick and muffled as the beat of the laboring heart. "Six men to a gang, and they aren't allowed to work alone. They make six-foot drives through the coal—two and sometimes three men working together. The rest clear away the stuff and load it into the tubs. We have no props in this gallery because we have a roof as good as a ceiling. The coal lies under the sandstone here. It's beautiful sandstone." It *was* beautiful sandstone—as hard as a billiard table and devoid of any nasty little bumps and jags which cut into the hat.

There was a roaring down one road—the roaring of infernal fires. This is not a pleasant thing to hear in the dark. It is too suggestive. "That's our ventilating shaft. Can't you feel the air getting brisker? Come and look."

Imagine a great iron-bound crate of burning coal, hanging over a gulf of darkness faintly showing the brickwork of the base of a chimney. "We're at the bottom of the shaft. That fire makes a draught that sucks up the foul air from the bottom of the pit. There's another down-draw shaft in another part of the mine where the clean air comes in. We aren't going to set the mines on fire. There's an earth and *kutcha* brick floor at the bottom of the pit; the crate hangs over. It isn't so deep as you think." Then a devil—a naked devil—came in with a pitchfork and fed the spouting flames. This was perfectly in keeping with the landscape, but it was not pretty. "That's only a little shaft. We've got one, an oval, eighteen feet by twelve, and four hundred and fifty feet deep. They aren't sunk like wells. Our sandstones are stronger than any bricks. We brick through the twenty feet of surface soil, but we can sink straight through the sandstone, knowing that the sinkings will stand. Now we'll go to the place where they are taking out the coal."

More trucks, more muffled noises, more darkness made visible, and more devils—male and female—coming out of darkness and vanishing. Then a picture to be remembered. A great Hall of Eblis, twenty feet from inky-black floor to grey roof, upheld by huge pillars of shining coal and filled with flitting and passing devils. On a shattered pillar near the roof stood a naked man, his flesh olive-colored in the light of the lamps, hewing down a mass of coal that still clove to the roof. Behind him was the wall of darkness and when the lamps shifted he disappeared like a ghost. The devils were shouting directions, and the man howled in reply, resting on his pick and wiping the sweat from his brow. When he smote the coal crushed and slid and rumbled from the darkness into the darkness, and the devils cried *shabash!* The man stood erect like a bronze statue, he twisted and bent himself like a Japanese grotesque, and anon threw himself on his side after the manner of the dying gradiator. Then spoke the still small voice of fact: "A first-class workman if he would only stick to it. But as soon as he makes a little money he lies off and spends it. That's the last of a pillar that we've knocked out. See here. These pillars of coal are square, about thirty feet each way. As you can see, we make the pillar first by cutting out all the coal between.

Then we drive a square tunnel, about seven feet wide, through and across the pillar, propping it with baulks. There's one fresh cut."

Two tunnels crossing at right angles had been driven through a pillar which in its under-cut condition seemed like the rough draft of a statue for an elephant. "When the pillar stands only on four legs we chip away one leg at a time from a square to an hour-glass shape, and then either the whole of the pillar crashes down from the roof or else a quarter or a half. If the coal lies against the sandstones it carries away clear, but in some places it brings down stone and rubbish with it. The chipped-away legs of the pillars are called stooks." "Who has to make the last cut that breaks a leg through?" "Oh! Englishmen of all sorts. We can't trust natives for the job unless it's very easy. The natives take kindly to the pillar work though. They are paid just as much for their coal as though they had hewed it out of the solid. Of course we take very good care to see that the roof doesn't come in on us. You would never understand how and why we prop our roofs with those piles of sleepers. Anyway, you can see that we cannot take out a whole line of pillars. We work 'em *en echelon,* and those big beams you see running from floor to roof are our indicators. They show when the roof is going to give. Oh! dear no, there's no dramatic effect about it. No splash, you know. Our roofs give plenty of warning by cracking and then *baito* slowly. The parts of the work that we have cleared out and allowed to fall in are called goafs'. You're on the edge of a goaf' now. All that darkness there marks the limit of the mine. We have worked that out piece-meal, and the props are gone and the place is down. The roof of any pillar-working is tested every morning by tapping—pretty hard tapping."

"Hi yi! yi!" shout all the devils in chorus, and the Hall of Eblis is full of rolling sound. The olive man has brought down an *avalanche* of coal. "It is a sight to see the whole of one of the pillars come away. They make an awful noise. It would startle you out of your wits. Some of 'em are ninety feet square. But there's not an atom of risk."

("Not an atom of risk." Oh, genial and courteous host, when you turned up next day blacker than any sweep that ever swept, with a neat, half-inch gash on your forehead—won by cutting a "stook" and getting caught by a bounding coal-knob—how long and earnestly did you endeavor to show that "stook-cutting" was an employment as harmless and unexciting as wool-sampling?)

"If you knew about mining, you'd see that our ways are rather primitive, but they're cheap, and they're safe as houses. Doms and Bauris, Kols and Beldars don't understand refinements in mining. They'd startle an English pit where there was fire-damp. Do you know it's a solemn fact that if you drop a Davy lamp or snatch it quickly you can blow a whole English pit inside out with all the miners? Good for us that we don't know what fire-damp is here. We can use the flare-lamps."

After the first feeling of awe and wonder is worn out, a mine becomes monotonous. How could a mine be anything but monotonous. Mile after mile of blackness stretching before the eyes as far as sight will carry, which is not saying much, even when one has been some time accustomed to the lack of light. There is only the humming, palpitating darkness, the rumble of the tubs and the endless procession of galleries to arrest the attention. And one pit to the uninitiated is as like to another as two peas. Tell a miner this and he laughs—slowly and softly. To him the pits have each distinct personalities, and each must be dealt with a different way. A descent from the pit-bank, and not from the mouth of an incline, is sickening—channel-passage sickening. Over pulley-wheels, mounted on shearlegs thirty, forty, or fifty feet high, passes the wire rope that is fastened to the "cages"—the two lifts on which the empty coal tubs go down and the loaded ones come up. A cage either has wooden guides at the four corners of the shaft or grips wire guide-ropes to steady it as it is let down. An engine drives the drum on which the wire-rope hauling line is coiled.

Very curious is a pit-bank when the work is in full swing. A hammer close to the winding engine strikes one, the driver places his foot on the lever: there is a roar far down the shaft, and an iron-railed platform with the loaded tub on it flies up and settles with a clang on four catches. The tub is run out into a "tippler" and discharges itself into a coal-truck. By the time it is run back empty into the second cage, a loaded truck is made ready at the bottom of the shaft, and as the empty truck sinks the full rises.

The hammer strikes three. The "winder" by the engine pulls the lever thrice, no empty tub is put into the cage, and the speed of the rise is not so great. There springs up a miner. He is a man, if we could get through the coal dust, and on his account special precautions are taken, and woe betide the pit-men who neglect them. All these things are lovely to look at. But the actual descent is not so good. If you swing a child vehemently, the little innocent is likely to complain that he feels as though his "tummy were left in the air." Now this is the exact sensation of dropping into a pit. The hangman adjusts the white cap. That is to say, you cram your hat down and go— drop away from the day and every one you ever loved, *and* your "tummy." That comes down later. You arrive destitute of any inside, and are told for your comfort that in some of the English mines you can go down two thousand feet at the rate of sixty miles an hour. Two hundred feet at a considerably slower rate is enough—quite enough. Try it once or twice, and see what the air is like.

The return journey is said to possess an element of risk. For this reason. If the "winder" of the engine at the top stopped to think, or hunted for a flea, or got a fit, or was choked by a fly, his engine would continue to wind and wind until the cage was hauled up to the pulley-wheels thirty feet in the air, where it would have three courses open to it. It might jam, break the wire rope and fall back unbridled into the pit, or part into several pieces, or be hauled with one tremendous bound right over the pulley-wheels and come down a bundle of shattered ribs. In any case the occupant would not be in a position to describe the precise nature of the accident. But a native "winder" knows these things, and thinks of them every time the three taps come to his ears. For him "over-winding" would mean loss of post and pay. Therefore he does not overwind. He generally has a keen rivalry with a fellow-winder at another pit-bank, and lays himself out to see if he cannot bring more tons of coal to the bank than his *bhai*.

CHAPTER III

THE PERILS OF THE PITS

An engineer, who has built a bridge, can strike you nearly dead with professional facts; the captain of a seventy horse power Ganges river-steamer can, in one hour, tell legends about the Sand-heads and the James and Mary shoal sufficient to fill half a *Pioneer*, but a couple of days spent on, above, and in a coal mine yields more mixed information than two engineers and three captains. It is hopeless to pretend to understand it all.

When your host says: "Ah, such an one is a thundering good fault-reader!" you smile hazily, and by way of keeping up the conversation, adventure on the statement that fault-reading and palmistry are very popular amusements. Then men laugh consumedly, and enter into explanations.

Every one knows that coal strata, in common with women, horses, and official superiors, have "faults" caused by some colic of the earth in the days when things were settling into their places. A coal seam is suddenly sliced off as a pencil is cut through with one slanting blow of the penknife, and one-half is either pushed up or pushed down any number of feet. The miners work the seam till they come to this break-off, and then call for an expert to "read the fault." It is sometimes very hard to discover whether the sliced-off beam has gone up or down. Theoretically, the end of the broken piece should show the direction. Practically its indications are not always clear. Then a good "fault-reader," who must more than know geology, is a useful man, and is much prized, for the Giridih fields are full of faults and "dykes." Tongues of what was once molten lava thrust themselves sheer into the coal, and the disgusted miner finds that for about twenty feet on each side of the tongue all the coal has been burned away.

The head of the mine is supposed to foresee these things and ever so many more. He can tell you, without looking at the map, what is the geological formation of any thousand square miles of India; he knows as much about brickwork and the building of houses, arches, and shafts as an average P. W. D. man; he has not only to know the intestines of a pumping or winding engine, but must be able to take them to pieces with his own hands, indicate on the spot such parts as need repair, and make drawings of anything that requires renewal; he knows how to lay out and build railways with a grade of one in twenty-seven; he has to carry in his head all the signals and points between and over which his locomotive engines work; he has to be an electrician capable of controlling the appara-

tus that fires the dynamite charges in the pits, and must thoroughly understand boring operations with thousand-foot drills. Over and above this, he must know by name, at least, one thousand of the men on the works, and must fluently speak the vernaculars of the low castes. If he has Sonthali, which is more elaborate than Greek, so much the better for him. He must know how to handle men of all grades, and, while himself holding aloof, must possess sufficient grip of the men's private lives to be able to see at once the merits of a charge of attempted abduction preferred by a clucking, croaking Kol against a fluent English-speaking Brahmin. For he is literally the Light of Justice, and to him the injured husband or the wrathful father looks for redress. He must be on the spot and take all responsibility when any specially risky job is under way in the pit, and he can claim no single hour of the day or the night for his own. From eight in the morning till one in the afternoon he is coated with coal-dust and oil. From one till eight in the evening he has office work. After eight o'clock he is free to attend to anything that he may be wanted for.

This is a soberly-drawn picture of a life that *Sahibs* on the mines actually enjoy. They are spared all private socio-official worry, for the Company, in its mixture of State and private interest, is as perfectly cold-blooded and devoid of bias as any great, grinding Department of the Empire. If certain things be done, well and good. If certain things be not done the defaulter goes, and his place is filled by another. The conditions of service are graven on stone. There may be generosity: there undoubtedly is justice, but above all there is freedom within broad limits. No irrepressible shareholder cripples the executive arm with suggestions and restrictions, and no private piques turn men's blood to gall within them. Therefore men work like horses and are happy.

When he can snatch a free hour, the grimy, sweating, cardigan-jacketed, ammunition-booted pick-bearing ruffian turns into a well-kept English gentleman, who plays a good game of billiards, and has a batch of new books from England every week. The change is sudden, but in Giridih nothing is startling. It is right and natural that a man should be alternately Valentine and Orson, specially Orson. It is right and natural to drive—always behind a mad horse—away and away toward the lonely hills till the flaming coke ovens become glow-worms on the dark horizon, and in the wilderness to find a lovely English maiden teaching squat, filthy Sonthal girls how to become Christians. Nothing is strange in Giridih, and the stories of the pits, the raffle of conversation that a man picks up as he passes, are quite in keeping with the place. Thanks to the law, which enacts that an Englishman must look after the native miners, and if any be killed, he and he alone has to explain satisfactorily that the accident was not due to preventable causes, the death-roll is kept astoundingly low. In one "bad" half-year six men out of the five thousand were killed, in another four, and in another none at all. Given "butcher bills" as small as these, it is not astonishing that the men in charge

do their best to cut them down at any cost of time and sleep. As has been said before, a big accident would scare off the workers, for, in spite of the age of the mines—nearly thirty years—the hereditary pitman has not yet been evolved. But to small accidents the men are orientally apathetic. Be pleased to read of a death among the five thousand.

A gang has been ordered to cut clay for the luting of the coke furnaces. The clay is piled in a huge bank in the open sunlight above ground. A coolie hacks and hacks till he has hewn out a small cave with twenty feet of clay above him. Why should he trouble to climb up the bank and bring down the eave of the cave? It is easier to cut in. The Sirdar of the gang is watching round the shoulder of the bank. The coolie cuts lazily as he stands: Sunday is very near, and he will get gloriously drunk in Giridih Bazar with his week's earnings. He digs his own grave stroke by stroke, for he has not sense enough to see that undercut clay is dangerous. He is a Sonthal from the hills. There is a smash and a dull thud, and his grave has shut down upon him in an *avalanche* of heavy-caked clay.

The Sirdar calls to the Babu of the Ovens, and with the promptitude of his race the Babu loses his head. He runs puffily, without giving orders, anywhere, everywhere. Finally he runs to the *Sahib's* house. The *Sahib* is at the other end of the collieries. He runs back. The *Sahib* has gone home to wash. Then his indiscretion strikes him. He should have sent runners—fleet-footed boys from the coal-screening gangs. He sends them and they fly. One catches the *Sahib* just changed after his bath. "There is a man dead at such a place"—he gasps, omitting to say whether it is a surface or a pit accident. On goes the grimy pit kit, and in three minutes the *Sahib's* dogcart is flying to the place indicated.

They have dug out the Sonthal. His head is smashed in, spine and breast-bone are broken, and the gang Sirdar, bowing double, throws the blame of the accident on the poor, shapeless, battered dead. "I had warned him, but he would not listen! *Twice* I warned him! These men are witnesses."

The Babu is shaking like a jelly. "Oh, sar, I have never seen a man killed before! Look at that eye, sar! I should have sent runners. I ran everywhere. I ran to your house. You were not in. I was running for hours. It was not my fault! It was the fault of the gang Sirdar." He wrings his hands and gurgles. The best of accountants, but the poorest of coroners is he. No need to ask how the accident happened. No need to listen to the Sirdar and his "witnesses." The Sonthal had been a fool, but it was the Sirdar's business to protect him against his own folly. "Has he any people here?"

"Yes, his *rukni*, his kept-woman, and his sister's brother-in-law. His home is far-off."

The sister's brother-in-law breaks through the crowd howling for vengeance on the Sirdar. He will send for the police, he will have the price of his *bhai's* blood full tale. The windmill arms and the angry eyes fall, for the *Sahib* is making the report of the death.

"Will this Sirdar give me *pensin?* I am his wife," a woman clamors, stamping her pewter-ankled feet. "He was killed in your service. Where is his *pensin? I* am his wife." "You lie! You're his *rukni*. Keep quiet! Go! The *pensin* somes to *us*." The sister's brother-in-law is not a refined man, but the *rukni* is his match. They are silenced. The *Sahib* takes the report, and the body is borne away. Before to-morrow's sun rises the Sirdar may find himself a simple "surface-coolie," earning nine pice a day; and, in a week some Sonthal woman behind the hills may discover that she is entitled to draw monthly great wealth from the coffers of the *Sirkar*. But this will not happen if the sister's brother-in-law can prevent it. He goes off swearing at the *rukni*.

But, in the meantime, what have the rest of the dead man's gang been doing? They have, if you please, abating not one stroke, dug out all the clay, and would have it verified. They have seen their comrade die. He is dead. *Bus!* Will the Sirdar take the tale of clay? And yet, were twenty men to be crushed by their own carelessness in the pit, these impassive workers would scatter like panic-stricken horses.

But, turning from this sketch, let us set in order some of the stories of the pits. These are quaint tales. The miner-folk laugh when they tell them. In some of the mines the coal is blasted out by the dynamite which is fired by electricity from a battery on the surface. Two men place the charges, and then signal to be drawn up in the cage which hangs in the pit-eye. On one occasion two natives were entrusted with the job. They performed their parts beautifully till the end, when the vaster idiot of the two scrambled into the cage, gave signal, and was hauled up before his friend could enter.

Thirty or forty yards up the shaft all possible danger for those in the cage was over, and the charge was accordingly exploded. Then it occurred to the man in the cage that his friend stood a very good chance of being by this time riven to pieces and choked.

But the friend was wise in his generation. He had missed the cage, but found a coal-tub—one of the little iron trucks—and turning this upside down, had crawled into it. His account of the explosion has never been published. When the charge went off, his shelter was battered in so much, that men had to hack him out, for the tub had made, as it were, a tinned sardine of its occupant. He was absolutely uninjured, but his feelings were lacerated. On reaching the pit-bank his first words were: "I do not desire to go down the pit with *that* man any more." His wish had been already gratified for "that man" had fled. Later on, the story goes, when "that man" found that the guilt of murder was not at his door, he returned, and was made a surface-coolie, and his *bhai-band* jeered at him as they passed to their better-paid occupation.

Occasionally there are mild cyclones in the pits. An old working, perhaps a mile away, will collapse: a whole gallery sinking in bodily. Then the displaced air rushes through the inhabited mine, and, to quote their own expression, blows the pitmen about "like dry leaves." Few things are more amusing than the spectacle of a burly Tyne-side

foreman who, failing to dodge round a corner in time, is "put down" by the wind, sitting fashion, on a knobby lump of coal.

But most impressive of all is a tale they tell of a fire in a pit many years ago. The coal caught—light. They had to send earth and bricks down the shaft and build great dams across the galleries to choke the fire. Imagine the scene, a few hundred feet underground, with the air growing hotter and hotter each moment, and the carbonic acid gas trickling through the dams. After a time the rough dams gaped, and the gas poured in afresh, and the Englishmen went down and leeped the cracks between roof and dam-sill with anything they could get. Coolies fainted, and had to be taken away, but no one died, and behind the kutcha dams they built great masonry ones, and bested that fire; though for a long time afterward, whenever they pumped water into it, the steam would puff out from crevices in the ground above.

It is a queer life that they lead, these men of the coal-fields, and a "big" life to boot. To describe one-half of their labors would need a week at the least, and would be incomplete then. "If you want to see anything," they say, "you should go over to the Baragunda copper-mines; you should look at the Barakar ironworks; you should see our boring operations five miles away; you should see how we sink pits; you should, above all, see Giridih Bazar on a Sunday. Why, you haven't seen anything. There's no end of a Sonthal Mission hereabouts. All the little dev— dears have gone on a picnic.

Wait till they come back, and see 'em learning to learn."

Alas! one cannot wait. At the most one can but thrust an impertinent pen skin-deep into matters only properly understood by specialists.

PART FOURTH
IN AN OPIUM FACTORY

On the banks of the Ganges, forty miles below Benares as the crow flies, stands the Ghazipur Factory, an opium mint as it were, whence issue the precious cakes that are to replenish the coffers of the Indian Government. The busy season is setting in, for with April the opium comes in from districts after having run the gauntlet of the district officers of the Opium Department, who will pass it as fit for use. Then the really serious work begins under a roasting sun. The opium arrives by *challans*, regiments of one hundred jars, each holding one maund and each packed in a basket and sealed atop. The district officer submits forms—never was such a place for forms as the Ghazipur Factory—showing the quality and weight of each pot, and with the jars come a ziladar responsible for the safe carriage of the *challans*, their delivery and their virginity. If any pots are broken or tampered with an unfortunate individual called the import officer, and appointed to work like a horse from dawn till dewy eve, must examine the ziladar in charge of the *challans* and reduce his statement to writing. Fancy getting any native to explain how a *matka* has been smashed. But the perfect flower is about as valuable as silver.

Then all the pots have to be weighed, and the weights—Calcutta Mint, if you please—and the beams must be daily tested. The weight of each pot is recorded on the pot, in a book, and goodness knows where else, and every one has to sign certificates that the weighing is correct. *Nota bene.* The pots have been weighed once in the district and once in the factory. Therefore a certain number of them are taken at random and weighed afresh before they are opened. This is only the beginning of the long series of checks. All sorts of inquiries are made about light pots, and then the testing begins. Every single, serially-numbered pot has to be tested for quality. A native called the *purkhea* drives his fist into the opium, rubs and smells it, and calls out the class for the benefit of the opium examiner. A sample picked between finger and thumb is thrown into a jar, and if the opium examiner thinks the *purkhea* has said sooth, the class of the jar is marked in chalk, and everything is entered in a book. Every ten samples are put in a locked box with duplicated keys, and sent over to the laboratory for assay. With the tenth boxful—and this marks the end of the *challan* of a hundred jars—the Englishman in charge of the testing signs the test paper, and enters the name of the native tester and sends it over to the laboratory. For convenience sake, it may be as well to say that, unless distinctly stated to the contrary, every single thing in Ghazipur is locked, and every operation is conducted under more than police supervision.

In the laboratory each set of ten samples is thoroughly mixed by hand, a quarter ounce lump is then tested for starch adulteration by iodine which turns the decoction blue, and, if necessary, for gum adulteration by alcohol which makes the decoction filmy. If adulteration be shown, all the ten pots of that set are tested separately. When the sinful pot is discovered, all the opium is tested in four-pound lumps. Over and above this test, three samples of one hundred grains each are taken from the *jummakaroed* set of ten samples, dried on a steam table and then weighed for consistence. The result is written down in a ten-columned form in the assay register, and by the mean result are those ten pots paid for. This, after everything has been done in duplicate and countersigned, completes the test and assay. If a district officer has classed the opium in a glaringly wrong way, he is thus caught and reminded of his error. No one trusts any one in Ghazipur. They are always weighing, testing and assaying.

Before the opium can be used it must be "alligated" in big vats. The pots are emptied into these, and special care is taken that none of the drug sticks to the hands of the coolies. Opium has a special knack of doing this, and therefore coolies are searched at most inopportune moments. There are a good many Mahomedans in Ghazipur, and they would all like a little opium. The pots after emptying are smashed up and scraped, and heaved down the steep river bank of the factory, where they help to keep the Ganges in its place, so many are they, and the little earthen bowls in which the opium cakes are made. People are forbidden to wander about the river front of the factory in search of remnants of opium on the strands. There are no remnants, but people will not credit this. After vatting, as has been said, the big vats, holding from one to three thousand maunds, are probed with test rods, and the samples are treated just like the samples of the *challans*, everybody writing everything in duplicate and signing it. Having secured the mean consistence of each vat, the requisite quantity of each blend—Calcutta Mint scales again, and an unlimited quantity of supervision—is weighed out, thrown into an alligation vat, of 250 maunds, and worked up by the feet of coolies, who hang on to ropes and drag their legs painfully through the probe. Try to wade in mud of 70° consistency, and see what it is like.

This completes the working of the opium. It is now ready to be made into cakes after a final assay. Man has done nothing to improve it since it streaked the capsule of the poppy—this mysterious drug. Perhaps half a hundred sinners have tried to adulterate it and been paid out accordingly, but that has been the utmost. April, May and June are the months for receiving and manufacturing opium, and in the winter months come the packing and the dispatch.

At the beginning of the cold weather Ghazipur holds locked up a trifle, say, of three and a half millions sterling in opium. Now, there may be only a paltry three-quarters of a million on hand, and that is going out at the rate of one Viceroy's salary for two and a half years per diem. For such a flea-bite it seems absurd to prohibit smoking in the factory or to stud the place with thanks and steam fire-engines. Really, Ghazipur is unnecessarily timid. A long time ago some one threatened to cast down a tree sacred to Mahadeo. In a very few days, just as soon as Mahadeo got news of the insult, a fire broke out and damaged thousands of pounds' worth of opium.

But all this time we have not gone through the factory. There are ranges and ranges of gigantic godowns, huge barns that can hold over half-a-million pounds' worth of opium. There are acres of bricked floor, regiments on regiments of chests; and yet more go downs and more godowns. The heart of the whole is the laboratory which is full of the sick faint smell of a *chandu-khana*. This makes Ghazipur indignant. "That's the smell of opium. We don't need *chandu* here. You don't know what real opium smells like. *Chandu-khana* indeed! That's refined opium under treatment for morphia, and *cocaine* and perhaps *narcoine*." "Very well, let's see some of the real opium made for the China market." "We shan't be making any for another six weeks at earliest; but we can show you one cake made, and you must imagine two hundred and fifty men making 'em as hard as they can up to one every four minutes." A *Sirdar* of cake-makers is called, and appears with a miniature *dhobi's* washing board on which he sits, a little square box of dark wood, a tin cup, an earthen bowl, and a mass of poppy petal *chupattis*. A larger earthen bowl holds a mass of what looks like bad Cape tobacco. "What's that?" "Trash—dried poppy leaves, not petals, broken up and used for packing cakes in. You'll see presently." The cake-maker sits down and

receives a lump of opium, weighed out, of one seer seven chittacks and a half, neither more nor less. "That's pure opium of seventy consistence." Every allowance is weighed. "What are they weighing that brown water for?" "That's *lewa*—thin opium at fifty consistence. It's the paste. He gets four chittacks and a half." "And do they weigh the *chupattis?*" "Of course. Five chittacks of *chupattis*—about sixteen *chupattis* of all three kinds." This is overwhelming. This *sirdar* takes a brass hemispherical cup and wets it with a rag. Then he tears a *chupatti* across so that it fits into the cup without a wrinkle, and pastes it with the thin opium, the *lewa*. After this his actions become incomprehensible, but there is evidently a deep method in them. *Chupatti* after *chupatti* is torn across, dressed with *lewa* and pressed down into the cup, the fringes hanging over the edge of the bowl. He takes half *chupattis* and fixes them skilfully, picking now first-class and now second-class ones. Everything is gummed into everything else with the *lewa,* and he presses all down by twisting his wrists inside the bowl. "He is making the *gattia* now." *Gattia* means a tight coat at any rate, so there is some ray of enlightenment. Torn *chupatti* follows torn *chupatti*, till the bowl is lined half-an-inch deep with them, and they all glisten with the greasy *lewa*. He now takes up an ungummed *chupatti* and fits in carefully all round. The opium is dropped tenderly upon this, and a curious washing motion of the hand follows. The opium is drawn up into a cone as one by one the *sirdar* picks up the overlapping portions of the *chupattis* that hung outside the bowl and plasters them against the drug. He makes a clever waist-belt while he keeps all the flags in place, and so strengthens the midriff of the lump. He tucks in the top of the cone with this thumbs, brings the fringe of *chupattis* over to close the opening, and pastes fresh leaves upon all. The cone has now taken a spherical shape, and he gives it the finishing touch by gumming a large *chupatti,* one of the "moon" kind, set aside from the first, on the top, so deftly that no wrinkle is visible. The cake is now complete, and all the Celestials of the middle kingdom shall not be able to disprove that it weighs two seers one and three-quarter chittacks, with a play of half a chittack for the personal equation.

The Sirdar takes it up and rubs it in the bran-like poppy trash in the big bowl, so that two-thirds of it are powdered with the trash and one-third is fair and shiny *chupatti.* "That is the difference between a Ghazipur and a Patna cake. Our cakes have always an unpowdered head. The Patna ones are rolled in trash all over. You can tell them anywhere by that mark. Now we'll cut this one open and you can see how a section looks." One-half of an inch as nearly as may be is the thickness of the *chupatti* shell all round the cake, and even in this short time so firmly has the *lewa* set that any attempt at sundering the skins of *chupatti* is followed by the rending of the poppy petals that compose the *chupatti.* "You've seen in detail what a cake is made of—that is to say, pure opium 70 consistence, poppy-petal pancakes, *lewa,* of 52'-50 consistence, and a powdering of poppy-trash." "But why are you so particular

about the shell?" "Because of the China market. The Chinaman likes every inch of the stuff we send him, and uses it. He boils the shell and gets out every grain of the *lewa* used to gum it together. He smokes that after he has dried it. Roughly speaking, the value of the cake we've just cut open is two pound ten. All the time it is in our hands we have to look after it and check it, and treat it as though it were gold. It mustn't have too much moisture in it, or it will swell and crack, and if it is too dry John Chinaman won't have it. He values his opium for qualities just the opposite of those in Smyrna opium. Smyrna opium gives as much as ten per cent. of morphia, and is nearly solid—90 consistence. Our opium does not give more than three or three and a half per cent. of morphia on the average, and, as you know it is only 70 or in Patna 75 consistence. That is the drug the Chinaman likes. He can get the maximum of extract out of it by soaking it in hot water, and he likes the flavor. He knows it is absolutely pure too, and it comes to him in good condition." "But has nobody found out any patent way of making these cakes and putting skins on them by machinery?" "Not *yet.* Poppy to poppy. There's nothing better. Here are a couple of cakes made in 1849, when they tried experiments in wrapping them in paper and cloth. You can see that they are beautifully wrapped and sewn like cricket balls, but it would take about half-an-hour to make such cakes, and we could not be sure of keeping the aroma in them. Nothing like poppy plant for poppy drug."

And this is the way the drug, which yields such a splendid income to the Indian Government, is prepared. To tell how it is thereafter kept in store, packed for export, put upon the market at certain fixed periods, and shipped away, for John Chinaman's consumption chiefly, would be a tame story. The interest lies in the actual manufacture and manipulation of the cakes, and we have seen how this is done in the busy factory at Ghazipur.

VOLUME IV

Plain Tales from the Hills

Lispeth

Look, you have cast out Love! What
    Gods are these
    You bid me please?
The Three in One, the One in Three?
    Not so!
    To my own Gods I go.
It may be they shall give me greater ease.
Than your cold Christ and tangled Trin-
    ities.
                    —*The Convert.*

SHE was the daughter of Sonoo, a Hill-
man of the Himalayas, and Jadéh his
wife. One year their maize failed, and
two bears spent the night in their only
opium poppy-field just above the Sutlej
Valley on the Kotgarh side; so, next season, they turned Christian, and brought
their baby to the Mission to be baptized.
The Kotgarh Chaplain christened her
Elizabeth, and "Lispeth" is the Hill or
pahari pronunciation.

Later, cholera came into the Kotgarh
Valley and carried off Sonoo and Jadéh,
and Lispeth became half servant, half
companion, to the wife of the then
Chaplain of Kotgarh. This was after the
reign of the Moravian missionaries in that
place, but before Kotgarh had quite forgotten her title of "Mistress of the
Northern Hills."

Whether Christianity improved Lispeth, or whether the gods of her own
people would have done as much for her
under any circumstances, I do not
know; but she grew very lovely. When
a Hill-girl grows lovely she is worth
traveling fifty miles over bad ground
to look upon. Lispeth had a Greek
face—one of those faces people paint
so often, and see so seldom. She was
of a pale, ivory color, and, for her
race, extremely tall. Also, she possessed eyes that were wonderful; and,
had she not been dressed in the abominable print-cloths affected by Missions,
you would, meeting her on the hillside
unexpectedly, have thought her the
original Diana of the Romans going
out to slay.

Lispeth took to Christianity readily,
and did not abandon it when she
reached womanhood, as do some Hill-
girls. Her own people hated her because she had, they said, become a
white woman and washed herself daily;
and the Chaplain's wife did not know
what to do with her. One cannot ask
a stately goddess, five foot ten in her
shoes, to clean plates and dishes. She
played with the Chaplain's children and
took classes in the Sunday-School, and
read all the books in the house, and
grew more and more beautiful, like the
Princesses in fairy tales. The Chaplain's wife said that the girl ought to
take service in Simla as a nurse or
something "genteel." But Lispeth did
not want to take service. She was very
happy where she was.

When travelers — there were not
many in those years—came in to Kot-

garh, Lispeth used to lock herself into her own room for fear they might take her away to Simla, or out into the unknown world.

One day, a few months after she was seventeen years old, Lispeth went out for a walk. She did not walk in the manner of English ladies—a mile and a half out, with a carriage-ride back again. She covered between twenty and thirty miles in her little constitutionals, all about and about, between Kotgarh and Narkunda. This time she came back at full dusk, stepping down the break-neck descent into Kotgarh with something heavy in her arms. The Chaplain's wife was dozing in the drawing-room when Lispeth came in breathing heavily and very exhausted with her burden. Lispeth put it down on the sofa, and said simply, "This is my husband. I found him on the Bagi Road. He has hurt himself. We will nurse him, and when he is well, your husband shall marry him to me."

This was the first mention Lispeth had ever made of her matrimonial views, and the Chaplain's wife shrieked with horror. However, the man on the sofa needed attention first. He was a young Englishman, and his head had been cut to the bone by something jagged. Lispeth said she had found him down the hillside, and had brought him in. He was breathing queerly and was unconscious.

He was put to bed and tended by the Chaplain, who knew something of medicine; and Lispeth waited outside the door in case she could be useful. She explained to the Chaplain that this was the man she meant to marry; and the Chaplain and his wife lectured her severely on the impropriety of her conduct. Lispeth listened quietly, and repeated her first proposition. It takes a great deal of Christianity to wipe out uncivilized Eastern instincts, such as falling in love at first sight. Lispeth, having found the man she worshipped, did not see why she should keep silent as to her choice. She had no intention of being sent away, either. She was going to nurse that Englishman until he was well enough to marry her. This was her programme.

After a fortnight of slight fever and inflammation, the Englishman recovered coherence and thanked the Chaplain and his wife, and Lispeth—especially Lispeth—for their kindness. He was a traveler in the East, he said—they never talked about "globe-trotters" in those days, when the P. & O. fleet was young and small—and had come from Dehra Dun to hunt for plants and butterflies among the Simla hills. No one at Simla, therefore, knew anything about him. He fancied that he must have fallen over the cliff while reaching out for a fern on a rotten tree-trunk, and that his coolies must have stolen his baggage and fled. He thought he would go back to Simla when he was a little stronger. He desired no more mountaineering.

He made small haste to go away, and recovered his strength slowly. Lispeth objected to being advised either by the Chaplain or his wife; therefore the latter spoke to the Englishman, and told him how matters stood in Lispeth's heart. He laughed a good deal, and said it was very pretty and romantic, but, as he was engaged to a girl at Home, he fancied that nothing would happen. Certainly he would behave with discretion. He did that. Still he found it very pleasant to talk to Lispeth, and walk with Lispeth, and say nice things to her, and call her pet names while he was getting strong enough to go away. It meant nothing at all to him, and everything in the world to Lispeth. She was very happy while the fortnight lasted, because she had found a man to love.

Being a savage by birth, she took no trouble to hide her feelings, and the Englishman was amused. When he went away, Lispeth walked with him up the Hill as far as Narkunda, very troubled and very miserable. The Chaplain's wife, being a good Christian and disliking anything in the shape of fuss or scandal—Lispeth was beyond her management entirely—had told the Englishman to tell Lispeth that he was coming back to marry her. "She is but a child you know, and, I fear, at heart a heathen," said the Chaplain's wife. So all the twelve miles up the Hill the Englishman, with his arm round Lispeth's waist, was assuring the girl that he would come back and marry her; and Lispeth made him promise over and over again. She wept on the Narkunda Ridge till he had passed out of sight along the Muttiani path.

Then she dried her tears and went into Kotgarh again, and said to the Chaplain's wife, "He will come back and marry me. He has gone to his own people to tell them so." And the Chaplain's wife soothed Lispeth and said, "He will come back." At the end of two months, Lispeth grew impatient, and was told that the Englishman had gone over the seas to England. She knew where England was, because she had read little geography primers; but, of course, she had no conception of the nature of the sea, being a Hill-girl. There was an old puzzle-map of the World in the house. Lispeth had played with it when she was a child. She unearthed it again, and put it together of evenings, and cried to herself, and tried to imagine where her Englishman was. As she had no ideas of distance or steam-boats, her notions were somewhat wild. It would not have made the least difference had she been perfectly correct; for the Englishman had no intention of coming back to marry a Hill-girl. He forgot all about her by the time he was butterfly-hunting in Assam. He wrote a book on the East afterward. Lispeth's name did not appear there.

At the end of three months Lispeth made daily pilgrimage to Narkunda to see if her Englishman was coming along the road. It gave her comfort, and the Chaplain's wife finding her happier thought that she was getting over her "barbarous and most indelicate folly." A little later, the walks ceased to help Lispeth and her temper grew very bad. The Chaplain's wife thought this a profitable time to let her know the real state of affairs—that the Englishman had only promised his love to keep her quiet—that he had never meant anything, and that it was wrong and improper of Lispeth to think of marriage with an Englishman, who was of a superior clay, besides being promised in marriage to a girl of his own people. Lispeth said that all this was clearly impossible because he had said he loved her, and the Chaplain's wife had, with her own lips, asserted that the Englishman was coming back.

"How can what he and you said be untrue?" asked Lispeth.

"We said it as an excuse to keep you quiet, child," said the Chaplain's wife.

"Then you have lied to me," said Lispeth, "you and he?"

The Chaplain's wife bowed her head, and said nothing. Lispeth was silent, too, for a little time; then she went out down the valley, and returned in the dress of a Hill-girl—infamously dirty, but without the nose-stud and earrings. She had her hair braided into the long pigtail, helped out with black thread, that Hill-women wear.

"I am going back to my own people," said she. "You have killed Lispeth. There is only left old Jadéh's daughter —the daughter of a *pahari* and the servan of *Tarka Devi*. You are all liars, you English."

By the time that the Chaplain's wife had recovered from the shock of the announcement that Lispeth had 'verted to her mother's gods, the girl had gone; and she never came back.

She took to her own unclean people savagely, as if to make up the arrears of the life she had stepped out of; and, in a little time, she married a woodcutter who beat her after the manner of *paharis*, and her beauty faded soon.

"There is no law whereby you can account for the vagaries of the heathen," said the Chaplain's wife, "and I believe that Lispeth was always at heart an infidel." Seeing she had been taken into the Church of England at the mature age of five weeks, this statement does not do credit to the Chaplain's wife.

Lispeth was a very old woman when she died. She had always a perfect command of English, and when she was sufficiently drunk, could sometimes be induced to tell the story of her first love-affair.

It was hard then to realize that the bleared, wrinkled creature, exactly like a wisp of charred rag, could ever have been "Lispeth of the Kotgarh Mission."

Three and—An Extra

When halter and heel-ropes are slipped, do not give chase with sticks but with *gram.—Punjabi Proverb.*

AFTER marriage arrives a reaction, sometimes a big, sometimes a little one; but it comes sooner or later, and must be tided over by both parties if they desire the rest of their lives to go with the current.

In the case of the Cusack-Bremmils this reaction did not set in till the third year after the wedding. Bremmil was hard to hold at the best of times; but he was a beautiful husband until the baby died and Mrs. Bremmil wore black, and grew thin, and mourned as though the bottom of the Universe had fallen out. Perhaps Bremmil ought to have comforted her. He tried to do so, but the more he comforted the more Mrs. Bremmil grieved, and, consequently, the more uncomfortable grew Bremmil. The fact was that they both needed a tonic. And they got it. Mrs. Bremmil can afford to laugh now, but it was no laughing matter to her at the time.

Mrs. Hauksbee appeared on the horizon; and where she existed was fair chance of trouble. At Simla her by-name was the "Stormy Petrel." She had won that title five times to my own certain knowledge. She was a little, brown, thin, almost skinny, woman, with big, rolling, violet-blue eyes, and the sweetest manners in the world. You had only to mention her name at afternoon teas for every woman in the room to rise up, and call her not blessed. She was clever, witty, brilliant, and sparkling beyond most of her kind; but possessed of many devils of malice and mischievousness. She could be nice, though, even to her own sex. But that is another story.

Bremmil went off at score after the baby's death and the general discomfort that followed, and Mrs. Hauksbee annexed him. She took no pleasure in hiding her captives. She annexed him publicly, and saw that the public saw it. He rode with her, and walked with her, and talked with her, and picnicked with her, and tiffined at Peliti's with her, till people put up their eyebrows and said, "Shocking!" Mrs. Bremmil stayed at home turning over the dead baby's frocks and crying into the empty cradle. She did not care to do anything else. But some eight dear, affectionate ladyfriends explained the situation at length to her in case she should miss the cream of it. Mrs. Bremmil listened quietly, and thanked them for their good offices. She was not as clever as Mrs. Hauksbee, but she was no fool. She kept her own counsel, and did not speak to Bremmil of what she had heard. This is worth remembering. Speaking to, or crying over, a husband never did any good yet.

When Bremmil was at home, which was not often, he was more affectionate than usual; and that showed his hand. The affection was forced partly to soothe his own conscience and partly to soothe Mrs. Bremmil. It failed in both regards.

Then "the A.-D.-C. in Waiting was commanded by Their Excellencies, Lord and Lady Lytton, to invite Mr. and Mrs. Cusack-Bremmil to Peterhoff on July 26 at 9:30 p. m."—"Dancing" in the bottom-left-hand corner.

"I can't go," said Mrs. Bremmil, "it is too soon after poor little Florrie . . . but it need not stop you, Tom."

She meant what she said then, and Bremmil said that he would go just to put in an appearance. Here he spoke the thing which was not; and Mrs. Bremmil knew it. She guessed—a woman's guess is much more accurate than a man's certainty—that he had meant to go from the first, and with Mrs. Hauksbee. She sat down to think, and the outcome of her thoughts was that the memory of a dead child was worth considerably less than the affections of a living husband. She made her plan and staked her all upon it. In that hour she discovered that she knew Tom Bremmil thoroughly, and this knowledge she acted on.

"Tom," said she, "I shall be dining out at the Longmores' on the evening of the 26th. You'd better dine at the Club."

This saved Bremmil from making an excuse to get away and dine with Mrs. Hauksbee, so he was grateful, and felt small and mean at the same time—which was wholesome. Bremmil left the house at five for a ride. About half-past five in the evening a large leather-covered basket came in from Phelps's for Mrs. Bremmil. She was a woman who knew how to dress; and she had not spent a week on designing that dress and having it gored, and hemmed, and herring-boned, and tucked and rucked (or whatever the terms are), for nothing. It was a gorgeous dress—slight mourning. I can't describe it, but it was what *The Queen* calls "a creation"—a thing that hit you straight between the eyes and made you gasp. She had not much heart for what she was going to do; but as she glanced at the long mirror she had the satisfaction of knowing that she had never looked so well in her life. She was a large blond, and, when she chose, carried herself superbly.

After the dinner at the Longmores' she went on to the dance—a little late—and encountered Bremmil with Mrs. Hauksbee on his arm. That made her flush, and as the men crowded round her for dances she looked magnificent. She filled up all her dances except three, and those she left blank. Mrs. Hauksbee caught her eye once; and she knew it was war—real war—between them. She started handicapped in the struggle, for she had ordered Bremmil about just the least little bit in the

world too much; and he was beginning to resent it. Moreover, he had never seen his wife look so lovely. He stared at her from doorways, and glared at her from passages as she went about with her partners; and the more he stared, the more taken was he. He could scarcely believe that this was the woman with the red eyes and the black stuff gown who used to weep over the eggs at breakfast.

Mrs. Hauksbee did her best to hold him in play, but, after two dances, he crossed over to his wife and asked for a dance.

"I'm afraid you've come too late, *Mister* Bremmil," she said, with her eyes twinkling.

Then he begged her to give him a dance, and, as a great favor, she allowed him the fifth waltz. Luckily Five stood vacant on his programme. They danced it together, and there was a little flutter round the room. Bremmil had a sort of a notion that his wife could dance, but he never knew she danced so divinely. At the end of that waltz he asked for another—as a favor, not as a right; and Mrs. Bremmil said, "Show me your programme, dear!" He showed it as a naughty little schoolboy hands up contraband sweets to a master. There was a fair sprinkling of "H" on it, besides "H" at supper. Mrs. Bremmil said nothing, but she smiled contemptuously, ran her pencil through Seven and Nine—two "H's"—and returned the card with her own name written above—a pet name that only she and her husband used. Then she shook her finger at him, and said laughing, "Oh you silly, *silly* boy!"

Mrs. Hauksbee heard that, and—she

owned as much—felt she had the worst of it. Bremmil accepted Seven and Nine gratefully. They danced Seven, and sat out Nine in one of the little tents. What Bremmil said and what Mrs. Bremmil did is no concern of any one.

When the band struck up "The Roast Beef of Old England," the two went out into the verandah, and Bremmil began looking for his wife's dandy (this was before 'rickshaw days) while she went into the cloak-room. Mrs Hauksbee came up and said, "You take me in to supper, I think, Mr. Bremmil?" Bremmil turned red and looked foolish, "Ah—h'm! I'm going home with my wife, Mrs. Hauksbee. I think there has

been a little mistake." Being a man, he spoke as though Mrs. Hauksbee were entirely responsible.

Mrs. Bremmil came out of the cloak-room in a swansdown cloak with a white "cloud" round her head. She looked radiant; and she had a right to.

The couple went off into the darkness together, Bremmil riding very close to the dandy.

Then said Mrs. Hauksbee to me—she looked a trifle faded and jaded in the lamplight—"Take my word for it, the silliest woman can manage a clever man; but it needs a very clever woman to manage a fool."

Then we went in to supper.

Thrown Away

And some are sulky, while some will plunge.
  [*So ho! Steady! Stand still, you!*]
Some you must gentle, and some you must lunge.
  [*There! There! Who wants to kill you?*]
Some—there are losses in every trade—
Will break their hearts ere bitted and made,
Will fight like fiends as the rope cuts hard,
And die dumb-mad in the breaking-yard.
  —*Toolungala Stockyard Chorus.*

To rear a boy under what parents call the "sheltered life system" is, if the boy must go into the world and fend for himself, not wise. Unless he be one in a thousand he has certainly to pass through many unnecessary troubles; and may, possibly, come to extreme grief simply from ignorance of the proper proportions of things.

Let a puppy eat the soap in the bathroom or chew a newly-blacked boot. He chews and chuckles until, by and by, he finds out that blacking and Old Brown Windsor make him very sick; so he argues that soap and boots are not wholesome. Any old dog about the house will soon show him the unwisdom of biting big dogs' ears. Being young, he remembers and goes abroad, at six months, a well-mannered little beast with a chastened appetite. If he had been kept away from boots, and soap, and big dogs till he came to the trinity full-grown and with developed teeth, consider how fearfully sick and thrashed he would be! Apply that notion to the "sheltered life," and see how it works. It does not sound pretty, but it is the better of two evils.

There was a Boy once who had been brought up under the "sheltered life" theory; and the theory killed him dead. He stayed with his people all his days, from the hour he was born till the hour he went into Sandhurst nearly at the top of the list. He was beautifully taught in all that wins marks by a private tutor, and carried the extra weight of "never having given his parents an hour's anxiety in his life." What he learned at Sandhurst beyond the regular routine is of no great consequence. He looked about him, and he found soap and blacking, so to speak, very good. He ate a little, and came out of Sandhurst not so high as he went in. Then there was an interval and a scene with his people, who expected much from him. Next a year of living unspotted from the world in a third-rate depôt battalion where all the juniors were children and all the seniors old women; and lastly he came out to India where he was cut off from the support of his parents, and had no one to fall back on in time of trouble except himself.

Now India is a place beyond all others where one must not take things too seriously—the midday sun always excepted. Too much work and too much energy kill a man just as effectively as too much assorted vice or too much drink. Flirtation does not matter, because every one is being transferred and either you or she leave the Station, and never return. Good work does not matter, because a man is judged by his worst output and another man takes all the credit of his best as a rule. Bad work does not matter, because other

men do worse and incompetents hang on longer in India than anywhere else. Amusements do not matter, because you must repeat them as soon as you have accomplished them once, and most amusements only mean trying to win another person's money. Sickness does not matter, because it's all in the day's work, and if you die, another man takes over your place and your office in the eight hours between death and burial. Nothing matters except Home-furlough and acting allowances, and these only because they are scarce. It is a slack country where all men work with imperfect instruments; and the wisest thing is to escape as soon as ever you can to some place where amusement is amusement and a reputation worth the having.

But this Boy—the tale is as old as the Hills—came out, and took all things seriously. He was pretty and was petted. He took the pettings seriously and fretted over women not worth saddling a pony to call upon. He found his new free life in India very good. It does look attractive in the beginning, from a subaltern's point of view—all ponies, partners, dancing, and so on. He tasted it as the puppy tastes the soap. Only he came late to the eating, with a grown set of teeth. He had no sense of balance—just like the puppy—and could not understand why he was not treated with the consideration he received under his father's roof. This hurt his feelings.

He quarreled with other boys and, being sensitive to the marrow, remembered these quarrels, and they excited him. He found whist, and gymkhanas, and things of that kind (meant to amuse one after office) good; but he took them seriously too, just as seriously as he took the "head" that followed after drink. He lost his money over whist and gymkhanas because they were new to him.

He took his losses seriously, and wasted as much energy and interest over a two-goldmohur race for maiden *ekka*-ponies with their manes hogged, as if it had been the Derby. One half of this came from inexperience—much as the puppy squabbles with the corner of the hearth-rug—and the other half from the dizziness bred by stumbling out of his quiet life into the glare and excitement of a livelier one. No one told him about the soap and the blacking, because an average man takes it for granted that an average man is ordinarily careful in regard to them. It was pitiful to watch The Boy knocking himself to pieces, as an over-handled colt falls down and cuts himself when he gets away from the groom.

This unbridled license in amusements not worth the trouble of breaking line for, much less rioting over, endured for six months—all through one cold weather—and then we thought that the heat and the knowledge of having lost his money and health and lamed his horses would sober The Boy down, and he would stand steady. In ninety-nine cases out of a hundred this would have happened. You can see the principle working in any Indian Station. But this particular case fell through because The Boy was sensitive and took things seriously—as I may have said some seven times before. Of course, we could not tell how his excesses struck him

personally. They were nothing very heartbreaking or above the average. He might be crippled for life financially, and want a little nursing. Still the memory of his performances would wither away in one hot weather, and the bankers would help him to tide over the money-troubles. But he must have taken another view altogether and have believed himself ruined beyond redemption. His Colonel talked to him severely when the cold weather ended. That made him more wretched than ever; and it was only an ordinary "Colonel's wigging"!

What follows is a curious instance of the fashion in which we are all linked together and made responsible for one another. *The* thing that kicked the beam in The Boy's mind was a remark that a woman made when he was talking to her. There is no use in repeating it, for it was only a cruel little sentence, rapped out before thinking, that made him flush to the roots of his hair. He kept himself to himself for three days, and then put in for two days' leave to go shooting near a Canal Engineer's Rest House about thirty miles out. He got his leave, and that night at Mess was noisier and more offensive than ever. He said he was "going to shoot big game," and left at half-past ten o'clock in an *ekka*. Partridge—which was the only thing a man could get near the Rest House—is not big game; so every one laughed.

Next morning one of the Majors came in from short leave, and heard that The Boy had gone out to shoot "big game." The Major had taken an interest in The Boy, and had, more than once, tried to check him. The

Major put up his eyebrows when he heard of the expedition and went to The Boy's rooms where he rummaged.

Presently he came out and found me leaving cards on the Mess. There was no one else in the ante-room.

He said, "The Boy has gone out shooting. *Does* a man shoot *tetur* with a revolver and writing-case?"

I said, "Nonsense, Major!" for I saw what was in his mind.

He said, "Nonsense or no nonsense, I'm going to the Canal now—at once. I don't feel easy."

Then he thought for a minute, and said, "Can you lie?"

"You know best," I answered. "It's my profession."

"Very well," said the Major, "you must come out with me now—at once—in an *ekka* to the Canal to shoot black-buck. Go and put on *shikar*-kit—*quick* —and drive here with a gun."

The Major was a masterful man; and I knew that he would not give orders for nothing. So I obeyed, and on return found the Major packed up in an *ekka* —gun-cases and food slung below— all ready for a shooting-trip.

He dismissed the driver and drove himself. We jogged along quietly while in the station; but, as soon as we got to the dusty road across the plains, he made that pony fly. A country-bred can do nearly anything at a pinch. We covered the thirty miles in under three hours, but the poor brute was nearly dead.

Once I said, "What's the blazing hurry, Major?"

He said, quietly, "The Boy has been alone, by himself for—one, two, five, —fourteen hours now! I tell you, I don't feel easy."

This uneasiness spread itself to me, and I helped beat the pony.

When we came to the Canal Engineer's Rest House the Major called for The Boy's servant; but there was no answer. Then we went up to the house, calling for The Boy by name; but there was no answer.

"Oh, he's out shooting," said I.

Just then, I saw through one of the windows a little hurricane-lamp burning. This was at four in the afternoon. We both stopped dead in the veranda, holding our breath to catch every sound; and we heard, inside the room the *"brr—brr—brr"* of a multitude of flies. The Major said nothing, but he took off his helmet and we entered very softly.

The Boy was dead on the bed in the centre of the bare, lime-washed room. He had shot his head nearly to pieces with his revolver. The gun-cases were still strapped, so was the bedding, and on the table lay The Boy's writing-case with photographs. He had gone away to die like a poisoned rat!

The Major said to himself, softly, "Poor Boy! Poor, *poor* devil!" Then he turned away fom the bed and said, "I want your help in this business."

Knowing The Boy was dead by his own hand, I saw exactly what that help would be, so I passed over to the table, took a chair, lit a cheroot, and began to go through the writing-case; the Major looking over my shoulder and repeating to himself, "We came too late!—Like a rat in a hole!—Poor, *poor* devil!"

The Boy must have spent half the

night in writing to his people, to his Colonel, and to a girl at Home; and as soon as he had finished, must have shot himself, for he had been dead a long time when we came in.

I read all that he had written, and passed over each sheet to the Major as I finished it.

We saw from his accounts how very seriously he had taken everything. He wrote about "disgrace which he was unable to bear"—"indelible shame"—"criminal folly"—"wasted life," and so on; besides a lot of private things to his father and mother much too sacred to put into print. The letter to the girl at Home was the most pitiful of all; and I choked as I read it. The Major made no attempt to keep dry-eyed. I respected him for that. He read and rocked himself to and fro, and simply cried like a woman without caring to hide it. The letters were so dreary and hopeless and touching. We forgot all about The Boy's follies, and only thought of the poor Thing on the bed and the scrawled sheets in our hands. It was utterly impossible to let the letters go Home. They would have broken his father's heart and killed his mother after killing her belief in her son.

At last the Major dried his eyes openly, and said, "Nice sort of thing to spring on an English family! What shall we do?"

I said, knowing what the Major had brought me out for,—"The Boy died of cholera. We were with him at the time. We can't commit ourselves to half-measures. Come along."

Then began one of the most grimly comic scenes I have ever taken part in—the concoction of a big, written lie, bolstered with evidence, to soothe The Boy's people at Home. I began the rough draft of the letter, the Major throwing in hints here and there while he gathered up all the stuff that The Boy had written and burned it in the fireplace. It was a hot, still evening when we began, and the lamp burned very badly. In due course I made the draft to my satisfaction, setting forth how The Boy was the pattern of all virtues, beloved by his regiment, with every promise of a great career before him, and so on; how we had helped him through the sickness—it was no time for little lies you will understand —and how he had died without pain. I choked while I was putting down these things and thinking of the poor people who would read them. Then I laughed at the grotesqueness of the affair, and the laughter mixed itself up with the choke—and the Major said that we both wanted drinks.

I am afraid to say how much whiskey we drank before the letter was finished. It had not the least effect on us. Then we took off The Boy's watch, locket, and rings.

Lastly, the Major said, "We must send a lock of hair, too. A woman values that."

But there were reasons why we could not find a lock fit to send. The Boy was black-haired, and so was the Major, luckily. I cut off a piece of the Major's hair above the temple with a knife, and put it into the packet we were making. The laughing-fit and the chokes got hold of me again, and I had to stop. The Major was nearly as bad; and we both knew that the worst part of the work was to come.

We sealed up the packet, photographs, locket, seals, ring, letter, and lock of hair with The Boy's sealing-wax and The Boy's seal.

Then the Major said, "For God's sake, let's get outside—away from the room—and think!"

We went outside, and walked on the banks of the Canal for an hour, eating and drinking what we had with us, until the moon rose. I know now exactly how a murderer feels. Finally, we forced ourselves back to the room with the lamp and the Other Thing in it, and began to take up the next piece of work. I am not going to write about this. It was too horrible. We burned the bedstead and dropped the ashes into the Canal; we took up the matting of the room and treated that in the same way. I went off to a village and borrowed two big hoes,—I did not want the villagers to help,—while the Major arranged—the other matters. It took us four hours hard work to make the grave. As we worked, we argued out whether it was right to say as much as we remembered of the Burial of the Dead. We compromised things by saying the Lord's Prayer with a private unofficial prayer for the peace of the soul of The Boy. Then we filled in the grave and went into the veranda—not the house—to lie down to sleep. We were dead tired.

When we woke the Major said, wearily, "We can't go back till to-morrow. We must give him a decent time to die in. He died early *this* morning, remember. That seems more nat-

ural." So the Major must have been lying awake all the time, thinking.

I said, "Then why didn't we bring the body back to cantonments?"

The Major thought for a minute. "Because the people bolted when they heard of the cholera. And the *ekka* has gone!"

That was strictly true. We had forgotten all about the *ekka*-pony, and he had gone home.

So we were left there alone, all that stifling day, in the Canal Rest House, testing and retesting our story of The Boy's death to see if it was weak in any point. A native appeared in the afternoon, but we said that a *Sahib* was dead of cholera, and he ran away. As the dusk gathered, the Major told me all his fears about The Boy, and awful stories of suicide or nearly-carried-out suicide—tales that made one's hair crisp. He said that he himself had once gone into the same Valley of the Shadow as The Boy, when he was young and new to the country; so he understood how things fought together in The Boy's poor jumbled head. He also said that youngsters, in their repentant moments, consider their sins much more serious and ineffaceable than they really are. We talked together all through the evening and rehearsed the story of the death of The Boy. As soon as the moon was up and The Boy, theoretically, just buried, we struck across country for the Station. We walked from eight till six o'clock in the morning; but though we were dead-tired, we did not forget to go to The Boy's rooms and put away his revolver with the proper amount of cartridges in the pouch. Also to set his writing-case on the table. We found the Colonel and reported the death, feeling more like murderers than ever. Then we went to bed and slept the clock round; for there was no more in us.

The tale had credence as long as was necessary; for every one forgot about The Boy before a fortnight was over. Many people, however, found time to say that the Major had behaved scandalously in not bringing in the body for a regimental funeral. The saddest thing of all was the letter from The Boy's mother to the Major and me—with big inky blisters all over the sheet. She wrote the sweetest possible things about our great kindness, and the obligation she would be under to us as long as she lived.

All things considered, she was under an obligation; but not exactly as she meant.

Miss Youghal's Sais

When Man and Woman are agreed, what can the Kazi do?—*Proverb*.

SOME people say that there is no romance in India. Those people are wrong. Our lives hold quite as much romance as is good for us. Sometimes more.

Strickland was in the Police, and people did not understand him; so they said he was a doubtful sort of man and passed by on the other side. Strickland had himself to thank for this. He held the extraordinary theory that a Policeman in India should try to know as much about the natives as the natives themselves. Now, in the whole of Upper India, there is only one man who can pass for Hindu or Mohommedan, hide-dresser or priest, as he pleases. He is feared and respected by the natives from the Ghor Kathri to the Jamma Musjid; and he is supposed to have the gift of invisibility and executive control over many Devils. But this has done him no good in the eyes of the Indian Government.

Strickland was foolish enough to take that man for his model; and, following out his absurd theory, dabbled in unsavory places no respectable man would think of exploring—all among the native riff-raff. He educated himself in this peculiar way for seven years, and people could not appreciate it. He was perpetually "going Fantee" among natives, which, of course, no man with any sense believes in. He was initiated into the *Sat Bhai* at Allahabad once, when he was on leave; he knew the Lizzard-Song of the Sansis, and the *Hâlli-Hukk* dance, which is a religious can-can of a startling kind. When a man knows who dance the *Hâlli-Hukk*, and how, and when, and where, he knows something to be proud of. He has gone deeper than the skin. But Strickland was not proud, though he had helped once, at Jagadhri, at the Painting of the Death Bull, which no

Englishman must even look upon; had mastered the thieves'-patter of the *chángars;* had taken a Eusufzai horse-thief alone near Attock; and had stood under the sounding-board of a Border mosque and conducted service in the manner of a Sunni Mollah.

His crowning achievement was spending eleven days as a *faquir* or priest in the gardens of Baba Atal at Amritsar, and there picking up the threads of the great Nasiban Murder Case. But people said, justly enough, "Why on earth can't Strickland sit in his office and write up his diary, and recruit and keep quiet, instead of showing up the incapacity of his seniors?" So the Nasiban Murder Case did him no good departmentally; but, after his first feeling of wrath, he returned to his outlandish custom of prying into native life. When a man once acquires a taste for this particular amusement, it abides with him all his days. It is the most fascinating thing in the world; Love not excepted. Where other men took ten days to the Hills, Strickland took leave for what he called *shikar,* put on the disguise that appealed to him at the time, stepped down into the brown crowd, and was swallowed up for awhile. He was a quiet, dark young fellow—spare, black-eyed—and, when he was not thinking of something else, a very interesting companion. Strickland on Native Progress as he had seen it was worth hearing. Natives hated Strickland; but they were afraid of him. He knew too much.

When the Youghals came into the station, Strickland—very gravely, as he did everything—fell in love with Miss Youghal; and she, after a while fell in love with him because she could not understand him. Then Strickland told the parents; but Mrs. Youghal said she was not going to throw her daughter into the worst paid Department in the Empire, and old Youghal said, in so many words, that he mistrusted Strickland's ways and works, and would thank him not to speak or write to his daughter any more. "Very well," said Strickland, for he did not wish to make his lady-love's life a burden. After one long talk with Miss Youghal he dropped the business entirely.

The Youghals went up to Simla in April.

In July Strickland secured three months' leave on "urgent private affairs." He locked up his house—though not a native in the Province would wittingly have touched "Estreekin Sahib's" gear for the world—and went down to see a friend of his, an old dyer, at Tarn Taran.

Here all trace of him was lost, until a *sais* or groom met me on the Simla Mall with this extraordinary note:

DEAR OLD MAN,—Please give bearer a box of cheroots—Supers, No. 1, for preference. They are freshest at the Club. I'll repay when I reappear; but at present I'm out of society. Yours,

E. STRICKLAND.

I ordered two boxes, and handed them over to the *sais* with my love. That *sais* was Strickland, and he was in old Youghal's employ, attached to Miss Youghal's Arab. The poor fellow was suffering for an English smoke, and knew that, whatever happened, I should hold my tongue till the business was over.

Later on, Mrs. Youghal, who was wrapped up in her servants, began talking at houses where she called of her paragon among *saises*— the man who was never too busy to get up in the morning and pick flowers for the breakfast-table, and who blacked—actually *blacked*—the hoofs of his horse like a London coachman! The turnout of Miss Youghal's Arab was a wonder and a delight. Strickland—Dulloo, I mean —found his reward in the pretty things that Miss Youghal said to him when she went out riding. Her parents were pleased to find she had forgotten all her foolishness for young Strickland and said she was a good girl.

Strickland vows that the two months of his service were the most rigid mental discipline he has ever gone through. Quite apart from the little fact that the wife of one of his fellow-*saises* fell in love with him and then tried to poison him with arsenic because he would have nothing to do with her, he had to school himself into keeping quiet when Miss Youghal went out riding with some man who tried to flirt with her, and he was forced to trot behind carrying the blanket and hearing every word! Also, he had to keep his temper when he was slanged in the theatre porch by a policeman—especially once when he was abused by a Naik he had himself recruited from Isser Jang village—or, worse still, when a young subaltern called him a pig for not making way quickly enough.

But the life had its compensations. He obtained great insight into the ways and thefts of *saises*—enough he says to have summarily convicted half the population of the Punjab if he had been

on business. He became one of the leading players at knuckle-bones, which all *jhampánis* and many *saises* play while they are waiting outside the Government House or the Gaiety Theatre of nights; he learned to smoke tobacco that was three-fourths cowdung; and he heard the wisdom of the grizzled Jemadar of the Government House grooms. Whose words are valuable. He saw many things which amused him; and he states, on honor, that no man can appreciate Simla properly, till he has seen it from the *sais's* point of view. He also says that, if he chose to write all he saw, his head would be broken in several places.

Strickland's account of the agony he endured on wet nights, hearing the music and seeing the lights in "Benmore," with his toes tingling for a waltz and his head in a horse-blanket, is rather amusing. One of these days, Strickland is going to write a little book on his experiences. That book will be worth buying; and even more worth suppressing.

Thus, he served faithfully as Jacob served for Rachel; and his leave was nearly at an end when the explosion came. He had really done his best to keep his temper in the hearing of the flirtations I have mentioned; but he broke down at last. An old and very distinguished General took Miss Youghal for a ride, and began that specially offensive "you're-only-a-little-girl" sort of flirtation—most difficult for a woman to turn aside deftly, and most maddening to listen to. Miss Youghal was shaking with fear at the things he said in the hearing of her *sais*. Dulloo—Strickland —stood it as long as he could. Then he caught hold of the General's bridle, and, in most fluent English, invited him to step off and be flung over the cliff. Next minute, Miss Youghal began to cry; and Strickland saw that he had hopelessly given himself away, and everything was over.

The General nearly had a fit, while Miss Youghal was sobbing out the story of the disguise and the engagement that was not recognized by the parents. Strickland was furiously angry with himself, and more angry with the General for forcing his hand; so he said nothing, but held the horse's head and prepared to thrash the General as some sort of satisfaction. But when the General had thoroughly grasped the story, and knew who Strickland was, he began to puff and blow in the saddle, and nearly rolled off with laughing. He said Strickland deserved a V. C., if it were only for putting on a *sais's* blanket. Then he called himself names, and vowed that he deserved a thrashing, but he was too old to take it from Strickland. Then he complimented Miss Youghal on her lover. The scandal of the business never struck him; for he was a nice old man, with a weakness for flirtations. Then he laughed again, and said that old Youghal was a fool. Strickland let go of the cob's head, and suggested that the General had better help them, if that was his opinion. Strickland knew Youghal's weakness for men with titles and letters after their names and high official position. "It's rather like a forty-minute farce," said the General, "but, begad, I *will* help, if it's only to escape that tremendous thrashing I deserve. Go along to your home, my *sais*-Policeman, and change into de-

cent kit, and I'll attack Mr. Youghal. Miss Youghal, may I ask you to canter home and wait?"

* * * * * *

About seven minutes later, there was a wild hurroosh at the Club. A *sais*, with blanket and headrope, was asking all the men he knew: "For Heaven's sake lend me decent clothes!" As the men did not recognize him, there were some peculiar scenes before Strickland could get a hot bath, with soda in it, in one room, a shirt here, a collar there, a pair of trousers elsewhere, and so on. He galloped off, with half the Club wardrobe on his back, and an utter stranger's pony under him, to the house of old Youghal. The General, arrayed in purple and fine linen, was before him. What the General had said Strickland never knew, but Youghal received Strickland with moderate civility; and Mrs. Youghal, touched by the devotion of the transformed Dulloo, was almost kind. The General beamed and chuckled, and Miss Youghal came in, and, almost before old Youghal knew where he was, the parental consent had been wrenched out, and Strickland had departed with Miss Youghal to the Telegraph Office to wire for his European kit. The final embarrassment was when a stranger attacked him on the Mall and asked for the stolen pony.

In the end, Strickland and Miss Youghal were married, on the strict understanding that Strickland should drop his old ways, and stick to Departmental routine, which pays best and leads to Simla. Strickland was far too fond of his wife, just then, to break his word, but it was a sore trial to him; for the streets and the bazars, and the sounds in them, were full of meaning to Strickland, and these called to him to come back and take up his wanderings and his discoveries. Some day, I will tell you how he broke his promise to help a friend. That was long since, and he has, by this time, been nearly spoiled for what he would call *shikar*. He is forgetting the slang, and the beggar's cant, and the marks and the signs, and the drift of the under-currents, which, if a man would master, he must always continue to learn.

But he fills in his Departmental returns beautifully.

"Yoked With An Unbeliever"

I am dying for you, and you are dying for another.—Punjabi Proverb.

WHEN the Gravesend tender left the P. & O. steamer for Bombay and went back to catch the train to Town, there were many people in it crying. But the one who wept most, and most openly, was Miss Agnes Laiter. She had reason to cry, because the only man she ever loved—or ever could love, so she said—was going out to India; and India, as every one knows, is divided equally between jungle, tigers, cobras, cholera, and sepoys.

Phil Garron, leaning over the side of the steamer in the rain, felt very unhappy too; but he did not cry. He was sent out to "tea." What "tea" meant he had not the vaguest idea, but fancied that he would have to ride on a prancing horse over hills covered with tea-vines, and draw a sumptuous salary for doing so; and he was very grateful to his uncle for getting him the berth. He was really going to reform all his slack, shiftless ways, save a large proportion of his magnificent salary yearly, and, in a very short time, return to marry Agnes Laiter. Phil Garron had been lying loose on his friends' hands for three years, and, as he had nothing to do, he naturally fell in love. He was very nice; but he was not strong in his views and opinions and principles, and though he never came to actual grief his friends were thankful when he said good-bye, and went out to this mysterious "tea" business near Darjiling. They said, "God bless you, dear boy! Let us never see your face again,"—or at least that was what Phil was given to understand.

When he sailed, he was very full of a great plan to prove himself several hundred times better than any one had given him credit for—to work like a horse, and triumphantly marry Agnes Laiter. He had many good points besides his good looks; his only fault being that he was weak, the least little bit in the world weak. He had as much notion of economy as the Morning Sun; and yet you could not lay your hand on any one item, and say, "Herein Phil Garron is extravagant or reckless." Nor could you point out any particular vice in his character; but he was "unsatisfactory" and as workable as putty.

Agnes Laiter went about her duties at home—her family objected to the engagement—with red eyes, while Phil was sailing to Darjiling—a "port on the Bengal Ocean," as his mother used to tell her friends. He was popular enough on board-ship, made many acquaintances and a moderately large liquor-bill, and sent off huge letters to Agnes Laiter at each port. Then he fell to work on this plantation, somewhere between Darjiling and Kangra, and, though the salary and the horse and the work were not quite all he had fancied, he succeeded fairly well, and gave himself much unnecessary credit for his perseverance.

In the course of time, as he settled more into collar, and his work grew fixed before him, the face of Agnes Laiter went out of his mind and only came when he was at leisure, which was not often. He would forget all about her for a fortnight, and remember her with a start, like a schoolboy who has forgotten to learn his lesson. She did not forget Phil, because she was of the kind that never forgets. Only, another man—a really desirable young man—presented himself before Mrs. Laiter; and the chance of a marriage with Phil was as far off as ever; and his letters were so unsatisfactory; and there was a certain amount of domestic pressure brought to bear on the girl; and the young man really was an eligible person as incomes go; and the end of all things was that Agnes married him, and wrote a tempestuous whirlwind of a letter to Phil in the wilds of Darjiling, and said she should never know a happy moment all the rest of her life. Which was a true prophecy.

Phil received that letter, and held himself ill-treated. This was two years after he had come out; but by dint of thinking fixedly of Agnes Laiter, and looking at her photograph, and patting himself on the back for being one of the most constant lovers in history, and warming to the work as he went on, he really fancied that he had been very hardly used. He sat down and wrote one final letter—a really pathetic "world without end, amen," epistle; explaining how he would be true to Eternity, and that all women were very much alike, and he would hide his broken heart, etc., etc.; but if, at any future time, etc., etc., he could afford to wait, etc., etc., unchanged affections, etc., etc., return to her old love, etc., etc., for eight closely-written pages. From an artistic point of view, it was very neat work, but an ordinary Philistine, who knew the state of Phil's real feelings—not the ones he rose to as he went on writing—would have called it the thoroughly mean and selfish work of a thoroughly mean and selfish weak man. But this verdict would have been incorrect. Phil paid for the postage, and felt every word he had written for at least two days and a half. It was the last flicker before the light went out.

That letter made Agnes Laiter very unhappy, and she cried and put it away in her desk, and became Mrs. Somebody Else for the good of her family. Which is the first duty of every Christian maid.

Phil went his ways, and thought no more of his letter, except as an artist thinks of a neatly touched-in sketch. His ways were not bad, but they were not altogether good until they brought him across Dunmaya, the daughter of a

Rajput ex-Subadar-Major of our Native
Army. The girl had a strain of Hill
blood in her, and like the Hill-women,
was not a *purdah-nashin* or woman who
lives behind the veil. Where Phil met
her, or how he heard of her, does not
matter. She was a good girl and handsome, and, in her way, very clever and
shrewd; though, of course, a little hard.
It is to be remembered that Phil was
living very comfortably, denying himself no small luxury, never putting by a
penny, very satisfied with himself and
his good intentions, was dropping all his
English correspondents one by one, and
beginning more and more to look upon
India as his home. Some men fall this
way; and they are of no use afterward.
The climate where he was stationed was
good, and it really did not seem ot him
that there was any reason to return to
England.

He did what many planters have done
before him—that is to say, he made up
his mind to marry a Hill-girl and settle
down. He was seven-and-twenty then,
with a long life before him, but no
spirit to go through with it. So he married Dunmaya by the forms of the English Church, and some fellow-planters
said he was a fool, and some said he
was a wise man. Dunmaya was a thoroughly honest girl, and, in spite of her
reverence for an Englishman, had a reasonable estimate of her husband's weaknesses. She managed him tenderly, and
became, in less than a year, a very passable imitation of an English lady in
dress and carriage. It is curious to
think that a Hill-man after a lifetime's
education is a Hill-man still; but a Hill-
woman can in six months master most
of the ways of her English sisters.

There was a coolie-woman once. But
that is another story. Dunmaya dressed
by preference in black and yellow and
looked well.

Meantime Phil's letter lay in Agnes
Laiter's desk, and now and again she
would think of poor, resolute, hard-
working Phil among the cobras and
tigers of Darjiling, toiling in the vain
hope that she might come back to him.
Her husband was worth ten Phils, except that he had rheumatism of the
heart. Three years after he was married,—and after he had tried Nice and
Algeria for his complaint,—he went to
Bombay, where he died, and set Agnes
free. Being a devout woman, she looked
on his death and the place of it, as a
direct interposition of Providence, and
when she had recovered from the shock,
she took out and re-read Phil's letter
with the "etc., etc.," and the big dashes,
and the little dashes, and kissed it several times. No one knew her in Bombay; she had her husband's income,
which was a large one, and Phil was
close at hand. It was wrong and improper, of course, but she decided, as
heroines do in novels, to find her old
lover, to offer him her hand and her
gold, and with him spend the rest of her
life in some spot far from unsympathetic
souls. She sat for two months, alone in
Watson's Hotel, elaborating this decision, and the picture was a pretty one.
Then she set out in search of Phil Garron, Assistant on a tea plantation with
a more than usually unpronounceable
name.

* * * * * *

She found him. She spent a month
over it, for his plantation was not in

the Darjiling district at all, but nearer Kangra. Phil was very little altered, and Dunmaya was very nice to her.

Now the particular sin and shame of the whole business is that Phil, who really is not worth thinking of twice, was and is loved by Dunmaya, and more than loved by Agnes, the whole of whose life he seems to have spoiled.

Worst of all, Dunmaya is making a decent man of him; and he will ultimately be saved from perdition through her training.

Which is manifestly unfair.

False Dawn

To-night God-knows what thing shall tide,
  The Earth is racked and faint—
Expectant, sleepless, open-eyed;
And we, who from the Earth were made,
  Thrill with our Mother's pain.
                        —*In Durance.*

No man will ever know the exact truth of this story; though women may sometimes whisper it to one another after a dance, when they are putting up their hair for the night and comparing lists of victims. A man, of course, cannot assist at these functions. So the tale must be told from the outside—in the dark—all wrong.

Never praise a sister to a sister, in the hope of your compliments reaching the proper ears, and so preparing the way for you later on. Sisters are women first, and sisters afterward; and you will find that you do yourself harm.

Saumarez knew this when he made up his mind to propose to the elder Miss Copleigh. Saumarez was a strange man, with few merits so far as men could see, though he was popular with women, and carried enough conceit to stock a Viceroy's Council and leave a little over for the Commander-in-Chief's Staff. He was a Civilian. Very many women took an interest in Saumarez, perhaps, because his manner to them was offensive. If you hit a pony over the nose at the outset of your acquaintance, he may not love you, but he will take a deep interest in your movements ever afterward. The elder Miss Copleigh was nice, plump, winning, and pretty. The younger was not so pretty, and, from men disregarding the hint set forth above, her style was repellant and unattractive. Both girls had, practically, the same figure, and there was a strong likeness between them in look and voice; though no one could doubt for an instant which was the nicer of the two.

Saumarez made up his mind, as soon as they came into the station from Behar, to marry the elder one. At least, we all made sure that he would, which comes to the same thing. She was two-and-twenty, and he was thirty-three, with pay and allowances of nearly fourteen hundred rupees a month. So the match, as we arranged it, was in every way a good one. Saumarez was his name, and summary was his nature, as a man once said. Having drafted his Resolution, he formed a Select Committee of One to sit upon it, and resolved to take his time. In our unpleasant slang, the Copleigh girls "hunted in couples." That is to say, you could do nothing with one without the other. They were very loving sisters; but their mutual affection was sometimes inconvenient. Saumarez held the balance-hair true between them, and none but himself could have said to which side his heart inclined; though every one guessed. He rode with them a good deal and danced with them, but he never succeeded in detaching them from each other for any length of time.

Women said that the two girls kept together through deep mistrust, each fearing that the other would steal a march on her. But that has nothing to do with a man. Saumarez was silent for good or bad, and as business-likely attentive as he could be, having due regard to his work and his polo. Beyond doubt both girls were fond of him.

As the hot weather drew nearer and Saumarez made no sign, women said that you could see their trouble in the eyes of the girls—that they were looking strained, anxious, and irritable. Men are quite blind in these matters unless they have more of the woman than the man in their composition, in which case it does not matter what they say or think. I maintain it was the hot April days that took the color out of the Copleigh girls' cheeks. They should have been sent to the Hills early. No one— man or woman—feels an angel when the hot weather is approaching. The younger sister grew more cynical, not to say acid, in her ways; and the winningness of the elder wore thin. There was effort in it.

The Station wherein all these things happened was, though not a little one, off the line of rail, and suffered through want of attention. There were no gardens, or bands or amusements worth speaking of, and it was nearly a day's journey to come into Lahore for a dance. People were grateful for small things to interest them.

About the beginning of May, and just before the final exodus of Hill-goers, when the weather was very hot and there were not more than twenty people in the Station, Saumarez gave a moonlight riding-picnic at an old tomb, six miles away, near the bed of the river. It was a "Noah's Ark" picnic; and there was to be the usual arrangement of quarter-mile intervals between each couple, on account of the dust. Six couples came altogether, including chaperones. Moonlight picnics are useful just at the very end of the season, before all the girls go away to the Hills. They lead to understandings, and should be encouraged by chaperones; especially those whose girls look sweetest in riding-habits. I knew a case once. But that is another story. That picnic was called the "Great Pop Picnic," because every one knew Saumarez would propose then to the eldest Miss Copleigh; and, besides his affair, there was another which might possibly come to happiness. The social atmosphere was heavily charged and wanted clearing.

We met at the parade-ground at ten: the night was fearfully hot. The horses sweated even at walking-pace, but anything was better than sitting still in our own dark houses. When we moved off under the full moon we were four couples, one triplet, and Me. Saumarez rode with the Copleigh girls, and I loitered at the tail of the procession wondering with whom Saumarez would ride home. Every one was happy and contented; but we all felt that things were going to happen. We rode slowly; and it was nearly midnight before we reached the old tomb, facing the ruined tank, in the decayed gardens where we were going to eat and drink. I was late in coming up; and, before I went in to the garden, I saw that the horizon to the north carried a faint, dun-colored feather. But no one would have thanked me for spoiling so well-managed an entertainment as this picnic—and a dust storm, more or less, does no great harm.

We gathered by the tank. Some one had brought out a banjo—which is a most sentimental instrument—and three or four of us sang. You must not laugh at this. Our amusements in out-of-the-way Stations are very few indeed. Then we talked in groups or together, lying under the trees, with the sun-baked roses dropping their petals on our feet, until supper was ready. It was a beautiful supper, as cold and as iced as you could wish; and we stayed long over it.

I had felt that the air was growing hotter and hotter; but nobody seemed to notice it until the moon went out and a burning hot wind began lashing the orange-trees with a sound like the noise of the sea. Before we knew where we were, the dust-storm was on us and everything was roaring, whirling darkness. The supper-table was blown bodily into the tank. We were afraid of staying anywhere near the old tomb for fear it might be blown down. So we felt our way to the orange-trees where the horses were picketed and waited for the storm to blow over. Then the little light that was left vanished, and you could not see your hand before your face. The air was heavy with dust and sand from the bed of the river, that filled boots and pockets and drifted down necks and coated eyebrows and moustaches. It was one of the worst dust-storms of the year. We were all huddled together close to the trembling horses, with the thunder chattering overhead, and the lightning spurting like water from a sluice, all ways at once. There was no danger, of course, unless the horses broke loose. I was standing with my head downwind and my hands over my mouth, hearing the trees thrashing each other. I could not see who was next me till the flashes came. Then I found that I was packed near Saumarez and the eldest Miss Copleigh, with my own horse just in front of me. I recognized the eldest Miss Copleigh, because she had a puggree round her helmet, and the younger had not. All the electricity in the air had gone into my body and I was quivering and tingling from head to foot—exactly as a corn shoots and tingles before rain. It was a grand storm. The wind seemed to be picking up the earth and pitching it to leeward in great heaps; and the heat beat up from the ground like the heat of the Day of Judgment.

The storm lulled slightly after the first half-hour, and I heard a despairing little voice close to my ear, saying to itself, quietly and softly, as if some lost soul were flying about with the wind, "O my God!" Then the younger Miss Copleigh stumbled into my arms, saying, "Where is my horse? Get my horse. I want to go home. I want to go home. Take me home."

I thought that the lightning and the black darkness had frightened her; so I said there was no danger, but she must wait till the storm blew over. She answered, "It is not that! I want to go home! Oh, take me away from here!"

I said that she could not go till the light came; but I felt her brush past me and go away. It was too dark to see where. Then the whole sky was split open with one tremendous flash, as if the end of the world were coming, and all the women shrieked.

Almost directly after this, I felt a man's hand on my shoulder and heard Saumarez bellowing in my ear. Through the rattling of the trees and howling of the wind, I did not catch his words at once, but at last I heard him say, "I've proposed to the wrong one! What shall I do?" Saumarez had no occasion to make this confidence to me. I was never a friend of his, nor am I now; but I fancy neither of us were ourselves just then. He was shaking as he stood with excitement, and I was feeling queer all over with the electricity. I could not think of anything to say except, "More fool you for proposing in a dust-storm." But I did not see how that would improve the mistake.

Then he shouted, "Where's Edith— Edith Copleigh?" Edith was the younger sister. I answered out of my astonishment, "What do you want with *her?*" For the next two minutes, he and I were shouting at each other like maniacs,—he vowing that it was the younger sister he had meant to propose to all along, and I telling him till my throat was hoarse that he must have

made a mistake! I cannot account for this except, again, by the fact that we were neither of us ourselves. Everything seemed to me like a bad dream— from the stamping of the horses in the darkness to Saumarez telling me the story of his loving Edith Copleigh from the first. He was still clawing my shoulder and begging me to tell him where Edith Copleigh was, when another lull came and brought light with it, and we saw the dust-cloud forming on the plain in front of us. So we knew the worst was over. The moon was low down, and there was just the glimmer of the false dawn that comes about an hour before the real one. But the light was very faint, and the dun cloud roared like a bull. I wondered where Edith Copleigh had gone; and as I was wondering I saw three things together: First, Maud Copleigh's face come smiling out of the darkness and move toward Saumarez who was standing by me. I heard the girl whisper, "George," and slide her arm through the arm that was not clawing my shoulder, and I saw that look on her face which only comes once or twice in a lifetime—when a woman is perfectly happy and the air is full of trumpets and gorgeously-colored fire and the Earth turns into cloud because she loves and is loved. At the same time, I saw Saumarez's face as he heard Maud Copleigh's voice, and fifty yards away from the clump of orange-trees, I saw a brown holland habit getting upon a horse.

It must have been my state of over-excitement that made me so ready to meddle with what did not concern me. Saumarez was moving off to the habit; but I pushed him back and said, "Stop here and explain. I'll fetch her back!" And I ran out to get at my own horse. I had a perfectly unnecessary notion that everything must be done decently and in order, and that Saumarez's first care was to wipe the happy look out of Maud Copleigh's face. All the time I was linking up the curb-chain I wondered how he would do it.

I cantered after Edith Copleigh, thinking to bring her back slowly on some pretence or another. But she galloped away as soon as she saw me, and I was forced to ride after her in earnest. She called back over her shoulder—"Go away! I'm going home. Oh, go away!" two or three times; but my business was to catch her first, and argue later. The ride fitted in with the rest of the evil dream. The ground was very rough, and now and again we rushed through the whirling, choking "dust-devils" in the skirts of the flying storm. There was a burning hot wind blowing that brought up a stench of stale brick-kilns with it; and through the half light and through the dust-devils, across that desolate plain, flickered the brown holland habit on the grey horse. She headed for the Station at first. Then she wheeled round and set off for the river through beds of burned-down jungle-grass, bad even to ride pig over. In cold blood I should never have dreamed of going over such a country at night, but it seemed quite right and natural with the lightning crackling overhead, and a reek like the smell of the Pit in my nostrils. I rode and shouted, and she bent forward and lashed her horse, and the aftermath of the dust-storm came up, and caught us both, and drove us downwind like pieces of paper.

I don't know how far we rode; but the drumming of the horse-hoofs and the roar of the wind and the race of the faint blood-red moon through the yellow mist seemed to have gone on for years and years, and I was literally drenched with sweat from my helmet to my gaiters when the grey stumbled, recovered himself and pulled up dead lame. My brute was used up altogether. Edith Copleigh was bare headed, plastered with dust, and crying bitterly. "Why can't you let me alone?" she said. "I only wanted to get away and go home. Oh, *please* let me go!"

"You have got to come back with me, Miss Copleigh. Saumarez has something to say to you."

It was a foolish way of putting it; but I hardly knew Miss Copleigh; and, though I was playing Providence at the cost of my horse, I could not tell her in as many words what Saumarez had told me. I thought he could do that better himself. All her pretence about being tired and wanting to go home broke down, and she rocked herself to and fro in the saddle as she sobbed, and the hot wind blew her black hair to leeward. I am not going to repeat what she said, because she was utterly unstrung.

This was the cynical Miss Copleigh, and I, almost an utter stranger to her, was trying to tell her that Saumarez loved her and she was to come back to hear him say so. I believe I made myself understood, for she gathered the grey together and made him hobble somehow, and we set off for the tomb, while the storm went thundering down to Umballa and a few big drops of warm rain fell. I found out that she had been standing close to Saumarez when he proposed to her sister, and had wanted to go home to cry in peace, as an English girl should. She dabbed her eyes with her pocket-handkerchief as we went along, and babbled to me out of sheer lightness of heart and hysteria. That was perfectly unnatural; and yet, it seemed all right at the time and in the place. All the world was only the two Copleigh girls, Saumarez and I, ringed in with the lightning and the dark; and the guidance of this misguided world seemed to lie in my hands.

When we returned to the tomb in the deep dead stillness that followed the storm, the dawn was just breaking and nobody had gone away. They were waiting for our return. Saumarez most of all. His face was white and drawn. As Miss Copleigh and I limped up, he came forward to meet us, and, when he helped her down from her saddle, he kissed her before all the picnic. It was like a scene in a theatre, and the likeness was heightened by all the dust-white, ghostly-looking men and women under the orange-trees clapping their hands—as if they were watching a play

—at Saumarez's choice. I never knew anything so un-English in my life.

Lastly, Saumarez said we must all go home or the Station would come out to look for us, and would I be good enough to ride home with Maud Copleigh? Nothing would give me greater pleasure, I said.

So we formed up, six couples in all, and went back two by two; Saumarez walking at the side of Edith Copleigh, who was riding his horse. Maud Copleigh did not talk to me at any length.

The air was cleared; and, little by little, as the sun rose, I felt we were all dropping back again into ordinary men and women, and that the "Great Pop Picnic" was a thing altogether apart and out of the world—never to happen again. It had gone with the dust-storm and the tingle in the hot air.

I felt tired and limp, and a good deal ashamed of myself as I went in for a bath and some sleep.

There is a woman's version of this story, but it will never be written . . . unless Maud Copleigh cares to try.

------◆------

The Rescue of Pluffles

Thus, for a season, they fought it fair—
  She and his cousin May—
Tactful, talented, debonnaire,
Decorous foes were they;
But never can battle of man compare
With merciless feminine fray.
          —Two and One.

MRS. HAUKSBEE was sometimes nice to her own sex. Here is a story to

prove this; and you can believe just as much as ever you please.

Pluffles was a subaltern in the "Unmentionables." He was callow, even for a subaltern. He was callow all over—like a canary that had not finished fledging itself. The worst of it was that he had three times as much money as was good for him; Pluffles' Papa being a rich man and Pluffles being the only son. Pluffles' Mamma adored him. She was only a little less callow than Pluffles, and she believed everything he said.

Pluffles' weakness was not believing what people said. He preferred what he called trusting to his own judgment. He had as much judgment as he had seat or hands; and this preference tumbled him into trouble once or twice. But the biggest trouble Pluffles ever manufactured came about at Simla—some years ago, when he was four-and-twenty.

He began by trusting to his own judgment as usual, and the result was that, after a time, he was bound hand and foot to Mrs. Reiver's 'rick-shaw wheels.

There was nothing good about Mrs. Reiver, unless it was her dress. She was bad from her hair—which started life on a Brittany girl's head—to her boot-heels, which were two and three-eighth inches high. She was not honestly mischievous like Mrs. Hauksbee; she was wicked in a business-like way.

There was never any scandal—she had not generous impulses enough for that. She was the exception which proved the rule that Anglo-Indian ladies are in every way as nice as their sisters at Home. She spent her life in proving that rule.

Mrs. Hauksbee and she hated each other fervently. They hated far too much to clash; but the things they said of each other were startling—not to say original. Mrs. Hauksbee was honest—honest as her own front-teeth—and, but for her love of mischief, would have

been a woman's woman. There was no honesty about Mrs. Reiver; nothing but selfishness. And at the beginning of the season, poor little Pluffles fell a prey to her. She laid herself out to that end, and how was Pluffles to resist? He trusted to his judgment, and he got judged.

I have seen Captain Hayes argue with a tough horse—I have seen a tonga-driver coerce a stubborn pony—I have seen a riotous setter broken to gun by a hard keeper—but the breaking-in of Pluffles of the "Unmentionables" was beyond all these. He learned to fetch and carry like a dog, and to wait like one, too, for a word from Mrs. Reiver. He learned to keep appointments which Mrs. Reiver had no intention of keeping. He learned to take thankfully dances which Mrs. Reiver had no intention of giving him. He learned to shiver for an hour and a quarter on the windward side of Elysium while Mrs. Reiver was making up her mind to come for a ride. He learned to hunt for a 'rickshaw, in a light dress-suit under pelting rain, and to walk by the side of that 'rickshaw when he had found it. He learned what it was to be spoken to like a coolie and ordered about like a cook. He learned all this and many other things besides. And he paid for his schooling.

Perhaps, in some hazy way, he fancied that it was fine and impressive, that it gave him a status among men, and was altogether the thing to do. It was nobody's business to warn Pluffles that he was unwise. The pace that season was too good to inquire; and meddling with another man's folly is always thankless work. Pluffles Colonel should have ordered him back to his regiment when he heard how things were going. But Pluffles had got himself engaged to a girl in England the last time he went Home; and, if there was one thing more than another that the Colonel detested, it was a married subaltern. He chuckled when he heard of the education of Pluffles, and said it was good training for the boy. But it was not good training in the least. It led him into spending money beyond his means, which were good; above that, the education spoiled an average boy and made it a tenth-rate man of an objectionable kind. He wandered into a bad set, and his little bill at the jewelers was a thing to wonder at.

Then Mrs. Hauksbee rose to the occasion. She played her game alone, knowing what people would say of her; and she played it for the sake of a girl she had never seen. Pluffles' *fiancée* was to come out, under chaperonage of an aunt, in October, to be married to Pluffles.

At the beginning of August, Mrs. Hauksbee discovered that it was time to interfere. A man who rides much knows exactly what a horse is going to do next before he does it. In the same way, a woman of Mrs. Hauksbee's experience knows accurately how a boy will behave under certain circumstances—notably when he is infatuated with one of Mrs. Reiver's stamp. She said that, sooner or later, little Pluffles would break off that engagement for nothing at all—simply to gratify Mrs. Reiver, who, in return, would keep him at her feet and in her service just so long as she found it worth her while. She said

she knew the signs of these things. If she did not no one else could.

Then she went forth to capture Pluffles under the guns of the enemy; just as Mrs. Cusack-Bremmil carried away Bremmil under Mrs. Hauksbee's eyes.

This particular engagement lasted seven weeks—we called it the Seven Weeks' War—and was fought out inch by inch on both sides. A detailed account would fill a book, and would be incomplete then. Anyone who knows about these things can fit in the details for himself. It was a superb fight— there will never be another like it as long as Jakko Hill stands—and Pluffles was the prize of victory. People said shameful things about Mrs. Hauksbee. They did not know what she was playing for. Mrs. Reiver fought partly because Pluffles was useful to her, but mainly because she hated Mrs. Hauksbee, and the matter was a trial of strength between them. No one knows what Pluffles thought. He had not many ideas at the best of times, and the few he possessed made him conceited. Mrs. Hauksbee said, "The boy must be caught; and the only way of catching him is by treating him well."

So she treated him as a man of the world and of experience so long as the issue was doubtful. Little by little, Pluffles fell away from his old allegiance and came over to the enemy, by whom he was made much of. He was never sent on out-post duty after 'rickshaws any more, nor was he given dances which never came off, nor were the drains on his purse continued. Mrs. Hauksbee held him on the snaffle; and, after his treatment at Mrs. Reiver's hands, he appreciated the change.

Mrs. Reiver had broken him of talking about himself, and made him talk about her own merits. Mrs. Hauksbee acted otherwise, and won his confidence, till he mentioned his engagement to the girl at Home, speaking of it in a high and mighty way as a piece of boyish folly. This was when he was taking tea with her one afternoon, and discoursing in what he considered a gay and fascinating style. Mrs. Hauksbee had seen an earlier generation of his stamp bud and blossom, and decay into fat Captains and tubby Majors.

At a moderate estimate there were about three-and-twenty sides to that lady's character. Some men say more. She began to talk to Pluffles after the manner of a mother, and as if there had been three hundred years, instead of fifteen, between them. She spoke with a sort of throaty quaver in her voice which had a soothing effect, though what she said was anything but soothing. She pointed out the exceeding folly, not to say meanness, of Pluffles' conduct, and the smallness of his views. Then he stammered something about "trusting to his own judgment as a man of the world"; and this paved the way for what she wanted to say next. It would have withered up Pluffles had it come from any other woman; but, in the soft cooing style in which Mrs. Hauksbee put it, it only made him feel limp and repentant—as if he had been in some superior kind of church. Little by little, very softly and pleasantly, she began taking the conceit out of Pluffles, as they take the ribs out of an umbrella before re-covering it. She told him what she thought of him

and his judgment and his knowledge of the world; and how his performances had made him ridiculous to other people; and how it was his intention to make love to herself if she gave him the chance. Then she said that marriage would be the making of him; and drew a pretty little picture—all rose and opal —of the Mrs. Pluffles of the future going through life relying on the judgment and knowledge of the world of a husband who had nothing to reproach himself with. How she reconciled these two statements she alone knew. But they did not stirke Pluffles as conflicting.

Hers was a perfect little homily— much better than any clergyman could have given—and it ended with touching allusions to Pluffles' Mamma and Papa, and the wisdom of taking his bride Home.

Then she sent Pluffles out for a walk, to think over what she had said. Pluffles left, blowing his nose very hard and holding himself very straight. Mrs. Hauksbee laughed.

What Pluffles had intended to do in the matter of the engagement only Mrs. Reiver knew, and she kept her own counsel to her death. She would have liked it spoiled as a compliment, I fancy.

Pluffles enjoyed many talks with Mrs. Hauksbee during the next few days. They were all to the same end, and they helped Pluffles in the path of Virtue.

Mrs. Hauksbee wanted to keep him under her wing to the last. Therefore she discountenanced his going down to Bombay to get married. "Goodness only knows what might happen by the way!" she said. "Pluffles is cursed with the curse of Reuben, and India is no fit place for him!"

In the end, the *fiancée* arrived with her aunt; and Pluffles, having reduced his affairs to some sort of order—here again Mrs. Hauksbee helped him—was married.

Mrs. Hauksbee gave a sigh of relief when both the "I wills" had been said, and went her way.

Pluffles took her advice about going Home. He left the Service and is now raising speckled cattle inside green painted fences somewhere in England. I believe he does this very judiciously. He would have come to extreme grief in India.

For these reasons, if any one says anything more than usually nasty about Mrs. Hauksbee, tell him the story of the Rescue of Pluffles.

Cupid's Arrows

Pit where the buffalo cooled his hide,
By the hot sun emptied, and blistered and dried;
Log in the plume-grass, hidden and lone;
Dam where the earth-rat's mounds are strown;
Cave in the bank where the sly stream steals;
Aloe that stabs at the belly and heels,
Jump if you dare on a steed untried—
Safer it is to go wide—go wide!
Hark, from in front where the best men ride:
"Pull to the off, boys! Wide! Go wide!"
            —*The Peora Hunt.*

ONCE upon a time there lived at Simla a very pretty girl, the daughter of a poor but honest District and Sessions Judge. She was a good girl but could not help knowing her power and using it. Her Mamma was very anxious about her daughter's future, as all good Mammas should be.

When a man is a Commissioner and a bachelor and has the right of wearing open-work jam-tart jewels in gold and enamel on his clothes, and of going through a door before every one except a Member of Council, a Lieutenant-Governor, or a Viceroy, he is worth marrying. At least, that is what ladies say. There was a Commissioner in Simla, in those days, who was, and wore and did all I have said. He was a plain man—an ugly man—the ugliest man in Asia, with two exceptions. His was a face to dream about and try to carve on a pipe-head afterward. His name was Saggott — Bar-Saggott — Anthony Bar-Saggott and six letters to follow. Departmentally, he was one of the best men the Government of India owned. Socially, he was like unto a blandishing gorilla.

When he turned his attentions to Miss Beighton, I believe that Mrs. Beighton wept with delight at the reward Providence had sent her in her old age.

Mr. Beighton held his tongue. He was an easy-going man.

A Commissioner is very rich. His pay is beyond the dreams of avarice—is so enormous that he can afford to save and scrape in a way that would almost discredit a Member of Council. Most Commissioners are mean; but Barr-Saggott was an exception. He entertained royally; he horsed himself well; he gave dances; he was a power in the land; and he behaved as such.

Consider that everything I am writing of took place in an almost pre-historic era in the history of British India. Some folk may remember the years before lawn-tennis was born when we all played croquet. There were seasons before that, if you will believe me, when even croquet had not been invented, and archery—which was revived in England in 1844—was as great a pest as lawn-tennis is now. People talked learnedly about "holding" and "loosing," "steles," "reflexed bows," "56-pound bows," "backed" or "self-yew bows," as we talk about "rallies," "volleys," "smashes," "returns," and "16-ounce rackets."

Miss Beighton shot divinely over ladies' distance—sixty yards, that is—and was acknowledged the best lady archer in Simla. Men called her "Diana of Tara-Devi."

Barr-Saggott paid her great attention; and, as I have said, the heart of her mother was uplifted in consequence. Kitty Beighton took matters more calmly. It was pleasant to be singled out by a Commissioner with letters after his name, and to fill the hearts of other girls with bad feelings. But there was no denying the fact that Barr-Saggott was phenomenally ugly; and all his attempts to adorn himself only made him more grotesque. He was not christened "The *Langur*"—which means grey ape—for nothing. It was pleasant, Kitty thought, to have him at her feet, but it

was better to escape from him and ride with the graceless Cubbon—the man in a Dragoon Regiment at Umballa—the boy with a handsome face, and no prospects. Kitty liked Cubbon more than a little. He never pretended for a moment that he was anything less than head over heels in love with her; for he was an honest boy. So Kitty fled, now and again, from the stately wooings of Barr-Saggott to the company of young Cubbon, and was scolded by her Mamma in consequence. "But, Mother," she said, "Mr. Saggott is such—such a —is so *fearfully* ugly, you know!"

"My dear," said Mrs. Beighton, piously, "we cannot be other than an all-ruling Providence has made us. Besides, you will take precedence of your own Mother, you know! Think of that and be reasonable."

Then Kitty put up her little chin and said irreverent things about precedence, and Commissioners, and matrimony. Mr. Beighton rubbed the top of his head; for he was an easy-going man.

Late in the season, when he judged that the time was ripe, Barr-Saggott developed a plan which did great credit to his administrative powers. He arranged an archery-tournament for ladies, with a most sumptuous diamond-studded bracelet as prize. He drew up his terms skilfully, and every one saw that the bracelet was a gift to Miss Beighton; the acceptance carrying with it the hand and the heart of Commissioner Barr-Saggott. The terms were a St. Leonard's Round—thirty-six shots at sixty yards—under the rules of the Simla Toxophilite Society.

All Simla was invited. There were beautifully arranged tea-tables under the deodars at Annandale, where the Grand Stand is now; and, alone in its glory, winking in the sun, sat the diamond bracelet in a blue velvet case. Miss Beighton was anxious—almost too anxious—to compete. On the appointed afternoon all Simla rode down to Annandale to witness the Judgment of Paris turned upside down. Kitty rode with young Cubbon, and it was easy to see that the boy was troubled in his mind. He must be held innocent of everything that followed. Kitty was pale and nervous, and looked long at the bracelet. Barr-Saggott was gorgeously dressed, even more nervous than Kitty, and more hideous than ever.

Mrs. Beighton smiled condescendingly, as befitted the mother of a potential Commissioneress, and the shooting began: all the world standing a semicircle as the ladies came out one after the other.

Nothing is so tedious as an archery competition. They shot, and they shot, and they kept on shooting, till the sun left the valley, and little breezes got up in the deodars, and people waited for Miss Beighton to shoot and win. Cubbon was at one horn of the semicircle round the shooters, and Barr-Saggott at the other. Miss Beighton was last on the list. The scoring had been weak, and the bracelet, with Commissioner Barr-Saggott, was hers to a certainty.

The Commissioner strung her bow with his own sacred hands. She stepped forward, looked at the bracelet, and her first arrow went true to a hair—full into the heart of the "gold"—counting nine points.

Young Cubbon on the left turned white, and his Devil prompted Barr-Saggott to smile. Now horses used to shy when Barr-Saggott smiled. Kitty saw that smile. She looked to her left-front, gave an almost imperceptible nod to Cubbon, and went on shooting.

I wish I could describe the scene that followed. It was out of the ordinary and most improper. Miss Kitty fitted her arrows with immense deliberation, so that every one might see what she was doing. She was a perfect shot; and her forty-six pound bow suited her to a nicety. She pinned the wooden legs of the target with great care four successive times. She pinned the wooden top of the target once, and all the ladies looked at each other. Then she began some fancy shooting at the white, which if you hit it, counts exactly one point. She put five arrows into the white. It was wonderful archery; but, seeing that her business was to make "golds" and win the bracelet, Barr-Saggott turned a delicate green like young water-grass. Next, she shot over the target twice, then wide to the left twice—always with the same deliberation—while a chilly hush fell over the company, and Mrs. Beighton took out her handkerchief. Then Kitty shot at the ground in front of the target, and split several arrows. Then she made a red—or seven points—just to show what she could do if she liked, and she finished up her amazing performance with some more fancy shooting at the target supports. Here is her score as it was pricked off:

	Gold	Red	Blue	Black	White	Total Hits	Total Score
Miss Beighton	1	1	0	0	5	7	21

Barr-Saggott looked as if the last few arrowheads had been driven into his legs instead of the target's, and the deep stillness was broken by a little snubby, mottled, half-grown girl saying in a shrill voice of triumph, "Then *I've* won!"

Mrs. Beighton did her best to bear up; but she wept in the presence of the people. No training could help her through such a disappointment. Kitty unstrung her bow with a vicious jerk, and went back to her place, while Barr-Saggott was trying to pretend that he enjoyed snapping the bracelet on the snubby girl's raw, red wrist. It was an awkward scene—most awkward. Every one tried to depart in a body and leave Kitty to the mercy of her Mamma.

But Cubbon took her away instead, and—the rest isn't worth printing.

His Chance in Life

Then a pile of heads he laid—
Thirty thousands heaped on high—
All to please the Kafir maid,
Where the Oxus ripples by.
Grimly spake Atulla Khan:—
"Love hath made this thing a Man."
—*Oatta's Story.*

IF you go straight away from Levées and Government House Lists, past Trades' Balls—far beyond everything and everybody you ever knew in your respectable life—you cross, in time, the Borderline where the last drop of White blood ends and the full tide of Black sets in. It would be easier to talk to a new-made Duchess on the spur of the moment than to the Borderline folk without violating some of their conventions or hurting their feelings. The Black and the White mix very quaintly in their ways. Sometimes the White shows in spurts of fierce, childish pride—which is Pride of Race run crooked—and sometimes the Black in still fiercer abasement and humility, half-heathenish customs and strange, unaccountable impulses to crime. One of these days, this people—understand they are far lower than the class whence Derozio, the man who imitated Byron, sprung—will turn out a writer or a poet; and then we shall know how they live and what they feel. In the meantime, any stories about them cannot be absolutely correct in fact or inference.

Miss Vezzis came from across the Borderline to look after some children who belonged to a lady until a regularly ordained nurse could come out. The lady said Miss Vezzis was a bad, dirty nurse and inattentive. It never struck her that Miss Vezzis had her own life to lead and her own affairs to worry over, and that these affairs were the most important things in the world to Miss Vezzis. Very few mistresses admit this sort of reasoning. Miss Vezzis was as black as a boot, and, to our standard of taste, hideously ugly. She wore cotton-print gowns and bulged shoes; and when she lost her temper with the children, she abused them in the language of the Borderline—which is part English, part Portuguese, and part Native. She was not attractive; but she had her pride, and she preferred being called "Miss Vezzis."

Every Sunday, she dressed herself wonderfully and went to see her Mamma, who lived, for the most part, on an old cane chair in a greasy *tussur*-silk dressing-grown and a big rabbit-warren of a house full of Vezzises, Pereiras, Ribieras, Lisboas and Gonsalveses, and a floating population of loafers; besides fragments of the day's market, garlic, stale incense, clothes thrown on the floor, petticoats hung on strings for screens, old bottles, pewter crucifixes dried *immortelles,* pariah puppies, plaster images of the Virgin, and hats without crowns. Miss Vezzis drew twenty rupees a month for acting as nurse, and she squabbled weekly with her Mamma as to the percentage to be given toward housekeeping. When the quarrel was over, Michele D'Cruze used to shamble across the low mud wall of the compound and make love to Miss Vezzis after the fashion of the Borderline, which is hedged about with much ceremony. Michele was a poor, sickly weed and very black; but he had his pride. He would not be seen smoking a *huqa* for anything; and he looked down on natives as only a man with seven-eighths native blood in his veins can. The Vezzis Family had their pride too. They traced their descent from a mythical platelayer who had worked on the Sone Bridge when railways were new in India, and they valued their English origin. Michele was a Telegraph Signaller on Rs. 35 a month. The fact that he was in Government employ made Mrs. Vezzis lenient to the short-comings of his ancestors.

There was a compromising legend—Dom Anna the tailor brought it from Poonani—that a black Jew of Cochin had once married into the D'Cruze family; while it was an open secret that an uncle of Mrs. D'Cruze was, at that very time, doing menial work, connected with cooking, for a Club in Southern India! He sent Mrs. D'Cruze seven rupees eight annas a month; but she felt the disgrace to the family very keenly all the same.

However, in the course of a few Sundays, Mrs. Vezzis brought herself to overlook these blemishes and gave her consent to the marriage of her daughter with Michele, on condition that Michele should have at least fifty rupees a month to start married life upon. This wonderful prudence must have been a lingering touch of the mythical platelayer's Yorkshire blood; for across the Border-line people take a pride in marrying when they please—not when they can.

Having regard to his departmental prospects, Miss Vezzis might as well have asked Michele to go away and come back with the Moon in his pocket. But Michele was deeply in love with Miss Vezzis, and that helped him to endure. He accompanied Miss Vezzis to Mass one Sunday, and after Mass, walking home through the hot stale dust with her hand in his, he swore by several Saints whose names would not interest you, never to forget Miss Vezzis; and she swore by her Honor and the Saints —the oath runs rather curiously; *"In nomine Sanctissimæ"*—(whatever the name of the she-Saint is) and so forth, ending with a kiss on the forehead, a kiss on the left cheek, and a kiss on the mouth—never to forget Michele.

Next week Michele was transferred, and Miss Vezzis dropped tears upon the window-sash of the "Intermediate" compartment as he left the Station.

If you look at the telegraph-map of India you will see a long line skirting the coast from Backergunge to Madras. Michele was ordered to Tibasu, a little Sub-office one-third down this line, to send messages on from Berhampur to Chicacola, and to think of Miss Vezzis and his chances of getting fifty rupees a month out of office-hours. He had the noise of the Bay of Bengal and a Bengali Babu for company; nothing more. He sent foolish letters, with crosses tucked inside the flaps of the envelopes, to Miss Vezzis.

When he had been at Tibasu for nearly three weeks his chance came.

Never forget that unless the outward and visible signs of Our Authority are always before a native he is as incapable as a child of understanding what authority means, or where is the danger of disobeying it. Tibasu was a forgotten little place with a few Orissa Mahommedans in it. These, hearing nothing of the Collector-*Sahib* for some time and heartily despising the Hindu Sub-Judge, arranged to start a little Mohurrum riot of their own. But the Hindus turned out and broke their heads; when, finding lawlessness pleasant, Hindus and Mahommedans together raised an aimless sort of Donnybrook just to see how far they could go. They looted each others' shops, and paid off private grudges in the regular way. It was a nasty little riot, but not worth putting in the newspapers.

Michele was working in his office when he heard the sound that a man never forgets all his life—the "*ah-yah*" of an angry crowd. [When that sound drops about three tones, and changes to a thick, droning *us*, the man who hears it had better go away if he is alone.] The Native Police Inspector ran in and told Michele that the town was in an uproar and coming to wreck the Telegraph Office. The Babu put on his cap and quietly dropped out of the window; while the Police Inspector, afraid, but obeying the old race-instinct which recognizes a drop of White blood as far as it can be diluted, said, "What orders does the *Sahib* give?"

The "*Sahib*" decided Michele. Though horribly frightened, he felt that, for the hour, he, the man with the Cochin Jew and the menial uncle in his pedigree, was the only representative of English authority in the place. Then he thought of Miss Vezzis and the fifty rupees, and took the situation on himself. There were seven native policemen in Tibasu, and four crazy smoothbore muskets among them. All the men were grey with fear, but not beyond leading. Michele dropped the key of the telegraph instrument, and went out, at the head of his army, to meet the mob. As the shouting crew came round a corner of the road, he dropped and fired; the men behind him loosing instinctively at the same time.

The whole crowd—curs to the backbone—yelled and ran; leaving one man dead, and another dying in the road. Michele was sweating with fear; but he kept his weakness under, and went down into the town, past the house where the Sub-Judge had barricaded himself. The streets were empty. Tibasu was more frightened than Michele, for the mob had been taken at the right time.

Michele returned to the Telegraph-Office, and sent a message to Chicacola asking for help. Before an answer came, he received a deputation of the elders of Tibasu, telling him that the Sub-Judge said his actions generally were "unconstitutional," and trying to bully him. But the heart of Michele D'Cruze was big and white in his breast, because of his love for Miss Vezzis, the nurse-girl, and because he had tasted for the first time Responsibility and Success. Those two make an intoxicating drink, and have ruined more men than ever has Whisky. Michele answered that the Sub-Judge might say what he pleased, but, until the Assistant Collector came, the Telegraph Signaller was the Government of India in Tibasu, and the elders of the town would be held accountable for further rioting. Then they bowed their heads and said, "Show mercy!" or words to that effect, and went back in great fear; each accusing the other of having begun the rioting.

Early in the dawn, after a night's patrol with his seven policemen, Michele went down the road, musket in hand, to meet the Assistant Collector who had ridden in to quell Tibasu. But, in the presence of this young Englishman, Michele felt himself slipping back more and more into the native; and the tale of the Tibasu Riots ended, with the strain on the teller, in an hysterical outburst of tears, bred by sorrow that he had killed a man, shame that he could not feel as uplifted as he had felt through the night, and childish anger that his tongue could not do justice to his great deeds. It was the White drop in Michele's veins dying out, though he did not know it.

But the Englishman understood; and, after he had schooled those men of Tibasu, and had conferred with the Sub-Judge till that excellent official turned green, he found time to draft an official letter describing the conduct of Michele. Which letter filtered through the Proper Channels, and ended in the transfer of Michele up-country once more, on the Imperial salary of sixty-six rupees a month.

So he and Miss Vezzis were married with great state and ancientry; and now there are several little D'Cruzes sprawling about the verandas of the Central Telegraph Office.

But, if the whole revenue of the Department he serves were to be his reward, Michele could never, never repeat what he did at Tibasu for the sake of Miss Vezzis the nurse-girl.

Which proves that, when a man does good work out of all proportion to his pay, in seven cases out of nine there is a woman at the back of the virtue.

The two exceptions must have suffered from sunstroke.

Watches of the Night

> What is in the Brahman's books that is in the Brahman's heart. Neither you nor I knew there was so much evil in the world.
>
> —*Hindu Proverb.*

THIS began in a practical joke; but it has gone far enough now, and is getting serious.

Platte, the Subaltern, being poor, had a Waterbury watch and a plain leather guard.

The Colonel had a Waterbury watch also, and, for the guard, the lip-strap of a curb-chain. Lip-straps make the best watch-guards. They are strong and short. Between a lip-strap and an ordinary leather-guard there is no great difference; between one Waterbury watch and another none at all. Every one in the Station knew the Colonel's lip-strap. He was not a horsey man, but he liked people to believe he had been one once; and he wove fantastic stories of the hunting-bridle to which this particular lip-strap had belonged. Otherwise he was painfully religious.

Platte and the Colonel were dressing at the Club—both late for their engagements, and both in a hurry. That was *Kismet*. The two watches were on a shelf below the looking-glass—guards hanging down. That was carelessness. Platte changed first, snatched a watch, looked in the glass, settled his tie, and ran. Forty seconds later, the Colonel did exactly the same thing; each man taking the other's watch.

You may have noticed that many religious people are deeply suspicicus. They seem—for purely religious purposes, of course—to know more about iniquity than the Unregenerate. Perhaps they were specially bad before they became converted! At any rate, in the imputation of things evil, and in putting the worst construction on things innocent, a certain type of good people may be trusted to surpass all others. The Colonel and his Wife were of that type. But the Colonel's Wife was the worst. She manufactured the Station scandal, and—talked to her ayah. Nothing more need be said. The Colonel's Wife broke up the Laplace's home. The Colonel's Wife stopped the Ferris-Haughtrey engagement. The Colonel's Wife induced young Buxton to keep his wife down in the Plains through the first year of the marriage. Wherefore little Mrs. Buxton died, and the baby with her. These things will be remembered against the Colonel's Wife so long as there is a regiment in the country.

But to come back to the Colonel and Platte. They went their several ways from the dressing-room. The Colonel dined with two Chaplains, while Platte went to a bachelor-party, and whist to follow.

Mark how things happen! If Platte's groom had put the new saddle-pad on the mare, the butts of the territs would not have worked through the worn leather and the old pad into the mare's withers, when she was coming home at two o'clock in the morning. She would not have reared, bolted, fallen into a ditch, upset the cart, and sent Platte flying over an aloe hedge on to Mrs. Larkyn's well-kept lawn; and this tale would never have been written. But the mare did all these things, and while Platte was rolling over and over on the turf, like a shot rabbit, the watch and guard flew from his waistcoat—as an Infantry Major's sword hops out of the scabbard when they are fireing a *feu-de-joie*—and rolled and rolled in the moonlight, till it stopped under a window.

Platte stuffed his handkerchief under the pad, put the cart straight, and went home.

Mark again how *Kismet* works! This would not arrive once in a hundred years. Toward the end of his dinner with the two Chaplains, the Colonel let out his waistcoat and leaned over the table to look at some Mission Reports. The bar of the watch-guard worked through the buttonhole, and the watch —Platte's watch—slid quietly on to the carpet. Where the bearer found it next morning and kept it.

Then the Colonel went home to the wife of his bosom; but the driver of the carriage was drunk and lost his way. So the Colonel returned at an unseemly hour and his excuses were not accepted. If the Colonel's Wife had been an ordinary vessel of wrath appointed for destruction, she would have known that when a man stays away on purpose, his excuse is always sound and original. The very baldness of the Colonel's explanation proved its truth.

See once more the workings of *Kismet*. The Colonel's watch which came with Platte hurriedly on to Mrs.

Larkyn's lawn, chose to stop just under Mrs. Larkyn's window, where she saw it early in the morning, recognized it and picked it up. She had heard the crash of Platte's cart at two o'clock that morning, and his voice calling the mare names. She knew Platte and liked him. That day she showed him the watch and heard his story. He put his head on one side, winked and said, "How disgusting! Shocking old man! With his religious training, too! I should send the watch to the Colonel's Wife and ask for explanations."

Mrs. Larkyn thought for a minute of the Laplaces—whom she had known when Laplace and his wife believed in each other—and answered, "I will send it. I think it will do her good. But, remember, we must never tell her truth."

Platte guessed that his own watch was in the Colonel's possession, and thought that the return of the lipstrapped Waterbury with a soothing note from Mrs. Larkyn would merely create a small trouble for a few minutes. Mrs. Larkyn knew better. She knew that any poison dropped would find good holding-ground in the heart of the Colonel's Wife.

The packet, and a note containing a few remarks on the Colonel's calling hours, were sent over to the Colonel's Wife, who wept in her own room and took counsel with herself.

If there was one woman under Heaven whom the Colonel's Wife hated with holy fervor, it was Mrs. Larkyn. Mrs. Larkyn was a frivolous lady, and called the Colonel's Wife "old cat." The Colonel's Wife said that somebody in Revelations was remarkably like Mrs.

Larkyn. She mentioned other Scripture people as well. From the Old Testament. But the Colonel's Wife was the only person who cared or dared to say anything against Mrs. Larkyn. Every one else accepted her as an amusing, honest little body. Wherefore, to believe that her husband had been shedding watches under that "Thing's" window at ungodly hours coupled with the fact of his late arrival on the previous night, was . . .

At this point she rose up and sought her husband. He denied everything except the ownership of the watch. She besought him, for his Soul's sake to speak the truth. He denied afresh, with two bad words. Then a stony silence held the Colonel's Wife, while a man could draw his breath five times.

The speech that followed is no affair of mine or yours. It was made up of wifely and womanly jealousy; knowledge of old age and sunk cheeks; deep mistrust born of the text that says even little babies' hearts are as bad as they make them; rancorous hatred of Mrs. Larkyn, and the tenets of the creed of the Colonel's Wife's upbringing.

Over and above all, was the damning lip-strapped Waterbury, ticking away in the palm of her shaking, withered hand. At that hour, I think, the Colonel's Wife realized a little of the restless suspicion she had injected into old Laplace's mind, a little of poor Miss Haughtrey's misery, and some of the canker that ate into Buxton's heart as he watched his wife dying before his eyes. The Colonel stammered and tried to explain. Then he remembered that his watch had disappeared; and the mystery grew greater. The Colonel's

Wife talked and prayed by turns till she was tired, and went away to devise means for chastening the stubborn heart of her husband. Which, translated, means, in our slang, "tail-twisting."

Being deeply impressed with the doctrine of Original Sin, she could not believe in the face of appearances. She knew too much, and jumped to the wildest conclusions.

But it was good for her. It spoiled her life, as she had spoiled the life of the Laplaces. She had lost her faith in the Colonel, and—here the creed-suspicion came in—he might, she argued, have erred many times, before a merciful Providence, at the hands of so unworthy an instrument as Mrs. Larkyn, had established his guilt. He was a bad, wicked, grey-haired profligate. This may sound too sudden a revulsion for a long-wedded wife; but it is a venerable fact that, if a man or woman makes a practice of, and takes a delight in, believing and spreading evil of people indifferent to him or her, he or she will end in believing evil of folk very near and dear. You may think, also, that the mere incident of the watch was too small and trivial to raise this misunderstanding. It is another aged fact that, in life as well as racing, all the worst accidents happen at little ditches and cut-down fences. In the same way, you sometimes see a woman who would have made a Joan of Arc in another century and climate, threshing herself to pieces over all the mean worry of housekeeping. But that is another story.

Her belief only made the Colonel's Wife more wretched, because it insisted so strongly on the villainy of men. Remembering what she had done, it was pleasant to watch her unhappiness, and the penny-farthing attempts she made to hide it from the Station. But the Station knew and laughed heartlessly; for they had heard the story of the watch, with much dramatic gesture, from Mrs. Larkyn's lips.

Once or twice Platte said to Mrs. Larkyn, seeing that the Colonel had not cleared himself, "This thing has gone far enough. I move we tell the Colonel's Wife how it happened." Mrs. Larkyn shut her lips and shook her head, and vowed that the Colonel's Wife must bear her punishment as best she could. Now Mrs. Larkyn was a frivolous woman, in whom none would have suspected deep hate. So Platte took no action, and came to believe gradually, from the Colonel's silence, that the Colonel must have run off the line somewhere that night, and, therefore, preferred to stand sentence on the lesser count of rambling into other people's compounds out of calling-hours. Platte forgot about the watch business after a while, and moved down-country with his regiment. Mrs. Larkyn went home when her husband's tour of Indian service expired. She never forgot.

But Platte was quite right when he said that the joke had gone too far. The mistrust and the tragedy of it—which we outsiders cannot see and do not believe in—are killing the Colonel's Wife, and are making the Colonel wretched. If either of them read this story, they can depend upon its being a fairly true account of the case, and can kiss and make friends.

Shakespeare alludes to the pleasure of watching an Engineer being shelled by his own Battery. Now this shows that poets should not write about what they do not understand. Any one could have told him that Sappers and Gunners are perfectly different branches of the Service. But, if you correct the sentence, and substitute Gunner for Sapper, the moral comes just the same.

The Other Man

When the Earth was sick and the Skies were grey
And the woods were rotted with rain,
The Dead Man rode through the autumn day
To visit his love again.
—*Old Ballad.*

FAR back in the "seventies," before they had built any Public-Offices at Simla, and the broad road round Jakko lived in a pigeon-hole in the P. W. D. hovels, her parents made Miss Gaurey marry Colonel Schreiderling. He could not have been much more than thirty-five years her senior; and, as he lived on two hundred rupees a month and had money of his own, he was well off. He belonged to good people, and suffered in the cold weather from lung-complaints. In the hot weather he dangled on the brink of heat-apoplexy; but it never quite killed him.

Understand, I do not blame Schreiderling. He was a good husband according to his lights, and his temper only failed him when he was being nursed. Which was some seventeen days in each month. He was almost generous to his wife about money-matters, and that, for him, was a concession. Still Mrs. Schreiderling was not happy. They married her when she was this side of twenty and had given all her poor little heart to another man. I have forgotten his name, but we will call him the Other Man. He had no money and no prospects. He was not even good-looking; and I think he was in the Commissariat or Transport. But, in spite of all these things, she loved him very badly; and there was some sort of an engagement between the two when Schreiderling appeared and told Mrs. Gaurey that he wished to marry her daughter. Then the other engagement was broken off— washed away by Mrs. Gaurey's tears, for that lady governed her house by weeping over disobedience to her authority and the lack of reverence she received in her old age. The daughter did not take after her mother. She never cried. Not even at the wedding.

The Other Man bore his loss quietly, and was transferred to as bad a station as he could find. Perhaps the climate consoled him. He suffered from intermittent fever, and that may have distracted him from his other trouble. He was weak about the heart also. Both ways. One of the valves was affected, and the fever made it worse. This showed itself later on.

Then many months passed, and Mrs. Schreiderling took to being ill. She did not pine away like people in story-books, but she seemed to pick up every form of illness that went about a Station, from simple fever upwards. She was never more than ordinarily pretty at the best of times; and the illnesses made her ugly. Schreiderling said so. He prided himself on speaking his mind.

When she ceased being pretty, he left her to her own devices, and went back to the lairs of his bachelordom. She used to trot up and down Simla Mall in a forlorn sort of way, with a grey Terai hat well on the back of her head, and a shocking bad saddle under her. Schreiderling's generosity stopped at the horse. He said that any saddle would do for a woman as nervous as Mrs. Schreiderling. She never was asked to dance, because she did not dance well; and she was so dull and uninteresting, that her box very seldom had any cards in it. Schreiderling said that if he had known she was going to be such a scarecrow after her marriage, he would never have married her. He always prided himself on speaking his mind, did Schreiderling.

He left her at Simla one August, and went down to his regiment. Then she revived a little, but she never recovered her looks. I found out at the Club that the Other Man was coming up sick—very sick—on an off chance of recovery. The fever and the heart-valves had nearly killed him. She knew that too, and she knew—what I had no interest in knowing—when he was coming up. I suppose he wrote to tell her. They had not seen each other since a month before the wedding. And here comes the unpleasant part of the story.

A late call kept me down at the Dovedell Hotel till dusk one evening. Mrs.

Schreiderling had been flitting up and down the Mall all the afternoon in the rain. Coming up along the Cart-road, a tonga passed me, and my pony, tired with standing so long, set off at a canter. Just by the road down to the Tonga office Mrs. Schreiderling, dripping from head to foot, was waiting for the tonga. I turned uphill as the tonga was no affair of mine; and just then she began to shriek. I went back at once and saw, under the Tonga Office lamps, Mrs. Schreiderling kneeling in the wet road by the back seat of the newly-arrived tonga, screaming hideously. Then she fell face down in the dirt as I came up.

Sitting in the back seat, very square and firm, with one hand on the awning-stanchion and the wet pouring off his hat and moustache, was the Other Man —dead. The sixty-mile uphill jolt had been too much for his valve, I suppose. The tonga-driver said, "This Sahib died two stages out of Solon. Therefore, I tied him with a rope, lest he should fall out by the way, and so came to Simla. Will the Sahib give me *bukshish*? *It,*"pointing to the Other Man, "should have given one rupee."

The Other Man sat with a grin on his face, as if he enjoyed the joke of his arrival; and Mrs. Schreiderling, in the mud, began to groan. There was no one except us four in the office and it was raining heavily. The first thing was to take Mrs. Schreiderling home, and the second was to prevent her name from being mixed up with the affair. The tonga-driver received five rupees to find a bazar 'rickshaw for Mrs. Schreiderling. He was to tell the Tonga Babu afterward of the Other Man, and the Babu was to make such arrangements as seemed best.

Mrs. Schreiderling was carried into the shed out of the rain, and for three-quarters of an hour we two waited for the 'rickshaw. The Other Man was left exactly as he had arrived. Mrs. Schreiderling would do everything but cry, which might have helped her. She tried to scream as soon as her senses came back, and then she began praying for the Other Man's soul. Had she not been as honest as the day, she would have prayed for her own soul too. I waited to hear her do this, but she did not. Then I tried to get some of the mud off her habit. Lastly, the 'rickshaw came, and I got her away—partly by force. It was a terrible business from beginning to end; but most of all when the 'rickshaw had to squeeze between the wall and the tonga, and she saw by the lamplight that thin, yellow hand grasping the awning-stanchion.

She was taken home just as every one was going to a dance at Viceregal Lodge—"Peterhoff" it was then—and the doctor found out that she had fallen from her horse, that I had picked her up at the back of Jakko, and really deserved great credit for the prompt manner in which I had secured medical aid. She did not die—men of Schreiderling's stamp marry women who don't die easily. They live and grow ugly.

She never told of her one meeting, since her marriage, with the Other Man; and, when the chill and cough following the exposure of that evening, allowed her abroad, she never by word or sign alluded to having met me by the Tonga Office. Perhaps she never knew.

She used to trot up and down the Mall, on that shocking bad saddle, looking as if she expected to meet some one round the corner every minute. Two years afterward she went Home, and died—at Bournemouth, I think.

Schreiderling, when he grew maudlin at Mess, used to talk about "my poor dear wife." He always set great store on speaking his mind, did Schreiderling.

Consequences

Rosicrucian subtleties
In the Orient had rise;
Ye may find their teachers still
Under Jacatâlâ's Hill.
Seek ye Bombast Paracelsus,
Read what flood the Seeker tells us
Of the Dominant that runs
Through the Cycles of the Suns—
Read my story last, and see
Luna at her apogee.

THERE are yearly appointments, and two-yearly appointments, and five-yearly appointments at Simla, and there are, or used to be, permanent appointments, whereon you stayed up for the term of your natural life and secured red cheeks and a nice income. Of course, you could descend in the cold weather; for Simla is rather dull then.

Tarrion came from goodness knows where—all away and away in some forsaken part of Central India, where they call Pachmari a Sanitarium, and drive behind trotting-bullocks, I believe. He belonged to a regiment; but what he really wanted to do was to escape from his regiment and live in Simla forever and ever. He had no preference for anything in particular, beyond a good horse and a nice partner. He thought he could do everything well; which is a beautiful belief when you hold it with all your heart. He was clever in many ways, and good to look at, and always made people round him comfortable— even in Central India.

So he went up to Simla, and, because he was clever and amusing, he gravitated naturally to Mrs. Hauksbee, who could forgive everything but stupidity. Once he did her great service by changing the date on an invitation-card for a big dance which Mrs. Hauksbee wished to attend, but couldn't because she had quarreled with the A.-D.-C., who took care, being a mean man, to invite her to a small dance on the 6th instead of the big Ball of the 26th. It was a very clever piece of forgery; and when Mrs. Hauksbee showed the A.-D.-C., her invitation-card, and chaffed him mildly for not better managing his vendettas, he really thought that he had made a mistake; and—which was wise —realized that it was no use to fight with Mrs. Hauksbee. She was grateful to Tarrion and asked what she could do for him. He said simply, "I'm a Free-lance up here on leave, on the lookout for what I can loot. I haven't a square inch of interest in all Simla. My name isn't known to any man with an appointment in his gift, and I want an appointment—a good, sound one. I believe you can do anything you turn yourself to. Will you help me?" Mrs. Hauksbee thought for a minute, and passed the lash of her riding-whip through her lips, as was her custom when thinking. Then her eyes sparkled and she said, "I will;" and she shook hands on it. Tarrion, having perfect confidence in this great woman, took no further thought of the business at all. Except to wonder what sort of an appointment he would win.

Mrs. Hauksbee began calculating the prices of all the Heads of Departments and Members of Council she knew, and the more she thought the more she laughed, because her heart was in the game and it amused her. Then she took a Civil List and ran over a few of the appointments. There are some beautiful appointments in the Civil List. Eventually, she decided that, though Tarrion was too good for the Political Department, she had better begin by trying to place him there. Her own plans to this end do not matter in the least, for Luck or Fate played into her hands and she had nothing to do but to watch the course of events and take the credit of them.

All Viceroys, when the first come out, pass through the Diplomatic Secrecy craze. It wears off in time; but they all catch it in the beginning, because they are new to the country. The particular Viceroy who was suffering from the complaint just then—this was a long time ago, before Lord Dufferin ever came from Canada, or Lord Ripon from the bosom of the English Church—had it very badly; and the result was that men who were new to keeping official secrets went about looking unhappy;

and the Viceroy plumed himself on the way in which he had instilled notions of reticence into his Staff.

Now, the Supreme Government have a careless custom of committing what they do to printed papers. These papers deal with all sorts of things—from the payment of Rs. 200 to a "secret service" native, up to rebukes administered to Vakils and Motamids of Native States, and rather brusque letters to Native Princes, telling them to put their houses in order, to refrain from kidnapping women, or filling offenders with pounded red pepper, and eccentricities of that kind. Of course, these things could never be made public, because Native Princes never err officially, and their States are officially as well administered as Our territories. Also, the private allowances to various queer people are not exactly matters to put into newspapers, though they give quaint reading sometimes. When the Supreme Government is at Simla, these papers are prepared there, and go round to the people who ought to see them in office-boxes or by post. The principle of secrecy was to that Viceroy quite as important as the practice, and he held that a benevolent despotism like Ours should never allow even little things, such as appointments of subordinate clerks, to leak out till the proper time. He was always remarkable for his principles.

There was a very important batch of papers in preparation at that time. It had to travel from one end of Simla to the other by hand. It was not put into an official envelope, but a large, square, pale pink one; the matter being inMS. on soft crinkly paper. It was addressed to "The Head Clerk, etc., etc." Now, between "The Head Clerk, etc., etc." and "Mrs. Hauksbee" and a flourish, is no very great difference, if the address be written in a very bad hand, as this was. The orderly who took the envelope was not more of an idiot than most orderlies. He merely forgot where this most unofficial cover was to be delivered, and so asked the first Englishman he met, who happened to be a man riding down to Annandale in a great hurry. The Englishman hardly looked at it, said, "Mrs. Hauksbee," and went on. So did the orderly, because that letter was the last in stock and he wanted to get his work over. There was no book to sign; he thrust the letter into Mrs. Hauksbee's bearer's hands and went off to smoke with a friend. Mrs. Hauksbee was expecting some cut-out pattern things in flimsy paper from a friend. As soon as she got the big square packet, therefore, she said, "Oh, the dear creature!" and tore it open with a paper-knife, and all the MS. enclosures tumbled out on the floor.

Mrs. Hauksbee began reading. I have said the batch was rather important. That is quite enough for you to know. It referred to some correspondence, two measures, a peremptory order to a native chief and two dozen other things. Mrs. Hauksbee gasped as she read, for the first glimpse of the naked machinery of the Great Indian Government, stripped of its casings, and lacquer, and paint, and guard-rails, impresses even the most stupid man. And Mrs. Hauksbee was a clever woman. She was a little afraid at first, and felt as if she had taken hold of a lightning-flash by the tail, and did not quite know what to do with it. There were remarks and initials at the side of the papers; and some of the remarks were rather more severe than the papers. The initials belonged to men who are all dead or gone now; but they were great in their day. Mrs. Hauksbee read on and thought calmly as she read. Then the value of her trove struck her, and she cast about for the best method of using it. Then Tarrion dropped in, and they read through all the papers together, and Tarrion, not knowing how she had come by them, vowed that Mrs. Hauksbee was the greatest woman on earth. Which I believe was true or nearly so.

"The honest course is always the best," said Tarrion after an hour and a half of study and conversation. "All things considered, the Intelligence Branch is about my form. Either that or the Foreign Office. I go to lay seige to the High Gods in their Temples."

He did not seek a little man, or a little big man, or a weak Head of a strong Department, but he called on the biggest and strongest man that the Government owned, and explained that he wanted an appointment at Simla on a good salary. The compound insolence of this amused the Strong Man, and, as he had nothing to do for the moment, he listened to the proposals of the audacious Tarrion. "You have, I presume, some special qualifications, besides the gift of self-assertion, for the claims you put forward?" said the Strong Man. "That, Sir," said Tarrion, "is for you to judge." Then he began, for he had a good memory, quoting a few of the more important notes in the papers—slowly and one by one as a man drops chlorodyne into a glass.

When he had reached the peremptory order—and it was a very peremptory order—the Strong Man was troubled. Tarrion wound up—"And I fancy that special knowledge of this kind is at least as valuable for, let us say, a berth in the Foreign Office, as the fact of being the nephew of a distinguished officer's wife." That hit the Strong Man hard, for the last appointment to the Foreign Office had been by black favor, and he knew it.

"I'll see what I can do for you," said the Strong Man.

"Many thanks," said Tarrion. Then he left, and the Strong Man departed to see how the appointment was to be blocked.

* * * * * *

Followed a pause of eleven days; with thunders and lightnings and much telegraphing. The appointment was not a very important one, carrying only between Rs.500 and Rs.700 a month; but, as the Viceroy said, it was the principle of diplomatic secrecy that had to be maintained, and it was more than likely that a boy so well supplied with special information would be worth translating. So they translated Tarrion. They must have suspected him, though he protested that his information was due to singular talents of his own. Now, much of this story, including the after-history of the missing envelope, you must fill in for yourself, because there are reasons why it cannot be written. If you do not know about things Up Above, you won't understand how to fill in, and you will say it is impossible.

What the Viceroy said when Tarrion was introduced to him was—"This is the boy who 'rushed' the Government of India, is it? Recollect, Sir, that is not done twice." So he must have known something.

What Tarrion said when he saw his appointment gazetted was —"If Mrs. Hauksbee were twenty years younger, and I her husband, I should be Viceroy of India in fifteen years."

What Mrs. Hauksbee said, when Tarrion thanked her, almost with tears in his eyes, was first—"I told you so!" and next, to herself—"What fools men are!"

———•———

The Conversion of Aurelian McGoggin

Ride with an idle whip, ride with an
    unused heel,
But, once in a way, there will come a
    day
When the colt must be taught to feel
The lash that falls, and the curb that
    galls, and the sting of the rowelled
    steel.
                            —*Life's Handicap.*

THIS is not a tale exactly. It is a Tract; and I am immensely proud of it. Making a Tract is a Feat.

Every man is entitled to his own religious opinions; but no man—least of all a junior—has a right to thrust these down other men's throats. The Government sends out weird Civilians now and again; but McGoggin was the queerest exported for a long time. He was clever—brilliantly clever—but his cleverness worked the wrong way. Instead of keeping to the study of the vernaculars, he had read some books written by a man called Comte, I think, and a man called Spencer. [You will find these books in the Library.] They deal with people's insides from the point of view of men who have no stomachs. There was no order against his reading them; but his Mamma should have smacked him. They fermented in his head, and he came out to India with a rarefied religion over and above his work. It was not much of a creed. It only proved that men had no souls, and there was no God and no hereafter, and that you must worry along somehow for the good of Humanity.

One of its minor tenets seemed to be that the one thing more sinful than giving an order was obeying it. At least, that was what McGoggin said; but I suspect he had misread his primers.

I do not say a word against this creed. It was made up in Town where there is nothing but machinery and asphalt and building—all shut in by the fog. Naturally, a man grows to think that there is no one higher than himself, and that the Metropolitan Board of Works made everything. But in India, where you really see humanity —raw, brown, naked humanity—with nothing between it and the blazing sky, and only the used-up, over-handled earth underfoot, the notion somehow dies away, and most folk come back to simpler theories. Life, in India, is not long enough to waste in proving that there is no one in particular at the head

of affairs. For this reason. The Deputy is above the Assistant, the Commissioner above the Deputy, the Lieutenant-Governor above the Commissioner, and the Viceroy above all four, under the orders of the Secretary of State who is responsible to the Empress. If the Empress be not responsible to her Maker—if there is no Maker for her to be responsible to—the entire system of Our Administration must be wrong. Which is manifestly impossible. At Home men are to be excused. They are stalled up a good deal and get intellectually "beany." When you take a gross, "beany" horse to exercise, he slavers and slobbers over the bit till you can't see the horns. But the bit is there just the same. Men do not get "beany" in India. The climate and the work are against playing bricks with words.

If McGoggin had kept his creed, with the capital letters and the endings in "isms," to himself, no one would have cared; but his grandfathers on both sides had been Wesleyan preachers, and the preaching strain came out in his mind. He wanted every one at the Club to see that they had no souls too, and to help him to eliminate his Creator. As a good many men told him, *he* undoubtedly had no soul, because he was so young, but it did not follow that his seniors were equally undeveloped; and, whether there was another world or not, a man still wanted to read his papers in this. "But that is not the point—that is not the point!" Aurelian used to say. Then men threw sofa-cushions at him and told him to go to any particular place he might believe in. They christened him the

"Blastoderm,"— he said he came from a family of that name somewhere, in the prehistoric ages—and, by insult and laughter strove to choke him dumb, for he was an unmitigated nuisance at the Club; besides being an offence to the older men. His Deputy Commissioner, who was working on the Frontier when Aurelian was rolling on a bed-quilt, told him that, for a clever boy, Aurelian was a very big idiot. And, if he had gone on with his work, he would have been caught up to the Secretariat in a few years. He was of the type that goes there—all head, no physique and a hundred theories. Not a soul was interested in McGoggin's soul. He might have had two, or none, or somebody else's. His business was to obey orders and keep abreast of his files, instead of devastating the Club with "isms."

He worked brilliantly; but he could not accept any order without trying to better it. That was the fault of his creed. It made men too responsible and left too much to their honor. You can sometimes ride an old horse in a halter; but never a colt. McGoggin took more trouble over his cases than any of the men of his year. He may have fancied that thirty-page judgments on fifty-rupee cases—both sides perjured to the gullet—advanced the cause of Humanity. At any rate, he worked too much, and worried and fretted over the rebukes he received, and lectured away on his ridiculous creed out of office, till the Doctor had to warn him that he was overdoing it. No man can toil eighteen annas in the rupee in June without suffering. But McGoggin was still intellectually "beany" and proud of himself and his powers, and he would

take no hint. He worked nine hours a day steadily.

"Very well," said the Doctor, "you'll break down, because you are over-engined for your beam." McGoggin was a little man.

One day, the collapse came—as dramatically as if it had been meant to embellish a Tract.

It was just before the Rains. We were sitting in the veranda in the dead, hot, close air, gasping and praying that the black-blue clouds would let down and bring the cool. Very, very far away, there was a faint whisper, which was the roar of the Rains breaking over the river. One of the men heard it, got out of his chair, listened and said, naturally enough, "Thank God!"

Then the Blastoderm turned in his place and said, "Why? I assure you it's only the result of perfectly natural causes—atmospheric phenomena of the simplest kind. Why you should, therefore, return thanks to a Being who never did exist—who is only a figment"—

"Blastoderm," grunted the man in the next chair, "dry up, and throw me over the *Pioneer*. We know all about your figments." The Blastoderm reached out to the table, took up one paper, and jumped as if something had stung him. Then he handed the paper.

"As I was saying," he went on slowly and with an effort—"due to perfectly natural causes—perfectly natural causes. I mean"—

"Hi! Blastoderm, you've given me the *Calcutta Mercantile Advertiser*."

The dust got up in little whorls, while the tree-tops rocked and the kites whistled. But no one was looking at the coming of the Rains. We were all staring at the Blastoderm who had risen from his chair and was fighting with his speech. Then he said, still more slowly—

"Perfectly conceivable——dictionary ——red oak——amenable——cause—— retaining——shuttlecock——alone."

"Blastoderm's drunk," said one man. But the Blastoderm was not drunk. He looked at us in a dazed sort of way, and began motioning with his hands in the half light as the clouds closed overhead. Then—with a scream—

"What is it?——Can't——reserve —— attainable —— market —— obscure"——

But his speech seemed to freeze in him, and—just as the lightning shot two tongues that cut the whole sky into three pieces and the rain fell in quivering sheets—the Blastoderm was struck dumb. He stood pawing and champing like a hard-held horse, and his eyes were full of terror.

The Doctor came over in three minutes, and heard the story. "It's *aphasia*," he said. "Take him to his room. I knew the smash would come." We carried the Blastoderm across in the pouring rain to his quarters, and the Doctor gave him bromide of potassium to make him sleep.

Then the Doctor came back to us and told us that *aphasia* was like all the arrears of "Punjab Head" falling in a lump; and that only once before—in the case of a sepoy—had he met with so complete a case. I have seen mild *aphasia* in an overworked man, but this sudden dumbness was uncanny—though, as the Blastoderm himself might have said, due to "perfectly natural causes."

"He'll have to take leave after this," said the Doctor. "He won't be fit for work for another three months. No; it isn't insanity or anything like it. It's only complete loss of control over the speech and memory. I fancy it will keep the Blastoderm quiet, though."

Two days later, the Blastoderm found his tongue again. The first question he asked was—"what was it?" The Doctor enlightened him. "But I can't understand it!" said the Blastoderm. "I'm quite sane; but I can't be sure of my mind, it seems—my *own* memory—can I?"

"Go up into the Hills for three months, and don't think about it," said the Doctor.

"But I can't understand it," repeated the Blastoderm. "It was my *own* mind and memory."

"I can't help it," said the Doctor; "there are a good many things you can't understand; and, by the time you have put in my length of service, you'll know exactly how much a man dare call his own in this world."

The stroke cowed the Blastoderm. He could not understand it. He went into the Hills in fear and trembling, wondering whether he would be permitted to reach the end of any sentence he began.

This gave him a wholesome feeling of mistrust. The legitimate explanation, that he had been overworking himself, failed to satisfy him. Something had wiped his lips of speech, as a mother wipes the milky lips of her child, and he was afraid—horribly afraid.

So the Club had rest when he returned; and if ever you come across

Aurelian McGoggin laying down the law on things Human—he doesn't seem to know as much as he used to about things Divine—put your forefinger to your lip for a moment, and see what happens.

Don't blame me if he throws a glass at your head.

A Germ-Destroyer

Pleasant it is for the Little Tin Gods
  When great Jove nods;
But Little Tin Gods make their little
  mistakes
In missing the hour when great Jove
wakes.

As a general rule, it is inexpedient to meddle with questions of State in a land where men are highly paid to work them out for you. This tale is a justifiable exception.

Once in every five years, as you know, we indent for a new Viceroy; and each Viceroy imports, with the rest of his baggage, a Private Secretary, who may or may not be the real Viceroy, just as Fate ordains. Fate looks after the Indian Empire because it is so big and so helpless.

There was a Viceroy once, who brought out with him a turbulent Private Secretary—a hard man with a soft manner and a morbid passion for work. This Secretary was called Wonder—John Fennil Wonder. The Viceroy possessed no name—nothing but a string of counties and two-thirds of the alphabet after them. He said, in confidence, that he was the electro-plated figurehead of a golden administration, and he watched in a dreamy, amused way Wonder's attempts to draw matters which were entirely outside his province into his own hands. "When we are all cherubims together," said His Excellency once, "my dear, good friend Wonder will head the conspiracy for plucking out Gabriel's tail-feathers or stealing Peter's keys. *Then* I shall report him."

But, though the Viceroy did nothing to check Wonder's officiousness, other people said unpleasant things. Maybe the Members of Council began it; but, finally all Simla agreed that there was "too much Wonder, and too little Viceroy" in that rule. Wonder was always quoting "His Excellency." It was "His Excellency this," "His Excellency that," "In the opinion of His Excellency," and so on. The Viceroy smiled; but he did not heed. He said that, so long as his old men squabbled with his "dear, good Wonder," they might be induced to leave the immemorial East in peace.

"No wise man has a Policy," said the Viceroy. "A Policy is the blackmail levied on the Fool by the Unforseen. I am not the former, and I do not believe in the latter."

I do not quite see what this means, unless it refers to an Insurance Policy. Perhaps it was the Viceroy's way of saying, "Lie low."

That season, came up to Simla one of these crazy people with only a single idea. These are the men who make things move; but they are not nice to talk to. This man's name was Mellish, and he had lived for fifteen years on land of his own, in Lower Bengal, studying cholera. He held that cholera was a germ that propagated itself as it flew through a muggy atmosphere; and stuck in the branches of trees like a wool-flake. The germ could be rendered sterile, he said, by "Mellish's Own Invincible Fumigatory"—a heavy violet-black powder—"the result of fifteen years' scientific investigation, Sir!"

Inventors seem very much alike as a caste. They talk loudly, especially about "conspiracies of monopolists"; they beat upon the table with their fists; and they secrete fragments of their inventions about their persons.

Mellish said that there was a Medical "Ring" at Simla, headed by the Surgeon-General, who was in league, apparently, with all the Hospital Assistants in the Empire. I forget exactly how he proved it, but it had something to do with "skulking up to the Hills"; and what Mellish wanted was the independent evidence of the Viceroy—"Steward of our Most Gracious Majesty the Queen, Sir." So Mellish went up to Simla, with eighty-four pounds of Fumagatory in his trunk, to speak to the Viceroy and to show him the merits of the invention.

But it is easier to see a Viceroy than to talk to him, unless you chance to be as important as Mellishe of Madras. He was a six-thousand-rupee man, so great that his daughters never "married." They "contracted alliances." He himself was not paid. He "received emoluments," and his journeys about the

country were "tours of observation." His business was to stir up the people in Madras with a long pole—as you stir up tench in a pond—and the people had to come up out of their comfortable old ways and gasp—"This is Enlightenment and Progress. Isn't it fine!" Then they gave Mellishe statues and jasmine garlands, in the hope of getting rid of him.

Mellishe came up to Simla "to confer with the Viceroy." That was one of his perquisites. The Viceroy knew nothing of Mellishe except that he was "one of those middle-class deities who seem necessary to the spiritual comfort of this Paradise of the Middle-classes," and that, in all probability, he had "suggested, designed, founded, and endowed all the public institutions in Madras." Which proves that His Excellency, though dreamy, had experience of the ways of six-thousand-rupee men.

Mellishe's name was E. Mellishe, and Mellish's was E. S. Mellish, and they were both staying at the same hotel, and the Fate that looks after the Indian Empire ordained that Wonder should blunder and drop the final *"e"*; that the Chaprassi should help him, and that the note which ran:

DEAR MR. MELLISH,—Can you set aside your other engagements, and lunch with us at two to-morrow? His Excellency has an hour at your disposal then,

should be given to Mellish with the Fumigatory. He nearly wept with pride and delight, and at the appointed hour cantered to Peterhoff, a big paper-bag full of the Fumigatory in his coat-tail pockets. He had his chance, and he meant to make the most of it. Mellishe of Madras had been so portentously solemn about his "conference," that Wonder had arranged for a private tiffin,—no A.-D.-C.'s, no Wonder, no one but the Viceroy, who said plaintively that he feared being left alone with unmuzzled autocrats like the great Mellishe of Madras.

But his guest did not bore the Viceroy. On the contrary, he amused him. Mellish was nervously anxious to go straight to his Fumigatory, and talked at random until tiffin was over and His Excellency asked him to smoke. The Viceroy was pleased with Mellish because he did not talk "shop."

As soon as the cheroots were lit, Mellish spoke like a man; beginning with his cholera-theory, reviewing his fifteen years' "scientific labors," the machinations of the "Simla Ring," and the excellence of his Fumigatory, while the Viceroy watched him between half-shut eyes and thought—"Evidently this is the wrong tiger; but it is an original animal." Mellish's hair was standing on end with excitement, and he stammered. He began groping in his coat-tails and, before the Viceroy knew what was about to happen, he had tipped a bagful of his powder into the big silver ash-tray.

"J-j-judge for yourself, Sir," said Mellish. "Y' Excellency shall judge for yourself! Absolutely infallible, on my honor."

He plunged the lighted end of his cigar into the powder, which began to smoke like a volcano, and send up fat, greasy wreaths of copper-colored smoke. In five seconds the room was filled with a most pungent and sickening stench —a reek that took fierce hold of the trap of your windpipe and shut it. The powder hissed and fizzed, and sent out blue and green sparks, and the smoke rose till you could neither see, nor breathe, nor gasp. Mellish, however, was used to it.

"Nitrate of Strontia," he shouted; "baryta, bone-meal *etcetera!* Thousand cubic feet smoke per cubic inch. Not a germ could live—not a germ, Y' Excellency!"

But His Excellency had fled, and was coughing at the foot of the stairs, while all Peterhoff hummed like a hive. Red Lancers came in, and the head Chaprassi who speaks English, came in, and mace-bearers came in, and ladies ran downstairs screaming "Fire"; for the smoke was drifting through the house and oozing out of the windows, and bellying along the verandas, and wreathing and writhing across the gardens. No one could enter the room where Mellish was lecturing on his Fumigatory, till that unspeakable powder had burned itself out.

Then an Aide-de-Camp, who desired the V. C., rushed through the rolling clouds and hauled Mellish into the hall. The Viceroy was prostrate with laughter, and could only waggle his hands feebly at Mellish, who was shaking a fresh bagful of powder at him.

"Glorious! Glorious!" sobbed His Excellency. "Not a germ, as you justly observe, could exist! I can swear it. A magnificent success!"

Then he laughed till the tears came, and Wonder, who had caught the real Mellishe snorting on the Mall, entered and was deeply shocked at the scene. But the Viceroy was delighted, because he saw that Wonder would presently depart. Mellish with the Fumigatory was also pleased, for he felt that he had smashed the Simla Medical "Ring."

* * * * * *

Few men could tell a story like His Excellency when he took the trouble, and his account of "my dear, good Wonder's friend with the powder" went the round of Simla, and flippant folk made Wonder unhappy by their remarks.

But His Excellency told the tale once too often—for Wonder. As he meant to do. It was at a Seepee Picnic. Wonder was sitting just behind the Viceroy.

"And I really thought for a moment," wound up His Excellency, "that my dear good Wonder had hired an assassin to clear his way to the throne!"

Every one laughed; but there was a delicate sub-tinkle in the Viceroy's tone which Wonder understood. He found that his health was giving way; and the Viceroy allowed him to go, and presented him with a flaming "character" for use at Home among big people.

"My fault entirely," said His Excellency, in after seasons, with a twinkle in his eye. "My inconsistency must always have been distasteful to such a masterly man."

Kidnapped

There is a tide in the affairs of men,
Which, taken any way you please, is bad,
And strands them in forsaken guts and
      creeks
No decent soul would think of visiting.
You cannot stop the tide; but, now and
      then,
You may arrest some rash adventurer
W⸺h'm—will hardly thank you for
      your pains.
                    —*Vibart's Moralities.*

WE are a high-caste and enlightened race, and infant-marriage is very shocking and the consequences are sometimes peculiar; but, nevertheless, the Hindu notion—which is the Continental notion, which is the aboriginal notion—of arranging marriages irrespective of the personal inclinations of the married, is sound. Think for a minute, and you will see that it must be so; unless, of course, you believe in "affinities." In which case you had better not read this tale. How can a man who has never married; who cannot be trusted to pick up at sight a moderately sound horse; whose head is hot and upset with visions of domestic felicity, go about the choosing of a wife? He cannot see straight or think straight if he tries; and the same disadvantages exist in case of a girl's fancies. But when mature, married, and discreet people arrange a match between a boy and a girl, they do it sensibly, with a view to the future, and the young couple live happily ever afterward. As everybody knows.

Properly speaking, Government should establish a Matrimonial Department, efficiently officered, with a Jury of Matrons, a Judge of the Chief Court, a Senior Chaplain, and an Awful Warning, in the shape of a love-match that has gone wrong, chained to the trees in the courtyard. All marriages should be made through the Department, which might be subordinate to the Educational Department, under the same penalty as that attaching to the transfer of land without a stamped document. But Government won't take suggestions. It pretends that it is too busy. However, I will put my notion on record, and explain the example that illustrates the theory.

Once upon a time, there was a good young man—a first-class officer in his own Department—a man with a career before him and, possibly, a K.C.I.E. at the end of it. All his superiors spoke well of him, because he knew how to hold his tongue and his pen at the proper time. There are, to-day, only eleven men in India who possess this secret; and they have all, with one exception, attained great honor and enormous incomes.

This good young man was quiet and self-contained—too old for his years by far. Which always carries its own punishment. Had a Subaltern, or a Tea-Planter's Assistant, or anybody who enjoys life and has no care for to-morrow, done what he tried to do, not a soul would have cared. But when Peythroppe—the estimable, virtuous, economical, quiet, hard-working, young Peythroppe—fell, there was a flutter through five Departments.

The manner of his fall was in this way. He met a Miss Castries—d' Castries it was originally, but the family dropped the d' for administrative reasons—and he fell in love with her even more energetically than he worked. Understand clearly that there was not a

breath of a word to be said against Miss Castries—not a shadow of a breath. She was good and very lovely—possessed what innocent people at Home call a "Spanish" complexion, with thick blue-black hair growing low down on the forehead, into a "widow's peak," and big violet eyes under eyebrows as black and as straight as the borders of a *Gazette Extraordinary,* when a big man dies. But——but——but——Well, she was a *very* sweet girl and very pious, but for many reasons she was "impossible." Quite so. All good Mammas know what "impossible" means. It was obviously absurd that Peythroppe should marry her. The little opal-tinted onyx at the base of her finger-nails said this as plainly as print. Further, marriage with Miss Castries meant marriage with several other Castries—Honorary Lieutenant Castries her Papa, Mrs. Eulalie Castries her Mamma, and all the ramifications of the Castries family, on incomes ranging from Rs.175 to Rs. 470 a month, and *their* wives and connections again.

It would have been cheaper for Peythroppe to have assaulted a Commissioner with a dog whip, or to have burned the records of a Deputy-Commissioner's Office, than to have contracted an alliance with the Castries. It would have weighted his after-career less—even under a Government which never forgets and *never* forgives. Everybody saw this but Peythroppe. He was going to marry Miss Castries, he was—being of age and drawing a good income—and woe betide the house that would not afterward receive Mrs. Virginie Saulez Peythroppe with the deference due to her husband's rank. That was

Peythroppe's ultimatum, and any remonstrance drove him frantic.

These sudden madnesses most afflict the sanest men. There was a case once —but I will tell you of that later on. You cannot account for the mania except under a theory directly contradicting the one about the Place wherein marriages are made. Peythroppe was burningly anxious to put a millstone round his neck at the outset of his career; and argument had not the least effect on him. He was going to marry Miss Castries, and the business was his own business. He would thank you to keep your advice to yourself. With a man in this condition, mere words only fix him in his purpose. Of course he cannot see that marriage in India does not concern the individual but the Government he serves.

Do you remember Mrs. Hauksbee— the most wonderful woman in India? She saved Pluffles from Mrs. Reiver, won Tarrion his appointment in the Foreign Office, and was defeated in open field by Mrs. Cusack-Bremmil. She heard of the lamentable condition of Peythroppe, and her brain struck out the plan that saved him. She had the wisdom of the Serpent, the logical coherence of the Man, the fearlessness of the Child, and the triple intuition of the Woman. Never—no, never—as long as a tonga buckets down the Solon dip, or the couples go a-riding at the back of Summer Hill, will there be such a genius as Mrs. Hauksbee. She attended the consultation of Three Men on Peythroppe's case; and she stood up with the lash of her riding-whip between her lips and spake.

* * * * * *

Three weeks later, Peythroppe dined with the Three Men, and the *Gazette of India* came in. Peythroppe found to his surprise that he had been gazetted a month's leave. Don't ask me how this was managed. I believe firmly that, if Mrs. Hauksbee gave the order, the whole Great Indian Administration would stand on its head. The Three Men had also a month's leave each. Peythroppe put the *Gazette* down and said bad words. Then there came from the compound the soft "pad-pad" of camels—"thieves' camels," the Bikaneer breed that don't bubble and howl when they sit down and get up.

After that, I don't know what happened. This much is certain. Peythroppe disappeared—vanished like smoke—and the long foot-rest chair in the house of the Three Men was broken to splinters. Also a bedstead departed from one of the bedrooms.

Mrs. Hauksbee said that Mr. Peythroppe was shooting in Rajputana with the Three Men; so we were compelled to believe her.

At the end of the month, Peythroppe was gazetted twenty days' extension of leave; but there was wrath and lamentation in the house of Castries. The marriage-day had been fixed, but the bridegroom never came: and the D'Silvas, Pereiras, and Ducketts lifted their voices and mocked Honorary Lieutenant Castries as one who had been basely imposed upon. Mrs. Hauksbee went to the wedding, and was much astonished when Peythroppe did not appear. After seven weeks, Peythroppe and the Three Men returned from Rajputana. Peythroppe was in hard tough condition, rather white, and more self-contained than ever.

One of the Three Men had a cut on his nose, caused by the kick of a gun. Twelve-bores kick rather curiously.

Then came Honorary Lieutenant Castries, seeking for the blood of his perfidious son-in-law to be. He said things —vulgar and "impossible" things which showed the raw rough "ranker" below the "Honorary," and I fancy Peythroppe's eyes were opened. Anyhow, he held his peace till the end; when he spoke briefly. Honorary Lieutenant Castries asked for a "peg," before he went away to die or bring a suit for breach of promise.

Miss Castries was a *very* good girl. She said that she would have no breach of promise suits. She said that, if she was not a lady, she was refined enough to know that ladies kept their broken hearts to themselves; and, as she ruled her parents, nothing happened. Later on, she married a most respectable and gentlemanly person. He traveled for an enterprising firm in Calcutta, and was all that a good husband should be.

So Peythroppe came to his right mind again, and did much good work, and was honored by all who knew him. One of these days he will marry; but he will marry a sweet pink-and-white maiden, on the Government House List, with a little money and some influential connections, as every wise man should. And he will never, all his life, tell her what happened during the seven weeks of his shooting-tour in Rajputana.

But just think how much trouble and expense—for camel-hire is not cheap, and those Bikaneer brutes had to be fed like humans—might have been saved by a properly conducted Matrimonial Department, under the control of the Director-General of Education, but corresponding direct with the Viceroy.

———•———

The Arrest of Lieutenant Golightly

"I've forgotten the countersign," sez 'e.
"Oh! You 'ave, 'ave you?" sez I.
"But I'm the Colonel," sez 'e.
"Oh! You are, are you?" sez I.
"Colonel nor no Colonel, you waits 'ere till I'm relieved, an' the Sarjint reports on your ugly old mug. *Choop!*" sez I.
*   *   *   *   *   *
An' s'elp me soul, 'twas the Colonel after all! But I was a recruity then.
—*The Unedited Autobiography of Private Otheris.*

IF there was one thing on which Golightly prided himself more than another, it was looking like "an Officer and a Gentleman." He said it was for the honor of the Service that he attired himself so elaborately; but those who knew him best said that it was just personal vanity. There was no harm about Golightly—not an ounce. He recognized a horse when he saw one, and could do more than fill a cantle. He played a very fair game at billiards, and was a sound man at the whist-table. Every one liked him; and nobody ever dreamed of seeing him handcuffed on a station platform as a deserter. But this sad thing happened.

He was going down from Dalhousie, at the end of his leave—riding down. He had run his leave as fine as he dared, and wanted to come down in a hurry.

It was fairly warm at Dalhousie, and, knowing what to expect below, he descended in a new *khaki* suit—tight fitting—of a delicate olive-green; a peacock-blue tie, white collar, and a snowy white *solah* helmet. He prided himself on looking neat even when he was riding post. He did look neat, and he was so deeply concerned about his appearance before he started that he quite forgot to take anything but some small change with him. He left all his notes at the hotel. His servants had gone down the road before him, to be ready in waiting at Pathankote with a change of gear. That was what he called traveling in "light marching-order." He was proud of his faculty of organization—what we call *bundobust*.

Twenty-two miles out of Dalhousie it began to rain—not a mere hill-shower but a good, tepid, monsoonish downpour. Golightly bustled on, wishing that he had brought an umbrella. The dust on the roads turned into mud, and the pony mired a good deal. So did Golightly's *khaki* gaiters. But he kept on steadily and tried to think how pleasant the coolth was.

His next pony was rather a brute at starting, and, Golightly's hands being slippery with the rain, contrived to get rid of Golightly at a corner. He chased the animal, caught it, and went ahead briskly. The spill had not improved his clothes or his temper, and he had lost one spur. He kept the other one employed. By the time that stage was ended, the pony had had as much exercise as he wanted, and, in spite of the rain, Golightly was sweating freely. At the end of another miserable half hour Golightly found the world disappear before his eyes in clammy pulp. The rain had turned the pith of his huge and snowy *solah-topee* into an evil-smelling dough, and it had closed on his head like a half-opened mushroom. Also the green lining was beginning to run.

Golightly did not say anything worth recording here. He tore off and squeezed up as much of the brim as was in his eyes and ploughed on. The back of the helmet was flapping on his neck and the sides stuck to his ears, but the leather band and green lining kept things roughly together, so that the hat did not actually melt away where it flapped.

Presently, the pulp and the green stuff made a sort of slimy mildew which ran over Golightly in several directions— down his back and bosom for choice. The *khaki* color ran too—it was really shockingly bad dye—and sections of Golightly were brown, and patches were violet, and contours were ochre, and streaks were ruddy-red, and blotches were nearly white, according to the nature and peculiarities of the dye. When he took out his handkerchief to wipe his face, and the green of the hat-lining and the purple stuff that had soaked through on to his neck from the tie became thoroughly mixed, the effect was amazing.

Near Dhar the rain stopped and the evening sun came out and dried him up slightly. It fixed the colors, too. Three miles from Pathankote the last pony fell dead lame, and Golightly was forced to walk. He pushed on into Pathankote to find his servants. He did not know then that his *khitmatgar* had stopped by the roadside to get drunk, and would come on the next day saying that he had sprained his ankle. When he got into Pathankote he couldn't find his servants, his boots were stiff and ropy with mud, and there were large quantities of dust about his body. The blue tie had run as much as the *khaki*. So he took it off with the collar and threw it away. Then he said something about servants generally and tried to get a peg. He paid eight annas for the drink, and this revealed to him that he had only six annas more in his pocket—or in the world as he stood at that hour.

He went to the Station-Master to negotiate for a first-class ticket to Khasa, where he was stationed. The booking-clerk said something to the Station-Master, the Station-Master said something to the Telegraph Clerk, and the three looked at him with curiosity. They asked him to wait for half an hour, while they telegraphed to Umritsar for authority. So he waited and four constables came and grouped themselves picturesquely round him. Just as he was preparing to ask them to go away, the Station-Master said that he would give the *Sahib* a ticket to Umritsar, if the *Sahib* would kindly come inside the booking-office. Golightly stepped inside, and the next thing he knew was that a constable was attached to each of his legs and arms, while the Station-Master was trying to cram a mail-bag over his head.

There was a very fair scuffle all round the booking-office, and Golightly took a nasty cut over his eye through falling against a table. But the constables were too much for him, and they and the Station-Master handcuffed him securely. As soon as the mail-bag was slipped, he began expressing his opinions, and the head constable said, "Without doubt this is the soldier-Englishman we required. Listen to the abuse!" Then Golightly asked the Station-Master what the this and the that the proceedings meant. The Station-Master told him he was "Private John Binkle of the —— Regiment, 5 ft. 9 in., fair hair, grey eyes, and a dissipated appearance, no marks on the body," who had deserted a fortnight ago. Golightly began explaining at great length; and the more he explained the less the Station-Master believed him. He said that no Lieutenant could look such a ruffian as did Golightly, and that his instructions were to send his capture under proper escort to Umritsar. Golightly was feeling very damp and uncomfortable and the language he used was not fit for publication, even in an expurgated form. The four constables saw him safe to Umritsar in an "intermediate" compartment, and he spent the four-hour journey in abusing them as fluently as his knowledge of the vernaculars allowed.

At Umritsar he was bundled out on the platform into the arms of a Corporal and two men of the —— Regiment. Golightly drew himself up and tried to carry off matters jauntily. He did not feel too jaunty in handcuffs, with four constables behind him, and the blood from the cut on his forehead stiffening on his left cheek. The Corporal was not jocular either. Golightly got as far as—"This is a very absurd mistake, my men," when the Corporal told him to "stow his lip" and come along. Golightly did not want to come along. He desired to stop and explain. He explained very well indeed, until the Corporal cut in with—"*You* a orficer! It's the like o' *you* as brings disgrace on the likes of *us*. Bloomin' fine orficer you are! I know your regiment. The Rogue's March is the quick-step where you come from. You're a black shame to the Service."

Golightly kept his temper, and began explaining all over again from the beginning. Then he was marched out of the rain into the refreshment-room and told not to make a qualified fool of himself. The men were going to run him up to Fort Govindghar. And "running up" is a performance almost as undignified as the Frog March.

Golightly was nearly hysterical with rage and the chill and the mistake and the handcuffs and the headache that the cut on his forehead had given him. He really laid himself out to express what was in his mind. When he had quite finished and his throat was feeling dry, one of the men said, "I've 'eard a few beggars in the clink blind, stiff and crack on a bit; but I've never 'eard any one to touch this 'ere 'orficer.'" They were not angry with him. They rather admired him. They had some beer at the refreshment-room, and offered Golightly some too, because he had "swore won'erful." They asked him to tell them all about the adventures of Private John Binkle while he was loose on the country-side; and

that made Golightly wilder than ever. If he had kept his wits about him he would have been quiet until an officer came; but he attempted to run.

Now the butt of a Martini in the small of your back hurts a great deal, and rotten, rain-soaked *khaki* tears easily when two men are yerking at your collar.

Golightly rose from the floor feeling very sick and giddy, with his shirt ripped open all down his breast and nearly all down his back. He yielded to his luck, and at that point the down-train from Lahore came in, carrying one of Golightly's Majors.

This is the Major's evidence in full—

"There was the sound of a scuffle in the second-class refreshment-room, so I went in and saw the most villainous loafer that I ever set eyes on. His boots and breeches were plastered with mud and beer-stains. He wore a muddy-white dunghill sort of thing on his head, and it hung down in slips on his shoulders which were a good deal scratched. He was half in and half out of a shirt as nearly in two pieces as it could be, and he was begging the guard to look at the name on the tail of it. As he had rucked the shirt all over his head, I couldn't at first see who he was, but I fancied that he was a man in the first stage of D. T. from the way he swore while he wrestled with his rags. When he turned round, and I had made allowances for a lump as big as a pork-pie over one eye, and some green war-paint on the face, and some violet stripes round the neck, I saw that it was Golightly. He was very glad to see me," said the Major, "and he hoped I would not tell the Mess about it. *I* didn't, but you can, if you like, now that Golightly has gone Home."

Golightly spent the greater part of that summer in trying to get the Corporal and the two soldiers tried by Court-Martial for arresting an "officer and a gentleman." They were, of course, very sorry for their error. But the tale leaked into the regimental canteen, and thence ran about the Province.

In the House of Suddhoo

A stone's throw out on either hand
From that well-ordered road we tread,
  And all the world is wild and strange:
Churel and ghoul and *Djinn* and sprite
Shall bear us company to-night,
For we have reached the Oldest Land
  Wherein the Powers of Darkness range.
    —*From the Dusk to the Dawn.*

THE house of Suddhoo, near the Taksali Gate, is two-storied, with four carved windows of old brown wood, and a flat roof. You may recognize it by five red hand-prints arranged like the Five of Diamonds on the whitewash between the upper windows. Bhagwan Dass the grocer and a man who says he gets his living by seal-cutting live in the lower story with a troop of wives, servants, friends, and retainers. The two upper rooms used to be occupied by Janoo and Azizun and a little black-and-tan terrier that was stolen from an Englishman's house and given to Janoo by a soldier. To-day, only Janoo lives in the upper rooms. Suddhoo sleeps on the roof generally, except when he sleeps in the street. He used to go to Peshawar in the cold weather to visit his son who sells curiosities near the Edwardes' Gate, and then he slept under a real mud roof. Suddhoo is a great friend of mine, because his cousin had a son who secured, thanks to my recommendation, the post of head-messenger to a big firm in the Sttion. Suddhoo says that God will make me a Lieutenant-Governor one of these days. I dare say his prophecy will come true. He is very, very old, with white hair and no teeth worth showing, and he has outlived his wits—outlived nearly everything except his fondness for his son at Peshawar. Janoo and Azizun are Kashmiris, Ladies of the City, and theirs was an ancient and more or less honorable profession; but Azizun has since married a medical student from the Northwest and has settled down to a most respectable life somewhere near Bareilly. Bhagwan Dass is an extortionate and an adulterator. He is very rich. The man who is supposed to get his living by seal-cutting pretends to be very poor. This lets you know as much as is necessary of the four principal tenants in the house of Suddhoo. Then there is Me of course; but I am only the chorus that comes in at the end to explain things. So I do not count.

Suddhoo was not clever. The man who pretended to cut seals was the cleverest of them all—Bhagwan Dass only knew how to lie—except Janoo. She was also beautiful, but that was her own affair.

Suddhoo's son at Peshawar was attacked by pleurisy, and old Suddhoo was troubled. The seal-cutter man heard of Suddhoo's anxiety and made capital out of it. He was abreast of the times. He got a friend in Peshawar to telegraph daily accounts of the son's health. And here the story begins.

Suddhoo's cousin's son told me, one evening, that Suddhoo wanted to see me; that he was too old and feeble to come personally, and that I should be conferring an everlasting honor on the House of Suddhoo if I went to him. I went; but I think, seeing how well off Suddhoo was then, that he might have sent something better than an *ekka,* which jolted fearfully, to haul out a future Lieutenant--Governor to the City on a muggy April evening. The *ekka* did not run quickly. It was full dark when we pulled up opposite the door of Ranjit Singh's Tomb near the main gate of the Fort. Here was Suddhoo, and he said that, by reason of my condescension, it was absolutely certain that I should become a Lieutenant-Governor while my hair was yet black. Then we talked about the weather and the state of my health, and the wheat crops, for fifteen minutes, in the Huzuri Bagh, under the stars.

Suddhoo came to the point at last. He said that Janoo had told him that there was an order of the *Sirkar* against magic, because it was feared that magic might one day kill the Empress of India. I didn't know anything about the state of the law; but I fancied that something interesting was going to happen. I said that so far from magic being discouraged by the Government it was highly commended. The greatest officials of the State practiced it themselves. (If the Financial Statement isn't magic, I don't know what is.) Then, to encourage him further, I said that, if there was any *jadoo* afoot, I had not the least objection to giving it my countenance and sanction, and to seeing that it was clean *jadoo*—white magic, as distinguished from the unclean *jadoo* which kills folk. It took a long time before Suddhoo admitted that this was just what he had asked me to come for. Then he told me, in jerks and quavers, that the man who said he cut seals was a sorcerer of the cleanest kind; that every day he gave Suddhoo news of the sick son in Peshawar more quickly than the lightning could fly, and that this news was always corroborated by the letters. Further, that he had told Suddhoo how a great danger was threatening his son, which could be removed by clean *jadoo;* and, of course, heavy payment. I began to see exactly how the land lay, and told Suddhoo that I also understood a little *jadoo* in the Western line, and would go to his house to see that everything was done decently and in order. We set off together; and on the way Suddhoo told me that he had paid the seal-cutter between one hundred and two hundred rupees already; and the *jadoo* of that night would cost two hundred more. Which was cheap, he said, considering the greatness of his son's danger; but I do not think he meant it.

The lights were all cloaked in the front of the house when we arrived.

I could hear awful noises from behind the seal-cutter's shop-front, as if some one were groaning his soul out. Suddhoo shook all over, and while we groped our way upstairs told me that the *jadoo* had begun. Janoo and Azizun met us at the stair-head, and told us that the *jadoo*-work was coming off in their rooms, because there was more space there. Janoo is a lady of a free-thinking turn of mind. She whispeed that the *jadoo* was an invention to get money out of Suddhoo, and that the seal-cutter would go to a hot place when he died. Suddhoo was nearly crying with fear and old age. He kept walking up and down the room in the half-light, repeating his son's name over and over again, and asking Azizun if the seal-cutter ought not to make a reduction in the case of his own landlord. Janoo pulled me over to the shadow in the recess of the carved bow-windows. The boards were up, and the rooms were only lit by one tiny oil-lamp. There was no chance of my being seen if I stayed still.

Presently, the groans below ceased, and we heard steps on the staircase. That was the seal-cutter. He stopped outside the door as the terrier barked and Azizun fumbled at the chain, and he told Suddhoo to blow out the lamp. This left the place in jet darkness, except for the red glow from the two *huqas* that belonged to Janoo and Azizun. The seal-cutter came in, and I heard Suddhoo throw himself down on the floor and groan. Azizun caught her breath, and Janoo backed on to one of the beds with a shudder. There was a clink of something metallic, and then shot up a pale blue-green flame near

the ground. The light was just enough to show Azizun, pressed against one corner of the room with the terrier between her knees; Janoo, with her hands clasped, leaning forward as she sat on the bed; Suddhoo, face down, quivering, and the seal-cutter.

I hope I may never see another man like that seal-cutter. He was stripped to the waist, with a wreath of white jasmine as thick as my wrist round his forehead, a salmon colored loin-cloth round his middle, and a steel bangle on each ankle. This was not awe-inspiring. It was the face of the man that turned me cold. It was blue-grey in the first place. In the second, the eyes were rolled back till you could only see the whites of them; and, in the third, the face was the face of a demon—a ghoul —anything you please except of the sleek, oily old ruffian who sat in the daytime over his turning-lathe down-stairs. He was lying on his stomach with his arms turned and crossed behind him, as if he had been thrown down pinioned. His head and neck were the only parts of him off the floor. They were nearly at right angles to the body like the head of a cobra at spring. It was ghastly. In the centre of the room, on the bare earth floor, stood a big, deep, brass basin, with a pale blue-green light floating in the centre like a night-light. Round that basin the man on the floor wriggled himself three times. How he did it I do not know. I could see the muscles ripple along his spine and fall smooth again; but I could not see any other motion. The head seemed the only thing alive about him, except that slow curl and uncurl of the laboring back-muscles. Janoo from the bed was breathing seventy to the minute; Azizun held her hands before her eyes; and old Suddhoo, fingering at the dirt that had got into his white beard, was crying to himself. The horror of it was that the creeping, crawly thing made no sound—only crawled! And, remember, this lasted for ten minutes, while the terrier whined, and Azizun shuddered, and Janoo gasped, and Suddhoo cried.

I felt the hair lift at the back of my head, and my heart thump like a thermantidote paddle. Luckily, the seal-cutter betrayed himself by his most impressive trick and made me calm again. After he had finished that unspeakable triple crawl, he stretched his head away from the floor as high as he could, and sent out a jet of fire from his nostrils. Now I knew how fire-spouting is done—I can do it myself—so I felt at ease. The business was a fraud. If he had only kept to that crawl without trying to raise the effect, goodness knows what I might not have thought. Both the girls shrieked at the jet of fire and the head dropped, chin-down on the floor, with a thud; the whole body lying then like a corpse with its arms trussed. There was a pause of five full minutes after this, and the blue-green flame died down. Janoo stooped to settle one of her anklets, while Azizun turned her face to the wall and took the terrier in her arms. Suddhoo put out an arm mechanically to Janoo's *huqa,* and she slid across the floor with her foot. Directly above the body and on the wall, were a couple of flaming portraits, in stamped-paper frames, of the Queen and the Prince of Wales. They looked down on the performance, and to my

thinking, seemed to heighten the grotesqueness of it all.

Just when the silence was getting unendurable, the body turned over and rolled away from the basin to the side of the room, where it lay stomach-up. There was a faint "plop" from the basin —exactly like the noise a fish makes when it takes a fly—and the green light in the centre revived.

I looked at the basin, and saw, bobbing in the water, the dried, shrivelled, black head of a native baby—open eyes, open mouth, and shaved scalp. It was worse, being so very sudden, than the crawling exhibition. We had no time to say anything before it began to speak.

Read Poe's account of the voice that came from the mesmerized dying man, and you will realize less than one half of the horror of that head's voice.

There was an interval of a second or two between each word, and a sort of "ring, ring, ring," in the note of the voice, like the timbre of a bell. It pealed slowly, as if talking to itself, for several minutes before I got rid of my cold sweat. Then the blessed solution struck me. I looked at the body lying near the doorway, and saw, just where the hollow of the throat joins on the shoulders, a muscle that had nothing to do with any man's regular breathing twitching away steadily. The whole thing was a careful reproduction of the Egyptian teraphin that one reads about sometimes; and the voice was as clever and as appalling a piece of ventriloquism as one could wish to hear. All this time the head was "lip-lip-lapping" against the side of the basin, and speaking. It told Suddhoo, on his face again whining, of his son's illness and of the state of the illness up to the evening of that very night. I always shall respect the seal-cutter for keeping so faithfully to the time of the Peshawar telegrams. It went on to say that skilled doctors were night and day watching over the man's life; and that he would eventually recover if the fee to the potent sorcerer, whose servant was the head in the basin, were doubled.

Here the mistake from the artistic point of view came in. To ask for twice your stipulated fee in a voice that Lazarus might have used when he rose from the dead, is absurd. Janoo, who is really a woman of masculine intellect, saw this as quickly as I did. I heard her say *"Asli nahin! Fareib!"* scornfully under her breath; and just as she said so, the light in the basin died out, the head stopped talking, and we heard the room door creak on its hinges. Then Janoo struck a match, lit the lamp, and we saw that head, basin, and seal-cutter were gone. Suddhoo was wringing his hands and explaining to any one who cared to listen, that, if his chances of eternal salvation depended on it, he could not raise another two hundred rupees. Azizun was nearly in hysterics in the corner; while Janoo sat down composedly on one of the beds to discuss the probabilities of the whole thing being a *bunao,* or "make-up."

I explained as much as I knew of the seal-cutter's way of *jadoo;* but her argument was much more simple—"The magic that is always demanding gifts is no true magic," said she. "My mother told me that the only potent love-spells are those which are told you for love. This seal-cutter man is a liar and a devil. I dare not tell, do anything, or get anything done, because I am in debt to Bhagwan Dass the bunnia for two gold rings and a heavy anklet. I must get my food from his shop. The seal-cutter is the friend of Bhagwan Dass, and he would poison my food. A fool's *jadoo* has been going on for ten days, and has cost Suddhoo many rupees each night. The seal-cutter used black hens and lemons and *mantras* before. He never showed us anything like this till to-night. Azizun is a fool, and will be a *purdahnashin* soon. Suddhoo has lost his strength and his wits. See now! I had hoped to get from Suddhoo many rupees while he lived, and many more after his death; and behold, he is spending everything on that offspring of a devil and a she-ass, the seal-cutter!"

Here I said, "But what induced Suddhoo to drag me into the business? Of course I can speak to the seal-cutter, and he shall refund. The whole thing is child's talk—shame—and senseless."

"Suddhoo *is* an old child," said Janoo. "He has lived on the roofs these seventy years and is as senseless as a milch-goat. He brought you here to assure himself that he was not breaking any law of the *Sirkar,* whose salt he ate many years ago. He worships the dust off the feet of the seal-cutter, and that cow-devourer has forbidden him to go and see his son. What does Suddhoo know of your laws or the lightning-post? I have to watch his money going day by day to that lying beast below."

Janoo stamped her foot on the floor and nearly cried with vexation; while Suddhoo was whimpering under a blanket in the corner, and Azizun was trying to guide the pipe-stem to his foolish old mouth.

* * * * * *

Now, the case stands thus. Unthinkingly, I have laid myself open to the charge of aiding and abetting the seal-cutter in obtaining money under false pretences, which is forbidden by Section 420 of the Indian Penal Code. I am helpless in the matter for these reasons. I cannot inform the Police. What witnesses would support my statements? Janoo refuses flatly, and Azizun is a veiled woman somewhere near Bareilly —lost in this big India of ours. I dare not again take the law into my own hands, and speak to the seal-cutter; for certain am I that, not only would Suddhoo disbelieve me, but this step would end in the poisoning of Janoo, who is bound hand and foot by her debt to the

bunnia. Suddhoo is an old dotard; and whenever we meet mumbles my idiotic joke that the *Sirkar* rather patronizes the Black Art than otherwise. His son is well now; but Suddhoo is completely under the influence of the seal-cutter, by whose advice he regulates the affairs of his life. Janoo watches daily the money that she hoped to wheedle out of Suddhoo taken by the seal-cutter, and becomes daily more furious and sullen.

She will never tell, because she dare not; but, unless something happens to prevent her, I am afraid that the seal-cutter will die of cholera—the white arsenic kind—about the middle of May. And thus I shall be privy to a murder in the House of Suddhoo.

His Wedded Wife

Cry "Murder!" in the market-place, and each
Will turn upon his neighbor anxious eyes
That ask—"Art thou the man?" We hunted Cain,
Some centuries ago, across the world.
That bred the fear our own misdeeds maintain
To-day.

—*Vibart's Moralities.*

SHAKESPEARE says something about worms, or it may be giants or beetles, turning if you tread on them too severely. The safest plan is never to tread on a worm—not even on the last new subaltern from Home, with his buttons hardly out of their tissue-paper, and the red of sappy English beef in his cheeks. This is a story of the worm

that turned. For the sake of brevity, we will call Henry Augustus Ramsay Faizanne, "The Worm," though he really was an exceedingly pretty boy, without a hair on his face, and with a waist like a girl's, when he came out to the Second "Shikarris" and was made unhappy in several ways. The "Shikarris" are a high-caste regiment, and you must be able to do things well—play a banjo, or ride more than little, or sing, or act, —to get on with them.

The Worm did nothing except fall off his pony, and knock chips out of gate-posts with his trap. Even that became monotonous after a time. He objected to whist, cut the cloth at billiards, sang out of tune, kept very much to himself, and wrote to his Mamma and sisters at Home. Four of these five things were vices which the "Shikarris" objected to and set themselves to eradicate. Every one knows how subalterns are, by brother subalterns, softened and not permitted to be ferocious. It is good and wholesome, and does no one any harm, unless tempers are lost; and then there is trouble. There was a man once—

The "Shikarris" *shikarred* The Worm very much, and he bore everything without winking. He was so good and so anxious to learn, and flushed so pink, that his education was cut short, and he was left to his own devices by every one except the Senior Subaltern, who continued to make life a burden to The Worm. The Senior Subaltern meant no harm; but his chaff was coarse and he didn't quite understand where to stop. He had been waiting too long for his Company; and that always sours a man. Also he was in love, which made him worse.

One day, after he had borrowed The Worm's trap for a lady who never existed, had used it himself all the afternoon, had sent a note, to The Worm, purporting to come from the lady, and was telling the Mess all about it, The Worm rose in his place and said, in his quiet, lady-like voice—"That was a very pretty sell; but I'll lay you a month's pay to a month's pay when you get your step, that I work a sell on you that you'll remember for the rest of your days, and the Regiment after you when you're dead or broke." The Worm wasn't angry in the least, and the rest of the Mess shouted. Then the Senior Subaltern looked at The Worm from the boots upward, and down again, and said—"Done, Baby." The Worm held the rest of the Mess to witness that the bet had been taken, and retired into a book with a sweet smile.

Two months passed, and the Senior Subaltern still educated The Worm, who began to move about a little more as the hot weather came on. I have said that the Senior Subaltern was in love. The curious thing is that a girl was in love with the Senior Subaltern. Though the Colonel said awful things, and the Majors snorted, and the married Captains looked unutterable wisdom, and the juniors scoffed, those two were engaged.

The Senior Subaltern was so pleased with getting his Company and his acceptance at the same time that he forgot to bother The Worm. The girl was a pretty girl, and had money of her own. She does not come into this story at all.

One night, at the beginning of the hot weather, all the Mess, except The Worm who had gone to his own room to write Home letters, were sitting on the platform outside the Mess House. The Band had finished playing, but no one wanted to go in. And the Captains' wives were there also. The folly of a man in love is unlimited. The Senior Subaltern had been holding forth on the merits of the girl he was engaged to, and the ladies were purring approval while the men yawned, when there was a rustle of skirts in the dark, and a tired, faint voice lifted itself.

"Where's my husband?"

I do not wish in the least to reflect on the morality of the "Shikarris"; but it is on record that four men jumped up as if they had been shot. Three of them were married men. Perhaps they were afraid that their wives had come from Home unbeknownst. The fourth said that he had acted on the impulse of the moment. He explained this afterward.

Then the voice cried, "O Lionel!" Lionel was the Senior Subaltern's name. A woman came into the little circle of light by the candles on the peg-tables, stretching out her hands to the dark where the Senior Subaltern was, and sobbing. We rose to our feet, feeling that things were going to happen and ready to believe the worst. In this bad, small world of ours, one knows so little of the life of the next man—which, after all, is entirely his own concern— that one is not surprised when a crash comes. Anything might turn up any day for any one. Perhaps the Senior Subaltern had been trapped in his youth. Men are crippled that way, occasionally. We didn't know; we wanted to hear; and the Captains' wives were as anxious as we. If he had been trapped, he was to be excused; for the woman from nowhere, in the dusty shoes and grey traveling-dress, was very lovely, with black hair and great eyes full of tears. She was tall, with a fine figure, and her voice had a running sob in it pitiful to hear. As soon as the Senior Subaltern stood up, she threw her arms round his neck, and called him "my darling," and said she could not bear waiting alone in England, and his letters were so short and cold, and she was his to the end of the world, and would he forgive her? This did not sound quite like a lady's way of speaking. It was too demonstrative.

Things seemed black indeed, and the Captains' wives peered under their eyebrows at the Senior Subaltern, and the Colonel's face set like the Day of Judgment framed in grey bristles, and no one spoke for a while.

Next the Colonel said, very shortly, "Well, Sir?" and the woman sobbed afresh. The Senior Subaltern was half choked with the arms round his neck, but he gasped out—"It's a damned lie! I never had a wife in my life!"—"Don't swear," said the Colonel. "Come into the Mess. We must sift this clear somehow," and he sighed to himself, for he believed in his "Shikarris," did the Colonel.

We trooped into the ante-room, under the full lights, and there we saw how beautiful the woman was. She stood up in the middle of us all, sometimes choking with crying, then hard and proud, and then holding out her arms to the Senior Subaltern. It was like the fourth act of a tragedy. She told us how the Senior Subaltern had married her when he was Home on leave eighteen months before; and she seemed to know all that we knew, and more too, of his people and his past life. He was white and ashy-grey, trying now and again to break into the torrent of her words; and we, noting how lovely she was and what a criminal he looked, esteemed him a beast of the worst kind. We felt sorry for him, though.

I shall never forget the indictment of the Senior Subaltern by his wife. Nor will he. It was so sudden, rushing out of the dark, unannounced, into our dull lives. The Captains' wives stood back; but their eyes were alight, and you could see that they had already convicted and sentenced the Senior Subaltern. The Colonel seemed five years older. One Major was shading his eyes with his hand and watching the woman from underneath it. Another was chewing his moustache and smiling quietly as if he were witnessing a play. Full in the open space in the centre, by the whist-tables, the Senior Subaltern's terrier was hunting for fleas. I remember all this as clearly as though a photograph were in my hand. I remember the look of horror on the Senior Subaltern's face. It was rather like seeing a man hanged; but much more interesting. Finally the woman wound up by saying that the Senior Subaltern carried a double F. M. in tattoo on his left shoulder. We all knew that, and to our innocent minds it seemed to clinch the matter. But one of the bachelor Majors said very politely, "I presume that your marriage-certificate would be more to the purpose?"

That roused the woman. She stood up and sneered at the Senior Subaltern for a cur, and abused the Major and the Colonel and all the rest. Then she wept, and then she pulled a paper from her breast, saying imperially, "Take that! And let my husband—my lawfully wedded husband—read it aloud—if he dare!"

There was a hush, and the men looked into each other's eyes as the Senior Subaltern came forward in a dazed and dizzy way, and took the paper. We were wondering, as we stared, whether there was anything against any one of us that might turn up later on. The Senior Subaltern's throat was dry; but, as he ran his eye over the paper, he broke out into a hoarse cackle of

relief, and said to the woman, "You young blackguard!" But the woman had fled through a door, and on the paper was written, "This is to certify that I, The Worm, have paid in full my debts to the Senior Subaltern, and, further, that the Senior Subaltern is my debtor, by agreement on the 23d of February, as by the Mess attested, to the extent of one month's Captain's pay, in the lawful currency of the Indian Empire."

Then a deputation set off for The Worm's quarters and found him, betwixt and between, unlacing his stays, with the hat, wig, and serge dress, on the bed. He came over as he was, and the "Shikarris" shouted till the Gunners' Mess sent over to know if they might have a share of the fun. I think we were all, except the Colonel and the Senior Subaltern, a little disappointed that the scandal had come to nothing. But that is human nature. There could be no two words about The Worm's sting. It leaned as near to a nasty tragedy as anything this side of a joke can. When most of the Subalterns sat upon him with sofa-cushions to find out why he had not said that acting was his strong point, he answered very quietly, "I don't think you ever asked me. I used to act at Home with my sisters." But no acting with girls could account for The Worm's display that night. Personally, I think it was in bad taste. Besides being dangerous. There is no sort of use in playing with fire, ever for fun.

The "Shikarris" made him President of the Regimental Dramatic Club; and, when the Senior Subaltern paid up his debt, which he did at once, The Worm sank the money in scenery and dresses. He was a good Worm; and the "Shikarris" are proud of him. The only drawback is that he has been christened "Mrs. Senior Subaltern"; and, as there are now two Mrs. Senior Subalterns in the Station, this is sometimes confusing to strangers.

Later on, I will tell you of a case something like this, but with all the jest left out and nothing in it but rea trouble.

The Broken-Link Handicap

While the snaffle holds, or the long-neck
    stings,
While the big beam tilts, or the last bell
    rings,
While horses are horses to train and to
    race,
Then women and wine take a second place
    For me—for me—
While a short "ten-three"
Has a field to squander or fence to face!
        —*Song of the G. R.*

THERE are more ways of running a horse to suit your book than pulling his head off in the straight. Some men forget this. Understand clearly that all racing it rotten—as everything connected with losing money must be. In India, in addition to its inherent rottenness, it has the merit of being two-thirds sham; looking pretty on paper only. Every one knows every one else far too well for business purposes. How on earth can you rack and harry and post a man for his losings, when you are fond of his wife, and live in the same Station with him? He says, "On the Monday following," "I can't settle just yet." You say, "All right, old man," and think yourself lucky if you pull off nine hundred out of a two-thousand-rupee debt. Any way you look at it, Indian racing is immoral, and expensive-ly immoral. Which is much worse. If a man wants your money, he ought to ask for it, or send round a subscription-list, instead of juggling about the country, with an Australian larrikin; a "brumby," with as much breed as the boy; a brace of *chumars* in gold-laced caps; three or four *ekka*-ponies with hogged manes, and a switch-tailed demirep of a mare called Arab because she has a kink in her flag. Racing leads to the *shroff* quicker than anything else. But if you have no conscience and no sentiments, and good hands, and some knowledge of pace, and ten years' experience of horses, and several thousand rupees a month, I believe that you can occasionally contrive to pay your shoeing-bills.

Did you ever know Shackles—b. w. g., 15. 1 3-8—coarse, loose, mule-like ears —barrel as long as a gatepost—tough as a telegraph-wire—and the queerest brute that ever looked through a bridle? He was of no brand, being one of an ear-nicked mob taken into the *Bucephalus* at £4:10s., a head to make up freight, and sold raw and out of condition at Calcutta for Rs.275. People who lost money on him called him a "brumby"; but if ever any horse had Harpoon's shoulders and The Gin's temper, Shackles was that horse. Two miles was his own particular distance. He trained himself, ran himself, and rode himself; and, if his jockey insulted him by giving him hints, he shut up at once and bucked the boy off. He objected to dictation. Two or three of his owners did not understand this, and lost money in consequence. At last he was bought by a man who discovered that, if a race was to be won, Shackles, and Shackles only, would win it in his own way, so long as his jockey sat still. This man had a riding-boy called Brunt —a lad from Perth, West Australia— and he taught Brunt, with a trainer's whip, the hardest thing a jock can learn—to sit still, to sit still, and to keep on sitting still. When Brunt fairly grasped this truth, Shackles devastated the country. No weight could stop him at his own distance; and the fame of Shackles spread from Ajmir in the South, to Chedputter in the North. There was no horse like Shackles, so long as he was allowed to do his work in his own way. But he was beaten in the end; and the story of his fall is enough to make angels weep.

At the lower end of the Chedputter race-course, just before the turn into the straight, the track passes close to a couple of old brick-mounds enclosing a funnel-shaped hollow. The big end of the funnel is not six feet from the railings on the off-side. The astounding peculiarity of the course is that, if you stand at one particular place, about half a mile away, inside the course, and speak at ordinary pitch, your voice just hits the funnel of the brick-mounds and makes a curious whining echo there. A man discovered this one morning by ac-

cident while out training with a friend. He marked the place to stand and speak from with a couple of bricks, and he kept his knowledge to himself. *Every* peculiarity of a course is worth remembering in a country where rats play the mischief with the elephant-litter, and Stewards build jumps to suit their own stables. This man ran a very fairish country-bred, a long, racking high mare with the temper of a fiend, and the paces of an airy wandering seraph—a drifty, glidy stretch. The mare was, as a delicate tribute to Mrs. Reiver, called "The Lady Regula Baddun"—or for short, Regula Baddun.

Shackles' jockey, Brunt, was a quite well-behaved boy, but his nerve had been shaken. He began his career by riding jump-races in Melbourne, where a few Stewards want lynching, and was one of the jockeys who came through the awful butchery—perhaps you will recollect it—of the Maribyrnong Plate. The walls were colonial ramparts—logs of *jarrah* spiked into masonry—with wings as strong as Church buttresses. Once in his stride, a horse had to jump or fall. He couldn't run out. In the Maribyrnong Plate, twelve horses were jammed at the second wall. Red Hat, leading, fell this side, and threw out The Gled, and the ruck came up behind and the space between wing and wing was one struggling, screaming, kicking shambles. Four jockeys were taken out dead; three were very badly hurt, and Brunt was among the three. He told the story of the Maribyrnong Plate sometimes; and when he described how Whalley on Red Hat, said, as the mare fell under him—"God ha' mercy, I'm done for!" and how, next instant, Sithee

There and White Otter had crushed the life out of poor Whalley, and the dust hid a small hell of men and horses, no one marveled that Brunt had dropped jump-races and Australia together. Regula Baddun's owner knew that story by heart. Brunt never varied it in the telling. He had no education.

Shackles came to the Chedputter Autumn races one year, and his owner walked about insulting the sportsmen of Chedputter generally, till they went to the Honorary Secretary in a body and said, "Appoint handicappers, and arrange a race which shall break Shackles and humble the pride of his owner." The Districts rose against Shackles and sent up of their best; Ousel, who was supposed to be able to do his mile in 1-53; Petard, the stud-bred, trained by a cavalry regiment who knew how to train; Gringalet, the ewe-lamb of the 75th; Bobolink, the pride of Peshawar; and many others.

They called that race The Broken-Link Handicap, because it was to smash Shackles; and the Handicappers piled on the weights, and the Fund gave eight hundred rupees, and the distance was "round the course for all horses." Shackles' owner said, "You can arrange the race with regard to Shackles only. So long as you don't bury him under weight-cloths, I don't mind." Regula Baddun's owner said, "I throw in my mare to fret Ousel. Six furlongs is Regula's distance, and she will then lie down and die. So also will Ousel, for his jockey doesn't understand a waiting race." Now, this was a lie, for Regula had been in work for two months at Dehra, and her chances were good, always supposing that Shackles broke a

blood-vessel—or Brunt moved on him.

The plunging in the lotteries was fine. They filled eight thousand-rupee lotteries on the Broken-Link Handicap, and the account in the *Pioneer* said that "favoritism was divided." In plain English, the various contingents were wild on their respective horses; for the Handicappers had done their work well. The Honorary Secretary shouted himself hoarse through the din; and the smoke of the cheroots was like the smoke, and the rattling of the dice-boxes like the rattle of small-arm fire.

Ten horses started—very level—and Regula Baddun's owner cantered out on his hack to a place inside the circle of the course, where two bricks had been thrown. He faced towards the brick-mounds at the lower end of the course and waited.

The story of the running is in the *Pioneer*. At the end of the first mile, Shackles crept out of the ruck, well on the outside, ready to get round the turn, lay hold of the bit and spin up the straight before the others knew he had got away. Brunt was sitting still, perfectly happy, listening to the "drum-drum-drum" of the hoofs behind, and knowing that, in about twenty strides, Shackles would draw one deep breath and go up the last half-mile like the "Flying Dutchman." As Shackles went short to take the turn and came abreast of the brick-mound, Brunt heard, above the noise of the wind in his ears, a whining, wailing voice on the offside, saying—"God ha' mercy, I'm done for!" In one stride, Brunt saw the whole seething smash of the Maribyrnong Plate before him, started in his saddle and gave a yell of terror. The start brought the heels into Shackles' side, and the scream hurt Shackles' feelings. He couldn't stop dead; but he put out his feet and slid along for fifty yards, and then, very gravely and judicially, bucked off Brunt—a shaking, terror-stricken lump, while Regula Baddun made a neck-and-neck race with Bobolink up the straight, and won by a short head—Petard a bad third. Shackles' owner, in the Stand, tried to think that his field-glasses had gone wrong. Regula Baddun's owner, waiting by the two bricks, gave one deep sigh of relief, and cantered back to the Stand. He had won, in lotteries and bets, about fifteen thousand.

It was a Broken-Link Handicap with a vengeance. It broke nearly all the men concerned, and nearly broke the heart of Shackles' owner. He went down to interview Brunt. The boy lay, livid and gasping with fright, where he had tumbled off. The sin of losing the race never seemed to strike him. All he knew was that Whalley had "called" him, that the "call" was a warning; and, were he cut in two for it, he would never get up again. His nerve had gone altogether, and he only asked his master to give him a good thrashing, and let him go. He was fit for nothing, he said. He got his dismissal, and crept up to the paddock, white as chalk, with blue lips, his knees giving way under him. People said nasty things in the paddock; but Brunt never heeded. He changed into tweeds, took his stick and went down the road, still shaking with fright, and muttering over and over again—"God ha' mercy, I'm done for!" To the best of my knowledge and belief he spoke the truth.

So now you know how the Broken-Link Handicap was run and won. Of course you don't believe it. You would credit anything about Russia's designs on India, or the recommendations of the Currency Commission; but a little bit of sober fact is more than you can stand.

Beyond the Pale

Love heeds not caste nor sleep a broken bed. I went in search of love and lost myself.—*Hindue Proverb.*

A MAN should, whatever happens, keep to his own caste, race and breed. Let the White go to the White and the Black to the Black. Then, whatever trouble falls is in the ordinary course of things—neither sudden, alien nor unexpected.

This is the story of a man who wilfully stepped beyond the safe limits of decent everyday society, and paid for it heavily.

He knew too much in the first instance; and he saw too much in the second. He took too deep an interest in native life; but he will never do so again.

Deep away in the heart of the City, behind Jitha Megji's *bustee*, lies Amir Nath's Gully, which ends in a dead-wall pierced by one grated window. At the head of the Gully is a big cowbyre, and the walls on either side of the Gully are without windows. Neither Suchet Singh nor Gaur Chand approve of their women-folk looking into the world. If Durga Charan had been of their opinion, he would have been a happier man to-day, and little Bisesa would have been able to knead her own bread. Her room looked out through the grated window into the narrow dark Gully where the sun never came and where the buffaloes wallowed in the blue slime. She was a widow, about fifteen years old, and she prayed the Gods, day and night, to send her a lover; for she did not approve of living alone.

One day, the man—Trejago his name was—came into Amir Nath's Gully on an aimless wandering; and, after he had passed the buffaloes, stumbled over a big heap of cattle-food.

Then he saw that the Gully ended in a trap, and heard a little laugh from behind the grated window. It was a pretty little laugh, and Trejago, knowing that, for all practical purposes, the old *Arabian Nights* are good guides, went forward to the window, and whispered that verse of "The Love Song of Har Dyal" which begins:

Can a man stand upright in the face of the naked Sun; or a Lover in the Presence of his Beloved?
If my feet fail me, O Heart of my Heart, am I to blame, being blinded by the glimpse of your beauty?

There came the faint *tchink* of a woman's bracelets from behind the grating, and a little voice went on with the song at the fifth verse:

Alas! alas! Can the Moon tell the Lotus of her love when the Gate of Heaven is shut and the clouds gather for the rains?
They have taken my Beloved, and driven her with the pack-horses to the North.
There are iron chains on the feet that were set on my heart.
Call to the bowmen to make ready—

The voice stopped suddenly, and Trejago walked out of Amir Nath's Gully, wondering who in the world could have capped "The Love Song of Har Dyal" so neatly.

Next morning, as he was driving to office, an old woman threw a packet into his dog-cart. In the packet was the half of a broken glass-bangle, one flower of the blood-red *dhak,* a pinch of *bhusa* or cattle-food, and eleven cardamoms. That packet was a letter—not a clumsy compromising letter, but an innocent unintelligible lover's epistle.

Trejago knew far too much about these things, as I have said. No Englishman should be able to translate object-letters. But Trejago spread all the trifles on the lid of his office-box and began to puzzle them out.

A broken glass-bangle stands for a Hindu widow all India over; because, when her husband dies, a woman's bracelets are broken on her wrists. Trejago saw the meaning of the little bit of the glass. The flower of the *dhak* means diversely "desire," "come," "write," or "danger," according to the other things with it. One cardamom means "jealousy"; but when any article is duplicated in an object-letter, it loses its symbolic meaning and stands merely for one of a number indicating time, or, if incense, curds, or saffron be sent also, place. The message ran then—"A widow—*dhak* flower and *bhusa*,—at eleven o'clock." The pinch of *bhusa* enlightened Trejago. He saw—this kind of letter leaves much to instinctive knowledge—that the *bhusa* referred to the big heap of cattle-food over which he had fallen in Amir Nath's Gully, and that the message must come from the person behind the grating; she being a widow. So the message ran then—"A widow, in the Gully in which is the heap of *bhusa*, desires you to come at eleven o'clock."

Trejago threw all the rubbish into the fireplace and laughed. He knew that men in the East do not make love under windows at eleven in the forenoon, nor do women fix appointments a week in advance. So he went, that very night at eleven, into Amir Nath's Gully, clad in a *boorka*, which cloaks a man as well as a woman. Directly the gongs of the City made the hour, the little voice behind the grating took up "The Love Song of Har Dyal" at the verse where the Panthan girl calls upon Har Dyal to return. The song is really pretty in the Vernacular. In English you miss the wail of it. It runs something like this—

Alone upon the housetops, to the North
I turn and watch the lightning in the sky,—
The glamour of thy footsteps in the North,
Come back to me, Beloved, or I die!

Below my feet the still bazar is laid
Far, far, below the weary camels lie,—
The camels and the captives of thy raid,
Come back to me, Beloved, or I die!

My father's wife is old and harsh with years,

And drudge of all my father's house am I.—
My bread is sorrow and my drink is tears,
Come back to me, Beloved, or I die!

As the song stopped, Trejago stepped up under the grating and whispered—"I am here."

Bisesa was good to look upon.

That night was the beginning of many strange things, and of a double life so wild that Trejago to-day sometimes wonders if it were not all a dream. Bisesa, or her old handmaiden who had thrown the object-letter, had detached the heavy grating from the brick-work of the wall; so that the window slid inside, leaving only a square of raw masonry into which an active man might climb.

In the daytime, Trejago drove through his routine of office-work, or put on his calling-clothes and called on the ladies of the Station; wondering how long they would know him if they knew of poor little Bisesa. At night, when all the City was still, came the walk under the evil-smelling *boorka*, the patrol through Jitha Megji's *bustee*, the quick turn into Amir Nath's Gully between the sleeping cattle and the dead walls, and then, last of all, Bisesa, and the deep, even breathing of the old woman who slept outside the door of the bare little room that Durga Charan allotted to his sister's daughter. Who or what Durga Charan was, Trejago never inquired; and why in the world he was not discovered and knifed never occurred to him till his madness was over, and Bisesa . . . But this comes later.

Bisesa was an endless delight to Trejago. She was as ignorant as a bird;

and her distorted versions of the rumors from the outside world that had reached her in her room, amused Trejago almost as much as her lisping attempts to pronounce his name—"Christopher." The first syllable was always more than she could manage, and she made funny little gestures with her rose-leaf hands, as one throwing the name away, and then, kneeling before Trejago, asked him, exactly as an Englishwoman would do, if he were sure he loved her. Trejago swore that he loved her more than any one else in the world. Which was true.

After a month of this folly, the exigencies of his other life compelled Trejago to be especially attentive to a lady of his acquaintance. You may take it for a fact that anything of this kind is not only noticed and discussed by a man's own race but by some hundred and fifty natives as well. Trejago had to walk with this lady and talk to her at the Band-stand, and once or twice to drive with her; never for an instant dreaming that this would affect his dearer, out-of-the-way life. But the news flew, in the usual mysterious fashion, from mouth to mouth, till Bisesa's duenna heard of it and told Bisesa. The child was so troubled that she did the household work evilly, and was beaten by Durga Charan's wife in consequence.

A week later, Bisesa taxed Trejago with the flirtation. She understood no gradations and spoke openly. Trejago laughed and Bisesa stamped her little feet—little feet, light as marigold flowers, that could lie in the palm of a man's one hand.

Much that is written about Oriental passion and impulsiveness is exaggerated and compiled at second-hand, but a little of it is true; and when an Englishman finds that little, it is quite as startling as any passion in his own proper life. Bisesa raged and stormed, and finally threatened to kill herself if Trejago did not at once drop the alien *Memsahib* who had come between them. Trejago tried to explain, and to show her that she did not understand these things from a Western standpoint. Bisesa drew herself up, and said simply—

"I do not. I know only this—it is not good that I should have made you dearer than my own heart to me, *Sahib*. You are an Englishman. I am only a black girl"—she was fairer than bargold in the Mint,—"and the widow of a black man."

Then she sobbed and said—"But on my soul and my Mother's soul, I love you. There shall no harm come to you, whatever happens to me."

Trejago argued with the child, and tried to soothe her, but she seemed quite unreasonably disturbed. Nothing would satisfy her save that all relations between them should end. He was to go away at once. And he went. As he dropped out of the window, she kissed his forehead twice, and he walked home wondering.

A week, and then three weeks, passed without a sign from Bisesa. Trejago, thinking that the rupture had lasted quite long enough, went down to Amir Nath's Gully for the fifth time in the three weeks, hoping that his rap at the sill of the shifting grating would be answered. He was not disappointed.

There was a young moon, and one stream of light fell down into Amir

Nath's Gully, and struck the grating which was drawn away as he knocked. From the black dark, Bisesa held out her arms into the moonlight. Both hands had been cut off at the wrists, and the stumps were nearly healed.

Then, as Bisesa bowed her head between her arms and sobbed, some one in the room grunted like a wild beast, and something sharp—knife, sword, or spear,—thrust at Trejago in his *boorka*. The stroke missed his body, but cut into one of the muscles of the groin, and he limped slightly from the wound for the rest of his days.

The grating went into its place. There was no sign whatever from inside the house,—nothing but the moonlight strip on the high wall, and the blackness of Amir Nath's Gully behind.

The next thing Trejago remembers, after raging and shouting like a madman between those pitiless walls, is that he found himself near the river as the dawn was breaking, threw away his *boorka* and went home bareheaded.

*   *   *   *   *   *

What was the tragedy—whether Bisesa had, in a fit of causeless despair, told everything, or the intrigue had been discovered and she tortured to tell; whether Durga Charan knew his name and what became of Bisesa—Trejago does not know to this day. Something horrible had happened, and the thought of what it must have been, comes upon Trejago in the night now and again, and keeps him company till the morning. One special feature of the case is that he does not know where lies the front of Durga Charan's house. It may open on to a courtyard common to two or more houses, or it may lie behind any one of the gates of Jitha Megji's *bustee*. Trejago cannot tell. He cannot get Bisesa—poor little Bisesa—back again. He has lost her in the City where each man's house is as guarded and as unknowable as the grave; and the grating that opens into Amir Nath's Gully has been walled up.

But Trejago pays his calls regularly, and is reckoned a very decent sort of man.

There is nothing peculiar about him, except a slight stiffness, caused by a riding-strain, in the right leg.

In Error

They burned a corpse upon the sand—
   The light shone out afar;
It guided home the plunging boats
   That beat from Zanzibar.
Spirit of Fire, where'er Thy altars rise,
Thou art Light of Guidance to our eyes!
      —Salsette Boat-Song.

THERE is hope for a man who gets publicly and riotously drunk more often than he ought to do; but there is no hope for the man who drinks secretly and alone in his own house—the man who is never seen to drink.

This is a rule; so there must be an exception to prove it. Moriarty's case was that exception.

He was a Civil Engineer, and the Government, very kindly, put him quite by himself in an out-district, with nobody but natives to talk to and a great deal of work to do. He did his work well in the four years he was utterly alone; but he picked up the vice of secret and solitary drinking, and came up out of the wilderness more old and worn and haggard than the dead-alive life had any right to make him. You know the saying that a man who has been alone in the jungle for more than a year is never quite sane all his life after. People credited Moriarty's queerness of manner and moody ways to the solitude, and said that it showed how Government spoiled the futures of its best men. Moriarty had built himself the plinth of a very good reputation in the bridge-dam-girder line. But he knew, every night of the week, that he was taking steps to undermine that reputation with L. L. L. and Christopher and little nips of liquors, and filth of that kind. He had a sound constitution and a great brain, or else he would have broken down and died like a sick camel in the district. As better men have done before him.

Government ordered him to Simla after he had come out of the desert; and he went up meaning to try for a post then vacant. That season, Mrs. Reiver—perhaps you will remember her —was in the height of her power, and many men lay under her yoke. Everything bad that could be said has already been said about Mrs. Reiver, in another tale. Moriarty was heavily-built and handsome, very quiet and nervously anxious to please his neighbors when he wasn't sunk in a brown study. He started a good deal at sudden noises or if spoken to without warning; and, when

you watched him drinking his glass of water at dinner, you could see the hand shake a little. But all this was put down to nervousness, and the quiet, steady, sip-sip-sip, fill and sip-sip-sip again that went on in his own room when he was by himself, was never known. Which was miraculous, seeing how everything in a man's private life is public property in India.

Moriarty was drawn, not into Mrs. Reiver's set, because they were not his sort, but into the power of Mrs. Reiver, and he fell down in front of her and made a goddess of her. This was due to his coming fresh out of the jungle to a big town. He could not scale things properly or see who was what.

Because Mrs. Reiver was cold and hard, he said she was stately and dignified. Because she had no brains, and could not talk cleverly, he said she was reserved and shy. Mrs. Reiver shy! Because she was unworthy of honor or reverence from any one, he reverenced her from a distance and dowered her with all the virtues in the Bible and most of those in Shakespeare.

This big, dark, abstracted man who was so nervous when a pony cantered behind him, used to moon in the train of Mrs. Reiver, blushing with pleasure when she threw a word or two his way. His admiration was strictly platonic; even other women saw and admitted this. He did not move out in Simla, so he heard nothing against his idol: which was satisfactory. Mrs. Reiver took no special notice of him, beyond seeing that he was added to her list of admirers, and going for a walk with him now and then, just to show that he was her property, claimable as such. Moriarty must have done most of the talking, for Mrs. Reiver couldn't talk much to a man of his stamp; and the little she said could not have been profitable. What Moriarty believed in, as he had good reason to, was Mrs. Reiver's influence over him, and, in that belief, set himself seriously to try to do away with the vice that only he himself knew of.

His experiences while he was fighting with it must have been peculiar, but he never described them. Sometimes he would hold off from everything except water for a week. Then, on a rainy night, when no one had asked him out to dinner, and there was a big fire in his room, and everything comfortable, he would sit down and make a big night of it by adding little nip to little nip, planning big schemes of reformation meanwhile, until he threw himself on his bed hopelessly drunk. He suffered next morning.

One night the big crash came. He was troubled in his own mind over his attempts to make himself "worthy of the friendship" of Mrs. Reiver. The past ten days had been very bad ones, and the end of it all was that he received the arrears of two and three quarter years of sipping in one attack of *delirium tremens* of the subdued kind; beginning with suicidal depression, going on to fits and starts and hysteria, and ending with downright raving. As he sat in a chair in front of the fire, or walked up and down the room picking a handkerchief to pieces, you heard what poor Moriarty really thought of Mrs. Reiver, for he raved about her and his own fall for the most part; though he raveled some P. W. D. accounts into the same skein of thought. He talked and

talked, and talked in a low dry whisper to himself, and there was no stopping him. He seemed to know that there was something wrong, and twice tried to pull himself together and confer rationally with the Doctor; but his mind ran out of control at once, and he fell back to a whisper and the story of his troubles. It is terrible to hear a big man babbling like a child of all that a man usually locks up, and puts away in the deep of his heart. Moriarty read out his very soul for the benefit of any one who was in the room between ten-thirty that night and two-forty-five next morning.

From what he said, one gathered how immense an influence Mrs. Reiver held over him, and how thoroughly he felt for his own lapse. His whisperings cannot, of course, be put down here; but they were very instructive—as showing the errors of his estimates.

*   *   *   *   *   *

When the trouble was over, and his few acquaintances were pitying him for the bad attack of jungle-fever that had so pulled him down, Moriarty swore a big oath to himself and went abroad again with Mrs. Reiver till the end of the season, adoring her in a quiet and deferential way as an angel from heaven. Later on, he took to riding—not hacking, but honest riding—which was good proof that he was improving and you could slam doors behind him without his jumping to his feet with a gasp. That, again, was hopeful.

How he kept his oath, and what it cost him in the beginning nobody knows. He certainly managed to compass the hardest thing that a man who has drunk heavily can do. He took his peg and wine at dinner; but he never drank alone, and never let what he drank have the least hold on him.

Once he told a bosom-friend the story of his great trouble, and how the "influence of a pure honest woman, and an angel as well" had saved him. When the man—startled at anything good being laid to Mrs. Reiver's door—laughed, it cost him Moriarty's friendship. Moriarty, who is married now to a woman ten thousand times better than Mrs. Reiver—a woman who believes that there is no man on earth as good and clever as her husband—will go down to his grave vowing and protesting that Mrs. Reiver saved him from ruin in both worlds.

That she knew anything of Moriarty's weakness nobody believed for a moment. That she would have cut him dead, thrown him over, and acquainted all her friends with her discovery, if she had known of it, nobody who knew her doubted for an instant.

Moriarty thought her something she never was, and in that belief saved himself. Which was just as good as though she had been everything that he had imagined.

But the question is, What claim will Mrs. Reiver have to the credit of Moriarty's salvation, when her day of reckoning comes?

A Bank Fraud

He drank strong waters and his speech
   was coarse;
He purchased raiment and forbore to
   pay;
He stuck a trusting junior with a horse,
   And won Gymkhanas in a doubtful
   way.
Then, 'twixt a vice and folly, turned
   aside
To do good deeds and straight to cloak
   them, lied.
           —*The Mess Room.*

IF Reggie Burke were in India now, he would resent this tale being told; but as he is in Hongkong and won't see it, the telling is safe. He was the man who worked the big fraud on the Sind and Sialkote Bank. He was manager of an up-country Branch, and a sound practical man with a large experience of native loan and insurance work. He could combine the frivolities of ordinary life with his work, and yet do well. Reggie Burke rode anything that would let him get up, danced as neatly as he rode, and was wanted for every sort of amusement in the Station.

As he said himself, and as many men found out rather to their surprise, there were two Burkes, both very much at your service. "Reggie Burke," between four and ten, ready for anything from a hot-weather gymkhana to a riding-picnic, and, between ten and four, "Mr. Reginald Burke, Manager of the Sind and Sialkote Branch Bank." You might play polo with him one afternoon and hear him express his opinions when a man crossed; and you might call on him next morning to raise a two-thousand rupee loan on a five hundred pound insurance policy, eighty pounds paid in premiums. He would recognize you, but you would have some trouble in recognizing him.

The Directors of the Bank—it had its headquarters in Calcutta and its General Manager's word carried weight with the Government—picked their men well. They had tested Reggie up to a fairly severe breaking-strain. They trusted him just as much as Directors ever trust Managers. You must see for yourself whether their trust was misplaced.

Reggie's Branch was in a big Station, and worked with the usual staff—one Manager, one Accountant, both English, a Cashier, and a horde of native clerks; besides the Police patrol at nights outside. The bulk of its work, for it was in a thriving district, was *hoondi* and accommodation of all kinds. A fool has no grip of this sort of business; and a clever man who does not go about among his clients, and know more than a little of their affairs, is worse than a fool. Reggie was young-looking, clean-shaved, with a twinkle in his eye, and a head that nothing short of a gallon of the Gunners' Madeira could make any impression on.

One day, at a big dinner, he announced casually that the Directors had shifted on to him a Natural Curiosity, from England, in the Accountant line. He was perfectly correct. Mr. Silas Riley, Accountant, was a most curious animal—a long, gawky, rawboned Yorkshireman, full of the savage self-conceit that blossoms only in the best county in England. Arrogance was a mild word for the mental attitude of Mr. S. Riley. He had worked himself up, after seven

years, to a Cashier's position in a Huddersfield Bank; and all his experience lay among the factories of the North. Perhaps he would have done better on the Bombay side, where they are happy with one-half per cent. profits, and money is cheap. He was useless for Upper India and a wheat Province, where a man wants a large head and a touch of imagination if he is to turn out a satisfactory balance-sheet.

He was wonderfully narrow-minded in business, and, being new to the country, had no notion that Indian banking is totally distinct from Home work. Like most clever self-made men, he had much simplicity in his nature; and, somehow or other, had construed the ordinarily polite terms of his letter of engagement into a belief that the Directors had chosen him on account of his special and brilliant talents, and that they set great store by him. This notion grew and crystallized; thus adding to his natural North-country conceit. Further, he was delicate, suffered from some trouble in his chest, and was short in his temper.

You will admit that Reggie had reason to call his new Accountant a Natural Curiosity. The two men failed to hit it off at all. Riley considered Reggie a wild, feather-headed idiot, given to Heaven only knew what dissipation in low places called "Messes," and totally unfit for the serious and solemn vocation of banking. He could never get over Reggie's look of youth and "you-be-damned" air; and he couldn't understand Reggie's friends—clean-built, careless men in the Army—who rode over to big Sunday breakfasts at the Bank, and told sultry stories till Riley got up and left the room. Riley was always showing Reggie how the business ought to be conducted, and Reggie had more than once to remind him that seven years' limited experience between Huddersfield and Beverly did not qualify a man to steer a big up-country business. Then Riley sulked, and referred to himself as a pillar of the Bank and a cherished friend of the Directors, and Reggie tore his hair. If a man's English subordinates fail him in India, he comes to a hard time indeed, for native help has strict limitations. In the winter Riley went sick for weeks at a time with his lung complaint, and this threw more work on Reggie. But he preferred it to the everlasting friction when Riley was well.

One of the Traveling Inspectors of the Bank discovered these collapses and reported them to the Directors. Now Riley had been foisted on the Bank by an M.P., who wanted the support of Riley's father who, again, was anxious to get his son out to a warmer climate because of those lungs. The M.P., had interest in the Bank; but one of the Directors wanted to advance a nominee of his own; and, after Riley's father had died, he made the rest of the Board see that an Accountant who was sick for half the year, had better give place to a healthy man. If Riley had known the real story of his appointment, he might have behaved better; but, knowing nothing, his stretches of sickness alternated with restless, persistent, meddling irritation of Reggie, and all the hundred ways in which conceit in a subordinate situation can find play. Reggie used to call him striking and

hair-curling names behind his back as a relief to his own feelings; but he never abused him to his face, because he said, "Riley is such a frail beast that half of his loathsome conceit is due to pains in the chest."

Late one April, Riley went very sick indeed. The Doctor punched him and thumped him, and told him he would be better before long. Then the Doctor went to Reggie and said—"Do you know how sick your Accountant is?"— "No!" said Reggie—"The worse the better, confound him! He's a clacking nuisance when he's well. I'll let you take away the Bank Safe if you can drug him silent for this hot weather."

But the Doctor did not laugh—"Man, I'm not joking," he said. "I'll give him another three months in his bed and a week or so more to die in. On my honor and reputation that's all the grace he has in this world. Consumption has hold of him to the marrow."

Reggie's face changed at once into the face of "Mr. Reginald Burke," and he answered, "What can I do?"— "Nothing," said the Doctor. "For all practical purposes the man is dead already. Keep him quiet and cheerful, and tell him he's going to recover. That's all. I'll look after him to the end, of course."

The Doctor went away, and Reggie sat down to open the evening mail. His first letter was one from the Directors, intimating for his information that Mr. Riley was to resign, under a month's notice, by the terms of his agreement, telling Reggie that their letter to Riley would follow, and advising Reggie of the coming of a new Accountant, a man whom Reggie knew and liked.

Reggie lit a cheroot, and, before he had finished smoking, he had sketched the outline of a fraud. He put away—burked—the Directors' letter, and went in to talk to Riley, who was as ungracious as usual, and fretting himself over the way the Bank would run during his illness. He never thought of the extra work on Reggie's shoulders, but solely of the damage to his own prospects of advancement. Then Reggie assured him that everything would be well, and that he, Reggie, would confer with Riley daily on the management of the Bank. Riley was a little soothed, but he hinted in as many words that he did not think much of Reggie's business capacity. Reggie was humble. And he had letters in his desk from the Directors that a Gilbarte or a Hardie might have been proud of!

The days passed in the big darkened house, and the Directors' letter of dismissal to Riley came and was put away by Reggie, who, every evening, brought the books to Riley's room, and showed him what had been going forward, while Riley snarled. Reggie did his best to make statements pleasing to Riley, but the Accountant was sure that the Bank was going to rack and ruin without him. In June, as the lying in bed told on his spirit, he asked whether his absence had been noted by the Directors, and Reggie said that they had written most sympathetic letters, hoping that he would be able to resume his valuable service before long. He showed Riley the letters; and Riley said that the Directors ought to have written to him direct. A few days later, Reggie opened Riley's mail in the half-light of the room, and gave him the sheet—not the envelope—of a

letter to Riley from the Directors. Riley said he would thank Reggie not to interfere with his private papers, specially as Reggie knew he was too weak to open his own letters. Reggie apologized.

Then Riley's mood changed, and he lectured Reggie on his evil ways: his horses and his bad friends. "Of course lying here, on my back, Mr. Burke, I can't keep you straight; but when I'm well, I do hope you'll pay some heed to my words." Reggie, who had dropped polo, and dinners, and tennis and all, to attend to Riley, said that he was penitent and settled Riley's head on the pillow and heard him fret and contradict in hard, dry, hacking whispers, without a sign of impatience. This, at the end of a heavy day's office work, doing double duty, in the latter half of June.

When the new Accountant came, Reggie told him the facts of the case, and announced to Riley that he had a guest staying with him. Riley said that he might have had more consideration than to entertain his "doubtful friends" at such a time. Reggie made Carron, the new Accountant, sleep at the Club in consequence. Carron's arrival took some of the heavy work off his shoulders, and he had time to attend to Riley's exactions—to explain, soothe, invent, and settle and resettle the poor wretch in bed, and to forge complimentary letters from Calcutta. At the end of the first month Riley wished to send some money home to his mother. Reggie sent the draft. At the end of the second month Riley's salary came in just the same. Reggie paid it out of his own pocket, and, with it, wrote

Riley a beautiful letter from the Directors.

Riley was very ill indeed, but the flame of his life burned unsteadily. Now and then he would be cheerful and confident about the future, sketching plans for going Home and seeing his mother. Reggie listened patiently when the office-work was over, and encouraged him.

At other times Riley insisted on Reggie reading the Bible and grim "Methody" tracts to him. Out of these tracts he pointed morals directed at his Manager. But he always found time to worry Reggie about the working of the Bank, and to show him where the weak points lay.

This indoor, sickroom life and constant strains wore Reggie down a good deal, and shook his nerves, and lowered his billiard play by forty points. But the business of the Bank, and the business of the sickroom, had to go on, though the glass was 116° in the shade.

At the end of the third month Riley was sinking fast, and had begun to realize that he was very sick. But the conceit that made him worry Reggie kept him from believing the worst. "He wants some sort of mental stimulant if he is to drag on," said the Doctor. "Keep him interested in life if you care about his living." So Riley, contrary to all the laws of business and the finance, received a 25-per-cent. rise of salary from the Directors. The "mental stimulant" succeeded beautifully. Riley was happy and cheerful, and, as is often the case in consumption, healthiest in mind when the body was weakest. He lingered for a full month, snarling and fretting about the Bank, talking of the future, hearing the Bible read, lecturing Reggie on sin, and wondering when he would be able to move abroad.

But at the end of September, one mercilessly hot evening, he rose up in his bed with a little gasp, and said quickly to Reggie—"Mr. Burke, I am going to die. I know it in myself. My chest is all hollow inside, and there's nothing to breathe with. To the best of my knowledge I have done nowt,"— he was returning to the talk of his boyhood—"to lie heavy on my conscience. God be thanked, I have been preserved from the grosser forms of sin; and I counsel *you,* Mr. Burke . . ."

Here his voice died down, and Reggie stooped over him.

"Send my salary for September to my Mother . . . done great things with the Bank if I had been spared . . . mistaken policy . . . no fault of mine. . . ."

Then he turned his face to the wall and died.

Reggie drew the sheet over its face, and went out into the veranda, with his last "mental stimulant"—a letter of condolence and sympathy from the Directors—unused in his pocket.

"If I'd been only ten minutes earlier," thought Reggie, "I might have heartened him up to pull through another day."

Tods' Amendment

The World hath set its heavy yoke
Upon the old white-bearded folk
    Who strive to please the king.
God's mercy is upon the young,
God's wisdom in the baby tongue
    That fears not anything.
    —*The Parable of Chajju Bhagat.*

Now Tods' Mamma was a singularly charming woman, and every one in Simla knew Tods. Most men had saved him from death on occasions. He was beyond his *ayah's* control altogether, and periled his life daily to find out what would happen if you pulled a Mountain Battery mule's tail. He was an utterly fearless young Pagan, about six years old, and the only baby who ever broke the holy calm of the Supreme Legislative Council.

It happened this way: Tod's pet kid got loose, and fled up the hill, off the Boileaugunge Road, Tods after it, until it burst into the Viceregal Lodge lawn, then attached to "Peterhoff." The Council were sitting at the time, and the windows were open because it was warm. The Red Lancer in the porch told Tods to go away; but Tods knew the Red Lancer and most of the Members of Council personally. Moreover, he had firm hold of the kid's collar, and was being dragged all across the flower-beds. "Give my *salaam* to the long Councilor *Sahib*, and ask him to help me take *Moti* back!" gasped Tods. The Council heard the noise through the open windows; and, after an interval, was seen the shocking spectacle of a Legal Member and a Lieutenant-Governor helping, under the direct patron-age of a Commander-in-Chief and a Viceroy, one small and very dirty boy in a sailor's suit and a tangle of brown hair, to coerce a lively and rebellious kid. They headed it off down the path to the Mall, and Tods went home in triumph and told his Mamma that *all* the Councilor *Sahibs* had been helping him to catch *Moti*. Whereat his Mamma smacked Tods for interfering with the administration of the Empire; but Tods met the Legal Member the next day, and told him in confidence that if the Legal Member ever wanted to catch a goat, he, Tods, would give him all the help in his power. "Thank you, Tods," said the Legal Member.

Tods was the idol of some eighty *jhampanis,* and half as many *saises.* He saluted them all as "O Brother." It never entered his head that any living human being could disobey his orders; and he was the buffer between the servants and his Mamma's wrath. The working of that household turned on Tods, who was adored by every one from the *dhoby* to the dog-boy. Even Futteh Khan, the villainous loafer *khit* from Mussoorie, shirked risking Tods' displeasure for fear his co-mates should look down on him.

So Tods had honor in the land from Boileaugunge to Chota Simla, and ruled justly according to his lights. Of course, he spoke Urdu, but he had also mastered many queer side-speeches like the *chotee bolee* of the women, and held grave converse with shopkeepers and Hill-coolies alike. He was precocious for his age, and his mixing with natives

335

had taught him some of the more bitter truths of life: the meanness and the sordidness of it. He used, over his bread and milk, to deliver solemn and serious aphorisms, translated from the vernacular into the English, that made his Mamma jump and vow that Tods *must* go Home next hot weather.

Just when Tods was in the bloom of his power, the Supreme Legislature were hacking out a Bill for the Sub-Montane Tracts, a revision of the then Act, smaller than the Punjab Land Bill but affecting a few hundred thousand people none the less. The Legal Member had built and bolstered, and embroidered, and amended that Bill, till it looked beautiful on paper. Then the Council began to settle what they called the "minor details." As if any Englishman legislating for natives knows enough to know which are the minor and which are the major points, from the native point of view, of any measure! That Bill was a triumph of "safeguarding the interests of the tenant." One clause provided that land should not be leased on longer terms than five years at a stretch; because, if the landlord had a tenant bound down for, say, twenty years, he would squeeze the very life out of him. The notion was to keep up a stream of independent cultivators in the Sub-Montane Tracts; and ethnologically and politically the notion was correct. The only drawback was that it was altogether wrong. A native's life in India implies the life of his son. Wherefore, you cannot legislate for one generation at a time. You must consider the next from the native point of view. Curiously enough, the native now and then, and in Northern India more

particularly, hates being over-protected against himself. There was a Naga village once, where they lived on dead *and* buried Commissariat mules. . . . But that is another story.

For many reasons, to be explained later, the people concerned objected to the Bill. The Native member in Council knew as much about Punjabis as he knew about Charing Cross. He had said in Calcutta that "the Bill was entirely in accord with the desires of that large and important class, the cultivators;" and so on, and so on. The Legal Member's knowledge of natives was limited to English-speaking Durbaris, and his own red *chaprassis*, the Sub-Montane Tracts concerned no one in particular, the Deputy Commissioners were a good deal too driven to make representations, and the measure was one which dealt with small landholders only. Nevertheless, the Legal Member prayed that it might be correct, for he was a nervously conscientious man. He did not know that no man can tell what natives think unless he mixes with them with the varnish off. And not always then. But he did the best he knew. And the measure came up to the Supreme Council for the final touches, while Tods patroled the Burra Simla Bazar in his morning rides, and played with the monkey belonging to Ditta Mull, the *bunnia,* and listened, as a child listens, to all the stray talk about this new freak of the *Lord Sahib's.*

One day there was a dinner-party, at the house of Tods' Mamma, and the Legal Member came. Tods was in bed, but he kept awake till he heard the bursts of laughter from the men over the coffee. Then he paddled out in his little red flannel dressing-gown and his night-suit and took refuge by the side of his father, knowing that he would not be sent back. "See the miseries of having a family!" said Tods' father, giving Tods three prunes, some water in a glass that had been used for claret, and telling him to sit still. Tods sucked the prunes slowly, knowing that he would have to go when they were finished, and sipped the pink water like a man of the world, as he listened to the conversation. Presently, the Legal Member, talking "shop" to the Head of a Department, mentioned his Bill by its full name—"The Sub-Montane Tracts *Ryotwary* Revised Enactment." Tods caught the one native word and lifting up his small voice said—

"Oh, I know *all* about that! Has it been *murramutted* yet, Councilor *Sahib?*"

"How much?" said the Legal Member.

"*Murramutted* — mended. — Put *theek*, you know—made nice to please Ditta Mull!"

The Legal Member left his place and moved up next to Tods.

"What do you know about *ryotwari*, little man?" he said.

"I'm not a little man, I'm Tods, and I know *all* about it. Ditta Mull, and Choga Lall, and Amir Nath, and—oh, *lakhs* of my friends tell me about it in the bazars when I talk to them."

"Oh, they do—do they? What do they say, Tods?"

Tods tucked his feet under his red flannel dressing-gown and said—"I must *fink*."

The Legal Member waited patiently. Then Tods with infinite compassion—

"You don't speak my talk, do you, Councilor *Sahib?*"

"No; I am sorry to say I do not," said the Legal Member.

"Very well," said Tods, "I must *fink* in English."

He spent a minute putting his ideas in order, and began very slowly, translating in his mind from the vernacular to English, as many Anglo-Indian children do. You must remember that the Legal Member helped him on by questions when he halted, for Tods was not equal to the sustained flight of oratory that follows.

"Ditta Mull says, 'This thing is the talk of a child, and was made up by fools.' But *I* don't think you are a fool, Councilor *Sahib*," said Tods, hastily. "You caught my goat. This is what Ditta Mull says—'I am not a fool, and why should the Sirkar say I am a child? I can see if the land is good and if the landlord is good. If I am a fool, the sin is upon my own head. For five years I take my ground for which I have saved money, and a wife I take too, and a little son is born.' Ditta Mull has one daughter now, but he *says* he will have a son, soon. And he says, 'At the end of five years, by this new *bundobust*, I must go. If I do not go, I must get fresh seals and *takkus*-stamps on the papers, perhaps in the middle of the harvest, and to go to the law-courts once is wisdom, but to go twice is *Jehannum*.' That is *quite* true," explained Tods, gravely. "All my friends say so. And Ditta Mull says, 'Always fresh *takkus* and paying money to *vakils* and *chaprassis* and law-courts every five years, or else the landlord makes me go. Why do I want to go?

Am I a fool? If I am a fool and do not know, after forty years, good land when I see it, let me die! But if the new *bundobust* says for *fifteen* years, that it is good and wise. My little son is a man, and I am burned, and he takes the ground or another ground, paying only once for the *takkus*-stamps on the papers, and his little son is born, and at the end of fifteen years is a man too. But what profit is there in five years and fresh papers? Nothing but *dikh,* trouble, *dikh.* We are not young men who take these lands, but old ones—not farmers, but tradesmen with a little money—and for fifteen years we shall have peace. Nor are we children that the Sirkar should treat us so.' "

Here Tods stopped short, for the whole table were listening. The Legal Member said to Tods, "Is that all?"

"All I can remember," said Tods. "But you should see Ditta Mull's big monkey. It's just like a Councilor *Sahib.*"

"Tods! Go to bed," said his father.

Tods gathered up his dressing-gown tail and departed.

The Legal Member brought his hand down on the table with a crash—"By Jove!" said the Legal Member, "I believe the boy is right. The short tenure *is* the weak point."

He left early, thinking over what Tods had said. Now, it was obviously impossible for the Legal Member to play with a *bunnia's* monkey, by way of getting understanding; but he did better. He made inquiries, always bearing in mind the fact that the real native—not the hybrid, University-trained mule—is as timid as a colt, and, little by little, he coaxed some of the men whom the measure concerned most intimately to give in their views, which squared very closely with Tods' evidence.

So the Bill was amended in that clause; and the Legal Member was filled with an uneasy suspicion that Native Members represent very little except the Orders they carry on their bosoms. But he put the thought from him as illiberal. He was a most Liberal man.

After a time, the news spread through the bazars that Tods had got the B..l recast in the tenure-clause, and if Tod's Mamma had not interfered, Tods would have made himself sick on the baskets of fruits and pistachio nuts and Cabuli grapes and almonds that crowded the veranda. Till he went Home, Tods ranked some few degrees before the Viceroy in popular estimation. But for the little life of him Tods could not understand why.

In the Legal Member's private-paper-box still lies the rough draft of the Sub-Montane Tracts *Ryotwary* Revised Enactment; and, opposite the twenty-second clause, penciled in blue chalk, and signed by the Legal Member, are the words *"Tods' Amendment."*

In the Pride of His Youth

"Stopped in the straight when the race
    was his own!
Look at him cutting it—cur to the
    bone!"
"Ask, ere the youngster be rated and
    chidden,
What did he carry and how was he
    ridden?
Maybe they used him too much at the
    start;
Maybe Fate's weight-cloths are breaking
    his heart."
            —*Life's Handicap.*

WHEN I was telling you of the joke that The Worm played off on the Senior Subaltern, I promised a somewhat similar tale, but with all the jest left out. This is that tale.

Dicky Hatt was kidnapped in his early, early youth—neither by landlady's daughter, housemaid, barmaid, nor cook, but by a girl so nearly of his own caste that only a woman could have said she was just the least little bit in the world below it. This happened a month before he came out to India, and five days after his one-and-twentieth birthday. The girl was nineteen—six years older than Dicky in the things of this world, that is to say—and, for the time, twice as foolish as he.

Excepting, always, falling off a horse there is nothing more fatally easy than marriage before the Registrar. The ceremony costs less than fifty shillings, and is remarkably like walking into a pawn-shop. After the declaration of residence have been put in, four minutes will cover the rest of the proceedings— fees, attestation, and all. Then the Registrar slides the blotting-pad over the names, and says grimly with his pen between his teeth, "Now you're man and wife"; and the couple walk out into the street feeling as if something were horribly illegal somewhere.

But that ceremony holds and can drag a man to his undoing just as thoroughly as the "long as ye both shall live" curse from the altar-rails, with the bridesmaids giggling behind, and "The Voice that breathed o'er Eden" lifting the roof off. In this manner was Dicky Hatt kidnapped, and he considered it vastly fine, for he had received an appointment in India which carried a magnificent salary from the Home point of view. The marriage was to be kept secret for a year. Then Mrs. Dicky Hatt was to come out, and the rest of life was to be a glorious golden mist. That was how they sketched it under the Addison Road Station lamps; and, after one short month, came Gravesend and Dicky steaming out to his new life, and the girl crying in a thirty-shillings a week bed-and-living-room, in a back street off Montpelier Square near the Knightsbridge Barracks.

But the country that Dicky came to was a hard land where men of twenty-one were reckoned very small boys indeed, and life was expensive. The salary that loomed so large six thousand miles away did not go far. Particularly when Dicky divided it by two, and remitted more than the fair half, at 1-6 7/8, to Montpelier Square. One hundred and thirty-five rupees out of three hundred and thirty is not much to live on; but it was absurd to suppose that Mrs. Hatt could exist forever on the £20 held back by Dicky from his outfit allowance. Dicky saw this and remitted at once; always remembering that Rs. 700 were to be paid, twelve months later, for a first-class passage out for a lady. When you add to these trifling details the natural instincts of a boy beginning a new life in a new country and longing to go about and enjoy himself, and the necessity for grappling with strange work—which, properly speaking, should take up a boy's undivided attention—you will see that Dicky started handicapped. He saw it himself for a breath or two; but he did not guess the full beauty of his future.

As the hot weather began, the shackles settled on him and ate into his flesh. First would come letters—big, crossed, seven-shee letters—from his wife, telling him how she longed to see him, and what a Heaven upon earth would be their property when they met. Then some boy of the chummery wherein Dicky lodged would pound on the door of his bare little room, and tell him to come out to look at a pony—the very thing to suit him. Dicky could not afford ponies. He had to explain this. Dicky could not afford living in the chummery, modest as it was. He had to explain this before he moved to a single room next the office where he worked all day. He kept the house on a green oilcloth tablecover, one chair, one bedstead, one photograph, one tooth-glass very strong and thick, a seven-rupee eight-anna filter, and messing by contract at thirty-seven rupees a month. Which last item was extortion. He had no punkah, for a punkah costs fifteen rupees a month; but he slept on the roof of the office with all his wife's letters under his pillow. Now and again he was asked out to dinner, where he got both a punkah and an iced drink. But this was seldom, for people objected to recognizing a boy who had evidently the instincts of a Scotch tallow-chandler, and who lived in such a nasty fashion. Dicky could not subscribe to any amusement, so he found no amusement except the pleasure of turning over his Bank-book and reading what it said about "loans on approved security." That cost nothing. He remitted through a Bombay Bank, by the way, and the Station knew nothing of his private affairs.

Every month he sent Home all he could possibly spare for his wife and for another reason which was expected to explain itself shortly, and would require more money.

About this time Dicky was overtaken with the nervous, haunting fear that besets married men when they are out of sorts. He had no pension to look to. What if he should die suddenly, and leave his wife unprovided for? The thought used to lay hold of him in the still, hot nights on the roof, till the shaking of his heart made him think that he was going to die then and there of heart-disease. Now this is a frame of mind which no boy has a right to know. It is a strong man's trouble; but coming, when it did, it nearly drove poor punkah-less, perspiring Dicky Hatt mad. He could tell no one about it.

A certain amount of "screw" is as necessary for a man as for a billiard-ball. It makes them both do wonderful things. Dicky needed money badly, and he worked for it like a horse. But, naturally, the men who owned him knew that a boy can live very comfortable on a certain income—pay in India is a matter of age not merit, you see, and, if their particular boy wished to work like two boys, Business forbid that they should stop him. But Business forbid that they should give him an increase of pay at his present ridiculously immature age. So Dicky won certain rises of salary—ample for a boy—not enough for a wife and a child—certainly too little for the seven-hundred-rupee passage that he and Mr. Hatt had discussed so lightly once upon a time. And with this he was forced to be content.

Somehow, all his money seemed to fade away in Home drafts and the crushing Exchange, and the tone of the Home letters changed and grew querulous. "Why wouldn't Dicky have his wife and the baby out? Surely he had a salary—a fine salary—and it was too bad of him to enjoy himself in India. But would he—could he—make the next draft a little more elastic?" Here followed a list of baby's kit, as long as a Parsee's bill. Then Dicky, whose heart yearned to his wife and the little son he had never seen—which, again, is a feeling no boy is entitled to—enlarged the draft and wrote queer half-boy, half-man letters, saying that life was not so enjoyable after all and would the little wife wait yet a little longer? But the little wife, however much she approved of money, objected to waiting, and there was a strange, hard sort of ring in her letters that Dicky didn't understand. How could he, poor boy?

Later on still—just as Dicky had been told—*àpropos* of another youngster who had "made a fool of himself" as the

saying is—that matrimony would not only ruin his further chances of advancement, but would lose him his present appointment—came the news that the baby, his own little, little son, had died and, behind this, forty lines of an angry woman's scrawl, saying the death might have been averted if certain things, all costing money, had been done, or if the mother and the baby had been with Dicky. The letter struck at Dicky's naked heart; but, not being officially entitled to a baby, he could show no sign of trouble.

How Dicky won through the next four months, and what hope he kept alight to force him into his work, no one dare say. He pounded on, the seven-hundred-rupee passage as far away as ever, and his style of living unchanged, except when he launched into a new filter. There was the strain of his office-work, and the strain of his remittances, and the knowledge of his boy's death, which touched the boy more, perhaps, than it would have touched a man; and, beyond all, the enduring strain of his daily life. Grey-headed seniors who approved of his thrift and his fashion of denying himself everything pleasant, reminded him of the old saw that says—

"If a youth would be distinguished in his art, art, art,
He must keep the girls away from his heart, heart, heart."

And Dicky, who fancied he had been through every trouble that a man is permitted to know, had to laugh and agree; with the last line of his balanced Bankbook jingling in his head day and night.

But he had one more sorrow to digest before the end. There arrived a letter from the little wife—the natural sequence of the others if Dicky had only known it—and the burden of that letter was "gone with a handsomer man than you." It was a rather curious production, without stops, something like this —"She was not going to wait forever and the baby was dead and Dicky was only a boy and he would never set eyes on her again and why hadn't he waved his handkerchief to her when he left Gravesend and God was her judge she was a wicked woman but Dicky was worse enjoying himself in India and this other man loved the ground she trod on and would Dicky ever forgive her for she would never forgive Dicky; and there was no address to write to."

Instead of thanking his stars that he was free, Dicky discovered exactly how an injured husband feels—again, not at all the knowledge to which a boy is entitled—for his mind went back to his wife as he remembered her in the thirty-shilling "suite" in Montpelier Square, when the dawn of his last morning in England was breaking, and she was crying in the bed. Whereat he rolled about on his bed and bit his fingers. He never stopped to think whether, if he had met Mrs. Hatt after those two years, he would have discovered that he and she had grown quite different and new persons. This, theoretically, he ought to have done. He spent the night after the English Mail came in rather severe pain.

Next morning, Dicky Hatt felt disinclined to work. He argued that he had missed the pleasure of youth. He was tired, and he had tasted all the sorrow in life before three-and-twenty. His Honor was gone—that was the man; and now he, too, would go to the Devil —that was the boy in him. So he put his head down on the green oilcloth table-cover, and wept before resigning his post, and all it offered.

But the reward of his services came. He was given three days to reconsider himself, and the Head of the establishment, after some telegraphings, said that it was a most unusual step, but, in view of the ability that Mr. Hatt had displayed at such and such a time, at such and such junctures, he was in a position to offer him an infinitely superior post—first on probation and later, in the natural course of things, on confirmation. "And how much does the post carry?" said Dicky. "Six hundred and fifty rupees," said the Head, slowly, expecting to see the young man sink with gratitude and joy.

And it came then! The seven-hundred-rupee-passage, and enough to have saved the wife, and the little son and to have allowed of assured and open marriage, came then. Dicky burst into a roar of laughter—laughter he could not check—nasty, jangling merriment that seemed as if it would go on forever. When he had recovered himself he said, quite seriously, "I'm tired of work. I'm an old man now. It's about time I retired. And I will."

"The boys' mad!" said the Head.

I think he was right; but Dicky Hatt never reappeared to settle the question.

Pig

Go, stalk the red deer o'er the heather,
  Ride, follow the fox if you can!
But, for pleasure and profit together,
  Allow me the hunting of Man,—
The chase of the Human, the search for
  the Soul
To its ruin,—the hunting of Man.
                    —*The Old Shikarri.*

I BELIEVE the difference began in the matter of a horse, with a twist in his temper, whom Pinecoffin sold to Nafferton and by whom Nafferton was nearly slain. There may have been other causes of offence; the horse was the official stalking-horse. Nafferton was very angry; but Pinecoffin laughed, and said that he had never guaranteed the beast's manners. Nafferton laughed too, though he vowed that he would write off his fall against Pinecoffin if he waited five years. Now, a Dalesman from beyond Skipton will forgive a man live; but a South Devon man is as soft as a Dartmoor bog. You can see from their names that Nafferton had the race-advantage of Pinecoffin. He was a peculiar man, and his notions of humor were cruel. He taught me a new and fascinating form of *shikar.* He hounded Pinecoffin from Mithankot to Jagadri, and from Gurgaon to Abbottabad—up and across the Punjab, a large Province, and in places remarkably dry. He said that he had no intention of allowing Assistant Commissioners to "sell him pups," in the shape of ramping, screaming country-breds, without making their lives a burden to them.

Most Assistant Commissioners de-velop a bent for some special work after their first hot weather in the country. The boys with digestions hope to write their names large on the Frontier, and struggle for dreary places like Bannu and Kohat. The bilious ones climb into Secretariat. Which is very bad for the liver. Others are bitten with a mania for District work, Ghuznivide coins or Persian poetry; while some, who come of farmers' stock, find that the smell of the Earth after the Rains gets into their blood, and calls them to "develop the resources of the Province." These men are enthusiasts. Pinecoffin belonged to their class. He knew a great many facts bearing on the cost of bullocks and temporary wells, and opium-scrapers, and what happens if you burn too much rubbish on a field in the hope of enriching used-up soil. All the Pinecoffins come of a landholding breed, and so the land only took back her own again. Unfortunately— most unfortunately for Pinecoffin—he was a Civilian, as well as a farmer. Nafferton watched him, and thought about the horse. Nafferton said, "See me chase that boy till he drops!" I said, "You can't get your knife into an Assistant Commissioner." Nafferton told me that I did not understand the adminstration of the Province.

Our Government is rather peculiar. It gushes on the agricultural and general information side, and will supply a moderately respectable man with all sorts of "economic statistics," if he speaks to it prettily. For instance, you are inter-

343

ested in gold-washing in the sands of the Sutlej. You pull the string, and find that it wakes up half a dozen Departments, and finally communicates, say, with a friend of yours in the Telegraph, who once wrote some notes on the customs of the gold-washers when he was on construction-work in their part of the Empire. He may or may not be pleased at being ordered to write out everything he knows for your benefit. This depends on his temperament. The bigger man you are, the more information and the greater trouble can you raise.

Nafferton was not a big man; but he had the reputation of being very "earnest." An "earnest" man can do much with a Government. There was an earnest man once who nearly wrecked . . . but all India knows *that* story. I am not sure what real "earnestness" is. A very fair imitation can be manufactured by neglecting to dress decently, by mooning about in a dreamy, misty sort of way, by taking office-work home, after staying in office till seven, and by receiving crowds of native gentlemen on Sundays. That is one sort of "earnestness."

Nafferton cast about for a peg whereon to hang his earnestness, and for a string that would communicate with Pinecoffin. He found both. They were Pig. Nafferton became an earnest inquirer after Pig. He informed the Government that he had a scheme whereby a large percentage of the British Army in India could be fed, at a very large saving, on Pig. Then he hinted that Pinecoffin might supply him with the "varied information necessary to the proper inception of the scheme." So

the Government wrote on the back of the letter, "instruct Mr. Pinecoffin to furnish Mr. Nafferton with any information in his power." Government is very prone to writing things on the backs of letters which, later, lead to trouble and confusion.

Nafferton had not the faintest interest in Pig, but he knew that Pinecoffin would flounce into the trap. Pinecoffin was delighted at being consulted about Pig. The Indian Pig is not exactly an important factor in agricultural life; but Nafferton explained to Pinecoffin that there was room for improvement, and corresponded direct with that young man.

You may think that there is not much to be evolved from Pig. It all depends how you set to work. Pinecoffin being a Civilian and wishing to do things thoroughly, began with an essay on the Primitive Pig, the Mythology of the Pig, and the Dravidian Pig. Nafferton filed that information—twenty-seven foolscap sheets—and wanted to know about the distribution of the Pig in the Punjab, and how it stood the Plains in the hot weather. From this point onward, remember that I am giving you only the barest outlines of the affair—the guy-ropes, as it were, of the web that Nafferton spun round Pinecoffin.

Pinecoffin made a colored Pig-population map, and collected observations on the comparative longevity of Pig (*a*) in the sub-montane tracts of the Himalayas, and (*b*) in the Rechna Doab. Nafferton filed that, and asked what sort of people looked after Pig. This started an ethnological excursus on swineherds, and drew from Pinecoffin long tables showing the proportion per thousand of the caste in the Derajat. Nafferton filed that bundle, and explained that the figures which he wanted referred to the Cis-Sutlej states, where he understood that Pigs were very fine and large, and where he proposed to start a Piggery. By this time, Government had quite forgotten their instructions to Mr. Pinecoffin. They were like the gentlemen, in Keats' poem, who turned well-oiled wheels to skin other people. But Pinecoffin was just entering into the spirit of the Pig-hunt, as Nafferton well knew he would do. He had a fair amount of work of his own to clear away; but he sat up of nights reducing Pig to five places of decimals for the honor of his Service. He was not going to appear ignorant of so easy a subject as Pig.

Then Government sent him on special duty to Kohat, to "inquire into" the big, seven-foot, iron-shod spades of that District. People had been killing each other with those peaceful tools; and Government wished to know "whether a modified form of agricultural implement could not, tentatively and as a temporary measure, be introduced among the agricultural population without needlessly or unduly exacerbating the existing religious sentiments of the peasantry."

Between those spades and Nafferton's Pig, Pinecoffin was rather heavily burdened.

Nafferton now began to take up "(a) The food-supply of the indigenous Pig, with a view to the improvement of its capacities as a flesh-former. (b) The acclimatization of the exotic Pig, maintaining its distinctive pecularities."

Pinecoffin replied exhaustively that the exotic Pig would become merged in the indigenous type; and quoted horse-breeding statistics to prove this. The side-issue was debated, at great length on Pinecoffin's side, till Nafferton owned that he had been in the wrong, and moved the previous question. When Pinecoffin had quite written himself out about flesh-formers, and fibrins, and glucose and the nitrogenous constituents of maize and lucerne, Nafferton raised the question of expense. By this time Pinecoffin, who had been transferred from Kohat, had developed a Pig theory of his own, which he stated in thirty-three folio pages—all carefully filed by Nafferton. Who asked for more.

These things took ten months, and Pinecoffin's interest in the potential Piggery seemed to die down after he had stated his own views. But Nafferton bombarded him with letters on "the Imperial aspect of the scheme, as tending to officialize the sale of pork, and thereby calculated to give offence to the Mohammedan population of Upper India." He guessed that Pinecoffin would want some broad, free-hand work after his niggling, stippling, decimal details. Pinecoffin handled the latest development of the case in masterly style, and proved that no "popular ebullition of excitement was to be apprehended." Nafferton said that there was nothing like Civilian insight in matters of this kind, and lured him up a by-path—"the possible profits to accrue to the Government from the sale of hog-bristles." There is an extensive literature of hog-bristles, and the shoe, brush, and color-man's trades recognize more varieties of bristles than you would think possible. After Pinecoffin had wondered a little at Nafferton's rage for information, he sent back a monograph, fifty-one pages, on "Products of the Pig." This led him, under Nafferton's tender handling, straight to the Cawnpore factories, the trade in hog-skin for saddles—and thence to the tanners. Pinecoffin wrote that pomegranate-seed was the best cure for hog-skin, and suggested—for the past fourteen month had wearied him —that Nafferton should "raise his pigs before he tanned them."

Nafferton went back to the second section of his fifth question. How could the exotic Pig be brought to give as much pork as it did in the West and yet "assume the essentially hirsute characteristics of its Oriental congener"? Pinecoffin felt dazed, for he had forgotten what he had written sixteen months before, and fancied that he was about to reopen the entire question. He was too far involved in the hideous tangle to retreat, and, in a weak moment, he wrote, "Consult my first letter." Which related to the Dravidian Pig. As a matter of fact, Pinecoffin had still to reach the acclimatization stage; having gone off on a side-issue on the merging of types.

Then Nafferton really unmasked his batteries! He complained to the Government, in stately language, of "the paucity of help accorded to me in my earnest attempts to start a potentially remunerative industry, and the flippancy with which my requests for information are treated by a gentleman whose pseudo-scholarly attainments should at least have taught him the primary differences between the Dravidian and the Berkshire variety of the genus *Sus*.

If I am to understand that the letter to which he refers me, contains his serious views on the acclimatization of a valuable, though possibly uncleanly, animal, I am reluctantly compelled to believe, etc., etc.

There was a new man at the head of the Department of Castigan. The wretched Pinecoffin was told that the Service was made for the Country, and not the Country for the Service, and that he had better begin to supply information about Pigs.

Pinecoffin answered insanely that he had written everything that could be written about Pig, and that some furlough was due to him.

Nafferton got a copy of that letter, and sent it, with the essay on the Dravidian Pig, to a down-country paper which printed both in full. The essay was rather high-flown; but if the Editor had seen the stacks of paper, in Pinecoffin's handwriting, on Nafferton's table, he would not have been so sarcastic about the "nebulous discursiveness and blatant self-sufficiency of the modern Competition-*wallah*, and his utter inability to grasp the practical issues of a practical question." Many friends cut out these remarks and sent them to Pinecoffin.

I have already stated that Pinecoffin came of a soft stock. This last stroke frightened and shook him. He could not understand it; but he felt that he had been, somehow, shamelessly betrayed by Nafferton. He realized that he had wrapped himself up in the Pigskin without need, and that he could not well set himself right with his Government. All his acquaintances asked after his "nebulous discursiveness" or his "blatant self-sufficiency," and this made him miserable.

He took a train and went to Nafferton, whom he had not seen since the Pig business began. He also took the cutting from the paper, and blustered feebly and called Nafferton names, and then died down to a watery, weak protest of the "I-say-it's-too-bad-you-know" order.

Nafferton was very sympathetic.

"I'm afraid I've given you a good deal of trouble, haven't I?" said he.

"Trouble!" whimpered Pinecoffin; "I don't mind the trouble so much, though that was bad enough; but what I resent is this showing up in print. It will stick to me like a burr all through my service. And I *did* do my best for your interminable swine. It's too bad of you—on my soul it is!"

"I don't know," said Nafferton. "Have you ever been stuck with a horse? It isn't the money I mind, though that is bad enough; but what I resent is the chaff that follows, especially from the boy who stuck me. But I think we'll cry quits now."

Pinecoffin found nothing to say save bad words; and Nafferton smiled ever so sweetly, and asked him to dinner.

The Rout of the White Hussars

It was not in the open fight
We threw away the sword,
But in the lonely watching
In the darkness by the ford.
The waters lapped, the night-wind blew,
Full-armed the Fear was born and grew,
And we were flying ere we knew
From panic in the night.
                    —*Beoni Bar.*

SOME people hold that an English Cavalry regiment cannot run. This is a mistake. I have seen four hundred and thirty-seven sabres flying over the face of the country in abject terror—have seen the best Regiment that ever drew bridle wiped off the Army List for the space of two hours. If you repeat this tale to the White Hussars they will, in all probability, treat you severely. They are not proud of the incident.

You may know the White Hussars by their "side," which is greater than that of all the Cavalry Regiments on the roster. If this is not a sufficient mark, you may know them by their old brandy. It has been sixty years in the Mess and is worth going far to taste. Ask for the "McGaire" old brandy, and see that you get it. If the Mess Sergeant thinks that you are uneducated, and that the genuine article will be lost on you, he will treat you accordingly. He is a good man. But, when you are at Mess, you must never talk to your hosts about forced marches or long-distance rides. The Mess are very sensitive; and, if they think that you are laughing at them, will tell you so.

As the White Hussars say, it was all the Colonel's fault. He was a new man, and he ought never to have taken the Command. He said that the Regiment was not smart enough. This to the

White Hussars, who knew that they could walk round any Horse and through any Guns, and over any Foot on the face of the earth! That insult was the firse cause of offence.

Then the Colonel cast the Drum-Horse—the Drum-Horse of the White Hussars! Perhaps you do not see what an unspeakable crime he had committed. I will try to make it clear. The soul of the Regiment lives in the Drum-Horse who carries the silver kettle-drums. He is nearly always a big pie-bald Waler. That is a point of honor; and a Regiment will spend anything you please on a piebald. He is beyond the ordinary laws of casting. His work is very light, and he only manœuvres at a footpace. Wherefore, so long as he can step out and look handsome, his well-being is assured. He knows more about the Regiment than the Adjutant, and could not make a mistake if he tried.

The Drum-Horse of the White Hussars was only eighteen years old, and perfectly equal to his duties. He had at least six years' more work in him, and carried himself with all the pomp and dignity of a Drum-Major of the Guards. The Regiment had paid Rs. 1200 for him.

But the Colonel said that he must go, and he was cast in due form and replaced by a washy, bay beast, as ugly as a mule, with a ewe-neck, rat-tail, and cow-hocks. The Drummer detested that animal, and the best of the Band-horses put back their ears and showed the whites of their eyes at the very sight of him. They knew him for an up-start and no gentleman. I fancy that the Colonel's ideas of smartness ex-tended to the Band, and that he wanted to make it take part in the regular pa-rade movements. A Cavalry Band is a sacred thing. It only turns out for Commanding Officers' parades, and the Band Master is one degree more im-portant than the Colonel. He is a High Priest and the "Keel Row" is his holy song. The "Keel Row" is the Cavalry Trot; and the man who has never heard that tune rising, high and shrill, above the rattle of the Regiment going past the saluting-base, has something yet to hear and understand.

When the Colonel cast the Drum-Horse of the White Hussars, there was nearly a mutiny.

The officers were angry, the Regiment were furious, and the Bandsmen swore—like troopers. The Drum-Horse was going to be put up to auction—public auction—to be bought, perhaps, by a Parsee and put into a cart! It was worse than exposing the inner life of the Regi-ment to the whole world, or selling the Mess Plate to a Jew—a Black Jew.

The Colonel was a mean man and a bully. He knew what the Regiment thought about his action; and, when the troopers offered to buy the Drum-Horse, he said that their offer was mu-tinous and forbidden by the Regula-tions.

But one of the Subalterns—Hogan-Yale, an Irishman—bought the Drum-Horse for Rs.160 at the sale, and the Colonel was wrouth. Yale professed repentance—he was unnaturally submis-sive—and said that, as he had only made the purchase to save the horse from possible ill-treatment and starva-tion, he would now shoot him and end the business. This appeared to soothe

the Colonel, for he wanted the Drum-Horse disposed of. He felt that he had made a mistake, and could not of course acknowledge it. Meantime, the presence of the Drum-Horse was an annoyance to him.

Yale took to himself a glass of the old brandy, three cheroots, and his friends Martyn; and they all left the Mess together. Yale and Martyn conferred for two hours in Yale's quarters; but only the bull-terrier who keeps watch over Yale's boot-trees knows what they said. A horse, hooded and sheeted to his ears, left Yale's stables and was taken, very unwillingly, into the Civil Lines. Yale's groom went with him. Two men broke into the Regimental Theatre and took several paint-pots and some large scenery-brushes. Then night fell over the Cantonments, and there was a noise as of a horse kicking his loose-box to pieces in Yale's stables. Yale had a big, old white Waler trap-horse.

The next day was a Thursday, and the men, hearing that Yale was going to shoot the Drum-Horse in the evening, determined to give the beast a regular regimental funeral—a finer one than they would have given the Colonel had he died just then. They got a bullock-cart and some sacking, and mounds and mounds of roses, and the body, under sacking, was carried out to the place where the anthrax cases were cremated; two-thirds of the Regiment following. There was no Band, but they all sang "The Place where the old Horse died" as something respectful and appropriate to the occasion. When the corpse was dumped into the grave and the men began throwing down armfuls of roses

to cover it, the Farrier-Sergeant ripped out an oath and said aloud, "Why, it ain't the Drum-Horse any more than it's me!" The Troop Sergeant-Majors asked him whether he had left his head in the Canteen. The Farrier-Sergeant said that he knew the Drum-Horse's feet as well as he knew his own; but he was silenced when he saw the regimental number burned in on the poor stiff, upturned near-fore.

Thus was the Drum-Horse of the White Hussars buried; the Farrier-Sergeant grumbling. The sacking that covered the corpse was smeared in places with black paint; and the Farrier-Sergeant drew attention to this fact. But the Troop-Sergeant-Major of E Troop kicked him severely on the shin, and told him that he was undoubtedly drunk.

On the Monday following the burial, the Colonel sought revenge on the White Hussars. Unfortunately, being at that time temporarily in Command of the Station, he ordered a Brigade field-day. He said that he wished to make the Regiment "sweat for their damned insolence," and he carried out his notion thoroughly. That Monday was one of the hardest days in the memory of the White Hussars. They were thrown against a skeleton-enemy, and pushed forward, and withdrawn, and dismounted, and "scientifically handled" in every possible fashion over dusty country, till they sweated profusely. Their only amusement came late in the day when they fell upon the battery of Horse Artillery and chased it for two miles. This was a personal question, and most of the troopers had money on the event; the Gunners saying openly that they had the legs of the White Hussars. They were wrong. A march-past concluded the campaign, and when the Regiment got back to their Lines, the men were coated with dirt from spur to chin-strap.

The White Hussars have one great and peculiar privilege. They won it at Fontenoy, I think.

Many Regiments possess special rights such as wearing collars with undress uniform, or a bow of riband between the shoulders, or red and white roses in their helmets on certain days of the year. Some rights are connected with regimental saints, and some with regimental successes. All are valued highly; but none so highly as the right of the White Hussars to have the Band playing when their horses are being watered in the Lines. Only one tune is played, and that tune never varies. I don't know its real name, but the White Hussars call it, "Take me to London again." It sounds very pretty. The Regiment would sooner be struck off the roster than forego their distinction.

After the "dismiss" was sounded, the officers rode off home to prepare for stables; and the men filed into the lines riding easy. That is to say, they opened their tight buttons, shifted their helmets, and began to joke or to swear as the humor took them; the more careful slipping off and easing girths and curbs. A good trooper values his mount exactly as much as he values himself, and believes, or should believe, that the two together are irresistible where women or men, girls or guns, are concerned.

Then the Orderly-Officer gave the order, "Water horses," and the Regiment loafed off to the squadron-troughs which were in rear of the stables and between these and the barracks. There were four huge troughs, one for each squadron, arranged *en échelon*, so that the whole Regiment could water in ten minutes if it liked. But it lingered for seventeen, as a rule, while the Band played.

The Band struck up as the squadrons filed off to the troughs, and the men slipped their feet out of the stirrups and chaffed each other. The sun was just setting in a big, hot bed of red cloud, and the road to the Civil Lines seemed to run straight into the sun's eye. There was a little dot on the road. It grew and grew till it showed as a horse, with a sort of gridiron-thing on his back. The red cloud glared through the bars of the gridiron. Some of the troopers shaded their eyes with their hands and said—"What the mischief 'as that there 'orse got on 'im?"

In another minute they heard a neigh that every soul—horse and man—in the Regiment knew, and saw, heading straight toward the Band, the dead Drum-Horse of the White Hussars!

On his withers banged and bumped the kettle-drums draped in crape, and on his back, very stiff and soldierly, sat a bareheaded skeleton.

The Band stopped playing, and, for a moment, there was a hush.

Then some one in E Troop—men said it was the Troop-Sergeant-Major —swung his horse round and yelled. No one can account exactly for what happened afterward; but it seems that, at least, one man in each troop set an example of panic, and the rest followed like sheep. The horses that had barely put their muzzles into the troughs reared and capered; but as soon as the

Band broke, which it did when the ghost of the Drum-Horse was about a furlong distant, all hooves followed suit, and the clatter of the stampede—quite different from the orderly throb and roar of a movement on parade, or the rough horse-play of watering in camp— made them only more terrified. They felt that the men on their backs were afraid of something. When horses once know that, all is over except the butchery.

Troop after troop turned from the troughs and ran—anywhere and everywhere—like spilled quicksilver. It was a most extraordinary spectacle, for men and horses were in all stages of easiness, and the carbine-buckets flopping against their sides urged the horses on. Men were shouting and cursing, and trying to pull clear of the Band which was being chased by the Drum-Horse whose rider had fallen forward and seemed to be spurring for a wager.

The Colonel had gone over to the Mess for a drink. Most of the officers were with him, and the Subaltern of the Day was preparing to go down to the lines, and receive the watering reports from the Troop-Sergeant-Majors. When "Take me to London again" stopped, after twenty bars, every one in the Mess said, "What on earth has happened?" A minute later, they heard unmilitary noises, and saw, far across the plain, the White Hussars scattered, and broken, and flying.

The Colonel was speechless with rage, for he thought that the Regiment had risen against him or was unanimously drunk. The Band, a disorganized mob, tore past, and at its heels labored the Drum-Horse—the dead and buried Drum-Horse—with the jolting, clattering skeleton. Hogan-Yale whispered softly to Martyn—"No wire will stand that treatment," and the Band, which had doubled like a hare, came back again. But the rest of the Regiment was gone, was rioting all over the Province, for the dusk had shut in and each man was howling to his neighbor that the Drum-Horse was on his flank. Troop-horses are far too tenderly treated as a rule. They can, on emergencies, do a great deal, even with seventeen stone on their backs. As the troopers found out.

How long this panic lasted I cannot say. I believe that when the moon rose the men saw they had nothing to fear, and, by twos and threes and half-troops, crept back into Cantonments very much ashamed of themselves. Meantime, the Drum-Horse, disgusted at his treatment by old friends, pulled up, wheeled round, and trotted up to the Mess veranda-steps for bread. No one liked to run; but no one cared to go forward till the Colonel made a movement and laid hold of the skeleton's foot. The Band had halted some distance away, and now came back slowly. The Colonel called it, individually and collectively, every evil name that occurred to him at the time; for he had set his hand on the bosom of the Drum-Horse and found flesh and blood. Then he beat the kettle-drums with his clenched fist, and discovered that they were but made of silvered paper and bamboo. Next, still swearing, he tried to drag the skeleton out of the saddle, but found that it had been wired into the cantle. The sight of the Colonel, with his arms round the skeleton's pelvis and his knee in the old Drum-

Horse's stomach, was striking. Not to say amusing. He worried the thing off in a minute or two, and threw it down on the ground, saying to the Band—"Here, you curs, that's what you're afraid of." The skeleton did not look pretty in the twilight. The Band-Sergeant seemed to recognize it, for he began to chuckle and choke. "Shall I take it away, sir?" said the Band-Sergeant. "Yes," said the Colonel, "take it to Hell, and ride there yourselves!"

The Band-Sergeant saluted, hoisted the skeleton across his saddle-bow, and led off to the stables. Then the Colonel began to make inquiries for the rest of the Regiment, and the language he used was wonderful. He would disband the Regiment—he would court-martial every soul in it—he would not command such a set of rabble, and so on, and so on. As the men dropped in, his language grew wilder, until at last it exceeded the utmost limits of free speech allowed even to a Colonel of Horse.

Martyn took Hogan-Yale aside and suggested compulsory retirement from the Service as a necessity when all was discovered. Martyn was the weaker man of the two. Hogan-Yale put up his eyebrows and remarked, firstly, that he was the son of a Lord, and, secondly, that he was as innocent as the babe unborn of the theatrical resurrection of the Drum-Horse.

"My instructions," said Yale, with a singularly sweet smile, "were that the Drum-Horse should be sent back as impressively as possible. I ask you, *am* I responsible if a mule-headed friend sends him back in such a manner as to

disturb the peace of mind of a regiment of Her Majesty's Cavalry?"

Martyn said, "You are a great man, and will in time become a General; but I'd give my chance of a troop to be safe out of this affair."

Providence saved Martyn and Hogan-Yale. The Second-in-Command led the Colonel away to the little curtained alcove wherein the Subalterns of the White Hussars were accustomed to play poker of nights; and there, after many oaths on the Colonel's part, they talked together in low tones. I fancy that the Second-in-Command must have represented the scare as the work of some trooper whom it would be hopeless to detect; and I know that he dwelt upon the sin and the shame of making a public laughing-stock of the scare.

"They will call us," said the Second-in-Command, who had really a fine imagination—"they will call us the 'Fly-by-Nights'; they will call us the 'Ghost Hunters'; they will nickname us from one end of the Army List to the other. All the explanation in the world won't make outsiders understand that the officers were away when the panic began. For the honor of the Regiment and for your own sake keep this thing quiet."

The Colonel was so exhausted with anger that soothing him down was not so difficult as might be imagined. He was made to see, gently and by degrees, that it was obviously impossible to court-martial the whole Regiment and equally impossible to proceed against any subaltern who, in his belief, had any concern in the hoax.

"But the beast's alive! He's never been shot at all!" shouted the Colonel. "It's flat flagrant disobedience! I've known a man broke for less—dam sight less. They're mocking me, I tell you, Mutman! They're mocking me!"

Once more, the Second-in-Command set himself to soothe the Colonel, and wrestled with him for half an hour. At the end of that time, the Regimental Sergeant-Major reported himself. The situation was rather novel to him; but he was not a man to be put out by circumstances. He saluted and said, "Regiment all come back, Sir." Then, to propitiate the Colonel—"An' none of the 'orses any the worse, Sir!"

The Colonel only snorted and answered—"You'd better tuck the men into their cots, then, and see that they don't wake up and cry in the night." The Sergeant withdrew.

His little stroke of humor pleased the Colonel, and, further, he felt slightly ashamed of the language he had been using. The Second-in-Command worried him again, and the two sat talking far into the night.

Next day but one, there was a Commanding Officer's parade, and the Colonel harangued the White Hussars vigorously. The pith of his speech was that, since the Drum-Horse in his old age had proved himself capable of cutting up the whole Regiment, he should return to his post of pride at the head of the Band, but the regiment were a set of ruffians with bad consciences.

The White Hussars shouted, and threw everything movable about them into the air, and when the parade was over, they cheered the Colonel till they couldn't speak. No cheers were put up for Lieutenant Hogan-Yale, who smiled very sweetly in the background.

Said the Second-in-Command to the Colonel, unofficially—

"These little things ensure popularity, and do not the least affect discipline."

"But I went back on my word," said the Colonel.

"Never mind," said the Second-in-Command. "The White Hussars will follow you anywhere from to-day. Regiments are just like women. They will do anything for trinketry."

A week later, Hogan-Yale received an extraordinary letter from some one who signed himself "Secretary, *Charity and Zeal,* 3709, E. C.," and asked for "the return of our skelton which we have reason to believe is in your possession."

"Who the deuce is this lunatic who trades in bones?" said Hogan-Yale.

"Beg your pardon, Sir," said the Band-Sergeant, "but the skelton is with me, an' I'll return it if you'll pay the carriage into the Civil Lines. There's a coffin with it, Sir."

Hogan-Yale smiled and handed two rupees to the Band-Sergeant, saying, "Write the date on the skull, will you?"

If you doubt this story, and know where to go, you can see the date on the skeleton. But don't mention the matter to the White Hussars.

I happened to know something about it, because I prepared the Drum-Horse for his resurrection. He did not take kindly to the skeleton at all.

The Bronckhorst Divorce-Case

In the daytime, when she moved about
   me,
In the night, when she was sleeping at
   my side,—
I was wearied, I was wearied of her
   presence,
Day by day and night by night I grew
   to hate her—
Would God that she or I had died!
              —*Confessions.*

THERE was a man called Bronckhorst—a three-cornered, middle-aged
man in the Army—grey as a badger,
and, some people said, with a touch
of country-blood in him. That, however, cannot be proved. Mrs. Bronckhorst was not exactly young, though fifteen years younger than her husband.
She was a large, pale, quiet woman,
with heavy eyelids over weak eyes, and
hair that turned red or yellow as the
lights fell on it.

Bronckhorst was not nice in in any
way. He had no respect for the pretty
public and private lies that make life
a little less nasty than it is. His manner toward his wife was coarse. There
are many things—including actual assault with the clenched fist—that a wife
will endure; but seldom a wife can bear
—as Mrs. Bronckhorst bore—with a
long course of brutal, hard chaff, making light of her weaknesses, her headaches, her small fits of gaiety, her
dresses, her queer little attempts to make
herself attractive to her husband when
she knows that she is not what she has
been, and—worst of all—the love that
she spends on her children. That particular sort of heavy-handed jest was
specially dear to Bronckhorst. I suppose that he had first slipped into it,
meaning no harm, in the honeymoon,
when folk find their ordinary stock of
endearments run short, and so go to the
other extreme to express their feelings.
A similar impulse makes a man say,
"Hutt, you old beast!" when a favorite
horse nuzzles his coat-front. Unluckily,
when the reaction of marriage sets in,
the form of speech remains, and, the
tenderness having died out, hurts the
wife more than she cares to say. But
Mrs. Bronckhorst was devoted to her
"Teddy" as she called him. Perhaps
that was why he objected to her. Perhaps—this is only a theory to account
for his infamous behavior later on—he
gave way to the queer, savage feeling
that sometimes takes by the throat a
husband twenty years married, when he
sees, across the table, the same face
of his wedded wife, and knows that, as
he has sat facing it, so must he continue
to sit until the day of its death or his
own. Most men and all women know
the spasm. It only lasts for three
breaths as a rule, must be a "throwback" to times when men and women
were rather worse then they are now,
and is too unpleasant to be discussed.

Dinner at the Bronckhorsts' was an
infliction few men cared to undergo.
Bronckhorst took a pleasure in saying
things that made his wife wince. When
their little boy came in at dessert,
Bronckhorst used to give him half a
glass of wine, and naturally enough, the
poor little mite got first riotous, next

354

miserable, and was removed screaming. Bronckhorst asked if that was the way Teddy usually behaved, and whether Mrs. Bronckhorst could not spare some of her time "to teach the little beggar decency." Mrs. Bronckhorst, who loved the boy more than her own life, tried not to cry—her spirit seemed to have been broken by her marriage. Lastly, Bronckhorst used to say, "There! That'll do, that'll do. For God's sake try to behave like a rational woman. Go into the drawing-room." Mrs. Bronckhorst would go, trying to carry it all off with a smile; and the guest of the evening would feel angry and uncomfortable.

After three years of this cheerful life —for Mrs. Bronckhorst had no women-friends to talk to—the Station was startled by the news that Bronckhorst had instituted proceedings *on the criminal count,* against a man called Biel, who certainly had been rather attentive to Mrs. Bronckhorst whenever she had appeared in public. The utter want of reserve with which Bronckhorst treated his own dishonor helped us to know that the evidence against Biel would be entirely circumstantial and native. There were no letters; but Bronckhorst said openly that he would rack Heaven and Earth until he saw Biel superintending the manufacture of carpets in the Central Jail. Mrs. Bronckorst kept entirely to her house, and let charitable folks say what they pleased. Opinions were divided. Some two-thirds of the Station jumped at once to the conclusion that Biel was guilty; but a dozen men who knew and liked him held by him. Biel was furious and surprised. He denied the whole thing, and vowed that he would thrash Bronckhorst within an inch of his life. No jury, we knew, would convict a man on the criminal count on native evidence in a land where you can buy a murder-charge, including the corpse, all complete for fifty-four rupees; but Biel did not care to scrape through by the benefit of a doubt. He wanted the whole thing cleared; but, as he said one night—"He can prove anything with servants' evidence, and I've only my bare word." This was almost a month before the case came on; and beyond agreeing with Biel, we could do little. All that we could be sure of was that the native evidence would be bad enough to blast Biel's character for the rest of his service; for when a native begins perjury he perjures himself thoroughly. He does not boggle over details.

Some genius at the end of the table whereat the affair was being talked over, said, "Look here! I don't believe lawyers are any good. Get a man to wire to Strickland, and beg him to come down and pull us through."

Strickland was about a hundred and eighty miles up the line. He had not long been married to Miss Youghal, but he scented in the telegram a chance of return to the old detective work that his soul lusted after, and next night he came in and heard our story. He finished his pipe and said oracularly, "We must get at the evidence. *Oorya* bearer, Mussulman *khit* and sweeper *ayah,* I suppose, are the pillars of the charge. I am on in this piece; but I'm afraid I'm getting rusty in my talk."

He rose and went into Biel's bedroom, where his trunk had been put, and shut the door. An hour later, we heard him say, "I hadn't the heart to part with my old make-ups when I married. Will this do?" There was a lothely *faquir* salaaming in the doorway.

"Now lend me fifty rupees," said Strickland, "and give me your Words of Honor that you won't tell my wife."

He got all that he asked for, and left the house while the table drank his health. What he did only he himself knows. A *faquir* hung about Bronckhorst's compound for twelve days. Then a sweeper appeared, and when Biel heard of *him*, he said that Strickland was an angel full-fledged. Whether the sweeper made love to Janki, Mrs. Bronckhorst's ayah, is a question which concerns Strickland exclusively.

He came back at the end of three weeks, and said, quietly, "You spoke the truth, Biel. The whole business is put up from beginning to end. 'Jove! It almost astonishes *me!* That Bronckhorst-beast isn't fit to live."

There was uproar and shouting, and Biel said, "How are you going to prove it? You can't say that you've been trespassing on Bronckhorst's compound in disguise!"

"No," said Strickland. "Tell your lawyer-fool, whoever he is, to get up something strong about 'inherent improbabilities' and 'discrepancies of evidence.' He won't have to speak, but it will make him happy. *I'm* going to run this business."

Biel held his tongue, and the other men waited to see what would happen. They trusted Strickland as men trust quiet men. When the case came off the Court was crowded. Strickland hung about in the veranda of the Court, till he met the Mohammedan *khitmat-*

gar. Then he murmured a *faquir's* blessing in his ear, and asked him how his second wife did. The man spun round, and, as he looked into the eyes of "Estreeken *Sahib*," his jaw dropped. You must remember that before Strickland was married, he was, as I have told you already, a power among natives. Strickland whispered a rather coarse vernacular proverb to the effect that he was abreast of all that was going on and went into the Court armed with a gut trainer's-whip.

The Mohammedan was the first witness and Strickland beamed upon him from the back of the Court. The man moistened his lips with his tongue and, in his abject fear of "Estreeken *Sahib*" the *faquir*, went back on every detail of his evidence—said he was a poor man and God was his witness that he had forgotten everything that Bronckhorst *Sahib* had told him to say. Between his terror of Strickland, the Judge, and Bronckhorst he collapsed weeping.

Then began the panic among the witnesses. Janki, the *ayah*, leering chastely behind her veil, turned grey, and the bearer left the Court. He said that his Mamma was dying and that it was not wholesome for any man to lie unthriftily in the presence of "Estreeken *Sahib*."

Biel said politely to Bronckhorst, "Your witnesses don't seem to work. Haven't you any forged letters to produce?" But Bronckhorst was swaying to and fro in his chair, and there was a dead pause after Biel had been called to order.

Bronckhorst's Counsel saw the look on his client's face, and without more ado, pitched his papers on the little green baize table, and mumbled something about having been misinformed. The whole court applauded wildly, like soldiers at a theatre, and the Judge began to say what he thought.

* * * * * *

Biel came out of the court, and Strickland dropped a gut trainer's-whip in the veranda. Ten minutes later, Biel was cutting Bronckhorst into ribbons behind the old Court cells, quietly and without scandal. What was left of Bronckhorst was sent home in a carriage; and his wife wept over it and nursed it into a man again.

Later on, after Biel had managed to hush up the counter-charge against Bronckhorst of fabricating false evidence, Mrs. Bronckhorst, with her faint, watery smile, said that there had been a mistake, but it wasn't her Teddy's fault altogether. She would wait till her Teddy came back to her. Perhaps he had grown tired of her, or she had tried his patience, and perhaps we wouldn't cut her any more, and perhaps the mothers would let their children play with "little Teddy" again. He was so lonely. Then the Station invited Mrs. Bronckhorst everywhere, until Bronckhorst was fit to appear in public, when he went Home and took his wife with him. According to latest advices, her Teddy did come back to her, and they are moderately happy. Though, of course, he can never forgive her the thrashing that she was the indirect means of getting for him.

* * * * * *

What Biel wants to know is, "Why didn't I press home the charge against the Bronckhorst-brute, and have him run in?"

What Mrs. Strickland wants to know is, "How *did* my husband bring such a lovely, lovely Waler from your Station? I know *all* his money-affairs; and I'm *certain* he didn't *buy* it."

What I want to know is, "How do women like Mrs. Bronckhorst come to marry men like Bronckhorst?"

And my conundrum is the most. unanswerable of the three.

Venus Annodomini

And the years went on, as the years must do ;
But our great Diana was always new—
Fresh, and blooming, and blonde, and fair,
With azure eyes and with aureate hair ;
And all the folk, as they came or went,
Offered her praise to her heart's content.
—*Diana of Ephesus.*

SHE had nothing to do with Number Eighteen in the Braccio Nuovo of the Vatican, between Visconti's Ceres and the God of the Nile. She was purely an Indian deity—an Anglo-Indian deity, that is to say—and we called her *the* Venus Annodomini, to distinguish her from other Annodominis of the same everlasting order. There was a legend among the Hills that she had once been young; but no living man was prepared to come forward and say boldly that the legend was true. Men rode up to

Simla, and stayed, and went away and made their name and did their life's work, and returned again to find the Venus Annodomini exactly as they had left her. She was as immutable as the Hills. But not quite so green. All that a girl of eighteen could do in the way of riding, walking, dancing, picnicking and over-exertion generally, the Venus Annodomini did, and showed no sign of fatigue or trace of weariness. Besides perpetual youth, she had discovered, men said, the secret of perpetual health; and her fame spread about the land. From a mere woman, she grew to be an Institution, insomuch that no young man could be said to be properly formed, who had not, at some time or another, worshipped at the shrine of the Venus Annodomini. There was no one like her, though there were many imitations. Six years in her eyes were no more than six months to ordinary women; and ten made less visible impression on her than does a week's fever on an ordinary woman. Every one adored her, and in return she was pleasant and courteous to nearly every one. Youth had been a habit of hers for so long, that she could not part with it—never realized, in fact, the necessity of parting with it—and took for her more chosen associates young people.

Among the worshippers of the Venus Annodomini was young Gayerson. "Very Young Gayerson" he was called to distinguish him from his father, "Young" Gayerson, a Bengal Civilian, who affected the customs—as he had the heart —of youth. "Very Young" Gayerson was not content to worship placidly and for form's sake, as the other young men did, or to accept a ride or a dance, or

a talk from the Venus Annodomini in a properly humble and thankful spirit. He was exacting, and, therefore, the Venus Annodomini repressed him. He worried himself nearly sick in a futile sort of way over her; and his devotion and earnestness made him appear either shy or boiterous or rude, as his mood might vary, by the side of the older men who, with him, bowed before the Venus Annodomini. She was sorry for him. He reminded her of a lad who, three-and-twenty years ago, had professed a boundless devotion for her, and for whom in return she had felt something more than a week's weakness. But that lad had fallen away and married another woman less than a year after he had worshipped her; and the Venus Annodomini had almost—not quite— forgotten his name. "Very Young Gayerson had the same big blue eyes and the same way of pouting his underlip when he was excited or troubled. But the Venus Annodomini checked him sternly none the less. Too much zeal was a thing that she did not approve of; preferring instead, a tempered and sober tenderness.

"Very Young" Gayerson was miserable, and took no trouble to conceal his wretchedness. He was in the Army —a Line regiment I think, but am not certain—and, since his face was a looking-glass and his forehead an open book, by reason of his innocence, his brothers-in-arms made his life a burden to him and embittered his naturally sweet disposition. No one except "Very Young" Gayerson, and he never told his views, knew how old "Very Young" Gayerson believed the Venus Annodomini to be. Perhaps he thought her five-and-twenty, or perhaps she told him that she was this age. "Very Young" Gayerson would have forded the Indus in flood to carry her lightest word, and had implicit faith in her. Every one liked him, and every one was sorry when they saw him so bound a slave of the Venus Annodomini. Every one, too, admitted that it was not her fault; for the Venus Annodomini differed from Mrs. Hauksbee and Mrs. Reiver in this particular —she never moved a finger to attract any one; but, like Ninon de L'Enclos, all men were attracted to her. One could admire and respect Mrs. Hauksbee, despise and avoid Mrs. Reiver, but one was forced to adore the Venus Annodomini.

"Very Young" Gayerson's papa held a Division or a Collectorate or something administrative in a particularly unpleasant part of Bengal—full of Babus who edited newspapers proving that "Young" Gayerson was a "Nero" and a "Scylla" and a "Charybdis"; and, in addition to the Babus, there was a good deal of dysentery and cholera abroad for nine months of the year. "Young" Gayerson—he was about five-and-forty—rather liked Babus, they amused him, but he objected to dysentery, and when he could get away, went to Darjiling for the most part. This particular season he fancied that he would come up to Simla and see his boy. The boy was not altogether pleased. He told the Venus Annodomini that his father was coming up, and she flushed a little and said that she should be delighted to make his acquaintance. Then she looked long and thoughtfully at "Very Young" Gayerson, because

she was very, very sorry for him, and he was a very, very big idiot.

"My daughter is coming out in a fortnight, Mr. Gayerson," she said.

"Your *what?*" said he.

"Daughter," said the Venus Annodomini. "She's been out for a year at Home already, and I want her to see a little of India. She is nineteen and a very sensible nice girl I believe."

"Very Young" Gayerson, who was a short twenty-two years old, nearly fell out of his chair with astonishment; for he had persisted•in believing, against all belief, in the youth of the Venus Annodomini. She, with her back to the curtained window, watched the effect of her sentences and smiled.

"Very Young" Gayerson's papa came up twelve days later, and had not been in Simla four-and-twenty hours, before two men, old acquaintances of his, had told him how "Very Young" Gayerson had been conducting himself.

"Young" Gayerson laughed a good deal, and inquired who the Venus Annodomini might be. Which proves that he had been living in Bengal where nobody knows anything except the rate of Exchange. Then he said boys will be boys, and spoke to his son about the matter. "Very Young" Gayerson said that he felt wretched and unhappy; and "Young" Gayerson said that he repented of having helped to bring a fool into the world. He suggested that his son had better cut his leave short and go down to his duties. This led to an unfilial answer, and relations were strained, until "Young" Gayerson demanded that they should call on the Venus Annodomini. "Very Young" Gayerson went with his papa, feeling, somehow, uncomfortable and small.

The Venus Annodomini received them graciously and "Young" Gayerson said, "By Jove! It's Kitty!" "Very Young" Gayerson would have listened for an explanation, if his time had not been taken up with trying to talk to a large, handsome, quiet, well-dressed girl—introduced to him by the Venus Annodomini as her daughter. She was far older in manner, style, and repose than "Very Young" Gayerson; and, as he realized this thing, he felt sick.

Presently, he heard the Venus Annodomini saying, "Do you know that your son is one of my most devoted admirers?"

"I don't wonder," said "Young" Gayerson. Here he raised his voice, "He follows his father's footsteps. Didn't I worship the ground you trod on, ever so long ago, Kitty—and you haven't changed since then. How strange it all seems!"

"Very Young" Gayerson said nothing. His conversation with the daughter of the Venus Annodomini was, through the rest of the call, fragmentary and disjointed.

* * * * * *

"At five to-morrow then," said the Venus Annodomini. "And mind you are punctual."

"At five punctually," said "Young" Gayerson. "You can lend your old father a horse I dare say, youngster, can't you? I'm going for a ride to-morrow afternoon."

"Certainly," said "Very Young" Gayerson. "I am going down to-morrow morning. My ponies are at your service, Sir."

The Venus Annodomini looked at him across the half-light of the room, and her big grey eyes filled with moisture. She rose and shook hands with him.

"Good-bye, Tom," whispered the Venus Annodomini.

———•———

The Bisara of Pooree

Little Blind Fish, thou art marvelous
    wise,
Little Blind Fish, who put out thy eyes?
Open thy ears while I whisper my wish—
Bring me a lover, thou little Blind Fish.
    —*The Charm of the Bisara.*

SOME natives say that it came from the other side of Kulu, where the eleven-inch Temple Sapphire is. Others that it was made at the Devil-Shrine of Ao-Chung in Thibet, was stolen by a Kafir, from him by a Gurkha, from him again by a Lahouli, from him by a *khitmatgar*, and by this latter sold to an Englishman, so all its virtue was lost; because, to work properly, the Bisara of Pooree must be stolen—with bloodshed if possible, but, at any rate, stolen.

These stories of the coming into India are all false. It was made at Pooree ages since—the manner of its making would fill a small book—was stolen by one of the Temple dancing-girls there, for her own purposes, and then passed on from hand to hand, steadily northward, till it reached Hanlé: always bearing the same name—the Bisara of Pooree. In shape it is a tiny square box of silver, studded outside with eight small balas-rubies. Inside the box, which opens with a spring, is a little eyeless fish, carved from some sort of dark, shiny nut and wrapped in a shred of faded gold-cloth. That is the Bisara of Pooree, and it were better for a man to take a king-cobra in his hand than to touch the Bisara of Pooree.

All kinds of magic are out of date, and done away with except in India where nothing changes in spite of the shiny, top-scum stuff that people call "civilization." Any man who knows about the Bisara of Pooree will tell you what its powers are—always supposing that it has been honestly stolen. It is the only regularly working, trustworthy love-charm in the country, with one exception. [The other charm is in the hands of a trooper of the Nizam's Horse, at a place called Tuprani, due north of Hyderabad.] This can be depended upon for a fact. Some one else may explain it.

If the Bisara be not stolen, but given or bought or found, it turns against its owner in three years, and leads to ruin or death. This is another fact which you may explain when you have time. Meanwhile, you can laugh at it. At present, the Bisara is safe on a hack-pony's neck, inside the blue bead-necklace that keeps off the Evil-Eye. If the pony-driver ever finds it, and wears it, or gives it to his wife, I am sorry for him.

A very dirty hill-cooly woman, with goitre, owned it at Theog in 1884. It came into Simla from the north before Churton's *khitmatgar* bought it, and sold it, for three times its silver-value, to Churton, who collected curiosities. The servant knew no more what he had bought than the master; but a man looking over Churton's collection of curiosities—Churton was an Assistant Commissioner by the way—saw and held his tongue. He was an Englishman; but knew how to believe. Which shows that he was different from most Englishmen. He knew that it was dangerous to have any share in the little box when working or dormant; for Love unsought is a terrible gift.

Pack—"Grubby" Pack, as we used to call him—was, in every way, a nasty little man who must have crawled into the Army by mistake. He was three inches taller than his sword, but not half so strong. And the sword was a fifty-shilling, tailor-made one. Nobody liked him, and, I suppose, it was his wizenedness and worthlessness that made him fall so hopelessly in love with Miss Hollis, who was good and sweet, and five-foot-seven in her tennis-shoes. He was not content with falling in love quietly, but brought all the strength of his miserable little nature into the business. If he had not been so objectionable, one might have pitied him. He vapored, and fretted, and fumed, and trotted up and down, and tried to make himself pleasing in Miss Hollis' big, quiet grey eyes, and failed. It was one of the cases that you sometimes meet, even in our country where we marry by Code, of a really blind attachment all on one side, without the faintest possibility of return. Miss Hollis looked on Pack as some sort of vermin running about the road. He had no prospects beyond Captain's pay, and no wits to help that out by one penny. In a large-sized man, love like his would have been touching. In a good man it would have been grand. He being what he was, it was only a nuisance. You will believe this much. What you will not believe is what follows: Churton, and The Man who Knew what the Bisara was, were lunching at the Simla Club together. Churton was complaining of life in general. His best mare had rolled out of stable down the cliff and had broken her back; his decisions were being reversed by the upper Courts more than an Assistant Commissioner of eight years' standing has a right to expect; he knew liver and fever, and, for weeks past, had felt out of sorts. Altogether, he was disgusted and disheartened.

Simla Club dining-room is built, as all the world knows, in two sections, with an arch-arrangement dividing them. Come in, turn to your left, take the table under the window, and you cannot see any one who has come in, turned to the right, and taken a table on the right side of the arch. Curiously enough, every word that you say can be heard, not only by the other diner, but by the servants beyond the screen through which they bring dinner. This is worth knowing; an echoing-room is a trap to be forewarned against.

Half in fun, and half hoping to be believed, the Man who Knew told Churton the story of the Bisara of Pooree at rather greater length than I have told it to you in this place; winding up with a suggestion that Churton might as well throw the little box down the hill and see whether all his troubles would go with it. In ordinary ears, English ears, the tale was only an interesting bit of folklore. Churton laughed, said that he felt better for his tiffin, and went out. Pack had been tiffining by himself to the right of the arch, and had heard everything. He was nearly mad with his absurd infatuation for Miss Hollis, that all Simla had been laughing about.

It is a curious thing that, when a man hates or loves beyond reason, he is ready to go beyond reason to gratify his feelings. Which he would not do for money or power merely. Depend upon it, Solomon would never have built altars to Ashtaroth and all those ladies with queer names, if there had not been trouble of some kind in his *zenana*, and nowhere else. But this is beside the story. The facts of the case are these: Pack called on Churton next day when Churton was out, left his card, and stole the Bisara of Pooree from its place under the clock on the mantelpiece! Stole it like the thief he was by nature. Three days later all Simla was electrified by the news that Miss Hollis had accepted Pack—the shrivelled rat, Pack! Do you desire clearer evidence than this? The Bisara of Pooree had been stolen, and it worked as it had always done when won by foul means.

There are three or four times in a man's life when he is justified in meddling with other people's affairs to play Providence.

The Man who Knew felt that he was justified; but believing and acting on a belief are quite different things. The insolent satisfaction of Pack as he ambled by the side of Miss Hollis, and

Churton's striking release from liver, as soon as the Bisara of Pooree had gone, decided The Man. He explained to Churton, and Churton laughed, because he was not brought up to believe that men on the Government House List steal—at least little things. But the miraculous acceptance by Miss Hollis of that tailor, Pack, decided him to take steps on suspicion. He vowed that he only wanted to find out where his ruby-studded silver box had vanished too. You cannot accuse a man on the Government House List of stealing. And if you rifle his room, you are a thief yourself. Churton, prompted by The Man who Knew, decided on burglary. If he found nothing in Pack's room . . . but it is not nice to think of what would have happened in that case.

Pack went to a dance at Benmore— Benmore was Benmore in those days, and not an office—and danced fifteen waltzes out of twenty-two with Miss Hollis. Churton and The Man took all the keys that they could lay hands on, and went to Pack's room in the hotel, certain that his servants would be away. Pack was a cheap soul. He had not purchased a decent cash-box to keep his papers in, but one of those native imitations that you buy for ten rupees. It opened to any sort of key, and there at the bottom, under Pack's Insurance Policy, lay the Bisara of Pooree!

Churton called Pack names, put the Bisara of Pooree in his pocket, and went to the dance with The Man. At least, he came in time for supper, and saw the beginning of the end in Miss Hollis' eyes. She was hysterical after supper, and was taken away by her Mamma.

At the dance, with the abominable Bisara in his pocket, Churton twisted his foot on one of the steps leading down to the old Rink, and had to be sent home in a 'rickshaw, grumbling. He did not believe in the Bisara of Pooree any the more for this manifestation, but he sought out Pack and called him some ugly names; and "thief" was the mildest of them. Pack took the names with the nervous smile of a little man who wants both soul and body to resent an insult, and went his way. There was no public scandal.

A week later, Pack got his definite dismissal from Miss Hollis. There had been a mistake in the placing of her affections, she said. So he went away to Madras, where he can do no great harm even if he lives to be a Colonel.

Churton insisted upon The Man who Knew taking the Bisara of Pooree as a gift. The Man took it, went down to the Cart-Road at once, found a cart-pony with a blue bead-necklace, fastened the Bisara of Pooree inside the necklace with a piece of shoe-string and thanked Heaven that he was rid of a danger. Remember, in case you ever find it, that you must not destroy the Bisara of Pooree. I have not time to explain why just now, but the power lies in the little wooden fish. Mister Gubernatis or Max Müller could tell you more about it than I.

You will say that all this story is made up. Very well. If ever you come across a little, silver, ruby-studded box, seven-eighths of an inch long by three-quarters wide, with a dark brown wooden fish, wrapped in gold cloth, inside it, keep it. Keep it for three years, and then you will discover for yourself whether my story is true or false.

Better still, steal it as Pack did, and you will be sorry that you had not killed yourself in the beginning.

---·---

A Friend's Friend

Wherefore slew you the stranger? He
  brought me dishonor.
I saddled my mare Bijli. I set him upon
  her.
I gave him rice and goat's flesh. He bared
  me to laughter;
When he was gone from my tent, swift
  I followed after,
Taking a sword in my hand. The hot
  wine had filled him:
Under the stars he mocked me. There-
  fore I killed him.
            —*Hadramauti.*

THIS tale must be told in the first person for many reasons. The man whom I want to expose is Tranter of the Bombay side. I want Tranter black-balled at his Club, divorced from his wife, turned out of Service, and cast into prison, until I get an apology from him in writing. I wish to warn the world against Tranter of the Bombay side.

You know the casual way in which men pass on acquaintances in India? It is a great convenience, because you can get rid of a man you don't like by writing a letter of introduction and putting him, with it, into the train. T. G.'s are best treated thus. If you keep them moving, they have no time to say insulting and offensive things about "Anglo-Indian Society."

One day, late in the cold weather, I got a letter of preparation from Tranter of the Bombay side, advising me of the advent of a T. G., a man called Jevon; and saying, as usual, that any kindness shown to Jevon would be a kindness to Tranter. Every one knows the regular form of these communications.

Two days afterward, Jevon turned up with his letter of introduction, and I did what I could for him. He was lint-haired, fresh-colored, and very English. But he held no views about the Government of India. Nor did he insist on shooting tigers on the Station Mall, as some T. G.'s do. Nor did he call us "colonists," and dine in a flannel-shirt and tweeds, under that delusion as other T. G.'s do. He was well-behaved and very grateful for the little I won for him —most grateful of all when I secured him an invitation for the Afghan Ball, and introduced him to a Mrs. Deemes, a lady for whom I had a great respect and admiration, who danced like the shadow of a leaf in a light wind. I set great store by the friendship of Mrs. Deemes; but, had I known what was coming, I would have broken Jevon's neck with a curtain-pole before getting him that invitation.

But I did not know, and he dined, at the Club, I think, on the night of the ball. I dined at home. When I went to the dance, the first man I met asked me whether I had seen Jevon. "No," said I. "He's at the Club.

Hasn't he come?" —"Come!" said the man. "Yes, he's very much come. You'd better look at him."

I sought for Jevon. I found him sitting on a bench and smiling to himself and a programme. Half a look was enough for me. On that one night, of all others, he had begun a long and thirsty evening, by taking too much! He was breathing heavily through his nose, his eyes were rather red, and he appeared very satisfied with all the earth. I put up a little prayer that the waltzing would work off the wine, and went about programme-filling, feeling uncomfortable. But I saw Jevon walk up to Mrs. Deemes for the first dance, and I knew that all the waltzing on the card was not enough to keep Jevon's rebellious legs steady. That couple went round six times. I counted. Mrs. Deemes dropped Jevon's arm and came across to me.

I am not going to repeat what Mrs. Deemes said to me; because she was very angry indeed. I am not going to write what I said to Mrs. Deemes, because I didn't say anything. I only wished that I had killed Jevon first and been hanged for it. Mrs. Deemes drew her pencil through all the dances that I had booked with her, and went away, leaving me to remember that what I ought to have said was that Mrs. Deemes had asked to be introduced to Jevon because he danced well; and that I really had not carefully worked out a plot to get her insulted. But I felt that argument was no good, and that I had better try to stop Jevon from waltzing me into more trouble. He, however, was gone, and about every third dance I set off to hunt for him.

This ruined what little pleasure I expected from the entertainment.

Just before supper I caught Jevon, at the buffet with his legs wide apart, talking to a very fat and indignant chaperone. "If this person is a friend of yours, as I understand he is, I would recommend you to take him home," said she. "He is unfit for decent society." Then I knew that goodness only knew what Jevon had been doing, and I tried to get him away.

But Jevon wasn't going; not he. He knew what was good for him, he did; and he wasn't going to be dictated to by any laconical nigger-driver, he wasn't; and I was the friend who had formed his infant mind and brought him up to buy Benares brassware and fear God, so I was; and we would have many more blazing good drunks together, so we would; and all the she-camels in black silk in the world shouldn't make him withdraw his opinion that there was nothing better than Benedictine to give one an appetite. And then . . . but he was my guest.

I set him in a quiet corner of the supper-room, and went to find a wall-prop that I could trust. There was a good and kindly Subaltern—may Heaven bless that Subaltern, and make him a Commander-in-Chief!—who heard of my trouble. He was not dancing himself, and he owned a head like five-year-old teak-baulks. He said that he would look after Jevon till the end of the ball.

" 'Don't suppose you much mind what I do with him?" said he.

"Mind!" said I. "No! You can murder the beast if you like."

But the Subaltern did not murder

him. He trotted off to the supper-room, and sat down by Jevon, drinking peg for peg with him. I saw the two fairly established, and went away, feeling more easy.

When "The Roast Beef of Old England" sounded, I heard of Jevon's performances between the first dance and my meeting with him at the buffet. After Mrs. Deemes had cast him off, it seems that he had found his way into the gallery, and offered to conduct the Band or to play any instrument in it just as the Bandmaster pleased.

When the Bandmaster refused, Jevon said that he wasn't appreciated, and he yearned for sympathy. So he trundled downstairs and sat out four dances with four girls, and proposed to three of them. One of the girls was a married woman by the way. Then he went into the whist-room, and fell face-down and wept on the hearth-rug in front of the fire, because he had fallen into a den of card-sharpers, and his Mamma had always warned him against bad company. He had done a lot of other things, too, and had taken about three quarts of mixed liquors. Besides, speaking of me in the most scandalous fashion!

All the women wanted him turned out, and all the men wanted him kicked. The worst of it was, that every one said it was my fault. Now, I put it to you how on earth could I have known that this innocent, fluffy T. G. would break out in this disgusting manner? You see he had gone round the world nearly, and his vocabulary of abuse was cosmopolitan, though mainly Japanese which he had picked up in a low tea-house at Hakodate. It sounded like whistling.

While I was listening to first one man and then another telling me of Jevon's shameless behavior and asking me for his blood, I wondered where he was. I was prepared to sacrifice him to Society on the spot.

But Jevon was gone, and, far away in the corner of the supper-room, sat my dear, good Subaltern, a little flushed, eating salad. I went over and said, "Where's Jevon?"—"In the cloakroom," said the Subaltern. "He'll keep till the women have gone. Don't you interfere, with my prisoner." I didn't want to interfere but I peeped into the cloakroom, and found my guest put to bed on some rolled-up carpets, all comfy, his collar free, and a wet swab on his head.

The rest of the evening I spent in making timid attempts to explain things to Mrs. Deemes and three or four other ladies, and trying to clear my character —for I am a respectable man—from the shameful slurs that my guest had cast upon it. Libel was no word for what he had said.

When I wasn't trying to explain, I was running off to the cloakroom to see that Jevon wasn't dead of apoplexy. I didn't want him to die on my hands. He had eaten my salt.

At last that ghastly ball ended, though I was not in the least restored to Mrs. Deemes' favor. When the ladies had gone, and some one was calling for songs at the second supper, that angelic Subaltern told the servants to bring in the *Sahib* who was in the cloakroom, and clear away one end of the supper-table. While this was being done, we formed ourselves into a Board of Punishment with the Doctor for President.

Jevon came in on four men's shoulders, and was put down on the table like a corpse in a dissecting-room, while the Doctor lectured on the evils of intemperance and Jevon snored. Then we set to work.

We corked the whole of his face. We filled his hair with meringue-cream till it looked like a white wig. To protect everything till it dried, a man in the Ordnance Department, who understood the work, luted a big blue paper cap from a cracker, with meringue-cream, low down on Jevon's forehead. This was punishment, not play, remember. We took gelatine off crackers, and stuck blue gelatine on his nose, and yellow gelatine on his chin, and green and red gelatine on his cheeks, pressing each dab down till it held as firm as goldbeaters' skin.

We put a ham-frill round his neck, and tied it in a bow in front. He nodded like a mandarin.

We fixed gelatine on the back of his hands, and burned-corked them inside, and put small cutlet-frills round his wrists, and tied both wrists together with string. We waxed up the ends of his moustache with isinglass. He looked very martial.

We turned him over, pinned up his coat-tails between his shoulders, and put a rosette of cutlet-frills there. We took up the red cloth from the ball-room to the supper-room, and wound him up in it. There were sixty feet of red cloth, six feet broad; and he rolled up into a big fat bundle, with only that amazing head sticking out.

Lastly, we tied up the surplus of the cloth beyond his feet with cocoanut-fibre string as tightly as we knew how. We were so angry that we hardly laughed at all.

Just as we finished, we heard the rumble of bullock-carts taking away some chairs and things that the General's wife had loaned for the ball. So we hoisted Jevon, like a roll of carpets, into one of the carts, and the carts went away.

Now the most extraordinary part of this tale is that never again did I see or hear anything of Jevon, T. G. He vanished utterly. He was not delivered at the General's house with the carpets. He just went into the black darkness of the end of the night, and was swallowed up. Perhaps he died and was thrown into the river.

But, alive or dead, I have often wondered how he got rid of the red cloth and the meringue-cream. I wonder still whether Mrs. Deemes will ever take any notice of me again, and whether I shall live down the infamous stories that Jevon set afloat about my manners and customs between the first and the ninth waltz of the Afghan Ball. They stick closer than cream.

Wherefore, I want Tranter of the Bombay side, dead or alive. But dead for preference.

The Gate of the Hundred Sorrows

If I can attain Heaven for a pice, why
should you be envious?
—*Opium Smoker's Proverb.*

THIS is no work of mine. My friend,
Gabral Misquitta, the half-caste, spoke
it all, between moonset and morning,
six weeks before he died; and I took
it down from his mouth as he answered
my questions. So:

It lies between the Coppersmith's
Gully and the pipe-stem sellers' quarter, within a hundred yards, too, as the
crow flies, of the Mosque of Wazir
Khan. I don't mind telling any one this
much, but I defy him to find the Gate,
however well he may think he knows
the City. You might even go through
the very gully it stands in a hundred
times, and be none the wiser. We used
to call the gully, "The Gully of the
Black Smoke," but its native name is
altogether different of course. A loaded
donkey couldn't pass between the walls;
and, at one point, just before you reach
the Gate, a bulged house-front makes
people go along all sideways.

It isn't really a gate though. It's a
house. Old Fung-Tching had it first five
years ago. He was a boot-maker in Calcutta. They say that he murdered his
wife there when he was drunk. That
was why he dropped bazar-rum and took
to the Black Smoke instead. Later on,
he came up north and opened the Gate
as a house where you could get your
smoke in peace and quiet. Mind you,
it was a *pukka*, respectable opium-house
and not one of those stifling, sweltering *chandoo-khanas*, that you can find
all over the City. No; the old man

knew his business thoroughly, and he
was most clean for a Chinaman. He
was a one-eyed little chap, not much
more than five feet high, and both his
middle fingers were gone. All the same,
he was the handiest man at rolling black
pills I have ever seen. Never seemed
to be touched by the Smoke, either; and
what he took day and night, night and
day, was a caution. I've been at it five
years, and I can do my fair share of
the Smoke with any one; but I was a
child to Fung-Tching that way. All the
same, the old man was keen on his
money: very keen; and that's what I
can't understand. I heard he saved a
good deal before he died, but his nephew
has got all that now; and the old man's
gone back to China to be buried.

He kept the big upper room, where
his best customers gathered, as neat as
a new pin. In one corner used to stand
Fung-Tching's Joss—almost as ugly as
Fung-Tching—and there were always
sticks burning under his nose; but you
never smelled 'em when the pipes were
going thick. Opposite the Joss was
Fung-Tching's coffin. He had spent a
good deal of his savings on that, and
whenever a new man came to the Gate
he was always introduced to it. It was
lacquered black, with red and gold writings on it, and I've heard that Fung-
Tching brought it out all the way from
China. I don't know whether that's true
or not, but I know that, if I came first
in the evening, I used to spread my mat
just at the foot of it. It was a quiet
corner, you see, and a sort of breeze
from the gully came in at the window

now and then. Besides the mats, there was no other furniture in the room— only the coffin, and the old Joss all green and blue and purple with age and polish.

Fung-Tching never told us why he called the place "The Gate of the Hundred Sorrows." (He was the only Chinaman I know who used bad-sounding fancy names. Most of them are flowery. As you'll see in Calcutta.) We used to find that out for ourselves. Nothing grows on you so much, if you're white, as the Black Smoke. A yellow man is made different. Opium doesn't tell on him scarcely at all; but white and black suffer a good deal. Of course, there are some people that the Smoke doesn't touch any more than tobacco would at first. They just doze a bit, as one would fall asleep naturally, and next morning they are almost fit for work. Now, I was one of that sort when I began, but I've been at it for five years pretty steadily, and it's different now. There was an old aunt of mine, down Agra way, and she left me a little at her death. About sixty rupees a month secured. Sixty isn't much. I can recollect a time, 'seems hundreds and hundreds of years ago, that I was getting my three hundred a month, and pickings, when I was working on a big timber-contract in Calcutta.

I didn't stick to that work for long. The Black Smoke does not allow of much other business; and even though I am very little affected by it, as men go I couldn't do a day's work now to save my life. After all, sixty rupees is what I want. When old Fung-Tching was alive he used to draw the money for me, give me about half of it to live

on (I eat very little), and the rest he kept himself. I was free of the Gate at any time of the day and night, and could smoke and sleep there when I liked, so I didn't care. I know the old man made a good thing out of it; but that's no matter. Nothing matters much to me; and besides, the money always came fresh and fresh each month.

There was ten of us met at the Gate when the place was first opened. Me, and two Baboos from a Government Office somewhere in Anarkulli, but they got the sack and couldn't pay (no man who has to work in the daylight can do the Black Smoke for any length of time straight on); a Chinaman that was Fung-Tching's nephew; a bazar-woman that had got a lot of money somehow; an English loafer—Mac-Somebody I think, but I have forgotten,—that smoked heaps, but never seemed to pay anything (they said he had saved Fung-Tching's life at some trial in Calcutta when he was a barrister); another Eurasian, like myself, from Madras; a half-caste woman, and a couple of men who said they had come from the North. I think they must have been Persians or Afghans or something. There are not more than five of us living now, but we come regular. I don't know what happened to the Baboos; but the bazar-woman she died after six months of the Gate, and I think Fung-Tching took her bangles and nose-ring for himself. But I'm not certain. The Englishman, he drank as well as smoked, and he dropped off. One of the Persians got killed in a row at night by the big well near the mosque a long time ago, and the Police shut up the well, because they said it was full of foul air. They found him dead at the bottom of it. So you see, there is only me, the Chinaman, the half-caste woman that we call the *Memsahib* (she used to live with Fung-Tching), the other Eurasian, and one of the Persians. The *Memsahib* looks very old now. I think she was a young woman when the Gate was opened; but we are all old for the matter of that. Hundreds and hundreds of years old. It is very hard to keep count of time in the Gate, and, besides, time doesn't matter to me. I draw my sixty rupees fresh and fresh every month. A very, very long while ago, when I used to be getting three hundred and fifty rupees a month, and pickings, on a big timber-contract at Calcutta, I had a wife of sorts. But she's dead now. People said that I killed her by taking to the Black Smoke. Perhaps I did, but it's so long since that it doesn't matter. Sometimes when I first came to the Gate, I used to feel sorry for it; but that's all over and done with long ago, and I draw my sixty rupees fresh and fresh every month, and am quite happy. Not *drunk* happy, you know, but always quiet and soothed and contented.

How did I take to it? It began at Calcutta. I used to try it in my own house, just to see what it was like. I never went very far, but I think my wife must have died then. Anyhow, I found myself here, and got to know Fung-Tching. I don't remember rightly how that came about; but he told me of the Gate and I used to go there, and, somehow, I have never got away from it since. Mind you, though, the Gate was a respectable place in Fung-Tching's time where you could be comfortable, and not at all like the *chandoo-*

khanas where the niggers go. No; it was clean and quiet, and not crowded. Of course, there were others beside us ten and the man; but we always had a mat apiece, with a wadded woolen headpiece, all covered with black and red dragons and things; just like the coffin in the corner.

At the end of one's third pipe the dragons used to move about and fight. I've watched 'em many and many a night through. I used to regulate my Smoke that way, and now it takes a dozen pipes to make 'em stir. Besides, they are all torn and dirty, like the mats, and old Fung-Tching is dead. He died a couple of years ago, and gave me the pipe I always use now—a silver one, with queer beasts crawling up and down the receiver-bottle below the cup. Before that, I think, I used a big bamboo stem with a copper cup, a very small one, and a green jade mouthpiece. It was a little thicker than a walking-stick stem, and smoked sweet, very sweet. The bamboo seemed to suck up the smoke. Silver doesn't, and I've got to clean it out now and then, that's a great deal of trouble, but I smoke it for the old man's sake. He must have made a good thing out of me, but he always gave me clean mats and pillows, and the best stuff you could get anywhere.

When he died, his nephew Tsin-ling took up the Gate, and he called it the "Temple of the Three Possessions"; but we old ones speak of it as the "Hundred Sorrows," all the same. The nephew does things very shabbily, and I think the *Memsahib* must help him. She lives with him; same as she used to do with the old man. The two let in all sorts of low people, niggers and all, and the Black Smoke isn't as good as it used to be. I've found burned bran in my pipe over and over again. The old man would have died if that had happened in his time. Besides, the room is never cleaned, and all the mats are torn and cut at the edges. The coffin is gone —gone to China again—with the old man and two ounces of Smoke inside it, in case he should want 'em on the way.

The Joss doesn't get so many sticks burned under his nose as he used to; that's a sign of ill-luck, as sure as Death. He's all brown, too, and no one ever attends to him. That's the *Memsahib's* work, I know; because, when Tsin-ling tried to burn gilt paper before him, she said it was a waste of money, and, if he kept a stick burning very slowly, the Joss wouldn't know the difference. So now we've got the sticks mixed with a lot of glue, and they take half an hour longer to burn, and smell stinky. Let alone the smell of the room by itself. No business can get on if they try that sort of thing. The Joss doesn't like it. I can see that. Late at night, sometimes, he turns all sorts of queer colors—blue and green and red— just as he used to do when old Fung-Tching was alive; and he rolls his eyes and stamps his feet like a devil.

I don't know why I don't leave the place and smoke quietly in a little room of my own in the bazar. Most like, Tsin-ling would kill me if I went away—he draws my sixty rupees now—and besides, it's so much trouble, and I've grown to be very fond of the Gate. It's not much to look at. Not what it was in the old man's time, but I couldn't leave it. I've seen so many come in and out. And I've seen so many die

here on the mats that I should be afraid of dying in the open now. I've seen some things that people would call strange enough; but nothing is strange when you're on the Black Smoke, except the Black Smoke. And if it was, it wouldn't matter. Fung-Tching used to be very particular about his people, and never got in any one who'd give trouble by dying messy and such. But the nephew isn't half so careful. He tells everywhere that he keeps a "first-chop" house. Never tries to get men in quietly, and make them comfortable like Fung-Tching did. That's why the Gate is getting a little bit more known than it used to be. Among the niggers of course. The nephew daren't get a white, or, for matter of that, a mixed skin into the place. He has to keep us three of course—me and the *Memsahib* and the other Eurasian. We're fixtures. But he wouldn't give us credit for a pipeful—not for anything.

One of these days, I hope, I shall die in the Gate. The Persian and the Madras man are terribly shaky now. They've got a boy to light their pipes for them. I always do that myself. Most like, I shall see them carried out before me. I don't think I shall ever outlive the *Memsahib* or Tsin-ling. Women last longer than men at the Black Smoke, and Tsin-ling has a deal of the old man's blood in him, though he does smoke cheap stuff. The bazar-woman knew when she was going two days before her time; and she died on a clean mat with a nicely wadded pillow, and the old man hung up her pipe just above the Joss. He was always fond of her, I fancy. But he took her bangles just the same.

I should like to die like the bazar-woman—on a clean, cool mat with a pipe of good stuff between my lips. When I feel I'm going, I shall ask Tsin-ling for them, and he can draw my sixty rupees a month, fresh and fresh, as long as he pleases. Then I shall lie back, quiet and comfortable, and watch the black and red dragons have their last big fight together; and then . . .

Well, it doesn't matter. Nothing matters much to me—only I wish Tsin-ling wouldn't put bran into the Black Smoke.

———•———

The Story of Muhammad Din

Who is the happy man? He that sees in his own house at home, little children crowned with dust, leaping and falling and crying.—*Munichandra,* translated by Professor Peterson.

THE polo-ball was an old one, scarred, chipped, and dinted. It stood on the mantelpiece among the pipe-stems which Imam Din, *khitmatgar,* was cleaning for me.

"Does the Heaven-born want this ball?" said Imam Din, deferentially.

The Heaven-born set no particular store by it; but of what use was a polo-ball to a *khimatgar?*

"By your Honor's favor, I have a little son. He has seen this ball, and desires it to play with. I do not want it for myself."

No one would for an instant accuse portly old Imam Din of wanting to play with polo-balls. He carried out the battered thing into the veranda; and there followed a hurricane of joyful squeaks, a patter of small feet, and the *thud-thud-thud* of the ball rolling along the ground. Evidently the little son had been waiting outside the door to secure his treasure. But how had he managed to see that polo-ball?

Next day, coming back from office half an hour earlier than usual, I was aware of a small figure in the dining-room—a tiny, plump figure in a ridiculously inadequate shirt which came, perhaps, half-way down the tubby stomach. It wandered round the room, thumb in mouth, crooning to itself as it took stock of the pictures. Undoubtedly this was the "little son."

He had no business in my room, of course; but was so deeply absorbed in his discoveries that he never noticed me in the doorway. I stepped into the room and startled him nearly into a fit. He sat down on the ground with a gasp. His eyes opened, and his mouth followed suit. I knew what was coming, and fled, followed by a long, dry howl which reached the servants' quarters far more quickly than any command of mine had ever done. In ten seconds Imam Din was in the dining-room. Then despairing sobs arose, and I returned to find Imam Din admonishing the small sinner who was using most of his shirt as a handkerchief.

"This boy," said Imam Din, judicially, "is a *budmash*—a big *budmash.* He will, without doubt, go to the *jail-*

khana for his behavior." Renewed yells from the penitent, and an elaborate apology to myself from Imam Din.

"Tell the baby," said I, that the *Sahib* is not angry, and take him away." Imam Din conveyed my forgiveness to the offender, who had now gathered all his shirt round his neck, stringwise, and the yell subsided into a sob. The two set off for the door. "His name," said Imam Din, as though the name were part of the crime, "is Muhammad Din, and he is a *budmash*. Freed from present danger, Muhammad Din turned round in his father's arms, and said gravely, "It is true that my name is Muhammad Din, *Tahib*, but I am not a *budmash*, I am a *man!*"

From that day dated my acquaintance with Muhammad Din. Never again did he come into my dining-room, but on the neutral ground of the garden, we greeted each other with much state, though our conversation was confined to *"Talaam, Tahib"* from his side, and *"Salaam, Muhammad Din"* from mine. Daily on my return from office, the little white shirt, and the fat little body used to rise from the shade of the creeper-covered trellis where they had been hid; and daily I checked my horse here, that my salutation might not be slurred over or given unseemly.

Muhammad Din never had any companions. He used to trot about the compound, in and out of the castor-oil bushes, on mysterious errands of his own. One day I stumbled upon some of his handiwork far down the grounds. He had half buried the polo-ball in dust, and stuck six shriveled old marigold flowers in a circle round it. Outside that circle again was a rude square, traced out in bits of red brick alternating with fragments of broken china; the whole bounded by a little bank of dust. The water-man from the well-curb put in a plea for the small architect, saying that it was only the play of a baby and did not much disfigure my garden.

Heaven knows that I had no intention of touching the child's work then or later; but, that evening, a stroll through the garden brought me unawares full on it; so that I trampled, before I knew, marigold-heads, dust-bank, and fragments of broken soap-dish into confusion past all hope of mending. Next morning, I came upon Muhammad Din crying softly to himself over the ruin I had wrought. Some one had cruelly told him that the *Sahib* was very angry with him for spoiling the garden, and had scattered his rubbish, using bad language the while. Muhammad Din labored for an hour at effacing every trace of the dust-bank and pottery fragments, and it was with a tearful and apologetic face that he said *"Talaam, Tahib,"* when I came home from office. A hasty inquiry resulted in Imam Din informing Muhammad Din that, by my singular favor, he was permitted to disport himself as he pleased. Whereat the child took heart and fell to tracing the ground-plan of an edifice which was to eclipse the marigold-polo-ball creation.

For some months, the chubby little eccentricity revolved in his humble orbit among the castor-oil bushes and in the dust; always fashioning magnificent palaces from stale flowers thrown away by the bearer, smooth water-worn pebbles, bits of broken glass, and feathers pulled, I fancy, from my fowls—always alone, and always crooning to himself.

A gaily-spotted sea-shell was dropped one day close to the last of his little buildings; and I looked that Muhammad Din should build something more than ordinarily splendid on the strength of it. Nor was I disappointed. He meditated for the better part of an hour, and his crooning rose to a jubilant song. Then he began tracing in the dust. It would certainly be a wondrous palace, this one, for it was two yards long and a yard broad in ground-plan. But the palace was never completed.

Next day there was no Muhammad Din at the head of the carriage-drive, and no "Talaam, Tahib" to welcome my return. I had grown accustomed to the greeting, and its omission troubled me. Next day Imam Din told me that the child was suffering slightly from fever and needed quinine. He got the medicine, and an English Doctor.

"They have no stamina, these brats," said the Doctor, as he left Imam Din's quarters.

A week later, though I would have given much to have avoided it, I met on the road to the Mussulman burying-ground Imam Din, accompanied by one other friend, carrying in his arms, wrapped in a white cloth, all that was left of little Muhammad Din.

On the Strength of a Likeness

If your mirror be broken, look into still water; but have a care that you do not fall in.—*Hindu Proverb.*

NEXT to a requited attachment, one of the most convenient things that a young man can carry about with him at the beginning of his career, is an unrequited attachment. It makes him feel important and business-like, and *blasé*, and cynical; and whenever he has a touch of liver, or suffers from want of exercise, he can mourn over his lost love, and be very happy in a tender, twilight fashion.

Hannasyde's affair of the heart had been a godsend to him. It was four years old, and the girl had long since given up thinking of it. She had married and had many cares of her own. In the beginning, she had told Hannasyde that, "while she could never be anything more than a sister to him, she would always take the deepest interest in his welfare." This startlingly new and original remark gave Hannasyde something to think over for two years; and his own vanity filled in the other twenty-four months. Hannasyde was quite different from Phil Garron, but, none the less, had several points in common with that far too lucky man.

He kept his unrequited attachment by him as men keep a well-smoked pipe—for comfort's sake, and because it had grown dear in the using. It brought him happily through one Simla season. Hannasyde was not lovely. There was a crudity in his manners, and a roughness in the way in which he helped a lady on to her horse, that did not attract the other sex to him. Even if he had cast about for their favor, which he did not. He kept his wounded heart all to himself for a while.

Then trouble came to him. All who go to Simla know the slope from the Telegraph to the Public Works Office. Hannasyde was loafing up the hill, one September morning between calling hours, when a 'rickshaw came down in a hurry, and in the 'rickshaw sat the living, breathing image of the girl who had made him so happily unhappy. Hannasyde leaned against the railings and gasped. He wanted to run downhill after the 'rickshaw, but that was impossible; so he went forward with most of his blood in his temples. It was impossible, for many reasons, that the woman in the 'rickshaw could be the girl he had known. She was, he discovered later, the wife of a man from Dindigul, or Coimbatore, or some out-of-the-way place, and she had come up to Simla early in the season for the good of her health. She was going back to Dindigul, or wherever it was, at the end of the season; and in all likelihood would never return to Simla again; her proper Hill-station being Ootacamund. That night Hannasyde, raw and savage from the raking up of all old feelings, took counsel with himself for one measured hour. What he decided upon was this; and you must decide for yourself how much genuine affection for the old Love, and how much a very natural inclination to go abroad and enjoy himself, affected the decision. Mrs. Landys-Haggert would never in all human likelihood cross his path again. So whatever he did didn't much matter. She was marvelously like the girl who "took a deep interest" and the rest of the formula. All things considered, it would be pleasant to make the acquaintance of Mrs. Landys-Haggert, and for a little time—only a very little time—to make believe that he was with Alice Chisane again. Every one is more or less mad on one point. Hannasyde's particular monomania was his old love, Alice Chisane.

He made it his business to get introduced to Mrs. Haggert, and the introduction prospered. He also made it his business to see as much as he could of that lady. When a man is in earnest as to interviews, the facilities which Simla offers are startling. There are garden-parties, and tennis-parties, and picnics, and luncheons at Annandale, and rifle-matches, and dinners and balls; besides rides and walks, which are matters of private arrangement. Hannasyde had started with the intention of seeing a likeness, and he ended by doing much more. He wanted to be deceived, he meant to be deceived, and he deceived himself very thoroughly. Not only were the face and figure the face and figure of Alice Chisane, but the voice and lower tones were exactly the same, and so were the turns of speech; and the little mannerisms, that every woman has, of gait and gesticulation, were absolutely and identically the same. The turn of the head was the same; the tired look in the eyes at the end of a long walk was the same; the stoop-and-wrench over the saddle to hold in a pulling horse was the same; and once, most marvelous of all, Mrs. Landys-Haggert singing to herself in the next room, while Hannasyde was waiting to take her for a ride, hummed, note for note, with a throaty quiver of the voice in the second line, "Poor Wandering One!" exactly as Alice Chisane had hummed it for Hannasyde in the dusk of an English drawing-room. In the actual woman herself—in the soul of her—there was not the least likeness; she and Alice Chisane being cast in different moulds. But all that Hannasyde wanted to know and see and think about, was this maddening and perplexing likeness of face and voice and manner. He was bent on making a fool of himself that way; and he was in no sort disappointed.

Open and obvious devotion from any sort of man is always pleasant to any sort of woman; but Mrs. Landys-Haggert, being a woman of the world, could make nothing of Hannasyde's admiration.

He would take any amount of trouble—he was a selfish man habitually—to meet and forestall, if possible, her wishes. Anything she told him to do was law; and he was, there could be no doubting it, fond of her company so long as she talked to him, and kept on talking about trivialities. But when she launched into expression of her personal views and her wrongs, those small social differences that make the spice of Simla life, Hannasyde was neither pleased nor interested. He didn't want to know anything about Mrs. Landys-Haggert, or her experiences in the past—she had traveled nearly all over the world, and could talk cleverly—he wanted the likeness of Alice Chisane before his eyes and her voice in his ears. Anything outside that, reminding him of another personality, jarred, and he showed that it did.

Under the new Post Office, one evening, Mrs. Landys-Haggert turned on him, and spoke her mind shortly and without warning. "Mr. Hannasyde," said she, "will you be good enough to explain why you have appointed yourself my special *cavalier servente*? I

don't understand it. But I am perfectly certain, somehow or other, that you don't care the least little bit in the world for *me*." This seems to support, by the way, the theory that no man can act or tell lies to a woman without being found out. Hannasyde was taken off his guard. His defence never was a strong one, because he was always thinking of himself, and he blurted out, before he knew what he was saying, this inexpedient answer, "No more I do."

The queerness of the situation and the reply, made Mrs. Landys-Haggert laugh. Then it all came out; and at the end of Hannasyde's lucid explanation Mrs. Haggert said, with the least little touch of scorn in her voice, "So I'm to act as the lay-figure for you to hang the rags of your tattered affections on, am I?"

Hannasyde didn't see what answer was required, and he devoted himself generally and vaguely to the praise of Alice Chisane, which was unsatisfactory. Now it is to be thoroughly made clear that Mrs. Haggert had not the shadow of a ghost of an interest in Hannasyde. Only . . . only no woman likes being made love through instead of to—specially on behalf of a musty divinity of four years' standing.

Hannasyde did not see that he had made any very particular exhibition of himself. He was glad to find a sympathetic soul in the arid wastes of Simla.

When the season ended, Hannasyde went down to his own place and Mrs. Haggert to hers. "It was like making love to a ghost," said Hannasyde to himself, "and it doesn't matter; and now I'll get to my work." But he found himself thinking steadily of the Haggert-Chisane ghost; and he could not be certain whether it was Haggert or Chisane that made up the greater part of the pretty phantom.

*   *   *   *   *   *

He got understanding a month later.

A peculiar point of this peculiar country is the way in which a heartless Government transfers men from one end of the Empire to the other. You can never be sure of getting rid of a friend or an enemy till he or she dies. There was a case once—but that's another story.

Haggert's Department ordered him up from Dindigul to the Frontier at two days' notice, and he went through, losing money at every step, from Dindigul to his station. He dropped Mrs. Haggert at Lucknow, to stay with some friends there, to take part in a big ball at the Chutter Munzil, and to come on when he had made the new home a little comfortable. Lucknow was Hannasyde's station, and Mrs. Haggert stayed a week there. Hannasyde went to meet her. As the train came in, he discovered what he had been thinking of for the past month. The unwisdom of his conduct also struck him. The Lucknow week, with two dances, and an unlimited quantity of rides together, clinched matters; and Hannasyde found himself pacing this circle of thought:—He adored Alice Chisane, at least he *had* adored her. *And* he admired Mrs. Landys-Haggert because she was like Alice Chisane. *But* Mrs. Landys-Haggert was not in the least like Alice Chisane, being a thousand times more adorable. *Now* Alice Chisane was "the bride of another," and so was Mrs. Landys-Haggert, and a good and honest wife too. *Therefore* he, Hannasyde, was . . . here he

called himself several hard names, and wished that he had been wise in the beginning.

Whether Mrs. Landys-Haggert saw what was going on in his mind, she alone knows. He seemed to take an unqualified interest in everything connected with herself, as distinguished from the Alice-Chisane likeness, and he said one or two things which, if Alice Chisane had been still betrothed to him, could scarcely have been excused, even on the grounds of the likeness. But Mrs. Haggert turned the remarks aside, and spent a long time in making Hannasyde see what a comfort and a pleasure she had been to him because of her strange resemblance to his old love. Hannasyde groaned in his saddle and said, "Yes, indeed," and busied himself with preparations for her departure to the Frontier, feeling very small and miserable.

The last day of her stay at Lucknow came, and Hannasyde saw her off at the Railway Station. She was very grateful for his kindness and the trouble he had taken, and smiled pleasantly and sympathetically as one who knew the Alice-Chisane reason of that kindness. And Hannasyde abused the coolies with the luggage, and hustled the people on the platform, and prayed that the roof might fall in and slay him.

As the train went out slowly, Mrs. Landys-Haggert leaned out of the window to say good-bye—"On second thoughts, *au revoir*, Mr. Hannasyde. I go Home in the Spring, and perhaps I may meet you in Town."

Hannasyde shook hands, and said very earnestly and adoringly—"I hope to Heaven I shall never see your face again!"

And Mrs. Haggert understood.

Wressley of the Foreign Office

I closed and drew for my Love's sake,
    That now is false to me,
And I slew the Riever of Tarrant Moss,
    And set Dumeny free.

And ever they give me praise and gold,
    And ever I moan my loss;
For I struck the blow for my false Love's
    sake,
And not for the men of the Moss!
                    —*Tarrant Moss.*

ONE of the many curses of our life in India is the want of atmosphere in the painters' sense. There are no half-tints worth noticing. Men stand out all crude and raw, with nothing to tone them down, and nothing to scale them against. They do their work, and grow to think that there is nothing but their work, and nothing like their work, and that they are the real pivots on which the Administration turns. Here is an instance of this feeling. A half-caste clerk was ruling forms in a Pay Office. He said to me, "Do you know what would happen if I added or took away one single line on this sheet?" Then, with the air of a conspirator, "It would disorganize the whole of the Treasury payments throughout the whole of the Presidency Circle! Think of that!"

If men had not this delusion as to the ultra-importance of their own particular employments, I suppose that they would sit down and kill themselves. But their weakness is wearisome, particularly when the listener knows that he himself commits exactly the same sin.

Even the Secretariat believes that it does good when it asks an over-driven Executive Officer to take a census of wheat-weevils through a district of five thousand square miles.

There was a man once in the Foreign Office—a man who had grown middle-aged in the Department, and was commonly said, by irreverent juniors, to be able to repeat Aitchison's *Treaties and Sunnuds* backward in his sleep. What he did with his stored knowledge only the Secretary knew; and he, naturally, would not publish the news abroad. This man's name was Wressley, and it was the Shibboleth, in those days, to say— "Wressley knows more about the Central Indian States than any living man." If you did not say this, you were considered one of mean understanding.

Nowadays, the man who says that he knows the ravel of the inter-tribal complications across the Border is more of use; but, in Wressley's time, much attention was paid to the Central Indian States. They were called "foci" and "factors," and all manner of imposing names.

And here the curse of Anglo-Indian life fell heavily. When Wressley lifted up his voice, and spoke about such-and-such a succession to such-and-such a throne, the Foreign Office were silent, and Heads of Departments repeated the last two or three words of Wressley's sentences, and tacked "yes, yes," on to them, and knew that they were assisting the Empire to grapple with serious political contingencies. In most big undertakings, one or two men do the work while the rest sit near and talk till the ripe decorations begin to fall.

Wressley was the working-member of

378

the Foreign Office firm, and, to keep him up to his duties when he showed signs of flagging, he was made much of by his superiors and told what a fine fellow he was. He did not require coaxing, because he was of tough build, but what he received confirmed him in the belief that there was no one quite so absolutely and imperatively necessary to the stability of India as Wressley of the Foreign Office. There might be other good men, but the known, honored and trusted man among men was Wressley of the Foreign Office. We had a Viceroy in those days who knew exactly when to "gentle" a fractious big man, and to hearten-up a collar-galled little one, and so keep all his team level. He conveyed to Wressley the impression which I have just set down; and even tough men are apt to be disorganized by a Viceroy's praise. There was a case once—but that is another story.

All India knew Wressley's name and office—it was in Thacker and Spink's Directory—but who he was personally, or what he did, or what his special merits were, not fifty men knew or cared. His work filled all his time, and he found no leisure to cultivate acquaintances beyond those of dead Rajput chiefs with *Ahir* blots in their scutcheons. Wressley would have made a very good Clerk in the Herald's College had he not been a Bengal Civilian.

Upon a day, between office and office, great trouble came to Wressley—overwhelmed him, knocked him down, and left him gasping as though he had been a little schoolboy. Without reason, against prudence, and at a moment's notice, he fell in love with a frivolous, golden-haired girl who used to tear about Simla Mall on a high, rough waler, with a blue velvet jockey-cap crammed over her eyes. Her name was Venner—Tillie Venner—and she was delightful. She took Wressley's heart at a hand-gallop, and Wressley found that it was not good for man to live alone; even with half the Foreign Office Records in his presses.

Then Simla laughed, for Wressley in love was slightly ridiculous. He did his best to interest the girl in himself— that is to say, his work—and she, after the manner of women, did her best to appear interested in what, behind his back, she called "Mr. W'essley's Wajahs"; for she lisped very prettily. She did not understand one little thing about them, but she acted as if she did. Men have married on that sort of error before now.

Providence, however, had care of Wressley. He was immensely struck with Miss Venner's intelligence. He would have been more impressed had he heard her private and confidential accounts of his calls. He held peculiar notions as to the wooing of girls. He said that the best work of a man's career should be laid reverently at their feet. Ruskin writes something like this somewhere, I think; but in ordinary life a few kisses are better and save time.

About a month after he had lost his heart to Miss Venner, and had been doing his work vilely in consequence, the first idea of his *Native Rule in Central India* struck Wressley and filled him with joy. It was, as he sketched it, a great thing—the work of his life—a really comprehensive survey of a most fascinating subject—to be written with all the special and laboriously acquired knowledge of Wressley of the Foreign Office—a gift fit for an Empress.

He told Miss Venner that he was going to take leave, and hoped, on his return, to bring her a present worthy of her acceptance. Would she wait? Certainly she would. Wressley drew seventeen hundred rupees a month. She would wait a year for that. Her Mamma would help her to wait.

So Wressley took one year's leave and all the available documents, about a truck-load, that he could lay hands on, and went down to Central India with his notion hot in his head. He began his book in the land he was writing of. Too much official correspondence had made him a frigid workman, and he must have guessed that he needed the white light of local color on his palette. This is a dangerous paint for amateurs to play with.

Heavens, how that man worked! He caught his Rajahs, analyzed his Rajahs, and traced them up into the mists of Time and beyond, with their queens and their concubines. He dated and cross-dated, pedigreed and triple-pedigreed, compared, noted, connoted, wove, strung, sorted, selected, inferred, calendared and counter-calendared for ten hours a day. And, because this sudden and new light of Love was upon him, he turned those dry bones of history and dirty records of misdeeds into things to weep or to laugh over as he pleased. His heart and soul were at the end of his pen, and they got into the ink. He was dowered with sympathy, insight, humor, and style for two hundred and thirty days and nights; and his book was a Book. He had his vast special knowledge with him, so to speak; but

the spirit, the woven-in human Touch, the poetry and the power of the output, were beyond all special knowledge. But I doubt whether he knew the gift that was in him then, and thus he may have lost some happiness. He was toiling for Tillie Venner, not for himself. Men often do their best work blind, for some one else's sake.

Also, though this has nothing to do with the story, in India where every one knows every one else, you can watch men being driven, by the women who govern them, out of the rank-and-file and sent to take up points alone. A good man, once started, goes forward; but an average man, so soon as the woman loses interest in his success as a tribute to her power, comes back to the battalion and is no more heard of.

Wressley bore the first copy of his book to Simla, and, blushing and stammering, presented it to Miss Venner. She read a little of it. I give her review *verbatim*—"Oh your book? It's all about those howwid Wajahs. I didn't understand it."

*   *   *   *   *   *

Wressley of the Foreign Office was broken, smashed,—I am not exaggerating—by this one frivolous little girl. All that he could say feebly was—"But—but it's my *magnum opus!* The work of my life." Miss Venner did not know what *magnum opus* meant; but she knew that Captain Kerrington had won three races at the last Gymkhana. Wressley didn't press her to wait for him any longer. He had sense enough for that.

Then came the reaction after the year's strain, and Wressley went back to the Foreign Office and his "Wajahs," a compiling, gazetteering, report-writing hack, who would have been dear at three hundred rupees a month. He abided by Miss Venner's review. Which proves that the inspiration in the book was purely temporary and unconnected with himself. Nevertheless, he had no right to sink, in a hill-tarn, five packing-cases, brought up at enormous expense from Bombay, of the best book of Indian history ever written.

When he sold off before retiring, some years later, I was turning over his shelves, and came across the only existing copy of *Native Rule in Central India*—the copy that Miss Venner could not understand. I read it, sitting on his mule-trunks, as long as the light lasted, and offered him his own price for it. He looked over my shoulder for a few pages and said to himself drearily—

"Now, how in the world did I come to write such damned good stuff as that?"

Then to me—

"Take it and keep it. Write one of your penny-farthing yarns about its birth. Perhaps—perhaps—the whole business may have been ordained to that end."

Which, knowing what Wressley of the Foreign Office was once, struck me as about the bitterest thing that I had ever heard a man say of his own work.

By Word of Mouth

Not though you die to-night, O Sweet,
    and wail,
  A spectre at my door,
Shall mortal Fear make Love immortal
    fail—
  I shall but love you more,
Who, from Death's house returning, give
    me still
One moment's comfort in my matchless
    ill.
            —*Shadow Houses.*

THIS tale may be explained by those who know how souls are made, and where the bounds of the Possible are put down. I have lived long enough in this India to know that it is best to know nothing, and can only write the story as it happened.

Dumoise was our Civil Surgeon at Meridki, and we called him "Dormouse," because he was a round little, sleepy little man. He was a good Doctor and never quarreled with any one, not even with our Deputy Commissioner who had the manners of a bargee and the tact of a horse. He married a girl as round and as sleepy-looking as himself. She was a Miss Hillardyce, daughter of "Squash" Hillardyce of the Berars, who married his Chief's daughter by mistake. But that is another story.

A honeymoon in India is seldom more than a week long; but there is nothing to hinder a couple from extending it over two or three years. India is a delightful country for married folk who are wrapped up in one another. They can live absolutely alone and without interruption—just as the Dormice did. Those two little people retired from the world after their marriage, and were very happy. They were forced, of course, to give occasional dinners, but they made no friends thereby, and the Station went its own way and forgot them; only saying, occasionally, that Dormouse was the best of good fellows though dull. A Civil Surgeon who never quarrels is a rarity, appreciated as such.

Few people can afford to play Robinson Crusoe anywhere—least of all in India, where we are few in the land and very much dependent on each other's kind offices. Dumoise was wrong in shutting himself from the world for a year, and he discovered his mistake when an epidemic of typhoid broke out in the Station in the heart of the cold weather, and his wife went down. He was a shy little man, and five days were wasted before he realized that Mrs. Dumoise was burning with something worse than simple fever, and three days more passed before he ventured to call on Mrs. Shute, the Engineer's wife, and timidly speak about his trouble. Nearly every household in India knows that Doctors are very helpless in typhoid. The battle must be fought out between Death and the Nurses minute by minute and degree by degree. Mrs. Shute almost boxed Dumoise's ears for what she called his "criminal delay," and went off at once to look after the poor girl. We had seven cases of typhoid in the Station that winter and, as the average of death is about one in every five cases, we felt certain that we should have to lose somebody. But all did their best. The women sat up nursing the women, and the men turned to and tended the bachelors who were down, and we wrestled with those typhoid cases for fifty-six days, and brought them through the Valley of the Shadow in triumph. But,

just when we thought all was over, and were going to give a dance to celebrate the victory, little Mrs. Dumoise got a relapse and died in a week and the Station went to the funeral. Dumoise broke down utterly at the brink of the grave, and had to be taken away.

After the death, Dumoise crept into his own house and refused to be comforted. He did his duties perfectly, but we all felt that he should go on leave, and the other men of his own Service told him so. Dumoise was very thankful for the suggestion—he was thankful for anything in those days—and went to Chini on a walking-tour. Chini is some twenty marches from Simla, in the heart of the Hills, and the scenery is good if you are in trouble. You pass through big, still deodar-forests, and under big, still cliffs, and over big, still grass-downs swelling like a woman's breasts; and the wind across the grass, and the rain among the deodars says—"Hush—hush —hush." So little Dumoise was packed off to Chini, to wear down his grief with a full-plate camera and a rifle. He took also a useless bearer, because the man had been his wife's favorite servant. He was idle and a thief, but Dumoise trusted everything to him.

On his way back from Chini, Dumoise turned aside to Bagi, through the Forest Reserve which is on the spur of Mount Huttoo. Some men who have traveled more than a little say that the march from Kotegarh to Bagi is one of the finest in creation. It runs through dark wet forest, and ends suddenly in bleak, nipped hillside and black rocks. Bagi dâk-bungalow is open to all the winds and is bitterly cold. Few people go to Bagi. Perhaps that was the reason why

Dumoise went there. He halted at seven in the evening, and his bearer went down the hillside to the village to engage coolies for the next day's march. The sun had set, and the night-winds were beginning to croon among the rocks. Dumoise leaned on the railing of the veranda, waiting for his bearer to return. The man came back almost immediately after he had disappeared, and at such a rate that Dumoise fancied he must have crossed a bear. He was running as hard as he could up the face of the hill.

But there was no bear to account for his terror. He raced to the veranda and fell down, the blood spurting from his nose and his face iron-grey. Then he gurgled—"I have seen the *Memsahib!* I have seen the *Memsahib!*"

"Where?" said Dumoise.

"Down there, walking on the road to the village. She was in a blue dress, and she lifted the veil of her bonnet and said—'Ram Dass, give my *salaams* to the *Sahib,* and tell him that I shall meet him next month at Nuddea.' Then I ran away, because I was afraid."

What Dumoise said or did I do not know. Ram Dass declares that he said nothing, but walked up and down the veranda all the cold night, waiting for the *Memsahib* to come up the hill and stretching out his arms into the dark like a madman. But no *Memsahib* came, and, next day, he went on to Simla cross-questioning the bearer every hour.

Ram Dass could only say that he had met Mrs. Dumoise and that she had lifted up her veil and given him the message which he had faithfully repeated to Dumoise. To this statement Ram Dass adhered. He did not know where Nuddea was, had no friends at Nuddea, and would most certainly never go to Nuddea; even though his pay were doubled.

Nuddea is in Bengal and has nothing whatever to do with a Doctor serving in the Punjab. It must be more than twelve hundred miles south of Meridki.

Dumoise went through Simla without halting, and returned to Meridki, there to take over charge from the man who had been officiating for him during his tour. There were some Dispensary accounts to be explained, and some recent orders of the Surgeon-General to be noted, and, altogether, the taking-over was a full day's work. In the evening, Dumoise told his *locum tenens,* who was an old friend of his bachelor days, what had happened at Bagi; and the man said that Ram Dass might as well have chosen Tuticorin while he was about it.

At that moment, a telegraph-peon came in with a telegram from Simla, ordering Dumoise not to take over charge at Meridki, but to go at once to Nuddea on special duty. There was a nasty outbreak of cholera at Nuddea, and the Bengal Government, being short-handed, as usual, had borrowed a Surgeon from the Punjab.

Dumoise threw the telegram across the table and said—"Well?"

The other Doctor said nothing. It was all that he could say.

Then he remembered that Dumoise had passed through Simla on his way from Bagi; and thus might, possibly, have heard first news of the impending transfer.

He tried to put the question, and the implied suspicion into words, but Dumoise stopped him with—"If I had desired *that*, I should never have come back from Chini. I was shooting there. I wish to live, for I have things to do . . . but I shall not be sorry."

The other man bowed his head, and helped, in the twilight, to pack up Dumoise's just opened trunks. Ram Dass entered with the lamps.

"Where is the *Sahib* going?" he asked.

"To Nuddea," said Dumoise, softly.

Ram Dass clawed Dumoise's knees and boots and begged him not to go. Ram Dass wept and howled till he was turned out of the room. Then he wrapped up all his belongings and came back to ask for a character. He was not going to Nuddea to see his *Sahib* die and, perhaps, to die himself.

So Dumoise gave the man his wages and went down to Nuddea alone; the other Doctor bidding him good-bye as one under sentence of death.

Eleven days later he had joined his *Memsahib;* and the Bengal Government had to borrow a fresh Doctor to cope with that epidemic at Nuddea. The first importation lay dead in Chooadanga Dâk-Bungalow.

To Be Filed for Reference

By the hoof of the Wild Goat up-tossed
From the Cliff where She lay in the Sun,
  Fell the Stone
To the Tarn where the daylight is lost;
So She fell from the light of the Sun,
  And alone.

Now the fall was ordained from the first,
With the Goat and the Cliff and the Tarn,
  But the Stone
Knows only Her life is accursed,
As She sings in the depths of the Tarn,
  And alone.

Oh, Thou who hast builded the world!
Oh, Thou who hast lighted the Sun!
Oh, Thou who hast darkened the Tarn!
  Judge Thou
The sin of the Stone that was hurled
By the Goat from the light of the Sun,
As She sinks in the mire of the Tarn,
  Even now—even now—even now!
—*From the Unpublished Papers of Mc-
Intosh Jellaludin.*

"SAY is it dawn, is it dusk in thy
    Bower,
Thou whom I long for, who longest
    for me?
Oh, be it night—be it"—

Here he fell over a little camel-colt that was sleeping in the Serai where the horse-traders and the best of the blackguards from Central Asia live; and, because he was very drunk indeed and the night was dark, he could not rise again till I helped him. That was the beginning of my acquaintance with McIntosh Jellaludin. When a loafer, and drunk, sings "The Song of the Bower," he must be worth cultivating. He got off the camel's back and said, rather thickly, "I—I—I'm a bit screwed, but a dip in Loggerhead will put me right again; and, I say, have you spoken to Symonds about the mare's knees?"

Now Loggerhead was six thousand weary miles away from us, close to Mesopotamia, where you mustn't fish and poaching is impossible, and Charley Symonds' stable a half mile farther across the paddocks. It was strange to hear all the old names, on a May night, among the horses and camels of the Sultan Caravanserai. Then the man seemed to remember himself and sober down at the same time. We leaned against the camel and pointed to a corner of the Serai where a lamp was burning.

"I live there," said he, "and I should be extremely obliged if you would be good enough to help my mutinous feet thither; for I am more than usually drunk—most—most phenomenally tight. But not in respect to my head. 'My brain cries out against'—how does it go? But my head rides on the—rolls on the dunghill I should have said, and controls the qualm."

I helped him through the gangs of tethered horses and he collapsed on the edge of the veranda in front of the line of native quarters.

"Thanks—a thousand thanks! O Moon and little, little Stars! To think that a man should so shamelessly · · · Infamous liquor too. Ovid in exile drank no worse. Better. It was frozen. Alas! I had no ice. Good-night. I would introduce you to my wife were I sober—or she civilized."

A native woman came out of the darkness of the room, and began calling the man names; so I went away. He was the most interesting loafer that I had had the pleasure of knowing for a long time; and later on, he became a friend of mine. He was a tall, well-built, fair man, fearfully shaken with drink, and he looked nearer fifty than the thirty-five which, he said, was his real age. When a man begins to sink in India, and is not sent Home by his friends as soon as may be, he falls very low from a respectable point of view. By the time

that he changes his creed, as did McIntosh, he is past redemption.

In most big cities, natives will tell you of two or three *Sahibs*, generally low-caste, who have turned Hindu or Mussulman, and who live more or less as such. But it is not often that you can get to know them. As McIntosh himself used to say, "If I change my religion for my stomach's sake, I do not seek to become a martyr to missionaries, nor am I anxious for notoriety."

At the outset of acquaintance McIntosh warned me. "Remember this. I am not an object for charity. I require neither your money, your food, nor your cast-off raiment. I am that rare animal, a self-supporting drunkard. If you choose, I will smoke with you, for the tobacco of the bazars does not, I admit, suit my palate; and I will borrow any books which you may not specially value. It is more than likely that I shall sell them for bottles of excessively filthy country liquors. In return, you shall share such hospitality as my house affords. Here is a charpoy on which two can sit, and it is possible that there may, from time to time, be food in that platter. Drink, unfortunately, you will find on the premises at any hour: and thus I make you welcome to all my poor establishment."

I was admitted to the McIntosh household—I and my good tobacco. But nothing else. Unluckily, one cannot visit a loafer in the Serai by day. Friends buying horses would not understand it. Consequently, I was obliged to see McIntosh after dark. He laughed at this, and said simply, "You are perfectly right. When I enjoyed a position in society, rather higher than yours,

I should have done exactly the same thing. Good heavens! I was once"—he spoke as though he had fallen from the Command of a Regiment—"an Oxford Man!" This accounted for the reference to Charley Symonds' stable.

"You," said McIntosh, slowly, "have not had that advantage; but, to outward appearance, you do not seem possessed of a craving for strong drinks. On the whole, I fancy that you are the luckier of the two. Yet I am not certain. You are—forgive my saying so even while I am smoking your excellent tobacco—painfully ignorant of many things."

We were sitting together on the edge of his bedstead, for he owned no chairs, watching the horses being watered for the night, while the native woman was preparing dinner. I did not like being patronized by a loafer, but I was his guest for the time being, though he owned only one very torn alpaca-coat and a pair of trousers made out of gunny-bags. He took the pipe out of his mouth, and went on judicially, "All things considered, I doubt whether you are the luckier. I do not refer to your extremely limited classical attainments, or your excruciating quantities, but to your gross ignorance of matters more immediately under your notice. That, for instance," he pointed to a woman cleaning a samovar near the well in the centre of the Serai. She was flicking the water out of the spout in regular cadenced jerks.

"There are ways and ways of cleaning samovars. If you knew why she was doing her work in that particular fashion, you would know what the Spanish Monk meant when he said—

I the Trinity illustrate,
　Drinking watered orange-pulp—
In three sips the Arian frustrate,
　While he drains his at one gulp—

and many other things which now are hidden from your eyes. However, Mrs. McIntosh has prepared dinner. Let us come and eat after the fashion of the people of the country—of whom, by the way, you know nothing."

The native woman dipped her hand in the dish with us. This was wrong. The wife should always wait until the husband has eaten. McIntosh Jellaludin apologized, saying—

"It is an English prejudice which I have not been able to overcome; and she loves me. Why, I have never been able to understand. I foregathered with her at Jullundur, three years ago, and she has remained with me ever since. I believe her to be moral, and know her to be skilled in cookery."

He patted the woman's head as he spoke, and she cooed softly. She was not pretty to look at.

McIntosh never told me what position he had held before his fall. He was, when sober, a scholar and a gentleman. When drunk, he was rather more of the first than the second. He used to get drunk about once a week for two days. On those occasions the native woman tended him while he raved in all tongues except his own. One day, indeed, he began reciting *Atalanta in Calydon*, and went through it to the end, beating time to the swing of the verse with a bedstead-leg. But he did most of his ravings in Greek or German. The man's mind was a perfect rag-bag of useless things. Once, when he was beginning to get sober, he told me that I was the only rational being in the Inferno into which he had descended—a Virgil in the Shades, he said—and that, in return for my tobacco, he would, before he died, give me the materials of a new Inferno that should make me greater than Dante. Then he fell asleep on a horse-blanket and woke up quite calm.

"Man," said he, "when you have reached the uttermost depths of degradation, little incidents which would vex a higher life, are to you of no consequence. Last night, my soul was among the Gods; but I make no doubt that my bestial body was writhing down here in the garbage."

"You were abominably drunk if that's what you mean," I said.

"I *was* drunk—filthily drunk. I who am the son of a man with whom you have no concern—I who was once Fellow of a College whose buttery-hatch you have not seen. I was loathsomely drunk. But consider how lightly I am touched. It is nothing to me. Less than nothing; for I do not even feel the headache which should be my portion. Now, in a higher life, how ghastly would have been my punishment, how bitter my repentance! Believe me my friend with the neglected education, the highest is as the lowest—always supposing each degree extreme."

He turned round on the blanket, put his head between his fists and continued—

"On the Soul which I have lost and on the Conscience which I have killed, I tell you that I cannot feel! I am as the Gods, knowing good and evil, but untouched by either. Is this enviable or is it not?"

When a man has lost the warning of "next morning's head," he must be in a bad state. I answered, looking at McIntosh on the blanket, with his hair over his eyes and his lips blue-white, that I did not think the insensibility good enough.

"For pity's sake, don't say that! I tell you, it *is* good and most enviable. Think of my consolations!"

"Have you so many, then, McIntosh?"

"Certainly; your attempts at sarcasm which is essentially the weapon of a cultured man, are crude. First, my attainments, my classical and literary knowledge, blurred, perhaps, by immoderate drinking—which reminds me that before my soul went to the Gods last night, I sold the Pickering Horace you so kindly loaned me. Ditta Mull the clothesman has it. It fetched ten annas, and may be redeemed for a rupee—but still infinitely superior to yours. Secondly, the abiding affection of Mrs. McIntosh, best of wives. Thirdly, a monument, more enduring than brass, which I have built up in the seven years of my degadation."

He stopped here, and crawled across the room for a drink of water. He was very shaky and sick.

He referred several times to his "treasure"—some great possession that he owned—but I held this to be the raving of drink. He was as poor and as proud as he could be. His manner was not pleasant, but he knew enough about the natives, among whom seven years of his life had been spent, to make his acquaintance worth having. He used ac-

tually to laugh at Strickland as an ignorant man—"ignorant West and East"
—he said. His boast was, first, that he
was an Oxford man of rare and shining
parts, which may or may not have been
true—I did not know enough to check
his statements—and, secondly, that he
"had his hand on the pulse of native
life"—which was a fact. As an Oxford
Man, he struck me as a prig: he was
always throwing his education about. As
a Mohammedan *faquir*—as McIntosh
Jellaludin—he was all that I wanted
for my own ends. He smoked several
pounds of my tobacco, and taught me
several ounces of things worth knowing;
but he would never accept any gifts, not
even when the cold weather came, and
gripped the poor thin chest under the
poor thin alpaca-coat. He grew very
angry, and said that I had insulted him,
and that he was not going into hospital.
He had lived like a beast and he would
die rationally, like a man.

As a matter of fact, he died of pneumonia; and on the night of his death
sent over a grubby note asking me to
come and help him to die.

The native woman was weeping by
the side of the bed. McIntosh, wrapped
in a cotton cloth, was too weak to resent
a fur coat being thrown over him. He
was very active as far as his mind was
concerned, and his eyes were blazing.
When he had abused the Doctor who
came with me, so foully that the indignant old fellow left, he cursed me for a
few minutes and calmed down.

Then he told his wife to fetch out
"The Book" from a hole in the wall.
She brought out a big bundle, wrapped
in the tail of a petticoat, of old sheets
of miscellaneous note-paper, all num-

bered and covered with fine cramped
writing. McIntosh ploughed his hand
through the rubbish and stirred it up
lovingly.

"This," he said, "is my work—the
Book of McIntosh Jellaludin, showing
what he saw and how he lived, and
what befell him and others; being also
an account of the life and sins and death
of Mother Maturin. What Mirza Murad
Ali Beg's book is to all other books on
native life, will my work be to Mirza
Murad Ali Beg's!"

This, as will be conceded by any one
who knows Mirza Murad Ali Beg's
book, was a sweeping statement. The
papers did not look specially valuable;
but McIntosh handled them as if they
were currency-notes. Then said he
slowly—

"In despite the many weaknesses of
your education, you have been good to
me. I will speak of your tobacco when
I reach the Gods. I owe you much
thanks for many kindnesses. But I
abominate indebtedness. For this reason, I bequeath to you now the monument more enduring than brass—my one
book—rude and imperfect in parts, but
oh how rare in others! I wonder if you
will understand it. It is a gift more
honorable than . . . Bah! where is
my brain rambling to? You will mutilate it horribly. You will knock out
the gems you call Latin quotations, you
Philistine, and you will butcher the style
to carve into your own jerky jargon;
but you cannot destroy the whole of it.
I bequeath it to you. Ethel . . . My
brain again! . . . Mrs. McIntosh,
bear witness that I give the *Sahib* all
these papers. They would be of no use
to you, Heart of my Heart; and I lay

it upon you," he turned to me here, "that you do not let my book die in its present form. It is yours unconditionally —the story of McIntosh Jellaludin, which is *not* the story of McIntosh Jellaludin, but of a greater man than he, and of a far greater woman. Listen now! I am neither mad nor drunk! That book will make you famous."

I said, "Thank you," as the native woman put the bundle into my arms.

"My only baby!" said McIntosh, with a smile. He was sinking fast, but he continued to talk as long as breath remained. I waited for the end; knowing that, in six cases out of ten a dying man calls for his mother. He turned on his side and said—

"Say how it came into your possession. No one will believe you, but my name, at least, will live. You will treat it brutally, I know you will. Some of it must go; the public are fools and prudish fools. I was their servant once. But do your mangling gently—very gently. It is a great work, and I have paid for it in seven years' damnation."

His voice stopped for ten or twelve breaths, and then he began mumbling a prayer of some kind in Greek. The native woman cried every bitterly. Lastly, he rose in bed and said, as loudly as slowly—"Not guilty, my Lord!"

Then he fell back, and the stupor held him till he died. The native woman ran into the Serai among the horses, and screamed and beat her breasts; for she had loved him.

Perhaps his last sentence in life told what McIntosh had once gone through; but, saving the big bundle of old sheets in the cloth, there was nothing in his room to say who or what he had been.

The papers were in a hopeless muddle.

Strickland helped me to sort them, and he said that the writer was either an extreme liar or a most wonderful person. He thought the former. One of these days, you may be able to judge for yourselves. The bundle needed much expurgation and was full of Greek nonsense, at the head of the chapters, which has all been cut out.

If the thing is ever published, some one may perhaps remember this story, now printed as a safeguard to prove that McIntosh Jellaludin and not I myself wrote the Book of Mother Maturin.

I don't want the *Giant's Robe* to come true in my case.

The Last Relief

"He rode to death across the moor—
　Oh, false to me and mine!
But the naked ghost came to my door
　And bade me tend the kine.

*The naked ghost came to my door,
　And flickered to and fro,
And syne it whimpered through the crack
　Wi' 'Jeanie, let me go.'"
　　　　—*Old Ballad.*

NOTHING is easier than the administration of an empire so long as there is a supply of administrators. Nothing, on the other hand, is more difficult than short-handed administration. In India, where every man holding authority above a certain grade must be specially imported from England, this difficulty crops up at unexpected seasons. Then the great empire staggers along, like a North Sea fishing-smack, with a crew of two men and a boy, until a fresh supply of food for fever arrives from England, and the gaps are filled up. Some of the provinces are permanently short-handed, because their rulers know that if they give a man just a little more work than he can do, he contrives to do it. From the man's point of view this is wasteful, but it helps the empire forward, and flesh and blood are very cheap. The young men—and young men are always exacting—expect too much at the outset. They come to India desiring careers and money and a little success, and sometimes a wife. There is no limit to their desires, but in a few years it is explained to them by the sky above, the earth beneath, and the men around, that they are of far less importance than their work, and that it really does not concern themselves whether they live or die so long as that work continues. After they have learned this lesson, they become men worth consideration.

Many seasons ago the gods attacked the administration of the government of India in the heart of the hot season. They caused pestilences and famines, and killed the men who were deputed to deal with each pestilence and every famine. They rolled the smallpox across a desert, and it killed four Englishmen, one after the other, leaving thirty thousand square miles masterless for many days. They even caused the cholera to attack the reserve depots—the sanitaria in the Himalayas—where men were waiting on leave till their turn should come to go down into the heat. They

killed men with sunstroke who otherwise might have lived for three months longer, and—this was mean—they caused a strong man to tumble from his horse and break his neck just when he was most needed. It will not be long, that is to say, five or six years will pass, before those who survived forget that season of tribulation, when they danced at Simla with wives who feared that they might be widows before the morning, and when the daily papers from the plains confined themselves entirely to one kind of domestic occurrence.

Only the Supreme government never blanched. It sat upon the hilltops of Simla among the pines, and called for returns and statements as usual. Sometimes it called to a dead man, but it always received the returns as soon as his successor could take his place.

Ricketts of Myndonie died, and was relieved by Carter. Carter was invalided home, but he worked to the last minute, and left no arrears. He was relieved by Morten-Holt, who was too young for the work. Holt died of sunstroke when the famine was in Myndonie. He was relieved by Damer, a man borrowed from another province, who did all he could, but broke down from overwork. Cromer, in London on a year's leave, was dragged out by telegram from the cool darkness of a Brompton flat to the white heat of Myndonie, and he held fast. That is the record of Myndonie alone.

On the Moonee Canal three men went down; in the Kahan district, when cholera was at its worst, three more. In the Divisional Court of Halimpur two good men were accounted for; and so the record ran, exclusive of the wives and little children. It was a great game of general post, with death in all the corners, and it drove the Government to their wits' end to tide over the trouble till autumn should bring the new drafts.

The gods had no mercy, but the Government and the men it employed had no fear. This annoyed the gods, who are immortal, for they perceived, that the men whose portion was death were greater than they. The gods are always troubled, even in their paradises, by this sense of inferiority. They know that it is so easy for themselves to be strong and cruel, and they are afraid of being laughed at. So they smote more furiously than ever, just as a swordsman slashes at a chain to prove the temper of his blade. The chain of men parted for an instant at the stroke, but it closed up again, and continued to drag the empire forward, and not one living link of it rang false or was weak. All desired life, and love, and the light, and liquor, and larks, but none the less they died without whimpering. Therefore the gods would have continued to slay them till this very day had not one man failed.

His name was Haydon, and being young, he looked for all that young men desire; most of all, he looked for love. He had been at work in the Girdhauri district for eleven months, till fever and pressure had shaken his nerve more than he knew. At last he had taken the holiday that was his right—the holiday for which he had saved up one month a year for three years past. Keyte, a junior, relieved him one hot afternoon. Haydon shut his ink-stained office box, packed himself some thick clothes—he

had been living in cotton ducks for four months—gave his files of sweat-dotted papers, saw Keyte slide a piece of blotting-paper between the naked arm and the desk, and left that parched station of roaring dust storms for Simla and the cool of the snows. There he found rest, and the pink blotches of prickly heat faded from his body, and being idle, he went a-courting without knowing it. After a decent interval he found himself drifting very gently along the road that leads to the church, and a pretty girl helped him. He enjoyed his meals, was free from the intolerable strain of bodily discomfort, and as he looked from Simla upon the torment of the silver-wrapped plains below, laughed to think he had escaped honorably, and could talk prettily to a pretty girl, who, he felt sure, would in a little time answer an important question as it should be answered.

But out of natural perversity and an inferior physique, Keyte, at Girdhauri, one evening laid his head upon his table and never lifted it up again, and news was flashed up to Simla that the district of Girdhauri called for a new head. It never occurred to Haydon that he would be in any way concerned till Hamerton, a secretary of the Government, stopped him on the Mall, and said:

"I'm afraid—I'm very much afraid—that you will have to drop your leave and go back to Girdhauri. You see Keyte's dead, and—and we have no one else to send except yourself. The roster's a very short one this season, and you look much better than when you came up. Of course I'll do all I can to spare you, but I'm afraid—I'm very much afraid—that you will have to go down."

The Government, on the other hand, was not in the least afraid. It was quite certain that Haydon must go down. He was in moderately good health, had enjoyed nearly a month's holiday, and the needs of the state were urgent. Let him, they said, return to his work at Girdhauri. He must forego his leave, but some time, in the years to come, the Government might repay him the lost months, if it were not too short-handed. In the meantime he would return to duty.

The assistants in the *hara-kiri* of Japan are all intimate friends of the man who must die. They like him immensely, and they bring him the news of his doom with polite sorrow. But he must die, for that is required of him.

Hamerton would have spared Haydon had it been possible, but, indeed, he was the healthiest man in the ranks, and he knew the district. "You will go 'lown to-morrow," said Hamerton. "The regular notification will appear in the *Gazette* later on. We can't stand on forms this year."

Haydon said nothing, because those who govern India obey the law. He looked—it was evening—at the line of the sun-flushed snows forty miles to the east, and the palpitating heat haze of the plains fifty miles to the west, and his heart sank. He wished to stay in Simla to continue his wooing, and he knew too well the torments that were in store for him in Girdhauri. His nerve was broken. The coolness, the dances, the dinners that were to come, the scent of the Simla pines and the wood smoke, the canter of horses' feet on the crowded Mall, turned his heart to water. He could have wept passionately, like a little child, for his lost holiday and his lost love, and, like a little child balked of its play, he became filled with cheap spite that can only hurt the owner. The men at the Club were sorry for him, but he did not want to be condoled with. He was angry and afraid. Though he recognized the necessity of the injustice that had been done to him, he conceived that it could all be put right by yet another injustice, and then—and then somebody else would have to do his work, for he would be out of it forever.

He reflected on this while he was hurrying down the hillsides, after a last interview with the pretty girl, to whom he had said nothing that was not commonplace and inconclusive. This last failure made him the more angry with himself, and the spite and the rage increased. The air grew warmer and warmer as the cart rattled down the mountain road, till at last the hot, stale stillness of the plains closed over his head like heated oil, and he gasped for breath among the dry date-palms at kalka. Then came the long level ride into Umballa; the stench of dust which breeds despair; the lime-washed walls of Umballa station, hot to the hand though it was eleven at night; the greasy, rancid meal served by the sweating servants; the badly trimmed lamps in the oven-like waiting-room; and the whining of innumerable mosquitoes. That night, he remembered, there would be a dance at Simla. He was a very weak man.

That night Hamerton sat at work till late in the old Simla Foreign Office, which was a rambling collection of match-boxes packed away in a dark by-path under the pines. One of the wandering storms that run before the regular breaking of the monsoon had wrapped Simla in white mist. The rain was roaring on the shingled, tin-patched roof, and the thunder rolled to and fro among the hills as a ship rolls in the seaways. Hamerton called for a lamp and a fire to drive out the smell of mould and forest undergrowth that crept in from the woods. The clerks and secretaries had left the office two hours ago, and there remained only one native orderly, who set the lamp and went away. Hamerton returned to his papers, and the voice of the rain rose and fell. In the pauses he could catch the crunching of 'rickshaw wheels and the clatter of horses' feet going to the dance at the Viceroy's. These ceased at last, and the rain with them. The thunder drew off, muttering, toward the plains, and all the dripping pine-trees sighed with relief.

"Orderly," said Hamerton. He fancied that he heard somebody moving about the rooms. There was no answer, except a deep-drawn breath at the door. It might come from a panther prowling about the verandas in search of a pet dog, but panthers generally snuffed in a deeper key. This was a thick, gasping breath, as of one who had been running swiftly, or lay in deadly pain. Hamerton listened again. There certainly was somebody moving about the Foreign Office. He could hear boards creaking in far-off rooms, and uncertain steps on the rickety staircase. Since the clock marked close upon midnight, no one had a right to be in the office. Hamer-

ton had picked up the lamp, and was going to make a search, when the steps and the heavy breathing came to the door again, and staid.

"Who's there?" said Hamerton. "Come in."

Again the heavy breathing, and a thick, short cough.

"Who relieves Haydon?" said a voice outside. "Haydon! Haydon! Dying at Umballa. He can't go till he is relieved. Who relieves Haydon?"

Hamerton dashed to the door and opened it, to find a stolid messenger from the telegraph office, breathing through his nose, after the manner of natives. The man held out a telegram. "I could not find the room at first," he said. "Is there an answer?"

The telegram was from the Station-master at Umballa, and said: "English-man killed; up mail 42; slipped from platform. Dying. Haydon. Civilian. Inform Government."

"There is no answer," said Hamerton; and the man went away. But the fluttering whisper at the door continued. "Haydon! Haydon! Who relieves Haydon? He must not go till he is relieved. Haydon! Haydon! Dying at Umballa. For pity's sake, be quick!"

Hamerton thought for a minute of the pitifully short roster of men available, and answered, quietly, "Flint, of Degauri." Then, and not till then, did the hair begin to rise on his head; and Hamerton, secretary to Government, neglecting the lamp and the papers, went out very quickly from the Foreign Office into the cool wet night. His ears were tingling with the sound of a dry death-rattle, and he was afraid to continue his work.

Now only the gods know by whose design and intention Haydon had slipped from the dimly lighted Umballa platform under the wheels of the mail that was to take him back to his district; but since they lifted the pestilence on his death, we may assume that they had proved their authority over the minds of men, and found one man in India who was afraid of present pain.

Bitters Neat

THE oldest trouble in the world comes from want of understanding. And it is entirely the fault of the woman. Somehow, she is built incapable of speaking the truth, even to herself. She only finds it out about four months later, when the man is dead, or has been transferred. Then she says she never was so happy in her life, and marries some one else, who again touches some woman's heart elsewhere, and did not know it, but was mixed up with another man's wife, who only used him to pique a third man. And so round again—all crisscross.

Out here, where life goes quicker than at Home, things are more obviously tangled, and therefore more pitiful to look at. Men speak the truth as they understand it, and women as they think men would like to understand it; and then they all act lies which would deceive Solomon, and the result is a heart-rending muddle that half a dozen open words would put straight.

This particular muddle did not differ from any other muddle you may see, if you are not busy playing cross-purposes yourself going on in a big Station any cold season. Its only merit was that it did not come all right in the end; as

muddles are made to do in the third volume.

I've forgotten what the man was—he was an ordinary sort of man—'man you meet any day at the A.-D.-C.'s end of the table, and go away and forget about. His name was Surrey; but whether he was in the Army or the P. W. D., or the Commissariat, or the Police, or a factory, I don't remember. He wasn't a Civilian. He was just an ordinary man, of the light-colored variety, with a fair moustache and with the average amount of pay that comes between twenty-seven and thirty-two—from six to nine hundred a month.

He didn't dance, and he did what little riding he wanted to do by himself, and was busy in office all day, and never bothered his head about women. No man ever dreamed he would. He was of the type that doesn't marry, just because it doesn't think about marriage. He was one of the plain cards, whose only use is to make up the pack, and furnish background to put the Court cards against.

Then there was a girl—ordinary girl—the dark-colored variety—daughter of a man in the Army, who played a little, sang a little, talked a little, and furnished the background, exactly as Surrey did. She had been sent out here to get married if she could, because there were many sisters at Home, and Colonel's allowances aren't elastic. She lived with an Aunt. She was a Miss Tallaght, and men spelled her name "Tart" on the programmes when they couldn't catch what the introducer said.

Surrey and she were thrown together in the same Station one cold weather; and the particular Devil who looks after muddles prompted Miss Tallaght to fall in love with Surrey. He had spoken to her perhaps twenty times—certainly not more—but she fell as unreasonably in love with him as if she had been Elaine and he Lancelot.

She, of course, kept her own counsel; and, equally of course, her manner to Surrey, who never noticed manner or style or dress any more than he noticed a sunset, was icy, not to say repellent. The deadly dullness of Surrey struck her as reserve of force, and she grew to believe he was wonderfully clever in some secret and mysterious sort of line. She did not know what line; but she believed, and that was enough. No one suspected anything of any kind, for the simple reason that no one took any deep interest in Miss Tallaght except her Aunt; who wanted to get the girl off her hands.

This went on for some months, till a man suddenly woke up to the fact that Miss Tallaght was the one woman in the world for him, and told her so. She jawabed him—without rhyme or reason; and that night there followed one of those awful bedroom conferences that men know nothing about. Miss Tallaght's Aunt, querulous, indignant, and merciless, with her mouth full of hair-

pins, and her hands full of false hair-plaits, set herself to find out by cross-examination what in the name of everything wise, prudent, religious and dutiful, Miss Tallaght meant by jawabing her suitor. The conference lasted for an hour and a half, with question on question, insult and reminders of poverty—appeals to Providence, then a fresh mouthful of hairpins—then all the questions over again, beginning with:—"But what do you see to dislike in Mr. ——?" then, a vicious tug at what was left of the mane; then impressive warnings and more appeals to Heaven; and then the collapse of poor Miss Tallaght, a rumpled, crumpled, tear-stained arrangement in white on the couch at the foot of the bed, and, between sobs and gasps, the whole absurd little story of her love for Surrey.

Now, in all the forty-five years' experience of Miss Tallaght's Aunt, she had never heard of a girl throwing over a real genuine lover with an appointment, for a problematical, hypothetical lover, to whom she had spoken merely in the course of the ordinary social visiting rounds. So Miss Tallaght's Aunt was struck dumb, and, merely praying that Heaven might direct Miss Tallaght into a better frame of mind, dismissed the *ayah,* and went to bed; leaving Miss Tallaght to sob and moan herself to sleep.

Understand clearly, I don't for a moment defend Miss Tallaght. She was wrong — absurdly wrong — but attachments like hers must sprout by the law of averages, just to remind people that Love is as nakedly unreasoning as when Venus first gave him his kit and told him to run away and play.

Surrey must be held innocent—innocent as his own pony. Could he guess that, when Miss Tallaght was as curt and as unpleasing as she knew how, she would have risen up and followed him from Colombo to Dadar at a word? He didn't know anything, or care anything about Miss Tallaght. He had his work to do.

Miss Tallaght's Aunt might have respected her niece's secret. But she didn't. What we call "Talking rank scandal," she called "seeking advice"; and she sought advice on the case of Miss Tallaght, from the Judge's wife "in strict confidence, my dear," who told the Commissioner's wife, "of course you won't repeat it, my dear," who told the Deputy Commissioner's wife, "you understand it is to go no further, my dear," who told the newest bride, who was as delighted at being in possession of a secret concerning real grown-up men and women, that she told any one and every one who called on her. So the tale went all over the Station, and from being no one in particular, Miss Tallaght came to take precedence of the last interesting squabble between the Judge's wife and the Civil Engineer's wife. Then began a really interesting system of persecution worked by women—soft and sympathetic and intangible, but calculated to drive a girl off her head. They were all so sorry for Miss Tallaght, and they cooed together and were exaggeratedly kind and sweet in their manner to her, as those who said: "You may confide in us, my stricken deer!"

Miss Tallaght was a woman and sensitive. It took her less than one evening at the Band Stand to find that her poor little, precious little secret, that had been wrenched from her on the rack, was known as widely as if it had been written on her hat. I don't know what she went through. Women don't speak of these things, and men ought not to guess; but it must have been some specially refined torture, for she told her Aunt she would go Home and die as a Governess sooner than stay in this hateful—hateful—place. Her Aunt said she was a rebellious girl, and sent her Home to her people after a couple of months; and said no one knew what the pains of a chaperone's life were.

Poor Miss Tallaght had one pleasure just at the last. Half way down the line, she caught a glimpse of Surrey, who had gone down on duty, and was in the up-train. And he took off his hat to her. She went Home, and if she is not dead by this time must be living still.

* * * * * *

Months afterward, there was a lively dinner at the Club for the Races. Surrey was mooning about as usual, and there was a good deal of idle talk flying every way. Finally, one man, who had taken more than was good for him, said, *àpropos* of something about Surrey's reserved ways,—"Ah, you old fraud. It's all very well for you to pretend. I know a girl who was awf'ly mashed on you—once. Dead nuts she was on old Surrey. What had you been doing, eh?"

Surrey expected some sort of sell, and said with a laugh:

"Who was she?"

Before any one could kick the man, he plumped out with the name; and the Honorary Secretary tactfully upset the half of a big brew of shandy-gaff all over the table. After the mopping up, the men went out to the Lotteries.

But Surrey sat on, and, after ten minutes, said very humbly to the only other man in the deserted dining-room: "On your honor, was there a word of truth in what the drunken fool said?"

Then the man who is writing this story, who had known of the thing from the beginning, and now felt all the hopelessness and tangle of it—the waste and the muddle—said, a good deal more energetically than he meant:

"Truth! O man, man, couldn't you see it?"

Surrey said nothing, but sat still, smoking and smoking and thinking, while the Lottery tent babbled outside, and the *khitmutgars* turned down the lamps.

To the best of my knowledge and belief that was the first thing Surrey ever knew about love. But his awakening did not seem to delight him. It must have been rather unpleasant, to judge by the look on his face. He looked like a man who had missed a train and had been half stunned at the same time.

When the men came in from the Lotteries, Surrey went out. He wasn't in the mood for bones and "horse" talk. He went to his tent, and the last thing he said, quite aloud to himself, was: "I didn't see. I didn't see. If I had only known!"

Even if he had known I don't believe . . .

But these things are kismet, and we only find out all about them just when any knowledge is too late.

Haunted Subalterns

So long as the "Inextinguishables" confined themselves to running picnics, gymkhanas, flirtations and innocences of that kind, no one said anything. But when they ran ghosts, people put up their eyebrows. 'Man can't feel comfy with a regiment that entertains ghosts on its establishment. It is against General Orders. The "Inextinguishables" said that the ghosts were private and not Regimental property. They referred you to Tesser for particulars; and Tesser told you to go to—the hottest cantonment of all. He said that it was bad enough to have men making hay of his bedding and breaking his banjo-strings when he was out, without being chaffed

afterward; and he would thank you to keep your remarks on ghosts to yourself. This was before the "Inextinguishables" had sworn by their several lady loves that they were innocent of any intrusion into Tesser's quarters. Then Horrocks mentioned casually at Mess, that a couple of white figures had been bounding about his room the night before, and he didn't approve of it. The "Inextinguishables" denied, energetically, that they had had any hand in the manifestations, and advised Horrocks to consult Tesser.

I don't suppose that a Subaltern believes in anything except his chances of a Company; but Horrocks and Tesser were exceptions. They came to believe in their ghosts. They had reason.

Horrocks used to find himself, at about three o'clock in the morning staring wide-awake, watching two white Things hopping about his room and jumping up to the ceiling. Horrocks was of a placid turn of mind. After a week or so spent in watching his servants, and lying in wait for strangers, and trying to keep awake all night, he came to the conclusion that he was haunted, and that, consequently, he need not bother. He wasn't going to encourage these ghosts by being frightened of them. Therefore, when he awoke—as usual—with a start and saw these Things jumping like kangaroos, he only murmured: "Go on! Don't mind me!" and went to sleep again.

Tesser said: "It's all very well for you to make fun of your show. You can see your ghosts. Now I can't see mine, and I don't half like it."

Tesser used to come into his room of nights, and find the whole of his bedding neatly stripped, as if it had been done with one sweep of the hand, from the top right-hand corner of the charpoy to the bottom left-hand corner. Also his lamp used to lie weltering on the floor, and generally his pet screw-head, inlaid, nickel-plated banjo was lying on the charpoy, with all its strings broken. Tesser took away the strings on the occasion of the third manifestation, and the next night a man complimented him on his playing the best music ever got out of a banjo, for half an hour.

"Which half hour?" said Tesser.

"Between nine and ten," said the man. Tesser had gone out to dinner at 7:30 and had returned at midnight.

He talked to his bearer and threatened him with unspeakable things. The bearer was grey with fear: "I'm a poor man," said he. "If the *Sahib* is haunted by a Devil, what can I do?"

"Who says I'm haunted by a Devil?" howled Tesser, for he was angry.

"I have seen It," said the bearer, "at night, walking round and round your bed; and that is why everything is ulta-pulta in your room. I am a poor man, but I never go into your room alone. The bhisti comes with me."

Tesser was thoroughly savage at this, and he spoke to Horrocks, and the two laid traps to catch that Devil, and threatened their servants with dog-whips if any more "shaitan-ke-hanky-panky" took place. But the servants were soaked with fear, and it was no use adding to their tortures. When Tesser went out for a night, four of his men, as a rule, slept in the veranda of his quarters, until the banjo without the strings struck up, and then they fled.

One day, Tesser had to put in a month at a Fort with a detachment of "Inextinguishables." The Fort might have been Govindghar, Jumrood or Phillour; but it wasn't. He left Cantonments rejoicing, for his Devil was preying on his mind; and with him went another Subaltern, a junior. But the Devil came too. After Tesser had been in the Fort about ten days he went out to dinner. When he came back he found his Subaltern doing sentry on a banquette across the Fort Ditch, as far removed as might be from the Officers' Quarters.

"What's wrong?" said Tesser.

The Subaltern said, "Listen!" and the two, standing under the stars heard from the Officers' Quarters, high up in the wall of the Fort, the "strumty, tumty, tumty" of the banjo; which seemed to have an oratorio on hand.

"That performance," said the Subaltern, "has been going on for three mortal hours. I never wished to desert before, but I do now. I say, Tesser, old man, you are the best of good fellows, I'm sure, but . . . I say . . . look here, now, you are quite unfit to live with. 'Tisn't in my Commission, you know, that I'm to serve under a . . . a . . . man with Devils."

"Isn't it?" said Tesser. "If you make an ass of yourself I'll put you under arrest . . . and in my room!"

"You can put me where you please, but I'm not going to assist at these infernal concerts. 'Tisn't right. 'Tisn't natural. Look here, I don't want to hurt your feelings, but—try to think now—haven't you done something—committed some — murder that has slipped your memory—or forged something . . .?"

"Well! For an all-round, double-shotted, half-baked fool you are the . . ."

"I dare say I am," said the Subaltern. "But you don't expect me to keep my wits with that row going on, do you?"

The banjo was rattling away as if it had twenty strings. Tesser sent up a stone, and a shower of broken window-pane fell into the Fort Ditch; but the banjo kept on. Tesser hauled the other Subaltern up to the quarters, and found his room in frightful confusion—lamp upset, bedding all over the floor, chairs overturned and table tilted side-ways.

He took stock of the wreck and said despairingly: "Oh, this is lovely!"

The Subaltern was peeping in at the door.

"I'm glad you think so," he said. "'Tisn't lovely enough for me. I locked up your room directly after you had gone out. See here, I think you'd better apply for Horrocks to come out in my place. He's troubled with your complaint, and this business will make me a jabbering idiot if it goes on."

Tesser went to bed amid the wreckage, very angry, and next morning he rode into Cantonments and asked Horroks to arrange to relieve "that fool with me now."

"You've got 'em again, have you?" said Horrocks. "So've I. Three white figures this time. We'll worry through the entertainment together."

So Horrocks and Tesser settled down in the Fort together, and the "Inextinguishables" said pleasant things about "seven other Devils." Tesser didn't see where the joke came in. His room was thrown upside down three nights out of the seven. Horrocks was not troubled in any way, so his ghosts must have been purely local ones. Tesser, on the other hand, was personally haunted; for his Devil had moved with him from Cantonments to the Fort. Those two boys spent three parts of their time trying to find out who was responsible for the riot in Tesser's rooms. At the end of a fortnight they tried to find out what was responsible; and seven days later they gave it up as a bad job. Whatever It was, It refused to be caught; even when Tesser went out of the Fort ostentatiously, and Horrocks lay under Tesser's charpoy with a revolver. The servants were afraid—more afraid than ever—and all the evidence showed that they had been playing no tricks. As Tesser said to Horrocks: "A haunted Subaltern is a joke, but s'pose this keeps on. Just think what a haunted Colonel would be! And, look here—s'pose I marry! D' you s'pose a girl would live a week with me and this Devil?"

"I don't know," said Horrocks. "I haven't married often; but I knew a woman once who lived with her husband when he had D. T. He's dead now and I dare say she would marry you if you asked her. She isn't exactly a girl though, but she has a large experience of the other devils—the blue variety. She's a Government pensioner now, and you might write, y' know. Personally, if I hadn't suffered from ghosts of my own, I should rather avoid you."

"That's just the point," said Tesser. "This Devil will end in getting me bud-named, and you know I've lived on lemon-squashes and gone to bed at ten for weeks past."

"Tisn't that sort of Devil," said Horrocks. "It's either a first-class fraud for which some one ought to be killed or else you've offended one of these Indian Devils. It stands to reason that such a beastly country should be full of fiends of all sorts."

"But why should the creature fix on me," said Tesser, "and why don't he show himself and have it out like a—like a Devil?"

They were talking outside the Mess after dark, and, even as they spoke, they heard the banjo begin to play in Tesser's room, about twenty yards off.

Horrocks ran to his own quarters for a shotgun and a revolver, and Tesser and he crept up quietly, the banjo still playing, to Tesser's door.

"Now we've got It!" said Horrocks, as he threw the door open and let fly with the twelve-bore; Tesser squibbling off all six barrels into the dark, as hard as he could pull the trigger.

The furniture was ruined, and the whole Fort was awake; but that was all. No one had been killed and the banjo was lying on the disheveled bedclothes as usual.

Then Tesser sat down in the veranda, and used language that would have qualified him for the companionship of unlimited Devils. Horrocks said things too; but Tesser said the worst.

When the month in the Fort came to an end, both Horrocks and Tesser were glad. They held a final council of war, but came to no conclusion.

" 'Seems to me, your best plan would be to make your Devil stretch himself. Go down to Bombay with the time-expired men," said Horrocks. "If he really is a Devil, he'll come in the train with you."

" 'Tisn't good enough," said Tesser. "Bombay's no fit place to live in at this time of the year. But I'll put in for Depôt duty at the Hills." And he did.

Now here the tale rests. The Devil stayed below, and Tesser went up and was free. If I had invented this story, I should have put in a satisfactory ending—explained the manifestations as somebody's practical joke. My business being to keep facts, I can only say what I have said. The Devil may have been a hoax. If so, it was one of the best ever arranged. If it was not a hoax . . . but you must settle that for yourselves.

VOLUME V
Soldiers Three

The Incarnation of Krishna Mulvaney

Wohl auf, my bully cavaliers,
  We ride to church to-day,
The man that hasn't got a horse
  Must steal one straight away.

. . . . . .

Be reverent, men, remember
  This is a Gottes haus.
Du, Conran, cut along der aisle
  And schenck der whiskey aus.

Hans Breitmann's Ride to Church.

ONCE upon a time, very far from England, there lived three men who loved each other so greatly that neither man nor woman could come between them. They were in no sense refined, nor to be admitted to the outer-door mats of decent folk, because they happened to be private soldiers in Her Majesty's Army; and private soldiers of our service have small time for self-culture. Their duty is to keep themselves and their accoutrements speck-lessly clean, to refrain from getting drunk more often than is necessary, to obey their superiors, and to pray for a war. All these things my friends accomplished; and of their own motion threw in some fighting-work for which the Army Regulations did not call. Their fate sent them to serve in India, which is not a golden country, though poets have sung otherwise. There men die with great swiftness, and those who live suffer many and curious things. I do not think that my friends concerned themselves much with the social or political aspects of the East. They attended a not unimportant war on the northern frontier, another one on our western boundary, and a third in Upper Burma. Then their regiment sat still to recruit, and the boundless monotony of cantonment life was their portion. They were drilled morning and evening on the same dusty parade-ground. They wandered up and down the same stretch of dusty white road, attended the same church and the same grog-shop, and slept in the same lime-washed barn of a barrack for two long years. There was Mulvaney, the father in the craft, who had served with various regiments from Bermuda to Halifax, old in war, scarred, reckless, resourceful, and in his pious hours an unequalled soldier. To him turned for help and comfort six and a half feet of slow-moving, heavy-footed Yorkshiremen, born on the wolds, bred in the dales, and educated chiefly among the carriers' carts at the back of York railway-station. His name was Learoyd, and his chief virtue an unmitigated patience which helped him to win fights. How Ortheris, a fox-terrier of a Cockney, ever came to be one of the trio, is a mystery which even to-day I cannot explain. "There was always three av us," Mulvaney used to say. "An' by the grace av God, so long as our service lasts, three av us they'll always be. 'Tis bether so."

They desired no companionship beyond their own, and it was evil for any man of the regiment who attempted dispute with them. Physical argument was out of the question as regarded Mulvaney and the Yorkshiremen; and assault on Ortheris meant a combined attack from these twain—a business which no five men were anxious to have on their hands. Therefore they flourished, sharing their drinks, their tobacco, and their money; good luck and evil; battle and the chances of death; life and the chances of happiness from Calicut in southern, to Peshawur in northern India.

Through no merit of my own it was my good fortune to be in a measure admitted to their friendship—frankly by Mulvaney from the beginning, sullenly and with reluctance by Learoyd, and suspiciously by Ortheris, who held to it that no man not in the Army could fraternize with a red-coat. "Like to like," said he. "I'm a bloomin' sodger—he's a bloomin' civilian. 'Taint natural—that's all.

But that was not all. They thawed progressively, and in the thawing told me more of their lives and adventures than I am ever likely to write.

Omitting all else, this tale begins with the Lamentable Thirst that was at the beginning of First Causes. Never was such a thirst—Mulvaney told me so They kicked against their compulsory virtue, but the attempt was only successful in the case of Ortheris. He, whose talents were many, went forth into the highways and stole a dog from a "civilian"—*videlicet*, some one, he knew not who, not in the Army. Now that civilian was but newly connected by marriage with the colonel of the regiment, and outcry was made from quarters least anticipated by Ortheris, and,

in the end, he was forced, lest a worse thing should happen, to dispose at ridiculously unremunerative rates of as promising a small terrier as ever graced one end of a leading string. The purchase-money was barely sufficient for one small outbreak which led him to the guard-room. He escaped, however, with nothing worse than a severe reprimand, and a few hours of punishment drill. Not for nothing had he acquired the reputation of being "the best soldier of his inches" in the regiment. Mulvaney had taught personal cleanliness and efficiency as the first articles of his companions' creed. "A dhirty man," he was used to say, in the speech of his kind, "goes to Clink for a weakness in the knees, an' is coort-martialled for a pair av socks missin'; but a clane man, such as is an ornament to his service—a man whose buttons are gold, whose coat is wax upon him, an' whose 'coutrements are widout a speck—*that* man may, spakin' in reason, do fwhat he likes an' dhrink from day to divil. That's the pride av bein' dacint."

We sat together, upon a day, in the shade of a ravine far from the barracks, where a water-course used to run in rainy weather. Behind us was the scrub jungle, in which jackals, peacocks, the grey wolves of the Northwestern Provinces, and occasionally a tiger estrayed from Central India, were supposed to dwell. In front lay the cantonment, glaring white under a glaring sun; and on either side ran the broad road that led to Delhi.

It was the scrub that suggested to my mind the wisdom of Mulvaney taking a day's leave and going upon a shooting-tour. The peacock is a holy bird through-

out India, and he who slays one is in
danger of being mobbed by the nearest
villagers; but on the last occasion that
Mulvaney had gone forth, he had contrived, without in the least offending
local religious susceptibilities, to return
with six beautiful peacock skins which
he sold to profit. It seemed just possible then—

"But fwhat manner av use is ut to
me goin' out widout a dhrink? The
ground's powdherdhry underfoot, an' ut
gets unto the throat fit to kill," wailed
Mulvaney, looking at me reproachfully.
"An' a peacock is not a bird you can
catch the tail av onless ye run. Can a
man run on wather—an' jungle-wather
too?"

Ortheris had considered the question
in all its bearings. He spoke, chewing
his pipe-stem meditatively the while:

"Go forth, return in glory,
  To Clusium's royal 'ome:
An' round these bloomin' temples 'ang
  The bloomin' shields o' Rome.

You better go. You ain't like to shoot
yourself—not while there's a chanst of
liquor. Me an' Learoyd'll stay at 'ome
an' keep shop—'case o' anythin' turnin'
up. But you go out with a gas-pipe
gun an' ketch the little peaockses or
somethin'. You kin get one day's leave
easy as winkin'. Go along an' get it,
an' get peacockses or somethin'."

"Jock," said Mulvaney, turning to
Learoyd, who was half asleep under the
shadow of the bank. He roused slowly.

"Sitha, Mulvaney, go," said he.

And Mulvaney went; cursing his allies
with Irish fluency and barrack-room
point.

"Take note," said he, when he had

won his holiday, and appeared dressed
in his roughest clothes with the only
other regimental fowling piece in his
hand. "Take note, Jock, an' you Orth'ris,
I am goin' in the face av my own will—
all for to please you. I misdoubt anythin' will come av permiscuous huntin'
afther peacockses in a desolit lan'; an'
I know that I will lie down an' die wid
th'rrrst. Me catch peacockses for you,
ye lazy scutts—an' be sacrificed by the
peasanthry—Ugh!"

He waved a huge paw and went
away.

At twilight, long before the appointed
hour, he returned empty-handed, much
begrimed with dirt.

"Peacockses?" queried Ortheris from
the safe rest of a barrack-room table
whereon he was smoking cross-legged,
Learoyd fast asleep on a bench.

"Jock," said Mulvaney, without answering, as he stirred up the sleeper.
"Jock, can ye fight? Will ye fight?"

Very slowly the meaning of the words
communicated itself to the half-roused
man. He understood—and again—what
might these things mean? Mulvaney
was shaking him savagely. Meantime
the men in the room howled with delight. There was war in the confederacy
at last—war and the breaking of bonds.

Barrack-room etiquette is stringent.
On the direct challenge must follow the
direct reply. This is more binding than
the ties of tried friendship. Once again
Mulvaney repeated the question. Learoyd answered by the only means in his
power, and so swiftly that the Irishman
had barely time to avoid the blow. The
laughter around increased. Learoyd
looked bewilderingly at his friend—himself as greatly bewildered. Ortheris

dropped from the table because his world was falling.

"Come outside," said Mulvaney, and as the occupants of the barrack-room prepared joyously to follow, he turned and said furiously, "There will be no fight this night—onless any wan av you is wishful to assist. The man that does, follows on."

No man moved. The three passed out into the moonlight, Learoyd fumbling with the buttons of his coat. The parade-ground was deserted except for the scurrying jackals. Mulvaney's impetuous rush carried his companions far into the open ere Learoyd attempted to turn round and continue the discussion.

"Be still now. 'Twas my fault for beginnin' things in the middle av an end, Jock. I should ha' comminst wid an explanation; but Jock, dear, on your sowl are ye fit, think you, for the finest fight that iver was—betther than fightin' me? Considher before ye answer."

More than ever puzzled, Learoyd turned round two or three times, felt an arm, kicked tentatively, and answered, "Ah'm fit." He was accustomed to fight blindly at the bidding of the superior mind.

They sat them down, the men looking on from afar, and Mulvaney untangled himself in mighty words.

"Followin' your fools' scheme I wint out into the thrackless desert beyond the barricks. An' there I met a pious Hindu dhriving a bullock-kyart. I tuk ut for granted he wud be delighted for to convoy me a piece, an' I jumped in"—

"You long, lazy, black-haired swine," drawled Otheris, who would have done the same thing under similar circumstances.

" 'Twas the height av policy. That naygur-man dhruv miles an' miles—as far as the new railway line they're buildin' now back av the Tavi river. ' 'Tis a kyart for dhirt only,' saye he now an' again timoreously, to get me out av ut. 'Dhirt I am,' sez I, 'an' the dhryest that you iver kyarted. Dhrive on, me son, an' glory be wid you.' At that I wint to slape, an' took no heed till he pulled up on the embankmint av the line where the coolies were pilin' mud. There was a matther av two thousand coolies on that line—you remimber that. Prisintly a bell rang, an' they throops off to a big pay-shed. 'Where's the white man in charge?' sez I to my kyart-dhriver. 'In the shed,' sez he, 'engaged on a riffle.'—'A fwhat?' sez I. 'Riffle,' sez he. 'You take ticket. He take money. You get nothin'.'—'Oho!' sez I, 'that's fwhat the shuperior an' cultivated man calls a raffle, me misbeguided child av darkness an' sin. Lead on to that raffle, though fwhat the mischief 'tis doin' so far away from uts home—which is the charity-bazar at Christmas, an' the colonel's wife grinnin' behind the tea-table—'s more than I know.' Wid that I wint to the shed an' found 'twas payday among the coolies. Their wages was on a table forninst a big, fine, red buk av a man—sivun fut high, four fut wide, an' three fut thick, wid a fist on him like a corn-sack. He was payin' the coolies fair an' easy, but he wud ask each man if he wud raffle that month, an' each man sez, 'Yes,' av course. Thin he wud deduct from their wages accordin'. Whin all was paid, he filled an ould cigar-box full av gun-wads an' scatthered ut among the coolies. They did not take much joy av that performince, an' small wondher. A man close to me picks up a black gun-wad an' sings out, 'I have ut.'—'Good may ut do you,' sez I. The coolie wint forward to this big, fine, red man, who threw a cloth off av the most sumpshus, jooled enamelled an' variously bedivilled sedanchair I iver saw."

"Sedan-chair! Put your 'ead in a bag. That was a palanquin. Don't yer know a palanquin when you see it?" said Ortheris with great scorn.

"I chuse to call ut sedan chair, an' chair ut shall be, little man," continued the Irishman. " 'Twas a most amazin' chair—all lined wid pink silk an' fitted wid red silk curtains. 'Here ut is,' sez the red man. 'Here ut is,' sez the coolie, an' he grinned weakly-ways. 'Is ut any use to you?' sez the red man. 'No,' sez the coolie; 'I'd like to make a presint av ut to you.'—'I am graciously pleased to accept that same,' sez the red man; an' at that all the coolies cried aloud in fwhat was mint for cheerful notes, an' wint back to their diggin', lavin' me alone in the shed. The red man saw me, an' his face grew blue on his big, fat neck. 'Fwhat d'you want here?' sez he. 'Standin'-room an' no more,' sez I, 'onless it may be fwhat ye niver had, an' that's manners, ye rafflin' ruffian,' for I was not goin' to have the Service throd upon. 'Out of this,' sez he. 'I'm in charge av this section av construction.'—'I'm in charge av mesilf,' sez I, 'an' it's like I will stay a while. D'ye raffle much in these parts?'—'Fwhat's that to you?' sez he. 'Nothin',' sez I, 'but a great dale to you, for begad I'm thinkin' you get the full half av your

revenue from that sedan-chair. Is ut always raffled so?' I sez, an' wid that I wint to a coolie to ask questions. Bhoys, that man's name is Dearsley, an' he's been rafflin' that ould sedan-chair monthly this matther av nine months. Ivry coolie on the section takes a ticket —or he gives 'em the go—wanst a month on pay-day. Ivry coolie that wins ut gives ut back to him, for 'tis too big to carry away, an' he'd sack the man that thried to sell ut. That Dearsley has been makin' the rowlin' wealth av Roshus by nefarious rafflin'. Think av the burnin' shame to the sufferin' coolieman that the army in Injia are bound to protect an' nourish in their bosoms! Two thousand coolies defrauded wanst a month!"

"Dom t' coolies. Has't gotten t' cheer, man?" said Learoyd.

"Hould on. Havin' onearthed this amazin' an' stupenjus fraud committed by the man Dearsley, I hild a council av war; he thryin' all the time to sejuce me into a fight wid opprobrious language. That sedan-chair niver belonged by right to any foreman av coolies. 'Tis a king's chair or a quane's. There's gold on ut an' silk an' all manner av trapesemints. Bhoys, 'tis not for me to countenance any sort av wrong-doin' —me bein' the ould man—but—anyway he has had ut nine months, an' he dare not make throuble av ut was taken from him. Five miles away, or ut may be six"—

There was a long pause, and the jackals howled merrily. Learoyd bared one arm, and contemplated it in the moonlight. Then he nodded partly to himself and partly to his friends. Ortheris wriggled with suppressed emotion.

"I thought ye wud see the reasonableness av ut," said Mulvaney. "I make bould to say as much to the man before. He was for a direct front attack—fut, horse, an' guns—an' all for nothin', seein' that I had no thransport to convey the machine away. 'I will not argue wid you,' sez I, 'this day, but subsequintly, Mister Dearsley, me rafflin, jool, we talk ut out lengthways. 'Tis no good policy to swindle the naygur av his hard-earned emolumints, an' by presint informashin' '—'twas the kyart man that tould me—'ye've been perpethrating that same for nine months. But I'm a just man,' sez I, 'an' over-lookin' the presumpshin that yondher settee wid the gilt top was not come by honust'—at that he turned sky-green, so I knew things was more thrue than tellable—'not come by honust, I'm willin' to compound the felony for this month's winnin's.' "

"Ah! Ho!" from Learoyd and Ortheris.

"That man Dearsley's rushin' on his fate," continued Mulvaney, solemnly wagging his head. "All Hell had no name for me that tide. Faith, he called me a robber! Me! that was savin' him from continuin' in his evil ways widout a remonstrince—an' to a man av conscience a remonstrince may change the chune av his life. ' 'Tis not for me to argue,' sez I, 'fwhatever ye are, Mister Dearsley, but, by my hand, I'll take away the temptation for you that lies in that sedan-chair.'—'You will have to fight me for ut,' sez he, 'for well I know you will never dare make report to any one.'—'Fight I will,' sez I, 'but not this day, for I'm rejuced for want av nourishment.'—'Ye're an ould bould hand,'

sez he, sizin' me up an' down; 'an' a jool av a fight we will have. Eat now an' dhrink, an' go your way.' Wid that he gave me some hump an' whisky—good whisky—an' we talked av this an' that the while. 'It goes hard on me now,' sez I, wipin' my mouth, 'to confiscate that piece av furniture, but justice is justice.'—'Ye've not got ut yet,' sez he; 'there's the fight between.'—'There is,' sez I, 'an' a good fight. Ye shall have the pick av the best quality in my rigimint for the dinner you have given this day.' Thin I came hot-foot to you two. Hould your tongue, the both. 'Tis this way. To-morrow we three will go there an' he shall have his pick betune me an' Jock. Jock's a deceivin' fighter, for he is all fat to the eye, an' he moves slow. Now I'm all beef to the look, an' I move quick. By my reckonin' the Dearsley man won't take me; so me an' Orth'ris see fair play. Jock, I tell you, 'twill be big fightin'—whipped, wid the cream above the jam. After the business 'twill take a good three av us—Jock'll be very hurt—to haul away that sedan-chair."

"Palanquin." This from Ortheris.

"Fwhatever ut is, we must have ut. 'Tis the only sellin' piece av property widin reach that we can get so cheap. An' fwhat's a fight afther all? He has robbed the naygur-man, dishonust. We rob him honust for the sake av the whisky he gave me."

"But wot'll we do with the bloomin' article when we've got it? Them palanquins are as big as 'ouses, an' uncommon 'ard to sell, as McCleary said when ye stole the sentry-box from the Curragh."

"Who's goin' to do t' fightin'?" said

Learoyd, and Ortheris subsided. The three returned to barracks without a word. Mulvaney's last argument clinched the matter. This palanquin was property, vendible, and to be attained in the simplest and least embarrassing fashion. It would eventually become beer. Great was Mulvaney.

Next afternoon a procession of three formed itself and disappeared into the scrub in the direction of the new railway line. Learoyd alone was without care, for Mulvaney dived darkly into the future, and little Ortheris feared the unknown. What befell at that interview in the lonely pay-shed by the side of the half-built embankment, only a few hundred coolies know, and their tale is a confusing one, running thus—

"We were at work. Three men in red coats came. They saw the Sahib—Dearsley Sahib. They made oration; and noticeably the small man among the red-coats. Dearsley Sahib also made oration, and used many very strong words. Upon this talk they departed together to an open space, and there the fat man in the red coat fought with Dearsley Sahib after the custom of white men—with his hands, making no noise, and never at all pulling Dearsley Sahib's hair. Such of us as were not afraid beheld these things for just so long a time as a man needs to cook the midday meal. The small man in the red coat had possessed himself of Dearsley Sahib's watch. No, he did not steal that watch. He held it in his hand, and at certain seasons made outcry, and the twain ceased their combat, which was like the combat of young bulls in spring. Both men were soon all red, but Dearsley Sahib was much more red than the other. Seeing this, and fearing for his life—because we greatly loved him—some fifty of us made shift to rush upon the red-coats. But a certain man—very black as to the hair, and in no way to be confused with the small man, or the fat man who fought—that man, we affirm, ran upon us, and of us he embraced some ten or fifty in both arms, and beat our heads together, so that our livers turned to water, and we ran away. It is not good to interfere in the fightings of white men. After that Dearsley Sahib fell and did not rise, these men jumped upon his stomach and despoiled him of all his money, and attempted to fire the pay-shed, and departed. Is it true that Dearsley Sahib makes no complaint of these latter things having been done? We were senseless with fear, and do not at all remember. There was no palanquin near the pay-shed. What do we know about palanquins? Is it true that Dearsley Sahib does not return to this place, on account of his sickness, for ten days? This is the fault of those bad men in the red coats, who should be severely punished; for Dearsley Sahib is both our father and mother, and we love him much. Yet, if Dearsley Sahib does not return to this place at all, we will speak the truth. There was a palanquin, for the up-keep of which we were forced to pay nine-tenths of our monthly wage. On such mulctings Dearsley Sahib allowed us to make obeisance to him before the palanquin. What could we do? We were poor men. He took a full half of our wages. Will the Government repay us those moneys? Those three men in red coats bore the palanquin upon their shoulders and departed.

All the money that Dearsley Sahib had taken from us was in the cushions of that palanquin. Therefore they stole it. Thousands of rupees were there—all our money. It was our bank-box, to fill which we cheerfully contributed to Dearsley Sahib three-sevenths of our monthly wage. Why does the white man look upon us with the eye of disfavor? Before God, there was a palanquin, and now there is no palanquin; and if they send the police here to make inquisition, we can only say that there never has been any palanquin. Why should a palanquin be near these works? We are poor men, and we know nothing."

Such is the simplest version of the simplest story connected with the descent upon Dearsley. From the lips of the coolies I received it. Dearsley himself was in no condition to say anything, and Mulvaney preserved a massive silence, broken only by the occasional licking of the lips. He had seen a fight so gorgeous that even his power of speech was taken from him. I respected that reserve until, three days after the affair, I discovered in a disused stable in my quarters a palanquin of unchastened splendor—evidently in past days the litter of a queen. The pole whereby it swung between the shoulders of the bearers was rich with the painted *papier-maché* of Cashmere. The shoulder-pads were of yellow silk. The panels of the litter itself were ablaze with the loves of all the gods and goddesses of the Hindu Pantheon— lacquer on cedar. The cedar sliding doors were fitted with hasps of translucent Jaipur enamel and ran in grooves shod with silver. The cushions were of brocaded Delhi silk, and the curtains which once hid any glimpse of the beauty of the king's palace were stiff with gold. Closer investigation showed that the entire fabric was everywhere rubbed and discolored by time and wear; but even thus it was sufficiently gorgeous to deserve housing on the threshold of a royal zezana. I found no fault with it, except that it was in my stable. Then, trying to lift it by the silver-shod shoulder-pole, I laughed. The road from Dearsley's pay-shed to the cantonment was a narrow and uneven one, and, traversed by three very inexperienced palanquin-bearers, one of whom was sorely battered about the head, must have been a path of torment. Still I did not quite recognize the right of the three musketeers to turn me into a "fence" for stolen property.

"I'm askin' you to warehouse ut," said Mulvaney when he was brought to consider the question. "There's no steal in ut. Dearsley tould us we cud have ut if we fought. Jock fought—an', oh, sorr, when the throuble was at uts finest an' Jock was bleedin' like a stuck pig, an' little Orth'ris was shquelin' on one leg chewin' big bites out av Dearsley's watch, I wud ha' given my place at the fight to have had you see wan round. He tuk Jock, as I suspicioned he would, an' Jock was deceptive. Nine roun's they were even matched, an' at the tenth—About that palanquin now. There's not the least throuble in the world, or we wud not ha' brought ut here. You will ondherstand that the Queen—God bless her!—does not reckon for a privit soldier to kape elephints an' palanquins an' sich in barricks. Afther we had dhragged ut down from Dearsley's through that cruel scrub that near broke Orth'ris's heart, we set ut in the ravine for a night; an' a thief av a porcupine an' a civet-cat av a jackal roosted in ut, as well we knew in the mornin'. I put ut to you, sorr, is an elegint palanquin, fit for the princess, the natural abidin' place av all the vermin in cantonmints? We brought ut to you, afther dark, and put ut in your shtable. Do not let your conscience prick. Think av the rejoicin' men in the pay-shed yonder—lookin' at Dearsley wid his head tied up in a towel—an' well knowin' that they can dhraw their pay ivry month widout stoppages for riffles. Indirectly, sorr, you have rescued from an onprincipled son av a tight-hawk the peasanthry av a numerous village. An' besides, will I let that sedan-chair rot on our hands? Not I. 'Tis not every day a piece av pure joolry comes into the market. There's not a king widin these forty miles"—he 'vaved his hand round the dusty horizon —"not a king wud not be glad to buy ut. Some day meself, whin I have leisure, I'll take ut up along the road an' dishpose av ut."

"How?" said I, for I knew the man was capable of anything.

"Get into ut, av coorse, and keep wan eye open through the curtains. Whin I see a likely man av the native persuasion, I will descind blushin' from my canopy and say, 'Buy a palanquin, ye black scutt?' I will have to hire four men to carry me first, though; and that's impossible till next pay-day."

Curiously enough, Learoyd, who had fought for the prize, and in the winning secured the highest pleasure life had to offer him, was altogether disposed to undervalue it, while Ortheris openly said

it would be better to break the thing up. Dearsley, he argued, might be a many-sided man, capable, despite his magnificent fighting qualities, of setting in motion the machinery of the civil law—a thing much abhorred by the soldier. Under any circumstances their fun had come and passed; the next pay-day was close at hand, when there would be beer for all. Wherefore longer conserve the painted palanquin?

"A first-class rifle-shot an' a good little man av your inches you are," said Mulvaney. "But you niver had a head worth a soft-boiled egg. 'Tis me has to lie awake av nights schamin' an' plottin' for the three av us. Orth'ris, me son, 'tis no matther av a few gallons av beer —no, nor twenty gallons—but tubs an' vats an' firkins in that sedan-chair. Who ut was, an' what ut was, an' how ut got there, we do not know; but I know in my bones that you an' me an' Jock wid his sprained thumb will get a fortune thereby. Lave me alone, an' let me think."

Meantime the palanquin stayed in my stall, the key of which was in Mulvaney's hands.

Pay-day came, and with it beer. It was not in experience to hope that Mulvaney, dried by four weeks' drought, would avoid excess. Next morning he and the palanquin had disappeared. He had taken the precaution of getting three days' leave "to see a friend on the railway," and the colonel, well knowing that the seasonal outburst was near, and hoping it would spend its force beyond the limits of his jurisdiction, cheerfully gave him all he demanded. At this point Mulvaney's history, as recorded in the mess-room, stopped.

Ortheris carried it not much further. "No, 'e wasn't drunk," said the little man loyally, "the liquor was no more than feelin' its way round inside of 'im; but 'e went an' filled that 'ole bloomin' palanquin with bottles 'fore 'e went off. 'E's gone an' 'ired six men to carry 'im, an' I 'ad to 'elp 'im into 'is nupshal couch, 'cause 'e wouldn't 'ear reason. 'E's gone off in 'is shirt an' trousies, swearin' tremenjus—gone down the road in the palanquin, wavin' 'is legs out 'o windy."

"Yes," said I, "but where?"

"Now you arx me a question. 'E said 'e was goin' to sell that palanquin, but from observations what happened when I was stuffin' 'im through the door, I fancy 'e's gone to the new embankment to mock at Dearsley. 'Soon as Jock's off duty I'm goin' there to see if 'e's safe—not Mulvaney, but t'other man. My saints, but I pity 'im as 'elps Terence out o' the palanquin when 'e's once fair drunk!"

"He'll come back without harm," I said.

"'Corse 'e will. On'y question is, what'll 'e be doin' on the road? Killing Dearsley, like as not. 'E shouldn't 'a gone without Jock or me."

Reinforced by Learoyd, Ortheris sought the foreman of the coolie-gang. Dearsley's head was still embellished with towels. Mulvaney, drunk or sober, would have struck no man in that condition, and Dearsley indignantly denied that he would have taken advantage of the intoxicated brave.

"I had my pick o' you two," he explained to Learoyd, "and you got my palanquin—not before I'd made my profit on it. Why'd I do harm when everything's settled? Your man *did*

come here—drunk as Davy's sow on a frosty night—came a-purpose to mock me—stuck his head out of the door an' called me a crucified hodman. I made him drunker, an' sent him along. But I never touched him."

To these things Learoyd, slow to perceive the evidences of sincerity, answered only, "if owt comes to Mulvaney 'long o' you, I'll gripple you, clouts or no clouts on your ugly head, an' I'll draw t' throat twistyways, man. See there now."

The embassy removed itself, and Dearsley, the battered, laughed alone over his supper that evening.

Three days passed—a fourth and a fifth. The week drew to a close and Mulvaney did not return. He, his royal palanquin, and his six attendants, had vanished into air. A very large and very tipsy soldier, his feet sticking out of the litter of a reigning princess, is not a thing to travel along the ways without comment. Yet no man of all the country round had seen any such wonder. He was, and he was not; and Learoyd suggested the immediate smashment of Dearsley as a sacrifice to his ghost. Ortheris insisted that all was well, and in the light of past experience his hopes seemed reasonable.

"When Mulvaney goes up the road," said he, "'e's like to go a very long ways up, specially when 'e's so blue drunk as 'e is now. But what gits me is 'is not bein' 'eard of pullin' wool off the niggers somewheres about. That don't look good. The drink must ha' died out in 'im by this, unless 'e's broke a bank, an' then—Why don't e' come back? 'E didn't ought to ha' gone off without us."

Even Ortheris's heart sank at the end of the seventh day, for half the regiment were out scouring the countryside, and Learoyd had been forced to fight two men who hinted openly that Mulvaney had deserted. To do him justice, the colonel laughed at the notion, even when it was put forward by his much-trusted adjutant.

"Mulvaney would as soon think of deserting as you would," said he. "No; he's either fallen into a mischief among the villagers—and yet that isn't likely, for he'd blarney himself out of the Pit; or else he is engaged on urgent private affairs—some stupendous devilment that we shall hear of at mess after it has been the round of the barrack-rooms. The worst of it is that I shall have to give him twenty-eight days' confinement at least for being absent without leave, just when I most want him to lick the new batch of recruits into shape. I never knew a man who could put a polish on young soldiers as quickly as Mulvaney can. How does he do it?"

"With blarney and the buckle-end of a belt, sir," said the adjutant. "He is worth a couple of non-commissioned officers when we are dealing with an Irish draft, and the London lads seem to adore him. The worst of it is that if he goes to the cells the other two are neither to hold nor to bind till he comes out again. I believe Ortheris preaches mutiny on those occasions, and I know that the mere presence of Learoyd mourning for Mulvaney kills all the cheerfulness of his room. The sergeants tell me that he allows no man to laugh when he feels unhappy. They are a queer gang."

"For all that, I wish we had a few more of them. I like a well-conducted regiment, but these pasty-faced, shifty-eyed, mealy-mouthed young slouchers from the depot worry me sometimes with their offensive virtue. They don't seem to have backbone enough to do anything but play cards and prowl round the married quarters. I believe I'd forgive that old villain on the spot if he turned up with any sort of explanation that I could in decency accept."

"Not likely to be much difficulty about that, sir," said the adjutant. "Mulvaney's explanations are only one degree less wonderful than his performances. They say that when he was in the Black Tyrone, before he came to us, he was discovered on the banks of the Liffey trying to sell his colonel's charger to a Donegal dealer as a perfect lady's hack. Shackbolt commanded the Tyrone then."

"Shackbolt must have had apoplexy at the thought of his ramping war-horses answering to that description. He used to buy unbacked devils, and tame them on some pet theory of starvation. What did Mulvaney say?"

"That he was a member of the Society for the Prevention of Cruelty to Animals, anxious to 'sell the poor baste where he would get something to fill out his dimples.' Shackbolt laughed, but I fancy that was why Mulvaney exchanged to ours."

"I wish he were back," said the colonel; "for I like him and believe he likes me."

That evening, to cheer our souls, Learoyd, Ortheris, and I went into the waste to smoke out a porcupine. All the dogs attended, but even their clamor—and they began to discuss the shortcomings of porcupines before they left can-

tonments—could not take us out of ourselves. A large, low moon turned the
tops of the plume-grass to silver, and
the stunted camelthorn bushes and sour
tamarisks into the likenesses of trooping devils. The smell of the sun had
not left the earth, and little aimless
winds blowing across the rose-gardens to
the southward brought the scent of dried
roses and water. Our fire once started,
and the dogs craftily disposed to wait
the dash of the porcupine, we climbed
to the top of a rain-scarred hillock of
earth, and looked across the scrub
seamed with cattle paths, white with the
long grass, and dotted with spots of
level pond-bottom, where the snipe
would gather in winter.

"This," said Ortheris, with a sigh, as
he took in the unkempt desolation of
it all, "this is sanguinary. This is unusually sanguinary. Sort o' mad
country. Like a grate when the fire's
put out by the sun." He shaded his
eyes against the moonlight. "An' there's
a loony dancin' in the middle of it all.
Quite right. I'd dance too if I wasn't
so downheart."

There pranced a Portent in the face
of the moon—a huge and ragged spirit
of the waste, that flapped its wings from
afar. It had risen out of the earth; it
was coming toward us, and its outline
was never twice the same. The toga,
table-cloth, or dressing-gown, whatever
the creature wore, took a hundred
shapes. Once it stopped on a neighbor-
ing mound and flung all its legs and
arms to the winds.

"My, but that scarecrow 'as got 'em
bad!" said Ortheris. "Seems like if 'e
comes any furder we'll 'ave to argify
with 'im."

Learoyd raised himself from the dirt
as a bull clears his flanks of the wallow.
And as a bull bellows, so he, after a
short minute at gaze, gave tongue to the
stars.

"MULVAANEY! MULVAANEY! A-hoo!"

Oh then it was that we yelled, and
the figure dipped into the hollow, till,
with a crash of rending grass, the lost
one strode up to the light of the fire,
and disappeared to the waist in a wave
of joyous dogs! Then Learoyd and Ortheris gave greeting, bass and falsetto
together, both swallowing a lump in the
throat.

"You damned fool!" said they, and
severally pounded him with their fists.

"Go easy!" he answered; wrapping a
huge arm around each. "I would have
you to know that I am a god, to be
treated as such—tho', by my faith, I
fancy I've got to go to the guardroom
just like a privit soldier."

The latter part of the sentence destroyed the suspicions raised by the
former. Any one would have been justified in regarding Mulvaney as mad.
He was hatless and shoeless, and his
shirt and trousers were dropping off
him. But he wore one wondrous garment—a gigantic cloak that fell from
collar-bone to heel—of pale pink silk,
wrought all over in cunningest needle-
work of hands long since dead, with the
loves of the Hindu gods. The monstrous
figures leaped in and out of the light
of the fire as he settled the folds round
him.

Ortheris handled the stuff respectfully
for a moment while I was trying to remember where I had seen it before.
Then he screamed, "What 'ave you done

with the palanquin? You're wearin' the linin'."

"I am," said the Irishman, "an' by the same token the 'broidery is scrapin' my hide off. I've lived in this sumpshus counterpane for four days. Me son, I begin to ondherstand why the naygur is no use. Widout me boots, an' me trousies like an openwork stocking on a gyurl's leg at a dance, I begin to feel like a naygur-man—all fearful an' timerous. Give me a pipe an' I'll tell on."

He lit a pipe, resumed his grip of his two friends, and rocked to and fro in a gale of laughter.

"Mulvaney," said Ortheris sternly, " 'tain't no time for laughin'. You've given Jock an' me more trouble than you're worth. You 'ave been absent without leave an' you'll go into cells for that; an' you 'ave come back disgustin'ly dressed an' most improper in the linin' o' that bloomin' palanquin. Instid of which you laugh. An' we thought you was dead all the time."

"Bhoys," said the culprit, still shaking gently, "whin I've done my tale you may cry if you like, an' little Orth'ris here can thrample my inside out. Ha' done an' listen. My performances have been stupenjus: my luck has been the blessed luck av the British Army—an' there's no betther than that. I went out dhrunk an' dhrinkin' in the palanquin, and I have come back a pink god. Did any of you go to Dearsley afther my time was up? He was at the bottom of ut all."

"Ah said so," murmured Learoyd. "Tomorrow ah'll smash t' face in upon his heead."

"Ye will not. Dearsley's a jool av a man. Afther Ortheris had put me into

the palanquin an' the six bearer-men were gruntin' down the road, I tuk thought to mock Dearsley for that fight. So I tould thim, 'Go to the embankmint,' and there, bein' most amazin' full, I shtuck my head out av the concern an' passed compliments wid Dearsley. I must ha' miscalled him outrageous, for whin I am that way the power av the tongue comes on me. I can bare remimber tellin' him that his mouth opened endways like the mouth av a skate, which was thrue afther Learoyd had handled ut; an' I clear remimber his takin' no manner nor matter av offence, but givin' me a big dhrink of beer. 'Twas the beer did the thrick, for I crawled back into the palanquin, steppin' on me right ear wid me left foot, an' thin I slept like the dead. Wanst I half-roused, an' begad the noise in my head was tremenjus—roarin' and rattlin' an' poundin', such as was quite new to me. 'Mother av Mercy,' thinks I, 'phwat a concertina I will have on my shoulders whin I wake!' An' wid that I curls mysilf up to sleep before ut should get hould on me. Bhoys, that noise was not dhrink, 'twas the rattle av a thrain!"

There followed an impressive pause.

"Yes, he had put me on a thrain—put me, palanquin, an' all, an' six black assassins av his own coolies that was in his nefarious confidence, on the flat av a ballast-thruck and we were rowlin' an' bowlin' along to Benares. Glory be that I did not wake up thin an' introjuce mysilf to the coolies. As I was sayin', I slept for the betther part of a day an' a night. But remimber you, that that man Dearsley had packed me off on wan av his material-thrains to

Benares, all for to make me overstay my leave an' get me into the cells."

The explanation was an eminently rational one. Benares lay at least ten hours by rail from the cantonments, and nothing in the world could have saved Mulvaney from arrest as a deserter had he appeared there in the apparel of his orgies. Dearsley had not forgotten to take his revenge. Learoyd, drawing back a little, began to place soft blows over selected portions of Mulvaney's body. His thoughts were away on the embankment, and they meditated evil for Dearsley. Mulvaney continued—

"Whin I was full awake the palanquin was set down in a street, I suspicioned, for I cud hear people passin' an' talkin'. But I knew well I was far from home. There is a queer smell upon our cantonments—a smell av cavalry stable-litter. This place smelt marigold flowers an' bad water, an' wanst somethin' alive came an' blew heavy with his muzzle at the chink av the shutter. 'It's in a village I am,' thinks I to myself, 'an' the parochial buffalo is investigatin' the palanquin.' But anyways I had no desire to move. Only lie still whin you're in foreign parts an' the standin' luck av the British Army will carry ye through. That is an epigram. I made ut."

"Thin a lot av whishperin' divils surrounded the palanquin. 'Take ut up,' sez wan man. 'But who'll pay us?' sez another. 'The Maharanee's minister, av coorse,' sez the man. 'Oho!' sez I to mysilf, 'I'm a quane in me own right, wid a minister to pay me expenses. I'll be an emperor if I lie still long enough; but this is no village I've found.' I lay quiet, but I gummed me right eye to a crack av the shutters, an' I saw that the whole street was crammed wid palanquins an' horses, an' a sprinklin' av naked priests all yellow powder an' tigers tails. But I may tell you, Orth'ris, an' you, Learoyd, that av all the palanquins ours was the most imperial an' magnificent. Now a palanquin means a native lady all the world over, except whin a soldier av the Quane happens to be takin' a ride. 'Women an' priests!' sez I. 'Your father's son is in the right pew this time, Terence. There will be proceedin's.' Six black divils in pink muslin tuk up the palanquin, an' oh! but the rowlin' an' the rockin' made me sick. Thin we got fair jammed among the palanquins—not more than fifty av them—an' we grated an' bumped like Queenstown potatosmacks in a runnin' tide. I cud hear the women gigglin' and squirkin' in their palanquins, but mine was the royal equipage. They made way for ut, an', begad, the pink muslin men o' mine were hawlin', 'Room for the Maharanee av Kokral-Seetarun.' Do you know aught av the lady, sorr?"

"Yes," said I. "She is a very estimable old queen of the Central Indian States, and they say she is fat. How on earth could she go to Benares without all the city knowing her palanquin?"

" 'Twas the eternal foolishness av the naygur-man. They saw the palanquin lying loneful an' forlornsome, an' the beauty av ut, after Dearsley's men had dhropped ut and gone away, an' they gave ut the best name that occurred to thim. Quite right too. For aught we know the ould lady was travelin' *incog*—like me. I'm glad to hear she's fat. I was no light weight mysilf, an' my men were mortial anxious to dhrop me under a great big archway promiscuously ornamented wid the most improper carvin's an' cuttin's I iver saw. Begad! they made me blush—like a—like a Maharanee."

"The temple of Prithi-Devi," I murmured, remembering the monstrous horrors of that sculptured archway at Benares.

"Pretty Devilskins, savin' your presence, sorr! There was nothin' pretty about ut, except me. 'Twas all half dhark, an' whin the coolies left they shut a big black gate behind av us, an' half a company av fat yellow priests began pully-haulin' the palanquins into a dharker place yet—a big stone hall full av pillars, an' gods, an' incense, an' all manner av similar thruck. The gate disconcerted me, for I perceived I wud have to go forward to get out, my retreat bein' cut off. By the same token a good priest makes a bad palanquin-coolie. Begad! they nearly turned me inside out draggin' the palanquin to the temple. Now the disposishin av the forces inside was this way. The Maharanee av Gokral-Seetarun—that was me—lay by the favor av Providence on the far left flank behind the dhark av a pillar carved with elephints' heads. The remainder av the palanquins was in a big half circle facing in to the biggest, fattest, an' most amazin' she-god that iver I dreamed av. Her head ran up into the black above us, an' her feet stuck out in the light av a little fire av melted butter that a priest was feedin' out av a butter-dish. Thin a man began to sing an' play on somethin' back in the dhark, an' 'twas a queer song. Ut made my hair lift on the back av my neck. Thin the doors av all the palanquins slid back, an' the women bundled out. I saw what I'll niver see again. 'Twas more glorious than thransformations at a pantomime, for they was in pink an' blue an' silver an' red an' grass green, wid di'monds an' im'ralds an' great red rubies all over thim. But that was the least part av the glory. O bhoys, they were more lovely than the like av any loveliness in hiven; a, their little bare feet were better than the white hands av a lord's lady, an' their mouths were like puckered roses, an' their eyes were bigger an' dharker than the eyes av any livin' women I've seen. Ye may laugh, but I'm speakin' truth. I niver saw the like, an' niver I will again."

"Seeing that in all probability you were watching the wives and daughters of most of the kings of India, the chances are that you won't," I said, for it was dawning on me that Mulvaney had stumbled upon a big Queen's Praying at Benares.

"I niver will," he said, mournfully. "That sight doesn't come twist to any man. It made me ashamed to watch. A fat priest knocked at my door. I didn't think he'd have the insolince to disturb the Maharanee av Gokral-Seetarun, so I lay still. 'The old cow's asleep,' sez he to another. 'Let her be,' sez that. ''Twill be long before she has a calf!' I might ha' known before he spoke that all a woman prays for in Injia—an' for that matter o' that in England too—is childher. That made me more sorry I'd come, me bein', as you well know, a childless man."

He was silent for a moment, thinking of his little son, dead many years ago.

"They prayed, an' the butter-fires blazed up an' the incense turned everything blue, an' between that an' the fires the women looked as tho' they were all ablaze an' twinklin'. They took hold av the she-god's knees, they cried out an' they threw themselves about, an' that world-without-end-amen music was dhrivin' thim mad. Mother av Hiven! how they cried, an' the ould she-god grinnin' above thim all so scornful! The dhrink was dyin' out in me fast, an' I was thinkin' harder than the thoughts wud go through my head—thinkin' how to get out, an' all manner of nonsense as well. The women were rockin' in rows, their di'mond belts clickin', an' the tears runnin' out betune their hands, an' the lights were goin' lower an' dharker. Thin there was a blaze like lightnin' from the roof, an' that showed me the inside av the palanquin, an' at the end where my foot was, stood the livin' spit an' image o' mysilf worked on the linin'. This man here, ut was."

He hunted in the folds of his pink cloak, ran a hand under one, and thrust into the firelight a foot-long embroidered presentment of the great god Krishna, playing on a flute. The heavy jowl, the staring eye, and the blue-black mustache of the god made up a far-off resemblance to Mulvaney.

"The blaze was gone in a wink, but the whole schame came to me thin. I believe I was mad too. I slid the off-shutter open an' rowled out into the dhark behind the elephint-head pillar, tucked up my trousies to my knees, slipped off my boots an' tuk a general hould av all the pink linin' av the palan-

quin. Glory be, ut ripped out like a woman's dhriss whin you tread on ut at a sergeants' ball, and a bottle came with ut. I tuk the bottle an' the next minut I was out av the dhark av the pillar, the pink linin' wrapped round me most graceful, the music thunderin' like kettledrums, an' a could draft blowin' round my bare legs. By this hand that did ut, I was Khrishna tootlin' on the flute—the god that the rig'mental chaplain talks about. A sweet sight I must ha' looked. I knew my eyes were big, and my face was wax-white, an' at the worst I must ha' looked like a ghost. But they took me for the livin' god. The music stopped, and the women were dead dumb an' I crooked my legs like a shepherd on a china basin, an' I did the ghost-waggle with my feet as I had done ut at the rig'mental theatre many times, an' I slid acrost the width av that temple in front av the she-god tootlin' on the beer bottle."

"Wot did you toot?" demanded Ortheris the practical.

"Me? Oh!" Mulvaney sprang up, suiting the action to the word, and sliding gravely in front of us, a dilapidated but imposing deity in the half light. "I sang—

> "Only say
> You'll be Mrs. Brallaghan.
> Don't say nay,
> Charmin' Judy Callaghan.

I didn't know me own voice when I sang. An' oh! 'twas pitiful to see the women. The darlin's were down on their faces. Whin I passed the last wan I cud see her poor little fingers workin' one in another as if she wanted to touch my feet. So I dhrew the tail av this pink overcoat over her head for the greater honor, an' I slid into the dhark on the otherside av the temple, and fetched up in the arms av a big fat priest.. All I wanted was to get away clear. So I tuk him by his greasy throat an' shut the speech out av him. 'Out!' sez I. 'Which way, ye fat heathen?'—'Oh!' sez he. 'Man,' sez I. 'White man, soldier man, common soldier man. Where in the name av confusion is the back door?' The women in the temple were still on their faces, an' a young priest was holdin' out his arms above their heads.

" 'This way,' sez my fat friend, duckin' behind a big bull-god an' divin' into a passage. Thin I remembered that I must ha' made the miraculous reputation av that temple for the next fifty years. 'Not so fast,' I sez, an' I held out both my hands wid a wink. That ould thief smiled like a father. I tuk him by the back av the neck in case he should be wishful to put a knife into me unbeknownst, an' I ran him up an' down the passage twice to collect his sensibilities! 'Be quiet,' sez he, in English. 'Now you talk sense,' I sez. 'Fwhat'll you give me for the use av that most iligant palanquin I have no time to take away?'—'Don't tell,' sez he. 'Is ut like?' sez I. 'But ye might give me my railway fare. I'm far from my home an' I've done you a service.' Bhoys, 'tis a good thing to be a priest. The ould man niver throubled himself to dhraw from a bank. As I will prove to you subsequint, he philandered all round the slack av his clothes an' began dribblin' ten-rupee notes, old gold mohurs, and rupees into my hand till I could hould no more."

"You lie!" said Ortheris. "You're mad

or sunstrook. A native don't give coin unless you cut it out o' 'im. 'Tain't nature."

"Then my lie an' my sunstroke is concealed under that lump av sod yonder," retorted Mulvaney, unruffled, nodding across the scrub. "An' there's a dale more in nature than your squidgy little legs have iver taken you to, Orth-'ris, me son. Four hundred an' thirty-four rupees by my reckonin', *an'* a big fat gold necklace that I took from him as a remimbrancer, was our share in that business."

"An' 'e give it you for love?" said Ortheris.

"We were alone in that passage. Maybe I was a trifle too pressin', but considher fwhat I had done for the good av the temple an' iverlastin' joy av those women. 'Twas cheap at the price. I wud ha' taken more if I cud ha' found ut. I turned the ould man upside down at the last, but he was milked dhry. Thin he opened a door in another passage an' I found mysilf up to my knees in Benares river-water, an' bad smellin' ut is. More by token I had come out on the river-line close to the burnin' ghat and contagious to a crackin' corpse. This was in the heart av the night, for I had been four hours in the temple. There was a crowd av boats tied up, so I tuk wan an' wint across the river. Thin I came home acrost country, lyin' up by day."

'How on earth did you manage?" I said.

"How did Sir Frederick Roberts get from Cabul to Candahar? He marched an' he niver tould how near he was to breakin' down. That's why he is fwhat he is. An' now"—Mulvaney yawned portentously. 'Now I will go an' give myself up for absince widout leave. It's eight an' twenty days an' the rough end of the colonel's tongue in orderly room, any way you look at ut. But 'tis cheap at the price."

"Mulvaney," said I, softly. "If there happens to be any sort of excuse that the colonel can in any way accept, I have a notion that you'll get nothing more than the dressing-gown. The new recruits are in, and"—

'Not a word more, sorr. Is ut excuses the old man wants? 'Tis not my way, but he shall have thim. I'll tell him I was engaged in financial operations connected wid a church," and he flapped his way to cantonments and the cells, singing lustily—

"So they sent a corp'ril's file,
And they put me in the gyard-room
For conduck unbecomin' of a soldier."

And when he was lost in the midst of the moonlight we could hear the refrain—

"Bang upon the big drum, bash upon the cymbals,
As we go marchin' along, boys, oh!
For although in this campaign
There's no whiskey nor champaign,
We'll keep our spirits goin' with a song, boys!"

Therewith he surrendered himself to the joyful and almost weeping guard, and was made much of by his fellows. But to the colonel he said that he had ben smitten with sunstroke and had lain insensible on a villager's cot foi untold hours, and between laughter and good-will the affair was smoothed over, so that he could, next day, teach the new recruits how to "Fear God, Honor the Queen, Shoot Straight, and Keer Clean."

The Three Musketeers

An' when the war began, we chased the
　　bold Afghan,
An' we made the bloomin' Ghazi for to
　　flee, boys O!
An' we marched into Kabul, an' we tuk
　　the Balar 'Issar
An' we taught 'em to respec' the British
　　Soldier.
　　　　　　　Barrack Room Ballad.

MULVANEY, Ortheris and Learoyd are Privates in B Company of a Line Regiment, and personal friends of mine. Collectively I think, but am not certain, they are the worst men in the regiment so far as genial blackguardism goes.

They told me this story, in the Um-balla Refreshment Room while we were waiting for an up-train. I supplied the beer. The tale was cheap at a gallon and a half.

All men know Lord Benira Trig. He is a Duke, or an Earl, or something unofficial; also a Peer; also a Globe-trotter. On all three counts, as Ortheris says, " 'e didn't deserve no consideration." He was out in India for three months collecting materials for a book on "Our Eastern Impedimenta," and quartering himself upon everybody, like a Cossack in evening-dress.

His particular vice—because he was

a Radical, men said—was having garrisons turned out for his inspection. He would then dine with the Officer Commanding, and insult him, across the Mess table, about the appearance of the troops. That was Benira's way.

He turned out troops once too often. He came to Helanthami Cantonment on a Tuesday. He wished to go shopping in the Bazars on Wednesday, and he "desired" the troops to be turned out on a Thursday. *On—a—Thursday.* The Officer Commanding could not well refuse; for Benira was a Lord. There was an indignation-meeting of subalterns in the Mess Room, to call the Colonel pet names.

"But the rale dimonstrashin," said Mulvaney, "was in B Comp'ny barrick; we three headin' it."

Mulvaney climbed on to the refreshment-bar, settled himself comfortably by the beer, and went on, "Whin the row was at ut's foinest an' B Comp'ny was fur goin' out to murther this man Thrigg on the p'rade-groun', Learoyd here takes up his helmut an' sez—fwhat was ut ye said?"

"Ah said," said Learoyd, "gie us t' brass. Tak oop a subscripshun, lads, for to put off t' p'rade, an' if t' p'rade's not put off, ah'll gie t' brass back agean. Thot's what ah said. All B Coomp'ny knawed me. Ah took oop a big subscripshun—fower rupees eight annas 'twas—an' ah went oot to turn t' job over. Mulvaney an' Orth'ris coom with me."

"We three raises the Divil in couples gin'rally," explained Mulvaney.

Here Ortheris interrupted. " 'Ave you read the papers?" said he.

"Sometimes," I said.

"We 'ad read the papers, an' we put hup a faked decoity, a—a sedukshun."

"*Ab*dukshin, ye cockney," said Mulvaney.

"*Ab*dukshun or *se*dukshun—no great odds. Any'ow, we arranged to taik an' put Mister Benhira out o' the way till Thursday was hover, or 'e too busy to rux 'isself about p'raids. *Hi* was the man wot said, "We'll make a few rupees off o' the business.' "

"We hild a Council av War," continued Mulvaney, "walkin' roun' by the Artill'ry Lines. I was Prisidint, Learoyd was Minister av Finance, an' little Orth'ris here was"—

"A bloomin' Bismarck! *Hi* made the 'ole show pay."

"This intereferin' bit av a Benira man," said Mulvaney, "did the thrick for us himself; for, on me sowl, we hadn't a notion av what was to come afther the next minut. He was shoppin' in the bazar on fut. 'Twas dhrawin' dusk thin, an' we stud watchin' the little man hoppin' in an' out av the shops, thryin' to injuce the naygurs to *mallum* his *bat.* Prisintly, he sthrols up, his arrums full av thruck, an' he sez in a consiquinshal way, shticking out his little belly, 'Me good men,' sez he, 'have ye seen the Kernel's b'roosh?'— 'B'roosh?' says Learoyd. 'There's no b'roosh here—nobbut a *'hekka.'*— 'Fwhat's that?' sez Thrigg. Learoyd shows him wan down the sthreet, an' he sez, 'How thruly Orientil! I will ride on a *hekka.*' I saw thin that our Rigimintal Saint was for givin' Thrigg over to us neck an' brisket. I purshued a *hekka,* and' I sez to the dhriver-divil, I sez, 'Ye black limb, there's a *Sahib* comin' for this *hekka*. He wants to go *jildi* to the Padsahi Jhil'—'twas about tu moiles away—' to shoot snipe—*chirria*. You dhrive *Jehannum ke marfik, mallum*—like Hell? 'Tis no manner av use *bukkin'* to the *Sahib*, bekaze he doesn't *samjao* your talk. Av he *bolos* anything, just you *choop* and *chel*. *Dekker?* Go *arsty* for the first *arder*-mile from cantonmints. Thin *chel, Shaitan ke marfik*, an' the *chooper* you *choops* an' the *jildier* you *chels* the better *kooshy* will that Sahib be; an' here's a rupee for ye?'

"The *hekka*-man knew there was somethin' out av the common in the air. He grinned an' sez, '*Bote achee!* I goin' damn fast.' I prayed that the Kernel's b'roosh wudn't arrive till me darlin' Benira by the grace av God was undher weigh. The little man puts his thruck into the *hekka* an' scuttles in like a fat guinea-pig; niver offerin' us the price av a dhrink for our services in helpin' him home. 'He's off to the Padsahi *jhil*,' sez I to the others."

Ortheris took up the tale—

"Jist then, little Buldoo kim up, 'oo was the son of one of the Artillery grooms—'e would 'av made a 'evinly newspaper-boy in London, bein' sharp an' fly to all manner o' games. 'E 'ad bin watchin' us puttin' Mister Benhira into 'is temporary baroush, an' 'e sez, 'What *'ave* you been a doin of' *Sahibs?*' sez 'e. Learoyd 'e caught 'im by the ear an 'e sez"—

"Ah says," went on Learoyd, 'Young mon, that mon's gooin' to have t' goons out o' Thursday—to-morrow—an' thot's more work for you, young mon. Now, sitha, tak' a *tat* an' a *lookri*, an' ride that domdest to t' Padsahi Jhil. Cotch

thot there *hekka,* and tell t' driver iv your lingo thot you've coom to tak' his place. T' *Sahib* doesn't speak t' *bat,* an' he's a little mon. Drive t' *hekka* into t' Padsahi Jhil into t' watter. Leave t' *Sahib* theer an' room hoam; an' here's a rupee for tha'."

Then Mulvaney and Ortheris spoke together in alternate fragments: Mulvaney leading [You must pick out the two speakers' as best you can]: —'He was a knowin' little divil was Bhuldoo,—'e sez *bote achee* an' cuts—wid a wink in his oi—but *Hi* sez there's money to be made—an' I wanted to see the ind av the campaign—so *Hi* says we'll double hout to the Padsahi Jhil—an' save the little man from bein' dacoited by the murtherin' Bhuldoo— an' turn hup like reskooers in a Vic'oria Melodrama—so we doubled for the *jhil,* an' prisintly there was the divil av a hurroosh behind us an' three bhoys on grasscuts' ponies come by, poundin' along for the dear life—s'elp me Bob, hif Buldoo 'adn't raised a rig'lar *harmy* of decoits—to do the job in shtile. An' we ran, an' they ran, shplittin' with laughin', till we gets near the *jhil*—and 'ears sounds of distress floatin' molloncolly on the hevenin' hair." [Ortheris was growing poetical under the influence of the beer. The duet recommenced: Mulvaney leading again.]

"Thin we heard Bhuldoo, the decoit, shoutin' to the *hekka* man, an' wan of the young divils brought his stick down on the top av the *hekka*-cover, an' Benira Thrigg inside howled 'Murther an' Death.' Buldoo takes the reins and dhrives like mad for the *jhil*, havin' dishpersed the *hekka*-dhriver—'oo cum up to us an' 'e sez, sez 'e, 'That *Sahib's* nigh mad with funk! Wot devil's work 'ave you led me into?'—'Hall right,' sez we, 'you catch that there pony an' come along. This *Sahib's* been decoited, an' we're going to resky 'im!' Says the driver, 'Decoits! Wot decoits? That's Buldoo the *budmash*'—'Bhuldoo be shot!' sez we. ' 'Tis a woild dissolute Pathan frum the hills. There's about eight av thim coercin' the *Sahib*. You remimber that an' you'll get another rupee!' Thin we heard the *whop-whop-whop* av the *hekka* turnin' over, an a splash av water an' the voice av Benira Thrigg callin' upon God to forgive his sins—an' Buldoo an' 'is friends squotterin' in the water like boys in the Serpentine."

Here the Three Musketeers retired simultaneously into the beer.

"Well? What came next?" said I.

"Fwhat nex'?" answered Mulvaney, wiping his mouth. "Wud ye let three bould sodger-bhoys lave the ornamint av the House av Lords to be dhrowned an' dacoited in a *jhil*? We formed line av quarther-column an' we discinded upon the inimy. For the better part av tin minutes you could not hear yerself spake. The *tattoo* was screamin' in chune wid Benira Thrigg an' Bhuldoo's army, an' the shticks was whistlin' roun' the *hekka*, an' Orth'ris was beatin' the *hekka*-cover wid his fistes, an' Learoyd yellin', 'Look out for their knives!' an' me cuttin' into the dark, right an' lef', dishpersin' army corps av Pathans. Holy Mother av Moses! 'twas more disp'rit than Ahmid Kheyl wid Maiwund thrown in. Afther a wihle Bhuldoo an' his bhoys flees. Have ye iver seen a rale live Lord thryin' to hide his nobility undher a fut an' a half av

brown swamp-wather? 'Tis the livin' image av a water-carrier's goatskin wid the shivers. It tuk toime to pershuade me frind Benira he was not disimbowilled: an' more toime to get out the *hekka*. The dhriver come up afther the battle, swearin' he tuk a hand in repulsin' the inimy. Benira was sick wid the fear. We escorted him back, very slow, to cantonmints, for that an' the chill to soak into him. It suk! Glory be to the Rigimintil Saint, but it suk to the marrow av Lord Benira Thrigg!"

Here Ortheris, slowly, with immense pride—" 'E sez, You har my noble preservers,' sez 'e. 'You har a *honor* to the British Harmy,' sez 'e. With that e' describes the hawful band of dacoits wot set on 'im. There was about forty of 'em an' 'e was hoverpowered by numbers, so 'e was; but 'e never lorst 'is presence of mind, so 'e didn't. 'E guv the *hekka*-driver five rupees for 'is noble assistance, an' 'e said 'e would see to us after 'e 'ad spoken to the Kernul. For we was a *honor* to the Regiment, we was."

"An' we three," said Mulvaney, with a seraphic smile, "have dhrawn the parti-cu-lar attinshin av Bobs Bahadur more than wanst. But he's a rale good little man is Bobs. Go on, Orth'ris, my son."

"Then we leaves 'im at the Kernul's 'ouse, werry sick, an' we cuts hover to B Comp'ny barrick an' we sez we 'ave saved Benira from a bloody doom, an' the chances was agin there bein' p'raid on Thursday. About ten minutes later come three envelicks, one for each of us. S'elp me Bob, if the old bloke 'adn't guv us a fiver apiece—sixty-four rupees in the bazar! On Thursday 'e was in 'orspital recoverin' from 'is sanguinary encounter with a gang of Pathans, an' B Comp'ny was drinkin' 'emselves into Clink by squads. So there never was no Thursday p'raid. But the Kernul, when 'e 'eard of our galliant conduct, 'e sez, 'Hi know there's been some devilry somewheres,' sez 'e, 'but I can't bring it 'ome to you three.' "

"An' my privit imprisshin is," said Mulvaney, getting off the bar and turning his glass upside down, "that, av they had known they wudn't have brought ut home. 'Tis flyin' in the face, firstly av Nature, secon' av the Rig'lations, an' third the will av Terence Mulvaney, to hold p'rades av Thursdays."

"Good, ma son!" said Learoyd; "but, young mon, what's t' notebook for?"

"Let be," said Mulvaney; "this time next month we're in the *Sherapis*. 'Tis immortial fame the gentleman's goin' to give us. But kape it dhark till we're out av the range av me little frind Bobs Bahadur."

And I have obeyed Mulvaney's order.

The Courting of Dinah Shadd

What did the colonel's lady think?
  Nobody never knew.
Somebody asked the sergeant's wife
  An' she told 'em true.
When you git to a man in the case
  They're like a row o' pins,
For the colonel's lady an' Judy O'Grady
  Are sisters under their skins.
                    Barrack Room Ballad.

ALL day I had followed at the heels of a pursuing army engaged on one of the finest battles that ever camp of exercise beheld. Thirty thousand troops had by the wisdom of the Government of India been turned loose over a few thousand square miles of country to practice in peace what they would never attempt in war. Consequently cavalry charged unshaken infantry at the trot. Infantry captured artillery by frontal attacks delivered in line of quarter columns, and mounted infantry skirmished up to the wheels of an armored train which carried nothing more deadly than a twenty-five pounder Armstrong, two Nordenfeldts, and a few score volunteers all cased in three-eighths-inch boiler-plate. Yet it was a very lifelike camp. Operations did not cease at sundown; nobody knew the country and nobody spared man or horse. There was unending cavalry scouting and almost unending forced work over broken ground. The Army of the South had finally pierced the centre of the Army of the North, and was pouring through the gap hot-foot to capture a city of strategic importance. Its front extended fanwise, the sticks being represented by regiments strung out along the line of route backward to the divisional transport columns and all the lumber that trails behind an army on the move. On its right the broken left of the Army of the North was flying in mass, chased by the Southern horse and hammered by the Southern guns till these had been pushed far beyond the limits of their last support. Then the flying sat down to rest, while the elated commandant of the pursuing force telegraphed that he held all in check and observation.

Unluckily he did not observe that three miles to his right flank a flying column of Northern horse with a detachment of Ghoorkhas and British troops had been pushed round, as fast as the failing light allowed, to cut across the entire rear of the Southern Army, to break, as it were, all the ribs of the fan where they converged by striking at the transport, reserve ammunition, and artillery supplies. Their instructions were to go in, avoiding the few scouts who might not have been drawn off by the pursuit, and create sufficient excitement to impress the Southern Army with the wisdom of guarding their own flank and rear before they captured cities. It was a pretty manœuvre, neatly carried out.

Speaking for the second division of the Southern Army, our first intimation of the attack was at twilight, when the artillery were laboring in deep sand, most of the escort were trying to help them out, and the main body of the infantry had gone on. A Noah's Ark of elephants, camels, and the mixed menagerie of an India transport-train bubbled and squealed behind the guns, when there appeared from nowhere in particular British infantry to the extent of three companies, who sprang to the heads of the gun-horses and brought all to a standstill amid oaths and cheers.

"How's that, umpire?" said the major commanding the attack, and with one voice the drivers and limber gunners answered 'Hout!" while the colonel of artillery sputtered.

"All your scouts are charging our main body," said the major. 'Your flanks are unprotected for two miles. I think we've broken the back of this division. And listen,—there go the Ghoorkhas!"

A weak fire broke from the rearguard more than a mile away, and was answered by cheerful howlings. The Ghoorkhas, who should have swung clear of the second division, had stepped on its tail in the dark, but drawing off hastened to reach the next line of attack, which lay almost parallel to us five or six miles away.

Our column swayed and surged irresolutely,—three batteries, the divisional ammunition reserve, the baggage, and a section of the hospital and bearer corps. The commandant ruefully promised to report himself "cut up" to the nearest umpire, and commending his cavalry and all other cavalry to the special care of Eblis, toiled on to resume touch with the rest of the division.

"We'll bivouac here to-night," said the major, "I have a notion that the Ghoorkhas will get caught. They may want us to re-form on. Stand easy till the transport gets away."

A hand caught my beast's bridle and led him out of the choking dust; a larger hand deftly canted me out of the saddle; and two of the hugest hands in the world received me sliding. Pleasant is the lot of the special correspondent who falls into such hands as those of Privates Mulvaney, Ortheris, and Learoyd.

"An' that's all right," said the Irishman, calmly. "We thought we'd find you somewheres here by. Is there anything av yours in the transport? Orth'ris'll fetch ut out."

Ortheris did "fetch ut out," from under the trunk of an elephant, in the shape of a servant and an animal both laden with medical comforts. The little man's eyes sparkled.

"If the brutil an' licentious soldiery av these parts gets sight av the thruck," said Mulvaney, making practiced investigation, "they'll loot ev'rything. They're bein' fed on iron-filin's an' dog-biscuit these days, but glory's no compensation for a belly-ache. Praise be, we're here to protect you, sorr. Beer, sausage, bread (soft an' that's a cur'osity), soup in a tin, whisky by the smell av ut, an' fowls! Mother av Moses, but ye take the field like a confectioner! 'Tis scand'lus."

"'Ere's a orficer" said Ortheris, significantly. "When the sergent's done lushin' the privit may clean the pot."

I bundled several things into Mulvaney's haversack before the major's hand fell on my shoulder and he said, tenderly, "Requisitioned for the Queen's service. Wolseley was quite wrong about special correspondents: they are the soldier's best friends. Come and take pot-luck with us to-night."

And so it happened amid laughter and shoutings that my well-considered commissariat melted away to reappear later at the mess-table, which was a waterproof sheet spread on the ground. The flying column had taken three days' rations with it, and there be few things nastier than government rations—especially when government is experimenting with German toys. Erbsen-wurst, tinned beef of surpassing tinniness, compressed vegetables, and meat-biscuits may be nourishing, but what Thomas Atkins needs is bulk in his inside. The major, assisted by his brother officers, purchased goats for the camp and so made the experiment of no effect. Long before the fatigue-party sent to collect brushwood had returned, the men were settled down by their valises, kettles and pots had appeared from the surrounding country and were dangling over fires as the kid and the compressed vegetable bubbled together; there rose a cheerful clinking of mess-tins; outrageous demands for "a little more stuffin' with that there liver-wing;" and gust on gust of chaff as pointed as a bayonet and as delicate as a gun-butt.

"The boys are in a good temper," said the major. "They'll be singing presently. Well, a night like this is enough to keep them happy."

Over our heads burned the wonderful Indian stars, which are not all pricked in on one plane, but, preserving an orderly perspective, draw the eye through the velvet darkness of the void up to the barred doors of heaven itself. The earth was a grey shadow more unreal than the sky. We could hear her breathing lightly in the pauses between the howling of the jackals, the movement of the wind in the tamarisks, and the fitful mutter of musketry-fire leagues away to the left. A native woman from some unseen hut began to sing, the mail-train thundered past on its way to Delhi, and a roosting crow cawed drowsily. Then there was a belt-loosening silence about the fires, and the even breathing of the crowded earth took up the story.

The men, full fed, turned to tobacco and song,—their officers with them. The subaltern is happy who can win the approval of the musical critics in his regiment, and is honored among the more intricate step-dancers. By him, as by him who plays cricket cleverly, Thomas Atkins will stand in time of need, when he will let a better officer go on alone. The ruined tombs of forgotten Mussulman saints heard the ballad of *Agra Town, The Buffalo Battery, Marching to Kabul, The long, long Indian Day, The Place where the Punkah-coolie died,* and that crashing chorus which announces,

Youth's daring spirit, manhood's fire,
    Firm hand and eagle eye,
Must he acquire who would aspire
    To see the grey boar die.

To-day, of all those jovial thieves who appropriated my commissariat and lay and laughed round that waterproof sheet, not one remains. They went to camps that were not of exercise and battles without umpires. Burmah, the Soudan, and the frontier,—fever and fight,—took them in their time.

I drifted across to the men's fires in search of Mulvaney, whom I found strategically greasing his feet by the blaze. There is nothing particularly lovely in the sight of a private thus engaged after a long day's march, but when you reflect on the exact proportion of the "might, majesty, dominion, and power" of the British Empire which stands on those feet you take an interest in the proceedings.

"There's a blister, bad luck to ut, on the heel," said Mulvaney. "I can't touch ut. Prick ut out, little man."

Ortheris took out his house-wife, eased the trouble with a needle, stabbed Mulvaney in the calf with the same weapon, and was swiftly kicked into the fire.

"I've bruk the best av my toes over you, ye grinnin' child av disruption," said Mulvaney, sitting cross-legged and nursing his feet; then seeing me, "Oh, ut's you, sorr! He welkim, an' take that maraudin' scutt's place. Jock, hold him down on the cindhers for a bit."

But Ortheris escaped and went elsewhere, as I took possession of the hollow he had scraped for himself and lined with his greatcoat. Learoyd on the other side of the fire grinned affably and in a minute fell fast asleep.

"There's the height av politeness for you," said Mulvaney, lighting his pipe with a flaming branch. "But Jock's eaten half a box av your sardines at wan gulp, an' I think the tin too. What's the best wid you, sorr, an' how did you happen to be on the losin' side this day whin we captured you?"

"The Army of the South is winning all along the line," I said.

"Then that line's the hangman's rope, savin' your presence. You'll learn tomorrow how we rethreated to dhraw thim on before we made him trouble, an' that's what a woman does. By the same tokin' we'll be attacked before the dawnin' an' ut would be betther not to slip your boots. How do I know that? By the light av pure reason. Here are three companies av us ever so far inside av the enemy's flank an' a crowd av roarin', tarin', squealin' cavalry gone on just to turn out the whole hornet's nest av them. Av course the enemy will pursue, by brigades like as not, an' thin we'll have to run for ut. Mark my words. I am av the opinion av Polonius whin he said, 'Don't fight wid ivry scutt for the pure joy av fightin', but if you do, knock the nose av him first an' frequent.' We ought to ha' gone on an' helped the Ghoorkhas."

"But what do you know about Polonius?" I demanded. This was a new side of Mulvaney's character.

"All that Shakespeare iver wrote an' a dale more that the gallery shouted," said the man of war, carefully lacing his boots. "Did I not tell you av Silver's theatre in Dublin, whin I was younger than I am now an' a patron av the drama? Ould Silver wud never pay actor-man or woman their just dues, an' by consequince his comp'nies was collapsible at the last minut. Thin the bhoys wud clamor to take a part, an' oft as not ould Silver made them pay for the fun. Faith, I've seen Hamlut played wid a new black eye an' the queen as full as a cornucopia. I remimber wanst Hogin that 'listed in the Black Tyrone an' was shot in South Africa, he sejuced ould Silver into givin' him Hamlut's part instid av me that had a fine fancy for rhetoric in those days. Av course I wint into the gallery an' began to fill the pit wid other people's hats, an' I passed the time av day to Hogin walkin' through Denmark like a hamstrung mule wid a pall on his back. 'Hamlut,' sez I, 'there's a hole in your heel. Pull up your shtockin's, Hamlut,' sez I. 'Hamlut, Hamlut, for the love av decincy dhrop that skull an' pull up your shtockin's.' The whole house begun to tell him that. He stopped his soliloquishms mid-between. 'My shtockin's may be comin' down or they may not,' sez he, screwin' his eye into the gallery, for well he knew who I was. 'But

after this performince is over me an' the Ghost 'll trample the tripes out av you, Terence, wid your ass's bray!' An' that's how I come to know about Hamlut. Eyah! Those days, those days! Did you iver have onendin' devilmint an' nothin' to pay for it in your life, sorr?"

"Never, without having to pay," I said.

"That's thrue! 'Tis mane whin you considher on ut; but ut's the same wid horse or fut. A headache if you dhrink, an' a belly-ache if you eat too much, an' a heart-ache to kape all down. Faith, the beast only gets the colic, an' he's the lucky man."

He dropped his head and stared into the fire, fingering his moustache the while. From the far side of the bivouac the voice of Corbet-Nolan, senior subaltern of B Company, uplifted itself in an ancient and much appreciated song of sentiment, the men moaning melodiously behind him.

The north wind blew coldly, she dropped from that hour,
My own little Kathleen, my sweet little Kathleen,
Kathleen, my Kathleen, Kathleen O'Moore!

With forty-five O's in the last word: even at that distance you might have cut the soft South Irish accent with a shovel.

"For all we take we must pay, but the price is cruel high," murmured Mulvaney when the chorus had ceased.

"What's the trouble?" I said gently, for I knew that he was a man of an inextinguishable sorrow.

"Hear now," said he. "Ye know what I am now. I know what I mint to be at the beginnin' av my service. I've tould you time an' again, an' what I have not Dinah Shadd has. An' what am I? Oh, Mary Mother av Hiven, an ould dhrunken, untrustable baste av a privit that has seen the reg'ment change out from colonel to drummer-boy, not wanst or twice, but scores av times! Ay, scores! An' me not so near gettin' promotion as in the first! An' me livin' on an' kapin' clear av clink, not by my own good conduck, but the kindness av some orf'cer-bhoy young enough to be son to me! Do I not know ut? Can I not tell whin I'm passed over at p'rade, tho' I'm rockin' full av liquor an' ready to fall all in wan piece, such as even a suckin' child might see, bekaze, 'Oh, 'tis only ould Mulvaney!' An' whin I'm let off in ord'ly-room through some thrick of the tongue an' a ready answer an' the ould man's mercy, is ut smilin' I feel whin I fall away an' go back to Dinah Shadd, thryin' to carry ut all off as a joke? Not I! 'Tis hell to me, dumb hell through ut all; an' next time whin the fit comes I will be as bad again. Good cause the reg'ment has to know me for the best soldier in ut. Better cause have I to know mesilf for the worst man. I'm only fit to tache the new drafts what I'll niver learn me-silf; an' I am sure, as tho' I heard ut, that the minut wan av these pink-eyed recruities gets away from my 'Mind ye now,' an' 'Listen to this, Jim, bhoy,'— sure I am that the sergint houlds me up to him for a warnin'. So I tache, as they say at musketry-instruction, by direct and ricochet fire. Lord be good to me, for I have stud some trouble!"

"Lie down and go to sleep," said I, not being able to comfort or advise. "You're the best man in the regiment, and, next to Ortheris, the biggest fool. Lie down and wait till we're attacked. What force will they turn out? Guns, think you?"

"Try that wid your lorrds an' ladies, twistin' an' turnin' the talk, tho' you mint ut well. Ye cud say nothin' to help me, an' yet ye niver knew what cause I had to be what I am."

"Begin at the beginning and go on to the end," I said, royally. "But rake up the fire a bit first."

I passed Ortheris's bayonet for a poker.

"That shows how little we know what we do," said Mulvaney, putting it aside. "Fire takes all the heart out av the steel, an' the next time, may be, that our little man is fighting for his life his bradawl 'll break, an' so you'll ha' killed him, manin' no more than to kape your-self warm. 'Tis a recruity's thrick that. Pass the clanin'-rod, sorr."

I snuggled down abased; and after an interval the voice of Mulvaney began.

"Did I iver tell you how Dinah Shadd came to be wife av mine?"

I dissembled a burning anxiety that I had felt for some months—ever since Dinah Shadd, the strong, the patient, and the infinitely tender, had of her own good love and free will washed a shirt for me, moving in a barren land where washing was not.

"I can't remember," I said, casually. "Was it before or after you made love to Annie Bragin, and got no satisfaction?"

The story of Annie Bragin is written in another place. It is one of the many less respectable episodes in Mulvaney's checkered career.

"Before—before—long before, was that business av Annie Bragin an' the corp'ril's ghost. Niver woman was the worse for me whin I had married Dinah. There's a time for all things, an' I know how to kape all things in place—barrin' the dhrink, that kapes me in my place wid no hope av comin' to be aught else."

"Begin at the beginning," I insisted. "Mrs. Mulvaney told me that you married her when you were quartered in Krab Bokhar barracks."

"An' the same is a cess-pit," said Mulvaney, piously. "She spoke thrue, did Dinah. 'Twas this way. Talkin' av that, have ye iver fallen in love, sorr?"

I preserved the silence of the damned. Mulvaney continued—

"Thin I will assume that ye have not. _I_ did. In the days av my youth, as I have more than wanst tould you, I was a man that filled the eye an' delighted the sowl av women. Niver man was hated as I have bin. Niver man was loved as I—no, not within half a day's march av ut! For the first five years av my service, whin I was what I wud give my sowl to be now, I tuk whatever was within my reach an' digested ut— an' that's more than most men can say. Dhrink I tuk, an' ut did me no harm. By the Hollow av Hiven, I cud play wid four women at wanst, an' kape them from findin' out anythin' about the other three, an' smile like a full-blown marigold through ut all. Dick Coulhan, av the battery we'll have down on us to-night, could drive his team no better than I mine, an' I hild the worser cattle!

An' so I lived, an' so I was happy till afther that business wid Annie Bragin— she that turned me off as cool as a meat-safe, an' taught me where I stud in the mind av an honest woman. 'Twas no sweet dose to swallow."

"After that I sickened awhile an' tuk thought to my reg'mental work; conceiting mesilf I wud study an' be a sargint, an' a major-gineral twinty minutes afther that. But on top av my ambitiousness there was an empty place in my sowl, an' me own opinion av mesilf cud not fill ut. Sez I to mesilf, 'Terence, you're a great man an' the best set-up in the reg'mint. Go on an' get promotion.' Sez mesilf to me. 'What for?' Sez I to mesilf, 'For the glory av ut!' Sez mesilf to me, 'Will that fill these two strong arrums av yours, Terence?' 'Go to the devil,' sez I to mesilf. 'Go to the married lines,' sez mesilf to me. ' 'Tis the same thing,' sez I to mesilf. 'Av you're the same man, ut is,' said mesilf to me; an' wid that I considhered on ut a long while. Did you iver feel that way, sorr?"

I snored gently, knowing tha if Mulvaney were uninterrupted he would go on. The clamor from the bivouac fires beat up to the stars, as the rival singers of the companies were pitted against each other.

"So I felt that way an' a bad time ut was. Wanst, bein' a fool, I wint into the married linse more for the sake av spakin' to our ould color-sergint Shadd than for any thruck wid women-folk. I was a corp'ril then—rejuced afterward, but a corp'ril then. I've got a photograft av mesilf to prove ut. 'You'll take a cup av tay wid us?' sez Shadd.

'I will that,' I sez, 'tho' tay is not my diversion.'

"'"Twud be better for you if ut were,' sez ould Mother Shadd, an' she had ought to know, for Shadd, in the ind av his service, dhrank bung-full each night.

"Wid that I tuk off my gloves—there was pipe-clay in thim, so that they stud alone—an' pulled up my chair, lookin' round at the china ornaments an' bits av things in the Shadd's quarters. They were things that belonged to a man, an' no camp-kit, here to-day an' dishipated next. 'You're comfortable in this place, sergint,' sez I. ' 'Tis the wife that did ut, boy,' sez he, pointin' the stem av his pipe to ould Mother Shadd, an' she smacked the top av his bald head apon the compliment. 'That manes you want money,' sez she.

"An' thin—an' thin whin the kettle was to be filled, Dinah came in—my Dinah—her sleeves rowled up to the elbow an' her hair in a winkin' glory over her forehead, the big blue eyes beneath twinklin' like stars on a frosty night, an' the tread av her two feet lighter than waste-paper from the colonel's basket in ord'ly-room whin ut's emptied. Bein' but a shlip av a girl she went pink at seein' me, an' I twisted me moustache an' looked at a picture forninst the wall. Niver show a woman that ye care the snap av a finger for her, an' begad she'll come bleatin' to your boot-heels!"

"I suppose that's why you followed Annie Bragin till everybody in the married quarters laughed at at you," said I, remembering that unhallowed wooing and casting off the disguise of drowsiness.

"I'm layin' down the gin'ral theory av the attack," said Mulvaney, driving his boot into the dying fire. "If you read the *Soldier's Pocket Book*, which niver any soldier reads, you'll see that there are exceptions. Whin Dinah was out av the door (an' 'twas as tho' the sunlight had shut too)—'Mother av Hiven, sergint,' sez I, 'but is that your daughter?'—'I've believed that way these eighteen years,' sez ould Shadd, his eyes twinklin'; 'but Mrs. Shadd has her own opinion, like iv'ry woman.'— ' 'Tis wid yours this time, for a mericle,' sez Mother Shadd. 'Thin why in the name av fortune did I niver see her before?' sez I. 'Bekaze you've been thrapesin' round wid the married women these three years past. She was a bit av a child till last year, an' she shot up wid the spring,' sez ould Mother Shadd. 'I'll thrapese no more,' sez I. 'D'you mane that?' sez ould Mother Shadd, lookin' at me side-ways like a hen looks at a hawk whin the chickens are runnin' free. 'Try me, an' tell,' sez I. Wid that I pulled on my gloves, dhrank off the tay, an' went out av the house as stiff as at gin'ral p'rade, for well I knew that Dinah Shadd's eyes were in the small av my back out av the scullery window. Faith! that was the only time I mourned I was not a cav'lry man for the pride av the spurs to jingle.

"I wint out to think, an' I did a powerful lot av thinkin', but ut all came round to that shlip av a girl in the dotted blue dhress, wid the blue eyes an' the sparkil in them. Thin I kept off canteen, an' I kept to the married quar-thers, or near by, on the chanst av meetin' Dinah. Did I meet her? Oh, my time past, did I not; wid a lump in my throat as big as my valise an' my heart goin' like a farrier's forge on a Saturday morning? 'Twas 'Good day to ye, Miss Dinah,' an' 'Good day t'you, corp'ril,' for a week or two, and divil a bit further could I get bakaze av the respect I had to that girl that I cud ha' broken betune finger an' thumb.''

Here I giggled as I recalled the gigantic figure of Dinah Shadd when she handed me my shirt.

"Ye may laugh," grunted Mulvaney. "But I'm speakin' the trut', an' 'tis you that are in fault. Dinah was a girl that wud ha' taken the imperiousness out av the Duchess av Clonmel in those days. Flower hand, foot av shod air, an' the eyes av the livin' mornin' she had that is my wife to-day—ould Dinah, and niver aught else than Dinah Shadd to me.

" 'Twas after three weeks standin' off an' on, an' niver makin' headway excipt through the eyes, that a little drummer boy grinned in me face whin I had admonished him wid the buckle av my belt for riotin' all over the place. 'An' I'm not the only wan that doesn't kape to barricks,' sez he. I tuk him by the scruff av his neck,—my heart was hung on a hair-thrigger those days, you will onderstand—an' 'Out wid ut,' sez I, 'or I'll lave no bone av you unbreakable.'— 'Speak to Dempsey,' sez he howlin'. 'Dempsey which?' sez I, 'ye unwashed limb av Satan.'—'Av the Bob-tailed D'hragoons,' sez he. 'He's seen her home from her aunt's house in the civil lines four times this fortnight.'—'Child!' sez I, dhroppin' him, 'your tongue's stronger than your body. Go to your quarters. I'm sorry I dhressed you down.'

"At that I went four ways to wanst huntin' Dempsey. I was mad to think that wid all my airs among women I shud ha' been chated by a basin-faced fool av a cav'lryman not fit to trust on a trunk. Presintly I found him in our lines—the Bobtails was quartered next us—an' a tallowy, topheavy son av a she-mule he was wid his big brass spurs an' his plastrons on his epigastrons an' all. But he niver flinched a hair.

" 'A word wid you, Dempsey,' sez I. 'You've walked wid Dinah Shadd four times this fortnight gone.'

" 'What's that to you?' sez he. 'I'll walk forty times more, an' forty on top av that, ye shovel-futted clod-breakin' infantry lance-corp'ril.'

"Before I cud gyard he had his gloved fist home on my cheek an' down I went full-sprawl. 'Will that content you?' sez he, blowin' on his knuckles for all the world like a Scots Greys or'ficer. 'Content!' sez I. 'For your own sake, man, take off your spurs, peel your jackut, an' onglove. 'Tis the beginnin' av the overture; stand up!'

"He stud all he know, but he niver peeled his jacket, an' his shoulders had no fair play. I was fightin' for Dinah Shadd an' that cut on my cheek. What hope had he forninst me? 'Stand up,' sez I, time an' aagin whin he was beginnin' to quarter the ground an' gyard high an' go large. 'This isn't ridin'-school,' I sez. 'O man, stand up an' let me in at ye.' But whin I saw he would be running' about, I grup his shock in my left an' his waist-belt in my right an' swung him clear to my right front, head under her, he hammerin' my nose till the wind was knocked out av him on the bare ground. 'Stand up,' sez

I, 'or I'll kick your head into your chest!' and I wud ha' done ut too, so ragin' mad I was.

"'My collar-bone's bruk,' sez he. 'Help me back to lines. I'll walk wid her no more.' So I helped him back."

"And was his collar-bone broken?" I asked, for I fancied that only Learoyd could neatly accomplish that terrible throw.

"He pitched on his left shoulder point. Ut was. Next day the news was in both barricks, an' whin I met Dinah Shadd wid a cheek on me like all the reg'mintal tailor's samples there was no 'Good mornin', corp'ril,' or aught else. 'An' what have I done, Miss Shadd,' sez I, very bould, platin' myself fornist her, 'that ye should not pass the time of day?'

"'Ye've half-killed rough-rider Dempsey,' sez she, her dear blue eyes fillin' up.

"'May be,' sez I. 'Was he a friend av yours that saw ye home four times in the fortnight?'

"'Yes,' sez she, but her mouth was down at the corners. 'An'—an' what's that to you?' she sez.

"'Ask Dempsey,' sez I, pretendin' to go away.

"'Did you fight for me then, ye silly man?' she sez, tho' she knew ut all along.

"'Who else?' sez I, an' I tuk wan pace to the front.

"'I wasn't worth ut,' sez she, fingerin' in her apron.

"'That's for me to say,' sez I. 'Shall I say ut?'

"'Yes,' sez she, in a saint's whisper an' at that I explained mesilf; and she tould me what ivry man that is a man, an' many that is a woman, hears wanst in his life.

"'But what made ye cry at startin', Dinah, darlin'?' sez I.

"'Your—your bloody cheek,' sez she,

"'But what made ye cry at startin'', duckin' her little head down on my sash (I was on duty for the day) an' whimperin' like a sorrowful angil.

"Now a man cud take that two ways. I tuk ut as pleased me best an' my first kiss wid ut. Mother av Innocence; but I kissed her on the tip av the nose and undher the eye; an' a girl that let's a kiss come tumble-ways like that has never been kissed before. Take note av that, sorr. Thin we wint hand in hand to ould Mother Shadd like two little childher, an' she said 'twas no bad thing, an' ould Shadd nodded behind his pipe, an' Dinah ran away to her own room. That day I throd on rollin' clouds. All earth was too small to hould me. Begad, I cud ha' hiked the sun out av the sky for a live coal to my pipe, so magnificent I was. But I tuk recruities at squad-drill instid an' began wid general battalion advance whin I shud ha' been balance-steppin' them. Eyah! that day! that day!"

A very long pause. "Well?" said I.

"'Twas all wrong," said Mulvaney, with an enormous sigh. "An' I know that ev'ry bit av ut was my own foolishness. That night I tuk maybe the half av three pints—not enough to turn the hair of a man in his natural senses. But I was more than half drunk wid pure joy, an' that canteen beer was so much whisky to me. I can't tell how it came about, but bekaze I had no thought for anywan except Dinah, bekaze I hadn't slipped her little white arms from my neck five minutes, *bekaze* the breath of her kiss was not gone from my mouth, I must go through the married lines on my way to quarters an' I must stay talkin' to a red-headed Mullingar heifer av a girl, Judy Sheehy, that was daughter to Mother Sheehy, the wife of Nick Sheehy, the canteen-sergint—the Black Curse av Shielygh be on the whole brood that are above groun' this day!

"An' what are ye houldin' your head that high for, corp'ril?' sez Judy. 'Come in an' thry a cup av tay,' she sez, standin' in the doorway. Bein' an ontrustable fool, an' thinkin' av anything but tay, I wint.

"'Mother's at canteen,' sez Judy, smoothin' the hair av hers that was like red snakes, an' lookin' at me cornerways out av her green cats' eyes. 'Ye will not mind, corp'ril?'

"'I can endure,' sez I; ould Mother Sheehy bein' no divarsion av mine, nor her daughter too. Judy fetched the tea things an' put thim on the table, leanin' over me very close to get thim square. I dhrew back, thinkin' av Dinah.

"'Is ut afraid you are av a girl alone?' sez Judy.

"'No,' sez I. 'Why should I be?'

"'That rests wid the girl,' sez Judy, dhrawin' her chair next to mine.

"'Thin there let ut rest,' sez I; an' thinkin' I'd been a trifle onpolite, I sez, 'The tay's not quite sweet enough for my taste. Put your little finger in the cup, Judy. 'Twill make ut necthar.'

"'What's necthar?' sez she.

"'Somethin' very sweet,' sez I; an' for the sinful life av me I cud not help lookin' at her out av the corner av my eye, as I was used to look at a woman

"'Go on wid ye, corp'ril,' sez she. 'You're a flirt.'

"'On me sowl I'm not,' sez I.

"'Then you're a cruel handsome man, an' that's worse,' sez she, heavin' big sighs an' lookin' crossways.

"'You know your own mind,' sez I.

"''Twud be better for me if I did not, 'she sez.

"'There's a dale to be said on both sides av that,' sez I, unthinkin'.

"'Say your own part av ut, then, Terence, darlin',' sez she; 'for begad I'm thinkin' I've said too much or too little for an honest girl,' an' wid that she put her arms round my neck an' kissed me.

"'There's no more to be said afther that,' sez I, kissin' her back again—Oh the mane scutt that I was, my head ringin' wid Dinah Shadd! How does ut come about, sorr, that when a man has put the comether on wan woman, he's sure bound to put it on another? 'Tis the same thing at musketry. Wan day ivry shot goes wide or into the bank, an' the next day, lay high lay low, sight ox snap, ye can't get off the bull's-eye for ten shots runnin'."

'That only happens to a man who has had a good deal of experience. He does it without thinking," I replied.

"Thankin' you for the complimint, sorr, ut may be so. But I'm doubtful whether you mint ut for a complimint. Hear now; I sat there wid Judy on my knee tellin' me all manner av nonsinse an' only sayin' 'yes' an' 'no,' when I'd much better ha' kept tongue betune teeth. An' that was not an hour afther I had left Dinah! What I was thinkin' av I cannot say. Presently, quiet as a cat, ould Mother Sheehy came in velvet-dhrunk. She had her daughter's red hair, but 'twas bald in patches, an' I cud see in her wicked ould face, clear as lightnin', what Judy wud be twenty years to come. I was for jumpin' up, but Judy niver moved.

" 'Terence has promust, mother,' sez she, an' the could sweat bruk out all over me. Ould Mother Sheehy sat down of a heap an' began playin' wid the cups. 'Thin you're a well-matched pair,' she sez, very thick. 'For he's the biggest rogue that iver spoiled the queen's shoe-leather,' an'—

" 'I'm off, Judy,' sez I. 'Ye should not talk nonsinse to your mother. Get her to bed, girl.'

" 'Nonsinse!' sez the old woman, prickin' up her ears like a cat an' grippin' the table-edge. 'Twill be the most nonsinsical nonsinse for you, ye grinnin' badger, if nonsinse 'tis. Git clear, you. I'm goin' to bed.'

'I ran out into the dhark, my head in a stew an' my heart sick, but I had sinse enough to see that I'd brought ut all on mysilf. 'It's this to pass the time av day to a panjandhrum av hellcats,' sez I. 'What I've said, an' what I've not said do not matther. Judy an' her dam will hould me for a promust man, an' Dinah will give me the go an' I desarve ut. I will go an' get dhrunk,' sez I, 'an' forget about ut, for 'tis plain I'm not a marrin' man.'

"On my way to canteen I ran against Lascelles, color-sergeant that was av E Comp'ny, a hard, hard man, wid a torment av a wife. 'You've the head av a drowned man on your shoulders,' sez he; 'an' you're goin' where you'll get a worse wan. Come back,' sez he. 'Let me go,' sez I. 'I've thrown my luck over the wall wid my own hand!'— 'Then that's not the way to get ut back again,' sez he. 'Have out wid your throuble, ye fool-bhoy.' An' I tould him how the matther was.

"He sucked in his lower lip. 'You've been thrapped,' sez he. 'Ju Sheehy wud be the betther for a man's name to hers as soon as can. An ye thought ye'd put the comether on her,—that's the natural vanity of the baste. Terence, you're a big born fool, but you're not bad enough to marry into that comp'ny. If you said anythin' an' for all your protestations I'm sure ye did—or did not, which is worse,—eat ut all—lie like the father of all lies, but come out av ut free av Judy. Do I not know what ut is to marry a woman that was the very spit an' image av Judy whin she was young? I'm gettin' old an' I've larnt patience, but you, Terence, you'd raise hand on Judy an' kill her in a year. Never mind if Dinah gives you the go, you've desarved ut; never mind if the whole reg'mint laughs you all day. Get shut av Judy an' her mother. They can't dhrag you to church, but if they do, they'll dhrag you to hell. Go back to your quarters and lie down,' sez he. Thin over his shoulder, 'You *must* ha' done with thim.'

"Next day I wint to see Dinah, but there was no tucker in me as I walked. I knew the throuble wud come soon enough widout any hnadlin' av mine, an' I dreaded ut sore.

"I heard Judy callin' me, but I hild straight on to the Shadds' quarthers, an' Dinah wud ha' kissed me but I put her back.

" 'Whin all's said, darlin', 'sez I, 'you can give ut me if ye will. tho' I misdoubt 'twill be so easy to come by then.'

"I had scarce begun to put the explanation into shape before Judy an' her mother came to the door. I think there was a veranda, but I'm forgettin'.

" 'Will ye not step in?' sez Dinah, pretty and polite, though the Shadds had no dealin's with the Sheehys. Old Mother Shadd looked up quick, an' she was the fust to see the throuble; for Dinah was her daughter.

" 'I'm pressed for time to-day,' sez Judy as bould as brass; 'an' I've only come for Terence,—my promust man. 'Tis strange to find him here the day afther the day.'

"Dinah looked at me as though I had hit her, an' I answered straight.

" 'There was some nonsinse last night at the Sheehys' quarthers, an' Judy's carryin' on the joke, darlin',' sez I.

" 'At the Sheehys' quarthers?' sez Dinah very slow, an' Judy cut in wid: 'He was there from nine till ten, Dinah Shadd, an' the betther half av that time I was sittin' on his knee, Dinah Shadd. Ye may look and ye may look an' ye may look me up an' down, but ye won't look away that Terence is my promust man. Terence, darlin', 'tis time for us to be comin' home.'

"Dinah Shadd niver said word to Judy. 'Ye left me at half-past eight,' she sez to me, 'an' I niver thought that ye'd leave me for Judy,—promises or no promises. Go back wid her, you that have to be fetched by a girl! I'm done with you,' sez she, and she ran into her own room, her mother followin'. So I was alone wid those two women and at liberty to spake my sentiments.

" 'Judy Sheehy,' sez I, 'if you made a fool av me betune the lights you shall not do ut in the day. I niver promised you words or lines.'

" 'You lie,' sez ould Mother Sheehy, 'an' may ut choke you where you stand!' She was far gone in dhrink.

" 'An' tho' ut choked me where I stud I'd not change,' sez I. 'Go home, Judy. I take shame for a decent girl like you dhraggin' your mother out bareheaded on this errand. Hear now, and have ut for an answer. I gave my word to Dinah Shadd yesterday, an', more blame to me, I was wid you last night talkin' nonsinse but nothin' more. You've chosen to thry to hould me on ut. I will not be held thereby for anythin' in the world. Is that enough?'

"Judy wint pink all over. 'An' I wish you joy av the perjury,' sez she, duckin' a curtsey. 'You've lost a woman that would ha' wore her hand to the bone for your pleasure; an' 'deed, Terence, ye were not thrapped. . . .' Lascelles must ha' spoken plain to her. 'I am such as Dinah is—'deed I am! Ye've lost a fool av a girl that'll niver look at you again, an' ye've lost what he niver had,—your common honesty. If you manage your men as you manage your love-makin', small wondher they call you the worst corp'ril in the comp'ny. Come away, mother,' sez she.

"But divil a fut would the ould woman budge! 'D'you hould by that?' sez she, peerin' up under her thick grey eyebrows.

" 'Ay, an' wud,' sez I, 'tho' Dinah give me the go twinty times. I'll have no thruck with you or yours,' sez I. 'Take your child away, ye shameless woman.'

" 'An' am I shameless?' sez she, bringin' her hands up above her head.

'Thin what are you, ye lyin', schamin', weak-kneed, dhirty-souled son av a sutler? Am *I* shameless? Who put the open shame on me an' my child that we shud go beggin' through the lines in the broad daylight for the broken word of a man? Double portion of my shame be on you, Terence Mulvaney, that think yourself so strong! By Mary and the saints, by blood and water an' by ivry sorrow that came into the world since the beginnin', the black blight fall on you and yours, so that you may niver be free from pain for another when ut's not your own! May your heart bleed in your breast drop by drop wid all your friends laughin' at the bleedin'! Strong you think yourself? May your strength be a curse to you to dhrive you into the divil's hands against your own will! Clear-eyed you are? May your eyes see clear evry step av the dark path you take till the hot cindhers av hell put thim out! May the ragin' dry thirst in my own ould bones go to you that you shall niver pass bottle full nor glass empty. God preserve the light av your onderstandin' to you, my jewel av a bhoy, that ye may niver forget what you mint to be an' do, whin you're wallowin' in the muck! May ye see the betther and follow the worse as long as there's breath in your body; an' may ye die quick in a strange land, watchin' your death before ut takes you, an' onable to stir hand or foot!'

"I heard a scufflin' in the room behind, and thin Dinah Shadd's hand dhropped into mine like a rose-leaf into a muddy road.

" 'The half av that I'll take,' sez she, 'an' more too if I can. Go home, ye silly talkin' woman,—go home an' confess.'

" 'Come away! Come away!' sez Judy, pullin' her mother by the shawl. ''Twas none av Terence's fault. For the love av Mary stop the talkin'!'

" 'An' you!' said ould Mother Sheehy, spinnin' round forninst Dinah. 'Will ye take the half av that man's load? Stand off from him, Dinah Shadd, before he takes you down too—you that look to be a quarther-master-sergeant's wife in five years. You look too high, child. You shall *wash* for the quarthermaster-sergeant, whin he plases to give you the job out av charity; but a privit's wife you shall be to the end, an' evry sorrow of a privit's wife you shall know and nivir a joy but wan, that shall go from you like the running tide from a rock. The pain av bearin' you shall know but niver the pleasure av giving the breast; an' you shall put away a man-child into the common ground wid never a priest to say a prayer over him, an' on that man-child ye shall think ivry day av your life. Think long, Dinah Shadd, for you'll niver have another tho' you pray till your knees are bleedin'. The mothers av childer shall mock you behind your back when you're wringing over the washtub. You shall know what ut is to help a dhrunken husband home an' see him go to the gyard-room. Will that plase you, Dinah Shadd, that won't be seen talkin' to my daughter? You shall talk to worse than Judy before all's over. The sergints' wives shall look down on you contemptuous, daughter av a sergint, an' you shall cover ut all up wid a smiling face when your heart's burstin'. Stand off av him, Dinah

Shadd, for I've put the Black Curse of Shielygh upon him an' his own mouth shall make ut good.'

"She pitched forward on her head an' began foamin' at the mouth. Dinah Shadd ran out wid water, an' Judy dhragged the ould woman into the veranda till she sat up.

" 'I'm old an' forlore,' she sez, thremblin' an' cryin', 'and 'tis like I say a dale more than I mane.'

" 'When you're able to walk,—go,' says ould Mother Shadd. 'This house has no place for the likes av you that have cursed my daughter.'

" 'Eyah!' said the ould woman. 'Hard words break no bones, an' Dinah Shadd 'll keep the love av her husband till my bones are green corn. Judy darlin', I misremember what I came here for. Can you lend us the bottom av a taycup av tay, Mrs. Shadd?'

"But Judy dhragged her off cryin' as tho' her heart wud break. An' Dinah Shadd an' I, in ten minutes we had forgot ut all."

"Then why do you remember it now?" said I.

"Is ut like I'd forget? Ivry word that wicked ould woman spoke fell thrue in my life aftherward, an' I cud ha' stud ut all—stud ut all—excipt when my little Shadd was born. That was on the line av march three months afther the regiment was taken with cholera. We were betune Umballa an' Kalka thin, an' I was on picket. Whin I came off duty the women showed me the child, an' ut turned out uts side an' died as I looked. We buried him by the road, an' Father Victor was a day's march behind wid the heavy baggage, so the comp'ny captain read a prayer. An' since then I've been a childless man, an' all else that ould Mother Sheehy put upon me an' Dinah Shadd. What do you think, sorr?"

I thought a good deal, but it seemed better then to reach out for Mulvaney's hand. The demonstration nearly cost me the use of three fingers. Whatever he knows of his weaknesses, Mulvaney is entirely ignorant of his strength.

"But what do you think?" he repeated, as I was straightening out the crushed fingers.

My reply was drowned in yells and outcries from the next fire, where ten men were shouting for "Orth'ris," "Privit Orth'ris," "Mistah Or—ther—ris!" "Deah boy," "Cap'n Orth'ris," "Field-Marshal Orth'ris," "Stanley, you pen'-north o' pop, come 'ere to your own comp'ny!" And the cockney, who had been delighting an other audience with recondite and Rabelaisian yarns, was shot down among his admirers by the major force.

"You've crumpled my dress-shirt 'orrid," said he, "an' I shan't sing no more to this 'ere bloomin' drawin'-room."

Learoyd, roused by the confusion, uncoiled himself, crept behind Ortheris, and slung him aloft on his shoulders.

"Sing, ye bloomin' hummin' bird!" said he, and Ortheris, beating time on Learoyd's skull, delivered himself, in the raucous voice of the Ratcliffe Highway, of this song:—

My girl she give me the go onst,
  When I was a London lad,
An' I went on the drink for a fortnight,
  An' then I went to the bad.
The Queen she give me a shillin'
  To fight for 'er over the seas;
But Guv'ment built me a fever-trap,
  An' Injia give me disease.

Chorus.

Ho! don't you 'eed what a girl says,
An' don't you go for the beer;
But I was an ass when I was at grass
An' that is why I'm here.

I fired a shot at a Afghan,
The begger 'e fired again,
An' I lay on my bed with a 'ole in my 'ed
An' missed the next campaign!

I up with my gun at a Burman
Who carried a bloomin' *dah,*
But the cartridge stuck and the bay'nit
bruk,
An' all I got was the scar.

Chorus.

Ho! don't you aim at a Afghan
When you stand on the sky-line clear;
An' don't you go for a Burman
If none o' your friends is near.

I served my time for a sergeant;
An' wetted my stripes with pop,
For I went on the bend with a intimate
friend.
An' finished the night in the "shop."
I served my time for a sergeant;
The colonel 'e sez "No!
The most you'll see is a full C. B." [1]
An' . . . very next night 'twas so.

Chorus.

Ho! don't you go for a corp'ral
Unless your 'ed is clear;
But I was an ass when I was at grass,
An' that is why I'm 'ere.

I've tasted the luck o' the army
In barrack an' camp an' clink,
An' I lost my tip through the bloomin'
trip
Along o' the women an' drink.
I'm down at the heel o' my service
An' when I am laid on the shelf,
My very wust friend from beginning to
end
By the blood of a mouse was myself!
[1] Confined to barracks.

Chorus.

Ho! don't you 'eed what a girl says,
An' don't you go for the beer:
But I was an ass when I was at grass,
An' that is why I'm 'ere.

"Ay, listen to our little man now,
singin' an' shoutin' as tho' trouble had
niver touched him. D' you remember
when he went mad with the homesick-
ness?" said Mulvaney, recalling a never-
to-be-forgotten season when Ortheris
waded through the deep waters of affliction and behaved abominably. "But he's
talkin' bitter truth, though. Eyah!

"My very worst frind from beginnin'
to ind
By the blood av a mouse was mesilf!"

.   .   .   .   .   .

When I woke I saw Mulvaney, the
night-dew gemming his moustache, leaning on his rifle at picket, lonely as
Prometheus on his rock, with I know
not what vultures tearing his liver.

On Greenhow Hill

To Love's low voice she lent a careless
ear;
Her hand within his rosy fingers lay,
A chilling weight. She would not turn or
hear;

But with averted face went on her way.
But when pale Death, all featureless and
grim,
Lifted his bony hand, and beckoning
Held out his cypress-wreath, she followed
him.

And Love was left forlorn and wondering,
That she who for his bidding would
not stay,
At Death's first whisper rose and went
away.
                              Rivals.

"OHE, *Ahmed Din! Shafiz Ulla
ahoo!* Bahadur Khan, where are you?
Come out of the tents, as I have done,
and fight against the English. Don't
kill your own kin! Come out to me!"

The deserter from a native corps was
crawling round the outskirts of the
camp, firing at intervals, and shouting
invitations to his old comrades. Misled by the rain and the darkness, he
came to the English wing of the camp,
and with his yelping and rifle-practice
disturbed the men. They had been
making roads all day, and were tired.

Ortheris was sleeping at Learoyd's
feet. "Wot's all that?" he said thickly.
Learoyd snored, and a Snider bullet
ripped its way through the tent wall.
The men swore. "It's that bloomin' deserter from the Aurangabadis," said
Ortheris. "Git up, some one, an' tell
'im 'e's come to the wrong shop."

"Go to sleep, little man," said Mulvaney, who was steaming nearest the
door. "I can't arise and expaytiate with
him. 'Tis rainin' entrenchin' tools outside."

"'Tain't because you bloomin' can't.
It's 'cause you bloomin' won't, ye long,
limp, lousy, lazy beggar, you. 'Ark to
'im 'owlin'!"

"Wot's the good of argifying? Put a
bullet into the swine! 'E's keepin' us
awake!" said another voice.

A subaltern shouted angrily, and a
dripping sentry whined from the darkness—

"'Tain't no good, sir. I can't see 'im.
'E's 'idin' somewhere down 'ill."

Ortheris tumbled out of his blanket.
"Shall I try to get 'im, sir?" said he.

"No," was the answer. "Lie down. I
won't have the whole camp shooting all
round the clock. Tell him to go and
pot his friends."

Ortheris considered for a moment.
Then, putting his head under the tent
wall, he called, as a 'bus conductor calls
in a block, "'lgher up, there! 'lgher up!"

The men laughed, and the laughter
was carried down wind to the deserter,
who, hearing that he had made a mistake, went off to worry his own regiment half a mile away. He was received with shots; the Aurangabadis
were very angry with him for disgracing
their colors.

"An' that's all right," said Ortheris,
withdrawing his head as he heard the
hiccough of the Sniders in the distance.
"S'elp me Gawd, tho', that man's not fit
to live—messin' with my beauty-sleep
this way."

"Go out and shoot him in the morning,
then," said the subaltern incautiously.
"Silence in the tents now. Get your
rest, men."

Ortheris lay down with a happy little
sigh, and in two minutes there was no
sound except the rain on the canvas and
the all-embracing and elemental snoring
of Learoyd.

The camp lay on a bare ridge of the
Himalayas, and for a week had been
waiting for a flying column to make
connection. The nightly rounds of the

deserter and his friends had become a nuisance.

In the morning the men dried themselves in hot sunshine and cleaned their grimy accoutrements. The native regiment was to take its turn of road-making that day while the Old Regiment loafed.

"I'm goin' to lay for a shot at that man," said Ortheris, when he had finished washing out his rifle. "'E comes up the watercourse every evenin' about five o'clock. If we go and lie out on the north 'ill a bit this afternoon we'll get 'im."

"You're a bloodthirsty little mosquito," said Mulvaney, blowing blue clouds into the air. "But I suppose I will have to come wid you. Fwhere's Jock?"

"Gone out with the Mixed Pickles, 'cause 'e thinks 'isself a bloomin' marksman," said Ortheris, with scorn.

The "Mixed Pickles" were a detachment of picked shots, generally employed in clearing spurs of hills when the enemy were too impertinent. This taught the young officers how to handle men, and did not do the enemy much harm. Mulvaney and Ortheris strolled out of camp, and passed the Aurangabadis going to their road-making.

"You've got to sweat to-day," said Ortheris, genially. "We're going to get your man. You didn't knock 'im out last night by any chance, any of you?"

"No. The pig went away mocking us. I had one shot at him," said a private. "He's my cousin, and I ought to have cleared our dishonor. But good luck to you."

They went cautiously to the north hill, Ortheris leading, because, as he explained, "this is a long-range show, an' I've got to do it." His was an almost passionate devotion to his rifle, which, by barrack-room report, he was supposed to kiss every night before turning in. Charges and scuffles he held in contempt, and, when they were inevitable, slipped between Mulvaney and Learoyd, bidding them to fight for his skin as well as their own. They never failed him. He trotted along, questing like a hound on a broken trail, through the wood of the north hill. At last he was satisfied, and threw himself down on the soft pine-needle slope that commanded a clear view of the watercourse and a brown, bare hillside beyond it. The trees made a scented darkness in which an army corps could have hidden from the sun-glare without.

"'Ere's the tail o' the wood," said Ortheris. "'E's got to come up the watercourse, 'cause it gives 'im cover. We'll lay 'ere. 'Tain't not arf so bloomin' dusty neither."

He buried his nose in a clump of scentless white violets. No one had come to tell the flowers that the season of their strength was long past, and they had bloomed merrily in the twilight of the pines.

"This is something like," he said, luxuriously. "Wot a 'evinly clear drop for a bullet acrost! How much d'you make it, Mulvaney?"

"Seven hunder. Maybe a trifle less, bekaze the air's so thin."

Wop! Wop! Wop! went a volley of musketry on the rear face of the north hill.

"'Curse them Mixed Pickles firin' at nothin'! They'll scare 'arf the country."

"Thry a sightin' shot in the middle

of the row," said Mulvaney, the man of many wiles. "There's a red rock yonder he'll be sure to pass. Quick!"

Ortheris ran his sight up to six hundred yards and fired. The bullet threw up a feather of dust by a clump of gentians at the base of the rock.

"Good enough!" said Ortheris, snapping the scale down. "You snick your sights to mine or a little lower. You're always firin' high. But remember, first shot to me. O Lordy! but it's a lovely afternoon."

The noise of the firing grew louder, and there was a tramping of men in the wood. The two lay very quiet, for they knew that the British soldier is desperately prone to fire at anything that moves or calls. Then Learoyd appeared, his tunic ripped across the breast by a bullet, looking ashamed of himself. He flung down on the pine-needles, breathing in snorts.

"One o' them damned gardeners o' th' Pickles," said he, fingering the rent. "Firin' to th' right flank, when he knowed I was there. If I knew who he was I'd 'a' rippen the hide offan him. Look at ma tunic!"

"That's the spishil trustability av a marksman. Train him to hit a fly wid a stiddy rest at seven hunder, an' he loose on anythin' he sees or hears up to th' mile. You're well out av that fancy-firin' gang, Jock. Stay here."

"Bin firin' at the bloomin' wind in the bloomin' treetops," said Ortheris, with a chuckle. "I'll show you some firin' later on."

They wallowed in the pine-needles, and the sun warmed them where they lay. The Mixed Pickles ceased firing, and returned to camp. and left the wood

to a few scared apes. The watercourse lifted up its voice in the silence, and talked foolishly to the rocks. Now and again the dull thump of a blasting charge three miles away told that the Aurangabadis were in difficulties with their road-making. The men smiled as they listened and lay still, soaking in the warm leisure. Presently Learoyd, between the whiffs of his pipe—

"Seems queer—about 'im yonder—desertin' at all."

" 'E'll be a bloomin' side queerer when I've done with 'im," said Ortheris. They were talking in whispers, for the stillness of the wood and the desire of slaughter lay heavy upon them.

"I make no doubt he had his reasons for desertin'; but, my faith! I make less doubt ivry man has good reason for killin' him," said Mulvaney.

"Happen there was a lass tewed up wi' it. Men do more than more for th' sake of a lass."

"They make most av us 'list. They've no manner av right to make us desert.'

"Ah; they make us 'list, or their fathers do," said Learoyd, softly, his helmet over his eyes.

Ortheris's brows contracted savagely. He was watching the valley. "If it's a girl I'll shoot the beggar twice over, an' second time for bein' a fool. You're blasted sentimental all of a sudden. Thinkin' o' your last near shave?"

"Nay, lad; ah was but thinkin' o' what had happened."

"An' fwhat has happened, ye lumberin' child av calamity, that you're lowing like a cow-calf at the back av the pasture, an' suggestin' invidious excuses for the man Stanley's goin' to kill. Ye'll have to wait another hour yet, little man. Split it out, Jock, an' bellow melojus to the moon. It takes an earthquake or a bullet graze to fetch aught out av you. Discourse, Don Juan! The a-moors av Lotharius Learoyd! Stanley, kape a rowlin' rig'mental eye on the valley."

"It's along o' yon hill there," said Learoyd, watching the bare sub-Himalayan spur that reminded him of his Yorkshire moors. He was speaking more to himself than his fellows. "Ay," said he, "Rumbolds Moor stands up ower Skipton town, an' Greenhow Hill stands up ower Pately Brig. I reckon you've never heeard tell o' Greenhow Hill, but yon bit o' bare stuff if there was nobbut a white road windin' is like ut; strangely like. Moors an' moors an' moors, wi' never a tree for shelter, an' grey houses wi' flagstone rooves, and pewits cryin', an' a windhover goin' to and fro just like these kites. And cold! A wind that cuts you like a knife. You could tell Greenhow Hill folk by the red-apple color o' their cheeks an' nose tips, and their blue eyes, driven into pin-points by the wind. Miners mostly, burrowin' for lead i' th' hillsides, followin' the trail of th' ore vein same as a field-rat. It was the roughest minin' I ever seen. Yo'd come on a bit o' creakin' wood windlass like a wellhead, an' you was let down i' th' bight of a rope, fendin' yoursen off the side wi' one hand, carryin' a candle stuck in a lump o' clay with t'other, an' clickin' hold of a rope with t'other hand."

"An' that's three of them," said Mulvaney. "Must be a good climate in those parts."

Learoyd took no heed.

"An' then yo' came to a level, where you crept on your hands and knees through a mile o' windin' drift, an' you come out into a cave-place as big as Leeds Townhall, with a engine pumpin' water from workin's 'at went deeper still. It's a queer country, let alone minin', for the hill is full of those natural caves, an' the rivers an' the becks drops into what they call pot-holes, an' come out again miles away."

"Wot was you doin' there?" said Ortheris.

"I was a young chap then, an' mostly went wi' 'osses, leadin' coal and lead ore; but at th' time I'm tellin' on I was drivin' the waggon-team i' th' big sumph. I didn't belong to that country-side by rights. I went there because of a little difference at home, an' at fust I took up wi' a rough lot. One night we'd been drinkin', an' I must ha' hed more than I could stand, or happen th' ale was none so good. Though i' them days, By for God, I never seed bad ale." He flung his arms over his head, and gripped a vast handful of white violets. "Nah," said he, "I never seed the ale I could not drink, the bacca I could not smoke, nor the lass I could not kiss. Well, we mun have a race home, the lot on us. I lost all th' others, an' when I was climbin' ower one of them walls built o' loose stones, I comes down into the ditch, stones and all, an' broke my arm. Not as I knawed much about it, for I fell on th' back of my head, an' was knocked stupid like. An' when I come to mysen it were mornin', an' I were lyin' on the settle i' Jesse Roantree's houseplace, an' 'Liza Roantree was settin' sewin'. I ached all ovver, and my mouth were like a lime-kiln. She gave me a drink out of a china mug wi' gold letters—'A Present from Leeds'—as I looked at many and many a time at after. 'Yo're to lie still while Dr. Warbottom comes, because your arm's broken, and father has sent a lad to fetch him. He found yo' when he was goin' to work, an' carried you here on his back,' sez she. 'Oa!' sez I; an' I shet my eyes, for I felt ashamed o' mysen. 'Father's gone to his work these three hours, an' he said he' tell 'em to get somebody to drive the tram.' The clock ticked, an' a bee comed in the house, an' they rung i' my head like mill-wheels. An' she give me another drink an' settled the pillow. 'Eh, but yo're young to be getten drunk an' such like, but yo' won't do it again, will yo'?'—'Noa,' sez I, 'I wouldn't if she'd not but stop they mill-wheels clatterin'.'"

"Faith, it's a good thing to be nursed by a woman when you're sick!" said Mulvaney. "Dir' cheap at the price av twenty broken heads."

Ortheris turned to frown across the valley. He had not been nursed by many women in his life.

"An' then Dr. Warbottom comes ridin' up, an' Jesse Roantree along with 'im. He was a high-larned doctor, but he talked wi' poor folk same as theirsens. 'What's ta bin agaate on naa?' he sings out. 'Brekkin' tha thick head?' An' he felt me all ovver. 'That's none broken. Tha' nobbut knocked a bit sillier than ordinary, an' that's daaft eneaf.' An' soa he went on, callin' me all the names he could think on, but settin' my arm, wi's Jesse's help, as careful as could be. 'Yo' mun let the big oaf bide here a bit, Jesse,' he says, when he hed strapped me up an' given

me a dose o' physic; 'an' you an' 'Liza will tend him, though he's scarcelins worth the trouble. An' tha'll lose tha work,' sez he, 'an' tha'll be upon th' Sick Club for a couple o' months an' more. Doesn't tha think tha's a fool?'"

"But whin was a young man, high or low, the other av a fool, I'd like to know?" said Mulvaney. "Sure, folly's the only safe way to wisdom, for I've thried it."

"Wisdom!" grinned Ortheris, scanning his comrades with uplifted chin. "You're bloomin' Solomons, you two, ain't you?"

Learoyd went calmly on, with a steady eye like an ox chewing the cud.

"And that was how I come to know 'Liza Roantree. There's some tunes as she used to sing—aw, she were always singin'—that fetches Greenhow Hill before my eyes as fair as yon brow across there. And she would learn me to sing bass, an' I was to go to th' chapel wi' 'em where Jesse and she led the singin', th' old man playin' the fiddle. He was a strange chap, old Jesse, fair mad wi' music, an' he made me promise to learn the big fiddle when my arm was better. It belonged to him, and it stood up in a big case alongside o' th' eight-day clock, but Willie Satterthwaite, as played it in the chapel, had gotten deaf as a door-post, and it vexed Jesse, as he had to rap him ower his head wi' th' fiddle-stick to make him give ower sawin' at th' right time.

"But there was a black drop in it all, an' it was a man in a black coat that brought it. When th' primitive Methodist preacher came to Greenhow, he would always stop wi' Jesse Roantree, an' he laid hold of me from th' beginning. It seemed I wor a soul to be saved, and he meaned to do it. At th' same time I jealoused 'at he were keen o' savin' 'Liza Roantree's soul as well, and I could ha' killed him many a time. An' this went on till one day I broke out, an' borrowed th' brass for a drink from 'Liza. After fower days I come back, wi' my tail between my legs, just to see 'Liza again. But Jesse were at home an' th' preacher—th' Reverend Amos Barraclough. 'Liza said naught, but a bit o' red come into her face as were white of a regular thing. Says Jesse, tryin' his best to be civil, 'Nay, lad, it's like this. You've getten to choose which way it's goin' to be. I'll ha' nobody across ma doorstep as goes a-drinkin', an' borrows my lass's money to spend i' their drink. Ho'd tha tongue, 'Liza,' sez he, when she wanted to put in a word 'at I were welcome to th' brass, and she were none afraid that I wouldn't pay it back. Then the Reverend cuts in, seein' as Jesse were losin' his temper, an' they fair beat me among them. But it were 'Liza, as looked an' said naught, as did more than either o' their tongues, an' soa I concluded to get converted."

"Fwhat?" shouted Mulvaney. Then, checking himself, he said softly, "Let be! Let be! Sure the Blessed Virgin is the mother of all religion an' most women; an' there's a dale av piety in a girl if the men would only let ut stay there. I'd ha' been converted myself under the circumstances."

"Nay, but," pursued Learoyd with a blush, "I meaned it."

Ortheris laughed as loudly as he dared, having regard to his business at the time.

"Ay, Ortheris, you may laugh, but you didn't know yon preacher Barraclough —a little white-faced chap, wi' a voice as 'ud wile a bird off an a bush, and a way o' layin' hold of folks as made them think they'd never had a live man for a friend before. You never saw him, an'—an'—you never seed 'Liza Roantree—never seed 'Liza Roantree. . . . Happen it was as much 'Liza as th' preacher and her father, but anyways they all meaned it, an' I was fair shamed o' mysen, an' so I become what they call a changed chàracter. And when I think on, it's hard to believe as yon chap going to prayermeetin's, chapel, and class-meetin's were me. But I nevet had naught to say for mysen, though there was a deal o' shoutin', and old Sammy Strother, as were almost clemmed to death and doubled up with the rheumatics, would sing out, 'Joyful! Joyful!' and 'at it were better to go up to heaven in a coal-basket than down to hell i' a coach an' six. And he would put his poor old claw on my shoulder, sayin', 'Doesn't tha feel it, tha great lump? Doesn't tha feel it?' An' sometimes I thought I did, and then again I thought I didn't, an' how was that?"

"The iverlastin' nature av mankind," said Mulvaney. "An', furthermore, I misdoubt you were built for the Primitive Methodians. They're a new corps anyways. I hold by the Ould Church, for she's the mother of them all—ay, an' the father, too. I like her bekase she's most remarkable regimental in her fittings. I may die in Honolulu, Nova Zambra, or Cape Cayenne, but wherever I die, me bein' fwhat I am, an' a priest handy, I go under the same orders an' the same words an' the same unction as tho' the Pope himself come down from the roof av St. Peter's to see me off. There's neither high nor low, nor broad nor deep, nor betwixt nor between wid her, an' that's what I like. But mark you, she's no manner av Church for a wake man, bekaze she takes the body and the soul av him, onless he has his proper work to do. I remember when my father died that was three months comin' to his grave; begad he'd ha' sold the she-been above our heads for ten minutes' quittance of purgathory. An' he did all he could. That's why I say ut takes a strong man to deal with the Ould Church, an' for that reason you'll find so many women go there. An' that same's a conundrum."

"Wot's the use o' worritin' 'bout these things?" said Ortheris. "You're bound to find all out quicker nor you want to, any'ow." He jerked the cartridge out of the breech-block into the palm of his hand. "Ere's my chaplain," he said, and made the venomous blackheaded bullet bow like a marionette. "'E's goin' to teach a man all about which is which, an' wot's true, after all, before sundown. But wot 'appened after that, Jock?"

"There was one thing they boggled at, and almost shut th' gate i' my face for, and that were my dog Blast, th' only one saved out o' a litter o' pups as was blowed up when a keg o' minin' powder loosed off in th' storekeeper's hut. They liked his name no better than his business, which were fightin' every dog he comed across; a rare good dog, wi' spots o' black and pink on his face, one ear gone, and lame o' one side wi' being driven

in a basket through an iron roof, a matter of half a mile.

"They said I mum give him up 'cause he were worldly and low; and would I let mysen be shut out of heaven for the sake on a dog? 'Nay,' says I, 'if th' door isn't wide enough for th' pair on us, we'll stop outside, for we'll none be parted.' And th' preacher spoke up for Blast, as had a likin' for him from th' first—I reckon that was why I come to like th' preacher—and wouldn't hear o' changin' his name to Bless, as some o' them wanted. So th' pair on us became reg'lar chapelmembers. But it's hard for a young chap o' my build to cut traces from the world, th' flesh, an' the devil all uv a heap. Yet I stuck to it for a long time, while th' lads as used to stand about th' town-end an' lean ower th' bridge, spittin' into th' beck o' a Sunday, would call after, 'Sitha, Learoyd, when's ta bean to preach, 'cause we're comin' to hear tha.'—'Ho'd that jaw. He hasn't getten th' white choaker on ta morn,' another lad would say, and I had to double my fists hard i' th' bottom of my Sunday coat, and say to mysen, 'If 'twere Monday and I warn't a member o' the Primitive Methodists, I'd leather all th' lot of yond'.' That was th' hardest of all—to know that I could fight and I mustn't fight."

Sympathetic grunts from Mulvaney.

"So what wi' singin', practicin', and class-meetin's, and th' big fiddle, as he made me take between my knees, I spent a deal o' time i' Jesse Roantree's house-place. But often as I was there, th' preacher fared to me to go oftener, and both th' old man an' th' young woman were pleased to have him. He lived i' Pately Brig, as were a goodish step off, but he come. He come all the same. I liked him as well or better as any man I'd ever seen i' one way, and yet I hated him wi' all my heart i' t'other, and we watched each other like cat and mouse, but civil as you please, for I was on my best behavior, and he was that fair and open that I was bound to be fair with him. Rare good company he was, if I hadn't wanted to wring his cliver little neck half of the time. Often and often when he was goin' from Jesse's I'd set him a bit on the road."

"See 'im 'ome, you mean?" said Ortheris.

"Ay. It's a way we have i' Yorkshire o' seein' friends off. You was a friend as I didn't want to come back, and he didn't want me to come back neither, and so we'd walk together toward Pately, and then he'd set me back again, and there we'd be wal two o'clock i' the mornin' settin' each other to an' fro like a blasted pair o' pendulums twixt hill and valley, long after th' light had gone out i' 'Liza's window, as both on us had been looking at, pretending to watch the moon."

"Ah!" broke in Mulvaney, "ye'd no chanst against the maraudin' psalm-singer. They'll take the airs an' the graces instid av the man nine times out av ten, an' they only find the blunder later—the wimmen."

"That's just where yo're wrong," said Learoyd, reddening under the freckled tan of his cheeks. "I was th' first wi' 'Liza, an' you'd think that were enough. But th' parson were a steady-gaited sort o' chap, and Jesse were strong o' his side, and all th' women i' the congre-gation dinned it to 'Liza 'at she were fair fond to take up wi' a wastrel ne'er-do-weel like me, as was scarcelins respectable an' a fighting dog at his heels. It was all very well for her to be doing me good and saving my soul, but she must mind as she didn't do herself harm. They talk o' rich folk bein' stuck up an' genteel, but for cast-iron pride o' respectability there's naught like poor chapel folk. It's as cold as th' wind o' Greenhow Hill—ay, and colder for 'twill never change. And now I come to think on it, one at strangest things I know is 'at they couldn't abide th' thought o' soldiering. There's a vast o' fightin' i' th' Bible, and there's a deal of Methodists i' th' army; but to hear chapel folk talk you'd think that soldierin' were next door, an' t'other side, to hangin'. I' their meetin's all their talk is o' fightin'. When Sammy Strother were stuck for summat to say in his prayers, he'd sing out, 'Th' sword o' th' Lord and o' Gideon.' They were allus at it about puttin' on th' whole armor o' righteousness, an' fightin' the good fight o' faith. And then, atop o' 't all, they held a prayer-meetin' ower a young chap as wanted to 'list, and nearly deafened him till he picked up his hat and fair ran away. And they'd tell tales in th' Sunday-school o' bad lads as had been thumped and brayed for bird-nesting o' Sundays and playin' truant o' week days, and how they took to wrestlin', dog-fightin', rabbit-runnin', and drinkin', till at last, as if 'twere a hepitaph on a gravestone, they damned him across th' moors wi', 'an' then he went and 'listed for a soldier,' an' they'd all fetch a deep breath, and throw up their eyes like a hen drinkin'."

"Fwhy is ut?" said Mulvaney, bringing down his hand on his thigh with a crack. "In the name av God, fwhy is ut? I've seen ut, tu. They cheat an' they swindle an' they lie an' they slander, an' fifty things fifty times worse; but the last an' the worst by their reckonin' is to serve the Widdy honest. It's like the talk av childer—seein' things all round."

"Plucky lot of fightin' good fights of whatsername they'd do if we didn't see they had a quiet place to fight in. And such fightin' as theirs is! Cats on the tiles. T'other callin' to which to come on. I'd give a month's pay to get some o' them broad-backed beggars in London sweatin' through a day's road-makin' an' a night's rain. They'd carry on a deal afterward—same as we're supposed to carry on. I've bin turned out of a measly arf-license pub down Lambeth way, full o' greasy kebmen, 'fore now," said Ortheris with an oath.

"Maybe you were dhrunk," said Mulvaney, soothingly.

"Worse nor that. The Forders were drunk. *I* was wearin' the Queen's uniform."

"I'd no particular thought to be a soldier i' them days," said Learoyd, still keeping his eye on the bare hill opposite, "but this sort o' talk put it i' my head. They was so good, th' chapel folk, that they tumbled ower t'other side. But I stuck to it for 'Liza's sake, specially as she was learning me to sing the bass part in a horotorio as Jesse were gettin' up. She sung like a throstle hersen, and we had practicin's night after night for a matter of three months." ·

"I know what a horotorio is," said Ortheris, pertly. "It's a sort of chaplain's sing-song—words all out of the Bible, and hullabalooiah choruses."

"Most Greenhow Hill Folks played some instrument or t'other, an' they all sung so you might have heard them miles away, and they were so pleased wi' the noise they made they didn't fair to want anybody to listen. The preacher sung high seconds when he wasn't playin' the flute, an' they set me, as hadn't got far with big fiddle, again Willie Satterthwaite, to jog his elbow when he had to get a' gate playin'. Old Jesse was happy if ever a man was, for he were th' conductor an' th' first fiddle an' th' leadin' singer, beatin' time wi' his fiddle-stick, till at times he'd rap with it on the table, and cry out, 'Now, you mun all stop; it's my turn.' And he'd face round to his front, fair sweating wi' pride, to sing th' tenor solos. But he were grandest i' th' choruses, waggin' his head, flingin' his arms round like a windmill, and singin' hisself black in the face. A rare singer were Jesse.

"Yo' see, I was not o' much account wi' 'em all exceptin' to 'Liza Roantree, and I had a deal o' time settin' quiet at meetings and horotorio practices to hearken their talk, and if it were strange to me at beginnin', it got stranger still at after, when I was shut on it, and could study what it meaned.

"Just after th' horotorios come off, 'Liza, as had allus been weakly like, was took very bad. I walked Dr. Warbottom's horse up and down a deal of times while he were inside, where they wouldn't let me go, though I fair ached to see her.

"'She'll be better i' noo, lad—better i' noo,' he used to say. 'Tha mun ha' patience.' Then they said if I was quiet I might go in, and th' Reverend Amos Barraclough used to read to her lyin' propped up among th' pillows. Then she began to mend a bit, and they let me carry her on to th' settle, and when it got warm again she went about same as afore. Th' preacher and me and Blast was a deal together i' them days, and i' one way we was rare good comrades. But I could ha' stretched him time and again with a good will. I mind one day he said he would like to go down into th' bowels o' th' earth, and see how th' Lord had builded th' framework o' th' everlastin' hills. He were one of them chaps as had a gift o' sayin' things. They rolled off the tip of his clever tongue, same as Mulvaney here, as would ha' made a rare good preacher if he had nobbut given his mind to it. I lent him a suit o' miner's kit as almost buried th' little man, and his white face down i' th' coat-collar and hatflap looked like the face of a boggart, and he cowered down i' th' bottom o' the waggon. I was drivin' a tram as led up a bit of an incline up to th' cave where the engine was pumpin', and where th' ore was brought up and put into th' waggons as went down o' themselves, me puttin' th' brake on and th' horses a-trottin' after. Long as it was daylight we were good friends, but when we got fair into th' dark, and could nobbut see th' day shinin' at the hole like a lamp at a street-end, I feeled downright wicked. Ma religion dropped all away from me when I looked back at him as were always comin' between me and 'Liza. The talk was 'at they were to be wed when she got better, an' I couldn't get her to say yes or nay to it. He

began to sing a hymn in his thin voice, and I came out wi' a chorus that was all cussin' an' swearin' at my horses, an' I began to know how I hated him. He were such a little chap, too. I could drop him wi' one hand down Garstang's Copper-hole—a place where th' beck slithered ower th' edge on a rock, and fell wi' a bit of a whisper into a pit as no rope i' Greenhow could plump."

Again Learoyd rooted up the innocent violets. "Ay, he should see th' bowels o' th' earth an' never naught else. I could take him a mile or two along th' drift, and leave him wi' his candle doused to cry hallelujah, wi' none to hear him and say amen. I was to lead him down th' ladder-way to th' drift where Jesse Roantree was workin', and why shouldn't he slip on th' ladder, wi' my feet on his fingers till they loosed grip, and I put him down wi' my heel? If I went fust down th' ladder I could click hold on him and chuck him over my head, so as he should go squshin' down the shaft, breakin' his bones at ev'ry timberin' as Bill Appleton did when he was fresh, and hadn't a bone left when he wrought to th' bottom. Niver a blasted leg to walk from Pately. Niver an arm to put round 'Liza Roantree's waist. Niver no more—niver no more."

The thick lips curled back over the yellow teeth, and that flushed face was not pretty to look upon. Mulvaney nodded sympathy, and Ortheris, moved by his comrade's passion, brought up the rifle to his shoulder, and searched the hillside for his quarry, muttering ribaldry about a sparrow, a spout, and a thunderstorm. The voice of the watercourse supplied the neecssary small talk till Learoyd picked up his story.

"But it's none so easy to kill a man like yon. When I'd given up my horses to th' lad as took my place and I was showin' th' preacher th' workin's, shoutin' into his ear across th' clang o' th' pumpin' engines, I saw he were afraid o' naught; and when the lamplight showed his black eyes, I could feel as he was masterin' me again. I were no better nor Blast chained up short and growlin' i' the depths of him while a strange dog went safe past.

" 'Th'art a coward and a fool,' I said to mysen; an' I wrestled i' my mind again' him till, when we come to Garstang's Copper-hole, I laid hold o' the preacher and lifted him up over my head and held him into the darkest on it. 'Now, lad,' I says, 'it's to be one or t'other on us—thee or me—for 'Liza Roantree. Why, isn't thee afraid for thysen?' I says, for he were still i' my arms as a sack. 'Nay; I'm but afraid for thee, my poor lad, as knows naught,' says he. I set him down on th' edge, an' th' beck run stiller, an' there was no more buzzin' in my head like when th' bee come through th' window o' Jesse's house. 'What dost tha mean?' says I.

" 'I've often though as thou ought to know,' says he, 'but 'twas hard to tell thee. 'Liza Roantree's for neither on us, nor for nobody o' this earth. Dr. Warbottom says—and he knows her, and her mother before her—that she is in a decline, and she cannot live six months longer. He's known it for many a day. Steady, John! Steady!' says he. And that weak little man pulled me further back and set me again' him, and talked it all over quiet and still, me turnin' a bunch o' candles in my hand, and counting them ower and ower again as I listened. A deal on it were th' regular preachin' talk, but there were a vast lot as made me begin to think as he were more of a man than I'd ever given him credit for, till I were cut as deep for him as I were for mysen.

"Six candles we had, and we crawled and climbed all that day while they lasted, and I said to mysen, ' 'Liza Roantree hasn't six months to live.' And when we came into th' daylight again we were like dead men to look at, an' Blast came behind us without so much as waggin' his tail. When I saw 'Liza again she looked at me a minute and says, 'Who's telled tha? For I see tha knows.' And she tried to smile as she kissed me, and I fair broke down.

"Yo' see, I was a young chap i' them days, and had seen naught o' life, let alone death, as is allus a-waitin'. She telled me as Dr. Warbottom said as Greenhow air was too keen, and they were goin' to Bradford, to Jesse's brother David, as worked i' a mill, and I mun hold up like a man and a Christian, and she'd pray for me. Well, and they went away, and the preacher that same back end o' th' year were appointed to another circuit, as they call it, and I were left alone on Greenhow Hill.

"I tried, and I tried hard, to stick tc th' chapel, but 'tweren't th' same thing at after. I hadn't 'Liza's voice to follow i' th' singin', nor her eyes a-shinin' acrost their heads. And i' th' class-meetings they said as I mun have some experiences to tell, and I hadn't a word to say for mysen.

"Blast and me moped a good deal, and happen we didn't behave ourselves over well, for they dropped us and wondered however they'd come to take us up. I can't tell how we got through th' time, while i' th' winter I gave up my job and went to Bradford. Old Jesse were at th' door o' th' house, in a long street o' little houses. He'd been sendin' th' children 'way as were clatterin' their clogs in th' causeway, for she were asleep.

"'Is it thee?' he says; 'but you're not to see her. I'll none have her wakened for a nowt like thee. She's goin' fast, and she mun go in peace. Thou'lt never be good for naught i' th' world, and as long as thou lives thou'll never play the big fiddle. Get away, lad, get away!' So he shut the door softly i' my face.

"Nobody never made Jesse my master, but it seemed to me he was about right, and I went away into the town and knocked up against a recruiting sergeant. The old tales o' th' chapel folk came buzzin' into my head. I was to get away, and this were th' regular road for the likes o' me. I 'listed there and then, took th' Widow's shillin', and had a bunch o' ribbons pinned i' my hat.

"But next day I found my way to David Roantree's door, and Jesse came to open it. Says he, 'Thou's come back again wi' th' devil's colors flyin'—thy true colors, as I always telled thee.'

"But I begged and prayed of him to let me see her nobbut to say good-bye, till a woman calls down th' stairway, 'She says John Learoyd's to come up.' Th' old man shifts aside in a flash, and lays his hand on my arm, quite gentle like. 'But thou'lt be quiet, John,' says

he, 'for she's rare and weak. Thou was allus a good lad.'

"Her eyes were all alive wi' light, and her hair was thick on the pillow round her, but her cheeks were thin—thin to frighten a man that's strong. 'Nay, father, yo' mayn't say th' devil's colors. Them ribbons is pretty.' An' she held out her hands for th' hat, an' she put all straight as a woman will wi' ribbons. 'Nay, but what they're pretty,' she says. 'Eh, but I'd ha' liked to see thee i' thy red coat, John, for thou was allus my own lad—my very own lad, and none else.'

"She lifted up her arms, and they come round my neck i' a gentle grip, and they slacked away, and she seemed fainting. 'Now yo' mun get away, lad,' says Jesse, and I picked up my hat and I came downstairs.

"Th' recruiting sergeant were waitin' for me at th' corner public-house. 'You've seen your sweetheart?' says he. 'Yes, I've seen her,' says I. 'Well, we'll have a quart now, and you'll do your best to forget her,' says he, bein' one o' them smart, bustlin' chaps. 'Ay, sergeant,' says I. 'Forget her.' And I've been forgettin' her ever since."

He threw away the wilted clump of white violets as he spoke. Ortheris suddenly rose to his knees, his rifle at his shoulder, and peered across the valley in the clear afternoon light. His chin cuddled the stock, and there was a twitching of the muscles of the right cheek as he sighted; Private Stanley Ortheris was engaged on his business. A speck of white crawled up the water-course.

"See that beggar? . . . Got 'im."

Seven hundred yards away, and a full two hundred down the hillside, the deserter of the Aurangabadis pitched forward, rolled down a red rock, and lay very still, with his face in a clump of blue gentians, while a big raven flapped out of the pine wood to make investigation.

"That's a clean shot, little man," said Mulvaney.

Learoyd thoughtfully watched the smoke clear away. "Happen there was a lass tewed up wi' him, too," said he.

Ortheris did not reply. He was staring across the valley, with the smile of the artist who looks on the completed work.

The Taking of Lungtungpen

So we loosed a bloomin' volley,
　An' we made the beggars cut,
An' when our pouch was emptied out,
We used the bloomin' butt,
　　Ho! My!
　Don't yer come anigh,
When Tommy is a playin' with the bay-
　　nit an' the butt.
　　　　Barrack Room Ballad.

My friend Private Mulvaney told me this, sitting on the parapet of the road to Dagshai, when we were hunting butterflies together. He had theories about the Army, and colored clay pipes perfectly. He said that the young soldier is the best to work with, "on account av the surpassing innocinse av the child."

"Now, listen!" said Mulvaney, throwing himself full length on the wall in the sun. "I'm a born scutt av the barrick-room! The Army's mate an' dhrink to me, bekaze I'm wan av the few that can't quit ut. I've put in sivinteen years, an' the pipeclay's in the marrow av me. Av I cud have kept out av wan big dhrink a month, I wud have been a Hon'ry Lift'nint by this time— a nuisance to my betthers, a laughin'-shtock to my equils, an' a curse to meself. Bein' fwhat I am, I'm Privit Mulvaney, wid no good-conduc' pay an' a devourin' thirst. Always barrin' me little frind Bobs Bahadur, I know as much about the Army as most men."

I said something here.

"Wolseley be shot! Betune you an' me an' that butterfly net, he's a ramblin', incoherent sort av a divil, wid wan oi on the Quane an' the Coort, an' the other on his blessed silf—everlastin'ly playing Saysar an' Alexandrier rowled into a lump. Now Bobs is a sinsible little man. Wid Bobs an' a few three-year-olds, I'd swape any army av the earth into a towel, an' throw it away afther-ward. Faith, I'm not jokin'! 'Tis the bhoys—the raw bhoys—that don't know fwhat a bullut manes, an' wudn't care av they did—that dhu the work. They're crammed wid bull-mate till they fairly *ramps* wid good livin'; and thin, av they don't fight, they blow each other's hids off. 'Tis the trut' I'm tellin' you. They shud be kept on water an' rice in the hot weather; but ther'd be a mut'ny av 'twas done.

"Did ye iver hear how Privit Mulvaney tuk the town av Lungtungpen? I thought not! 'Twas the Lift'nint got the credit; but 'twas me planned the schame. A little before I was inviladed from Burma, me an' four-an'-twenty young wans undher a Lift'nint Brazenose, was ruinin' our dijeshins thryin' to catch dacoits. An' such double-ended divils I niver knew! 'Tis only a *dah* an' a Snider that makes a dacoit. Widout thim, he's a paceful cultivator, an' felony for to shoot. We hunted, an' we hunted, an' tuk fever an' elephints now an' again; but no dacoits. Evenshually, we *puckarowed* wan man. 'Trate him tinderly,' sez the Lift'nint. So I tuk him away into the jungle, wid the Burmese Interprut'r an' my clanin'-rod. Sez I to the man, 'My paceful squireen,' sez I, 'you shquot on your hunkers an' dimonstrate to *my* frind here, where *your* frinds are whin they're at home?' Wid that I introjuced him to the clanin'-rod, an' he comminst to jabber; the Interprut'r interprutin' in betweens, an' me helpin' the Intilligince Departmint wid my clanin'-rod whin the man misremimbered.

"Prisintly, I learn that, acrost the river, about nine miles away, was a town just dhrippin' wid dahs, an' bohs an' arrows, an' dacoits, and elephints, an' *jingles*. 'Good!' sez I; 'this office will now close!'

"That night, I went to the Lift'nint an' communicates my information. I never thought much of Lift'nint Brazenose till that night. He was shtiff wid books an' the-ouries, an' all manner av thrimmin's no manner av use. 'Town did ye say?' sez he. 'Accordin' to the the—ouries av War, we shud wait for reinforcemints.'—'Faith!' thinks I, 'we'd betther dig our graves thin;' for the nearest throops was up to their shtocks in the marshes out Mimbu way. 'But,' says the Lift'nint, 'since 'tis a speshil case, I'll make an excepshin. We'll visit this Lungtungpen to-night.'

"The bhoys was fairly woild wid deloight whin I tould 'em; an', by this an' that, they wint through the jungle like buck-rabbits. About midnight we come to the shtrame which I had clane forgot to minshin to my orficer. I was on, ahead, wid four bhoys, an' I thought that the Lift'nint might want to theourise. 'Shtrip boys!' sez I. 'Shtrip to the buff, an' shwim in where glory waits!'—'But I *can't* shwim!' sez two av thim. 'To think I should live to hear that from a bhoy wid a board-school edukashin!' sez I. 'Take a lump av timber, an' me an' Conolly here will ferry ye over, ye young ladies!'

"We got an ould tree-trunk, an' pushed off wid the kits an' the rifles on it. The night was chokin' dhark, an' just as we was fairly embarked, I heard the Lift'nint behind av me callin' out. 'There's a bit av a *nullah* here, sorr,' sez I, 'but I can feel the bottom already.' So I cud, for I was not a yard from the bank.

"'Bit av a *nullah!* Bit av an eshtuary!' sez the Lift'nint. 'Go on, ye mad Irishman! Shtrip bhoys!' I heard him laugh; an' the bhoys begun shtrippin' an' rollin' a log into the wather to put their kits on. So me an' Conolly shtruck out through the warm wather wid our log, an' the rest come on behind.

"That shtrame was miles woide! Orth'ris, on the rear-rank log, whispers we had got into the Thames below

Sheerness by mistake. 'Kape on shwim-min', ye little blayguard,' sez I, 'an' don't go pokin' your dirty jokes at the Irriwaddy.'—'Silince, men!' sings out the Lift'nint. So we shwum on into the black dhark, wid our chests on the logs, trustin' in the Saints an' the luck av the British Army.

"Evenshually, we hit ground—a bit av sand—an' a man. I put my heel on the back av him. He skreeched an' ran. "'Now we've done it!' sez Lift'nint Brazenose. 'Where the Divil *is* Lung-tungpen?' There was about a minute and a half to wait. The bhoys laid a hould av their rifles an' some thried to put their belts on; we was marchin' wid fixed baynits av coorse. Thin we knew where Lungtungpen was; for we had hit the river-wall av it in the dhark, an' the whole town blazed wid thim messin' *jingles* an' Sniders like a cat's back on a frosty night. They was firin' all ways at wanst; but over our hids into the shtrame.

"'Have you got your rifles?' sez Brazenose. 'Got 'em!' sez Orth'ris. 'I've got that thief Mulvaney's for all my back-pay, an' she'll kick my heart sick wid that blunderin' long shtock av hers.' —'Go on!' yells Brazenose, whippin' his sword out. 'Go on an' take the town! An' the Lord have mercy on our sowls!'

"Thin the bhoys gave wan divastatin' howl, an' pranced into the dhark, feelin' for the town, an' blindin' an' stiffin' like Cavalry Ridin' Masters whin the grass pricked their bare legs. I ham-mered wid the butt at some bamboo-thing that felt wake, an' the rest come an' hammered contagious, while the *jin-gles* was jinglin', an' feroshus yells from inside was shplittin' our ears. We was too close under the wall for thim to hurt us.

"Eventually, the thing, whatever ut was, bruk; an' the six-and-twinty av us tumbled, wan after the other, naked as we was borrun, into the town of Lung-tungpen. There was a *melly* av a sump-shus kind for a whoile; but whether they tuk us, all white an' wet, for a new breed av divil, or a new kind av dacoit, I don't know. They ran as though we was both, an' we wint into thim, baynit an' butt, shriekin' wid laughin'. There was torches in the shtreets, an' I saw little Orth'ris rubbin' his showlther ivry time he loosed my long-shtock Martini; an' Brazenose walkin' into the gang wid his sword, like Diarmid av the Gowlden Collar—bar-ring he hadn't a stitch av clothin' on him. We diskivered elephints wid da-coits under their bellies, an', what wid wan thing an' other, we was busy till mornin' takin' possession av the town of Lungtungpen.

"Thin we halted an' formed up, the wimmen howlin' in the houses an' Lift'-nint Brazenose blushin' pink in the light av the mornin' sun. 'Twas the most ondasint p'rade I iver tuk a hand in. Foive-and-twenty privits an' a orficer av the Line in review ordher, an' not as much as wud dust a fife betune 'em all in the way of clothin'! Eight av us had their belts an' pouches on; but the rest had gone in wid a handful av cartridges an' the skin God gave them. *They* was as nakid as Vanus.

"'Number off from the right!' sez the Lift'nint. 'Odd numbers fall out to dress; even numbers pathrol the town till relieved by the dressing party.' Let me tell you, pathrollin' a town wid nothin' on is an ex*payr*ience. I patrolled for tin minutes, an' begad, before 'twas over, I blushed. The women laughed so. I niver blushed before or since; but I blushed all over my carkiss thin. Orth'ris didn't pathrol. He saz only, 'Portsmouth Barricks an' the 'Ard av a Sunday!' Thin he lay down an' rolled any ways wid laughin'.

"Whin we was all dhressed, we counted the dead—sivinty-foive dacoits besides wounded. We tuk five elephints, a hunder' an' sivinty Sniders, two hunder' dahs, and a lot av other burglarious thruck. Not a man av us was hurt—excep' maybe the Lift'nint, an' he from the shock to his dasincy.

"The Headman av Lungtungpen, who surrinder'd himself, asked the Interprut'r—' 'Av the English fight like that wid their clo'es off, what in the wurruld do they do wid their clo'es on?' Orth'ris began rowlin' his eyes an' crackin' his fingers an' dancin' a step-dance for to impress the Headman. He ran to his house; an' we spint the rest av the day carryin' the Lift'nint on our showlthers round the town, an' playin' wid the Burmese babies—fat, little, brown little divils, as pretty as picturs.

"Whin I was inviladed for the dysent'ry to India, I sez to the Lift'nint, 'Sorr,' sez I, 'you've the makin's in you av a great man; but, av you'll let an ould sodger spake, you're too fond of the-ourisin'. He shuk hands wid me and sez, 'Hit high, hit low, there's no plasin' you, Mulvaney. You've seen me waltzin' through Lungtungpen like a Red Injin widout the warpaint, an' you say I'm too fond av the-ourisin'?'—'Sorr,' sez I, for I loved the bhoy; 'I wud waltz wid you in that condishin through *Hell,* an' so wud the rest av the men!' Thin I wint downshtrame in the flat an' left him my blessin'. May the Saints carry ut where ut shud go, for he was a fine upstandin' young orficer.

"To reshume. Fwhat I've said jist shows the use av three-year-olds. Wud fifty seasoned sodgers have taken Lungtungpen in the dhark that way? No! They'd know the risk av fever and chill. Let alone the shootin'. Two hundher' might have done ut. But the three-year-olds know little an' care less; an' where there's no fear, there's no danger. Catch thim young, feed thim high, an' by the honor av that great, little man Bobs, behind a good orficer, 'tisn't only dacoits they'd smash wid their clo'es off—'tis Con-ti-nental Ar-r-r-mies! They tuk Lungtungpen nakid; an' they'd take St. Petersburg in their dhrawers' Begad, they would that!

"Here's your pipe, sorr. Shmoke her tinderly wid honey-dew, afther letting the reek av the Canteen plug die away. But 'tis no good, thanks to you all the same, fillin' my pouch wid your chopped hay. Canteen, baccy's like the Army. It shpoils a man's taste for moilder things."

So saying, Mulvaney took up his butterfly-net, and returned to barracks.

The Daughter of the Regiment

Jain 'Ardin' was a Sarjint's wife,
  A Sarjint's wife wus she.
She married of 'im in Orldershort
  An' comed across the sea.
(*Chorus*) 'Ave you never 'eard tell o'
    Jain 'Ardin'?
    Jain 'Ardin'?
    Jain 'Ardin'?
  'Ave you never 'eard tell o'
    Jain 'Ardin'?
The pride o' the Compan*ee?*
      Old Barrack Room Ballad.

"A GENTLEMAN who doesn't know the Circasian Circle ought not to stand up for it—puttin' everybody out." That was what Miss McKenna said, and the Sergeant who was my *vis-à-vis* looked the same thing. I was afraid of Miss McKenna. She was six feet high, all yellow freckles and red hair, and was simply clad in white satin shoes, a pink muslin dress, an apple-green stuff sash, and black silk gloves, with yellow roses in her hair. Wherefore I fled from Miss McKenna and sought my friend Private Mulvaney, who was at the cant—re-freshment-table.

"So you've been dancin' with little Jhansi McKenna, sorr—she that's goin' to marry Corp'ril Slane? Whin you next conversh wid your lorruds an' your ladies, tell thim you've danced wid little Jhansi. 'Tis a thing to be proud av."

But I wasn't proud. I was humble. I saw a story in Private Mulvaney's eye; and besides, if he stayed too long at the bar, he would, I knew, qualify for more pack-drill. Now to meet an esteemed friend doing pack-drill outside the guardroom is embarrassing, especially if you happen to be walking with his Commanding Officer.

"Come on to the parade-ground, Mulvaney, it's cooler there, and tell me about Miss McKenna. What is she, and who is she, and why is she called 'Jhansi'?"

"D'ye mane to say you've niver heard av Ould Pummeloe's daughter? An' you thinkin' you know things! I'm wid ye in a minut whin me poipe's lit."

We came out under the stars. Mulvaney sat down on one of the artillery bridges, and began in the usual way: his pipe between his teeth, his big hands clasped and dropped between his knees, and his cap well on the back of his head—

"Whin Mrs. Mulvaney, that is, was Miss Shadd that was, you were a dale younger than you are now, an' the Army was dif'rint in sev'ril e-sen-shuls. Bhoys have no call for to marry nowadays, an' that's why the Army has so few rale, good, honust, swearin', strapagin', tin-der-hearted, heavy-futted wives as u used to have whin I was a Corp'ril. was rejuced afterward—but no matther —I was a Corp'ril wanst. In thim times, a man lived *an'* died wid his regiment; an' by natur', he married when he was a *man.* Whin I was Corp'ril— Mother av Hivin, how the rigimint has died an' been borrun since that day!— my Color-Sar'jint was Ould McKenna, an' a married man tu. An' his woife—his first woife, for he married three times did McKenna—was Bridget McKenna, from Portarlington, like mesilf. I've misremembered fwhat her first name was; but in B Comp'ny we called her 'Ould Pummeloe,' by reason av her fig-

454

ure, which was entirely circum-fe-ren shill. Like the big dhrum! Now that woman—God rock her sowl to rest in glory!—was tor everlastin' havin' childher; an' McKenna, whin the fifth or sixth come squallin' on to the musther-roll, swore he wud number thim off in future. But Ould Pummeloe she prayed av him to christen them after the names av the stations they was borrun in. So there was Colaba McKenna, an' Muttra McKenna, an' a whole Presidincy av other McKennas, an' little Jhansi, dancin' over yonder. Whin the childher wasn't bornin', they was dying; for, av our childher die like sheep in these days, they died like flies thin. I lost me own little Shadd—but no matther. 'Tis long ago, and Mrs. Mulvaney niver had another.

"I'm digresshin. Wan divil's hot summer, there come an order from some mad ijjit, whose name I misremember, for the rigimint to go up-country. Maybe they wanted to know how the new rail carried throops. They knew! On me sowl, they knew before they was done! Old Pummeloe had just buried Muttra McKenna; an', the season bein' onwholesim, only little Jhansi McKenna, who was four year ould thin, was left on hand.

"Five children gone in fourteen months. 'Twas harrd, wasn't ut?"

"So we wint up to our new station in that blazin' heat—may the curse av Saint Lawrence conshume the man who gave the ordher! Will I iver forget that move? They gave us two wake thrains to the rigimint; an' we was eight hundher' and sivinty strong. There was A, B, C, an' D Companies in the secon' thrain, wid twelve women, no orficers'

ladies, an' thirteen childher. We was to go six hundher' miles, an' railways was new in thim days. Whin we had been a night in the belly av the thrain—the men ragin' in their shirts an' dhrinkin' anything they cud find, an' eatin' bad fruit-stuff whin they cud, for we cudn't stop 'em—I was a Corp'ril thin—the cholera bruk out wid the dawnin' av the day.

"Pray to the Saints, you may niver see cholera in a throop-thrain! 'Tis like the judgmint av God hittin' down from the nakid sky! We run into a· rest-camp—as ut might have been Ludianny, but not by any means so comfortable. The Orficer Commandin' sent a telegrapt up the line, three hundher' mile up, askin' for help. Faith, we wanted ut, for ivry sowl av the followers ran for the dear life as soon as the thrain stopped; an' by the time that telegrapt was writ, there wasn't a naygur in the station exceptin' the telegrapt-clerk—an' he only bekaze he was held down to his chair by the scruff av his sneakin' black neck. Thin the day began wid the noise in the carr'ges, an' the rattle av the men on the platform fallin' over, arms an' all, as they stud for to answer the Comp'ny muster-roll before goin' over to the camp. 'Tisn't for me to say what like the cholera was like. Maybe the Doctor cud ha' tould, av he hadn't dropped on to the platform from the door av a carriage where we was takin' out the dead. He died wid the rest. Some bhoys had died in the night. We tuk out siven, and twenty more was sickenin' as we tuk thim. The women was huddled up anyways, screamin' wid fear.

"Sez the Commandin' Orficer whose

name I misremember, 'Take the women over to that tope av trees yonder. Get thim out av the camp. 'Tis no place for thim.'

"Ould Pummeloe was sittin' on her beddin'-rowl, thryin' to kape little Jhansi quiet. 'Go off to that tope!' sez the Officer. 'Go out av the men's way!'

" 'Be damned av I do!' sez Ould Pummeloe, an' little Jhansi, squattin' by her mother's side, squeaks out, 'Be damned av I do,' tu. Thin Ould Pummeloe turns to the women an' she sez, 'Are ye goin' to let the bhoys die while you're picnickin' ye sluts?' sez she. ' 'Tis wather they want. Come on an' help.'

"Wid that, she turns up her sleeves an' steps out for a well behind the rest-camp—little Jhansi trottin' behind wid a *lotah* an' string, an' the other women followin' like lambs, wid horse-buckets and cookin' pots. Whin all the things was full, Ould Pummeloe marches back into camp—'twas like a battlefield wid all the glory missin'—at the hid av the rigimint av women.

" 'McKenna, me man!' she sez, wid a voice on her like grand-roun's challenge, 'tell the bhoys to be quiet. Ould Pummeloe's comin' to look afther thim—wid free dhrinks.'

"Thin we cheered, an' the cheerin' in the lines was louder than the noise av the poor divils wid the sickness on thim. But not much.

"You see, we was a new an' raw rigimint in those days, an' we cud make neither head nor tail av the sickness; an' so we was useless. The men was goin' roun' an' about like dumb sheep, waitin' for the nex' man to fall over, an' sayin' undher their spache, 'Fwhat is ut? In the name av God, *fwhat* is ut?'

'Twas horrible. But through ut all, up an' down, an' down an' up, wint Ould Pummeloe an' little Jhansi—all we cud see av the baby, undher a dead man's helmut wid the chin-strap swingin' about her little stummick—up an' down wid the wather an' fwhat brandy there was.

"Now an' thin Ould Pummeloe, the tears runnin' down her fat, red face, sez, 'Me bhoys, me poor, dead, darlin' bhoys!' But, for the most, she was thryin' to put heart into the men an' kape thim stiddy; and little Jhansi was tellin' thim all they wud be 'betther in the mornin'.' 'Twas a thrick she's picked up from hearin' Ould Pummeloe whin Muttra was burnin' out wid fever. In the mornin'! 'Twas the iverlastin' mornin' at St. Pether's Gate was the mornin' for seven-an'-twenty good men; and twenty more was sick to the death in that bitter, burnin' sun. But the women worked like angils as I've said, an' the men like divils, till two doctors come down from above, an' we was rescued.

"But, just before that, Ould Pummeloe, on her knees over a bhoy in my squad—right-cot man to me he was in the barrick—tellin' him the worrud av the Church that niver failed a man yet, sez, 'Hould me up, bhoys! I'm feelin' bloody sick!' 'Twas the sun, not the cholera, did ut. She mis-remembered she was only wearin' her ould black bonnet, an' she died wid 'McKenna, me man,' houldin' her up, an' the bhoys howled whin they buried her.

"That night, a big wind blew, an' blew, an' blew, an' blew the tents flat. But it blew the cholera away an' niver another case there was all the while we was waitin'—ten days in quarintin'. Av you will belave me the thrack av the sickness in the camp was for all the wurruld the thrack av a man walkin' four times in a figur-av-eight through the tents. They say 'tis the Wandherin' Jew takes the cholera wid him. I believe it.

"An' *that*," said Mulvaney, illogically, "is the cause why little Jhansi McKenna is fwhat she is. She was brought up by the Quartermaster Sergeant's wife whin McKenna died, but she b'longs to B Comp'ny; and this tale I'm tellin' you— *wid* a proper appreciashin av Jhansi Mc-Kenna—I've belted into ivry recruity av the Comp'ny as he was drafted. 'Faith, 'twas me belted Corp'ril Slane into askin' the girl!"

"Not really?"

"Man, I did! She's no beauty to look at, but she's Ould Pummeloe's daughter, an' 'tis my juty to provide for her. Just before Slane got his promotion I sez to him, 'Slane,' sez I, 'to-morrow 'twill be insubordinashin av me to chastise you; but, by the sowl av Ould Pummeloe, who is now in glory, av you don't give me your wurrud to ask Jhansi McKenna at wanst, I'll peel the flesh off yer bones wid a brass huk to-night. 'Tis a dishgrace to B Comp'ny she's been single so long!' sez I. Was I goin' to let a three-year-ould preshume to discoorse wid me—my will bein' set? No! Slane wint an' asked her. He's a good bhoy is Slane. Wan av these days he'll get into the Com'ssariat an' dhrive a buggy wid his—savin's. So I provided for Ould Pummeloe's daughter; an' now you go along an' dance again wid her."

And I did.

I felt a respect for Miss Jhansi Mc-Kenna; and I went to her wedding later on.

Perhaps I will tell you about that one of these days.

The Madness of Private Ortheris

Oh! Where would I be when my froat
    was dry?
Oh! Where should I be when the bul-
    lets fly?
Oh! Where would I be when I come to
    die?
        Why,
Somewheres anigh my chum.
  If 'e's liquor 'e'll give me some,
  If I'm dyin' 'e'll 'old my 'ead,
  An' 'e'll write 'em 'Ome when I'm
    dead.—
  Gawd send us a trusty chum!
      Barrack Room Ballad.

My friends Mulvaney and Ortheris had gone on a shooting-expedition for one day. Learoyd was still in hospital, recovering from fever picked up in Burma. They sent me an invitation to join them, and were genuinely pained when I brought beer—almost enough beer to satisfy two Privates of the Line . . . and Me.

" 'Twasn't for that we bid you wekim, sorr," said Mulvaney, sulkily. " 'Twas for the pleasure av your comp'ny."

Ortheris came to the rescue with— "Well, 'e won't be none the worse for bringin' liquor with 'im. We ain't a file o' Dooks. We're bloomin' Tommies, ye cantankris Hirishman; an' 'eres your very good 'ealth!"

We shot all the forenoon, and killed two pariah-dogs, four green parrots, sitting, one kite by the burning-ghaut, one snake flying, one mud-turtle, and eight crows. Game was plentiful. Then we sat down to tiffin—"bull-mate an' branbread." Mulvaney called it—by the side of the river, and took pot shots at the crocodiles in the intervals of cutting up the food with our only pocketknife. Then we drank up all the beer, and threw the bottles into the water and fired at them. After that, we eased belts and stretched ourselves on the warm sand and smoked. We were too lazy to continue shooting.

Ortheris heaved a big sigh, as he lay on his stomach with his head between his fists. Then he swore quietly into the blue sky.

"Fwhat's that for?" said Mulvaney. "Have ye not drunk enough?"

"Tott'nim Court Road, an' a gal I fancied there. Wot's the good of sodgerin'?"

"Orth'ris, me son," said Mulvaney, hastily, " 'tis more than likely you've got throuble in your inside wid the beer. I feel that way mesilf whin my liver gets rusty."

Ortheris went on slowly, not heeding the interruption—

"I'm a Tommy—a bloomin', eight, anna, dog-stealin' Tommy, with a number instead of a decent name. Wot's the good o' me? If I 'ad a stayed at 'Ome, I might a married that gal and a kep' a little shorp in the 'Ammersmith 'Igh.—'S. Orth'ris, Prac-ti-cal Taxi-dermist.' With a stuff' fox, like they 'as in the Haylesbury Dairies, in the win-

der, an' a little case of blue and yaller glass-heyes, an' a little wife to call 'shorp!' 'shorp!' when the door bell rung. As it his, I'm on'y a Tommy—a Bloomin', Gawd-forsaken, Beer-swillin' Tommy. 'Rest on your harms—'versed, Stan' at—hease; 'Shun. 'Verse—harms. Right an' lef'—tarrn. Slow—march. 'Alt—front. Rest on your harms— 'versed. With blank-cartridge—load.' An' that's the end o' me." He was quoting fragments from Funeral Parties' Orders.

"Stop ut!" shouted Mulvaney. "Whin you've fired into nothin' as often as me, over a better man than yoursilf, you will not make a mock av thim orders. 'Tis worse than whistlin' the Dead March in barricks. An' you full as a tick, an' the sun cool, an' all an' all! I take shame for you. You're no better than a Pagin—you an' your firin'-parties an' your glass-eyes. Won't you stop ut, sorr?"

What could I do? Could I tell Ortheris anything that he did not know of the pleasures of his life? I was not a Chaplain nor a Subaltern, and Ortheris had a right to speak as he thought fit.

"Let him run, Mulvaney," I said. "It's the beer."

"No! 'Tisn't the beer," said Mulvaney. "I know fwhat's comin'. He's tuk this way now an' agin', an' it's bad— it's bad—for I'm fond av the bhoy."

Indeed, Mulvaney seemed needlessly anxious; but I knew that he looked after Ortheris in a fatherly way.

"Let me talk, let me talk," said Ortheris, dreamily. "D'you stop your parrit screamin' of a 'ot day, when the cage is a-cookin' is pore little pink toes orf, Mulvaney?"

"Pink toes! D'ye mane to say you're pink toes undher your bullswools, ye blandanderin'," — Mulvaney gathered himself together for a terrific denunciation—"school-misthress! Pink toes! How much Bass wid the label did that ravin' child dhrink?"

" 'Tain't Bass," said Ortheris. "It's a bitterer beer nor that. It's 'omesickness!"

"Hark to him! An' he goin' Home in the *Sherapis* in the inside av four months!"

"I don't care. It's all one to me. 'Ow d'you know I ain't 'fraid o' dyin' 'fore I gets my discharge paipers?" He recommenced, in a sing-song voice, the Orders.

I had never seen this side of Ortheris' character before, but evidently Mulvaney had, and attached serious importance to it. While Ortheris babbled, with his head on his arms, Mulvaney whispered to me—

"He's always tuk this way whin he's been checked overmuch by the childher they make Sarjints nowadays. That an' havin' nothin' to do. I can't make ut out anyways."

"Well, what does it matter? Let him talk himself through."

Ortheris began singing a parody of "The Ramrod Corps," full of cheerful allusions to battle, murder, and sudden death. He looked out across the river as he sang; and his face was quite strange to me. Mulvaney caught me by the elbow to ensure attention.

"Matther? It matthers everything! 'Tis some sort av fit that's on him. I've seen ut. 'Twill hould him all this night, an' in the middle av it he'll get out av his cot an' go rakin' in the rack

for his 'coutremints. Thin he'll come over to me an' say, 'I'm goin' to Bombay. Answer for me in the mornin'.' Thin me an' him will fight as we've done before—him to go an' me to hould him—an' so we'll both come on the books for disturbin' in barricks. I've belted him, an' I've bruk his head, an' I've talked to him, but 'tis no manner av use whin the fit's on him. He's as good a bhoy as ever stepped whin his mind's clear. I know fwhat's comin', though, this night in barricks. Lord send he doesn't loose on me whin I rise to knock him down. 'Tis that that's in my mind day an' night."

This put the case in a much less pleasant light, and fully accounted for Mulvaney's anxiety. He seemed to be trying to coax Ortheris out of the fit; for he shouted down the bank where the boy was lying—

"Listen now, you wid the 'pore pink toes' an' the glass eyes! Did you shwim the Irriwaddy at night, behin' me, as a bhoy shud; or were you hidin' undei a bed, as you was at Ahmid Kheyl?"

This was at once a gross insult and a direct lie, and Mulvaney meant it to bring on a fight. But Ortheris seemed shut up in some sort of trance. He answered slowly, without a sign of irritation, in the same cadenced voice as he had used for his firing-party orders—

"*Hi* swum the Irriwaddy in the night, as you know, for to take the town of Lungtungpen, nakid an' without fear. *Hand* where I was at Ahmed Kheyl you know, and four bloomin' Pathans know too. But that was summat to do, an' I didn't think o' dyin'. Now I'm sick to go 'Ome—go 'Ome—go 'Ome! No, I ain't mammay-sick, because my uncle brung me up, but I'm sick for London again; sick for the sounds of 'er an' the sights of 'er, and the stinks of 'er; orange peel and hasphalte an' gas comin' in over Vaux'all Bridge. Sick for the rail goin' down to Box'll, with your gal on your knee an' a new clay pipe in your face. That, an' the Stran' lights where you knows ev'ry one, an' the Copper that takes you up is a old friend that tuk you up before, when you was a little, smitchy boy lying loose 'tween the Temple an' the Dark Harches. No bloomin' guard-mountin', no bloomin' rottenstone, nor khaki, an' yourself your own master with a gal to take an' see the Humaners practicin' a-hookin' dead corpses out of the Serpentine o' Sundays. An' I lef' all that for to serve the Widder beyond the seas, where there ain't no women and there ain't no liquor worth 'avin', and there ain't nothin' to see, nor do, nor say, nor feel, nor think. Lord love you, Stanley Orth'ris, but you're a bigger bloomin' fool than the rest o' the reg'-ment and Mulvaney wired together! There's the Widder sittin' at 'Ome with a gold crownd on 'er 'ead; and 'ere am Hi, Stanley Orth'ris, the Widder's property, a rottin' FOOL!"

His voice rose at the end of the sentence, and he wound up with a six-shot Anglo-Vernacular oath. Mulvaney said nothing, but looked at me as if he expected that I could bring peace to poor Ortheris' troubled brain.

I remembered once at Rawal Pindi having seen a man, nearly mad with drink, sobered by being made a fool of. Some regiments may know what I mean. I hoped that we might slake off

Ortheris in the same way, though he was perfectly sober. So I said—

"What's the use of grousing there, and speaking against The Widow?"

"I didn't!" said Ortheris. "S'elp me, Gawd, I never said a word agin 'er, an' I wouldn't—not if I was to desert this minute!"

Here was my opening. "Well, you meant to, anyhow. What's the use of cracking-on for nothing? Would you slip it now if you got the chance?"

"On'y try me!" said Ortheris, jumping to his feet as if he had been stung.

Mulvaney jumped too. "Fwhat are you going to do?" said he.

"Help Ortheris down to Bombay or Karachi, whichever he likes. You can report that he separated from you before tiffin, and left his gun on the bank here!"

"I'm to report that—am I?" said Mulvaney, slowly. "Very well. If Orth'ris manes to desert now, and will desert now, an' you, sorr, who have been a frind to me an' to him, will help him to ut, I, Terence Mulvaney, on my oath which I've never bruk yet, will report as you say. But"—here he stepped up to Ortheris, and shook the stock of the fowling-piece in his face—"your fists help you, Stanley Orth'ris, if ever I come across you agin!"

"I don't care!" said Ortheris. "I'm sick o' this dorg's life. Give me a chanst. Don't play with me. Le' me go!"

"Strip," said I, "and change with me, and then I'll tell you what to do."

I hoped that the absurdity of this would check Ortheris; but he had kicked off his ammunition-boots and got rid of his tunic almost before I had loosed my shirt-collar. Mulvaney gripped me by the arm—

"The fit's on him: the fit's workin' on him still! By my Honor and Sowl, we shall be accessiry to a desartion yet. Only, twenty-eight days, as you say, sorr, or fifty-six, but think o' the shame —the black shame to him an' me!" I had never seen Mulvaney so excited.

But Ortheris was quite calm, and, as soon as he had exchanged clothes with me, and I stood up a Private of the Line, he said shortly, "Now! Come on. What nex'? D'ye mean fair. What must I do to get out o' this 'ere a-Hell?"

I told him that, if he would wait for two or three hours near the river, I would ride into the Station and come back with one hundred rupees. He would, with that money in his pocket, walk to the nearest side-station on the line, about five miles away, and would there take a first-class ticket for Karachi. Knowing that he had no money on him when he went out shooting, his regiment would not immediately wire to the seaports, but would hunt for him in the native villages near the river. Further, no one would think of seeking a deserter in a first-class carriage. At Karachi, he was to buy white clothes and ship, if he could, on a cargo-steamer.

Here he broke in. If I helped him to Karachi, he would arrange all the rest. Then I ordered him to wait where he was until it was dark enough for me to ride into the station without my dress being noticed. Now God in His wisdom has made the heart of the British Soldier, who is very often an unlicked ruffian, as soft as the heart of a little child, in order that he may believe in and follow his officers into

tight and nasty places. He does not so readily come to believe in a "civilian," but, when he does, he believes implicitly and like a dog. I had had the honor of the friendship of Private Ortheris, at intervals, for more than three years, and we had dealt with each other as man by man. Consequently, he considered that all my words were true, and not spoken lightly.

Mulvaney and I left him in the high grass near the river-bank, and went away, still keeping to the high grass, toward my horse. The shirt scratched me horribly.

We waited nearly two hours for the dusk to fall and allow me to ride off. We spoke of Ortheris in whispers, and strained our ears to catch any sound from the spot where we had left him. But we heard nothing except the wind in the plume-grass.

"I've bruk his head," said Mulvaney, earnestly, "time an' agin. I've nearly kilt him wid the belt, an' *yet* I can't knock thim fits out av his soft head. No! An' he's not soft, for he's reasonable an' likely by natur'. Fwhat is ut? Is ut his breedin' which is nothin', or his edukashin which he niver got? You that think ye know things, answer me that."

But I found no answer. I was wondering how long Ortheris, in the bank of the river, would hold out, and whether I should be forced to help him to desert, as I had given my word.

Just as the dusk shut down and, with a very heavy heart, I was beginning to saddle up my horse, we heard wild shouts from the river.

The devils had departed from Private Stanley Ortheris, No. 22639, B Company. The loneliness, the dusk, and the waiting had driven them out as I had hoped. We set off at the double and found him plunging about wildly through the grass, with his coat off—my coat off, I mean. He was calling for us like a madman.

When we reached him he was dripping with perspiration, and trembling like a startled horse. We had great difficulty in soothing him. He complained that he was in civilian kit, and wanted to tear my clothes off his body. I ordered him to strip, and we made a second exchange as quickly as possible.

The rasp of his own "greyback"shirt and the squeak of his boots seemed to ·bring him to himself. He put his hands before his eyes and said—

"Wot was it? I ain't mad, I ain't sunstrook, an' I've bin an' gone an' said, an' bin an' gone an' done. . . . Wot 'ave I bin an' done!"

"Fwhat have you done?" said Mulvaney. "You've dishgraced yourself—

though that's no matter. You've dishgraced B Comp'ny, an' worst av all, you've dishgraced *Me!* Me that taught you how for to walk abroad like a man —whin you was a dhirty little, fishbacked little, whimperin' little recruity. As you are now, Stanley Orth'ris!"

Ortheris said nothing for a while. Then he unslung his belt, heavy with the badges of half a dozen regiments that his own had lain with, and handed it over to Mulvaney.

"I'm too little for to mill you, Mulvaney," said he, "an' you've strook me before; but you can take an' cut me in two with this 'ere if you like."

Mulvaney turned to me.

"Lave me to talk to him, sorr," said Mulvaney.

I left, and on my way home thought a good deal over Ortheris in particular, and my friend Private Thomas Atkins whom I love, in general.

But I could not come to any conclusion of any kind whatever.

The God from the Machine

Hit a man an' help a woman, an' ye can't be far wrong anyways.—*Maxims of Private Mulvaney.*

THE Inexpressibles gave a ball. They borrowed a seven-pounder from the Gunners, and wreathed it with laurels, and made the dancing-floor plate-glass and provided a supper, the like of which had never been eaten before, and set two sentries at the door of the room to hold the trays of programme-cards. My friend, Private Mulvaney, was one

of the sentries, because he was the tallest man in the regiment. When the dance was fairly started the sentries were released, and Private Mulvaney went to curry favor with the Mess Sergeant in charge of the supper. Whether the Mess Sergeant gave or Mulvaney took, I cannot say. All that I am certain of is that, at supper-time, I found Mulvaney with Private Ortheris, two-thirds of a ham, a loaf of bread, half a *pâté-de-foie-gras,* and two magnums of champagne, sitting on the roof of my carriage. As I came up I heard him saying—

"Praise be a danst doesn't come as often as Ord'ly-room, or, by this an' that, Orth-ris, me son, I wud be the dishgrace av the rig'mint instid av the brightest jool in uts crown."

"*Hand* the Colonel's pet noosance," said Ortheris. "But wot makes you curse your rations? This 'ere fizzy stuff's good enough."

"Stuff, ye oncivilized pagin! 'Tis champagne we're dhrinkin' now. 'Tisn't that I am set ag'in. 'Tis this quare stuff wid the little bits av black leather in it. I misdoubt I will be distressin'ly sick wid it in the mornin'. Fwhat is ut?"

"Goose liver," I said, climbing on the top of the carriage, for I knew that it was better to sit out with Mulvaney than to dance many dances.

"Goose liver is ut?" said Mulvaney. "Faith, I'm thinkin' thim that makes it wud do betther to cut up the Colonel. He carries a power av liver undher his right arrum whin the days are warm an' the nights chill. He wud give thim tons an' tons av liver. 'Tis he sez so. 'I'm all liver to-day,' sez he; an' wid that he ordhers me ten days C. B. for as moild a dhrink as iver a good sodger took betune his teeth."

"That was when 'e wanted for to wash 'isself in the Fort Ditch," Ortheris explained. "Said there was too much beer in the Barrack water-butts for a God-fearing man. You was lucky in gettin' orf with wot you did, Mulvaney."

"Say you so? Now I'm pershuaded I was cruel hard trated, seein' fwhat I've done for the likes av him in the days whin my eyes were wider opin than they are now. Man alive, for the Colonel to whip *me* on the peg in that way! Me that have saved the repitation av a ten times betther man than him! 'Twas ne-farious—an' that means a power av evil!"

"Never mind the nefariousness," I said. "Whose reputation did you save?"

"More's the pity, 'twasn't my own, but I tuk more trouble wid ut than av ut was. 'Twas just my way, messin' wid fwhat was no business av mine. Hear now!" He settled himself at ease on the top of the carriage. "I'll tell you all about ut. Av coorse I will name no names, for there's wan that's an orf'cer's lady now, that was in ut, and no more will I name places, for a man is thracked by a place."

"Eyah!" said Ortheris, lazily, "but this is a mixed story wot's comin'."

"Wanst upon a time, as the childer-books say, I was a recruity."

"Was you though?" said Ortheris; "now that's extryordinary!"

"Orth'ris," said Mulvaney, "av you opin thim lips av yours again, I will, savin' your presince, sorr, take you by the slack av your trousers an' heave you."

"I'm mum," said Ortheris. "Wot 'appened when you was a recruity?"

"I was a betther recruity than you iver was or will be, but that's neither here nor there. Thin I became a man, an' the divil of a man I was fifteen years ago. They called me Buck Mulvaney in thim days, an', begad, I tuk a woman's eye. I did that! Ortheris, ye scrub, fwhat are ye sniggerin' at? Do you misdoubt me?"

"Devil a doubt!" said Ortheris; "but I've 'eard summat like that before!"

Mulvaney dismissed the impertinence with a lofty wave of his hand and continued—

"An' the orf'cers av the rig'mint I was in in thim days *was* orf'cers—gran' men, wid a manner on 'em, an' a way wid 'em such as is not made these days —all but wan—wan o' the capt'ns. A bad dhrill, a wake voice, an' a limp leg—thim three things are the signs av a bad man. You bear that in your mind, Orth'ris, me son.

"An' the Colonel av the rig'mint had a daughter—wan av thim lamblike, bleatin', pick-me-up-an'-carry-me-or-I'll —die gurls such as was made for the natural prey av men like the Capt'n, who was iverlastin' payin' coort to her, though the Colonel he said time an' over, 'Kape out av the brute's way, my dear.' But he niver had the heart for to send her away from the throuble, bein' as he was a widower, an' she their wan child."

"Stop a minute, Mulvaney," said I; "how in the world did you come to know these things?"

"How did I come?" said Mulvaney, with a scornful grunt; "bekaze I'm turned durin' the Quane's pleasure to a lump av wood, lookin' out straight forninst me, wid a—a—candelabbrum in my hand, for you to pick your cards out av, must I not see nor feel? Av coorse I du! Up my back, an' in my boots, an' in the short hair av the neck— that's where I kape my eyes whim I'm on duty an' the reg'lar wans are fixed. Know! Take my word for it, sorr, ivrything an' a great dale more is known in a rig'mint; or fwhat wud be

the use av a Mess Sargint, or a Sargint's wife doin' wet-nurse to the Major's baby? To reshume. He was a bad dhrill was this Capt'n—a rotten bad dhrill—an' whin first I ran me eye over him, I sez to myself: 'My Militia bantam!' I sez, 'My cock av a Gosport dunghill'—'twas from Portsmouth he came to us—'there's combs to be cut,' sez I, 'an' by the grace av God, 'tis Terence Mulvaney will cut thim.'

"So he wint menowderin', and minanderin', an' blandandhering roun' an' about the Colonel's daughter, an' she, poor innocint, lookin' at him like a Comm'ssariat bullock looks at the Comp'ny cook. He'd a dhirty little scrub av a black moustache, an' he twisted an' turned ivry wurrd he used as av he found ut too sweet for to spit out. Eyah! He was a tricky man an' a liar by natur'. Some are born so. He was wan. I knew he was over his belt in money borrowed from natives; besides a lot av other matthers which, in regard for your presince, sorr, I will obliterate. A little av fwhat I knew, the Colonel knew, for he wud have none av him, an' that, I'm thinkin', by fwhat happened afterward, the Capt'in knew.

"Wan day, bein' mortial idle, or they wud never ha' thried ut, the rig'mint gave amsure theatricals—orf'cers an' orf'cers' ladies. You've seen the likes time an' again, sorr, an' poor fun 'tis for them that sit in the back row an' stamp wid their boots for the honor av the rig'mint. I was told off for to shif' the scenes, haulin' up this an' draggin' down that. Light work ut was, wid lashins av beer and the gurl that dhressed the orf'cers' ladies—but she died in Aggra twelve years gone, an' my tongue's gettin' the betther av me. They was actin' a play thing called *Sweethearts*, which you may ha' heard av, an' the Colonel's daughter she was a lady's maid. The Capt'n was a boy called Broom—Spread Broom was his name in the play. Thin I saw—ut come out in the actin'—fwhat I niver saw before, an' that was that he was no gentleman. They was too much together, thim two, a-whishperin' behind the scenes I shifted, an' some av what they said I heard; for I was death—blue death an' ivy—on the comb-cuttin'. He was iverlastin'ly oppressing her to fall in wid some sneakin' schame av his, an' she was thryin' to stand out against him, but not as though she was set in her will. I wonder now in thim days that my ears did not grow a yard on me head wid list'nin.' But I looked straight forninst me an' hauled up this an' dragged down that, such as was my duty, an' the orf'cers' ladies sez one to another, thinkin' I was out av listen-reach: 'Fwhat an obligin' young man is this Corp'ril Mulvaney!' I was a Corp'ril then. I was rejuced afth)erward, but, no matther, I was Corp'ril wanst.

"Well, this *Sweethearts'* business wint on like most amshure theatricals, an' barrin' fwhat I suspicioned, 'twasn't till the dhress-rehearsal that I saw for certain that thim two—he the blackguard, an' she no wiser than she should ha' been—had put up an evasion."

"A what?" said I.

"E-vasion! Fwhat you call an elopemint. E-vasion I calls it, bekaze, exceptin' whin 'tis right an' natural an' proper, 'tis wrong an' dhirty to steal a man's wan child she not knowin' her own mind. There was a Sargint in the

Comm'ssariat who set my face upon e-vasions. I'll tell you about that"—

"Stick to the bloomin' Captains, Mulvaney," said Ortheris; "Comm'ssariat Sargints is low."

Mulvaney accepted the amendment and went on:—

"Now I knew that the Colonel was no fool, any more than me, for I was hild the smartest man in the rig'mint, an' the Colonel was the best orf'cer commandin' in Asia; so fwhat he said an' *I* said was a mortial truth. We knew that the Capt'n was bad, but, for reasons which I have already oblitherated, I knew more than me Colonel. I wud ha' rolled out his face wid the butt av my gun before permittin' av him to steal the gurl. Saints knew av he wud ha' married her, and av he didn't she wud be in great tormint, an' the divil av a 'scandal.' But I niver sthruck, niver raised me hand on my shuperior orf'cer; an' that was a merricle now I come to considher it."

"Mulvaney, the dawn's risin'," said Ortheris, "an' we're no nearer 'ome than we was at the beginnin'. Lend me your pouch. Mine's all dust."

Mulvaney pitched his pouch over, and filled his pipe afresh.

"So the dhress-rehearsal came to an end, an', bekaze I was curious, I stayed behind whin the scene-shiftin' was ended, an' I shud ha' been in barricks, lyin' as flat as a toad under a painted cottage thing. They was talkin' in whispers, an' she was shiverin' an' gaspin' like a fresh-hukked fish. 'Are you sure you've got the hang av the manewvers?' sez he, or wurrds to that effec', as the coort-martial sez. 'Sure as death,' sez she, 'but I misdoubt 'tis cruel hard on my father.' 'Damn your father,' sez he, or anyways 'twas fwhat he thought, 'the arrangement is as clear as mud. Jungi will drive the carri'ge afther all's over, an' you come to the station, cool an' aisy, in time for the two o'clock thrain, where I'll be wid your kit.' 'Faith,' thinks I to myself, 'thin there's a ayah in the business tu!'

"A powerful bad thing is a ayah. Don't you niver have any thruck wid wan. Thin he began sootherin' her, an' all the orf'cers an' orf'cers' ladies left, an' they put out the lights. To explain the theory av the flight, as they say at Muskthry, you must understand that after this *Sweethearts'* nonsinse was ended, there was another little bit av a play called *Couples*—some kind av couple or another. The gurl was actin' in this, but not the man. I suspicioned he'd go to the station with the gurl's kit at the end av the first piece. 'Twas the kit that flusthered me, for I knew for a Capt'n to go trapesing about the impire wid 'the Lord knew what av a *truso* on his arrum was nefarious, an' wud be worse than easin' the flag, so far as the talk aftherward wint."

" 'Old on, Mulvaney. Wot's *truso?*" said Ortheris.

"You're an oncivilized man, me son. When a gurl's married, all her kit an' 'coutrements are *truso,* which manes weddin'-portion. An' 'tis the same whin she's runnin' away, even with the biggest blackguard on the Arrmy List.

"So I made my plan av campaign. The Colonel's house was a good two miles away. 'Dennis,' sez I to my color-sargint, 'av you love me lend me your kyart, for me heart is bruk an' me feet is sore wid trampin' to and from this foolishness at the Gaff.' An' Dennis lent ut, wid a rampin', stampin' red stallion in the shafts. Whin they was all settled down to their *Sweethearts* for the first scene, which was a long wan, I slips outside and into the kyart. Mother av Hivin! but I made the horse walk, an' we came into the Colonel's compound as the divil wint through Athlone—in standin' leps. There was no one there excipt the servints, an' I wint round to the back an' found the girl's ayah.

" 'Ye black brazen Jezebel,' sez I, 'sellin' your masther's honor for five rupees—pack up all the Miss Sahib's kit an' look slippy! *Capt'n Sahib's* order,' sez I. 'Going to the station we are,' I sez, an' wid that I laid my finger to my nose an' looked the schamin' sinner I was.

" '*Bote acchy,*' says she; so I knew she was in the business, an' I piled up all the sweet talk I'd iver learned in the bazars on to this she-bullock, an' prayed av her to put all the quick she knew into the thing. While she packed, I stud outside an' sweated, for I was wanted for to shif' the second scene. I tell you, a young gurl's e-vasion manes as much baggage as a rig'mint on the line av march! 'Saints help Dennis's springs,' thinks I, as I bundled the stuff into the thrap, 'for I'll have no mercy!'

" 'I'm comin' too,' says the ayah.

" 'No, you don't,' sez I, 'later—*pechy!* You *baito* where you are. I'll *pechy* come an' bring you *sart,* along with me, you maraudin' '—niver mind fwhat I called her.

"Thin I wint for the Gaff, an' by the special ordher av Providence, for I was doin' a good work you will ondersthand,

Dennis's springs hild toight. 'Now, whin the Capt'n goes for that kit,' thinks I, 'he'll be throubled.' At the end av *Sweethearts* off the Capt'n runs in his kyart to the Colonel's house, an' I sits on the steps and laughs. Wanst an' again I slipped in to see how the little piece was goin', an' whin ut was near endin' I stepped out all among the carriages an' sings out very softly, 'Jungi!' Wid that a carr'ge began to move, an' I waved to the dhriver. '*Hitherao!*' sez I, an' he *hitheraoed* till I judged he was at proper distance, an' thin I tuk him, fair an' square betune the eyes, all I knew for good or bad, an' he dhropped with a guggle like the canteen beer-engine whin ut's runnin' low. Thin I ran to the kyart an' tuk out all the kit an' piled it into the carr'ge, the sweat runnin' down my face in dhrops. 'Go home,' sez I, to the *sais;* 'you'll find a man close here. Very sick he is. Take him away, an' av you iver say wan wurrd about fwhat you've *dekkoed,* I'll *marrow* you till your own wife won't *sumjao* who you are!' Thin I heard the stampin' av feet at the ind av the play, an' I ran in to let down the curtain. Whin they all came out the gurl thried to hide herself behind wan av the pillars, an' sez 'Jungi' in a voice that wouldn't ha' scared a hare. I run over to Jungi's carr'ge an' tuk up the lousy old horse-blanket on the box, wrapped my head an' the rest av me in ut, an' dhrove up to where she was.

" 'Miss Sahib,' sez I; 'going to the station? *Captain Sahib's* order!' an' widout a sign she jumped in all among her own kit.

"I laid to an' dhruv like steam to the Colonel's house before the Colonel was

there, an' she screamed an' I thought she was goin' off. Out comes the ayah, saying all sorts av things about the Capt'n havin' come for the kit an' gone to the station.

" 'Take out the luggage, you divil,' sez I, 'or I'll murther you!'

"The lights av the thraps people comin' from the Gaff was showin' across the parade ground, an', by this an' that, the way thim two women worked at the bundles an' thrunks was a caution! I was dyin' to help, but, seein' I didn't want to be known, I sat wid the blanket roun' me an' coughed an' thanked the Saints there was no moon that night.

"Whin all was in the house again, 1 niver asked for *bukshish* but dhruv tremenjus in the opp'site way from the other carr'ge an' put out my lights. Presently, I saw a naygur-man wallowin' in the road. I slipped down before I got to him, for I suspicioned Providence was wid me all through that night. 'Twas Jungi, his nose smashed in flat, all dumb sick as you pleae. Dennis's man must have tilted him out av the thrap. Whin he came to, 'Hutt!' sez I, but he began to howl.

" 'You black lump av dirt,' I sez, 'is this the way you dhrive your *gharri?* That *tikka* has been *owin'* an' *fere-owin'* all over the bloomin' country this whole bloomin' night, an' you as *mut-walla* as Davey's sow. Get up, you hog!' sez I, louder, for I heard the wheels av a thrap in the dark; 'get up an' light your lamps, or you'll be run into!' This was on the road to the Railway Station.

" 'Fwhat the divil's this?' sez the Capt'n's voice in the dhark, an' I could judge he was in a lather av rage.

" '*Gharri* dhriver here, dhrunk, sorr,'

sez I; 'I've found his *gharri* sthrayin' about cantonmints, an' now I've found him.'

" 'Oh!' sez the Capt'n; 'fwhat's his name?' I stooped down an' pretended to listen.

" 'He sez his name's Jungi, sorr,' sez I.

" 'Hould my harse,' sez the Capt'n to his man, an' wid that he gets down wid the whip an' lays into Jungi, just mad wid rage an' swearin' like the scutt he was.

"I thought, afther a while, he wud kill the man, so I sez:—'Stop, sorr, or you'll murdher him!' That dhrew all his fire on me, an' he cursed me into Blazes, an' out again. I stud to attenshin an' saluted:—'Sorr,' sez I, 'av ivry man in this wurruld had his rights, I'm thinkin' that more than wan wud be beaten to a jelly for this night's work— that niver came off at all, sorr, as you see?' 'Now,' thinks I to myself, 'Terence Mulvaney, you've cut your own throat, for he'll sthrike, an' you'll knock him down for the good av his sowl an' your own iverlastin' dishgrace!'

"But the Capt'n never said a single wurrd. He choked where he stud, an' thin he went into his thrap widout sayin' good-night, an' I wint back to barricks."

"And then?" said Ortheris and I together.

"That was all," said Mulvaney;" niver another word did I hear av the whole thing. All I know was that there was no e-vasion, an' that was fwhat I wanted. Now, I put ut to you, sorr, is ten days' C.B. a fit an' a proper tratement for a man who has behaved as me?"

"Well, any'ow," said Ortheris, " 'twern't this 'ere Colonel's daughter, an' you *was* blazin' copped when you tried to wash in the Fort Ditch."

"That," said Mulvaney, finishing the champagne, "is a shuparfluous an' impert'nint observation."

———•———

Private Learoyd's Story

And he told a tale.—*Chronicles of Gautama Buddha.*

FAR from the haunts of Company Officers who insist upon kit-inspections, far from keen-nosed Sergeants who sniff the pipe stuffed into the bedding-roll, two miles from the tumult of the barracks, lies the Trap. It is an old dry well, shadowed by a twisted *pipal* tree and fenced with high grass. Here, in the years gone by, did Private Ortheris establish his depot and menagerie for such possessions, dead and living, as could not safely be introduced to the barrack-room. Here were gathered Houdin pullets, and fox-terriers of undoubted pedigree and more than doubtful ownership, for Ortheris was an inveterate poacher and preëminent among a regiment of neat-handed dog-stealers.

Never again will the long lazy evenings return wherein Ortheris, whistling softly, moved surgeon-wise among the captives of his craft at the bottom of the well; when Learoyd sat in the niche, giving sage counsel on the management cf "tykes," and Mulvaney, from the crook of the overhanging *pipal,* waved his enormous boots in benediction above our heads, delighting us with tales of Love and War, and strange experiences of cities and men.

Ortheris—landed at last in the "little stuff bird-shop" for which your soul longed; Learoyd—back again in the smoky, stone-ribbed North, amid the clang of the Bradford looms; Mulvaney —grizzled, tender, and very wise Ulysses, 'sweltering on the earthwork of a Central India line—judge if I have forgotten old days in the Trap!

Orth'ris, as allus thinks he knaws more than other foaks, said she wasn't a real lady, but nobbut a Hewrasian. I don't gainsay as her culler was a bit doosky like. But she *was* a laady. Why, she rode iv a carriage, an' good 'osses, too, an' her 'air was that oiled as you could see your faice in it, an' she wore dimond rings an' a goold chain, an' silk an' satin dresses as mun 'a' cost a deal, for it isn't a cheap shop as keeps enough o' one pattern to fit a figure like hers. Her name was Mrs. DeSussa, an' t' waay I coom to be acquainted wi' her 'was along of our Colonel's Laady's dog Rip.

I've seen a vast o' dogs, but Rip was t' prettiest picter of a cliver fox-tarrier 'at iver I set eyes on. He could do owt you like but speeak, an' t' Colonel Laady set more store by him than if he hed been a Christian. She hed bairns of her awn, but they was i' England, and Rip seemed to get all t' coodlin' and pettin' as belonged to a bairn by good right.

But Rip were a bit on a rover, an' hed a habit o' breakin' out o' barricks like, and trottin' round t' plaice as if he were t' Cantonment Magistrate coom round inspectin'. The Colonel leathers him once or twice, but Rip didn't care an' kept on gooin' his rounds, wi' his taail a-waggin' as if he were flag-signallin' to t' world at large 'at he was "gettin' on nicely, thank yo', and how's yo'sen?" An' then t' Colonel, as was noa sort of a hand wi' a dog, tees him oop. A real clipper of a dog, an' it's noa wonder yon laady, Mrs. DeSussa, should tek a fancy tiv him. Theer's one o' t' Ten Commandments says yo maun't cuvvet your neebor's ox nor his jackass, but it doesn't say nowt about his tarrier dogs, an' happen thot's t' reason why Mrs. DeSussa cuvveted Rip, tho' she went to church reg'lar along wi' her husband who was so mich darker 'at if he hedn't such a good coaat tiv his back yo' might ha' called him a black man and nut tell a lee nawther. They said he addled his brass i' jute, an' he'd a rare lot on it.

Well, you seen, when they teed Rip up, t' poor awd lad didn't enjoy very good 'elth. So t' Colonel's Laady sends for me as 'ad a naame for bein' knowledgeable about a dog, an' axes what's ailin' wi' him.

"Why," says I, "he's getten t' mopes, an' what he wants is his libbaty an' coompany like t' rest on us; wal happen a rat or two 'ud liven him oop. It's low, mum," sez I, "is rats, but it's t' nature of a dog; an' soa's cuttin' round an' meetin' another dog or two an' passin' t' time o' day, an' hevvin' a bit of a turn-up wi' him like a Christian."

So she says *her* dog maunt niver fight an' noa Christians iver fought.

"Then what's a soldier for?" says I;

an' I explains to her t' contrairy qualities of a dog, 'at when yo' 'coom to think on't, is one o' t' curusest things as is. For they larn to behave theirsens like gentlemen born, fit for t' fost o' coompany—they tell me t' widdy herself is fond of a good dog and knaws one when she sees it as well as onny body: then on t' other hand a-tewin' round after cats an' gettin' mixed oop i' all manners o' blackguardly street- rows, an' killin' rats, an' fightin' like divils.

T' Colonel's Laady says:—"Well, Learoyd, I doan't agree wi' you, but you're right in a way o' speeakin', an' I should like yo' to tek Rip out a-walkin' wi' you sometimes; but yo' maun't let him fight, nor chase cats, nor do nowt 'orrid;" an' them was her very wods.

Soa Rip an' me gooes out a-walkin' o' evenin's, he bein' a dog as did credit tiv a man, an' I catches a lot o' rats an' we hed a bit of a match on in an awd dry swimmin'-bath at back o' t' cantonments, an' it was none so long afore he was as bright as a button again. He hed a way o' flyin' at them big yaller pariah dogs as if he was a harrow offan a bow, an' though his weight were nowt, he tuk 'em so suddint-like they rolled over like skittles in a halley an' when they coot he stretched after 'em as if he were rabbit-runnin'. Saame with cats when he cud get t' cat agaate o' runnin'.

One evenin', him an' me was trespassin' ovver a compound wall after one of them mongooses 'at he'd started, an' we was busy grubbin' round a prickle-bush, an' when we looks up there was Mrs. DeSussa wi' a parasel ovver her shoulder, a-watchin' us. "Oh my!" she sings out: "there's that lovelee dog!

Would he let me stroke him, Mister Soldier?"

"Ay, he would, mum," sez I, "for he's fond o' laady's coompany. Coom here, Rip, an' speeak to this kind laady." An' Rip, seein' 'at t' mongoose hed getten clean awaay, cooms up like t' gentleman he was, nivver a hauporth shy or okkord.

"Oh, you beautiful—you prettee dog!" she says, clippin' an' chantin' her speech in a way them sooart has o' their awn; "I would like a dog like you. You are so veree lovelee—so awfullee prettee," an' all thot sort o' talk, 'at a dog o' sense mebbe thinks nowt on, tho' he bides it by reason o' his breedin'.

An' then I meks him joomp ovver my swagger-cane, an' shek hands, an' beg, an' lie dead, an' a lot o' them tricks as laadies teeaches dogs, though I doan't haud with it mysen, for it's makin' a fool o' a good dog to do such like.

An' at lung length it cooms out 'at she'd been thrawin' sheep's eyes, as t' sayin' is, at Rip for many a day. Yo' see, her childer was grown up, an' she'd nowt mich to do, an' were allus fond of a dog. Soa she axes me if I'd tek somethin' to dhrink. An' we gooes into t' drawn-room wheer her 'usband was a-settin'. They meks a gurt fuss ovver t' dog an' I has a bottle o' aale, an' he gave me a handful o' cigars.

Soa I coomed away, but t' awd lass sings out—"Oh, Mister Soldier, please coom again and bring that prettee dog."

I didn't let on to t' Colonel's Lady about Mrs. DeSussa, and Rip, he says nowt nawther; an' I gooes again, an' ivry time there was a good dhrink an' a handful o' good smooaks. An' I telled t' awd lass a heeap more about Rip than

I'd ever heeared; how he tuk t' fost prize at Lunnon dog-show and cost thotty-three pounds fower shillin' from t' man as bred him; 'at his own brother was t' propputty o' t' Prince o' Wailes, an' 'at he had a pedigree as long as a Dook's. An' she lapped it all oop an' were niver tired o' admirin' him. But when t' awd lass took to givin' me money an' I seed 'at she were gettin' fair fond about t' dog, I began to suspicion summat. Onny body may give a soldier t' price of a pint in a friendly way an' theer's no 'arm done, but when it cooms to five rupees slipt into your hand, sly like, why, it's what t' 'lectioneerin' fellows calls bribery an' corruption. Specially when Mrs. DeSussa threwed hints how t' cold weather would soon be ovver an' she was goin' to Munsooree Pahar an' we was goin' to Rawalpindi, an' she would niver see Rip any more onless somebody she knowed on would be kind tiv her.

Soa I tells Mulvaney an' Ortheris all t' taale thro', beginnin' to end.

" 'Tis larceny that wicked ould laady manes," says t' Irishman, " 'tis felony she is sejuicin' ye into, my 'frind Learoyd, but I'll purtect your innocince. I'll save ye from the wicked wiles av that wealthy ould woman, an' I'll go wid ye this evenin' and spake to her the wurrds av truth an' honesty. But Jock," says he, waggin' his heead, " 'twas not like ye to kape all that good dhrink an' thim fine cigars to yerself, while Orth'ris here an' me have been prowlin' round wid throats as dry as lime-kilns, and nothin' to smoke but Canteen plug. 'Twas a dhirty thrick to play on a comrade, for why should you, Learoyd, be balancin' yourself on the

butt av a satin chair, as if Terence Mulvaney was not the aquil av anybody who thrades in jute!"

"Let alone me," sticks in Orth'ris, "but that's like life. Them wot's really fitted to decorate society get no show while a blunderin' Yorkshireman like you"—

"Nay," says I, "it's none o' t' blunderin' Yorkshireman she wants; it's Rip. He's t' gentleman this journey."

Soa t' next day, Mulvaney an' Rip an' me goes to Mrs. DeSussa's, an' t' Irishman bein' a strainger she wor a bit shy at fost. But yo've heeard Mulvaney talk, an' you' may believe as he fairly bewitched t' awd lass wal she let out 'at she wanted to tek Rip away wi' her to Munsooree Pahar. Then Mulvaney changes his tune an' axes her solemn-like if she'd thought o' t' consequences o' gettin' two poor but honest soldiers sent t' Andamning Islands. Mrs. DeSussa began to cry, so Mulvaney turns round oppen t' other tack and smooths her down, allowin' 'at Rip ud be a vast better off in t' Hills than down i' Bengal, and 'twas a pity he shouldn't go wheer he was so well beliked. And soa he went on, backin' an' fillin' an' workin' up t' awd lass wal she felt as if her life warn't worth nowt if she didn't hev t' dog.

Then all of a suddint he says:—"But ye *shall* have him, marm, for I've a feelin' heart, not like this could-blooded Yorkshireman; but 'twill cost ye not a penny less than three hundher rupees."

"Don't yo' believe him, mum," says I; "t' Colonel's Laady wouldn't tek five hundred for him."

"Who said she would?" says Mulvaney; "it's not buyin' him I mane, but for the sake o' this kind, good laady, I'll do what I never dreamt to do in my life. I'll stale him!"

"Don't say steal," says Mrs. DeSussa; "he shall have the happiest home. Dogs often get lost, you know, and then they stray, an' he likes me and I like him as I niver liked a dog yet, an' I *must* hev him. If I got him at t' last minute I could carry him off to Munsooree Pahar and nobody would niver knaw."

Now an' again Mulvaney looked acrost at me, an' though I could mak nowt o' what he was after, I concluded to take his leead.

"Well, mum," I says, "I never thowt to coom down to dog-steealin', but if my comrade sees how it could be done to oblige a laady like yo'sen, I'm nut t' man to hod back, tho' it's a bad business I'm thinkin', an' three hundred rupees is a poor set-off again t' chance of them Damning Islands as Mulvaney talks on."

"I'll mek it three fifty," says Mrs. DeSussa; "only let me hev t' dog!"

So we let her persuade us, an' she teks Rip's measure theer an' then, an' sent to Hamilton's to order a silver collar again t' time when he was to be her awn, which was to be t' day she set off for Munsooree Pahar.

"Sitha, Mulvaney," says I, when we was outside, "you're niver goin' to let her hev Rip!"

"An' would ye disappoint a poor old woman?" says he; "she shall have *a* Rip."

"An' wheer's he to come through?" says I.

"Learoyd, my man," he sings out, "you're a pretty man av your inches an' a good comrade, but your head is made av duff. Isn't our friend Orth'ris a Taxi-dermist, an' a rale artist wid his nimble white fingers? An' what's a Taxidermist but a man who can thrate shkins? Do ye mind the white dog that belongs to the Canteen Sargint, bad cess to him —he that's lost half his time an' snarlin' the rest? He shall be lost for *good* now; an' do ye mind that he's the very spit in shape an' size av the Colonel's, barrin' that his tail is an inch too long, an' he has none av the color that divarsifies the rale Rip, an' his timper is that av his masther an' worse. But fwhat is an inch on a dog's tail? An' fwhat to a professional like Orth'ris is a few ring-straked shpots av black, brown, an' white? Nothin' at all, at all."

Then we meets Orth'ris, an' that little man, bein' sharp as a needle, seed his way through t' business in a minute. An' he went to work a-practicin' 'air-dyes the very next day, beginnin' on some white rabbits he had, an' then he drored all Rip's markin's on t' back of a white Commissariat bullock, so as to get his 'and in an' be sure of his colors; shadin' off brown into black as nateral as life. If Rip *hed* a fault it was too mich markin', but it was straingely reg'lar an' Orth'ris settled himself to make a fost-rate job on it when he got haud o' t' Canteen Sargint's dog. Theer niver was sich a dog as thot for bad temper, an' it did nut get no better when his tail hed to be fettled an inch an' a half shorter. But they may talk o' theer Royal Academies as they like. *I* niver seed a bit o' animal paintin' to beat t' copy as Orth'ris made of Rip's marks, wal t' picter itself was snarlin' all t' time an' tryin' to get at Rip standin' theer to be copied as good as goold.

Orth'ris allus hed as mich conceit on

himsen 'as would lift a balloon, an' he wor so pleeased wi' his sham Rip he wor for tekking him to Mrs. DeSussa before she went away. But Mulvaney an' me stopped thot, knowin' Orth'ris's work, though niver so cliver, was nobbut skin-deep.

An' at last Mrs. DeSussa fixed t' day for startin' to Munsooree Pahar. We was to tek Rip to t' stayshun i' a basket an' hand him ovver just when they was ready to start, an' then she'd give us t' brass—as was agreed upon.

An' my wod! It were high time she were off, for them 'air-dyes upon t' cur's back took a vast of paintin' to keep t' reet culler, tho' Orth'ris spent a matter o' seven rupees six annas i' t' best drooggist shops i' Calcutta.

An' t' Canteen Sargint was lookin' for 'is dog everywhere; an', wi' bein' tied up, t' beast's timper got waur nor ever.

It wor i' t' evenin' when t' train started thro' Howrah, an' we 'elped Mrs. DeSussa wi' about sixty boxes, an' then we gave her t' basket. Orth'ris, for pride av his work, axed us to let him coom along wi' us, an' he couldn't help liftin' t' lid an' showin' t' cur as he lay coiled oop.

"Oh!" says t' awd lass; "the beautee! How sweet he looks!" An' just then t' beauty snarled an' showed his teeth, so Mulvaney shuts down t' lid and says: "Ye'll be careful, marm, whin ye tek him out. He's disaccustomed to travel-ing by t' railway, an' he'll be sure to want his rale mistress an' his friend Learoyd, so ye'll make allowance for his feelings at fost."

She would do all thot an' more for the dear, good Rip, an' she would nut oppen t' basket till they were miles away, for fear anybody should recognize him, an' we were real good and kind soldier-men, we were, an' she honds me a bundle o' notes, an' then cooms up a few of her relations an' friends to say good-bye —not more than seventy-five there wasn't—an' we cuts away.

What coom to t' three hundred and fifty rupees? Thot's what I can scar-celins tell yo', but we melted it—we melted it. It was share an' share alike, for Mulvaney said: "If Learoyd got hold of Mrs. DeSussa first, sure, 'twas I that remimbered the Sargint's dog just in the nick av time, an' Orth'ris was the artist av janius that made a work av art out av that ugly piece av ill-nature. Yet, by way av a thank-offerin' that I was not led into felony by that wicked ould woman, I'll send a thrifle to Father Victor for the poor people he's always beggin' for."

But me an' Orth'ris, he bein' Cock-ney, an' I bein' pretty far north, did nut see it i' t' saame way. We'd getten t' brass, an' we meaned to keep it. An' soa we did—for a short time.

Noa, noa, we niver heeard a wod more o' t' awd lass. Our reg'mint went to Pindi, an' t' Canteen Sargint he got himself another tyke insteead o' t' one 'at got lost so reg'lar, an' was lost for good at last.

———————◆———————

The Solid Muldoon

Did ye see John Malone, wid his shinin',
  brand-new hat?
Did ye see how he walked like a grand
  aristocrat?
There was flags an' banners wavin' high,
  an' dhress and shtyle were shown,
But the best av all the company was
  Misther John Malone.
                                John Malone.

There had been a royal dog-fight in
the ravine at the back of the rifle-butts,
between Learoyd's *Jock* and Otheris's
Blue Rot—both mongrel Rampur
hounds, chiefly ribs and teeth. It lasted
for twenty happy, howling minutes, and
then *Blue Rot* collapsed and Ortheris
paid Learoyd three rupees, and we were
all very thirsty. A dog-fight is a most
heating entertainment, quite apart from
the shouting, because Rampurs fight
over a couple of acres of ground. Later,
when the sound of belt-badges clicking
against the necks of beer-bottles had
died away, conversation drifted from
dog to man-fights of all kinds. Humans
resemble red-deer in some respects. Any
talk of fighting seems to wake up a sort
of imp in their breasts, and they bell
one to the other, exactly like challeng-
ing bucks. This is noticeable even in
men who consider themselves superior
to Privates of the Line: it shows the
Refining Influence of Civilization and
the March of Progress.

Tale provoked tale, and each tale
more beer. Even dreamy Learoyd's eyes
began to brighten, and he unburdened
himself of a long history in which a trip
to Malham Cove, a girl at Pateley Brigg,
a ganger, himself and a pair of clogs
were mixed in drawling tangle.

"An' so Ah coot's yead oppen from t'
chin to t' hair, an' he was abed for t'
matter o' a month," concluded Learoyd, pensively.

Mulvaney came out of a revery—he
was lying down—and flourished his heels
in the air. "You're a man, Learoyd,"
said he, critically, "but you've only
fought wid men, an' that's an ivry-day
expayrience; but I've stud up to a
ghost an' that was *not* an ivry-day expayrience."

"No?" said Ortheris, throwing a cork
at him. "You git up an' address the
'ouse—you an' yer expayriences. Is it
a bigger one nor usual?"

" 'Twas the livin' trut'!" answered
Mulvaney, stretching out a huge arm
and catching Ortheris by the collar.
"Now where are ye, me son? Will ye
take the wurrud av the Lorrd out av my
mouth another time?" He shook him to
emphasize the question.

"No, somethin' else, though," said
Ortheris, making a dash at Mulvaney's
pipe, capturing it and holding it at arm's
length; "I'll chuck it across the ditch if
you don't let me go!"

"You maraudin' hathen! 'Tis the
only cutty I iver loved. Handle her
tinder or I'll chuck *you* across the
nullah. If that poipe was bruk—Ah!
Give her back to me, sorr!"

Ortheris had passed the treasure to
my hand. It was an absolutely perfect
clay, as shiny as the black ball at Pool.
I took it reverently, but I was firm.

"Will you tell us about the ghost-
fight if I do?" I said.

"Is ut the shtory that's troublin' you?

Ave course I will. I mint to all along.
I was only gettin' at ut my own way, as
Popp Doggle said whin they found him
thrying to ram a cartridge down the
muzzle. Orth'ris, fall away!''

He released the little Londoner, took
back his pipe, filled it, and his eyes
twinkled. He has the most eloquent
eyes of any one that I know.

"Did I iver tell you," he began, "that
I was wanst the divil of a man?"

"You did," said Learoyd, with a childish gravity that made Ortheris yell with
laughter, for Mulvaney was always impressing upon us his great merits in the
old days.

"Did I iver tell you," Mulvaney continued, calmly, "that I was wanst more
av a divil than I am now?"

"Mer—ria! You don't mean it?" said
Ortheris.

"Whin I was Corp'ril—I was rejuced
afterward—but, as I say, *whin* I was
Corp'ril, I was a divil of a man."

He was silent for nearly a minute,
while his mind rummaged among old
memories and his eye glowed. He bit
upon the pipe-stem and charged into his
tale.

"Eyah! They was great times. I'm
ould now; me hide's wore off in patches;
sinthrygo has disconceited me, an' I'm a
married man tu. But I've had my day
—I've had my day, an' nothin' can take
away the taste av that! Oh my time
past, whin I put me fut through ivry
livin' wan av the Tin Commandmints
between Revelly and Lights Out, blew
the froth off a pewter, wiped me moustache wid the back av me hand, an'
slept on ut all as quiet as a little child!
But ut's over—ut's over, an' 'twill niver
come back to me; not though I prayed

for a week av Sundays. Was there *any*
wan in the Ould Rig'mint to touch
Corp'ril Terence Mulvaney whin that
same was turned out for sedukshin? I
niver met him. Ivry woman that was
not a witch was worth the runnin' afther
in those days, an' ivry man was my
dearest frind or—I had stripped to him
an' we knew which was the betther av
the tu.

"Whin I was Corp'ril I wud not ha'
changed wid the Colonel—no, nor yet
the Commandher-in-Chief. I wud be a
Sargint. There was nothin' I wud not
be! Mother av Hivin, look at me!
Fwhat am I *now?*

"We was quartered in a big cantonmint—'tis no manner av use namin'
names, for ut might give the barricks
disrepitation—an' I was the Imperor av
the Earth to my own mind, an' wan or
tu women thought the same. Small
blame to thim. Afther we had lain there
a year, Bragin, the Color Sargint av E
Comp'ny, wint an' took a wife that was
lady's maid to some big lady in the
Station. She's dead now is Annie Bragin
—died in child-bed at Kirpa Tal, or ut
may ha' been Almorah—seven—nine
years gone, an' Bragin he married agin.
But she was a pretty woman whin
Bragin inthrojuced her to cantonmint
society. She had eyes like the brown
av a butterfly's wing whin the sun
catches ut, an' a waist no thicker than
my arm, an' a little sof' button av a
mouth I would ha' gone through all Asia
bristlin' wid bay'nits to get the kiss av.
An' her hair was as long as the tail av
the Colonel's charger—forgive me men-
tionin' that blunderin' baste in the same
mouthful with Annie Bragin—but 'twas
all shpun gold, an' time was when ut

was more than di'monds to me. There was niver pretty woman yet, an' I've had thruck wid a few, cud open the door to Annie Bragin.

" 'Twas in the Cath'lic Chapel I saw her first, me oi rolling round as usual to see fwhat was to be seen. 'You're too good for Bragin, my love,' thinks I to mesilf, 'but that's a mistake I can put straight, or my name is not Terence Mulvaney.'

"Now take my wurrd for ut, you Orth'ris there an' Learoyd, an' kape out av the Married Quarters—as I did not. No good iver comes av ut, an' there's always the chance av your bein' found wid your face in the dirt, a long picket in the back av your head, an' your hands playing the fifes on the tread av another man's doorstep. 'Twas so we found O'Hara, he that Rafferty killed six years gone, when he wint to his death wid his hair oiled, whistlin' *Larry O'Rourke* betune his teeth. Kape out av the Married Quarters, I say, as I did not. 'Tis onwholesim, 'tis dangerous, an' 'tis ivrything else that's bad, but— O my sowl, 'tis swate while ut lasts!

"I was always hangin' about there whin I was off duty an' Bragin wasn't, but niver a sweet word beyon' ordinar' did I get from Annie Bragin. ' 'Tis the pervarsity av the sect,' sez I to mesilf, an' gave my cap another cock on my head an' straightened my back—'twas the back av a Dhrum Major in those days—an' wint off as tho' I did not care, wid all the women in the Married Quarters laughin'. I was pershuaded —most bhoys *are* I'm thinkin'—that no women born av woman cud stand against me av I hild up my little finger.

I had reason fer thinkin' that way— till I met Annie Bragin.

"Time an' agin whin I was blandan-dherin' in the dusk a man wud go past me as quiet as a cat. 'That's quare,' thinks I, 'for I am, or I should be, the only man in these parts. Now what divilment can Annie be up to?' Thin I called myself a blayguard for thinkin' such things; but I thought thim all the same. An' that, mark you, is the way av a man.

"Wan evenin' I said:—'Mrs. Bragin, manin' no disrespect to you, who is that Corp'ril man'—I had seen the stripes though I cud niver get sight av his face—'*who* is that Corp'ril man that comes in always whin I'm goin' away?'

" 'Mother av God!' sez she, turnin' as white as my belt; 'have *you* seen him too?'

" 'Seen him!' sez I; 'av coorse I have. Did ye want me not to see him, for'— we were standin' talkin' in the dhark, outside the veranda av Bragin's quar-ters—'you'd betther tell me to shut me eyes. Onless I'm mistaken, he's come now.'

"An', sure enough, the Corp'ril man was walkin' to us, hangin' his head down as though he was ashamed av himsilf.

" 'Good-night, Mrs. Bragin,' sez I, very cool; ' 'tis not for me to interfere wid your *a-moors*; but you might man-age some things wid more dacincy. I'm off to canteen,' I sez.

"I turned on my heel an' wint away, swearin' I wud give that man a dhressin' that wud shtop him messin' about the Married Quarters for a month an' a week. I had not tuk ten paces before Annie Bragin was hangin' on to my arm, an' I cud feel that she was shakin' all over.

" 'Stay wid me, Mister Mulvaney,' sez she; 'you're flesh an' blood, at the least—are ye not?'

" 'I'm *all* that," sez I, an' my anger wint away in a flash. 'Will I want to be asked twice, Annie?'

"Wid that I slipped my arm round her waist, for, begad, I fancied she had surrindered at discretion, an' the honors av war were mine.

" 'Fwhat nonsinse is this?' sez she, dhrawin' hersilf up on the tips av her dear little toes. 'Wid the mother's milk not dhry on your impident mouth? Let go!' she sez.

" 'Did ye not say just now that I was flesh and blood?' sez I. 'I have not changed since,' I sez; an' I kep' my arm where ut was.

" 'Your arms to yourself!' sez she, an' her eyes sparkild.

" 'Sure, 'tis only human nature,' sez I, an' I kep' my arm where ut was.

" 'Nature or no nature,' sez she, 'you take your arm away or I'll tell Bragin, an' he'll alter the nature av your head. Fwhat d'you take me for?' she sez.

" 'A woman,' sez I; 'the prettiest in barricks.'

" 'A *wife*,' sez she; 'the straightest in cantonmints!'

"Wid that I dropped my arm, fell back tu paces, an' saluted, for I saw that she mint fwhat she said."

"Then you know something that some men would give a good deal to be certain of. How could you tell?" I demanded in the interest of Science.

"Watch the hand," said Mulvaney; "av she shut her hand tight, thumb down over the knuckle, take up your

hat an' go. You'll only make a fool av yourself av you shtay. But av the hand lies opin on the lap, or av you see her thryin' to shut ut, an' she can't, —go on! She's not past reasonin' wid.

"Well, as I was sayin', I fell back, saluted, an' was goin' away.

" 'Shtay wid me,' she sez. 'Look! He's comin' again.'

"She pointed to the veranda, an' by the Hoight av Impart'nince, the Corp'ril man was comin' out av Bragin's quarters.

" 'He's done that these five evenin's past,' sez Annie Bragin. 'Oh, fwhat will I do!'

" 'He'll not do ut again,' sez I, for I was fightin' mad.

"Kape way from a man that has been a thrifle crossed in love till the fever's died down. He rages like a brute beast.

"I wint up to the man in the veranda, manin', as sure as I sit, to knock the life out av' him. He slipped into the open. 'Fwhat are you doin' philanderin' about here, ye scum av the gutter?' sez I polite, to give him his warnin', for I wanted him ready.

"He niver lifted his head, but sez, all mournful an' melancolius, as if he thought I wud be sorry for him: 'I can't find her,' sez he.

" 'My troth,' sez I, 'you've lived too long—you an' your seekin's an' findin's in a dacint married woman's quarters! Hould up your head, ye frozen thief av Genesis,' sez I, 'an' you'll find all you want an' more!'

"But he niver hild up, an' I let go from the shoulder to where the hair is short over the eyebrows.

" 'That'll do your business,' sez I, but it nearly did mine instid. I put my bodyweight behind the blow, but I hit nothing at all, an' near put my shoulther out. The Corp'ril man was not there, an' Annie Bragin, who had been watchin' from the veranda, throws up her heels, an' carries on like a cock whin his neck's wrung by the dhrummer-bhoy. I wint back to her, for a livin' woman, an' a woman like Annie Bragin, is more than a p'rade-groun' full av ghosts. I'd never seen a woman faint before, an' I stud like a shtuck calf, askin' her whether she was dead, an' prayin' her for the love av me, an' the love av her husband, an' the love av the Virgin, to opin her blessed eyes again, an' callin' mesilf all the names undher the canopy av Hiven for plaguin' her wid my miserable *a-moors* whin I ought to ha' stud betune her an' this Corp'ril man that had lost the number av his mess.

"I misremimber fwhat nonsinse I said, but I was not so far gone that I cud not hear a fut on the dirt outside. 'Twas Bragin comin' in, an' by the same token Annie was comin' to. I jumped to the far end av the veranda an' looked as if butter wudn't melt in my mouth. But Mrs. Quinn, the Quarter-Master's wife that was, had tould Bragin about my hangin' round Annie.

" 'I'm not pleased wid you, Mulvaney,' sez Bragin, unbucklin' his sword, for he had been on duty.

" 'That's bad hearin',' I sez, an' I knew that the pickets were dhriven in. 'What for, Sargint?' sez I.

" 'Come outside,' sez he, 'an' I'll show you why.'

" 'I'm willin',' I sez; 'but my stripes are none so ould that I can afford to lose thim. Tell me now, *who* do I go out wid?' sez I.

"He was a quick man an' a just, an' saw fwhat I wud be afther. 'Wid Mrs. Bragin's husband,' sez he. He might ha' known by me askin' that favor that I had done him no wrong.

"We wint to the back av the arsenal an' I stripped to him, an' for ten minutes 'twas all I cud do to prevent him killin' himself against my fistes. He was mad as a dumb dog—just frothing wid rage; but he had no chanst wid me in reach, or learnin', or anything else.

" 'Will ye hear reason?' sez I, whin his first wind was run out.

" 'Not whoile I can see,' sez he. Wid that I gave him both, one after the other, smash through the low gyard that he'd been taught whin he was a boy, an' the eyebrow shut down on the cheek-bone like the wing av a sick crow.

" 'Will you hear reason now, ye brave man?' sez I.

" 'Not while I can speak,' sez he, staggerin' up blind as a stump. I was loath to do ut, but I wint round an' swung into the jaw side-on an' shifted ut a half pace to the lef'.

" 'Will ye hear reason now?' sez I; 'I can't keep my timper much longer, an' tis like I will hurt you.'

" 'Not whoile I can stand,' he mumbles out av one corner av his mouth. So I closed an' threw him—blind, dumb, an' sick, an' jammed the jaw straight.

" 'You're an ould fool, *Mister* Bragin,' sez I.

" 'You're a young thief,' sez he, 'an' you've bruk my heart, you an' Annie betune you!'

"Thin he began cryin' like a child as he lay. I was sorry as I had niver

been before. 'Tis an awful thing to
see a strong man cry.

" 'I'll swear on the Cross!' sez I.

" 'I care for none av your oaths,'
sez he.

" 'Come back to your quarters,' sez
I, 'an' if you don't believe the livin',
begad, you shall listen to the dead,' I
sez.

"I hoisted him an' tuk him back to
his quarters. 'Mrs. Bragin,' sez I,
'here's a man that you can cure quicker
than me.'

" 'You've shamed me before my wife,'
he whimpers.

" 'Have I so?' sez I. 'By the look
on Mrs. Bragin's face I think I'm for
a dhressin'-down worse than I gave you.'

"An' I was! Annie Bragin was woild
wid indignation. There was not a name
that a dacint woman cud use that was
not given my way. I've had my Colonel
walk roun' me like a cooper roun' a
cask for fifteen minutes in Ord'ly Room,
bekaze I wint into the Corner Shop an
unstrapped lewnatic; but all that I iver
tuk from his rasp av a tongue was gin-
ger-pop to fwhat Annie tould me. An'
that, mark you, is the way av a woman.

"Whin ut was done for want av
breath, an' Annie was bendin' over her
husband, I sez: ' 'Tis all thrue, an' I'm
a blayguard an' you're an honest
woman; but will you tell him of wan
service that I did you?'

"As I finished speakin' the Corp'ril
man came up to the veranda, an' Annie
Bragin shquealed. The moon was up,
an' we cud see his face.

" 'I can't find her,' sez the Corp'ril
man, an' wint out like the puff av a
candle.

" "Saints stand betune us an' evil!'
sez Bragin, crossin' himself; 'that's
Flahy av the Tyrone.'

" 'Who was he?' I sez, 'for he has
given me a dale av fightin' this day.'

"Bragin tould us that Flahy was a
Corp'ril who lost his wife av cholera
in those quarters three years gone, an'
wint mad, an' *walked* afther they buried
him, huntin' for her.

" 'Well,' sez I to Bragin, 'he's been
hookin' out av Purgathory to kape company wid Mrs. Bragin ivry evenin' for
the last fortnight. You may tell Mrs.
Quinn, wid my love, for I know that
she's been talkin' to you, an' you've
been listenin', that she ought to ondherstand the differ 'twixt a man an' a
ghost. She's had three husbands,' sez
I, 'an' *you*'ve got a wife too good for
you. Instid av which you lave her to
be bodered by ghosts an'—an' all manner av evil spirruts. I'll niver go talkin'
in the way av politeness to a man's wife
again. Good-night to you both,' sez I;
an' wid that I wint away, havin' fought
wid woman, man and Divil all in the
heart av an hour. By the same token
I gave Father Victor wan rupee to say
a mass for Flahy's soul, me havin' discommoded him by shticking my fist
into his systim."

"Your ideas of politeness seem rather
large, Mulvaney," I said.

"That's as you look at ut," said Mulvaney, calmly; "Annie Bragin niver
cared for me. For all that, I did not
want to leave anything behin' me that
Bragin could take hould av to be angry
wid her about—whin an honust wurrd
cud ha' cleared all up. There's nothing
like opin-speakin'. Orth'ris, ye scutt,
let me put me oi to that bottle, for my

throat's as dhry as whin I thought I wud get a kiss from Annie Bragin. An' that's fourteen years gone! Eyah! Cork's own city an' the blue sky above ut—an' the times that was—the times that was!"

With the Main Guard

Der jungere Uhlanen
Sit round mit open mouth
While Breitmann tell dem stdories
Of fightin' in the South;
Und gif dem moral lessons,
How before der battle pops,
Take a little prayer to Himmel
Und a goot long drink of Schnapps.
Hans Breitmann's Ballads.

"MARY, Mother av Mercy, fwhat the divil possist us to take an' kepe this melancolius counthry? Answer me that, sorr."

It was Mulvaney who was speaking. The time was one o'clock of a stifling June night, and the place was the main gate of Fort Amara, most desolate and least desirable of all fortresses in India. What I was doing there at that hour is a question which only concerns M'Grath the Sergeant of the Guard, and the men on the gate.

"Slape," said Mulvaney, "is a shuparfluous necessity. This gyard'll shtay lively till relieved." He himself was stripped to the waist; Learoyd on the next bedstead was dripping from the skinful of water which Ortheris, clad only in white trousers, had just sluiced over his shoulders; and a fourth private was muttering uneasily as he dozed open-mouthed in the glare of the great guard-lantern. The heat under the bricked archway was terrifying.

"The worrst night that iver I re-mimber. Eyah! Is all Hell loose this tide?" said Mulvaney. A puff of burning wind lashed through the wicket-gate like a wave of the sea, and Ortheris swore.

"Are ye more heasy, Jock?" he said to Learoyd. "Put yer 'ead between your legs. It'll go orf in a minute."

"Ah don't care. Ah would not care, but ma heart is plaayin' tivvy-tivvy on ma ribs. Let me die! Oh, leave me die!" groaned the huge Yorkshireman, who was feeling the heat acutely, being of fleshly build.

The sleeper under the lantern roused for a moment and raised himself on his elbow.—"Die and be damned then!" he said. "*I'm* damned and I can't die!"

"Who's that?" I whispered, for the voice was new to me.

"Gentleman born," said Mulvaney; "Corp'ril wan year, Sargint nex'. Redhot on his C'mission, but dhrinks like a fish. He'll be gone before the cowld weather's here. So!"

He slipped his boot, and with the naked toe just touched the trigger of his Martini. Ortheris misunderstood the movement, and the next instant the Irishman's rifle was dashed aside, while Ortheris stood before him, his eyes blazing with reproof.

"You!" said Ortheris. "My Gawd, *you! If* it was you, wot would *we* do?"

"Kape quiet, little man," said Mulvaney, putting him aside, but very gently; "'tis not me nor will ut be me whoile Dinah Shadd's here. I was but showin' something."

Learoyd, bowed on his bedstead, groaned, and the gentleman-ranker sighed in his sleep. Ortheris took Mulvaney's tendered pouch, and we three smoked gravely for a space while the dust-devils danced on the glacis and scoured the red-hot plain.

"Pop?" said Ortheris, wiping his forehead.

"Don't tantalize wid talkin' av dhrink, or I'll shtuff you into your own breechblock an'—fire you off!" grunted Mulvaney.

Ortheris chuckled, and from a niche in the veranda produced six bottles of gingerade.

"Where did ye get ut, ye Machiavel?" said Mulvaney. " 'Tis no bazar pop."

"Owdo *Hi* know wot the Orf'cers drink?" answered Ortheris. "Arst the mess-man."

"Ye'll have a Disthrict Coort-martial settin' on ye yet, me son," said Mulvaney, "but"—he opened a bottle—"I will not report ye this time. Fwhat's in the mess-kid is mint for the belly, as they say, 'specially whin that mate is dhrink. Here's luck! A bloody war or a—no, we've got the sickly season. War, thin!"—he waved the innocent "pop" to the four quarters of Heaven. "Bloody war! North, East, South, an' West! Jock, ye quakin' hayrick, come an' dhrink."

But Learoyd, half mad with the fear of death presaged in the swelling veins of his neck, was pegging his Maker to strike him dead, and fighting for more air between his prayers. A second time Ortheris drenched the quivering body with water, and the giant revived.

"An' Ah divn't see thot a mon is i' fettle for gooin' on to live; an' Ah divn't see thot there is owt for t' livin' for. Hear now, lads! Ah'm tired—tired. There's nobbut watter i' ma bones. Let me die!"

The hollow of the arch gave back Learoyd's broken whisper in a bass boom. Mulvaney looked at me hopelessly, but I remembered how the madness of despair had once fallen upon Ortheris, that weary, weary afternoon in the banks of the Khemi River, and how it had been exorcised by the skilful magician Mulvaney.

"Talk, Terence!" I said, "or we shall have Learoyd slinging loose, and he'll be worse than Ortheris was. Talk! He'll answer to your voice."

Almost before Ortheris had deftly thrown all the rifles of the Guard on Mulvaney's bedstead, the Irishman's voice was uplifted as that of one in the middle of a story, and, turning to me, he said—

"In barracks or out of it, as *you* say, sorr, an' Oirish rig'mint is the divil an' more. 'Tis only fit for a young man wid eddicated fistesses. Oh the crame av disruption is an Oirish rig'mint, an' rippin', tearin', ragin' scattherers in the field av war! My first rig'mint was Oirish—Faynians an' rebils to the heart av their marrow was they, an' *so* they fought for the Widdy betther than most, bein' contrairy—Oirish. They was the Black Tyrone. You've heard av thim, sorr?"

Heard of them! I knew the Black Tyrone for the choicest collection of unmitigated blackguards, dog-stealers, robbers of hen-roosts, assaulters of innocent citizens, and recklessly daring heroes in the Army List. Half Europe and half Asia has had cause to know the Black Tyrone—good luck be with their tattered Colors as Glory has ever been!

"They *was* hot pickils an' ginger! I cut a man's head tu deep wid my belt in the days av my youth, an', afther some circumstances which I will oblitherate, I came to the Ould Rig'mint, bearin' the character av a man wid hands an' feet. But, as I was goin' to tell you, I fell acrost the Black Tyrone agin wan day whin we wanted thim powerful bad. Orth'ris, me son, fwhat was the name av that place where they sint wan comp'ny av us an' wan av the Tyrone roun' a hill an' down again, all for to tache the Paythans something they'd niver learned before? Afther Ghuzni 'twas."

"Don't know what the bloomin' Paythans called it. We call it Silver's Theayter. You know that, sure!"

"Silver's Theatre—so 'twas. A gut betune two hills, as black as a bucket, an' as thin as a girl's waist. There was over-many Paythans for our convaynience in the gut, an' begad they called thimselves a Reserve—bein' impident by natur! Our Scotchies an' lashins av Gurkys was poundin' into some Paythan rig'mints, I think 'twas. Scotchies an' Gurkys are twins bekaze they're so onlike, an' they get dhrunk together whin God plazes. As I was sayin', they sint wan comp'ny av the Ould an wan av the Tyrone to double up the hill an' clane out the Paythan Reserve. Orf'cers was scarce in thim days, fwhat with dysintry an' not takin'

care av thimselves, an' we was sint out wid only wan orf'cer for the comp'ny; but he was a Man that had his feet beneath him, an' all his teeth in their sockuts."

"Who was he?" I asked.

"Captain O'Neil—Old Crook—Cruikna-bulleen—him that I tould ye that tale av whin he was in Burma.[1] Hah! He was a Man. The Tyrone tuk a little orf'cer bhoy, but divil a bit was he in command, as I'll dimonstrate presintly. We an' they came over the brow av the hill, wan on each side av the gut, an' there was that ondacint Reserve waitin' down below like rats in a pit.

" 'Howld on, men,' sez Crook, who tuk a mother's care av us always. 'Rowl some rocks on thim by way av visitin'-kyards.' We hadn't rowled more than twinty bowlders, an' the Paythans was beginnin' to swear tremenjus, whin the little orf'cer bhoy av the Tyrone shqueaks out acrost the valley:—'Fwhat the devil an' all are you doin', shpoilin' the fun for my men? Do ye not see they'll stand?'

" 'Faith, that's a rare pluckt wan!' sez Crook. 'Niver mind the rocks, men. Come along down an' take tay wid thim!'

" 'There's damned little sugar in ut!' ses my rear-rank man; but Crook heard.

" 'Have ye not all got spoons?' he sez, laughin', an' down we wint as fast as we cud. Learoyd bein' sick at the Base, he, av coorse, was not there."

"Thot's a lie!" said Learoyd, dragging his bedstead nearer. "Ah gotten *thot*

[1] Now first of the foemen of Boh Da Thone
Was Captain O'Neil of the Black Tyrone.
The Ballad of Boh Da Thone.

theer, an' you knaw it, Mulvaney." He threw up his arms and from the right arm-pit ran, diagonally through the fell of his chest, a thin white line terminating near the fourth left rib.

"My mind's goin'," said Mulvaney, the unabashed. "Ye were there. Fwhat I was thinkin' of! 'Twas another man, av coorse. Well, you'll remimber thin, Jock, how we an' the Tyrone met wid a bang at the bottom an' got jammed past all movin' among the Paythans."

"Ow! It *was* a tight 'ole. I was squeezed till I thought I'd bloomin' well bust," said Ortheris, rubbing his stomach meditatively.

" 'Twas no place for a little man, but *wan* little man"—Mulvaney put his hand on Ortheris's shoulder—"saved the life av me. There we shtuck, for divil a bit did the Paythans flinch, an' divil a bit dare we; our business bein' to clear 'em out. An' the most exthryordinar' thing av all was that we an' they just rushed into each other's arrums, an' there was no firing for a long time. Nothin' but knife an' bay'nit when we cud get our hands free: an' that was not often. We was breast-on to thim, an' the Tyrone was yelpin' behind av us in a way I didn't see the lean av at first. But I knew later, an' so did the Paythans.

" 'Knee to knee!' sings out Crook, wid a laugh whin the rush av our comin' into the gut shtopped, an' he was huggin' a hairy great Paythan, neither bein' able to do anything to the other, tho' both was wishful.

" 'Breast to breast!' he sez, as the Tyrone was pushin' us forward closer an' closer.

" 'An' hand over back!' sez a Sargint

that was behin'. I saw a sword lick out past Crook's ear, an' the Paythan was tuk in the apple av his throat like a pig at Dromeen fair.

" 'Thank ye, Brother Inner Guard,' sez Crook, cool as a cucumber widout salt. 'I wanted that room.' An' he wint forward by the thickness av a man's body, havin' turned the Paythan undher him. The man bit the heel off Crook's boot in his death-bite.

" 'Push, men!' sez Crook. 'Push, ye paper-backed beggars!' he sez. 'Am I to pull ye through?' So we pushed, an' we kicked, an' we swung, an' we swore, an' the grass bein' slippery, our heels wouldn't bite, an' God help the front-rank man that wint down that day!"

" 'Ave you ever bin in the Pit hentrance o' the Vic. on a thick night?" interrupted Ortheris. "It was worse nor that, for they was goin' one way an' we wouldn't 'ave it. Leastaways, I 'adn't much to say."

"Faith, me son, ye said ut, thin. I kep' the little man betune my knees as long as I cud, but he was pokin' roun' wid his bay'nit, blindin' an' stiffin' feroshus. The devil of a man is Orth'ris in a ruction—aren't ye?" said Mulvaney.

"Don't make game!" said the Cockney. "I knowed I wasn't no good then, but I guv 'em compot from the lef' flank when we opened out. No!" he said, bringing down his hand with a thump on the bedstead, "a bay'nit ain't no good to a little man—might as well 'ave a bloomin' fishin'-rod! I 'ate a clawin', maulin' mess, but gimme a breech that's wore out a bit, an' hamminition one year in store, to let the powder kiss the bullet, an' put me somewheres where I ain't trod on by

'ulkin swine like you, an' s'elp me Gawd,
I could bowl you over five times outer
seven at height 'undred. Would yer
try, you lumberin' Hirishman."

"No, ye wasp. I've seen ye do ut.
I say there's nothin' better than the
bay'nit, with a long reach, a double
twist av ye can, an' a slow recover."

"Dom the bay'nit," said Learoyd, who
had been listening intently. "Look a-
here!" He picked up a rifle an inch
below the foresight with an underhand
action, and used it exactly as a man
would use a dagger.

"Sitha," said he, softly, "thot's better than owt, for a mon can bash t'
faace wi' thot, an', if he divn't, he can
breeak t' forearm o' t' gaard. 'Tis not
i' t' books, though. Gie me t' butt."

"Each does ut his own way, like
makin' love," said Mulvaney, quietly;
"the butt or the bay'nit or the bullet
accordin' to the natur' av the man.
Well, as I was sayin', we shtruck there
breathin' in each other's faces and
swearin' powerful; Orth'ris cursin' the
mother that bore him bekaze he was not
three inches taller.

"Prisintly he sez:—'Duck, ye lump,
an' I can get at a man over your shoul-
dher!'

"'You'll blow me head off,' I sez,
throwin' my arm clear; 'go through under my arm-pit, ye bloodthirsty little
scutt,' sez I, 'but don't shtick me or I'll
wring your ears round.'

"Fwhat was ut ye gave the Paythan
man forninst me, him that cut at me
whin I cudn't move hand or foot? Hot
or cowld was ut?"

"Cold," said Ortheris, "up an' under
the rib-jint. 'E come down flat. Best
for you 'e did."

"Thrue, my son! This jam thing that
I'm talkin' about lasted for five minutes
good, an' thin we got our arms clear
an' wint in. I misremimber exactly
fwhat I did, but I didn't want Dinah
to be a widdy at the Depôt. Thin, after
some promishkuous hackin' we shtuck
again, an' the Tyrone behin' was callin'
us dogs an' cowards an' all manner av
names; we barrin' their way.

"'Fwhat ails the Tyrone?' thinks I;
'they've the makin's av a most con-
vanient fight here.'

"A man behind me sez beseechful
an' in a whisper:—'Let me get at thim!
For the Love av Mary give me room
beside ye, ye tall man!'

"'An' who are you that's so anxious
to be kilt?' sez I, widout turnin' my
head, for the long knives was dancin'
in front like the sun on Donegal Bay
whin ut's rough.

"'We've seen our dead,' he sez,
squeezin' into me; 'our dead that was
men two days gone! An' me that was
his cousin by blood could not bring
Tim Coulan off! Let me get on,' he
sez, 'let me get to thim or I'll run ye
through the back!'

"'My troth,' thinks I, 'if the Tyrone
have seen their dead, God help the Paythans this day!' An' thin I knew why
the Oirish was ragin' behind us as they
was.

"I gave room to the man, an' he ran
forward wid the Haymaker's Lift on his
bay'nit an' swung a Paythan clear off
his feet by the belly-band av the brute,
an' the iron bruk at the lockin'-ring.

"'Tim Coulan 'll slape easy to-night,'
sez he, wid a grin; an' the next minut
his head was in two halves and he wint
down grinnin' by sections.

The Tyrone was pushin' an' pushin' in, an' our men was swearin' at thim, an' Crook was workin' away in front av us all, his sword-arm swingin' like a pump-handle an' his revolver spittin' like a cat. But the strange thing av ut was the quiet that lay upon. 'Twas like a fight in a drame—except for thim that was dead.

"Whin I gave room to the Oirishman I was expinded an' forlorn in my inside. 'Tis a way I have, savin' your presince, sorr, in action. 'Let me out, bhoys,' sez I, backin' in among thim. 'I'm goin' to be onwell!' Faith they gave me room at the wurrud, though they would not ha' given room for all Hell wid the chill off. When I got clear, I was, savin' your presince, sorr, outragis sick bekaze I had dhrunk heavy that day.

"Well an' far out av harm was a Sargint av the Tyrone sittin' on the little orf'cer bhoy who had stopped Crook from rowlin' the rocks. Oh, he was a beautiful bhoy, an' the long black curses was slidin' out av his innocint mouth like mornin'-jew from a rose!

"Fwhat have you got there?' sez I to the Sargint.

"'Wan av Her Majesty's bantams wid his spurs up,' sez he. 'He's goin' to Coort-martial me.'

"'Let me go!' sez the little orf'cer bhoy. 'Let me go and command my men!' manin' thereby the Black Tyrone which was beyond any command—ay, even av they had made the Divil a Field orf'cer.

"'His father howlds my mother's cow-feed in Clonmel,' sez the man that was sittin' on him. 'Will I go back to *his* mother an' tell her that I've let him throw himself away? Lie still, ye little pinch av dynamite, an' Coort-martial me afterward.'

"'Good,' sez I; ''tis the likes av him makes the likes av the Commandher-in-Chief, but we must presarve thim. Fwhat d'you want to do, sorr?' sez I, very politeful.

"'Kill the beggars—kill the beggars!' he shqueaks; his big blue eyes brimmin' wid tears.

"'An' how'll ye do that?' sez I. 'You've shquibbed off your revolver like a child wid a cracker; you can make no play wid that fine large sword av yours; an' your hand's shakin' like an asp on a leaf. Lie still an' grow,' sez I.

"'Get back to your comp'ny,' sez he; 'you're insolint!'

"'All in good time,' sez I, 'but I'll have a dhrink first.'

"Just thin Crook comes up, blue an' white all over where he wasn't red.

"'Wather!' sez he; 'I'm dead wid drouth! Oh, but it's a gran' day!'

"He dhrank half a skinful, and the rest he tilts into his chest, an' it fair hissed on the hairy hide av him. He sees the little orf'cer bhoy undher the Sargint.

"'Fwhat's yonder?' sez he.

"'Mutiny, sorr,' sez the Sargint, an' the orf'cer bhoy begins pleadin' pitiful to Crook to be let go: but divil a bit wud Crook budge.

"'Kape him there,' he sez, ''tis no child's work this day. By the same token,' sez he, 'I'll confishcate that iligant nickel-plated scent-sprinkler av yours, for my own has been vomitin' dishgraceful!'

"The fork av his hand was black wid the backspit av the machine. So he tuk the orf'cer bhoy's revolver. Ye may look, sorr, but, by my faith, *there's a dale more done in the field than iver gets into Field Ordhers!*

" 'Come on, Mulvaney,' sez Crook; 'is this a Coort-martial?' The two av us wint back together into the mess an' the Paythans were still standin' up. They was not *too* impart'nint though, for the Tyrone was callin' wan to another to remimber Tim Coulan.

"Crook stopped outside av the strife an' looked anxious, his eyes rowlin' roun'.

" 'Fwhat is ut, sorr?' sez I; 'can I get ye anything?'

" 'Where's a bugler?' sez he.

"I wint into the crowd—our men was dhrawin' breath behin' the Tyrone who was fightin' like sowls in tormint—an' prisintly I came acrost little Frehan, our bugler bhoy, pokin' roun' among the best wid a rifle an' bay'nit.

" 'Is amusin' yoursilf fwhat you're paid for, ye limb?' sez I, catchin' him by the scruff. 'Come out av that an' attind to your duty,' I sez; but the bhoy was not pleased.

" 'I've got wan,' sez he, grinnin', 'big as you, Mulvaney, an' fair half as ugly. Let me go get another.'

"I was dishpleased at the personability av that remark, so I tucks him under my arm an' carries him to Crook who was watchin' how the fight wint. Crook cuffs him till the bhoy cries, an' thin sez nothin' for a whoile.

"The Paythans began to flicker onaisy, an' our men roared. 'Opin ordher! Double!' sez Crook. 'Blow, child, blow for the honor av the British Arrmy!'

"That bhoy blew like a typhoon, an' the Tyrone an' we opined out as the Paythans broke, an' I saw that fwhat had gone before wud be kissin' an' huggin' to fwhat was to come. We'd dhruv thim into a broad part av the gut whin they gave, an' thin we opined out an' fair danced down the valley, dhrivin' thim before us. Oh, 'twas lovely, an' stiddy, too! There was the Sargints on the flanks av what was left av us, kapin' touch, an' the fire was runnin' from flank to flank, an' the Paythans was dhroppin'. We opined out wid the widenin' av the valley, an' whin the valley narrowed we closed again like the shticks on a lady's fan, an' at the far ind av the gut where they thried to stand, we fair blew them off their feet, for we had expinded very little ammunition by reason av the knife work."

"Hi used thirty rounds goin' down that valley," said Ortheris, "an' it was gentleman's work. Might 'a' done it in a white 'andkerchief an' pink silk stockin's, that part. Hi was on in that piece."

"You could ha' heard the Tyrone yellin' a mile away," said Mulvaney, "an' 'twas all their Sargints cud do to get thim off. They was mad—mad—mad! Crook sits down in the quiet that fell whin we had gone down the valley, an' covers his face wid his hands. Prisintly we all came back again accordin' to our natures and disposishins, for they, mark you, show through the hide av a man in that hour.

" 'Bhoys! bhoys!' sez Crook to himself. 'I misdoubt we could ha' engaged at long range an' saved betther men than me.' He looked at our dead an' said no more.

" 'Captain dear,' sez a man av the

Tyrone, comin' up wid his mouth bigger than iver his mother kissed ut, spittin' blood like a whale; 'Captain dear,' sez he, 'if wan or two in the shtalls have been discommoded, the gallery have enjoyed the performinces av a Roshus.'

"Thin I knew that man for the Dublin dock-rat he was—wan av the bhoys that made the lessee av Silver's Theatre grey before his time wid tearin' out the bowils av the benches an' t'rowin' thim into the pit. So I passed the wurrud that I knew when I was in the Tyrone an' we lay in Dublin. 'I don't know who ' twas,' I whispers, 'an' I don't care, but anyways I'll knock the face av you, Tim Kelly.'

" 'Eyah!' sez the man, 'was you there too? We'll call ut Silver's Theatre.' Half the Tyrone, knowin' the ould place, tuk ut up: so we called ut Silver's Theatre.

"The little orf'cer bhoy av the Tyrone was thremblin' an' cryin'.' He had no heart for the Coort-martials that he talked so big upon. 'Ye'll do well later,' sez Crook, very quiet, 'for not bein' allowed to kill yourself for amusemint.'

" 'I'm a dishgraced man!' sez the little orf'cer bhoy.

" 'Put me undher arrest, sorr, if you will, but, by my sowl, I'd do ut again sooner than face your mother wid you dead,' sez the Sargint that had sat on his head, standin' to attention an' salutin'. But the young wan only cried as tho' his little heart was breakin'.

"Thin another man av the Tyrone came up, with the fog av fightin' on him."

"The what, Mulvaney?"

"Fog av fightin'. You know, sorr, that, like makin' love, ut takes each man diff'rint. Now I can't help bein' powerful sick whin I'm in action. Orth'ris, here, niver stops swearin' from ind to ind, an' the only time that Learoyd opins his mouth to sing is whin he is messin' wid other people's heads; for he's a dhirty fighter is Jock. Recruities sometime cry, an' sometime they don't know fwhat they do, an' sometime they are all for cuttin' throats an' such like dirtiness; but some men get heavy-dead-dhrunk on the fightin'. This man was. He was staggerin', an' his eyes were half shut, an' we cud hear him dhraw breath twinty yards away. He sees the little orf'cer bhoy, an' comes up, talkin' thick an' drowsy to himsilf. 'Blood young whelp;' an' wid that he threw up his arms, shpun roun', an' dropped at our feet, dead as a Paythan, an' there was niver sign or scratch on him. They said 'twas his heart was rotten, but oh, 'twas a quare thing to see!

"Thin we wint to bury our dead, for we wud not lave thim to the Paythans, an' in movin' among the haythen we nearly lost that little orf'cer bhoy. He was for givin' wan divil wather and layin' him aisy against a rock. 'Be careful, sorr,' sez I; 'a wounded Paythan's worse than a live wan.' My troth, before the words was out of my mouth, the man on the ground fires at the orf'cer bhoy lanin' over him, an' I saw the helmit fly. I dropped the butt on the face av the man an' tuk his pistol. The little orf'cer bhoy turned very white, for the hair av half his head was singed away.

" 'I tould you so, sorr!' sez I; an'. afther that, whin he wanted to help a Paythan I stud wid the muzzle contagious to the ear. They dare not do anythin' but curse. The Tyrone was growlin' like dogs over a bone that had been taken away too soon, for they had seen their dead an' they wanted to kill ivry sowl on the ground. Crook tould thim that he'd blow the hide off any man that misconducted himself; but, seeing that ut was the first time the Tyrone had iver seen their dead, I do not wondher they were on the sharp. 'Tis a shameful sight! Whin I first saw ut I wud nivar ha' given quarter to any man north of the Khaibar—no, nor woman either, for the women used to come out afther dhark—Auggrh!

"Well, evenshually we buried our dead an' tuk away our wounded, an' come over the brow av the hills to see the Scotchies an' the Gurkys taking tay with the Paythans in bucketfuls. We were a gang av dissolute ruffians, for the blood had caked the dust, an' the sweat had cut the cake, an' our bay'-nits was hangin' like butchers' steels betune ur legs, an' most av us were marked one way or another.

"A Staff Orf'cer man, clean as a new rifle, rides up an' sez: 'What damned scarecrows are you?'

" 'A comp'ny av Her Majesty's Black Tyrone an' wan av the Ould Rig'mint,' sez Crook very quiet, givin' our visitors the flure as 'twas.

" 'Oh!' sez the Staff Orf'cer; 'did you dislodge that Reserve?'

" 'No!' sez Crook, an' the Tyrone laughed.

" 'Thin fwhat the divil have ye done?'

" 'Disthroyed ut,' sez Crook, an' he took us on, but not before Toomey that was in the Tyrone sez aloud, his voice somewhere in his stummick: 'Fwhat in

the name av misfortune does this parrit widout a tail mane by shtoppin' the road av his betthers?'

"The Staff Orf'cer wint blue, an' Toomey makes him pink by changin' to the voice av a minowderin' woman an' sayin': 'Come an' kiss me, Major, dear, for me husband's at the wars an' I'm all alone at the Depôt.'

"The Staff Orf'cer wint away, an' I cud see Crook's shoulthers shakin'.

"His Corp'ril checks Toomey. 'Lave me alone,' sez Toomey, widout a wink. 'I was his bâtman before he was married an' he knows fwhat I mane, av you don't. There's nothin' like livin' in the hoight av society.' D'you remimber that, Orth'ris!"

"Hi do. Toomey, 'e died in 'orspital, next week it was, 'cause I bought 'arf his kit; an' I remember after that"—

"GUARRD, TURN OUT!"

The Relief had come; it was four o'clock. "I'll catch a kyart for you, sorr," said Mulvaney, diving hastily into his accoutrements. "Come up to the top av the Fort an' we'll pershue our invistigations into M'Grath's shtable." The relieved Guard strolled round the main bastion on its way to the swimming-bath, and Learoyd grew almost talkative. Ortheris looked into the Fort ditch and across the plain. "Ho! it's weary waitin' for Ma-ary!" he hummed; "but I'd like to kill some more bloomin' Paythans before my time's up. War! Bloody war! North, East, South and West."

"Amen," said Learoyd, slowly.

"Fwhat's here?" said Mulvaney, checking at a blurr of white by the foot of the old sentry-box. He stooped and touched it. "It's Norah—Norah M'Taggart! Why, Nonie, darlin', fwhat are ye doin' out av your mother's bed at this time?"

The two-year-old child of Sergeant M'Taggart must have wandered for a breath of cool air to the very verge of the parapet of the Fort ditch. Her tiny night-shift was gathered into a wisp round her neck and she moaned in her sleep. "See there!" said Mulvaney; "poor lamb! Look at the heat-rash on the innocint skin av her. 'Tis hard—crool hard even for us. Fwhat must it be for these? Wake up, Nonie, your mother will be woild about you. Begad, the child might ha' fallen into the ditch!"

He picked her up in the growing light, and set her on his shoulder, and her fair curls touched the grizzled stubble of his temples. Ortheris and Learoyd followed snapping their fingers, while Norah smiled at them a sleepy smile. Then carolled Mulvaney, clear as a lark, dancing the baby on his arm—

"If any young man should marry you,
    Say nothin' about the joke;
That iver ye slep' in a sinthry-box,
    Wrapped up in a soldier's cloak."

"Though, on my sowl, Nonie," he said, gravely, "there was not much cloak about you. Niver mind, you won't dhress like this ten years to come. Kiss your friends an' run along to your mother."

Nonie, set down close to the Married Quarters, nodded with the quiet obedience of the soldier's child, but, ere she pattered off over the flagged path, held up her lips to be kissed by the Three Musketeers. Ortheris wiped his mouth with the back of his hand and swore sentimentally; Learoyd turned pink; and the two walked away together. The Yorkshireman lifted up his voice and gave in thunder the chorus of *The Sentry-Box,* while Ortheris piped at his side.

" 'Bin to a bloomin' sing-song, you two?" said the Artilleryman, who was taking his cartridge down to the Morning Gun. "You're over merry for these dashed days."

"I bid ye take care o' the brat," said he,
    "For it comes of a noble race,"

Learoyd bellowed. The voices died out in the swimming-bath.

"Oh, Terence!" I said, dropping into Mulvaney's speech, when we were alone. "it's you that have the Tongue!"

He looked at me wearily; his eyes were sunk in his head, and his face was drawn and white. "Eyah!" said he; "I've blandandhered thim through the night somehow, but can thim that helps others help thimselves? Answer me that, sorr!"

And over the bastions of Fort-Amara broke the pitiless day.

Black Jack

To the wake av Tim O'Hara
    Came company,
All St. Patrick's Alley
    Was there to see.
        Robert Buchanan.

As the Three Musketeers share their silver, tobacco, and liquor together, as they protect each other in barracks or camp, and as they rejoice together over the joy of one, so do they divide their sorrows. When Ortheris's irrepressible tongue has brought him into cells for a season, or Learoyd has run amok through his kit and accoutrements, or Mulvaney has indulged in strong waters, and under their influence reproved his Commanding officer, you can see the trouble in the faces of the untouched two. And the rest of the regiment know that comment or jest is unsafe. Generally the three avoid Orderly Room and the Corner Shop that follows, leaving both to the young bloods who have not sown their wild oats; but there are occasions—

For instance, Ortheris was sitting on the drawbridge of the main gate of Fort Amara, with his hands in his pockets and his pipe, bowl down, in his mouth. Learoyd was lying at full length on the turf of the glacis, kicking his heels in the air, and I came round the corner and asked for Mulvaney.

Ortheris spat into the ditch and shook his head. "No good seein' 'im now," said Ortheris; "'e's a bloomin' camel. Listen."

I heard on the flags of the veranda opposite to the cells, which are close to the Guard-Room, a measured step that I could have identified in the tramp of an army. There were twenty paces *crescendo,* a pause, and then twenty *diminuendo.*

"That's 'im," said Ortheris; "my Gawd, that's 'im! All for a bloomin' button you could see your face in an' a bit o' lip that a bloomin' Hark-angel would 'a' guv back."

Mulvaney was doing pack-drill—was compelled, that is to say, to walk up and down for certain hours in full marching order, with rifle, bayonet, ammunition, knapsack, and overcoat. And his offence was being dirty on parade! I nearly fell into the Fort Ditch with astonishment and wrath, for Mulvaney is the smartest man that ever mounted guard, and would as soon think of turning out uncleanly as of dispensing with his trousers.

"Who was the Sergeant that checked him?" I asked.

"Mullins, o' course," said Ortheris. "There ain't no other man would whip 'im on the peg so. But Mullins ain't a man. 'E's a dirty little pigscraper, that's wot 'e is."

"What did Mulvaney say? He's not the make of man to take that quietly."

"Said! Bin better for 'im if 'e'd shut 'is mouth. Lord, 'ow we laughed! 'Sargint,' 'e sez, 'ye say I'm dirty. Well,' sez 'e, 'when your wife lets you blow your own nose for yourself, perhaps you'll know wot dirt is. You're himperfectly eddicated, Sargint,' sez 'e, an' then we fell in. But after p'rade, 'e was up an' Mullins was swearin' 'imself black in the face at Ord'ly Room that

490

Mulvaney 'ad called 'im a swine an'
Lord knows wot all. You know Mullins. 'E'll 'ave 'is 'ead broke in one o'
these days. 'E's too big a bloomin' liar
for ord'nary consumption. 'Three
hours' can an' kit,' sez the Colonel; 'not
for bein' dirty on p'rade, but for 'avin'
said somthin' to Mullins, tho' I do not
believe,' sez 'e, 'you said wot 'e said you
said.' An' Mulvaney fell away sayin'
nothin'. You know 'e never speaks to
the Colonel for fear o' gettin' 'imself
fresh copped."

Mullins, a very young and very much
married Sergeant, whose manners were
partly the result of innate depravity and
partly of imperfectly digested Board
School, came over the bridge, and most
rudely asked Ortheris what he was
doing.

"Me?" said Ortheris. "Ow! I'm
waiting for my C'mission. 'Seed it
comin' along yit?"

Mullins turned purple and passed on.
There was the sound of a gentle chuckle
from the glacis where Learoyd lay.

" 'E expects to get 'is C'mission some
day," explained Orth'ris; "Gawd 'elp the
Mess that 'ave to put their 'ands into
the same kiddy as 'im! Wot time d'you
make it, sir? Fower! Mulvaney'll be
out in 'arf an hour. You don't want
to buy a dorg, sir, do you? A pup you
can trust—'arf Rampore by the Colonel's grey'ound."

"Ortheris," I answered, sternly, for I
knew what was in his mind, "do you
mean to say that"—

"I didn't mean to arx money o' you,
any'ow," said Ortheris; "I'd 'a' sold you
the dorg good an' cheap, but—but—I
know Mulvaney'll want somethin' after
we've walked 'im orf, an' I ain't got

nothin', nor 'e 'asn't neither. I'd sooner
sell you the dorg, sir. 'S trewth I
would!"

A shadow fell on the drawbridge,
and Ortheris began to rise into the air,
lifted by a huge hand upon his collar.

"Onything but t' braass," said Learoyd, quietly, as he held the Londoner
over the ditch. "Onything but t' braass.
Orth'ris, ma son! Ah've got one rupee
eight annas of ma own." He showed
two coins, and replaced Ortheris on the
drawbridge rail.

"Very good," I said; "where are you
going to?"

"Goin' to walk 'im orf wen 'e comes
out—two miles or three or fower," said
Ortheris.

The footsteps within ceased. I heard
the dull thud of a knapsack falling on
a bedstead, followed by the rattle of
arms. Ten minutes later, Mulvaney,
faultlessly dressed, his lips tight and
his face as black as a thunderstorm,
stalked into the sunshine on the drawbridge. Learoyd and Ortheris sprang
from my side and closed in upon him,
both leaning toward as horses lean upon
the pole. In an instant they had disappeared down the sunken road to the
cantonments, and I was left alone. Mulvaney had not seen fit to recognize me;
so I knew that his trouble must be
heavy upon him.

I climbed one of the bastions and
watched the figures of the Three Musketeers grow smaller and smaller across
the plain. They were walking as fast
as they could put foot to the ground,
and their heads were bowed. They
fetched a great compass round the
parade-ground, skirted the Cavalry
lines, and vanished in the belt of trees

that fringes the low land by the river.

I followed slowly, and sighted them—dusty, sweating, but still keeping up their long, swinging tramp—on the river bank. They crashed through the Forest Reserve, headed toward the Bridge of Boats, and presently established themselves on the bow of one of the pontoons. I rode cautiously till I saw three puffs of white smoke rise and die out in the clear evening air, and knew that peace had come again. At the bridge-head they waved me forward with gestures of welcome.

"Tie up your 'orse," shouted Ortheris, "an' come on, sir. We're all goin' 'ome in this 'ere bloomin' boat."

From the bridge-head to the Forest Officer's bungalow is but a step. The mess-man was there, and would see that a man held my horse. Did the Sahib require aught else—a peg, or beer? Ritchie Sahib had left half a dozen bottles of the latter, but since the Sahib was a friend of Ritchie Sahib, and he, the mess-man, was a poor man—

I gave my order quietly, and returned to the bridge. Mulvaney had taken off his boots, and was dabbling his toes in the water; Learoyd was lying on his back on the pontoon; and Ortheris was pretending to row with a big bamboo.

"I'm an ould fool," said Mulvaney, reflectively, "dhraggin' you two out here bekaze I was undher the Black Dog—sulkin' like a child. Me that was soldierin' when Mullins, an' be damned to him, was shqualin' on a counterpin for five shillin' a week—an' that not paid! Bhoys, I've took you five miles out av natural pervasity, Phew!"

"Wot's the odds so long as you're 'appy?" said Ortheris, applying himself afresh to the bamboo. "As well 'ere as anywhere else."

Learoyd held up a rupee and an eight-anna bit, and shook his head sorrowfully. "Five mile from t' Canteen, all along o' Mulvaney's blaasted pride."

"I know ut," said Mulvaney, penitently. "Why will ye come wid me? An' yet I wud be mortial sorry if ye did not—any time—though I am ould enough to know betther. But I will do penance. I will take a dhrink av wather."

Ortheris squeaked shrilly. The butler of the Forest bungalow was standing near the railings with a basket, uncertain how to clamber down to the pontoon. "Might 'a' know'd you'd 'a' got liquor out o' bloomin' desert, sir," said Ortheris, gracefully, to me. Then to the mess-man: "Easy with them there bottles. They're worth their weight in gold. Jock, ye long-armed beggar, get out o' that an' hike 'em down."

Learoyd had the basket on the pontoon in an instant, and the Three Musketeers gathered round it with dry lips. They drank my health in due and ancient form, and thereafter tobacco tasted sweeter than ever. They absorbed all the beer, and disposed themselves in picturesque attitudes to admire the setting sun—no man speaking for a while.

Mulvaney's head dropped upon his chest, and we thought that he was asleep.

"What on earth did you come so far for?" I whispered to Ortheris.

"To walk 'im orf, o' course. When 'e's been checked we allus walks 'im orf. 'E ain't fit to be spoke to those times—nor 'e ain't fit to leave alone neither. So we takes 'im till 'e is."

Mulvaney raised his head, and stared straight into the sunset. "I had my rifle," said he, dreamily, "an' I had my bay'nit, an' Mullins came round the corner, an' he looked in my face an' grinned dishpiteful. '*You* can't blow your own nose,' sez he. Now, I cannot tell fwhat Mullins's expayrience may ha' been, but, Mother av God, he was nearer to his death that minut' than I have iver been to mine—and that's less than the thick-nuss av a hair!"

"Yes," said Ortheris, calmly, "you'd look fine with all your buttons took orf, an' the Band in front o' you, walkin' roun' slow time. We're both front-rank men, me an' Jock, when the rig'ment's in 'ollow square. Bloomin' fine you'd look. 'The Lord giveth an' the Lord takᵉth awai,—Heasy with that there drop!—Blessed be the naime o' the Lord,'" he gulped in a quaint and suggestive fashion.

"Mullins! Wot's Mullins?" said Learoyd, slowly. "Ah'd take a coomp'ny o' Mullinses—ma hand behind me. Sitha, Mulvaney, don't be a fool."

"*You* were not checked for fwhat you did not do, an' made a mock av afther. 'Twas for less than that the Tyrone wud ha' sent O'Hara to hell, instid av lettin' him go by his own choosin', whin Rafferty shot him," retorted Mulvaney.

"And who stopped the Tyrone from doing it?" I asked.

"That ould fool who's sorry he didn't stick the pig Mullins." His head dropped again. When he raised it he shivered and put his hands on the shoulders of his two companions.

"Ye've walked the Divil out av me, bhoys," said he.

Ortheris shot out the red-hot dottel of his pipe on the back of the hairy fist. "They say 'Ell's 'otter than that," said he, as Mulvaney swore aloud. "You be warned so. Look yonder!"—he pointed across the river to a ruined temple—"Me an' you an' '*im*'—he indicated me by a jerk of his head—"was there one day when Hi made a bloomin' show o' myself. You an' 'im stopped me doin' such—an' Hi was on'y wishful for to desert. You are makin' a bigger bloomin' show o' yourself now."

"Don't mind him, Mulvaney," I said; "Dinah Shadd won't let you hang yourself yet awhile, and you don't intend to try it either. Let's hear about the Tyrone and O'Hara. Rafferty shot him for fooling with his wife. What happened before that?"

"There's no fool like an ould fool. You know you can do anythin' wid me whin I'm talkin'. Did I say I wud like to cut Mullins's liver out? I deny the imputashin, for fear that Orth'ris here wud report me—Ah! You wud tip me into the river, wud you? Sit quiet, little man. Anyways, Mullins is not worth the trouble av an extry p'rade, an' I will trate him wid outrajis contimpt. The Tyrone an' O'Hara! O'Hara an' the Tyrone, begad! Ould days are hard to bring back into the mouth, but they're always inside the head."

Followed a long pause.

"O'Hara was a Divil. Though I saved him, for the honor av the rig'-mint, from his death that time, I say it now. He was a Divil—a long, bould, black-haired Divil."

"Which way?" asked Ortheris.

"Women."

"Then I know another."

"Not more than in reason, if you mane me, yo warped walkin'-shtick. I have been young, an' for why should I not have tuk what I cud? Did I iver, whin I was Corp'ril, use the rise av my rank—wan step an' that taken away, more's the sorrow an' the fault av me!—to prosecute a nefarious inthrigue, as O'Hara did? Did I, whin I was Corp'ril, lay my spite upon a man an' make his life a dog's life from day to day? Did I lie, as O'Hara lied, till the young wans in the Tyrone turned white wid the fear av the Judgment av God killin' thim all in a lump, as ut killed the woman at Devizes? I did not! I have sinned my sins an' I have made my confesshin, an' Father Victor knows knows the worst av me. O'Hara was tuk, before he cud spake, on Rafferty's doorstep, an' no man knows the worst av him. But this much I know!

"The Tyrone was recruited any fashion in the ould days. A draf' from Connemara—a draf' from Portsmouth—a draf' from Kerry, an' that was a blazin' bad draf'—here, there and iverywhere—but the large av thim was Oirish—Black Oirish. Now there are Oirish an' Oirish. The good are good as the best, but the bad are wurrst than the wurrst. 'Tis this way. They clog together in pieces as fast as thieves, an' no wan knows fwhat they will do till wan turns informer an' the gang is bruk. But ut begins again, a day later, meetin' in holes an' corners an' swearin' bloody oaths an' shtickin' a man in the back an' runnin' away, an' thin waitin' for the blood-money on the reward papers—to see if ut's worth enough. Those are

the Black Oirish, an' 'tis they that bring dishgrace upon the name av Oireland, an' thim I wud kill—as I nearly killed wan wanst.

"But to reshume. My room—'twas before I was married—was with twelve av the scum av the earth—the pickin's av the gutter—mane men that wud neither laugh nor talk nor yet get dhrunk as a man shud. They thried some av their dog's thricks on me, but I dhrew a line round my cot, an' the man that thransgressed ut wint into hospital for three days good.

"O'Hara had put his spite on the room—he was my Color Sargint—an' nothin' cud we do to plaze him. I was younger than I am now, an' I tuk what I got in the way av dressing down and punishment-dhrill wid my tongue in my cheek. But it was diff'rint wid the others, an' why I cannot say, excipt that some men are borrun mane an' go to dhirty murdher where a fist is more than enough. Afther a whoile, they changed their chune to me an' was desp'rit frien'ly—all twelve av thim cursin' O'Hara in chorus.

" 'Eyah,' sez I, 'O'Hara's a divil an' I'm not for denyin' ut, but is he the only man in the wurruld? Let him go. He'll get tired av findin' our kit foul an' our 'coutrements onproperly kep'.'

" 'We will *not* let him go,' sez they.

" 'Thin take him,' sez I, 'an' a dashed poor yield you will get for your throuble.'

" 'Is he not misconductin' himself wid Slimmy's wife?' sez another.

" 'She's common to the rig'mint,' sez I. 'Fwhat has made ye this partic'lar on a suddint?'

" 'Has he not put his spite on the

roomful av us? Can we do anythin' that he will not check us for?' sez another.

" 'That's thrue,' sez I.

" 'Will ye not help us to do aught,' sez another—'a big bould man like you?'

" 'I will break his head upon his shoulthers av he puts hand on me,' sez I. 'I will give him the lie av he says that I'm dhirty, an' I wud not mind duckin' him in the Artillery troughs if ut was not that I'm thryin' for my shtripes.'

" 'Is that all ye will do?' sez another. 'Have ye no more spunk than that, ye blood-dhrawn calf?'

" 'Blood-dhrawn I may be,' sez I, gettin' back to my cot an' makin' my line round ut; 'but ye know that the man who comes acrost this mark will be more blood-dhrawn than me. No man gives me the name in my mouth,' I sez. 'Ondersthand, I will have no part wid you in anythin' ye do, nor will I raise my fist to my shuperior. Is any wan comin' on?' sez I.

"They made no move, tho' I gave them full time, but stud growlin' an' snarlin' together at wan ind av the room. I tuk up my cap and wint out to Canteen, thinkin' no little av mesilf, and there I grew most ondacintly dhrunk in my legs. My head was all reasonable.

" 'Houligan,' I sez to a man in E Comp'ny that was by way av bein' a frind av mine; 'I'm overtuk from the belt down. Do you give me the touch av your shoulther to presarve my formation an' march me acrost the ground into the high grass. I'll sleep ut off there,' sez I; an' Houligan—he's dead now, but good he was while he lasted—

walked wid me, givin' me the touch whin I wint wide, ontil we came to the high grass, an', my faith, the sky an' the earth was fair rowlin' undher me. I made for where the grass was thickust, an' there I slep' off my liquor wid an easy conscience. I did not desire to come on books too frequent; my charachter havin' been shpotless for the good half av a year.

"Whin I roused, the dhrink was dyin' out in me, an' I felt as though a she-cat had littered in my mouth. I had not learned to hould my liquor wid comfort in thim days. 'Tis little betther I am now. 'I will get Houligan to pour a bucket over my head,' thinks I, an' I wud ha' risen, but I heard some wan say: 'Mulvaney can take the blame av ut for the backslidin' hound he is.'

" 'Oho!' sez I, an' my head rang like a guard-room gong: 'fwhat is the blame that this young man must take to oblige Tim Vulmea?' For 'twas Tim Vulmea that shpoke.

"I turned on my belly an' crawled through the grass, a bit at a time, to where the spache came from. There was the twelve av my room sittin' down in a little patch, the dhry grass wavin' above their heads an' the sin av black murdher in their hearts. I put the stuff aside to get a clear view.

" 'Fwhat's that?' sez wan man, jumpin' up.

" 'A dog,' says Vulmea. 'You're a nice hand to this job! As I said, Mulvaney will take the blame—av ut comes to a pinch.'

" " 'Tis harrd to swear a man's life away,' sez a young wan.

" 'Thank ye for that,' thinks I. 'Now,

fwhat the divil are you paragins con-thrivin' against me?'

" ' 'Tis as easy as dhrinkin' your quart,' sez Vulmea. 'At seven or there-on, O'Hara will come acrost to the Married Quarters, goin' to call on Slimmy's wife, the swine! Wan av us'll pass the wurrd to the room an' we shtart the divil an' all av a shine—laughin' an' crackin' on an' t'rowin' our boots about. Thin O'Hara will come to give us the ordher to be quiet, the more by token bekaze the room-lamp will be knocked over in the larkin'. He will take the straight road to the ind door where there's the lamp in the veranda, an' that'll bring him clear against the light as he sthands. He will not be able to look into the dhark. Wan av us will loose off, an' a close shot ut will be, an' shame to the man that misses. 'Twill be Mulvaney's rifle, she that is at the head av the rack—there's no mis-takin' long-shtocked, cross-eyed bitch even in the dhark.'

"The thief misnamed my ould firin'-piece out av jealousy—I was pershuad-ed av that—an' ut made me more an-gry than all.

"But Vulmea goes on: 'O'Hara will dhrop, an' by the time the light's lit again, there'll be some six av us on the chest av Mulvaney, cryin' murdher an' rape. Mulvaney's cot is near the ind door, an' the shmokin' rifle will be lyin' undher him whin we've knocked him over. We know, an' all the rig'mint knows, that Mulvaney has given O'Hara more lip than any man av us. Will there be any doubt at the Coort-martial? Wud twelve honust sodger-bhoys swear away the life av a dear, quiet, swate-timpered man such as is Mulvaney—

wid his line av pipe-clay roun' his cot, threatenin' us wid murdher av we over-shtepped ut, as we can truthful testify?'

" 'Mary, Mother av Mercy!' thinks I to mesilf; 'it is this to have an unruly mimber an' fistes fit to use! Oh the sneakin' hounds!'

"The big dhrops ran down my face, for I was wake wid the liquor an' had not the full av my wits about me. I laid shtill an' heard thim workin' them-selves up to swear my life by tellin' tales av ivry time I put my mark on wan or another; an' my faith, they was few that was not so dishtinguished. 'Twas all in the way av fair fight, though, for niver did I raise my hand excipt whin they had provoked me to ut.

" ' 'Tis all well,' sez wan av thim, 'but who's to do this shootin'?'

" 'Fwhat matter?' sez Vulmea. ' 'Tis Mulvaney will do that—at the Coort-martial.'

" 'He will so,' sez the man, 'but whose hand is put to the trigger—*in the room?*'

" 'Who'll do ut?' sez Vulmea, lookin' round, but divil a man answeared. They began to dishpute till Kiss, that was always playin' Shpoil Five, sez: 'Thry the kyards!' Wid that he opined his tunic an' tuk out the greasy palammers, an' they all fell in wid the notion.

" 'Deal on!' sez Vulmea, wid a big rattlin' oath, 'an' the Black Curse av Shielygh come to the man that will not do his duty as the kyards say. Amin!'

" 'Black Jack is the masther,' sez Kiss, dealin'. Black Jack, sorr, I shud expaytiate to you, is the Ace av Shpades which from time immimorial has been intimately connect wid battle, murdher an' suddin death.

"*Wanst* Kiss dealt an' there was no sign, but the men was whoite wid the workin's av their sowls. *Twice* Kiss dealt, an' there was a grey shine on their cheeks like the mess av an egg. *Three* times Kiss dealt an' they was blue. 'Have ye not lost him?' sez Vulmea, wipin' the sweat on him. Let's ha' done Quick! 'Quick ut is,' says Kiss, t'rowin' him, the kyard; an' ut fell face up on his knee—Black Jack!

"Thin they all cackled wid laughin'. 'Duty thrippence,' sez wan av thim, 'an' damned cheap at that price!' But I cud see they all dhrew a little away from Vulmea an' lef' him sittin' playin' wid the kyard. Vulmea sez no word for a whoile but licked his lips—cat-ways. Thin he threw up his head an' made the men swear by ivry oath known to stand by him not alone in the room but at the Coort-martial that was to set on *me!* He tould off five av the biggest to stretch me on my cot whin the shot was fired, an' another man he tould off to put out the light, an' yet another to load my rifle. He wud not do that himself; an' that was quare, for 'twas but a little thing considerin'.

"Thin they swore over again that they wud not bethray wan another, an' crep' out av the grass in diff'rint ways, two by two. A mercy ut was that they did not come on me. I was sick wid fear in the pit av my stummick—sick, sick, sick! Afther they was all gone, I wint back to Canteen an' called for a quart to put a thought in me. Vulmea was there, dhrinkin' heavy, an' politeful to me beyond reason. 'Fwhat will I do—fwhat will I do?' thinks I to mesilf whin Vulmea wint away.

"Prisintly the Arm'rer Sargint comes in stiffin' an' crackin' on, not pleased wid any wan, bekaze the Martini Henri bein' new to the rig'mint in those days we used to play the mischief wid her arrangemints. 'Twas a long time before I cud get out av the way av thryin' to pull back the back-sight an' turnin' her over after firin'—as if she was a Snider.

"'Fwhat tailor-man do they give me to work wid?' sez the Arm'rer Sargint. 'Here's Hogan, his nose flat as a table, laid by for a week, an' ivry Comp'ny sendin' their arrums in knocked to small shivreens.'

"'Fwhat's wrong wid Hogan, Sargint?' sez I.

"'Wrong!' sez the Arm'rer Sargint; 'I showed him, as though I had been his mother, the way av shtrippin' a 'Tini, an' he shtrup her clane an' easy. I tould him to put her to again an' fire a blank into the blow-pit to show how the dirt hung on the groovin'. He did that, but he did not put in the pin av the fallin'-block, an' av coorse whin he fired he was strook by the block jumpin' clear. Well for him 'twas but a blank—a full charge wud ha' cut his oi out.'

"I looked a thrifle wiser than a boiled sheep's head. 'How's that, Sargint?' sez I.

"'This way, ye blundherin' man, an' don't you be doin' ut,' sez he. Wid that he shows me a Waster action—the breech av her all cut away to show the inside—an' so plazed he was to grumble that he dimonstrated fwhat Hogan had done twice over. 'An' that comes av not knowin' the wepping you're purvided wid,' sez he.

"'Thank ye, Sargint,' sez I; 'I will come to you again for further information.'

"'Ye will not,' sez he. 'Kape your clanin'-rod away from the breech-pin or you will get into throuble.'

"I wint outside an' I could ha' danced wid delight for the grandeur av ut. 'They will load my rifle, good luck to thim, whoile I'm away,' thinks I, and back I wint to the Canteen to give them their clear chanst.

"The Canteen was fillin' wid men at the ind av the day. I made feign to be far gone in dhrink, an', wan by wan, all my roomful came in wid Vulmea. I wint away, walkin' thick an' heavy, but not so thick an' heavy that any wan cud ha' tuk me. Sure and thrue, there was a kyartridge gone from my pouch an' lyin' snug in my rifle. I was hot wid rage against thim all, an' I worried the bullet out wid my teeth as fast as I cud, the room bein' empty. Then I tuk my boot an' the clainin'-rod and knocked out the pin av the fallin'-block. Or, 'twas music when that pin rowled on the flure! I put ut into my pouch an' stuck a dab av dirt on the holes in the plate, puttin' the fallin'-block back. 'That'll do your business, Vulmea,' sez I, lyin' easy on the cot. 'Come an' sit on my chest the whole room av you, an' I will take you to my bosom for the biggest divils that iver cheated halter.' I would have no mercy on Vulmea. His oi or his life—little I cared!

"At dusk they came back, the twelve av thim, an' they had all been dhrinkin'. I was shammin' sleep on the cot. Wan man wint outside in the veranda. Whin he whishtled they began to rage roun' the room an' carry on tremenjus. But I niver want to hear men laugh as they did—skylarkin' too! 'Twas like mad jackals.

"'Shtop that blasted noise!' sez O'Hara in the dark, an' pop goes the room lamp. I cud hear O'Hara runnin' up an' the rattlin' av my rifle in the rack an' the men breathin' heavy as they stud roun' my cot. I cud see O'Hara in the light av the veranda lamp, an' thin I heard the crack av my rifle. She cried loud, poor darlint, bein' mishandled. Next minut' five men were houldin' me down. 'Go easy, I sez; 'fwhat's ut all about?'

"Thin Vulmea, on the flure, raised a howl you cud hear from wan ind av cantonmints to the other. 'I'm dead, I'm butchered, I'm blind!' sez he. 'Saints have mercy on my sinful sowl! Sind for Father Constant! Oh sind for Father Constant an' let me go clean!' By that I knew he was not so dead as I cud ha' wished.

"O'Hara picks up the lamp in the veranda wid a hand as stiddy as a rest. 'Fwhat damned dog's thrick is this av yours?' sez he, and turns the light on Tim Vulmea that was shwimmin' in blood from top to toe. The fallin'-block had sprung free behin' a full charge av powther—good care I took to bite down the brass afther takin' out the bullet that there might be somethin' to give ut full worth—an' had cut Tim from the lip to the corner av the right eye, lavin' the eyelid in tatthers, an' so up an' along by the forehead to the hair. 'Twas more av a rakin' plough, if you will ondherstand, than a clean cut; an' niver did I see a man bleed as Vulmea did. The dhrink an' the stew that he was in pumped the blood strong. The minut' the men sittin' on my chest heard O'Hara spakin' they scatthered each

wan to his cot, an' cried out very politeful: 'Fwhat is ut, Sargint?'

" 'Fwhat is ut!' sez O'Hara, shakin'
Tim. 'Well an' good do you know fwhat
ut is, ye skulkin' ditch-lurkin' dogs! Get
a *doolie,* an' take this whimperin' scutt
away. There will be more heard av ut
than any av you will care for.'

"Vulmea sat up rockin' his head in
his hand an' moanin' for Father Constant.

" 'Be done!' sez O'Hara, dhraggin'
him up by the hair. 'You're none so
dead that you cannot go fifteen years
for thryin' to shoot me.'

" 'I did not,' sez Vulmea; 'I was
shootin' mesilf.'

" 'That's quare,' sez O'Hara, 'for the
front av my jackut is black wid your
powther.' He tuk up the rifle that was
still warm an' began to laugh. 'I'll
make your life Hell to you,' sez he, 'for
attempted murdher an' kapin' your rifle
onproperly. You'll be hanged first an'
thin put undher stoppages for four fifteen. The rifle's done for,' sez he.

" 'Why, 'tis my rifle!' sez I, comin' up
to look; 'Vulmea, ye divil, fwhat were
you doin' wid her—answer me that?'

" 'Lave me alone,' sez Vulmea; 'I'm
dyin'!'

" 'I'll wait till you're betther,' sez
I, 'an' thin we two will talk ut out um-
brageous.'

"O'Hara pitched Tim into the *doolie,*
none too tinder, but all the bhoys kep'
by their cots, which was not the sign av
innocint men. I was huntin' ivrywhere
for my fallin'-block, but not findin' ut
at all. I niver found ut.

" '*Now* fwhat will I do?' sez O'Hara,
swinging the veranda light in his hand
an' lookin' down the room. I had hate

and contimpt av O'Hara an' I have now,
dead tho' he is, but, for all that, will
I say he was a brave man. He is baskin'
in Purgathory this tide, but I wish he
cud hear that, whin he stud lookin' down
the room an' the bhoys shivered before
the oi av him, I knew him for a brave
man an' I liked him *so.*

" 'Fwhat will I do?' sez O'Hara again,
an' we heard the voice av a woman low
an' sof' in the veranda. 'Twas Slimmy's
wife, come over at the shot, sittin' on
wan av the benches an' scarce able to
walk.

" 'O Denny!—Denny, dear,' sez she,
'have they kilt you?'

"O'Hara looked down the room again
an' showed his teeth to the gum. Then
he spat on the flure.

" 'You're not worth ut,' sez he. 'Light
that lamp, ye dogs,' an' wid that he
turned away, an' I saw him walkin' off
wid Slimmy's wife; she thryin' to wipe
off the powther-black on the front av
his jacket wid her handkerchief. 'A
brave man you are,' thinks I—'a brave
man an' a bad woman.'

"No wan said a word for a time. They
was all ashamed, past spache.

" 'Fwhat d'you think he will do?'
sez wan av thim at last. 'He knows
we're all in ut.'

" 'Are we so?' sez I from my cot.
'The man that sez that to me will be
hurt. I do not know,' sez I, 'fwhat
onderhand divilmint you have con-
thrived, but by what I've seen I know
that you cannot commit murdher wid
another man's rifle—such shakin' cowards you are. I'm goin' to slape,' I
sez, 'an' you can blow my head off
whoile I lay.' I did not slape, though,
for a long time. Can ye wonder?

"Next morn the news was through all the rig'mint, an' there was nothin' that the men did not tell. O'Hara reports, fair an' easy, that Vulmea was come to grief through tamperin' wid his rifle in barricks, all for to show the mechanism. An' by my sowl, he had the impart'nince to say that he was on the sphot at the time an' cud certify that ut was an accident! You might ha' knocked my roomful down wid a straw whin they heard that. 'Twas lucky for thim that the bhoys were always thryin' to find out how the new rifle was made, an' a lot av thim had come up for easin' the pull by shtickin' bits av grass an' such in the part av the lock that showed near the thrigger. The first issues of the 'Tinis was not covered in, an' I mesilf have eased the pull av mine time an' agin. A light pull is ten points on the range to me.

" 'I will not have this foolishness!' sez the Colonel. 'I will twist the tail off Vulmea!' sez he; but whin he saw him, all tied up an' groanin' in hospital, he changed his will. 'Make him an early convalescint,' sez he to the Doctor, an' Vulmea was made so for a warnin'. His big bloody bandages an' face puckered up to wan side did more to kape the bhoys from messin' wid the insides av their rifles than any punishmint.

"O'Hara gave no reason for fwhat he'd said, an' all my roomful were too glad to inquire, tho' he put his spite upon thim more wearin' than before. Wan day, howiver, he tuk me apart very polite, for he cud be that at the choosin'.

" 'You're a good sodger, tho' you're a damned insolint man,' sez he.

" 'Fair words, Sargint,' sez I, 'or I may be insolint again.'

" ' 'Tis not like you,' sez he, 'to lave your rifle in the rack widout the breech-pin, for widout the breech-pin she was whin Vulmea fired. I should ha' found the break av ut in the eyes av the holes, else,' he sez.

" 'Sargint,' sez I, 'fwhat wud your life ha' been worth av the breech-pin had been in place, for, on my sowl, my life wud be worth just as much to me av I tould you whether ut was or was not. Be thankful the bullet was not there,' I sez.

" 'That's thrue,' sez he, pulling his moustache; 'but I do not believe that you, for all your lip, was in that business.'

" 'Sargint,' sez I, 'I cud hammer the life out av a man in ten minuts wid my fistes if that man dishpleased me; for I am a good sodger, an' I will be threated as such, an' whoile my fistes are my own they're strong enough foi all work I have to do. They do not fly back toward me!' sez I, lookin' him betune the eyes.

" 'You're a good man,' sez he, lookin' me betune the eyes—an' oh he was a gran'-built man to see!—'you're a good man,' he sez, 'an' I cud wish, for the pure frolic av ut, that I was not a Sargint, or that you were not a Privit; an' you will think me no coward whin I say this thing.'

" 'I do not,' sez I. 'I saw you whin Vulmea mishandled the rifle. But, Sargint,' I sez, 'take the wurrd from me now, spakin' as man to man wid the shtripes off, tho' 'tis little right I have to talk, me being fwhat I am by natur'. This time ye tuk no harm, an' next time ye may not, but, in the ind, so sure as Slimmy's wife came into the veranda, so sure will ye take harm—an' bad harm. Have thought, Sargint,' sez I. 'Is ut worth ut?'

" 'Ye're a bould man,' sez he, breathin' harrd. 'A very bould man. But I am a bould man tu. Do you go your way, Privit Mulvaney, an' I will go mine.'

"We had no further spache thin or afther, but, wan by another, he drafted the twelve av my room out into other rooms, an' got thim spread among the Comp'nies, for they was not a good breed to live together, an' the Comp'ny orf'cers saw ut. They wud ha' shot me in the night av they had known fwhat I knew; but that they did not.

"An', in the ind, as I said, O'Hara met his death from Rafferty for foolin' wid his wife. He wint his own way too well —Eyah, too well! Shtraight to that affair, widout turnin' to the right or to the lef', he wint, an' may the Lord have mercy on his sowl. Amin!"

" 'Ear! 'Ear!" said Ortheris, pointing the moral with a wave of his pipe. "An' this is 'im 'oo would be a bloomin' Vulmea all for the sake of Mullins an' a bloomin' button! Mullins never went after a woman in his life. Mrs. Mullins, she saw 'im one day"—

"Ortheris," I said, hastily, for the romances of Private Ortheris are all too daring for publication, "look at the sun. It's quarter past six!"

"O Lord! Three quarters of an hour for five an' a 'arf miles! We'll 'ave to run like Jimmy O."

The Three Musketeers clambered on to the bridge, and departed hastily in the direction of the cantonment road. When I overtook them I offered them two stirrups and a tail, which they accepted enthusiastically. Ortheris held the tail, and in this manner we trotted steadily through the shadows by an unfrequented road.

At the turn into the cantonments we heard carriage wheels. It was the Colonel's barouche, and in it sat the Colonel's wife and daughter. I caught a suppressed chuckle, and my beast sprang forward with a lighter step.

The Three Musketeers had vanished into the night.

The Big Drunk Draf'

We're goin' 'ome ,we're goin' 'ome—
Our ship is *at* the shore,
An' you mus' pack your 'aversack,
For we won't come back no more.
Ho, don't you grieve for me,
My lovely Mary Ann,
For I'll marry you yet on a fourp'ny bit,
As a time-expired ma-a-an!
          Barrack Room Ballad.

AN awful thing has happened! My friend, Private Mulvaney, who went home in the *Serapis,* time-expired, not very long ago, has come back to India as a civilian! It was all Dinah Shadd's fault. She could not stand the poky little lodgings, and she missed her servant Abdullah more than words could tell. The fact was that the Mulvaneys had been out here too long, and had lost touch of England.

Mulvaney knew a contractor on one

of the new Central India lines, and wrote to him for some sort of work. The contractor said that if Mulvaney could pay the passage he would give him command of a gang of coolies for old sake's sake. The pay was eighty-five rupees a month, and Dinah Shadd said that if Terence did not accept she would make his life a "basted purgathory." Therefore the Mulvaneys came out as "civilians," which was a great and terrible fall; though Mulvaney tried to disguise it, by saying that he was "Ker'nel on the railway line, an' a consequinshal man."

He wrote me an invitation, on a tool-indent form, to visit him; and I came down to the funny little "construction" bungalow at the side of the line. Dinah Shadd had planted peas about and about, and nature had spread all manner of green stuff round the place. There was no change in Mulvaney except the change of clothing, which was deplorable, but could not be helped. He was standing upon his trolly, haranguing a gangman, and his shoulders were as well drilled, and his big, thick chin was as clean-shaven as ever.

"I'm a civilian now," said Mulvaney. "Cud you tell that I was iver a martial man? Don't answer, sorr, av you're strainin' betune a complimint an' a lie. There's no houldin' Dinah Shadd now she's got a house av her own. Go inside, an' dhrink tay out av chiny in the drrrawin'-room, an' thin we'll dhrink like Christians undher the tree here. Scutt, ye naygur-folk! There's a Sahib come to call on me, an' that's more than he'll iver do for you onless you run! Get out, an' go on pilin' up the earth, quick, till sundown."

When we three were comfortably settled under the big *sisham* in front of the bungalow, and the first rush of questions and answers about Privates Ortheris and Learoyd and old times and places had died away, Mulvaney said, reflectively—"Glory be there's no p'rade to-morrow, an' no bun-headed Corp'ril-bhoy to give you his lip. An' yit I don't know. 'Tis harrd to be something ye niver were an' niver meant to be, an' all the ould days shut up along wid your papers. Eyah! I'm growin' rusty, an' 'tis the will av God that a man mustn't serve his Quane for time an' all."

He helped himself to a fresh peg, and sighed furiously.

"Let your beard grow, Mulvaney," said I, "and then you won't be troubled with those notions. You'll be a real civilian."

Dinah Shadd had told me in the drawing-room of her desire to coax Mulvaney into letting his beard grow—" 'Twas so civilian-like," said poor Dinah, who hated her husband's hankering for his old life.

"Dinah Shadd, you're a dishgrace te an honust, clane-scraped man!" said Mulvaney, without replying to me. "Grow a beard on your own chin, darlint, and lave my razors alone. They're all that stand betune me and dis-rispect-ability. Av I didn't shave, I wud be torminted wid an outrajis thirst; for there's nothin' so dhryin to the throat as a big billy-goat beard waggin' undher the chin. Ye wudn't have me dhrink *always*, Dinah Shadd? By the same token, you're kapin' me crool dhry now. Let me look at that whiskey."

The whiskey was lent and returned, but Dinah Shadd, who had been just as eager as her husband in asking after old friends, rent me with—

"I take shame for you, sorr, coming down here—though the Saints know you're as welkim as the daylight whin you *do* come—an' upsettin' Terence's head wid your nonsense about—about fwhat's much better forgotten. He bein' a civilian now, an' you niver was aught else. Can you not let the Arrmy rest? 'Tis not good for Terence."

I took refuge by Mulvaney, for Dinah Shadd has a temper of her own.

"Let be—let be," said Mulvaney. " 'Tis only wanst in a way I can talk about the ould days." Then to me:— "Ye say Dhrumshticks is well, an' his lady tu? I niver knew how I liked the grey garron till I was shut av him an' Asia."—"Dhrumshticks" was the nickname of the Colonel commanding Mulvaney's old regiment.—"Will you be seein' him again? You will. Thin tell him"—Mulvaney's eyes began to twinkle—"tell him wid Privit"—

"*Mister,* Terence," interrupted Dinah Shadd.

"Now the Divil an' all his angils an' the Firmament av Hiven fly away wid the 'Mister,' an' the sin av making me swear be on your confession, Dinah Shadd! *Privit,* I tell ye. Wid *Privit* Mulvaney's best obedience, that but for me the last time-expired wud be still pullin' harr on their way to the sea."

He threw himself back in the chair, chuckled, and was silent.

"Mrs. Mulvaney," I said, "please take up the whiskey, and don't let him have it until he has told the story."

Dinah Shadd dexterously whipped the bottle away, saying at the same time, " 'Tis nothing to be proud av," and thus

captured by the enemy, Mulvaney spake:—

" 'Twas on Chuseda week. I was be-haderin' round wid the gangs on the 'bankmint—I've taught the hoppers how to kape step an' stop screechin'—whin a head-gangman comes up to me, wid about two inches av shirt-tail hanging round his neck an' a disthressful light in his oi. 'Sahib,' sez he, 'there's a reg'-mint an' a half av soldiers up at the junction, knockin' red cinders out av ivrything an' ivrybody! They thried to hang me in my cloth,' he sez, 'an' there will be murder an' ruin an' rape in the place before nightfall! They say they're comin' down here to wake us up. What will we do wid our women-folk?'

" 'Fetch my throlly!' sez I; 'my heart's sick in my ribs for a wink at anything wid the Quane's uniform on ut. Fetch my throlly, an' six av the jildiest men, and run me up in shtyle.' "

"He tuk his best coat," said Dinah Shadd, reproachfully.

" 'Twas to do honor to the Widdy. I cud ha' done no less, Dinah Shadd. You and your digressins interfere wid the coorse av the narrative. Have you iver considhered fwhat I fud look like wid me *head* shaved as well as my chin? You bear that in your mind, Dinah darlin'."

"I was throllied up six miles, all to get a shquint at that draf'. I *knew* 'twas a spring draf' goin' home, for there's no rig'mint hereabouts, more's the pity."

"Praise the Virgin!" murmured Dinah Shadd. But Mulvaney did not hear.

"Whin I was about three-quarters av a mile off the rest-camp, powtherin' along fit to burst, I heard the noise av the men an', on my sowl, sorr, I cud catch the voice av Peg Barney bellowin' like a bison wid the belly-ache. You remimber Peg Barney that was in D Comp'ny—a red, hairy scraun, wid a scar on his jaw? Peg Barney that cleared out the Blue Lights Jubilee meeting wid the cook-room mop last year?

"Thin I knew ut was a draf' of the ould rig'mint, an' I was conshumed wid sorrow for the bhoy that was in charge. We was harrd scrapin's at any time. Did I iver tell you how Horker Kelley went into clink nakid as Phœbus Apollonius, wid the shirts av the Corp'ril an' file undher his arrum? An' he was a moild man! But I'm digreshin'. 'Tis a shame both to the rig'mints and the Arrmy sendin' down little orf'cer bhoys wid a draf' av strong men mad wid liquor an' the chanst av gettin' shut av India, an' niver a punishment that's fit to be given right down an' away from cantonmints to the dock! 'Tis this nonsince. Whin I am servin' my time, I'm undher the Articles av War, an' can be whipped on the peg for thim. But whin I've served my time, I'm a Reserve man, an' the Articles av War haven't any hould on me. An orf'cer can't do anythin' to a time-expired savin' confinin' him to barricks. 'Tis a wise rig'-lation bekaze a time-expired does not have any barricks; bein' on the move all the time. 'Tis a Solomon av a rig'lation, is that. I wud like to be introduced to the man that made ut. 'Tis easier to get colts from a Kibbereen horse-fair into Galway than to take a bad draf' over ten miles av country. Consiquintly that rig'lation—for fear that the men wud be hurt by the little orf'cer bhoy. No matther. The nearer

my throll came to the rest-camp, the woilder was the shine, an' the louder was the voice av Peg Barney. ' 'Tis good I am here,' thinks I to myself, 'for Peg alone is employmint for two or three.' He bein', I well knew, as cooped as a dhrover.

"Faith, that rest-camp was a sight! The tent-ropes was all skew-nosed, an' the pegs looked as dhrunk as the men—fifty av thim—the scourin's, an' rinsin's, an' Divil's lavin's av the Ould Rig'mint. I tell you, sorr, they were dhrunker than any men you've ever seen in your mortial life. How does a draf' get dhrunk? How does a frog get fat? The suk ut in through their shkins.

"There was Peg Barney sittin' on the groun' in his shirt—wan shoe off an' wan shoe on—whackin' a tent-peg over the head wid his boot, an' singin' fit to wake the dead. 'Twas no clane song that he sung, though. 'Twas the Divil's Mass."

"What's that?" I asked.

"Whin a bad egg is shut av the Army, he sings the Divil's Mass for a good riddance; an' that manes swearin' at ivrything from the Commandher-in-Chief down to the Room-Corp'ril, such as you niver in your days heard. Some men can swear so as to make green turf crack! Have you iver heard the Curse in an Orange Lodge? The Divil's Mass is ten times worse, an' Peg Barney was singin' ut, whackin' the tent-peg on the head wid his boot for each man that he cursed. A powerful big voice had Peg Barney, an' a hard swearer he was whin sober. I stood forninst him, an' 'twas not me oi alone that cud tell Peg was dhrunk as a coot.

" 'Good mornin', Peg,' I sez, whin he dhrew breath afther cursin' the Adj'tint

Gen'ral; 'I've put on my best coat to see you, Peg Barney,' sez I.

" 'Thin take ut off again,' sez Peg Barney, latherin' away wid the boot; 'take ut off an' dance, ye lousy civilian!'

"Wid that he begins cursin' ould Dhrumshticks, being so full he clean disremimbers the Brigade-Major an' the Judge Advokit Gen'ral.

" 'Do you not know me, Peg?' sez I, though me blood was hot in me wid being called a civilian."

"An' him a decent married man!" wailed Dinah Shadd.

" 'I do not,' sez Peg, 'but dhrunk or sober I'll tear the hide off your back wid a shovel whin I've stopped singin'.'

" 'Say you so, Peg Barney?' sez I. ' 'Tis clear as mud you've forgotten me. I'll assist your autobiography.' Wid that I stretched Peg Barney, boot an' all, an' wint into the camp. An awful sight ut was!

" 'Where's the orf'cer in charge av the detachment?' sez I to Scrub Greene— the manest little worm that ever walked.

" 'There's no orf'cer, ye ould cook,' sez Scrub; 'we're a bloomin' Republic.'

" 'Are you that?' sez I; 'thin I'm O'Connell the Dictator, an' by this you will larn to kape a civil tongue in your rag-box.'

"Wid that I stretched Scrub Greene an' wint to the orf'cer's tent. 'Twas a new little bhoy—not wan I'd iver seen before. He was sittin' in his tent, purtendin' not to 'ave ear av the racket.

"I saluted—but for the life av me I mint to shake hands whin I went in. 'Twas the sword hangin' on the tent-pole changed my will.

" 'Can't I help, sorr?' sez I; ' 'tis a strong man's job they've given you, an' you'll be wantin' help by sundown.' He was a bhoy wid bowils, that child, an' a rale gintleman.

" 'Sit down,' sez he.

" 'Not before my orf'cer,' sez I; an' I tould him fwhat my service was.

" 'I've heard av you,' sez he. 'You tuk the town av Lungtungpen nakid.'

" 'Faith,' thinks I, 'that's Honor an' Glory;' for 'twas Lift'nint Brazenose did that job. 'I'm wid ye, sorr,' sez I, 'if I'm av use. They shud niver ha' sent you down wid the draf'. Savin' your presince, sorr,' I sez, 'tis only Lift'nint Hackerston in the Ould Rig'mint can manage a Home draf'.'

" 'I've niver had charge of men like this before,' sez he, playin' wid the pens on the table; 'an' I see by the Rig-la-tions'—

" 'Shut your oi to the Rig'lations, sorr,' I sez, 'till the throoper's into blue wather. By the Rig'lations you've got to tuck thim up for the night, or they'll be runnin' foul av my coolies an' makin' a shiverarium half through the country. Can you trust your noncoms, sorr?'

" 'Yes,' sez he.

" 'Good,' sez I; 'there'll be throuble before the night. Are you marchin', sorr?'

" 'To the next station,' sez he.

" 'Better still,' sez I; 'there'll be big throuble.'

" 'Can't be too hard on a Home draf',' sez he; 'the great thing is to git thim in-ship.'

" 'Faith you've larnt the half av your lesson, sorr,' sez I, 'but av you shtick to the Rig'lations you'll niver get thim in-ship at all, at all. Or there won't be a rag iv kit betune thim whin you do.'

" 'Twas a dear little orf'cer bhoy, an' by way av kapin' his heart up, I tould him fwhat I saw wanst in a draf' in Egypt."

"What was that, Mulvaney?" said I.

"Sivin an' fifty men sittin' on the bank av a canal, laughin' at a poor little squidgereen av an orf'cer that they'd made wade into the slush an' pitch the things out av the boats for their Lord High Mightinesses. That made me orf'cer bhoy woild wid indignation.

" 'Soft an' aisy, sor,' sez I; 'you've niver had your draf' in hand since you left cantonmints. Wait till the night, an' your work will be ready to you. Wid your permission, sorr, I will investigate the camp, an' talk to my ould friends. 'Tis no manner av use thryin' to shtop the divilmint *now*.'

"Wid that I wint out into the camp an' inthrojuced mysilf to ivry man sober enough to remimber me. I was some wan in the ould days, an' the bhoys was glad to see me—all excipt Peg Barney wid a eye like a tomata five days in the bazar, an' a nose to match. They come round me an' shuk me, an' I tould thim I was in privit employ wid an in-come av me own, an' a drrrawin'-room fit to bate the Quane's; an' wid me lies an' me shtories an' nonsinse gin'rally, I kept 'em quiet in wan way an' another, knockin' roun' the camp. 'Twas *bad* even thin whin I was the Angil av Peace.

"I talked to me ould non-coms—*they* was sober—an' betune me an' thim we wore the draf' over into their tents at the proper time. The little orf'cer bhoy he comes round, decint an' civil-spoken as might be.

" 'Rough quarters, men,' sez he, 'but you can't look to be as comfortable as in barricks. We must make the best av things. I've shut my eyes to a dale av dog's tricks to-day, an' now there must be no more av ut.'

" 'No more we will. Come an' have a dhrink, me son,' sez Peg Barney, stag-gerin' where he stud. Me little orf'cer bhoy kep' his timper.

" 'You're a sulky swine, you are,' sez Peg Barney, an' at that the men in the tent began to laugh.

"I tould you me orf'cer bhoy had bowils. He cut Peg Barney as near as might be on the oi that I'd squshed whin we first met. Peg wint spinnin' acrost the tent.

" 'Peg him out, sorr,' sez I, in a whish-per.

" 'Peg him out!' sez me orf'cer bhoy, up loud, just as if 'twas battalion-p'rade an' he pickin' his wurrds from the Sar-gint.

"The non-coms tuk Peg Barney—a howlin' handful he was—an' in three minuts he was pegged out—chin down, tight-dhrawn—on his stummick—a tent-peg to each arm an' leg, swearin' fit to turn a naygur white.

"I tuk a peg an' jammed ut into his ugly jaw.—'Bite on that, Peg Barney,' I sez; 'the night is settin' frosty, an' you'll be wantin' divarsion before the mornin'. But for the Rig'lations you'd be bitin' on a bullet now at the thriangles, Peg Barney,' sez I.

"All the draf' was out av their tents watchin' Barney bein' pegged.

" ' 'Tis agin the Rig'lations! He strook him!' screeches out Scrub Greene, who was always a lawyer; an' some of the men tuk up the shoutin'.

" 'Peg out that man!' sez my orf'cer

bhoy, niver losin' his timper; an' the non-coms wint in and pegged out Scrub Greene by the side av Peg Barney.

"I cud see that the draf' was comin' roun'. The men stud not knowin' fwhat to do.

"'Get to your tents!' sez me orf'cer bhoy. 'Sargint, put a sintry over these two men.'

"The men wint back into the tents like jackals, an' the rest av the night there was no noise at all excipt the stip av the sintry over the two, an' Scrub Greene blubberin' like a child. 'Twas a chilly night, an' faith, ut sobered Peg Barney.

"Just before Revelly, my orf'cer bhoy comes out an' sez: 'Loose those men an' send thim to their tents!' Scrub Greene wint away widout a word, but Peg Barney, stiff wid the cowld, stud like a sheep, tryin' to make his orf'cer understhand he was sorry for playin' the goat.

"There was no tucker in the draf' whin ut fell in for the march, an' divil a wurrd about 'illegality' cud I hear.

"I wint to the ould Color Sargint and I sez:—'Let me die in glory,' sez I. 'I've seen a man this day!'

"'A man he is,' sez ould Hother; 'the draf's as sick as a herrin'. They'll all go down to the sea like lambs. That bhoy has the bowils av a cantonmint av Gin'rals.'

"'Amin,' sez I, 'an' good luck go wid him, wheriver he be, by land or by sea. Let me know how the draf' gets clear.'

"An' do you know how they *did?* That bhoy, so I was tould by letter from Bombay, bullydamned 'em down to the dock, till they cudn't call their sowls their own. From the time they left me oi till they was 'tween decks, not wan av thim was more than dacintly dhrunk. An', by the Holy Articles av War, whin they wint aboard they cheered him till they cudn't spake, an' *that,* mark you, has not come about wid a draf' in the mim'ry av livin' man! You look to that little orf'cer bhoy. He has bowils. 'Tis not ivry child that wud chuck the Rig'- lations to Flanders an' stretch Peg Bar- ney on a wink from a brokin' an' dilapi- dated ould carkiss like mesilf. I'd be proud to serve"—

"Terence, you're a civilian," said Dinah Shadd, warningly.

"So I am—so I am. Is ut likely I wud forget ut? But he was a gran' bhoy all the same, an' I'm only a mudtipper wid a hod on my shoulthers. The whis- key's in the heel av my hand, sorr. Wid your good lave we'll dhrink to the Ould Rig'mint—three fingers—standin' up!"

And we drank.

———•———

L'Envoi

And they were stronger hands than
    mine
  That digged the Ruby from the
    earth—
  More cunning brains that made it
    worth
  The large desire of a King;
And bolder hearts that through the brine
  Went down the Perfect Pearl to bring.

Lo, I have wrought in common clay
  Rude figures of a rough-hewn race;
  For Pearls strew not the market-
    place
  In this my town of banishment,
Where with the shifting dust I play
  And eat the bread of Discontent.

Yet is there life in that I make,—
  Oh, Thou who knowest, turn and
    see,
  As Thou hast power over me,
  So have I power over these,
Because I wrought them for Thy sake,
  And breathe in them mine agonies.

Small mirth was in the making. Now
  I lift the cloth that cloaks the clay,
  And, wearied, at Thy feet I lay
  My wares ere I go forth to sell.
The long *bazar* will praise—but Thou—
  Heart of my heart, have I done well?

VOLUME VI

Mine Own People

Bimi

THE orang-outang in the big iron cage lashed to the sheep-pen began the discussion. The night was stiflingly hot, and as Hans Breitmann and I passed him, dragging our bedding to the fore-peak of the steamer, he roused himself and chattered obscenely. He had been caught somewhere in the Malayan Archipelago, and was going to England to be exhibited at a shilling a head. For four days he had struggled, yelled, and wrenched at the heavy iron bars of his prison without ceasing, and had nearly slain a Lascar incautious enough to come within reach of the great hairy paw.

"It would be well for you, mine friend, if you was a liddle seasick," said Hans Breitmann, pausing by the cage. "You haf too much Ego in your Cosmos."

The orang-outang's arm slid out negligently from between the bars. No one would have believed that it would make a sudden snake-like rush at the German's breast. The thin silk of the sleeping-suit tore out: Hans stepped back unconcernedly, to pluck a banana from a bunch hanging close to one of the boats.

"Too much Ego," said he, peeling the fruit and offering it to the caged devil, who was rending the silk to tatters.

Then we laid out our bedding in the bows, among the sleeping Lascars, to catch any breeze that the pace of the ship might give us. The sea was like smoky oil, except where it turned to fire under our forefoot and whirled back into the dark in smears of dull flame. There was a thunderstorm some miles away: we could see the glimmer of the lightning. The ship's cow, distressed by the heat and the smell of the ape-beast in the cage, lowed unhappily from time to time in exactly the same key as the lookout man at the bows answered the hourly call from the bridge. The trampling tune of the engines was very distinct, and the jarring of the ash-lift, as it was tipped into the sea, hurt the procession of hushed noise. Hans lay down by my side and lighted a good-night cigar. This was naturally the beginning of conversation. He owned a voice as soothing as the wash of the sea, and stores of experiences as vast as the sea itself; for his business in life was to wander up and down the world, collecting orchids and wild beasts and ethnological specimens for German and American dealers. I watched the glowing end of his cigar wax and wane in the gloom, as the sentences rose and fell, till I was nearly asleep. The orang-outang, troubled by some dream of the forests of his freedom, began to yell like a soul in purgatory, and to wrench madly at the bars of the cage.

"If he was out now dere would not be much of us left hereabouts," said Hans, lazily. "He screams good. See, now, how I shall tame him when he stops himself."

There was a pause in the outcry, and

from Hans' mouth came an imitation of a snake's hiss, so perfect that I almost sprung to my feet. The sustained murderous sound ran along the deck, and the wrenching at the bars ceased. The orang-outang was quaking in an ecstasy of pure terror.

"Dot stop him," said Hans. "I learned dot trick in Mogoung Tanjong when I was collecting liddle monkeys for some peoples in Berlin. Efery one in der world is afraid of der monkeys —except der snake. So I blay snake against monkey, and he keep quite still. Dere was too much Ego in his Cosmos. Dot is der soul-custom of monkeys. Are you asleep, or will you listen, and I will tell a dale dot you shall not pelief?"

"There's no tale in the wide world that I can't believe," I said.

"If you have learned pelief you haf learned somedings. Now I shall try your pelief. Good! When I was collecting dose liddle monkeys—it was in '79 or '80, und I was in der islands of der Archipelago—over dere in der dark"—he pointed southward to New Guinea generally—"Mein Gott! I would sooner collect life red devils than liddle monkeys. When dey do not bite off your thumbs dey are always dying from nostalgia—homesick—for dey haf der imperfect soul, which is midway arrested in defelopment—und too much Ego. I was dere for nearly a year, und dere I found a man dot was called Bertran. He was a Frenchman, und he was a goot man—naturalist to the bone. Dey said he was an escaped convict, but he was a naturalist, und dot was enough for me. He would call all her life beasts from der forest, und dey

would come. I said he was St. Francis of Assisi in a new dransmigration produced, und he laughed und said he haf never preach to der fishes. He sold dem for tripang—*bêche-de-mer*.

"Und dot man, who was king of beasts-tamer men, he had in der house shush such anoder as dot devil-animal in der cage—a great orang-outang dot thought he was a man. He haf found him when he was a child—der orang-outang—und he was child and brother and opera comique all round to Bertran. He had his room in dot house— not a cage, but a room—mit a bed and sheets, and he would go to bed and get up in der morning and smoke his cigar und eat his dinner mit Bertran, und walk mit him hand-in-hand, which was most horrible. Herr Gott! I haf seen dot beast throw himself back in his chair and laugh when Bertran haf made fun of me. He was *not* a beast; he was a man; and he talked to Bertran, und Bertran comprehended, for I have seen dem. Und he was always politeful to me except when I talk too long to Bertran und say nodings at all to him. Den he would pull me away—dis great, dark devil; mit his enormous paws—shush as if I was a child. He was not a beast, he was a man. Dis I saw pefore I know him three months, und Bertran he haf saw the same; and Bimi, der orang-outang, haf understood us both, mit his cigar between his big-dog teeth und der blue gum.

"I was dere a year, dere und at dere oder islands—somedimes for monkeys and somedimes for butterflies und orchits. One time Bertran says to me dot he will be married, because he haf found a girl dot was goot, and he inquire if this marrying idea was right. I would not say, pecause it was not me dot was going to be married. Den he go off courting der girl—she was a half-caste French girl—very pretty. Haf you got a new light for my cigar? Oof! Very pretty. Only I say: 'Haf you thought of Bimi? If he pulls me away when I talk to you, what will he do to your wife? He will pull her in pieces. If I was you, Bertran, I would gif my wife for wedding present der stuff figure of Bimi.' By dot time I had learned somedings about der monkey peoples. 'Shoot him?' says Bertran. 'He is your beast,' I said; 'if he was mine he would be shot now.'

"Den I felt at der back of my neck der fingers of Bimi. Mein Gott! I tell you dot he talked through dose fingers. It was der deaf-and-dumb alphabet all gomplete. He slide his hairy arm round my neck, and he tilt up my chin und look into my face, shust to see if I understood his talk so well as he understood mine.

" 'See now dere!' says Bertran, 'und you would shoot him while he is cuddling you? Dot is der Teuton ingrate!'

"But I knew dot I had made Bimi a life's enemy, pecause his fingers haf talk murder through the back of my neck. Next dime I see Bimi dere was a pistol in my belt, und he touch it once, and I open de breech to show him it was loaded. He haf seen der liddle monkeys killed in der woods, and he understood.

"So Bertran he was married, and he forgot clean about Bimi dot was skippin' alone on the beach mit der haf of a human soul in his belly. I was see him skip, und he took a big bough und thrash der sand till he haf made a great hole like a grave. So I says to Bertran: 'For any sakes, kill Bimi. He is mad mit der jealousy.'

"Bertran haf said: 'He is not mad at all. He haf obey and love my wife, und if she speaks he will get her slippers,' und he looked at his wife across der room. She was a very pretty girl.

"Den I said to him: 'Dost thou pretend to know monkeys und dis beast dot is lashing himself mad upon der sands, pecause you do not talk to him? Shoot him when he comes to der house, for he haf der light in his eyes dot means killing—und killing.' Bimi come to der house, but dere was no light in his eyes. It was all put away, cunning —so cunning—und he fetch der girl her slippers, and Bertran turn to me und say: 'Dost thou know him in nine months more dan I haf known him in twelve years? Shall a child stab his fader? I have fed him, und he was my child. Do not speak this nonsense to my wife or to me any more.'

"Dot next day Bertran came to my house to help me make some wood cases for der specimens, und he tell me dot he haf left his wife a liddle while mit Bimi in der garden. Den I finish my cases quick, und I say: 'Let us go to your house und get a trink.' He laugh und say: 'Come along, dry mans.'

"His wife was not in der garden, und Bimi did not come when Bertran called. Und his wife did not come when he called, und he knocked at her bedroom door und dot was shut tight—locked. Den he look at me, und his face was white. I broke down der door mit my shoulder, und der thatch of der roof was torn into a great hole, und der sun came in upon der floor. Haf you ever seen paper in der waste-basket, or cards at whist on der table scattered? Dere was no wife dot could be seen. I tell you dere was noddings in dot room dot might be a woman. Dere was stuff on der floor, und dot was all. I looked at dese things und I was very sick; but Bertran looked a liddle longer at what was upon the floor und der walls, und der hole in der thatch. Den he pegan to laugh, soft and low, und I know und thank God dot he was mad. He nefer cried, he nefer prayed. He stood still in der doorway und laugh to himself. Den he said: 'She haf locked herself in dis room, and he haf torn up der thatch. *Fi donc.* Dot is so. We will mend der thatch und wait for Bimi. He will surely come.'

"I tell you we waited ten days in dot house, after der room was made into a room again, and once or twice we saw Bimi comin' a liddle way from der woods. He was afraid pecause he haf done wrong. Bertran called him when he was come to look on the tenth day, und Bimi come skipping along der beach und making noises, mit a long piece of black hair in his hands. Den Bertran laugh and say, *'Fi donc!'* shust as if it was a glass broken upon der table; und Bimi come nearer, und Bertran was honey-sweet in his voice and laughed to himself. For three days he made love to Bimi, pecause Bimi would not let himself be touched. Den

Bimi come to dinner at der same table mit us, und der hair on his hands was all black und thick mit—mit what had dried on his hands. Bertran gave him sangaree till Bimi was drunk and stupid, und den—

Hans paused to puff at his cigar.

"And then?" said I.

"Und den Bertran kill him with his hands, und I go for a walk upon der beach. It was Bertran's own piziness. When I come back der ape he was dead, und Bertran he was dying abofe him; but still he laughed a liddle und low, and he was quite content. Now you know der formula uf der strength of der orang-outang—it is more as seven to one in relation to man. But Bertran, he haf killed Bimi mit sooch dings as Gott gif him. Dot was der mericle."

The infernal clamor in the cage recommenced. "Aha! Dot friend of ours haf still too much Ego in his Cosmos. Be quiet, thou!"

Hans hissed long and venomously. We could hear the great beast quaking in his cage.

"But why in the world didn't you help Bertran instead of letting him be killed?" I asked.

"My friend," said Hans, composedly stretching himself to slumber, "it was not nice even to mineself dot I should lif after I had seen dot room wit der hole in der thatch. Und Bertran, he was her husband. Goot-night, und sleep well."

Namgay Doola

ONCE upon a time there was a king who lived on the road to Thibet, very many miles in the Himalaya Mountains. His kingdom was 11,000 feet above the sea, and exactly four miles square, but most of the miles stood on end, owing to the nature of the country. His revenues were rather less than £400 yearly, and they were expended on the maintenance of one elephant and a standing army of five men. He was tributary to the Indian government, who allowed him certain sums for keeping a section of the Himalaya-Thibet road in repair. He further increased his revenues by selling timber to the railway companies, for he would cut the great deodar trees in his own forest and they fell thundering into the Sutlej River and were swept down to the Plains, 300 miles away, and became railway ties. Now and again this king, whose name does not matter, would mount a ring-streaked horse and ride scores of miles to Simlatown to confer with the lieutenant-governor on matters of state, or assure the viceroy that his sword was at the service of the queen-empress. Then the viceroy would cause a ruffle of drums to be sounded and the ring-streaked horse and the cavalry of the state—two men in tatters—and the herald who bore the Silver Stick before the king would trot back to their own place, which was between the tail of a heaven-climbing glacier and a dark birch forest.

Now, from such a king, always remembering that he possessed one veritable elephant and could count his descent for 1,200 years, I expected, when it was my fate to wander through his dominions, no more than mere license to live.

The night had closed in rain, and rolling clouds blotted out the lights of the villages in the valley. Forty miles away, untouched by cloud or storm, the white shoulder of Dongo Pa—the Mountain of the Council of the Gods—upheld the evening star. The monkeys sung sorrowfully to each other as they hunted for dry roots in the fern-draped trees, and the last puff of the day-wind brought from the unseen villages the scent of damp wood smoke, hot cakes, dripping undergrowth, and rotting pine-cones. That smell is the true smell of the Himalayas, and if it once gets into the blood of a man he will, at the last, forgetting everything else, return to the Hills to die. The clouds closed and the smell went away, and there remained nothing in all the world except chilling white mists and the boom of the Sutlej River.

A fat-tailed sheep, who did not want to die, bleated lamentably at my tent-door. He was scuffling with the prime minister and the director-general of public education, and he was a royal gift to me and my camp servants. I expressed my thanks suitably and inquired if I might have audience of the king. The prime minister readjusted his turban—it had fallen off in the struggle—and assured me that the king would be very pleased to see me. Therefore I dispatched two bottles as a foretaste, and when the sheep had entered upon

513

another incarnation, climbed up to the king's palace through the wet. He had sent his army to escort me, but it stayed to talk with my cook. Soldiers are very much alike all the world over.

The palace was a four-roomed, whitewashed mud-and-timber house, the finest in all the Hills for a day's journey. The king was dressed in a purple velvet jacket, white muslin trousers, and a saffron-yellow turban of price. He gave me audience in a little carpeted room opening off the palace court-yard, which was occupied by the elephant of state. The great beast was sheeted and anchored from trunk to tail, and the curve of his back stood out against the sky line.

The prime minister and the director-general of public instruction were present to introduce me; but all the court had been dismissed lest the two bottles aforesaid should corrupt their morals. The king cast a wreath of heavy, scented flowers round my neck as I bowed, and inquired how my honored presence had the felicity to be. I said that through seeing his auspicious countenance the mists of the night had turned into sunshine, and that by reason of his beneficent sheep his good deeds would be remembered by the gods. He said that since I had set my magnificent foot in his kingdom the crops would probably yield seventy per cent. more than the average. I said that the fame of the king had reached to the four corners of the earth, and that the nations gnashed their teeth when they heard daily of the glory of his realm and the wisdom of his moon-like prime minister and lotus-eyed director-general of public education.

Then we sat down on clean white cushions, and I was at the king's right hand. Three minutes later he was telling me that the condition of the maize crop was something disgraceful, and that the railway companies would not pay him enough for his timber. The talk shifted to and fro with the bottles. We discussed very many quaint things, and the king became confidential on the subject of government generally. Most of all he dwelt on the shortcomings of one of his subjects, who, from what I could gather, had been paralyzing the executive.

"In the old days," said the king, "I could have ordered the elephant yonder to trample him to death. Now I must e'en send him seventy miles across the hills to be tried, and his keep for that time would be upon the state. And the elephant eats everything."

"What be the man's crimes, Rajah Sahib?" said I.

"Firstly, he is an 'outlander,' and no man of mine own people. Secondly, since of my favor I gave him land upon his coming, he refuses to pay revenue. Am I not the lord of the earth, above and below—entitled by right and custom to one-eighth of the crop? Yet this devil, establishing himself, refuses to pay a single tax . . . and he brings a poisonous spawn of babes."

"Cast him into jail," I said.

"Sahib," the king answered, shifting a little on the cushions, "once and only once in these forty years sickness came upon me so that I was not able to go abroad. In that hour I made a vow to my God that I would never again cut man or woman from the light of the sun and the air of God, for I perceived the nature of the punishment. How can I break my vow? Were it only the lopping off of a hand or a foot, I should not delay. But even that is impossible now that the English have rule. One or another of my people"—he looked obliquely at the director-general of public education—"would at once write a letter to the viceroy, and perhaps I should be deprived of that ruffle of drums."

He unscrewed the mouthpiece of his silver water-pipe, fitted a plain amber one, and passed the pipe to me. "Not content with refusing revenue," he continued, "this outlander refuses also to beegar" (this is the corvee or forced labor on the roads), "and stirs my people up to the like treason. Yet he is, if so he wills, an expert log-snatcher. There is none better or bolder among my people to clear a block of the river when the logs stick fast."

"But he worships strange gods," said the prime minister, deferentially.

"For that I have no concern," said the king, who was as tolerant as Akbar in matters of belief. "To each man his own god, and the fire or Mother Earth for us all at the last. It is the rebellion that offends me."

"The king has an army," I suggested. "Has not the king burned the man's house, and left him naked to the night dews?"

"Nay. A hut is a hut, and it holds the life of a man. But once I sent my army against him when his excuses became wearisome. Of their heads he brake three across the top with a stick. The other two men ran away. Also the guns would not shoot."

I had seen the equipment of the infantry. One-third of it was an old muzzle-loading fowling-piece with ragged rust holes where the nipples should have been; one-third a wirebound matchlock with a worm-eaten stock, and one-third a four-bore flint duck-gun, without a flint.

"But it is to be remembered," said the king, reaching out for the bottle, "that he is a very expert log-snatcher and a man of a merry face. What shall I do to him, sahib?"

This was interesting. The timid hillfolk would as soon have refused taxes to their king as offerings to their gods. The rebel must be a man of character.

"If it be the king's permission," I said, "I will not strike my tents till the third day, and I will see this man. The mercy of the king is godlike, and rebellion is like unto the sin of witchcraft. Moreover, both the bottles, and another, be empty."

"You have my leave to go," said the king.

Next morning the crier went through the stare proclaiming that there was a log-jam on the river and that it behooved all loyal subjects to clear it. The people poured down from their villages to the moist, warm valley of poppy fields, and the king and I went with them.

Hundreds of dressed deodar logs had caught on a snag of rock, and the river was bringing down more logs every minute to complete the blockade. The water snarled and wrenched and worried at the timber, while the population of the state prodded at the nearest logs with poles, in the hope of easing the pressure. Then there went up a shout of "Namgay Doola! Namgay Doola!"

and a large, red-haired villager hurried up, stripping off his clothes as he ran.

"That he is. That is the rebel!" said the king. "Now will the dam be cleared."

"But why has he red hair?" I asked, since red hair among hill-folk is as uncommon as blue or green.

"He is an outlander," said the king. "Well done! Oh, well done!"

Namgay Doola had scrambled on the jam and was clawing out the butt of a log with a rude sort of a boat-hook. It slid forward slowly, as an alligator moves, and three or four others followed it. The green water spouted through the gaps. Then the villagers howled and shouted and leaped among the logs, pulling and pushing the obstinate timber, and the red head of Namgay Doola was chief among them all. The logs swayed and chafed and groaned as fresh consignments from up-stream battered the now weakening dam. It gave way at last in a smother of foam, racing butts, bobbing black heads, and a confusion indescribable, as the river tossed everything before it. I saw the red head go down with the last remnants of the jam and disappear between the great grinding tree trunks. It rose close to the bank, and blowing like a grampus, Namgay Doola wiped the water out of his eyes and made obeisance to the king.

I had time to observe the man closely. The virulent redness of his shock head and beard was most startling, and in the thicket of hair twinkled above high cheek-bones two very merry blue eyes. He was indeed an outlander, but yet a Thibetan in language, habit and attire. He spoke the Lepcha dialect with an indescribable softening of the gutturals. It was not so much a lisp as an accent.

"Whence comest thou?" I asked, wondering.

"From Thibet." He pointed across the hills and grinned. That grin went straight to my heart. Mechanically I held out my hand and Namgay Doola took it. No pure Thibetan would have understood the meaning of the gesture. He went away to look for his clothes, and as he climbed back to his village, I heard a joyous yell that seemed unaccountably familiar. It was the whooping of Namgay Doola.

"You see now," said the king, "why I would not kill him. He is a bold man among my logs, but," and he shook his head like a schoolmaster, "I know that before long there will be complaints of him in the court. Let us return to the palace and do justice."

It was that king's custom to judge his subjects every day between eleven and three o'clock. I heard him do justice equitably on weighty matters of trespass, slander, and a little wife-stealing. Then his brow clouded and he summoned me.

"Again it is Namgay Doola," he said, despairingly. "Not content with refusing revenue on his own part, he has bound half his village by an oath to the like treason. Never before has such a thing befallen me! Nor are my taxes heavy."

A rabbit-faced villager, with a blush-rose stuck behind his ear, advanced trembling. He had been in Namgay Doola's conspiracy, but had told everything and hoped for the king's favor.

"Oh, king!" said I, "if it be the king's

will, let this matter stand over till the morning. Only the gods can do right in a hurry, and it may be that yonder villager has lied."

"Nay, for I know the nature of Namgay Doola; but since a guest asks, let the matter remain. Wilt thou, for my sake, speak harshly to this red-headed outlander? He may listen to thee."

I made an attempt that very evening, but for the life of me I could not keep my countenance. Namgay D o o l a grinned so persuasively and began to tell me about a big brown bear in a poppy field by the river. Would I care to shoot that bear? I spoke austerely on the sin of detected conspiracy and the certainty of punishment. Namgay Doola's face clouded for a moment. Shortly afterward he withdrew from my tent, and I heard him singing softly among the pines. The words were unintelligible to me, but the tune, like his liquid, insinuating speech, seemed the ghost of something strangely familiar.

"Dir hane mard-i-yemen dir
To weeree ala gee,"

crooned Namgay Doola again and again, and I racked my brain for that lost tune. It was not till after dinner that I discovered some one had cut a square foot of velvet from the centre of my best camera-cloth. This made me so angry that I wandered down the valley in the hope of meeting the big brown bear. I could hear him grunting like a discontented pig in the poppy field as I waited shoulder deep in the dew-dripping Indian corn to catch him after his meal. The moon was at full and drew out the scent of the tasseled crop. Then I heard the anguished bellow of a Himalayan cow—one of the little black crummies no bigger than Newfoundland dogs. Two shadows that looked like a bear and her cub hurried past me. I was in the act of firing when I saw that each bore a brilliant red head. The lesser animal was trailing something rope-like that left a dark track on the path. They were within six feet of me, and the shadow of the moonlight lay velvet-black on their faces. Velvet-black was exactly the word, for by all the powers of moonlight they were masked in the velvet of my camera-cloth. I marveled, and went to bed.

Next morning the kingdom was in an uproar. Namgay Doola, men said, had gone forth in the night and with a sharp knife had cut off the tail of a cow belonging to the rabbit-faced villager who had betrayed him. It was sacrilege unspeakable against the holy cow! The state desired his blood, but he had retreated into his hut, barricaded the doors and windows with big stones, and defied the world.

The king and I and the populace approached the hut cautiously. There was no hope of capturing our man without loss of life, for from a hole in the wall projected the muzzle of an extremely well-cared-for gun—the only gun in the state that could shoot. Namgay Doola had narrowly missed a villager just before we came up.

The standing army stood.

It could do no more, for when it advanced pieces of sharp shale flew from the windows. To these were added from time to time showers of scalding water. We saw red heads bobbing up and down within. The family of Namgay Doola were aiding their sire. Blood-curdling yells of defiance were the only answer to our prayers.

"Never," said the king, puffing, "has such a thing befallen my state. Next year I will certainly buy a little cannon." He looked at me imploringly.

"Is there any priest in the kingdom to whom he will listen?" said I, for a light was beginning to break upon me.

"He worships his own god," said the prime minister. "We can but starve him out."

"Let the white man approach," said Namgay Doola from within. "All others I will kill. Send me the white man."

The door was thrown open and I entered the smoky interior of a Thibetan hut crammed with children. And every child had flaming red hair. A fresh-gathered cow's tail lay on the floor, and by its side two pieces of black velvet—my black velvet—rudely hacked into the semblance of masks.

"And what is this shame, Namgay Doola?" I asked.

He grinned more charmingly than ever. "There is no shame," said he. "I did but cut off the tail of that man's cow. He betrayed me. I was minded to shoot him, sahib, but not to death. Indeed, not to death; only in the legs."

"And why at all, since it is the custom to pay revenue to the king? Why at all?"

"By the god of my father, I cannot tell," said Namgay Doola.

"And who was thy father?"

"The same that had this gun." He showed me his weapon, a Tower musket, bearing date 1832 and the stamp of the Honorable East India Company.

"And thy father's name?" said I.

"Timlay Doola," said he. "At the first, I being then a little child, it is in my mind that he wore a red coat."

"Of that I have no doubt; but repeat the name of thy father twice or thrice."

He obeyed, and I understood whence the puzzling accent in his speech came. "Thimla Dhula!" said he, excitedly. "To this hour I worship his god."

"May I see that god?"

"In a little while—at twilight time."

"Rememberest thou aught of thy father's speech?"

"It is long ago. But there was one word which he said often. Thus, ''Shun!' Then I and my brethren stood upon our feet, our hands to our sides, thus."

"Even so. And what was thy mother?"

"A woman of the Hills. We be Lepchas of Darjiling, but me they call an outlander because my hair is as thou seest."

The Thibetan woman, his wife, touched him on the arm gently. The long parley outside the .fort had lasted far into the day. It was now close upon twilight—the hour of the Angelus. Very solemnly the red-headed brats rose from the floor and formed a semicircle. Namgay Doola laid his gun aside, lighted a little oil-lamp, and set it before a recess in the wall. Pulling back a whisp of dirty cloth, he revealed a worn brass crucifix leaning against the helmet badge of a long-forgotten East India Company's regiment. "Thus did my father," he said, crossing himself clumsily. The wife and children followed suit. Then, all together, they struck up the wailing chant that I heard on the hillside:

"Dir hane mard-i-yemen dir
To weeree ala gee."

I was puzzled no longer. Again and again they sung, as if their hearts would break, their version of the chorus of "The Wearing of the Green":

"They're hanging men and women, too,
For the wearing of the green."

A diabolical inspiration came to me. One of the brats, a boy about eight years old—could he have been in the fields last night?—was watching me as he sung. I pulled out a rupee, held the coin between finger and thumb, and looked—only looked—at the gun leaning against the wall. A grin of brilliant and perfect comprehension overspread his porringer-like face. Never for an instant stopping the song, he held out his hand for the money, and then slid the gun to my hand. I might have shot Namgay Doola dead as he chanted, but I was satisfied. The inevitable blood-instinct held true. Namgay Doola drew the curtain across the recess. Angelus was over.

"Thus my father sung. There was much more, but I have forgotten, and I do not know the purport of even these words, but it may be that the god will understand. I am not of this people, and I will not pay revenue."

"And why?"

Again that soul-compelling grin. "What occupation would be to me between crop and crop? It is better than scaring bears. But these people do not understand."

He picked the masks off the floor and looked in my face as simply as a child.

"By what road didst thou attain knowledge to make those deviltries?" I said, pointing.

"I cannot tell. I am but a Lepcha of Darjiling, and yet the stuff"—

"Which thou hast stolen," said I.

"Nay, surely. Did I steal? I desired it so. The stuff—the stuff. What else should I have done with the stuff?" He twisted the velvet between his fingers.

"But the sin of maiming the cow—consider that."

"Oh, sahib, the man betrayed me; the heifer's tail waved in the moonlight, and I had my knife. What else should I have done? The tail came off ere I was aware. Sahib, thou knowest more than I."

"That is true," said I. "Stay within the door. I go to speak to the king." The population of the state were ranged on the hillside. I went forth and spoke.

"O king," said I, "touching this man, there be two courses open to thy wisdom. Thou canst either hang him from a tree—he and his brood—till there remains no hair that is red within thy land."

"Nay," said the king. "Why should I hurt the little children?"

They had poured out of the hut and were making plump obeisances to everybody. Namgay Doola waited at the door with his gun across his arm.

"Or thou canst, discarding their impiety of the cow-maiming, raise him to honor in thy army. He comes of a race that will not pay revenue. A red flame is in his blood which comes out at the top of his head in that glowing hair. Make him chief of thy army. Give him honor as may befall and full allowance of work, but look to it, oh, king, that neither he nor his hold a foot of earth from thee henceforward. Feed him with words and favor, and also liquor from certain bottles that thou knowest of, and he will be a bulwark of defense. But deny him even a tuftlet of grass for his own. This is the nature that God has given him. Moreover, he has brethren"—

The state groaned unanimously.

"But if his brethren come they will surely fight with each other till they die; or else the one will always give information concerning the other. Shall he be of thy army, oh, king? Choose."

The king bowed his head, and I said: "Come forth, Namgay Doola, and command the king's army. Thy name shall no more be Namgay in the mouths of men, but Patsay Doola, for, as thou hast truly said, I know."

Then Namgay Doola, new-christened Patsay Doola, son of Timlay Doola—which is Tim Doolan—clasped the king's feet, cuffed the standing army, and hurried in an agony of contrition from temple to temple making offerings for the sin of the cattle-maiming.

And the king was so pleased with my perspicacity that he offered to sell me a village for £20 sterling. But I buy no village in the Himalayas so long as one red head flares between the tail of the heaven-climbing glacier and the dark birch forest.

I know that breed.

The Recrudescence of Imray

IMRAY had achieved the impossible. Without warning, for no conceivable motive, in his youth and at the threshold of his career he had chosen to disappear from the world—which is to say, the little Indian station where he lived. Upon a day he was alive, well, happy, and in great evidence at his club, among the billiard-tables. Upon a morning he was not, and no manner of search could make sure where he might be. He had stepped out of his place; he had not appeared at his office at the proper time, and his dog-cart was not upon the public roads. For these reasons and because he was hampering in a microscopical degree the administration of the Indian Empire, the Indian Empire paused for one microscopical moment to make inquiry into the fate of Imray. Ponds were dragged, wells were plumbed, telegrams were dispatched down the lines of railways and to the nearest seaport town—1,200 miles away—but Imray was not at the end of the drag-ropes nor the telegrams. He was gone, and his place knew him no more. Then the work of the great Indian Empire swept forward, because it could not be delayed, and Imray, from being a man, became a mystery—such a thing as men talk over at their tables in the club for a month and then forget utterly. His guns, horses, and carts were sold to the highest bidder. His superior officer wrote an absurd letter to his mother, saying that Imray had unaccountably disappeared and his bungalow stood empty on the road.

After three or four months of the scorching hot weather had gone by, my friend Strickland, of the police force, saw fit to rent the bungalow from the native landlord. This was before he was engaged to Miss Youghai—an affair which has been described in another place—and while he was pursuing his investigations into native life. His own life was sufficiently peculiar, and men complained of his manners and customs. There was always food in his house, but there were no regular times for meals. He eat, standing up and walking about, whatever he might find on the sideboard, and this is not good for the insides of human beings. His domestic equipment was limited to six rifles, three snotguns, five saddles, and a collection of stiff-jointed masheer rods, bigger and stronger than the largest salmon rods. These things occupied one half of his bungalow, and the other half was given up to Strickland and his dog Tietjens— an enormous Rampur slut, who sung when she was ordered, and devoured daily the rations of two men. She spoke to Strickland in a language of her own, and whenever, in her walks abroad she saw things calculated to destroy the peace of Her Majesty the Queen Empress, she returned to her master and gave him information. Strickland would take steps at once, and the end of his labors was trouble and fine and imprisonment for other people. The natives believed that Tietjens was a familiar spirit, and treated her with the great reverence that is born of hate and fear. One room in the bungalow was set apart for her special use. She owned a bedstead, a blanket, and a drinking-trough, and if any one came into Strickland's room at night, her custom was to knock down the invader and give tongue till some one came with a light. Strickland owes his life to her. When he was on the frontier in search of the local murderer who came in the grey dawn to send Strickland much further than the Andaman Islands, Tietjens caught him as he was crawling into Strickland's tent with a dagger between his teeth, and after his record of iniquity was established in the eyes of the law, he was hanged. From that date Tietjens wore a collar of rough silver and employed a monogram on her night blanket, and the blanket was double-woven Kashmir cloth, for she was a delicate dog.

Under no circumstances would she be separated from Strickland, and when he was ill with fever she made great trouble for the doctors because she did not know how to help her master and would not allow another creature to attempt aid. Macarnaght, of the Indian Medical Service, beat her over the head with a gun, before she could understand that she must give room for those who could give quinine.

A short time after Strickland had taken Imray's bungalow, my business took me through that station, and naturally, the club quarters being full, I quartered myself upon Strickland. It was a desirable bungalow, eight-roomed, and heavily thatched against any chance of leakage from rain. Under the pitch of the roof ran a ceiling cloth, which looked just as nice as a whitewashed ceiling. The landlord had repainted it when Strickland took the bungalow, and unless you knew how Indian bungalows were built you would never have suspected that above the cloth lay the dark, three-cornered cavern of the roof, where the beams and the under side of the thatch harbored all manner of rats, bats, ants, and other things.

Tietjens met me in the veranda with a bay like the boom of the bells of St. Paul's, and put her paws on my shoulders and said she was glad to see me. Strickland had contrived to put together that sort of meal which he called lunch, and immediately after it was finished went out about his business. I was left alone with Tietjens and my own affairs. The heat of the summer had broken up and given place to the warm damp of the rains. There was no motion in the heated air, but the rain fell like bayonet rods on the earth, and flung up a blue mist where it splashed back again. The bamboos and the custard apples, the poinsettias and the mango-trees in the garden stood still while the warm water lashed through them, and the frogs began to sing among the aloe hedges. A little before the light failed, and when the rain was at its worst, I sat in the back veranda and heard the water roar from the eaves, and scratched myself because I was covered with the thing they called prickly heat. Tietjens came out with me and put her head in my lap, and was very sorrowful, so I gave her biscuits when tea was ready, and I took tea in the back veranda on account of the little coolness I found there. The rooms of the house were dark behind me. I could smell Strickland's saddlery and the oil on his guns, and I did not

the least desire to sit among these things. My own servant came to me in the twilight, the muslin of his clothes clinging tightly to his drenched body, and told me that a gentleman had called and wished to see some one. Very much against my will, and because of the darkness of the rooms, I went into the naked drawing-room, telling my man to bring the lights. There might or might not have been a caller in the room— it seems to me that I saw a figure by one of the windows, but when the lights came there was nothing save the spikes of the rain without and the smell of the drinking earth in my nostrils. I explained to my man that he was no wiser than he ought to be, and went back to the veranda to talk to Tietjens. She had gone out into the wet and I could hardly coax her back to me—even with biscuits with sugar on top. Strickland rode back, dripping wet, just before dinner, and the first thing he said was:

"Has any one called?"

I explained, with apologies, that my servant had called me into the drawing-room on a false alarm; or that some loafer had tried to call on Strickland, and, thinking better of it, fled after giving his name. Strickland ordered dinner without comment, and since it was a real dinner, with white table-cloth attached, we sat down.

At nine o'clock Strickland wanted to go to bed, and I was tired too. Tietjens, who had been lying underneath the table, rose up and went into the least-exposed veranda as soon as her master moved to his own room, which was next to the stately chamber set apart for Tietjens. If a mere wife had wished to sleep out-of-doors in that pelting rain, it would not have mattered, but Tietjens was a dog, and therefore the better animal. I looked at Strickland, expecting to see him flog her with a whip. He smiled queerly, as a man would smile after telling some hideous domestic tragedy. "She has done this ever since I moved in here."

The dog was Strickland's dog, so I said nothing, but I felt all that Strickland felt in being made light of. Tietjens encamped outside my bedroom window, and storm after storm came up, thundered on the thatch, and died away. The lightning spattered the sky as a thrown egg spattered a barn door, but the light was pale blue, not yellow; and looking through my slit bamboo blinds, I could see the great dog standing, not sleeping, in the veranda, the hackles alift on her back, and her feet planted as tensely as the drawn wire rope of a suspension bridge. In the very short pauses of the thunder I tried to sleep, but it seemed that some one wanted me very badly. He, whoever he was, was trying to call me by name, but his voice was no more than a husky whisper. Then the thunder ceased and Tietjens went into the garden and howled at the low moon. Somebody tried to open my door, and walked about and through the house, and stood breathing heavily in the verandas, and just when I was falling asleep I fancied that I heard a wild hammering and clamoring above my head or on the door.

I ran into Strickland's room and asked him whether he was ill and had been calling for me. He was lying on the bed half-dressed, with a pipe in his mouth. "I thought you'd come," he said. "Have I been walking around the house at all?"

I explained that he had been in the dining-room and the smoking-room and two or three other places; and he laughed and told me to go back to bed. I went back to bed and slept till the morning, but in all my dreams I was sure I was doing some one an injustice in not attending to his wants. What those wants were I could not tell, but a fluttering, whispering, bolt-fumbling, luring, loitering some one was reproaching me for my slackness, and through all the dreams I heard the howling of Tietjens in the garden and the thrashing of the rain.

I was in that house for two days, and Strickland went to his office daily, leaving me alone for eight or ten hours a day, with Tietjens for my only companion. As long as the full light lasted I was comfortable, and so was Tietjens; but in the twilight she and I moved into the back veranda and cuddled each other for company. We were alone in the house, but for all that it was fully occupied by a tenant with whom I had no desire to interfere. I never saw him, but I could see the curtains between the rooms quivering where he had just passed through; I could hear the chairs creaking as the bamboos sprung under a weight that had just quitted them; and I could feel when I went to get a book from the dining-room that somebody was waiting in the shadows of the front veranda till I should have gone away. Tietjens made the twilight more interesting by glaring into the darkened rooms, with every hair erect, and following the motions of something that I could not see. She never entered the rooms, but her eyes moved, and that was quite sufficient. Only when my servant came to trim the lamps and make all light and habitable, she would come in with me and spend her time sitting on her haunches watching an invisible extra man as he moved about behind my shoulder. Dogs are cheerful companions.

I explained to Strickland, gently as might be, that I would go over to the club and find for myself quarters there. I admired his hospitality, was pleased with his guns and rods, but I did not much care for his house and its atmosphere. He heard me out to the end, and then smiled very wearily, but without contempt, for he is a man who understands things. "Stay on," he said, "and see what this thing means. All you have talked about I have known since I took the bungalow. Stay on and wait. Tietjens has left me. Are you going too?"

I had seen him through one little affair connected with an idol that had brought me to the doors of a lunatic asylum, and I had no desire to help him through further experiences. He was a man to whom unpleasantnesses arrived as do dinners to ordinary people.

Therefore I explained more clearly than ever that I liked him immensely, and would be happy to see him in the daytime, but that I didn't care to sleep under his roof. This was after dinner, when Tietjens had gone out to lie in the veranda.

"'Pon my soul, I don't wonder," said Strickland, with his eyes on the ceiling-cloth. "Look at that!"

The tails of two snakes were hanging between the cloth and the cornice of the wall. They threw long shadows in the lamp-light. "If you are afraid of snakes, of course"—said Strickland. "I hate and fear snakes, because if you look into the eyes of any snake you will see that it knows all and more of man's fall, and that it feels all the contempt that the devil felt when Adam was evicted from Eden. Besides which its bite is generally fatal, and it bursts up trouser legs."

"You ought to get your thatch overhauled," I said. "Give me a masheer rod, and we'll poke 'em down."

"They'll hide among the roof beams," said Strickland. "I can't stand snakes overhead. I'm going up. If I shake 'em down, stand by with a cleaning-rod and break their backs."

I was not anxious to assist Strickland in his work, but I took the loading-rod and waited in the dining-room, while Strickland brought a gardener's ladder from the veranda and set it against the side of the room. The snake tails drew themselves up and disappeared. We could hear the dry rushing scuttle of long bodies running over the baggy cloth. Strickland took a lamp with him, while I tried to make clear the danger of hunting roof snakes between a ceiling cloth and a thatch, apart from the deterioration of property caused by ripping out ceiling-cloths.

"Nonsense!" said Strickland. "They're sure to hide near the walls by the cloth. The bricks are too cold for 'em, and the heat of the room is just what they like." He put his hand to the corner of the cloth and ripped the rotten stuff from the cornice. It gave a great sound of tearing, and Strickland put his head through the opening into the dark of the angle of the roof beams. I set my teeth and lifted the loading-rod, for I had not the least knowledge of what might descend.

"H'm," said Strickland; and his voice rolled and rumbled in the roof. "There's room for another set of rooms up here, and, by Jove! some one is occupying 'em."

"Snakes?" I said down below.

"No. It's a buffalo. Hand me up the two first joints of a masheer rod, and I'll prod it. It's lying on the main beam."

I handed up the rod.

"What a nest for owls and serpents! No wonder the snakes live here," said Strickland, climbing further into the roof. I could see his elbow thrusting with the rod. "Come out of that, whoever you are! Look out! Heads below there! It's tottering."

I saw the ceiling-cloth nearly in the centre of the room bag with a shape that was pressing it downward and downward toward the lighted lamps on the table. I snatched a lamp out of danger and stood back. Then the cloth ripped out from the walls, tore, split, swayed, and shot down upon the table something that I dared not look at till Strickland had slid down the ladder and was standing by my side.

He did not say much, being a man of few words, but he picked up the loose end of the table-cloth and threw it over the thing on the table.

"It strikes me," said he, pulling down the lamp, "our friend Imray has come back. Oh! you would, would you?"

There was a movement under the cloth, and a little snake wriggled out, to be back-broken by the butt of the masheer rod. I was sufficiently sick to make no remarks worth recording.

Strickland meditated and helped himself to drinks liberally. The thing under the cloth made no more signs of life.

"Is it Imray?" I said.

Strickland turned back the cloth for a moment and looked. "It is Imray," he said, "and his throat is cut from ear to ear."

Then we spoke both together and to ourselves:

"That's why he whispered about the house."

Tietjens, in the garden, began to bay furiously. A little later her great nose heaved upon the dining-room door.

She sniffed and was still. The broken and tattered ceiling-cloth hung down almost to the level of the table, and there was hardly room to move away from the discovery.

Then Tietjens came in and sat down, her teeth bared and her forepaws planted. She looked at Strickland.

"It's bad business, old lady," said he. "Men don't go up into the roofs of their bungalows to die, and they don't fasten up the ceiling-cloth behind 'em. Let's think it out."

"Let's think it out somewhere else," I said.

"Excellent idea! Turn the lamps out. We'll get into my room."

I did not turn the lamps out. I went into Strickland's room first and allowed him to make the darkness. Then he followed me, and we lighted tobacco and thought. Strickland did the thinking. I smoked furiously because I was afraid.

"Imray is back," said Strickland. "The question is, who killed Imray? Don't talk—I have a notion of my own. When I took this bungalow I took most of Imray's servants. Imray was guileless and inoffensive, wasn't he?"

I agreed, though the heap under the cloth looked neither one thing nor the other.

"If I call the servants they will stand fast in a crowd and lie like Aryans. What do you suggest?"

"Call 'em in one by one," I said.

"They'll run away and give the news to all their fellows," said Strickland.

"We must segregate 'em. Do you suppose your servant knows anything about it?"

"He may, for aught I know, but I don't think it's likely. He has only been here two or three days."

"What's your notion?" I asked.

"I can't quite tell. How the dickens did the man get the wrong side of the ceiling-cloth?"

There was a heavy coughing outside Strickland's bedroom door. This showed that Bahadur Khan, his bodyservant, had waked from sleep and wished to put Strickland to bed.

"Come in," said Strickland. "It is a very warm night, isn't it?"

Bahadur Khan, a great, green-turbaned, six-foot Mohammedan, said that it was a very warm night, but that there was more rain pending, which, by his honor's favor, would bring relief to the country.

"It will be so, if God pleases," said Strickland, tugging off his boots. "It is in my mind, Bahadur Khan, that I

have worked thee remorselessly for many days—ever since that time when thou first camest into my service. What time was that?"

"Has the heaven-born forgotten? It was when Imray Sahib went secretly to Europe without warning given, and I —even I—came into the honored service of the protector of the poor."

"And Imray Sahib went to Europe?"

"It is so said among the servants."

"And thou wilt take service with him when he returns?"

"Assuredly, sahib. He was a good master and cherished his dependents."

"That is true. I am very tired, but I can go buck-shooting to-morrow. Give me the little rifle that I use for black buck; it is in the case yonder."

The man stooped over the case, handed barrels, stock, and fore-end to Strickland, who fitted them together. Yawning dolefully, then he reached down to the gun-case, took a solid drawn cartridge, and slipped it into the breech of the .360 express.

"And Imray Sahib has gone to Europe secretly? That is very strange, Bahadur Khan, is it not?"

"What do I know of the ways of the white man, heaven-born?"

"Very little, truly. But thou shalt know more. It has reached me that Imray Sahib has returned from his so long journeyings, and that even now he lies in the next room, waiting his servant."

"Sahib!"

The lamp-light slid along the barrels of the rifle as they leveled themselves against Bahadur Khan's broad breast.

"Go, then, and look!" said Strickland.

"Take a lamp. Thy master is tired, and he waits. Go!"

The man picked up a lamp and went into the dining-room, Strickland following, and almost pushing him with the muzzle of the rifle. He looked for a moment at the black depths behind the ceiling-cloth, at the carcass of the mangled snake under foot, and last, a grey glaze setting on his face, at the thing under the table-cloth.

"Hast thou seen?" said Strickland, after a pause.

"I have seen. I am clay in the white man's hands. What does the presence do?"

"Hang thee within a month! What else?"

"For killing him? Nay, sahib, consider. Walking among us, his servants, he cast his eyes upon my child, who was fours years old. Him he bewitched, and in ten days he died of the fever. My child!"

"What said Imray Sahib?"

"He said he was a handsome child, and patted him on the head; wherefore my child died. Wherefore I killed Imray Sahib in the twilight, when he came back from office and was sleeping. The heaven-born knows all things. I am the servant of the heaven-born."

Strickland looked at me above the rifle, and said, in the vernacular: "Thou art witness to this saying. He has killed."

Bahadur Khan stood ashen grey in the light of the one lamp. The need for justification came upon him very swiftly.

"I am trapped," he said, "but the offence was that man's. He cast an evil eye upon my child, and I killed and hid him. Only such as are served by devils," he glared at Tietjens, crouched stolidly before him, "only such could know what I did."

"It was clever. But thou shouldst have lashed him to the beam with a rope. Now, thou thyself wilt hang by a rope. Orderly!"

A drowsy policeman answered Strickland's call. He was followed by another, and Tietjens sat still.

"Take him to the station," said Strickland. "There is a case toward."

"Do I hang, then?" said Bahadur Khan, making no attempt to escape and keeping his eyes on the ground.

"If the sun shines, or the water runs, thou wilt hang," said Strickland. Bahadur Khan stepped back one pace, quivered, and stood still. The two policemen waited further orders.

"Go!" said Strickland.

"Nay; but I go very swiftly," said Bahadur Khan. "Look! I am even now a dead man."

He lifted his foot, and to the little toe there clung the head of the halfkilled snake, firm fixed in the agony of death.

"I come of land-holding stock," said Bahadur Khan, rocking where he stood. "It were a disgrace for me to go to the public scaffold, therefore I take this way. Be it remembered that the sahib's shirts are correctly enumerated, and that there is an extra piece of soap in his washbasin. My child was bewitched, and I slew the wizard. Why should you seek to slay me? My honor is saved, and—and—I die."

At the end of an hour he died as they die who are bitten by the little kariat, and the policemen bore him and the thing under the table-cloth to their appointed places. They were needed to make clear the disappearance of Imray.

"This," said Strickland, very calmly, as he climbed into bed, "is called the nineteenth century. Did you hear what that man said?"

"I heard," I answered. "Imray made a mistake."

"Simply and solely through not knowing the nature and the coincidence of a little seasonal fever. Bahadur Khan has been with him for four years."

I shuddered. My own servant had been with me for exactly that length of time. When I went over to my own room I found him waiting, impassive as the copper head on a penny, to pull off my boots.

"What has befallen Bahadur Khan?" said I.

"He was bitten by a snake and died; the rest the sahib knows," was the answer.

"And how much of the matter hast thou known?"

"As much as might be gathered from one coming in the twilight to seek satisfaction. Gently, sahib. Let me pull off those boots."

I had just settled to the sleep of exhaustion when I heard Strickland shouting from his side of the house:

"Tietjens has come back to her room!"

And so she had. The great deerhound was couched on her own bedstead, on her own blanket, and in the next room the idle, empty ceiling-cloth wagged light-heartedly as it flailed on the table.

Moti Guj--Mutineer

ONCE upon a time there was a coffee-planter in India who wished to clear some forest land for coffee-planting. When he had cut down all the trees and burned the underwood, the stumps still remained. Dynamite is expensive and slow fire slow. The happy medium for stump-clearing is the lord of all beasts, who is the elephant. He will either push the stump out of the ground with his tusks, if he has any, or drag it out with ropes. The planter, therefore, hired elephants by ones and twos and threes, and fell to work. The very best of all the elephants belonged to the very worst of all the drivers or mahouts; and this superior beast's name was Moti Guj. He was the absolute property of his mahout, which would never have been the case under native rule: for Moti Guj was a creature to be desired by kings, and his name, being translated, meant the Pearl Elephant. Because the British government was in the land, Deesa, the mahout, enjoyed his property undisturbed. He was dissipated. When he had made much money through the strength of his elephant, he would get extremely drunk and give Moti Guj a beating with a tent-peg over the tender nails of the forefeet. Moti Guj never trampled the life out of Deesa on these occasions, for he knew that after the beating was over, Deesa would embrace his trunk and weep and call him his love and his life and the liver of his soul, and give him some liquor. Moti Guj was very fond of liquor—arrack for choice, though he would drink palm-tree toddy if nothing better offered. Then Deesa would go to sleep between Moti Guj's forefeet, and as Deesa generally chose the middle of the public road, and as Moti Guj mounted guard over him, and would not permit horse, foot, or cart to pass by, traffic was congested till Deesa saw fit to wake up.

There was no sleeping in the daytime on the planter's clearing: the wages were too high to risk. Deesa sat on Moti Guj's neck and gave him orders, while Moti Guj rooted up the stumps—for he owned a magnificent pair of tusks: or pulled at the end of a rope—for he had a magnificent pair of shoulders—while Deesa kicked him behind the ears and said he was the king of elephants. At evening time Moti Guj would wash down his three hundred pounds' weight of green food with a quart of arrack, and Deesa would take a share, and sing songs between Moti Guj's legs till it was time to go to bed. Once a week Deesa led Moti Guj down to the river, and Moti Guj lay on his side luxuriously in the shallows, while Deesa went over him with a coir swab and a brick. Moti Guj never mistook the pounding blow of the latter for the smack of the former that warned him to get up and turn over on the other side. Then Deesa would look at his feet and examine his eyes, and turn up the fringes of his mighty

ears in case of sores or budding ophthalmia. After inspection the two would "come up with a song from the sea," Moti Guj, all black and shining, waving a torn tree branch twelve feet long in his trunk, and Deesa knotting up his own long wet hair.

It was a peaceful, well-paid life till Deesa felt the return of the desire to drink deep. He wished for an orgy. The little draughts that led nowhere were taking the manhood out of him.

He went to the planter, and "My mother's dead," said he, weeping.

"She died on the last plantation two months ago, and she died once before that when you were working for me last year," said the planter, who knew something of the ways of nativedom.

"Then it's my aunt, and she was just the same as a mother to me," said Deesa, weeping more than ever. "She has left eighteen small children entirely without bread, and it is I who must fill their little stomachs," said Deesa, beating his head on the floor.

"Who brought the news?" said the planter.

"The post," said Deesa.

"There hasn't been a post here for the past week. Get back to your lines!"

"A devastating sickness has fallen on my village, and all my wives are dying," yelled Deesa, really in tears this time.

"Call Chihun, who comes from Deesa's village," said the planter. "Chihun, has this man got a wife?"

"He?" said Chihun. "No. Not a woman of our village would look at him. They'd sooner marry the elephant."

Chihun snorted. Deesa wept and bellowed.

"You will get into a difficulty in a

minute," said the planter. "Go back to your work!"

"Now I will speak Heaven's truth," gulped Deesa, with an inspiration. "I haven't been drunk for two months. I desire to depart in order to get properly drunk afar off and distant from this heavenly plantation. Thus I shall cause no trouble."

A flickering smile crossed the planter's face. "Deesa," said he, "you've spoken the truth, and I'd give you leave on the spot if anything could be done with Moti Guj while you're away. You know that he will only obey your orders."

"May the light of the heavens live forty thousand years. I shall be absent but ten little days. After that, upon my faith and honor and soul, I return. As to the inconsiderable interval, have I the gracious permission of the heaven-born to call up Moti Guj?"

Permission was granted, and in answer to Deesa's shrill yell, the mighty tusker swung out of the shade of a clump of trees where he had been squirting dust over himself till his master should return.

"Light of my heart, protector of the drunken, mountain of might, give ear!" said Deesa, standing in front of him.

Moti Guj gave ear, and saluted with his trunk. "I am going away," said Deesa.

Moti Guj's eyes twinkled. He liked jaunts as well as his master. One could snatch all manner of nice things from the roadside then.

"But you, you fussy old pig, must stay behind and work."

The twinkle died out as Moti Guj tried to look delighted. He hated stump-hauling on the plantation. It hurt his teeth.

"I shall be gone for ten days, oh, delectable one! Hold up your near fore-foot and I'll impress the fact upon it, warty toad of a dried mud-puddle." Deesa took a tent-peg and banged Moti Guj ten times on the nails. Moti Guj grunted and shuffled from foot to foot.

"Ten days," said Deesa, "you will work and haul and root the trees as Chihun here shall order you. Take up Chihun and set him on your neck!" Moti Guj curled the tip of his trunk, Chihun put his foot there, and was swung on to the neck. Deesa handed Chihun the heavy *ankus*—the iron elephant goad.

Chihun thumped Moti Guj's bald head as a paver thumps a curbstone.

Moti Guj trumpeted.

"Be still, hog of the backwoods! Chihun's your mahout for ten days. And now bid me good-bye, beast after mine own heart. Oh, my lord, my king! Jewel of all created elephants, lily of the herd, preserve your honored health; be virtuous. Adieu!"

Moti Guj lapped his trunk round Deesa and swung him into the air twice. That was his way of bidding him good-bye.

"He'll work now," said Deesa to the planter. "Have I leave to go?"

The planter nodded, and Deesa dived into the woods. Moti Guj went back to haul stumps.

Chihun was very kind to him, but he felt unhappy and forlorn for all that. Chihun gave him a ball of spices, and tickled him under the chin, and Chihun's little baby cooed to him after work was over, and Chihun's wife called him a darling; but Moti Guj was a bachelor by instinct, as Deesa was. He did not understand the domestic emotions. He wanted the light of his universe back again—the drink and the drunken slumber, the savage beatings and the savage caresses.

None the less he worked well, and the planter wondered. Deesa had wandered along the roads till he met a marriage procession of his own caste, and, drinking, dancing, and tippling, had drifted with it past all knowledge of the lapse of time.

The morning of the eleventh day dawned, and there returned no Deesa. Moti Guj was loosed from his ropes for the daily stint. He swung clear, looked round, shrugged his shoulders, and began to walk away, as one having business elsewhere.

"Hi! ho! Come back you!" shouted Chihun. "Come back and put me on your neck, misborn mountain! Return, splendor of the hillsides! Adornment of all India, heave to, or I'll bang every toe off your fat forefoot!"

Moti Guj gurgled gently, but did not obey. Chihun ran after him with a rope and caught him up. Moti Guj put his ears forward, and Chihun knew what that meant, though he tried to carry it off with high words.

"None of your nonsense with me," said he. "To your pickets, devil-son!"

"Hrrump!" said Moti Guj, and that was all—that and the forebent ears.

Moti Guj put his hands in his pockets, chewed a branch for a toothpick, and strolled about the clearing, making fun of the other elephants who had just set to work.

Chihun reported the state of affairs to the planter, who came out with a dog-whip and cracked it furiously. Moti Guj paid the white man the compliment of charging him nearly a quarter of a mile across the clearing and "Hrrumphing" him into his veranda. Then he stood outside the house, chuckling to himself and shaking all over with the fun of it, as an elephant will.

"We'll thrash him," said the planter. "He shall have the finest thrashing ever elephant received. Give Kala Nag and Nazim twelve foot of chain apiece, and tell them to lay on twenty."

Kala Nag—which means Black Snake —and Nazim were two of the biggest elephants in the lines, and one of their duties was to administer the graver punishment, since no man can beat an elephant properly.

They took the whipping-chains and rattled them in their trunks as they sidled up to Moti Guj, meaning to hustle him between them. Moti Guj had never, in all his life of thirty-nine years, been whipped, and he did not intend to begin a new experience. So he waited, waving his head from right to left, and measuring the precise spot in Kala Nag's fat side where a blunt tusk could sink deepest. Kala Nag had no tusks; the chain was the badge of his authority; but for all that, he swung wide of Moti Guj at the last minute, and tried to appear as if he had brought the chain out for amusement. Nazim turned round and went home early. He did not feel fighting fit that morning, and so Moti Guj was left standing alone with his ears cocked.

That decided the planter to argue no more, and Moti Guj rolled back to his amateur inspection of the clearing. An elephant who will not work and is not tied up is about as manageable as an eighty-one-ton gun loose in a heavy seaway. He slapped old friends on the back and asked them if the stumps were coming away easily; he talked nonsense concerning labor and the inalienable rights of elephants to a long "nooning"; and, wandering to and fro, he thoroughly demoralized the garden till sundown, when he returned to his picket for food.

"If you won't work, you sha'n't eat," said Chihun, angrily. "You're a wild elephant, and no educated animal at all. Go back to your jungle."

Chihun's little brown baby was rolling on the floor of the hut, and stretching out its fat arms to the huge shadow in the doorway. Moti Guj knew well that it was the dearest thing on earth to Chihun. He swung out his trunk with a fascinating crook at the end, and the brown baby threw itself, shouting, upon it. Moti Guj made fast and pulled up till the brown baby was crowing in the air twelve feet above his father's head.

"Great Lord!" said Chihun. "Flour cakes of the best, twelve in number, two feet across and soaked in rum, shall be yours on the instant, and two hundred pounds weight of fresh-cut young sugar-cane therewith. Deign only to put down safely that insignificant brat who is my heart and my life to me!"

Moti Guj tucked the brown baby comfortably between his forefeet, that could have knocked into toothpicks all Chihun's hut, and waited for his food. He ate it, and the brown baby crawled away. Moti Guj dozed and thought of Deesa. One of many mysteries connected with the elephant is that his huge body needs less sleep than anthing else that lives. Four or five hours in the night suffice—two just before midnight, lying down on one side; two just after one o'clock, lying down on the other. The rest of the silent hours are filled with eating and fidgeting, and long grumbling soliloquies.

At midnight, therefore, Moti Guj strode out of his pickets, for a thought had come to him that Deesa might be lying drunk somewhere in the dark forest with none to look after him. So all that night he chased through the undergrowth, blowing and trumpeting and shaking his ears. He went down to the river and blared across the shallows where Deesa used to wash him, but there was no answer. He could not find Deesa, but he disturbed all the other elephants in the lines, and nearly frightened to death some gypsies in the woods.

At dawn Deesa returned to the plantation. He had been very drunk indeed, and he expected to get into trouble for outstaying his leave. He drew a long breath when he saw that the bungalow and the plantation were still uninjured, for he knew something of Moti Guj's temper, and reported himself with many lies and salaams. Moti Guj had gone to his pickets for breakfast. The night exercise had made him hungry.

"Call up your beast," said the planter; and Deesa shouted in the mysterious elephant language that some mahouts believe came from China at the birth of the world, when elephants and not men were masters. Moti Guj heard and came. Elephants do not gallop. They move from places of varying rates of speed. If an elephant wished to catch an express train he could not gallop, but he could catch the train. So Moti Guj was at the planter's door almost before Chihun noticed that he had left his pickets. He fell into Deesa's arms trumpeting with joy, and the man and beast wept and slobbered over each other, and handled each other from head to heel to see that no harm had befallen.

"Now we will get to work," said Deesa. "Lift me up, my son and my joy!"

Moti Guj swung him up, and the two went to the coffee-clearing to look for difficult stumps.

The planter was too astonished to be very angry.

The Mutiny of the Mavericks

WHEN three obscure gentlemen in San Francisco argued on insufficient premises, they condemned a fellow-creature to a most unpleasant death in a far country which had nothing whatever to do with the United States. They foregathered at the top of a tenement-house in Tehama Street, an unsavory quarter of the city, and there calling for certain drinks, they conspired because they were conspirators by trade, officially known as the Third Three of the I. A. A.—an institution for the propagation of pure light, not to be confounded with any others, though it is affiliated to many. The Second Three live in Montreal and work among the poor there; the First Three have their home in New York, not far from Castle Garden, and write regularly once a week to a small house near one of the big hotels at Boulogne. What happens after that, a particular section of Scotland Yard knows too well and laughs at. A conspirator detests ridicule. More men have been stabbed with Lucrezia Borgia daggers and dropped into the Thames for laughing at head centres and triangles than for betraying secrets; for this is human nature.

The Third Three conspired over whisky cocktails and a clean sheet of note-paper against the British Empire and all that lay therein. This work is very like what men without discernment call politics before a general election. You pick out and discuss in the company of congenial friends all the weak points in your opponents' organization, and unconsciously dwell upon and exaggerate all their mishaps, till it seems to you a miracle that the party holds together for an hour.

"Our principle is not so much active demonstration—that we leave to others —as passive embarrassment to weaken and unnerve," said the first man. "Wherever an organization is crippled, wherever a confusion is thrown into any branch of any department, we gain a step for those who take on the work; we are but the forerunners." He was a German enthusiast, and editor of a newspaper, from whose leading articles he quoted frequently.

"That cursed empire makes so many

blunders of her own that unless we doubled the year's average I guess it wouldn't strike her anything special had occurred," said the second man. "Are you prepared to say that all our resources are equal to blowing off the muzzle of a hundred-ton gun or spiking a ten-thousand-ton ship on a plain rock in clear daylight? They can beat us at our own game. Better join hands with the practical branches; we're in funds now. Try and direct a scare in a crowded street. They value their greasy hides." He was the drag upon the wheel, and an Americanized Irishman of the second generation, despising his own race and hating the other. He had learned caution.

The third man drank his cocktail and spoke no word. He was the strategist, but unfortunately his knowledge of life was limited. He picked a letter from his breast-pocket and threw it across the table. That epistle to the heathen contained some very concise directions from the First Three in New York. It said:

"The boom in black iron has already affected the eastern markets, where our agents have been forcing down the English-held stock among the smaller buyers who watch the turn of shares. Any immediate operations, such as western bears, would increase their willingness to unload. This, however, cannot be expected till they see clearly that foreign iron-masters are willing to coöperate. Mulcahy should be dispatched to feel the pulse of the market, and act accordingly. Mavericks are at present the best for our purpose—P. D. Q."

As a message referring to an iron crisis in Pennsylvania it was interesting, if not lucid. As a new departure in organized attack on an outlying English dependency, it was more than interesting.

The first man read it through, and murmured:

"Already? Surely they are in too great a hurry. All that Dhulip Singh could do in India he has done, down to the distribution of his photographs among the peasantry. Ho! ho! The Paris firm arranged that, and he has no substantial money backing from the Other Power. Even our agents in India know he hasn't. What is the use of our organization wasting men on work that is already done? Of course, the Irish regiments in India are half mutinous as they stand."

This shows how near a lie may come to the truth. An Irish regiment, for just so long as it stands still, is generally a hard handful to control, being reckless and rough. When, however, it is moved in the direction of musketry-fire, it becomes strangely and unpatriotically content with its lot. It has even been heard to cheer the queen with enthusiasm on these occasions.

But the notion of tampering with the army was, from the point of view of Tehama Street, an altogether sound one. There is no shadow of stability in the policy of an English government, and the most sacred oaths of England would, even if embossed on vellum, find very few buyers among colonies and dependencies that have suffered from vain beliefs. But there remains to England always her army. That cannot change, except in the matter of uniform and equipment. The officers may write to the papers demanding the heads of the Horse Guards in default of cleaner re-

.lress for grievances; the men may break loose across a country town, and seriously startle the publicans, but neither officers nor men have it in their composition to mutiny after the Continental manner. The English people, when they trouble to think about the army at all, are, and with justice, absolutely assured that it is absolutely trustworthy. Imagine for a moment their emotions on realizing that such and such a regiment was in open revolt from causes directly due to England's management of Ireland. They would probably send the regiment to the polls forthwith, and examine their own consciences as to their duty to Erin, but they would never be easy any more. And it was this vague, unhappy mistrust that the I. A. A. was laboring to produce.

"Sheer waste of breath," said the second man, after a pause in the council. "I don't see the use of tampering with their fool-army, but it has been tried before, and we must try it again. It looks well in the reports. If we send one man from here, you may bet your life that other men are going too. Order up Mulcahy."

They ordered him up—a slim, slight, dark-haired young man, devoured with that blind, rancorous hatred of England that only reaches its full growth across the Atlantic. He had sucked it from his mother's breast in the little cabin at the back of the northern avenues of New York; he had been taught his rights and his wrongs, in German and Irish, on the canal fronts of Chicago; and San Francisco held men who told him strange and awful things of the great blind power over the seas. Once, when business took him across the At-

lantic, he had served in an English regiment, and being insubordinate, had suffered extremely. He drew all his ideas of England that were not bred by the cheaper patriotic print, from one iron-fisted colonel and an unbending adjutant. He would go to the mines if need be to teach his gospel. And he went as his instructions advised *p. d. q.*— which means "with speed"—to introduce embarrassment into an Irish regiment, "already half mutinous, quartered among Sikh peasantry, all wearing miniatures of His Highness Dhulip Singh, Maharaja of the Punjab, next their hearts, and all eagerly expecting his arrival." Other information equally valuable was given him by his masters. He was to be cautious, but never to grudge expense in winning the hearts of the men in the regiment. His mother in New York would supply funds, and he was to write to her once a month. Life is pleasant for a man who has a mother in New York to send him £200 a year over and above his regimental pay.

In process of time, thanks to his intimate knowledge of drill and musketry exercise, the excellent Mulcahy, wearing the corporal's stripe, went out in a troop-ship and joined Her Majesty's Royal Loyal Musketeers, commonly known as the "Mavericks," because they were masterless and unbranded cattle —sons of small farmers in County Clare, shoeless vagabonds of Kerry, herders of Ballyvegan, much wanted "moon-lighters" from the bare rainy headlands of the south coast, officered by O'Mores, Bradys, Hills, Kilreas, and the like. Never, to outward seeming, was there more promising material to work on. The First Three had chosen their regi-

ment well. It feared nothing that moved
or talked save the colonel and the regimental Roman Catholic chaplain, the fat
Father Dennis, who held the keys of
heaven and hell, and glared like an angry bull when he desired to be convinc-
ing. Him also it loved because on occasions of stress he was wont to tuck up
his cassock and charge with the rest
into the merriest of the fray, where he
always found, good man, that the saints
sent him a revolver when there was a
fallen private to be protected or—but
this came as an after-thought—his own
grey head to be guarded.

Cautiously as he had been instructed,
tenderly and with much beer, Mulcahy
opened his projects to such as he
deemed fittest to listen. And these
were, one and all, of that quaint,
crooked, sweet, profoundedly irresponsible, and profoundly lovable race that
fights like fiends, argue like children,
reason like women, obey like men, and
jest like their own goblins of the wrath
through rebellion, loyalty, want, woe, or
war. The underground work of a conspiracy is always dull, and very much
the same the world over. At the end of
six months—the seed always falling on
good ground—Mulcahy spoke almost explicitly, hinting darkly in the approved
fashion at dread powers behind him, and
advising nothing more nor less than mutiny. Were they not dogs, evilly treated?
had they not all their own and the natural revenges to satisfy? Who in these
days could do aught to nine hundred
men in rebellion? who, again, could
stay them if they broke for the sea, licking up on their way other regiments only
too anxious to join? And afterward
. . . here followed windy promises of

gold and preferment, office and honor,
ever dear to a certain type of Irishman.

As he finished his speech, in the dusk
of a twilight, to his chosen associates,
there was a sound of a rapidly unslung
belt behind him. The arm of one Dan
Grady flew out in the gloom and arrested something. Then said Dan:

"Mulcahy, you're a great man, an'
you do credit to whoever sent you.
Walk about a bit while we think of it."
Mulcahy departed elated. He knew his
words would sink deep.

"Why the triple-dashed asterisks did
ye not let me curl the tripes out of
him?" grunted a voice.

"Because I'm not a fat-headed fool.
Boys, 'tis what he's been driving at
these six months—our superior corpril,
with his education, and his copies of
the Irish papers, and his everlasting
beer. He's been sent for the purpose,
and that's where the money comes from.
Can ye not see? That man's a gold-
mine, which Horse Egan here would
have destroyed with a belt-buckle. It
would be throwing away the gifts of
Providence not to fall in with his little
plans. Of course we'll mutiny till all's
dry. Shoot the colonel on the parade-
ground, massacre the company officers,
ransack the arsenal, and then—boys, did
he tell you what next? He told me the
other night, when he was beginning to
talk wild. Then we're to join with the
niggers, and look for help from Dhulip
Singh and the Russians!"

"And spoil the best campaign that
ever was this side of hell! Danny, I'd
have lost the beer to ha' given him the
belting he requires."

"Oh, let him go this awhile, man!
He's got no—no constructiveness; but

that's the egg-meat of his plan, and you must understand that I'm in with it, an' so are you. We'll want oceans of beer to convince us—firmaments full. We'll give him talk for his money, and one by one all the boys'll come in, and he'll have a nest of nine hundred mutineers to squat in an' give drink to."

"What makes me killing mad is his wanting us to do what the niggers did thirty years gone. That an' his pig's cheek in saying that other regiments would come along," said a Kerry man.

"That's not so bad as hintin' we should loose off at the colonel."

"Colonel be sugared! I'd as soon as not put a shot through his helmet, to see him jump and clutch his old horse's head. But Mulcahy talks o' shootin' our comp'ny orf'cers accidental."

"He said that, did he?" said Horse Egan.

"Somethin' like that, anyways. Can't ye fancy ould Barber Brady wid a bullet in his lungs, coughin' like a sick monkey an' sayin': 'Bhoys, I do not mind your gettin' dhrunk, but you must hould your liquor like men. The man that shot me is dhrunk. I'll suspend investigations for six hours, while I get this bullet cut out, and then'"—

"An' then," continued Horse Egan, for the pepper major's peculiarities of speech and manner were as well known as his tanned face—"an' then, ye dissolute, half-baked, putty-faced scum o' Connemara, if I find a man so much as lookin' confused, bedad I'll coortmartial the whole company. A man that can't get over his liquor in six hours is not fit to belong to the Mavericks!"

A shout of laughter bore witness to the truth of the sketch.

"It's pretty to think of," said the Kerry man slowly. "Mulcahy would have us do all the devilment, and get clear himself, someways. He wudn't be takin' all this fool's throuble in shpoilin' the reputation of the regiment."

"Reputation of your grandmother's pig!" said Dan.

"Well, an' he had a good reputation too; so it's all right. Mulcahy must see his way clear out behind him, or he'd not ha' come so far, talkin' powers of darkness."

"Did you hear anything of a regimental court-martial among the Black Boneens, these days? Half a company of 'em took one of the new draft an' hanged him by his arms with a tent-rope from a third-story veranda. They gave no reason for so doin', but he was half dead. I'm thinking that the Boneens are short-sighted. It was a friend of Mulcahy's, or a man in' the same trade. They'd a deal better hà' taken his beer," returned Dan, reflectively.

"Better still ha' handed him up to the colonel," said Horse Egan, "onless— But sure the news wud be all over the counthry an' give the reg'ment a bad name."

"An' there'd be no reward for that man—but he went about talkin'," said the Kerry man, artlessly.

"You speak by your breed," said Dan, with a laugh. "There was never a Kerry man yet that wudn't sell his brother for a pipe o' tobacco an' a pat on the back from a policeman."

"Thank God I'm not a bloomin' Orangeman," was the answer.

"No, nor never will be," said Dan. "They breed men in Ulster. Would you like to thry the taste of one?"

The Kerry man looked and longed, but forbore. The odds of battle were too great.

"Then you'll not even give Mulcahy a—a strike for his money," said the voice of Horse Egan, who regarded what he called "trouble" of any kind as the pinnacle of felicity.

Dan answered not at all, but crept on tiptoe, with large strides, to the mess-room, the men following. The room was empty. In a corner, cased like the King of Dahomey's state umbrella, stood the regimental colors. Dan lifted them tenderly, and unrolled in the light of the candles the record of the Mavericks—tattered, worn, and hacked. The white satin was darkened everywhere with big brown stains, the gold threads on the crowned harp were frayed and discolored, and the red bull, the totem of the Mavericks, was coffee-hued. The stiff, embroidered folds, whose price is human life, rustled down slowly. The Mavericks keep their colors long and guard them very sacredly.

"Vittoria, Salamanca, Toulouse, Waterloo, Moodkee, Ferozshah, and Sobraon—that was fought close next door here, against the very beggars he wants us to join. Inkermann, the Alma, Sebastopol! What are those little businesses compared to the campaigns of General Mulcahy? The mut'ny, think o' that; the mut'ny an' some dirty little matters in Afghanistan, and for that an' these and those"—Dan pointed to the names of glorious battles—"that Yankee man with the partin' in his hair comes and says as easy as 'have a drink' . . . Holy Moses! there's the captain!"

But it was the mess-sergeant who came in just as the men clattered out, and found the colors uncased.

From that day dated the mutiny of the Mavericks, to the joy of Mulcahy and the pride of his mother in New York—the good lady who sent the money for the beer. Never, as far as words went, was such a mutiny. The conspirators, led by Dan Grady and Horse Egan poured in daily. They were sound men, men to be trusted, and they all wanted blood; but first they must have beer. They cursed the queen, they mourned over Ireland, they suggested hideous plunder of the Indian countryside, and then, alas! some of the younger men would go forth and wallow on the ground in spasms of unholy laughter. The genius of the Irish for conspiracies is remarkable. None the less, they would swear no oaths but those of their own making, which were rare and curious, and they were always at pains to impress Mulcahy with the risks they ran. Naturally the flood of beer wrought demoralization. But Mulcahy confused the causes of things, and when a pot-valiant Maverick smote a servant on the nose or called his commanding officer a bald-headed old lard-bladder, and even worse names, he fancied that rebellion and not liquor was at the bottom of the outbreak. Other gentlemen who have concerned themselves in larger conspiracies have made the same error.

The hot season, in which they protested no man could rebel, came to an end, and Mulcahy suggested a visible return for his teachings. As to the actual upshot of the mutiny, he cared nothing. It would be enough if the English, infatuatedly trusting to the integrity of their army, should be startled

with news of an Irish regiment revolting from political considerations. His
persistent demands would have ended,
at Dan's instigation, in a regimental
belting which in all probability would
have killed him and cut off the supply
of beer, had not he been sent on special duty some fifty miles away from the
cantonment to cool his heels in a mud
fort and dismount obsolete artillery.
Then the colonel of the Mavericks, reading his newspaper diligently and scenting frontier trouble from afar, posted to
the army headquarters and pleaded with
the commander-in-chief for certain privileges, to be granted under certain contingencies; which contingencies came
about only a week later when the annual little war on the border developed
itself and the colonel returned to carry
the good news to the Mavericks. He
held the promise of the chief for active
service, and the men must get ready.

On the evening of the same day, Mulcahy, an unconsidered corporal—yet
great in conspiracy—returned to cantonments, and heard sounds of strife and
howlings from afar off. The mutiny had
broken out, and the barracks of the
Mavericks were one whitewashed pandemonium. A private tearing through
the barrack square gasped in his ear:
"Service! Active service! It's a burnin' shame." Oh, joy, the Mavericks had
risen on the eve of battle! They would
not—noble and loyal sons of Ireland!—
serve the queen longer. The news
would flash through the country-side
and over to England, and he—Mulcahy
—the trusted of the Third Three, had
brought about the crash. The private
stood in the middle of the square and
cursed colonel, regiment, officers, and

doctor, particularly the doctor, by his
gods. An orderly of the native cavalry
regiment clattered through the mob of
soldiers. He was half lifted, half
dragged from his horse, beaten on the
back with mighty hand-claps till his
eyes watered, and called all manner of
endearing names. Yes, the Mavericks
had fraternized with the native troops.
Who, then, was the agent among the
latter that had blindly wrought with
Mulcahy so well?

An officer slunk, almost ran, from
the mess to a barrack. He was mobbed
by the infuriated soldiery, who closed
round but did not kill him, for he fought
his way to shelter, flying for his life.
Mulcahy could have wept with pure joy
and thankfulness. The very prisoners in
the guard-room were shaking the bars
of their cells and howling like wild
beasts, and from every barrack poured
the booming as of a big war-drum.

Mulcahy hastened to his own barrack.
He could hardly hear himself speak.
Eighty men were pounding with fist and
heel the tables and trestles—eighty men
flushed with mutiny, stripped to their
shirt-sleeves, their knapsacks half-
packed for the march to the sea, made
the two-inch boards thunder again as
they chanted to a tune that Mulcahy
knew well, the Sacred War Song of the
Mavericks:

"Listen in the north, my boys, there's
    trouble on the wind;
  Tramp o' Cossack's hoofs in front, grey
      great-coats behind,
  Trouble on the frontier of a most
      amazin' kind,
    Trouble on the water o' the Oxus!"

Then as a table broke under the furious accompaniment:

"Hurrah! hurrah! it's north by west we
go;
Hurrah! hurrah! the chance we wanted
so;
Let 'em hear the chorus from Umballa
to Moscow,
As we go marching to the Kremlin."

"Mother of all the saints in bliss and
all the devils in cinders, where's my
fine new sock widout the heel?" howled
Horse Egan, ransacking everybody's
knapsack but his own. He was engaged
in making up deficiencies of kit preparatory to a campaign, and in that employ,
he steals best who steals last. "Ah,
Mulcahy, you're in good time," he
shouted. "We've got the route, and
we're off on Thursday for a picnic wid
the Lancers next door."

An ambulance orderly appeared with
a huge basket full of lint rolls, provided
by the forethought of the queen, for
such as might need them later on.
Horse Egan unrolled his bandage and
flicked it under Mulcahy's nose, chanting:

" 'Sheep's skin an' bees'-wax, thunder,
pitch and plaster;
The more you try to pull it off, the
more it sticks the faster.
As I was goin' to New Orleans'—

You know the rest of it, my Irish-
American Jew boy. By gad, ye have to
fight for the queen in the inside av a
fortnight, my darlin'."

A roar of laughter interrupted. Mulcahy looked vacantly down the room.
Bid a boy defy his father when the
pantomime-cab is at the door, or a girl
develop a will of her own when her
mother is putting the last touches to
the first ball-dress, but do not ask an

Irish regiment to embark upon mutiny
on the eve of a campaign; when it has
fraternized with the native regiment
that accompanies it, and driven its officers into retirement with ten thousand
clamorous questions, and the prisoners
dance for joy, and the sick men stand
in the open, calling down all known diseases on the head of the doctor who has
certified that they are "medically unfit
for active service." And even the Mavericks might have been mistaken for mutineers by one so unversed in their natures as Mulcahy. At dawn a girls'
school might have learned deportment
from them. They knew that their colonel's hand had closed, and that he who
broke that iron discipline would not go
to the front. Nothing in the world will
persuade one of our soldiers when he
is ordered to the north on the smallest
of affairs, that he is not immediately
going gloriously to slay Cossacks and
cook his kettles in the palace of the czar.
A few of the younger men mourned for
Mulcahy's beer, because the campaign
was to be conducted on strict temperance principles, but, as Dan and Horse
Egan said sternly: "We've got the beer-
man with us; he shall drink now on his
own hook."

Mulcahy had not taken into account
the possibility of being sent on active
service. He had made up his mind that
he would not go under any circumstances; but fortune was against him.

"Sick—you?" said the doctor, who
had served an unholy apprenticeship to
his trade in Tralee poorhouses. "You're
only homesick, and what you call vari-
cose veins come from overeating. A
little gentle exercise will cure that." And
later: "Mulcahy, my man, everybody is

allowed to apply for a sick certificate *once*. If he tries it twice, we call him by an ugly name. Go back to your duty, and let's hear no more of your diseases."

I am ashamed to say that Horse Egan enjoyed the study of Mulcahy's soul in those days, and Dan took an equal interest. Together they would communicate to their corporal all the dark lore of death that is the portion of those who have seen men die. Egan had the larger experience, but Dan the finer imagination. Mulcahy shivered when the former spoke of the knife as an intimate acquaintance, or the latter dwelt with loving particularity on the fate of those who, wounded and helpless, had been overlooked by the ambulances, and had fallen into the hands of the Afghan women-folk.

Mulcahy knew that the mutiny, for the present at least, was dead. Knew, too, that a change had come over Dan's usually respectful attitude toward him, and Horse Egan's laughter and frequent allusions to abortive conspiracies, emphasized all that the conspirator had guessed. The horrible fascination of the death-stories, however, made him seek their society. He learned much more than he had bargained for; and in this manner. It was on the last night before the regiment entrained to the front. The barracks were stripped of everything movable, and the men were too excited to sleep. The bare walls gave out a heavy hospital smell of chloride of lime—a stench that depresses the soul.

"And what," said Mulcahy, in an awe-stricken whisper, after some conversation on the eternal subject, "are you going to do to me, Dan?" This might

have been the language of an able conspirator conciliating a weak spirit.

"You'll see," said Dan, grimly, turning over in his cot, "or I rather shud say you'll not see."

This was hardly the language of a weak spirit. Mulcahy shook under the bedclothes.

"Be easy with him," put in Egan from the next cot. "He has got his chanst o' goin' clean. Listen, Mulcahy: all we want is for the good sake of the regiment that you take your death standing up, as a man shud. There be heaps an' heaps of enemy—plenshus heaps. Go there an' do all you can and die decent. You'll die with a good name *there*. 'Tis not a hard thing considerin'."

Again Mulcahy shivered.

"And how could a man wish to die better than fightin'?" added Dan, consolingly.

"And if I won't?" said the corporal in a dry whisper.

"There'll be a dale of smoke," returned Dan, sitting up and ticking off the situation on his fingers, "sure to be, an' the noise of the firin' 'll be tremenjous, an' we'll be running about up and down, the regiment will. But we, Horse and I—we'll stay by you, Mulcahy, and never let you go. Maybe there'll be an accident."

"It's playing it low on me. Let me go. For pity's sake, let me go! I never did you harm, and—and I stood you as much beer as I could. Oh, don't be hard on me, Dan! You are—you were in it, too. You won't kill me up there, will you?"

"I'm not thinkin' of the treason; though you shud be glad any honest boys drank with you. It's for the regiment. We can't have the shame o' you bringin' shame on us. You went to the doctor quiet as a sick cat to get and stay behind an' live with the women at the depot—you that wanted us to run to the sea in wolf-packs like the rebels none of your black blood dared to be! But we knew about your goin' to the doctor, for he told it in mess, and it's all over the regiment. Bein' as we are your best friends, we didn't allow any one to molest you yet. We will see to you ourselves. Fight which you will— us or the enemy—you'll never lie in that cot again, and there's more glory and maybe less kicks from fighting the enemy. That's fair speakin'."

"And he told us by word of mouth to go and join with the niggers—you've forgotten that, Dan," said Horse Egan, to justify sentence.

"What's the use plaguin' the man? One shot pays for all. Sleep ye sound, Mulcahy. But you onderstand, do ye not?"

Mulcahy for some weeks understood very little of anything at all save that ever at his elbow, in camp, or at parade, stood two big men with soft voices adjuring him to commit *hari kari* lest a worse thing should happen—to die for the honor of the regiment in decency among the nearest knives. But Mulcahy dreaded death. He remembered certain things that priests had said in his infancy, and his mother—not the one at New York—starting from her sleep with shrieks to pray for a husband's soul in torment. It is well to be of a cultured intelligence, but in time of trouble the weak human mind returns to the creed it sucked in at the breast, and if that creed be not a pretty one, trouble fol-

lows. Also, the death he would have to face would be physically painful. Most conspirators have large imaginations. Mulcahy could see himself, as he lay on the earth in the night, dying by various causes. They were all horrible; the mother in New York was very far away, and the regiment, the engine that, once you fall in its grip, moves you forward whether you will or won't, was daily coming closer to the enemy!

* * * * * *

They were brought to the field of Marzun-Katai, and with the Black Boneens to aid, they fought a fight that has never been set down in the newspapers. In response, many believe, to the fervent prayers of Father Dennis, the enemy not only elected to fight in the open, but made a beautiful fight, as many weeping Irish mothers knew later. They gathered behind walls or flickered across the open in shouting masses, and were pot-valiant in artillery. It was expedient to hold a large reserve and wait for the psychological moment that was being prepared by the shrieking shrapnel. Therefore the Mavericks lay down in open order on the brow of a hill to watch the play till their call should come. Father Dennis, whose place was in the rear, to smooth the trouble of the wounded, had naturally managed to make his way to the foremost of his boys, and lay, like a black porpoise, at length on the grass. To him crawled Mulcahy, ashen-grey, demanding absolution.

"Wait till you're shot," said Father Dennis, sweetly. "There's a time for everything."

Dan Grady chuckled as he blew for

the fiftieth time into the breech of his speechless rifle. Mulcahy groaned and buried his head in his arms till a stray shot spoke like a snipe immediately above his head, and a general heave and tremor rippled the line. Other shots followed, and a few took effect, as a shriek or a grunt attested. The officers, who had been lying down with the men, rose and began to walk steadily up and down the front of their companies.

This manœuvre, executed not for publication, but as a guarantee of good faith, to soothe men, demands nerve. You must not hurry, you must not look nervous, though you know that you are a mark for every rifle within extreme range; and, above all, if you are smitten you must make as little noise as possible and roll inward through the files. It is at this hour, when the breeze brings the first salt whiff of the powder to noses rather cold at the tips, and the eye can quietly take in the appearance of each red casualty, that the strain on the nerves is strongest. Scotch regiments can endure for half a day, and abate no whit of their zeal at the end; English regiments sometimes sulk under punishment, while the Irish, like the French, are apt to run forward by ones and twos, which is just as bad as running back. The truly wise commandment of highly strung troops allows them in seasons of waiting to hear the sound of their own voices uplifted in song. There is a legend of an English regiment that lay by its arms under fire chanting "Sam Hall," to the horror of its newly appointed and pious colonel. The Black Boneens, who were suffering more than the Mavericks on a hill half

a mile away, began presently to explain to all who cared to listen:

"We'll sound the jubilee, from the centre to the sea,
    And Ireland shall be free, says the Shan-van-Voght."

"Sing, boys," said Father Dennis, softly. "It looks as if we cared for their Afghan peas."

Dan Grady raised himself to his knees and opened his mouth in a song imparted to him, as to most of his comrades, in the strictest confidence by Mulcahy—that Mulcahy then lying limp and fainting on the grass, the chill fear of death upon him.

Company after company caught up the words which, the I. A. A. say, are to herald the general rising of Erin, and to breathe which, except to those duly appointed to hear, is death. Wherefore they are printed in this place:

"The Saxon in heaven's just balance is weighed,
    His doom, like Belshazzar's, in death has been cast,
And the hand of the 'venger shall never be stayed
    Till his race, faith, and speech are a dream of the past."

They were heart-filling lines, and they ran with a swirl; the I. A. A. are better served by pens than their petards. Dan clapped Mulcahy merrily on the back, asking him to sing up. The officers lay down again. There was no need to walk any more. Their men were soothing themselves thunderously, thus:

"St. Mary in heaven has written the vow
    That the land shall not rest till the
        heretic blood,
From the babe at the breast to the
        hand at the plow,
Has rolled to the ocean like Shannon
        in flood!"

"I'll speak to you after all's over," said Father Dennis, authoritatively, in Dan's ear. "What's the use of confessing to me when you do this foolishness? Dan, you've been playing with fire! I'll lay you more penance in a week than"—

"Come along to purgatory with us, father, dear. The Boneens are on the move; they'll let us go now!"

The regiment rose to the blast of the bugle as one man; but one man there was who rose more swiftly than all the others, for half an inch of bayonet was in the fleshy part of his leg.

"You've got to do it," said Dan, grimly. "Do it decent, anyhow;" and the roar of the rush drowned his words as the rear companies thrust forward the first, still singing as they swung down the slope:

"From the child at the breast to the hand
        at the plow
    Has rolled to the ocean like Shannon
        in flood!"

They should have sung it in the face of England, not of the Afghans, whom it impressed as much as did the wild Irish yell.

"They came down singing," said the unofficial report of the enemy, borne from village to village next day. "They continued to sing, and it was written that our men could not abide when they came. It is believed that there was magic in the aforesaid song."

Dan and Horse Egan kept themselves in the neighborhood of Mulcahy. Twice

the man would have bolted back in the confusion. Twice he was heaved like a half-drowned kitten into the unpaintable inferno of a hotly contested charge.

At the end, the panic excess of his fear roved him into madness beyond all human courage. His eyes staring at nothing, his mouth open and frothing, and breathing as one in a cold bath, he went forward demented, while Dan toiled after him. The charge was checked at a high mud wall. It was Mulcahy that scrambled up tooth and nail and heaved down among the bayonets the amazed Afghan who barred his way. It was Mulcahy, keeping to the straight line of the rabid dog, led a collection of ardent souls at a newly unmasked battery, and flung himself on the muzzle of a gun as his companions danced among the gunners. It was Mulcahy who ran wildly on from that battery into the open plain where the enemy were retiring in sullen groups. His hands were empty, he had lost helmet and belt, and he was bleeding from a wound in the neck. Dan and Horse Egan, panting and distressed, had thrown themselves down on the ground by the captured guns, when they noticed Mulcahy's flight.

"Mad," said Horse Egan, critically. "Mad with fear! He's going straight to his death, an' shouting's no use."

"Let him go. Watch now! If we fire we'll hit him maybe."

The last of a hurrying crowd of Afghans turned at the noise of shod feet behind him, and shifted his knife ready to hand. This, he saw, was no time to take prisoners. Mulcahy ran on, sobbing, and the straight-held blade went home through the defenceless breast, and the body pitched forward almost before a shot from Dan's rifle brought down the slayer and still further hurried the Afghan retreat. The two Irishmen went out to bring in their dead.

"He was given the point, and that was an easy death," said Horse Egan, viewing the corpse. "But would you ha' shot him, Danny, if he had lived?"

"He didn't live, so there's no sayin'. But I doubt I wud have, bekase of the fun he gave us—let alone the beer. Hike up his legs, Horse, and we'll bring him in. Perhaps 'tis better this way."

They bore the poor limp body to the mass of the regiment, lolling openmouthed on their rifles; and there was a general snigger when one of the younger subalterns said: "That was a good man!"

"Phew!" said Horse Egan, when a burial party had taken over the burden. "I'm powerful dhry, and this reminds me, there'll be no more beer at all."

"Fwhy not?" said Dan, with a twinkle in his eye as he stretched himself for rest. "Are we not conspirin' all we can, an' while we conspire are we not entitled to free dhrinks? Sure his ould mother in New York would not let her son's comrades perish of drouth —if she can be reached at the end of a letter."

"You're a janius," said Horse Egan. "'O' coorse she will not. I wish this crool war was over, an' we'd get back to canteen. Faith, the commander-in-chief ought to be hanged on his own little sword-belt for makin' us work on wather."

The Mavericks were generally of Horse Egan's opinion. So they made haste to get their work done as soon as possible, and their industry was rewarded by unexpected peace. "We can fight the sons of Adam," said the tribesmen, "but we cannot fight the sons of Eblis, and this regiment never stays still in one place. Let us therefore come in." They came in, and "this regiment" withdrew to conspire under the leadership of Dan Grady.

Excellent as a subordinate, Dan failed altogether as a chief-in-command—possibly because he was too much swayed by the advice of the only man in the regiment who could perpetrate more than one kind of handwriting. The same mail that bore to Mulcahy's mother in New York a letter from the colonel, telling her how valiantly her son had fought for the queen, and how assuredly he would have been recommended for the Victoria Cross had he survived, carried a communication signed, I grieve to say, by that same colonel and all the officers of the regiment, explaining their willingness to do "anything which is contrary to the regulations and all kinds of revolutions" if only a little money could be forwarded to cover incidental expenses. Daniel Grady, Esquire, would receive funds, *vice* Mulcahy, who "was unwell at this present time of writing."

Both letters were forwarded from New York to Tehema Street, San Francisco, with marginal comments as brief as they were bitter. The Third Three read and looked at each other. Then the Second Conspirator—he who believed in "joining hands with the practical branches"—began to laugh, and on recovering his gravity, said: "Gentlemen, I consider this will be a lesson to us. We're left again. Those cursed Irish have let us down. I knew they would, but"—here he laughed afresh—"I'd give considerable to know what was at the back of it all."

His curiosity would have been satisfied had he seen Dan Grady, discredited regimental conspirator, trying to explain to his thirsty comrades in India the non-arrival of funds from New York.

At the End of the Passage

FOUR men, theoretically entitled to "life, liberty, and the pursuit of happiness," sat at a table playing whist. The thermometer marked—for them—one hundred and one degrees of heat. The room was darkened till it was only just possible to distinguish the pips of the cards and the very white faces of the players. A tattered, rotten punkah of whitewashed calico was puddling the hot air and whining dolefully at each stroke. Outside lay gloom of a November day in London. There was neither sky, sun, nor horizon—nothing but a brown-purple haze of heat. It was as though the earth were dying of apoplexy.

From time to time clouds of tawny dust rose from the ground without wind or warning, flung themselves table-cloth-wise among the tops of the parched trees, and came down again. Then a whirling dust-devil would scutter across the plain for a couple of miles, break, and fall outward, though there was nothing to check its flight save a long low line of piled railway-sleepers white with the dust, a cluster of huts made of mud, condemned rails and canvas, and the one squat four-roomed bungalow that belonged to the assistant engineer in charge of a section of the Gandhari State line then under construction.

The four men, stripped to the thinnest of sleeping-suits, played whist crossly, with wranglings as to leads and returns. It was not the best kind of whist, but they had taken some trouble to arrive at it. Mottram, of the India Survey, had ridden thirty and railed one hundred miles from his lonely post in the desert since the previous night; Lowndes, of the Civil Service, on special duty in the political department, had come as far to escape for an instant the miserable intrigues of an impoverished native state whose king alternately fawned and blustered for more money from the pitiful revenues contributed by hard-wrung peasants and despairing camel-breeders; Spurstow, the doctor of the line, had left a cholera-stricken camp of coolies to look after itself for forty-eight hours while he associated with white men once more. Hummil, the assistant engineer, was the host. He stood fast, and received his friends thus every Sunday if they could come in. When one of them failed to appear, he would send a telegram to his last address, in order that he might know whether the defaulter was dead or alive. There be very many places in the East where it is not good or kind to let your acquaintances drop out of sight even for one short week.

The players were not conscious of any special regard for each other. They squabbled whenever they met; but they ardently desired to meet, as men without water desire to drink. They were lonely folk who understood the dread meaning of loneliness. They were all under thirty years of age—which is too soon for any man to possess that knowledge.

"Pilsener," said Spurstow, after the second rubber, mopping his forehead.

"Beer's out, I'm sorry to say, and there's hardly enough soda-water for to-night," said Hummil.

"What filthy bad management!" snarled Spurstow.

"Can't help it. I've written and wired; but the trains don't come through regularly yet. Last week the ice ran out—as Lowndes knows."

"Glad I didn't come. I could ha' sent you some if I had known, though. Phew! it's too hot to go on playing bumblepuppy."

This was a savage growl at Lowndes, who only laughed. He was a hardened offender.

Mottram rose from the table and looked out of a chink in the shutters.

"What a sweet day!" said he.

The company yawned unanimously and betook themselves to an aimless investigation of all Hummil's possessions—guns, tattered novels, saddlery, spurs, and the like. They had fingered them a score of times before, but there was really nothing else to do.

"Got anything fresh?" said Lowndes.

"Last week's 'Gazette of India,' and a cutting from a home paper. My father sent it out. It's rather amusing."

"One of those vestrymen that call 'emselves M. P.'s again, is it?" said Spurstow, who read his newspapers when he could get them.

"Yes. Listen to this. It's to your address, Lowndes. The man was making a speech to his constituents, and he piled it on. Here's a sample: 'And I assert unhesitatingly that the Civil Service in India is the preserve—the pet preserve—of the aristocracy of England. What does the democracy—what do the masses—get from that country, which we have step by step fraudulently annexed? I answer, nothing whatever. It is farmed, with a single eye to their own interests, by the scions of the aristocracy. They take good care to maintain their lavish scale of incomes, to avoid or stifle any inquiries into the nature and conduct of their administration, while they themselves force the unhappy peasant to pay with the sweat of his brow for all the luxuries in which they are lapped.'" Hummil waved the cutting above his head. "'Ear! 'ear!" said his audience.

Then Lowndes, meditatively: "I'd give—I'd give three months' pay to have that gentleman spend one month with me and see how the free and independent native prince works things. Old Timbersides"—this was his flippant title for an honored and decorated prince—"has been wearing my life out this week past for money. By Jove! his latest performance was to send me one of his women as a bribe!"

"Good for you. Did you accept it?" said Mottram.

"No. I rather wish I had, now. She was a pretty little person, and she yarned away to me about the horrible destitution among the king's womenfolk. The darlings haven't had any new clothes for nearly a month, and the old man wants to buy a new drag from Calcutta—solid silver railings and silver lamps, and trifles of that kind. I've tried to make him understand that he has played the deuce with the revenues for the last twenty years, and must go slow. He can't see it."

"But he has the ancestral treasure-vault to draw on. There must be three millions at least in jewels and coin under his palace," said Hummil.

"Catch a native king disturbing the family treasure! The priests forbid it, except as the last resort. Old Timbersides has added something like a quarter of a million to the deposit in his reign."

"Where the mischief does it all come from?" said Mottram.

"The country. The state of the people is enough to make you sick. I've known the tax-men wait by a milch-camel till the foal was born, and then hurry off the mother for arrears. And what can I do? I can't get the court clerks to give me any accounts; I can't raise anything more than a fat smile from the commander-in-chief when I find out the troops are three months in arrears; and old Timbersides begins to weep when I speak to him. He has taken to the king's peg heavily—liquor brandy for whisky and Heidsieck for soda-water."

"That's what the Rao of Jubela took to. Even a native can't last long at that," said Spurstow. "He'll go out."

"And a good thing, too. Then I suppose we'll have a council of regency, and a tutor for the young prince, and hand him back his kingdom with ten years' accumulations."

"Whereupon that young prince, having been taught all the vices of the English, will play ducks and drakes with the money, and undo ten years' work in eighteen months. I've seen that business before," said Spurstow. "I should tackle the king with a light hand, if I were you, Lowndes. They'll hate you quite enough under any circumstances."

"That's all very well. The man who looks on can talk about the light hand; but you can't clean a pig-sty with a pen dipped in rosewater. I know my risks; but nothing has happened yet. My servant's an old Pathan, and he cooks for me. They are hardly likely to bribe him, and I don't accept food from my true friends, as they call themselves. Oh, but it's weary work! I'd sooner be with you, Spurstow. There's shooting near your camp."

"Would you? I don't think it. About fifteen deaths a day don't incite a man to shoot anything but himself. And the worst of it is that the poor devils look at you as though you ought to save them. Lord knows, I've tried everything. My last attempt was empirical, but it pulled an old man through. He was brought to me apparently past hope, and I gave him gin and Worcester sauce with cayenne. It cured him; but I don't recommend it."

"How do the cases run generally?" said Hummil.

"Very simply indeed. Chlorodyne, opium pill, chlorodyne, collapse, nitre, bricks to the feet, and then—the burning-ghat. The last seems to be the only thing that stops the trouble. It's black cholera you know. Poor devils! But, I will say, little Bunsee Lal, my apothecary, works like a demon. I've recommended him for promotion if he comes through it all alive."

"And what are your chances, old man?" said Mottram.

"Don't know; don't care much; but I've sent the letter in. What are you doing with yourself generally?"

"Sitting under a table in the tent and spitting on the sextant to keep it cool," said the man of the survey. "Washing my eyes to avoid ophthalmia, which I shall certainly get, and trying to make a sub-surveyor understand that an error of five degrees in an angle isn't quite so small as it looks. I'm altogether alone, y' know, and shall be till the end of the hot weather."

"Hummil's the lucky man," said Lowndes, flinging himself into a long chair. "He has an actual roof—torn as to the ceiling-cloth, but still a roof—over his head. He sees one train daily. He can get beer and soda-water, and ice it when God is good. He has books, pictures"—they were torn from the "Graphic"—"and the society of the excellent sub-contractor Jevins, besides the pleasure of receiving us weekly."

Hummil smiled grimly. "Yes, I'm the lucky man, I suppose. Jevins is luckier."

"How? Not"—

"Yes. Went out. Last Monday."

"*Ap se?*" said Spurstow, quickly, hinting the suspicion that was in everybody's mind. There was no cholera near Hummil's section. Even fever gives a man at least a week's grace, and sudden death generally implied self-slaughter.

"I judge no man this weather," said Hummil. "He had a touch of the sun, I fancy; for last week, after you fellows

had left, he came into the veranda and told me that he was going home to see his wife, in Market Street, Liverpool, that evening. I got the apothecary in to look at him, and we tried to make him lie down. After an hour or two he rubbed his eyes and said he believed he had had a fit—hoped he hadn't said anything rude. Jevins had a great idea of bettering himself socially. He was very like Chucks in his language."

"Well?"

"Then he went to his own bungalow and began cleaning a rifle. He told the servant that he was going after buck in the morning. Naturally he fumbled with the trigger, and shot himself through the head accidentally. The apothecary sent in a report to my chief, and Jevins is buried somewhere out there. I'd have wired to you, Spurstow, if you could have done anything."

"You're a queer chap," said Mottram. "If you killed the man yourself you couldn't have been more quiet about the business."

"Good Lord! what does it matter?" said Hummil, calmly. "I've got to do a lot of his overseeing work in addition to my own. I'm the only person that suffers. Jevins is out of it—by pure accident, of course, but out of it. The apothecary was going to* write a long screed on suicide. Trust a babu to drivel when he gets the chance."

"Why didn't you let it go in as suicide?" said Lowndes.

"No direct proof. A man hasn't many privileges in this country, but he might at least be allowed to mishandle his own rifle. Besides, some day I may need a man to smother up an accident to myself. Live and let live. Die and let die."

"You take a pill," said Spurstow, who had been watching Hummil's white face narrowly. "Take a pill, and don't be an ass. That sort of talk is skittles. Anyhow, suicide is shirking your work. If I was a Job ten times over, I should be so interested in what was going to happen next that I'd stay on and watch."

"Ah! I've lost that curiosity," said Hummil.

"Liver out of order?" said Lowndes, feelingly.

"No. Can't sleep. That's worse."

"By Jove, it is!" said Mottram. "I'm that way every now and then, and the fit has to wear itself out. What do you take for it?"

"Nothing. What's the use? I haven't had ten minutes' sleep since Friday morning."

"Poor chap! Spurstow, you ought to attend to this," said Mottram. "Now you mention it, your eyes are rather gummy and swollen."

Spurstow, still watching Hummil, laughed lightly. "I'll patch him up later on. Is it too hot, do you think, to go for a ride?"

"Where to?" said Lowndes, wearily. "We shall have to go away at eight, and there'll be riding enough for us then. I hate a horse, when I have to use him as a necessity. Oh, heavens! what is there to do?"

"Begin whist again, at chick points" (a "chick" is supposed to be eight shillings), "and a gold mohur on the rub," said Spurstow, promptly.

"Poker. A month's pay all round for the pool—no limit—and fifty-rupee raises. Somebody would be broken before we got up," said Lowndes.

"Can't say that it would give me any pleasure to break any man in this company," said Mottram. "There isn't enough excitement in it, and it's foolish." He crossed over to the worn and battered little camp-piano—wreckage of a married household that had once held the bungalow—and opened the case.

"It's used up long ago," said Hummil. "The servants have picked it to pieces."

The piano was indeed hopelessly out of order, but Mottram managed to bring the rebellious notes into a sort of agreement, and there rose from the ragged key-board something that might once have been the ghost of a popular music-hall song. The men in the long chairs turned with evident interest as Mottram banged the more lustily.

"That's good!" said Lowndes. "By Jove! the last time I heard that song was in '79, or thereabouts, just before I came out."

"Ah!" said Spurstow, with pride, "I was home in '80." And he mentioned a song of the streets popular at that date.

Mottram executed it indifferently well. Lowndes criticised, and volunteered emendations. Mottram dashed into another ditty, not of the music-hall character, and made as if to rise.

"Sit down," said Hummil. "I didn't know that you had any music in your composition. Go on playing until you can't think of anything more. I'll have that piano tuned up before you come again. Play something festive."

Very simple indeed were the tunes to which Mottram's art and the limitations of the piano could give effect, but the men listened with pleasure, and in the pauses talked all together of what they had seen or heard when they were last at home. A dense dust-storm sprung up outside and swept roaring over the house, enveloping it in the choking darkness of midnight, but Mottram continued unheeding, and the crazy tinkle reached the ears of the listeners above the flapping of the tattered ceiling-cloth.

In the silence after the storm he glided from the more directly personal songs of Scotland, half humming them as he played, into the "Evening Hymn."

"Sunday," said he, nodding his head.

"Go on. Don't apologize for it," said Spurstow.

Hummil laughed long and riotously. "Play it, by all means. You're full of surprises to-day. I didn't know you had such a gift of finished sarcasm. How does that thing go?"

Mottram took up the tune.

"Too slow by half. You miss the note of gratitude," said Hummil. "It ought to go to the 'Grasshopper's Polka' —this way." And he chanted, *prestissimo:*

"'Glory to Thee, my God, this night,
    For all the blessings of the light.'

That shows we really feel our blessings. How does it go on?—

"'If in the night I sleepless lie,
    My soul with sacred thoughts
        supply;
    May no ill dreams disturb my
        rest,'—

Quicker, Mottram!—

"'Or powers of darkness me
    molest!'"

"Bah! what an old hypocrite you are."

"Don't be an ass," said Lowndes. "You are at full liberty to make fun of anything else you like, but leave that hymn alone. It's associated in my mind with the most sacred recollections"—

"Summer evenings in the country— stained-glass window—light going out, and you and she jamming your heads together over one hymn-book," said Mottram.

"Yes, and a fat old cockchafer hitting you in the eye when you walked home. Smell of hay, and a moon as big as a band-box sitting on the top of a haycock; bats—roses—milk and midges," said Lowndes.

"Also mothers. I can just recollect my mother singing me to sleep with that when I was a little chap," said Spurstow.

The darkness had fallen on the room. They could hear Hummil squirming in his chair.

"Consequently," said he, testily, "you sing it when you are seven fathoms deep in hell! It's an insult to the intelligence of the Deity to pretend we're anything but tortured rebels."

"Take *two*.. pills," said Spurstow: that's tortured liver."

"The usually placid Hummil is in a vile bad temper. I'm sorry for the coolies to-morrow," said Lowndes, as the servants brought in the lights and prepared the table for dinner.

As they were settling into their places about the miserable goat-chops, the curried eggs, and the smoked tapioca pudding, Spurstow took occasion to whisper to Mottram: "Well done, David!"

"Look after Saul, then," was the reply.

"What are you two whispering about?" said Hummil, suspiciously.

"Only saying that you are a d——d poor host. This fowl can't be cut," returned Spurstow, with a sweet smile. "Call this a dinner?"

"I can't help it. You don't expect a banquet, do you?"

Throughout that meal Hummil contrived laboriously to insult directly and pointedly all his guests in succession, and at each insult Spurstow kicked the aggrieved person under the table; but he dared not exchange a glance of intelligence with either of them. Hummil's face was white and pinched, while his eyes were unnaturally large. No man dreamed for a moment of resenting his savage personalities, but as soon as the meal was over they made haste to get away.

"Don't go. You're just getting amusing, you fellows. I hope I haven't said anything that annoyed you. You're such touchy devils." Then, changing the note into one of almost abject entreaty: "I say, you surely aren't going?"

"Where I dines, I sleeps, in the language of the blessed Jorrocks," said Spurstow. "I want to have a look at your coolies to-morrow, if you don't mind. You can give me a place to lie down in, I suppose?"

The others pleaded the urgency of their several employs next day, and, saddling up, departed together, Hummil begging them to come next Sunday. As they jogged off together, Lowndes unbosomed himself to Mottram: ". . . And I never felt so like kicking a man at his own table in my life. Said I cheated at whist, and reminded me I was in debt! Told you you were as good as a liar to your face! You aren't half indignant enough over it."

"Not I," said Mottram. "Poor devil! Did you ever know old Hummy behave like that before? Did you ever know him go within a hundred miles of it?"

"That's no excuse. Spurstow was hacking my shin all the time, so I kept a hand on myself. Else I should have"—

"No, you wouldn't. You'd have done as Hummy did about Jevins: judge no man this weather. By Jove! the buckle of my bridle is hot in my hand! Trot out a bit, and mind the rat-holes."

Ten minutes' trotting jerked out of Lowndes one very sage remark when he pulled up, sweating from every pore:

"Good thing Spurstow's with him to-night."

"Ye-es. Good man, Spurstow. Our roads turn here. See you again next Sunday, if the sun doesn't bowl me over."

"S'pose so, unless old Timbersides' finance minister manages to dress some of my food. Good-night, and—God bless you!"

"What's wrong now?"

"Oh, nothing." Lowndes gathered up his whip, and, as he flicked Mottram's mare on the flank, added: "You're a good little chap—that's all." And the mare bolted half a mile across the sand on the word.

In the assistant engineer's bungalow Spurstow and Hummil smoked the pipe of silence together, each narrowly watching the other. The capacity of a bachelor's establishment is as elastic as its arrangements are simple. A servant cleared away the dining-room table, brought in a couple of rude native bedsteads made of tape strung on a light wood frame, flung a square of cool Calcutta matting over each, set them side by side, pinned two towels to the punkah so that their fringes should just sweep clear of each sleeper's nose and mouth, and announced that the couches were ready.

The men flung themselves down, adjuring the punkah-coolies by all the powers of Eblis to pull. Every door and window was shut, for the outside air was that of an oven. The atmosphere within was only 104°, as the thermometer attested, and heavy with the foul smell of badly trimmed kerosene lamps; and this stench, combined with that of native tobacco, baked brick, and dried earth, sends the heart of many a strong man down to his boots, for it is the smell of the great Indian Empire when she turns herself for six months into a house of torment. Spurstow packed his pillows craftily, so that he reclined rather than lay, his head at a safe elevation above his feet. It is not good to sleep on a low pillow in the hot weather if you happen to be of thick-necked build, for you may pass with lively snores and gurglings from natural sleep into the deep slumber of heat-apoplexy.

"Pack your pillows," said the doctor, sharply, as he saw Hummil preparing to lie down at full length.

The night-light was trimmed; the shadow of the punkah wavered across the room, and the *flick* of the punkah-towel and the soft whine of the rope through the wall-hole followed it. Then the punkah flagged, almost ceased. The sweat poured from Spurstow's brow. Should he go out and harangue the coolie? It started forward again with a savage jerk, and a pin came out of the towels. When this was replaced, a tom-tom in the coolie lines began to beat with the steady throb of a swollen artery inside some brain-fevered skull. Spurstow turned on his side and swore gently. There was no movement on Hummil's part. The man had composed himself as rigidly as a corpse, his hands clinched at his sides. The respiration was too hurried for any suspicion of sleep. Spurstow looked at the set face. The jaws were clinched, and there was a pucker round the quivering eyelids.

"He's holding himself as tightly as ever he can," thought Spurstow. "What a sham it is! and what in the world is the matter with him?—Hummil!"

"Yes."

"Can't you get to sleep?"

"No."

"Head hot? Throat feeling bulgy? or how?"

"Neither, thanks. I don't sleep much, you know."

"Feel pretty bad?"

"Pretty bad, thanks. There is a tom-tom outside, isn't there? I thought it was my head at first. Oh, Spurstow, for pity's sake, give me something that will put me asleep—sound sleep—if it's only for six hours!" He sprung up. "I haven't been able to sleep naturally for days, and I can't stand it!—I can't stand it!"

"Poor old chap!"

"That's no use. Give me something to make me sleep. I tell you I'm nearly mad. I don't know what I say half my time. For three weeks I've had to think and spell out every word that has come through my lips before I dared say it. I had to get my sentences out down to the last word, for fear of talking drivel if I didn't. Isn't that enough to drive a man mad? I can't see things correctly now, and I've lost my sense of touch. Make me sleep. Oh, Spurstow, for the love of God, make me sleep sound. It isn't enough merely to let me dream. Let me sleep!"

"All right, old man, all right. Go slow. You aren't half as bad as you think." The flood-gates of reserve once broken, Hummil was clinging to him like a frightened child.

"You're pinching my arm to pieces."

"I'll break your neck if you don't do something for me. No, I didn't mean that. Don't be angry, old fellow." He wiped the sweat off himself as he fought to regain composure. "As a matter of fact, I'm a bit restless and off my oats, and perhaps you could recommend some sort of sleeping-mixture—bromide of potassium."

"Bromide of skittles! Why didn't you tell me this before? Let go of my arm, and I'll see if there's anything in my cigarette-case to suit your complaint." He hunted among his day-clothes, turned up the lamp, opened a little silver cigarette-case, and advanced on the expectant Hummil with the daintiest of fairy squirts.

"The last appeal of civilization," said he, "and a thing I hate to use. Hold out your arm. Well, your sleeplessness hasn't ruined your muscle; and what a thick hide it is! Might as well inject a buffalo subcutaneously. Now in a few minutes the morphia will begin working. Lie down and wait."

A smile of unalloyed and idiotic delight began to creep over Hummil's face. "I think," he whispered—"I think I'm going off now. Gad! it's positively heavenly! Spurstow, you must give me that case to keep; you"— The voice ceased as the head fell back.

"Not for a good deal," said Spurstow to the unconscious form. "And now, my friend, sleeplessness of your kind being very apt to relax the moral fibre in little matters of life and death, I'll just take the liberty of spiking your guns."

He paddled into Hummil's saddle-room in his bare feet, and uncased a twelve-bore, an express, and a revolver. Of the first he unscrewed the nipples and hid them in the bottom of a saddlery-case; of the second he abstracted the lever, placing it behind a big wardrobe. The third he merely opened, and knocked the doll-head bolt of the grip up with the heel of a riding-boot.

"That's settled," he said, as he shook the sweat off his hands. "These little precautions will at least give you time to turn. You have too much sympathy with gun-room accidents."

And as he rose from his knees, the thick muffled voice of Hummil cried in the doorway: "You fool!"

Such tones they use who speak in the lucid intervals of delirium to their friends a little before they die.

Spurstow jumped with sheer fright. Hummil stood in the doorway, rocking with helpless laughter.

"That was awf'ly good of you, I'm sure," he said, very slowly, feeling for his words. "I don't intend to go out by my own hand at present. I say, Spurstow, that stuff won't work. What shall I do? What shall I do?" And panic terror stood in his eyes.

"Lie down and give it a chance. Lie down at once."

"I daren't. It will only take me halfway again, and I sha'n't be able to get away this time. Do you know it was all I could do to come out just now? Generally I am as quick as lightning; but you have clogged my feet. I was nearly caught."

"Oh, yes, I understand. Go and lie down."

"No, it isn't delirium; but it was an awfully mean trick to play on me. Do you know I might have died?"

As a sponge rubs a slate clean, so some power unknown to Spurstow had wiped out of Hummil's face all that stamped it for the face of a man, and he stood at the doorway in the expression of his lost innocence. He had slept back into terrified childhood.

"Is he going to die on the spot?" thought Spurstow. Then, aloud: "All right, my son. Come back to bed, and tell me all about it. You couldn't sleep; but what was all the rest of the nonsense?"

"A place—a place down there," said Hummil, with simple sincerity. The drug was acting on him by waves, and he was flung from the fear of a strong man to the fright of a child as his nerves gathered sense or were dulled.

"Good God! I've been afraid of it for months past, Spurstow. It has made every night hell to me; and yet I'm not conscious of having done anything wrong."

"Be still, and I'll give you another dose. We'll stop your nightmares, you unutterable idiot!"

"Yes, but you must give me so much that I can't get away. You must make me quite sleepy—not just a little sleepy. It's so hard to run then."

"I know it; I know it. I've felt it myself. The symptoms are exactly as you describe."

"Oh, don't laugh at me, confound you! Before this awful sleeplessness came to me I've tried to rest on my elbow and put a spur in the bed to sting me when I fell back. Look!"

"By Jove! the man has been roweled like a horse! Ridden by the nightmare with a vengeance! And we all thought him sensible enough. Heaven send us understanding! You like to talk, don't you, old man?"

"Yes, sometimes. Not when I'm frightened. *Then* I want to run. Don't you?"

"Always. Before I give you your second dose, try to tell me exactly what your trouble is."

Hummil spoke in broken whispers for nearly ten minutes, while Spurstow looked into the pupils of his eyes and passed his hand before them once or twice.

At the end of the narrative the silver cigarette-case was produced, and the last words that Hummil said as he fell back for the second time were: "Put me quite to sleep; for if I'm caught, I die—I die!"

"Yes, yes; we all do that sooner or later, thank Heaven! who has set a term to our miseries," said Spurstow, settling the cushions under the head. "It occurs to me that unless I drink something I shall go out before my time. I've stopped sweating, and I wear a seventeen-inch collar." And he brewed himself scalding hot tea, which is an excellent remedy against heat-apoplexy if you take three or four cups of it in time. Then he watched the sleeper.

"A blind face that cries and can't wipe its eyes. H'm! Decidedly, Hummil ought to go on leave as soon as possible; and, sane or otherwise, he undoubtedly did rowel himself most cruelly. Well, Heaven send us understanding!"

At midday Hummil rose, with an evil taste in his mouth, but an unclouded eye and a joyful heart.

"I was pretty bad last night, wasn't I?" said he.

"I have seen healthier men. You must have had a touch of the sun. Look here: if I write you a swingeing medical certificate, will you apply for leave on the spot?"

"No."

"Why not? You want it."

"Yes, but I can hold on till the weather's a little cooler."

"Why should you, if you can get relieved on the spot?"

"Burkett is the only man who could be sent; and he's a born fool."

"Oh, never mind about the line. You aren't so important as all that. Wire for leave, if necessary."

Hummil looked very uncomfortable.

"I can hold on till the rains," he said, evasively.

"You can't. Wire to headquarters for Burkett."

"I won't. If you want to know why, particularly, Burkett is married, and his wife's just had a kid, and she's up at Simla, in the cool, and Burkett has a very nice billet that takes him into Simla from Saturday to Monday. That little woman isn't at all well. If Burkett was transferred she'd try to follow him. If she left the baby behind she'd fret herself to death. If she came—and Burkett's one of those selfish little beasts who are always talking about a wife's place being with her husband—she'd die. It's murder to bring a woman here just now. Burkett has got the physique of a rat. If he came here he'd go out; and I know she hasn't any money, and I'm pretty sure she'd go out too. I'm salted in a sort of way, and I'm not married. Wait till the rains, and then Burkett can get thin down here. It'll do him heaps of good."

"Do you mean to say that you intend to face—what you have faced, for the next fifty-six nights?"

"Oh, it won't be so bad, now you've shown me a way out of it. I can always wire to you. Besides, now I've once got into the way of sleeping, it'll be all right. Anyhow, I sha'n't put in for leave. That's the long and the short of it."

"My great Scott! I thought all that sort of thing was dead and done with."

"Bosh! You'd do the same yourself. I feel a new man, thanks to that cigarette-case. You're going over to camp now, aren't you?"

"Yes; but I'll try to look you up every other day, if I can."

"I'm not bad enough for that. I don't want you to bother. Give the coolies gin and ketchup."

"Then you feel all right?"

"Fit to fight for my life, but not to stand out in the sun talking to you.

Go along, old man, and bless you!"

Hummil turned on his heel to face the echoing desolation of his bungalow, and the first thing he saw standing in the veranda was the figure of himself. He had met a similar apparition once before, when he was suffering from overwork and the strain of the hot weather.

"This is bad—already," he said, rubbing his eyes. "If the thing slides away from me all in one piece, like a ghost, I shall know it is only my eyes and stomach that are out of order. If it walks, I shall know that my head is going."

He walked to the figure, which naturally kept at an unvarying distance from him, as is the use of all spectres that are born of overwork. It slid through the house and dissolved into swimming specks within the eyeball as soon as it reached the burning light of the garden. Hummil went about his business till even. When he came into dinner he found himself sitting at the table. The thing rose and walked out hastily.

No living man knows what that week held for Hummil. An increase of the epidemic kept Spurstow in camp among the coolies, and all he could do was to telegraph to Mottram, bidding him go to the bungalow and sleep there. But Mottram was forty miles away from the nearest telegraph, and knew nothing of anything save the needs of the survey till he met early on Sunday morning Lowndes and Spurstow heading toward Hummil's for the weekly gathering.

"Hope the poor chap's in a better temper," said the former, swinging himself off his horse at the door. "I suppose he isn't up yet."

"I'll just have a look at him," said the doctor. "If he's asleep there's no need to wake him."

And an instant later, by the tone of Spurstow's voice calling upon them to enter, the men knew what had happened.

The punkah was still being pulled over the bed, but Hummil had departed this life at least three hours before.

The body lay on its back, hands clinched by the side, as Spurstow had seen it lying seven nights previously. In the staring eyes was written terror beyond the expression of any pen.

Mottram, who had entered behind Lowndes, bent over the dead and touched the forehead lightly with his lips. "Oh, you lucky, lucky devil!" he whispered.

But Lowndes had seen the eyes, and had withdrawn shuddering to the other side of the room.

"Poor chap! poor chap! And the last time I met him I was angry. Spurstow, we should have watched him. Has he"—

Deftly Spurstow continued his investigations, ending by a search round the room.

"No, he hasn't," he snapped. "There's no trace of anything. Call in the servants."

They came, eight or ten of them, whispering and peering over each other's shoulders.

"When did your sahib go to bed?" said Spurstow.

"At eleven or ten, we think," said Hummil's personal servant.

"He was well then? But how should you know?"

"He was not ill, as far as our comprehension extended. But he had slept very little for three nights. This I know, because I saw him walking much, and especially in the heart of the night."

As Spurstow was arranging the sheet, a big, straight-necked hunting-spur tumbled on the ground. The doctor groaned. The personal servant peeped at the body.

"What do you think, Chuma?" said Spurstow, catching the look in the dark face.

"Heaven-born, in my poor opinion, this that was my master has descended into the Dark Places, and there has been caught, because he was not able to escape with sufficient speed. We have the spur for evidence that he fought with Fear. Thus have I seen men of my race do with thorns when a spell was laid upon them to overtake them in their sleeping hours and they dared not sleep."

"Chuma, you're a mud-head. Go out and prepare seals to be set on the sahib's property."

"God has made the heaven-born. God has made me. Who are we, to inquire into the dispensations of God? I will bid the other servants hold aloof while you are reckoning the tale of the sahib's property. They are all thieves, and would steal."

"As far as I can make out, he died from—oh, anything: stopping of the heart's action, heat-apoplexy, or some other visitation," said Spurstow to his companions. "We must make an inventory of his effects, and so on."

"He was scared to death," insisted Lowndes. "Look at those eyes! For pity's sake, don't let him be buried with them open!"

"Whatever it was, he's out of all the trouble now," said Mottram, softly.

Spurstow was peering into the open eyes.

"Come here," said he. "Can you see anything there?"

"I can't face it!" whimpered Lowndes. "Cover up the face! Is there any fear on earth that can turn a man into that likeness? It's ghastly. Oh, Spurstow, cover him up!"

"No fear—on earth," said Spurstow. Mottram leaned over his shoulder and looked intently.

"I see nothing except some grey blurs in the pupil. There can be nothing there, you know."

"Even so. Well, let's think. It'll take half a day to knock up any sort of coffin; and he must have died at midnight. Lowndes, old man, go out and tell the coolies to break ground next to Jevins' grave. Mottram, go round the house with Chuma and see that the seals are put on things. Send a couple of men to me here, and I'll arrange."

The strong-armed servants when they returned to their own kind told a strange story of the doctor sahib vainly trying to call their master back to life by magic arts—to wit, the holding of a little green box opposite each of the dead man's eyes, of a frequent clicking of the same, and of a bewildered muttering on the part of the doctor sahib, who subsequently took the little green box away with him.

The resonant hammering of a coffin-lid is no pleasant thing to hear, but those who have experience maintain that much more terrible is the soft swish of the bed-linen, the reeving and unreeving of the bed-tapes, when he who has fallen by the roadside is appareled for burial, sinking gradually as the tapes are tied over, till the swaddled shape touches the floor and there is no protest against the indignity of hasty disposal.

At the last moment Lowndes was seized with scruples of conscience. "Ought you to read the service—from beginning to end?" said he.

"I intend to. You're my senior as a civilian. You can take it, if you like."

"I didn't mean that for a moment. I only thought if we could get a chaplain from somewhere—I'm willing to ride anywhere—and give poor Hummil a better chance. That's all."

"Bosh!" said Spurstow, as he framed his lips to the tremendous words that stand at the head of the burial service.

After breakfast they smoked a pipe in silence to the memory of the dead. Then said Spurstow, absently:

" 'Tisn't in medical science."

"What?"

"Things in a dead man's eyes."

"For goodness' sake, leave that horror alone!" said Lowndes. "I've seen a native die of fright when a tiger chivied him. I know what killed Hummil."

"The deuce you do! I'm going to try to see." And the doctor retreated into the bath-room with a Kodak camera, splashing and grunting for ten minutes. Then there was the sound of something being hammered to pieces, and Spurstow emerged, very white indeed.

"Have you got a picture?" said Mottram. "What does the thing look like?"

"Nothing there. It was impossible, of course. You needn't look, Mottram. I've torn up the films. There was nothing there. It was impossible."

"That," said Lowndes, very distinctly, watching the shaking hand striving to relight the pipe, "is a damned lie."

There was no further speech for a long time. The hot wind whistled without, and the dry trees sobbed. Presently the daily train, winking brass, burnished steel, and spouting steam, pulled up panting in the intense glare. "We'd better go on on that," said Spurstow. "Go back to work. I've written my certificate. We can't do any more good here. Come on."

No one moved. It is not pleasant to face railway journeys at midday in June. Spurstow gathered up his hat and whip, and turning in the doorway, said:

"There may be heaven—there must be hell.
Meantime, there is our life here. We-ell?"

But neither Mottram nor Lowndes had any answer to the question.

The Man Who Was

LET it be clearly understood that the Russian is a delightful person till he tucks his shirt in. As an Oriental he is charming. It is only when he insists upon being treated as the most easterly of Western peoples, instead of the most westerly of Easterns, that he becomes a racial anomaly extremely difficult to handle. The host never knows which side of his nature is going to turn up next.

Dirkovitch was a Russian—a Russian of the Russians, as he said—who appeared to get his bread by serving the czar as an officer in a Cossack regiment, and corresponding for a Russian newspaper with a name that was never twice the same. He was a handsome young Oriental, with a taste for wandering through unexplored portions of the earth, and he arrived in India from nowhere in particular. At least no living man could ascertain whether it was by way of Balkh, Budukhshan, Chitral, Beloochistan, Nepaul, or anywhere else. The Indian government, being in an unusually affable mood, gave orders that he was to be civilly treated, and shown everything that was to be seen; so he drifted, talking bad English and worse French, from one city to another till he foregathered with her Majesty's White Hussars in the city of Peshawur, which stands at the mouth of that narrow swordcut in the hills that men call the Khyber Pass. He was undoubtedly an officer, and he was decorated, after the manner of the Russians, with little enameled crosses, and he could talk, and (though this has nothing to do with her merits), he had been given up as a hopeless task or case by the Black Tyrones, who, individually and collectively, with hot whisky and honey, mulled brandy and mixed spirits of all kinds, had striven in all hospitality to make him drunk. And when the Black Tyrones, who are exclusively Irish, fail to disturb the peace of the head of a foreigner, that foreigner is certain to be a superior man. This was the argument

of the Black Tyrones, but they were ever an unruly and self-opinionated regiment, and they allowed junior subalterns of four years' service to choose their wines. The spirits were always purchased by the colonel and a committee of majors. And a regiment that would so behave may be respected but cannot be loved.

The White Hussars were as conscientious in choosing their wine as in charging the enemy. There was a brandy that had been purchased by a cultured colonel a few years after the battle of Waterloo. It has been maturing ever since, and it was a marvelous brandy at the purchasing. The memory of that liquor would cause men to weep as they lay dying in the teak forests of Upper Burmah or the slime of the Irrawaddy. And there was a port which was notable; and there was a champagne of an obscure brand, which always came to mess without any labels, because the White Hussars wished none to know where the source of supply might be found. The officer on whose head the champagne-choosing lay was forbidden the use of tobacco for six weeks previous to sampling.

This particularity of detail is necessarily to emphasize the fact that that champagne, that port, and, above all, that brandy—the green and yellow and white liquors did not count—was placed at the absolute disposition of Dirkovitch, and he enjoyed himself hugely—even more than among the Black Tyrones.

But he remained distressingly European through it all. The White Hussars were—"My dear true friends," "Fellow-soldiers glorious," and "Brothers inseparable." He would unburden himself by the hour on the glorious future that awaited the combined arms of England and Russia when their hearts and their territories should run side by side, and the great mission of civilizing Asia should begin. That was unsatisfactory, because Asia is not going to be civilized after the methods of the West. There is too much Asia, and she is too old. You cannot reform a lady of many lovers, and Asia has been insatiable in her flirtations aforetime. She will never attend Sunday-school, or learn to vote save with swords for tickets.

Dirkovitch knew this as well as any one else, but it suited him to talk special correspondently and to make himself as genial as he could. Now and then he volunteered a little, a very little, information about his own Sotnia of Cossacks, left apparently to look after themselves somewhere at the back of beyond. He had done rough work in Central Asia, and had seen rather more help-yourself fighting than most men of his years. But he was careful never to betray his superiority, and more than careful to praise on all occasions the appearance, drill, uniform, and organization of her Majesty's White Hussars. And, indeed, they were a regiment to be admired. When Mrs. Durgan, widow of the late Sir John Durgan, arrived in their station, and after a short time had been proposed to by every single man at mess, she put the public sentiment very neatly when she explained that they were all so nice that unless she could marry them all, including the colonel and some majors who were already married, she was not going to content herself with one of them. Wherefore she wedded a little man in a rifle regiment—being by nature contradictious—and the White Hussars were going to wear crepe on their arms, but compromised by attending the wedding in full force, and lining the aisle with unutterable reproach. She had jilted them all—from Basset-Holmer, the senior captain, to Little Mildred, the last subaltern, and he could have given her four thousand a year and a title. He was a viscount, and on his arrival the mess had said he had better go into the Guards, because they were all sons of large grocers and small clothiers in the Hussars, but Mildred begged very hard to be allowed to stay, and behaved so prettily that he was forgiven, and became a man, which is much more important than being any sort of viscount.

The only persons who did not share the general regard for the White Hussars were a few thousand gentlemen of Jewish extraction who lived across the border, and answered to the name of Pathan. They had only met the regiment officially, and for something less than twenty minutes, but the interview, which was complicated with many casualties, had filled them with prejudice. They even called the White Hussars "children of the devil," and sons of persons whom it would be perfectly impossible to meet in decent society. Yet they were not above making their aversion fill their money-belts. The regiment possessed carbines, beautiful Martini-Henry carbines, that would cob a bullet into an enemy's camp at one thousand yards, and were even handier than the long rifle. Therefore they were coveted all along the border, and, since demand inevitably breeds supply, they were supplied at the risk of life and limb for exactly their weight in coined silver—seven and one half pounds of rupees, or sixteen pounds and a few shillings each, reckoning the rupee at par. They were stolen at night by snaky-thieves that crawled on their stomachs under the nose of the sentries; they disappeared mysteriously from arm-racks; and in the hot weather, when all the doors and windows were open, they vanished like puffs of their own smoke. The border people desired them first for their own family vendettas, and then for contingencies. But in the long cold nights of the Northern Indian winter they were stolen most extensively. The traffic of murder was liveliest among the hills at that season, and prices ruled high. The regimental guards were first doubled and then trebled. A trooper does not much care if he loses a weapon—government must make it good—but he deeply resents the loss of his sleep. The regiment grew very angry, and one night-thief who managed to limp away bears the visible marks of their anger upon him to this hour. That incident stopped the burglaries for a time, and the guards were reduced accordingly, and the regiment devoted itself to polo with unexpected results, for it beat by two goals to one that very terrible polo corps the Lushkar Light Horse, though the latter had four ponies a piece for a short hour's fight, as well as a native officer who played like a lambent flame across the ground.

Then they gave a dinner to celebrate the event. The Lushkar team came, and Dirkovitch came, in the fullest full uniform of a Cossack officer, which is as full as a dressing-gown, and was introduced to the Lushkars, and opened his eyes as he regarded them. They were lighter men that the Hussars, and they carried themselves with the swing that is the peculiar right of the Punjab frontier force and all irregular horse. Like everything else in the service, it has to be learned; but, unlike many things, it is never forgotten, and remains on the body till death.

The great beam-roofed mess-room of the White Hussars was a sight to be remembered. All the mess-plate was on the long table—the same table that had served up the bodies of five dead officers in a forgotten fight long and long ago—the dingy, battered standards faced the door of entrance, clumps of winter roses lay between the silver candlesticks, the portraits of eminent officers deceased looked down on their successors from between the heads of sambhur, nilghai, maikhor, and, pride of all the mess, two grinning snow-leopards that had cost Basset-Holmer four months' leave that he might have spent in England instead of on the road to Thibet, and the daily risk of his life on ledge, snow-slide, and glassy grass-slope.

The servants, in spotless white muslin and the crest of their regiments on the brow of their turbans, waited behind their masters, who were clad in the scarlet and gold of the White Hussars and the cream and silver of the Lushkar Light Horse. Dirkovitch's dull green uniform was the only dark spot at the board, but his big onyx eyes made up for it. He was fraternizing effusively with the captain of the Lushkar team, who was wondering how many of Dirkovitch's Cossacks his own long, lathy down-countrymen could account for in a fair charge. But one does not speak of these things openly.

The talk rose higher and higher, and the regimental band played between the courses, as is the immemorial custom, till all tongues ceased for a moment with the removal of the dinner slips and the First Toast of Obligation, when the colonel, rising, said: "Mr. Vice, the Queen," and Little Mildred from the bottom of the table answered: "The Queen, God bless her!" and the big spurs clanked as the big men heaved themselves up and drank the Queen, upon whose pay they were falsely supposed to pay their mess-bills. That sacrament of the mess never grows old, and never ceases to bring a lump into the throat of the listener wherever he be, by land, or by sea. Dirkovitch rose with his "brothers glorious," but he could not understand. No one but an officer can understand what the toast means; and the bulk have more sentiment than comprehension. It all comes to the same in the end, as the enemy said when he was wriggling on a lance-point. Immediately after the little silence that follows on the ceremony there entered the native officer who had played for the Lushkar team. He could not of course eat with the alien, but he came in at dessert, all six feet of him, with the blue-and-silver turban atop and the big black top-boots below. The mess rose joyously as he thrust forward the hilt of his sabre, in token of realty, for the colonel of the White Hussars to touch, and dropped into a vacant chair amid shouts of *Rung Ho!* "Hira Singh!" (which being translated means "Go in and win!"). "Did I whack you over the knee, old man?"

"Ressaidar Sahib, what the devil made you play that kicking pig of a pony in the last ten minutes?" "Shabash, Ressaidar Sahib!" Then the voice of the colonel: "The health of Ressaidar Hira Singh!"

After the shouting had died away Hira Singh rose to reply, for he was the cadet of a royal house, the son of a king's son, and knew what was due on these occasions. Thus he spoke in the vernacular:

"Colonel Sahib and officers of this regiment, much honor have you done me. This will I remember. We came down from afar to play you; but we were beaten." ("No fault of yours, Ressaidar Sahib. Played on your own ground, y' know. Your ponies were cramped from the railway. Don't apologize.") "Therefore perhaps we will come again if it be so ordained." ("Hear! Hear, hear, indeed! Bravo! H'sh!") "Then we will play you afresh" ("Happy to meet you"), "till there are left no feet upon our ponies. Thus far for sport." He dropped one hand on his sword-hilt, and his eyes wandered to Dirkovitch lolling back in his chair. "But if by the will of God there arises any other game which is not the polo game, then be assured, Colonel Sahib and officers, that we shall play it out side by side, though *they*"—again his eye sought Dirkovitch—"though *they,* I say, have fifty ponies to our one horse." And with a deep-mouthed *Rung ho!* that rang like a musket-butt on flag-stones, he sat down amid shoutings.

Dirkovitch, who had devoted himself steadily to the brandy—the terrible brandy aforementioned—did not understand, nor did the expurgated translations offered to him at all convey the point. Decidedly the native officer's was the speech of the evening, and the clamor might have continued to the dawn had it not been broken by the noise of a shot without that sent every man feeling at his defenseless left side. It is notable that Dirkovitch "reached back," after the American fashion—a gesture that set the captain of the Lushkar team wondering how Cossack officers were armed at mess. Then there was a scuffle and a yell of pain.

"Carbine-stealing again!" said the adjutant, calmly sinking back in his chair. "This comes of reducing the guards. I hope the sentries have killed him."

The feet of armed men pounded on the veranda flags, and it sounded as though something was being dragged.

"Why don't they put him in the cells till the morning?" said the colonel, testily. "See if they've damaged him, sergeant."

The mess-sergeant fled out into the darkness, and returned with two troopers and a corporal, all very much perplexed.

"Caught a man stealin' carbines, sir," said the corporal. "Leastways 'e was crawlin' toward the barracks, sir, past the main-road sentries; an' the sentry 'e says, sir"—

The limp heap of rags upheld by the three men groaned. Never was seen so destitute and demoralized an Afghan. He was turbanless, shoeless, caked with dirt, and all but dead with rough handling. Hira Singh started slightly at the sound of the man's pain. Dirkovitch took another liquor glass of brandy.

"What does the sentry say?" said the colonel.

"Sez he speaks English, sir," said the corporal.

"So you brought him into mess instead of handing him over to the sergeant! If he spoke all the tongues of the Pentecost, you've no business"—

Again the bundle groaned and muttered. Little Mildred had risen from his place to inspect. He jumped back as though he had been shot.

"Perhaps it would be better, sir, to send the men away," said he to the colonel, for he was a much-privileged subaltern. He put his arms round the ragbound horror as he spoke, and dropped him into a chair. It may not have been explained that the littleness of Mildred lay in his being six feet four, and big in proportion. The corporal, seeing that an officer was disposed to look after the capture, and that the colonel's eye was beginning to blaze, promptly removed himself and his men. The mess was left alone with the carbine thief, who laid his head on the table and wept bitterly, hopelessly, and inconsolably, as little children weep.

Hira Singh leaped to his feet with a long-drawn vernacular oath. "Colonel Sahib," said he, "that man is no Afghan, for they weep 'Ai! Ai!' Nor is he of Hindoostan, for they weep 'Oh! Ho!' He weeps after the fashion of the white men, who say 'Ow! Ow!' "

"Now where the dickens did you get that knowledge, Hira Singh?" said the captain of the Lushkar team.

"Hear him!" said Hira Singh, simply, pointing at the crumpled figure, that wept as though it would never cease.

"He said, 'My God!'" said Little Mildred. "I heard him say it."

The colonel and the mess-room looked at the man in silence. It is a horrible thing to hear a man cry. A woman can sob from the top of her palate, or her lips, or anywhere else, but a man cries from his diaphragm, and it rends him to pieces. Also, the exhibition causes the throat of the on-looker to close at the top.

"Poor devil!" said the colonel, coughing tremendously. "We ought to send him to hospital. He's been man-handled."

Now the adjutant loved his rifles. They were to him as his grandchildren—the men standing in the first place. He grunted rebelliously: "I can understand an Afghan stealing, because he's made that way. But I can't understand his crying. That makes it worse."

The brandy must have affected Dirkovitch, for he lay back in his chair and stared at the ceiling. There was nothing special in the ceiling beyond a shadow as of a huge black coffin. Owing to some peculiarity in the construction of the mess-room, this shadow was always thrown when the candles were lighted. It never disturbed the digestion of the White Hussars. They were, in fact, rather proud of it.

"Is he going to cry all night," said the colonel, "or are we supposed to sit up with Little Mildred's guest until he feels better?"

The man in the chair threw up his head and stared at the mess. Outside, the wheels of the first of those bidden to the festivities crunched the roadway.

"Oh, my God!" said the man in the chair, and every soul in the mess rose to his feet. Then the Lushkar captain did a deed for which he ought to have been given the Victoria Cross—distinguished gallantry in a fight against overwhelming curiosity. He picked up his team with his eyes as the hostess picks up the ladies at the opportune moment, and pausing only by the colonel's chair to say: "This isn't *our* affair, you know, sir," led the team into the veranda and the gardens. Hira Singh was the last, and he looked at Dirkovitch as he moved. But Dirkovitch had departed into a brandy paradise of his own. His lips moved without sound, and he was studying the coffin on the ceiling.

"White—white all over," said Basset-Holmer, the adjutant. "What a pernicious renegade he must be! I wonder where he came from?"

The colonel shook the man gently by the arm, and "Who are you?" said he.

There was no answer. The man stared round the mess-room and smiled in the colonel's face. Little Mildred, who was always more of a woman than a man till "Boot and saddle" was sounded, repeated the question in a voice that would have drawn confidences from a geyser. The man only smiled. Dirkovitch, at the far end of the table, slid gently from his chair to the floor. No son of Adam, in this present imperfect world, can mix the Hussars' champagne with the Hussars' brandy by five and eight glasses of each without remembering the pit whence he has been digged and descended thither. The band began to play the tune with which the White Hussars, from the date of their formation, preface all their functions. They would sooner be disbanded than abandon that tune. It is a part of their system. The man straightened himself in his chair and drummed on the table with his fingers.

"I don't see why we should entertain lunatics," said the colonel; "call a guard and send him off to the cells. We'll look into the business in the morning. Give him a glass of wine first, though."

Little Mildred filled a sherry glass with the brandy and thrust it over to the man. He drank, and the tune rose louder, and he straightened himself yet more. Then he put out his long-taloned hands to a piece of plate opposite and fingered it lovingly. There was a mystery connected with that piece of plate in the shape of a spring, which converted what was a seven-branched candlestick, three springs each side and one in the middle, into a sort of wheel-spoke candelabrum. He found the spring, pressed it, and laughed weakly. He rose from his chair and inspected a picture on the wall, then moved on to another picture, the mess watching him without a word. When he came to the mantelpiece he shook his head and seemed distressed. A piece of plate representing a mounted hussar in full uniform caught his eye. He pointed to it, and then to the mantelpiece, with inquiry in his eyes.

"What is it—oh, what is it?" said Little Mildred. Then, as a mother might speak to a child, "That is a horse—yes, a horse."

Very slowly came the answer, in a thick, passionless guttural: "Yes, I—have seen. But—where is *the* horse."

He could have heard the hearts of the mess beating as the men drew back to give the stranger full room in his wanderings. There was no question of calling the guard.

Again he spoke, very slowly: "Where is *our* horse?"

There is no saying what happened after that. There is but one horse in the White Hussars, and his portrait hangs outside the door of the mess-room. He is the piebald drum-horse, the king of the regimental band, that served the regiment for seven-and-thirty years, and in the end was shot for old age. Half the mess tore the thing down from its place and thrust it into the man's hands. He placed it above the mantelpiece; it clattered on the ledge, as his poor hands dropped it, and he staggered toward the bottom of the table, falling into Mildred's chair. The band began to play the "River of Years" waltz, and the laughter from the gardens came into the tobacco-scented mess-room. But nobody, even the youngest, was thinking of waltzes. They all spoke to one another something after this fashion: "The drum-horse hasn't hung over the mantelpiece since '67." •"How does he know?" "Mildred, go and speak to him again." "Colonel, what are you going to do?" "Oh, dry up, and give the poor devil a chance to pull himself together!" "It isn't possible, anyhow. The man's a lunatic."

Little Mildred stood at the colonel's side talking into his ear. "Will you be good enough to take your seats, please, gentlemen?" he said, and the mess dropped into the chairs.

Only Dirkovitch's seat, next to Little Mildred's was blank, and Little Mildred himself had found Hira Singh's place. The wide-eyed mess-sergeant filled the glasses in dead silence. Once more the colonel rose, but his hand shook, and the port spilled on the table as he looked straight at the man in Little Mildred's chair and said, hoarsely: "Mr. Vice, the Queen." There was a little pause, but the man sprung to his feet and answered, without hesitation: "The Queen, God bless her!" and as he emptied the thin glass he snapped the shank between his fingers.

Long and long ago, when the Empress of India was a young woman, and there were no unclean ideals in the land, it was the custom in a few messes to drink the queen's toast in broken glass, to the huge delight of the mess contractors. The custom is now dead, because there is nothing to break anything for, except now and again the word of a government, and that has been broken already.

"That settles it," said the colonel, with a gasp. "He's not a sergeant. What in the world is he?"

The entire mess echoed the word, and the volley of questions would have scared any man. Small wonder that the ragged, filthy invader could only smile and shake his head.

From under the table, calm and smiling urbanely, rose Dirkovitch, who had been roused from healthful slumber by feet upon his body. By the side of the man he rose, and the man shrieked and groveled at his feet. It was a horrible sight, coming so swiftly upon the pride and glory of the toast that had brought the strayed wits together.

Dirkovitch made no offer to raise him, but Little Mildred heaved him up in an instant. It is not good that a gentleman who can answer to the queen's toast should lie at the feet of a subaltern of Cossacks.

The hasty action tore the wretch's upper clothing nearly to the waist, and his body was seamed with dry black scars. There is only one weapon in the world that cuts in parallel lines, and it is neither the cane nor the cat. Dirkovitch saw the marks, and the pupils of his eyes dilated—also, his face changed. He said something that sounded like "Shto ve takete"; and the man, fawning, answered, "Chetyre."

"What's that?" said everybody together.

"His number. That is number four, you know." Dirkovitch spoke very thickly.

"What has a queen's officer to do with a qualified number?" said the colonel, and there rose an unpleasant growl round the table.

"How can I tell?" said the affable Oriental, with a sweet smile. "He is a —how you have it?—escape—runaway, from over there."

He nodded toward the darkness of the night.

"Speak to him, if he'll answer you, and speak to him gently," said Little Mildred, settling the man in a chair. It seemed most improper to all present that Dirkovitch should sip brandy as he talked in purring, spitting Russian to the creature who answered so feebly and with such evident dread. But since Dirkovitch appeared to understand, no man said a word. They breathed heavily, leaning forward in the long gaps of the conversation. The next time that they have no engagements on hand the White Hussars intend to go to St. Petersburg and learn Russian.

"He does not know how many years ago," said Dirkovitch, facing the mess, "but he says it was very long ago, in a war. I think that there was an accident. He says he was of this glorious and distinguished regiment in the war."

"The rolls! The rolls! Holmer, get the rolls!" said Little Mildred, and the adjutant dashed off bareheaded to the orderly-room where the rolls of the regiment were kept. He returned just in time to hear Dirkovitch conclude: "Therefore I am most sorry to say there was an accident, which would have been reparable if he had apologized to that our colonel, which he had insulted."

Another growl, which the colonel tried to beat down. The mess was in no mood to weigh insults to Russian colonels just then.

"He does not remember, but I think that there was an accident, and so he was not exchanged among the prisoners, but he was sent to another place—how do you say?—the country. So, he says, he came here. He does not know how he came. Eh? He was at Chepany"—the man caught the word, nodded, and shivered—"at Zhingansk and Irkutsk. I cannot understand how he escaped. He says, too, that he was in the forests for many years, but how many years he has forgotten—that with many things. It was an accident; done because he did not apologize to that our colonel. Ah!"

Instead of echoing Dirkovitch's sigh of regret, it is sad to record that the White Hussars livelily exhibited unchristian delight and other emotions, hardly restrained by their sense of hospitality. Holmer flung the frayed and yellow regimental rolls on the table, and the men flung themselves atop of these.

"Steady! Fifty-six—fifty-five—fifty-four," said Holmer. "Here we are. 'Lieutenant Austin Limmason—*missing*.' That was before Sebastopol. What an infernal shame! Insulted one of their colonels, and was quietly shipped off. Thirty years of his life wiped out."

"But he never apologized. Said he'd see him—first," chorused the mess.

"Poor devil! I suppose he never had the chance afterward. How did he come here?" said the colonel.

The dingy heap in the chair could give no answer.

"Do you know who you are?"

It laughed weakly.

"Do you know that you are Limmason—Lieutenant Limmason, of the White Hussars?"

Swift as a shot came the answer, in a slightly surprised tone: "Yes, I'm Limmason, of course." The light died out in his eyes, and he collapsed afresh, watching every motion of Dirkovitch with terror. A flight from Siberia may fix a few elementary facts in the mind, but it does not lead to continuity of thought. The man could not explain how, like a homing pigeon, he had found his way to his own old mess again. Of what he had suffered or seen he knew nothing. He cringed before Dirkovitch as instinctively as he had pressed the spring of the candlestick, sought the picture of the drum-horse, and answered to the queen's toast. The rest was a blank that the dreaded Russian tongue could only in part remove. His head bowed on his breast, and he giggled and cowered alternately.

The devil that lived in the brandy prompted Dirkovitch at this extremely inopportune moment to make a speech. He rose, swaying slightly, gripped the table-edge, while his eyes glowed like opals, and began:

"Fellow-soldiers glorious—true friends and hospitables. It was an accident, and deplorable—most deplorable." Here he smiled sweetly all round the mess. "But you will think of this little—little thing. So little, is it not? The czar! Posh! I slap my fingers—I snap my fingers at him. Do I believe in him? No! But the Slav who has done nothing, *him* I believe. Seventy—how much?—millions that have done nothing—not one thing. Napoleon was an episode." He banged a hand on the table. "Hear you, old peoples, we have done nothing in the world—out here. All our work is to do: and it shall be done, old peoples. Get away!" He waved his hand imperiously, and pointed to the man. "You see him. He is not good to see. He was just one little—oh, so little—accident, that no one remembered. Now he is *That*. So will you be, brother-soldiers so brave—so will you be. But you will never come back. You will all go where he is gone, or"—he pointed to the great coffin shadow on the ceiling, and muttering, "Seventy millions—get away, you old people," fell asleep.

"Sweet, and to the point," said Little Mildred. "What's the use of getting wroth? Let's make the poor devil comfortable."

But that was a matter suddenly and swiftly taken from the loving hands of the White Hussars. The lieutenant had returned only to go away again three days later, when the wail of the "Dead March" and the tramp of the squadrons told the wondering station, that saw no gap in the table, an officer of the regiment had resigned his new found commission.

And Dirkovitch—bland, supple, and always genial—went away too by a night train. Little Mildred and another saw him off, for he was the guest of the mess, and even had he smitten the colonel with the open hand, the law of the mess allowed no relaxation of hospitality.

"Good-bye, Dirkovitch, and a pleasant journey," said Little Mildred.

"*Au revoir*, my true friends," said the Russian.

"Indeed! But we thought you were going home?"

"Yes; but I will come again. My friends, is that road shut?" He pointed to where the north star burned over the Khyber Pass.

"By Jove! I forgot. Of course. Happy to meet you, old man, any time you like. Got everything you want—cheroots, ice, bedding? That's all right. Well, *au revoir*, Dirkovitch."

"Um," said the other man, as the tail-lights of the train grew small. "Of—all—the—unmitigated"—

Little Mildred answered nothing, but watched the north star, and hummed a selection from a recent burlesque that had much delighted the White Hussars. It ran:

> "I'm sorry for Mr. Bluebeard,
> I'm sorry to cause him pain;
> But a terrible spree there's sure
> to be
> When he comes back again."

A Conference of the Powers

"Life liveth best in life, and doth not
  roam
To other realms if all be well at home.
'Solid as ocean foam,' quoth ocean
  foam."

THE room was blue with the smoke of three pipes and a cigar. The leave season had opened in India, and the first-fruits on the English side of the water were "Tick" Boileau, of the Forty-fifth Bengal Cavalry, who called on me after three years' absence to discuss old things which had happened. Fate, who always does her work handsomely, sent up the same staircase within the same hour the Infant, fresh from Upper Burmah, and he and Boileau, looking out of my window, saw walking in the street one Nevin, late in a Ghoorkha regiment and the Black Mountain expedition. They yelled to him to come up, and the whole street was aware that they desired him to come up; and he came up, and there followed pandemonium, because we had foregathered from the ends of the earth, and three of us were on a holiday, and none of us was twenty-five, and all the delights of all London lay waiting our pleasure.

Boileau took the only other chair; and the Infant, by right of his bulk, the sofa; and Nevin, being a little man, sat cross-legged on the top of the revolving book-case; and we all said: "Who'd ha' thought it?" and "What are *you* doing here?" till speculation was exhausted, and the talk went over to inevitable "shop." Boileau was full of a great scheme for securing military attaché-

ship at St. Petersburg; Nevin had hopes of the Staff College; and the Infant had been moving heaven and earth and the Horse Guards for a commission in the Egyptian army.

"What's the use o' that?" said Nevin, twirling round on the book-case.

"Oh, heaps! Course if you get stuck with a Fellaheen regiment, you're sold; but if you are appointed to a Soudanese lot, you're in clover. They are first-class fighting men, and just think of the eligible central position of Egypt in the next row!"

This was putting the match to a magazine. We all began to explain the Central-Asian question off-hand, flinging army corps from the Helmund to Cashmir with more than Russian recklessness. Each of the boys made for himself a war to his own liking, and when we had settled all the details of Armageddon, killed all our senior officers, handled a division apiece, and nearly torn the atlas in two in attempts to explain our theories, Boileau needs must lift up his voice above the clamor and cry: "Anyhow, it'll be the —— of a row!" in tones that carried conviction far down the staircase.

Entered unperceived in the smoke William the Silent. "Gen'elman to see you, sir," said he, and disappeared, leaving in his stead none other than Mr. Eustace Cleever. William would have introduced the dragon of Wantley with equal disregard of present company.

"I—I beg your pardon! I didn't know that there was anybody—with you. I"—

570

But it was not seemly to allow Mr. Cleever to depart, for he was a great man. The boys remained where they were, because any movement would block the little room. Only when they saw his grey hairs they stood up on their feet, and when the Infant caught the name, he said: "Are you—did you write that book called 'As it was in the Beginning'?"

Mr. Cleever admitted that he had written the book.

"Then—then I don't know how to thank you, sir," said the Infant, flushing pink. "I was brought up in the country you wrote about. All my people live there, and I read the book in camp out in Burmah on the Hlinedatalone, and I knew every stick and stone, and the dialect, too; and, by Jove! it was just like being at home and hearing the country people talk. Nevin, you know 'As it was in the Beginning?' So does Ti—Boileau."

Mr. Cleever has tasted as much praise, public and private, as one man may safely swallow, but it seemed to me that the outspoken admiration in the Infant's eyes and the little stir in the little company came home to him very nearly indeed.

"Won't you take the sofa?" said the Infant. "I'll sit on Boileau's chair, and"— Here he looked at me to spur me to my duties as a host, but I was watching the novelist's face. Cleever had not the least intention of going away, but settled himself on the sofa. Following the first great law of the army, which says: "All property is common except money, and you've only got to ask the next man for that," the Infant offered tobacco and drink. It was

the least he could do, but not four columns of the finest review in the world held half as much appreciation and reverence as the Infant's simple: "Say when, sir," above the long glass.

Cleever said "when," and more thereto, for he was a golden talker, and he sat in the midst of hero-worship devoid of all taint of self-interest. The boys asked him of the birth of his book and whether it was hard to write, and how his notions came to him, and he answered with the same absolute simplicity as he was questioned. His big eyes twinkled, he dug his long, thin hands into his grey beard, and tugged it as he grew animated and dropped little by little from the peculiar pinching of the broader vowels—the indefinable "euh" that runs through the speech of the pundit caste—and the elaborate choice of words to freely mouthed ows and ois, and for him, at least, unfettered colloquialisms. He could not altogether understand the boys who hung upon his words so reverently. The line of the chin-strap that still showed white and untanned on cheek-bone and jaw, the steadfast young eyes puckered at the corners of the lids with much staring through red-hot sunshine, the deep, troubled breathing, and the curious crisp, curt speech seemed to puzzle him equally. He could create men and women, and send them to the uttermost ends of the earth to help, delight, and comfort; he knew every mood of the fields, and could interpret them to the cities, and he knew the hearts of many in the city and country, but he had hardly in forty years come into contact with the thing which is called a Subaltern of the Line. He told the boys this.

"Well, how should you?" said the Infant. "You—you're quite different, y' see, sir."

The Infant expressed his ideas in his tone rather than his words, and Cleever understood the compliments.

"We're only subs," said Nevin, "and we aren't exactly the sort of men you'd meet much in your life, I s'pose."

"That's true," said Cleever. "I live chiefly among those who write and paint and sculp and so forth. We have our own talk and our own interests, and the outer world doesn't trouble us much."

"That must be awf'ly jolly," said Boileau, at a venture. "We have our own shop too, but 'tisn't half as interesting as yours, of course. You know all the men who've ever done anything, and we only knock about from place to place, and we do nothing."

"The army's a very lazy profession, if you choose to make it so," said Nevin. "When there's nothing going on, there *is* nothing going on, and you lie up."

"Or try to get a billet somewhere so as to be ready for the next show," said the Infant, with a chuckle.

"To me," said Cleever, softly, "the whole idea of warfare seems so foreign and unnatural—so essentially vulgar, if I may say so—that I can hardly appreciate your sensations. Of course, though, any change from idling in garrison towns must be a godsend to you."

Like not a few home-staying Englishmen, Cleever believed that the newspaper phrase he quoted covered the whole duty of the army, whose toil enabled him to enjoy his many-sided life in peace. The remark was not a happy one, for Boileau had just come off the Indian frontier, the Infant had been on the war-path for nearly eighteen months, and the little red man, Nevin, two months before had been sleeping under the stars at the peril of his life. But none of them tried to explain till I ventured to point out that they had all seen service, and were not used to idling. Cleever took in the idea slowly.

"Seen service?" said he. Then, as a child might ask, "Tell me—tell me everything about everything."

"How do you mean, sir?" said the Infant, delighted at being directly appealed to by the great man.

"Good heavens! how am I to make you understand if you can't see? In the first place, what is your age?"

"Twenty-three next July," said the Infant, promptly.

Cleever questioned the others with his eyes.

"I'm twenty-four," said Nevin.

"I'm twenty-two," said Boileau.

"And you've all seen service?"

"We've all knocked about a little bit, sir, but the Infant's the war-worn veteran. He's had two years' work in Upper Burmah," said Nevin.

"When you say work, what do you mean, you extraordinary creatures?"

"Explain it, Infant," said Nevin.

"Oh, keeping things in order generally, and running about after little *dakus* —that's—Dacoits—and so on. There's nothing to explain."

"Make that young leviathan speak," said Cleever, impatiently.

"How can he speak?" said I. "He's done the work. The two don't go together. But, Infant, you are requested to *bukh*."

"What about? I'll try."

"*Bukh* about a *daur*. You've been on heaps of 'em," said Nevin.

"What in the world does that mean? Has the army a language of its own?"

The Infant turned very red. He was afraid he was being laughed at, and he detested talking before outsiders; but it was the author of "As it was in the Beginning" who waited.

"It's all so new to me," pleaded Cleever. "And—and you said you liked my book."

This was a direct appeal that the Infant could understand. He began, rather flurriedly, with "Pull me up, sir, if I say anything you don't follow. 'Bout six months before I took my leave out of Burmah I was on the Hlinedatalone up near the Shan states with sixty Tommies—private soldiers, that is—and another subaltern, a year senior to me. The Burmese business was a subaltern war, and our forces were split up into little detachments, all running about the country and trying to keep the Dacoits quiet. The Dacoits were having a first-class time, y' know—filling women up with kerosene and setting 'em alight, and burning villages, and crucifying people."

The wonder in Eustace Cleever's eyes deepened. He disbelieved wholly in a book which describes crucifixion at length, and he could not quite realize that the custom still existed.

"Have you ever seen a crucifixion?" said he.

"Of course not. Shouldn't have allowed it if I had. But I've seen the corpses. The Dacoits had a nice trick of sending a crucified corpse down the river on a raft, just to show they were keeping their tail up and enjoying themselves. Well, that was the kind of people I had to deal with."

"Alone?" said Cleever. Solitude of the soul he knew—none better; but he had never been ten miles away from his fellow-men in his life.

"I had my men, but the rest of it was pretty much alone. The nearest military post that could give me orders was fifteen miles away, and we used to heliograph to them, and they used to give us orders same way. Too many orders."

"Who was your C. O.?" said Boileau.

"Bounderby. Major. *Pukka* Bounderby. More Bounder than *pukka*. He went out up Bhamo way. Shot or cut down last year," said the Infant.

"What mean these interludes in a strange tongue?" said Cleever to me.

"Professional information, like the Mississippi pilots' talk. He did not approve of his major, who has since died a violent death," said I. "Go on, Infant."

"Far too many orders. You couldn't take the Tommies out for a two-days' daur—that means expedition, sir—without being blown up for not asking leave. And the whole country was humming with Dacoits. I used to send out spies and act on their information. As soon as a man came in and told me of a gang in hiding, I'd take thirty men, with some grub, and go out and look for them, while the other subaltern lay doggo in camp."

"Lay? Pardon me, but how did he lie?" said Cleever.

"Lay doggo. Lay quiet with the other thirty men. When I came back, he'd take out his half of the command, and have a good time of his own."

"Who was he?" said Boileau.

"Carter-Deecy, of the Aurangabadis. Good chap, but too *zubberdusty*, and went *bokhar* four days out of seven. He's gone out too. Don't interrupt a man."

Cleever looked helplessly at me.

"The other subaltern," I translate swiftly, "came from a native regiment and was over-bearing in his demeanor. He suffered much from the fever of the country, and is now dead. Go on, Infant."

"After a bit we got into trouble for using the men on frivolous occasions, and so I used to put my signaler under arrest to prevent him reading the helio orders. Then I'd go out, and leave a message to be sent an hour after I got clear of the camp; something like this: 'Received important information; start in an hour, unless countermanded.' If I was ordered back, it didn't much matter. I swore that the C. O.'s watch was wrong or something, when I came back. The Tommies enjoyed the fun, and—oh, yes—there was one Tommy who was the bard of the detachment. He used to make up verses on everything that happened."

"What sort of verses?" said Cleever.

"Lovely verses; and the Tommies used to sing 'em. There was one song with a chorus, and it said something like this." The Infant dropped into the barrack-room twang:

" 'Theebau, the Burmah king, did a very
        foolish thing
    When 'e mustered 'ostile forces in
        ar-rai.
  'E littul thought that *we,* from far
        across the sea,
    Would send our armies up to Man-
        dalai!' "

"Oh, gorgeous!" said Cleever. "And how magnificently direct! The notion of a regimental bard is new to me. It's epic."

"He was awf'ly popular with the men," said the Infant. "He had them all down in rhyme as soon as ever they had done anything. He was a great bard. He was always on time with a eulogy when we picked up a Boh—that's a leader of Dacoits."

"How did you pick him up?" said Cleever.

"Oh, shot him if he wouldn't surrender."

"You! Have you shot a man?"

There was a subdued chuckle from all three, and it dawned on the questioner that one experience in life which was denied to himself—and he weighed the souls of men in a balance—had been shared by three very young gentlemen of engaging appearance. He turned round on Nevin, who had climbed to the top of the book-case and was sitting cross-legged as before.

"And have *you,* too?"

"Think so," said Nevin, sweetly. "In the Black Mountain, sir. He was rolling cliffs on to my half-company and spoiling our formation. I took a rifle from a man and brought him down at the second shot."

"Good heavens! And how did you feel afterward?"

"Thirsty. I wanted a smoke, too."

Cleever looked at Boileau, the youngest. Surely his hands were guiltless of blood. Boileau shook his head and laughed. "Go on, Infant," said he.

"And you, too?" said Cleever.

"Fancy so. It was a case of cut—cut or be cut—with me, so I cut at one. I couldn't do any more, sir," said Boileau.

Cleever looked as though he would like to ask many questions, but the Infant swept on in the full tide of his tale.

"Well, we were called insubordinate young whelps at last, and strictly forbidden to take the Tommies out any more without orders. I wasn't sorry, because Tommy is such an exacting sort of creature, though he works beautifully. He wants to live as though he were in barracks all the time. I was grubbing on fowls and boiled corn, but the Tommies wanted their pound of fresh meat, and their half ounce of this, and their two ounces of t'other thing, and they used to come to me and badger me for plug tobacco when we were four days in jungle! I said: 'I can get you Burmah tobacco, but I don't keep a canteen up my sleeve.' They couldn't see it. They wanted all the luxuries of the season, confound 'em!"

"You were alone when you were dealing with these men?" said Cleever, watching the Infant's face under the palm of his hand. He was receiving new ideas, and they seemed to trouble him.

"Of course. Unless you count the mosquitoes. They were nearly as big as the men. After I had to lie doggo I began to look for something to do, and I was great pals with a man called Hicksey, in the Burmah police—the best man that ever stepped on earth; a first-class man."

Cleever nodded applause. He knew something of enthusiasm.

"Hicksey and I were as thick as thieves. He had some Burmah mounted police—nippy little chaps, armed with sword and Snider carbine. They rode punchy Burmah ponies, with string stirrups, red cloth saddles, and red bell-rope head-stalls. Hicksey used to lend me six or eight of them when I asked him—nippy little devils, keen as mustard. But they told their wives too much, and all my plans got known, till I learned to give false marching orders over night, and take the men to quite a different village in the morning. Then we used to catch the simple *dakus* before breakfast, and make them very sick. It's a ghastly country on the Hlinedatalone; all bamboo jungle, with paths about four feet wide winding through it. The *dakus* knew all the paths, and used to pot at us as we came round a corner; but the mounted police knew the paths as well as the *dakus,* and we used to go stalking 'em in and out among the paths. Once we flushed 'em—the men on the ponies had the pull of the man on foot. We held all the country absolutely quiet for ten miles round in about a month. Then we took Boh Na-ghee—Hicksey and I and the civil officer. That was a lark!"

"I think I am beginning to understand a little," said Cleever. "It was a pleasure to you to administer and fight, and so on."

"Rather. There's nothing nicer than a satisfactory little expedition, when you find all your plans fit together and your conformations *teek*—correct, you know—and the whole *subchiz*—I mean when everything works out like formulæ on a blackboard. Hicksey had all the information about the Boh. He had been burning villages and murdering people right and left, and cutting up government convoys, and all that. He was lying doggo in a village about fifteen miles off, waiting to get a fresh gang together. So we arranged to take thirty mounted police, and turn him out before he could plunder into the newly settled villages. At the last minute the civil officer in our part of the world thought he'd assist in the performance."

"Who was he?" said Nevin.

"His name was Dennis," said the Infant, slowly; "and we'll let it stay so. He's a better man now than he was then."

"But how old was the civil power?" said Cleever. "The situation is developing itself." Then, in his beard: "Who are you, to judge men?"

"He was about six-and-twenty," said the Infant; "and he was awf'ly clever. He knew a lot of literary things, but I don't think he was quite steady enough for Dacoit-hunting. We started over night for Boh Na-ghee's village, and we got there just before the morning, without raising an alarm. Dennis had turned out armed to the teeth—two revolvers, a carbine, and all sorts of things. I was talking to Hicksey about posting our men, and Dennis edged his pony in between us, and said: 'What shall I do? What shall I do? Tell me what to do, you fellows.' We didn't take much notice, but his pony tried to bite me in the leg, and I said: 'Pull out a bit, old man, till we've settled the attack.' He kept edging in, and fiddling with his reins and the revolvers, and saying: 'Dear me! dear me! Oh, dear me! What do you think I'd better do?' The man was in a blue funk and his teeth were chattering."

"I sympathize with the civil power," said Cleever. "Continue, young Clive."

"The fun of it was that he was supposed to be our superior officer. Hicksey took a good look at him, and told him to attach himself to my party. Beastly mean of Hicksey, that. The chap kept on edging in and bothering, instead of asking for some men and taking up his own position, till I got angry. The carbines began popping on the other side of the village. Then I said: 'For God's sake, be quiet, and sit down where you are! If you see anybody come out of the village, shoot at him.' I knew he couldn't hit a hayrick at a yard. Then I took my men over the garden wall—over the palisades, y' know—somehow or other, and the fun began. Hicksey had found the Boh in bed under a mosquito curtain, and he had taken a flying jump on to him."

"A flying jump!" said Cleever. "Is that also war?"

"Yes," said the Infant, now thoroughly warmed. "Don't you know how you take a flying jump on to a fellow's head at school when he snores in the dormitory? The Boh was sleeping in a regular bedful of swords and pistols, and Hicksey came down à la Zazel through the netting, and the net got mixed up with the pistols and the Bob and Hicksey, and they all rolled on the floor together. I laughed till I couldn't stand, and Hicksey was cursing me for not helping him, so I left him to fight it out, and went into the village. Our men were slashing about and firing, and so were the Dacoits, and in the thick of the mess some ass set fire to a house, and we all had to clear out. I froze on to the nearest *daku* and ran to the palisade, shoving *him* in front of me. He wriggled clear and bounded over to the other side. I came after him, but when I had one leg one side and one leg the other of the palisade, I saw that my friend had fallen flat on Dennis's head. That man had never moved from where I left him. The two rolled on the ground together, and Dennis's carbine went off and nearly shot me. The *daku* picked himself up and ran, and Dennis heaved his carbine after him, and it caught him on the back of his head and knocked him silly. You never saw anything so funny in your life. I doubled up on the top of the palisade and hung there, yelling with laughter. But Dennis began to weep like anything. 'Oh, I've killed a man!' he said—'I've killed a man, and I shall never know another peaceful hour in my life! Is he dead? Oh, *is* he dead? Good God! I've killed a man!' I came down and said: 'Don't be a fool!' But he kept on shouting 'Is he dead?' till I could have kicked him. The *daku* was only knocked out of time with the carbine. He came to after a bit, and I said: 'Are you hurt much?' He grinned and said no. His chest was all cut with scrambling over the palisade. 'The white man's gun didn't do that,' he said. 'I did that myself, and I knocked the white man over.' Just like a Burman, wasn't it? Dennis wouldn't be happy at any price. He said: 'Tie up his wounds. He'll bleed to death. Oh, my God, he'll bleed to death!' 'Tie 'em up yourself,' I said, 'if you're so anxious.' 'I can't touch him,' said Dennis, 'but here's my shirt.' He took off his shirt, and he fixed his braces again over his bare shoulders. I ripped the shirt up and bandaged the Dacoit quite professionally. He was grinning at Dennis all the time; and Dennis's haver-

sack was lying on the ground, bursting full of sandwiches. Greedy hog! I took some and offered some to Dennis. 'How can I eat?' he said. 'How can you ask me to eat? His very blood is on your hands, oh, God! and you're eating *my* sandwiches!' 'All right,' I said. 'I'll give 'em to the *daku*.' So I did, and the little chap was quite pleased, and wolfed 'em down like one o'clock."

Cleever brought his hand down on the tablecloth a thump that made the empty glasses dance. "That's art," he said. "Flat, flagrant mechanism. Don't tell me that happened on the spot!"

The pupils of the Infant's eyes contracted to pin points. "I beg your pardon," he said slowly and a little stiffly, "but I am telling this thing as it happened."

Cleever looked at him for a moment. "My fault entirely," said he. "I should have known. Please go on."

"Oh, then Hicksey came out of what was left of the village with his prisoners and captives all neatly tied up. Boh Na-ghee was first, and one of the villagers, as soon as he saw the old ruffian helpless, began kicking him quietly. The Boh stood it as long as he could, and then groaned, and we saw what was going on. Hicksey tied the villager up and gave him half a dozen good ones to remind him to leave a prisoner alone. You should have seen the old Boh grin. Oh, but Hicksey was in a furious rage with everybody. He'd got a wipe over the elbow that had tickled up his funny bone, and he was simply rabid with me for not having helped him with the Boh and the mosquito net. I had to explain that I couldn't do anything. If you'd seen 'em both tangled up together on the floor, like a blaspheming cocoon, you'd have laughed for a week. Hicksey swore that the only decent man of his acquaintance was the Boh, and all the way back to camp Hicksey was talking to him, and the Boh was grumbling about the soreness of his bones. When we got home and had had a bath, the Boh wanted to know when he was going to be hanged. Hicksey said he couldn't oblige him on the spot, but had to send him to Rangoon. The Boh went down on his knees and reeled off a catalogue of his crimes—he ought to have been hanged seventeen times over by his own confession—and implored Hicksey to settle the business out of hand. 'If I'm sent to Rangoon,' said he, 'they'll keep me in jail all my life, and that is a death every time the sun gets up or the wind blows.' But we had to send him to Rangoon; and, of course, he was let off down there and given penal servitude for life. When I came to Rangoon I went over the jail—I had helped to fill it, y' know—and the old Boh was there and recognized me at once. He begged for some opium first, and I tried to get him some; but that was against the rules. Then he asked me to have his sentence changed to death, because he was afraid of being sent to the Andamans. I couldn't do that, either; but I tried to cheer him, and told him how the row was going up country. And the last thing he said was: 'Give my compliments to the fat white man who jumped on me. If I'd been awake I'd have killed him.' I wrote that to Hicksey next mail, and—that's all. I'm 'fraid I've been gassing awf'ly, sir."

Cleever said nothing for a long time. The Infant looked uncomfortable. He feared that, misled by enthusiasm, he had filled up the novelist's time with unprofitable recital of trivial anecdotes.

Then said Cleever: "I can't understand it. Why should *you* have seen and done all these things before you have cut your wisdom-teeth?"

"Don't know," said the Infant, apologetically. "I haven't seen much—only Burmese jungle."

"And dead men and war and power and responsibility," said Cleever, under his breath. "You won't have any sensations left at thirty if you go on as you have done. But I want to hear more tales—more tales." He seemed to forget that even subalterns might have engagements of their own.

"We're thinking of dining out somewhere, the lot of us, and going on to the Empire afterward," said Nevin, with hesitation. He did not like to ask Cleever to come too. The invitation might be regarded as "cheek." And Cleever, anxious not to wag a grey beard unbidden among boys at large, said nothing on his side.

Boileau solved the little difficulty by blurting out: "Won't you come too, sir?"

Cleever almost shouted "Yes," and while he was being helped into his coat, continued to murmur "Good heavens!" at intervals, in a manner that the boys could not understand.

"I don't think I've been to the Empire in my life," said he. "But, good heavens! what is my life, after all? Let us go back."

So they went out with Eustace Cleever, and I sulked at home, because the boys had come to see me, but had gone over to the better man, which was humiliating. They packed him into a cab with utmost reverence, for was he not the author of "As it was in the Beginning," and a person in whose company it was an honor to go abroad? From all I gathered later, he had taken no less interest in the performance before him than in the boys' conversation, and they protested with emphasis that he was "as good a man as they make, knew what a man was driving at almost before he said it, and yet he's so dashed simple about things any man knows." That was one of many comments made afterward.

At midnight they returned, announcing that they were highly respectable gondoliers, and that oysters and stout were what they chiefly needed. The eminent novelist was still with them, and I think he was calling them by their shorter names. I am certain that he said he had been moving in worlds not realized, and that they had shown him the Empire in a new light. Still sore at recent neglect, I answered shortly: "Thank Heaven, we have within the land ten thousand as good as they!" and when Cleever departed, asked him what he thought of things generally.

He replied with another quotation, to the effect that though singing was a remarkably fine performance, I was to be quite sure that few lips would be moved to song if they could find a sufficiency of kissing.

Whereat I understood that Eustace Cleever, decorator and color man in words, was blaspheming his own art, and that he would be sorry for this in the morning.

Without Benefit of Clergy

I

"But if it be a girl?"

"Lord of my life, it cannot be! I have prayed for so many nights, and sent gifts to Sheikh Badl's shrine so often, that I know God will give us a son—a man-child that shall grow into a man. Think of this and be glad. My mother shall be his mother till I can take him again, and the mullah of the Pattan Mosque shall cast his nativity—God send he be born in an auspicious hour!—and then, and then thou wilt never weary of me, thy slave."

"Since when hast thou been a slave, my queen?"

"Since the beginning—till this mercy came to me. How could I be sure of thy love when I knew that I had been bought with silver?"

"Nay, that was the dowry. I paid it to thy mother."

"And she has buried it, and sits upon it all day long like a hen. What talk is yours of dowry? I was bought as though I had been a Lucknow dancing-girl instead of a child."

"Art thou sorry for the sale?"

"I have sorrowed; but to-day I am

glad. Thou wilt never cease to love me now? Answer, my king."

"Never—never. No."

"Not even though the *mem-log*—the white women of thy own blood—love thee? And remember, I have watched them driving in the evening; they are very fair."

"I have seen fire-balloons by the hundred, I have seen the moon, and then— I saw no more fire-balloons."

Ameera clapped her hands and laughed. "Very good talk," she said. Then, with an assumption of great stateliness: "It is enough. Thou hast my permission to depart—if thou wilt."

The man did not move. He was sitting on a low red-lacquered couch in a room furnished only with a blue-and-white floor-cloth, some rugs, and a very complete collection of native cushions. At his feet sat a woman of sixteen, and she was all but all the world in his eyes. By every rule and law she should have been otherwise, for he was an Englishman and she a Mussulman's daughter, bought two years before from her mother, who, being left without money would have sold Ameera, shrieking, to the Prince of Darkness, if the price had been sufficient.

It was a contract entered into with a light heart. But even before the girl had reached her bloom she came to fill the greater portion of John Holden's life. For her and the withered hag her mother he had taken a little house overlooking the great red-walled city, and found, when the marigolds had sprung up by the well in the courtyard, and Ameera had established herself according to her own ideas of comfort, and her mother had ceased grumbling at the inadequacy of the cooking-places, the distance from the daily market, and matters of housekeeping in general, that the house was to him his home. Any one could enter his bachelor's bungalow by day or night, and the life that he led there was an unlovely one. In the house in the city his feet only could pass beyond the outer court-yard to the women's rooms; and when the big wooden gate was bolted behind him he was king in his own territory, with Ameera for queen. And there was going to be added to this kingdom a third person, whose arrival Holden felt inclined to resent. It interfered with his perfect happiness. It disarranged the orderly peace of the house that was his own. But Ameera was wild with delight at the thought of it, and her mother not less so. The love of a man, and particularly a white man, was at the best an inconstant affair, but it might, both women argued, be held fast by a baby's hands. "And then," Ameera would always say—"then he will never care for the white *mem-log*. I hate them all—I hate them all!"

"He will go back to his own people in time," said the mother, "but, by the blessing of God, that time is yet afar off."

Holden sat silent on the couch, thinking of the future, and his thoughts were not pleasant. The drawbacks of a double life are manifold. The government, with singular care, had ordered him out of the station for a fortnight on special duty, in the place of a man who was watching by the bedside of a sick wife. The verbal notification of the transfer had been edged by a cheerful remark that Holden ought to think himself lucky in being a bachelor and a free man. He came to break the news to Ameera.

"It is not good," she said, slowly, "but it is not all bad. There is my mother here, and no harm will come to me—unless, indeed, I die of pure joy. Go thou to thy work, and think no troublesome thoughts. When the days are done, I believe . . . nay, I am sure. And—and then I shall lay *him* in thy arms, and thou wilt love me forever. The train goes to-night—at midnight, is it not? Go now, and do not let thy heart be heavy by cause of me. But thou wilt not delay in returning! Thou wilt not stay on the road to talk to the bold white *mem-log!* Come back to me swiftly, my life!"

As he left the court-yard to reach his horse, that was tethered to the gatepost, Holden spoke to the white-haired old watchman who guarded the house, and bid him under certain contingencies dispatch the filled-up telegraph form that Holden gave him. It was all that could be done, and, with the sensations of a man who has attended his own funeral, Holden went away by the night mail to his exile. Every hour of the day he dreaded the arrival of the telegram, and every hour of the night he pictured to himself the death of Ameera. In consequence, his work for the state was not of first-rate quality, nor was his temper toward his colleagues of the most amiable. The fortnight ended without a sign from his home, and, torn to pieces by his anxieties, Holden returned to be swallowed up for two precious hours by a dinner at the club, wherein he heard, as a man hears in a swoon, voices telling him how execrably

he had performed the other man's duties, and how he had endeared himself to all his associates. Then he fled on horseback through the night with his heart in his mouth. There was no answer at first to his blows on the gate, and he had just wheeled his horse round to kick it in, when Pir Khan appeared with a lantern and held his stirrup.

"Has aught occurred?" said Holden.

"The news does not come from my mouth, Protector of the Poor, but"—He held out his shaking hand, as befitted the bearer of good news who is entitled to a reward.

Holden hurried through the court-yard. A light burned in the upper room. His horse neighed in the gateway, and he heard a pin-pointed wail that sent all the blood into the apple of his throat. It was a new voice, but it did not prove that Ameera was alive.

"Who is there?" he called up the narrow brick staircase.

There was a cry of delight from Ameera, and then the voice of her mother, tremulous with old age and pride. "We be two women, and—the—man—thy son."

On the threshold of the room Holden stepped on a naked dagger that was laid there to avert ill-luck, and it broke at the hilt under his impatient heel.

"God is great!" cooed Ameera in the half-light. "Thou hast taken his misfortunes on thy head."

"Ay, but how is it with thee, life of my life? Old woman, how is it with her?"

"She has forgotten her sufferings for joy that the child is born. There is no harm; but speak softly," said the mother.

"It only needed thy presence to make me all well," said Ameera. "My king, thou hast been very long away. What gifts hast thou for me? Ah! ah! It is I that bring gifts this time. Look, my life, look! Was there ever such a babe? Nay, I am too weak even to clear my arm from him."

"Rest, then, and do not talk. I am here, *bachheri*" (little woman).

"Well said, for there is a bond and a heel-rope [*peecharee*] between us now that nothing can break. Look—canst thou see in this light? He is without spot or blemish. Never was such a man-child. *Ya illah!* he shall be a pundit—no, a trooper of the queen. And, my life, dost thou love me as well as ever, though I am faint and sick and worn? Answer truly."

"Yea. I love as I have loved, with all my soul. Lie still, pearl, and rest."

"Then do not go. Sit by my side here—so. Mother, the lord of this house needs a cushion. Bring it." There was an almost imperceptible movement on the part of the new life that lay in the hollow of Ameera's arm. "Aho!" she said, her voice breaking with love. "The babe is a champion from his birth. He is kicking me in the side with mighty kicks. Was there ever such a babe? And he is ours to us—thine and mine. Put thy hand on his head, but carefully, for he is very young, and men are unskilled in such matters."

Very cautiously Holden touched with the tips of his fingers the downy head.

"He is of the Faith," said Ameera; "for, lying here in the night-watches, I whispered the Call to Prayer and the Profession of Faith into his ears. And it is most marvelous that he was born upon a Friday, as I was born. Be careful of him, my life; but he can almost grip with his hands."

Holden found one helpless little hand that closed feebly on his finger. And the clutch ran through his limbs till it settled about his heart. Till then his sole thought had been for Ameera. He began to realize that there was some one else in the world, but he could not feel that it was a veritable son with a soul. He sat down to think, and Ameera dozed lightly.

"Get hence, sahib," said her mother, under her breath. "It is not good that she should find you here on waking. She must be still."

"I go," said Holden, submissively. "Here be rupees. See that my *baba* gets fat and finds all that he needs."

The chink of the silver roused Ameera. "I am his mother, and no hireling," she said, weakly. "Shall I look to him more or less for the sake of money? Mother, give it back. I have borne my lord a son."

The deep sleep of weakness came upon her almost before the sentence was completed. Holden went down to the court-yard very softly, with his heart at ease. Pir Khan, the old watchman, was chuckling with delight.

"This house is now complete," he said, and without further comment thrust into Holden's hands the hilt of a sabre worn many years ago, when Pir Khan served the queen in the police. The bleat of a tethered goat came from the well-curb.

"There be two," said Pir Khan—"two goats of the best. I bought them, and they cost much money; and since there is no birth-party assembled, their flesh will be all mine. Strike craftily, sahib. 'Tis an ill-balanced sabre at the best. Wait till they raise their heads from cropping the marigolds."

"And why?" said Holden, bewildered.

"For the birth sacrifice. What else? Otherwise the child, being unguarded from fate, may die. The Protector of the Poor knows the fitting words to be said."

Holden had learned them once, with little thought that he would ever say them in earnest. The touch of the cold sabre-hilt in his palm turned suddenly to the clinging grip of the child upstairs— the child that was his own son—and a dread of loss filled him.

"Strike!" said Pir Khan. "Never life came into the world but life was paid for it. See, the goats have raised their heads. Now! With a drawing cut!"

Hardly knowing what he did, Holden cut twice as he muttered the Mohammedan prayer that runs: "Almighty! In place of this my son I offer life for life, blood for blood, head for head, bone for bone, hair for hair, skin for skin." The waiting horse snorted and bounded in his pickets at the smell of the raw blood that spurted over Holden's riding-boots.

"Well smitten!" said Pir Khan, wiping the sabre. "A swordsman was lost in thee. Go with a light heart, heaven born. I am thy servant and the servant of thy son. May the Presence live a thousand years, and . . . the flesh of the goats is all mine?"

Pir Khan drew back richer by a month's pay. Holden swung himself into the saddle and rode off through the low-hanging wood smoke of the evening. He was full of riotous exultation, alternating with a vast vague tenderness directed toward no particular object, that made him choke as he bent over the neck of his uneasy horse. "I never felt like this in my life," he thought. "I'll go to the club and pull myself together."

A game of pool was beginning, and the room was full of men. Holden entered, eager to get to the light and the company of his fellows, singing at the top of his voice:

" 'In Baltimore a-walking, a lady I did
    meet.' "

"Did you?" said the club secretary from his corner. "Did she happen to tell you that your boots were wringing wet. Great goodness, man, it's blood!"

"Bosh!" said Holden, picking his cue from the rack. "May I cut in? It's dew. I've been riding through high crops. My faith! my boots are in a mess, though!

" 'And if it be a girl, she shall wear a
    wedding-ring;
And if it be a boy, he shall fight for
    his king;
With his dirk and his cap, and his lit-
    tle jacket blue,
He shall walk the quarter-deck' "—

"Yellow and blue—green next player," said the marker, monotonously.

" 'He shall walk the quarter-deck'— am I green, marker?—'he shall walk the quarter-deck'—ouch! that's a bad shot! —'as his daddy used to do!' "

"I don't see that you have anything to crow about," said a zealous junior civilian, acidly. "The government is not exactly pleased with your work when you relieved Sanders."

"Does that mean a wigging from headquarters?" said Holden, with an abstracted smile. "I think I can stand it."

The talk beat up round the ever-fresh subject of each man's work, and steadied Holden till it was time to go to his dark, empty bungalow, where his butler received him as one who knew all his affairs. Holden remained awake for the greater part of the night, and his dreams were pleasant ones.

II

"How old is he now?"

"*Ya illah!* What a man's question! He is all but six weeks old; and on this night I go up to the house-top with thee, my life, to count the stars. For that is auspicious. And he was born on a Friday, under the sign of the Sun, and it has been told to me that he will outlive us both and get wealth. Can we wish for aught better, beloved?"

"There is nothing better. Let us go up to the roof, and thou shalt count the stars—but a few only, for the sky is heavy with cloud."

"The winter rains are late, and maybe they come out of season. Come, before all the stars are hid. I have put on my richest jewels."

"Thou hast forgotten the best of all."

"Ai! *Ours.* He comes also. He has never yet seen the skies."

Ameera climbed the narrow staircase that led to the flat roof. The child, placid and unwinking, lay in the hollow of her right arm, gorgeous in silver-fringed muslin, with a small skull-cap on his head. Ameera wore all that she valued most. The diamond nose-stud that takes the place of the Western patch in drawing attention to the curve of the nostril, the gold ornament in the

centre of the forehead studded with tallow-drop emeralds and flawed rubies, the heavy circlet of beaten gold that was fastened round her neck by the softness of the pure metal, and the chinking curb-patterned silver anklets hanging low over the rosy ankle-bone. She was dressed in jade-green muslin, as befitted a daughter of the Faith, and from shoulder to elbow and elbow to wrist ran bracelets of silver tied with floss silk, frail glass bangles slipped over the wrist in proof of the slenderness of the hand, and certain heavy gold bracelets that had no part in her country's ornaments, but since they were Holden's gift, and fastened with a cunning European snap, delighted her immensely.

They sat down by the low white parapet of the roof, overlooking the city and its lights.

"They are happy down there," said Ameera. "But I do not think that they are as happy as we. Nor do I think the white *mem-log* are as happy. And thou?"

"I know they are not."

"How dost thou know?"

"They give their children over to the nurses."

"I have never seen that," said Ameera, with a sigh; "nor do I wish to see. Ahi!"—she dropped her head on Holden's shoulder—"I have counted forty stars, and I am tired. Look at the child, love of my life. He is counting, too."

The baby was staring with round eyes at the dark of the heavens. Ameera placed him in Holden's arms, and he lay there without a cry.

"What shall we call him among ourselves?" she said. "Look! Art thou ever tired of looking? He carries thy very eyes! But the mouth"—

"Is thine, most dear. Who should know better than I?"

" 'Tis such a feeble mouth. Oh, so small! And yet it holds my heart between its lips. Give him to me now. He has been too long away."

"Nay, let him lie; he has not yet begun to cry."

"When he cries thou wilt give him back, eh? What a man of mankind thou art! If he cried, he were only the dearer to me. But, my life, what little name shall we give him?"

The small body lay close to Holden's heart. It was utterly helpless and very soft. He scarcely dared to breathe for fear of crushing it. The caged green parrot, that is regarded as a sort of guardian spirit in most native households, moved on its perch and fluttered a drowsy wing.

"There is the answer," said Holden. "Mian Mittu has spoken. He shall be the parrot. When he is ready he will talk mightily, and run about. Mian Mittu is the parrot in thy—in the Mussulman tongue, is it not?"

"Why put me so far off?" said Ameera, fretfully. "Let it be like unto some English name—but not wholly. For he is mine."

"Then call him Tota, for that is likest English."

"Ay, Tota; and that is still the parrot. Forgive me, my lord, for a minute ago; but, in truth, he is too little to wear all the weight of Mian Mittu for name. He shall be Tota—our Tota to us. Hearest thou, oh, small one? Littlest, thou art Tota."

She touched the child's cheek, and, he

waking, wailed, and it was necessary to return him to his mother, who soothed him with the wonderful rhyme of *"Aré koko, Ja ré koko!"* which says:

"Oh, crow! Go crow! Baby's sleeping
          sound,
And the wild plums grow in the jungle,
     only a penny a pound—
Only a penny a pound, *Baba*—only a
     penny a pound."

Reassured many times as to the price of those plums. Tota cuddled himself down to sleep. The two sleek white well-bullocks in the court-yard were steadily chewing the cud of their evening meal; old Pir Khan squatted at the head of Holden's horse, his police sabre across his knees, pulling drowsily at a big water-pipe that croaked like a bullfrog in a pond. Ameera's mother sat spinning in the lower veranda, and the wooden gate was shut and barred. The music of a marriage procession came to the roof above the gentle hum of the city, and a string of flying-foxes crossed the face of the low moon.

"I have prayed," said Ameera, after a long pause, with her chin in her hand— "I have prayed for two things. First, that I may die in thy stead, if thy death is demanded; and in the second, that I may die in the place of the child. I have prayed to the Prophet and to Beebee Miriam.[1] Thinkest thou either will hear?"

"From thy lips who would not hear the lightest word?"

"I asked for straight talk, and thou has given me sweet talk. Will my prayers be heard?"

"How can I say? God is very good."

---

[1] The Virgin Mary.

"Of that I am not sure. Listen now. When I die or the child dies, what is thy fate? Living, thou wilt return to the bold white *mem-log,* for kind calls to kind."

"Not always."

"With a woman, no. With a man it is otherwise. Thou wilt in this life, later on, go back to thine own folk. That I could almost endure, for I should be dead. But in thy very death thou wilt be taken away to a strange place and a paradise that I do not know."

"Will it be paradise?"

"Surely; for what God would harm thee? But we two—I and the child—shall be elsewhere, and we cannot come to thee, nor canst thou come to us. In the old days, before the child was born, I did not think of these things; but now I think of them perpetually. It is very hard talk."

"It will fall as it will fall. To-morrow we do now know, but to-day and love we know well. Surely we are happy now."

"So happy that it were well to make our happiness assured. And thy Beebee Miriam should listen to me; for she is also a woman. But then she would envy me— It is not seemly for men to worship a woman."

Holden laughed aloud at Ameera's little spasm of jealousy.

"Is it not seemly? Why didst thou not turn me from worship of thee, then?"

"Thou a worshipper! And of me! My king, for all thy sweet words, well I know that I am thy servant and thy slave, and the dust under thy feet. And I would not have it otherwise. See!"

Before Holden could prevent her she stooped forward and touched his feet; recovering herself with a little laugh, she hugged Tota closer to her bosom. Then, almost savagely:

"Is it true that the bold white *mem-log* live for three times the length of my life? Is it true that they make their marriages not before they are old women?"

"They marry as do others—when they are women."

"That I know, but they wed when they are twenty-five. Is that true?"

"That is true."

"*Ya illah!* At twenty-five! Who would of his own will take a wife even of eighteen? She is a woman—aging every hour. Twenty-five! I shall be an old woman at that age, and— Those *mem-log* remain young forever. How I hate them!"

"What have they to do with us?"

"I cannot tell. I know only that there may now be alive on this earth a woman ten years older than I who may come to thee and take thy love ten years after I am an old woman, grey-headed, and the nurse of Tota's son. That is unjust and evil. They should die too."

"Now, for all thy years thou art a child, and shalt be picked up and carried down the staircase."

"Tota! Have a care for Tota, my lord! Thou, at least, art as foolish as any babe!" Ameera tucked Tota out of harm's way in the hollow in her neck, and was carried downstairs, laughing, in Holden's arms, while Tota opened his eyes and smiled, after the manner of the lesser angels.

He was a silent infant, and almost before Holden could realize that he was in the world, developed into a small gold-colored godling and unquestioned despot of the house overlooking the city. Those were months of absolute happiness to Holden and Ameera—happiness withdrawn from the world, shut in behind the wooden gate that Pir Khan guarded. By day Holden did his work, with an immense pity for such as were not so fortunate as himself, and a sympathy for small children that amazed and amused many mothers at the little station gatherings. At nightfall he returned to Ameera—Ameera full of the wondrous doings of Tota: how he had been seen to clap his hands together and move his fingers with intention and purpose, which was manifestly a miracle; how, later, he had of his own initiative crawled out of his low bedstead on to the floor, and swayed on both feet for the space of three breaths. "And they were long breaths, for my heart stood still with delight," said Ameera.

Then he took the beasts into his councils—the well-bullocks, the little grey squirrels, the mongoose that lived in a hole near the well, and especially Mian Mittu, the parrot, whose tail he grievously pulled, and Mian Mittu screamed till Ameera and Holden arrived.

"Oh, villain! Child of strength! This is to thy brother on the house-top! *Tobah, tobah!* Fy! fy! But I know a charm to make him wise as Suleiman and Aflatoun.[1] Now look, said Ameera. She drew from an embroidered bag a handful of almonds. "See! we count seven. In the name of God!" She placed Mian Mittu, very angry and rumpled, on the top of his cage, and,

_____
[1]Solomon and Plato.

seating herself between the babe and the bird, cracked and peeled an almond less white than her teeth. "This is a true charm, my life; and do not laugh. See! I give the parrot one-half and Tota the other." Mian Mittu, with careful beak, took his share from between Ameera's lips, and she kissed the other half into the mouth of the child, who eat it slowly, with wondering eyes. "This I will do each day of seven, and without doubt he who is ours will be a bold speaker and wise. Eh, Tota, what wilt thou be when thou art a man and I am grey-headed?" Tota tucked his fat legs into adorable creases. He could crawl, but he was not going to waste the spring of his youth in idle speech. He wanted Mian Mittu's tail to tweak.

When he was advanced to the dignity of a silver belt—which, with a magic square engraved on silver and hung round his neck, made up the greater part of his clothing—he staggered on a perilous journey down the garden to Pir Khan, and proffered him all his jewels in exchange for one little ride on Holden's horse. He had seen his mother's mother chaffering with peddlers in the veranda. Pir Khan wept, set the untried feet on his own grey head in sign of fealty, and brought the bold adventurer to his mother's arms, vowing that Tota would be a leader of men ere his beard was grown.

One hot evening, while he sat on the roof between his father and mother watching the never-ending warfare of the kites that the city boys flew, he demanded a kite of his own, with Pir Khan to fly it, because he had a fear of dealing with anything larger than himself; and when Holden called him a "spark," he rose to his feet and answered slowly, in defense of his new-found individuality: *"Hum 'park nahin hai. Hum admi hai."* (I am no spark, but a man.)

The protest made Holden choke, and devote himself very seriously to a consideration of Tota's future.

He need hardly have taken the trouble. The delight of that life was too perfect to endure. Therefore it was taken away, as many things are taken away in India, suddenly and without warning. The little lord of the house, as Pir Khan called him, grew sorrowful and complained of pains, who had never known the meaning of pain. Ameera, wild with terror, watched him through the night, and in the dawning of the second day the life was shaken out of him by fever—the seasonal autumn fever. It seemed altogether impossible that he could die, and neither Ameera nor Holden at first believed the evidence of the body on the bedstead. Then Ameera beat her head against the wall, and would have flung herself down the well in the garden had Holden not restrained her by main force.

One mercy only was granted to Holden. He rode to his office in broad daylight, and found waiting him an unusually heavy mail that demanded concentrated attention and hard work. He was not, however, alive to this kindness of the gods.

III

The first shock of a bullet is no more than a brisk pinch. The wrecked body does not send in its protest to the soul till ten or fifteen seconds later. Then comes thirst, throbbing, and agony, and a ridiculous amount of screaming. Holden realized his pain slowly, exactly as he had realized his happiness, and with the same imperious necessity for hiding all trace of it. In the beginning he only felt that there had been a loss, and that Ameera needed comforting where she sat with her head on her knees, shivering as Mian Mittu, from the house-top, called "Tota! Tota! Tota!" Later all his world and the daily life of it rose up to hurt him. It was an outrage that any one of the children at the bandstand in the evening should be alive and clamorous when his own child lay dead. It was more than mere pain when one of them touched him, and stories told by overfond fathers of their children's latest performances cut him to the quick. He could not declare his pain. He had neither help, comfort, nor sympathy, and Ameera, at the end of each weary day, would lead him through the hell of self-questioning reproach which is reserved for those who have lost a child, and believe that with a little—just a little—more care it might have been saved. There are not many hells worse than this, but he knows one who has sat down temporarily to consider whether he is or is not responsible for the death of his wife.

"Perhaps," Ameera would say, "I did not take sufficient heed. Did I, or did I not? The sun on the roof that day when he played so long alone, and I was—*ahi!* braiding my hair—it may be that the sun then bred the fever. If I had warned him from the sun he might have lived. But, oh, my life, say that I am guiltless! Thou knowest that I loved him as I loved thee! Say that

there is no blame on me, or I shall die—
I shall die!"

"There is no blame. Before God, none. It was written, and how could we do aught to save? What has been, has been. Let it go, beloved."

"He was all my heart to me. How can I let the thought go when my arm tells me every night that he is not here? *Ahi! ahi!* Oh, Tota, come back to me—come back again, and let us be together as it was before!"

"Peace! peace! For thine own sake, and for mine also, if thou lovest me, rest."

"By this I know thou dost not care; and how shouldst thou? The white men have hearts of stone and souls of iron. Oh, that I had married a man of mine own people—though he beat me—and had never eaten the bread of an alien!"

"Am I an alien, mother of my son?"

"What else, sahib? . . . Oh, forgive me—forgive! The death has driven me mad. Thou art the life of my heart, and the light of my eyes, and the breath of my life, and—and I have put thee from me, though it was but for a moment. If thou goest away, to whom shall I look for help? Do not be angry. Indeed, it was the pain that spoke, and not thy slave."

"I know—I know. We be two who were three. The greater need, therefore, that we should be one."

They were sitting on the roof, as of custom. The night was a warm one in early spring, and sheet-lightning was dancing on the horizon to a broken tune played by far-off thunder. Ameera settled herself in Holden's arms.

"The dry earth is lowing like a cow for the rain, and I—I am afraid. It was not like this when we counted the stars. But thou lovest me as much as before, though a bond is taken away? Answer."

"I love more, because a new bond has come out of the sorrow that we have eaten together; and that thou knowest."

"Yea, I know," said Ameera, in a very small whisper. "But it is good to hear thee say so, my life, who art so strong to help. I will be a child no more, but a woman and an aid to thee. Listen. Give me my *sitar,* and I will sing bravely."

She took the light silver-studded *sitar,* and began a song of the great hero Raja Rasalu. The hand failed on the strings, the tune halted, checked, and at a low note turned off to the poor little nursery rhyme about the wicked crow:

" 'And the wild plums grow in the
        jungle—
  Only a penny a pound,
  Only a penny a pound, *Baba*—only' "—

Then came the tears and the piteous rebellion against fate, till she slept, moaning a little in her sleep, with the right arm thrown clear of the body, as though it protected something that was not there.

It was after this night that life became a little easier for Holden. The ever-present pain of loss drove him into his work, and the work repaid him by filling up his mind for eight or nine hours a day. Ameera sat alone in the house and brooded, but grew happier when she understood that Holden was more at ease, according to the custom of women. They touched happiness again, but this time with caution.

"It was because we loved Tota that

he died. The jealousy of God was upon us," said Ameera. "I have hung up a large black jar before our window to turn the Evil Eye from us, and we must make no protestations of delight, but go softly underneath the stars, lest God find us out. Is that not good talk, worthless one?"

She had shifted the accent of the word that means "beloved," in proof of the sincerity of her purpose. But the kiss that followed the new christening was a thing that any deity might have envied. They went about henceforth saying: "It is naught—it is naught," and hoping that all the powers heard.

The powers were busy on other things. They had allowed thirty million people four years of plenty, wherein men fed well and the crops were certain and the birth-rate rose year by year; the districts reported a purely agricultural population varying from nine hundred to two thousand to the square mile of the overburdened earth. It was time to make room. And the Member of the Lower Tooting, wandering about India in top-hat and frock-coat, talked largely of the benefits of British rule, and suggested as the one thing needful the establishment of duly qualified electoral system and a general bestowal of the franchise. His long-suffering hosts smiled and made him welcome, and when he paused to admire, with pretty picked words, the blossom of the blood-red dhak-tree, that had flowered untimely for a sign of the sickness that was coming, they smiled more than ever.

It was the Deputy Commissioner of Kot-Kumharsen, staying at the club for a day, who lightly told a tale that made Holden's blood run cold as he overheard the end.

"He won't bother any one any more. Never saw a man so astonished in my life. By Jove! I thought he meant to ask a question in the House about it. Fellow-passenger in his ship—dined next him—bowled over by cholera, and died in eighteen hours. You needn't laugh, you fellows. The Member for Lower Tooting is awfully angry about it; but he's more scared. I think he's going to take his enlightened self out of India."

"I'd give a good deal if he were knocked over. It might keep a few vestrymen of his kidney to their parish. But what's this about cholera? It's full early for anything of that kind," said a warden of an unprofitable salt-lick.

"Dunno," said the deputy commissioner, reflectively. "We've got locusts with us. There's sporadic cholera all along the north—at least, we're calling it sporadic for decency's sake. The spring crops are short in five districts, and nobody seems to know where the winter rains are. It's nearly March now. I don't want to scare anybody, but it seems to me that Nature's going to audit her accounts with a big red pencil this summer."

"Just when I wanted to take leave, too," said a voice across the room.

"There won't be much leave this year, but there ought to be a great deal of promotion. I've come in to persuade the government to put my pet canal on the list of famine-relief works. It's an ill wind that blows no good. I shall get that canal finished at last."

"Is it the old programme, then?"

said Holden—"famine, fever, and cholera?"

"Oh, no! Only local scarcity and an unusual prevalence of seasonal sickness. You'll find it all in the reports if you live till next year. You're a lucky chap. You haven't got a wife to put you out of harm's way. The hill-stations ought to be full of women this year."

"I think you're inclined to exaggerate the talk in the bazaars," said a young civilian in the secretariat. "Now, I have observed"—

"I dare say you have," said the deputy commissioner, "but you've a great deal more to observe, my son. In the meantime, I wish to observe to you"— And he drew him aside to discuss the construction of the canal that was so dear to his heart.

Holden went to his bungalow, and began to understand that he was not alone in the world, and also that he was afraid for the sake of another, which is the most soul-satisfying fear known to man.

Two months later, as the deputy had foretold, Nature began to audit her accounts with a red pencil. On the heels of the spring reapings came a cry for bread, and the government, which had decreed that no man should die of want, sent wheat. Then came the cholera from all four quarters of the compass. It struck a pilgrim gathering of half a million at a sacred shrine. Many died at the feet of their god, the others broke and ran over the face of the land, carrying the pestilence with them. It smote a walled city and killed two hundred a day. The people crowded the trains, hanging on to the foot-boards and squatting on the roofs of the car-

riages; and the cholera followed them, for at each station they dragged out the dead and the dying on the platforms reeking of lime-wash and carbolic acid. They died by the roadside, and the horses of the Englishmen shied at the corpses in the grass. The rains did not come, and the earth turned to iron lest man should escape by hiding in her. The English sent their wives away to the Hills, and went about their work, coming forward as they were hidden to fill the gaps in the fighting line. Holden, sick with fear of losing his chiefest treasure on earth, had done his best to persuade Ameera to go away with her mother to the Himalayas.

"Why should I go?" said she one evening on the roof.

"There is sickness, and the people are dying, and all the white *mem-log* have gone."

"All of them?"

"All—unless, perhaps, there remain some old scald-head who vexes her husband's heart by running risk of death."

"Nay; who stays is my sister, and thou must not abuse her, for I will be a scald-head too. I am glad all the bold white *mem-log* are gone."

"Do I speak to a woman or a babe? Go to the Hills, and I will see to it that thou goest like a queen's daughter. Think, child! In a red-lacquered bullock-cart, veiled and curtained, with brass peacocks upon the pole and red-cloth hangings. I will send two orderlies for guard, and"—

"Peace! Thou art the babe in speaking thus. What use are those toys to me? *He* would have patted the bullocks and played with the housings. For his sake, perhaps—thou hast made me very English—I might have gone. Now I will not. Let the *mem-log* run."

"Their husbands are sending them, beloved."

"Very good talk. Since when hast thou been my husband to tell me what to do? I have but borne thee a son. Thou art only all the desire of my soul to me. How shall I depart when I know that if evil befall thee by the breadth of so much as my littlest finger-nail—is that not small?—I should be aware of it though I were in Paradise? And here, this summer thou mayest die —ai, Janee, die!—and in dying they might call to tend thee a white woman, and she would rob me in the last of thy love."

"But love is not born in a moment, or on a deathbed."

"What dost thou know of love, stone-heart? She would take thy thanks at least, and, by God and the Prophet and Beebee Miriam, the mother of thy Prophet, that I will never endure. My lord and my love, let there be no more foolish talk of going away. Where thou art, I am. It is enough." She put an arm round his neck and a hand on his mouth.

There are not many happinesses so complete as those that are snatched under the shadow of the sword. They sat together and laughed, calling each other openly by every pet name that could move the wrath of the gods. The city below them was locked up in its own torments. Sulphur-fires blazed in the streets; the conches in the Hindoo temples screamed and bellowed, for the gods were inattentive in those days. There was a service in the great Mohammedan shrine, and the call to prayer from the minarets was almost unceasing. They heard the wailing in the houses of the dead, and once the shriek of a mother who had lost a child and was calling for its return. In the grey dawn they saw the dead borne out through the city gates, each litter with its own little knot of mourners. Wherefore they kissed each other and shivered.

It was a red and heavy audit, for the land was very sick and needed a little breathing-space ere the torrent of cheap life should flood it anew. The children of immature fathers and undeveloped mothers made no resistance. They were cowed and sat still, waiting till the sword should be sheathed in November, if it were so willed. There were gaps among the English, but the gaps were filled. The work of superintending famine relief, cholera-sheds, medicine distribution, and what little sanitation was possible, went forward because it was so ordered.

Holden had been told to hold himself in readiness to move to replace the next man who should fall. There were twelve hours in each day when he could not see Ameera, and she might die in three. He was considering what his pain would be if he could not see her for three months, or if she died out of his sight. He was absolutely certain that her death would be demanded—so certain that, when he looked up from the telegram and saw Pir Khan breathless in the doorway, he laughed aloud, "And?"—said he.

"When there is a cry in the night and the spirit flutters into the throat, who has a charm that will restore? Come swiftly, heaven born. It is the black cholera."

Holden galloped to his home. The

sky was heavy with clouds, for the long-deferred rains were at hand, and the heat was stifling. Ameera's mother met him in the court-yard, whimpering: "She is dying. She is nursing herself into death. She is all but dead. What shall I do, sahib?"

Ameera was lying in the room in which Tota had been born. She made no sign when Holden entered, because the human soul is a very lonely thing, and when it is getting ready to go away hides itself in a misty border-land where the living may not follow. The black cholera does its work quietly and without explanation. Ameera was being thrust out of life as though the Angel of Death had himself put his hand upon her. The quick breathing seemed to show that she was either afraid or in pain, but neither eyes nor mouth gave any answer to Holden's kisses. There was nothing to be said or done. Holden could only wait and suffer. The first drops of the rain began to fall on the roof, and he could hear shouts of joy in the parched city.

The soul came back a little and the lips moved. Holden bent down to listen. "Keep nothing of mine," said Ameera. "Take no hair from my head. *She* would make thee burn it later on. That flame I should feel. Lower! Stoop lower! Remember only that I was thine and bore thee a son. Though thou wed a white woman to-morrow, the pleasure of taking in thy arms thy first son is taken from thee forever. Remember me when thy son is born—the one that shall carry thy name before all men. His misfortunes be on my head. I bear witness—I bear witness"—the lips were forming the words on his ear—"that there is no God but—thee, beloved."

Then she died. Holden sat still, and thought of any kind was taken from him till he heard Ameera's mother lift the curtain.

"Is she dead, sahib?"

"She is dead."

"Then I will mourn, and afterward take an inventory of the furniture in this house; for that will be mine. The sahib does not mean to resume it. It is so little, so very little, sahib, and I am an old woman. I would like to lie softly."

"For the mercy of God, be silent awhile! Go out and mourn where I cannot hear."

"Sahib, she will be buried in four hours."

"I know the custom. I shall go ere she is taken away. That matter is in thy hands. Look to it that the bed—on which—on which—she lies"—

"Aha! That beautiful red-lacquered bed. I have long desired"—

—"That the bed is left here untouched for my disposal. All else in the house is thine. Hire a cart, take everything, go hence, and before sunrise let there be nothing in this house but that which I have ordered thee to respect."

"I am an old woman. I would stay at least for the days of mourning, and the rains have just broken. Whither shall I go?"

"What is that to me? My order is that there is a going. The house-gear is worth a thousand rupees, and my orderly shall bring thee a hundred rupees to-night."

"That is very little. Think of the cart-hire."

"It shall be nothing unless thou goest, and with speed. Oh, woman, get hence, and leave me to my dead!"

The mother shuffled down the staircase, and in her anxiety to take stock of the house-fittings forgot to mourn. Holden stayed by Ameera's side, and the rain roared on the roof. He could not think connectedly by reason of the noise, though he made many attempts to do so. Then four sheeted ghosts glided dripping into the room and stared at him through their veils. They were the washers of the dead. Holden left the room and went out to his horse. He had come in a dead, stifling calm, through ankle-deep dust. He found the court-yard a rain-lashed pond alive with frogs, a torrent of yellow water ran under the gate, and a roaring wind drove the bolts of the rain like buckshot against the mud walls. Pir Khan was shivering in his little hut by the gate, and the horse was stamping uneasily in the water.

"I have been told the sahib's order," said he. "It is well. This house is now desolate. I go also, for my monkey face would be a reminder of that which has been. Concerning the bed, I will bring that to thy house yonder in the morning. But remember, sahib, it will be to thee as a knife turned in a green wound. I go upon a pilgrimage and I will take no money. I have grown fat in the protection of the Presence, whose sorrow is my sorrow. For the last time I hold his stirrup."

He touched Holden's foot with both hands, and the horse sprung out into the road, where the creaking bamboos were whipping the sky and all the frogs were chuckling. Holden could not see for the rain in his face. He put his hands before his eyes and muttered: "Oh, you brute! You utter brute!"

The news of his trouble was already in his bungalow. He read the knowledge in his butler's eyes when Ahmed Khan brought in food, and for the first and last time in his life laid a hand upon his master's shoulder, saying: "Eat, sahib, eat. Meat is good against sorrow. I also have known. Moreover, the shadows come and go, sahib. The shadows come and go. These be curried eggs."

Holden could neither eat nor sleep. The heavens sent down eight inches of rain in that night and scoured the earth clean. The waters tore down walls, broke roads, and washed open the shallow graves in the Mohammedan burying-ground. All next day it rained, and Holden sat still in his house considering his sorrow. On the morning of the third day he received a telegram which said only: "Ricketts, Myndonie. Dying. Holden. Relieve. Immediate." Then he thought that before he departed he would look at the house wherein he had been master and lord. There was a break in the weather. The rank earth steamed with vapor, and Holden was vermilion from head to heel with the prickly-heat born of sultry moisture.

He found that the rains had torn down the mud-pillars of the gateway, and the heavy wooden gate that had guarded his life hung drunkenly from one hinge. There was grass three inches high in the court-yard; Pir Khan's lodge was empty and the sodden thatch sagged between the beams. A grey squirrel was in possession of the veranda, as if the house had been untenanted for thirty years instead of three days. Ameera's mother had removed everything except some mildewed matting. The *tick-tick* of the little scorpions as they hurried across the floor was the only sound in the house. Ameera's room and that other one where Tota had lived were heavy with mildew, and the narrow staircase leading to the roof was streaked and stained with rain-borne mud. Holden saw all these things, and came out again to meet in the road Durga Dass, his landlord—portly, affable, clothed in white muslin, and driving a C-spring buggy. He was overlooking his property, to see how the roofs withstood the stress of the first rains.

"I have heard," said he, "you will not take this place any more, sahib?"

"What are you going to do with it?"

"Perhaps I shall let it again."

"Then I will keep it on while I am away."

Durga Dass was silent for some time. "You shall not take it on, sahib," he said. "When I was a young man I also — But to-day I am a member of the municipality. Ho! ho! No. When the birds have gone, what need to keep the nest? I will have it pulled down; the timber will sell for something always. It shall be pulled down, and the municipality shall make a road across, as they desire, from the burning-ghat to the city wall. So that no man may say where this house stood."

———— • ————

The Mark of the Beast

Your Gods and my Gods—do you or I
 know which are the stronger?
   —*Native Proverb.*

EAST of Suez, some hold, the direct control of Providence ceases; Man being there handed over to the power of the Gods and Devils of Asia, and the Church of England Providence only exercising an occasional and modified supervision in the case of Englishmen.

This theory accounts for some of the more unnecessary horrors of life in India: it may be stretched to explain my story.

My friend Strickland of the Police, who knows as much of natives of India as is good for any man, can bear witness to the facts of the case. Dumoise,

our doctor, also saw what Strickland and I saw. The inference which he drew from the evidence was entirely incorrect. He is dead now; he died in a rather curious manner, which has been elsewhere described.

When Fleete came to India he owned a little money and some land in the Himalayas, near a place called Dharmsala. Both properties had been left him by an uncle, and he came out to finance them. He was a big, heavy, genial, and inoffensive man. His knowledge of natives was, of course, limited, and he complained of the difficulties of the language.

He rode in from his place in the hills to spend New Year in the station, and he stayed with Strickland. On New Year's Eve there was a big dinner at the club, and the night was excusably wet. When men foregather from the uttermost ends of the Empire, they have a right to be riotous. The Frontier had sent down a contingent o' Catch-'em-Alive-O's who had not see twenty white faces for a year, and were used to ride fifteen miles to dinner at the next Fort at the risk of a Khyberee bullet where their drinks should lie. They profited by their new security, for they tried to play pool with a curled-up hedge-hog found in the garden, and one of them carried the marker round the room in his teeth. Half a dozen planters had come in from the south and were talking "horse" to the Biggest Liar in Asia, who was trying to cap all their stories at once. Everybody was there, and there was a general closing up of ranks and taking stock of our losses in dead or disabled that had fallen during the past year. It was a very wet night, and I remember that we sang "Auld Lang Syne" with our feet in the Polo Championship Cup, and our heads among the stars, and swore that we were all dear friends. Then some of us went away and annexed Burma, and some tried to open up the Soudan and were opened up by Fuzzies in that cruel scrub outside Suakim, and some found stars and medals, and some were married, which was bad, and some did other things which were worse, and the others of us stayed in our chains and strove to make money on insufficient experiences.

Fleete began the night with sherry and bitters, drank champagne steadily up to dessert, then raw, rasping Capri with all the strength of whisky, took

Benedictine with his coffee, four or five whiskies and sodas to improve his pool strokes, beer and bones at half-past two, winding up with old brandy. Consequently, when he came out, at half-past three in the morning, into fourteen degrees of frost, he was very angry with his horse for coughing, and tried to leap-frog into the saddle. The horse broke away and went to his stables; so Strickland and I formed a Guard of Dishonor to take Fleete home.

Our road lay through the bazaar, close to a little temple of Hanuman, the Monkey-god, who is a leading divinity worthy of respect. All gods have good points, just as have all priests. Personally, I attach much importance to Hanuman, and am kind to his people— the great grey apes of the hills. One never knows when one may want a friend.

There was a light in the temple, and as we passed, we could hear voices of men chanting hymns. In a native temple, the priests rise at all hours of the night to do honor to their god. Before we could stop him, Fleete dashed up the steps, patted two priests on the back, and was gravely grinding the ashes of his cigar-butt into the forehead of the red, stone image of Hanuman. Strickland tried to drag him out, but he sat down and said solemnly:

"Shee that? 'Mark of the B— beasht! I made it. Ishn't it fine?"

In half a minute the temple was alive and noisy, and Strickland, who knew what came of polluting gods, said that things might occur. He, by virtue of his official position, long residence in the country, and weakness for going among the natives, was known to the priests and he felt unhappy. Fleete sat on the ground and refused to move. He said that "good old Hanuman" made a very soft pillow.

Then, without any warning, a Silver Man came out of a recess behind the image of the god. He was perfectly naked in that bitter, bitter cold, and his body shone like frosted silver, for he was what the Bible calls "a leper as white as snow." Also he had no face, because he was a leper of some years' standing, and his disease was heavy upon him. We two stooped to haul Fleete up, and the temple was filling and filling with folk who seemed to spring from the earth, when the Silver Man ran in under our arms, making a noise exactly like the mewing of an otter, caught Fleete round the body and dropped his head on Fleete's breast before we could wrench him away. Then he retired to a corner and sat mewing while the crowd blocked all the doors.

The priests were very angry until the Silver Man touched Fleete. That nuzzling seemed to sober them.

At the end of a few minutes' silence one of the priests came to Strickland and said, in perfect English, "Take your friend away. He has done with Hanuman, but Hanuman has not done with him." The crowd gave room and we carried Fleete into the road.

Strickland was very angry. He said that we might all three have been knifed, and that Fleete should thank his stars that he had escaped without injury.

Fleete thanked no one. He said that he wanted to go to bed. He was gorgeously drunk.

We moved on, Strickland silent and wrathful, until Fleete was taken with violent shivering fits and sweating. He said that the smells of the bazaar were overpowering, and he wondered why slaughter-houses were permitted so near English residences. "Can't you smell the blood?" said Fleete.

We put him to bed at last, just as the dawn was breaking, and Strickland invited me to have another whisky and soda. While we were drinking he talked of the trouble in the temple, and admitted that it baffled him completely. Strickland hates being mystified by natives, because his business in life is to overmatch them with their own weapons. He has not yet succeeded in doing this, but in fifteen or twenty years he will have made some small progress.

"They should have mauled us," he said, "instead of mewing at us. I wonder what they meant. I don't like it one little bit."

I said that the Managing Committee of the temple would in all probability bring a criminal action against us for insulting their religion. There was a section of the Indian Penal Code which exactly met Fleete's offence. Strickland said he only hoped and prayed that they would do this. Before I left I looked into Fleete's room, and saw him lying on his right side, scratching his left breast. Then I went to bed cold, depressed, and unhappy, at seven o'clock in the morning.

At one o'clock I rode over to Strickland's house to inquire after Fleete's head. I imagined that it would be a sore one. Fleete was breakfasting and seemed unwell. His temper was gone, for he was abusing the cook for not supplying him with an underdone chop. A man who can eat raw meat after a wet night is a curiosity. I told Fleete this and he laughed.

"You breed queer mosquitoes in these parts," he said. "I've been bitten to pieces, but only in one place."

"Let's have a look at the bite," said Strickland. "It may have gone down since this morning."

While the chops were being cooked, Fleete opened his shirt and showed us, just over his left breast, a mark, the perfect double of the black rosettes— the five or six irregular blotches arranged in a circle—on a leopard's hide. Strickland looked and said, "It was only pink this morning. It's grown black now."

Fleete ran to a glass.

"By Jove!" he said, "this is nasty. What is it?"

We could not answer. Here the chops came in, all red and juicy, and Fleete bolted three in a most offensive manner. He ate on his right grinders only, and threw his head over his right shoulder as he snapped the meat. When he had finished, it struck him that he had been behaving strangely, for he said, apologetically, "I don't think I ever felt so hungry in my life. I've bolted like an ostrich."

After breakfast Strickland said to me, "Don't go. Stay here, and stay for the night."

Seeing that my house was not three miles from Strickland's, this request was absurd. But Strickland insisted, and was going to say something when Fleete interrupted by declaring in a shame-faced way that he felt hungry again. Strickland sent a man to my house to fetch over my bedding and a horse, and we three went down to Strickland's stables to pass the hours until it was time to go out for a ride. The man who has a weakness for horses never wearies of inspecting them; and when two men are killing time in this way they gather knowledge and lies the one from the other.

There were five horses in the stables, and I shall never forget the scene as we tried to look them over. They seemed to have gone mad. They reared and screamed and nearly tore up their pickets; they sweated and shivered and lathered and were distraught with fear. Strickland's horses used to know him as well as his dogs; which made the matter more curious. We left the stable for fear of the brutes throwing themselves in their panic. Then Strickland turned back and called me. The horses were still frightened, but they let us "gentle" and make much of them, and put their heads in our bosoms.

"They aren't afraid of *us*," said Strickland. "D' you know, I'd give three months' pay if *Outrage* here could talk."

But *Outrage* was dumb, and could only cuddle up to his master and blow out his nostrils, as is the custom of horses when they wish to explain things but can't. Fleete came up when we were in the stalls, and as soon as the horses saw him, their fright broke out afresh. It was all that we could do to escape from the place unkicked. Strickland said, "They don't seem to love you, Fleete."

"Nonsense," said Fleete; "my mare will follow me like a dog." He went to her; she was in a loose-box; but as he slipped the bars she plunged, knocked him down, and broke away into the garden. I laughed, but Strickland was not amused. He took his moustache in both fists and pulled at it till it nearly came out. Fleete, instead of going off to chase his property, yawned, saying that he felt sleepy. He went to the house to lie down, which was a foolish way of spending New Year's Day.

Strickland sat with me in the stables and asked if I had noticed anything peculiar in Fleete's manner. I said that he ate his food like a beast; but that this might have been the result of living alone in the hills out of the reach of society as refined and elevating as ours for instance. Strickland was not amused. I do not think that he listened to me, for his next sentence referred to the mark on Fleete's breast, and I said that it might have been caused by blister-flies, or that it was possibly a birth-mark newly born and now visible for the first time. We both agreed that it was unpleasant to look at, and Strickland found occasion to say that I was a fool.

"I can't tell you what I think now," said he, "because you would call me a madman; but you must stay with me for the next few days, if you can. I want you to watch Fleete, but don't tell me what you think till I have made up my mind."

"But I am dining out to-night," I said.

"So am I," said Strickland, "and so is Fleete. At least if he doesn't change his mind."

We walked about the garden smoking, but saying nothing—because we were friends, and talking spoils good tobacco

—till our pipes were out. Then we went to wake up Fleete. He was wide awake and fidgeting about his room.

"I say, I want some more chops," he said. "Can I get them?"

We laughed and said, "Go and change. The ponies will be round in a minute."

"All right," said Fleete. "I'll go when I get the chops—underdone ones, mind."

He seemed to be quite in earnest. It was four o'clock, and we had had breakfast at one; still, for a long time, he demanded those underdone chops. Then he changed into riding clothes and went out into the veranda. His pony—the mare had not been caught—would not let him come near. All three horses were unmanageable—mad with fear—and finally Fleete said that he would stay at home and get something to eat. Strickland and I rode out wondering. As we passed the temple of Hanuman, the Silver Man came out and mewed at us.

"He is not one of the regular priests of the temple," said Strickland. "I think I should peculiarly like to lay my hands on him."

There was no spring in our gallop on the race-course that evening. The horses were stale, and moved as though they had been ridden out.

"The fright after breakfast has been too much for them," said Strickland.

That was the only remark he made through the remainder of the ride. Once or twice I think he swore to himself; but that did not count.

We came back in the dark at seven o'clock, and saw that there were no lights in the bungalow. "Careless ruffians my servants are!" said Strickland. My horse reared at something on the carriage drive, and Fleete stood up under its nose.

"What are you doing, grovelling about the garden?" said Strickland.

But both horses bolted and nearly threw us. We dismounted by the stables and returned to Fleete, who was on his hands and knees under the orange-bushes.

"What the devil's wrong with you?" said Strickland.

"Nothing, nothing in the world," said Fleete, speaking very quickly and thickly. "I've been gardening—botanizing, you know. The smell of the earth is delightful. I think I'm going for a walk —a long walk—all night."

Then I saw that there was something excessively out of order somewhere, and I said to Strickland, "I am not dining out."

"Bless you!" said Strickland. "Here, Fleete, get up. You'll catch fever there. Come in to dinner and let's have the lamps lit. We'll all dine at home."

Fleete stood up unwillingly, and said, "No lamps—no lamps. It's much nicer here. Let's dine outside and have some more chops—lots of 'em and underdone —bloody ones with gristle."

Now a December evening in Northern India is bitterly cold, and Fleete's suggestion was that of a maniac.

"Come in," said Strickland, sternly. "Come in at once."

Fleete came, and when the lamps were brought, we saw that he was literally plastered with dirt from head to foot. He must have been rolling in the garden. He shrank from the light and went to his room. His eyes were horrible to look at. There was a green light behind them, not in them, if you understand, and the man's lower lip hung down.

Strickland said, "There is going to be trouble—big trouble—to-night. Don't you change your riding-things."

We waited and waited for Fleete's reappearance, and ordered dinner in the meantime. We could hear him moving about his own room, but there was no light there. Presently from the room came the long-drawn howl of a wolf.

People write and talk lightly of blood running cold and hair standing up and things of that kind. Both sensations are too horrible to be trifled with. My heart stopped as though a knife had been driven through it, and Shrickland turned as white as the table-cloth.

The howl was repeated, and was answered by another howl far across the fields.

That set the gilded roof on the horror. Strickland dashed into Fleete's room. I followed, and we saw Fleete getting out of the window. He made beast-noises in the back of his throat. He could not answer us when we shouted at him. He spat.

I don't quite remember what followed, but I think that Strickland must have stunned him with the long boot-jack or else I should never have been able to sit on his chest. Fleete could not speak, he could only snarl, and his snarls were those of a wolf, not of a man. The human spirit must have been giving way all day and have died out with the twilight. We were dealing with a beast that had once been Fleete.

The affair was beyond any human and rational experience. I tried to say "Hydrophobia," but the word wouldn't come, because I knew that I was lying.

We bound this beast with leather thongs of the punkah-rope, and tied its thumbs and big toes together, and gagged it with a shoe-horn, which makes a very efficient gag if you know how to arrange it. Then we carried it into the dining-room, and sent a man to Dumoise, the doctor, telling him to come over at once. After we had despatched the messenger and were drawing breath, Strickland said, "It's no good. This isn't any doctor's work." I, also, knew that he spoke the truth.

The beast's head was free, and it threw it about from side to side. Any one entering the room would have believed that we were curing a wolf's pelt. That was the most loathsome accessory of all.

Strickland sat with his chin in the heel of his fist, watching the beast as it wriggled on the ground, but saying nothing. The shirt had been torn open in the scuffle and showed the black rosette mark on the left breast. It stood out like a blister.

In the silence of the watching we heard something without mewing like a she-otter. We both rose to our feet, and, I answer for myself, not Strickland, felt sick—actually and physically sick. We told each other, as did the men in *Pinafore*, that it was the cat.

Dumoise arrived, and I never saw a little man so unprofessionally shocked. He said that it was a heart-rending case of hydrophobia, and that nothing could be done. At least any palliative measures would only prolong the agony. The beast was foaming at the mouth. Fleete, as we told Dumoise, had been bitten by dogs once or twice. Any man who keeps half a dozen terriers must expect a nip now and again. Dumoise could offer no help. He could only certify that Fleete was dying of hydrophobia. The beast was then howling, for it had managed to spit out the shoe-horn. Dumoise said that he would be ready to certify to the cause of death, and that the end was certain. He was a good little man, and he offered to remain with us; but Strickland refused the kindness. He did not wish to poison Dumoise's New Year. He would only ask him not to give the real cause of Fleete's death to the public.

So Dumoise left, deeply agitated; and as soon as the noise of the cart wheels had died away, Strickland told me, in a whisper, his suspicions. They were so wildly improbable that he dared not say them out aloud; and I, who entertained all Strickland's beliefs, was so ashamed of owning to them that I pretended to disbelieve.

"Even if the Silver Man had bewitched Fleete for polluting the image of Hanuman, the punishment could not have fallen so quickly."

As I was whispering this the cry outside the house rose again, and the beast fell into a fresh paroxysm of struggling till we were afraid that the thongs that held it would give way.

"Watch!" said Strickland. "If this happens six times I shall take the law into my own hands. I order you to help me."

He went into his room and came out in a few minutes with the barrels of an old shot-gun, a piece of fishing-line, some thick cord, and his heavy wooden bedstead. I reported that the convulsions had followed the cry by two seconds in each case, and the beast seemed perceptibly weaker.

Strickland muttered, "But he can't take away the life! He can't take away the life!"

I said, though I knew that I was arguing against myself, "It may be a cat. It must be a cat. If the Silver Man is responsible, why does he dare to come here?"

Strickland arranged the wood on the hearth, put the gun-barrels into the glow of the fire, spread the twine on the table and broke a walking stick in two. There was one yard of fishing line, gut, lapped with wire, such as is used for *mahseer-fishing*, and he tied the two ends together in a loop.

Then he said, "How can we catch him? He must be taken alive and unhurt."

I said that we must trust in Providence, and go out softly with polo-sticks into the shrubbery at the front of the house. The man or animal that made the cry was evidently moving round the house as regularly as a night-watchman. We could wait in the bushes till he came by and knock him over.

Strickland accepted this suggestion, and we slipped out from a bath-room window into the front veranda and then across the carriage drive into the bushes. In the moonlight we could see the leper coming round the corner of the house. He was perfectly naked, and from time to time he mewed and stopped to dance with his shadow. It was an unattractive sight, and thinking of poor Fleete, brought to such degradation by so foul a creature, I put away all my doubts and resolved to help Strickland from the heated gun-barrels to the loop of

twine—from the loins to the head and back again—with all tortures that might be needful.

The leper halted in the front porch for a moment and we jumped out on him with the sticks. He was wonderfully strong, and we were afraid that he might escape or be fatally injured before we caught him. We had an idea that lepers were frail creatures, but this proved to be incorrect. Strickland knocked his legs from under him and I put my foot on his neck. He mewed hideously, and even through my riding-boots I could feel that his flesh was not the flesh of a clean man.

He struck at us with his hand and feet-stumps. We looped the lash of a dog-whip round him, under the armpits, and dragged him backward into the hall and so into the dining-room where the beast lay. There we tied him with trunkstraps. He made no attempt to escape, but mewed.

When we confronted him with the beast the scene was beyond description. The beast doubled backward into a bow as though he had been poisoned with strychnine, and moaned in the most pitiable fashion. Several other things happened also, but they cannot be put down here.

"I think I was right," said Strickland. "Now we will ask him to cure this case."

But the leper only mewed. Strickland wrapped a towel round his hand and took the gun-barrels out of the fire. I put the half of the broken walking stick through the loop of the fishing-line and buckled the leper comfortably to Strickland's bedstead. I understood then how men and women and little children can endure to see a witch burned alive; for the beast was moaning on the floor, and though the Silver Man had no face, you could see horrible feelings passing through the slab that took its place, exactly as waves of heat play across red-hot iron—gun-barrels for instance.

Strickland shaded his eyes with his hands for a moment and we got to work. This part is not to be printed.

* * * * *

The dawn was beginning to break when the leper spoke. His mewings had not been satisfactory up to that point. The beast had fainted from exhaustion and the house was very still. We unstrapped the leper and told him to take away the evil spirit. He crawled to the beast and laid his hand upon the left breast. That was all. Then he fell face down and whined, drawing in his breath as he did so.

We watched the face of the beast, and saw the soul of Fleete coming back into the eyes. Then a sweat broke out on the forehead and the eyes—they were human eyes—closed. We waited for an hour but Fleete still slept. We carried him to his room and bade the leper go, giving him the bedstead, and the sheet on the bedstead to cover his nakedness, the gloves and the towels with which we had touched him, and the whip that had been hooked round his body. He put the sheet about him and went out into the early morning without speaking or mewing.

Strickland wiped his face and sat down. A night-gong, far away in the city, made seven o'clock.

"Exactly four-and-twenty hours!"

said Strickland. "And I've done enough to ensure my dismissal from the service, besides permanent quarters in a lunatic asylum. Do you believe that we are awake?"

The red-hot gun-barrel had fallen on the floor and was singeing the carpet. The smell was entirely real.

That morning at eleven we two together went to wake up Fleete. We looked and saw that the black leopard-rosette on his chest had disappeared. He was very drowsy and tired, but as soon as he saw us, he said, "Oh! Confound you fellows. Happy New Year to you. Never mix your liquors. I'm nearly dead."

"Thanks for your kindness, but you're over time," said Strickland. "To-day is the morning of the second. You've slept the clock round with a vengeance."

The door opened, and little Dumoise put his head in. He had come on foot, and fancied that we were laying out Fleete.

"I've brought a nurse," said Dumoise. "I suppose that she can come in for . . . what is necessary."

"By all means," said Fleete, cheerily, sitting up in bed. "Bring on your nurses."

Dumoise was dumb. Strickland led him out and explained that there must have been a mistake in the diagnosis. Dumoise remained dumb and left the house hastily. He considered that his professional reputation had been injured, and was inclined to make a personal matter of the recovery. Strickland went out too. When he came back, he said that he had been to call on the Temple of Hanuman to offer redress for the pollution of the god, and had been solemnly assured that no white man had ever touched the idol and that he was an incarnation of all the virtues laboring under a delusion. "What do you think?" said Strickland.

"I said, "There are more things. . . .'"

But Strickland hates that quotation. He says that I have worn it threadbare.

One other curious thing happened which frightened me as much as anything in all the night's work. When Fleete was dressed he came into the dining-room and sniffed. He had a quaint trick of moving his nose when he sniffed. "Horrid doggy smell, here," said he. "You should really keep those terriers of yours in better order. Try sulphur, Strick."

But Strickland did not answer. He caught hold of the back of a chair, and, without warning, went into an amazing fit of hysterics. It is terrible to see a strong man overtaken with hysteria. Then it struck me that we had fought with Fleete's soul with the Silver Man in that room, and had disgraced ourselves as Englishmen forever, and I laughed and gasped and gurgled just as shamefully as Strickland, while Fleete thought that we had both gone mad. We never told him what we had done.

Some years later, when Strickland had married and was a church-going member of society for his wife's sake, we reviewed the incident dispassionately, and Strickland suggested that I should put it before the public.

I cannot myself see that this step is likely to clear up the mystery; because, in the first place, no one will believe a rather unpleasant story, and, in the second, it is well known to every right-minded man that the gods of the heathen are stone and brass, and any attempt to deal with them otherwise is justly condemned.

The Head of the District

There's a convict more in the Central Jail,
  Behind the old mud wall;
There's a lifter less on the Border trail,
And the Queen's Peace over all,
          Dear boys,
    The Queen's Peace over all.

For we must bear our leader's blame,
  On us the shame will fall,
If we lift our hand from a fettered land
  And the Queen's Peace over all,
          Dear boys,
    The Queen's Peace over all!
  —*The Running of Shindand.*

I

THE Indus had risen in flood without warning. Last night it was a fordable shallow; to-night five miles of raving muddy water parted bank and caving bank, and the river was still rising under the moon. A litter borne by six bearded men, all unused to the work, stopped in the white sand that bordered the whiter plain.

"It's God's will," they said. "We

dare not cross to-night, even in a boat. Let us light a fire and cook food. We be tired men."

They looked at the litter inquiringly. Within, the Deputy Commissioner of the Kot-Kumharsen district lay dying of fever. They had brought him across country, six fighting-men of a frontier clan that he had won over to the paths of a moderate righteousness, when he had broken down at the foot of their inhospitable hills. And Tallantire, his assistant, rode with them, heavy-hearted as heavy-eyed with sorrow and lack of sleep. He had served under the sick man for three years, and had learned to love him as men associated in toil of the hardest learn to love—or hate. Dropping from his horse he parted the curtains of the litter and peered inside. "Orde—Orde, old man, can you hear? We have to wait till the river goes down, worse luck."

"I hear," returned a dry whisper. "Wait till the river goes down. I thought we should reach camp before the dawn. Polly knows. She'll meet me."

One of the litter-men stared across the river and caught a faint twinkle of light on the far side. He whispered to Tallantire, "There are his camp-fires, and his wife. They will cross in the morning, for they have better boats. Can he live so long?"

Tallantire shook his head. Yardley-Orde was very near to death. What need to vex his soul with hopes of a meeting that could not be? The river gulped at the banks, brought down a cliff of sand, and snarled the more hungrily. The litter-men sought for fuel in the waste— dried camel-thorn and refuse of the camps that had waited at the ford. Their sword-belts clinked as they moved softly in the haze of the moonlight, and Tallantire's horse coughed to explain that he would like like a blanket.

"I'm cold too," said the voice from the litter. "I fancy this is the end. Poor Polly!"

Tallantire rearranged the blankets; Khoda Dad Khan, seeing this, stripped off his own heavywadded sheepskin coat and added it to the pile. "I shall be warm by the fire presently," said he. Tallantire took the wasted body of his chief into his arms and held it against his breast. Perhaps if they kept him very warm Orde might live to see his wife once more. If only blind Providence would send a three-foot fall in the river!

"That's better," said Orde, faintly. "Sorry to be a nuisance, but is—is there anything to drink?"

They gave him milk and whisky, and Tallantire felt a little warmth against his own breast. Orde began to mutter.

"It isn't that I mind dying," he said. "It's leaving Polly and the district. Thank God! we have no children. Dick, you know, I'm dipped—awfully dipped —debts in my first five years' service. It isn't much of a pension, but enough for her. She has her mother at home. Getting there is the difficulty. And— and—you see, not being a soldier's wife"—

"We'll arrange the passage home, of course," said Tallantire, quietly.

"It's not nice to think of sending round the hat; but, good Lord! how many men I lie here and remember that had to do it! Morten's dead—he was of my year. Shaughnessy is dead, and he had children; I remember he used to read us their school-letters; what a bore we thought him! Evans is dead—Kot-Kumharsen killed him! Rickett's of Myndonie is dead—and I'm going too. 'Man that is born of woman is small potatoes and few in the hill.' That reminds me, Dick; the four Khusru Kheyl villages in our border want a one-third remittance this spring. That's fair; their crops are bad. See that they get it, and speak to Ferris about the canal. I should like to have lived till that was finished; it means so much for the North-Indus villages—but Ferris is an idle beggar—wake him up. You'll have charge of the district till my successor comes. I wish they would appoint you permanently; you know the folk. I suppose it will be Bullows, though. 'Good man, but too weak for frontier work; and he doesn't understand the priests. The blind priest at Jagai will bear watching. You'll find it in my papers,—in the uniform-case, I think. Call the Khusru Kheyl men up; I'll hold my last public audience. Khoda Dad Khan!"

The leader of the men sprang to the side of the litter, his companions following.

"Men, I'm dying," said Orde, quickly, in the vernacular; "and soon there will be no more Orde Sahib to twist your tails and prevent you from raiding cattle."

"God forbid this thing!" broke out the deep bass chorus. "The Sahib is not going to die."

"Yes, he is; and then he will know whether Mahomed speaks truth, or Moses. But you must be good men, when I am not here. Such of you as

live in our borders must pay your taxes quietly as before. I have spoken of the villages to be gently treated this year. Such of you as live in the hills must refrain from cattle-lifting, and burn no more thatch, and turn a deaf ear to the voice of the priests, who, not knowing the strength of the Government, would lead you into foolish wars, wherein you will surely die and your crops be eaten by strangers. And you must not sack any caravans, and must leave your arms at the police-post when you come in; as has been your custom, and my order. And Tallantire Sahib will be with you, but I do not know who takes my place. I speak now true talk, for I am as it were already dead, my children,—for though ye be strong men, ye are children."

"And thou art our father and our mother," broke in Khoda Dad Khan with an oath. "What shall we do, now there is no one to speak for us, or to teach us to go wisely!"

"There remains Tallantire Sahib. Go to him; he knows your talk and your heart. Keep the young men quiet, listen to the old men, and obey. Khoda Dad Khan, take my ring. The watch and chain go to thy brother. Keep those things for my sake, and I will speak to whatever God I may encounter and tell him that the Khusru Kheyl are good men. Ye have my leave to go."

Khoda Dad Khan, the ring upon his finger, choked audibly as he caught the well-known formula that closed an interview. His brother turned to look across the river. The dawn was breaking, and a speck of white showed on the dull silver of the stream. "She comes," said the man under his breath. "Can he live for another two hours?" And he pulled the newly-acquired watch out of his belt and looked uncomprehendingly at the dial, as he had seen Englishmen do.

For two hours the bellying sail tacked and blundered up and down the river, Tallantire still clasping Orde in his arms, and Khoda Dad Khan chafing his feet. He spoke now and again of the district, and his wife, but, as the end neared, more frequently of the latter. They hoped he did not know that she was even then risking her life in a crazy native boat to regain him. But the awful foreknowledge of the dying deceived them. Wrenching himself forward, Orde looked through the curtains and saw how near was the sail. "That's Polly," said he, simply, though his mouth was wried with agony. "Polly and—the grimmest practical joke ever played on a man. Dick—you'll—have—to—explain."

And an hour later Tallantire met on the bank a woman in a gingham riding-habit and a sun-hat who cried out to him for her husband—her boy and her darling—while Khoda Dad Khan threw himself face-down on the sand and covered his eyes.

II

THE very simplicity of the notion was its charm. What more easy to win a reputation for far-seeing statesmanship, originality, and, above all, deference to the desires of the people, than by appointing a child of the country to the rule of that country? Two hundred millions of the most loving and grateful folk under Her Majesty's dominion would laud the fact, and their praise would endure forever. Yet he was indifferent to praise or blame, as befitted the Very Greatest of All the Viceroys. His administration was based upon principle, and the principle must be enforced in season and out of season. His pen and tongue had created the New India, teeming with possibilities—loud-voiced, insistent, a nation among nations—all his very own. Wherefore the Very Greatest of All the Viceroys took another step in advance, and with it counsel of those who should have advised him on the appointment of a successor to Yardley-Orde. There was a gentleman and a member of the Bengal Civil Service who had won his place and a university degree to boot in fair and open competition with the sons of the English. He was cultured, of the world, and, if report spoke truly, had wisely and, above all, sympathetically ruled a crowded district in Southeastern Bengal. He had been to England and charmed many drawingrooms there. His name, if the Viceroy recollected aright, was Mr. Grish Chunder Dé, M. A. In short, did anybody see any objection to the appointment, always on principle, of a man of the people to rule the people? The district in Southeastern Bengal might with advantage, he apprehended, pass over to a younger civilian of Mr. G. C. Dé's nationality (who had written a remarkably clever pamphlet on the political value of sympathy in administration); and Mr. G. C. Dé could be transferred northward to Kot-Kumharsen. The Viceroy was averse, on principle, to interfering with appointments under control of the Provincial Governments. He wished it to be understood that he merely recommended and advised in this instance. As regarded the mere question of race, Mr. Grish Chunder Dé was more English than the English, and yet possessed of that peculiar sympathy and insight which the best among the best Service in the world could only win to at the end of their service.

The stern, black-bearded kings who sit about the Council-board of India divided on the step,•with the inevitable result of driving the Very Greatest of All the Viceroys into the borders of hysteria, and a bewildered obstinacy pathetic as that of a child.

"The principle is sound enough," said the weary-eyed Head of the Red Provinces in which Kot-Kumharsen lay, for he too held theories. "The only difficulty is"—

"Put the screw on the District officials; brigade Dé with a very strong Deputy Commissioner on each side of him; give him the best assistant in the Province; rub the fear of God into the people beforehand; and if anything goes wrong, say that his colleagues didn't back him up. All these lovely little experiments recoil on the District-Officer in the end," said the Knight of the Drawn Sword with a truthful brutality that made the Head of the Red Provinces shudder. And on a tacit understanding of this kind the transfer was accomplished, as quietly as might be for many reasons.

It is sad to think that what goes for public opinion in India did not generally see the wisdom of the Viceroy's appointment. There were not lacking indeed hireling organs, notoriously in the pay of a tyrannous bureaucracy, who

more than hinted that His Excellency was a fool, a dreamer of dreams, a doctrinaire, and, worst of all, a trifler with the lives of men. "The Viceroy's Excellence Gazette," published in Calcutta, was at pains to thank "Our beloved Viceroy for once more and again thus gloriously vindicating the potentialities of the Bengali nations for extended executive and administrative duties in foreign parts beyond our ken. We do not at all doubt that our excellent fellow-townsman, Mr. Grish Chunder Dé, Esq., M. A., will uphold the prestige of the Bengali, notwithstanding what underhand intrigue and *peshbundi* may be set on foot to insidiously nip his fame and blast his prospects among the proud civilians, some of which will now have to serve under a despised native and take orders too. How will you like that, Misters? We entreat our beloved Viceroy still to substantiate himself superiorly to race-prejudice and color-blindness, and to allow the flower of this now *our* Civil Service all the full pays and allowances granted to his more fortunate brethren."

III

"WHEN does this man take over charge? I'm alone just now, and I gather that I'm to stand fast under him."

"Would you have cared for a transfer?" said Bullows, keenly. Then, laying his hand on Tallantire's shoulder: "We're all in the same boat; don't desert us. And yet, why the devil should you stay, if you can get another charge?"

"It was Orde's," said Tallantire, simply.

"Well, it's Dé's now. He's a Bengali of the Bengalis, crammed with code and case law; a beautiful man so far as routine and guesswork go, and pleasant to talk to. They naturally have always kept him in his own home district, where all his sisters and his cousins and his aunts lived, somewhere south of Dacca. He did no more than turn the place into a pleasant little family preserve, allowed his subordinates to do what they liked, and let everybody have a chance at the shekels. Consequently he's immensely popular down there."

"I've nothing to do with that. How on earth am I to explain to the district that they are going to be governed by a Bengali? Do you—does the Government, I mean—suppose that the Khusru Kheyl will sit quiet when they once know? What will the Mahommed heads of villages say? How will the police —Muzbi Sikhs and Pathans—how will *they* work under him? We couldn't say anything if the Government appointed a sweeper; but my people will say a good deal, you know that. It's a piece of cruel folly!"

"My dear boy, I know all that, and more. I've represented it, and have been told that I am exhibiting 'culpable and puerile prejudice.' By Jove, if the Khusru Kheyl don't exhibit something worse than that I don't know the Border! The chances are that you will have the district alight on your hands, and I shall have to leave my work and help you pull through. I needn't ask you to stand by the Bengali man in every possible way. You'll do that for your own sake."

"For Orde's. I can't say that I care two pence personally."

"Don't be an ass. It's grievous enough, God knows, and the Government will know later on; but that's no reason for your sulking. *You* must try to run the district; *you* must stand between him and as much insult as possible; *you* must show him the rope; *you* must pacify the Khusru Kheyl, and just warn Curbar of the Police to look out for trouble by the way. I'm always at the end of a telegraph-wire, and willing to peril my reputation to hold the district together. You'll lose yours, of course. If you keep things straight, and he isn't actually beaten with a stick when he's on tour, he'll get all the credit. If anything goes wrong, you'll be told that you didn't support him loyally."

"I know what I've got to do," said Tallantire, wearily, "and I'm going to do it. But it's hard."

"The work is with us, the event is with Allah—as Orde used to say when he was more than usually in hot water." And Bullows rode away.

That two gentlemen in Her Majesty's Bengal Civil Service should thus discuss a third, also in that service, and a cultured and affable man withal, seems strange and saddening. Yet listen to the artless babble of the Blind Mullah of Jagai, the priest of the Khusru Kheyl, sitting upon a rock overlooking the Border. Five years before, a chance-hurled shell from a screw-gun battery had dashed earth in the face of the Mullah, then urging a rush of Ghazis against half a dozen British bayonets. So he became blind, and hated the English none the less for the little accident. Yardley-Orde knew his failing, and had many times laughed at him therefore.

"Dogs you are," said the Blind Mullah to the listening tribesmen round the fire. "Whipped dogs! Because you listened to Orde Sahib and called him father and behaved as his children, the British Government have proven how they regard you. Orde Sahib ye know is dead."

"Ai! ai! ai!" said half a dozen voices.

"He was a man. Comes now in his stead, whom think ye? A Bengali of Bengal—an eater of fish from the South."

"A lie!" said Khoda Dad Khan. "And but for the small matter of thy priesthood, I'd drive my gun butt-first down thy throat."

"Oho, art thou there, lickspittle of the English? Go in to-morrow across the Border to pay service to Orde Sahib's successor, and thou shalt slip thy shoes at the tent-door of a Bengali, as thou shalt hand thy offering to a Bengali's black fist. This I know; and in my youth, when a young man spoke evil to a Mullah holding the doors of Heaven and Hell, the gun-butt was not rammed down the Mullah's gullet. No!"

The Blind Mullah hated Khoda Dad Khan with Afghan hatred; both being rivals for the headship of the tribe; but the latter was feared for bodily as the other for spiritual gifts. Khoda Dad Khan looked at Orde's ring and grunted: "I go in to-morrow because I am not an old fool, preaching war against the English. If the Government, smitten with madness, have done this, then . . ."

"Then," croaked the Mullah, "thou wilt take out the young men and strike at the four villages within the Border?"

"Or wring thy neck, black raven of Jehannum, for a bearer of ill-tidings."

Khoda Dad Khan oiled his long locks with great care, put on his best Bokhara belt, a new turban cap and fine green shoes, and accompanied by a few friends came down from the hills to pay a visit to the new Deputy Commissioner of Kot-Kumharsen. Also he bore tribute—four or five priceless gold mohurs of Akbar's time in a white handkerchief. These the Deputy Commissioner would touch and remit. The little ceremony used to be a sign that, so far as Khoda Dad Khan's personal influence went, the Khusru Kheyl would be good boys,—till the next time; especially if Khoda Dad Khan happened to like the new Deputy Commissioner. In Yardley-Orde's counsulship his visit concluded with a sumptuous dinner and perhaps forbidden liquors; certainly with some wonderful tales and great goodfellowship. Then Khoda Dad Khan would swagger back to his hold, vowing that Orde Sahib was one prince and Tallantire Sahib another, and that whosoever went a-raiding into British territory would be flayed alive. On this occasion he found the Deputy Commissioner's tents looking much as usual. Regarding himself as privileged he strode through the open door to confront a suave, portly Bengali in English costume writing at a table. Unversed in the elevating influence of education, and not in the least caring for university degrees, Khoda Dad Khan promptly set the man down for a Babu—the native clerk of the Deputy Commissioner —a hated an despised animal.

"Ugh!" said he, cheerfully. "Where's your master, Babujee?"

"I am the Deputy Commissioner," said the gentleman in English.

Now he overvalued the effects of university degrees, and stared Khoda Dad Khan in the face. But if from your earliest infancy you have been accustomed to look on battle, murder, and sudden death, if spilt blood affects your nerves as much as red paint, and, above all, if you have faithfully believed that the Bengali was the servant of all Hindustan, and that all Hindustan was vastly inferior to your own large, lustful self, you can endure, even though uneducated, a very large amount of looking over. You can even stare down a graduate of an Oxford college if the latter has been born in a hothouse, of stock bred in a hothouse, and fearing physical pain as some men fear sin; especially if your opponent's mother has frightened him to sleep in his youth with horrible stories of devils inhabitating Afghanistan, and dismal legends of the black North. The eyes behind the gold spectacles sought the flood. Khoda Dad Khan chuckled, and swung out to find Tallantire hard by. "Here," said he, roughly, thrusting the coins before him, "touch and remit. That answers for *my* good behavior. But, O Sahib, has the Government gone mad to send a black Bengali dog to us? And am I to pay service to such an one? And are you to work under him? What does it mean?"

"It is an order," said Tallantire. He had expected something of this kind. "He is a very clever S-sahib."

"He a Sahib! He's a *kala admi*—a black man—unfit to run at the tail of a potter's donkey. All the peoples of the earth have harried Bengal. It is

written. Thou knowest when we of the North wanted women or plunder whither went we? To Bengal—where else? What child's talk is this of Sahibdom— after Orde Sahib too! Of a truth the Blind Mullah was right."

"What of him?" asked Tallantire, uneasily. He mistrusted that old man with his dead eyes and his deadly tongue.

"Nay, now, because of the oath that I sware to Orde Sahib when we watched him die by the river yonder, I will tell. In the first place, is it true that the English have set the heel of the Bengali on their own neck, and that there is no more English rule in the land?"

"I am here," said Tallantire, "and I serve the Maharanee of England."

"The Mullah said otherwise, and further that because we loved Orde Sahib the Government sent us a pig to show that we were dogs, who till now have been held by the strong hand. Also that they were taking away the white soldiers, that more Hindustanis might come, and that all was changing."

This is the worst of ill-considered handling of a very large country. What looks so feasible in Calcutta, so right in Bombay, so unassailable in Madras, is misunderstood by the North and entirely changes its complexion on the banks of the Indus. Khoda Dad Khan explained as clearly as he could that, though he himself intended to be good, he really could not answer for the more reckless members of his tribe under the leadership of the Blind Mullah. They might or they might not give trouble, but they certainly had no intention whatever of obeying the new Deputy Commissioner. Was Tallantire perfectly sure that in the event of any systematic border-raiding the force in the district could put it down promptly?

"Tell the Mullah if he talks any more fool's talk," said Tallantire, curtly, "that he takes his men on to certain death, and his tribe to blockade, trespass-fine, and blood-money. But why do I talk to one who no longer carries weight in the counsels of the tribe?"

Khoda Dad Khan pocketed that insult. He had learned something that he much wanted to know and returned to his hills to be sarcastically complimented by the Mullah, whose tongue raging round the camp-fires was deadlier flame than ever dung-cake fed.

IV

BE pleased to consider here for a moment the unknown district of Kot-Kumharsen. It lay cut lengthways by the Indus under the line of the Khursu hills—ramparts of useless earth and tumbled stone. It was seventy miles long by fifty broad, maintained a population of something less than two hundred thousand, and paid taxes to the extent of forty thousand pounds a year on an area that was by rather more than half sheer, hopeless waste. The cultivators were not gentle people, the miners for salt were less gentle still, and the cattle-breeders least gentle of all. A police-post in the top right-hand corner and a tiny mud fort in the top left-hand corner prevented as much salt-smuggling and cattle-lifting as the influence of the civilians could not put down; and in the bottom right-hand corner lay Jumala, the district head-quarters—a pitiful knot of lime-washed

barns facetiously rented as houses, reeking with frontier fever, leaking in the rain, and ovens in the summer.

It was to this place that Grish Chunder Dé was traveling, there formally to take over charge of the district. But the news of his coming had gone before. Bengalis were as scarce as poodles among the simple Borderers, who cut each other's heads open with their long spades and worshipped impartially at Hindu and Mahommedan shrines. They crowded to see him, pointing at him, and diversely comparing him tó a gravid milch-buffalo, or a broken-down horse, as their limited range of metaphor prompted. They laughed at his police-guard, and wished to know how long the burly Sikhs were going to lead Bengali apes. They inquired whether he had brought his women with him, and advised him explicitly not to tamper with theirs. It remained for a wrinkled hag by the roadside to slap her lean breasts as he passed, crying, "I have suckled six that could have eaten six thousand of *him*. The Government shot them, and made this That a king!" Whereat a blue-turbaned huge-boned plough-mender shouted, "Have hope, mother o' mine! He may yet go the way of thy wastrels." And the children, the little brown puff-balls, regarded curiously. It was generally a good thing for infancy to stray into Orde Sahib's tent, where copper coins were to be won for the mere wishing, and tales of the most authentic, such as even their mothers knew but the first half of. No! This fat black man could never tell them how Pir Prith hauled the eye-teeth out of ten devils; how the big stones came to lie all in a row on top of the Khusru hills, and what happened if you shouted through the village-gate to the grey wolf at even "Badl Khas is dead." Meantime Grish Chunder Dé talked hastily and much to Tallantire, after the manner of those who are "more English than the English,"—of Oxford and "home," with much curious book-knowledge of bump-suppers, cricket-matches, hunting-runs, and other unholy sports of the alien. "We must get these fellows in hand," he said once or twice, uneasily; "get them well in hand, and drive them on a tight rein. No use, you know, being slack with your district."

And a moment later Tallantire heard Debendra Nath Dé, who brotherliwise had followed his kinsman's fortune and hoped for the shadow of his protection as a pleader, whisper in Bengali, "Better are dried fish at Dacca than drawn swords at Delhi. Brother of mine, these men are devils, as our mother said. And you will always have to ride upon a horse!"

That night there was a public audience in a broken-down little town thirty miles from Jumala, when the new Deputy Commissioner, in reply to the greetings of the subordinate native officials, delivered a speech. It was a carefully thought-out speech, which would have been very valuable had not his third sentence begun with three innocent words, "*Hamara hookum hai*—It is my order." Then there was a laugh, clear and bell-like, from the back of the big tent, where a few Border landholders sat, and the laugh grew and scorn mingled with it, and the lean, keen face of Debendra Nath Dé paled, and Grish Chunder turning to Tallantire spake:

"*You*—you put up this arrangement." Upon that instant the noise of hoofs rang without, and there entered Curbar, the District Superintendent of Police, sweating and dusty. The State had tossed him into a corner of the province for seventeen weary years, there to check smuggling of salt, and to hope for promotion that never came. He had forgotten how to keep his white uniform clean, had screwed rusty spurs into patent-leather shoes, and clothed his head indifferently with a helmet or a turban. Soured, old, worn with heat and cold, he waited till he should be entitled to sufficient pension to keep him from starving.

"Tallantire," said he, disregarding Grish Chunder Dé, "come outside. I want to speak to you." They withdrew. "It's this," continued Curbar. "The Khusru Kheyl have rushed and cut up half a dozen of the coolies on Ferris's new canal-embankment; killed a couple of men and carried off a woman. I wouldn't trouble you about that—Ferris is after them and Hugonin, my assistant, with ten mounted police. But that's only the beginning, I fancy. Their fires are out on the Hassan Ardeb heights, and unless we're pretty quick there'll be a flare-up all along our Border. They are sure to raid the four Khusru villages on our side of the line; there's been bad blood between them for years; and you know the Blind Mullah has been preaching a holy war since Orde went out. What's your notion?"

"Damn!" said Tallantire, thoughtfully. "They've begun quick. Well, it seems to me I'd better ride off to Fort Ziar and get what men I can there to picket among the lowland villages, if it's not too late. Tommy Dodd commands at Fort Ziar, I think. Ferris and Hugonin ought to teach the canal-thieves a lesson, and— No, we can't have the Head of the Police ostentatiously guarding the Treasury. You go back to the canal. I'll wire Bullows to come into Jumala with a strong police-guard, and sit on the Treasury. They won't touch the place, but it looks well."

"I—I—I insist upon knowing what this means," said the voice of the Deputy Commissioner, who had followed the speakers.

"Oh!" said Curbar, who being in the Police cound not understand that fifteen years of education, must, on principle, change the Bengali into a Briton. "There has been a fight on the Border, and heaps of men are killed. There's going to be another fight, and heaps more will be killed."

"What for?"

"Because the teeming millions of this district don't exactly approve of you, and think that under your benign rule they are going to have a good time. It strikes me that you had better make arrangements. I act, as you know, by your orders. What do you advise?"

"I—I take you all to witness that I have not yet assumed charge of the district," stammered the Deputy Commissioner, not in the tones of the "more English."

"Ah, I thought so. Well, as I was saying, Tallantire, your plan is sound. Carry it out. Do you want an escort?"

"No; only a decent horse. But how about wiring to headquarters?"

"I fancy, from the color of his cheeks, that your superior officers will send some wonderful telegrams before the night's over. Let him do that, and we shall have half the troops of the province coming up to see what's the trouble. Well, run along, and take care of yourself—the Khusru Kheyl jab upward from below, remember. Ho! Mir Khan, give Tallantire Sahib the best of the horses, and tell five men to ride to Jumala with the Deputy Commissioner Sahib Bahadur. There is a hurry toward."

There was; and it was not in the least bettered by Debendra Nath Dé clinging to a policeman's bridle and demanding the shortest, the very shortest way to Jumala. Now originality is fatal to the Bengali. Debendra Nath should have stayed with his brother, who rode steadfastly for Jumala on the railway-line, thanking gods entirely unknown to the most catholic of universities that he had not taken charge of the district, and could still—happy resource of a fertile race!—fall sick.

And I grieve to say that when he reached his goal two policemen, not devoid of rude wit, who had been conferring together as they bumped in their saddles, arranged an entertainment for his behoof. It consisted of first one and then the other entering his room with prodigious details of war, the massing of bloodthirsty and devilish tribes, and the burning of towns. It was almost as good, said these scamps, as riding with Curbar after evasive Afghans. Each invention kept the hearer at work for half an hour on telegrams which the sack of Delhi would hardly have justified. To every power that could move a bayonet or transfer a terrified man, Grish Chunder Dé appealed telegraphically. He was alone, his assistants had fled, and in truth he had not taken over charge of the district. Had the telegrams been despatched many things would have occurred; but since the only signaller in Jumala had gone to bed, and the station-master, after one look at the tremendous pile of paper, discovered that railway regulations forbade the forwarding of imperial messages, Policeman Ram Singh and Nihal Singh were fain to turn the stuff into a pillow and slept on it very comfortably.

Tallantire drove his spurs into a rampant skew-bald stallion with china-blue eyes, and settled himself for the forty-mile ride to Fort Ziar. Knowing his district blindfold, he wasted no time hunting for short cuts, but headed across the richer grazing-ground to the ford where Orde had died and been buried. The dusty ground deadened the noise of his horse's hoofs, the moon threw his shadow, a restless goblin, before him, and the heavy dew drenched him to the skin. Hillock, scrub that brushed against the horse's belly, unmetalled road where the whip-like foliage of the tamarisks lashed his forehead, illimitable levels of lowland furred with bent and speckled and drowsing cattle, waste, and hillock anew, dragged themselves past, and the skew-bald was laboring in the deep sand of the Indusford. Tallantire was conscious of no distinct thought till the nose of the dawdling ferry-boat grounded on the farther side, and his horse shied snorting at the white headstone of Orde's grave. Then he uncovered, and shouted that the dead might hear, "They're out, old man! Wish me luck." In the chill of the dawn he was hammering with a stirrup-iron at the gate of Fort Ziar,

where fifty sabres of that tattered regiment, the Belooch Beshaklis were supposed to guard Her Majesty's interests along a few hundred miles of Border. This particular fort was commanded by a subaltern, who, born of the ancient family of the Derouletts, naturally answered to the name of Tommy Dodd. Him Tallantire found robed in a sheepskin coat, shaking with fever like an aspen, and trying to read the native apothecary's list of invalids.

"So you've come, too," said he. "Well, we're all sick here, and I don't think I can horse thirty men; but we're bub—bub—bub blessed willing. Stop, does this impress you as a trap or a lie?" He tossed a scrap of paper to Tallantire, on which was written painfully in crabbed Gurmukhi, "We cannot hold young horses. They will feed after the moon goes down in the four Border villages issuing from the Jagai pass on the next night." Then in English round hand—"Your sincere friend."

"Good man!" said Tallantire. "That's Khoda Dad Khan's work, I know. It's the only piece of English he could ever keep in his head, and he is immensely proud of it. He is playing against the Blind Mullah for his own hand—the treacherous young ruffian!"

"Don't know the politics of the Khusru Kheyl, but if you're satisfied, I am. That was pitched in over the gatehead last night, and I thought we might pull ourselves together and see what was on. Oh, but we're sick with fever here and no mistake! Is this going to be a big business, think you?" said Tommy Dodd.

Tallantire gave him briefly the outlines of the case, and Tommy Dodd whistled and shook with fever alternately. That day he devoted to strategy, the art of war, and the enlivenment of the invalids, till at dusk there stood ready forty-two troopers, lean, worn, and disheveled, whom Tommy Dodd surveyed with pride, and addressed thus: "O men! If you die you will go to Hell. Therefore endeavor to keep alive. But if you go to Hell that place cannot be hotter than this place, and we are not told that we shall there suffer from fever. Consequently be not afraid of dying. File out there!" They grinned, and went.

V

IT will be long ere the Khusru Kheyl forget their night attack on the lowland villages. The Mullah had promised an easy victory and unlimited plunder; but behold, armed troopers of the Queen had risen out of the very earth, cutting, slashing, and riding down under the stars, so that no man knew where to turn, and all feared that they had brought an army about their ears, and ran back to the hills. In the panic of that flight more men were seen to drop from wounds inflicted by an Afghan knife jabbed upward, and yet more from long-range carbine-fire. Then there rose a cry of treachery, and when they reached their own guarded heights, they had left, with some forty dead and sixty wounded, all their confidence in the Blind Mullah on the plains below. They clamored, swore, and argued round the fires; the women wailing for the lost, and the Mullah shrieking curses on the returned.

Then Khoda Dad Khan, eloquent and unbreathed, for he had taken no part in the fight, rose to improve the occasion. He pointed out that the tribe owed every item of its present misfortune to the Blind Mullah, who had lied in every possible particular and talked them into a trap. It was undoubtedly an insult that a Bengali, the son of a Bengali, should presume to administer the Border, but that fact did not, as the Mullah, pretended, herald a general time of license and lifting; and the inexplicable madness of the English had not in the least impaired their power of guarding their marches. On the contrary, the baffled and out-generaled tribe would now, just when their food-stock was lowest, be blockaded from any trade with Hindustan until they had sent hostages for good behavior, paid compensation for disturbance, and blood-money at the rate of thirty-six English pounds per head for every villager that they might have slain. "And ye know that those lowland dogs will make oath that we have slain scores. Will the Mullah pay the fines or must we sell our guns?" A low growl ran round the fires. "Now, seeing that all this is the Mullah's work, and that we have gained nothing but promises of Paradise thereby, it is in my heart that we of the Khusru Kheyl lack a shrine whereat to pray. We are weakened, and henceforth how shall we dare to cross into the Madar Kheyl border, as has been our custom, to kneel to Pir Saji's tomb? The Madar men will fall upon us, and rightly. But our Mullah is a holy man. He has helped two score of us into Paradise this night. Let him therefore accompany his flock, and we will build over his body a dome of the blue tiles of Mooltan, and burn lamps at his feet every Friday night.

He shall be a saint: we shall have a shrine; and there our women shall pray for fresh seed to fill the gaps in our fighting-tale. How think you?"

A grim chuckle followed the suggestion, and the soft *wheep, wheep,* of unscabbarded knives followed the chuckle. It was an excellent notion, and met a long felt want of the tribe. The Mullah sprang to his feet, glaring with withered eyeballs at the drawn death he could not see, and calling down the curses of God and Mahomed on the tribe. Then began a game of blind man's buff round and between the fires, whereof Khuruk Shah, the tribal poet, has sung in verse that will not die.

They tickled him gently under the armpit with the knife-point. He leaped aside screaming, only to feel a cold blade drawn lightly over the back of his neck, or a rifle-muzzle rubbing his beard. He called on his adherents to aid him, but most of these lay dead on the plains, for Khoda Dad Khan had been at some pains to arrange their decease. Men described to him the glories of the shrine they would build, and the little children clapping their hands cried, "Run, Mullah, run! There's a man behind you!" In the end, when the sport wearied, Khoda Dad Khan's brother sent a knife home between his ribs. "Wherefore," said Khoda Dad Khan with charming simplicity, "I am now Chief of the Khusru Kheyl!" No man gainsaid him; and they all went to sleep very stiff and sore.

On the plain below Tommy Dodd was lecturing on the beauties of a cavalry charge by night, and Tallantire, bowed on his saddle, was gasping hysterically because there was a sword dangling from his wrist flecked with the blood of the Khusru Kheyl, the tribe that Orde had kept in leash so well. When a Rajpoot trooper pointed out that the skewbald's right ear had been taken off at the root by some blind slash of its unskilled rider, Tallantire broke down altogether, and laughed and sobbed till Tommy Dodd made him lie down and rest.

"We must wait about till the morning," said he. I wired to the Colonel just before we left, to send a wing of the Beshaklis after us. He'll be furious with me for monopolizing the fun, though. Those beggars in the hills won't give us any more trouble."

"Then tell the Beshaklis to go on and see what has happened to Curbar on the canal. We must patrol the whole line of the Border. You're quite sure, Tommy, that—that stuff was—was only the skewbald's ear?"

"Oh, quite," said Tommy. "You just missed cutting off his head. *I* saw you when we went into the mess. Sleep, old man."

Noon brought two squadrons of Beshaklis and a knot of furious brother officers demanding the court-martial of Tommy Dodd for "spoiling the picnic," and a gallop across country to the canal-works where Ferris, Curbar, and Hugonin were haranguing the terror-stricken coolies on the enormity of abandoning good work and high pay, merely because half a dozen of their fellows had been cut down. The sight of a troop of the Beshaklis restored wavering confidence, and the police-hunted section of the Khusru Kheyl had the joy of watching the canal-bank humming with life as usual, while such of their men as had taken refuge in the water-courses and ravines were being driven out by the troopers. By sundown began the remorseless patrol of the Border by police and trooper, most like the cow-boys' eternal ride round restless cattle.

"Now," said Khoda Dad Khan to his fellows, pointing out a line of twinkling fires below, "ye may see how far the old order changes. After their horse will come the little devil-guns that they can drag up to the tops of the hills, and, for aught I know, to the clouds when we crown the hills. If the tribe-council thinks good, I will go to Tallantire Sahib—who loves me—and see if I can stave off at least the blockade. Do I speak for the tribe?"

"Ay, speak for the tribe in God's name. How those accursed fires wink! Do the English send their troops on the wire—or is this the work of the Bengali?"

As Khoda Dad Khan went down the hill he was delayed by an interview with a hard-pressed tribesman, which caused him to return hastily for something he had forgotten. Then, handing himself over to the two troopers who had been chasing his friend, he claimed escort to Tallantire Sahib, then with Bullows at Jumala. The Border was safe, and the time for reasons in writing had begun.

"Thank Heaven!" said Bullows, "that the trouble came at once. Of course we can never put down the reason in black and white, but all India will understand. And it is better to have a sharp short outbreak than five years of impotent administration inside the Border. It costs less. Grish Chunder Dé has reported himself sick, and has been transferred to his own province without any sort of reprimand. He was strong

on not having taken over the district."

"Of course," said Tallantire, bitterly. "Well, what am I supposed to have done that was wrong?"

"Oh, you will be told that you exceeded all your powers, and should have reported, and written, and advised for three weeks until the Khusru Kheyl could really come down in force. But I don't think the authorities will dare to make a fuss about it. They've had their lesson. Have you seen Curbar's version of the affair? He can't write a report, but he can speak the truth."

"What's the use of the truth? He'd much better tear up the report. I'm sick and heart-broken over it all. It was so utterly unnecessary—except in that it rid us of that Babu."

Entered unabashed Khoda Dad Khan, a stuffed forage-net in his hand, and the troopers behind him.

"May you never be tired!" said he, cheerily. "Well, Sahibs, that was a good fight, and Naim Shah's mother is in debt to you, Tallantire Sahib. A clean cut, they tell me, through jaw, wadded coat, and deep into the collar-bone. Well done! But I speak for the tribe. There has been a fault—a great fault. Thou knowest that I and mine Tallantire Sahib, kept the oath we sware to Orde Sahib on the banks of the Indus."

"As an Afghan keeps his knife—sharp on one side, blunt on the other," said Tallantire.

"The better swing in the blow, then. But I speak God's truth. Only the Blind Mullah carried the young men on the tip of his tongue, and said that there was no more Border-law because a Bengali had been sent, and we need not fear the English at all. So they came down to avenge that insult and get plunder. Ye know what befell, and how far I helped. Now five score of us are dead or wounded, and we are all shamed and sorry and desire no further war. Moreover, that ye may better listen to us, we have taken off the head of the Blind Mullah, whose evil counsels have led us to folly. I bring it for proof,"— and he heaved on the floor the head. "He will give no more trouble, for *I* am chief now, and so I sit in a higher place at all audiences. Yet there is an offset to this head. That was another fault. One of the men found that black Bengali beast, through whom this trouble arose, wandering on horseback and weeping. Reflecting that he had caused loss of much good life, Alla Dad Khan, whom, if you choose, I will to-morrow shoot, whipped off this head, and I bring it to you to cover your shame, that ye may bury it. See, no man kept the spectacles, though they were of gold."

Slowly rolled to Tallantire's feet the crop-haired head of a spectacled Bengali gentleman, open-eyed, open-mouthed —the head of Terror incarnate. Bullows bent down. "Yet another blood-fine and a heavy one, Khoda Dad Khan, for this is the head of Debendra Nath, the man's brother. The Babu is safe long since. All but the fools of the Khusru Kheyl know that."

"Well, I care not for carrion. Quick meat for me. The thing was under our hills asking the road to Jumala and Alla Dad Khan showed him the road to Jehannum, being, as thou sayest, but a fool. Remains now what the Government will do to us. As to the blockade"—

"Who art thou, seller of dog's flesh," thundered Tallantire, "to speak of terms and treaties? Get hence to the hills—go, and wait there starving, till it shall please the Government to call thy people out for punishment—children and fools that ye be! Count your dead, and be still. Rest assured that the Government will send you a *man!*"

"Ay," returned Khoda Dad Khan, "for we also be men."

As he looked Tallantire between the eyes, he added, "And by God, Sahib, may thou be that man!"

VOLUME VII

In Black and White

Introduction

BY KADIR BAKSH, KHITMATGAR

HAZUR,—Through your favor this is a book written by my sahib. I know that he wrote it, because it was his custom to write far into the night; I greatly desiring to go to my house. But there was no order; therefore it was my fate to sit without the door until the work was accomplished. Then came I and made shut all the papers in the office-box, and these papers, by the peculiar operation of Time and owing to the skilful manner in which I picked them up from the floor, became such a book as you now see. God alone knows what is written therein, for I am a poor man and the sahib is my father and my mother, and I have no concern with his writings until he has left his table and gone to bed.

Nabi Baksh, clerk, says that it is a book about the black men—common people. This is a manifest lie, for by what road can my sahib have acquired knowledge of common people? Have I not, for several years, been perpetually with the sahib; and throughout that time have I not stood between him and the other servants who would persecute him with complaints or vex him with idle tales about my work? Did I not smite Dunnoo, the groom, only yesterday in the matter of the badness of the harness-composition which I had procured? I am the head of the sahib's household and hold his purse. Without me he does not know where are his rupees or his clean collars. So great is my power over the sahib and the love that he bears to me! Have I ever told the sahib about the customs of servants or black men? Am I a fool? I have said "very good talk" upon all occasions. I have always cut smooth his wristbands with scissors, and timely warned him of the passing away of his tobacco that he might not be left smokeless upon a Sunday. More than this I have not done. The sahib cannot go out to dinner lacking my aid. How then should he know aught that I did not tell him? Certainly Nabi Baksh is a liar.

None the less this is a book, and the sahib wrote it, for his name is in it, and it is not his washing-book. Now, such is the wisdom of the sahib-log, that, upon opening this thing, they will instantly discover the purport. Yet I would of their favor beg them to observe how correct is the order of the pages, which I have counted, from the first to the last. Thus, One is followed by Two and Two by Three, and so forward to the end of the book. Even as I picked the pages one by one with great trouble from the floor when the sahib had gone to bed, so have they been placed; and there is not a fault in the whole account. And this is my work. It was a great burden, but I accomplished it; and if the sahib gains honor by that which he has written—and God knows what he is always writing about— I, Kadir Baksh, his servant, also have a claim to honor.

Dray Wara Yow Dee

For jealousy is the rage of a man: therefore he will not spare in the day of vengeance.—*Prov*. vi. 34.

ALMONDS and raisins, Sahib? Grapes from Kabul? Or a pony of the rarest if the Sahib will only come with me. He is thirteen three, Sahib, plays polo, goes in a cart, carries a lady and—Holy Kurshed and the Blessed Imams, it is the Sahib himself! My heart is made fat and my eye glad. May you never be tired! As is cold water in the Tirah, so is the sight of a friend in a far place. And what do *you* in this accursed land? South of Delhi, Sahib, you know the saying—"Rats are the men and trulls the women." It was an order? Ahoo! An order is an order till one is strong enough to disobey. O my brother, O my friend, we have met in an auspicious hour! Is all well in the heart and the body and the house? In a lucky day have we two come together again.

I am to go with you? Your favor is great. Will there be picket-room in the compound? I have three horses and the bundles and the horse-boy. Moreover, remember that the police here hold me a horse-thief. What do these Lowland bastards know of horse-thieves? Do you remember that time in Peshawur when Kamal hammered on the gates of Jumrud—mountebank that he was—and lifted the Colonel's horses all in one night? Kamal is dead now, but his nephew has taken up the matter, and there will be moie horses amissing if the Khaiber Levies do not look to it.

The Peace of God and the favor of His Prophet be upon this house and all that is in it! Shafizullah, rope the mottled mare under the tree and draw water. The horses can stand in the sun, but double the felts over the loins. Nay, my friend, do not trouble to look them over. They are to sell to the Officer fools who know so many things of the horse. The mare is heavy in foal; the grey is a devil unlicked; and the dun—but you know the trick of the peg. When they are sold I go back to Pubbi, or, it may be, the Valley of Peshawur.

O friend of my heart, it is good to see you again. I have been bowing and lying all day to the Officer-Sahibs in respect to those horses; and my mouth is dry for straight talk. *Auggrh!* Before a meal tobacco is good. Do not join me, for we are not in our own country. Sit in the veranda and I will spread my cloth here. But first I will drink. *In the name of God returning thanks, thrice!* This is sweet water, indeed—sweet as the water of Sheoran when it comes from the snows.

They are all well and pleased in the North—Khoda Baksh and the others. Yar Khan has come down with the horses from Kurdistan—six and thirty head only, and a full half pack-ponies—and has said openly in the Kashmir Serai that you English should send guns and blow the Amir into Hell. There are *fifteen* tolls now on the Kabul road; and at Dakka, when he thought he was

622

clear, Yar Khan was stripped of all his Balkh stallions by the Governor! This is a great injustice, and Yar Khan is not with rage. And of the others: Mahbub Ali is still at Pubbi, writing God knows what. Tugluq Khan is in jail for the business of the Kohat Police Post. Faiz Beg came down from Ismail-ki-Dhera with a Bok-hariot belt for thee, my brother, at the closing of the year, but none knew whither thou hadst gone: there was no news left behind. The Cousins have taken a new run near Pak-pattan to breed mules for the Government carts, and there is a story in Bazar of a priest. Oho! Such a salt tale! Listen—

Sahib, why do you ask that? My clothes are fouled because of the dust on the road. My eyes are sad because of the glare of the sun. My feet are swollen because I have washed them in bitter water; and my cheeks are hollow because the food here is bad. Fire burn your money! What do I want with it? I am rich and I thought you were my friend; but you are like the others—a Sahib. Is a man sad? Give him money, say the Sahibs. Is he dishonored? Give him money, say the Sahibs. Hath he a wrong upon his head? Give him money, say the Sahibs. Such are the Sahibs, and such art thou—even thou.

Nay, do not look at the feet of the dun. Pity it is that I ever taught you to know the legs of a horse. Footsore? Be it so. What of that? The roads are hard. And the mare footsore? She bears a double burden, Sahib.

And now I pray you, give me permission to depart. Great favor and honor has the Sahib done me, and graciously has he shown his belief that the horses are stolen. Will it please him to send me to the Thana? To call a sweeper and have me led away by one of these lizard-men? I am the Sahib's friend. I have drunk water in the shadow of his house, and he has blackened my face. Remains there anything more to do? Will the Sahib give me eight annas to make smooth the injury and—complete the insult?—

Forgive me, my brother. I knew not —I know not now—what I say. Yes, I lied to you! I will put dust on my head—and I am an Afridi! The horses have been marched footsore from the Valley to this place, and my eyes are dim, and my body aches for the want of sleep, and my heart is dried up with sorrow and shame. But as it was my shame, so by God the Dispenser of Justice—by Allah-al-Mumit—it shall be my own revenge!

We have spoken together with naked hearts before this, and our hands have dipped into the same dish and thou hast been to me as a brother. Therefore I pay thee back with lies and ingratitude —as a Pathan. Listen now! When the grief of the soul is too heavy for endurance it may be a little eased by speech, and, moreover, the mind of a true man is as a well, and the pebble of confession dropped therein sinks and is no more seen. From the Valley have I come on foot, league by league, with a fire in my chest like the fire of the Pit. And why? Hast thou, then, so quickly forgotten our customs, among this folk who sell their wives and their daughters for silver? Come back with me to the North and be among men once more. Come back, when this matter is accomplished and I call for thee!

The bloom of the peach-orchards is upon all the Valley, and *here* is only dust and a great stink. There is a pleasant wind among the mulberry trees, and the streams are bright with snow-water, and the caravans go up and the caravans go down, and a hundred fires sparkle in the gut of the Pass, and tent-peg answers hammer-nose, and pack-horse squeals to pack-horse across the drift smoke of the evening. It is good in the North now. Come back with me. Let us return to our own people! Come!

*   *   *   *   *   *

Whence is my sorrow? Does a man tear out his heart and make fritters thereof over a slow fire for aught other than a woman? Do not laugh, friend of mine, for your time will also be. A woman of the Abazai was she, and I took her to wife to staunch the feud between our village and the men of Ghor. I am no longer young? The lime has touched my beard? True. I had no need of the wedding? Nay, but I loved her. What saith Rahman: "Into whose heart Love enters, there is Folly *and naught else*. By a glance of the eye she hath blinded thee; and by the eyelids and the fringe of the eyelids taken thee into the captivity without ransom, *and naught else*." Dost thou remember that song at the sheep-roasting in the Pindi camp among the Uzbegs of the Amir?

The Abazai are dogs and their women the servants of sin. There was a lover of her own people, but of that her father told me naught. My friend, curse for me in your prayers, as I curse at each praying from the Fakr to the Isha, the name of Daoud Shah, Abazai, whose

head is still upon his neck, whose hands are still upon his wrists, who has done me dishonor, who has made my name a laughing-stock among the women of Little Malikand.

I went into Hindustan at the end of two months—to Cherat. I was gone twelve days only; but I had said that I would be fifteen days absent. This I did to try her, for it is written: "Trust not the incapable." Coming up the gorge alone in the falling of the light, I heard the voice of a man singing at the door of my house; and it was the voice of Daoud Shah, and the song that he sang was *"Dray wara yow dee"*—"All three are one." It was as though a heel-rope had been slipped round my heart and all the Devils were drawing it tight past endurance. I crept silently up the hill-road, but the fuse of my matchlock was wetted with the rain, and I could not slay Daoud Shah from afar. Moreover, it was in my mind to kill the woman also. Thus he sang, sitting outside my house, and, anon, the woman opened the door, and I came nearer, crawling on my belly among the rocks. I had only my knife to my hand. But a stone slipped under my foot, and the two looked down the hillside, and he, leaving his matchlock, fled from my anger, because he was afraid for the life that was in him. But the woman moved not till I stood in front of her, crying: "O woman, what is this that thou hast done?" And she, void of fear, though she knew my thought, laughed, saying: "It is a little thing. I loved him, and *thou* art a dog and cattle-thief coming by night. Strike!" And I, being still blinded by her beauty, for, O my friend, the women of the Abazai are very fair, said: "Hast thou no fear?" And she answered: "None—but only the fear that I do not die." Then said I: "Have no fear." And she bowed her head, and I smote it off at the neck-bone so that it leaped between my feet. Thereafter the rage of our people came upon me, and I hacked off the breasts, that the men of Little Malikand might know the crime, and cast the body into the water-course that flows to the Kabul river. *Dray wara yow dee! Dray wara yow dee!* The body without the head, the soul without light, and my own darkling heart—all three are one—all three are one!

That night, making no halt, I went to Ghor and demanded news of Daoud Shah. Men said: "He is gone to Pubbi for horses. What wouldst thou of him? There is peace between the villages." I made answer: "Aye! The peace of treachery and the love that the Devil Atala bore to Gurel." So I fired thrice into the gate and laughed and went my way.

In those hours, brother and friend of my heart's heart, the moon and the stars were as blood above me, and in my mouth was the taste of dry earth. Also, I broke no bread, and my drink was the rain of the Valley of Ghor upon my face.

At Pubbi I found Mahbub Ali, the writer, sitting upon his charpoy and gave up my arms according to your Law. But I was not grieved, for it was in my heart that I should kill Daoud Shah with my bare hands thus—as a man strips a bunch of raisins. Mahbub Ali said: "Daoud Shah has even now gone hot-foot to Peshawur, and he will pick up his horses upon the road to Delhi,

for it is said that the Bombay Tramway Company are buying horses there by the truckload; eight horses to the truck." And that was a true saying.

Then I saw that the hunting would be no little thing, for the man was gone into your borders to save himself against my wrath. And shall he save himself so? Am I not alive? Though he run northward to the Dora and the snow, or southerly to the Black Water, I will follow him, as a lover follows the footsteps of his mistress, and coming upon him I will take him tenderly—Aho! so tenderly!—in my arms, saying: "Well hast thou done and well shalt thou be repaid." And out of that embrace Daoud Shah shall not go forth with the breath in his nostrils. *Auggrh!* Where is the pitcher? I am as thirsty as a mother-mare in the first month.

Your Law! What is your Law to me? When the horses fight on the runs do they regard the boundary pillars; or do the kites of Ali Musjid forbear because the carrion lies under the shadow of the Ghort Kuttri? The matter began across the Border. It shall finish where God pleases. Here, in my own country, or in Hell. All three are one.

Listen now, sharer of the sorrow of my heart, and I will tell of the hunting. I followed to Peshawur from Pubbi, and I went to and fro about the streets of Peshawur like a houseless dog, seeking for my enemy. Once I thought that I saw him washing his mouth in the conduit in the big square, but when I came up he was gone. It may be that it was he, and, seeing my face, he had fled.

A girl of the bazar said that he would go to Nowshera. I said: "O heart's heart, does Daoud Shah visit thee?" And she said: "Even so." I said: "I would fain see him, for we be friends parted for two years. Hide me, I pray, here in the shadow of the window shutter, and I will wait for his coming." And the girl said: "O Pathan, look into my eyes!" And I turned, leaning upon her breast, and looked into her eyes, swearing that I spoke the very Truth of God. But she answered: "Never friend waited friend with such eyes. Lie to God and the Prophet, but to a woman ye cannot lie. Get hence! There shall no harm befall Daoud Shah by cause of me."

I would have strangled that girl but for the fear of your Police; and thus the hunting would have come to naught. Therefore I only laughed and departed, and she leaned over the window-bar in the night and mocked me down the street. Her name is Jamun. When I have made my account with the man I will return to Peshawur and—her lovers shall desire her no more for her beauty's sake. She shall not be *Jamun* but *Ak,* the cripple among trees. Ho! Ho! *Ak* shall she be!

At Peshawur I bought the horses and grapes, and the almonds and dried fruits, that the reason of my wanderings might be open to the Government, and that there might be no hindrance upon the road. But when I came to Nowshera he was gone, and I knew not where to go. I stayed one day at Nowshera, and in the night a Voice spoke in my ears as I slept among the horses. All night it flew round my head and would not cease from whispering. I was upon my belly, sleeping as the Devils sleep, and it may have been that the Voice

was the voice of a Devil. It said: "Go south, and thou shalt come upon Daoud Shah." Listen, my brother and chiefest among friends—listen! Is the tale a long one? Think how it was long to me. I have trodden every league of the road from Pubbi to this place; and from Nowshera my guide was only the Voice and the lust of vengeance.

To the Uttock I went, but that was no hindrance to me. Ho! Ho! A man may turn the word twice, even in his trouble. The Uttock was no *uttoc* (obstacle) to me; and I heard the Voice above the noise of the waters beating on the big rock, saying: "Go to the right." So I went to Pindigheb, and in those days my sleep was taken from me utterly, and the head of the woman of the Abazai was before me night and day, even as it had fallen between my feet. *Dray wara yow dee! Dray wara yow dee!* Fire, ashes, and my couch, all three are one—all three are one!

Now I was far from the winter path of the dealers who had gone to Sialkot and so south by the rail and the Big Road to the line of cantonments; but there was a Sahib in camp at Pindigheb who bought from me a white mare at a good price, and told me that one Daoud Shah had passed to Shahpur with horses. Then I saw that the warning of the Voice was true, and made swift to come to the Salt Hills. The Jhelum was in flood, but I could not wait, and, in the crossing, a bay stallion was washed down and drowned. Herein was God hard to me—not in respect of the beast, of that I had no care—but in this snatching. While I was upon the right bank urging the horses into the water, Daoud Shah was upon the left; for—*Alghias! Alghias!* —the hoofs of my hare scattered the hot ashes of his fires when we came up the hither bank in the light of morning. But he had fled. His feet were made swift by the terror of Death. And I went south from Shahpur as the kite flies. I dared not turn aside, lest I should miss my vengeance—which is my right. From Shahpur I skirted by the Jhelum, for I thought that he would avoid the Desert of the Rechna. But, presently, at Sahiwal, I turned away upon the road to Jhang, Samundri, and Gugera, till, upon a night, the mottled mare breasted the fence of the rail that runs to Montgomery. And that place was Okara, and the head of the woman of the Abazai lay upon the sand between my feet.

Thence I went to Fazilka, and they said that I was mad to bring starved horses there. The Voice was with me, and I was *not* mad, but only wearied, because I could not find Daoud Shah. It was written that I should not find him at Rania nor Bahadurgarh, and I came into Delhi from the west, and there also I found him not. My friend, I have seen many strange things in my wanderings. I have seen Devils rioting across the Rechna as the stallions riot in spring. I have heard the *Djinns* calling to each other from holes in the sand, and I have seen them pass before my face. There are no Devils, say the Sahibs? They are very wise, but they do not know all things about devils or —horses. Ho! Ho! I say to you who are laughing at my misery, that I have seen the Devils at high noon whooping and leaping on the shoals of the Chenab. And was I afraid? My

brother, when the desire of a man is set upon one thing alone, he fears neither God nor Man nor Devil. If my vengeance failed, I would splinter the Gates of Paradise with the butt of my gun, or I would cut my way into Hell with my knife, and I would call upon Those who Govern there for the body of Daoud Shah. What love so deep as hate?

Do not speak. I know the thought in your heart. Is the white of this eye clouded? How does the blood beat at the wrist? There is no madness in my flesh, but only the vehemence of the desire that has eaten me up. Listen! South of Delhi I knew not the country at all. Therefore I cannot say where I went, but I passed through many cities. I knew only that it was laid upon me to go south. When the horses could march no more, I threw myself upon the earth, and waited till the day. There was no sleep with me in that journeying; and that was a heavy burden. Dost thou know, brother of mine, the evil of wakefulness that cannot break—when the bones are sore for lack of sleep, and the skin of the temples twitches with weariness, and yet—there is no sleep—there is no sleep? *Dray wara yow dee! Dray wara yow dee!* The eye of the Sun, the eye of the Moon, and my own unrestful eyes— all three are one—all three are one!

There was a city the name whereof I have forgotten, and there the Voice called all night. That was ten days ago. It has cheated me afresh.

I have come hither from a place called Hamirpur, and, behold, it is my Fate that I should meet with thee to my comfort, and the increase of friendship. This is a good omen. By the joy of looking upon thy face the weariness has gone from my feet, and the sorrow of my so long travel is forgotten. Also my heart is peaceful; for I know that the end is near.

It may be that I shall find Daoud Shah in this city going northward, since a Hillman will ever head back to his Hills when the spring warns. And shall he see those hills of our country? Surely I shall overtake him! Surely my vengeance is safe! Surely God hath him in the hollow of His hand against my claiming. There shall no harm befall Daoud Shah till I come; for I would fain kill him quick and whole with the life sticking firm in his body. A pomegranate is sweetest when the cloves break away unwilling from the rind. Let it be in the daytime, that I may see his face, and my delight may be crowned.

And when I have accomplished the matter and my Honor is made clean, I shall return thanks unto God, the Holder of the Scale of the Law, and I shall sleep. From the night, through the day, and into the night again I shall sleep; and no dream shall trouble me.

And now, O my brother, the tale is all told. *Ahi! Ahi! Alghias! Ahi!*

The Judgment of Dungara

See the pale martyr with his shirt cn fire.—*Printer's Error.*

THEY tell the tale even now among the groves of the Berbulda Hill, and for corroboration point to the roofless and windowless Mission-house. The great God Dungara, the God of Things as They Are, Most Terrible, One-eyed, Bearing the Red Elephant Tusk, did it all; and he who refuses to believe in Dungara will assuredly be smitten by the Madness of Yat—the madness that fell upon the sons and the daughters of the Buria Kol when they turned aside from Dungara and put on clothes. So says Athon Dazé, who is High Priest of the shrine and Warden of the Red Elephant Tusk. But if you ask the Assistant Collector and Agent in Charge of the Buria Kol, he will laugh—not because he bears any malice against missions, but because he himself saw the vengeance of Dungara executed upon the spiritual children of the Reverend Justus Krenk, Pastor of the Tubingen Mission, and upon Lotta, his virtuous wife.

Yet if ever a man merited good treatment of the Gods it was the Reverend Justus, one time of Heidelberg, who, on the faith of a call, went into the wilderness and took the blonde, blue-eyed Lotta with him. "We will these Heathen now by idolatrous practices so darkened better make," said Justus in the early days of his career. "Yes," he added with conviction, "they shall be good and shall with their hands to work learn. For all good Christians must work." And upon a stipend more modest even than that of an English lay-reader, Justus Krenk kept house beyond Kamala and the gorge of Malair, beyond the Berbulda River close to the foot of the blue hill of Panth on whose summit stands the Temple of Dungara—in the heart of the country of the Buria Kol—the naked, good-tempered, timid, shameless, lazy Buria Kol.

Do you know what life at a Mission outpost means? Try to imagine a loneliness exceeding that of the smallest station to which Government has ever sent you—isolation that weighs upon the waking eyelids and drives you by force headlong into the labors of the day. There is no post, there is no one of your own color to speak to, there are no roads: there is, indeed, food to keep you alive, but it is not pleasant to eat; and whatever of good or beauty or interest there is in your life, must come from yourself and the grace that may be planted in you.

In the morning, with a patter of soft feet, the converts, the doubtful, and the open scoffers, troop up to the veranda. You must be infinitely kind and patient, and, above all, clear-sighted, for you deal with the simplicity of childhood, the experience of man, and the subtlety of the savage. Your congregation have a hundred material wants to be considered; and it is for you as you believe in your personal responsibility to your Maker, to pick out of the clamoring crowd any grain of spirituality that may lie therein. If to the cure of souls you add that of bodies, your task will be all the more difficult, for the sick and the maimed will profess any and every creed for the sake of healing, and will laugh at you because you are simple enough to believe them.

As the day wears and the impetus of the morning dies away, there will come upon you an overwhelming sense of the uselessness of your toil. This must be striven against, and the only spur in your side will be the belief that you are playing against the Devil for the living soul. It is a great, a joyous belief; but he who can hold it unwavering for four and twenty consecutive hours, must be blessed with an abundantly strong physique and equable nerve.

Ask the grey heads of the Bannockburn Medical Crusade what manner of life their preachers lead; speak to the Racine Gospel Agency, those lean Americans whose boast is that they go where no Englishman dare follow; get a Pastor of the Tubingen Mission to talk of his experiences—if you can. You will be referred to the printed reports, but these contain no mention of the men who have lost youth and health, all that a man may lose except faith, in the wilds; of English maidens who have gone forth and died in the fever-stricken jungle of the Panth Hills, knowing from the first that death was almost a certainty. Few Pastors will tell you of these things any more than they will speak of that young David of St. Bees, who, set apart for the Lord's work, broke down in the utter desolation, and returned half distraught to the Head Mission, crying: "There is no God, but I have walked with the Devil!"

The reports are silent here, because heroism, failure, doubt, despair, and self-abnegation on the part of a mere cultured white man are things of no weight as compared to the saving of one half-human soul from a fantastic faith in wood-spirits, goblins of the rock, and river-fiends.

And Gallio, the Assistant Collector of the country side, "cared for none of these things." He had been long in the district, and the Buria Kol loved him and brought him offerings of speared fish, orchids from the dim moist heart of the forests, and as much game as he could eat. In return he gave them quinine, and with Athon Dazé, the High Priest, controlled their simple policies.

"When you have been some years in the country," said Gallio at the Krenks' table, "you grow to find one creed as good as another. I'll give you all the assistance in my power, of course, but don't hurt my Buria Kol. They are a good people and they trust me."

"I will them the Word of the Lord teach," said Justus, his round face beaming with enthusiasm, "and I will assuredly to their prejudices no wrong hastily without thinking make. But, O my friend, this in the mind impartiality-of-creed-judgment-be-looking is very bad."

"Heigh-ho!" said Gallio, "I have their bodies and the district to see to, but you can try what you can do for their souls. Only don't behave as your predecessor did, or I'm afraid that I can't guarantee your life."

"And that?" said Lotta, sturdily, handing him a cup of tea.

"He went up to the Temple of Dungara—to be sure he was new to the country—and began hammering old Dungara over the head with an umbrella; so the Buria Kol turned out and hammered *him* rather savagely. I was in the district, and he sent a runner to me with a note saying: 'Persecuted for

the Lord's sake. Send wing of regiment.' The nearest troops were about two hundred miles off, but I guessed what he had been doing. I rode to Panth and talked to old Athon Dazé like a father, telling him that a man of his wisdom ought to have known that the Sahib had sunstroke and was mad. You never saw a people more sorry in your life. Athon Dazé apologized, sent wood and milk and fowls and all sorts of things; and I gave five rupees to the shrine and told Macnamara that he had been injudicious. He said that I had bowed down in the House of Rimmon; but if he had only just gone over the brow of the hill and insulted Palin Deo, the idol of the Suria Kol, he would have been impaled on a charred bamboo long before I could have done anything, and then I should have had to have hanged some of the poor brutes. Be gentle with them, Padri—but I don't think you'll do much."

"Not I," said Justus, "but my Master. We will with the little children begin. Many of them will be sick—that is so. After the children the mothers; and then the men. But I would greatly that you were in internal sympathies with us prefer."

Gallio departed to risk his life in mending the rotten bamboo bridges of his people, in killing a too persistent tiger here or there, in sleeping out in the reeking jungle, or in tracking the Suria Kol raiders who had taken a few heads from their brethren of the Buria clan. He was a knock-kneed, shambling young man, naturally devoid of creed or reverence, with a longing for absolute power which his undesirable district gratified.

"No one wants my post," he used to say, grimly, "and my Collector only pokes his nose in when he's quite certain that there is no fever. I'm monarch of all I survey, and Athon Dazé is my viceroy."

Because Gallio prided himself on his supreme disregard of human life—though he never extended the theory beyond his own—he naturally rode forty miles to the Mission with a tiny brown girl-baby on his saddle-bow.

"Here is something for you, Padri," said he. "The Kols leave their surplus children to die. 'Don't see why they shouldn't, but you may rear this one. I picked it up beyond the Berbulda fork. I've a notion that the mother has been following me through the woods ever since."

"It is the first of the fold," said Justus, and Lotta caught up the screaming morsel to her bosom and hushed it craftily; while, as a wolf hangs in the field, Matui, who had borne it and in accordance with the law of her tribe had exposed it to die, panted weary and footsore in the bamboo-brake, watching the house with hungry mother-eyes. What would the omnipotent Assistant Collector do? Would the little man in the black coat eat her daughter alive as Athon Dazé said was the custom of all men in black coats?

Matui waited among the bamboos through the long night; and, in the morning, there came forth a fair white woman, the like of whom Matui had never seen, and in her arms was Matui's daughter clad in spotless raiment. Lotta knew little of the tongue of the Buria Kol, but when mother calls to mother, speech is easy to follow. By the hands stretched timidly to the hem of her gown, by the passionate gutturals and the longing eyes, Lotta understood with whom she had to deal. So Matui took her child again—would be a servant, even a slave, to this wonderful white woman, for her own tribe would recognize her no more. And Lotta wept with her exhaustively, after the German fashion, which includes much blowing of the nose.

"First the child, then the mother, and last the man, and to the Glory of God all," said Justus the Hopeful. And the man came, with a bow and arrows, very angry indeed, for there was no one to cook for him.

But the tale of the Mission is a long one, and I have no space to show how Justus, forgetful of his injudicious predecessor, grievously smote Moto, the husband of Matui, for his brutality; how Moto was startled, but being released from the fear of instant death, took heart and became the faithful ally and first convert of Justus; how the little gathering grew, to the huge disgust of Athon Dazé; how the Priest of the God of Things as They Are argued subtilely with the Priest of the God of Things as They Should Be, and was worsted; how the dues of the Temple of Dungara fell away in fowls and fish and honeycomb; how Lotta lightened the Curse of Eve among the women, and how Justus did his best to introduce the Curse of Adam; how the Buria Kol rebelled at this, saying that their God was an idle God, and how Justus partially overcame their scruples against work, and taught them that the black earth was rich in other produce than pignuts only.

All these things belong to the history of many months, and throughout those months the white-haired Athon Dazé meditated revenge for the tribal neglect of Dungara. With savage cunning he feigned friendship toward Justus, even hinting at his own conversion; but to the congregation of Dungara he said darkly: "They of the Padri's flock have put on clothes and worship a busy God. Therefore Dungara will afflict them grievously till they throw themselves, howling into the waters of the Berbulda." At night the Red Elephant Tusk boomed and groaned among the hills, and the faithful waked and said: "The God of Things as They Are matures revenge against the backsliders. Be merciful, Dungara, to us Thy children, and give us all their crops!"

Late in the cold weather, the Collector and his wife came into the Buria Kol country. "Go and look at Krenk's Mission," said Gallio. "He is doing good work in his own way, and I think he'd be pleased if you opened the bamboo chapel that he has managed to run up. At any rate you'll see a civilized Buria Kol."

Great was the stir in the Mission. "Now he and the gracious lady will that we have done good work with their own eyes see, and—yes—we will him our converts in all their new clothes by their own hands constructed exhibit. It will a great day be—for the Lord always," said Justus, and Lotta said "Amen."

Justus had, in his quiet way, felt jealous of the Basel Weaving Mission, his own converts being unhandy; but

Athon Dazé had latterly induced some of them to hackle the glossy silky fibres of a plant that grew plenteously on the Panth Hills. It yielded a cloth white and smooth almost as the *tappa* of the South Seas, and that day the converts were to wear for the first time clothes made therefrom. Justus was proud of his work.

"They shall in white clothes clothed to meet the Collector and his well-born lady come down, singing '*Now thank we all our God.*' Then he will the Chapel open, and—yes—even Gallio to believe will begin. Stand so my children, two by two, and—Lotta, why do they thus themselves bescratch? It is not seemly to wriggle, Nala, my child. The Collector will be here and be pained."

The Collector, his wife, and Gallio climbed the hill to the Mission-station. The converts were drawn up in two lines, a shining band nearly forty strong. "Hah!" said the Collector, whose acquisitive bent of mind led him to believe that he had fostered the institution from the first. "Advancing, I see, by leaps and bounds."

Never was truer word spoken! The Mission *was* advancing exactly as he had said—at first by little hops and shuffles of shamefaced uneasiness, but soon by the leaps of fly-stung horses and the bounds of maddened kangaroos. From the hill of Panth the Red Elephant Tusk delivered a dry and anguished blare. The ranks of the converts wavered, broke and scattered with yells and shrieks of pain, while Justus and Lotta stood horror-stricken.

"It is the Judgment of Dungara!" shouted a voice. "I burn! I burn! To the river or we die!"

The mob wheeled and headed for the rocks that overhung the Berbulda, writhing, stamping, twisting and shedding its garments as it ran, pursued by the thunder of the trumpet of Dungara. Justus and Lotta fled to the Collector almost in tears.

"I cannot understand! Yesterday," panted Justus, "they had the Ten Commandments— What is this? Praise the Lord all good spirits by land and by sea. Nala! Oh, shame!"

With a bound and a scream there alighted on the rocks above their heads, Nala, once the pride of the Mission, a maiden of fourteen summers, good, docile, and virtuous—now naked as the dawn and spitting like a wild-cat.

"Was it for this!" she raved, hurling her petticoat at Justus; "was it for this I left my people and Dungara—for the fires of your Bad Place? Blind ape, little earthworm, dried fish that you are, you said that I should never burn! O Dungara, I burn now! I burn now! Have mercy, God of Things as They Are!"

She turned and flung herself into the Berbulda, and the trumpet of Dungara bellowed jubilantly. The last of the converts of the Tubingen Mission had put a quarter of a mile of rapid river between herself and her teachers.

"Yesterday," gulped Justus, "she taught in the school A, B, C, D.—Oh! It is the work of Satan!"

But Gallio was curiously regarding the maiden's petticoat where it had fallen at his feet. He felt its texture, drew back his shirt-sleeve beyond the deep tan of his wrist and pressed a fold of the cloth against the flesh. A blotch of angry red rose on the white skin.

"Ah!" said Gallio, calmly, "I thought so."

"What is it?" said Justus.

"I should call it the Shirt of Nessus, but— Where did you get the fibre of this cloth from?"

"Athon Dazé," said Justus. "He showed the boys how it should manufactured be."

"The old fox! Do you know that he has given you the Nilgiri Nettle— scorpion—*Girardenia Heterophylla*—to work up? No wonder they squirmed! Why, it stings even when they make bridge-ropes of it, unless it's soaked for six weeks. The cunning brute! It would take about half an hour to burn through their thick hides, and then!"—

Gallio burst into laughter, but Lotta was weeping in the arms of the Collector's wife, and Justus had covered his face with his hands.

"*Girardenia Heterophylla!*" repeated Gallio. "Krenk, why *didn't* you tell me? I could have saved you this. Woven fire! Anybody but a naked Kol would have known it, and, if I'm a judge of their ways, you'll never get them back."

He looked across the river to where the converts were still wallowing and wailing in the shallows, and the laughter died out of his eyes, for he saw that the Tubingen Mission to the Buria Kol was dead.

Never again, though they hung mournfully round the deserted school for three months, could Lotta or Justus coax back even the most promising of their flock. No! The end of conversion was the fire of the Bad Place— fire that ran through the limbs and gnawed into the bones. Who dare a second time tempt the anger of Dungara? Let the little man and his wife go elsewhere. The Buria Kol would have none of them. An unofficial message to Athon Dazé that if a hair of their heads were touched, Athon Dazé and the priests of Dungara would be hanged by Gallio at the temple shrine, protected Justus and Lotta from the stumpy poisoned arrows of the Buria Kol, but neither fish nor fowl, honeycomb, salt nor young pig were brought to their doors any more. And, alas! man cannot live by grace alone if meat be wanting.

"Let us go, mine wife," said Justus; "there is no good here, and the Lord has willed that some other man shall the work take—in good time—in His own good time. We will go away, and I will—yes—some botany bestudy."

If any one is anxious to convert the Buria Kol afresh, there lies at least the core of a mission-house under the hill of Panth. But the chapel and school have long since fallen back into jungle.

At Howli Thana

His own shoe, his own head.—Native Proverb.

As a messenger, if the heart of the Presence be moved to so great favor. And on six rupees. Yes, Sahib, for I have three little little children whose stomachs are always empty, and corn is now but forty pounds to the rupee. I will make so clever a messenger that you shall all day long be pleased with me, and, at the end of the year, bestow a turban. I know all the roads of the Station and many other things. Aha, Sahib! I am clever. Give me service. I was aforetime in the Police. A bad character? Now without doubt an enemy has told this tale. Never was I a scamp. I am a man of clean heart, and all my words are true. They knew this when I was in the Police. They said: "Afzal Khan is a true speaker in whose words men may trust." I am a Delhi Pathan, Sahib—all Delhi Pathans are good men. You have seen Delhi? Yes, it is true that there be many scamps among the Delhi Pathans. How wise is the Sahib! Nothing is hid from his eyes, and he will make me his messenger, and I will take all his notes secretly and without ostentation. Nay, Sahib, God is my witness that I meant no evil. I have long desired to serve under a true Sahib—a virtuous Sahib. Many young Sahibs are as devils unchained. With these Sahibs I would take no service—not though all the stomachs of my little children were crying for bread.

Why am I not still in the police? I will speak true talk. An evil came to the Thana—to Ram Baksh, the Havildar, and Maula Baksh, and Juggut Ram and Bhim Singh and Suruj Bul. Ram Baksh is in the jail for a space, and so also is Maula Baksh.

It was at the Thana of Howli, on the road that leads to Gokral-Seetarun wherein are many dacoits. We were all brave men—Rustums. Wherefore we were sent to that Thana which was eight miles from the next Thana. All day and all night we watched for dacoits. Why does the Sahib laugh? Nay, I will make a confession. The dacoits were too clever, and seeing this, we made no further trouble. It was in the hot weather. What can a man do in the hot days? Is the Sahib who is so strong—is he, even, vigorous in that hour? We made an arrangement with the dacoits for the sake of peace. That was the work of the Havildar who was fat. Ho! Ho! Sahib, he is now getting thin in the jail among the carpets. The Havildar said: "Give us no trouble, and we will give you no trouble. At the end of the reaping send us a man to lead before the judge, a man of infirm mind against whom the trumped-up case will break down. Thus we shall save our honor." To this talk the dacoits agreed, and we had no trouble at the Thana, and could eat melons in peace, sitting upon our charpoys all day long. Sweet as sugar-cane are the melons of Howli.

Now there was an assistant commissioner—a Stunt Sahib, in that district, called Yunkum Sahib. Aha! He was hard—hard even as is the Sahib who, without doubt, will give me the shadow of his protection. Many eyes had Yunkum Sahib, and moved quickly through his district. Men called him The Tiger of Gokral-Seetarun, because he would arrive unannounced and make his kill, and, before sunset, would be giving trouble to the Tehsildars, thirty miles away. No one knew the comings or the goings of Yunkum Sahib. He had

no camp, and when his horse was weary he rode upon a devil carriage. I do not know its name, but the Sahib sat in the midst of three silver wheels that made no creaking, and drave them with his legs, prancing like a bean-fed horse —thus. A shadow of a hawk upon the fields was not more without noise than the devil-carriage of Yunkum Sahib. It was here: it was there: it was gone: and the rapport was made, and there was trouble. Ask the Tehsildar of Rohestri how the hen-stealing came to be known, Sahib.

It fell upon a night that we of the Thana slept according to custom upon our charpoys, having eaten the evening meal and drunk tobacco. When we awoke in the morning, behold, of our six rifles not one remained! Also, the big Police-book that was in the Havildar's charge was gone. Seeing these things, we were very much afraid, thinking on our parts that the dacoits, regardless of honor, had come by night, and put us to shame. Then said Ram Baksh, the Havildar: "Be silent! The business is an evil business, but it may yet go well. Let us make the case complete. Bring a kid and my tulwar. See you not *now*, O fools? A kick for a horse, but a word is enough for a man."

We of the Thana, perceiving quickly what was in the mind of the Havildar, and greatly fearing that the service would be lost, made haste to take the kid into the inner room, and attended to the words of the Havildar. "Twenty dacoits came," said the Havildar, and we, taking his words, repeated after him according to custom. "There was a great fight," said the Havildar, "and of us no man escaped unhurt. The bars of the window were broken. Suruj Bul, see thou to that; and, O men, put speed into your work, for a runner must go with the news to The Tiger of Gokral-Seetarun." Thereon, Suruj Bul, leaning with his shoulder, brake in the bars of the window, and I, beating her with a whip, made the Havildar's mare skip among the melon-beds till they were much trodden with hoof-prints.

These things being made, I returned to the Thana, and the goat was slain, and certain portions of the walls were blackened with fire, and each man dipped his clothes a little into the blood of the goat. Know, O Sahib, that a wound made by man upon his own body can, by those skilled, be easily discerned from a wound wrought by another man. Therefore, the Havildar, taking his tulwar, smote one of us lightly on the forearm in the fat, and another on the leg, and a third on the back of the hand. Thus dealt he with all of us till the blood came; and Suruj Bul, more eager than the others, took out much hair. O Sahib, never was so perfect an arrangement. Yea, even I would have sworn that the Thana had been treated as we said. There was smoke and breaking and blood and trampled earth.

"Ride now, Maula Baksh," said the Havildar, "to the house of the Stunt Sahib, and carry the news of the dacoity. Do you also, O Afzal Khan, run there, and take heed that you are mired with sweat and dust on your in-coming. The blood will be dry on the clothes. I will stay and send a straight report to the Dipty Sahib, and we will catch certain that ye know of, villagers, so

that all may be ready against the Dipty Sahib's arrival."

Thus Maula Baksh rode and I ran hanging on the stirrup, and together we came in an evil plight before The Tiger of Gokral-Seetarun in the Rohestri tehsil. Our tale was long and correct, Sahib, for we gave even the names of the dacoits and the issue of the fight and besought him to come. But The Tiger made no sign, and only smiled after the manner of Sahibs when they have a wickedness in their hearts. "Swear ye to the rapport?" said he, and we said: "Thy servants swear. The blood of the fight is but newly dry upon us. Judge thou if it be the blood of the servants of the Presence, or not." And he said: "I see. Ye have done well." But he did not call for his horse or his devil-carriage, and scour the land as was his custom. He said: "Rest now and eat bread, for ye be wearied men. I will wait the coming of the Dipty Sahib."

Now it is the order that the Havildar of the Thana should send a straight report of all dacoities to the Dipty Sahib. At noon came he, a fat man and an old, and overbearing withal, but we of the Thana had no fear of his anger; dreading more the silences of The Tiger of Gokral-Seetarun. With him came Ram Baksh, the Havildar, and the others, guarding ten men of the village of Howli—all men evil affected toward the Police of the Sirkar. As prisoners they came, the irons upon their hands, crying for mercy—Imam Baksh, the farmer, who had denied his wife to the Havildar, and others, ill-conditioned rascals against whom we of the Thana bore spite. It was well done, and the

Havildar was proud. But the Dipty Sahib was angry with the Stunt for lack of zeal, and said "Dam-Dam" after the custom of the English people, and extolled the Havildar. Yunkum Sahib lay still in his long chair. "Have the men sworn?" said Yunkum Sahib. "Aye, and captured ten evil-doers," said the Dipty Sahib. "There be more abroad in *your* charge. Take horse—ride, and go in the name of the Sirkar!" "Truly there be more evil-doers abroad," said Yunkum Sahib, "but there is no need of a horse. Come all men with me."

I saw the mark of a string on the temples of Imam Baksh. Does the Presence know the torture of the Cold Draw? I saw also the face of The Tiger of Gokral-Seetarun, the evil smile was upon it, and I stood back ready for what might befall. Well it was, Sahib, that I did this thing. Yunkum Sahib unlocked the door of his bathroom, and smiled anew. Within lay the six rifles and the big Police-book of the Thana of Howli! He had come by night in the devil-carriage that is noiseless as a ghoul, and moving among us asleep, had taken away both the guns and the book! Twice had he come to the Thana, taking each time three rifles. The lever of the Havildar was turned to water, and he fell scrabbling in the dirt about the boots of Yunkum Sahib, crying—"Have mercy!"

And I? Sahib, I am a Delhi Pathan, and a young man with little children. The Havildar's mare was in the compound. I ran to her and rode: the black wrath of the Sirkar was behind me, and I knew not whither to go. Till she dropped and died I rode the red mare; and by the blessing of God, who is without doubt on the side of all just men, I escaped. But the Havildar and the rest are now in jail.

I am a scamp? It is as the Presence pleases. God will make the Presence a Lord, and give him a rich *Memsahib* as fair as a Peri to wife, and many strong sons, if he makes me his orderly. The Mercy of Heaven be upon the Sahib! Yes, I will only go to the bazar and bring my children to these so-palace-like quarters, and then—the Presence is my Father and my Mother, and I, Afzal Khan, am his slave.

Ohe, *Sidar-ji!* I also am of the household of the Sahib.

Gemini

Great is the justice of the White Man—greater the power of a lie.—*Native Proverb.*

THIS is your English Justice, Protector of the Poor. Look at my back and loins which are beaten with sticks—heavy sticks! I am a poor man, and there is no justice in Courts.

There were two of us, and we were born of one birth, but I swear to you that I was born the first, and Ram Dass is the younger by three full breaths.

The astrologer said so, and it is written in my horoscope—the horoscope of Durga Dass.

But we were alike—I and my brother who is a beast without honor—so alike that none knew, together ar apart, which was Durga Dass. I am a Mahajun of Pali in Marwar, and an honest man. This is true talk. When we were men, we left our father's house in Pali, and went to the Punjab, where all the people are mud-heads and sons of asses. We took shop together in Isser Jang—I and my brother—near the big well where the Governor's camp draws water. But Ram Dass, who is without truth, made quarrel with me, and we were divided. He took his books, and his pots, and his Mark, and became a *bunnia*—a money-lender—in the long street of Isser Jang, near the gateway of the road that goes to Montgomery. It was not my fault that we pulled each other's turbans. I am a Mahajun of Pali, and I *always* speak true talk. Ram Dass was the thief and the liar.

Now no man, not even the little children, could at one glance see which was Ram Dass and which was Durga Dass. But all the people of Isser Jang —may they die without sons!—said that we were thieves. They used much bad talk, but I took money on their bedsteads and their cooking-pots and the standing crop and the calf unborn, from the well in the big square to the gate of the Montgomery road. They were fools, these people—unfit to cut the toe-nails of a Marwari from Pali. I loaned money to them all. A little, very little only—here a pice and there a pice. God is my witness that I am a poor man! The money is all with

Ram Dass—may his sons turn Christian, and his daughter be a burning fire and a shame in the house from generation to generation! May she die unwed, and be the mother of a multitude of bastards! Let the light go out in the house of Ram Dass, my brother. This I pray daily twice—with offerings and charms.

Thus the trouble began. We divided the town of Isser Jang between us— I and my brother. There was a landholder beyond the gates, living but one short mile out, on the road that leads to Montgomery, and his name was Muhammad Shah, son of a Nawab. He was a great devil and drank wine. So long as there were women in his house, and wine and money for the marriage-feasts, he was merry and wiped his mouth. Ram Dass loaned him the money, a lakh or half a lakh—how do I know?—and so long as the money was loaned, the landholder cared not what he signed.

The people of Isser Jang were my portion, and the landholder and the out-town was the portion of Ram Dass; for so we had arranged. I was the poor man, for the people of Isser Jang were without wealth. I did what I could, but Ram Dass had only to wait without the door of the landholder's garden-court, and to lend him the money; taking the bonds from the hand of the steward.

In the autumn of the year after the lending, Ram Dass said to the landholder: "Pay me my money," but the landholder gave him abuse. But Ram Dass went into the Courts with the papers and the bonds—all correct—and took out decrees against the landholder;

and the name of the Government was across the stamps of the decrees. Ram Dass took field by field, and mango-tree by mango-tree, and well by well; putting in his own men—debtors of the out-town of Isser Jang—to cultivate the crops. So he crept up across the land, for he had the papers, and the name of the Government was across the stamps, till his men held the crops for him on all sides of the big white house of the landholder. It was well done; but when the landholder saw these things he was very angry and cursed Ram Dass after the manner of the Muhammadans.

And thus the landholder was angry, but Ram Dass laughed and claimed more fields, as was written upon the bonds. This was in the month of Phagun. I took my horse and went out to speak to the man who makes lac-bangles upon the road that leads to Montgomery, because he owed me a debt. There was in front of me, upon his horse, my brother Ram Dass. And when he saw me, he turned aside into the high crops, because there was hatred between us. And I went forward till I came to the orange-bushes by the land-holder's house. The bats were flying, and the evening smoke was low down upon the land. Here met me four men —swash-bucklers and Muhammadans— with their faces bound up, laying hold of my horse's bridle and crying out: "This is Ram Dass! Beat!" Me they beat with their staves—heavy staves bound about with wire at the end, such weapons as those swine of Punjabis use —till, having cried for mercy, I fell down senseless. But these shameless ones still beat me, saying: "O Ram Dass, this is your interest—well weighed and counted into your hand, Ram Dass." I cried aloud that I was not Ram Dass but Durga Dass, his brother, yet they only beat me the more, and when I could make no more outcry they left me. But I saw their faces. There was Elahi Baksh who runs by the side of the landholder's white horse, and Nur Ali the keeper of the door, and Wajib Ali the very strong cook, and Abdul Latif the mes-senger—all of the household of the landholder. These things I can swear on the Cow's Tail if need be, but—*Ahi! Ahi!*—it has been already sworn, and I am a poor man whose honor is lost.

When these four had gone away laughing, my brother Ram Dass came out of the crops and mourned over me as one dead. But I opened my eyes, and prayed him to get me water. When I had drunk, he carried me on his back, and by byways brought me into the town of Isser Jang. My heart was turned to Ram Dass, my brother, in that hour, because of his kindness, and I lost my enmity.

But a snake is a snake till it is dead; and a liar is a liar till the Judgment of the Gods takes hold of his heel. I was wrong in that I trusted my brother— the son of my mother.

When we had come to his house and I was a little restored, I told him my tale, and he said: "Without doubt it is me whom they would have beaten. But the Law Courts are open, and there is the Justice of the Sirkar above all; and to the Law Courts do thou go when this sickness is overpast."

Now when we two had left Pali in the old years, there fell a famine that ran from Jeysulmir to Gurgaon and touched Gogunda in the south. At that time the sister of my father came away and lived with us in Isser Jang; for a man must above all see that his folk do not die of want. When the quarrel between us twain came about, the sister of my father—a lean she-dog without teeth—said that Ram Dass had the right, and went with him. Into her hands—because she knew medicines and many cures—Ram Dass, my brother, put me faint with the beating, and much bruised even to the pouring of blood from the mouth. When I had two days' sickness the fever came upon me; and I set aside the fever to the account written in my mind against the landholder.

The Punjabis of Isser Jang are all the sons of Belial and a she-ass, but they are very good witnesses, bearing testimony unshakingly whatever the pleaders may say. I would purchase witnesses by the score, and each man should give evidence, not only against Nur Ali, Wajib Ali, Abdul Latif and Elahi Baksh, but against the landholder, saying that he upon his white horse had called his men to beat me; and, further, that they had robbed me of two hundred rupees. For the latter testimony, I would remit a little of the debt of the man who sold the lac-bangles, and he should say that he had put the money into my hands, and had seen the robbery from afar, but, being afraid, had run away. This plan I told to my brother Ram Dass; and he said that the arrangement was good, and bade me take comfort and make swift work to be abroad again. My heart was opened to my brother in my sickness, and I told him the names of those whom

I would call as witnesses—all men in my debt, but of that the Magistrate Sahib could have no knowledge, nor the landholder. The fever stayed with me, and after the fever, I was taken with colic, and gripings very terrible. In that day I thought that my end was at hand, but I know now that she who gave me the medicines, the sister of my father—a widow with a widow's heart— had brought about my second sickness. Ram Dass, my brother, said that my house was shut and locked, and brought me the big doorkey and my books, together with all the moneys that were in my house—even the money that was buried under the floor; for I was in great fear lest thieves should break in and dig. I speak true talk; there was but very little money in my house. Perhaps ten rupees—perhaps twenty. How can I tell? God is my witness that I am a poor man.

One night, when I had told Ram Dass all that was in my heart of the lawsuit that I would bring against the landholder, and Ram Dass had said that he had made the arrangements with the witnesses, giving me their names written, I was taken with a new great sickness, and they put me on the bed. When I was a little recovered—I cannot tell how many days afterward—I made enquiry for Ram Dass, and the sister of my father said that he had gone to Montgomery upon a lawsuit. I took medicine and slept very heavily without waking. When my eyes were opened, there was a great stillness in the house of Ram Dass, and none answered when I called—not even the sister of my father. This filled me with fear, for I knew not what had happened.

Taking a stick in my hand, I went out slowly, till I came to the great square by the well, and my heart was hot in me against the landholder because of the pain of every step I took.

I called for Jowar Singh, the carpenter, whose name was first upon the list of those who should bear evidence against the landholder, saying: "Are all things ready, and do you know what should be said?"

Jowar Singh answered: "What is this, and whence do you come, Durga Dass?"

"I said: "From my bed, where I have so long lain sick because of the landholder. Where is Ram Dass, my brother, who was to have made the arrangement for the witnesses? Surely you and yours know these things!"

Then Jowar Singh said: "What has this to do with us, O Liar? I have borne witness and I have been paid, and the landholder has, by the order of the Court, paid both the five hundred rupees that he robbed from Ram Dass and yet other five hundred because of the great injury he did to your brother."

The well and the jujube-tree above it and the square of Isser Jang became dark in my eyes, but I leaned on my stick and said: "Nay! This is child's talk and senseless. It was I who suffered at the hands of the landholder, and I am come to make ready the case. Where is my brother Ram Dass?"

But Jowar Singh shook his head, and a woman cried: "What lie is here? What quarrel had the landholder with you, *bunnia?* It is only a shameless one and one without faith, who profits by his brother's smarts. Have these *bunnias* no bowels?"

I cried again, saying: "By the Cow —by the Oath of the Cow, by the Temple of the Blue-throated Mahadeo, I and I only was beaten—beaten to the death! Let your talk be straight, O people of Isser Jang, and I will pay for the witnesses." And I tottered where I stood, for the sickness and the pain of the beating were heavy upon me.

Then Ram Narain, who has his carpet spread under the jujube-tree by the well, and writes all letters for the men of the town, came up and said: "To-day is the one and fortieth day since the beating, and since these six days the case has been judged in the Court, and the Assistant Commissioner Sahib has given it for your brother Ram Dass, allowing the robbery, to which, too, I bore witness, and all things else as the witnesses said. There were many witnesses, and twice Ram Dass became senseless in the Court because of his wounds, and the Stunt Sahib—the *baba* Stunt Sahib—gave him a chair before all the pleaders. Why do you howl, Durga Dass? These things fell as I have said. Was it not so?"

And Jowar Singh said: "That is truth. I was there, and there was a red cushion in the chair."

And Ram Narain said: "Great shame has come upon the landholder because of this judgment, and fearing his anger, Ram Dass and all his house have gone back to Pali. Ram Dass told us that you also had gone first, the enmity being healed between you, to open a shop in Pali. Indeed, it were well for you that you go even now, for the landholder has sworn that if he catch any one of your house, he will hang him by the heels from the well-beam, and, swinging him to and fro, will beat him with staves till the blood runs from his ears. What I have said in respect to the case is true, as these men here can testify—even to the five hundred rupees."

I said: "Was it five hundred?" And Kirpa Ram, the *jat*, said: "Five hundred; for I bore witness also."

And I groaned, for it had been in my heart to have said two hundred only.

Then a new fear came upon me and my bowels turned to water, and, running swiftly to the house of Ram Dass, I sought for my books and my money in the great wooden chest under my bedstead. There remained nothing: not even a cowrie's value. All had been taken by the devil who said he was my brother. I went to my own house also and opened the boards of the shutters; but there also was nothing save the rats among the grain-baskets. In that hour my senses left me, and, tearing my clothes, I ran to the well-place, crying out for the Justice of the English on my brother Ram Dass, and, in my madness, telling all that the books were lost. When men saw that I would have jumped down the well, they believed the truth of my talk; more especially because upon my back and bosom were still the marks of the staves of the landholder.

Jowar Singh the carpenter withstood me, and turning me in his hands—for he is a very strong man—showed the scars upon my body, and bowed down with laughter upon the well-curb. He cried aloud so that all heard him, from the well-square to the Caravanserai of the Pilgrims: "Oho! The jackals have quarreled, and the grey one has been caught in the trap. In truth, this man has been grievously beaten, and his brother has taken the money which the Court decreed! Oh, *bunnia*, this shall be told for years against you! The jackals have quarreled, and, moreover, the books are burned. O people indebted to Durga Dass—and I know that ye be many—the books are burned!"

Then all Isser Jang took up the cry that the books were burned—*Ahi! Ahi!* that in my folly I had let that escape my mouth—and they laughed throughout the city. They gave me the abuse of the Punjabi, which is a terrible abuse and very hot; pelting me also with sticks and cow-dung till I fell down and cried for mercy.

Ram Narain, the letter-writer, bade the people cease, for fear that the news should get into Montgomery, and the Policemen might come down to inquire. He said, using many bad words: "This much mercy will I do to you, Durga Dass, though there was no mercy in your dealings with my sister's son over the matter of the dun heifer. Has any man a pony on which he sets no store, that this fellow may escape? If the landholder hears that one of the twain (and God knows whether he beat one or both, but this man is certainly beaten) be in the city, there will be a murder done, and then will come the Police, making inquisition into each man's house and eating the sweet-seller's stuff all day long."

Kirpa Ram the *jat*, said: I have a pony very sick. But with beating he can be made to walk for two miles. If he dies, the hide-sellers will have the body."

Then Chumbo, the hide-seller, said: "I will pay three annas for the body, and will walk by this man's side till such time as the pony dies. If it be more than two miles, I will pay two annas only."

Kirpa Ram said: "Be it so." Men brought out the pony, and I asked leave to draw a little water from the well, because I was dried up with fear.

Then Ram Narain said: "Here be four annas. God has brought you very low, Durga Dass, and I would not send you away empty, even though the matter of my sister's son's dun heifer be an open sore between us. It is a long way to your own country. Go, and if it be so willed, live; but, above all, do not take the pony's bridle, for that is mine."

And I went out of Isser Jang, amid the laughing of the huge-thighed Jats, ànd the hide-seller walked by my side waiting for the pony to fall dead. In one mile it died, and being full of fear of the landholder, I ran till I could run no more and came to this place.

But I swear by the Cow, I swear by all things whereon Hindus and Musalmans, and even the Sahibs swear, that I, and not my brother, was beaten by the landholder. But the case is shut and the doors of the Law Courts are shut, and God knows where the *baba* Stunt Sahib—the mother's milk is not yet dry upon his hairless lip—is gone. *Ahi! Ahi!* I have no witnesses, and the scars will heal, and I am a poor man. But, on my Father's Soul, on the oath of a Mahajun from Pali, I, and not my brother, I was beaten by the landholder.

What can I do? The Justice of the English is as a great river. Having gone forward, it does not return. Howbeit, do you, Sahib, take a pen and write clearly what I have said, that the Dipty Sahib may see, and reprove the Stunt Sahib, who is a colt yet unlicked by the mare, so young is he. I, and not my brother, was beaten, and he is gone to the west—I do not know where.

But, above all things, write—so that Sahibs may read, and his disgrace be accomplished—that Ram Dass, my brother, son of Purun Dass, Hahajun of Pali, is a swine and a night-thief, a taker of life, an eater of flesh, a jackal-spawn without beauty, or faith, or cleanliness, or honor!

At Twenty-Two

Narrow as the womb, deep as the Pit, and dark as the heart of a man.—*Sonthal Miner's Proverb.*

"A WEAVER went out to reap but stayed to unravel the corn-stalks. Ha! Ha! Ha! Is there any sense in a weaver?"

Janki Meah glared at Kundoo, but, as Janki Meah was blind, Kundoo was not impressed. He had come to argue with Janki Meah, and, if chance favored, to make love to the old man's pretty young wife.

This was Kundoo's grievance, and he

spoke in the name of all the five men who, with Janki Meah, composed the gang in Number Seven gallery of Twenty-Two. Janki Meah had been blind for the thirty years during which he had served the Jimahari Collieries with pick and crowbar. All through those thirty years he had regularly, every morning before going down, drawn from the overseer his allowance of lamp-oil—just as if he had been an eyed miner. What Kundoo's gang resented, as hundreds of gangs had resented before, was Janki Meah's selfishness. He would not add the oil to the common stock of his gang, but would save and sell it.

"I knew these workings before you were born," Janki Meah used to reply: "I don't want the light to get my coal out by, and I am not going to help you. The oil is mine, and I intend to keep it."

A strange man in many ways was Janki Meah, the white-haired, hot tempered, sightless weaver who had turned pitman. All day long—except on Sundays and Mondays when he was usually drunk—he worked in the Twenty-Two shaft of the Jimahari Colliery as cleverly as a man with all the senses. At evening he went up in the great steam-hauled cage to the pit-bank, and there called for his pony—a rusty, coal-dusty beast, nearly as old as Janki Meah. The pony would come to his side, and Janki Meah would clamber on to its back and be taken at once to the plot of land which he, like the other miners, received from the Jimahari Company. The pony knew that place, and when, after six years, the Company changed all the allotments to prevent

the miners from acquiring proprietary rights, Janki Meah represented, with tears in his eyes, that were his holdings shifted, he would never be able to find his way to the new one. "My horse only knows that place," pleaded Janki Meah, and so he was allowed to keep his land.

On the strength of this concession and his accumulated oil-savings, Janki Meah took a second wife—a girl of the Jolaha main stock of the Meahs, and singularly beautiful. Janki Meah could not see her beauty; wherefore he took her on trust, and forbade her to go down the pit. He had not worked for thirty years in the dark without knowing that the pit was no place for pretty women. He loaded her with ornaments—not brass or pewter, but real silver ones— and she rewarded him by flirting outrageously with Kundoo of Number Seven gallery gang. Kundoo was really the gang-head, but Janki Meah insisted upon all the work being entered in his own name, and chose the men that he worked with. Custom—stronger even than the Jimahari Company—dictated that Janki, by right of his years, should manage these things, and should, also, work despite his blindness. In Indian mines where they cut into the solid coal with the pick and clear it out from floor to ceiling, he could come to no great harm. At Home, where they undercut the coal and bring it down in crashing avalanches from the roof, he would never have been allowed to set foot in a pit. He was not a popular man, because of his oil-savings; but all the gangs admitted that Janki knew all the *khads*, or workings, that had ever been sunk or worked since the Jimahari

Company first started operations on the Tarachunda fields.

Pretty little Unda only knew that her old husband was a fool who could be managed. She took no interest in the collieries except in so far as they swallowed up Kundoo five days out of the seven, and covered him with coal-dust. Kundoo was a great workman, and did his best not to get drunk, because, when he had saved forty rupees, Unda was to steal everything that she could find in Janki's house and run with Kundoo to a land where there were no mines, and every one kept three fat bullocks and a milch-buffalo. While this scheme ripened it was his custom to drop in upon Janki and worry him about the oil savings. Unda sat in a corner and nodded approval. On the night when Kundoo had quoted that objectionable proverb about weavers, Janki grew angry.

"Listen, you pig," said he, "blind I am, and old I am, but, before ever you were born I was grey among the coal. Even in the days when the Twenty-Two *khad* was unsunk and there were not two thousand men here, I was known to have all knowledge of the pits. What *khad* is there that I do not know, from the bottom of the shaft to the end of the last drive? Is it the Baromba *khad*, the oldest, or the Twenty-Two where Tibu's gallery runs up to Number Five?"

"Hear the old fool talk!" said Kundoo, nodding to Unda. "No gallery of Twenty-Two will cut into Five before the end of the Rains. We have a month's solid coal before us. The Babuji says so."

"Babuji! Pigji! Dogji! What do

these fat slugs from Calcutta know? He draws and draws and draws, and talks and talks and talks, and his maps are all wrong. I, Janki, know that this is so. When a man has been shut up in the dark for thirty years, God gives him knowledge. The old gallery that Tibu's gang made is not six feet from Number Five."

"Without doubt God gives the blind knowledge," said Kundoo, with a look at Unda. "Let it be as you say. I, for my part, do not know where lies the gallery of Tibu's gang, but *I* am not a withered monkey who needs oil to grease his joints with."

Kundoo swung out of the hut laughing, and Unda giggled. Janki turned his sightless eyes toward his wife and swore. "I have land, and I have sold a great deal of lamp-oil," mused Janki; "but I was a fool to marry this child."

A week later the Rains set in with a vengeance, and the gangs paddled about in coal-slush at the pit-banks. Then the big mine-pumps were made ready, and the Manager of the Colliery ploughed through the wet toward the Tarachunda River swelling between its soppy banks. "Lord send that this beastly beck doesn't misbehave," said the Manager, piously, and he went to take counsel with his Assistant about the pumps.

But the Tarachunda misbehaved very much indeed. After a fall of three inches of rain in an hour it was obliged to do something. It topped its bank and joined the flood water that was hemmed between two low hills just where the embankment of the Colliery main line crossed. When a large part of a rain-fed river, and a few acres of flood-water, made a dead set for a nine-foot culvert, the culvert may spout its finest, but the water cannot *all* get out. The Manager pranced upon one leg with excitement, and his language was improper.

He had reason to swear, because he knew that one inch of water on land meant a pressure of one hundred tons to the acre; and here were about five feet of water forming, behind the railway embankment, over the shallower workings of Twenty-two. You must understand that, in a coal-mine, the coal nearest the surface is worked first from the central shaft. That is to say, the miners may clear out the stuff to within ten, twenty, or thirty feet of the surface, and, when all is worked out, leave only a skin of earth upheld by some few pillars of coal. In a deep mine where they know that they have any amount of material at hand, men prefer to get all their mineral out at one shaft, rather than make a number of little holes to tap the comparatively unimportant surface-coal.

And the Manager watched the flood.

The culvert spouted a nine-foot gush; but the water still formed, and word was sent to clear the men out of Twenty-Two. The cages came up crammed and crammed again with the men nearest the pit-eye, as they call the place where you can see daylight from the bottom of the main shaft. All away and away up the long black galleries the flare-lamps were winking and dancing like so many fireflies, and the men and the women waited for the clanking, rattling, thundering cages to come down and fly up again. But the outworkings were very far off, and word could not be passed quickly, though the heads of the gangs and the Assistant shouted and swore and tramped and stumbled. The Manager kept one eye on the great troubled pool behind the embankment, and prayed that the culvert would give way and let the water through in time. With the other eye he watched the cages come up and saw the headmen counting the roll of the gangs. With all his heart and soul he swore at the winder who controlled the iron drum that wound up the wire rope on which hung the cages.

In a little time there was a down-draw in the water behind the embankment—a sucking whirlpool, all yellow and yeasty. The water had smashed through the skin of the earth and was pouring into the old shallow workings of Twenty-Two.

Deep down below, a rush of black water caught the last gang waiting for the cage, and as they clambered in, the whirl was about their waists. The cage reached the pit-bank, and the Manager called the roll. The gangs were all safe except Gang Janki, Gang Mogul, and Gang Rahim, eighteen men, with perhaps ten basket-women who loaded the coal into the little iron carriages that ran on the tramways of the main galleries. These gangs were in the outworkings, three-quarters of a mile away, on the extreme fringe of the mine. Once more the cage went down, but with only two English men in it, and dropped into a swirling, roaring current that had almost touched the roof of some of the lower side-galleries. One of the wooden balks with which they had propped the old workings shot past on the current, just missing the cage.

"If we don't want our ribs knocked out, we'd better go," said the Manager. "We can't even save the Company's props."

The cage drew out of the water with a splash, and a few minutes later, it was officially reported that there were at least ten feet of water in the pit's eye. Now ten feet of water there meant that all other places in the mine were flooded except such galleries as were more than ten feet above the level of the bottom of the shaft. The deep workings would be full, the main galleries would be full, but in the high workings reached by inclines from the main roads, there would be a certain amount of air cut off, so to speak, by the water and squeezed up by it. The little science-primers explain how water behaves when you pour it down test-tubes. The flooding of Twenty-Two was an illustration on a large scale.

* * * * * *

"By the Holy Grove, what has happened to the air!" It was a Sonthal gangman of Gang Mogul in Number Nine gallery, and he was driving a six-foot way through the coal. Then there was a rush from the other galleries, and Gang Janki and Gang Rahim stumbled up with their basket-women.

"Water has come in the mine," they said, "and there is no way of getting out."

"I went down," said Janki—"down the slope of my gallery, and I felt the water."

"There has been no water in the cutting in our time," clamored the women. "Why cannot we go away?"

"Be silent!" said Janki. "Long ago, when my father was here, water came

to Ten—no, Eleven—cutting, and there was great trouble. Let us get away to where the air is better."

The three gangs and the basket-women left Number Nine gallery and went further up Number Sixteen. At one turn of the road they could see the pitchy black water lapping on the coal. It had touched the roof of a gallery that they knew well—a gallery where they used to smoke their *huqas* and manage their flirtations. Seeing this, they called aloud upon their Gods, and the Mehas, who are thrice bastered Muhammadans, strove to recollet the name of the Prophet. They came to a great open square whence nearly all the coal had been extracted. It was the end of the out-workings, and the end of the mine. Far away down the gallery a small pumping-engine, used for keeping dry a deep working and fed with steam from above, was throbbing faithfully. They heard it cease.

"They have cut off the steam," said Kundoo, hopefully. "They have given the order to use all the steam for the pit-bank pumps. They will clear out the water."

"If the water has reached the smoking-gallery," said Janki, "all the Company's pumps can do nothing for three days."

"It is very hot," moaned Jasoda, the Meah basket-woman. "There is a very bad air here because of the lamps."

"Put them out," said Janki; "why do you want lamps?" The lamps were put out and the company sat still in the utter dark. Somebody rose quietly and began walking over the coals. It was Janki, who was touching the walls with his hands. "Where is the ledge?" he murmured to himself.

"Sit, sit!" said Kundoo. "If we die, we die. The air is very bad."

But Janki still stumbled and crept and tapped with his pick upon the walls. The women rose to their feet.

"Stay all where you are. Without the lamps you cannot see, and I—I am always seeing," said Janki. Then he paused, and called out: "Oh, you who have been in the cutting more than ten years, what is the name of this open place? I am an old man and I have forgotten."

"Bullia's Room," answered the Sonthal, who had complained of the vileness of the air.

"Again," said Janki.

"Bullia's Room.

"Then I have found it," said Janki. "The name only had slipped my memory. Tibu's gang's gallery is here."

"A lie," said Kundoo. "There have been no galleries in this place since my day."

"Three paces was the depth of the ledge," muttered Janki, without heeding —"and—oh, my poor bones!—I have found it! It is here, up this ledge. Come all you, one by one, to the place of my voice, and I will count you."

There was a rush in the dark, and Janki felt the first man's face hit his knees as the Sonthal scrambled up the ledge.

"Who?" cried Janki.

"I, Sunua Manji."

"Sit you down," said Janki. "Who next?"

One by one the women and the men crawled up the ledge which ran along one side of "Bullia's Room." Degraded Muhammadan, pig-eating Musahr and wild Sonthal, Janki ran his hand over them all.

"Now follow after," said he, "catching hold of my heel, and the women catching the men's clothes." He did not ask whether the men had brought their picks with them. A miner, black or white, does not drop his pick. One by one, Janki leading, they crept into the old gallery—a six-foot way with a scant four feet from thill to roof.

"The air is better here," said Jasoda. They could hear her heart beating in thick, sick bumps.

"Slowly, slowly," said Janki. "I am an old man, and I forget many things. This is Tibu's gallery, but where are the four bricks where they used to put their *huqa* fire on when the Sahibs never saw? Slowly, slowly, O you people behind."

They heard his hands disturbing the small coal on the floor of the gallery and then a dull sound. "This is one unbaked brick, and this is another and another. Kundoo is a young man—let him come forward. Put a knee upon this brick and strike here. When Tibu's gang were at dinner on the last day before the good coal ended, they heard the men of Five on the other side, and Five worked *their* gallery two Sundays later —or it may have been one. Strike there, Kundoo, but give me room to go back."

Kundoo, doubting, drove the pick, but the first soft crush of the coal was a call to him. He was fighting for his life and for Unda—pretty little Unda with rings on all her toes—for Unda and the forty rupees. The women sang the Song of the Pick—the terrible, slow, swinging melody with the muttered chorus that repeats the sliding of the loosened coal, and to each cadence, Kundoo smote in the black dark. When he could do no more, Sunua Manji took the pick, and struck for his life and his wife, and his village beyond the blue hills over the Tarachunda River. An hour the men worked, and then the women cleared away the coal.

"It is farther than I thought," said Janki. "The air is very bad; but strike, Kundoo, strike hard."

For the fifth time Kundoo took up the pick as the Sonthal crawled back. The song had scarcely recommenced when it was broken by a yell from Kundoo that echoed down the gallery: *"Par hua! Par hua!* We are through, we are through!" The imprisoned air in the mine shot through the opening, and the women at the far end of the gallery heard the water rush through the pillars of "Bullia's Room" and roar against the ledge. Having fulfilled the law under which it worked, it rose no farther. The women screamed and pressed forward. "The water has come —we shall be killed! Let us go."

Kundoo crawled through the gap and found himself in a propped gallery by the simple process of hitting his head against a beam.

"Do I know the pits or do I not?" chuckled Janki. "This is the Number Five; go you out slowly, giving me your names. Ho! Rahim, count your gang! Now let us go forward, each catching hold of the other as before."

They formed a line in the darkness and Janki led them—for a pit-man in a strange pit is only one degree less liable to err than an ordinary mortal underground for the first time. At last they

saw a flare-lamp, and Gangs, Janki, Mogul, and Rahim of Twenty-Two stumbled dazed into the glare of the draught-furnace at the bottom of Five; Janki feeling his way and the rest behind.

"Water has come into Twenty-Two. God knows where are the others. I have brought these men from Tibu's gallery in our cutting; making connection through the north side of the gallery. Take us to the cage," said Janki Meah.

* * * * * *

At the pit-bank of Twenty-Two, some thousand people clamored and wept and, shouted. One hundred men—one thousand men—had been drowned in the cutting. They would all go to their homes to-morrow. Where were their men? Little Unda, her cloth drenched with the rain, stood at the pit-mouth calling down the shaft for Kundoo. They had swung the cages clear of the mouth, and her only answer was the murmur of the flood in the pit's eye two hundred and sixty feet below.

"Look after that woman! She'll chuck herself down the shaft in a minute," shouted the Manager.

But he need not have troubled; Unda was afraid of Death. She wanted Kundoo. The Assistant was watching the flood and seeing how far he could wade into it. There was a lull in the water, and the whirlpool had slackened. The mine was full, and the people at the pit-bank howled.

"My faith, we shall be lucky if we have five hundred hands on the place to-morrow!" said the Manager. "There's some chance yet of running a temporary dam across that water. Shove in anything—tubs and bullock-carts if you haven't enough bricks. Make them work *now* if they never worked before. Hi! you gangers, make them work."

Little by little the crowd was broken into detachments, and pushed toward the water with promises of overtime. The dam-making began, and when it was fairly under way, the Manager thought that the hour had come for the pumps. There was no fresh inrush into the mine. The tall, red, iron-clamped pump-beam rose and fell, and the pumps snored and guttered and shrieked as the first water poured out of the pipe.

"We must run her all to-night," said the Manager, wearily, "but there's no hope for the poor devils down below. Look here, Gur Sahai, if you are proud of your engines, show me what they can do now."

Gur Sahai grinned and nodded, with his right hand upon the lever and an oil-can in his left. He could do no more than he was doing, but he could keep that up till the dawn. Were the Company's pumps to be beaten by the vagaries of that troublesome Tarachunda River? Never, never! And the pumps sobbed and panted: "Never, never!" The Manager sat in the shelter of the pit-bank roofing, trying to dry himself by the pump-boiler fire, and, in the dreary dusk, he saw the crowds on the dam scatter and fly.

"That's the end," he groaned. " 'Twill take us six weeks to persuade 'em that we haven't tried to drown their mates on purpose. Oh, for a decent, rational Geordie!"

But the flight had no panic in it.

Men had run over from Five with astounding news, and the foremen could not hold their gangs together. Presently, surrounded by a clamorous crew, Gangs Rahim, Mogul, and Janki, and ten basket-women, walked up to report themselves, and pretty little Unda stole away to Janki's hut to prepare his evening meal.

"Alone I found the way," explained Janki Meah, "and now will the Company give me pension?"

The simple pit-folk shouted and leaped and went back to the dam, reassured in their old belief that, whatever happened, so great was the power of the Company whose salt they ate, none of them could be killed. But Gur Sahai only bared his white teeth and kept his hand upon the lever and proved his pumps to the uttermost.

*   *   *   *   *   *

"I say," said the Assistant to the Manager, a week later, "do you recollect *Germinal?*"

"Yes. 'Queer thing. I thought of it in the cage when that balk went by. Why?"

"Oh, this business seems to be *Germinal* upside down. Janki was in my veranda all this morning, telling me that Kundo had eloped with his wife— Unda or Anda, I think her name was."

"Hillo! And those were the cattle that you risked your life to clear out of Twenty-Two!"

"No—I was thinking of the Company's props, not the Company's men."

"Sounds better to say so *now;* but I don't believe you, old fellow."

In Flood Time

Tweed said tae Till:
"What gars ye rin sae Still?"
Till said tae Tweed:
"Though ye rin wi' speed
An' I rin slaw—
Yet where ye droon ae man
I droon twa."

THERE is no getting over the river to-night, Sahib. They say that a bullock-cart has been washed down already, and the *ekka* that went over a half hour before you came, has not yet reached the far side. Is the Sahib in haste? I will drive the ford-elephant in to show him. *Ohe, mahout* there in the shed! Bring out Ram Pershad, and if he will face the current, good. An elephant never lies, Sahib, and Ram Pershad is separated from his friend Kala Nag. He, too, wishes to cross to the far side. Well done! Well done! my King! Go half way across, *mahoutji,* and see what the river says. Well done, Ram Pershad! Pearl among elephants, go into the river! Hit him on the head, fool! Was the goad made only to scratch thy own fat back with, bastard? Strike! Strike! What are the boulders to thee, Ram Pershad, my Rustum, my mountain of strength? Go in! Go in!

No, Sahib! It is useless. You can hear him trumpet. He is telling Kala Nag that he cannot come over. See! He has swung round and is shaking his head. He is no fool. He knows what the Barhwi means when it is angry. Aha! Indeed, thou art no fool, my child! *Salaam,* Ram Pershad, Bahadur! Take him under the trees, *mahout,* and

see that he gets his spices. Well done, thou chiefest among tuskers. *Salaam* to the Sirkar and go to sleep.

What is to be done? The Sahib must wait till the river goes down. It will shrink to-morrow morning, if God pleases, or the day after at the latest. Now why does the Sahib get so angry? I am his servant. Before God, *I* did not create this stream! What can I do? My hut and all that is therein is at the service of the Sahib, and it is beginning to rain. Come away, my Lord. How will the river go down for your throwing abuse at it? In the old days the English people were not thus. The fire-carriage has made them soft. In the old days, when they drave behind horses by day or by night, they said naught if a river barred the way, or a carriage sat down in the mud. It was the will of God—not like a fire-carriage which goes and goes and goes, and would go though all the devils in the land hung on to its tail. The fire-carriage hath spoiled the English people. After all, what is a day lost, or, for that matter, what are two days? Is the Sahib going to his own wedding, that he is so mad with haste? Ho! Ho! Ho! I am an old man and see few Sahibs. Forgive me if I have forgotten the respect that is due to them. The Sahib is not angry?

His own wedding! Ho! Ho! Ho! The mind of an old man is like the *numah*-tree. Fruit, bud, blossom, and the dead leaves of all the years of the

651

past flourish together. Old and new and that which is gone out of remembrance, all three are there! Sit on the bedstead, Sahib, and drink mink. Or—would the Sahib in truth care to drink my tobacco? It is good. It is the tobacco of Nuklao. My son, who is in service there sent it to me. Drink, then, Sahib, if you know how to handle the tube. The Sahib takes it like a Musalman. Wah! Wah! Where did he learn that? His own wedding! Ho! Ho! Ho! The Sahib says that there is no wedding in the matter at all? Now *is* it likely that the Sahib would speak true talk to me who am only a black man? Small wonder, then, that he is in haste. Thirty years have *I* beaten the gong at this ford, but never have I seen a Sahib in such haste. Thirty years, Sahib! That is a very long time. Thirty years ago this ford was on the track of the *bunjaras,* and I have seen two thousand pack-bullocks cross in one night. Now the rail has come, and the fire-carriage says *buz-buz-buz,* and a hundred lakhs of maunds slide across that big bridge. It is very wonderful; but the ford is lonely now that there are no *bunjaras* to camp under the trees.

Nay, do not trouble to look at the sky without. It will rain till the dawn. Listen! The boulders are talking tonight in the bed of the river. Hear them! They would be husking your bones, Sahib, had you tried to cross. See, I will shut the door and no rain can enter. *Wahi! Ahi!! Ugh!* Thirty years on the banks of the ford! An old man am I and—where is the oil for the lamp?

*   *   *   *   *   *

Your pardon, but, because of my years, I sleep no sounder than a dog; and you moved to the door. Look then, Sahib. Look and listen. A full half *kos* from bank to bank is the stream now—you can see it under the stars—and there are ten feet of water therein. It will not shrink because of the anger in your eyes, and it will not be quiet on account of your curses. Which is louder, Sahib—your voice or the voice of the river? Call to it—perhaps it will be ashamed. Lie down and sleep afresh, Sahib. I know the anger of the Barhwi when there has fallen rain in the foot-hills. I swam the flood, once, on a night tenfold worse than this, and by the Favor of God I was released from Death when I had come to the very gates thereof.

May I tell the tale? Very good talk. I will fill the pipe anew.

Thirty years ago it was, when I was a young man and had but newly come to the ford. I was strong then, and the *bunjaras* had no doubt when I said "this ford is clear." I have toiled all night up to my shoulder-blades in running water amid a hundred bullocks mad with fear, and have brought them across losing not a hoof. When all was done I fetched the shivering men, and they gave me for reward the pick of their cattle—the bell-bullock of the drove. So great was the honor in which I was held But, to-day when the rail falls and the river rises, I creep into by hut and whimper like a dog. My strength is gone from me. I am an old man and the fire-carriage has made the ford desolate. They were wont to call me the Strong One of the Barhwi.

Behold my face, Sahib—it is the face

of a monkey. And my arm—it is the arm of an old woman. I swear to you, Sahib, that a woman has loved this face and has rested in the hollow of this arm. Twenty years ago, Sahib. Believe me, this was true talk—twenty years ago.

Come to the door and look across. Can you see a thin fire very far away down the stream? That is the temple-fire, in the shrine of Hanuman, of the village of Pateera. North, under the big star, is the village itself, but it is hidden by a bend of the river. Is that far to swim, Sahib? Would you take off your clothes and adventure? Yet I swam to Pateera—not once but many times; and there are *muggers* in the river too.

Love knows no caste; else why should I, a Musalman and the son of a Musalman, have sought a Hindu woman—a widow of the Hindus—the sister of the headman of Pateera? But it was even so. They of the headman's household came on a pilgrimage to Muttra when She was but newly a bride. Silver tires were upon the wheels of the bullock-cart, and silken curtains hid the woman. Sahib, I made no haste in their conveyance, for the wind parted the curtains and I saw Her. When they returned from pilgrimage the boy that was Her husband had died, and I saw Her again in the bullock-cart. By God, these Hindus are fools! What was it to me whether She was Hindu or Jain —scavenger, leper, or whole? I would have married Her and made Her a home by the ford. The Seventh of the Nine Bars says that a man may not marry one of the idolaters? Is that truth? Both Shiahs and Sunnis say that a Musalman may not marry one of the idolaters? Is the Sahib a priest, then, that he knows so much? I will tell him something that he does not know. There is neither Shiah nor Sunni, forbidden nor idolater, in Love; and the Nine Bars are but nine little fagots that the flame of Love utterly burns away. In truth, I would have taken Her; but what could I do? The headman would have sent his men to break my head with staves. I am not—I was not—afraid of any five men; but against half a village who can prevail?

Therefore it was my custom, these things having been arranged between us twain, to go by night to the village of Pateera, and there we met among the crops; no man knowing aught of the matter. Behold, now! I was wont to cross here, skirting the jungle to the river bend where the railway bridge is, and thence across the elbow of land to Pateera. The light of the shrine was my guide when the nights were dark. That jungle near the river is very full of snakes—little *karaits* that sleep on the sand—and moreover, Her brothers would have slain me had they found me in the crops. But none knew—none knew save She and I; and the blown sand of the river-bed covered the track of my feet. In the hot months it was an easy thing to pass from the ford to Pateera, and in the first Rains, when the river rose slowly, it was an easy thing also. I set the strength of my body against the strength of the stream, and nightly I ate in my hut here and drank at Pateera yonder. She had said that one Hirnam Singh, a thief, had sought Her, and he was of a village up the river but on the same bank. All Sikhs are dogs, and they have refused in their folly that good gift of God—tobacco. I was ready to destroy Hirnam Singh that ever he had come nigh Her; and the more because he had sworn to Her that She had a lover, and that he would lie in wait and give the name to the headman unless She went away with him. What curs are these Sikhs!

After that news, I swam always with a little sharp knife in my belt, and evil would it have been for a man had he stayed me. I knew not the face of Hirnam Singh, but I would have killed any who came between me and Her.

Upon a night in the beginning of the Rains, I was minded to go across to Pateera, albeit the river was angry. Now the nature of the Barhwi is this, Sahib. In twenty breaths it comes down from the Hills, a wall three feet high, and I have seen it, between the lighting of a fire and the cooking of a *chupatty*, grow from a runnel to a sister of the Jumna.

When I left this bank there was a shoal a half mile down, and I made shift to feth it and draw breath there ere going forward; for I felt the hands of the river heavy upon my heels. Yet what will a young man not do for Love's sake? There was but little light from the stars, and midway to the shoal a branch of the stinking deodar tree brushed my mouth as I swam. That was a sign of heavy rain in the foot-hills and beyond, for the deodar is a strong tree, not easily shaken from the hillsides. I made haste, the river aiding me, but ere I had touched the shoal, the pulse of the stream beat, as it were, within me and around, and, behold, the shoal was gone and I rode high on the crest of a wave that ran from bank to bank. Has the Sahib ever been cast into much water that fights and will not let a man use his limbs? To me my head upon the water, it seemed as though there were naught but water to the world's end, and the river drave me with its driftwood. A man is a very little thing in the belly of a flood. And *this* flood, though I knew it not, was the Great Flood about which men talk still. My liver was dissolved and I lay like a log upon my back in the fear of Death. There were living things in the water, crying and howling grievously—beasts of the forest and cattle, and once the voice of a man asking for help. But the rain came and lashed the water white, and I heard no more save the roar of the boulders below and the roar of the rain above. Thus I was whirled down-stream, wrestling for the breath in me. It is very hard to die when one is young. Can the Sahib, standing here, see the railway bridge? Look, there are the lights of the mail-train going to Peshawur! The bridge is now twenty feet above the river, but upon that night the water was roaring against the lattice-work and against the lattice came I feet first. But much driftwood was piled there and upon the piers, and I took no great hurt. Only the river pressed me as a strong man presses a weaker. Scarcely could I take hold of the lattice-work and crawl to the upper boom. Sahib, the water was foaming across the rails a foot deep! Judge therefore what manner of flood it must have been. I could not hear. I could not see. I could but lie on the boom and pant for breath.

After a while the rain ceased and

there came out in the sky certain new washed stars, and by their light I saw that there was no end to the black water as far as the eye could travel, and the water had risen upon the rails. There were dead beasts in the driftwood on the piers, and others caught by the neck in the lattice-work, and others not yet drowned who strove to find a foothold on the lattice-work—buffaloes and kine, and wild pig, and deer one or two, and snakes and jackals past all counting. Their bodies were black upon the left side of the bridge, but the smaller of them were forced through the lattice-work and whirled down-stream.

Thereafter the stars died and the rain came down afresh and the river rose yet more, and I felt the bridge begin to stir under men as a man stirs in his sleep ere he wakes. But I was not afraid, Sahib. I swear to you that I was not afraid, though I had no power in my limbs. I knew that I should not die till I had seen Her once more. But I was very cold, and I felt that the bridge must go.

There was a trembling in the water, such a trembling as goes before the coming of a great wave, and the bridge lifted its flank to the rush of that coming so that the right lattice dipped under water and the left rose clear. On my beard, Sahib, I am speaking God's truth! As a Mirzapore stone-boat careens to the wind, so the Barhwi Bridge turned. Thus and in no other manner.

I slid from the boom into deep water, and behind me came the wave of the wrath of the river. I heard its voice and the scream of the middle part of the bridge as it moved from the piers and sank, and I knew no more till I rose in the middle of the great flood. I put forth my hand to swim, and lo! it fell upon the knotted hair of the head of a man. He was dead, for no one but I, the Strong One of Barhwi, could have lived in that race. He had been dead full two days, for he rode high, wallowing, and was an aid to me. I laughed then, knowing for a surety that I should yet see Her and take no harm; and I twisted my fingers in the hair of the man, for I was far spent, and together we went down the stream—he the dead and I the living. Lacking that help I should have sunk: the cold was in my marrow, and my flesh was ribbed and sodden on my bones. But *he* had no fear who had known the uttermost of the power of the river; and I let him go where he chose. At last we came into the power of a side-current that set to the right bank, and I strove with my feet to draw with it. But the dead man swung heavily in the whirl, and I feared that some branch had struck him and that he would sink. The tops of the tamarisk brushed my knees, so I knew we were come into flood-water above the crops, and, after I let down my legs and felt bottom—the ridge of a field—and, after, the dead man stayed upon a knoll under a fig-tree, and I drew my body from the water rejoicing.

Does the Sahib know whither the backwash of the flood had borne me? To the knoll which is the eastern boundary-mark of the village of Pateera! No other place. I drew the dead man up on the grass for the service that he had done me, and also because I knew not whether I should need him again. Then I went, crying thrice like a jackal, to the appointed place which was near the byre of the headman's house. But my Love was already there, weeping. She feared that the flood had swept my hut at the Barhwi Ford. When I came softly through the ankle-deep water, She thought it was a ghost and would have fled, but I put my arms round Her, and—I was no ghost in those days, though I am an old man now. Ho! Ho! Dried corn, in truth. Maize without juice. Ho! Ho![1]

I told Her the story of the breaking of the Barhwi Bridge, and She said that I was greater than mortal man, for none may cross the Barhwi in full flood, and I had seen what never man had seen before. Hand in hand we went to the knoll where the dead lay, and I showed Her by what help I had made the ford. She looked also upon the body under the stars, for the latter end of the night was clear, and hid Her face in Her hands, crying: "It is the body of Hirnam Singh!" I said: "The swine is of more use dead than living, my Beloved," and She said: "Surely, for he has saved the dearest life in the world to my love. None the less, he cannot stay here, for that would bring shame upon me." The body was not a gunshot from her door.

Then said I, rolling the body with my hands: "God hath judged between us, Hirnam Singh, that thy blood might not be upon my head. Now, whether I have done thee a wrong in keeping thee from the burning-ghat do thou and the crows settle together." So I cast him adrift into the flood-water, and he was

drawn out to the open, ever wagging his thick black beard like a priest under the pulpit-board. And I saw no more of Hirnam Singh.

Before the breaking of the day we two parted, and I moved toward such of the jungle as was not flooded. With the full light I saw what I had done in the darkness, and the bones of my body were loosened in my flesh, for there ran two *kos* of raging water between the village of Pateera and the trees of the far bank, and, in the middle, the piers of the Barhwi Bridge showed like broken teeth in the jaw of an old man. Nor was there any life upon the waters —neither birds nor boats, but only an army of drowned things—bullocks and horses and men—and the river was redder than blood from the clay of the foothills. Never had I seen such a flood —never since that year have I seen the like—and, O Sahib, no man living had done what I had done. There was no return for me that day. Not for all the lands of the headman would I venture a second time without the shield of darkness that cloaks danger. I went a *kos* up the river to the house of a blacksmith, saying that the flood had swept me from my hut, and they gave me food. Seven days I stayed with the blacksmith, till a boat came and I returned to my house. There was no trace of wall, or roof, or floor—naught but a patch of slimy mud. Judge, therefore, Sahib, how far the river must have risen.

It was written that I should not die either in my house, or in the heart of the Barhwi, or under the wreck of the Barhwi Bridge, for God sent down Hirnam Singh two days dead, though I

[1] I grieve to say that the Warden of Barhwi ford is responsible here for two very bad puns in the vernacular.—R. K.

know not how the man died, to be my buoy and support. Hirnam Singh has been in Hell these twenty years, and the thought of that night must be the flower of his torment.

Listen, Sahib! The river has changed its voice. It is going to sleep before the dawn, to which there is yet one hour. With the light it will come down afresh. How do I know? Have I been here thirty years without knowing the voice of the river as a father knows the voice of his son? Every moment it is talking less angrily. I swear that there will be no danger for one hour or, perhaps, two. I cannot answer for the morning. Be quick, Sahib! I will call Ram Pershad, and he will not turn back this time. Is the paulin tightly corded upon all the baggage? *Ohe, mahout* with a mud head, the elephant for the Sahib, and tell them on the far side that there will be no crossing after daylight.

Money? Nay, Sahib. I am not of that kind. No, not even to give sweetmeats to the baby-folk. My house, look you, is empty, and I am an old man.

Dutt, Ram Pershad! *Dutt! Dutt! Dutt!* Good luck go with you, Sahib.

The Sending of Dana Da

When the Devil rides on your chest remember the *chamar.—Native Proverb.*

ONCE upon a time, some people in India made a new Heaven and a new Earth out of broken tea-cups, a missing brooch or two, and a hair-brush. These were hidden under brushes, or stuffed into holes in the hillside, and an entire Civil Service of subordinate Gods used to find or mend them again; and every one said: "There are more things in Heaven and Earth than are dreamed of in our philosophy." Several other things happened also, but the Religion never seemed to get much beyond its first manifestations; though it added an air-line postal service, and orchestral effects in order to keep abreast of the times, and choke off competition.

This Religion was too elastic for ordinary use. It stretched itself and embraced pieces of everything that the medicine-men of all ages have manufactured. It approved of and stole from Freemasonry; looted the Latter-day Rosicrucians of half their pet words; took any fragments of Egyptian philosophy that it found in the *Encyclopoedia Britannica;* annexed as many of the Vedas as had been translated into French or English, and talked of all the rest; built in the German versions of what is left of the Zend Avesta; encouraged White, Grey and Black Magic, including spiritualism, palmistry, fortune-telling by cards, hot chestnuts, double-kerneled nuts and tallow droppings; would have adopted Voodoo and Oboe had it known anything about them, and showed itself, in every way, one of the most accommodating arrangements that had ever been invented since the birth of the Sea.

When it was in thorough working order, with all the machinery, down to the subscriptions, complete, Dana Da came from nowhere, with nothing in his hands, and wrote a chapter in its history which has hitherto been unpublished. He said that his first name was Dana, and his second was Da. Now, setting aside Dana of the New York *Sun*, Dana is a Bhil name, and Da fits no native of India unless you except the Bengali Dé as the original spelling. Da is Lap or Finnish; and Dana Da was neither Finn, Chin, Bhil, Bengali, Lap, Nair, Gond, Romaney, Magh, Bokhariot, Kurd, Armenian, Levantine, Jew, Persian, Punjabi, Madrasi, Parsee, nor anything else known to ethnologists. He was simply Dana Da, and declined to give further information. For the sake of brevity and as roughly indicating his origin, he was called "The Native." He might have been the original Old Man of the Mountains, who is said to be the only authorized head of the Tea-cup Creed. Some people said that he was; but Dana Da used to smile and deny any connection with the cult; explaining that he was an "Independent Experimenter."

As I have said, he came from nowhere, with his hands behind his back, and studied the Creed for three weeks; sitting at the feet of those best competent to explain its mysteries. Then he laughed aloud and went away, but the laugh might have been either of devotion or derision.

When he returned he was without money, but his pride was unabated. He declared that he knew more about the Things in Heaven and Earth than those who taught him, and for this contumacy was abandoned altogether.

His next appearance in public life was at a big cantonment in Upper India, and he was then telling fortunes with the help of three leaden dice, a very dirty old cloth, and a little tin box of opium pills. He told better fortunes when he was allowed half a bottle of whiskey; but the things which he invented on the opium were quite worth the money. He was in reduced circumstances. Among other people's he told the fortune of an Englishman who had once been interested in the Simla Creed, but who, later on, had married and forgotten all his old knowledge in the study of babies and things. The Englishman allowed Dana Da to tell a fortune for charity's sake, and gave him five rupees, a dinner, and some old clothes. When he had eaten, Dana Da professed gratitude, and asked if there were anything he could do for his host —in the esorteric line.

"Is there any one that you love?" said Dana Da. The Englishman loved his wife, but had no desire to drag her name into the conversation. He therefore shook his head.

"Is there any one that you hate?" said Dana Da. The Englishman said that there were several men whom he hated deeply.

"Very good," said Dana Da, upon whom the whiskey and the opium were beginning to tell. "Only give me their names, and I will despatch a Sending to them and kill them."

Now a Sending is a horrible arrangement, first invented, they say, in Iceland. It is a Thing sent by a wizard, and may take any form, but, most generally, wanders about the land in the shape of a little purple cloud till it finds the Sendee, and him it kills by changing into the form of a horse, or a cat, or a man without a face. It is not strictly a native patent, though *chamars* of the skin and hide castes can, if irritated, despatch a Sending which sits on the breast of their enemy by night and nearly kills him. Very few natives care to irritate *chamars* for this reason.

"Let me despatch a Sending," said Dana Da; "I am nearly dead now with want, and drink, and opium; but I should like to kill a man before I die. I can send a Sending anywhere you choose, and in any form except in the shape of a man."

The Englishman had no friends that he wished to kill, but partly to soothe Dana Da, whose eyes were rolling, and partly to see what would be done, he asked whether a modified Sending could not be arranged for—such a Sending as should make a man's life a burden to him, and yet do him no harm. If this were possible, he notified his willingness to give Dana Da ten rupees for the job.

"I am not what I was once," said Dana Da, "and I must take the money because I am poor. To what Englishman shall I send it?"

"Send a Sending to Lone Sahib," said the Englishman, naming a man who had been most bitter in rebuking him for his apostasy from the Tea-cup Creed. Dana Da laughed and nodded.

"I could have chosen no better man myself," said he. "I will see that he finds the Sending about his path and

about his bed."

He lay down on the hearth-rug, turned up the whites of his eyes, shivered all over and began to snort. This was Magic, or Opium, or the Sending, or all three. When he opened his eyes he vowed that the Sending had started upon the war-path, and was at that moment flying up to the town where Lone Sahib lives.

"Give me my ten rupees," said Dana Da, wearily, "and write a letter to Lone Sahib telling him, and all who believe with him, that you and a friend are using a power greater than theirs. They will see that you are speaking the truth."

He departed unsteadily, with the promise of some more rupees if anything came of the Sending.

The Englishman sent a letter to Lone Sahib, couched in what he remembered of the terminology of the Creed. He wrote: "I also, in the days of what you held to be my backsliding, have obtained Enlightenment, and with Enlightenment has come Power." Then he grew so deeply mysterious that the recipient of the letter could make neither head nor tail of it, and was proportionately impressed; for he fancied that his friend had become a "fifth-rounder." When a man is a "fifth-rounder" he can do more than Slade and Houdin combined.

Lone Sahib read the letter in five different fashions, and was beginning a sixth interpretation when his bearer dashed in with the news that there was a cat on the bed. Now if there was one thing that Lone Sahib hated more than another, it was a cat. He scolded the bearer for not turning it out of the house. The bearer said that he was afraid. All the doors of the bedroom had been shut throughout the morning, and no *real* cat could possibly have entered the room. He would prefer not to meddle with the creature.

Lone Sahib entered the room gingerly, and there, on the pillow of his bed, sprawled and whimpered a wee white kitten; not a jumpsome, frisky little beast, but a slug-like crawler with its eyes barely opened and its paws lacking strength or direction—a kitten that ought to have been in a basket with its mamma. Lone Sahib caught it by the scurff of its neck, handed it over to the sweeper to be drowned, and fined the bearer four annas.

That evening, as he was reading in his room, he fancied that he saw something moving about on the hearth-rug, outside the circle of light from his reading-lamp. When the thing began to myowl, he realized that it was a kitten—a wee white kitten, nearly blind and very miserable. He was seriously angry, and spoke bitterly to his bearer, who said that there was no kitten in the room when he brought it in the lamp, and *real* kittens of tender age generally had mother-cats in attendance.

"If the Presence will go out into the veranda and listen," said the bearer, "he will hear no cats. How, therefore, can the kitten on the bed and the kitten on the hearth-rug be real kittens?"

Lone Sahib went out to listen, and the bearer followed him, but there was no sound of any one mewing for her children. He returned to his room, having hurled the kitten down the hillside, and wrote out the incidents of the day for the benefit of his co-religionists.

Those people were so absolutely free from superstition that they ascribed anything a little out of the common to Agencies. As it was their business to know all about the Agencies, they were on terms of almost indecent familiarity with Manifestations of every kind. Their letters dropped from the ceiling —unstamped—and Spirits used to squatter up and down their staircases all night; but they had never come into contact with kittens. Lone Sahib wrote out the facts, noting the hour and the minute, as every Psychical Observer is bound to do, and appending the Englishman's letter because it was the most mysterious document and might have had a bearing upon anything in this world or the next. An outsider would have translated all the tangle thus: "Look out! You laughed at me once, and now I am going to make you sit up."

Lone Sahib's co-religionists found that meaning in it; but their translation was refined and full of four-syllable words. They held a sederunt, and were filled with tremulous joy, for, in spite of their familiarity with all the other worlds and cycles, they had a very human awe of things sent from Ghostland. They met in Lone Sahib's room in shrouded and sepulchral gloom, and their conclave was broken up by clinking among the photo-frames on the mantelpiece. A wee white kitten, nearly blind, was looping and writhing itself between the clock and the candlesticks. That stopped all investigations or doubtings. Here was the Manifestation in the flesh. It was, so far as could be seen, devoid of purpose, but it was a Manifestation of undoubted authenticity.

They drafted a Round Robin to the Englishman, the backslider of old days, adjuring him in the interests of the Creed to explain whether there was any connection between the embodiment of some Egyptian God or other (I have forgotten the name) and his communication. They called the kitten Ra, or Toth, or Tum, or some thing; and when Lone Sahib confessed that the first one had, at his most misguided instance, been drowned by the sweeper, they said consolingly that in his next life he would be a "bounder," and not even a "rounder" of the lowest grade. These words may not be quite correct, but they accurately express the sense of the house.

When the Englishman received the Round Robin—it came by post—he was startled and bewildered. He sent into the bazar for Dana Da, who read the letter and laughed. "That is my Sending," said he. "I told you I would work well. Now give me another ten rupees."

"But what in the world is this gibberish about Egyptian Gods?" asked the Englishman.

"Cats," said Dana Da, with a hiccough, for he had discovered the Englishman's whiskey bottle. "Cats, and cats, and cats! Never was such a Sending. A hundred of cats. Now give me ten more rupees and write as I dictate."

Dana Da's letter was a curiosity. It bore the Englishman's signature, and hinted at cats—at a Sending of Cats. The mere words on paper were creepy and uncanny to behold.

"What have you done, though?" said the Englishman; "I am as much in the dark as ever. Do you mean to say that you can actually send this absurd Sending you talk about?"

"Judge for yourself," said Dana Da. "What does that letter mean? In a little time they will all be at my feet and yours, and I—O Glory!—will be drugged or drunk all day long."

Dana Da knew his people.

When a man who hates cats wakes up in the morning and finds a little squirming kitten on his breast, or puts his hands into his ulster-pocket and finds a little half-dead kitten where his gloves should be, or opens his trunk and finds a vile kitten among his dress-shirts, or goes for a long ride with his mackintosh strapped on his saddle-bow and shakes a little squawling kitten from its folds when he opens it, or goes out to dinner and finds a little blind kitten under his chair, or stays at home and finds a writhing kitten under the quilt, or wriggling among his boots, or hanging, head downward, in his tobacco-jar, or being mangled by his terrier in the veranda,—when such a man finds one kitten, neither more nor less, once a day in a place where no kitten rightly could or should be, he is naturally upset. When he dare not murder his daily trove because he believes it to be a Manifestation, and Emissary, an Embodiment, and half a dozen other things all out of the regular course of nature, he is more than upset. He is actually distressed. Some of Lone Sahib's co-religionists thought that he was a highly favored individual; but many said that if he had treated the first kitten with proper respect—as suited a Toth-Ra

Tum-Sennacherib Embodiment—all this trouble would have been averted. They compared him to the Ancient Mariner, but none the less they were proud of him and proud of the Englishman who had sent the Manifestation. They did not call it a Sending because Icelandic magic was not in their programme.

After sixteen kittens, that is to say after one fortnight, for there were three kittens on the first day to impress the fact of the Sending, the whole camp was uplifted by a letter—it came flying through a window—from the Old Man of the Mountains—the Head of all the Creed—explaining the Manifestation in the most beautiful language and soaking up all the credit of it for himself. The Englishman, said the letter, was not there at all. He was a backslider without Power or Asceticism, who couldn't even raise a table by force of volition, much less project an army of kittens through space. The entire arrangement, said the letter, was strictly orthodox, worked and sanctioned by the highest Authorities within the pale of the Creed. There was great joy at this, for some of the weaker brethren seeing that an outsider who had been working on independent lines could create kittens, whereas their own rulers had never gone beyond crockery—and broken at best—were showing a desire to break line on their own trail. In fact, there was the promise of a schism. A second Round Robin was drafted to the Englishman, beginning "O Scoffer," and ending with a selection of curses from the Rites of Mizraim and Memphis and the Commination of Jugana, who was a "fifth-rounder," upon whose name an unstart "third-

rounder" once traded. A papal excommunication is a *billet-doux* compared to the Commination of Jugana. The Englishman had been proved, under the hand and seal of the Old Man of the Mountains, to have appropriated Virtue and pretended to have Power which, in reality, belonged only to the Supreme Head. Naturally the Round Robin did not spare him.

He handed the letter to Dana Da to translate into decent English. The effect on Dana Da was curious. At first he was furiously angry, and then he laughed for five minutes.

"I had thought," he said, "that they would have come to me. In another week I would have shown that I sent the Sending, and they would have discrowned the Old Man of the Mountains who has sent this Sending of mine. Do you do nothing. The time has come for me to act. Write as I dictate, and I will put them to shame. But give me ten more rupees."

At Dana Da's dictation the Englishman wrote nothing less than a formal challenge to the Old Man of the Mountains. It wound up: "And if this Manifestation be from your hand, then let it go forward; but if it be from my hand, I will that the Sending shall cease in two days' time. On that day there shall be twelve kittens and thenceforward none at all. The people shall judge between us." This was signed by Dana Da, who added pentacles and pentagrams, and a *crux ansata*, and half a dozen *swastikas*, and a Triple Tau to his name, just to show that he was all he laid claim to be.

The challenge was read out to the gentlemen and ladies, and they remembered then that Dana Da had laughed at them some years ago. It was officially announced that the Old Man of the Mountains would treat the matter with contempt; Dana Da being an Independent Investigator without a single "round" at the back of him. But this did not soothe his people. They wanted to see a fight. They were very human for all their spirituality. Lone Sahib, who was really being worn out with kittens, submitted meekly to his fate. He felt that he was being "kittened to prove the power of Dana Da," as the poet says.

When the stated day dawned, the shower of kittens began. Some were white and some were tabby, and all were about the same loathsome age. Three were on his hearth-rug, three in his bath-room, and the other six turned up at intervals among the visitors who came to see the prophecy break down. Never was a more satisfactory Sending. On the next day there were no kittens, and the next day and all the other days were kittenless and quiet. The people murmured and looked to the Old Man of the Mountains for an explanation. A letter, written on a palm-leaf, dropped from the ceiling, but every one except Lone Sahib felt that letters were not what the occasion demanded. There should have been cats, there should have been cats,—full-grown ones. The letter proved conclusively that there had been a hitch in the Psychic Current which, colliding with a Dual Identity, had interfered with the Percipient Activity all along the main line. The kittens were still going on, but owing to some failure in the Developing Fluid, they were not materialized. The air

was thick with letters for a few days afterward. Unseen hands played Glück and Beethoven on finger-bowls and clock-shades; but all men felt that Psychic Life was a mockery without materialized Kittens. Even Lone Sahib shouted with the majority on this head. Dana Da's letters were very insulting, and if he had then offered to lead a new departure, there is no knowing what might not have happened.

But Dana Da was dying of whiskey and opium in the Englishman's go-down, and had small heart for honors.

"They have been put to shame," said he. "Never was such a Sending. It has killed me."

"Nonsense," said the Englishman, "you are going to die, Dana Da, and that sort of stuff must be left behind. I'll admit that you have made some queer things come about. Tell me honestly, now, how was it done?"

"Give me ten more rupees," said Dana Da, faintly, "and if I die before I spend them, bury them with me." The silver was counted out while Dana Da was fighting with Death. His hand closed upon the money and he smiled a grim smile.

"Bend low," he whispered. The Englishman bent.

"*Bunnia*—Mission-school—expelled— *box-wallah* (peddler)—Ceylon pearl-merchant—all mine English education —out-casted, and made up name Dana Da—England with American thought-reading man and—and—you gave me ten rupees several times—I gave the Sahib's bearer two-eight a month for cats—little, little cats. I wrote, and he put them about—very clever man. Very few kittens now in the *bazar*. Ask Lone Sahib's sweeper's wife."

So saying, Dana Da gasped and passed away into a land where, if all be true, there are no materializations and the making of new creeds is discouraged.

But consider the gorgeous simplicity of it all!

———•———

On the City Wall

Then she let them down by a cord through the window; for her house was upon the town-wall, and she dwelt upon the wall.—*Joshua* ii. 15.

LALUN is a member of the most ancient profession in the world. Lilith was her very-great-grandmamma, and that was before the days of Eve as every one knows. In the West, people say rude things about Lalun's profession, and write lectures about it, and distribute the lectures to young persons in order that Morality may be preserved. In the East where the profession is hereditary, descending from mother to daughter, nobody writes lectures or takes any notice; and that is a distinct proof of the inability of the East to manage its own affairs.

Lalun's real husband, for even ladies of Lalun's profession in the East must have husbands, was a big jujube-tree. Her Mamma, who had married a fig-tree, spent ten thousand rupees on Lalun's wedding, which was blessed by forty-seven clergymen of Mamma's church, and distributed five thousand rupees in charity to the poor. And that was the custom of the land. The advantages of having a jujube-tree for a husband are obvious. You cannot hurt his feelings, and he looks imposing.

Lalun's husband stood on the plain outside the City walls, and Lalun's house was upon the east wall facing the river. If you fell from the broad window-seat you dropped thirty feet sheer into the City Ditch. But if you stayed where you should and looked forth, you saw all the cattle of the City being driven down to water, the students of the Government College playing cricket, the high grass and trees that fringed the river-bank, the great sand bars that ribbed the river, the red tombs of dead Emperors beyond the river, and very far away through the blue heat-haze, a glint of the snows of the Himalayas.

Wali Dad used to lie in the window-seat for hours at a time watching this view. He was a young Muhammadan who was suffering acutely from education of the English variety and knew it. His father had sent him to a Mission-school to get wisdom, and Wali Dad had absorbed more than ever his father or the Missionaries intended he should. When his father died, Wali Dad was independent and spent two years experimenting with the creeds of the Earth and reading books that are of no use to anybody.

After he had made an unsuccessful attempt to enter the Roman Catholic

Church and the Presbyterian fold at the same time (the Missionaries found him out and called him names, but they did not understand his trouble), he discovered Lalun on the City wall and became the most constant of her few admirers. He possessed a head that English artists at home would rave over and paint amid impossible surroundings —a face that female novelists would use with delight through nine hundred pages. In reality he was only a clean-bred young Muhammadan, with penciled eyebrows, small-cut nostrils, little feet and hands, and a very tired look in his eyes. By virtue of his twenty-two years he had grown a neat black beard which he stroked with pride and kept delicately scented. His life seemed to be divided between borrowing books from me and making love to Lalun in the window-seat. He composed songs about her, and some of the songs are sung to this day in the City from the Street of the Mutton-Butchers to the Copper-Smiths' ward.

One song, the prettiest of all, says that the beauty of Lalun was so great that it troubled the hearts of the British Government and caused them to lose their peace of mind. That is the way the song is sung in the streets; but, if you examine it carefully and know the key to the explanation, you will find that there are three puns in it—on "beauty," "heart," and "peace of mind,"—so that it runs: "By the subtlety of Lalun the administration of the Government was troubled and it lost such and such a man." When Wali Dad sings that song his eyes glow like hot coals, and Lalun leans back

among the cushions and throws bunches of jasmine-buds at Wali Dad.

But first it is necessary to explain something about the Supreme Government which is above all and below all and behind all. Gentlemen come from England, spend a few weeks in India, walk round this great Sphinx of the Plains, and write books upon its ways and its works, denouncing or praising it as their own ignorance prompts. Consequently all the world knows how the Supreme Government conducts itself. But no one, not even the Supreme Government, knows everything about the administration of the Empire. Year by year England sends out fresh drafts for the first fighting-line, which is officially called the Indian Civil Service. These die, or kill themselves by overwork, or are worried to death or broken in health and hope in order that the land may be protected from death and sickness, famine and war, and may eventually become capable of standing alone. It will never stand alone, but the idea is a pretty one, and men are willing to die for it, and yearly the work of pushing and coaxing and scolding and petting the country into good living goes forward. If an advance be made all credit is given to the native, while the Englishmen stand back and wipe their foreheads. If a failure occurs the Englishmen step forward and take the blame. Overmuch tenderness of this kind has bred a strong belief among many natives that the native is capable of administering the country, and many devout Englishmen believe this also, because the theory is stated in beautiful English with all the latest political color.

There be other men who, though uneducated, see visions and dream dreams, and they, too, hope to administer the country in their own way—that is to say, with a garnish of Red Sauce. Such men must exist among two hundred million people, and, if they are not attended to, may cause trouble and even break the great idol called *Pax Britannic,* which, as the newspapers say, lives between Peshawur and Cape Comorin. Were the Day of Doom to dawn to-morrow, you would find the Supreme Government "taking measures to allay popular excitement" and putting guards upon the graveyards that the Dead might troop forth orderly. The Youngest Civilian would arrest Gabriel on his own responsibility if the Archangel could not produce a Deputy Commissioner's to "make music or other noises" as the license says.

Whence it is easy to see that mere men of the flesh who would create a tumult must fare badly at the hands of the Supreme Government. And they do. There is no outward sign of excitement; there is no confusion; there is no knowledge. When due and sufficient reasons have been given, weighed and approved, the machinery moves forward, and the dreamer of dreams and the seer of visions is gone from his friends and following. He enjoys the hospitality of Government; there is no restriction upon his movements within certain limits; but he must not confer any more with his brother dreamers. Once in every six months the Supreme Government assures itself that he is well and takes formal acknowledgment of his existence. No one protests against his detention, because the few people who know about it are in deadly fear of seeming to know him; and never a single newspaper "takes up his case" or organizes demonstrations on his behalf, because the newspapers of India have got behind that lying proverb which says the Pen is mightier than the Sword, and can walk delicately.

So now you know as much as you ought about Wali Dad, the educational mixture, and the Supreme Government.

Lalun has not yet been described. She would need, so Wali Dad says, a thousand pens of gold and ink scented with musk. She has been variously compared to the Moon, the Dil Sagar Lake, a spotted quail, a gazelle, the Sun on the Desert of Kutch, the Dawn, the Stars, and the young bamboo. These comparisons imply that she is beautiful exceedingly according to the native standards, which are practically the same as those of the West. Her eyes are black and her hair is black, and her eyebrows are black as leeches; her mouth is tiny and says witty things; her hands are tiny and have saved much money; her feet are tiny and have trodden on the naked hearts of many men. But, as Wali Dad sings: "Lalun *is* Lalun, and when you have said that, you have only come to the Beginnings of Knowledge."

The little house on the City wall was just big enough to hold Lalun, and her maid, and a pussy-cat with a silver collar. A big pink and blue cut-glass chandelier hung from the ceiling of the reception room. A petty Nawab had given Lalun the horror, and she kept it for politeness' sake. The floor of the room was of polisheed chunam, white as curds. A latticed window of carved wood was set in one wall; there was a profusion of squabby pluffy cushions and fat carpets everywhere, and Lalun's silver *huqa*, studded with turquoises, had a special little carpet all to its shining self. Wali Dad was nearly as permanent a fixture as the chandelier. As I have said, he lay in the window-seat and meditated on Life and Death and Lalun—specially Lalun. The feet of the young men of the City tended to her doorways and then—retired, for Lalun was a particular maiden, slow of speech, reserved of mind, and not in the least inclined to orgies which were nearly certain to end in strife. "If I am of no value, I am unworthy of this honor," said Lalun. "If I am of value, they are unworthy of Me." And that was a crooked sentence.

In the long hot nights of latter April and May all the City seemed to assemble in Lalun's little white room to smoke and to talk. Shiahs of the grimmest and most uncompromising persuasion; Sufis who had lost all belief in the Prophet and retained but little in God; wandering Hindu priests passing southward on their way to the Central India fairs and other affairs; Pundits in black gowns, with spectacles on their noses and undigested wisdom in their insides; bearded headmen of the wards; Sikhs with all the details of the latest ecclesiastical scandal in the Golden Temple; red-eyed priests from beyond the Border, looking like trapped wolves and talking like ravens; M. A.'s of the University, very superior and very voluble—all these people and more also you might find in the white

room. Wali Dad lay in the window-seat and listened to the talk.

"It is Lalun's salon," said Wali Dad to me, "and it is electic—is not that the word? Outside of a Freemason's Lodge I have never seen such gatherings. *There* I dined once with a Jew—a Yahoudi!" He spat into the City Ditch with apologies for allowing national feelings to evercome him. "Though I have lost every belief in the world," said he, "and try to be proud of my losing, I cannot help hating a Jew. Lalun admits no Jews here."

"But what in the world do all these men do?" I asked.

"The curse of our country," said Wali Dad. "They talk. It is like the Athenians—always hearing and telling some new thing. Ask the Pearl and she will show you how much she knows of the news of the City and the Province. Lalun knows everything."

"Lalun," I said at random—she was talking to a gentleman of the Kurd persuasion who had come in from God-knows-where—"when does the 175th Regiment go to Agra?"

"It does not go at all," said Lalun, without turning her head. "They have ordered the 118th to go in its stead. That Regiment goes to Lucknow in three months, unless they give a fresh order."

"That is so," said Wali Dad without a shade of doubt. "Can you, with your telegrams and your newspapers, do better? Always hearing and telling some new thing," he went on. "My friend, has your God ever smitten a European nation for gossiping in the bazars? India has gossiped for centuries—always standing in the bazars until the soldiers go by. Therefore—you are here to-day instead of starving in your own country, and I am not a Muhammadan—I am a Product—a Demnition Product. That also I owe to you and yours: that I cannot make an end to my sentence without quoting from your authors." He pulled at the *huqa* and mourned, half feelingly, half in earnest, for the shattered hopes of his youth. Wali Dad was always mourning over something or other—the country of which he despaired, or the creed in which he had lost faith, or the life of the English which he could by no means understand.

Lalun never mourned. She played little songs on the *sitar,* and to hear her sing, *"O Peacock, cry again,"* was always a fresh pleasure. She knew all the songs that have ever been sung, from the war-songs of the South that men and the young men angry with the State, to the love-songs of the North where the swords whinny-whicker like angry kites in the pauses between the kisses, and the Passes fill with armed men, and the Lover is torn from his Beloved and cries *Ai, Ai, Ai!* evermore. She knew how to make up tobacco for the *huqa* so that it smelled like the Gates of Paradise and wafted you gently through them. She could embroider strange things in gold and silver, and dance softly with the moonlight when it came in at the window. Also she knew the hearts of men, and the heart of the City, and whose wives were faithful and whose untrue, and more of the secrets of the Government officees than are good to be set down in this place. Nasiban, her maid, said

that her jewelry was worth ten thousand pounds, and that, some night, a thief would enter and murder her for its possession; but Lalun said that all the City would tear that thief limb from limb, and that he, whoever he was, knew it.

So she took her *sitar* and sat in the window-seat and sang a song of old days that had been sung by a girl of her profession in an armed camp on the eve of a great battle—the day before the Fords of the Jumna ran red and Sivaji fled fifty miles to Delhi with a Toorkh stallion at his horse's tail and another Lalun on his saddle-bow. It was what men call a Mahratta *laonee,* and it said:

> Their warrior forces Chimnajee
> Before the Peishwa led,
> The Children of the Sun and Fire
> Behind him turned and fled.

And the chorus said:

> With them there fought who rides so free
> With sword and turban red,
> The warrior-youth who earns his fee
> At peril of his head.

"At peril of his head," said Wali Dad in English to me. "Thanks to your Government, all our heads are protected, and with the educational facilities at my command"—his eyes twinkled wickedly—"I might be a distinguished member of the local administration. Perhaps, in time, I might even be a member of a Legislative Council."

"Don't speak English," said Lalun, bending over her *sitar* afresh. The chorus went out from the City wall to the blackened wall of Fort Amara which dominates the City. No man knows the precise extent of Fort Amara. Three kings built it hundreds of years ago, and they say that there are miles of underground rooms beneath its walls. It is peopled with many ghosts, a detachment of Garrison Artillery and a Company of Infantry. In its prime it held ten thousand men and filled its ditches with corpses.

"At peril of his head," sang Lalun, again and again.

A head moved on one of the Ramparts—the grey head of an old man—and a voice, rough as shark-skin on a sword-hilt, sent back the last line of the chorus and broke into a song that I could not understand, though Lalun and Wali Dad listened intently.

"What is it?" I asked "Who is it?"

"A consistent man," said Wali Dad. "He fought you in '46, when he was a warrior-youth; refought you in '57, and he tried to fight you in '71, but you had learned the trick of blowing men from guns too well. Now he is old; but he would still fight if he could."

"Is he a Wahabi, then? Why should he answer to a Mahratta *laonee* if he be Wahabi—or Sikh?" said I.

"I do not know," said Wali Dad. "He has lost perhaps, his religion. Perhaps he wishes to be a King. Perhaps he is King. I do not know his name."

"That is a lie, Wali Dad. If you know his career you must know his name."

"That is quite true. I belong to a nation of liars. I would rather not tell you his name. Think for yourself."

Lalun finished her song, pointed to the Fort, and said simply: "Khem Singh."

"Hm," said Wali Dad. "If the Pearl chooses to tell you the Pearl is a fool."

I translated to Lalun, who laughed. "I choose to tell what I choose to tell. They kept Khem Singh in Burma," said she. "They kept him there for many years until his mind was changed in him. So great was the kindness of the Government. Finding this, they sent him back to his own country that he might look upon it before he died. He is an old man, but when he looks upon this his country his memory will come. Moreover, there be many who remember him."

"He is an Interesting Survival," said Wali Dad, pulling at the *huqo*. "He returns to a country now full of educational and political reform, but, as the Pearl says, there are many who remember him. He was once a great man. There will never be any more great men in India. They will all, when they are boys, go whoring after strange gods, and they will become ciitzens—'fellow-citizens'—'iilustrious fellow-citizens.' What is it that the native papers call them?"

Wali Dad seemed to be in a very bad temper. Lalun loked out of the window and smiled into the dust-haze. I went away thinking about Khem Singh who had once made history with a thousand followers, and would have been a princeling but for the power of the Supreme Government aforesaid.

The Senior Captain Commanding Fort Amara was away on leave, but the Subaltern, his Deputy, had drifted down to the Club, where I found him and inquired of him whether it was really true that a political prisoner had been added to the attractions of the Fort. The

Subaltern explained at great length, for this was the first time that he had held Command of the Fort, and his glory lay heavy upon him.

"Yes," said he, "a man was sent in to me about a week ago from down the line—a thorough gentleman whoever he is. Of course I did all I could for him. He had his two servants and some silver cooking-pots, and he looked for all the world like a native officer. I called him Subadar Sahib; just as well to be on the safe side, y'know. 'Look here, Subadar Sahib,' I said, 'you're handed over to my authority, and I'm supposed to guard you. Now I don't want to make your life hard, but you must make things easy for me. All the Fort it at your disposal, from the flagstaff to the dry ditch, and I shall be happy to entertain you in any way I can, but you mustn't take advantage of it. Give me your word that you won't try to escape, Subadar Sahib, and I'll give you my word that you shall have no heavy guard put over you.' I thought the best way of getting him was by going at him straight, y'know, and it was, by Jove! The old man gave me his word, and moved about the Fort as contented as a sick crow. He's a rummy chap—always asking to be told where he is and what the buildings about him are. I had to sign a slip of blue paper when he turned up, acknowledging receipt of his body and all that, and I'm responsible, y'know, that he doesn't get away. Queer thing, though, looking after a Johnnie old enough to be your grandfather, isn't it? Come to the Fort one of these days and see him?"

For reasons which will appear, I never went to the Fort while Khem Singh was then within its walls. I knew him only as a grey head seen from Lalun's window—a grey head and a harsh voice. But natives told me that, day by day, as he looked upon the fair lands round Amara, his memory came back to him and, with it, the old hatred against the Government that had been nearly effaced in far-off Burma. So he raged up and down the West face of the Fort from morning till noon and from evening till the night, devising vain things in his heart, and croaking war-songs when Lalun sang on the City wall. As he grew more acquainted with the Subaltern he unburdened his old heart of some of the passions that had withered it. "Sahib," he used to say, tapping his stick against the parapet, "when I was a young man I was one of twenty thousand horsemen who came out of the City and rode round the plain here. Sahib, I was the leader of a hundred, then of a thousand, then of five thousand, and now!"—he pointed to his two servants. "But from the beginning to to-day I would cut the throats of all the Sahibs in the land if I could. Hold me fast, Sahib, lest I get away and return to those who would follow me. I forgot them when I was in Burma, but now that I am in my own country again, I remember everything."

"Do you remember that you have given me your Honor not to make your tendance a hard matter?" said the Subaltern.

"Yes, to you, only to you, Sahib," said Khem Singh. "To you, because you are of a pleasant countenance. If my turn comes again, Sahib, I will not hang you nor cut your throat."

"Thank you," said the Subaltern, gravely, as he looked along the line of guns that could pound the City to powder in half an hour. "Let us go into our own quarters, Khem Singh. Come and talk with we after dinner."

Khem Singh would sit on his own cushion at the Subaltern's feet, drinking heavy, scented anise-seed brandy in great gulps, and telling strange stories of Fort Amara, which had been a palace in the old days, of Begums and Ranees tortured to death—aye, in the very vaulted chamber that now served as a Mess-room; would tell stories of Sobraon that made the Subaltern's cheeks flush and tingle with pride of race, and of the Kuka rising from which so much was expected and the foreknowledge of which was shared by a hundred thousand souls. But he never told tales of '57, because, as he said, he was the Subaltern's guest, and '57 is a year that no man, Black or White, cares to speak of. Once only, when the anise-seed brandy had slightly affected his head, he said: "Sahib, speaking now of a matter which lay between Sobraon and the affair of the Kukas, it was ever a wonder to us that you stayed your hand at all, and that, having stayed it, you did not make the land one prison. Now I hear from without that you do great honor to all men of our country and by your own hands are destroying the Terror of your Name which is your strong rock and defence. This is a foolish thing. Will oil and water mix? Now in '57"—

"I was not born then, Subadar Sahib," said the Subaltern, and Khem Singh reeled to his quarters.

The Subaltern would tell me of these conversations at the Club, and my desire to see Khem Singh increased. But Wali Dad, sitting in the window-seat of the house on the City wall, said that it would be a cruel thing to do, and Lalun pretended that I preferred the society of a grizzled old Sikh to hers.

"Here is tobacco, here is talk, here are many friends and all the news of the City, and, above all, here is myself. I will tell you stories and sing you songs, and Wali Dad will talk his English nonsense in your ears. Is that worse than watching the caged animal yonder? Go to-morrow then, if you must, but to-day such and such an one will be here, and he will speak of wonderful things."

It happened that To-morrow never came, and the warm heat of the latter Rains gave place to the chill of early October almost before I was aware of the flight of the year. The Captain commanding the Fort returned from leave and took over charge of Khem Singh according to the laws of seniority. The Captain was not a nice man. He called all natives "niggers," which, besides being extreme bad form, shows gross ignorance.

"What's the use of telling off two Tommies to watch that old nigger?" said he.

"I fancy it soothes his vanity," said the Subaltern. "The men are ordered to keep well out of his way, but he takes them as a tribute to his importance, poor old wretch."

"I won't have Line men taken off regular guards in this way. Put on a couple of Native Infantry."

"Sikhs?" said the Subaltern, lifting his eyebrows.

"Sikhs, Pathans, Dogras—they're all

alike, these black vermin," and the Captain talked to Khem Singh in a manner which hurt that old gentleman's feelings. Fifteen years before, when he had been caught for the second time, every one looked upon him as a sort of tiger. He liked being regarded in this light. But he forgot that the world goes forward in fifteen years, and many Subalterns are promoted to Captaincies.

"The Captain-pig is in charge of the Fort?" said Khem Singh to his native guard every morning. And the native guard said: "Yes, Subadar Sahib," in deference to his age and his air of distinction; but they did not know who he was.

In those days the gathering in Lalun's little white room was always large and talked more than before.

"The Greeks," said Wali Dad who had been borrowing my books, "the inhabitants of the city of Athens, where they were always hearing and telling some new thing, rigorously secluded their women—who were fools. Hence the glorious institution of the heterodox woman—is it not?—who were amusing and *not* fools. All the Greek philosophers delighted in their company. Tell me, my friend, how it goes now in Greece and the other places upon the Continent of Europe. Are your womenfolk also fools?"

"Wali Dad," I said, "you never speak to us about your women-folk and we never speak about ours to you. That is the bar between us."

"Yes," said Wali Dad, "it is curious to think that our common meeting-place should be here, in the house of a common—how do you call *her?*" He pointed with the pipe-mouth to Lalun.

"Lalun is nothing but Lalun," I said, and that was perfectly true. "But if you took your place in the world, Wali Dad, and gave up dreaming dreams"—

"I might wear an English coat and trouser. I might be a leading Muhammadan pleader. I might be received even at the Commissioner's tennis-parties where the English stand on one side and the natives on the other, in order to promote social intercourse throughout the Empire. Heart's Heart," said he to Lalun quickly, "the Sahib says that I ought to quit you."

"The Sahib is always talking stupid talk," returned Lalun, with a laugh. "In this house I am a Queen and thou art a King. The Sahib"—she put her arms above her head and thought for a moment—"the Sahib shall be our Vizier —thine and mine, Wali Dad—because he has said that thou shouldst leave me."

Wali Dad laughed immoderately, and I laughed too. "Be it so," said he. "My friend, are you willing to take this lucrative Government appointment? Lalun, what shall his pay be?"

But Lalun began to sing, and for the rest of the time there was no hope of getting a sensible answer from her or Wali Dad. When the one stopped, the other began to quote Persian poetry with a triple pun in every other line. Some of it was not strictly proper, but it was all very funny, and it only came to an end when a fat person in black, with gold *pince-nez*, sent up his name to Lalun, and Wali Dad dragged me into the twinkling night to walk in a big rose-garden and talk heresies about Religion and Governments and a man's career in life.

The Mohurrum, the great mourning-festival of the Muhammadans, was close at hand, and the things that Wali Dad said about religious fanaticism would have secured his expulsion from the loosest-thinking Muslim sect. There were the rose-bushes round us, the stars above us, and from every quarter of the City came the boom of the big Bohurrum drums. You must know that the City is divided in fairly equal proportions between the Hindus and the Musalmans, and where both creeds belong to the fighting races, a big religious festival gives ample chance for trouble. When they can—that is to say when the authorities are weak enough to allow it—the Hindus do their best to arrange some minor feast-day of their own in time to clash with the period of general mourning for the martyrs Hasan and Hussain, the heroes of the Mohurrum. Gilt and painted paper presentations of their tombs are borne with shouting and wailing, music, torches, and yells, through the principal thoroughfares of the City, which fakements are called *tazias*. Their passage is rigorously laid down beforehand by the Police, and detachments of Police accompany each *tazia*, lest the Hindus should throw bricks at it and the peace of the Queen and the heads of Her loyal subjects should thereby be broken. Mohurrum time in a "fighting" town means anxiety to all the officials, because, if a riot breaks out, the officials and not the rioters are held responsible. The former must foresee everything, and while not making their precautions ridiculously elaborate, must see that they are at least adequate.

"Listen to the drums!" said Wali Dad. "That is the heart of the people—empty and making much noise. How, think you, will the Mohurrum go this year. *I* think that there will be trouble."

He turned down a side-street and left me alone with the stars and a sleepy Police patrol. Then I went to bed and dreamed that Wali Dad had sacked the City and I was made Vizier, with Lalun's silver *huqa* for mark of office.

All day the Mohurrum drums beat in the City, and all day deputations of tearful Hindu gentlemen besieged the Deputy Commissioner with assurances that they would be murdered ere next dawning by the Muhammadans. "Which," said the Deputy Commissioner, in confidence to the Head of Police, "is a pretty fair indication that the Hindus are going to make 'emselves unpleasant. I think we can arrange a little surprise for them. I have given the heads of both Creeds fair warning. If they choose to disregard it, so much the worse for them."

There was a large gathering in Lalun's house that night, but of men that I had never seen before, if I except the fat gentleman in black with the gold *pincenez*. Wali Dad lay in the window-seat, more bitterly scornful of his Faith and its manifestations than I had ever known him. Lalun's maid was very busy cutting up and mixing tobacco for the guests. We could hear the thunder of the drums as the processions accompanying each *tazia* marched to the central gathering-place in the plain outside the City, preparatory to their triumphant reëntry and circuit within the walls. All the streets seemed ablaze with torches, and only Fort Amara was black and silent.

When the noise of the drums ceased, no one in the white room spoke for a time. "The first *tazia* has moved off," said Wali Dad, looking to the plain.

"That is very early," said the man with the *prince-nez.*

"It is only half-past eight." The company rose and departed.

"Some of them were men from Ladakh," said Lalun, when the last had gone. "They brought me brick-tea such as the Russians sell, and a tea-urn from Peshawur. Show me, now, how the English *Memsahibs* make tea."

The brick-tea was abominable. When it was finished Wali Dad suggested going into the streets. "I am nearly sure that there will be trouble to-night," he said. "All the City thinks so, and *Vox Populi* is *Vox Dei,* as the Babus say. Now I tell you that at the corner of the Padshahi Gate you will find my horse all this night if you want to go about and to see things. It is a most disgraceful exhibition. Where is the pleasure of saying '*Ya Hasan, Ya Hussain,*' twenty thousand times in a night?"

All the processions—there were two and twenty of them—were now well within the City walls. The drums were beating afresh, the crowd were howling "*Ya Hasan! Ya Hussain!*" and beating their breasts, the brass bands were playing their loudest, and at every corner where space allowed, Muhammadan preachers were telling the lamentable story of the death of the Martyrs. It was impossible to move except with the crowd, for the streets were not more than twenty feet wide. In the Hindu quarters the shutters of all the shops were up and cross-barred. As the first *tazia,* a gorgeous erection ten feet high,

was borne aloft on the shoulders of a score of stout men into the semi-darkness of the Gully of the Horsemen, a brickbat crashed through its talc and tinsel sides.

"Into thy hands, O Lord?" murmured Wali Dad, profanely, as a yell went up from behind and a native officer of Police jammed his horse through the crowd. Another brickbat followed, and the *tazia* staggered and swayed where it had stopped.

"Go on! In the name of the *Sirkar,* go forward!" shouted the Policemen; but there was an ugly cracking and splintering of shutters, and the crowd halted, with oaths and growlings, before the house whence the brickbat had been thrown.

Then, without any warning, broke the storm—not only in the Gully of the Horsemen, but in half a dozen other places. The *tazias* rocked like ships at sea, the long pole-torches dipped and rose round them while the men shouted: "The Hindus are dishonoring the *tazias!* Strike! Strike! Into their temples for the faith!" The six or eight Policemen with each *tazia* drew their batons, and struck as long as they could in the hope of forcing the mob forward, but they were overpowered, and as contingents of Hindus poured into the streets, the fight became general. Half a mile away where the *tazias* were yet untouched the drums and the shrieks of "*Ya Hasan! Ya Hussain!*" continued, but not for long. The priests at the corners of the streets knocked the legs from the bedsteads that supported their pulpits and smote for the Faith, while stones fell from the silent houses upon friend and foe, and the packed streets bellowed:

"*Din! Din! Din!*" A *tazia* caught fire, and was dropped for a flaming barrier between Hindu and Musalman at the corner of the Gully. Then the crowd surged forward, and Wali Dad drew me close to the stone pillar of a well.

"It was intended from the beginning!" he shouted in my ear, with more heat than blank unbelief should be guilty of. "The bricks were carried up to the houses beforehand. These swine of Hindus! We shall be gutting kine in their temples to-night!"

Tazia after *tazia*, some burning, others torn to pieces, hurried past us and the mob with them, howling, shrieking, and striking at the house doors in their flight. At last we saw the reason of the rush. Hugonin the Assistant District Superintendent of Police, a boy of twenty, had got together thirty constables and was forcing the crowd through the streets. His old grey Police-horse showed no sign of uneasiness as it was spurred breast-on into the crowd, and the long dog-whip with which he had armed himself was never still.

"They know we haven't enough Police to hold 'em," he cried as he passed me, mopping a cut on his face. "They *know* we haven't! Aren't any of the men from the Club coming down to help? Get on, you sons of burned fathers!" The dog-whip cracked across the writhing backs, and the constables smote afresh with baton and gun-butt. With these passed the lights and the shouting, and Wali Dad began to swear under his breath. From Fort Amara shot up a single rocket; then two side by side. It was the signal for troops.

Petitt, the Deputy Commissioner, covered with dust and sweat, but calm and gently smiling, cantered up the clean-swept street in rear of the main body of the rioters. "No one killed yet," he shouted. "I'll keep 'em on the run till dawn! Don't let 'em halt, Hugonin! Trot 'em about till the troops come."

The science of the defence lay solely in keeping the mob on the move. If they had breathing-space they would halt and fire a house, and then the work of restoring order would be more difficult to say the least of it. Flames have the same effect on a crowd as blood has on a wild beast.

Word had reached the Club and men in evening-dress were beginning to show themselves and lend a hand in heading off and breaking up the shouting masses with stirrup-leathers, whips, or chance-found staves. They were not very often attacked, for the rioters had sense enough to know that the death of a European would not mean one hanging but many, and possibly the appearance of the thrice-dreaded Artillery. The clamor in the City redoubled. The Hindus had descended into the streets in real earnest and ere long the mob returned. It was a strange sight. There were no *tazias*—only their riven platforms—and there were no Police. Here and there a City dignitary, Hindu or Muhammadan, was vainly imploring his co-religionists to keep quiet and behave themselves—advice for which his white beard was pulled. Then a native officer of Police, unhorsed but still using his spurs with effect, would be borne along, warning all the crowd of the danger of insulting the Government. Everywhere men struck aimlessly with sticks, grasping each other by the throat, howling and foaming with rage, or beat with their bare hands on the doors of the houses.

"It is a lucky thing that they are fighting with natural weapons," I said to Wali Dad, "else we should have half the City killed."

I turned as I spoke and looked at his face. His nostrils were distended, his eyes were fixed, and he was smiting himself softly on the breast. The crowd poured by with renewed riot—a gang of Musalmans hard-pressed by some hundred Hindu fanatics. Wali Dad left my side with an oath, and shouting: "*Ya Hasan! Ya Hussain!*" plunged into the thick of the fight where I lost sight of him.

I fled by a side alley to the Padshahi Gate where I found Wali Dad's house, and thence rode to the Fort. Once outside the City wall, the tumult sank to a dull roar, very impressive under the stars and reflecting great credit on the fifty thousand angry able-bodied men who were making it. The troops who, at the Deputy Commissioner's instance, had been ordered to rendezvous quietly near the Fort, showed no signs of being impressed. Two companies of Native Infantry, a squadron of Native Cavalry and a company of British Infantry were kicking their heels in the shadow of the East face, waiting for orders to march in. I am sorry to say that they were all pleased, unholily pleased, at the chance of what they called "a little fun." The senior officers, to be sure, grumbled at having been kept out of bed, and the English troops pretended to be sulky, but there was joy in the hearts of all the subalterns, and whispers ran up and down the line: "No ball-cart-

ridge—what a beastly shame!" "D'you think the beggars will really stand up to us?" " 'Hope I shall meet my money-lender there. I owe him more than I can afford." "Oh, they won't let us even unsheathe swords." "Hurrah! Up goes the fourth rocket. Fall in, there!"

The Garrison Artillery, who to the last cherished a wild hope that they might be allowed to bombard the City at a hundred yards' range, lined the parapet above the East gateway and cheered themselves hoarse as the British Infantry doubled along the road to the Main Gate of the City. The Cavalry cantered on to the Padshahi Gate, and the Native Infantry marched slowly to the Gate of the Butchers. The surprise was intended to be of a distinctly unpleasant nature, and to come on top of the defeat of the Police who had been just able to keep the Muhammadans from firing the houses of a few leading Hindus. The bulk of the riot lay in the north and northwest wards. The east and southeast were by this time dark and silent, and I rode hastily to Lalun's house for I wished to tell her to send some one in search of Wali Dad. The house was unlighted, but the door was open, and I climbed upstairs in the darkness. One small lamp in the white room showed Lalun and her maid leaning half out of the window, breathing heavily and evidently pulling at something that refused to come.

"Thou art late—very late," gasped Lalun, without turning her head. "Help us now, O Fool, if thou hast not spent thy strength howling among the *tazias*. Pull! Nasiban and I can do no more! O Sahib, is it you? The Hindus have been hunting an old Muhammadan round the Ditch with clubs. If they find him again they will kill him. Help us to pull him up."

I put my hands to the long red silk waist-cloth that was hanging out of the window, and we three pulled and pulled with all the strength at our command. There was something very heavy at the end, and it swore in an unknown tongue as it kicked against the City wall.

"Pull, oh, pull!" said Lalun, at the last. A pair of brown hands grasped the window-sill and a venerable Muhammadan tumbled upon the floor, very much out of breath. His jaws were tied up, his turban had fallen over one eye, and he was dusty and angry.

Lalun hid her face in her hands for an instant and said something about Wali Dad that I could not catch.

Then, to my extreme gratification, she threw her arms round my neck and murmured pretty things. I was in no haste to stop her; and Nasiban, being a handmaiden of tact, turned to the big jewelchest that stands in the corner of the white room and rummaged among the contents. The Muhammadan sat on the floor and glared.

"One service more, Sahib, since thou hast come so opportunely," said Lalun. "Wilt thou"—it is very nice to be thou-ed by Lalun—"take this old man across the City—the troops are everywhere, and they might hurt him for he is old—to the Kumsharen Gate? There I think he may find a carriage to take him to his house. He is a friend of mine, and thou art—more than a friend —therefore I ask this."

Nasiban bent over the old man, tucked something into his belt, and I raised him up, and led him into the streets. In crossing from the east to the west of the City there was no chance of avoiding the troops and the crowd. Long before I reached the Gully of the Horsemen I heard the shouts of the British Infantry crying cheeringly: "Hutt, ye beggars! Hutt, ye devils! Get along! Go forward, there!" Then followed the ringing of rifle-butts and shrieks of pain. The troops were banging the bare toes of the mob with their gun-butts— for not a bayonet had been fixed. My companion mumbled and jabbered as we walked on until we were carried back by the crowd and had to force our way to the troops. I caught him by the wrist and felt a bangle there—the iron bangle of the Sikhs—but I had no suspicions, for Lalun had only ten minutes before put her arms round me. Thrice we were carried back by the crowd, and when we made our way past the British Infantry it was to meet the Sikh Cavalry driving another mob before them with the butts of their lances.

"What are these dogs?" said the old man.

"Sikhs of the Cavalry, Father," I said, and we edged our way up the line of horses two abreast and found the Deputy Commissioner, his helmet smashed on his head, surrounded by a knot of men who had come down from the Club as amateur constables and had helped the Police mightily.

"We'll keep 'em on the run till dawn," said Petitt. "Who's your villainous friend?"

I had only time to say: "The Protection of the *Sirkar!*" when a fresh crowd flying before the Native Infantry carried us a hundred yards nearer to the Kumharsen Gate, and Petitt was swept away like a shadow.

"I do not know—I cannot see—this is all new to me!" moaned my companion. "How many troops are there in the City?"

"Perhaps five hundred," I said.

"A lakh of men beaten by five hundred—and Sikhs among them! Surely, surely, I am an old man, but—the Kumharsen Gate is new. Who pulled down the stone lions? Where is the conduit? Sahib, I am a very old man, and, alas, I—I cannot stand." He dropped in the shadow of the Kumharsen Gate where there was no disturbance. A fat gentleman wearing gold *pincenez* came out of the darkness.

"You are most kind to bring my old friend," he said, suavely. "He is a landholder of Akala. He should not be in a big City when there is religious excitement. But I have a carriage here. You are quite truly kind. Will you help me to put him into the carriage? It is very late."

We bundled the old man into a hired victoria that stood close to the gate, and I turned back to the house on the City wall. The troops were driving the people to and fro, while the Police shouted, "To your houses! Get to your houses!" and the dog-whip of the Assistant District Superintendent cracked remorselessly. Terror-stricken *bunnias* clung to the stirrups of the cavalry, crying that their houses had been robbed (which was a lie), and the burly Sikh horsemen patted them on the shoulder, and bade them to return to those houses lest a worse thing should happen. Parties of five or six British soldiers, joining arms, swept down the side-gullies, their rifles on their backs, stamping, with shouting and song, upon the toes of Hindu and Musalman. Never was religious enthusiasm more systematically squashed; and never were poor breakers of the peace more utterly weary and footsore. They were routed out of holes and corners, from behind well-pillars and byres, and bidden to go to their houses. If they had no houses to go to, so much the worse for their toes.

On returning to Lalun's door I stumbled over a man at the threshold. He was sobbing hysterically and his arms flapped like the wings of a goose. It was Wali Dad, Agnostic and Unbeliever, shoeless, turbanless, and frothing at the mouth, the flesh on his chest bruised and bleeding from the vehemence with which he had smitten himself. A broken torch-handle lay by his side, and his quivering lips murmured, "*Ya Hasan! Ya Hussain!*" as I stooped over him. I pushed him a few steps up the staircase, threw a pebble at Lalun's City window and hurried home.

Most of the streets were very still, and the cold wind that comes before the dawn whistled down them. In the centre of the Square of the Mosque a man was bending over a corpse. The skull had been smashed in by gun-butt or bamboo-stave.

"It is expedient that one man should die for the people," said Petitt, grimly, raising the shapeless head. "These brutes were beginning to show their teeth too much."

And from afar we could hear the soldiers singing "Two Lovely Black Eyes," as they drove the remnant of the rioters within doors.

*   *   *   *   *

Of course you can guess what happened? I was not so clever. When the news went abroad that Khem Singh had escaped from the Fort, I did not, since I was then living this story, not writing it, connect myself, or Lalun, or the fat gentleman of the gold *pince-nez* with his disappearance. Nor did it strike me that Wali Dad was the man who should have convoyed him across the City, or that Lalun's arms round my neck were put there to hide the money that Nasiban gave to Kehm Singh, and that Lalun had used me and my white face as even a better safe-guard than Wali Dad who proved himself so untrustworthy. All that I knew at the time was that, when Fort Amara was taken up with the riots, Khem Singh profited by the confusion to get away, and this his own Sikh guards also escaped.

But later on I received full enlightenment; and so did Khem Singh. He fled to those who knew him in the old days, but many of them were dead and more were changed, and all knew something of the Wrath of the Government. He went to the young men, but the glamour of his name had passed away, and they were entering native regiments of Government offices, and Khem Singh could not give them neither pension, decoraitons, nor influence—nothing but a glorious death with their backs to the mouth of a gun. He wrote letters and made promises, and the letters fell into bad hands, and a wholly insignificant subordinate officer of Police tracked them down and gained promotion thereby.

Moreover, Khem Singh was old, and anise-seed brandy was scarce, and he had left his silver cooking-pots in Fort Amara with his nice warm bedding, and the gentleman with the gold *pince-nez* was told by those who had employed him that Khem Singh as a popular leader was not worth the money paid.

"Great is the mercy of these fools of English!" said Khem Singh when the situation was put before him. "I will go back to Fort Amara of my own free will and gain honor. Give me good clothes to return in."

So, at his own time, Khem Singh knocked at the wicket-gate of the Fort and walked to the Captain and the Sub-altern, who were nearly grey-headed on account of correspondence that daily arrived from Simla marked "Private."

"I have come back, Captain Sahib," said Khem Singh. "Put no more guards over me. It is no good out yonder."

A week later I saw him for the first time to my knowledge, and he made as though there were an understanding between us.

"It was well done, Sahib," said he, "and greatly I admired your astuteness in thus boldly facing the troops when I, whom they would have doubtless torn to pieces, was with you. Now there is a man in Fort Ooltagarh whom a bold man could with ease help to escape. This is the position of the Fort as I draw it on the sand"—

But I was thinking how I had become Lalun's Vizier after all.

VOLUME VIII

The Phantom 'Rickshaw and Other
Ghost Stories

The Phantom 'Rickshaw

May no ill dreams disturb my rest,
Nor Powers of Darkness me molest.
—Evening Hymn.

ONE of the few advantages that India has over England is a great Knowability. After five years' service a man is directly or indirectly acquainted with the two or three hundred Civilians in his Province, all the Messes of ten or twelve Regiments and Batteries, and some fifteen hundred other people of the non-official caste. In ten years his knowledge should be doubled, and at the end of twenty he knows, or knows something about, every Englishman in the Empire, and may travel anywhere and everywhere without paying hotel-bills.

Globe-trotters who expect entertainment as a right, have, even within my memory, blunted this open-heartedness, but none the less to-day, if you belong to the Inner Circle and are neither a Bear nor a Black Sheep, all houses are open to you, and our small world is very, very kind and helpful.

Rickett of Kamartha stayed with Polder of Kumaon some fifteen years ago. He meant to stay two nights, but was knocked down by rheumatic fever, and for six weeks disorganized Polder's establishment, stopped Polder's work, and nearly died in Polder's bedroom. Polder behaves as though he had been placed under eternal obligation by Rickett, and yearly sends the little Ricketts a box of presents and toys. It is the same everywhere. The men who do not take the trouble to conceal from you their opinion that you are an incompetent ass, and the women who blacken your character and misunderstand your wife's amusements, will work themselves to the bone in your behalf if you fall sick or into serious trouble.

Heatherlegh, the Doctor, kept, in addition to his regular practice, a hospital on his private account—an arrangement of loose boxes for Incurables, his friend called it—but it was really a sort of fitting-up shed for craft that had been damaged by stress of weather. The weather in India is often sultry, and since the tale of bricks is always a fixed quantity, and the only liberty allowed is permission to work overtime and get no thanks, men occasionally break down and become as mixed as the metaphors in this sentence.

Heatherlegh is the dearest doctor that ever was, and his invariable prescription to all his patients is, "lie low, go slow, and keep cool." He says that more men are killed by overwork than the importance of this world justifies. He maintains that overwork slew Pansay, who died under his hands about three years ago. He has, of course, the right to speak authoritatively, and he laughs at my theory that there was a crack in Pansay's head and a little bit of the Dark World came through and pressed him to death. "Pansay went off the handle," says Heatherlegh, "after the stimulus of long leave at Home. He may or he may not have behaved like a blackguard to Mrs. Keith-Wessington. My notion is that the work of the Kata- bundi Settlement ran him off his legs, and that he took to brooding and mak- ing much of an ordinary P. & O. flirta- tion. He certainly was engaged to Miss Mannering, and she certainly broke off the engagement. Then he took a fever- ish chill and all that nonsense about ghosts developed. Overwork started his illness, kept it alight, and killed him, poor devil. Write him off to the Sys- tem—one man to take the work of two and a half men."

I do not believe this. I used to sit up with Pansay sometimes when Heath- erlegh was called out to patients, and I happened to be within claim. The man would make me most unhappy by de- scribing in a low, even voice, the pro- cession that was always passing at the bottom of his bed. He had a sick man's command of language. When he recov- ered I suggested that he should write out the whole affair from beginning to end, knowing that ink might assist him to ease his mind. When little boys have learned a new bad word they are never happy till they have chalked it up on a door. And this also is Literature.

He was in a high fever while he was writing, and the blood-and-thunder Magazine diction he adopted did not calm him. Two months afterward he was reported fit for duty, but, in spite of the fact that he was urgently needed to help an undermanned Commission stagger through a deficit, he preferred to die; vowing at the last that he was hag-ridden. I got his manuscript before he died, and this is his version of the affair, dated 1885:

My doctor tells me that I need rest and change of air. It is not improbable that I shall get both ere long—rest that neither the red-coated messenger nor the midday gun can break, and change of air far beyond that which any home- ward-bound steamer can give me. In the meantime I am resolved to stay where I am; and, in flat defiance of my doctor's orders, to take all the world into my confidence. You shall learn for yourselves the precise nature of my malady; and shall, too, judge for your- selves whether any man born of woman on this weary earth was ever so tor- mented as I.

Speaking now as a condemned crim- inal might speak ere the drop-bolts are drawn, my story, wild and hideously improbable as it may appear, demands at least attention. That it will ever receive credence I utterly disbelieve. Two months ago I should have scouted as mad or drunk the man who had dared tell me the like. Two months ago I was the happiest man in India. To-day, from Peshawur to the sea, there is no one more wretched. My doctor and I are the only two who know this. His explanation is, that my brain, digestion, and eyesight are all slightly affected; giving rise to my fre- quent and persistent "delusions." De- lusions, indeed! I call him a fool; but he attends me still with the same un- wearied smile, the same bland profes- sional manner, the same neatly trimmed red whiskers, till I begin to suspect that I am an ungrateful, evil-tempered invalid. But you shall judge for your- selves.

Three years ago it was my fortune— my great misfortune—to sail from

Gravesend to Bombay, on return from long leave, with one Agnes Keith-Wessington, wife of an officer on the Bombay side. It does not in the least concern you to know what manner of woman she was. Be content with the knowledge that, ere the voyage had ended, both she and I were desperately and unreasoningly in love with one another. Heaven knows that I can make the admission now without one particle of vanity. In matters of this sort there is always one who gives and another who accepts. From the first day of our ill-omened attachment, I was conscious that Agnes's passion was a stronger, a more dominant, and—if I may use the expression—a purer sentiment than mine. Whether she recognized the fact then, I do not know. Afterward it was bitterly plain to both of us.

Arrived at Bombay in the spring of the year, we went our respective ways, to meet no more for the next three or four months, when my leave and her love took us both to Simla. There we spent the season together; and there my fire of straw burned itself out to a pitiful end with the closing year. I attempt no excuse. I make no apology. Mrs. Wessington had given up much for my sake, and was prepared to give up all. From my own lips, in August, 1882, she learned that I was sick of her presence, tired of her company, and weary of the sound of her voice. Ninety-nine women out of a hundred would have wearied of me as I wearied of them; seventy-five of that number would have promptly avenged themselves by active and obtrusive flirtation with other men. Mrs. Wessington was

the hundredth. On her neither my openly expressed aversion nor the cutting brutalities with which I garnished our interviews had the least effect.

"Jack, darling!" was her one eternal cuckoo cry: "I'm sure it's all a mistake —a hideous mistake; and we'll be good friends again some day. *Please* forgive me, Jack, dear."

I was the offender, and I knew it. That knowledge transformed my pity into passive endurance, and, eventually, into blind hate—the same instinct, I suppose, which prompts a man to savagely stamp on the spider he has but half killed. And with this hate in my bosom the season of 1882 came to an end.

Next year we met again at Simla—she with her monotonous face and timid attempts at reconciliation, and I with loathing of her in every fibre of my frame. Several times I could not avoid meeting her alone; and on each occasion her words were identically the same. Still the unreasoning wail that it was all a "mistake"; and still the hope of eventually "making friends." I might have seen had I cared to look, that that hope only was keeping her alive. She grew more wan and thin month by month. You will agree with me, at least, that such conduct would have driven any one to despair. It was uncalled for; childish; unwomanly. I maintain that she was much to blame. And again, sometimes, in the black, fever-stricken night-watches, I have begun to think that I might have been a little kinder to her. But that really *is* a "delusion." I could not have continued pretending to love her when I didn't; could !? It would have been unfair to us both.

Last year we met again—on the same terms as before. The same weary appeals, and the same curt answers from my lips. At least I would make her see how wholly wrong and hopeless were her attempts at resuming the old relationship. As the season wore on, we fell apart—that is to say, she found it difficult to meet me, for I had other and more absorbing interests to attend to. When I think it over quietly in my sick-room, the season of 1884 seems a confused nightmare wherein light and shade were fantastically intermingled— my courtship of little Kitty Mannering; my hopes, doubts, and fears; our long rides together; my trembling avowal of attachment; her reply; and now and again a vision of a white face flitting by in the 'rickshaw with the black and white liveries I once watched for so earnestly; the wave of Mrs. Wessington's gloved hand; and, when she met me alone, which was but seldom, the irksome monotony of her appeal. I loved Kitty Mannering; honestly, heartily loved her, and with my love for her grew my hatred for Agnes. In August Kitty and I were engaged. The next day I met those accursed "magpie" jhampanies at the back of Jakko, and, moved by some passing sentiment of pity, stopped to tell Mrs. Wessington everything. She knew it already.

"So I hear you're engaged, Jack dear." Then, without a moment's pause:—"I'm sure it's all a mistake—a hideous mistake. We shall be as good friends some day, Jack, as we ever were."

My answer might have made even a man wince. It cut the dying woman before me like the blow of a whip. "Please forgive me, Jack; I didn't mean to make you angry; but it's true, it's true!"

And Mrs. Wessington broke down completely. I turned away and left her to finish her journey in peace, feeling, but only for a moment or two, that I had been an unutterably mean hound. I looked back, and saw that she had turned her 'rickshaw with the idea, I suppose, of overtaking me.

The scene and its surroundings were photographed on my memory. The rain-swept sky (we were at the end of the wet weather), the sodden, dingy pines, the muddy road, and the black powder-riven cliffs formed a gloomy background against which the black and white liveries of the jhampanies, the yellow-paneled 'rickshaw and Mrs. Wessington's down-bowed golden head stood out clearly. She was holding her handkerchief in her left hand and was leaning back exhausted against the 'rickshaw cushions. I turned my horse up a by-path near the Sanjowlie Reservoir and literally ran away. Once I fancied I heard a faint call of "Jack!" This may have been imagination. I never stopped to verify it. Ten minutes later I came across Kitty on horseback; and, in the delight of a long ride with her, forgot all about the interview.

A week later Mrs. Wessington died, and the inexpressible burden of her existence was removed from my life. I went Plainsward perfectly happy. Before three months were over I had forgotten all about her, except that at times the discovery of some of her old letters reminded me unpleasantly of our bygone relationship. By January I had disinterred what was left of our correspondence from among my scattered belongings and had burned it. At the beginning of April of this year, 1885, I was at Simla—semi-deserted Simla—once more, and was deep in lover's talks and walks with Kitty. It was decided that we should be married at the end of June. You will understand, therefore, that, loving Kitty as I did, I am not saying too much when I pronounce myself to have been, at that time, the happiest man in India.

Fourteen delightful days passed almost before I noticed their flight. Then, aroused to the sense of what was proper among mortals circumstanced as we were, I pointed out to Kitty that an engagement ring was the outward and visible sign of her dignity as an engaged girl; and that she must forthwith come to Hamilton's to be measured for one. Up to that moment, I give you my word, we had completely forgotten so trivial a matter. To Hamilton's we accordingly went on the 15th of April, 1885. Remember that—whatever my doctor may say to the contrary—I was then in perfect health, enjoying a well-balanced mind and an *absolute* tranquil spirit. Kitty and I entered Hamilton's shop together, and there, regardless of the order of affairs, I measured Kitty for the ring in the presence of the amused assistant. The ring was a sapphire with two diamonds. We then rode out down the slope that leads to the Combermere Bridge and Peliti's shop.

While my Waler was cautiously feeling his way over the loose shale, and Kitty was laughing and chattering at my side—while all Simla, that is to say as much of it as had then come from the Plains, was grouped round the Reading-room and Peliti's veranda,—I was aware that some one, apparently at a vast distance, was calling me by my Christian name. It struck me that I had heard the voice before, but when and where I could not at once determine. In the short space it took to cover the road between the path from Hamilton's shop and the first plank of the Combermere Bridge I had thought over half a dozen people who might have committed such a solecism, and had eventually decided that it must have been singing in my ears. Immediately opposite Peliti's shop my eye was arrested by the sight of four *jhampanies* in "magpie" livery, pulling a yellow-paneled, cheap, bazar 'rickshaw. In a moment my mind flew back to the previous season and Mrs. Wessington with a sense of irritation and disgust. Was it not enough that the woman was dead and done with, without her black and white servitors reappearing to spoil the day's happiness? Whoever employed them now I thought I would call upon, and as a personal favor to change her *Jhampanies'* livery. I would hire the men myself, and, if necessary, buy their coats from off their backs. It is impossible to say here what a flood of undesirable memories their presence evoked.

"Kitty," I cried, "there are poor Mrs. Wessington's *jhampanies* turned up again! I wonder who has them now?"

Kitty had known Mrs. Wessington slightly last season, and had always been interested in the sickly woman.

"What? Where?" she asked. "I can't see them anywhere."

Even as she spoke, her horse, swerving from a laden mule, threw himself directly in front of the advancing 'rickshaw. I had scarcely time to utter a word of warning when, to my unutterable horror, horse and rider passed *through* men and carriage as if they had been thin air.

"What's the matter?" cried Kitty; "what made you call out so foolishly, Jack? If I *am* engaged I don't want all creation to know about it. There was lots of space between the mule and the veranda; and, if you think I can't ride — There!"

Whereupon wilful Kitty set off, her dainty little head in the air, at a handgallop in the direction of the Bandstand; fully expecting, as she herself afterward told me, that I should follow her. What was the matter? Nothing indeed. Either that I was mad or drunk, or that Simla was haunted with devils. I reined in my impatient cob, and turned round. The 'rickshaw had turned too, and now stood immediately facing me, near the left railing of the Combermere Bridge.

"Jack! Jack, darling!" (There was no mistake about the words this time: they rang through my brain as if they had been shouted in my ear.) "It's some hideous mistake, I'm sure. *Please* forgive me, Jack, and let's be friends again."

The 'rickshaw-hood had fallen back, and inside, as I hope and pray daily for the death I dread by night, sat Mrs. Keith-Wessington, handkerchief in hand, and golden head bowed on her breast.

How long I stared motionless I do not know. Finally, I was aroused by my ysce taking the Waler's bridle and asking whether I was ill. From the hor-

rible to the commonplace is but a step. I tumbled off my horse and dashed, half fainting, into Peliti's for a glass of cherry-brandy. There two or three couples were gathered round the coffee-tables discussing the gossip of the day. Their trivialities were more comforting to me just then than the consolations of religion could have been. I plunged into the midst of the conversation at once; chatted, laughed, and jested with a face (when I caught a glimpse of it in a mirror) as white and drawn as that of a corpse. Three or four men noticed my condition; and, evidently setting it down to the results of over-many pegs, charitably endeavored to draw me apart from the rest of the loungers. But I refused to be led away. I wanted the company of my kind—as a child rushes into the midst of the dinner-party after a fright in the dark. I must have talked for about ten minutes or so, though it seemed an eternity to me, when I heard Kitty's clear voice outside inquiring for me. In another minute she had entered the shop, prepared to roundly upbraid me for failing so signally in my duties. Something in my face stopped her.

"Why, Jack," she cried, "what *have* you been doing? What *has* happened? Are you ill?" Thus driven into a direct lie, I said that the sun had been a little too much for me. It was close upon five o'clock of a cloudy April afternoon, and the sun had been hidden all day. I saw my mistake as soon as the words were out of my mouth: attempted to recover it; blundered hopelessly and followed Kitty in a regal rage, out of doors, amid the smiles of my acquaintances. I made some excuse

(I have forgotten what) on the score of my feeling faint; and cantered away to my hotel, leaving Kitty to finish the ride by herself.

In my room I sat down and tried calmly to reason out the matter. Here was I, Theobald Jack Pansay, a well-educated Bengal Civilian in the year of grace, 1885, presumably sane, certainly healthy, driven in terror from my sweetheart's side by the apparition of a woman who had been dead and buried eight months ago. These were facts that I could not blink. Nothing was further from my thought than any memory of Mrs. Wessington when Kitty and I left Hamilton's shop. Nothing was more utterly commonplace than the stretch of wall opposite Peliti's. It was broad daylight. The road was full of people; and yet here, look you, in defiance of every law of probability, in direct outrage of Nature's ordinance, there had appeared to me a face from the grave.

Kitty's Arab had gone *through* the 'rickshaw: so that my first hope that some woman marvelously like Mrs. Wessington had hired the carriage and the coolies with their old livery was lost. Again and again I went round this treadmill of thought; and again and again gave up baffled and in despair. The voice was as inexplicable as the apparition. I had originally some wild notion of confiding it all to Kitty; of begging her to marry me at once; and in her arms defying the ghostly occupant of the 'rickshaw. "After all," I argued, "the presence of the 'rickshaw is in itself enough to prove the existence of a spectral illusion. One may see ghosts of men and women, but surely never of

coolies and carriages. The whole thing is absurd. Fancy the ghost of a hillman!"

Next morning I sent a penitent note to Kitty, imploring her to overlook my strange conduct of the previous afternoon. My Divinity was still very wroth, and a personal apology was necessary. I explained, with a fluency born of night-long pondering over a falsehood, that I had been attacked with a sudden palpitation of the heart—the result of indigestion. This eminently practical solution had its effect; and Kitty and I rode out that afternoon with the shadow of my first lie dividing us.

Nothing would please her save a canter round Jakko. With my nerves still unstrung from the previous night I feebly protested against the notion, suggesting Observatory Hill, Jutogh, the Boileaugunge road—anything rather than the Jakko round. Kitty was angry and a little hurt: so I yielded from fear of provoking further misunderstanding, and we set out together toward Chota Simla. We walked a greater part of the way, and, according to our custom, cantered from a mile or so below the Convent to the stretch of level road by the Sanjowlie Reservoir. The wretched horses appeared to fly, and my heart beat quicker and quicker as we neared the crest of the ascent. My mind had been full of Mrs. Wessington all the afternoon; and every inch of the Jakko road bore witness to our oldtime walks and talks. The bowlders were full of it; the pines sang it aloud overhead; the rain-fed torrents giggled and chuckled unseen over the shameful story; and the wind in my ears chanted the iniquity aloud.

As a fitting climax, in the middle of the level men call the Ladies' Mile the Horror was awaiting me. No other 'rickshaw was in sight—only the four black and white *jhampanies,* the yellow-paneled carriage, and the golden head of the woman within—all apparently just as I had left them eight months and one fortnight ago! For an instant I fancied that Kitty *must* see what I saw—we were so marvelously sympathetic in all things. Her next words undeceived me—"Not a soul in sight! Come along, Jack, and I'll race you to the Reservoir buildings!" Her wiry little Arab was off like a bird, my Waler following close behind, and in this order we dashed under the cliffs. Half a minute brought us within fifty yards of the 'rickshaw. I pulled my Waler and fell back a little. The 'rickshaw was directly in the middle of the road; and once more the Arab passed through it, my horse following. "Jack! Jack dear! *Please* forgive me," rang with a wail in my ears, and, after an interval:— "It's all a mistake, a hideous mistake!"

I spurred my horse like a man possessed. When I turned my head at the Reservoir works, the black and white liveries were still waiting—patiently waiting—under the grey hillside, and the wind brought me a mocking echo of the words I had just heard. Kitty bantered me a good deal on my silence throughout the remainder of the ride. I had been talking up till then wildly and at random. To save my life I could not speak afterward naturally, and from Sanjowlie to the Church wisely held my tongue.

I was to dine with the Mannerings that night, and had barely time to canter home to dress. On the road to Elysium Hill I overheard two men talking together in the dusk.—"It's a curious thing," said one, "how completely all trace of it disappeared. You know my wife was insanely fond of the woman ('never could see anything in her myself), and wanted me to pick up her old 'rickshaw and coolies if they were to be got for love or money. Morbid sort of fancy I call it; but I've got to do what the *Memsahib* tells me. Would you believe that the man she hired it from tells me that all four of the men—they were brothers—died of cholera on the way to Hardwar, poor devils; and the 'rickshaw has been broken up by the man himself. 'Told me he never used a dead *Memsahib's* 'rickshaw. 'Spoiled his luck. Queer notion, wasn't it? Fancy poor little Mrs. Wessington spoiling any one's luck except her own!" I laughed aloud at this point; and my laugh jarred on me as I uttered it. So there *were* ghosts of 'rickshaws after all, and ghostly employments in the other world! How much did Mrs. Wessington give her men? What were their hours? Where did they go?

And for visible answer to my last question I saw the infernal Thing blocking my path in the twilight. The dead travel fast, and by short cuts unknown to ordinary coolies. I laughed aloud a second time and checked my laughter suddenly, for I was afraid I was going mad. Mad to a certain extent I must have been, for I recollect that I reined in my horse at the head of the 'rickshaw, and politely wished Mrs. Wessington "Good-evening." Her answer was one I knew only too well. I listened to the end; and replied that I had heard it all before, but should be delighted if she had anything further to say. Some malignant devil stronger than I must have entered into me that evening, for I have a dim recollection of taking the commonplaces of the day for five minutes to the Thing in front of me.

"Mad as a hatter, poor devil—or drunk. Max, try and get him to come home."

Surely *that* was not Mrs. Wessington's voice! The two men had overheard me speaking to the empty air, and had returned to look after me. They were very kind and considerate, and from their words evidently gathered that I was extremely drunk. I thanked them confusedly and cantered away to my hotel, there changed, and arrived at the Mannerings' ten minutes late. I pleaded the darkness of the night as an excuse; was rebuked by Kitty for my unlover-like tardiness; and sat down.

The conversation had already become general; and under cover of it, I was addressing some tender small talk to my sweetheart when I was aware that at the further end of the table a short red-whiskered man was describing, with much broidery, his encounter with a mad unknown that evening.

A few sentences convinced me that he was repeating the incident of half an hour ago. In the middle of the story he looked round for applause, as professional story-tellers do, caught my eye, and straightway collapsed. There was a moment's awkward silence, and the red-whiskered man muttered something to the effect that he had "forgotten the rest," thereby sacrificing a reputation as a good story-teller which he had built up for six seasons past. I blessed him from the bottom of my heart, and—went on with my fish.

In the fulness of time that dinner came to an end; and with genuine regret I tore myself away from Kitty—as certain as I was of my own existence that It would be waiting for me outside the door. The red-whiskered man, who had been introduced to me as Doctor Heatherlegh, of Simla, volunteered to bear me company as far as our roads lay together. I accepted his offer with gratitude.

My instinct had not deceived me. It lay in readiness in the Mall, and, in what seemed devilish mockery of our ways, with a lighted head-lamp. The red-whiskered man went to the point at once, in a manner that showed he had been thinking it over all dinner time.

"I say, Pansay, what the deuce was the matter with you this evening on the Elysium road?" The suddenness of the question wrenched an answer from me before I was aware.

"That!" said I, pointing to It.

"*That* may be either D. T. or Eyes for aught I know. Now you don't liquor. I saw as much at dinner, so it can't be *D. T.* There's nothing whatever where you're pointing, though you're sweating and trembling with fright like a scared pony. Therefore, I conclude that it's Eyes. And I ought to understand all about them. Come along home with me. I'm on the Blessington lower road."

To my intense delight the 'rickshaw instead of waiting for us kept about twenty yards ahead—and this, too, whether we walked, trotted, or cantered. In the course of that long night ride I had told my companion almost as much as I have told you here.

"Well, you've spoiled one of the best tales I've ever laid tongue to," said he, "but I'll forgive you for the sake of what you've gone through. Now come home and do what I tell you; and when I've cured you, young man, let this be a lesson to you to steer clear of women and indigestible food till the day of your death."

The 'rickshaw kept steady in front; and my red-whiskered friend seemed to derive great pleasure from my account of its exact whereabouts.

"Eyes, Pansay—all Eyes, Brain, and Stomach. And the greatest of these three is Stomach. You've too much conceited Brain, too little Stomach, and thoroughly unhealthy Eyes. Get your Stomach straight and the rest follows. And all that's French for a liver pill. I'll take sole medical charge of you from this hour! for you're too interesting a phenomenon to be passed over."

By this time we were deep in the shadow of the Blessington lower road and the 'rickshaw came to a dead stop under a pine-clad, over-hanging shale cliff. Instinctively I halted too, giving my reason. Heatherlegh rapped out an oath.

"Now, if you think I'm going to spend a cold night on the hillside for the sake of a Stomach-*cum*-Brain-*cum*-Eye illusion . . . Lord, ha' mercy! What's that?"

There was a muffled report, a blinding smother of dust just in front of us, a crack, the noise of rent boughs, and

about ten yards of the cliff-side—pines, undergrowth, and all—slid down into the road below, completely blocking it up. The uprooted trees swayed and tottered for a moment like drunken giants in the gloom, and then fell prone among their fellows with a thunderous crash. Our two horses stood motionless and sweating with fear. As soon as the rattle of falling earth and stone had subsided, my companion muttered:—"Man, if we'd gone forward we should have been ten feet deep in our graves by now. 'There are more things in heaven and earth.' . . . Come home, Pansay, and thank God. I want a peg badly."

We retraced our way over the Church Ridge, and I arrived at Dr. Heatherlegh's house shortly after midnight.

His attempts toward my cure commenced almost immediately, and for a week I never left his sight. Many a time in the course of that week did I bless the good-fortune which had thrown me in contact with Simla's best and kindest doctor. Day by day my spirits grew lighter and more equable. Day by day, too, I became more and more inclined to fall in with Heatherlegh's "spectral illusion" theory, implicating eyes, brain, and stomach. I wrote to Kitty, telling her that a slight sprain caused by a fall from my horse kept me indoors for a few days; and that I should be recovered before she had time to regret my absence.

Heatherlegh's treatment was simple to a degree. It consisted of liver pills, cold-water baths, and strong exercise, taken in the dusk or at early dawn— for, as he sagely observed:—"A man with a sprained ankle doesn't walk a dozen miles a day, and your young woman might be wondering if she saw you."

At the end of the week, after much examination of pupil and pulse, and strict injunctions as to diet and pedestrianism, Heatherlegh dismissed me as brusquely as he had taken charge of me. Here is his parting benediction:— "Man, I can certify to your mental cure, and that's as much as to say I've cured most of your bodily ailments. Now, get your traps out of this as soon as you can; and be off to make love to Miss Kitty."

I was endeavoring to express my thanks for his kindness. He cut me short.

"Don't think I did this because I like you. I gather that you've behaved like a blackguard all through. But, all the same, you're a phenomenon, and as queer a phenomenon as you are a blackguard. No!"—checking me a second time—"not a rupee please. Go out and see if you can find the eyes-brain-and-stomach business again. I'll give you a lakh for each time you see it."

Half an hour later I was in the Mannerings' drawing-room with Kitty—drunk with the intoxication of present happiness and the fore-knowledge that I should never more be troubled with Its hideous presence. Strong in the sense of my new-found security, I proposed a ride at once; and, by preference, a canter round Jakko.

Never had I felt so well, so overladen with vitality and mere animal spirits, as I did on the afternoon of the 30th of April. Kitty was delighted at the change in my appearance, and complimented me on it in her delightfully frank and outspoken manner. We left the Mannerings' house together, laughing and talking, and cantered along the Chota Simla road as of old.

I was in haste to reach the Sanjowlie Reservoir and there make my assurance doubly sure. The horses did their best, but seemed all too slow to my impatient mind. Kitty was astonished at my boisterousness. "Why, Jack!" she cried at last, "you are behaving like a child. What are you doing?"

We were just below the Convent, and from sheer wantonness I was making my Waler plunge and curvet across the road as I tickled it with the loop of my riding-whip.

"Doing?" I answered; "nothing, dear. That's just it. If you'd been doing nothing for a week except lie up, you'd be as riotous as I."

"'Singing and murmuring in your feast-
    ful mirth,
  Joying to feel yourself alive;
Lord over Nature, Lord of the visible
    Earth,
  Lord of the senses five.'"

My quotation was hardly out of my lips before we had rounded the corner above the Convent; and a few yards further on could see across to Sanjowlie. In the centre of the level road stood the black and white liveries, the yellow-paneled 'rickshaw, and Mrs. Keith-Wessington. I pulled up, looked, rubbed my eyes, and, I believe, must have said something. The next thing I knew was that I was lying face down-ward on the road with Kitty kneeling above me in tears.

"Has it gone, child!" I gasped. Kitty only wept more bitterly.

"Has what gone, Jack dear? what

does It all mean? There must be a mistake somewhere, Jack. A hideous mistake." Her last words brought me to my feet—mad—raving for the time being.

"Yes, there *is* a mistake somewhere," I repeated, "a hideous mistake. Come and look at It."

I have an indistinct idea that I dragged Kitty by the wrist along the road up to where It stood, and implored her for pity's sake to speak to It; to tell It that we were betrothed; that neither Death nor Hell could break the tie between us: and Kitty only knows how much more to the same effect. Now and again I appealed passionately to the Terror in the 'rickshaw to bear witness to all I had said, and to release me from a torture that was killing me. As I talked I suppose I must have told Kitty of my old relations with Mrs. Wessington, for I saw her listen intently with white face and blazing eyes.

"Thank you, Mr. Pansay," she said, "that's *quite* enough. *Syce ghora láo.*"

The syces, impassive as Orientals always are, had come up with the recaptured horses; and as Kitty sprang into her saddle I caught hold of the bridle, entreating her to hear me out and forgive. My answer was the cut of her riding-whip across my face from mouth to eye. and a word or two of farewell that even now I cannot write down. So I judged, and judged rightly, that Kitty knew all; and I staggered back to the side of the 'rickshaw. My face was cut and bleeding, and the blow of the riding-whip had raised a livid blue wheal on it. I had no self-respect. Just then, Heatherlegh, who must have been following Kitty and me at a distance, cantered up.

"Doctor," I said, pointing to my face, "here's Miss Mannering's signature to my order of dismissal and . . . I'll thank you for that lakh as soon as convenient.

Heatherlegh's face, even in my abject misery, moved me to laughter.

"I'll stake my professional reputation" —he began. "Don't be a fool," I whispered. "I've lost my life's happiness and you'd better take me home."

As I spoke the 'rickshaw was gone. Then I lost all knowledge of what was passing. The crest of Jakko seemed to heave and roll like the crest of a cloud and fall in upon me.

Seven days later (on the 7th of May, that is to say) I was aware that I was lying in Heatherlegh's room as weak as a little child. Heatherlegh was watching me intently from behind the papers on his writing-table. His first words were not encouraging; but I was too far spent to be much moved by them.

"Here's Miss Kitty has sent back your letters. You corresponded a good deal, you young people. Here's a packet that looks like a ring, and a cheerful sort of a note from Mannering Papa, which I've taken the liberty of reading and burning. The old gentleman's not pleased with you."

"And Kitty?" I asked, dully.

"Rather more drawn than her father from what she says. By the same token you must have been letting out any number of queer reminiscences just before I met you. 'Says that a man who would have behaved to a woman as you did to Mrs. Wessington ought to kill himself out of sheer pity for his kind. She's a hot-headed little virago, your mash. 'Will have it too that you were suffering from *D. T.* when that row on the Jakko road turned up. 'Says she'll die before she ever speaks to you again."

I groaned and turned over on the other side.

"Now you've got your choice, my friend. This engagement has to be broken off; and the Mannerings don't want to be too hard on you. Was it broken through *D. T.* or epileptic fits? Sorry I can't offer you a better exchange unless you'd prefer hereditary insanity. Say the word and I'll tell 'em it's fits. All Simla knows about that scene on the Ladies' Mile. Come! I'll give you five minutes to think over it."

During those five minutes I believe that I explored thoroughly the lowest circles of the Inferno which it is permitted man to tread on earth. And at the same time I myself was watching myself faltering through the dark labyrinths of doubt, misery, and utter despair. I wondered, as Heatherlegh in his chair might have wondered, which dreadful alternative I should adopt. Presently I heard myself answering in a voice that I hardly recognized,—

"They're confoundedly particular about morality in these parts. Give 'em fits, Heatherlegh, and my love. Now let me sleep a bit longer."

Then my two selves joined, and it was only I (half crazed, devil-driven I) that tossed in my bed, tracing step by step the history of the past month.

"But I am in Simla," I kept repeating to myself. "I, Jack Pansay, am in Simla, and there are no ghosts here. It's

unreasonable of that woman to pretend there are. Why couldn't Agnes have left me alone? I never did her any harm. It might just as well have been me as Agnes. Only I'd never have come back on purpose to kill *her.* Why can't I be left alone—left alone and happy?"

It was high noon when I first awoke: and the sun was low in the sky before I slept—slept as the tortured criminal sleeps on his rack, too worn to feel further pain.

Next day I could not leave my bed. Heatherlegh told me in the morning that he had received an answer from Mr. Mannering, and that, thanks to his (Heatherlegh's) friendly offices, the story of my affliction had traveled through the length and breadth of Simla, where I was on all sides much pitied.

"And that's rather more than you deserve," he concluded, pleasantly, "though the Lord knows you've been going through a pretty severe mill. Never mind; we'll cure you yet, you perverse phenomenon."

I declined firmly to be cured. "You've been much too good to me already, old man," said I; "but I don't think I need trouble you further."

In my heart I knew that nothing Heatherlegh could do would lighten the burden that had been laid upon me.

With that knowledge came also a sense of hopeless, impotent rebellion against the unreasonableness of it all. There were scores of men no better than I whose punishments had at least been reserved for another world; and I felt that it was bitterly, cruelly unfair that I alone should have been singled out for so hideous a fate. This mood would in time give place to another where it seemed that the 'rickshaw and I were the only realties in a world of shadows; that Kitty was a ghost; that Mannering, Heatherlegh, and all the other men and women I knew were all ghosts; and the great, grey hills themselves but vain shadows devised to torture me. From mood to mood I tossed backward and forward for seven weary days; by body growing daily stronger and stronger, until the bedroom looking-glass told me that I had returned to everyday life, and was as other men once more. Curiously enough my face showed no signs of the struggle I had gone through. It was pale indeed, but as expressionless and commonplace as ever. I had expected some permanent alteration—visible evidence of the disease that was eating me away. I found nothing.

On the 15th of May I left Heatherlegh's house at eleven o'clock in the morning; and the instinct of the bachelor drove me to the Club. There I found that every man knew my story as told by Heatherlegh, and was, in clumsy fashion, abnormally kind and attentive. Nevertheless I recognized that for the rest of my natural life I should be among but not of my fellows; and I envied very bitterly indeed the laughing coolies on the Mall below. I lunched at the Club, and at four o'clock wandered aimlessly down the Mall in the vague hope of meeting Kitty. Close to the Band-stand the black and white liveries joined me; and I heard Mrs. Wessington's old appeal at my side. I had been expecting this ever since I came out; and was only surprised at her delay. The phantom 'rickshaw and I went side by side along the Chota Simla road in silence. Close to the bazar, Kitty and a man on horseback overtook and passed us. For any sign she gave I might have been a dog in the road. She did not even pay me the compliment of quickening her pace; though the rainy afternoon had served for an excuse.

So Kitty and her companion, and I and my ghostly Light-o'-Love, crept round Jakko in couples. The road was streaming with water; the pines dripped like roof-pipes on the rocks below, and the air was full of fine, driving rain. Two or three times I found myself saying to myself almost aloud: "I'm Jack Pansay on leave at Simla—*at Simla!* Everyday, ordinary Simla. I mustn't forget that—I mustn't forget that." Then I would try to recollect some of the gossip I had heard at the Club: the prices of So-and-So's horses—anything, in fact, that related to the workaday Anglo-Indian world I knew so well. I even repeated the multiplication-table rapidly to myself, to make quite sure that I was not taking leave of my senses. It gave me much comfort; and must have prevented my hearing Mrs. Wessington for a time.

Once more I wearily climbed the Convent slope and entered the level road. Here Kitty and the man started off at a canter, and I was left alone with Mrs. Wessington. "Agnes," said I, "will you put back your hood and tell me what it all means?" The hood dropped noiselessly, and I was face to face with my dead and buried mistress. She was wearing the dress in which I had last seen her alive; carried the same tiny handkerchief in her right hand; and the same cardcase in her left. (A woman eight months dead with a cardcase!) I had to pin myself down to the multiplication-table, and to set both hands on the stone parapet of the road, to assure myself that that at least was real.

"Agnes," I repeated, "for pity's sake tell me what it all means." Mrs. Wessington leaned forward, with that odd, quick turn of the head I used to know so well, and spoke.

If my story had not already so madly overleaped the bounds of all human belief I should apologize to you now. As I know that no one—no, not even Kitty, for whom it is written as some sort of justification of my conduct—will believe me, I will go on. Mrs. Wessington spoke and I walked with her from the Sanjowlie road to the turning below the Commander-in-Chief's house as I might walk by the side of any living woman's 'rickshaw, deep in conversation. The second and most tormenting of my moods of sickness had suddenly laid hold upon me, and like the Prince in Tennyson's poem, "I seemed to move amid a world of ghosts." There had been a garden-party at the Commander-in-Chief's, and we two joined the crowd of homeward-bound folk. As I saw them then it seemed that *they* were the shadows—impalpable, fantastic shadows—that divided for Mrs. Wessington's 'rickshaw to pass through. What we said during the course of that weird interview I cannot—indeed, I dare not—tell. Heatherlegh's comment would have been a short laugh and a remark that I had been "mashing a brain-eye-and-stomach chimera." It was a ghastly and yet in some indefinable way a marvelously dear experience. Could it be

possible, I wondered, that I was in this life to woo a second time the woman I had killed by my own neglect and cruelty?

I met Kitty on the homeward road—a shadow among shadows.

If I were to describe all the incidents of the next fortnight in their order, my story would never come to an end; and your patience would be exhausted. Morning after morning and evening after evening the ghostly 'rickshaw and I used to wander through Simla together. Wherever I went there the four black and white liveries followed me and bore me company to and from my hotel. At the Theatre I found them amid the crowd of yelling *jhampanies;* outside the Club veranda, after a long evening of whist; at the Birthday Ball, waiting patiently for my reappearance; and in broad daylight when I went calling. Save that it cast no shadow, the 'rickshaw was in every respect as real to look upon as one of wood and iron. More than once, indeed, I have had to check myself from warning some hard-riding friend against cantering over it. More than once I have walked down the Mall deep in conversation with Mrs. Wessington to the unspeakable amazement of the passers-by.

Before I had been out and about a week I learned that the "fit" theory had been discarded in favor of insanity. However, I made no change in my mode of life. I called, rode, and dined out as freely as ever. I had a passion for the society of my kind which I had never felt before; I hungered to be among the realities of life; and at the same time I felt vaguely unhappy when I had been separated too long from my ghostly companion. It would be almost impossible to describe my varying moods from the 15th of May up to to-day.

The presence of the 'rickshaw filled me by turns with horror, blind fear, a dim sort of pleasure, and utter despair. I dared not leave Simla; and I knew that my stay there was killing me. I knew, moreover, that it was my destiny to die slowly and a little every day. My only anxiety was to get the penance over as quietly as might be. Alternately I hungered for a sight of Kitty and watched her outrageous flirtations with my successor—to speak more accurately, my successors—with amused interest. She was as much out of my life as I was out of hers. By day I wandered with Mrs. Wessington almost content. By night I implored Heaven to let me return to the world as I used to know it. Above all these varying moods lay the sensation of dull, numbling wonder that the Seen and the Unseen should mingle so strangely on this earth to hound one poor soul to its grave.

*   *   *   *   *   *

August 27.—Heatherlegh has been indefatigable in his attendance on me; and only yesterday told me that I ought to send in an application for sick leave. An application to escape the company of a phantom! A request that the Government would graciously permit me to get rid of five ghosts and an airy 'rickshaw by going to England! Heatherlegh's proposition moved me to almost hysterical laughter. I told him that I should await the end quietly at Simla; and I am sure that the end is not far off. Believe me that I dread its advent more than any word can say; and I torture myself nightly with a thousand speculations as to the manner of my death.

Shall I die in my bed decently and as an English gentleman should die; or, in one last walk on the Mall, will my soul be wrenched from me to take its place forever and ever by the side of that ghastly phantasm? Shall I return to my old lost allegiance in the next world, or shall I meet Agnes loathing her and bound to her side through all eternity? Shall we two hover over the scene of our lives till the end of Time? As the day of my death draws nearer, the intense horror that all living flesh feels toward escaped spirits from beyond the grave grows more and more powerful. It is an awful thing to go down quick among the dead with scarcely one-half of your life completed. It is a thousand times more awful to wait as I do in your midst, for I know not what unimaginable terror. Pity me, at least on the score of my "delusion," for I know you will never believe what I have written here. Yet as surely as ever a man was done to death by the Powers of Darkness I am that man.

In justice, too, pity her. For as surely as ever woman was killed by man, I killed Mrs. Wessington. And the last portion of my punishment is even now upon me.

My Own True Ghost Story

As I came through the Desert thus it
was—
As I came through the Desert.
—*The City of Dreadful Night.*

SOMEWHERE in the Other World,
where there are books and pictures and
plays and shop-windows to look at, and
thousands of men who spend their lives
in building up all four, lives a gentleman
who writes real stories about the real
insides of people; and his name is Mr.
Walter Besant. But he will insist upon
treating his ghosts—he has published
half a workshopful of them—with levity.
He makes his ghost-seers talk familiarly,
and, in some cases, flirt outrageously,
with the phantoms. You may treat anything, from a Viceroy to a Vernacular
Paper, with levity; but you must behave
reverently toward a ghost, and particularly an Indian one.

There are, in this land, ghosts who
take the form of fat, cold, pobby
corpses, and hide in trees near the roadside till a traveler passes. Then they
drop upon his neck and remain. There
are also terrible ghosts of women who
have died in child-bed. These wander
along the pathways at dusk, or hide in
the crops near a village, and call se-
ductively. But to answer their call is
death in this world and the next. Their
feet are turned backward that all sober
men may recognize them. There are
ghosts of little children who have been
thrown into wells. These haunt well-
curbs and the fringes of jungles, and
wail under the stars, or catch women by
the wrist and beg to be taken up and

carried. These and the corpse-ghosts,
however, are only vernacular articles
and do not attack Sahibs. No native
ghost has yet been authentically reported to have frightened an Englishman; but many English ghosts have
scared the life out of both white and
black.

Nearly every other Station owns a
ghost. There are said to be two at
Simla, not counting the woman who
blows the bellows at Syree dâk-bungalow
on the Old Road; Mussoorie has a
house haunted of a very lively Thing;
a White Lady is supposed to do night-
watchman round a house in Lahore;
Dalhousie says that one of her houses
"repeats" on autumn evenings all the
incidents of a horrible horse-and-preci-
pice accident; Murree has a merry
ghost, and, now that she has been swept
by cholera, will have room for a sorrowful one; there are Officers' Quarters in
Mian Mir whose doors open without
reason, and whose furniture is guaranteed to creak, not with the heat of
June but with the weight of Invisibles
who come to lounge in the chair; Peshawur possesses houses that none will will-
ingly rent; and there is something—not
fever—wrong with a big bungalow in
Allahabad. The older Provinces simply
bristle with haunted houses, and march
phantom armies along their main
thoroughfares.

Some of the dâk-bungalows on the
Grand Trunk Road have handy little
cemeteries in their compound—witnesses
to the "changes and chances of this

607

mortal life" in the days when men drove from Calcutta to the Northwest. These bungalows are objectionable places to put up in. They are generally very old, always dirty, while the *khansamah* is as ancient as the bungalow. He either chatters senilely, or falls into the long trances of age. In both moods he is useless. If you get angry with him, he refers to some Sahib dead and buried these thirty years, and says that when he was in that Sahib's service not a *khansamah* in the Province could touch him. Then he jabbers and mows and trembles and fidgets among the dishes, and you repent of your irritation.

In these dâk-bungalows, ghosts are most likely to be found, and when found, they should be made a note of. Not long ago it was my business to live in dâk-bungalows. I never inhabited the same house for three nights running, and grew to be learned in the breed. I lived in Government-built ones with red brick walls and rail ceilings, an inventory of the furniture posted in every room, and an excited snake at the threshold to give welcome. I lived in "converted" ones—old houses officiating as dâk-bungalows—where nothing was in its proper place and there wasn't even a fowl for dinner. I lived in second-hand palaces where the wind blew through open-work marble tracery just as uncomfortably as through a broken pane. I lived in dâk-bungalows where the last entry in the visitors' book was fifteen months old, and where they slashed off the curry-kid's head with a sword. It was my good-luck to meet all sorts of men, from sober traveling missionaries and deserters flying from British Regiments, to drunken loafers who threw whiskey bottles at all who passed; and my still greater good-fortune just to escape a maternity case. Seeing that a fair proposition of the tragedy of our lives out here acted itself in dâk-bungalows, I wondered that I had met no ghosts. A ghost that would voluntarily hang about a dâk-bungalow would be mad of course; but so many men have died mad in dâk-bungalows that there must be a fair percentage of lunatic ghosts.

In due time I found my ghost, or ghosts rather, for there were two of them. Up till that hour I had sympathized with Mr. Besant's method of handling them, as shown in *"The Strange Case of Mr. Lucraft and other Stories."* I am now in the Opposition.

We will call the bungalow Katmal dâk-bungalow. But *that* was the smallest part of the horror. A man with a sensitive hide has no right to sleep in dâk-bungalows. He should marry. Katmal dâk-bungalow was old and rotten and unrepaired. The floor was of worn brick, the walls were filthy, and the windows were nearly black with grime. It stood on a by-path largely used by native Sub-Deputy Assistants of all kinds, from Finance to Forests; but real Sahibs were rare. The *khansamah*, who was nearly bent double with old age, said so.

When I arrived, there was a fitful, undecided rain on the face of the land, accompanied by a restless wind, and every gust made a noise like the ratling of dry bones in the stiff toddy-palms outside. The *khansamah* completely lost his head on my arrival. He had served as Sahib once. Did I know that Sahib? He gave me the name of a well-known man who has been buried for more than a quarter of a century, and showed me an ancient daguerrotype of that man in his prehistoric youth. I had seen a steel engraving of him at the head of a double volume of Memoirs a month before, and I felt ancient beyond telling.

The day shut in and the *khansamah* went to get me food. He did not go through the pretence of calling it *"khana"*—man's victuals. He said *"ratub,"* and that means, among other things, "grub"—dog's rations. There was no insult in his choice of the term. He had forgotten the other word, I suppose.

While he was cutting up the dead bodies of animals, I settled myself down, after exploring the dâk-bungalow. There were three rooms, beside my own, which was a corner kennel, each giving into the other through dingy white doors fastened with long iron bars. The bungalow was a very solid one, but the partition-walls of the rooms were almost jerry-built in their flimsiness. Every step or bang of a trunk echoed from my room down the other three, and every footfall came back tremulously from the far walls. For this reason I shut the door. There were no lamps—only candles in long glass shades. An oil wick was set in the bath-room.

For bleak, unadulterated misery that dâk-bungalow was the worst of the many that I had ever set foot in. There was no fireplace, and the windows would not open; so a brazier of charcoal would have been useless. The rain and the wind splashed and gurgled and moaned round the house, and the toddy-palms rattled and roared. Half a dozen jackals went through the compound singing, and a hyena stood afar off and mocked them. A hyena would convince a Sadducee of the Resurrection of the Dead—the worst sort of Dead. Then came the *ratub*—a curious meal, half native and half English in composition—with the old *khansamah* babbling behind my chair about dead and gone English people, and the wind-blown candles playing shadow-bo-peep with the bed and the mosquito-curtains. It was just the sort of dinner and evening to make a man think of every single one of his past sins, and of all the others that he intended to commit if he lived.

Sleep, for several hundred reasons, was not easy. The lamp in the bath-room threw the most absurd shadows into the room, and the wind was beginning to talk nonsense.

Just when the reasons were drowsy with blood-sucking I heard the regular— "Let-us-take-and-heave-him-over" grunt of doolie-bearers in the compound. First one doolie came in, then a second, and then a third. I heard the doolies dumped on the ground, and the shutter in front of my door shook. "That's some one trying to come in," I said. But no one spoke, and I persuaded myself that it was the gusty wind. The shutter of the room next to mine was attacked, flung back, and the inner door opened. "That's some Sub-Deputy Assistant," I said, "and he has brought his friends with him. Now they'll talk and spit and smoke for an hour."

But there were no voices and no footsteps. No one was putting his luggage into the next room. The door shut, and I thanked Providence that I was to be left in peace. But I was curious to know where the doolies had gone. I got out of bed and looked into the darkness. There was never a sign of a doolie. Just as I was getting into bed again, I heard, in the next room, the sound that no man in his senses can possibly mistake—the whir of a billiard ball down the length of the slates when the striker is stringing for break. No other sound is like it. A minute afterward there was another whir, and I got into bed. I was not frightened—indeed I was not. I was very curious to know what had become of the doolies. I jumped into bed for that reason.

Next minute I heard the double click of a cannon and my hair sat up. It is a mistake to say that hair stands up. The skin of the head tightens and you can feel a faint, prickly bristling all over the scalp. That is the hair sitting up.

There was a whir and a click, and both sounds could only have been made by one thing—a billiard ball. I argued the matter out at great length with myself; and the more I argued the less probable it seemed that one bed, one table, and two chairs—all the furniture of the room next to mine—could so exactly duplicate the sounds of a game of billiards. After another cannon, a three-cushion one to judge by the whir, I argued no more. I had found my ghost and would have given worlds to have escaped from that dâk-bungalow. I listened, and with each listen the game grew clearer. There was whir on whir and click on click. Sometimes there was a double click and a whir and another click. Beyond any sort of doubt, people were playing billiards in the next room. And the next

room was not big enough to hold a billiard table!

Between the pauses of the wind I heard the game go forward—stroke after stroke. I tried to believe that I could not hear voices; but that attempt was a failure.

Do you know what fear is? Not ordinary fear of insult, injury or death, but abject, quivering dread of something that you cannot see—fear that dries the inside of the mouth and half of the throat—fear that makes you sweat on the palms of the hands, and gulp in order to keep the uvula at work? This is a fine Fear—a great cowardice, and must be felt to be appreciated. The very improbability of billiards in a dâk-bungalow proved the reality of the thing. No man—drunk or sober—could imagine a game at billiards, or invent the spitting crack of a "screw-cannon."

A severe course of dâk-bungalows has this disadvantage—it breeds infinite credulity. If a man said to a confirmed dâk-bungalow-haunter:—"There is a corpse in the next room, and there's a mad girl in the next but one, and the woman and man on that camel have just eloped from a place sixty miles away," the hearer would not disbelieve because he would know that nothing is too wild, grotesque, or horrible to happen in a dâk-bungalow.

This credulity, unfortunately, extends to ghosts. A rational person fresh from his own house would have turned on his side and slept. I did not. So surely as I was given up as a bad carcass by the scores of things in the bed because the bulk of my blood was in my heart, so surely did I hear every stroke of a long game at billiards played in the echoing room behind the iron-barred door. My dominant fear was that the players might want a maker. It was an absurd fear; because creatures who could play in the dark would be above such superfluities. I only know that that was my terror; and it was real.

After a long long while, the game stopped, and the door banged. I slept because I was dead tired. Otherwise I should have preferred to have kept awake. Not for everything in Asia would I have dropped the door-bar and peered into the dark of the next room.

When the morning came, I considered that I had done well and wisely, and inquired for the means of departure.

"By the way, *khansamah*," I said, "what were those three doolies doing in my compound in the night?"

"There were no doolies," said the *khansamah*.

I went into the next room and the daylight streamed through the open door. I was immensely brave. I would, at that hour, have played Black Pool with the owner of the big Black Pool down below.

"Has this place always been a dâk-bungalow?" I asked.

"No," said the *khansamah*. "Ten or twenty years ago, I have forgotten how long, it was a billiard-room."

"A how much?"

"A billiard-room for the Sahibs who built the Railway. I was *khansamah* then in the big house where all the Railway-Sahibs lived, and I used to come across with brandy-*shrab*. These three rooms were all one, and they held a big table on which the Sahibs played every evening. But the Sahibs are all dead now, and the Railway runs, you say, nearly to Kabul."

"Do you remember anything about the Sahibs?"

"It is long ago, but I remember that one Sahib, a fat man and always angry, was playing here one night, and he said to me:—'Mangal Khan, brandy-*pani do*,' and I filled the glass, and he bent over the table to strike, and his head fell lower and lower till it hit the table, and his spectacles came off, and when we— the Sahibs and I myself—ran to lift him he was dead. I helped to carry him out. Aha, he was a strong Sahib! But he is dead and I, old Mangal Khan, am still living, by your favor."

That was more than enough! I had my ghost—a first-hand, authenticated article. I would write to the Society for Psychical Research—I would paralyze the Empire with the news! But I would, first of all, put eighty miles of assessed crop-land between myself and that dâk-bungalow before nightfall. The Society might send their regular agent to investigate later on.

I went into my own room and prepared to pack after noting down the facts of the case. As I smoked I heard the game begin again—with a miss in balk this time, for the whir was a short one.

The door was open and I could see into the room. *Click—click!* That was a cannon. I entered the room without fear, for there was sunlight within and a fresh breeze without. The unseen game was going on at a tremendous rate. And well it might, when a restless little rat was running to and fro inside the dingy ceiling-cloth, and a piece of loose window-sash was making fifty breaks off the window-bolt as it shook in the breeze!

Impossible to mistake the sound of billiard balls! Impossible to mistake the whir of a ball over the slate! But I was to be excused. Even when I shut my enlightened eyes the sound was marvelously like that of a fast game.

Entered angrily the faithful partner of my sorrows, Kadir Baksh.

"This bungalow is very bad and low-caste! No wonder the Presence was disturbed and is speckled. Three sets of doolie-bearers came to the bungalow late last night when I was sleeping outside, and said that it was their custom to rest in the rooms set apart for the English people! What honor has the khansamah? They tried to enter, but I told them to go. No wonder, if these Oorias have been here, that the Presence is sorely spotted. It is shame, and the work of a dirty man!"

Kadir Baksh did not say that he had taken from each gang two annas for rent in advance, and then, beyond my earshot, had beaten them with the big green umbrella whose use I could never before divine. But Kadir Baksh has no notions of morality.

There was an interview with the khansamah, but as he promptly lost his head, wrath gave place to pity, and pity led to a long conversation, in the course of which he put the fat Engineer-Sahib's tragic death in three separate stations—two of them fifty miles away. The third shift was to Calcutta, and there the Sahib died while driving a dog-cart.

If I had encouraged him the khansamah would have wandered all through Bengal with his corpse.

I did not go away as soon as I intended. I stayed for the night, while the wind and the rat and the sash and the window-bolt played a ding-dong "hundred and fifty up." Then the wind ran out and the billiards stopped, and I felt that I had ruined my one genuine, hall-marked ghost story.

Had I only stopped at the proper time, I could have made anything out of it.

That was the bitterest thought of all!

The Strange Ride of Morrowbie Jukes

Alive or dead—there is no other way.—
Native Proverb.

THERE is, as the conjurers say, no deception about this tale. Jukes by accident stumbled upon a village that is well known to exist, though he is the only Englishman who has been there. A somewhat similar institution used to flourish on the outskirts of Calcutta, and there is a story that if you go into the heart of Bikanir, which is in the heart of the Great Indian Desert, you shall come across not a village but a town where the Dead who did not die but may not live have established their headquarters. And, since it is perfectly true that in the same Desert is a wonderful city where all the rich moneylenders retreat after they have made their fortunes (fortunes so vast that the owners cannot trust even the strong hand of the Government to protect them, but take refuge in the waterless sands), and drive sumptuous C-spring barouches, and buy beautiful girls and decorate their palaces with gold and ivory and Minton tiles and mother-o'-pearl, I do not see why Jukes's tale should not be true. He is a Civil Engineer, with a head for plans and distances and things of that kind, and he certainly would not take the trouble to invent imaginary traps. He could earn more by doing his legitimate work. He never varies the tale in the telling, and grows very hot and indignant when he thinks of the disrespectful treatment he received. He wrote this quite straightforwardly at first, but he has since touched it up in places and introduced Moral Reflections, thus:

In the beginning it all arose from a slight attack of fever. My work necessitated my being in camp for some months between Pakpattan and Mubarakpur—a desolate sandy stretch of country as every one who has had the misfortune to go there may know. My coolies were neither more nor less exasperating than other gangs, and my work demanded sufficient attention to keep me from moping, had I been inclined to so unmanly a weakness.

On the 23d December, 1884, I felt a little feverish. There was a full moon at the time, and, in consequence, every dog near my tent was baying it. The brutes assembled in twos and threes and drove me frantic. A few days previously I had shot one loud-mouthed singer and suspended his carcass *in terrorem* about fifty yards from my tent-door. But his friends fell upon, fought for, and ultimately devoured the body; and, as it seemed to me, sang their hymns of thanksgiving afterward with renewed energy.

The light-heartedness which accompanies fever acts differently on different men. My irritation gave way, after a short time, to a fixed determination to slaughter one huge black and white beast who had been foremost in song and first in flight throughout the evening. Thanks to a shaking hand and a giddy head I had already missed him twice with both barrels of my shot-gun, when it struck me that my best plan would be to ride him down in the open and finish him off with a hog-spear. This, of course, was merely the semi-delirious notion of a fever patient; but I remember that it struck me at the time as being eminently practical and feasible.

I therefore ordered my groom to saddle Pornic and bring him round quietly to the rear of my tent. When the pony was ready, I stood at his head prepared to mount and dash out as soon as the dog should again lift up his voice. Pornic, by the way, had not been out of his pickets for a couple of days; the night air was crisp and chilly; and I was armed with a specially long and sharp pair of persuaders with which I had been rousing a sluggish cob that afternoon. You will easily believe, then, that when he was let go he went quickly. In one moment, for the brute bolted as straight as a die, the tent was left far behind, and we were flying over the smooth sandy soil at racing speed.

In another we had passed the wretched dog, and I had almost forgotten why it was that I had taken horse and hog-spear.

The delirium of fever and the excitement of rapid motion through the air must have taken away the remnant of my senses. I have a faint recollection of standing upright in my stirrups, and of brandishing my hog-spear at the great white Moon that looked down so calmly on my mad gallop; and of shouting challenges to the camel-thorn bushes as they whizzed past. Once or twice, I believe, I swayed forward on Pornic's neck, and literally hung on by my spurs —as the marks next morning showed.

The wretched beast went forward like a thing possessed, over what seemed to be a limitless expanse of moonlit sand. Next, I remember, the ground rose suddenly in front of us, and as we topped the ascent I saw the waters of the Sutlej shining like a silver bar below. Then Pornic blundered heavily on his nose, and we rolled together down some unseen slope.

I must have lost consciousness, for when I recovered I was lying on my stomach in a heap of soft white sand, and the dawn was beginning to break dimly over the edge of the slope down which I had fallen. As the light grew stronger I saw that I was at the bottom of a horseshoe-shaped crater of sand, opening on one side directly on to the shoals of the Sutlej. My fever had altogether left me, and, with the exception of a slight dizziness in the head, I felt no bad effects from the fall over night.

Pornic, who was standing a few yards away, was naturally a good deal ex-hausted, but had not hurt himself in the least. His saddle, a favorite polo one, was much knocked about, and had been twisted under his belly. It took me some time to put him to rights, and in the meantime I had ample opportunities of observing the spot into which I had so foolishly dropped.

At the risk of being considered tedious, I must describe it at length; inasmuch as an accurate mental picture of its peculiarities will be of material assistance in enabling the reader to understand what follows.

Imagine then, as I have said before, a horseshoe-shaped crater of sand with steeply graded sand walls about thirty-five feet high. (The slope, I fancy, must have been about 65°.) This crater enclosed a level piece of ground about fifty yards long by thirty at its broadest part, with a rude well in the centre. Round the bottom of the crater, about three feet from the level of the ground proper, ran a series of eighty-three semi-circular, ovoid, square, and multilateral holes, all about three feet at the mouth. Each hole on inspection showed that it was carefully shored internally with drift-wood and bamboos, and over the mouth a wooden drip-board projected, like the peak of a jockey's cap, for two feet. No sign of life was visible in these tunnels, but a most sickening stench pervaded the entire amphitheatre—a stench fouler than any which my wanderings in Indian villages have introduced me to.

Having remounted Pornic, who was as anxious as I to get back to camp, I rode round the base of the horseshoe to find some place whence an exit would be practicable. The inhabitants, whoever they might be, had not thought fit to put in an appearance, so I was left to my own devices. My first attempt to "rush" Pornic up the steep sandbanks showed me that I had fallen into a trap exactly on the same model as that which the ant-lion sets for its prey. At each step the shifting sand poured down from above in tons, and rattled on the drip-boards of the holes like small shot. A couple of ineffectual charges sent us both rolling down to the bottom, half choked with the torrents of sand; and I was constrained to turn my attention to the river-bank.

Here everything seemed easy enough. The sand hills ran down to the river edge, it is true, but there were plenty of shoals and shallows across which I could gallop Pornic, and find my way back to *terra firma* by turning sharply to the right or the left. As I led Pornic over the sands I was startled by the faint pop of a rifle across the river; and at the same moment a bullet dropped with a sharp *"whit"* close to Pornic's head.

There was no mistaking the nature of the missile—a regulation Martini-Henry "picket." About five hundred yards away a country-boat was anchored in midstream; and a jet of smoke drifting away from its bows in the still morning air showed me whence the delicate attention had come. Was ever a respectable gentleman in such an *impasse?* The treacherous sand slope allowed no escape from a spot which I had visited most involuntarily, and a promenade on the river frontage was the signal for a bombardment from some insane native in a boat. I'm afraid that I lost my temper very much indeed.

Another bullet reminded me that I had better save my breath to cool my porridge; and I retreated hastily up the sands and back to the horseshoe, where I saw that the noise of the rifle had drawn sixty-five human beings from the badger-holes which I had up till that point supposed to be untenanted. I found myself in the midst of a crowd of spectators—about forty men, twenty women, and one child who could not have been more than five years old. They were all scantily clothed in that salmon-colored cloth which one associates with Hindu mendicants, and, at first sight, gave me the impression of a band of loathsome *fakirs*. The filth and repulsiveness of the assembly were beyond all description, and I shuddered to think what their life in the badger-holes must be.

Even in these days, when local self-government has destroyed the greater part of a native's respect for a Sahib, I have been accustomed to a certain amount of civility from my inferiors, and on approaching the crowd naturally expected that there would be some recognition of my presence. As a matter of fact there was; but it was by no means what I had looked for.

The ragged crew actually laughed at me—such laughter I hope I may never hear again. They cackled, yelled, whistled, and howled as I walked into their midst; some of them literally throwing themselves down on the ground in convulsions of unholy mirth. In a moment I had let go Pornic's head, and, irritated beyond expression at the morning's adventure, commenced cuffing those nearest to me with all the force I could. The wretches dropped under my blows like nine-pins, and the laughter gave place to wails for mercy; while those yet untouched clasped me round the knees, imploring me in all sorts of uncouth tongues to spare them.

In the tumult, and just when I was feeling very much ashamed of myself for having thus easily given way to my temper, a thin, high voice murmured in English from behind my shoulder:—"Sahib! Sahib! Do you not know me? Sahib, it is Gunga Dass, the telegraph-master."

I spun round quickly and faced the speaker.

Gunga Dass (I have, of course, no hesitation in mentioning the man's real name) I had known four years before as a Deccanee Brahmin loaned by the Punjab Government to one of the Khalsia States. He was in charge of a branch telegraph-office there, and when I had last met him was a jovial, full-stomached, portly Government servant with a marvelous capacity for making bad puns in English—a peculiarity which made me remember him long after I had forgotten his services to me in his official capacity. It is seldom that a Hindu makes English puns.

Now, however, the man was changed beyond all recognition. Caste-mark, stomach, slate-colored continuations, and unctuous speech were all gone. I looked at a withered skeleton, turbanless and almost naked, with long matted hair and deep-set codfish-eyes. But for a crescent-shaped scar on the left cheek —the result of an accident for which I was responsible—I should never have known him. But it was indubitably Gunga Dass, and—for this I was thankful—an English-speaking native who

might at least tell me the meaning of all that I had gone through that day.

The crowd retreated to some distance as I turned toward the miserable figure, and ordered him to show me some method of escaping from the crater. He held a freshly plucked crow in his hand, and in reply to my question climbed slowly on a platform of sand which ran in front of the holes, and commenced lighting a fire there in silence. Dried bents, sand-poppies, and driftwood burn quickly; and I derived much consolation from the fact that he lit them with an ordinary sulphur-match. When they were in a bright glow, and the crow was neatly spitted in front thereof, Gunga Dass began without a word of preamble:

"There are only two kinds of men, Sar. The alive and the dead. When you are dead you are dead, but when you are alive you live." (Here the crow demanded his attention for an instant as it twirled before the fire in danger of being burned to a cinder.) "If you die at home and do not die when you come to the ghât to be burned you come here."

The nature of the reeking village was made plain now, and all that I had known or read of the grotesque and the horrible paled before the fact just communicated by the ex-Brahmin. Sixteen years ago, when I first landed in Bombay, I had been told by a wandering Armenian of the existence, somewhere in India, of a place to which such Hindus as had the misfortune to recover from trance or catalepsy were conveyed and kept, and I recollect laughing heartily at what I was then pleased to consider a traveler's tale.

Sitting at the bottom of the sand-trap, the memory of Watson's Hotel, with its swinging punkahs, white-robed attendants, and the sallow-faced Armenian, rose up in my mind as vividly as a photograph, and I burst into a loud fit of laughter. The contrast was too absurd!

Gunga Dass, as he bent over the unclean bird, watched me curiously. Hindus seldom laugh, and his surroundings were not such as to move Gunga Dass to any undue excess of hilarity. He removed the crow solemnly from the wooden spit and as solemnly devoured it. Then he continued his story, which I give in his own words:

"In epidemics of the cholera you are carried to be burned almost before you are dead. When you come to the riverside the cold air, perhaps, makes you alive, and then, if you are only little alive, mud is put on your nose and mouth and you die conclusively. If you are rather more alive, more mud is put; but if you are too lively they let you go and take you away. I was too lively, and made protestation with anger against the indignities that they endeavored to press upon me. In those days I was Brahmin and proud man. Now I am dead man and eat"—here he eyed the well-gnawed breast bone with the first sign of emotion that I had seen in him since we met—"crows, and other things. They took me from my sheets when they saw that I was too lively and gave me medicines for one week, and I survived successfully. Then they sent me by rail from my place to Okara Station, with a man to take care of me; and at Okara Station we met two other men, and they conducted we three

on camels, in the night, from Okara Station to this place, and they propelled me from the top to the bottom, and the other two succeeded, and I have been here ever since two and a half years. Once I was Brahmin and proud man, and now I eat crows."

"There is no way of getting out?"

"None of what kind at all. When I first came I made experiments frequently and all the others also, but we have always succumbed to the sand which is precipitated upon our heads."

"But surely," I broke in at this point, "the river-front is open, and it is worth while dodging the bullets; while at night"—

I had already matured a rough plan of escape which a natural instinct of selfishness forbade me sharing with Gunga Dass. He, however, divined my unspoken thought almost as soon as it was formed; and, to my intense astonishment, gave vent to a long low chuckle of derision—the laughter, be it understood, of a superior or at least of an equal.

"You will not"—he had dropped the Sir completely after his opening sentence—"make any escape that way. But you can try. I have tried. Once only."

The sensation of nameless terror and abject fear which I had in vain attempted to strive against overmastered me completely. My long fast—it was now close upon ten o'clock, and I had eaten nothing since tiffin on the previous day—combined with the violent and unnatural agitation of the ride had exhausted me, and I verily believe that, for a few minutes, I acted as one mad. I hurled myself against the pitiless sand-slope. I ran round the base of the crater, blaspheming and praying by turns. I crawled out among the sedges of the river-front, only to be driven back each time in an agony of nervous dread by the rifle-bullets which cut up the sand round me—for I dared not face the death of a mad dog among that hideous crowd—and finally fell, spent and raving, at the curb of the well. No one had taken the slightest notice of an exhibition which makes me blush hotly even when I think of it now.

Two or three men trod on my panting body as they drew water, but they were evidently used to this sort of thing, and had no time to waste upon me. The situation was humiliating. Gunga Dass, indeed, when he had banked the embers of his fire with sand, was at some pains to throw half a cupful of fetid water over my head, an attention for which I could have fallen on my knees and thanked him, but he was laughing all the while in the same mirthless, wheezy key that greeted me on my first attempt to force the shoals. And so, in a semi-comatose condition, I lay till noon. Then, being only a man after all, I felt hungry, and intimated as much to Gunga Dass, whom I had begun to regard as my natural protector. Following the impulse of the outer world when dealing with natives, I put my hand into my pocket and drew out four annas. The absurdity of the gift struck me at once, and I was about to replace the money.

Gunga Dass, however, was of a different opinion. "Give me the money," said he; "all you have, or I will get help, and we will kill you!" All this as if it were the most natural thing in the world!

A Briton's first impulse, I believe, is to guard the contents of his pockets; but a moment's reflection convinced me of the futility of differing with the one man who had it in his power to make me comfortable; and with whose help it was possible that I might eventually escape from the crater. I gave him all the money in my possession, Rs. 9-8-5— nine rupees eight annas and five pie— for I always keep small change as *bakshish* when I am in camp. Gunga Dass clutched the coins, and hid them at once in his ragged loin-cloth, his expression changing to something diabolical as he looked round to assure himself that no one had observed us.

"*Now* I will give you something to eat," said he.

What pleasure the possession of my money could have afforded him I am unable to say; but inasmuch as it did give him evident delight I was not sorry that I had parted with it so readily, for I had no doubt that he would have had me killed if I had refused. One does not protest against the vagaries of a den of wild beasts; and my companions were lower than any beasts. While I devoured what Gunga Dass had provided, a coarse *chapatti* and a cupful of the foul well-water, the people showed not the faintest sign of curiosity —that curiosity which is so rampant, as a rule, in an Indian village.

I could even fancy that they despised me. At all events they treated me with the most chilling indifference, and Gunga Dass was nearly as bad. I plied him with questions about the terrible village, and received extremely unsatisfactory answers. So far as I could gather, it had been in existence from time immemorial—whence I concluded· that it was at least a century old—and during that time no one had ever been known to escape from it. [I had to control myself here with both hands, lest the blind terror should lay hold of me a second time and drive me raving round the crater.] Gunga Dass took a malicious pleasure in emphasizing this point and in watching me wince. Nothing that I could do would induce him to tell me who the mysterious "They" were.

"It is so ordered," he would reply, "and I do not yet know any one who has disobeyed the orders."

"Only wait till my servants find that I am missing," I retorted, "and I promise you that this place shall be cleared off the face of the earth, and I'll give you a lesson in civility, too, my friend."

"Your servants would be torn in pieces before they came near this place; and, besides, you are dead, my dear friend. It is not your fault, of course, but none the less you are dead *and* buried."

At irregular intervals supplies of food, I was told, were dropped down from the land side into the amphitheatre, and the inhabitants fought for them like wild beasts. When a men felt his death coming on he retreated to his lair and died there. The body was sometimes dragged out of the hole and thrown on to the sand, or allowed to rot where it lay.

The phrase "thrown on to the sand" caught my attention, and I asked Gunga Dass whether this sort of thing was not likely to breed a pestilence.

"That," said he, with another of his wheezy chuckles, "you may see for yourself subsequently. You will have much time to make observations."

Whereat, to his great delight, I winced once more and hastily continued the conversation:—"And how do you live here from day to day? What do you do?" The question elicited exactly the same answer as before—coupled with the information that "this place is like your European heaven; there is neither marrying nor giving in marriage."

Gunga Dass has been educated at a Mission School, and, as he himself admitted, had he only changed his religion "like a wise man," might have avoided the living grave which was now his portion. But as long as I was with him I fancy he was happy.

Here was a Sahib, a representative of the dominant race, helpless as a child and completely at the mercy of his native neighbors. In a deliberate lazy way he set himself to torture me as a schoolboy would devote a rapturous half-hour to watching the agonies of an impaled beetle, or as a ferret in a blind burrow might glue himself comfortably to the neck of a rabbit. The burden of his conversation was that there was no escape "of no kind whatever," and that I should stay here till I died and was "thrown on to the sand." If it were possible to forejudge the conversation of the Damned on the advent of a new soul in their abode, I should say that they would speak as Gunga Dass did to me throughout that long afternoon. I was powerless to protest or answer; all my energies being devoted to a struggle against the inexplicable terror that threatened to overwhelm me again and again. I can compare the feeling to nothing except the struggles of a man against the overpowering nausea of the Channel passage—only my agony was of the spirit and infinitely more terrible.

As the day wore on, the inhabitants began to appear in full strength to catch the rays of the afternoon sun, which were now sloping in at the mouth of the crater. They assembled in little knots, and talked among themselves without even throwing a glance in my direction. About four o'clock, as far as I could judge, Gunga Dass rose and dived into his lair for a moment, emerging with a live crow in his hands. The wretched bird was in a most draggled and deplorable condition, but seemed to be in no way afraid of its master. Advancing cautiously to the river front, Gunda Dass stepped from tussock to tussock until he had reached a smooth patch of sand directly in the line of the boat's fire. The occupants of the boat took no notice. Here he stopped, and, with a couple of dexterous turns of the wrist, pegged the bird on its back with outstretched wings. As was only natural, the crow began to shriek at once and beat the air with its claws. In a few seconds the clamor had attracted the attention of a bevy of wild crows on a shoal a few hundred yards away, where they were discussing something that looked like a corpse. Half a dozen crows flew over at once to see what was going on, and also, as it proved, to attack the pinioned bird. Gunga Dass, who had lain down on a tussock, motioned to me to be quiet, though I fancy this was a needless precaution. In a moment,

and before I could see how it happened, a wild crow, who had grappled with the shrieking and helpless bird, was entangled in the latter's claws, swiftly disengaged by Gunga Dass, and pegged down beside its companion in adversity. Curiosity, it seemed, overpowered the rest of the flock, and almost before Gunga Dass and I had time to withdraw to the tussock, two more captives were struggling in the upturned claws of the decoys. So the chase—if I can give it so dignified a name—continued until Gunga Dass had captured seven crows. Five of them he throttled at once, reserving two for further operations another day. I was a good deal impressed by this to me, novel method of securing food, and complimented Gunga Dass on his skill.

"It is nothing to do," said he. "Tomorrow you must do it for me. You are stronger than I am."

This calm assumption of superiority upset me not a little, and I answered peremptorily;—"Indeed, you old ruffian! What do you think I have given you money for?"

"Very well," was the unmoved reply. "Perhaps not to-morrow, nor the day after, nor subsequently; but in the end, and for many years, you will catch crows and eat crows, and you will thank your European God that you have crows to catch and eat."

I could have cheerfully strangled him for this; but judged it best under the circumstances to smother my resentment. An hour later I was eating one of the crows; and, as Gunga Dass had said, thanking my God that I had a crow to eat. Never as long as I live shall I forget that evening meal. The whole population were squatting on the hard sand platform opposite their dens, huddled over tiny fires of refuse and dried rushes. Death, having once laid his hand upon these men and forborne to strike, seemed to stand aloof from them now; for most of our company were old men, bent and worn and twisted with years, and women aged to all appearance as the Fates themselves. They sat together in knots and talked—God only knows what they found to discuss—in low equable tones, curiously in contrast to the strident babble with which natives are accustomed to make day hideous. Now and then an access of that sudden fury which had possessed me in the morning would lay hold on a man or woman; and with yells and imprecations the sufferer would attack the steep slope until, baffled and bleeding, he fell back on the platform incapable of moving a limb. The others would never even raise their eyes when this happened, as men too well aware of the futility of their fellows' attempts and wearied with their useless repetition. I saw four such outbursts in the course of that evening.

Gunga Dass took an eminently business-like view of my situation, and while we were dining—I can afford to laugh at the recollection now, but it was painful enough at the time—propounded the terms on which he would consent to "do" for me. My nine rupees eight annas, he argued, at the rate of three annas a day, would provide me with food for fifty-one days, or about seven weeks; that is to say, he would be willing to cater for me for that length of time. At the end of it I was to look after myself. For a

further consideration—*videlicet* my boots—he would be willing to allow me to occupy the den next to his own, and would supply me with as much dried grass for bedding as he could spare.

"Very well, Gunga Dass," I replied; "to the first terms I cheerfully agree, but, as there is nothing on earth to prevent my killing you as you sit here and taking everything that you have" (I thought of the two invaluable crows at the time), "I flatly refuse to give you my boots and shall take whichever den I please."

The stroke was a bold one, and I was glad when I saw that it had succeeded. Gunga Dass changed his tone immediately, and disavowed all intention of asking for my boots. At the time it did not strike me as at all strange that I, a Civil Engineer, a man of thirteen years' standing in the Service, and I trust, an average Englishman, should thus calmly threaten murder and violence against the man who had, for a consideration it is true, taken me under his wing. I had left the world, it seemed, for centuries. I was as certain then as I am now of my own existence, that in the accursed settlement there was no law save that of the strongest; that the living dead men had thrown behind them every canon of the world which had cast them out; and that I had to depend for my own life on my strength and vigilance alone. The crew of the ill-fated Mignonette are the only men who would understand my frame of mind. "At present," I argued to myself, "I am strong and a match for six of these wretches. It is imperatively necessary that I should, for my own sake, keep both health and strength

until the hour of my release comes—
if it ever does."

Fortified with these resolutions, I ate
and drank as much as I could, and made
Gunga Dass understand that I intended
to be his master, and that the least sign
of insubordination on his part would
be visited with the only punishment I
had it in my power to inflict—sudden
and violent death. Shortly after this
I went to bed. That is to say, Gunga
Dass gave me a double armful of dried
bents which I thrust down the mouth of
the lair to the right of his, and followed myself, feet foremost; the hole
running about nine feet into the sand
with a slight downward inclination, and
being neatly shored with timbers. From
my den, which faced the river-front, I
was able to watch the waters of the
Sutlej flowing past under the light of a
young moon and compose myself to
sleep as best I might.

The horrors of that night I shall
never forget. My den was nearly as
narrow as a coffin, and the sides had
been worn smooth and greasy by the
contact of innumerable naked bodies,
added to which it smelled abominably.
Sleep was altogether out of question
to one in my excited frame of mind.
As the night wore on, it seemed that
the entire amphitheatre was filled with
legions of unclean devils that, trooping
up from the shoals below, mocked the
unfortunates in their lairs.

Personally I am not of an imaginative
temperament,—very few Engineers are,
—but on that occasion I was as completely prostrated with nervous terror as
any woman. After half an hour or so,
however, I was able once more to calmly
review my chances of escape. Any

exit by the steep sand walls was, of
course, impracticable. I had been thoroughly convinced of this some time
before. It was possible, just possible,
that I might, in the uncertain moonlight, safely run the gauntlet of the
rifle shots. The place was so full of
terror for me that I was prepared to
undergo any risk in leaving it. Imagine
my delight, then, when after creeping
stealthily to the river-front I found
that the infernal boat was not there.
My freedom lay before me in the next
few steps!

By walking out to the first shallow
pool that lay at the foot of the pro-
jecting left horn of the horseshoe, I
could wade across, turn the flank of
the crater, and make my way inland.
Without a moment's hesitation I
marched briskly past the tussocks where
Gunga Dass had snared the crows, and
out in the direction of the smooth white
sand beyond. My first step from the
tufts of dried grass showed me how utterly futile was any hope of escape;
for, as I put my foot down, I felt an
indescribable drawing, sucking motion
of the sand below. Another moment
and my leg was swallowed up nearly
to the knee. In the moonlight the whole
surface of the sand seemed to be shaken
with devilish delight at my disappointment. I struggled clear, sweating with
terror and exertion, back to the tussocks
behind me and fell on my face.

My only means of escape from the
semicircle was protected with a quicksand!

How long I lay I have not the faintest
idea; but I was roused at last by the
malevolent chuckle of Gunga Dass at
my ear. "I would advise you, Pro-

tector of the Poor" (the ruffian was speaking English) "to return to your house. It is unhealthy to lie down here. Moreover, when the boat returns, you will most certainly be rifled at." He stood over me in the dim light of the dawn, chuckling and laughing to himself. Suppressing my first impulse to catch the man by the neck and throw him on to the quicksand, I rose sullenly and followed him to the platform below the burrows.

Suddenly, and futiley as I thought while I spoke, I asked:—"Gunga Dass, what is the good of the boat if I can't get out *anyhow?*" I recollect that even in my deepest trouble I had been speculating vaguely on the waste of ammunition in guarding an already well protected foreshore.

Gunga Dass laughed again and made answer:—"They have the boat only in daytime. It is for the reason that *there is a way.* I hope we shall have the pleasure of your company for much longer time. It is a pleasant spot when you have been here some years and eaten roast crow long enough."

I staggered, numbed and helpless, toward the fetid burrow alloted to me, and fell asleep. An hour or so later I was awakened by a piercing scream— the shrill, high-pitched scream of a horse in pain. Those who have once heard that will never forget the sound. I found some little difficulty in scrambling out of the burrow. When I was in the open, I saw Pornic, my poor old Pornic, lying dead on the sandy soil. How they had killed him I cannot guess. Gunga Dass explained that horse was better than crow, and "greatest good of greatest number is

political maxim. We are now Republic, Mister Jukes, and you are entitled to a fair share of the beast. If you like, we will pass a vote of thanks. Shall I propose?"

Yes, we were a Republic indeed! A Republic of wild beasts penned at the bottom of a pit, to eat and fight and sleep till we died. I attempted no protest of any kind, but sat down and stared at the hideous sight in front of me. In less time almost than it takes me to write this, Pornic's body was divided, in some unclean way or other; the men and women had dragged the fragments on to the platform and were preparing their morning meal. Gunga Dass cooked mine. The almost irresistible impulse to fly at the sand walls until I was wearied laid hold of me afresh, and I had to struggle against it with all my might. Gunga Dass was offensively jocular till I told him that if he addressed another remark of any kind whatever to me I should strangle him where he sat. This silenced him till silence became insupportable, and I bade him say something.

"You will live here till you die like the other Feringhi," he said, coolly, watching me over the fragment of gristle that he was gnawing.

"What other Sahib, you swine? Speak at once, and don't stop to tell me a lie."

"He is over there," answered Gunga Dass, pointing to a burrow-mouth about four doors to the left of my own. "You can see for yourself. He died in the burrow as you will die, and I will die, and as all these men and women and the one child will also die."

"For pity's sake tell me all you

know about him. Who was he? When did he come, and when did he die?"

This appeal was a weak step on my part. Gunga Dass only leered and replied:—"I will not—unless you give me something first."

Then I recollected where I was, and struck the man between the eyes, partially stunning him. He stepped down from the platform at once, and, cringing and fawning and weeping and attempting to embrace my feet, led me round to the burrow which he had indicated.

"I know nothing whatever about the gentleman. Your God be my witness that I do not. He was as anxious to escape as you were, and he was shot from the boat, though we all did all things to prevent him from attempting. He was shot here." Gunga Dass laid his hand on his lean stomach and bowed to the earth.

"Well, and what then? Go on!"

"And then—and then, Your Honor, we carried him in to his house and gave him water, and put wet cloths on the wound, and he laid down in his house and gave up the ghost."

"In how long? In how long?"

"About half an hour, after he received his wound. I call Vishn to witness," yelled the wretched man, "that I did everything for him. Everything which was possible, that I did!"

He threw himself down on the ground and clasped my ankles. But I had my doubts about Gunga Dass's benevolence, and kicked him off as he lay protesting.

"I believe you robbed him of everything he had. But I can find out in a minute or two. How long was the Sahib here?"

"Nearly a year and a half. I think he must have gone mad. But hear me swear, Protector of the Poor! Won't Your Honor hear me swear that I never touched an article that belonged to him? What is Your Worship going to do?"

I had taken Gunga Dass by the waist and had hauled him on to the platform opposite the deserted burrow. As I did so I thought of my wretched fellow-prisoner's unspeakable misery among all these horrors for eighteen months, and the final agony of dying like a rat in a hole, with a bullet-wound in the stomach. Gunga Dass fancied I was going to kill him and howled pitifully. The rest of the population, in the plethora that follows a full flesh meal, watched us without stirring.

"Go inside, Gunga Dass," said I, "and fetch it out."

I was feeling sick and faint with horror now. Gunga Dass nearly rolled off the platform and howled aloud.

"But I am Brahmin, Sahib—a high-caste Brahmin. By your soul, by your father's soul, do not make me do this thing!"

"Brahmin or no Brahmin, by my soul and my father's soul, in you go!" I said, and, seizing him by the shoulders, I crammed his head into the mouth of the burrow, kicked the rest of him in, and, sitting down, covered my face with my hands.

At the end of a few minutes I heard a rustle and a creak; then Gunga Dass in a sobbing, choking whisper speaking to himself; then a soft thud—and I uncovered my eyes.

The dry sand had turned the corpse entrusted to its keeping into a yellow-brown mummy. I told Gunga Dass to stand off while I examined it. The body—clad in an olive-green hunting-suit much stained and worn, with leather pads on the shoulders—was that of a man between thirty and forty, above middle height, with light, sandy hair, long mustache, and a rough unkempt beard. The left canine of the upper jaw was missing, and a portion of the lobe of the right ear was gone. On the second finger of the left hand was a ring—a shield-shaped bloodstone set in gold, with a monogram that might have been either "B.K." or "B.L." On the third finger of the right hand was a silver ring in the shape of a coiled cobra, much worn and tarnished. Gunga Dass deposited a handful of trifles he had picked out of the burrow at my feet, and, covering the face of the body with my handkerchief, I turned to examine these. I give the full list in the hope that it may lead to the identification of the unfortunate man:

1. Bowl of a briarwood pipe, serrated at the edge; much worn and blackened; bound with string at the screw.

2. Two patent-lever keys; wards of both broken.

3. Tortoise - shell - handled penknife, silver or nickel, name-plate, marked with monogram "B.K."

4. Envelope, postmark undecipherable, bearing a Victorian stamp, addressed to "Miss Mon—" (rest illegible) —"ham"—"nt."

5. Imitation crokodile-skin notebook with pencil. First forty-five pages blank; four and a-half illegible; fifteen others filled with private memoranda relating chiefly to three persons—a Mrs.

L. Singleton, abbreviated several times to "Lot Single," "Mrs. S. May," and "Garmison," referred to in places as "Jerry" or "Jack."

6. Handle of small-sized hunting-knife. Blade snapped short. Buck's horn, diamond cut, with swivel and ring on the butt; fragment of cotton cord attached.

It must not be supposed that I inventoried all these things on the spot as fully as I have here written them down. The notebook first attracted my attention, and I put it in my pocket with a view to studying it later on. The rest of the articles I conveyed to my burrow for safety's sake, and there, being a methodical man, I inventoried them. I then returned to the corpse and ordered Gunga Dass to help me to carry it out to the river-front. While we were engaged in this, the exploded shell of an old brown cartridge dropped out of one of the pockets and rolled at my feet. Gunga Dass had not seen it; and I fell to thinking that a man does not carry exploded cartridge-cases, especially "browns," which will not bear loading twice, about with him when shooting. In other words, that cartridge-case has been fired inside the crater. Consequently there must be a gun somewhere. I was on the verge of asking Gunga Dass, but checked myself, knowing that he would lie. We laid the body down on the edge of the quicksand by the tussocks. It was my intention to push it out and let it be swallowed up—the only possible mode of burial that I could think of. I ordered Gunga Dass to go away.

Then I gingerly put the corpse out on the quicksand. In doing so, it was lying face downward, I tore the frail and rotten khaki shooting-coat open, disclosing a hideous cavity in the back. I have already told you that the dry sand had, as it were, mummified the body. A moment's glance showed that the gaping hole had been caused by a gun-shot wound; the gun must have been fired with the muzzle almost touching the back. The shooting-coat, being intact, had been drawn over the body after death, which must have been instantaneous. The secret of the poor wretch's death was plain to me in a flash. Some one of the crater, presumably Gunga Dass, must have shot him with his own gun—the gun that fitted the brown cartridges. He had never attempted to escape in the face of the rifle-fire from the boat.

I pushed the corpse out hastily, and saw it sink from sight literally in a few seconds. I shuddered as I watched. In a dazed, half-conscious way I turned to peruse the notebook. A stained and discolored slip of paper had been inserted between the binding and the back, and dropped out as I opened the pages. This is what it contained:—
"*Four out from crow-clump: three left; nine out; two right; three back; two left; fourteen out; two left; seven out; one left; nine back; two right; six back; four right; seven back.*" The paper had been burned and charred at the edges. What it meant I could not understand. I sat down on the dried bents turning it over and over between my fingers, until I was aware of Gunga Dass standing immediately behind me with glowing eyes and outstretched hands.

"Have you got it?" he panted. "Will you not let me look at it also? I swear that I will return it."

"Got what? Return what?" I asked.

"That which you have in your hands. It will help us both." He stretched out his long, bird-like talons, trembling with eagerness.

"I could never find it," he continued. "He had secreted it about his person. Therefore I shot him, but nevertheless I was unable to obtain it."

Gunga Dass had quite forgotten his little fiction about the rifle-bullet. I received the information perfectly calmly. Morality is blunted by consorting with the Dead who are alive.

"What on earth are you raving about? What is it you want me to give you?"

"The piece of paper in the notebook. It will help us both. Oh, you fool! You fool! Can you not see what it will do for us? We shall escape!"

His voice rose almost to a scream, and he danced with excitement before me. I own I was moved at the chance of getting away.

"Don't skip!. Explain yourself. Do you mean to say that this slip of paper will help us? What does it mean?"

"Read it aloud! Read it aloud! I beg and I pray you to read it aloud."

I did so. Gunga Dass listened delightedly, and drew an irregular line in the sand with his fingers.

"See now! It was the length of his gun-barrels without the stock. I have those barrels. Four gun-barrels out from the place where I caught crows. Straight out; do you follow me? Then three left— Ah! how well I remember when that man worked it out night after night. Then nine out, and so on. Out is always straight before you across the quicksand. He told me so before I killed him."

"But if you knew all this why didn't you get out before?"

"I did *not* know it. He told me that he was working it out a year and a half ago, and how he was working it out night after night when the boat had gone away, and he could get out near the quicksand safely. Then he said that we would get away together. But I was afraid that he would leave me behind one night when he had worked it all out, and so I shot him. Besides, it is not advisable that the men who once get in here should escape. Only I, and *I* am a Brahmin."

The prospect of escape had brought Gunga Dass's caste back to him. He stood up, walked about and gesticulated violently. Eventually I managed to make him talk soberly, and he told me how this Englishman had spent six months night after night in exploring, inch by inch, the passage across the quicksand; how he had declared it to be simplicity itself up to within about twenty yards of the river bank after turning the flank of the left horn of the horseshoe. This much he had evidently not completed when Gunga Dass shot him with his own gun.

In my frenzy of delight at the possibilities of escape I recollect shaking hands effusively with Gunga Dass, after we had decided that we were to make an attempt to get away that very night. It was weary work waiting throughout the afternoon.

About ten o'clock, as far as I could judge, when the Moon had just risen above the lip of the crater, Gunga Dass made a move for his burrow to bring out the gun-barrels whereby to measure our path. All the other wretched inhabitants had retired to their lairs long ago. The guardian boat drifted downstream some hours before, and we were utterly alone by the crow-clump. Gunga Dass, while carrying the gun-barrels, let slip the piece of paper which was to be our guide. I stooped down hastily to recover it, and, as I did so, I was aware that the diabolical Brahmin was aiming a violent blow at the back of my head with the gun-barrels. It was too late to turn round. I must have received the blow somewhere on the nape of my neck. A hundred thousand fiery stars danced before my eyes, and I fell forwards senseless at the edge of the quicksand.

When I recovered consciousness, the Moon was going down, and I was sensible of intolerable pain in the back of my head. Gunga Dass had disappeared and my mouth was full of blood. I lay down again and prayed that I might die without more ado. Then the unreasoning fury which I have before mentioned laid hold upon me, and I staggered inland toward the walls of the crater. It seemed that some one was calling to me in a whisper—"Sahib! Sahib! Sahib!" exactly as my bearer used to call me in the morning. I fancied that I was delirious until a handful of sand fell at my feet. Then I looked up and saw a head peering down into the amphitheatre—the head of Dunnoo, my dog-boy, who attended to my collies. As soon as he had attracted my attention, he held up his hand and showed a rope. I motioned, staggering to and fro the while, that he should throw it down. It was a couple of leather punkah-ropes knotted together, with a loop at one end. I slipped the loop over my head and under my arms; heard Dunnoo urge something forward; was conscious that I was being dragged, face downward, up the steep sand slope, and the next instant found myself choked and half fainting on the sand hills overlooking the crater. Dunnoo, with his face ashy grey in the moonlight, implored me not to stay but to get back to my tent at once.

It seems that he had tracked Pornic's footprints fourteen miles across the sands to the crater; had returned and told my servants, who flatly refused to meddle with any one, white or black, once fallen into the hideous Village of the Dead; whereupon Dunnoo had taken one of my ponies and a couple of pukah-ropes, returned to the crater, and hauled me out as I have described.

To cut a long story short, Dunnoo is now my personal servant on a gold mohur a month—a sum which I still think far too little for the services he has rendered. Nothing on earth will induce me to go near that devilish spot again, or to reveal its whereabouts more clearly than I have done. Of Gunga Dass I have never found a trace, nor do I wish to do. My sole motive in giving this to be published is the hope that some one may possibly identify, from the details and the inventory which I have given above, the corpse of the man in the olive-green hunting-suit.

The Man Who Would Be King

"Brother to a Prince and fellow to a beggar if he be found worthy."

THE Law, as quoted, lays down a fair conduct of life, and one not easy to follow. I have been fellow to a beggar again and again under circumstances which prevented either of us finding out whether the other was worthy. I have still to be brother to a Prince, though I once came near to kinship with what might have been a veritable King and was promised the reversion of a Kingdom—army, law-courts, revenue and policy all complete. But, to-day, I greatly fear that my King is dead, and if I want a crown I must go and hunt it for myself.

The beginning of everything was in a railway train upon the road to Mhow from Ajmir. There had been a Deficit in the Budget, which necessitated traveling, not Second-class, which is only half as dear as First-class, but by Intermediate, which is very awful indeed. There are no cushions in the Intermediate class, and the population are either Intermediate, which is Eurasian, or native, which for a long night journey is nasty, or Loafer, which is amusing though intoxicated. Intermediates do not patronize refreshment-rooms. They carry their food in bundles and pots, and buy sweets from the native sweet-meat-sellers, and drink the roadside water. That is why in the hot weather Intermediates are taken out of the carriages dead, and in all weathers are most properly looked down upon.

My particular Intermediate happened to be empty till I reached Nasirabad, when a huge gentleman in shirt-sleeves entered, and, following the custom of Intermediates, passed the time of day. He was a wanderer and a vagabond like myself, but with an educated taste for whiskey. He told tales of things he had seen and done, of out-of-the-way corners of the Empire into which he had penetrated, and of adventures in which he risked his life for a few days' food. "If India was filled with men like you and me, not knowing more than the crows where they'd get their next day's rations, it isn't seventy millions of revenue the land would be paying—it's seven hundred millions," said he; and as I looked at his mouth and chin I was disposed to agree with him. We talked politics—the politics of Loaferdom that sees things from the underside where the lath and plaster is not smoothed off—and we talked postal arrangements because my friend wanted to send a telegram back from the next station to Ajmir, which is the turning-off place from the Bombay to the Mhow line as you travel westward. My friend had no money beyond eight annas which he wanted for dinner, and I had no money at all, owing to the hitch in the Budget before mentioned. Further, I was going into a wilderness where, though I should resume touch with the Treasury, there were no telegraph offices. I was, therefore, unable to help him in any way.

"We might threaten a Station-master, and make him send a wire on tick," said my friend, "but that'd mean inquiries for you and for me, and I've got my hands full these days. Did you say you are traveling back along this line within any days?"

"Within ten," I said.

"Can't you make it eight?" said he. "Mine is rather urgent business."

"I can send your telegram within ten days if that will serve you," I said.

"I couldn't trust the wire to fetch him now I think of it. It's this way. He leaves Delhi on the 23d for Bombay. That means he'll be running through Ajmir about the night of the 23d."

"But I am going into the Indian Desert," I explained.

"Well *and* good," said he. "You'll be changing at Marwar Junction to get into Jodhpore territory—you must do that—and he'll be coming through Marwar Junction in the early morning of the 24th by the Bombay Mail. Can you be at Marwar Junction on that time? 'Twon't be inconveniencing you because I know that there's precious few pickings to be got out of these Central India States—even though you pretend to be correspondent of the *Backwoodsman*."

"Have you ever tried that trick?" I asked.

"Again and again, but the Residents find you out, and then you get escorted to the Border before you've time to get your knife into them. But about my friend here. I *must* give him a word o'mouth to tell him what's come to me or else he won't know where to go. I would take it more than kind of you if you was to come out of Central India in time to catch him at Marwar Junction, and say to him:—'He has

gone South for the week.' He'll know
what that means. He's a big man with
a red beard, and a great swell he is.
You'll find him sleeping like a gentleman with all his luggage round him in
a Second-class compartment. But don't
you be afraid. Slip down the window,
and say:—'He has gone South for the
week," and he'll tumble. It's only cutting your time of stay in those parts by
two days. I ask you as a stranger—
going to the West," he said, with emphasis.

"Where have *you* come from?" said
J.

"From the East," said he, "and I am
hoping that you will give him the
message on the Square—for the sake of
my Mother as well as your own."

Englishmen are not usually softened
by appeals to the memory of their
mothers, but for certain reasons, which
will be fully apparent, I saw fit to agree.

"It's more than a little matter," said
he, "and that's why I ask you to do
it—and now I know that I can depend
on you doing it. A Second-class
carriage at Marwar Junction, and a red-
haired man asleep in it. You'll be sure
to remember. I get out at the next
station, and I must hold on there till
he comes or sends me what I want."

"I'll give the message if I catch him,"
I said, "and for the sake of your Mother
as well as mine I'll give you a word of
advice. Don't try to run the Central
India States just now as the correspondent of the *Backwoodsman*. There's
a real one knocking about here, and it
might lead to trouble."

"Thank you," said he, simply, "and
when will the swine be gone? I can't
starve because he's ruining my work.

I wanted to get hold of the Degumber
Rajah down here about his father's
widow, and give him a jump."

"What did he do to his father's
widow, then?"

"Filled her up with red pepper and
slippered her to death as she hung from
a beam. I found that out myself and
I'm the only man that would dare going
into the State to get hush-money for
it. They'll try to poison me, same as
they did in Chortumna when I went on
the loot there. But you'll give the man
at Marwar Junction my message?"

He got out at a little roadside station,
and I reflected. I had heard, more than
once, of men personating correspondents
of newspapers and bleeding small Native
States with threats of exposure, but I
had never met any of the caste before.
They lead a hard life, and generally die
with great suddenness. The Native
States have a wholesome horror of
English newspapers, which may throw
light on their peculiar methods of government, and do their best to choke
correspondence with champagne, or
drive them out of their mind with four-
in-hand barouches. They do not understand that nobody cares a straw for the
internal administration of Native States
so long as oppression and crime are kept
within decent limits, and the ruler is
not drugged, drunk, or diseased from
one end of the year to the other. Native
States were created by Providence in
order to supply picturesque scenery,
tigers, and tall-writing. They are the
dark places of the earth, full of unimaginable cruelty, touching the Railway and the Telegraph on one side, and,
on the other, the days of Harun-al-
Raschid. When I left the train I did

business with divers Kings, and in eight days passed through many changes of life. Sometimes I wore dress-clothes and consorted with Princes and Politicals, drinking from crystal and eating from silver. Sometimes I lay out upon the ground and devoured what I could get, from a plate made of a flapjack, and drank the running water, and slept under the same rug as my servant. It was all in the day's work.

Then I headed for the Great Indian Desert upon the proper date, as I had promised, and the night Mail set me down at Marwar Junction, where a funny little, happy-go-lucky, native-managed railway runs to Jodhpore. The Bombay Mail from Delhi makes a short halt at Marwar. She arrived as I got in, and I had just time to hurry to her platform and go down the carriages. There was only one Second-class on the train. I slipped the window and looked down upon a flaming red beard, half covered by a railway rug. That was my man, fast asleep, and I dug him gently in the ribs. He woke with a grunt and I saw his face in the light of the lamps. It was a great and shining face.

"Tickets again?" said he.

"No," said I. "I am to tell you that he is gone South for the week. He is gone South for the week!"

The train had begun to move out. The red man rubbed his eyes. "He has gone South for the week," he repeated. "Now that's just like his impidence. Did he say that I was to give you anything?—'Cause I won't."

"He didn't," I said, and dropped away, and watched the red lights die out in the dark. It was horribly cold because the wind was blowing off the sands. I climbed into my own train— not an Intermediate Carriage this time —and went to sleep.

If the man with the beard had given me a rupee I should have kept it as a memento of a rather curious affair. But the consciousness of having done my duty was my only reward.

Later on I reflected that two gentlemen like my friends could not do any good if they foregathered and personated correspondents of newspapers, and might, if they "stuck up" one of the little rat-trap states of Central India or Southern Rajputana, get themselves into serious difficulties. I therefore took some trouble to describe them as accurately as I could remember to people who would be interested in deporting them: and succeeded, so I was later informed, in having them headed back from the Degumber border.

Then I became respectable, and returned to an Office where there were no Kings and no incidents except the daily manufacture of a newspaper. A newspaper office seems to attract every conceivable sort of person, to the prejudice of discipline. Zenana-mission ladies arrive, and beg that the Editor will instantly abandon all his duties to describe a Christian prize-giving in a back-slum of a perfectly inaccessible village; Colonels who have been over-passed for commands sit down and sketch the outline of a series of ten, twelve, or twenty-four leading articles on Seniority *versus* Selection; missionaries wish to know why they have not been permitted to escape from their regular vehicles of abuse and swear at a brother-missionary under special patronage of the editorial We; stranded theatrical companies troop up to explain that they cannot pay for their advertisements, but on their return from New Zealand or Tahiti will do so with interest; inventors of patent punkah-pulling machines, carriage couplings and unbreakable swords and axletrees call with specifications in their pockets and hours at their disposal; tea-companies enter and elaborate their prospectuses with the office pens; secretaries of ball-committees clamor to have the glories of their last dance more fully expounded; strange ladies rustle in and say:—"I want a hundred lady's cards printed *at once,* please," which is manifestly part of an Editor's duty; and every dissolute ruffian that ever tramped the Grand Trunk Road makes it his business to ask for employment as a proof-reader. And, all the time, the telephone-bell is ringing madly, and Kings are being killed on the Continent, and Empires are saying—"You're another," and Mister Gladstone is calling down brimstone upon the British Dominions, and the little black copy-boys are whining, *"kaa-pi chay-ha-yeh"* (copy wanted) like tired bees, and most of the paper is as blank as Modred's shield.

But that is the amusing part of the year. There are other six months wherein none ever come to call, and the thermometer walks inch by inch up to the top of the glass, and the office is darkened to just above reading-light, and the press machines are red-hot of touch, and nobody writes anything but accounts of amusements in the Hill-stations or obituary notices. Then the telephone becomes a tinkling terror, be-

cause it tells you of the sudden deaths of men and women that you knew intimately, and the prickly-heat covers you as with a garment, and you sit down and write:—"A slight increase of sickness is reported from the Khuda Janta Khan District. The outbreak is purely sporadic in its nature, and, thanks to the energetic efforts of the District authorities, is now almost at an end. It is, however, with deep regret we record the death, etc."

Then the sickness really breaks out, and the less recording and reporting the better for the peace of the subscribers. But the Empires and the Kings continue to divert themselves as selfishly as before, and the Foreman thinks that a daily paper really ought to come out once in twenty-four hours, and all the people at the Hill-stations in the middle of their amusements say: —"Good gracious! Why can't the paper be sparkling? I'm sure there's plenty going on up here."

That is the dark half of the moon, and, as the advertisements say, "must be experienced to be appreciated."

It was in that season, and a remarkably evil season, that the paper began running the last issue of the week on Saturday night, which is to say Sunday morning, after the custom of a London paper. This was a great convenience, for immediately after the paper was put to bed, the dawn would lower the thermometer from 96° to almost 84° for half an hour, and in that chill— you have no idea how cold is 84° on the grass until you begin to pray for it— a very tired man could set off to sleep ere the heat roused him.

One Saturday night it was my

pleasant duty to put the paper to bed alone. A King or courtier or a courtesan or a community was going to die or get a new Constitution, or do something that was important on the other side of the world, and the paper was to be held open till the latest possible minute in order to catch the telegram. It was a pitchy black night, as stifling as a June night can be, and the *loo,* the red-hot wind from the westward, was booming among the tinder-dry trees and pretending that the rain was on its heels. Now and again a spot of almost boiling water would fall on the dust with the flop of a frog, but all our weary world knew that was only pretence. It was a shade cooler in the press-room than the office, so I sat there, while the type ticked and clicked, and the night-jars hooted at the windows, and the all but naked compositors wiped the sweat from their foreheads and called for water. The thing that was keeping us back, whatever it was, would not come off, though the *loo* dropped and the last type was set, and the whole round earth stood still in the choking heat, with its finger on its lip, to wait the event. I drowsed, and wondered whether the telegraph was a blessing, and whether this dying man, or struggling people, was aware of the inconvenience the delay was causing. There was no special reason beyond the heat and worry to make tension, but, as the clock hands crept up to three o'clock and the machines spun their fly-wheels two and three times to see that all was in order, before I said the word that would set them off, I could have shrieked aloud.

Then the roar and rattle of the wheels shivered the quiet into little bits. I rose to go away, but two men in white clothes stood in front of me. The first one said:—"It's him!" The second said:—"So it is!" And they both laughed almost as loudly as the machinery roared, and mopped their foreheads. "We see there was a light burning across the road and we were sleeping in that ditch there for coolness, and I said to my friend here, The office is open. Let's come along and speak to him as turned us back from the Degumber State," said the smaller of the two. He was the man I had met in the Mhow train, and his fellow was the red-bearded man of Marwar Junction. There was no mistaking the eyebrows of the one or the beard of the other.

I was not pleased, because I wished to go to sleep, not to squabble with loafers. "What do you want?" I asked.

"Half an hour's talk with you cool and comfortable, in the office," said the red-bearded man. "We'd *like* some drink—the Contrack doesn't begin yet, Peachey, so you needn't look—but what we really want is advice. We don't want money. We ask you as a favor, because you did us a bad turn about Degumber."

I led from the press-room to the stifling office with the maps on the walls, and the red-haired man rubbed his hands. "That's something like," said he. "This was the proper shop to come to. Now, Sir, let me introduce to you Brother Peachey Carnehan, that's him, and Brother Daniel Dravot, that is *me,* and the less said about our professions the better, for we have been most things in our time. Soldier, sailor, compositor, photographer, proof-reader, street-preacher, and correspondents of the *Backwoodsman* when we thought the paper wanted one. Carnehan is sober, and so am I. Look at us first and see that's sure. It will save you cutting into my talk. We'll take one of your cigars apiece, and you shall see us light."

I watched the test. The men were absolutely sober, so I gave them each a tepid peg.

"Well *and* good," said Carnehan of the eyebrows, wiping the froth from his moustache. "Let me talk now, Dan. We have been all over India, mostly on foot. We have been boiler-fitters, engine-drivers, petty contractors, and all that, and we have decided that India isn't big enough for such as us."

They certainly were too big for the office. Dravot's beard seemed to fill half the room and Carnehan's shoulders the other half, as they sat on the big table. Carnehan continued:—"The country isn't half worked out because they that governs it won't let you touch it. They spend all their blessed time in governing it, and you can't lift a spade, nor chip a rock, nor look for oil, nor anything like that without all the Government saying—'Leave it alone and let us govern.' Therefore, such as it is, we will let it alone, and go away to some other place where a man isn't crowded and can come to his own. We are not little men, and there is nothing that we are afraid of except Drink, and we have signed a Contrack on that. *Therefore,* we are going away to be Kings."

"Kings in our own right," muttered Dravot.

"Yes, of course," I said. "You've been tramping in the sun, and it's a very warm night, and hadn't you better sleep over the notion? Come to-morrow."

"Neither drunk nor sunstruck," said Dravot. "We have slept over the notion half a year, and require to see Books and Atlases, and we have decided that there is only one place now in the world that two strong men can Sar-a-*whack.* They call it Kafiristan. By my reckoning it's the top right-hand corner of Afghanistan, not more than three hundred miles from Peshawur. They have two and thirty heathen idols there, and we'll be the thirty-third. It's a mountaineous country, and the women of those parts are very beautiful."

"But that is provided against in the Contrack," said Carnehan. "Neither Women nor Liqu-or, Daniel."

"And that's all we know, except that no one has gone there, and they fight, and in any place where they fight a man who knows how to drill men can always be a King. We shall go to those parts and say to any King we find—'D' you want to vanquish your foes?' and we will show him how to drill men; for that we know better than anything else. Then we will subvert that King and seize his Throne and establish a Dynasty."

"You'll be cut to pieces before you're fifty miles across the Border," I said. "You have to travel through Afghanistan to get to that country. It's one mass of mountains and peaks and glaciers, and no Englishman has been through it. The people are utter brutes, and even if you reached them you couldn't do anything."

"That's more like," said Carnehan. "If you could think us a little more mad we would be more pleased. We have come to you to know about this country, to read a book about it, and to be shown maps. We want you to tell us that we are fools and to show us your books." He turned to the bookcases.

"Are you at all in earnest?" I said.

"A little," said Dravot, sweetly. "As big a map as you have got, even if it's all blank where Kafiristan is, and any books you've got. We can read, though we aren't very educated."

I uncased the big thirty-two-miles-to-the-inch-map of India, and two smaller Frontier maps, hauled down volume INFKAN of the *Encyclopædia Britannica*, and the men consulted them.

"See here!" said Dravot, his thumb on the map. "Up to Jagdallak, Peachey and me know the road. We was there with Roberts's Army. We'll have to turn off to the right at Jagdallak through Laghmann territory. Then we get among the hills—fourteen thousand feet—fifteen thousand—it will be cold work there, but it don't look very far on the map."

I handed him Wood on the *Sources of the Oxus*. Carnehan was deep in the *Encyclopædia*.

"They're a mixed lot," said Dravot, reflectively; "and it won't help us to know the names of their tribes. The more tribes the more they'll fight, and the better for us. From Jagdallak to Ashang. H'mm!"

"But all the information about the country is as sketchy and inaccurate as can be," I protested. "No one knows anything about it really. Here's the file of the *United Services' Institute*. Read what Bellew says."

"Blow Bellew!" said Carnehan. "Dan they're an all-fired lot of heathens, but this book here says they think they're related to us English."

I smoked while the men pored over *Raverty, Wood*, the maps and the *Encyclopædia*.

"There is no use your waiting," said Dravot, politely. "It's about four o'clock now. We'll go before six o'clock if you want to sleep, and we won't steal any of the papers. Don't you sit up. We're two harmless lunatics, and if you come, to-morrow evening, down to the Serai we'll say good-bye to you."

"You *are* two fools," I answered. "You'll be turned back at the Frontier or cut up the minute you set foot in Afghanistan. Do you want any money or a recommendation down-country? I can help you to the chance of work next week."

"Next week we shall be hard at work ourselves, thank you," said Dravot. "It isn't so easy being a King as it looks. When we've got our Kingdom in going order we'll let you know, and you can come up and help us to govern it."

"Would two lunatics make a Contrack like that?" said Carnehan, with subdued pride, showing me a greasy half-sheet of note-paper on which was written the following. I copied it, then and there, as a curiosity:

This Contract between me and you persuing witnesseth in the name of God —Amen and so forth.

(*One*)   *That me and you will settle this matter together: i. e., to be Kings of Kafiristan.*

(*Two*)   *That you and me will not, while this matter is being settled, look at any Liquor, nor any Woman, black, white or brown, so as to get mixed up with one or the other harmful.*

(**Three**)   *That we conduct ourselves with dignity and discretion, and if one of us gets into trouble the other will stay by him.*

Signed by you and me this day.
    Peachey Taliaferro Carnehan.
    Daniel Dravot.
    Both Gentlemen at Large.

"There was no need for the last article," said Carnehan, blushing modestly; "but it looks regular. Now you know the sort of men that loafers are— we *are* loafers, Dan, until we get out of India—and *do* you think that we would sign a Contrack like that unless we was in earnest? We have kept away from the two things that make life worth having."

"You won't enjoy your lives much longer if you are going to try this idiotic adventure. Don't set the office on fire," I said, "and go away before nine o'clock."

I left them still poring over the maps and making notes on the back of the "Contrack." "Be sure to come down to the Serai to-morrow," were their parting words.

The Kumharsen Serai is the great four-square sink of humanity where the strings of camels and horses from the North load and unload. All the nationalities of Central Asia may be found there, and most of the folk of India

proper. Balkh and Bokhara there meet Bengal and Bombay, and try to draw eye-teeth. You can buy ponies, turquoises, Persian pussy-cats, saddle-bags, fat-tailed sheep and musk in the Kumharsen Serai, and get many strange things for nothing. In the afternoon I went down there to see whether my friends intended to keep their word or were lying about drunk.

A priest attired in fragments of ribbons and rags stalked up to me, gravely twisting a child's paper whirligig. Behind him was his servant bending under the load of a crate of mud toys. The two were loading up two camels, and the inhabitants of the Serai watched them with shrieks of laughter.

"The priest is mad," said a horse-dealer to me. "He is going up to Kabul to sell toys to the Amir. He will either be raised to honor or have his head cut off. He came in here this morning and has been behaving madly ever since."

"The witless are under the protection of God," stammered a flat-cheeked Usbeg in broken Hindi. "They foretell future events."

"Would they could have foretold that my caravan would have been cut up by the Shinwaris almost within shadow of the Pass!" grunted the Eusufzai agent of a Rajputana trading-house whose goods had been feloniously diverted into the hands of other robbers just across the Border, and whose misfortunes were the laughing-stock of the bazar. "Ohé, priest, whence come you and whither do you go?"

"From Roum have I come," shouted the priest, waving his whirligig; "from Roum, blown by the breath of a hundred devils across the sea! O thieves, robbers, liars, the blessing of Pir Khan on pigs, dogs, and perjurers! Who will take the Protected of God to the North to sell charms that are never still to the Amir? The camels shall not gall, the sons shall not fall sick, and the wives shall remain faithful while they are away, of the men who give me place in their caravan. Who will assist me to slipper the King of the Roos with a golden slipper with a silver heel? The protection of Pir Khan be upon his labors!" He spread out the skirts of his gaberdine and pirouetted between the lines of tethered horses.

"There starts a caravan from Peshawur to Kabul in twenty days, *Huzrut,*" said the Eusufzai trader. "My camels go therewith. Do thou also go and bring us good-luck."

"I will go even now!" shouted the priest. "I will depart upon my winged camels, and be at Pashawur in a day! Ho! Hazar Mir Khan," he yelled to his servant, "drive out the camels, but let me first mount my own."

He leaped on the back of his beast as it knelt, and, turning round to me, cried:—"Come thou also, Sahib, a little along the road and I will sell thee a charm—an amulet that shall make thee King of Kafiristan."

Then the light broke upon me and I followed the two camels out of the Serai till we reached open road and the priest halted.

"What d' you think o' that?" said he in English. "Carnehan can't talk their patter, so I've made him my servant. He makes a handsome servant. 'Tisn't for nothing that I've been knocking about the country for fourteen years. Didn't I do that talk neat? We'll

hitch on to a caravan at Peshawur till we get to Jagdallak, and then we'll see if we can get donkeys for our camels, and strike into Kafiristan. Whirligigs for the Amir, O Lor! Put your hand under the camel-bags and tell me what you feel."

I felt the butt of a Martini, and another and another.

"Twenty of 'em," said Dravot, placidly. "Twenty of 'em, and ammunition to correspond, under the whirligigs and the mud dolls."

"Heaven help you if you are caught with those things!" I said. "A Martini is worth her weight in silver among the Pathans."

"Fifteen hundred rupees of capital— every rupee we could beg, borrow, or steal—are invested on these two camels," said Dravot. "We won't get caught. We're going through the Khaiber with a regular caravan. Who'd touch a poor mad priest?"

"Have you got everything you want?" I asked, overcome with astonishment.

"Not yet, but we shall soon. Give us a memento of your kindness, *Brother.* You did me a service yesterday, and that time in Marwar. Half my Kingdom shall you have, as the saying is." I slipped a small charm compass from my watch-chain and handed it up to the priest.

"Good-bye," said Dravot, giving me hand cautiously. "It's the last time we'll shake hands with an Englishman these many days. Shake hands with him, Carnehan," he cried, as the second camel passed me.

Carnehan leaned down and shook hands. Then the camels passed away along the dusty road, and I was left alone to wonder. My eye could detect no failure in the disguises. The scene in Serai attested that they were complete to the native mind. There was just the chance, therefore, that Carnehan and Dravot would be able to wander through Afghanistan without detection. But, beyond, they would find death, certain and awful death.

Ten days later a native friend of mine, giving me the news of the day from Peshawur, wound up his letter with:—"There has been much laughter here on account of a certain mad priest who is going in his estimation to sell petty gauds and insignificant trinkets which he ascribes as great charms to H. H. the Amir of Bokhara. He passed through Peshawur and associated himself to the Second Summer caravan that goes to Kabul. The merchants are pleased because through superstition they imagine that such mad fellows bring good-fortune.

The two, then, were beyond the Border. I would have prayed for them, but, that night, a real King died in Europe and demanded an obituary notice.

*   *   *   *   *   *

The wheel of the world swings through the same phases again and again. Summer passed and winter thereafter, and came and passed again. The daily paper continued and I with it, and upon the third summer there fell a hot night, a night-issue, and a strained waiting for something to be telegraphed from the other side of the world, exactly as had happened before. A few great men had died in the past two years, the machines worked with more clatter, and some of the trees in

the Office garden were a few feet taller. But that was all the difference.

I passed over to the press-room, and went through just such a scene as I have already described. The nervous tension was stronger than it had been two years before, and I felt the heat more acutely. At three o'clock I cried, "Print off," and turned to go, when there crept to my chair what was left of a man. He was bent into a circle, his head was sunk between his shoulders, and he moved his feet one over the other like a bear. I could hardly see whether he walked or crawled—this rag-wrapped, whining cripple who addressed me by name, crying that he was come back, "Can you give me a drink?" he whimpered. "For the Lord's sake, give me a drink!"

I went back to the office, the man following with groans of pain, and I turned up the lamp.

"Don't you know me?" he gasped, dropping into a chair, and he turned his drawn face, surmounted by a shock of grey hair, to the light.

I looked at him intently. Once before had I seen eyebrows that met over the nose in an inch-broad black band, but for the life of me I could not tell where.

"I don't know you," I said, handing him the whiskey. "What can I do for you?"

He took a gulp of the spirit raw, and shivered in spite of the suffocating heat.

"I've come back," he repeated; "and I was the King of Kafiristan—me and Dravot—crowned Kings we was! In this office we settled it—you setting there and giving us the books. I am Peachey—Peachey Taliaferro Carnehan, and you've been setting here ever since —O Lord!"

I was more than a little astonished, and expressed my feelings accordingly.

"It's true," said Carnehan, with a dry cackle, nursing his feet, which were wrapped in rags. "True as gospel. Kings we were, with crowns upon our heads—me and Dravot—poor Dan—oh, poor, poor Dan, that would never take advice, not though I begged of him!"

"Take the whiskey," I said, "and take your own time. Tell me all you can recollect of everything from beginning to end. You got across the border on your camels, Dravot dressed as a mad priest and you his servant. Do you remember that?"

"I ain't mad—yet, but I shall be that way soon. Of course I remember. Keep looking at me, or maybe my words will go all to pieces. Keep looking at me in my eyes and don't say anything."

I leaned forward and looked into his face as steadily as I could. He dropped one hand upon the table and I grasped it by the wrist. It was twisted like a bird's claw, and upon the back was a ragged, red, diamond-shaped scar.

"No, don't look there. Look at *me*," said Carnehan.

"That comes afterward, but for the Lord's sake don't distrack me. We left with that caravan, me and Dravot playing all sorts of antics to amuse the people we were with. Dravot used to make us laugh in the evenings when all the people were cooking their dinners—cooking their dinners, and . . . what did they do then? They lit little fires with sparks that went into Dravot's beard, and we all laughed—fit to die. Little red fires they was, going into Dravot's big red beard—so funny." His eyes left mine and he smiled foolishly.

"You went as far as Jagdallak with that caravan," I said, at a venture, "after you had lit those fires. To Jagdallak, where you turned off to try to get into Kafiristan."

"No, we didn't neither. What are you talking about? We turned off before Jagdallak, because we heard the roads was good. But they wasn't good enough for our two camels—mine and Dravot's. When we left the caravan, Dravot took off all his clothes and mine too, and said we would be heathen, because the Kafirs didn't allow Mohammedans to talk to them So we dressed betwixt and between, and such a sight as Daniel Dravot I never saw yet nor expect to see again. He burned half his beard, and slung a sheep-skin over his shoulder, and shaved his head into patterns. He shaved mine, too, and made me wear outrageous things to look like a heathen. That was in a most mountaineous country, and our camels couldn't go along any more because of the mountains. They were tall and black, and coming home I saw them fight like wild goats —there are lots of goats in Kafiristan. And these mountains, they never keep still, no more than the goats. Always fighting they are, and don't let you sleep at night."

"Take some more whiskey," I said, very slowly. "What did you and Daniel Dravot do when the camels could go no further because of the rough roads that led into Kafiristan?"

"What did which do? There was a party called Peachey Taliaferro Carnehan that was with Dravot. Shall I tell you about him? He died out there in the cold. Slap from the bridge fell old Peachey, turning and twisting in the air life a penny whirligig that you can sell to the Amir.—No; they was two for three ha'pence, those whirligigs, or I am much mistaken and woful sore. And then these camels were no use, and Peachey said to Dravot—'For the Lord's sake, let's get out of this before our heads are chopped off,' and with that they killed the camels all among the mountains, not having anything in particular to eat, but first they took off the boxes with the guns and the ammunition, till two men came along driving four mules. Dravot up and dances in front of them, singing,—'Sell me four mules.' Says the first man,—'If you are rich enough to buy, you are rich enough to rob;' but before ever he could put his hand to his knife, Dravot breaks his neck over his knee, and the other party runs away. So Carnehan loaded the mules with the rifles that was taken off the camels, and together we starts forward into those bitter cold mountaineous parts, and never a road broader than the back of your hand."

He paused for a moment, while I asked him if he could remember the nature of the country through which he had journeyed.

"I am telling you as straight as I can, but my head isn't as good as it might be. They drove nails through it to make me hear better how Dravot died. The country was mountaineous and the mules were most contrary, and the inhabitants was dispersed and solitary. They went up and up, and down and down, and that other party, Carnehan, was imploring of Dravot not to sing and whistle so loud, for fear of bringing down the tremenjus avalanches. But Dravot says that if a King couldn't sing it wasn't worth being King, and whacked the mules over the rump, and never took no heed for ten cold days. We came to a big level valley all among the mountains, and the mules were near dead, so we killed them, not having anything in special for them or us to eat. We sat upon the boxes, and played odd and even with the cartridges that was jolted out.

"Then ten men with bows and arrows ran down that valley, chasing twenty men with bows and arrows, and the row was tremenjus. They was fair men—fairer than you or me—with yellow hair and remarkable well built. Says Dravot, unpacking the guns—'This is the beginning of the business. We'll fight for the ten men,' and with that he fires two rifles at the twenty men, and drops one of them at two hundred yards from the rock where we was sitting. The other men began to run but Carnehan and Dravot sits on the boxes picking them off at all ranges, up and down the valley. Then we goes up to the ten men that had run across the snow too, and they fires a footy little arrow at us. Dravot he shoots above their heads and they all falls down flat. Then he walks over them and kicks them, and then he lifts them up and shakes hands all round to make them friendly like. He calls them and gives them the boxes to carry, and waves his hand for all the world as though he was King already. They takes the boxes and him across the valley and up the hill into a pine wood on the top, where there was half a dozen big stone idols. Dravot he goes to the biggest—a fellow they call Imbra—and lays a rifle and a cartridge at his feet, rubbing his nose respectful with his own nose, patting him on the head, and saluting in front of it. He turns round to the men and nods his head, and says,—'That's all right. I'm in the know too, and all these old jim-jams are my friends.' Then he opens his mouth and points down it, and when the first man brings him food, he says—'No,;' and when the second man brings him food, he says—'No;' but when one of the old priests and the boss of the village brings him food, he says—'Yes;' very haughty, and eats it slow. That was how we came to our first village, without any trouble, just as though we had tumbled from the skies. But we tumbled from one of those damned rope-bridges, you see, and you couldn't expect a man to laugh much after that."

"Take some more whiskey and go on," I said. "That was the first village you came into. How did you get to be King?"

"I wasn't King," said Carnehan. "Dravot he was the King, and a handsome man he looked with the gold crown on his head and all. Him and the other party stayed in that village, and every morning Dravot sat by the side of old Imbra, and the people came and worshipped. That was Dravot's order. Then a lot of men came into the valley, and Carnehan and Dravot picks them off with the rifles before they knew where they was, and runs down into the valley and up again the other side, and finds another village, same as the first one, and the people all falls down flat on their faces, and Dravot says,—'Now what is the trouble between you two villages?' and the people points to a woman, as fair as you or me, that was carried off, and Dravot takes her back to the first village and counts up the dead—eight there was. For each dead man Dravot pours a little milk on the ground and waves his arms like a whirligig and 'That's all right,' says he. Then he and Carnehan takes the big boss of each village by the arm and walks them down into the valley, and shows them how to scratch a line with a spear right down the valley, and gives each a sod of turf from both sides o' the line. Then all the people comes down and shouts like the devil and all, and Dravot says,—'Go and dig the land, and be fruitful and multiply,' which they did, though they didn't understand. Then we asks the names of things in their lingo—bread and water and fire and idols and such, and Dravot leads the priest of each village up to the idol, and says he must sit there and judge the people, and if anything goes wrong he is to be shot.

"Next week they was all turning up the land in the valley as quiet as bees and much prettier, and the priests heard all the complaints and told Dravot in dumb show what it was about. 'That's just the beginning,' said Dravot. 'They think we're Gods.' He and Carnehan picks out twenty good men and shows them how to click off a rifle, and form fours, and advance in line, and they was very pleased to do so, and clever to see the hang of it. Then he takes out his pipe and his baccy-pouch and leaves one at one village and one at the other, and off we two goes to see what was to be done in the next valley. That was all rock, and there was a little

village there, and Carnehan says,—
'Send 'em to the old valley to plant,'
and takes 'em there and gives 'em some
land that wasn't took before. They
were a poor lot, and we blooded 'em
with a kid before letting 'em into the
new Kingdom. That was to impress
the people, and then they settled down
quiet, and Carnehan went back to Dravot who had got into another valley,
all snow and ice and most mountaineous. There was no people there and
the Army got afraid, so Dravot shoots
one of them, and goes on till he finds
some people in a village, and the Army
explains that unless the people wants
to be killed they had better not shoot
their little matchlocks; for they had
matchlocks. We make friends with the
priest and I stays there alone with two
of the Army, teaching the men how to
drill, and a thundering big Chief comes
across the snow with kettle-drums and
horns twanging, because he heard there
was a new God kicking about. Carnehan sights for the brown of the men
half a mile across the snow and wings
one of them. Then he sends a message
to the Chief that, unless he wished to
be killed, he must come and shake
hands with me and leave his arms behind. The chief comes alone first, and
Carnehan shakes hands with him and
whirls his arms about, same as Dravot
used, and very much surprised that
Chief was, and strokes my eyebrows.
Then Carnehan goes alone to the Chief,
and asks him in dumb show if he had
an enemy he hated. 'I have,' says the
Chief. So Carnehan weeds out the pick
of his men, and sets the two of the
Army to show them drill and at the
end of two weeks the men can manœuvre

about as well as Volunteers. So he
marches with the Chief to a great big
plain on the top of a mountain, and
the Chief's men rushes into a village
and takes it; we three Martinis firing
into the brown of the enemy. So we
took that village too, and I gives the
Chief a rag from my coat and says,
'Occupy till I come:' which was scrip-
tural. By way of a reminder, when
me and the Army was eighteen hundred
yards away, I drops a bullet near him
standing on the snow, and all the people falls flat on their faces. Then I
sends a letter to Dravot, wherever he
be by land or by sea."

At the risk of throwing the creature
out of train I interrupted,—"How could
you write a letter up yonder?"

"The letter?—Oh!—The letter! Keep
looking at me between the eyes, please.
It was a string-talk letter, that we'd
learned the way of it from a blind beggar in the Punjab."

I remember that there had once come
to the office a blind man with a knotted
twig and a piece of string which he
wound round the twig according to some
cypher of his own. He could, after the
lapse of days or hours, repeat the sentence which he had reeled up. He had
reduced the alphabet to eleven primitive sounds; and tried to teach me his
method, but failed.

"I sent that letter to Dravot," said
Carnehan; "and told him to come back
because this Kingdom was growing too
big for me to handle, and then I struck
for the first valley, to see how the
priests were working. They called the
village we took along with the Chief,
Bashkai, and the first village we took,
Er-Heb. The priests at Er-Heb was

doing all right, but they had a lot of pending cases about land to show me, and some men from another village had been firing arrows at night. I went out and looked for that village and fired four rounds at it from a thousand yards. That used all the cartridges I cared to spend, and I waited for Dravot, who had been away two or three months, and I kept my people quiet.

"One morning I heard the devil's own noise of drums and horns, and Dan Dravot marches down the hill with his Army and a tail of hundreds of men, and, which was the most amazing—a great gold crown on his head. 'My Gord, Carnehan,' says Daniel, 'this is a tremendjus business, and we've got the whole country as far as it's worth having. I am the son of Alexander by Queen Semiramis, and you're my younger brother and a God too! It's the biggest thing we've ever seen. I've been marching and fighting for six weeks with the Army, and every footy little village for fifty miles has come in rejoiceful; and more than that, I've got the key of the whole show, as you'll see, and I've got a crown for you! I told 'em to make two of 'em at a place called Shu, where the gold lies in the rock like suet in mutton. Gold I've seen, and turquoise I've kicked out of the cliffs, and there's garnets in the sands of the river, and here's a chunk of amber that a man brought me. Call up all the priests and, here, take your crown.'

"One of the men opens a black hair bag and I slips the crown on. It was too small and too heavy, but I wore it for the glory. Hammered gold it

was—five pound weight, like a hoop of a barrel.

"'Peachey,' says Dravot, 'we don't want to fight no more. The Craft's the trick so help me!' and he brings forward that same Chief that I left at Bashkai—Billy Fish we called him afterward, because he was so like Billy Fish that drove the big tank-engine at Mach on the Bolan in the old days. 'Shake hands with him,' says Dravot, and I shook hands and nearly dropped, for Billy Fish gave me the Grip. I said nothing, but tried him with the Fellow Craft Grip. He answers, all right, and I tried the Master's Grip, but that was a slip. 'A Fellow Craft he is!' I says to Dan. 'Does he know the word?' 'He does,' says Dan, 'and all the priests know. It's a miracle! The Chiefs and the priests can work a Fellow Craft Lodge in a way that's very like ours, and they've cut the marks on the rocks, but they don't know the Third Degree, and they've come to find out. It's Gord's Truth. I've known these long years that the Afghans knew up to the Fellow Craft Degree, but this is a miracle. A God and a Grand-Master of the Craft am I, and a Lodge in the Third Degree I will open, and we'll raise the head priests and the Chiefs of the villages.'

"'It's against all the law,' I says, 'holding a Lodge without warrant from any one; and we never held office in any Lodge.'

"'It's a master-stroke of policy,' says Dravot. 'It means running the country as easy as a four-wheeled bogy on a down grade. We can't stop to inquire now, or they'll turn against us. I've forty Chiefs at my heel, and passed and raised according to their merit they shall be. Billet these men on the villages and see that we run up a Lodge of some kind. The temple of Imbra will do for the Lodge-room. The women must make aprons as you show them. I'll hold a levee of Chiefs tonight and Lodge to-morrow.''

"I was fair run off my legs, but I wasn't such a fool as not to see what a pull this Craft business gave us. I showed the priests' families how to make aprons of the degrees, but for Dravot's apron the blue border and marks was made of turquoise lumps on white hide, not cloth. We took a great square stone in the temple for the Master's chair, and little stones for the officers' chairs, and painted the black pavement with white squares, and did what we could to make things regular.

"At the levee which was held that night on the hillside with big bonfires, Dravot gives out that him and me were Gods and sons of Alexander, and Past Grand-Masters in the Craft, and was come to make Kafiristan a country where every man should eat in peace and drink in quiet, and specially obey us. Then the Chiefs come round to shake hands, and they was so hairy and white and fair it was just shaking hands with old friends. We gave them names according as they was like men we had known in India—Billy Fish, Holly Dilworth, Pikky Kergan that was Bazarmaster when I was at Mhow, and so on and so on.

"The *most* amazing miracle was at Lodge next night. One of the old priests was watching us continuous, and I felt uneasy, for I knew we'd have to fudge the Ritual, and I didn't know what the men knew. The old priest

was a stranger come in from beyond the village of Bashkai. The minute Dravot puts on the Master's apron that the girls had made for him, the priest fetches a whoop and a howl, and tries to overturn the stone that Dravot was sitting on. 'It's all up now,' I says. 'That comes of meddling with the Craft without warrant!' Dravot never winked an eye, not when ten priests took and tilted over the Grand-Master's chair—which was to say the stone of Imbra. The priest begins rubbing the bottom end of it to clear away the black dirt, and presently he shows all the other priests the Master's Mark, same as was on Dravot's apron, cut into the stone. Not even the priests of the temple of Imbra knew it was there. The old chap falls flat on his face at Dravot's feet and kisses 'em. 'Luck again,' says Dravot, across the Lodge to me, 'they say it's the missing Mark that no one could understand the why of. We're more than safe now.' Then he bangs the butt of his gun for a gavel and says:— 'By virtue of the authority vested in me by my own right hand and the help of Peachey, I declare myself Grand-Master of all Freemasonry in Kafiristan in this the Mother Lodge o' the country, and King of Kafiristan equally with Peachey!' At that he puts on his crown and I puts on mine—I was doing Senior Warden—and we opens the Lodge in most ample form. It was an amazing miracle! The priests moved in Lodge through the first two degrees almost without telling, as if the memory was coming back to them. After that, Peachey and Dravot raised such as was worthy—high priests and Chiefs of far-off villages. Billy Fish was the first, and I can tell you we scared the soul out of him. It was not in any way according to Ritual, but it served our turn. We didn't raise more than ten of the biggest men because we didn't want to make the Degree common. And they was clamoring to be raised.

" 'In another six months,' says Dravot, 'we'll hold another Communication and see how you are working.' Then he asks them about their villages, and learns that they was fighting one against the other and were fair sick and tired of it. And when they wasn't doing that they was fighting with the Mohammedans. 'You can fight those when they come into our country,' says Dravot. 'Tell off every tenth man of your tribes for a Frontier guard, and send two hundred at a time to this valley to be drilled. Nobody is going to be shot or speared any more so long as he does well, and I know that you won't cheat me because you're white people—sons of Alexander—and not like common, black Mohammedans. You are *my* people and by God,' says he, running off into English at the end—'I'll make a damned fine Nation of you, or I'll die in the making!'

"I can't tell all we did for the next six months because Dravot did a lot I couldn't see the hang of, and he learned their lingo in a way I never could. My work was to help the people plough, and now and again go out with some of the Army and see what the other villages were doing, and make 'em throw rope-bridges across the ravines which cut up the country horrid. Dravot was very kind to me, but when he walked up and down in the pine wood pulling that bloody red beard of his with both fists I knew he was thinking plans I could not advise him about, and I just waited for orders.

"But Dravot never showed me disrespect before the people. They were afraid of me and the Army, but they loved Dan. He was the best of friends with the priests and the Chiefs; but any one could come across the hills with a complaint and Dravot would hear him out fair, and call four priests together and say what was to be done. He used to call in Billy Fish from Bashkai, and Pikky Kergan from Shu, and an old Chief we called Kafuzelum—it was like enough to his real name—and hold councils with 'em when there was any fighting to be done in small villages. That was his Council of War, and the four priests of Bashkai, Shu, Khawak, and Madora was his Privy Council. Between the lot of 'em they send me, with forty men and twenty rifles, and sixty men carrying turquoises, into the Ghorband country to buy those hand-made Martini rifles, that come out of the Amir's workshops at Kabul, from one of the Amir's Herati regiments that would have sold the very teeth out of their mouths for turquoises.

"I stayed in Ghorband a month, and gave the Governor there the pick of my baskets for hush-money, and bribed the Colonel of the regiment some more, and, between the two and the tribespeople, we got more than a hundred hand-made Martinis, a hundred good Kohat Jezails, that'll throw to six hundred yards, and forty man-loads of very bad ammunition for the rifles. I came back with what I had, and distributed 'em among the men that the Chiefs sent to me to drill. Dravot was too busy to attend to those things, but the old Army that we first made helped me, and we turned out five hundred men that could drill, and two hundred that knew how to hold arms pretty straight. Even those cork-screwed, hand-made guns was a miracle to them. Dravot talked big about powder-shops and factories, walking up and down in the pine wood when the winter was coming on.

" 'I won't make a Nation,' says he, 'I'll make an Empire! These men aren't niggers; they're English! Look at their eyes—look at their mouths. Look at the way they stand up. They sit on chairs in their own houses. They're the Lost Tribes, or something like it, and they've grown to be English. I'll take a census in the spring if the priests don't get frightened. There must be a fair two million of 'em in these hills. The villages are full o' little children. Two million people— two hundred and fifty thousand fighting men—and all English! They only want the rifles and a little drilling. Two hundred and fifty thousand men, ready to cut in on Russia's right flank when she tries for India! Peachey, man,' he says, chewing his beard in great hunks, 'we shall be Emperors—Emperors of the Earth! Rajah Brooke will be a suckling to us. I'll treat with the Viceroy on equal terms. I'll ask him to send me twelve picked English—twelve that I know of—to help us govern a bit. There's Mackray, Sergeant-pensioner at Segowli—many's the good dinner he's given me, and his wife a pair of trousers. There's Donkin, the Warder of Tounghoo Jail; there's hundreds

that I could lay my hand on if I was in India. The Viceroy shall do it for me. I'll send a man through in the spring for those men, and I'll write for a dispensation from the Grand Lodge for what I've done as Grand-Master. That—and all the Sniders that'll be thrown out when the native troops in India take up the Martini. They'll be worn smooth, but they'll do for fighting in these hills. Twelve English, a hundred thousand Sniders run through the Amir's country in driblets—I'd be content with twenty thousand in one year —and we'd be an Empire. When everything was shipshape, I'd hand over the crown—this crown I'm wearing now— to Queen Victoria on my knees, and she'd say: "Rise up, Sir Daniel Dravot." Oh, it's big! It's big, I tell you! But there's so much to be done in every place—Bashkai, Khawak, Shu, and everywhere else.'

" 'What is it?' I says. 'There are no more men coming in to be drilled this autumn. Look at those fat, black clouds. They're bringing the snow.'

" 'It isn't that,' says Daniel, putting his hand very hard on my shoulder; 'and I don't wish to say anything that's against you, for no other living man would have followed me and made me what I am as you have done. You're a first-class Commander-in-Chief, and the people know you; but—it's a big country, and somehow you can't help me, Peachey, in the way I want to be helped.'

" 'Go to your blasted priests, then!' I said, and I was sorry when I made that remark, but it did hurt me sore to find Daniel talking so superior when

I'd drilled all the men, and done all he told me.

" 'Don't let's quarrel, Peachey,' says Daniel, without cursing. 'You're a King too, and the half of this Kingdom is yours; but can't you see, Peachey, we want cleverer men than us now—three or four of 'em, that we can scatter about for our Deputies. It's a hugeous great State, and I can't always tell the right thing to do, and I haven't time for all I want to do, and here's the winter coming on and all.' He put half his beard into his mouth, and it was as red as the gold of his crown.

" 'I'm sorry, Daniel,' says I. 'I've done all I could. I've drilled the men and shown the people how to stack their oats better; and I've brought in those tinware rifles from Ghorband—but I know what you're driving at. I take it Kings always feel oppressed that way.'

" 'There's another thing too,' says Dravot, walking up and down. 'The winter's coming and these people won't be giving much trouble, and if they do we can't move about. I want a wife.'

" 'For Gord's sake leave the women alone!' I says. 'We've both got all the work we can, though I *am* a fool. Remember the Contrak, and keep clear o' women.'

" 'The Contrack only lasted till such time as we was Kings; and Kings we have been these months past,' says Dravot, weighing his crown in his hand. 'You go get a wife too, Peachey—a nice, strappin', plump girl that'll keep you warm in the winter. They're prettier than English girls, and we can take the pick of 'em. Boil 'em once or twice in hot water, and they'll come as fair as chicken and ham.'

" 'Don't tempt me!' I says. 'I will not have any dealings with a woman not till we are a dam' side more settled than we are now. I've been doing the work o' two men, and you've been doing the work o' three. Let's lie off a bit, and see if we can get some better tobacco from Afghan country and run in some good liquor; but no women.'

" 'Who's talking o' *women?*' says Dravot. 'I said *wife*—a Queen to breed a King's son for the King. A Queen out of the strongest tribe, that'll make them your blood-brothers, and that'll lie by your side and tell you all the people thinks about you and their own affairs. That's what I want.'

" 'Do you remember that Bengali woman I kept at Mogul Serai when I was a plate-layer?' says I. 'A fat lot o' good she was to me. She taught me the lingo and one or two other things; but what happened? She ran away with the Station Master's servant and half my month's pay. Then she turned up at Dadur Junction in tow of a half-caste, and had the impidence to say I was her husband—all among the drivers in the running-shed!'

" 'We've done with that,' says Dravot. 'These women are whiter than you or me, and a Queen I will have for the winter months.'

" 'For the last time o' asking, Dan, do *not*,' I says. 'It'll only bring us harm. The Bible says that Kings ain't to waste their strength on women, 'specially when they've got a new raw Kingdom to work over.'

" 'For the last time of answering I will,' said Dravot, and he went away through the pine-trees looking like a big red devil. The low sun hit his crown and beard on one side and the two blazed like hot coals.

"But getting a wife was not as easy as Dan thought. He put it before the Council, and there was no answer till Billy Fish said that he'd better ask the girls. Dravot damned them all round. 'What's wrong with me?' he shouts, standing by the idol Imbra. 'Am I a dog or am I not enough of a man for your wenches? Haven't I put the shadow of my hand over this country? Who stopped the last Afghan raid? It was me really, but Dravot was too angry to remember. 'Who brought your guns? Who repaired the bridges? Who's the Grand-Master of the sign cut in the stone?' and he thumped his hand on the block that he used to sit on in Lodge, and at Council, which opened like Lodge always. Billy Fish said nothing and no more did the others. 'Keep your hair on, Dan,' said I; 'and ask the girls. That's how it's done at Home, and these people are quite English.'

" 'The marriage of the King is a matter of State,' says Dan, in a white-hot rage, for he could feel, I hope, that he was going against his better mind. He walked out of the Council-room, and the others sat still, looking at the ground.

" 'Billy Fish,' says I to the Chief of Bashkai, 'what's the difficulty here? A straight answer to a true friend.' 'You know,' says Billy Fish. 'How should a man tell you who knows everything? How can daughters of men marry Gods or Devils? It's not proper.'

"I remember something like that in the Bible; but, if, after seeing us as long as they had they still believed we were Gods, it wasn't for me to undeceive them.

" 'A God can do anything,' says I. 'If the King is fond of a girl he'll not let her die.' 'She'll have to,' said Billy Fish. 'There are all sorts of Gods and Devils in these mountains, and now and again a girl marries one of them and isn't seen any more. Besides, you two know the Mark cut in the stone. Only the Gods know that. We thought you were men till you showed the sign of the Master.'

"I wished then that we had explained about the loss of the genuine secrets of a Master-Mason at the first go-off; but I said nothing. All that night there was a blowing of horns in a little dark temple half-way down the hill, and I heard a girl crying fit to die. One of the priests told us that she was being prepared to marry the King.

" 'I'll have no nonsense of that kind,' says Dan. 'I don't want to interfere with your customs, but I'll take my own wife.' 'The girl's a little bit afraid,' says the priest. 'She thinks she's going to die, and they are a-heartening of her up down in the temple.'

" 'Hearten her very tender, then,' says Dravot, 'or I'll hearten you with the butt of a gun so that you'll never want to be heartened again.' He licked his lips, did Dan, and stayed up walking about more than half the night, thinking of the wife that he was going to get in the morning. I wasn't any means comfortable, for I knew that dealings with a woman in foreign parts, though you was a crowned King twenty times over, could not but be risky. I got up very early in the morning while Dravot was asleep, and I saw the priests talking together in whispers, and the Chiefs talking together too, and they looked at me out of the corners of their eyes.

" 'What is up, Fish?' I says to the Bashkai man, who was wrapped up in his furs and looking splendid to behold.

" 'I can't rightly say,' says he; 'but if you can induce the King to drop all this nonsense about marriage, you'll be doing him and me and yourself a great service.'

" 'That I do believe,' says I. 'But sure, you know, Billy, as well as me, having fought against and for us, that the King and me are nothing more than two of the finest men that God Almighty ever made. Nothing more, I do assure you.'

" 'That may be,' says Billy Fish, 'and yet I should be sorry if it was.' He sinks his head upon his great fur cloak for a minute and thinks. 'King,' says he, 'be you man or God or Devil, I'll stick by you to-day. I have twenty of my men with me, and they will follow me. We'll go to Bashkai until the storm blows over.'

"A little snow had fallen in the night, and everything was white except the greasy fat clouds that blew down and down from the north. Dravot came out with his crown on his head, swinging his arms and stamping his feet, and looking more pleased than Punch.

" 'For the last time, drop it, Dan,' says I, in a whisper. 'Billy Fish here says that there will be a row.'

" 'A row among my people!' says Dravot. 'Not much. Peachey, you're a fool not to get a wife too. Where's the girl?' says he, with a voice as loud as the braying of a jackass. 'Call up all the Chiefs and priests, and let the Emperor see if his wife suits him.'

"There was no need to call any one. They were all there leaning on their guns and spears round the clearing in the centre of the pine wood. A deputation of priests went down to the little temple to bring up the girl, and the horns blew up fit to wake the dead. Billy Fish saunters round and gets as close to Daniel as he could, and behind him stood his twenty men wtih match-locks. Not a man of them under six feet. I was next to Dravot, and behind me was twenty men of the regular Army. Up comes the girl, and a strapping wench she was, covered with silver and turquoises but white as death, and looking back every minute at the priests.

" 'She'll do,' said Dan, looking her over. 'What's to be afraid of, lass? Come and kiss me.' He puts his arm round her. She shuts her eyes, gives a bit of a squeak, and down goes her face in the side of Dan's flaming red beard.

" 'The slut's bitten me!' says he, clapping his hand to his neck, and, sure enough, his hand was red with blood. Billy Fish and two of his matchlock-men catches hold of Dan by the shoulders and drags him into the Bashkai lot, while the priests howls in their lingo,— 'Neither God nor Devil but a man!' I was all taken aback, for a priest cut at me in front, and the Army behind began firing into the Bashkai men.

" 'God A-mighty!' says Dan. 'What is the meaning o' this?'

" 'Come back! Come away!' says Billy Fish. 'Ruin and Mutiny is the matter. We'll break for Bashkai if we can.'

"I tried to give some sort of orders

to my men—the men o' the regular Army—but it was no use, so I fired into the brown of 'em with an English Martini and drilled three beggars in a line. The valley was full of shouting, howling creatures, and every soul was shrieking, 'Not a God nor a Devil but only a man!' The Bashkai troops stuck to Billy Fish all they were worth, but their matchlocks wasn't half as good as the Kabul breech-loaders, and four of them dropped. Dan was bellowing like a bull, for he was very wrathy; and Billy Fish had a hard job to prevent him running out at the crowd.

" 'We can't stand,' says Billy Fish. 'Make a run for it down the valley! The whole place is against us.' The matchlock-men ran, and we went down the valley in spite of Dravot's protestations. He was swearing horribly and crying out that he was a King. The priests rolled great stones on us, and the regular Army fired hard, and there wasn't more than six men, not counting Dan, Billy Fish, and Me, that came down to the bottom of the valley alive.

"Then they stopped firing and the horns in the temple blew again. 'Come away—for Gord's sake come away!' says Billy Fish. 'They'll send runners out to all the villages before ever we get to Bashkai. I can protect you there, but I can't do anything now.'

"My own notion is that Dan began to go mad in his head from that hour. He stared up and down like a stuck pig. Then he was all for walking back alone and killing the priests with his bare hands; which he could have done. 'An Emperor am I,' says Daniel, 'and next year I shall be a Knight of the Queen.'

" 'All right, Dan,' says I; 'but come along now while there's time.'

" 'It's your fault,' says he, 'for not looking after your Army better. There was mutiny in the midst, and you didn't know—you damned engine-driving, plate-laying, missionary's-pass-hunting hound!' He sat upon a rock and called me every foul name he could lay tongue to. I was too heart-sick to care, though it was all his foolishness that brought the smash.

" 'I'm sorry, Dan,' says I, 'but there's no accounting for natives. This business is our Fifty-Seven. Maybe we'll make something out of it yet, when we've got to Bashkai.'

" 'Let's get to Bashkai, then,' says Dan, 'and, by God, when I come back here again I'll sweep the valley so there isn't a bug in a blanket left!'

"We walked all that day, and all that night Dan was stumping up and down on the snow, chewing his beard and muttering to himself.

" 'There's no hope o' getting clear,' said Billy Fish. 'The priests will have sent runners to the villages to say that you are only men. Why didn't you stick on as Gods till things was more settled? I'm a dead man,' says Billy Fish, and he throws himself down on the snow and begins to pray to his Gods.

"Next morning we was in a cruel bad country—all up and down, no level ground at all, and no food either. The six Bashkai men looked at Billy Fish hungry-wise as if they wanted to ask something, but they said never a word. At noon we came to the top of a flat mountain all covered with snow, and when we climbed up into it, behold, there was an Army in position waiting in the middle!

"The runners have been very quick,' says Billy Fish, with a little bit of a laugh. 'They are waiting for us.'

"Three or four men began to fire from the enemy's side, and a chance shot took Daniel in the calf of the leg. That brought him to his senses. He looks across the snow at the Army, and sees the rifles that we had brought into the country.

" 'We're done for,' says he. 'They are Englishmen, these people,—and it's my blasted nonsense that has brought you to this. Get back, Billy Fish, and take your men away; you've done what you could, and now cut for it. Carnehan,' says he, 'shake hands with me and go along with Billy. Maybe they won't kill you. I'll go and meet 'em alone. It's me that did it. Me, the King!'

" 'Go!' says I. 'Go to Hell, Dan. I'm with you here. Billy Fish, you clear out, and we two will meet those folk.'

" 'I'm a Chief,' says Billy Fish, quite quiet. 'I stay with you. My men can go.'

"The Bashkai fellows didn't wait for a second word but ran off, and Dan and Me and Billy Fish walked across to where the drums were drumming and the horns were horning. It was cold—awful cold. I've got that cold in the back of my head now. There's a lump of it there."

The punkah-coolies had gone to sleep. Two kerosene lamps were blazing in the office, and the perspiration poured down my face and splashed on the blotter as I leaned forward. Carnehan was shiver-ing, and I feared that his mind might go. I wiped my face, took a fresh grip of the piteously mangled hands, and said:—"What happened after that?"

The momentary shift of my eyes had broken the clear current.

"What was you pleased to say?" whined Carnehan. "They took them without any sound. Not a little whisper all along the snow, not though the King knocked down the first man that set hand on him—not though old Peachey fired his last cartridge into the brown of 'em. Not a single solitary sound did those swines make. They just closed up tight, and I tell you their furs stunk. There was a man called Billy Fish, a good friend of us all, and they cut his throat, Sir, then and there, like a pig; and the King kicks up the bloody snow and says:—'We've had a dashed fine run for our money. What's coming next?' But Peachey, Peachey Taliaferro, I tell you, Sir, in confidence as betwixt two friends, he lost his head, Sir. No, he didn't neither. The King lost his head, so he did, all along o' one of those cunning rope-bridges. Kindly let me have the paper-cutter, Sir. It tilted this way. They marched him a mile across that snow to a rope-bridge over a ravine with a river at the bot-tom. You may have seen such. They prodded him behind like an ox. 'Damn your eyes!' says the King. 'D'you sup-pose I can't die like a gentleman?' He turns to Peachey—Peachey that was crying like a child. 'I've brought you to this, Peachey,' says he. 'Brought you out of your happy life to be killed in Kafiristan, where you was late Com-mander-in-Chief of the Emperor's forces. Say you forgive me, Peachey.'

'I do,' says Peachey. 'Fully and freely do I forgive you, Dan.' 'Shake hands, Peachey,' says he. 'I'm going now.' Out he goes, looking neither right nor left, and when he was plumb in the middle of those dizzy dancing ropes. 'Cut, you beggars,' he shouts; and they cut, and old Dan fell, turning round and round and round twenty thousand miles, for he took half an hour to fall till he struck the water, and I could see his body caught on a rock with the gold crown close beside.

"But do you know what they did to Peachey between two pine trees? They crucified him, Sir, as Peachey's hand will show. They used wooden pegs for his hands and his feet; and he didn't die. He hung there and screamed, and they took him down next day, and said it was a miracle that he wasn't dead. They took him down—poor old Peachey that hadn't done them any harm—that hadn't done them any. . . ."

He rocked to and fro and wept bitterly, wiping his eyes with the back of his scarred hands and moaning like a child for some ten minutes.

"They was cruel enough to feed him up in the temple, because they said he was more of a God than old Daniel that was a man. Then they turned him out on the snow, and told him to go home, and Peachey came home in about a year, begging along the roads quite safe; for Daniel Dravot he walked before and said:—'Come along, Peachey. It's a big thing we're doing.' The mountains they danced at night, and the mountains they tried to fall on Peachey's head, but Dan he held up his hand, and Peachey came along bent double. He never let go of Dan's hand,

and he never let go of Dan's head. They gave it to him as a present in the temple, to remind him not to come again, and though the crown was pure gold, and Peachey was starving, never would Peachey sell the same. You knew Dravot, Sir! You knew Right Worshipful Brother Dravot! Look at him now!"

He fumbled in the mass of rags round his bent waist; brought out a black horsehair bag embroidered with silver thread; and shook therefrom on to my table—the dried, withered head of Daniel Dravot! The morning sun that had long been paling the lamps struck the red beard and blind sunken eyes; struck, too, a heavy circlet of gold studded with raw turquoises, that Carnehan placed tenderly on the battered temples.

"You behold now," said Carnehan, "the Emperor in his habit as he lived—the King of Kafiristan with his crown upon his head. Poor old Daniel that was a monarch once!"

I shuddered, for, in spite of defacements manifold, I recognized the head of the man of Marwar Junction. Carnehan rose to go. I attempted to stop him. He was not fit to walk abroad. "Let me take away the whiskey and give me a little money," he grasped. "I was a King once. I'll go to the Deputy Commissioner and ask to set in the Poorhouse till I get my health. No, thank you, I can't wait till you get a carriage for me. I've urgent private affairs—in the south—at Marwar."

He shambled out of the office and departed in the direction of the Deputy Commissioner's house. That day at noon I had occasion to go down the blinding hot Mall, and I saw a crooked man crawling along the white dust of the roadside, his hat in his hand, quavering dolorously after the fashion of street-singers at Home. There was not a soul in sight and he was out of all possible earshot of the houses. And he sang through his nose, turning his head from right to left:

"The Son of Man goes forth to war,
  A golden crown to gain;
His blood-red banner streams afar—
  Who follows in his train?"

I waited to hear no more, but put the poor wretch into my carriage and drove him off to the nearest missionary for eventual transfer to the Asylum. He repeated the hymn twice while he was with me whom he did not in the least recognize, and I left him singing it to the missionary.

Two days later I inquired after his welfare of the Superintendent of the Asylum.

"He was admitted suffering from sunstroke. He died early yesterday morning," said the Superintendent. "Is it true that he was half an hour bareheaded in the sun at midday?"

"Yes," said I, "but do you happen to know if he had anything upon him by any chance when he died?"

"Not to my knowledge," said the Superintendent.

And there the matter rests.

"The Finest Story in the World"

"Or ever the knightly years were gone
  With the old world to the grave,
I was a king in Babylon
  And you were a Christian slave."
         —W. E. Henley.

His name was Charlie Mears; he was the only son of his mother who was a widow, and he lived in the north of London, coming into the City every day to work in a bank. He was twenty years old and suffered from aspirations. I met him in a public billiard-saloon where the marker called him by his given name, and he called the marker "Bullseyes." Charlie explained, a little nervously, that he had only come to the place to look on, and since looking on at games of skill is not a cheap amusement for the young, I suggested that Charlie should go back to his mother.

That was our first step toward better acquaintance. He would call on me sometimes in the evenings instead of running about London with his fellow-clerks; and before long, speaking of himself as a young man must, he told me of his aspirations, which were all literary. He desired to make himself an undying name chiefly through verse, though he was not above sending stories of love and death to the drop-a-penny-in-the-slot journals. It was my fate to sit still while Charlie read me poems of many hundred lines, and bulky fragments of plays that would surely shake the world. My reward was his unreserved confidence, and the self-revelations and troubles of a young man are almost as holy as those of a maiden. Charlie had never fallen in love, but was anxious to do so on the first opportunity; he believed in all things good and all things honorable, but, at the same time, was curiously careful to let me see that he knew his way about the world as befitted a bank clerk on twenty-five shillings a week. He rhymed "dove" with "love" and "moon" with "June," and devoutly believed that they had never so been rhymed before. The long lame gaps•in his plays he filled up with hasty words of apology and description and swept on, seeing all that he intended to do so clearly that he esteemed it already done, and turned to me for applause.

I fancy that his mother did not encourage his aspirations, and I know that his writing-table at home was the edge of his washstand. This he told me almost at the outset of our acquaintance; when he was ravaging my bookshelves, and a little before I was implored to speak the truth as to his chances of "writing something really great, you know." Maybe I encouraged him too much, for, one night, he called on me, his eyes flaming with excitement, and said breathlessly:

"Do you mind—can you let me stay here and write all this evening? I won't interrupt you, I won't really. There's no place for me to write in at my mother's."

"What's the trouble?" I said, knowing well what that trouble was.

"I've a notion in my head that would make the most splendid story that was ever written. Do let me write it out here. It's *such* a notion!"

There was no resisting the appeal. I set him a table; he hardly thanked me, but plunged into the work at once. For half an hour the pen scratched without stopping. Then Charlie sighed and tugged his hair. The scratching grew slower, there were more erasures, and at last ceased. The finest story in the world would not come forth.

"It looks such awful rot now," he said, mournfully. "And yet it seemed so good when I was thinking about it. What's wrong?"

I could not dishearten him by saying the truth. So I answered: "Perhaps you don't feel in the mood for writing."

"Yes I do—except when I look at this stuff. Ugh!"

"Read me what you've done," I said.

He read, and it was wondrous bad, and he paused at all the specially turgid sentences, expecting a little approval; for he was proud of those sentences, as I knew he would be.

"It needs compression," I suggested, cautiously.

"I hate cutting my things down. I don't think you could alter a word here without spoiling the sense. It reads better aloud than when I was writing it."

"Charlie, you're suffering from an alarming disease afflicting a numerous class. Put the thing by, and tackle it again in a week."

"I want to do it at once. What do you think of it?"

"How can I judge from a half-written tale? Tell me the story as it lies in your head."

Charlie told, and in the telling there was everything that his ignorance had so carefully prevented from escaping into the written word. I looked at him, and wondering whether it were possible that he did not know the originality, the power of the notion that had come in his way? It was distinctly a Notion among notions. Men had been puffed up with pride by notions not a tithe as excellent and practicable. But Charlie babbled on serenely, interrupting the current of pure fancy with samples of horrible sentences that he purposed to use. I heard him out to the end. It would be folly to allow his idea to remain in his own inept hands, when I could do so much with it. Not all that could be done indeed; but, oh so much!

"What do you think?" he said, at last. "I fancy I shall call it 'The Story of a Ship.'"

"I think the idea's pretty good; but you won't be able to handle it for ever so long. Now I"—

"Would it be of any use to you? Would you care to take it? I should be proud," said Charlie, promptly.

There are few things sweeter in this world than the guileless, hot-headed, intemperate, open admiration of a junior. Even a woman in her blindest devotion does not fall into the gait of the man she adores, tilt her bonnet to the angle at which he wears his hat, or interlard her speech with his pet oaths. And Charlie did all these things. Still it was necessary to salve my conscience before I possessed myself of Charlie's thoughts.

"Let's make a bargain. I'll give you a fiver for the notion," I said.

Charlie became a bank-clerk at once.

"Oh, that's impossible. Between two pals, you know, if I may call you so, and speaking as a man of the world, I couldn't. Take the notion if it's any use to you. I've heaps more."

He had—none knew this better than I

—but they were the notions of other men.

"Look at it as a matter of business— between men of the world," I returned. "Five pounds will buy you any number of poetry-books. Business is business, and you may be sure I shouldn't give that price unless"—

"Oh, if you put it *that way*," said Charlie, visibly moved by the thought of the books. The bargain was clinched with an agreement that he should at unstated intervals come to me with all the notions that he possessed, should have a table of his own to write at, and unquestioned right to inflict upon me all his poems and fragments of poems. Then I said, "Now tell me how you came by this idea."

"It came by itself." Charlie's eyes opened a little.

"Yes, but you told me a great deal about the hero that you must have read before somewhere."

"I haven't any time for reading, except when you let me sit here, and on Sundays I'm on my bicycle or down the river all day. There's nothing wrong about the hero, is there?"

"Tell me again and I shall understand clearly. You say that your hero went pirating. How did he live?"

"He was on the lower deck of this ship-thing that I was telling you about."

"What sort of ship?"

"It was the kind rowed with oars, and the sea spurts through the oar-holes and the men row sitting up to their knees in water. Then there's a bench running down between the two lines of oars and an overseer with a whip walks up and down the bench to make the men work.

"How do you know that?"

"It's in the table. There's a rope running overhead, looped to the upper deck, for the overseer to catch hold of when the ship rolls. When the overseer misses the rope once and falls among the rowers, remember the hero laughs at him and gets licked for it. He's chained to his oar of course—the hero."

"How is he chained?"

"With an iron band round his waist fixed to the bench he sits on, and a sort of handcuff on his left wrist chaining him to the oar. He's on the lower deck where the worst men are sent, and the only light comes from the hatchways and through the oar-holes. Can't you imagine the sunlight just squeezing through between the handle and the hole and wobbling about as the ship moves?"

"I can, but I can't imagine your imagining it."

"How could it be any other way? Now you listen to me. The long oars on the upper deck are managed by four men to each bench, the lower ones by three, and the lowest of all by two. Remember it's quite dark on the lowest deck and all the men there go mad. When a man dies at his oar on that deck he isn't thrown overboard, but cut up in his chains and stuffed through the oar-hole in little pieces."

"Why?" I demanded, amazed, not so much at the information as the tone of command in which it was flung out.

"To save trouble and to frighten the others. It needs two overseers to drag a man's body up to the top deck; and if the men at the lower deck oars were left alone, of course they'd stop rowing and try to pull up the benches by all standing up together in their chains."

"You've a most provident imagination. Where have you been reading about galleys and galley-slaves?"

"Nowhere that I remember. I row a little when I get the chance. But, perhaps, if you say so, I may have read something."

He went away shortly afterward to deal with booksellers, and I wondered how a bank clerk aged twenty could put into my hands with a profligate abundance of detail, all given with absolute assurance, the story of extravagant and bloodthirsty adventure, riot, piracy, and death in unnamed seas. He had led his hero a desperate dance through revolt against the overseas, to command of a ship of his own, and ultimate establishment of a kingdom on an island "somewhere in the sea, you know"; and, delighted with my paltry five pounds, had gone out to buy the notions of other men, that these might teach him how to write. I had the consolation of knowing that this notion was mine by right of purchase, and I thought that I could make something of it.

When next he came to me he was drunk—royally drunk on many poets for the first time revealed to him. His pupils were dilated, his words tumbled over each other, and he wrapped himself in quotations. Most of all was he drunk with Longfellow.

"Isn't it splendid? Isn't it superb?" he cried, after hasty greetings. "Listen to this—

" 'Wouldst thou,'—so the helmsman answered,
'Know the secret of the sea?
Only those who brave its dangers
Comprehend its mystery.

By gum!

" 'Only those who brave its dangers
  Comprehend its mystery.' "

he repeated twenty times, walking up
and down the room and forgetting me.
"But *I can* understand it too," he said
to himself. "I don't know how to thank
you for that fiver. And this; listen—

" 'I remember the black wharves and the
    ships
  And the sea-tides tossing free,
  And the Spanish sailors with bearded
    lips,
  And the beauty and mystery of the
    ships,
  And the magic of the sea.'

I haven't braved any dangers, but I feel
as if I knew all about it."

"You certainly seem to have a grip
of the sea. Have you ever seen it?"

"When I was a little chap I went to
Brighton once; we used to live in Cov-
entry, though, before we came to London. I never saw it,

" 'When descends on the Atlantic
    The gigantic
  Storm-wind of the Equinox.' "

He shook me by the shoulder to make
me understand the passion that was
shaking himself.

"When that storm comes," he continued, "I think that all the oars in the
ship that I was talking about get broken,
and the rowers have their chests
smashed in by the bucking oar-heads.
By the way, have you done anything
with that notion of mine yet?"

"No. I was waiting to hear more of
it from you. Tell me how in the world
you're so certain about the fittings of
the ship. You know nothing of ships."

"I don't know. It's as real as anything to me until I try to write it down.
I was thinking about it only last night
in bed, after you had loaned me
'Treasure Island'; and I made up a
whole lot of new things to go into the
story."

"What sort of things?"

"About the food the men ate; rotten
figs and black beans and wine in a skin
bag, passed from bench to bench."

"Was the ship built so long ago as
that?"

"As what? I don't know whether it
was long ago or not. It's only a notion, but sometimes it seems just as
real as if it was true. Do I bother you
with talking about it?"

"Not in the least. Did you make up
anything else?"

"Yes, but it's nonsense." Charlie
flushed a little.

"Never mind; let's hear about it."

"Well, I was thinking over the story,
and after awhile I got out of bed and
wrote down on a piece of paper the
sort of stuff the men might be supposed
to scratch on their oars with the edges
of their handcuffs. It seemed to make
the thing more lifelike. It *is* so real to
me, y'know."

"Have you the paper on you?"

"Ye-es, but what's the use of showing
it? It's only a lot of scratches. All
the same, we might have 'em reproduced
in the book on the front page."

"I'll attend to those details. Show
me what your men wrote."

He pulled out of his pocket a sheet of
note-paper, with a single line of
scratches upon it, and I put this carefully away.

"What is it supposed to mean in English?" I said.

"Oh, I don't know. Perhaps it means 'I'm beastly tired.' It's great nonsense," he repeated, "but all those men in the ship seem as real as people to me. Do do something to the notion soon; I should like to see it written and printed.'"

"But all you've told me would make a long book."

"Make it then. You've only to sit down and write it out."

"Give me a little time. Have you any more notions?"

"Not just now. I'm reading all the books I've bought. They're splendid."

When he had left I looked at the sheet of note-paper with the inscription upon it. Then I took my head tenderly between both hands, to make certain that it was not coming off or turning round. Then . . . but there seemed to be no interval between quitting my rooms and finding myself arguing with a policeman outside a door marked *Private* in a corridor of the British Museum. All I demanded, as politely as possible, was "the Greek antiquity man." The policeman knew nothing except the rules of the Museum, and it became necessary to forage through all the houses and offices inside the gates. An elderly gentleman called away from his lunch put an end to my search by holding the note-paper between finger and thumb and sniffing at it scornfully.

"What does this mean? H'mm," said he. "So far as I can ascertain it is an attempt to write extremely corrupt Greek on the part"—here he glared at me with intention—"of an extremely illiterate—ah—person." He read slowly from the paper, *"Pollock, Erckmann, Tauchnitz, Henniker"*—four names familiar to me.

"Can you tell me what the corruption is supposed to mean—the gist of the thing?" I asked.

"I have been—many times—overcome with weariness in this particular employment. That is the meaning." He returned me the paper, and I fled without a word of thanks, explanation, or apology.

I might have been excused for forgetting much. To me of all men had been given the chance to write the most marvelous tale in the world, nothing less than the story of a Greek galley-slave, as told by himself. Small wonder that his dreaming had seemed real to Charlie. The Fates that are so careful to shut the doors of each successive life behind us had, in this case, been neglectful, and Charlie was looking, though that he did not know where never man had been permitted to look with full knowledge since Time began. Above all he was absolutely ignorant of the knowledge sold to me for five pounds; and he would retain that ignorance, for bank-clerks do not understand metempsychosis, and a sound commercial education does not include Greek. He would supply me—here I capered among the dumb gods of Egypt and laughed in their battered faces—with material to make my tale sure—so sure that the world would hail it as an impudent and vamped fiction. And I—I alone would know that it was absolutely and literally true. I,—I alone held this jewel to my hand for the cutting and polishing. Therefore I danced again among the gods till a policeman saw me and took steps in my direction.

It remained now only to encourage Charlie to talk, and here there was no difficulty. But I had forgotten those accursed books of poetry. He came to me time after time, as useless as a sur-charged phonograph—drunk on Byron, Shelley, or Keats. Knowing now what the boy had been in his past lives, and desperately anxious not to lose one word of his babble, I could not hide from him my respect and interest. He miscon-strued both into respect for the present soul of Charlie Mears, to whom life was as new as it was to Adam, and interest in his readings; and stretched my pa-tience to breaking point •by reciting poetry—not his own now, but that of others. I wished every English poet blotted out of the memory of mankind. I blasphemed the mightiest names of song because they had drawn Charlie from the path of direct narrative, and would, later, spur him to imitate them; but I choked down my impatience until the first flood of enthusiasm should have spent itself and the boy returned to his dreams.

"What's the use of my telling you what *I* think, when these chaps wrote things for the angels to read?" he growled, one evening. "Why don't you write something like theirs?"

"I don't think you're treating me quite fairly," I said, speaking under strong restraint.

"I've given you the story," he said, shortly replunging into "Lara."

"But I want the details."

"The things I make up about that damned ship that you call a galley? They're quite easy. You can just make 'em up yourself. Turn up the gas a little, I want to go on reading."

I could have broken the gas globe over his head for his amazing stupidity. I could indeed make up things for my-self did I only know what Charlie did not know that he knew. But since the doors were shut behind me I could only wait his youthful pleasure and strive to keep him in good temper. One minute's want of guard might spoil a priceless revelation: now and again he would toss his books aside—he kept them in my rooms, for his mother would have been shocked at the waste of good money had she seen them—and launched into his sea dreams. Again I cursed all the poets of England. The plastic mind of the bank-clerk had been overlaid, col-ored and distorted by that which he had read, and the result as delivered was a confused tangle of other voices most like the muttered song through a City telephone in the busiest part of the day.

He talked of the galley—his own gal-ley had he but known it—with illustra-tions borrowed from the "Bride of Abydos." He pointed the experiences of his hero with quotations from "The Corsair," and threw in deep and des-perate moral reflections from "Cain" and "Manfred," expecting me to use them all. Only when the talk turned on Longfellow were the jarring cross-cur-rents dumb, and I knew that Charlie was speaking the truth as he remembered it.

"What do you think of this?" I said one evening, as soon as I understood the medium in which his memory worked best, and, before he could expostulate, read him the whole of "The Saga of King Olaf!"

He listened open-mouthed, flushed,

his hands drumming on the back of the sofa where he lay, till I came to the Song of Einar Tamberskelver and the verse:

"Einar then, the arrow taking
    From the loosened string,
 Answered: 'That was Norway breaking
    'Neath thy hand, O King.' "

He gasped with pure delight of sound.

"That's better than Byron, a little," I ventured.

"Better? Why it's *true!* How could he have known?"

I went back and repeated:

" 'What was that?' said Olaf, standing
    On the quarter-deck,
 'Something heard I like the standing
    Of a shattered wreck?' "

"How could he have known how the ships crash and the oars rip out and go *z-zzp* all along the line? Why only the other night. . . . But go back please and read 'The Skerry of Shrieks' again."

"No, I'm tired. Let's talk. What happened the other night?"

"I had an awful nightmare about that galley of ours. I dreamed I was drowned in a fight. You see we ran alongside another ship in harbor. The water was dead still except where our oars whipped it up. You know where I always sit in the galley?" He spoke haltingly at first, under a fine English fear of being laughed at.

"No. That's news to me," I answered, meekly, my heart beginning to beat.

"On the fourth oar from the bow on the right side on the upper deck. There were four of us at that oar, all chained. I remember watching the water and trying to get my handcuffs off before the row began. Then we closed up on the other ship, and all their fighting men jumped over our bulwarks, and my bench broke and I was pinned down with the three other fellows on top of me, and the big oar jammed across our backs."

"Well?" Charlie's eyes were alive and alight. He was looking at the wall behind my chair.

"I don't know how we fought. The men were trampling all over my back, and I lay low. Then our rowers on the left side—tied to their oars, you know—began to yell and back water. I could hear the water sizzle, and we spun round like a cockchafer and I knew, lying where I was, that there was a galley coming up bow-on, to ram us on the left side. I could just lift up my head and see her sail over the bulwarks. We wanted to meet her bow to bow, but it was too late. We could only turn a little bit because the galley on our right had hooked herself on to us and stopped our moving. Then, by gum! there was a crash! Our left oars began to break as the other galley, the moving one y'know, stuck her nose into them. Then the lower-deck oars shot up through the deck-planking, but first, and one of them jumped clean up into the air and came down again close to my head."

"How was that managed?"

"The moving galley's bow was plunking them back through their own oarholes, and I could hear the devil of a shindy in the decks below. Then her nose caught us nearly in the middle, and we tilted sideways, and the fellows in the right-hand galley unhitched their hooks and ropes, and threw things on to our upper deck—arrows, and hot pitch or something that stung, and we went up and up and up on the left side, and the right side dipped, and I twisted my head round and saw the water stand still as it topped the right bulwarks, and then it curled over and crashed down on the whole lot of us on the right side, and I felt it hit my back, and I woke."

"One minute, Charlie. When the sea topped the bulwarks, what did it look like?" I had my reasons for asking. A man of my acquaintance had once gone down with a leaking ship in a still sea, and had seen the water-level pause for an instant ere it fell on the deck.

"It looked just like a banjo-string drawn tight, and it seemed to stay there for years," said Charlie.

Exactly! The other man had said: "It looked like a silver wire laid down along the bulwarks, and I thought it was never going to break." He had paid everything except the bare life for this little valueless piece of knowledge, and I had traveled ten thousand weary miles to meet him and take his knowledge at second hand. But Charlie, the bank-clerk on twenty-five shillings a week, who had never been out of sight of a London omnibus, knew it all. It was no consolation to me that once in his lives he had been forced to die for his gains. I also must have died scores of times, but behind me, because I could have used my knowledge, the doors were shut.

"And then?" I said, trying to put away the devil of envy.

"The funny thing was, though, in all the mess I didn't feel a bit astonished or frightened. It seemed as if I'd been in a good many fights, because I told my next man so when the row began. But that cad of an overseer on my deck wouldn't unloose our chains and give us a chance. He always said that we'd all be set free after a battle, but we never were; we never were." Charlie shook his head mournfully.

"What a scoundrel!"

"I should say he was. He never gave us enough to eat, and sometimes we were so thirsty that we used to drink salt-water. I can taste that salt-water still."

"Now tell me something about the harbor where the fight was fought."

"I didn't dream about that. I know it was a harbor, though; because we were tied up to a ring on a white wall and all the face of the stone under water was covered with wood to prevent our ram getting chipped when the tide made us rock."

"That's curious. Our hero commanded the galley, didn't he?"

"Didn't he just! He stood by the bows and shouted like a good 'un. He was the man who killed the overseer."

"But you were all drowned together, Charlie, weren't you?"

"I can't make that fit quite," he said with a puzzled look. "The galley must have gone down with all hands and yet I fancy that the hero went on living afterward. Perhaps he climbed into the attacking ship. I wouldn't see that, of course. I was dead, you know."

He shivered slightly and protested that he could remember no more.

I did not press him further, but to satisfy myself that he lay in ignorance of the workings of his own mind, deliberately introduced him to Mortimer Collins's "Transmigration," and gave him a sketch of the plot before he opened the pages.

"What rot it all is!" he said, frankly, at the end of an hour. "I don't understand his nonsense about the Red Planet Mars and the King, and the rest of it. Chuck me the Longfellow again."

I handed him the book and wrote out as much as I could remember of his description of the sea-fight, appealing to him from time to time for confirmation of fact or detail. He would answer without raising his eyes from the book, as assuredly as though all his knowledge lay before him on the printed page. I spoke under the normal key of my voice that the current might not be broken, and I know that he was not aware of what he was saying, for his thoughts were out on the sea with Longfellow.

"Charlie," I asked, "when the rowers on the gallies mutinied how did they kill their overseers?"

"Tore up the benches and brained 'em. That happened when a heavy sea was running. An overseer on the lower deck slipped from the centre plank and fell among the rowers. They choked him to death against the side of the ship with their chained hands quite quietly, and it was too dark for the other overseer to see what had happened. When he asked, he was pulled down too and choked, and the lower deck fought their way up deck by deck, with the pieces of the broken benches banging behind 'em. How they howled!"

"And what happened after that?"

"I don't know. The hero went away —red hair and red beard and all. That was after he had captured our galley, I think."

The sound of my voice irritated him, and he motioned slightly with his left hand as a man does when interruption jars.

"You never told me he was redheaded before, or thaat he captured your galley," I said, after a discreet interval.

Charlie did not raise his eyes.

"He was as red as a red bear," said he, abstractedly. "He came from the north; they said so in the galley when he looked for rowers—not slaves, but free men. Afterward—years and years afterward—news came from another ship, or else he came back"—

His lips moved in silence. He was rapturously retasting some poem before him.

"Where had he been, then?" I was almost whispering that the sentence might come gentle to whichever section of Charlie's brain was working on my behalf.

"To the Beaches—the Long and Wonderful Beaches!" was the reply, after a minute of silence.

"To Furdurstrandi?" I asked, tingling from head to foot.

"Yes, to Furdurstrandi," he pronounced the word in a new fashion. "And I too saw"— The voice failed.

"Do you know what you have said?" I shouted, incautiously.

He lifted his eyes, fully roused now. "No!" he snapped. "I wish you'd let a chap go on reading. Hark to this:

" 'But Othere, the old sea captain,
   He neither paused nor stirred
      Till the king listened, and then
      Once more took up his pen
   And wrote down every word.

" 'And to the King of the Saxons
In witness of the truth,
    Raising his noble head,
    He stretched his brown hand and
        said,
"Behold this walrus tooth." '

By Jove, what chaps those must have been, to go sailing all over the shop never knowing where they'd fetch the land! Hah!"

"Charlie," I pleaded, "if you'll only be sensible for a minute or two I'll make our hero in our tale every inch as good as Othere."

"Umph! Longfellow wrote that poem. I don't care about writing things any more. I want to read." He was thoroughly out of tune now, and raging over my own ill-luck, I left him.

Conceive yourself at the door of the world's treasure-house guarded by a child—an idle irresponsible child playing knuckle-bones—on whose favor depends the gift of the key, and you will imagine one-half my torment. Till that evening Charlie had spoken nothing that might not lie within the experiences of a Greek galley-slave. But now, or there was no virtue in books, he had talked of some desperate adventure of the Vikings, of Thorfin Karlsefne's sailing to Wineland, which is America, in the ninth or tenth century. The battle in the harbor he had seen; and his own death he had described. But this was a much more startling plunge into the past. Was it possible that he had skipped half a dozen lives and was then dimly remembering some episode of a thousand years later? It was a maddening jumble, and the worst of it was that Charlie Mears in his normal condition was the last person in the world to

clear it up. I could only wait and watch, but I went to bed that night full of the wildest imaginings. There was nothing that was not possible if Charlie's detestable memory only held good.

I might rewrite the Saga of Thorfin Karlsefne as it had never been written before, might tell the story of the first discovery of America, myself the discoverer. But I was entirely at Charlie's mercy, and so long as there was a three-and-six-penny Bohn volume within his reach Charlie would not tell. I dared not curse him openly; I hardly dared jog his memory, for I was dealing with the experiences of a thousand years ago, told through the mouth of a boy of to-day; and a boy of to-day is affected by every change of tone and gust of opinion, so that he lies even when he desires to speak the truth.

I saw no more of him for nearly a week. When next I met him it was in Gracechurch Street with a billbook chained to his waist. Business took him over London Bridge and I accompanied him. He was very full of the importance of that book and magnified it. As we passed over the Thames we paused to look at a steamer unloading great slabs of white and brown marble. A barge drifted under the steamer's stern and a lonely cow in that barge bellowed. Charlie's face changed from the face of the bank-clerk to that of an unknown and—though he would not have believed this—a much shrewder man. He flung out his arm across the parapet of the bridge and laughing very loudly, said:

"When they heard our bulls bellow the Skrœlings ran away!"

I waited only for an instant, but the barge and the cow had disappeared under the bows of the steamer before I answered.

"Charlie, what do you suppose are Skrœlings?"

"Never heard of 'em before. They sound like a new kind of seagull. What a chap you are for asking questions!" he replied. "I have to go to the cashier of the Omnibus Company yonder. Will you wait for me and we can lunch somewhere together? I've a notion for a poem."

"No, thanks. I'm off. You're sure you know nothing about Skrœlings?"

"Not unless he's been entered for the Liverpool Handicap." He nodded and disappeared in the crowd.

Now it is written in the Saga of Eric the Red or that of Thorfin Karlsefne, that nine hundred years ago when Karlsefne's galleys came to Leif's booths, which Leif had erected in the unknown land called Markland, which may or may not have been Rhode Island, the Skrœlings—and the Lord He knows who these may or may not have been—came to trade with the Vikings, and ran away because they were frightened at the bellowing of the cattle which Thorfin had brought with him in the ships. But what in the world could a Greek slave know of that affair? I wandered up and down among the streets trying to unravel the mystery, and the more I considered it, the more baffling it grew. One thing only seemed certain and that certainty took away my breath for the moment. If I came to full knowledge of anything at all, it would not be one life of the soul in Charlie Mears's body, but half a dozen —half a dozen several and separate ex-

istences spent on blue water in the morning of the world!

Then I walked round the situation.

Obviously if I used my knowledge I should stand alone and unapproachable until all men were as wise as myself. That would be something, but manlike I was ungrateful. It seemed bitterly unfair that Charlie's memory should fail me when I needed it most. Great Powers above—I looked up at them through the fog smoke—did the Lords of Life and Death know what this meant to me? Nothing less than eternal fame of the best kind, that comes from One, and is shared by one alone. I would be content—remembering Clive, I stood astounded at my own moderation, —with the mere right to tell one story, to work out one little contribution to the light literature of the day. If Charlie were permitted full recollection for one hour—for sixty short minutes —of existences that had extended over a thousand years—I would forego all profit and honor from all that I should make of his speech. I would take no share in the commotion that would follow throughout the particular corner of the earth that calls itself "the world." The thing should be put forth anonymously. Nay, I would make other men believe that they had written it. They would hire bull-hided self-advertising Englishmen to bellow it abroad. Preachers would found a fresh conduct of life upon it, swearing that it was new and that they had lifted the fear of death from all mankind. Every Orientalist in Europe would patronize it discursively with Sanskrit and Pali texts. Terrible women would invent unclean variants of the men's belief for the elevation of their sisters. Churches and religions would war over it. Between the haiilng and re-starting of an omnibus I foresaw the scuffles that would arise among half a dozen denominations all professing "the doctrine of the True Metempsychosis as applied to the world and the New Era"; and saw, too, the respectable English newspapers shying, like frightened kine, over the beautiful simplicity of the tale. The mind leaped forward a hundred—two hundred—a thousand years. I saw with sorrow that men would mutilate and garble the story; that rival creeds would turn it upside down till, at last, the western world which clings to the dread of death more closely than the hope of life, would set it aside as an interesting superstition and stampede after some faith so long forgotten that it seemed altogether new. Upon this I changed the terms of the bargain that I would make with the Lords of Life and Death. Only let me know, let me write, the story with sure knowledge that I wrote the truth, and I would burn the manuscript as a solemn sacrifice. Five minutes after the last line was written I would destroy it all. But I must be allowed to write it with absolute certainty.

There was no answer. The flaming colors of an Aquarium poster caught my eye and I wondered whether it would be wise or prudent to lure Charlie into the hands of the professional mesmerist, and whether, if he were under his power, he would speak of his past lives. If he did, and if people believed him . . . but Charlie would be frightened and flustered, or made conceited by the interviews. In either case he would begin to lie,

through fear or vanity. He was safest in my own hands.

"They are very funny fools, your English," said a voice at my elbow, and turning round I recognized a casual acquaintance, a young Bengali law student, called Grish Chunder, whose father had sent him to England to become civilized. The old man was a retired native official, and on an income of five pounds a month contrived to allow his son two hundred pounds a year, and the run of his teeth in a city where he could pretend to be the cadet of a royal house, and tell stories of the brutal Indian bureaucrats who ground the faces of the poor.

Grish Chunder was a young, fat, full-bodied Bengali dressed with scrupulous care in frock coat, tall hat, light trousers and tan gloves. But I had known him in the days when the brutal Indian Government paid for his university education, and he contributed cheap sedition to *Sachi Durpan*, and intrigued with the wives of his schoolmates.

"That is very funny and very foolish," he said, nodding at the poster. "I am going down to the Northbrook Club. Will you come too?"

I walked with him for some time. "You are not well," he said. "What is there in your mind? You do not talk."

"Grish Chunder, you've been too well educated to believe in a God, haven't you?"

"Oah, yes, *here!* But when I go home I must conciliate popular superstition, and make ceremonies of purification, and my women will anoint idols."

"And hang up *tulsi* and feast the *purohit,* and take you back into caste again and make a good *khuttri* of you again, you advanced social Free-thinker. And you'll eat *desi* food, and like it all, from the smell in the courtyard to the mustard oil over you."

"I shall very much like it," said Grish Chunder, unguardedly. "Once a Hindu—always a Hindu. But I like to know what the English think they know."

"I'll tell you something that one Englishman knows. It's an old tale to you."

I began to tell the story of Charlie in English, but Grish Chunder put a question in the vernacular, and the history went forward naturally in the tongue best suited for its telling. After all it could never have been told in English. Grish Chunder heard me, nodding from time to time, and then came up to my rooms where I finished the tale.

"Beshak," he said, philisophically. *"Lekin darwaza band hai.* (Without doubt, but the door is shut.) I have heard of this remembering of previous existences among my people. It is of course an old tale with us, but, to happen to an Englishman—a cow-fed *Malechh*—an outcast. By Jove, that is most peculiar!"

"Outcast yourself, Grish Chunder! You eat cow-beef every day. Let's think the thing over. The boy remembers his incarnations."

"Does he know that?" said Grish Chunder, quietly, swinging his legs as he sat on my table. He was speaking in English now.

"He does not know anything. Would I speak to you if he did? Go on!"

"There is no going on at all. If you tell that to your friends they will say you are mad and put it in the papers. Suppose, now, you prosecute for libel."

"Let's leave that out of the question entirely. Is there any chance of his being made to speak?"

"There is a chance. Oah, yess! But *if* he spoke it would mean that all this world would end now—*instanto*—fall down on your head. These things are not allowed, you know. As I said, the door is shut."

"Not a ghost of a chance?"

"How can there be? You are a Christi-án, and it is forbidden to eat, in your books, of the Tree of Life, or else you would never die. How shall you all fear death if you all know what your friend does not know that he knows? I am afraid to be kicked, but I am not afraid to die, because I know what I know. You are not afraid to be kicked, but you are afraid to die. If you were not, by God! you English would be all over the shop in an hour, upsetting the balances of power, and making commotions. It would not be good. But no fear. He will remember a little and a little less, and he will call it dreams. Then he will forget altogether. When I passed my First Arts Examination in Calcutta that was all in the cram-book on Wordsworth. Trailing clouds of glory, you know."

"This seems to be an exception to the rule."

"There are no exceptions to rules. Some are not so hard-looking as others, but they are all the same when you touch. If this friend of yours said so-

and-so and so-and-so, indicating that he remembered all his lost lives, or one piece of a lost life, he would not be in the bank another hour. He would be what you called sack because he was mad, and they would send him to an asylum for lunatics. You can see that, my friend."

"Of course I can, but I wasn't thinking of him. His name need never appear in the story."

"Ah! I see. That story will never be written. You can try."

"I am going to."

"For your own credit and for the sake of money, of course?"

"No. For the sake of writing the story. On my honor that will be all."

"Even then there is no chance. You cannot play with the Gods. It is a very pretty story now. As they say, Let it go on that—I mean at that. Be quick; he will not last long."

"How do you mean?"

"What I say. He has never, so far, thought about a woman."

"Hasn't he though!" I remembered some of Charlie's confidences.

"I mean no woman has thought about him. When that comes; bus—hogya—all up!.... I know. There are millions of women here. Housemaids, for instance."

I winced at the thought of my story being ruined by a housemaid. And yet nothing was more probable.

Grish Chunder grinned.

"Yes—also pretty girls—cousins of his house, and perhaps not of his house. One kiss that he gives back again and remembers will cure all this nonsense, or else"—

"Or else what? Remember he does not know that he knows."

"I know that. Or else, if nothing happens he will become immersed in the trade and the financial speculations like the rest. It must be so. You can see that it must be so. But the woman will come first, I think."

There was a rap at the door, and Charlie charged in impetuously. He had been released from office, and by the look in his eyes I could see that he had come over for a long talk; most probably with poems in his pockets. Charlie's poems were very wearying, but sometimes they led him to talk about the galley.

Grish Chunder looked at him keenly for a minute.

"I beg your pardon," Charlie said, uneasily; "I didn't know you had any one with you."

"I am going," said Grish Chunder.

He drew me into the lobby as he departed.

"That is your man," he said, quickly. "I tell you he will never speak all you wish. That is rot—bosh. But he would be most good to make to see things. Suppose now we pretend that it was only play"—I had never seen Grish Chunder so excited—"and pour the ink-pool into his hand. Eh, what do you think? I tell you that he could see anything that a man could see. Let me get the ink and the camphor. He is a seer and he will tell us very many things."

"He may be all you say, but I'm not going to trust him to your gods and devils."

"It will not hurt him. He will only feel a little stupid and dull when he wakes up. You have seen boys look into the ink-pool before."

"That is the reason why I am not going to see it any more. You'd better go, Grish Chunder."

He went, declaring far down the staircase that it was throwing away my only chance of looking into the future.

This left me unmoved, for I was concerned for the past, and no peering of hypnotized boys into mirrors and ink-pools would help me to that. But I recognized Grish Chunder's point of view and sympathized with it.

"What a big black brute that was!" said Charlie, when I returned to him. "Well, look here, I've just done a poem; did it instead of playing dominoes after lunch. May I read it?"

"Let me read it to myself."

"Then you miss the proper expression. Besides, you always make my things sound as if the rhymes were all wrong."

"Read it aloud, then. You're like the rest of 'em."

Charlie mouthed me his poem, and it was not much worse than the average of his verses. He had been reading his books faithfully, but he was not pleased when I told him that I preferred my Longfellow undiluted with Charlie.

Then we began to go through the MS. line by line; Charlie parrying every objection and correction with:

"Yes, that may be better, but you don't catch what I'm driving at."

Charles was, in one way at least, very like one kind of poet.

There was a pencil scrawl at the back of the paper and "What's that?" I said.

"Oh that's not poetry at all. It's

some rot I wrote last night before I went to bed and it was too much bother to hunt for rhymes; so I made it a sort of blank verse instead."

Here is Charlie's "blank verse":

"We pulled for you when the wind was against us and the sails were low.
Will you never let us go?
We ate bread and onions when you took towns or ran aboard quickly when you were beaten back by the foe,
The captains walked up and down the deck in fair weather singing songs, but we were below,
We fainted with our chins on the oars and you did not see that we were idle for we still swung to and fro.
Will you never let us go?
The salt made the oar handles like sharkskin; our knees were cut to the bone with salt cracks; our hair was stuck to our foreheads; and our lips were cut to our gums and you whipped us because we could not row.
Will you never let us go?
But in a little time we shall run out of the portholes as the water runs along the oarblade, and though you tell the others to row after us you will never catch us till you catch the oar-thresh and tie up the winds in the belly of the sail. Aho!
Will you never let us go?"

"H'm. What's oar-thresh, Charlie?"

"The water washed up by the oars. That's the sort of song they might sing in the galley, y'know. Aren't you ever going to finish that story and give me some of the profits?"

"It depends on yourself. If you had only told me more about your hero in the first instance it might have been finished by now. You're so hazy in your notions."

"I only want to give you the general notion of it—the knocking about from place to place and the fighting and all that. Can't you fill in the rest yourself? Make the hero save a girl on a pirate-galley and marry her or do something."

"You're a really helpful collaborator. I suppose the hero went through some few adventures before he married."

"Well then, make him a very artful card—a low sort of man—a sort of political man who went about making treaties and breaking them—a black-haired chap who hid behind the mast when the fighting began."

"But you said the other day that he was red-haired."

"I couldn't have. Make him black-haired of course. You've no imagination."

Seeing that I had just discovered the entire principles upon which the half-memory falsely called imagination is based, I felt entitled to laugh, but forbore, for the sake of the tale.

"You're right. *You're* the man with imagination. A black-haired chap in a decked ship," I said.

"No, an open ship—like a big boat." This was maddening.

"Your ship has been built and designed, closed and decked in; you said so yourself," I protested.

"No, no, not that ship. That was open, or half decked because— By Jove you're right. You made me think of the hero as a red-haired chap. Of course if he were red, the ship would be an open one with painted sails."

Surely, I thought, he would remember now that he had served in two galleys at least—in a three-decked Greek one under the black-haired "political man," and again in a Viking's open sea-serpent under the man "red as a red bear" who

went to Markland. The devil prompted me to speak.

"Why, 'of course,' Charlie?" said I.

"I don't know. Are you making fun of me?"

The current was broken for the time being. I took up a notebook and pretended to make many entries in it.

"It's a pleasure to work with an imaginative chap like yourself," I said, after a pause. "The way that you've brought out the character of the hero is simply wonderful."

"Do you think so?" he answered, with a pleased flush. "I often tell myself that there's more in me than my mo—than people think."

"There's an enormous amount in you."

"Then, won't you let me send an essay on The Ways of Bank Clerks to *Tit-Bits*, and get the guinea prize?"

"That wasn't exactly what I meant, old fellow: perhaps it would be better to wait a little and go ahead with the galley-story."

"Ah, but I sha'n't get the credit of that. *Tit-Bits* would publish my name and address if I win. What are you grinning at? They *would*."

"I know it. Suppose you go for a walk. I want to look through my notes about our story."

Now this reprehensible youth who left me, a little hurt and put back, might for aught he or I knew have been one of the crew of the Argo—had been certainly slave or comrade to Thorfin Karlsefne. Therefore he was deeply interested in guinea competitions. Remembering what Grish Chunder had said I laughed aloud. The Lords of Life and Death would never allow

Charlie Mears to speak with full knowledge of his pasts, and I must even piece out what he had told me with my own poor inventions while Charlie wrote of the ways of bank-clerks.

I got together and placed on one file all my notes; and the net result was not cheering. I read them a second time. There was nothing that might not have been compiled at second-hand from other people's books—except, perhaps, the story of the fight in the harbor. The adventures of a Viking had been written many times before; the history of a Greek galley-slave was no new thing, and though I wrote both, who could challenge or confirm the accuracy of my details? I might as well tell a tale of two thousand years hence. The Lords of Life and Death were as cunning as Grish Chunder had hinted. They would allow nothing to escape that might trouble or make easy the minds of men. Though I was convinced of this, yet I could not leave the tale alone. Exaltation followed reaction, not once, but twenty times in the next few weeks. My moods varied with the March sunlight and flying clouds. By night or in the beauty of a spring morning I perceived that I could write that tale and shift continents thereby. In the wet, windy afternoons, I saw that the tale might indeed be written, but would be nothing more than a faked, false-varnished, sham-rusted piece of Wardour Street work at the end. Then I blessed Charlie in many ways—though it was no fault of his. He seemed to be busy with prize competitions, and I saw less and less of him as the weeks went by and the earth

cracked and grew ripe to spring, and the buds swelled in their sheaths. He did not care to read or talk of what he had read, and there was a new ring of self-assertion in his voice. I hardly cared to remind him of the galley when we met; but Charlie alluded to it on every occasion, always as a story from which money was to be made.

"I think I deserve twenty-five per cent., don't I, at least," he said, with beautiful frankness. "I supplied all the ideas, didn't I?"

This greediness for silver was a new side in his nature. I assumed that it had been developed in the City, where Charlie was picking up the curious nasal drawl of the underbred City man.

"When the thing's done we'll talk about it. I can't make anything of it at present. Red-haired or black-haired hero are equally difficult."

He was sitting by the fire staring at the red coals. "I can't understand what you find so difficult. It's all as clear as mud to me," he replied. A jet of gas puffed out between the bars, took light and whistled softly. "Suppose we take the red-haired hero's adventures first, from the time that he came south to my galley and captured it and sailed to the Beaches."

I knew better now than to interrupt Charlie. I was out of reach of pen and paper, and dared not move to get them lest I should break the current. The gas-jet puffed and whinnied, Charlie's voice dropped almost to a whisper, and he told a tale of the sailing of an open galley to Furdurstrandi, of sunsets on the open sea, seen under the curve of the one sail evening after evening when the galley's beak was notched into the centre of the sinking disc, and "we sailed by that for we had no other guide," quoth Charlie. He spoke of a landing on an island and explorations in its woods, where the crew killed three men whom they found asleep under the pines. Their ghosts, Charlie said, followed the galley, swimming and choking in the water, and the crew cast lots and threw one of their number overboard as a sacrifice to the strange gods whom they had offended. Then they ate sea-weed when their provisions failed, and their legs swelled, and their leader, the red-haired man, killed two rowers who mutinied, and after a year spent among the woods they set sail for their own country, and a wind that never failed carried them back so safely that they all slept at night. This, and much more Charlie told. Sometimes the voice fell so low that I could not catch the words, though every nerve was on the strain. He spoke of their leader, the red-haired man, as a pagan speaks of his God; for it was he who cheered them and slew them impartially as he thought best for thier needs; and it was he who steered them for three days among floating ice, each floe crowded with strange beasts that "tried to sail with us," said Charlie, "and we beat them back with the handles of the oars."

The gas-jet went out, a burned coal gave way, and the fire settled down with a tiny crash to the bottom of the grate. Charlie ceased speaking, and I said no word.

"By Jove!" he said, at last, shaking his head. "I've been staring at the fire till I'm dizzy. What was I going to say?"

"Something about the galley."

"I remember now. It's 25 per cent. of the profits, isn't it?"

"It's anything you like when I've done the tale."

"I wanted to be sure of that. I must go now. I've—I've an appointment." And he left me.

Had my eyes not been held I might have known that that broken muttering over the fire was the swan-song of Charlie Mears. But I thought it the prelude to fuller revelation. At last and at last I should cheat the Lords of Life and Death!

When next Charlie came to me I received him with rapture. He was nervous and embarrassed, but his eyes were very full of light, and his lips a little parted.

"I've done a poem," he said; and then, quickly: "it's the best I've ever done. Read it." He thrust it into my hand and retreated to the window.

I groaned inwardly. It would be the work of half an hour to criticise—that is to say praise—the poem sufficiently to please Charlie. Then I had good reason to groan, for Charlie, discarding his favorite centipede metres, had launched into shorter and choppier verse, and verse with a motive at the back of it. This is what I read:

"The day is most fair, the cheery wind
    Halloos behind the hill,
Where he bends the wood as seemeth good,
    And the sapling to his will!
Riot O wind; there is that in my blood
    That would not have thee still!

"She gave me herself, O Earth, O Sky;
    Grey sea, she is mine alone!
Let the sullen boulders hear my cry,
    And rejoice tho' they be but stone!

"Mine! I have won her O good brown
    earth,
Make merry! 'Tis hard on Spring;
Make merry; my love is doubly worth
All worship your fields can bring!
Let the hind that tills you feel my mirth
At the early harrowing."

"Yes, it's the early harrowing, past
a doubt," I said, with a dread at my
heart. Charlie smiled, but did not
answer.

"Red cloud of the sunset, tell it abroad;
    I am victor. Greet me O Sun,
Dominant master and absolute lord
    Over the soul of one!"

"Well?" said Charlie, looking over my
shoulder.

I thought it far from well, and very
evil indeed, when he silently laid a
photograph on the paper—the photograph of a girl with a curly head, and
a foolish slack mouth.

"Isn't it—isn't it wonderful?" he
whispered, pink to the tips of his ears,
wrapped in the rosy mystery of first
love. "I didn't know; I didn't think—
it came like a thunderclap."

"Yes. It comes like a thunderclap.
Are you very happy, Charlie?"

"My God—she—she loves me!" He
sat down repeating the last words to
himself. I looked at the hairless face,
the narrow shoulders already bowed by
desk-work, and wondered when, where,
and how he had loved in his past lives.

"What will your mother say?" I
asked, cheerfully.

"I don't care a damn what she says."

At twenty the things for which one
does not care a damn should, properly,
be many, but one must not include
mothers in the list. I told him this
gently; and he described Her, even as
Adam must have described to the newly
named beasts the glory and tenderness
and beauty of Eve. Incidentally I
learned that She was a tobacconist's
assistant with a weakness for pretty
dress, and had told him four or five
times already that She had never been
kissed by a man before.

Charlie spoke on, and on, and on;
while I, separated from him by thousands of years, was considering the beginnings of things. Now I understood
why the Lords of Life and Death shut
the doors so carefully behind us. It is
that we may not remember our first
wooings. Were it not so, our world
would be without inhabitants in a hundred years.

"Now, about that galley-story," I
said, still more cheerfully, in a pause
in the rush of the speech.

Charlie looked up as though he had
been hit. "The galley—what galley?
Good heavens, don't joke, man! This
is serious! You don't know how serious
it is!"

Grish Chunder was right. Charlie
had tasted the love of woman that
kills remembrance, and the finest story
in the world would never be written.

VOLUME IX

Under the Deodars

The Education of Otis Yeere

I

In the pleasant orchard-closes
"God bless all our gains," say we;
But "May God bless all our losses,"
Better suits with our degree.
—*The Lost Bower.*

THIS is the history of a failure; but the woman who failed said that it might be an instructive tale to put into print for the benefit of the younger generation. The younger generation does not want instruction, being perfectly willing to instruct if any one will listen to it. None the less, here begins the story where every right-minded story should begin, that is to say at Simla, where all things begin and many come to an evil end.

The mistake was due to a very clever woman making a blunder and not retrieving it. Men are licensed to stumble, but a clever woman's mistake is outside the regular course of Nature and Providence; since all good people know that a woman is the only infallible thing in this world, except Government Paper of the '79 issue, bearing interest at four and a half per cent. Yet, we have to remember that six consecutive days of rehearsing the leading part of *The Fallen Angel*, at the New Gaiety Theatre where the plaster is not yet properly dry, might have brought about an unhingement of spirits which, again, might have led to eccentricities.

Mrs. Hauksbee came to "The Foundry" to tiffin with Mrs. Mallowe, her one bosom friend, for she was in no sense "a woman's woman." And it was a woman's tiffin, the door shut to all the world; and they both talked *chiffons*, which is French for Mysteries.

"I've enjoyed an interval of sanity," Mrs. Hauksbee announced, after tiffin was over and the two were comfortably settled in the little writing-room that opened out of Mrs. Mallowe's bedroom.

"My dear girl, what has *he* done?" said Mrs. Mallowe, sweetly. It is noticeable that ladies of a certain age call each other "dear girl," just as commissioners of twenty-eight years' standing address their equals in the Civil List as "my boy."

"There's no *he* in the case. Who am I that an imaginary man should be always credited to me? Am I an Apache?"

"No, dear, but somebody's scalp is generally drying at your wigwam-door. Soaking, rather."

This was an allusion to the Hawley Boy, who was in the habit of riding all across Simla in the Rains, to call on Mrs. Hauksbee. That lady laughed.

"For my sins, the Aide at Tyrconnel last night told me off to The Mussuck. Hsh! Don't laugh. One of my most devoted admirers. When the duff came —some one really ought to teach them to make puddings at Tyrconnel—The Mussuck was at liberty to attend to me."

"Sweet soul! I know his appetite," said Mrs. Mallowe. "Did he, oh *did* he, begin his wooing?"

763

"By a special mercy of Providence, *no.* He explained his importance as a Pillar of the Empire. I didn't laugh."

"Lucy, I don't believe you."

"Ask Captain Sangar; he was on the other side. Well, as I was saying, The Mussuck dilated."

"I think I can see him doing it," said Mrs. Mallowe, pensively, scratching her fox-terrier's ears.

"I was properly impressed. Most properly. I yawned openly. 'Strict supervision, and play them off one against the other,' said The Mussuck, shoveling down his ice by *tureenfuls,* I assure you. *'That,* Mrs. Hauksbee, is the secret of our Government.'"

Mrs. Mallowe laughed long and merrily. "And what did you say?"

"Did you ever know me at loss for an answer yet? I said: 'So I have observed in my dealings with you.' The Mussuck swelled with pride. He is coming to call on me to-morrow. The Hawley Boy is coming too."

"'Strict supervision and play them off one against the other. *That,* Mrs. Hauksbee, is the secret of *our* Government.' And I dare say if we could get to The Mussuck's heart, we should find that he considers himself a man of the world."

"As he is of the other two things. I like The Mussuck, and I won't have you call him names. He amuses me."

"He has reformed you, too, by what appears. Explain the interval of sanity, and hit *Tim* on the nose with the paper-cutter, please. That dog is too fond of sugar. Do you take milk in yours?"

"No, thanks. Polly, I'm wearied of this life. It's hollow."

"Turn religious, then. I always said that Rome would be your fate."

"Only exchanging half a dozen *attachés* in red for one and in black, and if I fasted, the wrinkles would come and never, *never* go. Has it ever struck you, dear, that I'm getting old?"

"Thanks for your courtesy. I'll return it. Ye-es we are both not exactly —how shall I put it?"

"What we have been. 'I feel it in my bones,' as Mrs. Crossley says. Polly, I've wasted my life."

"As how?"

"Never mind how. I feel it. I want to be a Power before I die."

"Be a Power then. You've wits enough for anything—and beauty?"

Mrs. Hauksbee pointed a teaspoon straight at her hostess. "Polly, if you heap compliments on me life this, I shall cease to believe that you're a woman. Tell me how I am to be a Power."

"Inform The Mussuck that he is the most fascinating and slimmest man in Asia, and he'll tell you anything and everything you please."

"Bother The Mussuck! I mean an intellectual Power—not a gas-power. Polly, I'm going to start a *salon.*"

Mrs. Mallowe turned lazily on the sofa and rested her head on her hand. "Hear the words of the Preacher, the son of Baruch," she said.

"*Will* you talk sensibly?"

"I will, dear, for I see that you are going to make a mistake."

"I never made a mistake in my life —at least, never one that I couldn't explain away afterward."

"Going to make a mistake," went on Mrs. Mallowe, composedly. "It is impossible to start a *salon* in Simla. A bar would be much more to the point."

"Perhaps, but why? It seems so easy."

"Just what makes it so difficult. How many clever women are there in Simla."

"Myself and yourself," said Mrs. Hauksbee, without a moment's hesitation.

"Modest woman! Mrs. Feardon would thank you for that. And how many clever men?"

"Oh — er — hundreds," said Mrs. Hauksbee, vaguely.

"What a fatal blunder! Not one. They are all bespoke by the Government. Take my husband, for instance. Jack *was* a clever man, though I say so who shouldn't. Government has eaten him up. All his ideas and powers of conversation—he really used to be a good talker, even to his wife, in the old days—are taken from him by this —this kitchen-sink of a Government. That's the case with every man up here who is at work. I don't suppose a Russian convict under the knout is able to amuse the rest of his gang; and all our men-folk here are gilded convicts."

"But there are scores"—

"I know what you're going to say. Scores of idle men up on leave. I admit it, but they are all of two objectionable sets. The Civilian who'd be delightful if he had the military man's knowledge of the world and style, and the military man who'd be adorable if he had the Civilian's culture."

"Detestable word! *Have* Civilians culchaw? I never studied the breed deeply."

"Don't make fun of Jack's service. Yes. They're like the teapoys in the Lakka Bazar—good material but not polished. They can't help themselves, poor dears. A Civilian only begins to be tolerable after he has knocked about the world for fifteen years."

"And a military man?"

"When he has had the same amount of service. The young of both species are horrible. You would have scores of them in your *salon.*"

"I would *not!*" said Mrs. Hauksbee, fiercely. "I would tell the bearer to *darwaza band* them. I'd put their own colonels and commissioners at the door to turn them away. I'd give them to the Topsham girl to play with."

"The Topsham girl would be grateful for the gift. But to go back to the *salon.* Allowing that you had gathered all your men and women together, what would you do with them? Make them talk? They would all with one accord begin to flirt. Your *salon* would become a glorified Peliti's—a 'Scandal Point' by lamp-light."

"There's a certain amount of wisdom in that view."

"There's all the wisdom in the world in it. Surely, twelve Simla seasons ought to have taught you that you can't focus anything in India; and a *salon,* to be any good at all, must be permanent. In two seasons your roomful would be scattered all over Asia. We are only little bits of dirt on the hillsides—here one day and blown down the *khud* the next. We have lost the art of talking— at least our men have. We have no cohesion"—

"George Eliot in the flesh," interpolated Mrs. Hauksbee, wickedly.

"And collectively, my dear scoffer, we, men and women alike, have *no* influence.

Come into the veranda and look at the Mall!"

The two looked down on the now rapidly filling road, for all Simla was abroad to steal a stroll between a shower and a fog.

"How do you propose to fix that river? Look! There's The Mussack—head of goodness knows what. He is a power in the land, though he *does* eat like a costermonger. There's Colonel Blone, and General Grucher, and Sir Dugald Delane, and Sir Henry Haughton, and Mr. Jellalatty. All Heads of Departments, and all powerful."

"And all my fervent admirers," said Mrs. Hauksbee, piously. "Sir Henry Haughton raves about me. But go on."

"One by one, these men are worth something. Collectively, they're just a mob of Anglo-Indians. Who cares for what Anglo-Indians say? Your *salon* won't weld the Departments together and make you mistress of India, dear. And these creatures won't talk administrative 'shop' in a crowd—your *salon*—because they are so afraid of the men in the lower ranks overhearing it. They have forgotten what of Literature and Art they ever knew, and the women"—

"Can't talk about anything except the last Gymkhana, or the sins of their last nurse. I was calling on Mrs. Derwills this morning."

"You admit that? They can talk to the subalterns though, and the subalterns can talk to them. Your *salon* would suit their views admirably, if you respected the religious prejudices of the country and provided plenty of *kala juggahs.*"

"Plenty of *kala juggahs.* Oh my poor little idea! *Kala juggahs* in a *salon!* But who made you so awfully clever?"

"Perhaps I've tried myself; or perhaps I know a woman who has. I have preached and expounded the whole matter and the conclusion thereof"—

"You needn't go on. 'Is Vanity.' Polly, I thank you. These vermin"—Mrs. Hauksbee waved her hand from the veranda to two men in the crowd below who had raised their hats to her —"these vermin shall not rejoice in a new Scandal Point or an extra Peliti's. I will abandon the notion of a *salon.* It did seem so tempting, though. But what shall I do? I must do something."

"Why? Are not Abana and Pharphar"—

"Jack has made you nearly as bad as himself! I want to, of course. I'm tired of everything and everybody, from a moonlight picnic at Seepee to the blandishments of The Mussuck."

"Yes—that comes, too, sooner or later. Have you nerve enough to make your bow yet?"

Mrs. Hauksbee's mouth shut grimly. Then she laughed. "I think I see myself doing it. Big pink placards on the Mall: 'Mrs. Hauksbee! Positively her last appearance on *any* stage! This is to give notice!' No more dances; no more rides; no more luncheons; no more theatricals with supper to follow; no more sparring with one's dearest, dearest friend; no more fencing with an inconvenient man who hasn't wit enough to clothe what he's pleased to call his sentiments in passable speech; no more parading of The Mussuck while Mrs. Tarkass calls all round Simla, spreading horrible stories about me? No more

of anything that is thoroughly wearying, abominable and detestable, but, all
the same, makes life worth the having.
Yes! I see it all! Don't interrupt,
Polly, I'm inspired. A mauve and white
striped 'cloud' round my excellent shoulders, a seat in the fifth row of the
Gaiety, and *both* horses sold. Delightful vision! A comfortable armchair, sit-
uated in three different draughts, at
every ballroom; and nice, large, sensible shoes for all the couples to stumble
over as they go into the veranda! Then
at supper. Can't you imagine the scene?
The greedy mob gone away. Reluctant
subaltern, pink all over like a newly-
powdered baby,—they really ought to
tan subalterns before they are exported,
Polly—sent back by the hostess to do
his duty. Slouches up to me across the
room, tugging at a glove two sizes too
large for him—I *hate* a man who wears
gloves like overcoats—and trying to look
as if he'd thought of it from the first.
'May I ah-have the pleasure 'of takin'
you 'nt' supper?' Then I get up with
a hungry smile. Just like this."

"Lucy, how *can* you be so absurd?"

"And sweep out on his arm. So!
After supper I shall go away early, you
know, because I shall be afraid of
catching cold. No one will look for
my 'rickshaw. *Mine*, so please you! I
shall stand, always with that mauve and
white 'cloud' over my head, while the
wet soaks into my dear, old, venerable
feet and Tom swears and shouts for the
mem-sahib's gharri. Then home to bed
at half-past eleven! Truly excellent
life—helped out by the visits of the
Padri, just fresh from burying somebody
down below there." She pointed through
the pines, toword the Cemetery, and

continued with vigorous dramatic gesture—

"Listen! I see it all—down, down
even to the stays! *Such* stays! Six-
eight a pair, Polly, with red flannel—
or list is it?—that they put into the
tops of those fearful things. I can
draw you a picture of them."

"Lucy, for Heaven's sake, don't go
waving your arms about in that idiotic
manner! Recollect, every one can see
you from the Mall."

"Let them see! They'll think I am
rehearsing for *The Fallen Angel*. Look!
There's The Mussuck. How badly he
rides. There!"

She blew a kiss to the venerable Indian administrator with infinite grace.

"Now," she continued, "he'll be
chaffed about that at the Club in the
delicate manner those brutes of men
affect, and the Hawley Boy will tell me
all about it—softening the details for
fear of shocking me. That boy is too
good to live, Polly. I've serious thoughts
of recommending him to throw up his
Commission and go into the Church.
In his present frame of mind he would
obey me. Happy, happy child."

"Never again," said Mrs. Mallowe,
with an affectation of indignation, "shall
you tiffin here! 'Lucindy, your behavior
is scand'lus.' "

"All your fault," retorted Mrs. Hauksbee, "for suggesting such a thing as my
abdication. No! *Jamais*-nevaire! I
will act, dance, ride, frivol, talk scandal,
dine out, and appropriate the legitimate
captives of any woman I choose until i
d-r-r-rop or a better woman than I puts
me to shame before all Simla,—and it's
dust and ashes in my mouth while I'm
doing it!"

She swept into the drawing-room. Mrs. Mallowe followed and put an arm round her waist.

"I'm *not!*" said Mrs. Hauksbee, defiantly, rummaging for her handkerchief. "I've been dining out the last ten nights, and rehearsing in the afternoon. You'd be tired yourself. It's only because I'm tired."

Mrs. Mallowe did not offer Mrs. Hauksbee any pity or ask her to lie down, but gave her another cup of tea, and went on with the talk.

"I've been through that too, dear," she said.

"I remember," said Mrs. Hauksbee, a gleam of fun on her face. "In '84 wasn't it? You went out a great deal less next season."

Mrs. Mallowe smiled in a superior and Sphinx-like fashion.

"I became an Influence," said she.

"Good gracious, child, you didn't join the Theosophists and kiss Buddha's big toe, did you? I tried to get into their set once, but they cast me out for a skeptic—without a chance of improving my poor little mind, too."

"No, I didn't Theosophilander. Jack says"—

"Never mind Jack. What a husband says is known before. What did you do?"

"I made a lasting impression."

"So have I—for four months. But that didn't console me in the least. I hated the man. *Will* you stop smiling in that inscrutable way and tell me what you mean?"

Mrs. Mallowe told.

*   *   *   *   *

"And—you—mean—to—say that it is absolutely Platonic on both sides?"

"Absolutely, or I should never have taken it up."

"And his last promotion was due to you?"

Mrs. Mallowe nodded.

"And you warned him against the Topsham girl?"

Another nod.

"And told him of Sir Dugald Delane's private memo about him?"

A third nod.

"*Why?*"

"What a question to ask a woman! Because it amused me at first. I am proud of my property now. If I live he shall continue to be successful. Yes, I will put him upon the straight road to Knighthood, and everything else that a man values. The rest depends upon himself."

"Polly, you are a most extraordinary woman."

"Not in the least. I'm concentrated, that's all. You diffuse yourself, dear; and though all Simla knows your skill in managing a team"—

"Can't you choose a prettier word?"

"*Team,* of half a dozen, from The Mussuck to the Hawley Boy, you gain nothing by it. Not even amusement."

"And you?"

"Try my recipe. Take a man, not a boy, mind, but an almost mature, unattached man, and be his guide phisosopher, and friend. You'll find it *the* most interesting occupation that you ever embarked on. It can be done—you needn't look like that—because I've done it."

"There's an element of risk about it that makes the notion attractive. I'll get such a man and say to him. 'Now, understand that there must be no flirtation. Do exactly what I tell you, profit by my instruction and counsels, and all will yet be well.' Is that the idea?"

"More or less," said Mrs. Mallowe, with an unfathomable smile. "But be sure he understands."

II

Dribble-dribble—trickle-trickle—
What a lot of raw dust!
My dollie's had an accident
And out came all the sawdust!
                    —*Nursery Rhyme.*

So Mrs. Hauksbee, in "The Foundry" which overlooks Simla Mall, sat at the feet of Mrs. Mallowe and gathered wisdom. The end of the Conference was the Great Idea upon which Mrs. Hauksbee so plumed herself.

"I warn you," said Mrs. Mallowe, beginning to repent of her suggestion, "that the matter is not half so easy as it looks. Any woman—even the Topsham girl—can catch a man, but very, very few know how to manage him when caught."

"My child," was the answer, "I've been a female St. Simon Stylites looking down upon men for these—these years past. Ask The Mussuck whether I can manage them."

Mrs. Hauksbee departed humming, "*I'll go to him and say to him in manner most ironical.*" Mrs. Mallowe laughed to herself. Then she grew suddenly sober. "I wonder whether I've done well in advising that amusement? Lucy's a clever woman, but a thought too careless."

A week later, the two met at a Monday Pop. "Well?" said Mrs. Mallowe. "I've caught him!" said Mrs. Hauksbee; her eyes were dancing with merriment.

"Who is it, mad woman? I'm sorry I ever spoke to you about it."

"Look between the pillars. In the third row; fourth from the end. You can see his face now. Look!"

"Otis Yeere! Of *all* the improbable and impossible people!! I don't believe you."

"Hsh! Wait till Mrs. Tarkass begins murdering Milton Wellings; and I'll tell you all about it. *S-s-ss!* That woman's voice always reminds me of an Underground train coming into Earl's Court with the breaks on. Now listen. It is *really* Otis Yeere."

"So I see, but does it follow that he is your property."

"He *is!* By right of trove. I found him, lonely and unbefriended, the very next night after our talk, at the Dugald Delane's *burra-khana*. I liked his eyes, and I talked to him. Next day he called. Next day we went for a ride together, and to-day he's tied to my *'rickshaw*-wheels hand and foot. You'll see when the concert's over. He doesn't know I'm here yet."

"Thank goodness you haven't chosen a boy. What are you going to do with him, assuming that you've got him?"

"Assuming, indeed! Does a woman—do *I*—ever make a mistake in that sort of thing? First"—Mrs. Hauksbee ticked off the items ostentatiously on her little gloved fingers—"First, my dear, I shall dress him properly. At present his raiment is a disgrace, and he wears a dress-shirt like a crumpled sheet of the *Pioneer*. Secondly, after I have made him presentable, I shall form his manners—his morals are above reproach."

"You seem to have discovered a great deal about him considering the shortness of your acquaintance."

"Surely *you* ought to know that the first proof a man gives of his interest in a woman is by talking to her about his own sweet self. If the woman listens without yawning, he begins to like her. If she flatters the animal's vanity, he ends by adoring her."

"In some cases."

"Never mind the exceptions. I know which one you are thinking of. Thirdly, and lastly, after he is polished and made pretty, I shall, as you said, be his guide, philosopher and friend, and he shall become a success—as great a success as your friend. I always wondered how that man got on. *Did* The Mussuck come to you with the Civil List and, dropping on one knee—no, two knees, *à la Gibbon*—hand it to you and say, 'Adorable angel, choose your friend's appointment'?"

"Lucy, your long experiences of the Military Department have demoralized you. One doesn't do that sort of thing on the Civil Side."

"No disrespect meant to Jack's Service, my dear. I only asked for information. Give me three months, and see what changes I shall work in my prey."

"Go your own way since you must. But I'm sorry that I was weak enough to suggest the amusement."

" 'I am all discretion, and may be trusted to an in-fin-ite extent,' " quoted Mrs. Hauksbee from *The Fallen Angel;* and the conversation ceased with Mrs. Tarkass's last, long-drawn war-whoop.

Her bitterest enemies—and she had many—could hardly accuse Mrs. Hauksbee of wasting her time. Otis Yeere was one of those wandering "dumb" characters, foredoomed through life to be nobody's property. Ten years in Her Majesty's Bengal Civil Service, spent, for the most part, in undesirable Districts, had given him little to be proud of, and nothing to bring confidence. Old enough to have lost the first fine careless rapture that showers on the immature 'Stunt imaginary Commissionerships and Stars, and sends him into the collar with coltish earnestness and abandon; too young to be yet able to look back upon the progress he had made, and thank Providence that under the conditions of the day he had come even so far, he stood upon the dead-centre of his career. And when a man stands still, he feels the slightest impulse from without. Fortune had ruled that Otis Yeere should be, for the first part of his service, one of the rank and file who are ground up in the wheels of the Administration; losing heart and soul, and mind and strength, in the process. Until steam replaces manual power in the working of the Empire, there must always be this percentage—must always be the men who are used up, expended, in the mere mechanical routine. For these promotion is far off and the mill-grind of every day very instant. The Secretariats know them only by name; they are not the picked men of the Districts with Divisions and Collectorates awaiting them. They are simply the rank and file—the food for fever—sharing with the *ryot* and the plough-bullock the honor of being the plinth on which the State rests. The older ones have lost their aspirations; the younger are putting theirs aside with a sigh. Both learn to endure patiently until the end of the day. Twelve years in the rank and file, men say, will sap the hearts of the bravest and dull the wits of the most keen.

Out of this life Otis Yeere had fled for a few months; drifting, in the hope of a little masculine society, into Simla. When his leave was over he would return to his swampy, sour-green, under-manned Bengal district; to the native Assistant, the native Doctor, the native Magistrate, the steaming, sweltering Station, the ill-kempt City, and the undisguised insolence of the Municipality that babbled away the lives of men. Life was cheap however. The soil spawned humanity, as it bred frogs in the Rains, and the gap of the sickness of one season was filled to overflowing by the fecundity of the next. Otis was unfeignedly thankful to lay down his work for a little while and escape from the seething, whining, weakly hive, impotent to help itself, but strong in its power to cripple, thwart, and annoy the sunken-eyed man who, by official irony was said to be "in charge" of it.

*   *   *   *   *

"I knew there were women-dowdies in Bengal. They come up here sometimes. But I didn't know that there were men-dowds, too."

Then, for the first time, it occurred to Otis Yeere that his clothes wore the mark of the ages. It will be seen that his friendship with Mrs. Hauksbee had made great strides.

As that lady truthfully says, a man is never so happy as when he is talking about himself. From Otis Yeere's lips Mrs. Hauksbee, before long, learned everything that she wished to know about the subject of her experiment:

learned what manner of life he had led in what she vaguely called "those awful cholera districts"; learned too, but this knowledge came later, what manner of life he had purposed to lead and what dreams he had dreamed in the year of grace '77, before the reality had knocked the heart out of him. Very pleasant are the shady bridle-paths round Prospect Hill for the telling of such confidences.

"Not yet," said Mrs. Hauksbee to Mrs. Mallowe. "Not yet. I must wait until the man is properly dressed, at least. Great Heavens, is it possible that he doesn't know what an honor it is to be taken up by *Me!*"

Mrs. Hauksbee did not reckon false modesty as one of her failings.

"Always with Mrs. Hauksbee!" murmured Mrs. Mallowe, with her sweetest smile, to Otis. "Oh you men, you men! Here are our Punjabis growling because you've monopolized the nicest woman in Simla. They'll tear you to pieces on the Mall, some day, Mr. Yeere."

Mrs. Mallowe rattled down-hill, having satisfied herself, by a glance through the fringe of her sunshade, of the effect of her words.

The shot went home. Of a surety Otis Yeere was somebody in this bewildering whirl of Simla—had monopolized the nicest woman in it and the Punjabis were growling. The notion justified a mild glow of vanity. He had never looked upon his acquaintance with Mrs. Hauksbee as a matter for general interest.

The knowledge of envy was a pleasant feeling to the man of no account. It was intensified later in the day when a luncher at the Club said, spitefully, "Well, for a debilitated Ditcher, Yeere you *are* going it. Hasn't any kind friend told you that she's the most dangerous woman in Simla?"

Yeere chuckled and passed out. When, oh when, would his new clothes be ready? He descended into the Mall to inquire; and Mrs. Hauksbee, coming over the Church Ridge in her *'rickshaw*, looked down upon him approvingly. "He's learning to carry himself as if he were a man, instead of a piece of furniture,—and," she screwed up her eyes to see the better through the sunlight—"he *is* a man when he holds himself like that. Oh blessed Conceit, what should we be without you?"

With the new clothes came a new stock of self-confidence. Otis Yeere discovered that he could enter a room without breaking into a gentle perspiration—could cross one, even to talk to Mrs. Hauksbee, as though rooms were meant to be crossed. He was for the first time in nine years proud of himself, and contented with his life, satisfied with his new clothes, and rejoicing in the friendship of Mrs. Hauksbee.

"Conceit is what the poor fellow wants," she said in confidence to Mrs. Mallowe. "I believe they must use Civilians to plough the fields with in Lower Bengals. You see I have to begin from the very beginning—haven't I? But you'll admit, won't you, dear, that he is immensely improved since I took him in hand. Only give me a little more time and he won't know himself."

Indeed, Yeere was rapidly beginning to forget what he had been. One of his own rank and file put the matter brutally when he asked Yeere, in reference to nothing, "And who has been making *you* a Member of Council, lately? You

carry the side of half a dozen of 'em."

"I—I'm awf'ly sorry. I didn't mean it, you know," said Yeere, apologetically.

"There'll be no holding you," continued the old stager, grimly. "Climb down, Otis—climb down, and get all that beastly affectation knocked out of you with fever! Three thousand a month wouldn't support it."

Yeere repeated the incident to Mrs. Hauksbee. He had come to look upon her as his Mother Confessor.

"And you apologized!" she said. "Oh, shame! I *hate* a man who apologizes. Never apologize for what your friend called 'side.' *Never!* It's a man's business to be insolent and overbearing until he meets with a stronger. Now, you bad boy, listen to me."

Simply and straightforwardly, as the *'rickshaw* loitered round Jakko, Mrs. Hauksbee preached to Otis Yeere the Great Gospel of Conceit, illustrating it with living pictures encountered during their Sunday afternoon stroll.

"Good gracious!" she ended, with the personal argument, "you'll apologize next for being my *attaché?*"

"Never!" said Otis Yeere. "That's another thing altogether. I shall always be"—

"What's coming?" thought Mrs. Hauksbee.

"Proud of that," said Otis.

"Safe for the present," she said to herself.

"But I'm afraid I have grown conceited. Like Jeshurun, you know. When he waxed fat, then he kicked. It's the having no worry on one's mind and the Hill air, I suppose."

"Hill air, indeed!" said Mrs. Hauksbee to herself. "He'd have been hiding in the Club till the last day of his leave, if I hadn't discovered him." And aloud—

"Why shouldn't you be? You have every right to."

"I! Why?"

"Oh, hundreds of things. I'm not going to waste this lovely afternoon by explaining; but I know you have. What was that heap of manuscript you showed me about the grammar of the aboriginal —what's their names?"

"*Gullals.* A piece of nonsense. I've far too much work to do to bother over *Gullals* now. You should see my District. Come down with your husband some day and I'll show you round. Such a lovely place in the Rains! A sheet of water with the railway-embankment and the snakes sticking out, and, in the summer, green flies and green squash. The people would die of fear if you shook a dogwhip at 'em. But they know you're forbidden to do that, so they conspire to make your life a burden to you. My District's worked by some man at Darjiling, on the strength of a native pleader's false reports. Oh, it's a heavenly place!"

Otis Yeere laughed bitterly.

"There's not the least necessity that you should stay in it. Why do you?"

"Because I must. How'm I to get out of it?"

"How! In a hundred and fifty ways. If there weren't so many people on the road, I'd like to box your ears. Ask, my dear boy, *ask!* Look! There is young Hexarly with six years' service and half your talents. He asked for what he wanted, and he got it. See, down by the Convent! There's McAr-

thurson who has come to his present position by asking—sheer, downright asking—after he had pushed himself out of the rank and file. One man is as good as another in your service—believe me. I've seen Simla for more seasons than I care to think about. Do you suppose men are chosen for appointments because of their special fitness *beforehand?* You have all passed a high test—what do you call it?—in the beginning, and, except for the few who have gone altogether to the bad, you can all work hard. Asking does the rest. Call it cheek, call it insolence, call it anything you like, but *ask!* Men argue— yes, I know what men say—that a man, by the mere audacity of his request, *must* have some good in him. A weak man doesn't say: 'Give me this and that.' He whines: 'Why haven't I been given this and that?' If you were in the Army, I should say learn to spin plates or play a tambourine with your toes. As it is—*ask!* You belong to a Service that ought to be able to command the Channel Fleet, or set a leg at twenty minutes' notice, and *yet* you hesitate over asking to escape from a squashy green district where you admit you are not master. Drop the Bengal Government altogether. Even Darjiling is a little out-of-the-way hole. I was there once, and the rents were extortionate. Assert yourself. Get the Government of India to take you over. Try to get on the Frontier, where *every* man has a grand chance if he can trust himself. *Go* somewhere! *Do* something! You have twice the wits and three times the presence of the men up here, and, and"—Mrs. Hauksbee paused for breath; then continued—

"and in *any* way you look at it, you *ought* to. *You* who could go so far!"

"I don't know," said Yeere, rather taken aback by the unexpected eloquence. "I haven't such a good opinion of myself."

It was not strictly Platonic, but it was Policy. Mrs. Hauksbee laid her hand lightly upon the ungloved paw that rested on the turned-backed 'rickshaw hood, and, looking the man full in the face, said tenderly, almost too tenderly, "*I* believe in you if you mistrust yourself. Is that enough, my friend?"

"It is enough," answered Otis, very solemnly.

He was silent for a long time, redreaming the dreams that he had dreamed eight years ago, but through them all ran, as sheet-lightning through golden cloud, the light of Mrs. Hauksbee's violet eyes.

Curious and impenetrable are the mazes of Simla life—the only existence in this desolate land worth the living. Gradually it went abroad among men and women, in the pauses between dance, play and Gymkhana, that Otis Yeere, the man with the newly-lit light of self-confidence in his eyes, had "done something decent" in the wilds whence he came. He had brought an erring Municipality to reason, appropriated the funds on his own responsibility, and saved the lives of hundreds. He knew more about the *Gullals* than any living man. Had a vast knowledge of the aboriginal tribes; was, in spite of his juniority, the greatest authority on the aboriginal *Gullals*. No one quite knew who or what the *Gullals* were till The Mussuck, who had been calling on Mrs. Hauksbee, and prided himself upon picking peoples's brains, explained they were a tribe of ferocious hillmen, somewhere near Sikkim, whose friendship even the Great Indian Empire would find it worth her while to secure. Now we know that Otis Yeere had showed Mrs. Hauksbee his MS notes of six years' standing on the same *Gullals*. He had told her, too, how, sick and shaken with the fever their negligence had bred, crippled by the loss of his pet clerk, and savagely angry at the desolation in his charge, he had once damned the collective eyes of his "intelligent local board" for a set of *haramzadas*. Which act of "brutal and tyrannous oppression" won him a Reprimand Royal from the Bengal Government; but in the anecdote as amended for Northern consumption we find no record of this. Hence we are forced to conclude that Mrs. Hauksbee edited his reminiscences before sowing them in idle ears, ready, as she well knew, to exaggerate good or evil. And Otis Yeere bore himself as befitted the hero of many tales.

"You can talk to *me* when you don't fall into a brown study. Talk now, and talk your brightest and best," said Mrs. Hauksbee.

Otis needed no spur. Look to a man who has the counsel of a woman of or above the world to back him. So long as he keeps his head, he can meet both sexes on equal ground—an advantage never intended by Providence, who fashioned Man on one day and Woman on another, in sign that neither should know more than a very little of the other's life. Such a man goes far, or, the counsel being withdrawn, collapses suddenly while his world seeks the reason.

Generalled by Mrs. Hauksbee, who,

again, had all Mrs. Mallowe's wisdom at her disposal, proud of himself and, in the end, believing in himself because he was believed in, Otis Yeere stood ready for any fortune that might befall, certain that it would be good. He would fight for his own hand, and intended that this second struggle should lead to better issue than the first helpless surrender of the bewildered 'Stunt.

What might have happened, it is impossible to say. This lamentable thing befell, bred directly by a statement of Mrs. Hauksbee that she would spend the next season in Darjiling.

"Are you certain of that?" said Otis Yeere.

"Quite. We're writing about a house now."

Otis Yeere "stopped dead," as Mrs. Hauksbee put it in discussing the relapse with Mrs. Mallowe.

"He has behaved," she said, angrily, "just like Captain Kerrington's pany—only Otis is a donkey—at the last Gymkhana. Planted his forefeet and refused to go on another step. Polly, my man's going to disappoint me. What shall I do?"

As a rule, Mrs. Mallowe does not approve of staring, but on this occasion she opened her eyes to the utmost.

"You have managed cleverly so far," she said. "Speak to him, and ask him what he means."

"I will—at to-night's dance."

"No—o, not at a dance," said Mrs. Mallowe, cautiously. "Men are never themselves quite at dances. Better wait till to-morrow morning."

"Nonsense. If he's going to 'vert in this insane way, there isn't a day to lose. Are you going? No? Then sit up for me, there's a dear. I shan't stay longer than supper under any circumstances."

Mrs. Mallowe waited through the evening, looking long and earnestly into the fire, and sometimes smiling to herself.

* * * * *

"Oh! oh! oh! The man's an idiot! A raving, positive idiot! I'm sorry I ever saw him!"

Mrs. Hauksbee burst into Mrs. Mallowe's house, at midnight, almost in tears.

"What in the world has happened?" said Mrs. Mallowe, but her eyes showed that she had guessed an answer.

"Happened! Everything has happened! He was there. I went to him and said, 'Now, what does this nonsense mean?' Don't laugh, dear, I can't bear it. But you know what I mean I said. Then it was a square, and I sat it out with him and wanted an explanation, and *he* said— Oh! I haven't patience with such idiots! You know what I said about going to Darjiling next year? It doesn't matter to me *where* I go. I'd have changed the Station and lost the rent to have saved this. He said, in so many words, that he wasn't going to try to work up any more, because— because he would be shifted into a province away from Darjiling, and his own District, where these creatures are, is within a day's journey"—

"Ah—hh!" said Mrs. Mallowe, in a tone of one who has successfully tracked an obscure word through a large dictionary.

"Did you ever *hear* of anything so mad—so absurd? And he had the ball at his feet. He had only to kick it! I would have made him *anything!* Anything in the wide world. He could have gone to the world's end. I would have helped him. I made him, didn't I, Polly? Didn't I *create* that man? Doesn't he owe everything to me? And to reward me, just when everything was nicely arranged, by this lunacy that spoiled everything!"

"Very few men understand your devotion thoroughly."

"Oh, Polly, *don't* laugh at me! I give men up from this hour. I could have killed him then and there. What *right* had this man—this *Thing* I had picked out of his filthy paddy-fields—to make love to me?"

"He did that, did he?"

"He did. I don't remember half he said, I was so angry. .Oh, but such a funny thing happened! I can't help laughing at it now, though I felt nearly ready to cry with rage. He raved and I stormed—I'm afraid we must have made an awful noise in our *kala juggah*. Protect my character, dear, if it's all over Simla by to-morrow—and then he bobbed forward in the middle of this insanity—I *firmly* believe the man's demented—and kissed me!"

"Morals above reproach," purred Mrs. Mallowe.

"So they were—so they are! It was the most absurd kiss. I don't believe he'd ever kissed a woman in his life before. I threw my head back, and it was a sort of slidy, pecking dab, just on the end of the chin—here." Mrs. Hauksbee tapped her masculine little chin with her fan. "Then, of course, I was *furiously* angry, and told him that he was no gentleman, and I was sorry I'd ever met him, and so on. He was

crushed so easily that I couldn't be *very* angry. Then I came away straight to you."

"Was this before or after supper?"

"Oh! before—oceans before. Isn't it perfectly disgusting?"

"Let me think. I withhold judgment till to-morrow. Morning brings counsel."

But morning brought only a servant with a dainty bouquet of Annandale roses for Mrs. Hauksbee to wear at the dance at Viceregal Lodge that night."

"He doesn't seem to be very penitent," said Mrs. Mallowe. "What's the *billet-doux* in the centre?"

Mrs. Hauksbee opened the neatly folded note,—another accomplishment that she had taught Otis,—read it, and groaned tragically.

"Last wreck of a feeble intellect! Poetry! Is it his own, do you think? Oh, that I ever built my hopes on such a maudlin idiot!"

"No. It's a quotation from Mrs. Browning, and, in view of the facts of the case, as Jack says, uncommonly well chosen. Listen—

" 'Sweet thou has trod on a heart,
    Pass! There's a world full of men;
And women as fair as thou art,
    Must do such things now and then.

" 'Thou only hast stepped unaware—
    Malice not one can impute;
And why should a heart have been there,
    In the way of a fair woman's
        foot?' "

"I didn't—I didn't—I didn't!"—said Mrs. Hauksbee, angrily, her eyes filling with tears; "there was no malice at all. Oh, it's *too* vexatious!"

"You've misunderstood the compliment," said Mrs. Mallowe. "He clears you completely and—ahem—I should think by this, that *he* has cleared completely too. My experience of men is that when they begin to quote poetry, they are going to flit. Like swans singing before they die, you know."

"Polly, you take my sorrows in a most unfeeling way."

"Do I? Is it so terrible? If he's hurt your vanity, I should say that you've done a certain amount of damage to his heart."

"Oh, you never can tell about a man!" said Mrs. Hauksbee.

At the Pit's Mouth

Men say it was a stolen tide—
  The Lord that sent it he knows all,
But in mine ear will aye abide
  The message that the bells let fall,
And awesome bells they were to me,
That in the dark rang, "Enderby."
        —Jean Ingelow.

ONCE upon a time there was a man and his Wife and a Tertium Quid.

All three were unwise, but the Wife was the unwisest. The Man should have looked after his Wife, who should have avoided the Tertium Quid, who, again, should have married a wife of his own, after clean and open flirtations, to which nobody can possibly object, round Jakko or Observatory Hill. When you see a young man with his pony in a white lather, and his hat on the back of his head flying down-hill at fifteen miles an hour to meet a girl who will be properly surprised to meet him, you naturally approve of that young man, and wish him Staff Appointments, and take an interest in his welfare, and, as the proper time comes, give them sugar-tongs or side-saddles according to your means and generosity.

The Tertium Quid flew down-hill on horseback, but it was to meet the Man's Wife; and when he flew up-hill it was for the same end. The Man was in the Plains, earning money for his Wife to spend on dresses and four-hundred-rupee bracelets, and inexpensive luxuries of that kind. He worked very hard, and sent her a letter or a post-card daily. She also wrote to him daily, and said that she was longing for him to come up to Simla. The Tertium Quid used to lean over her shoulder and laugh as she wrote the notes. Then the two would ride to the Post Office together.

Now, Simla is a strange place and its customs are peculiar; nor is any man who has not spent at least ten seasons there qualified to pass judgment on circumstantial evidence, which is the most untrustworthy in the Courts. For these reasons, and for others which need not appear, I decline to state positively whether there was anything irretrievably wrong in the relations between the Man's Wife and the Tertium Quid. If there was, and hereon you must form your own opinion, it was the Man's Wife's fault. She was kittenish in her manners, wearing generally an air of soft and fluffy innocence. But she was deadlily learned and evil-instructed; and, now and again, when the mask dropped, men saw this, shuddered and—almost drew back. Men are occasionally particular, and the least particular men are always the most exacting.

Simla is eccentric in its fashion of treating friendships. Certain attachments which have set and crystallized through half a dozen seasons acquire almost the sanctity of the marriage bond, and are revered as such. Again, certain attachments equally old, and, to all appearance, equally venerable, never seem to win any recognized official status; while a chance-sprung acquaintance not two months born, steps into the place which by right belongs to the senior. There is no law reducible to print which regulates these affairs.

Some people have a gift which secures them infinite toleration, and others have not. The Man's Wife had not. If she looked over the garden wall, for instance, women taxed her with stealing their husbands. She complained pathetically that she was not allowed to choose her own friends. When she put up her big white muff to her lips, and gazed over it and under her eyebrows at you as she said this thing, you felt that she had been infamously misjudged, and that all the other women's instincts were all wrong; which was absurd. She was not allowed to own the Tertium Quid in peace; and was so strangely constructed that she would not have enjoyed peace had she been so permitted. She preferred some semblance of intrigue to cloak even her most commonplace actions.

After two months of riding, first round Jakko, then Elysium, then Summer Hill, then Observatory Hill, then under Jutogh, and lastly up and down the Cart Road as far as the Tara Devi gap in the dusk, she said to the Tertium Quid, "Frank, people say we are too much together, and people are so horrid."

The Tertium Quid pulled his moustache, and replied that horrid people were unworthy of the consideration of nice people.

"But they have done more than talk—they have written—written to my hubby—I'm sure of it," said the Man's Wife, and she pulled a letter from her husband out of her saddle-pocket and gave it to the Tertium Quid.

It was an honest letter, written by an honest man, then stewing in the Plains on two hundred rupees a month (for he allowed his wife eight hundred and fifty), and in a silk banian and cotton trousers. It is said that, perhaps, she had not thought of the unwisdom of allowing her name to be so generally coupled with the Tertium Quid's; that she was too much of a child to understand the dangers of that sort of thing; that he, her husband, was the last man in the world to interfere jealously with her little amusements and interests, but that it would be better were she to drop the Tertium Quid quietly and for her husband's sake. The letter was sweetened with many pretty little pet names, and it amused the Tertium Quid considerably. He and She laughed over it, so that you, fifty yards away, could see their shoulders shaking while the horses slouched along side by side.

Their conversation was not worth reporting. The upshot of it was that, next day, no one saw the Man's Wife and the Tertium Quid together. They had both gone down to the Cemetery, which, as a rule, is only visited officially by the inhabitants of Simla.

A Simla funeral with the clergyman riding, the mourners riding, and the coffin creaking as it swings between the bearers, is one of the most depressing things on this earth, particularly when the procession passes under the wet, dank dip beneath the Rockcliffe Hotel, where the sun is shut out, and all the hill streams are wailing and weeping together as they go down the valleys.

Occasionally, folk tend the graves, but we in India shift and are transferred so often that, at the end of the second year, the Dead have no friends—only acquaintances who are far too busy amusing themselves up the hill to attend to old partners. The idea of using a Cemetery as a rendezvous is distinctly a feminine one. A man would have said simply "Let people talk. We'll go down the Mall." A woman is made differently, especially if she be such a woman as the Man's Wife. She and the Tertium Quid enjoyed each other's society among the graves of men and women whom they had known and danced with aforetime.

They used to take a big horse-blanket and sit on the grass a little to the left of the lower end, where there is a dip in the ground, and where the occupied graves stop short and the ready-made ones are not ready. Each well-regulated Indian Cemetery keeps half a dozen graves permanently open for contingencies and incidental wear and tear. In the Hills these are more usually baby's size, because children who come up

weakened and sick from the Plains often succumb to the effects of the Rains in the Hills or get pneumonia from their *ayahs* taking them through damp pine-woods after the sun has set. In Cantonments, of course, the man's size is more in request; these arrangements varying with the climate and population.

One day when the Man's Wife and the Tertium Quid had just arrived in the Cemetery, they saw some coolies breaking ground. They had marked out a full-size grave, and the Tertium Quid asked them whether any *Sahib* was sick. They said that they did not know; but it was an order that they should dig a *Sahib's* grave.

"Work away," said the Tertium Quid, "and let's see how it's done."

The coolies worked away, and the Man's Wife and the Tertium Quid watched and talked for a couple of hours while the grave was being deepened. Then a coolie, taking the earth in blankets as it was thrown up, jumped over the grave.

"That's queer," said the Tertium Quid. "Where's my ulster?"

"What's queer?" said the Man's Wife.

"I have got a chill down my back— just as if a goose had walked over my grave."

"Why do you look at the thing, then?" said the Man's Wife. "Let us go."

The Tertium Quid stood at the head of the grave, and stared without answering for a space. Then he said, dropping a pebble down, "It is nasty—and cold; horribly cold. I don't think I shall come to the Cemetery any more. I don't think grave-digging is cheerful."

The two talked and agreed that the

Cemetery was depressing. They also arranged for a ride next day out from the Cemetery through the Mashobra Tunnel up to Fagoo and back, because all the world was going to a garden-party at Viceregal Lodge, and all the people of Mashobra would go too.

Coming up the Cemetery road, the Tertium Quid's horse tried to bolt up-hill, being tired with standing so long, and managed to strain a back sinew.

"I shall have to take the mare to-morrow," said the Tertium Quid, "and she will stand nothing heavier than a snaffle."

They made their arrangements to meet in the Cemetery, after allowing all the Mashobra people time to pass into Simla. That night it rained heavily, and next day, when the Tertium Quid came to the trysting-place, he saw that the new grave had a foot of water in it, the ground being a tough and sour clay.

"'Jove! That looks beastly," said the Tertium Quid. "Fancy being boarded up and dropped into that well!"

They then started off to Fagoo, the mare playing with the snaffle and picking her way as though she were shod with satin, and the sun shining divinely. The road below Mashobra to Fagoo is officially styled the Himalayan-Thibet Road; but in spite of its name it is not much more than six feet wide in most places, and the drop into the valley below must be anything between one and two thousand feet.

"Now we're going to Thibet," said the Man's Wife merrily, as the horses drew near to Fagoo. She was riding on the cliff-side.

"Into Thibet," said the Tetium Quid,

"ever so far from people who say horrid things, and hubbies who write stupid letters. With you—to the end of the world!"

A coolie carrying a log of wood came round a corner, and the mare went wide to avoid him—forefeet in and haunches out, as a sensible mare should go.

"To the world's end," said the Man's Wife, and looked unspeakable things over her near shoulder at the Tertium Quid.

He was smiling, but, while she looked, the smile froze stiff as it were on his face, and changed to a nervous grin—the sort of grin men wear when they are not quite easy in their saddles. The mare seemed to be sinking by the stern, and her nostrils cracked while she was trying to realize what was happening. The rain of the night before had rotted the drop-side of the Himalayan-Thibet Road, and it was giving way under her. "What are you doing?" said the Man's Wife. The Tertium Quid gave no answer. He grinned nervously and set his spurs into the mare, who rapped with her forefeet on the road, and the struggle began. The Man's Wife screamed, "Oh, Frank, get off!"

But the Tertium Quid was glued to the saddle—his face blue and white—and he looked into the Man's Wife's eyes. Then the Man's Wife clutched at the mare's head and caught her by the nose instead of the bridle. The brute threw up her head and went down with a scream, the Tertium Quid upon her, and the nervous grin still set on his face.

The Man's Wife heard the tinkle-tinkle of little stones and loose earth falling off the roadway, and the sliding roar of the man and horse going down. Then everything was quiet, and she called on Frank to leave his mare and walk up. But Frank did not answer. He was underneath the mare, nine hundred feet below, spoiling a patch of Indian corn.

As the revellers came back from Viceregal Lodge in the mists of the evening, they met a temporarily insane woman, on a temporarily mad horse, swinging round the corners, with her eyes and her mouth open, and her head like the head of the Medusa. She was stopped by a man at the risk of his life, and taken out of the saddle, a limp heap, and put on the bank to explain herself. This wasted twenty minutes, and then she was sent home in a lady's 'rickshaw, still with her mouth open and her hands picking at her riding-gloves.

She was in bed through the following three days, which were rainy; so she missed attending the funeral of the Tertium Quid, who was lowered into eighteen inches of water, instead of the twelve to which he had first objected.

•

A Wayside Comedy

Because to every purpose there is time
and judgment, therefore the misery
of man is great upon him.—
        —*Eccles.* viii. 6.

FATE and the Government of India have turned the Station of Kashima into a prison; and, because there is no help for the poor souls who are now lying there in torment, I write this story, praying that the Government of India may be moved to scatter the European population to the four winds.

Kashima is bounded on all sides by the rock-tipped circle of the Dosehri hills. In Spring, it is ablaze with roses; in Summer, the roses die and the hot winds blow from the hills; in Autumn, the white mists from the *jhils* cover the place as with water, and in Winter the frosts nip everything young and tender to earth-level. There is but one view in Kashima—a stretch of perfectly flat pasture and plough-land, running up to the grey-blue scrub of the Dosehri hills.

There are no amusements, except snipe and tiger shooting; but the tigers have been long since hunted from their lairs in the rock-caves, and the snipe only come once a year. Narkarra—one hundred and forty-three miles by road—is the nearest station to Kashima. But Kashima never goes to Narkarra, where there are at least twelve English people. It stays within the circle of the Dosehri hills.

All Kashima acquits Mrs. Vansuythen of any intention to do harm; but all Kashima knows that she, and she alone, brought about their pain.

Boulte, the Engineer, Mrs. Boulte, and Captain Kurrell know this. They are the English population of Kashima, if we except Major Vansuythen, who is of no importance whatever, and Mrs. Vansuythen, who is the most important of all.

You must remember, though you willl not understand, that all laws weaken in a small and hidden community where there is no public opinion. When a man is absolutely alone in a Station he runs a certain risk of falling into evil ways. This risk is multiplied by every addition to the population up to twelve —the Jury-number. After that, fear and consequent restraint begin, and human action becomes less grotesquely jerky.

There was deep peace in Kashima till Mrs. Vansuythen arrived. She was a charming woman, every one said so everywhere; and she charmed every one. In spite of this, or, perhaps, because of this, since Fate is so perverse, she cared only for one man, and he was Major Vansuythen. Had she been plain or stupid, this matter would have been intelligible to Kashima. But she was a fair woman, with very still grey eyes, the color of a lake just before the light of the sun touches it. No man who had seen those eyes could, later on, explain what fashion of woman she was to look upon. The eyes dazzled him. Her own sex said that she was "not bad looking, but spoiled by pretending to be so grave." And yet her gravity was natural. It was not her habit to smile. She merely went through life, looking at those who passed; and the women objected while the men fell down and worshipped.

She knows and is deeply sorry for the evil she has done to Kashima; but Major Vansuythen cannot understand why Mrs. Boulte does not drop in to afternoon tea at least three times a week. "When there are only two women in one Station, they ought to see a great deal of each other," says Major Vansuythen.

Long and long before ever Mrs. Vansuythen came out of those far-away places where there is society and amusement, Kurrell had discovered that Mrs. Boulte was the one woman in the world for him and—you dare not blame them. Kashima was as out of the world as Heaven or the Other Place, and the Dosehri hills kept their secret well. Boulte had no concern in the matter. He was in camp for a fortnight at a time. He was a hard, heavy man, and neither Mrs. Boulte nor Kurrell pitied him. They had all Kashima and each other for their very, very own; and Kashima was the Garden of Eden in those days. When Boulte returned from his wanderings he would slap Kurrell between the shoulders and call him "old fellow," and the three would dine together. Kashima was happy then when the judgment of God seemed almost as distant as Narkarra or the railway that ran down to the sea. But the Government sent Major Vansuythen to Kashima, and with him came his wife.

The etiquette of Kashima is much the same as that of a desert island. When a stranger is cast away there, all hands go down to the shore to make him welcome. Kashima assembled at the masonry platform close to the Narkarra Road, and spread tea for the Vansuythens. That ceremony was reckoned a formal call, and made them free of the Station, its rights and privileges. When the Vansuythens were settled down, they gave a tiny house-warming to all Kashima; and that made Kashima free of their house, according to the immemorial usage of the Station.

Then the Rains came, when no one

could go into camp, and the Narkarra Road was washed away by the Kasun River, and in the cup-like pastures of Kashima the cattle waded knee-deep. The clouds dropped down from the Dosehri hills and covered everything.

At the end of the Rains, Boulte's manner toward his wife changed and became demonstratively affectionate. They had been married twelve years, and the change startled Mrs. Boulte, who hated her husband with the hate of a woman who has met with nothing but kindness from her mate, and, in the teeth of this kindness, has done him a great wrong. Moreover, she had her own trouble to fight with—her watch to keep over her own property, Kurrell. For two months the Rains had hidden the Dosehri hills and many other things besides; but, when they lifted, they showed Mrs. Boulte that her man among men, her Ted—for she called him Ted in the old days when Boulte was out of earshot—was slipping the links of the allegiance.

"The Vansuythen Woman has taken him," Mrs. Boulte said to herself; and when Boulte was away, wept over her belief, in the face of the over-vehement blandishments of Ted. Sorrow in Kashima is as fortunate as Love, because there is nothing to weaken it save the flight of Time. Mrs. Boulte had never breathed her suspicion to Kurrell because she was not certain; and her nature led her to be very certain before she took steps in any direction. That is why she behaved as she did.

Boulte came into the house one evening, and leaned against the door-posts of the drawing-room, chewing his moustache. Mrs. Boulte was putting some flowers into a vase. There is a pretence of civilization even in Kashima.

"Little woman," said Boulte, quietly, "do you care for me?"

"Immensely," said she, with a laugh. "Can you ask it?"

"But I'm serious," said Boulte. "*Do* you care for me?"

Mrs. Boulte dropped the flowers, and turned round quickly. "Do you want an honest answer?"

"Ye-es, I've asked for it."

Mrs. Boulte spoke in a low, even voice for five minutes, very distinctly, that there might be no misunderstanding her meaning. When Samson broke the pillars of Gaza, he did a little thing, and one not to be compared to the deliberate pulling down of a woman's homestead about her own ears. There was no wise female friend to advise Mrs. Boulte, the singularly cautious wife, to hold her hand. She struck at Boulte's heart, because her own was sick with suspicion of Kurrell, and worn out with the long strain of watching alone through the Rains. There was no plan or purpose in her speaking. The sentences made themselves; and Boulte listened leaning against the door-post with his hands in his pockets. When all was over, and Mrs. Boulte began to breathe through her nose before breaking out into tears, he laughed and stared straight in front of him at the Dosehri hills.

"Is that all?" he said. "Thanks, I only wanted to know, you know."

"What are you going to do?" said the woman, between her sobs.

"Do! Nothing. What should I do? Kill Kurrell or send you Home, or apply for leave to get a divorce? It's two days' *dâk* into Narkarra." He laughed again and went on: "I'll tell you what *you* can do. You can ask Kurrell to dinner to-morrow—no, on Thursday, that will allow you time to pack—and you can bolt with him. I give you my word I won't follow."

He took up his helmet and went out of the room, and Mrs. Boulte sat till the moonlight streaked the floor, thinking and thinking and thinking. She had done her best upon the spur of the moment to pull the house down; but it would not fall. Moreover, she could not understand her husband, and she was afraid. Then the folly of her useless truthfulness struck her, and she was ashamed to write to Kurrell, saying: "I have gone mad and told everything. My husband says that I am free to elope with you. Get a *dâk* for Thursday, and we will fly after dinner." There was a cold-bloodedness about that procedure which did not appeal to her. So she sat still in her own house and thought.

At dinner-time Boulte came back from his walk, white and worn and haggard, and the woman was touched at his distress. As the evening wore on, she muttered some expression of sorrow, something approaching to contrition. Boulte came out of a brown study and said, "Oh, *that!* I wasn't thinking about that. By the way, what does Kurrell say to the elopement?"

"I haven't seen him," said Mrs. Boulte. "Good God! is that all?"

But Boulte was not listening, and her sentence ended in a gulp.

The next day brought no comfort to Mrs. Boulte, for Kurrell did not appear, and the new life that she, in the five minutes' madness of the previous evening, had hoped to build out of the ruins of the old, seemed to be no nearer.

Boulte ate his breakfast, advised her to see her Arab pony fed in the veranda, and went out. The morning wore through, and at midday the tension became unendurable. Mrs. Boulte could not cry. She had finished her crying in the night, and now she did not want to be left alone. Perhaps the Vansuythen Woman would talk to her; and, since talking opens the heart, perhaps there might be some comfort to be found in her company. She was the only other woman in the Station.

In Kashima there are no regular calling-hours. Every one can drop in upon every one else at pleasure. Mrs. Boulte put on a big *terai* hat, and walked across to the Vansuythen's house to borrow last week's *Queen.* The two compounds touched, and instead of going up the drive, she crossed through the gap in the cactus-hedge, entering the house from the back. As she passed through the dining-room, she heard, behind the *purdah* that cloaked the drawing-room door, her husband's voice, saying—

"But on my Honor! On my Soul and Honor, I tell you she doesn't care for me. She told me so last night. I would have told you then if Vansuythen hadn't been with you. If it is for *her* sake that you'll have nothing to say to me, you can make your mind easy. It's Kurrell"—

"What?" said Mrs. Vansuythen, with an hysterical little laugh. "Kurrell! Oh, it can't be! You two must have made some horrible mistake. Perhaps you—you lost your temper, or misunderstood, or something. Things *can't* be as wrong as you say."

Mrs. Vansuythen had shifted her defence to avoid the man's pleading, and was desperately trying to keep him to a side-issue.

"There must be some mistake," she insisted, "and it can be all put right again."

Boulte laughed grimly.

"It can't be Captain Kurrell! He told me that he had never taken the least—the least interest in your wife, Mr. Boulte. Oh, *do* listen! He said he had not. He swore he had not," said Mrs. Vansuythen.

The *purdah* rustled, and the speech was cut short by the entry of a little, thin woman, with big rings round her eyes. Mrs. Vansuythen stood up with a gasp.

"What was that you said?" asked Mrs. Boulte. "Never mind that man. What did Ted say to you? What did he say to you? What did he say to you?"

Mrs. Vansuythen sat down helplessly on the sofa, overborne by the trouble of her questioner.

"He said—I can't remember exactly what he said—but I understood him to say—that is —But, really, Mrs. Boulte, isn't it rather a strange question?"

"*Will* you tell me what he said?" repeated Mrs. Boulte. Even a tiger will fly before a bear robbed of her whelps, and Mrs. Vansuythen was only an ordinarily good woman. She began in a sort of desperation: "Well, he said that he never cared for you at all, and, of course, there was not the least reason why he should have, and—and—that was all."

"You said he *swore* he had not cared for me. Was that true?"

"Yes," said Mrs. Vansuythen, very softly.

Mrs. Boulte wavered for an instant where she stood, and then fell forward fainting.

"What did I tell you?" said Boulte, as though the conversation had been unbroken. "You can see for yourself. She cares for *him*." The light began to break into his dull mind, and he went on—"And he—what was *he* saying to you?"

But Mrs. Vansuythen, with no heart for explanations or impassioned protestations, was kneeling over Mrs. Boulte.

"Oh, you brute!" she cried. "Are *all* men like this? Help me to get her into my room—and her face is cut against the table. Oh, *will* you be quiet, and help me to carry her? I hate you, and I hate Captain Kurrell. Lift her up carefully and now—go! Go away!"

Boulte carried his wife into Mrs. Vansuythen's bedroom and departed before the storm of that lady's wrath and disgust, impenitent and burning with jealousy. Kurrell had been making love to Mrs. Vansuythen—would do Vansuythen as great a wrong as he had done Boulte, who caught himself considering whether Mrs. Vansuythen would faint if she discovered that the man she loved had foresworn her.

In the middle of these meditations, Kurrell came cantering along the road and pulled up with a cheery, "Good-mornin'. 'Been mashing Mrs. Vansuythen as usual, eh? Bad thing for a sober, married man, that. What will Mrs. Boulte say?"

Boulte raised his head and said, slowly, "Oh, you liar!" Kurrell's face changed. "What's that?" he asked, quickly.

"Nothing much," said Boulte. "Has my wife told you that you two are free to go off whenever you please? She has been good enough to explain the situation to me. You've been a true friend to me, Kurrell—old man—haven't you?"

Kurrell groaned, and tried to frame some sort of idiotic sentence about being willing to give "satisfaction." But his interest in the woman was dead, had died out in the Rains, and, mentally, he was abusing her for her amazing indiscretion. It would have been so easy to have broken off the thing gently and by degrees, and now he was saddled with— Boulte's voice recalled him.

"I don't think I should get any satisfaction from killing you, and I'm pretty sure you'd get none from killing me."

Then in a querulous tone, ludicrously disproportioned to his wrongs, Boulte added—

" 'Seems rather a pity that you haven't the decency to keep to the woman, now you've got her. You've been a true friend to *her* too, haven't you?"

Kurrell stared long and gravely. The situation was getting beyond him.

"What do you mean?" he said.

Boulte answered, more to himself than the questioner: "My wife came over to Mrs. Vansuythen's just now; and it seems you'd been telling Mrs. Vansuythen that you'd never cared for Emma. I suppose you lied, as usual. What had Mrs. Vansuythen to do with

you, or you with her? Try to speak the truth for once in a way."

Kurrell took the double insult without wincing, and replied by another question: "Go on. What happened?"

"Emma fainted," said Boulte, simply. "But, look here, what had you been saying to Mrs. Vansuythen?"

Kurrell laughed. Mrs. Boulte had, with unbridled tongue, made havoc of his plans; and he could at least retaliate by hurting the man in whose eyes he was humiliated and shown dishonorable.

"Said to her? What *does* a man tell a lie like that for? I suppose I said pretty much what you've said, unless I'm a good deal mistaken."

"I spoke the truth," said Boulte, again more to himself than Kurrell. "Emma told me she hated me. She has no right in me."

"No! I suppose not. You're only her husband, y'know. And what did Mrs. Vansuythen say after you had laid your disengaged heart at her feet?"

Kurrell felt almost virtuous as he put the question.

"I don't think that matters," Boulte replied; "and it doesn't concern you."

"But it does! I tell you it does"— began Kurrell, shamelessly.

The sentence was cut by a roar of laughter from Boulte's lips. Kurrell was silent for an instant, and then he, too, laughed—laughed long and loudly, rocking in his saddle. It was an unpleasant sound—the mirthless mirth of these men on the long, white line of the Narkarra Road. There were no strangers in Kashima, or they might have thought that captivity within the

Dosehri hills had driven half the European population mad. The laughter ended abruptly, and Kurrell was the first to speak.

"Well, what are you going to do?"

Boulte looked up the road, and at the hills. "Nothing," said he, quietly; "what's the use? It's too ghastly for anything. We must let the old life go on. I can only call you a hound and a liar, and I can't go on calling you names forever. Besides which, I don't feel that I'm much better. We can't get out of this place. What is there to do?"

Kurrell looked round the rat-pit of Kashima and made no reply. The injured husband took up the wondrous tale.

"Ride on, and speak to Emma if you want to. God knows *I* don't care what you do."

He walked forward, and left Kurrell gazing blankly after him. Kurrell did not ride on either to see Mrs. Boulte or Mrs. Vansuythen. He sat in his saddle and thought, while his pony grazed by the roadside.

The whir of approaching wheels roused him. Mrs. Vansuythen was driving home Mrs. Boulte, white and wan, with a cut on her forehead.

"Stop, please," said Mrs. Boulte, "I want to speak to Ted."

Mrs. Vansuythen obeyed, but as Mrs. Boulte leaned forward, putting her hand upon the splash-board of the dog-cart, Kurrell spoke.

"I've seen your husband, Mrs. Boulte."

There was no necessity for any further explanation. The man's eyes were fixed, not upon Mrs. Boulte, but

her companion. Mrs. Boulte saw the look.

"Speak to him!" she pleaded, turning to the woman at her side. "Oh, speak to him! Tell him what you told me just now. Tell him you hate him. Tell him you hate him!"

She bent forward and wept bitterly, while the *sais*, impassive, went forward to hold the horse. Mrs. Vansuythen turned scarlet and dropped the reins. She wished to be no party to such unholy explanations.

"I've nothing to do with it," she began, coldly; but Mrs. Boulte's sobs overcame her, and she addressed herself to the man. "I don't know what I am to say, Captain Kurrell. I don't know what I can call you. I think you've—you've behaved abominably, and she has cut her forehead terribly against the table."

"It doesn't hurt. It isn't anything," said Mrs. Boulte, feebly. "*That* doesn't matter. Tell him what you told me. Say you don't care for him. Oh, Ted, *won't* you believe her?"

"Mrs. Boulte has made me understand that you were—that you were fond of her once upon a time," went on Mrs. Vansuythen.

"Well!" said Kurrell, brutally. "It seems to me that Mrs. Boulte had better be fond of her own husband first."

"Stop!" said Mrs. Vansuythen. "Hear me first. I don't care—I don't want to know anything about you and Mrs. Boulte; but I want *you* to know that I hate you, that I think you are a cur, and that I'll never, *never* speak to you again. Oh, I don't dare to say what I think of you, you—man!"

"I want to speak to Ted," moaned Mrs. Boulte, but the dog-cart rattled on, and Kurrell was left on the road, shamed, and boiling with wrath against Mrs. Boulte.

He waited till Mrs. Vansuythen was driving back to her own house, and, she being freed from the embarrassment of Mrs. Boulte's presence, learned for the second time her opinion of himself and his actions.

In the evenings, it was the wont of all Kashima to meet at the platform on the Narkarra Road, to drink tea, and discuss the trivialities of the day. Major Vansuythen and his wife found themselves alone at the gathering-place for almost the first time in their remembrance; and the cheery Major, in the teeth of his wife's remarkably reasonable suggestion that the rest of the Station might be sick, insisted upon driving round to the two bungalows and unearthing the population.

"Sitting in the twilight!" said he, with great indignation, to the Boultes. "That'll never do! Hang it all, we're one family here! You *must* come out, and so must Kurrell. I'll make him bring his banjo." So great is the power of honest simplicity and a good digestion over guilty consciences that all Kashima did turn out, even down to the banjo; and the Major embraced the company in one expansive grin. As he grinned, Mrs. Vansuythen raised her eyes for an instant and looked at all Kashima. Her meaning was clear. Major Vansuythen would never know anything. He was to be the outsider in that happy family whose cage was the Dosehri hills.

"You're singing villainously out of tune, Kurrell," said the Major, truthfully. "Pass me that banjo."

And he sang in excruciating-wise till the stars came out and all Kashima went to dinner.

*   *   *   *   *   *

That was the beginning of the New Life of Kashima—the life that Mrs. Boulte made when her tongue was loosened in the twilight.

Mrs. Vansuythen has never told the Major; and since he insists upon keeping up a burdensome geniality, she has been compelled to break her vow of not speaking to Kurrell. This speech, which must of necessity preserve the semblance of politeness and interest, serves admirably to keep alight the flame of jealousy and dull hatred in Boulte's bosom, as it awakens the same passions in his wife's heart. Mrs. Boulte hates Mrs. Vansuythen because she has taken Ted from her, and, in some curious fashion, hates her because Mrs. Vansuythen—and here the wife's eyes see far more clearly than the husband's—detests Ted. And Ted—that gallant captain and honorable man—knows now that it is possible to hate a woman once loved, to the verge of wishing to silence her forever with blows. Above all, is he shocked that Mrs. Boulte cannot see the error of her ways.

Boulte and he go out tiger-shooting together in all friendship. Boulte has put their relationship on a most satisfactory footing.

"You're a blackguard," he says to Kurrell, "and I've lost any self-respect I may ever have had; but when you're with me, I can feel certain that you are not with Mrs. Vansuythen, or making Emma miserable."

Kurrell endures anything that Boulte may say to him. Sometimes they are away for three days together, and then the Major insists upon his wife going over to sit with Mrs. Boulte; although

Mrs. Vansuythen has repeatedly declared that she prefers her husband's company to any in the world. From the way in which she clings to him, she would certainly seem to be speaking the truth.

But of course, as the Major says, "in a little Station we must all be friendly."

The Hill of Illusion

What rendered vain their deep desire?
A God, a God their severance ruled,
And bade between their shores to be
The unplumbed, salt, estranging sea.
—*Matthew Arnold.*

HE. Tell your *jhampanis* not to hurry so, dear. They forget I'm fresh from the Plains.

SHE. Sure proof that *I* have not been going out with any one. Yes, they *are* an untrained crew. Where do we go?

HE. As usual—to the world's end. No, Jakko.

SHE. Have your pony led after you, then. It's a long round.

HE. And for the last time, thank Heaven!

SHE. Do you mean *that* still? I didn't dare to write to you about it—all these months.

HE. Mean it! I've been shaping my affairs to that end since Autumn. What makes you speak as though it had occurred to you for the first time?

SHE. I! Oh! I don't know. I've had long enough to think, too.

HE. And you've changed your mind?

SHE. No. You ought to know that I am a miracle of constancy. What are your—arrangements?

HE. *Ours*, Sweetheart, please.

SHE. Ours, be it then. My poor boy, how the prickly heat has marked your forehead! Have you ever tried sulphate of copper in water?

HE. It'll go away in a day or two up here. The arrangements are simple enough. Tonga in the early morning—reach Kalka at twelve—Umballa at seven—down, straight by night train, to Bombay, and then the steamer of the 21st for Rome. That's my idea. The Continent and Sweden—a ten-week honeymoon.

SHE. Ssh! Don't talk of it in that way. It makes me afraid. Guy, how long have we two been insane?

HE. Seven months and fourteen days, I forget the odd hours exactly, but I'll think.

SHE. I only wanted to see if you remembered. Who are those two on the Blessington Road?

HE. Eabrey and the Penner woman. What do they matter to *us?* Tell me everything that you've been doing and saying and thinking.

SHE. Doing little, saying less, and thinking a great deal. I've hardly been cut at all.

HE. That was wrong of you. You haven't been moping?

SHE. Not very much. Can you wonder that I'm disinclined for amusement?

HE. Frankly, I do. Where was the difficulty?

SHE. In this only. The more people I know and the more I'm known here, the wider spread will be the news of the crash when it comes. I don't like that.

HE. Nonsense. We shall be out of it.

SHE. You think so?

HE. I'm sure of it, if there is any power in steam or horse-flesh to carry us away. Ha! ha!

SHE. And the fun of the situation comes in—where, my Lancelot?

HE. Nowhere, Guinevere. I was only thinking of something.

SHE. They say men have a keener sense of humor than women. Now *I* was thinking of the scandal.

HE. Don't think of anything so ugly. We shall be beyond it.

SHE. It will be there all the same— in the mouths of Simla—telegraphed over India, and talked of at the dinners —and when He goes out they will stare at Him to see how He takes it. And we shall be dead, Guy dear—dead and cast into the outer darkness where there is—

HE. Love at least. Isn't that enough?

SHE. I have said so.

HE. And you think so still?

SHE. What do *you* think?

HE. What have I *done*? It means equal ruin to me, as the world reckons it—outcasting, the loss of my appointment, the breaking off my life's work. I pay my price.

SHE. And are you so much above the world that you can afford to pay it? Am I?

HE. My Divinity—what else?

SHE. A very ordinary woman I'm afraid, but, so far, respectable. How'd you do, Mrs. Middleditch? Your husband? I think he's riding down to Annandale with Colonel Statters. Yes, isn't it divine after the rain?—Guy, how long am I to be allowed to bow to Mrs. Middleditch? Till the 17th?

HE. Frowsy Scotchwoman? What is the use of bringing her into the discussion? You were saying?

SHE. Nothing. Have you ever seen a man hanged?

HE. Yes. Once.

SHE. What was it for?

HE. Murder, of course.

SHE. Murder. Is *that* so great a sin after all? I wonder how he felt before the drop fell.

HE. I don't think he felt much. What a gruesome little woman it is this evening! You're shivering. Put on your cape, dear.

SHE. I think I will. Oh! Look at the mist coming over Sanjaoli; and I thought we should have sunshine on the Ladies' Mile! Let's turn back.

HE. What's the good? There's a cloud on Elysium Hill, and that means it's foggy all down the Mall. We'll go on. It'll blow away before we get to the Convent, perhaps. 'Jove! It *is* chilly.

SHE. You feel 'it, fresh from below. Put on your ulster. What do you think of my cape?

HE. Never ask a man his opinion of a woman's dress when he is desperately and abjectly in love with the wearer. Let me look. Like everything else of yours it's perfect. Where did you get it from?

SHE. He gave it me, on Wednesday —our wedding-day, you know.

HE. The Deuce He did! He's growing generous in his old age. D'you like all that frilly, bunchy stuff at the throat? I don't.

SHE. Don't you?

Kind Sir, o' your courtesy,
  As you go by the town, Sir,
'Pray you o' your love for me,
  Buy me a russet gown, Sir.

HE. I won't say: "Keek into the draw-well, Janet, Janet." Only wait a little, darling, and you shall be stocked with russet gowns and everything else.

SHE. And when the frocks wear out, You'll get me new ones—and everything else?

HE. Assuredly.

SHE. I wonder!

HE. Look here, Sweetheart, I didn't spend two days and two nights in the train to hear you wonder. I thought we'd settled all that at Shaifazehat.

SHE (dreamily). At Shaifazehat? Does the Station go on still? That was ages and ages ago. It must be crumbling to pieces. All except the Amirtollah kutcha road. I don't believe that could crumble till the Day of Judgment.

HE. You think so? What is the mood now?

SHE. I can't tell. How cold it is! Let us get on quickly.

HE. 'Better walk a little. Stop your jhampanis and get out. What's the matter with you this evening, dear?

SHE. Nothing. You must grow accustomed to my ways. If I'm boring you I can go home. Here's Captain Congleton coming, I dare say he'll be willing to escort me.

HE. Goose! Between us, too! Damn Captain Congleton!

SHE. Chivalrous Knight. Is it your habit to swear much in talking? It jars a little, and you might swear at me.

HE. My angel! I didn't know what I was saying; and you changed so quickly that I couldn't follow. I'll apologize in dust and ashes.

SHE. There'll be enough of those later on—Good-night, Captain Congleton. Going to the singing-quadrilles already? What dances am I giving you next week? No! You must have written them down wrong. Five and Seven, I said. If you've made a mistake, I certainly don't intend to suffer for it. You must alter your programme.

HE. I thought you told me that you had not been going out much this season?

SHE. Quite true, but when I do I dance with Captain Congleton. He dances very nicely.

HE. And sit out with him, I suppose?

SHE. Yes. Have you any objection? Shall I stand under the chandelier in future?

HE. What does he talk to you about?

SHE. What do men talk about when they sit out?

HE. Ugh! Don't! Well now I'm up, you must dispense with the fascinating Congleton for a while. I don't like him.

SHE (*after a pause*). Do you know what you have said?

HE. 'Can't say that I do exactly. I'm not in the best of tempers.

SHE. So I see,—and feel. My true and faithful lover, where is your "eternal constancy," "unalterable trust," and "reverent devotion"? I remember those phrases; you seem to have forgotten them. I mention a man's name—

HE. A good deal more than that.

SHE. Well, speak to him about a dance—perhaps the last dance that I shall ever dance in my life before I,—before I go away; and you at once distrust and insult me.

HE. I never said a word.

SHE. How much did you imply? Guy, is *this* amount of confidence to be our stock to start the new life on?

HE. No, of course not. I didn't mean that. On my word and honor, I didn't. Let it pass, dear. Please let it pass.

SHE. This once—yes—and a second time, and again and again, all through the years when I shall be unable to resent it. You want too much, my Lancelot, and,—you know too much.

HE. How do you mean?

SHE. That is a part of the punishment. There *cannot* be perfect trust between us.

HE. In Heaven's name, why not?

SHE. Hush! The Other Place is quite enough. Ask yourself.

HE. I don't follow.

SHE. You trust me so implicitly that when I look at another man— Never mind, Guy. Have you ever made love to a girl—a *good* girl?

HE. Something of the sort. Centu-

ries ago—in the Dark Ages, before I ever met you, dear.

SHE. Tell me what you said to her.

HE. What does a man say to a girl? I've forgotten.

SHE. *I* remember. He tells her that he trusts her and worships the ground she walks on, and that he'll love and honor and protect her till her dying day; and so she marries in that belief. At least, I speak of one girl who was *not* protected.

HE. Well, and then?

SHE. And then, Guy, and then, that girl needs *ten* times the love and trust and honor—yes, *honor*—that was enough when she was only a mere wife if—if— the other life she chooses to lead is to be made even bearable. Do you understand?

HE. Even bearable! It'll be Paradise.

SHE. Ah! Can you give me all I've asked for—not now, nor a few months later, but when you begin to think of what you might have done if you had kept your own appointment and your caste here—when you begin to look upon me as a drag and a burden? I shall want it most, then, Guy, for there will be no one in the wide world but you.

HE. You're a little over-tired tonight, Sweetheart, and you're taking a stage view of the situation. After the necessary business in the Courts, the road is clear to—

SHE. "The holy state of matrimony!" Ha! ha! ha!

HE. Ssh! Don't laugh in that horrible way!

SHE. I—I c-c-c-can't help it! Isn't it too absurd! Ah! Ha! ha! ha! Guy,

-top me quick or I shall—l-l-laugh till
we get to the Church.

HE. For goodness' sake, stop! Don't
make an exhibition of yourself. What
is the matter with you?

SHE. N-nothing. I'm better now.

HE. That's all right. One moment,
dear. There's a little wisp of hair got
loose from behind your right ear and
it's straggling over your cheek. So!

SHE. Thank'oo. I'm 'fraid my hat's
on one side, too.

HE. What do you wear these huge
dagger bonnet-skewers for? They're big
enough to kill a man with.

SHE. Oh! Don't kill *me*, though.
You're sticking it into my head! Let
me do it. You men are so clumsy.

HE. Have you had many opportunities of comparing us—in this sort of
work?

SHE. Guy, what is my name?

HE. Eh! I don't follow.

SHE. Here's my cardcase. Can you
read?

HE. Yes. Well?

SHE. Well, that answers your question. You know the other man's name.
Am I sufficiently humbled, or would you
like to ask me if there is any one else?

HE. I see now. My darling, I never
meant that for an instant. I was only
joking. There! Lucky there's no one
on the road. They'd be scandalized.

SHE. They'll be more scandalized
before the end.

HE. Do-on't! I don't like you to
talk in that way.

SHE. Unreasonable man! Who asked
me to face the situation and accept it?
—Tell me, do I look like Mrs. Penner?
Do I look like a naughty woman? *Swear*
I don't! Give me your word of honor,

my *honorable* friend, that I'm not like
Mrs. Buzgago. That's the way she
stands, with her hands clasped at the
back of her head. D'you like that?

HE. Don't be affected.

SHE. I'm not. I'm Mrs. Buzgago.
Listen!

Pendant une anne' toute entière
Le régiment n'a pas r'paru.
Au Ministère de la Guerre
On le r'porta comme perdu.

On se r'noncait à r'trouver sa trace,
Quand un matin subitement,
On le vit r'paraitre sur la place,
L'Colonel toujours en avant.

That's the way she rolls her r's. *Am*
I like her?

HE. No, but I object when you go
on like an actress and sing stuff of that
kind. Where in the world did you pick
up the *Chanson du Colonel?* It isn't
a drawing-room song. It isn't proper.

SHE. Mrs. Buzgago taught it me.
She is both drawing-room and proper,
and in another month she'll shut her
drawing-room to me, and thank God she
isn't as improper as I am. Oh, Guy,
Guy! I wish I was like some women
and had no scruples about—what is it
Keene says?—"Wearing a corpse's hair
and being false to the bread they eat."

HE. I am only a man of limited intelligence, and, just now, very bewildered. When you have *quite* finished
flashing through all your moods tell me,
and I'll try to understand the last one.

SHE. Moods, Guy! I haven't any.
I'm sixteen years old and you're just
twenty, and you've been waiting for two
hours outside the school in the cold.
And now I've met you, and now we're

walking home together. Does *that* suit you, My Imperial Majesty?

HE. No. We aren't children. Why can't you be rational?

SHE. He asks me that when I'm going to commit suicide for his sake, and, and—I don't want to be French and rave about my mother, but have I ever told you that I have a mother, and a brother who was my pet before I married? He's married now. Can't you imagine the pleasure that the news of the elopement will give him? Have *you* any people at Home, Guy, to be pleased with your performances?

HE. One or two. One can't make omelets without breaking eggs.

SHE (*slowly*). I don't see the necessity—

HE. Hah! What do you mean?

SHE. Shall I speak the truth?

HE. Under the circumstances, perhaps it *would* be as well.

SHE. Guy, I'm afraid.

HE. I thought we'd settled all that. What of?

SHE. Of you.

HE. Oh, damn it all! The old business! This is *too* bad!

SHE. Of *you*.

HE. And what now?

SHE. What do you think of me?

HE. Beside the question altogether. What do you intend to do?

SHE. I daren't risk it. I'm afraid. If I could only cheat—

HE. *A la Buzgago?* No, *thanks.* That's the one point on which I have any notion of Honor. I won't eat his salt and steal too. I'll loot openly or not at all.

SHE. I never meant anything else.

HE. Then, why in the world do you pretend not to be willing to come?

SHE. It's *not* pretence, Guy. I *am* afraid.

HE. Please explain.

SHE. It can't last, Guy. It can't last. You'll get angry, and then you'll swear, and then you'll get jealous, and then you'll mistrust me—you do *now*—and you yourself will be the best reason for doubting. And I—what shall *I* do? I shall be no better than Mrs. Buzgago found out—no better than any one. And you'll *know* that. Oh, Guy, can't you *see?*

HE. I see that you are desperately unreasonable, little woman.

SHE. There! The moment I begin to object, you get angry. What will you do when I am only your property— stolen property? It can't be, Guy. It can't be! I thought it could, but it *can't*. You'll get tired of me.

HE. I tell you I shall *not*. Won't anything make you understand that?

SHE. There, can't you see? If you speak to me like that now, you'll call me horrible names later, if I don't do everything as you like. And if you were cruel to me, Guy, where should I go— where should I go? I can't trust you. Oh! I *can't* trust you!

HE. I suppose I ought to say that I *can* trust you. I've ample reason.

SHE. *Please* don't, dear. It hurts as much as if you hit me.

HE. It isn't exactly pleasant for *me*.

SHE. I can't help it. I wish I were dead! I can't trust you, and I don't trust myself. Oh, Guy, let it die away and be forgotten!

HE. Too late now. I don't understand you—I won't—and I can't trust myself to talk this evening. May I call to-morrow?

SHE. Yes. *No!* Oh, give me time! The day after. I get into my *'rickshaw* here and meet Him at Peliti's. You ride.

HE. I'll go on to Peliti's too. I think I want a drink. My world's knocked about my ears and the stars are falling. Who are those brutes howling in the Old Library?

SHE. They're rehearsing the singing-quadrilles for the Fancy Ball. Can't you hear Mrs. Buzgago's voice? She has a solo. It's quite a new idea. Listen.

MRS. BUZGAGO (*in the Old Library, con. molt. exp.*).

See saw! Margery Daw!
Sold her bed to lie upon straw.
Wasn't she a silly slut
To sell her bed and lie upon dirt?

Captain Congleton, I'm going to alter that to "flirt." It sounds better.

HE. No, I've changed my mind about the drink. Good-night, little lady. I shall see you to-morrow?

SHE. Ye—es. Good-night, Guy. *Don't* be angry with me.

HE. Angry! You *know* I trust you absolutely. Good-night and—God bless you!

(*Three seconds later. Alone.*) Hmm! I'd give something to discover whether there's another man at the back of all this.

A Second-Rate Woman

Est fuga, volvitur rota,
 On we drift; where looms the dim
  port?
One Two Three Four Five contribute
  their quota:
Something is gained if one caught but
  the import,
Show it us, Hugues of Saxe-Gotha.
 —*Master Hugues of Saxe-Gotha.*

"DRESSED! Don't tell me that woman ever dressed in her life. She stood in the middle of the room while her *ayah* —no, her husband—it *must* have been a man—threw her clothes at her. She then did her hair with her fingers, and rubbed her bonnet in the flue under the bed. I *know* she did, as well as if I had assisted at the orgie. Who is she?" said Mrs. Hauksbee.

"Don't!" said Mrs. Mallowe, feebly.

"You make my head ache. I'm miserable to-day. Stay me with *fondants*, comfort me with chocolates, for I am— Did you bring anything from Peliti's?"

"Questions to begin with. You shall have the sweets when you have answered them. Who and what is the creature? There were at least half a dozen men round her, and she appeared to be going to sleep in their midst."

"Delville," said Mrs. Mallowe, " 'Shady' Delville, to distinguish her from Mrs. Jim of that ilk. She dances as untidily as she dresses, I believe, and her husband is somewhere in Madras. Go and call, if you are so interested."

"What have I to do with Shigramitish women? She merely caught my attention for a minute, and I wondered at the attraction that a dowd has for a certain type of man. I expected to see her walk out of her clothes—until I looked at her eyes."

"Hooks and eyes, surely," drawled Mrs. Mallowe.

"Don't be clever, Polly. You make my head ache. And round this hayrick stood a crowd of men—a positive crowd!"

"Perhaps *they* also expected"—

"Polly, don't be Rabelaisian!"

Mrs. Mallowe curled herself up comfortably on the sofa, and turned her attention to the sweets. She and Mrs. Hauksbee shared the same house at Simla; and these things befell two seasons after the matter of Otis Yeere, which has been already recorded.

Mrs. Hauksbee stepped into the veranda and looked down upon the Mall, her forehead puckered with thought.

"Hah!" said Mrs. Hauksbee, shortly. "Indeed!"

"What is it?" said Mrs. Mallowe, sleepily.

"That dowd and The Dancing Master —to whom I object."

"Why to The Dancing Master? He is a middle-aged gentleman, of reprobate and romantic tendencies, and tries to be a friend of mine."

"Then make up your mind to lose him. Dowds cling by nature, and I should imagine that this animal—how terrible her bonnet looks from above!— is specially clingsome."

"She is welcome to The Dancing Master so far as I am concerned. I never could take an interest in a monotonous liar. The frustrated aim

of his life is to persuade people that he is a bachelor."

"O-oh! I think I've met that sort of man before. And isn't he?"

"No. He confided that to me a few days ago. Ugh! Some men ought to be killed."

"What happened then?"

"He posed as the horror of horrors—a misunderstood man. Heaven knows the *femme incomprise* is sad enough and bad enough—but the other thing!"

"And so fat too! *I* should have laughed in his face. Men seldom confide in me. How is it they come to you?"

"For the sake of impressing me with their careers in the past. Protect me from men with confidences!"

"And yet you encourage them?"

"What can I do? They talk, I listen, and they vow that I am sympathetic. I know I always profess astonishment even when the plot is—of the most old possible."

"Yes. Men are so unblushingly explicit if they are once allowed to talk, whereas women's confidences are full of reservations and fibs, except"—

"When they go mad and babble of the Unutterabilities after a week's acquaintance. Really, if you come to consider, we know a great deal more of men than of our own sex."

"And the extraordinary thing is that men will never believe it. They say we are trying to hide something."

"They are generally doing that on their own account. Alas! These chocolates pall upon me, and I haven't eaten more than a dozen. I think I shall go to sleep."

"Then you'll get fat, dear. If you

took more exercise and a more intelligent interest in your neighbors you would"—

"Be as much loved as Mrs. Hauksbee. You're a darling in many ways and I like you—you are not a woman's woman—but *why* do you trouble yourself about mere human beings?"

"Because in the absence of angels, who I am sure would be horribly dull, men and women are the most fascinating things in the whole wide world, lazy one. I am interested in The Dowd— I am interested in The Dancing Master —I am interested in the Hawley Boy— and I am interested in *you*."

"Why couple me with the Hawley Boy? He is your property."

"Yes, and in his own guileless speech, I'm making a good thing out of him. When he is slightly more reformed, and has passed his Higher Standard, or whatever the authorities think fit to exact from him, I shall select a pretty little girl, the Holt girl, I think, and"—here she waved her hands airily—"'whom Mrs. Hauksbee hath joined together let no man put asunder.' That's all."

"And when you have yoked May Holt with the most notorious detrimental in Simla, and earned the undying hatred of Mamma Holt, what will you do with me, Dispenser of the Destinies of the Universe?"

Mrs. Hauksbee dropped into a low chair in front of the fire, and, chin in hand, gazed long and steadfastly at Mrs. Mallowe.

"I do not know," she said, shaking her head, "*what* I shall do with you, dear. It's obviously impossible to marry you to some one else—your husband would object and the experiment might not be

successful after all. I think I shall begin by preventing you from—what is it? —'sleeping on ale-house benches and snoring in the sun.'"

"Don't! I don't like your quotations. They are so rude. Go to the Library and bring me new books."

"While you sleep? *No!* If you don't come with me, I shall spread your newest frock on my 'rickshaw-bow, and when any one asks me what I am doing, I shall say that I am going to Phelps's to get it let out. I shall take care that Mrs. MacNamara sees me. Put your things on, there's a good girl."

Mrs. Mallowe groaned and obeyed, and the two went off to the Library, where they found Mrs. Delville and the man who went by the nickname of The Dancing Master. By that time Mrs. Mallowe was awake and eloquent.

"That is the Creature!" said Mrs. Hauksbee, with the air of one pointing out a slug in the road.

"No," said Mrs. Mallowe. "The man is the Creature. Ugh! Good-evening, Mr. Bent. I thought you were coming to tea this evening."

"Surely it was for to-morrow, was it not?" answered The Dancing Master. "I understood . . . I fancied . . . I'm so sorry . . . How very unfortunate!" . . .

But Mrs Mallowe had passed on.

"For the practiced equivocator you said he was," murmured Mrs. Hauksbee, "he strikes *me* as a failure. Now wherefore should he have preferred a walk with The Dowd to tea with us? Elective affinities, I suppose—both grubby. Polly, I'd never forgive that woman as long as the world rolls."

"I forgive every woman everything,"

said Mrs. Mallowe. "He will be a sufficient punishment for her. What a common voice she has!"

Mrs. Delville's voice was not pretty,
her carriage was even less lovely, and
her raiment was strikingly neglected.
All these things Mrs. Mallowe noticed
over the top of a magazine.

"Now *what* is there in her?" said Mrs.
Hauksbee. "Do you see what I meant
about the clothes falling off? If I were
a man I would perish sooner than be
seen with that rag-bag. And yet, she
has good eyes, but— Oh!"

"What is it?"

"She doesn't know how to use them!
On my Honor, she does not. Look! Oh
look! Untidiness I can endure, but
ignorance never! The woman's a fool."

"Hsh! She'll hear you."

"All the women in Simla are fools.
She'll think I mean some one else. Now
she's going out. What a thoroughly objectionable couple she and The Dancing
Master make! Which reminds me. Do
you suppose they'll ever dance together?"

"Wait and see. I don't envy her the
conversation of The Dancing Master—
loathly man! His wife ought to be up
here before long."

"Do you know anything about him?"

"Only what he told me. It may be
all a fiction. He married a girl bred in
the country, I think, and, being an honorable, chivalrous soul, told me that he
repented his bargain and sent her to her
mother as often as possible—a person
who has lived in the Doon since the
memory of man and goes to Mussoorie
when other people go Home. The wife
is with her at present. So he says."

"Babies?"

"One only, but he talks of his wife
in a revolting way. I hated him for it.
He thought he was being epigrammatic
and brilliant."

"That is a vice peculiar to men. I
dislike him because he is generally in
the wake of some girl, disappointing the
Eligibles. He will persecute May Holt
no more, unless I am much mistaken."

"No. I think Mrs. Delville may occupy his attention for a while."

"Do you suppose she knows that he
is the head of a family?"

"Not from his lips. He swore me to
eternal secrecy. Wherefore I tell you.
Don't you know that type of man?"

"Not intimately, thank goodness! As
a general rule, when a man begins to
abuse his wife to me, I find that the
Lord gives me wherewith to answer him
according to his folly; and we part with
a coolness between us. I laugh."

"I'm different. I've no sense of
humor."

"Cultivate it, then. It has been my
mainstay for more years than I care to
think about. A well-educated sense of
Humor will save a woman when Religion, Training, and Home influences fail;
and we may all need salvation sometimes."

"Do you suppose that the Delville
woman has humor?"

"Her dress beways her. How can a
Thing who wears her *supplément* under
her left arm have any notion of the fitness of things—much less their folly?
If she discards The Dancing Master
after having once seen him dance, I may
respect her. Otherwise"—

"But are we not both assuming a
great deal too much, dear? You saw
the woman at Peliti's—half an hour

later you saw her walking with The Dancing Master—an hour later you met her here at the Library."

"Still with The Dancing Master, remember."

"Still with The Dancing Master, I admit, but why on the strength of that should you imagine"—

"I imagine nothing. I have no imagination. I am only convinced that The Dancing Master is attracted to The Dowd because he is objectionable in every way and she in every other. If I know the man as you have described him, he holds his wife in slavery at present."

"She is twenty years younger than he."

"Poor wretch! And, in the end, after he has posed and swaggered and lied—he has a mouth under that ragged moustache simply made for lies—he will be rewarded according to his merits."

"I wonder what those really are," said Mrs. Mallowe.

But Mrs. Hauksbee, her face close to the shelf of the new books, was humming softly: *"What shall he have who killed the Deer!"* She was a lady of unfettered speech.

One month later, she announced her intention of calling upon Mrs. Delville. Both Mrs. Hauksbee and Mrs. Mallowe were in morning wrappers, and there was a great peace in the land.

"I should go as I was," said Mrs. Mallowe. "It would be a delicate compliment to her style."

Mrs. Hauksbee studied herself in the glass.

"Assuming for a moment that she ever darkened these doors, I should put on this robe, after all the others, to show

her what a morning wrapper ought to be. It might enliven her. As it is, I shall go in the dove-colored—sweet emblem of youth and innocence—and shall put on my new gloves."

"If you really are going, dirty tan would be too good; and you know that dove-color spots with the rain."

"I care not. I may make her envious. At least I shall try, though one cannot expect very much from a woman who puts a lace tucker into her habit."

"Just Heavens! When did she do that?"

"Yesterday—riding with The Dancing Master. I met them at the back of Jakko, and the rain had made the lace lie down. To complete the effect, she was wearing an unclean *terai* with the elastic under her chin. I felt almost too well content to take the trouble to despise her."

"The Hawley Boy was riding with you. What did he think?"

"Does a boy ever notice these things? Should I like him if he did? He stared in the rudest way, and just when I thought he had seen the elastic, he said, 'There's something very taking about that face.' I rebuked him on the spot. I don't approve of boys being taken by faces."

"Other than your own. I shouldn't be in the least surprised if the Hawley Boy immediately went to call."

I forbade him. Let her be satisfied with The Dancing Master, and his wife when she comes up. I'm rather curious to see Mrs. Bent and the Delville woman together."

Mrs. Hauksbee departed and, at the end of an hour, returned slightly flushed.

"There is no limit to the treachery of

youth! I *ordered* the Hawley Boy, as he valued my patronage, not to call. The first person I stumble over—literally stumble over—in her poky, dark, little drawing-room is, of course, the Hawley Boy. She kept us waiting ten minutes, and then emerged as though she had been tipped out of the dirty-clothes basket. You know my way, dear, when I am at all put out. I was Superior, *crrrrushingly* Superior! 'Lifted my eyes to Heaven, and had heard of nothing—'dropped my eyes on the carpet and 'really didn't know'—'played with my cardcase and 'supposed so.' The Hawley Boy giggled like a girl, and I had to freeze him with scowls between the sentences."

"And she?"

"She sat in a heap on the edge of a couch, and managed to convey the impression that she was suffering from stomach-ache, at the very least. It was all I could do not to ask after her symptoms. When I rose she grunted just like a buffalo in the water—too lazy to move."

"Are you certain?"—

"Am I blind, Polly? Laziness, sheer laziness, nothing else—or her garments were only constructed for sitting down in. I stayed for a quarter of an hour trying to penetrate the gloom, to guess what her surroundings were like, while she stuck out her tongue."

"Lu—*cy!*"

"Well—I'll withdraw the tongue, though I'm sure if she didn't do it when I was in the room, she did the minute I was outside. At any rate, she lay in a lump and grunted. Ask the Hawley Boy, dear. I believe the grunts were meant for sentences, but she spoke so indistinctly that I can't swear to it."

"You are incorrigible, simply."

"I am *not!* Treat me civilly, give me peace with honor, don't put the only available seat facing the window, and a child may eat jam in my lap before Church. But I resent being grunted at. Wouldn't you? Do you suppose that she communicates her views on life and love to The Dancing Master in a set of modulated 'Grmphs'?"

"You attach too much importance to The Dancing Master."

"He came as we went, and The Dowd grew almost cordial at the sight of him. He smiled greasily, and moved about that darkened dog-kennel in a suspiciously familiar way."

"Don't be uncharitable. Any sin but that I'll forgive."

"Listen to the voice of History. I am only describing what I saw. He entered, the heap on the sofa revived slightly, and the Hawley Boy and I came away together. *He* is disillusioned, but I felt it my duty to lecture him severely for going there. And that's all."

"Now for Pity's sake leave the wretched creature and The Dancing Master alone. They never did you any harm."

"No harm? To dress as an example and a stumbling-block for half Simla, and then to find this Person who is dressed by the hand of God—not that I wish to disparage *Him* for a moment, but you know the *tikka dhurzie* way He attires those lilies of the field—this Person draws the eyes of men—and some of them nice men? It's almost enough to make one discard clothing. I told the Hawley Boy so."

"And what did that sweet youth do?"

"Turned shell-pink and looked across the far blue hills like a distressed cherub. *Am* I talking wildly, Polly? Let me say my say, and I shall be calm. Otherwise I may go abroad and disturb Simla with a few original reflections. Excepting always your own sweet self, there isn't a single woman in the land who understands me when I am—what's the word?"

"*Tête-Fêlée*," suggested Mrs. Mallowe.

"Exactly! And now let us have tiffin. The demands of Society are exhausting, and as Mrs. Delville says"— Here Mrs. Hauksbee, to the horror of the *khitmatgars*, lapsed into a series of grunts, while Mrs. Mallowe stared in lazy surprise.

" 'God gie us a gude conceit of oorselves,' " said Mrs. Hauksbee, piously, returning to her natural speech. "Now, in any other woman that would have been vulgar. I am consumed with curiosity to see Mrs. Bent. I expect complications."

"Woman of one idea," said Mrs. Mallowe, shortly; "all complications are as old as the hills! I have lived through or near all—*all*—ALL!"

"And yet do not understand that men and women never behave twice alike. I am old who was young—if ever I put my head in your lap, you dear, big sceptic, you will learn that my parting is gauze—but never, no never, have I lost my interest in men and women. Polly, I shall see this business out to the bitter end."

"I am going to sleep," said Mrs. Mallowe, calmly. "I never interfere with men or women unless I am compelled,"

and she retired with dignity to her own room.

Mrs. Hauksbee's curiosity was not long left ungratified, for Mrs. Bent came up to Simla a few days after the conversation faithfully reported above, and pervaded the Mall by her husband's side.

"Behold!" said Mrs. Hauksbee, thoughtfully rubbing her nose. "That is the last link of the chain, if we omit the husband of the Delville, whoever he may be. Let me consider. The Bents and the Delvilles inhabit the same hotel; and the Delville is detested by the Waddy—do you know the Waddy? —who is almost as big a dowd. The Waddy also abominates the male Bent, for which, if her other sins do not weigh too heavily, she will eventually go to Heaven."

"Don't be irreverent," said Mrs. Mallowe. "I like Mrs. Bent's face."

"I am discussing the Waddy," returned Mrs. Hauksbee, loftily. "The Waddy will take the female Bent apart, after having borrowed—yes!—everything that she can, from hairpins to babies' bottles. Such, my dear, is life in a hotel. The Waddy will tell the female Bent facts and fictions about The Dancing Master and The Dowd."

"Lucy, I should like you better if you were not always looking into people's back-bed-rooms."

"Anybody can look into their front drawing-rooms; and remember whatever I do, and whatever I look, I never talk —as the Waddy will. Let us hope that The Dancing Master's greasy smile and manner of the pedagogue will soften the heart of that cow, his wife. If mouths speak truth, I should think that little Mrs. Bent could get very angry on occasion."

"But what reason has she for being angry?"

"What reason! The Dancing Master in himself is a reason. How does it go? 'If in his life some trivial errors fall, Look in his face and you'll believe them all.' I am prepared to credit *any* evil of The Dancing Master, because I hate him so. And The Dowd is so disgustingly badly dressed"—

"That she, too, is capable of every iniquity? I always prefer to believe the best of everybody. It saves so much trouble."

"Very good. I prefer to believe the worst. It saves useless expenditure of sympathy. And you may be quite certain that the Waddy believes with me."

Mrs. Mallowe sighed and made no answer.

The conversation was holden after dinner while Mrs. Hauksbee was dressing for a dance.

"I am too tired to go," pleaded Mrs. Mallowe, and Mrs. Hauksbee left her in peace till two in the morning, when she was aware of emphatic knocking at her door.

"Don't be *very* angry, dear," said Mrs. Hauksbee. "My idiot of an *ayah* has gone home, and, as I hope to sleep to-night, there isn't a soul in the place to unlace me."

"Oh, this is too bad!" said Mrs. Mallowe sulkily.

" 'Can't help it. I'm a lone, lorn grass-widow, dear, but I will *not* sleep in my stays. And such news, too! Oh, *do* unlace me, there's a darling! The Dowd—The Dancing Master—I and the Hawley Boy— You know the North veranda?"

"How can I do anything if you spin round like this?" protested Mrs. Mallowe, fumbling with the knot of the laces.

"Oh, I forget. I must tell my tale without the aid of your eyes. Do you know you've lovely eyes, dear? Well, to begin with, I took the Hawley Boy to a *kala juggah*."

"Did he want much taking?"

"Lots! There was an arrangement of loose-boxes in *kanats*, and *she* was in the next one talking to *him*."

"Which? How? Explain."

"You know what I mean—The Dowd and The Dancing Master. We could hear every word and we listened shamelessly—'specially the Hawley Boy. Polly, I quite love that woman!"

"This is interesting. There! Now turn round. What happened?"

"One moment. Ah—h! Blessed relief. I've been looking forward to taking them off for the last half-hour—which is ominous at my time of life. But, as I was saying, we listened and heard The Dowd drawl worse than ever. She drops her final g's like a barmaid or a blue-blooded Aide-de-Camp. 'Look he-ere, you're gettin' too fond o' me,' she said, and The Dancing Master owned it was so in language that nearly made me ill. The Dowd reflected for a while. Then we heard her say, 'Look he-ere, Mister Bent, why are you such an aw-ful liar?' I nearly exploded while The Dancing Master denied the charge. It seems that he never told her he was a married man."

"I said he wouldn't."

"And she had taken this to heart, on

personal grounds, I suppose. She drawled along for five minutes, reproaching him with his perfidy and grew quite motherly. 'Now you've got a nice little wife of your own—you have,' she said. 'She's ten times too good for a fat old man like you, and, look he-ere, you never told me a word about her, and I've been thinkin' about it a good deal, and I think you're a liar.' Wasn't that delicious? The Dancing Master maundered and raved till the Hawley Boy suggested that he should burst in and beat him. His voice runs up into an impassioned squeak when he is afraid. The Dowd must be an extraordinary woman. She explained that had he been a bachelor she might not have objected to his devotion; but since he was a married man and the father of a very nice baby, she considered him a hypocrite, and this she repeated twice. She wound up her drawl with: 'An' I'm tellin' you this because your wife is angry with m?, an' I hate quarrellin' with any other woman, an' I like your wife. You know how you have behaved for the last six weeks. You shouldn't have done it, indeed you shouldn't. You're too old an' fat.' Can't you imagine how The Dancing Master would wince at that! 'Now go away,' she said. 'I don't want to tell you what I think of you, because I think you are not nice. I'll stay he-ere till the next dance begins.' Did you think that the creature had so much in her?"

"I never studied her as closely as you did. It sounds unnatural. What happened?"

"The Dancing Master attempted blandishment, reproof, jocularity, and the style of the Lord High Warden, and I had almost to pinch the Hawley Boy to make him keep quiet. She grunted at the end of each sentence and, in the end *he* went away swearing to himself, quite like a man in a novel. He looked more objectionable than ever. I laughed. I love that woman—in spite of her clothes. And now I'm going to bed. What do you think of it?"

"I sha'n't begin to think till the morning," said Mrs. Mallowe, yawning. "Perhaps she spoke the truth. They do fly into it by accident sometimes."

Mrs. Hauksbee's account of her eavesdropping was an ornate one but truthful in the main. For reasons best known to herself, Mrs. "Shady" Delville had turned upon Mr. Bent and rent him limb from limb, casting him away limp and disconcerted ere she withdrew the light of her eyes from him permanently. Being a man of resource, and anything but pleased in that he had been called both old and fat, he gave Mrs. Bent to understand that he had, during her absence in the Doon, been the victim of unceasing persecution at the hands of Mrs. Delville, and he told the tale so often and with such eloquence that he ended in believing it, while his wife marvelled at the manners and customs of "some women." When the situation showed signs of languishing, Mrs. Waddy was always on hand to wake the smouldering fires of suspicion in Mrs. Bent's bosom and to contribute generally to the peace and comfort of the hotel. Mr. Bent's life was not a happy one, for if Mrs. Waddy's story were true, he was, argued his wife, untrustworthy to the last degree. If his own statement was true, his charms of manner and conversation were so great that he needed constant surveillance. And he received it, till he repented genuinely of his marriage and neglected his personal appearance. Mrs. Delville alone in the hotel was unchanged. She removed her chair some six paces toward the head of the table, and occasionally in the twilight ventured on timid overtures of friendship to Mrs. Bent, which were repulsed.

"She does it for my sake," hinted the virtuous Bent.

"A dangerous and designing woman," purred Mrs. Waddy.

Worst of all, every other hotel in Simla was full!

*   *   *   *   *   *

"Polly, are you afraid of diphtheria?"

"Of nothing in the world except smallpox. Diphtheria kills, but it doesn't disfigure. Why do you ask?"

"Because the Bent baby has got it, and the whole hotel is upside down in consequence. The Waddy has 'set her five young on the rail' and fled. The Dancing Master fears for his precious throat, and that miserable little woman, his wife, has no notion of what ought to be done. She wanted to put it into a mustard bath—for croup!"

"Where did you learn all this?"

"Just now, on the Mall. Dr. Howlen told me. The Manager of the hotel is abusing the Bents, and the Bents are abusing the manager. They *are* a feckless couple."

"Well. What's on your mind?"

"This; and I know it's a grave thing to ask. Would you seriously object to my bringing the child over here, with its mother?"

"On the most strict understanding that we see nothing of The Dancing Master."

"He will be only too glad to stay away. Polly, you're an angel. The woman really is at her wits' end."

"And you know nothing about her, careless, and would hold her up to public scorn if it gave you a minute's amusement. Therefore you risk your life for the sake of her brat. No, Loo, *I'm* not the angel. I shall keep to my rooms and avoid her. But do as you please—only tell me why you do it."

Mrs. Hauksbee's eyes softened; she looked out of the window and back into Mrs. Mallowe's face.

"I don't know," said Mrs. Hauksbee, simply.

"You dear!"

"Polly!—and for aught you knew you might have taken my fringe off. Never do that again without warning. Now we'll get the rooms ready. I don't suppose I shall be allowed to circulate in society for a month."

"And I also. Thank goodness I shall at last get all the sleep I want."

Much to Mrs. Bent's surprise she and the baby were brought over to the house almost before she knew where she was. Bent was devoutly and undisguisedly thankful, for he was afraid of the infection, and also hoped that a few weeks in the hotel alone with Mrs. Delville might lead to explanations. Mrs. Bent had thrown her jealousy to the winds in her fear for her child's life.

"We can give you good milk," said Mrs. Haukebee to her, "and our house is much nearer to the Doctor's than the hotel, and you won't feel as though you were living in a hostile camp. Where is the dear Mrs. Waddy? She seemed to be a particular friend of yours."

"They've all left me," said Mrs. Bent, bitterly. "Mrs. Waddy went first. She said I ought to be ashamed of myself for introducing diseases there, and I am *sure* it wasn't my fault that little Dora"—

"How nice!" cooed Mrs. Hauksbee. "The Waddy is an infectious disease herself—'more quickly caught than the plague and the taker runs presently mad.' I lived next door to her at the Elysium, three years ago. Now see, you won't give us the *least* trouble, and I've ornamented all the house with sheets soaked in carbolic. It smells comforting, doesn't it? Remember I'm always in call, and my *ayah's* at your service when yours goes to her meals and—and —if you cry I'll *never* forgive you."

Dora Bent occupied her mother's unprofitable attention through the day and the night. The Doctor called thrice in the twenty-four hours, and the house reeked with the smell of the Condy's Fluid, chlorine-water, and carbolic acid washes. Mrs. Mallowe kept to her own rooms—she considered that she had made sufficient concessions in the cause of humanity—and Mrs. Hauksbee was more esteemed by the Doctor as a help in the sick-room than the half-distraught mother.

"I know nothing of illness," said Mrs. Hauksbee to the Doctor. "Only tell me what to do, and I'll do it."

"Keep that crazy woman from kissing the child, and let her have as little to do with the nursing as you possibly can," said the Doctor; "I'd turn her out of the sick-room, but that I honestly believe she'd die of anxiety. She is less

than no good, and I depend on you and the *ayahs*, remember."

Mrs. Hauksbee accepted the responsibility, though it painted olive hollows under her eyes and forced her to her oldest dresses. Mrs. Bent clung to her with more than childlike faith.

"I *know* you'll make Dora well, won't you?" she said at least twenty times a day; and twenty times a day Mrs. Hauksbee answered valiantly, "Of course I will."

But Dora did not improve, and the Doctor seemed to be always in the house.

"There's some danger of the thing taking a bad turn," he said; "I'll come over between three and four in the morning to-morrow."

"Good gracious!" said Mrs. Hauksbee. "He never told me what the turn would be! My education has been horribly neglected; and I have only this foolish mother-woman to fall back upon."

The night wore through slowly, and Mrs. Hauksbee dozed in a chair by the fire. There was a dance at the Viceregal Lodge, and she dreamed of it till she was aware of Mrs. Bent's anxious eyes staring into her own.

"Wake up! Wake up! Do something!" cried Mrs. Bent, piteously. "Dora's choking to death! Do you mean to let her die?"

Mrs. Hauksbee jumped to her feet and bent over the bed. The child was fighting for breath, while the mother wrung her hands despairing.

"Oh, what can I do? What can you do? She won't stay still! I can't hold her. Why didn't the Doctor say this was coming?" screamed Mrs. Bent. "*Won't* you help me? She's dying!"

"I—I've never seen a child die before!" stammered Mrs. Hauksbee, feebly, and then—let none blame her weakness after the strain of long watching—she broke down, and covered her face with her hands. The *ayahs* on the threshold snored peacefully.

There was a rattle of '*rickshaw* wheels below, the clash of an opening door, a heavy step on the stairs, and Mrs. Delville entered to find Mrs. Bent screaming for the Doctor as she ran round the room. Mrs. Hauksbee, her hands to her ears, and her face buried in the chintz of a chair, was quivering with pain at each cry from the bed, and murmuring, "Thank God, I never bore a child! Oh! thank God, I never bore a child!"

Mrs. Delville looked at the bed for an instant, took Mrs. Bent by the shoulders, and said, quietly, "Get me some caustic. Be quick."

The mother obeyed mechanically. Mrs. Delville had thrown herself down by the side of the child and was opening its mouth.

"Oh, you're killing her!" cried Mrs. Bent. "Where's the Doctor! Leave her alone!"

Mrs. Delville made no reply for a minute, but busied herself with the child.

"Now the caustic, and hold a lamp behind my shoulder. *Will* you do as you are told? The acid-bottle, if you don't know what I mean," she said.

A second time Mrs. Delville bent over the child. Mrs. Hauksbee, her face still hidden, sobbed and shivered. One of

the *ayahs* staggered sleepily into the room, yawning: "*Doctor Sahib* come."

Mrs. Delville turned her head.

"You're only just in time," she said. "It was chokin' her when I came in, an' I've burned it."

"There was no sign of the membrane getting to the air-passages after the last steaming. It was the general weakness, I feared," said the Doctor half to himself, and he whispered as he looked, "You've done what I should have been afraid to do without consultation."

"She was dyin'," said Mrs. Delville, under her breath. "Can you do anythin'? What a mercy it was I went to the dance!"

Mrs. Hauksbee raised her head.

"Is it all over?" she gasped. "I'm useless—I'm worse than useless! What are *you* doing here?"

She stared at Mrs. Delville, and Mrs. Bent, realizing for the first time who was the Goddess from the Machine, stared also.

Then Mrs. Delville made explanation, putting on a dirty long glove and smoothing a crumpled and ill-fitting ball-dress.

"I was at the dance, an' the Doctor was tellin' me about your baby bein' so ill. So I came away early, an' your door was open, an' I—I—lost my boy this way six months ago, an' I've been tryin' to forget it ever since, an' I—I—am very sorry for intrudin' an' anythin' that has happened."

Mrs. Bent was putting out the Doctor's eye with a lamp as he stooped over Dora.

"Take it away," said the Doctor. "I think the child will do, thanks to you, Mrs. Delville. *I* should have come too late, but, I assure you"—he was addressing himself to Mrs. Delville—"I had not the faintest reason to expect *this*. The membrane must have grown like a mushroom. Will one of you help me, please?"

He had reason for the last sentence. Mrs. Hauksbee had thrown herself into Mrs. Delville's arms, where she was weeping bitterly, and Mrs. Bent was unpicturesquely mixed up with both, while from the tangle came the sound of many sobs and much promiscuous kissing.

"Good gracious! I've spoilt all your beautiful roses!" said Mrs. Hauksbee, lifting her head from the lump of crushed gum and calico atrocities on Mrs. Delville's shoulder and hurrying to the Doctor.

Mrs. Delville picked up her shawl, and slouched out of the room, mopping her eyes with the glove that she had not put on.

"I always said she was more than a woman," sobbed Mrs. Hauksbee, hysterically, "and *that* proves it!"

* * * * * *

Six weeks later, Mrs. Bent and Dora had returned to the hotel. Mrs. Hauksbee had come out of the Valley of Humiliation, had ceased to reproach herself for her collapse in an hour of need, and was even beginning to direct the affairs of the world as before.

"So nobody died, and everything went off as it should, and I kissed The Dowd, Polly. I feel so old. Does it show in my face?"

"Kisses don't as a rule, do they? Of course you know what the result of The Dowd's providential arrival has been."

"They ought to build her a statue—only no sculptor dare copy those skirts."

"Ah!" said Mrs. Mallowe, quietly. "She has found another reward. The Dancing Master has been smirking through Simla, giving every one to understand that she came because of her undying love for him—for him—to save *his* child, and all Simla naturally believes this."

"But Mrs. Bent"—

"Mrs. Bent believes it more than any one else. She won't speak to The Dowd now. *Isn't* The Dancing Master an angel?"

Mrs. Hauksbee lifted up her voice and raged till bedtime. The doors of the two rooms stood open.

"Polly," said a voice from the darkness, "what did that American-heiress-globe-trotter girl say last season when she was tipped out of her 'rickshaw turning a corner? Some absurd adjective that made the man who picked her up explode."

"'Paltry,'" said Mrs. Mallowe. "Through her nose—like this—'Ha-ow pahltry!'"

"Exactly," said the voice. "Ha-ow pahltry it all is!"

"Which?"

"Everything. Babies, Diphtheria, Mrs. Bent and The Dancing Master, I whooping in a chair, and The Dowd dropping in from the clouds. I wonder what the motive was—*all* the motives."

"Um!"

"What do *you* think?"

"Don't ask me. Go to sleep."

Only a Subaltern

. . . Not only to enforce by command but to encourage by example the energetic discharge of duty and the steady endurance of the difficulties and privations inseparable from Military Service.—*Bengal Army Regulations.*

THEY made Bobby Wick pass an examination at Sandhurst. He was a gentleman before he was gazetted, so, when the Empress announced that "Gentleman-Cadet Robert Hanna Wick" was posted as Second Lieutenant to the Tyneside Tail Twisters at Kram Bokhar, he became an officer *and* a gentleman, which is an enviable thing; and there was joy in the house of Wick where Mamma Wick and all the little Wicks fell upon their knees and offered incense to Bobby by virtue of his achievements.

Papa Wick had been a Commissioner in his day, holding authority over three millions of men in the Chota-Buldana Division, building great works for the good of the land, and doing his best to make two blades of grass grow where there was but one before. Of course, nobody knew anything about this in the little English village where he was just "old Mr. Wick" and had forgotten that he was a Companion of the Order of the Star of India.

He patted Bobby on the shoulder and said: "Well done, my boy!"

There followed, while the uniform was being prepared, an interval of pure delight, during which Bobby took brevet-rank as a "man" at the women-swamped tennis-parties and tea-fights of the village, and, I dare say, had his joining-time been extended, would have fallen in love with several girls at once. Little country villages at Home are very full of nice girls, because all the young men come out to India to make their fortunes.

"India," said Papa Wick, "is the place. "I've had thirty years of it and, begad, I'd like to go back again. When you join the Tail Twisters you'll be among friends, if every one hasn't forgotten Wick of Chota-Buldana, and a lot of people will be kind to you for our sakes. The mother will tell you more about outfit than I can, but remember this. Stick to your Regiment, Bobby—stick to your Regiment. You'll see men all round you going into the Staff Corps, and doing every possible sort of duty but regimental, and you may be tempted to follow suit. Now so long as you keep within your allowance, and I haven't stinted you there, stick to the Line, the whole Line and nothing but the Line. Be careful how you back another young fool's bill, and if you fall in love with a woman twenty years older than yourself, don't tell *me* about it, that's all."

With these counsels, and many others equally valuable, did Papa Wick fortify Bobby ere that last awful night at Portsmouth when the Officers' Quarters held more inmates than were provided for by the Regulations, and the liberty-men of the ships fell foul of the drafts for India, and the battle raged from the Dockyard Gates even to the slums of

Longport, while the drabs of Fratton came down and scratched the faces of the Queen's Officers.

Bobby Wick, with an ugly bruise on his freckled nose, a sick and shaky detachment to manœuvre inship and the comfort of fifty scornful females to attend to, had no time to feel homesick till the *Malabar* reached mid-Channel, when he doubled his emotions with a little guard-visiting and a great many other matters.

The Tail Twisters were a most particular Regiment. Those who knew them least said that they were eaten up with "side." But their reserve and their internal arrangements generally were merely protective diplomacy. Some five years before, the Colonel commanding had looked into the fourteen fearless eyes of seven plump and juicy subalterns who had all applied to enter the Staff Corps, and had asked them why the three stars should he, a colonel of the Line, command a dashed nursery for double-dashed bottle-suckers who put on condemned tin spurs and rode qualified mokes at the hiatused heads of forsaken Black Regiments. He was a rude man and a terrible. Wherefore the remnant took measures [with the half-butt as an engine of public opinion] till the rumor went abroad that young men who used the Tail Twisters as a crutch to the Staff Corps, had many and varied trials to endure. However, a regiment had just as much right to its own secrets as a woman.

When Bobby came up from Deolali and took his place among the Tail Twisters, it was gently but firmly borne in upon him that the Regiment was his father and his mother and his indissolubly wedded wife, and that there was no crime under the canopy of heaven blacker than that of bringing shame on the Regiment, which was the best-shooting, best-drilled, best set-up, bravest, most illustrious, and in all respects most desirable Regiment within the compass of the Seven Seas. He was taught the legends of the Mess Plate from the great grinning Golden Gods that had come out of the Summer Palace in Pekin to the silver-mounted markhorhorn snuff-mull presented by the last C. O. [he who spake to the seven subalterns]. And every one of those legends told him of battles fought at long odds, without fear as without support; of hospitality catholic as an Arab's; of friendships deep as the sea and steady as the fighting-line; of honor won by hard roads for honor's sake; and of instant and unquestioning devotion to the Regiment—the Regiment that claims the lives of all and lives forever.

More than once, too, he came officially into contact with the Regimental colors, which looked like the lining of a bricklayer's hat on the end of a chewed stick. Bobby did not kneel and worship them, because British subalterns are not constructed in that manner. Indeed, he condemned them for their weight at the very moment that they were filling with awe and other more noble sentiments.

But best of all was the occasion when he moved with the Tail Twisters, in review order at the breaking of a November day. Allowing for duty-men and sick, the Regiment was one thousand and eighty strong, and Bobby belonged to them; for was he not a Subaltern of the Line—the whole Line and nothing but the Line—as the tramp of two thousand one hundred and sixty sturdy ammunition boots attested. He would not have changed places with Deighton of the Horse Battery, whirling by in a pillar of cloud to a chorus of "Strong right! Strong left!" or Hogan-Yale of the White Hussars, leading his squadron for all it was worth, with the price of horseshoes thrown in; or "Tick" Boileau, trying to live up to his fierce blue and gold turban while the wasps of the Bengal Cavalry stretched to a gallop in the wake of the long, lollopping Walers of the White Hussars.

They fought through the clear cool day, and Bobby felt a little thrill run down his spine when he heard the *tinkle-tinkle-tinkle* of the empty cartridge-cases hopping from the breech-blocks after the roar of the volleys; for he knew that he should live to hear that sound in action. The review ended in a glorious chase across the plain—batteries thundering after cavalry to the huge disgust of the White Hussars, and the Tyneside Tail Twisters hunting a Sikh Regiment, till the lean lathy Singhs panted with exhaustion. Bobby was dusty and dripping long before noon, but his enthusiasm was merely focused—not diminished.

He returned to sit at the feet of Revere, his "skipper," that is to say, the Captain of his Company, and to be instructed in the dark art and mystery of managing men, which is a very large part of the Profession of Arms.

"If you haven't a taste that way," said Revere, between his puffs of his cheroot, "you'll never be able to get the hang of it, but remember Bobby, 'tisn't the best drill, though drill is nearly everything, that hauls a Regiment through Hell and out on the other side. It's the man who knows how to handle men—goat-men, swine-men, dog-men, and so on."

"Dormer, for instance," said Bobby, "I think he comes under the head of fool-men. He mopes like a sick owl."

"That's where you make your mistake, my son. Dormer isn't a fool *yet*, but he's a dashed dirty soldier, and his room corporal makes fun of his socks before kit-inspection. Dormer, being two-thirds pure brute, goes into a corner and growls."

"How do you know?" said Bobby, admiringly.

"Because a Company commander has to know these things—because, if he does *not* know, he may have crime—ay, murder—brewing under his very nose and yet not see that it's there. Dormer is being badgered out of his mind—big as he is—and he hasn't intellect enough to resent it. He's taken to quiet boozing and, Bobby, when the butt of a room goes on the drink, or takes to moping by himself, measures are necessary to pull him out of himself."

"What measures? 'Man can't run round coddling his men forever."

"No. The men would precious soon show him that he was not wanted. You've got to"—

Here the Color-sergeant entered with some papers; Bobby reflected for a while as Revere looked through the Company forms.

"Does Dormer do anything, Sergeant?" Bobby asked, with the air of one continuing an interrupted conversation."

"No, sir. Does 'is dooty like a hor-tomato," said the Sergeant, who delighted in long words. "A dirty soldier, and 'e's under full stoppages for new kit. It's covered with scales, sir."

"Scales? What scales?"

"Fish-scales, sir. 'E's always pokin' in the mud by the river an' a-cleanin' them *muchly*-fish with 'is thumbs."

Revere was still absorbed in the Company papers, and the Sergeant, who was sternly fond of Bobby, continued,—

" 'E generally goes down there when 'e's got 'is skinful, beggin' your pardon, sir, an' they *do* say that the more lush —in-*he*-briated 'e is, the more fish 'e catches. They call 'im the Looney Fish-monger in the Comp'ny, sir."

Revere signed the last paper and the Sergeant retreated.

"It's a filthy amusement," sighed Bobby to himself. Then aloud to Revere: "Are you really worried about Dormer?"

"A little. You see he's never mad enough to send to hospital, or drunk enough to run in, but at any minute he may flare up, brooding and sulking as he does. He resents any interest being shown in him, and the only time I took him out shooting he all but shot *me* by accident."

"I fish," said Bobby, with a wry face. "I hire a country-boat and go down the river from Thursday to Sunday, and the amiable Dormer goes with me—if you can spare us both."

"You blazing young fool!" said Revere, but his heart was full of much more pleasant words.

Bobby, the Captain of a *dhoni*, with

Private Dormer for mate, dropped down the river on Thursday morning—the Private at the bow, the Subaltern at the helm. The Private glared uneasily at the Subaltern, who respected the reserve of the Private.

After six hours, Dormer paced to the stern, saluted, and said—"Beg y' pardon, sir, but *was* you ever on the Durh'm Canal?"

"No," said Bobby Wick. "Come and have some tiffin."

They ate in silence. As the evening fell, Private Dormer broke forth, speaking to himself—

"Hi was on the Durh'm Canal, jes' such a night, come next week twelve month, a-trailin' *of* my toes in the water." He smoked and said no more till bedtime.

The witchery of the dawn turned the grey river-reaches to purple, gold, and opal; and it was as though the lumbering *dhoni* crept across the splendors of a new heaven.

Private Dormer popped his head out of his blanket and gazed at the glory below and around.

"Well—damn—my eyes!" said Private Dormer, in an awed whisped. "This 'ere is like a bloomin' gallantry-show!" For the rest of the day he was dumb, but achieved an ensanguined filthiness through the cleaning of big fish.

The boat returned on Saturday evening. Dormer had been struggling with speech since noon. As the lines and luggage were being disembarked, he found tongue.

"Beg y' pardon, sir," he said, "but would you—would you min' shakin' 'ands with me, sir?"

"Of course not," said Bobby, and he

shook accordingly. Dormer returned to barracks and Bobby to mess.

"He wanted a little quiet and some fishing, I think," said Bobby. "My aunt, but he's a filthy sort of animal! Have you ever seen him clean 'them, *muchly-fish* with 'is thumbs'?"

"Anyhow," said Revere, three weeks later, "he's doing his best to keep his things clean."

When the spring died, Bobby joined in the general scramble for Hill leave, and to his surprise and delight secured three months.

"As good a boy as I want," said Revere, the admiring skipper.

"The best of the batch," said the Adjutant to the Colonel. "Keep back that young skrim-shanker Porkiss, sir, and let Revere make him sit up."

So Bobby departed joyously to Simla Pahar with a tin box of gorgeous raiment.

" 'Son of Wick—old Wick of Chota-Buldana? Ask him to dinner, dear," said the aged men.

"What a nice boy!" said the matrons and the maids.

"First-class place, Simla. Oh, ri—ipping!" said Bobby Wick, and ordered new white cord breeches on the strength of it.

"We're in a bad way," wrote Revere to Bobby at the end of two months. "Since you left, the Regiment has taken to fever and is fairly rotten with it—two hundred in hospital, about a hundred in cells—drinking to keep off fever—and the Companies on parade fifteen file strong at the outside. There's rather more sickness in the out-villages than I care for, but then I'm so blistered with prickly-heat that I'm ready to hang myself. What's the yarn about your mashing a Miss Haverley up there? Not serious, I hope? You're over-young to hang millstones round your neck, and the Colonel will turf you out of that in double-quick time if you attempt it."

It was not the Colonel that brought Bobby out of Simla, but a much more to be respected Commandant. The sickness in the out-villages spread, the Bazar was put out of bounds, and then came the news that the Tail Twisters must go into camp. The message flashed to the Hill stations.—"Cholera—Leave stopped—Officers recalled." Alas, for the white gloves in the neatly soldered boxes, the rides and the dances and picnics that were to be, the loves half spoken, and the debts unpaid! Without demur and without question, fast as tonga could fly or pony gallop, back to their Regiments and their Batteries, as though they were hastening to their weddings, fled the subalterns.

Bobby received his orders on returning from a dance at Viceregal Lodge where he had—but only the Haverley girl knows what Bobby had said or how many waltzes he had claimed for the next ball. Six in the morning saw Bobby at the Tonga Office in the drenching rain, the whirl of the last waltz still in his ears, and an intoxication due neither to wine nor waltzing in his brain.

"Good man!" shouted Deighton of the Horse Battery, through the mists. "Whar you raise dat tonga? I'm coming with you. Ow! But I've had a head and a half. *I* didn't sit out all night. They say the Battery's awful bad," and he hummed dolorously—

"Leave the what at the what's-its-name,
Leave the flock without shelter,
Leave the corpse uninterred,
Leave the bride at the altar!

"My faith! It'll be more bally corpse than bride, though, this journey. Jump in, Bobby. Get on, *Coachwan!*"

On the Umballa platform waited a detachment of officers discussing the latest news from the stricken cantonment, and it was here that Bobby learned the real condition of the Tail Twisters.

"They went into camp," said an elderly Major recalled from the whist-tables at Mussoorie to a sickly Native Regiment, "they went into camp with two hundred and ten sick in carts. Two hundred and ten fever cases only, and the balance looking like so many ghosts with sore eyes. A Madras Regiment could have walked through 'em."

"But they were as fit as be-damned when I left them!" said Bobby.

"Then you'd better make them as fit as be-damned when you rejoin," said the Major, brutally.

Bobby pressed his forehead against the rain-splashed windowpane as the train lumbered across the sodden Doab, and prayed for the health of the Tyneside Tail Twisters. Naini Tal had sent down her contingent with all speed; the lathering ponies of the Dalhousie Road staggered into Pathankot, taxed to the full stretch of their strength; while from cloudy Darjiling the Calcutta Mail whirled up the last straggler of the little army that was to fight a fight, in which was neither medal nor honor for the winning, against an enemy none other than "the sickness that destroyeth in the noonday."

And as each man reported himself, he said: "This is a bad business," and went about his own forthwith, for every Regiment and Battery in the cantonment was under canvas, the sickness bearing them company.

Bobby fought his way through the rain to the Tail Twisters' temporary mess, and Revere could have fallen on the boy's neck for the joy of seeing that ugly, wholesome phiz once more.

"Keep 'em amused and interested," said Revere. "They went on the drink, poor fools, after the first two cases, and there was no improvement. Oh, it's good to have you back, Bobby! Porkiss is a—never mind."

Deighton came over from the Artillery camp to attend a dreary mess dinner, and contributed to the general gloom by nearly weeping over the condition of his beloved Battery. Porkiss so far forgot himself as to insinuate that the presence of the officers could do no earthly good, and that the best thing would be to send the entire Regiment into hospital and "let the doctors look after them." Porkiss was demoralized with fear, nor was his peace of mind restored when Revere said coldly: "Oh! The sooner *you* go out the better, if that's your way of thinking. Any public school could send us fifty *good* men in your place, but it takes time, time, Porkiss, and money, and a certain amount of trouble, to make a Regiment. 'S'pose *you're* the person we go into camp for, eh?"

Whereupon Porkiss was overtaken with a great and chilly fear which a drenching in the rain did not allay, and, two days later, quitted this world for another where, men do fondly hope, allowances are made for the weaknesses of the flesh. The Regimental Sergeant-Major looked wearily across the Sergeants' Mess tent when the news was announced.

"There goes the worst of them," he said. "It'll take the best, and then, please God, it'll stop." The Sergeants were silent till one said: "It couldn't be *him!*" and all knew of whom Travis was thinking.

Bobby Wick stormed through the tents of his Company, rallying, rebuking, mildly, as is consistent with the Regulations, chaffing the faint-hearted: haling the sound into the watery sunlight when there was a break in the weather, and bidding them be of good cheer for their trouble was nearly at an end; scuttling on his dun pony round the outskirts of the camp and heading back men who, with the innate perversity of British soldiers, were always wandering into infected villages, or drinking deeply from rain-flooded marshes; comforting the panic-stricken with rude speech, and more than once tending the dying who had no friends— the men without "townies"; organizing, with banjos and burned cork, Sing-songs which should allow the talent of the Regiment full play; and generally, as he explained, "playing the giddy garden-goat all round."

"You're worth half a dozen of us, Bobby," said Revere in a moment of enthusiasm. "How the devil do you keep it up?"

Bobby made no answer, but had Revere looked into the breast-pocket of his coat he might have seen there a sheaf of badly-written letters which perhaps accounted for the power that possessed the boy. A letter came to Bobby every other day. The spelling was not above reproach, but the sentiments must have been most satisfactory, for on receipt Bobby's eyes softened marvelously, and he was wont to fall into a tender abstraction for a while ere, shaking his cropped head, he charged into his work.

By what power he drew after him the hearts of the roughest, and the Tail Twisters counted in their ranks some rough diamonds indeed, was a mystery to both skipper and C. O., who learned from the regimental chaplain that Bobby was considerably more in request in the hospital tents than the Reverend John Emery.

"The men seem fond of you. Are you in the hospitals much?" said the Colonel, who did his daily round and ordered the men to get well with a hardness that did not cover his bitter grief.

"A little, sir," said Bobby.

"Shouldn't go there too often if I were you. They say it's not contagious, but there's no use in running unnecessary risks. We can't afford to have you down, y' know."

Six days later, it was with the utmost difficulty that the post-runner plashed his way out to the camp with the mail-bags, for the rain was falling in torrents. Bobby received a letter, bore it off to his tent, and, the programme for the next week's Sing-song being satisfactorily disposed of, sat down to answer it. For an hour the unhandy pen toiled over the paper, and where sentiment rose to more than normal tide-level Bobby Wick stuck out his tongue and breathed heavily. He was not used to letter-writing.

"Beg y' pardon, sir," said a voice at the tent door; "but Dormer's 'orrid bad, sir, an' they've taken him orf, sir."

"Damn Private Dormer and you too!" said Bobby Wick, running the blotter over the half-finished letter. "Tell him I'll come in the morning."

" 'E's awful bad, sir," said the voice, hesitatingly. There was an undecided squelching of heavy boots.

"Well?" said Bobby, impatiently.

"Excusin' 'imself before'and for takin' the liberty, 'e says it would be a comfort for to assist 'im, sir, if"—

"*Tattoo lao!* Get my pony! Here, come in out of the rain till I'm ready. What blasted nuisances you are! That's brandy. Drink some; you want it. Hang on to my stirrup and tell me if I go too fast."

Strengthened by a four-finger "nip" which he swallowed without a wink, the Hospital Orderly kept up with the slipping, mud-stained, and very disgusted pony as it shambled to the hospital tent.

Private Dormer was certainly " 'orrid bad." He had all but reached the stage of collapse and was not pleasant to look upon.

"What's this, Dormer?" said Bobby, bending over the man. "You're not going out this time. You've got to come fishing with me once or twice more yet."

The blue lips parted and in the ghost of a whisper said,—"Beg y' pardon, sir, disturbin' of you now, but would you min' 'oldin' my 'and, sir?"

Bobby sat on the side of the bed, and the icy cold hand closed on his own like a vice, forcing a lady's ring which was on the little finger deep into the flesh. Bobby set his lips and waited, the water dripping from the hem of his trousers. An hour passed and the grasp of the hand did not relax, nor did the expression of the drawn face change. Bobby with infinite craft lit himself a cheroot with the left hand, his right arm was numbed to the elbow, and resigned himself to a night of pain.

Dawn showed a very white-faced Subaltern sitting on the side of a sick man's cot, and a Doctor in the doorway using language unfit for publication.

"Have you been here all night, you young ass?" said the Doctor.

"There or thereabouts," said Bobby, ruefully. "He's frozen on to me."

Dormer's mouth shut with a click. He turned his head and sighed. The clinging hand opened, and Bobby's arms fell useless at his side.

"He'll do," said the Doctor, quietly. "It must have been a toss-up all through the night. 'Think you're to be congratulated on this case."

"Oh, bosh!" said Bobby. "I thought the man had gone out long ago—only—only I didn't care to take my hand away. Rub my arm down, there's a good chap. What a grip the brute has! I'm chilled to the marrow!" He passed out of the tent shivering.

Private Dormer was allowed to celebrate his repulse of Death by strong waters. Four days later, he sat on the side of his cot and said to the patients mildly: "I'd 'a' liken to 'a' spoken to 'im—so I should."

But at that time Bobby was reading yet another letter—he had the most persistent correspondent of any man in camp—and was even then about to write that the sickness had abated, and in another week at the outside would be gone. He did not intend to say that the chill of a sick man's hand seemed to have struck into the heart whose capacities for affection he dwelt on at such length. He did intend to enclose the illustrated programme of the forthcoming Sing-song whereof he was not a little proud. He also intended to write on many other matters which do not concern us, and doubtless would have done so but for the slight feverish headache which made him dull and unresponsive at mess.

"You are overdoing it, Bobby," said his skipper. " 'Might give the rest of us credit of doing a little work. You go on as if you were the whole Mess rolled into one. Take it easy."

"I will," said Bobby. "I'm feeling done up, somehow." Revere looked at him anxiously and said nothing.

There was a flickering of lanterns about the camp that night, and a rumor that brought men out of their cots to the tent doors, a paddling of the naked feet of doolie-bearers and the rush of a galloping horse.

"Wot's up?" asked twenty tents; and through twenty tents ran the answer— "Wick, 'e's down."

They brought the news to Revere and he groaned. "Any one but Bobby and I shouldn't have cared! The Sergeant-Major was right."

"Not going out this journey," gasped Bobby, as he was lifted from the doolie. "Not going out this journey." Then with an air of supreme conviction—"I *can't*, you see."

"Not if I can do anything!" said the Surgeon-Major, who had hastened over from the mess where he had been dining.

He and the Regimental Surgeon fought together with Death for the life of Bobby Wick. Their work was interrupted by a hairy apparition in a blue-grey dressing-gown who stared in horror at the bed and cried—"Oh, my Gawd! It can't be *'im!*" until an indignant Hospital Orderly whisked him away.

If care of man and desire to live could have done aught, Bobby would have been saved. As it was, he made a fight of three days, and the Surgeon-Major's brow uncreased. "We'll save him yet," he said; and the Surgeon, who, though he ranked with the Captain, had a very youthful heart, went out upon the word and pranced joyously in the mud.

"Not going out this journey," whispered Bobby Wick, gallantly, at the end of the third day.

"Bravo!" said the Surgeon-Major. "That's the way to look at it, Bobby."

As evening fell a grey shade gathered round Bobby's mouth, and he turned his face to the tent wall wearily. The Surgeon-Major frowned.

"I'm awfully tired," said Bobby, very faintly. "What's the use of bothering me with medicine? I—don't—want—it. Let me alone."

The desire for life had departed, and Bobby was content to drift away on the easy tide of Death.

"It's no good," said the Surgeon-Major. "He doesn't want to live. He's meeting it, poor child." And he blew his nose.

Half a mile away, the regimental band was playing the overture to the Sing-song, for the men had been told that Bobby was out of danger. The clash of the brass and the wail of the horns reached Bobby's ears.

Is there a single joy or pain,
That I should never kno—ow?
You do not love me, 'tis in vain,
Bid me good-bye and go!

An expression of hopeless irritation crossed the boy's face, and he tried to shake his head.

The Surgeon-Major bent down— "What is it? Bobby?"—"Not that waltz," muttered Bobby. "That's our own—our very ownest own. . . . Mummy dear."

With this he sank into the stupor that gave place to death early next morning.

Revere, his eyes red at the rims and his nose very white, went into Bobby's tent to write a letter to Papa Wick which should bow the white head of the ex-Commissioner of Chota-Buldana in the keenest sorrow of his life. Bobby's little store of papers lay in confusion on the table, and among them a half-finished letter. The last sentence ran:

"So you see, darling, there is really no fear, because as long as I know you care for me and I care for you, nothing can touch me."

Revere stayed in the tent for an hour. When he came out, his eyes were redder than ever.

* * * * * *

Private Conklin sat on a turned-down bucket, and listened to a not unfamiliar tune. Private Conklin was a convalescent and should have been tenderly treated.

"Ho!" said Private Conklin. "There's another bloomin' orf'cer da—ed."

The bucket shot from under him, and his eyes filled with a smithyful of sparks. A tall man in a blue-grey bedgown was regarding him with deep disfavor.

"You ought to take shame for yourself, Conky! Orf'cer?—bloomin' orf'cer? I'll learn you to misname the likes of 'im. Hangel! _Bloomin'_ Hangel! That's wot 'e is!"

And the Hospital Orderly was so satisfied with the justice of the punishment that he did not even order Private Dormer back to his cot.

In the Matter of a Private

Hurrah! hurrah! a soldier's life for me!
Shout, boys, shout! for it makes you
jolly and free.
—_The Ramrod Corps._

PEOPLE who have seen, say that one of the quaintest spectacles of human frailty is an outbreak of hysterics in a girls' school. It starts without warning, generally on a hot afternoon, among the elder pupils. A girl giggles till the giggle gets beyond control. Then she throws up her head, and cries, _"Honk, honk, honk,"_ like a wild goose, and tears mix with the laughter. If the mistress be wise she will rap out something severe at this point to check matters. If she be tender-hearted, and send for a drink of water, the chances are largely in favor of another girl laughing at the afflicted one and herself collapsing. Thus the trouble spreads, and may end in half of what answers to the Lower Sixth of a boys' school rocking and whooping together. Given a week of warm weather, two stately promenades per diem, a heavy mutton and rice meal in the middle of the day, a certain amount of nagging from the teachers, and a few other things, some amazing effects develop. At least, this is what folk say who have had experience.

Now, the Mother Superior of a Convent and the Colonel of a British Infantry Regiment would be justly shocked at any comparison being made between their respective charges. But it is a fact that, under certain circumstances, Thomas in bulk can be worked up into dithering, rippling hysteria. He does not weep, but he shows his trouble unmistakably, and the consequences get into the newspapers, and all the good people who hardly know a Martini from a Snider say: "Take away the brute's ammunition!"

Thomas isn't a brute, and his business, which is to look after the virtuous people, demands that he shall have his ammunition to his hand. He doesn't wear silk stockings, and he really ought to be supplied with a new Adjective to help him to express his opinions; but, for all that, he is a great man. If you call him "the heroic defender of the national honor" one day, and "a brutal and licentious soldiery" the next, you naturally bewilder him, and he looks upon you with suspicion. There is nobody to speak for Thomas except people who have theories to work off on him; and nobody understands Thomas except

Thomas, and he does not always know what is the matter with himself.

That is the prologue. This is the story:

Corporal Slane was engaged to be married to Miss Jhansi M'Kenna, whose history is well known in the regiment and elsewhere. He had his Colonel's permission, and, being popular with the men, every arrangement had been made to give the wedding what Private Ortheris called "eeklar." It fell in the heart of the hot weather, and, after the wedding, Slane was going up to the Hills with the bride. None the less, Slane's grievance was that the affair would be only a hired-carriage wedding, and he felt that the "eeklar" of that was meagre. Miss M'Kenna did not care so much. The Sergeant's wife was helping her to make her wedding-dress, and she was very busy. Slane was, just then, the only moderately contented man in barracks. All the rest were more or less miserable.

And they had so much to make them happy, too. All their work was over at eight in the morning, and for the rest of the day they could lie on their backs and smoke Canteen-plug and swear at the punkah-coolies. They enjoyed a fine, full flesh meal in the middle of the day, and then threw themselves down on their cots and sweated and slept till it was cool enough to go out with their "towny," whose vocabulary contained less than six hundred words, and the Adjective, and whose views on every conceivable question they had heard many times before.

There was the Canteen, of course, and there was the Temperance Room with the second-hand papers in it; but a man of any profession cannot read for eight hours a day in a temperature of 96° or 98° in the shade, running up sometimes to 103° at midnight. Very few men, even though they get a pannikin of flat, stale, muddy beer and hide it under their cots, can continue drinking for six hours a day. One man tried, but he died, and nearly the whole regiment went to his funeral because it gave them something to do. It was too early for the excitement of fever or cholera. The men could only wait and wait and wait, and watch the shadow of the barrack creeping across the blinding white dust. That was a gay life.

They lounged about cantonments—it was too hot for any sort of game, and almost too hot for vice—and fuddled themselves in the evening, and filled themselves to distension with the healthy nitrogenous food provided for them, and the more they stoked the less exercise they took and more explosive they grew. Then tempers began to wear away, and men fell a-brooding over insults real or imaginary, for they had nothing else to think of. The tone of the repartees changed, and instead of saying light-heartedly: "I'll knock your silly face in," men grew laboriously polite and hinted that the cantonments were not big enough for themselves and their enemy, and that there would be more space for one of the two in another Place.

It may have been the Devil who arranged the thing, but the fact of the case is that Losson had for a long time been worrying Simmons in an aimless way. It gave him occupation. The two had their cots side by side, and would sometimes spend a long afternoon swearing at each other; but Simmons was afraid of Losson and dared not challenge him to a fight. He thought over the words in the hot still nights, and half the hate he felt toward Losson he vented on the wretched punkah-coolie.

Losson bought a parrot in the bazar, and put it into a little cage, and lowered the cage into the cool darkness of a well, and sat on the well-curb, shouting bad language down to the parrot. He taught it to say: "Simmons, ye so-oor," which means swine, and several other things entirely unfit for publication. He was a big gross man, and he shook like a jelly when the parrot had the sentence correctly. Simmons, however, shook with rage, for all the room were laughing at him—the parrot was such a disreputable puff of green feathers and it looked so human when it chattered. Losson used to sit, swinging his fat legs, on the side of the cot, and ask the parrot what it thought of Simmons. The parrot would answer: "Simmons, ye so-oor." "Good boy," Losson used to say, scratching the parrot's head; "ye 'ear that, Sim?" And Simmons used to turn over on his stomach and make answer: "I 'ear. Take 'eed you don't 'ear something one of these days."

In the restless nights, after he had been asleep all day, fits of blind rage came upon Simmons and held him till he trembled all over, while he thought in how many different ways he would slay Losson. Sometimes he would picture himself trampling the life out of the man, with heavy ammunition-boots, and at others smashing in his face with the butt, and at others jumping on his shoulders and dragging the head back till the neckbone cracked. Then his mouth would feel hot and fevered, and he would reach out for another sup of the beer in the pannikin.

But the fancy that came to him most frequently and stayed with him longest was one connected with the great roll of fat under Losson's right ear. He noticed it first on a moonlight night, and thereafter it was always before his eyes. It was a fascinating roll of fat. A man could get his hand upon it and tear away one side of the neck; or he could place the muzzle of a rifle on it and blow away all the head in a flash. Losson had no right to be sleek and contented and well-to-do, when he, Simmons, was the butt of the room. Some day, perhaps, he would show those who laughed at the "Simmons, ye *so-oor*" joke, that he was as good as the rest, and held a man's life in the crook of his forefinger. When Losson snored, Simmons hated him more bitterly than ever. Why should Losson be able to sleep when Simmons had to stay awake hour after hour, tossing and turning on the tapes, with the dull liver pain gnawing into his right side and his head throbbing and aching after Canteen? He thought over this for many nights, and the world became unprofitable to him. He even blunted his naturally fine appetite with beer and tobacco; and all the while the parrot talked at and made a mock of him.

The heat continued and the tempers wore away more quickly than before. A Sergeant's wife died of heat-apoplexy in the night, and the rumor ran abroad that it was cholera. Men rejoiced openly, hoping that it would spread and send them into camp. But that was a false alarm.

It was late on a Tuesday evening, and the men were waiting in the deep double verandas for "Last Posts," when Simmons went to the box at the foot of his bed, took out his pipe, and slammed the lid down with a bang that echoed through the deserted barrack like the crack of a rifle. Ordinarily speaking, the men would have taken no notice; but their nerves were fretted to fiddle-strings. They jumped up, and three or four clattered into the barrack-room only to find Simmons kneeling by his box.

"Ow! It's you, is it?" they said and laughed foolishly. "We t h o u g h t 'twas"—

Simmons rose slowly. If the accident had so shaken his fellows, what would not the reality do?

"You thought it was—did you? And what makes you think?" he said, lashing himself into madness as he went on; "to Hell with your thinking, ye dirty spies."

"Simmons, ye *so-oor*," chuckled the parrot in the veranda, sleepily, recognizing a well-known voice. Now that was absolutely all.

The tension snapped. Simmons fell back on the arm-rack deliberately,—the men were at the far end of the room,—and took out his rifle and packet of ammunition. "Don't go playing the goat, Sim!" said Losson. "Put it down," but there was a quaver in his voice. Another man stooped, slipped his boot and hurled it at Simmons's head. The prompt answer was a shot which, fired at random, found its billet in Losson's throat. Losson fell forward without a word, and the others scattered.

"You thought it was!" yelled Simmons. "You're drivin' me to it! I tell you you're drivin' me to it! Get up, Losson, an' don't lie shammin' there—you an' your blasted parrit that druv me to it!"

But there was an unaffected reality about Losson's pose that showed Simmons what he had done. The men were still clamoring in the veranda. Simmons appropriated two more packets of ammunition and ran into the moonlight, muttering: "I'll make a night of it. Thirty roun's, an' the last for myself. Take you that, you dogs!"

He dropped on one knee and fired into the brown of the men on the veranda, but the bullet flew high, and landed in the brickwork with a vicious *phwit* that made some of the younger ones turn pale. It is, as musketry theorists observe, one thing to fire and another to be fired at.

Then the instinct of the chase flared up. The news spread from barrack to barrack, and the men doubled out intent on the capture of Simmons, the wild beast, who was heading for the Cavalry parade-ground, stopping now and again to send back a shot and a curse in the direction of his pursuers.

"I'll learn you to spy on me!" he shouted; "I'll learn you to give me dorg's names! Come on the 'ole lot o' you! Colonel John Anthony Deever, C.B.!"—he turned toward the Infantry Mess and shook his rifle—"you think yourself the devil of a man—but I tell you that if you put your ugly old car-cass outside o' that door, I'll make you the poorest-lookin' man in the army. Come out, Colonel John Anthony Deever, C.B.! Come out and see me practiss on the rainge. I'm the crack shot of the 'ole bloomin' battalion." In proof of which statement Simmons fired at the lighted windows of the mess-house.

"Private Simmons, E Comp'ny, on the Cavalry p'rade-ground, Sir, with thirty rounds," said a Sergeant breathlessly to the Colonel. "Shootin' right and lef', Sir. Shot Private Losson. What's to be done, Sir?"

Colonel John Anthony Deever, C.B., sallied out, only to be saluted by a spurt of dust at his feet.

"Pull up!" said the Second in Command; "I don't want my step in that way, Colonel. He's as dangerous as a mad dog."

"Shoot him like one, then," said the Colonel, bitterly, "if he won't take his chance. *My* regiment, too! If it had been the Towheads I could have understood."

Private Simmons had occupied a strong position near a well on the edge of the parade-ground, and was defying the regiment to come on. The regiment was not anxious to comply, for there is small honor in being shot by a fellow-private. Only Corporal Slane, rifle in hand, threw himself down on the ground, and wormed his way toward the well.

"Don't shoot," said he to the men round him; "like as not you'll 'it me. I'll catch the beggar, livin'."

Simmons ceased shouting for a while, and the noise of trap-wheels could be heard across the plain. Major Oldyne,

Commanding the Horse Battery, was coming back from a dinner in the Civil Lines; was driving after his usual custom—that is to say, as fast as the horse could go.

"A orf'cer! A blooming spangled orf'cer!" shrieked Simmons; "I'll make a scarecrow of that orf'cer!" The trap stopped.

"What's this?" demanded the Major of Gunners. "You there, drop your rifle."

"Why, it's Jerry Blazes! I ain't got no quarrel with you, Jerry Blazes. Pass frien', an' all's well!"

But Jerry Blazes had not the faintest intention of passing a dangerous murderer. He was, as his adoring Battery swore long and fervently, without knowledge of fear, and they were surely the best judges, for Jerry Blazes, it was notorious, had done his possible to kill a man each time the Battery went out. He walked toward Simmons, with the intention of rushing him, and knocking him down.

"Don't make me do it, Sir," said Simmons; "I ain't got nothing agin you. Ah! you would?"—the Major broke into a run—"Take that then!"

The Major dropped with a bullet through his shoulder, and Simmons stood over him. He had lost the satisfaction of killing Losson in the desired way: but here was a helpless body to his hand. Should he slip in another cartridge, and blow off the head, or with the butt smash in the white face? He stopped to consider, and a cry went up from the far side of the parade-ground: "He's killed Jerry Blazes!" But in the shelter of the well-pillars Simmons was safe, except when he stepped

out to fire. "I'll blow yer 'andsome 'ead off, Jerry Blazes," said Simmons, reflectively. "Six an' three is nine an' one is ten, an' that leaves me another nineteen, an' one for myself." He tugged at the string of the second packet of ammunition. Corporal Slane crawled out of the shadow of a bank into the moonlight.

"I see you!" said Simmons. "Come a bit furder on an' I'll do for you."

"I'm comin'," said Corporal Slane, briefly; "you've done a bad day's work, Sim. Come out 'ere an' come back with me."

"Come to,"—laughed Simmons, sending a cartridge home with his thumb. "Not before I've settled you an' Jerry Blazes."

The Corporal was lying at full length in the dust of the parade-ground, a rifle under him. Some of the less-cautious men in the distance shouted: "Shoot 'im! Shoot 'im, Slane!"

"You move 'and or foot, Slane," said Simmons, "an' I'll kick Jerry Blazes' 'ead in, and shoot you after."

"I ain't movin'," said the Corporal, raising his head; "you daren't 'it a man on 'is legs. Let go o' Jerry Blazes an' come out o' that with your fistes. Come an' 'it me. You daren't, you bloomin' dog-shooter!"

"I dare."

"You lie, you man-sticker. You sneakin', Sheeny butcher, you lie. See there!" Slane kicked the rifle away, and stood up in the peril of his life. "Come on, now!"

The temptation was more than Simmons could resist, for the Corporal in his white clothes offered a perfect mark.

"Don't misname me," shouted Simmons, firing as he spoke. The shot missed, and the shooter, blind with rage, threw his rifle down and rushed at Slane from the protection of the well. Within striking distance, he kicked savagely at Slane's stomach, but the weedy Corporal knew something of Simmons's weakness, and knew, too, the deadly guard for that kick. Bowing forward and drawing up his right leg till the heel of the right foot was set some three inches above the inside of the left knee-cap, he met the blow standing on one leg—exactly as Gonds stand when they meditate—and ready for the fall that would follow. There was an oath, the Corporal fell over to his own left as shinbone met shinbone, and the Private collapsed, his right leg broken an inch above the ankle.

" 'Pity you don't know that guard, Sim," said Slane, spitting out the dust as he rose. Then raising his voice— "Come an' take him orf. I've bruk 'is leg." This was not strictly true, for the Private had accomplished his own downfall, since it is the special merit of that leg-guard that the harder the kick the greater the kicker's discomfiture.

Slane walked to Jerry Blazes and hung over him with ostentatious anxiety, while Simmons, weeping with pain, was carried away. " 'Ope you ain't 'urt badly, Sir," said Slane. The Major had fainted, and there was an ugly, ragged hole through the top of his arm. Slane knelt down and murmured: "S'elp me, I believe 'e's dead. Well, if that ain't my blooming luck all over!"

But the Major was destined to lead his Battery afield for many a long day with unshaken nerve. He was removed, and nursed and petted into convalescence, while the Battery discussed the wisdom of capturing Simmons, and blowing him from a gun. They idolized their Major, and his reappearance on parade brought about a scene nowhere provided for in the Army Regulations.

Great, too, was the glory that fell to Slane's share. The Gunners would have made him drunk thrice a day for at least a fortnight. Even the Colonel of his own regiment complimented him upon his coolness, and the local paper called him a hero. These things did not puff him up. When the Major offered him money and thanks, the virtuous Corporal took the one and put aside the other. But he had a request to make and prefaced it with many a "Beg y' pardon, Sir." Could the Major see his way to letting the Slane-M'Kenna wedding be adorned by the presence of four Battery horses to pull a hired barouche? The Major could, and so could the Battery. Excessively so. It was a gorgeous wedding.

*   *   *   *   *   *

"Wot did I do it for?" said Corporal Slane. "For the 'orses o' course. Jhansi ain't a beauty to look at, but I wasn't goin' to 'ave a hired turn-out. Jerry Blazes? If I 'adn't 'a' wanted something, Sim might ha' blowed Jerry Blazes' blooming 'ead into Hirish stew for aught I'd 'a' cared."

And they hanged Private Simmons— hanged him as high as Haman in hollow square of the regiment; and the Colonel said it was Drink; and the Chaplain was sure it was the Devil; and Simmons fancied it was both, but he didn't know, and only hoped his fate would be a warning to his companions; and half a dozen "intelligent publicists" wrote six beautiful leading articles on "The Prevalence of Crime in the Army."

But not a soul thought of comparing the "bloody-minded Simmons" to the squawking, gaping schoolgirl with which this story opens.

The Enlightenments of Pagett, M.P.

"Because half a dozen grasshoppers under a fern make the field ring with their importunate chink while thousands of great cattle, reposed beneath the shadow of the British oak, chew the cud and are silent, pray do not imagine that those who make the noise are the only inhabitants of the field—that, of course, they are many in number—or that, after all, they are other than the little, shrivelled, meagre, hopping, though loud and troublesome insects of the hour."— *Burke*: "Reflections on the Revolution in France."

THEY were sitting in the veranda of "the splendid palace of an Indian Pro-Consul"; surrounded by all the glory and mystery of the immemorial East. In plain English is was a one-storied, ten-roomed, whitewashed, mud-roofed bungalow, set in a dry garden of dusty tamarisk trees and divided from the road by a low mud wall. The green parrots screamed overhead as they flew in battalions to the river for their morning drink. Beyond the wall, clouds of fine dust showed where the cattle and goats of the city were passing afield to graze. The remorseless white light of the winter sunshine of Northern India lay upon everything and improved nothing, from the whining Persian-wheel by the lawn-tennis court to the long perspective of level road and the blue, domed tombs of Mohammedan saints just visible above the trees.

"A Happy New Year," said Orde to his guest. "It's the first you've ever spent out of England, isn't it?"

"Yes. 'Happy New Year," said Pagett, smiling at the sunshine. "What a divine climate you have here! Just think of the brown cold fog hanging over London now!" And he rubbed his hands.

It was more than twenty years since he had last seen Orde, his schoolmate, and their paths in the world had divided early. The one had quitted college to become a cog-wheel in the machinery of the great Indian Government; the other more blessed with goods, had been whirled into a similar position in the English scheme. Three successive elections had not affected Pagett's position with a loyal constituency, and he had grown insensibly to regard himself in some sort as a pillar of the Empire, whose real worth would be known later on. After a few years of conscientious attendance at many divisions, after newspaper battles innumerable and the publication of interminable correspondence, and more hasty oratory than in his calmer moments he cared to think upon, it occurred to him, as it had occurred to many of his fellows in Parliament, that a tour to India would enable him to sweep a larger lyre and address himself to the problems of Imperial administration with a firmer hand. Accepting, therefore, a general invitation extended to him by Orde some years before, Pagett had taken ship to Karachi, and only over-night had been received with joy by the Deputy-Commissioner of Amara. They had sat late, discussing the changes and chances of twenty years, recalling the names of the dead, and weighing the futures of the living, as is the custom of men meeting after intervals of action.

Next morning they smoked the after breakfast pipe in the veranda, still regarding each other curiously, Pagett, in a light grey frock-coat and garments much too thin for the time of the year, and a puggried sun-hat carefully and wonderfully made. Orde in a shooting coat, riding breeches, brown cowhide boots with spurs, and a battered flax helmet. He had ridden some miles in the early morning to inspect a doubtful river dam. The men's faces differed as much as their attire. Orde's worn and wrinkled about the eyes, and grizzled at the temples, was the harder and more square of the two, and it was with something like envy that the owner looked at the comfortable outlines of Pagett's blandly receptive countenance, the clear skin, the untroubled eye, and the mobile, clean-shaved lips.

"And this is India!" said Pagett for the twentieth time, staring long and intently at the grey feathering of the tamarisks.

"One portion of India only. It's very much like this for 300 miles in every direction. By the way, now that you have rested a little—I wouldn't ask the old question before—what d'you think of the country?"

" 'Tis the most pervasive country that ever yet was seen. I acquired several pounds of your country coming up from Karachi. The air is heavy with it, and for miles and miles along that distressful eternity of rail there's no horizon to show where air and earth separate."

"Yes. It isn't easy to see truly or far in India. But you had a decent passage out, hadn't you?"

"Very good on the whole. Your Anglo-Indian may be unsympathetic about one's political views; but he has reduced ship life to a science."

"The Anglo-Indian is a political orphan, and if he's wise he won't be in a hurry to be adopted by your party grandmothers. But how were your companions unsympathetic?"

"Well, there was a man called Dawlishe, a judge somewhere in this country it seems, and a capital partner at whist by the way, and when I wanted to talk to him about the progress of India in a political sense (Orde hid a grin, which might or might not have been sympathetic), the National Congress movement, and other things in which, as a Member of Parliament, I'm of course interested, he shifted the subject, and when I once cornered him, he looked me calmly in the eye, and said: 'That's all Tommy rot. Come and have a game at Bull.' You may laugh; but that isn't the way to treat a great and important question; and, knowing who I was, well, I thought it rather rude, don't you know; and yet Dawlishe is a thoroughly good fellow."

"Yes; he's a friend of mine, and one of the straightest men I know. I suppose, like many Anglo-Indians, he felt it was hopeless to give you any just idea of any Indian question without the documents before you, and in this case the documents you want are the country and the people."

"Precisely. That was why I came straight to you, bringing an open mind to bear on things. I'm anxious to know what popular feeling in India is really like y'know, now that it has wakened into political life. The National Congress, in spite of Dawlishe, must have caused great excitement among the masses?"

"On the contrary, nothing could be more tranquil than the state of popular feeling; and as to excitement, the people would as soon be excited over the 'Rule of Three' as over the Congress."

"Excuse me, Orde, but do you think you are a fair judge? Isn't the official Anglo-Indian naturally jealous of any external influences that might move the masses, and so much opposed to liberal ideas, truly liberal ideas, that he can scarcely be expected to regard a popular movement with fairness?"

"What did Dawlishe say about Tommy Rot? Think a moment, old man. You and I were brought up together; taught by the same tutors, read the same books, lived the same life, and new languages, and work among new races; while you, more fortunate, remain at home. Why should I change my mind—our mind—because I change my sky? Why should I and the few

hundred Englishmen in my service become unreasonable, prejudiced fossils, while you and your newer friends alone remain bright and open-minded? You surely don't fancy civilians are members of a Primrose League?"

"Of course not, but the mere position of an English official gives him a point of view which cannot but bias his mind on this question." Pagett moved his knee up and down a little uneasily as he spoke.

"That sounds plausible enough, but, like more plausible notions on Indian matters, I believe it's a mistake. You'll find when you come to consult the unofficial Briton that our fault, as a class —I speak of the civilian now—is rather to magnify the progress that has been made toward liberal institutions. It is of English origin, such as it is, and the stress of our work since the Mutiny— only thirty years ago—has been in that direction. No, I think you will get no fairer or more dispassionate view of the Congress business than such men as I can give you. But I may as well say at once that those who know most of India, from the inside, are inclined to wonder at the noise our scarcely begun experiment makes in England."

"But surely the gathering together of Congress delegates is of itself a new thing."

"There's nothing new under the sun. When Europe was a jungle half Asia flocked to the canonical conferences of Buddhism; and for centuries the people have gathered at Puri, Hurdwar, Trimbak, and Benares in immense numbers. A great meeting, what you call a mass meeting, is really one of the oldest and most popular of Indian institutions.

In the case of the Congress meetings, the only notable fact is that the priests of the altar are British, not Buddhist, Jain or Brahmanical, and that the whole thing is a British contrivance kept alive by the efforts of Messrs. Hume, Eardley, Norton, and Digby."

"You mean to say, then, it's not a spontaneous movement?"

"What movement was ever spontaneous in any true sense of the word? This seems to be more factitious than usual. You seem to know a great deal about it; try it by the touchstone of subscriptions, a coarse but fairly trustworthy criterion, and there is scarcely the color of money in it. The delegates write from England that they are out of pocket for working expenses, railway fares, and stationery—the mere pasteboard and scaffolding of their show. It is, in fact, collapsing from mere financial inanition."

"But you cannot deny that the people of India, who are, perhaps, too poor to subscribe, are mentally and morally moved by the agitation," Pagett insisted.

"That is precisely what I *do* deny. The native side of the movement is the work of a limited class, a microscopic minority, as Lord Dufferin described it, when compared with the people proper, but still a very interesting class, seeing that it is of our own creation. It is composed almost entirely of those of the literary or clerkly castes who have received an English education."

"Surely that's a very important class. Its members must be the ordained leaders of popular thought."

"Anywhere else they might be leaders, but they have no social weight in this topsy-turvy land, and though they have been employed in clerical work for generations they have no practical knowledge of affairs. A ship's clerk is a useful person, but he is scarcely the captain; and an orderly-room writer, however smart he may be, is not the colonel. You see, the writer class in India has never till now aspired to anything like command. It wasn't allowed to. The Indian gentleman, for thousands of years past, has resembled Victor Hugo's noble:

> 'Un vrai sire
> Chatelain
> Laisse ecrire
> Le vilain.
> Sa main digne
> Quand il signe
> Égratigne
> Le velin.'

And the little *egratignures* he most likes to make have been scored pretty deeply by the sword."

"But this is childish and mediæval nonsense!"

"Precisely; and from your, or rather our, point of view the pen *is* mightier than the sword. In this country it's otherwise. The fault lies in our Indian balances, not yet adjusted to civilized weights and measures."

"Well, at all events, this literary class represent the natural aspirations and wishes of the people at large, though it may not exactly lead them, and, in spite of all you say, Orde, I defy you to find a really sound English Radical who would not sympathize with those aspirations."

Pagett spoke with some warmth, and he had scarcely ceased when a well-appointed dog-cart turned into the compound gates, and Orde rose saying:

"Here is Edwards, the Master of the Lodge I neglect so diligently, come to talk about accounts, I suppose."

As the vehicle drove up under the porch Pagett also rose, saying with the trained effusion born of much practice:

"But this is also *my* friend, my old and valued friend Edwards. I'm delighted to see you. I knew you were in India, but not exactly where."

"Then it isn't accounts, Mr. Edwards," said Orde, cheerily.

"Why, no, sir; I heard Mr. Pagett was coming, and as our works were closed for the New Year I thought I would drive over and see him."

"A very happy thought. Mr. Edwards, you may not know, Orde, was a leading member of our Radical Club at Switchton when I was beginning political life, and I owe much to his exertions. There's no pleasure like meeting an old friend, except, perhaps, making a new one. I suppose, Mr. Edwards, you stick to the good old cause?"

"Well, you see, sir, things are different out here. There's precious little one can find to say against the Government, which was the main of our talk at home, and them that do say things are not the sort o' people a man who respects himself would like to be mixed up with. There are no politics, in a manner of speaking, in India. It's all work."

"Surely you are mistaken, my good friend. Why I have come all the way from England just to see the working of this great National movement."

"I don't know where you're going to find the nation as moves to begin with,

and then you'll be hard put to it to find what they are moving about. It's like this, sir," said Edwards, who had not quite relished being called "my good friend." "They haven't got any grievance—nothing to hit with, don't you see, sir; and then there's not much to hit against, because the Government is more like a kind of general Providence, directing an old-established state of things, than that at home, where there's something new thrown down for us to fight about every three months."

"You are probably, in your workshops, full of English mechanics, out of the way of learning what the masses think."

"I don't know so much about that. There are four of us English foremen, and between seven and eight hundred native fitters, smiths, carpenters, painters, and such like."

"And they are full of the Congress, of course?"

"Never hear a word of it from year's end to year's end, and I speak the talk, too. But I wanted to ask how things are going on at home—old Tyler and Brown and the rest?"

"We will speak of them presently, but your account of the indifference of your men surprises me almost as much as your own. I fear you are a backslider from the good old doctrine, Edwards. Pagett spoke as one who mourned the death of a near relative.

"Not a bit, sir, but I should be if I took up with a parcel of baboos, pleaders, and schoolboys, as never did a day's work in their lives, and couldn't if they tried. And if you was to poll us English railway men, mechanics, tradespeople, and the like of that all up and down the country from Pesha-wur to Calcutta, you would find us mostly in a tale together. And yet you know we're the same English you pay some respect to at home at 'lection time, and we have the pull o' knowing something about it."

"This is very curious, but you will let me come and see you, and perhaps you will kindly show me the railway works, and we will talk things over at leisure. And about all old friends and old times," added Pagett, detecting with quick insight a look of disappointment in the mechanic's face.

Nodding briefly to Orde, Edwards mounted his dog-cart and drove off.

"It's very disappointing," said the Member to Orde, who, while his friend discoursed with Edwards, had been looking over a bundle of sketches drawn on grey paper in purple ink, brought to him by a Chuprassee.

"Don't let it trouble you, old chap," said Orde, sympathetically. "Look here a moment, here are some sketches by the man who made the carved wood screen you admired so much in the dining-room, and wanted a copy of, and the artist himself is here too."

"A native?" said Pagett.

"Of course," was the reply, "Bishen Singh is his name, and he has two brothers to help him. When there is an important job to do, the three go into partnership, but they spend most of their time and all their money in litigation over an inheritance, and I'm afraid they are getting involved. Thor-oughbred Sikhs of the old rock, obsti-nate, touchy, bigoted, and cunning, but good men for all that. Here is Bishen Singh—shall we ask *him* about the Congress?"

But Bishen Singh, who approached with a respectful salaam, had never heard of it, and he listened with a puzzled face and obviously feigned in-terest to Orde's account of its aims and objects, finally shaking his vast white turban with great significance when he learned that it was promoted by cer-tain pleaders named by Orde, and by educated natives. He began with la-bored respect to explain how he was a poor man with no concern in such mat-ters, which were all under the control of God, but presently broke out of Urdu into familiar Punjabi, the mere sound of which had a rustic smack of village smoke-reek and plough-tail, as he denounced the wearers of white coats, the jugglers with words who filched his field from him, the men whose backs were never bowed in honest work; and poured ironical scorn on the Bengali. He and one of his brothers had seen Calcutta, and being at work there had Bengali carpenters given to them as assistants.

"Those carpenters!" said Bishen Singh. "Black apes were more efficient workmates, and as for the Bengali babu —tchick!" The guttural click needed no interpretation, but Orde translated the rest, while Pagett gazed with in-terest at the wood-carver.

"He seems to have a most illiberal prejudice against the Bengali," said the M.P.

"Yes, it's very sad that for ages outside Bengal there should be so bitter a prejudice. Pride of race, which also means race-hatred, is the plague and curse of India and it spreads far," Orde pointed with his riding-whip to the large map of India on the veranda wall.

"See! I begin with the North," said he. "There's the Afghan, and, as a highlander, he despises all the dwellers in Hindoostan—with the exception of the Sikh, whom he hates as cordially as the Sikh hates him. The Hindu loathes Sikh and Afghan, and the Rajput—that's a little lower down across this yellow blot of desert—has a strong objection, to put it mildly, to the Maratha who, by the way, poisonously hates the Afghan. Let's go North a minute. The Sindhi hates everybody I've mentioned. Very good, we'll take less warlike races. The cultivator of Northern India domineers over the man in the next province, and the Behari of the Northwest ridicules the Bengali. They are all at one on that point. I'm giving you merely the roughest possible outlines of the facts, of course."

Bishen Singh, his clean cut nostrils still quivering, watched the large sweep of the whip as it traveled from the frontier, through Sindh, the Junjab and Rajputana, till it rested by the valley of the Jumna.

"Hate—eternal and inextinguishable hate," concluded Orde, flicking the lash of the whip across the large map from East to West as he sat down. "Remember Canning's advice to Lord Granville, 'Never write or speak of Indian things without looking at a map.'"

Pagett opened his eyes, Orde resumed. "And the race-hatred is only a part of it. What's really the matter with Bishen Singh is class-hatred, which, unfortunately, is even more intense and more widely spread. That's one of the little drawbacks of caste, which some of your recent English writers find an impeccable system."

The wood-carver was glad to be recalled to the business of his craft, and his eyes shone as he received instructions for a carved wooden doorway for Pagett, which he promised should be splendidly executed and despatched to England in six months. It is an irrelevant detail, but in spite of Orde's reminders, fourteen months elapsed before the work was finished. Business over, Bishen Singh hung about, reluctant to take his leave, and at last joining his hands and approaching Orde with bated breath and whispering humbleness, said he had a petition to make. Orde's face suddenly lost all trace of expression. "Speak on, Bishen Singh," said he, and the carver in a whining tone explained that his case against his brothers was fixed for hearing before a native judge and—here he dropped his voice still lower till he was summarily stopped by Orde, who sternly pointed to the gate with an emphatic Begone!

Bishen Singh, showing but little sign of discomposure, salaamed respectfully to the friends and departed.

Pagett looked inquiry; Orde with complete recovery of his usual urbanity, replied: "It's nothing, only the old story, he wants his case to be tried by an English judge—they all do that—but when he began to hint that the other side were in improper relations with the native judge I had to shut him up. Gunga Ram, the man he wanted to make insinuations about, may not be very bright; but he's as honest as daylight on the bench. But that's just what one can't get a native to believe."

"Do you really mean to say these people prefer to have their cases tried by English judges?"

"Why, certainly."

Pagett drew a long breath. "I didn't know that before." At this point a phaeton entered the compound, and Orde rose with "Confound it, there's old Rasul Ali Khan come to pay one of his tiresome duty calls. I'm afraid we shall never get through our little Congress discussion."

Pagett was an almost silent spectator of the grave formalities of a visit paid by a punctilious old Mahommedan gentleman to an Indian official; and was much impressed by the distinction of manner and fine appearance of the Mohammedan landholder. When the exchange of polite banalities came to a pause, he expressed a wish to learn the courtly visitor's opinion of the National Congress.

Orde reluctantly interpreted, and with a smile which even Mohammedan politeness could not save from bitter scorn, Rasul Ali Khan intimated that he knew nothing about it and cared still less. It was a kind of talk encouraged by the Government for some mysterious purpose of its own, and for his own part he wondered and held his peace.

Pagett was far from satisfied with this, and wished to have the old gentleman's opinion on the propriety of managing all Indian affairs on the basis of an elective system.

Orde did his best to explain, but it was plain the visitor was bored and bewildered. Frankly, he didn't think much of committees; they had a Mu-

nicipal Committee at Lahore and had elected a menial servant, an orderly, as a member. He had been informed of this on good authority, and after that, committees had ceased to interest him. But all was according to the rule of Government, and, please God, it was all for the best.

"What an old fossil it is!" cried Pagett, as Orde returned from seeing his guest to the door; "just like some old blue-blooded hidalgo of Spain. What does he really think of the Congress after all, and of the elective system?"

"Hates it all like poison. When you are sure of a majority, election is a fine system; but you can scarcely expect the Mahommedans, the most masterful and powerful minority in the country, to contemplate their own extinction with joy. The worst of it is that he and his co-religionists, who are many, and the landed proprietors, also, of Hindu race, are frightened and put out by this election business and by the importance we have bestowed on lawyers, pleaders, writers, and the like, who have, up to now, been in abject submission to them. They say little, but after all they are the most important fagots in the great bundle of communities, and all the glib bunkum in the world would not pay for their estrangement. They have controlled the land."

"But I am assured that experience of local self-government in your municipalities has been most satisfactory, and when once the principle is accepted in your centres, don't you know, it is bound to spread, and these important—ah'm—people of yours would learn it like the rest. I see no difficulty at all," and the smooth lips closed with the complacent snap habitual to Pagett, M.P., the "man of cheerful yesterdays and confident to-morrows."

Orde looked at him with a dreary smile.

"The privilege of election has been most reluctantly withdrawn from scores of municipalities, others have had to be summarily suppressed, and, outside the Presidency towns, the actual work done has been badly performed. This is of less moment, perhaps—it only sends up the local death-rates—than the fact that the public interest in municipal elections, never very strong, has waned, and is waning, in spite of careful nursing on the part of Government servants."

"Can you explain this lack of interest?" said Pagett, putting aside the rest of Orde's remarks.

"You may find a ward of the key in the fact that only one in every thousand of our population can spell. Then they are infinitely more interested in religion and caste questions than in any sort of politics. When the business of mere existence is over, their minds are occupied by a series of interests, pleasures, rituals, superstitions, and the like, based on centuries of tradition and usage. You, perhaps, find it hard to conceive of people absolutely devoid of curiosity, to whom the book, the daily paper, and the printed speech are unknown, and you would describe their life as blank. That's a profound mistake. You are in another land, another century, down on the bed-rock of society, where the family merely, and not the community, is all-important. The average Oriental cannot be brought to look beyond his clan. His life, too, is more complete and self-sufficing, and

less sordid and low-thoughted than you might imagine. It is bovine and slow in some respects, but it is never empty. You and I are inclined to put the cart before the horse, and to forget that it is the man that is elemental, not the book.

'The corn and the cattle are all my care,
And the rest is the will of God.'

Why should such folk look up from their immemorially appointed round of duty and interests to meddle with the unknown and fuss with voting-papers. How would you, atop of all your interests care to conduct even one-tenth of your life according to the manners and customs of the Papuans, let's say? That's what it comes to."

"But if they won't take the trouble to vote, why do you anticipate that Mohammedans, proprietors, and the rest would be crushed by majorities of them?"

Again Pagett disregarded the closing sentence.

"Because, though the landholders would not move a finger on any purely political question, they could be raised in dangerous excitement by religious hatreds. Already the first note of this has been sounded by the people who are trying to get up an agitation on the cow-killing question, and every year there is trouble over the Mohammedan Muharrum processions."

"But who looks after the popular rights, being thus unrepresented?"

"The Government of Her Majesty the Queen, Empress of India, in which, if the Congress promoters are to be believed, the people have an implicit trust; for the Congress circular, specially prepared for rustic comprehension, says the movement is *'for the remission of tax, the advancement of Hindustan, and the strengthening of the British Government.'* This paper is headed in large letters—'MAY THE PROSPERITY OF THE EMPIRE OF INDIA ENDURE.' "

"Really!" said Pagett, "that shows some cleverness. But there are things better worth imitation in our English methods of—er—political statement than this sort of amiable fraud."

"Anyhow," resumed Orde, "you perceive that not a word is said about elections and the elective principle, and the reticence of the Congress promoters here shows they are wise in their generation."

"But the elective principle must triumph in the end, and the little difficulties you seem to anticipate would give way on the introduction of a well-balanced scheme, capable of indefinite extension."

"But is it possible to devise a scheme which, always assuming that the people took any interest in it, without enormous expense, ruinous dislocation of the administration and danger to the public peace, can satisfy the aspirations of Mr. Hume and his following, and yet safeguard the interests of the Mahommedans, the landed and wealthy classes, the Conservative Hindus, the Eurasians, Parsees, Sikhs, Rajputs, native Christians, domiciled Europeans and others, who are each important and powerful in their way?"

Pagett's attention, however, was diverted to the gate, where a group of cultivators stood in apparent hesitation.

"Here are the twelve Apostles, by Jove!—come straight out of Raffaele's cartoons," said the M.P., with the fresh appreciation of a newcomer.

Orde, loth to be interrupted, turned impatiently toward the villagers, and their leader, handing his long staff to one of his companions, advanced to the house.

"It is old Jelloo, the Lumberdar, or head-man of Pind Sharkot, and a very intelligent man for a villager."

The Jat farmer had removed his shoes and stood smiling on the edge of the veranda. His strongly marked features glowed with russet bronze, and his bright eyes gleamed under deeply set brows, contracted by lifelong exposure to sunshine. His beard and moustache streaked with grey swept from bold cliffs of brow and cheek in the large sweeps one sees drawn by Michael Angelo, and strands of long black hair mingled with the irregularity piled wreaths and folds of his turban. The drapery of stout blue cotton cloth thrown over his broad shoulders and girt round his narrow loins, hung from his tall form in broadly sculptured folds, and he would have made a superb model for an artist in search of a patriarch.

Orde greeted him cordially, and after a polite pause the countryman started off with a long story told with impressive earnestness. Orde listened and smiled, interrupting the speaker at times to argue and reason with him in a tone which Pagett could hear was kindly, and finally checking the flux of words was about to dismiss him, when Pagett suggested that he should be asked about the National Congress. But Jelloo had never heard of it.

He was a poor man and such things, by the favor of his Honor, did not concern him.

"What's the matter with your big friend that he was so terribly in earnest?" asked Pagett, when he had left.

"Nothing much. He wants the blood of the people in the next village, who have had smallpox and cattle plague pretty badly, and by the help of a wizard, a currier, and several pigs have passed it on to his own village. 'Wants to know if they can't be run in for this awful crime. It seems they made a dreadful charivari at the village boundary, threw a quantity of spell-bearing objects over the border, a buffalo's skull and other things; then branded a *chamár*—what you would call a currier—on his hinder parts and drove him and a number of pigs over into Jelloo's village. Jelloo says he can bring evidence to prove that the wizard directing these proceedings, who is a Sansi, has been guilty of theft, arson, cattle-killing, perjury and murder, but would prefer to have him punished for bewitching them and inflicting small-pox."

"And how on earth did you answer such a lunatic?"

"Lunatic! the old fellow is as sane as you or I; and he has some ground of complaint against those Sansis. I asked if he would like a native superintendent of police with some men to make inquiries, but he objected on the grounds the police were rather worse than smallpox and criminal tribes put together."

"Criminal tribes—er—I don't quite understand," said Pagett.

"We have in India many tribes of people who in the slack anti-British days became robbers, in various kind, and preyed on the people. They are being restrained and reclaimed little by little, and in time will become useful citizens, but they still cherish hereditary traditions of crime, and are a difficult lot to deal with. By the way what about the political rights of these folk under your schemes? The country people call them vermin, but I suppose they would be electors with the rest."

"Nonsense—special provision would be made for them in a well-considered electoral scheme, and they would doubtless be treated with fitting severity," said Pagett, with a magisterial air.

"Severity, yes—but whether it would be fitting is doubtful. Even those poor devils have rights, and, after all, they only practice what they have been taught."

"But criminals, Orde!"

"Yes, criminals with codes and rituals of crime, gods and godlings of crime, and a hundred songs and sayings in praise of it. Puzzling, isn't it?"

"It's simply dreadful. They ought to be put down at once. Are there many of them?"

"Not more than about sixty thousand in this province, for many of the tribes broadly described as criminal are really vagabond and criminal only on occasion, while others are being settled and reclaimed. They are of great antiquity, a legacy from the past, the golden, glorious Aryan past of Max Müller, Birdwood and the rest of your spindrift philosophers."

An orderly brought a card to Orde,

who took it with a movement of irritation at the interruption, and handed it to Pagett; a large card with a ruled border in red ink, and in the centre in schoolboy copper plate, *Mr. Dina Nath*. "Give salaam," said the civilian, and there entered in haste a slender youth, clad in a closely fitting coat of grey homespun, tight trousers, patent-leather shoes, and a small black velvet cap. His thin cheek twitched, and his eyes wandered restlessly, for the young man was evidently nervous and uncomfortable, though striving to assume a free and easy air.

"Your honor may perhaps remember me," he said in English, and Orde scanned him keenly.

"I know your face somehow. You belonged to the Shershah district I think, when I was in charge there?"

"Yes, sir, my father is writer at Shershah, and your honor gave me a prize when I was first in the Middle School examination five years ago. Since then I have prosecuted my studies, and I am now second year's student in the Mission College."

"Of course: you are Kedar Nath's son —the boy who said he liked geography better than play or sugar cakes, and I didn't believe you. How is your father getting on?"

"He is well, and he sends his salaam, but his circumstances are depressed, and he also is down on his luck."

"You learn English idioms at the Mission College, it seems."

"Yes, sir, they are the best idioms, and my father ordered me to ask your honor to say a word for him to the present incumbent of your honor's shoes, the latchet of which he is not worthy to open, and who knows not Joseph; for things are different at Shershah now, and my father wants promotion."

"Your father is a good man, and I will do what I can for him."

At this point a telegram was handed to Orde, who, after glancing at it, said he must leave his young friend whom he introduced to Pagett, "a member of the English House of Commons who wishes to learn about India."

Orde had scarcely retired with his telegram when Pagett began:

"Perhaps you can tell me something of the National Congress movement?"

"Sir, it is the greatest movement of modern times, and one in which all educated men like us *must* join. All our students are for the Congress."

"Excepting, I suppose, Mahommedans, and the Christians?" said Pagett, quick to use his recent instruction.

"These are some *mere* exceptions to the universal rule."

"But the people outside the College, the working classes, the agriculturists; your father and mother, for instance."

"My mother," said the young man, with a visible effort to bring himself to pronounce the word, "has no ideas, and my father is not agriculturist, nor working class; he is of the Kayeth caste; but he had not the advantage of a collegiate education, and he does not know much of the Congress. It is a movement for the educated young-man" —connecting adjective and noun in a sort of vocal hyphen.

"Ah, yes," said Pagett, feeling he was a little off the rails, "and what are the benefits you expect to gain by it?"

"Oh, sir, everything. England owes

its greatness to Parliamentary institutions, and we should *at once* gain the same high position in scale of nations. Sir, we wish to have the sciences, the arts, the manufactures, the industrial factories, with steam engines, and other motive powers and public meetings, and debates. Already we have a debating club in connection with the college, and elect a Mr. Speaker. Sir, the progress *must* come. You also are a Member of Parliament and worship the great Lord Ripon," said the youth, breathlessly, and his black eyes flashed as he finished his commaless sentences.

"Well," said Pagett, drily, "it has not yet occurred to me to worship his Lordship, although I believe he is a very worthy man, and I am not sure that England owes quite all the things you name to the House of Commons. You see, my young friend, the growth of a nation like ours is slow, subject to many influences, and if you have read your history aright"—

"Sir, I know it all—all! Norman Conquest, Magna Charta, Runnymede, Reformation, Tudors, Stuarts, Mr. Milton and Mr. Burke, and I have read something of Mr. Herbert Spencer and Gibbon's 'Decline and Fall,' Reynolds' 'Mysteries of the Court,' and"—

Pagett felt like one who had pulled the string of a shower-bath unawares, and hastened to stop the torrent with a question as to what particular grievances of the people of India the attention of an elected assembly should be first directed. But young Mr. Dina Nath was slow to particularize. There were many, very many demanding consideration. Mr. Pagett would like to hear of one or two typical examples.

The Repeal of the Arms Act was at last named, and the student learned for the first time that a license was necessary before an Englishman could carry a gun in England. Then natives of India ought to be allowed to become Volunteer Riflemen if they chose, and the absolute equality of the Oriental with his European fellow-subject in civil status should be proclaimed on principle, and the Indian Army should be considerably reduced. The student was not, however, prepared with answers to Mr. Pagett's mildest questions on these points, and he returned to vague generalities, leaving the M.P. so much impressed with the crudity of his views that he was glad on Orde's return to say good-bye to his "very interesting" young friend.

"What do you think of young India?" asked Orde.

"Curious, very curious—and callow."

"And yet," the civilian replied, "one can scarcely help sympathizing with him for his mere youth's sake. The young orators of the Oxford Union arrived at the same conclusions and showed doubtless just the same enthusiasm. If there were any political analogy between India and England, if the thousand races of this Empire were one, if there were any chance even of their learning to speak one language, if, in short, India were a Utopia of the debating-room, and not a real land, this kind of talk might be worth listening to, but it is all based on false analogy and ignorance of the facts."

"But he is a native and knows the facts."

"He is a sort of English schoolboy, but married three years, and the father of two weaklings, and knows less than most English schoolboys. You saw all he is and knows, and such ideas as he has acquired are directly hostile to the most cherished convictions of the vast majority of the people."

"But what does he mean by saying he is a student of a mission college? Is he a Christian?"

"He meant just what he said, and he is not a Christian, nor ever will he be. Good people in America, Scotland, and England, most of whom would never dream of collegiate education for their own sons, are pinching themselves to bestow it in pure waste on Indian youths. Their scheme is an oblique, subterranean attack on heathenism; the theory being that with the jam of secular education, leading to a University degree, the pill of moral or religious instruction may be coaxed down the heathen gullet."

"But does it succeed; do they make converts?"

"They make no converts, for the subtle Oriental swallows the jam and rejects the pill; but the mere example of the sober righteous, and godly lives of the principals and professors who are most excellent and devoted men, must have a certain moral value. Yet, as Lord Lansdowne pointed out the other day, the market is dangerously overstocked with graduates of our Universities who look for employment in the administration. An immense number are employed, but year by year the college mills grind out increasing lists of youths foredoomed to failure and disappointment, and meanwhile, trade, manufactures, and the industrial arts are neglected, and in fact regarded with contempt by our new literary mandarins *in posse*."

"But our young friend said he wanted steam-engines and factories," said Pagett.

"Yes, he would like to direct such concerns. He wants to begin at the top, for manual labor is held to be discreditable, and he would never defile his hands by the apprenticeship which the architects, engineers, and manufacturers of England cheerfully undergo; and he would be aghast to learn that the leading names of industrial enterprise in England belonged a generation or two since, or now belong, to men who wrought with their own hands. And, though he talks glibly of manufacturers, he refuses to see that the Indian manufacturer of the future will be the despised workman of the present. It was proposed, for example, a few weeks ago, that a certain municipality in this province should establish an elementary technical school for the sons of workmen. The stress of the opposition to the plan came from a pleader who owed all he had· to a college education bestowed on him gratis by Government and missions. You would have fancied some fine old crusted Tory squire of the last generation was speaking. 'These people,' he said, 'want no education, for they learn their trades from their fathers, and to teach a workman's son the elements of mathematics and physical science would give him ideas above his business. They must be kept in their place, and it was idle to imagine that there was any science in wood or iron work.' And he carried his point. But the Indian workman will rise in the social scale in spite of the new literary caste."

"In England we have scarcely begun to realize that there is an industrial class in this country, yet, I suppose, the example of men, like Edwards for instance, must tell," said Pagett, thoughtfully.

"That you shouldn't know much about it is natural enough, for there are but few sources of information. India in this, as in other respects, is like a badly kept ledger—not written up to date. And men like Edwards are, in reality, missionaries, who by precept and example are teaching more lessons than they know. Only a few, however, of their crowds of subordinates seem to care to try to emulate them, and aim at individual advancement; the rest drop into the ancient Indian caste groove."

"How do you mean?" asked Pagett.

"Well, it is found that the new railway and factory workmen, the fitter, the smith, the engine-driver, and the rest are already forming separate hereditary castes. You may notice this down at Jamalpur in Bengal, one of the oldest railway centres; and at other places, and in other industries, they are following the same inexorable Indian law."

"Which means?"—queried Pagett.

"It means that the rooted habit of the people is to gather in small self-contained, self-sufficing family groups with no thought or care for any interests but their own—a habit which is scarcely compatible with the right acceptation of the elective principle."

"Yet you must admit, Orde, that though our young friend was not able to expound the faith that is in him, your Indian army is too big."

"Not nearly big enough for its main purpose. And, as a side issue, there are certain powerful minorities of fighting folk whose interests an Asiatic Government is bound to consider. Arms is as much a means of livelihood as civil employ under Government and law. And it would be a heavy strain on British bayonets to hold down Sikhs, Jats, Bilochis, Rohillas, Rajputs, Bhils, Dogras, Pahtans, and Gurkhas to abide by the decisions of a numerical majority opposed to their interests. Leave the 'numerical majority' to itself without the British bayonets—a flock of sheep might as reasonably hope to manage a troop of collies."

"This complaint about excessive growth of the army is akin to another contention of the Congress party. They protest against the malversation of the whole of the moneys raised by additional taxes as a Famine Insurance Fund to other purposes. You must be aware that this special Famine Fund has all been spent on frontier roads and defences and strategic railway schemes as a protection against Russia."

"But there was never a special famine fund raised by special taxation and put by as in a box. No sane administrator would dream of such a thing. In a time of prosperity a finance minister, rejoicing in a margin, proposed to annually apply a million and a half to the construction of railways and canals for the protection of districts liable to scarcity, and to the reduction of the annual loans for public works. But times were not always prosperous, and the finance minister had to choose whether he would hang up the insurance scheme for a year or impose fresh taxation. When a farmer hasn't got the little surplus he hoped to have for buying a new wagon and draining a low-lying field corner, you don't accuse him of malversation, if he spends what he has on the necessary work of the rest of his farm."

A clatter of hoofs was heard, and Orde looked up with vexation, but his brow cleared as a horseman halted under the porch.

"Hello, Orde! just looked in to ask if you are coming to polo on Tuesday: we want you badly to help to crumple up the Krab Bokhar team."

Orde explained that he had to go out into the District, and while the visitor complained that though good men wouldn't play, duffers were always keen, and that his side would probably be beaten, Pagett rose to look at his mount, a red, lathered Biloch mare, with a curious lyre-like incurving of the ears. "Quite a little thoroughbred in all other respects," said the M.P., and Orde presented Mr. Reginald Burke, Manager of the Sind and Sialkote Bank to his friend.

"Yes, she's as good as they make 'em, and she's all the female I possess and spoiled in consequence, aren't you, old girl?" said Burke, patting the mare's glossy neck as she backed and plunged.

"Mr. Pagett," said Orde, "has been asking me about the Congress. What is your opinion?" Burke turned to the M.P. with a frank smile.

"Well, if it's all the same to you, sir, I should say, Damn the Congress, but then I'm no politician, but only a business man."

"You find it a tiresome subject?"

"Yes, it's all that, and worse than that, for this kind of agitation is anything but wholesome for the country."

"How do you mean?"

"It would be a long job to explain, and *Sara* here won't stand, but you know how sensitive capital is, and how timid investors are. All this sort of rot is likely to frighten them, and we can't afford to frighten them. The passengers aboard an Ocean steamer don't feel reassured when the ship's way is stopped, and they hear the workmen's hammers tinkering at the engines down below. The old Ark's going on all right as she is, and only wants quiet and room to move. Them's my sentiments, and those of some other people who have to do with money and business."

"Then you are a thick-and-thin supporter of the Government as it is."

"Why, no! The Indian Government is much too timid with its money—like an old maiden aunt of mine—always in a funk about her investments. They don't spend half enough on railways for instance, and they are slow in a general way, and ought to be made to sit up in all that concerns the encouragement of private enterprise, and coaxing out into use the millions of capital that lie dormant in the country."

The mare was dancing with impatience, and Burke was evidently anxious to be off, so the men wished him good-bye.

"Who is your genial friend who condemns both Congress and Government in a breath?" asked Pagett, with an amused smile.

"Just now he is Reggie Burke, keener on polo than on anything else, but if you go to the Sind and Sialkote Bank to-morrow you would find Mr. Reginald

Burke a very capable man of business, known and liked by an immense constituency North and South of this.

"Do you think he is right about the Government's want of enterprise?"

"I should hesitate to say. Better consult the merchants and chambers of commerce in Cawnpore, Madras, Bombay, and Calcutta. But though these bodies would like, as Reggie puts it, to make Government sit up, it is an elementary consideration in governing a country like India, which must be administered for the benefit of the people at large, that the counsels of those who resort to it for the sake of making money should be judiciously weighed and not allowed to overpower the rest. They are welcome guests here, as a matter of course, but it has been found best to restrain their influence. Thus the rights of plantation laborers, factory operatives, and the like, have been protected, and the capitalist, eager to get on, has not always regarded Government action with favor. It is quite conceivable that under an elective system the commercial communities of the great towns might find means to secure majorities on labor questions and on financial matters."

"They would act at least with intelligence and consideration."

"Intelligence, yes; but as to consideration, who at the present moment most bitterly resents the tender solicitude of Lancashire for the welfare and protection of the Indian factory operative? English and native capitalists running cotton mills and factories."

"But is the solicitude of Lancashire in this matter entirely disinterested?"

"It is no business of mine to say. I merely indicate an example of how a powerful commercial interest might hamper a Government intent in the first place on the larger interests of humanity."

Orde broke off to listen a moment. "There's Dr. Lathrop talking to my wife in the drawing-room," said he.

"Surely not; that's a lady's voice, and if my ears don't deceive me, an American."

"Exactly, Dr. Eva McCreery Lathrop, chief of the new Women's Hospital here, and a very good fellow forbye. Good-morning, Doctor," he said, as a graceful figure came out on the veranda, "you seem to be in trouble. I hope Mrs. Orde was able to help you."

"Your wife is real kind and good, I always come to her when I'm in a fix, but I fear it's more than comforting I want."

"You work too hard and wear yourself out," said Orde, kindly. "Let me introduce my friend, Mr. Pagett, just fresh from home, and anxious to learn his India. You could tell him something of that more important half of which a mere man knows so little."

"Perhaps I could if I'd any heart to do it, but I'm in trouble, I've lost a case, a case that was doing well, through nothing in the world but inattention on the part of a nurse I had begun to trust. And when I spoke only a small piece of my mind she collapsed in a whining heap on the floor. It is hopeless!"

The men were silent, for the blue eyes of the lady doctor were dim. Recovering herself she looked up with a smile, half sad, half humorous, "And I am in a whining heap, too; but what phase of Indian life are you particularly interested in, sir?"

"Mr. Pagett intends to study the political aspect of things and the possibility of bestowing electoral institutions on the people."

"Wouldn't it be as much to the purpose to bestow point-lace collars on them? They need many things more urgently than votes. Why it's like giving a bread-pill for a broken leg."

"Er—I don't quite follow," said Pagett, uneasily.

"Well, what's the matter with this country is not in the least political, but an all round entanglement of physical, social, and moral evils and corruptions, all more or less due to the unnatural treatment of women. You can't gather figs from thistles, and so long as the system of infant marriage, the prohibition of the remarriage of widows, the lifelong imprisonment of wives and mothers in a worse than penal confinement, and the witholding from them of any kind of education or treatment as rational beings continues, the country can't advance a step. Half of it is morally dead, and worse than dead, and that's just the half from which we have a right to look for the best impulses. It's right here where the trouble is, and not in any political considerations whatsoever."

"But do they marry so early?" said Pagett, vaguely.

"The average age is seven, but thousands are married still earlier. One result is that girls of twelve and thirteen have to bear the burden of wifehood and motherhood, and, as might be expected, the rate of mortality both for mothers and children is terrible. Pauperism, domestic unhappiness, and a low state of health are only a few of the consequences of this. Then, when, as frequently happens, the boy-husband dies prematurely, his widow is condemned to worse than death. She may not re-marry, must live a secluded and despised life, a life so unnatural that she sometimes prefers suicide; more often she goes astray. You don't know in England what such words as 'infant-marriage, baby-wife, girl-mother, and virgin-widow' mean; but they mean unspeakable horrors here."

"Well, but the advanced political party here will surely make it their business to advocate social reforms as well as political ones," said Pagett.

"Very surely they will do no such thing," said the lady doctor, emphatically. "I *wish* I could make you understand. Why, even of the funds devoted to the Marchioness of Dufferin's organization for medical aid to the women of India, it was said in print and in speech, that they would be better spent on more college scholarships for men. And in all the advanced parties' talk— God forgive them—and in all their programmes, they carefully avoid all such subjects. They will talk about the protection of the cow, for that's an ancient superstition—they can all understand that; but the protection of the women is a new and dangerous idea."

She turned to Pagett impulsively:

"You are a member of the English Parliament. Can you do nothing? The foundations of their life are rotten— utterly and bestially rotten   I could tell your wife things that I couldn't tell you. I know the life—the inner life that belongs to the native, and I know nothing else; and believe me you might as well try to grow golden-rod in a mushroom-pit as to make anything of a people that are born and reared as these—these things are. The men talk of their rights and privileges. I have seen the women that bear these very men, and again—may God forgive the men!"

Pagett's eyes opened with a large wonder. Dr. Lathrop rose tempestuously.

"I must be off to lecture," said she, "and I'm sorry that I can't show you my hospitals; but you had better believe, sir, that it's more necessary for India than all the elections in creation."

"That's a woman with a mission, and no mistake," said Pagett, after a pause.

"Yes; she believes in her work, and so do I," said Orde. "I've a notion that in the end it will be found that the most helpful work done for India in this generation was wrought by Lady Dufferin in drawing attention—what work that was, by the way, even with her husband's great name to back it!—to the needs of women here. In effect, native habits and beliefs are an organized conspiracy against the laws of health and happy life—but there is some dawning of hope now."

"How d' you account for the general indifference, then?"

"I suppose it's due in part to their fatalism and their utter indifference to all human suffering. How much do you imagine the great province of the Punjab with over twenty million people and half a score rich towns has contributed to the maintenance of civil dispen-

saries last year? About seven thousand rupees."

"That's seven hundred pounds," said Pagett, quickly.

"I wish it was," replied Orde; "but anyway, it's an absurdly inadequate sum, and shows one of the blank sides of Oriental character."

Pagett was silent for a long time. The question of direct and personal pain did not lie within his researches. He preferred to discuss the weightier matters of the law, and contented himself with murmuring: "They'll do better later on." Then, with a rush, returning to his first thought:

"But, my dear Orde, if it's merely a class movement of a local and temporary character, how d' you account for Bradlaugh, who is at least a man of sense, taking it up?"

"I know nothing of the champion of the New Brahmins but what I see in the papers. I suppose there is something tempting in being hailed by a large assemblage as the representative of the aspirations of two hundred and fifty millions of people. Such a man looks 'through all the roaring and the wreaths,' and does not reflect that it is a false perspective, which, as a matter of fact, hides the real complex and manifold India from his gaze. He can scarcely be expected to distinguish between the ambitions of a new oligarchy and the real wants of the people of whom he knows nothing. But it's strange that a professed Radical should come to be the chosen advocate of a movement which has for its aim the revival of an ancient tyranny. Shows how even Radicalism can fall into academic grooves and miss the essential truths of its own creed. Believe me, Pagett, to deal with India you want first-hand knowledge and experience. I wish he would come and live here for a couple of years or so."

"Is not this rather an *ad hominem* style of argument?"

"Can't help it in a case like this. Indeed, I am not sure you ought not to go further and weigh the whole character and quality and upbringing of the man. You must admit that the monumental complacency with which he trotted out his ingenious little Constitution for India showed a strange want of imagination and the sense of humor."

"No, I don't quite admit it," said Pagett.

"Well, you know him and I don't, but that's how it strikes a stranger." He turned on his heel and paced the veranda thoughtfully. "And, after all, the burden of the actual, daily unromantic toil falls on the shoulders of the men out here, and not on his own. He enjoys all the privileges of recommendation without responsibility, and we— well, perhaps, when you've seen a little more of India you'll understand. To begin with, our death rate's five times higher than yours—I speak now for the brutal bureaucrat—and we work on the refuse of worked-out cities and exhausted civilizations, among the bones of the dead."

Pagett laughed. "That's an epigrammatic way of putting it, Orde."

"Is it? Let's see," said the Deputy Commissioner of Amara, striding into the sunshine toward a half-naked gardener potting roses. He took the man's hoe, and went to a rain-scarped bank at the bottom of the garden.

"Come here, Pagett," he said, and cut at the sun-baked soil. After three strokes there rolled from under the blade of the hoe the half of a clanking skeleton that settled at Pagett's feet in an unseemly jumble of bones. The M.P. drew back.

"Our houses are built on cemeteries," said Orde. "There are scores of thousands of graves within ten miles."

Pagett was contemplating the skull with the awed fascination of a man who has but little to do with the dead. "India's a very curious place," said he, after a pause.

"Ah? You'll know all about it in three months. Come in to lunch," said Orde.

VOLUME X

Wee Willie Winkie and Other Child Stories

Wee Willie Winkie

"An officer and a gentleman."

His full name was Percival William Williams, but he picked up the other name in a nursery-book, and that was the end of the christened titles. His mother's *ayah* called him Willie-*Baba*, but as he never paid the faintest attention to anything that the *ayah* said, her wisdom did not help matters.

His father was the Colonel of the 195th, and as soon as Wee Willie Winkie was old enough to understand what Military Discipline meant, Colonel Williams put him under it. There was no other way of managing the child. When he was good for a week, he drew good-conduct pay; and when he was bad, he was deprived of his good-conduct stripe. Generally he was bad, for India offers so many chances to little six-year olds of going wrong.

Children resent familiarity from strangers, and Wee Willie Winkie was a very particular child. Once he accepted an acquaintance, he was graciously pleased to thaw. He accepted Brandis, a subaltern of the 195th, on sight. Brandis was having tea at the Colonel's, and Wee Willie Winkie entered strong in the possession of a good-conduct badge won for not chasing the hens round the compound. He regarded Brandis with gravity for at least ten minutes, and then delivered himself of his opinion.

"I like you," said he, slowly, getting off his chair and coming over to Brandis.

"I like you. I shall call you Coppy, because of your hair. Do you *mind* being called Coppy? it is because of ve hair, you know."

Here was one of the most embarrassing of Wee Willie Winkie's peculiarities. He would look at a stranger for some time, and then, without warning or explanation, would give him a name. And the name stuck. No regimental penalties could break Wee Willie Winkie of this habit. He lost his good-conduct badge for christening the Commissioner's wife "Pobs"; but nothing that the Colonel could do made the Station forego the nickname, and Mrs. Collen remained Mrs. "Pobs" till the end of her stay. So Brandis was christened "Coppy," and rose, therefore, in the estimation of the regiment.

If Wee Willie Winkie took an interest in any one, the fortunate man was envied alike by the mess and the rank and file. And in their envy lay no suspicion of self-interest. "The Colonel's son" was idolized on his own merits entirely. Yet Wee Willie Winkie was not lovely. His face was permanently freckled, as his legs were permanently scratched, and in spite of his mother's almost tearful remonstrances he had insisted upon having his long yellow locks cut short in the military fashion. "I want my hair like Sergeant Tummil's," said Wee Willie Winkie, and, his father abetting, the sacrifice was accomplished.

Three weeks after the bestowal of his youthful affections on Lieutenant Brandis—henceforward to be called "Coppy" for the sake of brevity—Wee Willie Winkie was destined to behold strange things and far beyond his comprehension.

Coppy returned his liking with interest. Coppy had let him wear for five rapturous minutes his own big sword--just as tall as Wee Willie Winkie. Coppy had promised him a terrier puppy; and Coppy had permitted him to witness the miraculous operation of shaving. Nay, more—Coppy had said that even he, Wee Willie Winkie, would rise in time to the ownership of a box of shiny knives, a silver soap-box and a silver-handled "sputter-brush," as Wee Willie Winkie called it. Decidedly, there was no one except his father, who could give or take away good-conduct badges at pleasure, half so wise, strong, and valiant as Coppy with the Afghan and Egyptian medals on his breast. Why, then, should Coppy be guilty of the unmanly weakness of kissing—vehemently kissing—a "big girl," Miss Allardyce to wit? In the course of a morning ride, Wee Willie Winkie had seen Coppy so doing, and, like the gentleman he was, had promptly wheeled round and cantered back to his groom, lest the groom should also see.

Under ordinary circumstances he would have spoken to his father, but he felt instinctively that this was a matter on which Coppy ought first to be consulted.

"Coppy," shouted Wee Willie Winkie, reining up outside that subaltern's bungalow early one morning—"I want to see you, Coppy!"

"Come in, young 'un," returned Coppy, who was at early breakfast in the midst of his dogs. "What mischief have you been getting into now?"

Wee Willie Winkie had done nothing notoriously bad for three days, and so stood on a pinnacle of virtue.

"I've been doing nothing bad," said he, curling himself into a long chair with a studious affectation of the Colonel's languor after a hot parade. He buried his freckled nose in a tea-cup and, with eyes staring roundly over the rim, asked:—"I say, Coppy, is it pwoper to kiss big girls?"

"By Jove! You're beginning early. Who do you want to kiss?"

"No one. My muvver's always kissing me if I don't stop her. If it isn't pwoper, how was you kissing Major Allardyce's big girl last morning, by ve canal?"

Coppy's brow wrinkled. He and Miss Allardyce had with great craft managed to keep their engagement secret for a fortnight. There were urgent and imperative reasons why Major Allardyce should not know how matters stood for at least another month, and this small marplot had discovered a great deal too much.

"I saw you," said Wee Willie Winkie, calmly. "But ve groom didn't see. I said, 'hut jao.'"

"Oh, you had that much sense, you young Rip," groaned poor Coppy, half amused and half angry. "And how many people may you have told about it?"

"Only me myself. You didn't tell when I twied to wide ve buffalo ven my pony was lame; and I fought you wouldn't like."

"Winkie," said Coppy, enthusiastically, shaking the small hand, "you're the best of good fellows. Look here, you can't understand all these things. One of these days—hang it, how can I make you see it!—I'm going to marry Miss Allardyce, and then she'll be Mrs. Coppy, as you say. If your young mind is so scandalized at the idea of kissing big girls, go and tell your father."

"What will happen?" said Wee Willie Winkie, who firmly believed that his father was omnipotent.

"I shall get into trouble," said Coppy, playing his trump card with an appealing look at the holder of the ace.

"Ven I won't," said Wee Willie Winkie, briefly. "But my faver says it's un-man-ly to be always kissing, and I didn't fink *you'd* do vat, Coppy."

"I'm not always kissing, old chap. It's only now and then, and when you're bigger you'll do it too. Your father meant it's not good for little boys."

"Ah!" said Wee Willie Winkie, now fully enlightened. "It's like ve sputterbrush?"

"Exactly," said Coppy, gravely.

"But I don't fink I'll ever want to kiss big girls, nor no one, 'cept my muvver. And I *must* vat, you know."

There was a long pause, broken by Wee Willie Winkie.

"Are you fond of vis big girl, Coppy?"

"Awfully!" said Coppy.

"Fonder van you are of Bell or ve Butcha—or me?"

"It's in a different way," said Coppy. "You see, one of these days Miss Allardyce will belong to me, but you'll grow up and command the Regiment and—all sorts of things. It's quite different, you see."

"Very well," said Wee Willie Winkie, rising. "If you're fond of ve big girl, I won't tell any one. I must go now."

Coppy rose and escorted his small guest to the door, adding: "You're the best of little fellows, Winkie. I tell you what. In thirty days from now you can tell if you like—tell any one you like."

Thus the secret of the Brandis-Allardyce engagement was dependent on a little child's word. Coppy, who knew Wee Willie Winkie's idea of truth, was at ease, for he felt that he would not break promises. Wee Willie Winkie betrayed a special and unusual interest in Miss Allardyce, and, slowly revolving round that embarrassed young lady, was used to regard her gravely with unwinking eye. He was trying to discover why Coppy should have kissed her. She was not half so nice as his own mother. On the other hand, she was Coppy's property, and would in time belong to him. Therefore it behooved him to treat her with as much respect as Coppy's big sword or shiny pistol.

The idea that he shared a great secret in common with Coppy kept Wee Willie Winkie unusually virtuous for three weeks. Then the Old Adam broke out, and he made what he called a "campfire" at the bottom of the garden. How could he have foreseen that the flying sparks would have lighted the Colonel's little hayrick and consumed a week's store for the horses? Sudden and swift was the punishment—deprivation of the good-conduct badge and, most sorrowful of all, two days' confinement to barracks—the house and veranda—coupled with the withdrawal of the light of his father's countenance.

He took the sentence like the man he strove to be, drew himself up with a quivering under-lip, saluted, and, once clear of the room, ran to weep bitterly in his nursery—called by him "my quarters." Coppy came in the afternoon and attempted to console the culprit.

"I'm under awwest," said Wee Willie Winkie, mournfully, "and I didn't ought to speak to you."

Very early the next morning he climbed on to the roof of the house— that was not forbidden—and beheld Miss Allardyce going for a ride.

"Where are you going?" cried Wee Willie Winkie.

"Across the river," she answered, and trotted forward.

Now the cantonment in which the 195th lay was bounded on the north by a river—dry in the winter. From his earliest years, Wee Willie Winkie had been forbidden to go across the river, and had noted that even Coppy—the almost almighty Coppy—had never set foot beyond it. Wee Willie Winkie had once been read to, out of a big blue book, the history of the Princess and the Goblins—a most wonderful tale of a land where the Goblins were always warring with the children of men until they were defeated by one Curdie. Ever since that date it seemed to him that the bare black and purple hills across the river were inhabited by Goblins, and, in truth, every one had said that there lived the Bad Men. Even in his own house the lower halves of the windows were covered with green paper on account of the Bad Men who might, if allowed clear view, fire into peaceful

drawing-rooms and comfortable bedrooms. Certainly, beyond the river, which was the end of all the Earth, lived the Bad Men. And here was Major Allardyce's big girl, Coppy's property, preparing to venture into their borders! What would Coppy say if anything happened to her? If the Goblins ran off with her as they did with Curdie's Princess? She must at all hazards be turned back.

The house was still. Wee Willie Winkie reflected for a moment on the very terrible wrath of his father; and then—broke his arrest! It was a crime unspeakable. The low sun threw his shadow, very large and very black, on the trim garden-paths, as he went down to the stables and ordered his pony. It seemed to him in the hush of the dawn that all the big world had been bidden to stand still and look at Wee Willie Winkie guilty of mutiny. The drowsy groom handed him his mount, and, since the one great sin made all others insignificant, Wee Willie Winkie said that he was going to ride over to Coppy Sahib, and went out at a foot-pace, stepping on the soft mould of the flowerborders.

The devastating track of the pony's feet was the last misdeed that cut him off from all sympathy of Humanity. He turned into the road, leaned forward, and rode as fast as the pony could put foot to the ground in the direction of the river.

But the liveliest of twelve-two ponies can do little against the long canter of a Waler. Miss Allardyce was far ahead, had passed through the crops, beyond the Police-post, when all the guards were asleep, and her mount was scattering the pebbles of the river-bed as Wee Willie Winkie left the cantonment and British India behind him. Bowed forward and still flogging, Wee Willie Winkie shot into Afghan territory, and could just see Miss Allardyce a black speck, flickering across the stony plain. The reason of her wandering was simple enough. Coppy, in a tone of too-hastily-assumed authority, had told her over night that she must not ride out by the river. And she had gone to prove her own spirit and teach Coppy a lesson.

Almost at the foot of the inhospitable hills, Wee Willie Winkie saw the Waler blunder and come down heavily. Miss Allardyce struggled clear, but her ankle had been severely twisted, and she could not stand. Having thus demonstrated her spirit, she wept copiously, and was surprised by the apparition of a white, wide-eyed child in khaki, on a nearly spent pony.

"Are you badly, badly hurted?" shouted Wee Willie Winkie, as soon as he was within range. "You didn't ought to be here."

"I don't know," said Miss Allardyce, ruefully, ignoring the reproof. "Good gracious, child, what are *you* doing here?"

"You said you was going acwoss ve wiver" panted Wee Willie Winkie, throwing himself off his pony. "And nobody—not even Coppy—must go acwoss ve wiver, and I came after you ever so hard, but you wouldn't stop, and now you've hurted yourself, and Coppy will be angwy wiv me, and—I've bwoken my awwest! I've bwoken my awwest!"

The future Colonel of the 195th sat down and sobbed. In spite of the pain in her ankle the girl was moved.

"Have you ridden all the way from cantonments, little man? What for?"

"You belonged to Coppy. Coppy told me so!" wailed Wee Willie Winkie, disconsolately. "I saw him kissing you, and he said he was fonder of you van Bell or ve Butcha or me. And so I came. You must get up and come back. You didn't ought to be here. Vis is a bad place, and I've bwoken my awwest."

"I can't move, Winkie," said Miss Allardyce, with a groan. "I've hurt my foot. What shall I do?"

She showed a readiness to weep afresh, which steadied Wee Willie Winkie, who had been brought up to believe that tears were the depth of unmanliness. Still, when one is as great a sinner as Wee Willie Winkie, even a man may be permitted to break down.

"Winkie," said Miss Allardyce, "when you've rested a little, ride back and tell them to send out something to carry me back in. It hurts fearfully."

The child sat still for a little time and Miss Allardyce closed her eyes; the pain was nearly making her faint. She was roused by Wee Willie Winkie tying up the reins of his pony's neck and setting it free with a vicious cut of his whip that made it whicker. The little animal headed toward the cantonments.

"Oh, Winkie! What are you doing?"

"Hush!" said Wee Willie Winkie. "Vere's a man coming—one of ve Bad Men. I must stay wiv you. My faver says a man must *always* look after a girl. Jack will go home, and ven vey'll come and look for us. Vat's why I let him go."

Not one man but two or three had appeared from behind the rocks of the hills, and the heart of Wee Willie Winkie sank within him, for just in this manner were the Goblins wont to steal out and vex Curdie's soul. Thus had they played in Curdie's garden, he had seen the picture, and thus had they frightened the Princess's nurse. He heard them talking to each other, and recognized with joy the bastard Pushto that he had picked up from one of his father's grooms lately dismissed. People who spoke that tongue could not be the Bad Men. They were only natives after all.

They came up to the bowlders on which Miss Allardyce's horse had blundered.

Then rose from the rock Wee Willie Winkie, child of the Dominant Race, aged six and three-quarters, and said briefly and emphatically *"Jao!"* The pony had crossed the river-bed.

The men laughed, and laughter from natives was the one thing Wee Willie Winkie could not tolerate. He asked them what they wanted and why they did not depart. Other men with most evil faces and crooked-stocked guns crept out of the shadows of the hills, till, soon, Wee Willie Winkie was face to face with an audience some twenty strong. Miss Allardyce screamed.

"Who are you?" said one of the men.

"I am the Colonel Sahib's son, and my order is that you go at once. You black men are frightening the Miss Sahib. One of you must run into cantonments and take the news that Miss Sahib has hurt herself, and that the Colonel's son is here with her."

"Put our feet into the trap?" was the laughing reply. "Hear this boy's speech!"

"Say that I sent you—I, the Colonel's son. They will give you money."

"What is the use of this talk? Take up the child and the girl, and we can at least ask for the ransom. Ours are the villages on the heights," said a voice in the background.

These *were* the Bad Men—worse than Goblins—and it needed all Wee Willie Winkie's training to prevent him from bursting into tears. But he felt that to cry before a native, excepting only his mother's *ayah*, would be an infamy greater than any mutiny. Moreover, he, as future Colonel of the 195th, had that grim regiment at his back.

"Are you going to carry us away?" said Wee Willie Winkie, very blanched and uncomfortable.

"Yes, my little *Sahib Bahadur*," said the tallest of the men, "and eat you afterward."

"That is child's talk," said Wee Willie Winkie. "Men do not eat men."

A yell of laughter interrupted him, but he went on firmly,—"And if you do carry us away, I tell you that all my regiment will come up in a day and kill you all without leaving one. Who will take my message to the Colonel Sahib?"

Speech in any vernacular—and Wee Willie Winkie had a colloquial acquaintance with three—was easy to the boy who could not yet manage his "r's" and the "th's" aright.

Another man joined the conference, crying:—"O foolish men! What this babe says is true. He is the heart's heart of those white troops. For the sake of peace let them go both, for if he be taken, the regiment will break loose and gut the valley. *Our* villages are in the valley, and we shall not escape. That regiment are devils. They broke Khoda Yar's breast-bone with kicks when he tried to take the rifles; and if we touch this child they will fire and rape and plunder for a month, till nothing remains. Better to send a man back to take the message and get a reward. I say that this child is their God, and that they will spare none of us, nor our women, if we harm him."

It was Din Mahommed, the dismissed groom of the Colonel, who made the diversion and an angry and heated discussion followed. Wee Willie Winkie, standing over Miss Allardyce, waited the upshot. Surely his "wegiment," his own "wegiment," would not desert him if they knew of his extremity.

* * * * * *

The riderless pony brought the news to the 195th, though there had been consternation in the Colonel's household for an hour before. The little beast came in through the parade ground in front of the main barracks, where the men were settling down to play Spoil-five till the afternoon. Devlin, the Color Sergeant of E Company, glanced at the empty saddle and tumbled through the barrack-rooms, kicking up each Room Corporal as he passed. "Up, ye beggars! There's something happened to the Colonel's son," he shouted.

"He couldn't fall off! S'elp me, 'e *couldn't* fall off," blubbered a drummer-boy. "Go an' hunt acrost the river. He's over there if he's anywhere, an' maybe those Pathans have got 'im. For the love o' Gawd don't look for 'im

in the nullahs! Let's go over the river."

"There's sense in Mott yet," said Devlin. "E Company, double out to the river—sharp!"

So E Company, in its shirt-sleeves mainly, doubled for the dear life, and in the rear toiled the perspiring Sergeant, adjuring it to double yet faster. The cantonment was alive with the men of the 195th hunting for Wee Willie Winkie, and the Colonel finally overtook E Company, far too exhausted to swear, struggling in the pebbles of the river-bed.

Up the hill under which Wee Willie Winkie's Bad Men were discussing the wisdom of carrying off the child and the girl, a look-out fired two shots.

"What have I said?" shouted Din Mahommed. "There is the warning! The *pulton* are out already and are coming across the plain! Get away! Let us not be seen with the boy!"

The men waited for an instant, and then, as another shot was fired, withdrew into the hills, silently as they had appeared.

"The wegiment is coming," said Wee Willie Winkie, confidently, to Miss Allardyce, "and it's all wight. Don't cwy!"

He needed the advice himself, for ten minutes later, when his father came up, he was weeping bitterly with his head in Miss Allardyce's lap.

And the men of the 195th carried him home with shouts and rejoicings; and Coppy, who had ridden a horse into a lather, met him, and, to his intense disgust, kissed him openly in the presence of the men.

But there was balm for his dignity.

His father assured him that not only would the breaking of arrest be condoned, but that the good-conduct badge would be restored as soon as his mother could sew it on his blouse-sleeve. Miss Allardyce had told the Colonel a story that made him proud of his son.

"She belonged to you, Coppy," said Wee Willie Winkie, indicating Miss Allardyce with a grimy forefinger. "I *knew* she didn't ought to go acwoss ve wiver, and I knew ve wegiment would come to me if I sent Jack home."

"You're a hero, Winkie," said Coppy —"a *pukka* hero!"

"I don't know what vat means," said Wee Willie Winkie, "but you mustn't call me Winkie any no more. I'm Percival Will'am Will'ams."

And in this manner did Wee Willie Winkie enter into his manhood.

Baa, Baa, Black Sheep

Baa Baa, Black Sheep,
Have you any wool?
Yes, Sir, yes, Sir, three bags full.
One for the Master, one for the Dame—
None for the Little Boy that cries down
    the lane.
                    —*Nursery Rhyme.*

THE FIRST BAG

"When I was in my father's house, I was in a better place."

THEY were putting Punch to bed— the *ayah* and the *hamal* and Meeta, the big *Surti* boy with the red and gold turban. Judy, already tucked inside her mosquito-curtains, was nearly asleep. Punch had been allowed to stay up for dinner. Many privileges had been accorded to Punch within the last ten days, and a greater kindness from the people of his world had encompassed his ways and works, which were mostly obstreperous. He sat on the edge of his bed and swung his bare legs defiantly.

"Punch-*baba* going to bye-lo?" said the *ayah*, suggestively.

"No," said Punch. "Punch-*baba* wants the story about the Ranee that was turned into a tiger. Meeta must tell it, and the *hamal* shall hide behind the door and make tiger-noises at the proper time."

"But Judy-*baba* will wake up," said the *ayah*.

"Judy-*baba* is waking," piped a small voice from the mosquito-curtains. "There was a Ranee that lived at Delhi. Go on, Meeta," and she fell fast asleep again while Meeta began the story.

Never had Punch secured the telling of that tale with so little opposition. He reflected for a long time. The *hamal* made the tiger-noises in twenty different keys.

" 'Top!" said Punch, authoritatively. "Why doesn't Papa come in and say he is going to give me *put-put?*"

"Punch-*baba* is going away," said the *ayah*. "In another week there will be no Punch-*baba* to pull my hair any more." She sighed softly, for the boy of the household was very dear to her heart.

"Up the Ghauts in a train?" said Punch, standing on his bed. "All the way to Nassick where the Ranee-Tiger lives?"

"Not to Nassick this year, little Sahib," said Meeta, lifting him on his shoulder. "Down to the sea where the cocoanuts are thrown, and across the sea in a big ship. Will you take Meeta with you to *Belait?*"

"You shall all come," said Punch, from the height of Meeta's strong arms. "Meeta and the *ayah* and the *hamal* and Bhini-in-the-Garden, and the salaam-Captain-Sahib-snake-man."

There was no mockery in Meeta's voice when he replied—"Great is the Sahib's favor," and laid the little man down in the bed, while the *ayah*, sitting in the moonlight at the doorway, lulled him to sleep with an interminable canticle such as they sing in the Roman Catholic Church at Parel. Punch curled himself into a ball and slept.

Next morning Judy shouted that there was a rat in the nursery, and thus he forgot to tell her the wonderful news. It did not much matter, for Judy was only three and she would not have understood. But Punch was five; and he knew that going to England would be much nicer than a trip to Nassick.

* * * * * *

And Papa and Mamma sold the brougham and the piano, and stripped the house, and curtailed the allowance of crockery for the daily meals, and took long council together over a bundle of letters bearing the Rocklington postmark.

"The worst of it is that one can't be certain of anything," said Papa, pulling his moustache. "The letters in themselves are excellent, and the terms are moderate enough."

"The worst of it is that the children will grow up away from me," thought Mamma: but she did not say it aloud.

"We are only one case among hundreds," said Papa, bitterly. "You shall go Home again in five years, dear."

"Punch will be ten then—and Judy eight. Oh, how long and long and long the time will be! And we have to leave them among strangers."

"Punch is a cheery little chap. He's sure to make friends wherever he goes."

"And who could help loving my Ju?"

They were standing over the cots in the nursery late at night, and I think that Mamma was crying softly. After Papa had gone away, she knelt down by the side of Judy's cot. The *ayah* saw her and put up a prayer that the *memsahib* might never find the love of her children taken away from her and given to a stranger.

Mamma's own prayer was a slightly illogical one. Summarized it ran:—"Let strangers love my children and be as good to them as I should be, but let *me* preserve their love and their confidence forever and ever. Amen." Punch scratched himself in his sleep, and Judy moaned a little. That seems to be the only answer to the prayer: and, next day, they all went down to the sea, and there was a scene at the Apollo Bunder when Punch discovered that Meeta could not come too, and Judy learned that the *ayah* must be left behind. But Punch found a thousand fascinating things in the rope, block, and steam-pipe line on the big P. and O. Steamer, long before Meeta and the *ayah* had dried their tears.

"Come back, Punch-*baba*," said the *ayah*.

"Come back," said Meeta, "and be a *Burra Sahib.*"

"Yes," said Punch, lifted up in his father's arms to wave good-bye. "Yes, I will come back, and I will be a *Burra Sahib Baha dur!*"

At the end of the first day Punch demanded to be set down in England, which he was certain must be close at hand. Next day there was a merry breeze, and Punch was very sick. "When I come back to Bombay," said Punch on his recovery, "I will come by the road—in a broom-*gharri*. This is a very naughty ship."

The Swedish boatswain consoled him, and he modified his opinions as the voyage went on. There was so much to see and to handle and ask questions about that Punch nearly forgot the *ayah* and Meeta and the *hamal*, and with difficulty remembered a few words of the Hindustan; once his second-speech.

But Judy was much worse. The day before the steamer reached Southampton, Mamma asked her if she would not like to see the *ayah* again. Judy's blue eyes turned to the stretch of sea that had swallowed all her tiny past, and she said: "*Ayah!* What *ayah?*"

Mamma cried over her and Punch marveled. It was then that he heard for the first time Mamma's passionate appeal to him never to let Judy forget Mamma. Seeing that Judy was young, ridiculously young, and that Mamma, every evening for four weeks past, had come into the cabin to sing her and Punch to sleep with a mysterious tune

that he called "Sonny, my soul," Punch could not understand what Mamma meant. But he strove to do his duty; for, the moment Mamma left the cabin, he said to Judy: "Ju, you bemember Mamma?"

"'Torse I do," said Judy.

"Then *always* bemember Mamma, 'r else I won't give you the paper ducks that the red-haired Captain Sahib cut out for me."

So Judy promised always to "bemember Mamma."

Many and many a time was Mamma's command laid upon Punch, and Papa would say the same thing with an insistence that awed the child.

"You must make haste and learn to write, Punch," said Papa, "and then you'll be able to write letters to us in Bombay."

"I'll come into your room," said Punch, and Papa choked.

Papa and Mamma were always choking in those days. If Punch took Judy to task for not "bemembering," they choked. If Punch sprawled on the sofa in the Southampton lodging-house and sketched his future in purple and gold, they choked; and so they did if Judy put up her mouth for a kiss.

Through many days all four were vagabonds on the face of the earth:— Punch with no one to give orders to, Judy too young for anything, and Papa and Mamma grave, distracted, and choking.

"Where," demanded Punch, wearied of a loathsome contrivance on four wheels with a mound of luggage atop— "*where* is our broom-*gharri*? This thing talks so much that *I* can't talk. Where is our *own* broom-*gharri*? When I was at Bandstand before we comed away, I asked Inverarity Sahib why he was sitting in it, and he said it was his own. And I said, 'I will *give* it you'—I like Inverarity Sahib—and I said, 'Can you put youg legs through the pully-wag loops by the windows?' And Inverarity Sahib said No, and laughed. *I* can put my legs through the pully-wag loops. I can put my legs through *these* pully-wag loops. Look! Oh, Mamma's crying again! I didn't know. I wasn't not to do *so*."

Punch drew his legs out of the loops of the four-wheeler: the door opened and he slid to the earth, in a cascade of parcels, at the door of an austere little vista whose gates bore the legend "Downe Lodge." Punch gathered himself together and eyed the house with disfavor. It stood on a sandy road, and a cold wind tickled his knickerbockered legs.

"Let us go away," said Punch. "This is not a pretty place."

But Mamma and Papa and Judy had quitted the cab, and all the luggage was being taken into the house. At the doorstep stood a woman in black, and she smiled largely, with dry chapped lips. Behind her was a man, big, bony, grey, and lame as to one leg—behind him a boy of twelve black-haired and oily in appearance. Punch surveyed the trio, and advanced without fear, as he had been accustomed to do in Bombay when callers came and he happened to be playing in the veranda.

"How do you do?" said he. "I am Punch." But they were all looking at the luggage—all except the grey man, who shook hands with Punch and said he was "a smart little fellow." There

was much running about and banging of boxes, and Punch curled himself up on the sofa in the dining-room and considered things.

"I don't like these people," said Punch. "But never mind. We'll go away soon. We have always went away soon from everywhere. I wish we was gone back to Bombay *soon*."

The wish bore no fruit. For six days Mamma wept at intervals, and showed the woman in black all Punch's clothes —a liberty which Punch resented. "But p'raps she's a new white *ayah*," he thought. "I'm to call her Antirosa, but she doesn't call *me* Sahib. She says just Punch," he confided to Judy. "What is Antirosa?"

Judy didn't know. Neither she nor punch had heard anything of an animal called an aunt. Their world had been Papa and Mamma, who knew everything, permitted everything, and loved everybody—even Punch when he used to go into the garden at Bombay and fill his nails with mould after the weekly nail-cutting, because, as he explained between two strokes of the slipper to his sorely tried Father, his fingers "felt so new at the ends."

In an undefined way Punch judged it advisable to keep both parents between himself and the woman in black and the boy in black hair. He did not approve of them. He liked the grey man, who had expressed a wish to be called "Uncleharri." They nodded at each other when they met, and the grey man showed him a little ship with rigging that took up and down.

"She is a model of the Brisk—the little Brisk that was sore exposed that day at Navarino." The grey man hummed the last words and fell into a reverie. "I'll tell you about Navarino, Punch, when we go for walks together; and you mustn't touch the ship, because she's the Brisk."

Long before that walk, the first of many, was taken, they roused Punch and Judy in the chill dawn of a February morning to say Good-bye: and of all people in the wide earth to Papa and Mamma—both crying this time. Punch was very sleepy and Judy was cross.

"Don't forget us," pleaded Mamma. "Oh, my little son, don't forget us, and see that Judy remembers too."

"I've told Judy to bemember," said Punch, wriggling, for his father's beard tickled his neck. "I've told Judy—ten—forty—'leven thousand times. But Ju's so young—quite a baby—isn't she?"

"Yes," said Papa, "quite a baby, and you must be good to Judy, and make haste to learn to write and—and—and" . . .

Punch was back in his bed again. Judy was fast asleep, and there was the rattle of a cab below. Papa and Mamma had gone away. Not to Nassick; that was across the sea. To some place much nearer, of course, and equally of course, they would return. They came back after dinner-parties, and Papa had come bock after he had been to a place called "The Snows," and Mamma with him, to Punch and Judy at Mrs. Inverarity's house in Marine Lines. Assuredly they would come back again. So Punch fell asleep till the true morning, when the black-haired boy met him with the information that Papa and Mamma had gone

to Bombay, and that he and Judy were to stay at Downe Lodge "forever." Antirosa, tearfully appealed to for a contradiction, said that Harry had spoken the truth, and that it behooved Punch to fold up his clothes neatly on going to bed. Punch went out and wept bitterly with Judy, into whose faid head he had driven some ideas of the meaning of separation.

When a matured man discovers that he has been deserted by Providence, deprived of his God, and cast without help, comfort, or sympathy, upon a world which is new and strange to him, his despair, which may find expression in evil-living, the writing of his experiences, or the more satisfactory diversion of suicide, is generally supposed to be impressive. A child, under exactly similar circumstances as far as its knowledge goes, cannot very well curse God and die. It howls till its nose is red, its eyes are sore, and its head aches. Punch and Judy, through no fault of their own, had lost all their world. They sat in the hall and cried; the black-haired boy looking on from afar.

The model of the ship availed nothing, though the grey man assured Punch that he might pull the rigging up and down as much as he pleased; and Judy was promised free entry into the kitchen. They wanted Papa and Mamma gone to Bombay beyond the seas, and their grief while it lasted was without remedy.

When the tears ceased the house was very still. Antirosa had decided it was better to let the children "have their cry out," and the boy had gone to school. Punch raised his head from the floor and sniffed mournfully. Judy was nearly asleep. Three short years had not taught her how to bear sorrow with full knowledge. There was a distant, dull boom in the air—a repeated heavy thud. Punch knew that sound in Bombay in the Monsoon. It was the sea— the sea that must be traversed before any one could get to Bombay.

"Quick, Ju!" he cried, "we're close to the sea. I can hear it! Listen! That's where they've went. P'raps we can catch them if we was in time. They didn't mean to go without us. They've only forgot."

"Iss," said Judy. "They've only forgotted. Less go to the sea."

The hall-door was open and so was the garden-gate.

"It's very, very big, this place," he said, looking cautiously down the road, "and we will get lost; but *I* will find a man and order him to take me back to my house—like I did in Bombay."

He took Judy by the hand, and the two fled hatless in the direction of the sound of the sea. Downe Villa was almost the last of a range of newly built houses running out, through a chaos of brick-mounds, to a heath where gypsies occasionally camped and where the Garrison Artillery of Rocklington practiced. There were few people to be seen, and the children might have been taken for those of the soldiery who ranged far. Half an hour the wearied little legs tramped across heath, potato-field, and sand-dune.

"I'se so tired," said Judy, "and Mamma will be angry."

"Mamma's *never* angry. I suppose she is waiting at the sea now while Papa gets tickets. We'll find them and go along with. Ju, you mustn't sit

down. Only a little more and we'll come to the sea. Ju, if you sit down I'll *thmack* you!" said Punch.

They climbed another dune, and came upon the great grey sea at low tide. Hundreds of crabs were scuttling about the beach, but there was no trace of Papa and Mamma, not even of a ship upon the waters—nothing but sand and mud for miles and miles.

And "Uncleharri" found them by chance—very muddy and very forlorn —Punch dissolved in tears, but trying to divert Judy with an "ickle trab," and Judy wailing to the pitiless horizon for "Mamma, Mamma!"—and again "Mamma!"

THE SECOND BAG

Ah, well-a-day, for we are souls bereaved!
Of all the creatures under Heaven's wide scope
We are most hopeless, who had once most hope,
And most beliefless, who had most believed.
—*The City of Dreadful Night.*

ALL this time not a word about Black Sheep. He came later, and Harry the black-haired boy was mainly responsible for his coming.

Judy—who could help loving little Judy?—passed, by special permit, into the kitchen and thence straight to Aunty Rosa's heart. Harry was Aunty Rosa's one child, and Punch was the extra boy about the house. There was no special place for him or his little affairs, and he was forbidden to sprawl on sofas and explain his ideas about the manufacture of this world and his hopes for his future. Sprawling was lazy and wore out sofas, and little boys were not expected to talk. They were talked to, and the talking to was intended for the benefit of their morals. As the unquestioned despot of the house at Bombay, Punch could not quite understand how he came to be of no account in this, his new life.

Harry might reach across the table and take when he wanted; Judy might point and get what she wanted. Punch was forbidden to do either. The grey man was his great hope and stand-by for many months after Mamma and Papa left, and he had forgotten to tell Judy to "bemember Mamma."

This lapse was excusable, because in the interval he had been introduced by Aunty Rosa to two very impressive things—an abstraction called God, the intimate friend and ally of Aunty Rosa, generally believed to live behind the kitchen range because it was hot there —and a dirty brown book filled with unintelligible dots and marks. Punch was always anxious to oblige everybody. He, therefore, welded the story of the Creation on to what he could recollect of his Indian fairy tales, and scandalized Aunty Rosa by repeating the result to Judy. It was a sin, a grievous sin, and Punch was talked to for a quarter of an hour. He could not understand where the iniquity came in, but was careful not to repeat the offence, because Aunty Rosa told him that God had heard every word he had said and was very angry. If this were true why didn't God come and say so, thought Punch, and dismissed the matter from his mind. Afterward he learned to know the Lord as the only thing in the

world more awful than Aunty Rosa— as a Creature that stood in the background and counted the strokes of the cane.

But the reading was, just then, a much more serious matter than any creed. Aunty Rosa sat him upon a table and told him that A B meant ab.

"Why?" said Punch. "A is a and B is bee. *Why* does A B mean ab?"

"Because I tell you it does," said Aunty Rosa, "and you've got to say it."

Punch said it accordingly, and for a month, hugely against his will, stumbled through the brown book, not in the least comprehending what it meant. But Uncle Harry, who walked much and generally alone, was wont to come into the nursery and suggest to Aunty Rosa that Punch should walk with him. He seldom spoke, but he showed Punch all Rocklington, from the mud-banks and the sand of the back-bay to the great harbors where ships lay at anchor, and the dockyards where the hammers were never still, and the marine-store shops, and the shiny brass counters in the Offices where Uncle Harry went once every three months with a slip of blue paper and received sovereigns in exchange; for he held a wound-pension. Punch heard, too from his lips the story of the battle of Navarino, where the sailors of the Fleet, for three days afterward, were deaf as posts and could only sign to each other. "That was because of the noise of the guns," said Uncle Harry, "and I have got the wadding of a bullet somewhere inside me now."

Punch regarded him with curiosity. He had not the least idea what wadding was, and his notion of a bullet was a dockyard cannon-ball bigger than his own head. How could Uncle Harry keep a cannon-ball inside him? He was ashamed to ask, for fear Uncle Haary might be angry.

Punch had never known what anger—real anger—meant until one terrible day when Harry had taken his paint-box to paint a boat with, and Punch had protested with a loud and lamentable voice. Then Uncle Harry had appeared on the scene and, muttering something about "strangers' children," had with a stick smitten the black-haired boy across the shoulders till he wept and yelled, and Aunty Rosa came in and abused Uncle Harry for cruelty to his own flesh and blood, and Punch shuddered to the tips of his shoes. "It wasn't my fault," he explained to the boy, but both Harry and Aunty Rosa said that it was, and that Punch had told tales, and for a week there were no more walks with Uncle Harry.

But that week brought a great joy to Punch.

He had repeated till he was thrice weary the statement that "the Cat lay on the Mat and the Rat came in."

"Now I can truly read," said Punch, "and now I will never read anything in the world."

He put the brown book in the cupboard where his school-books lived and accidentally tumbled out a venerable volume, without covers, labelled Sharpe's Magazine. There was the most portentious picture of a griffin on the first page, with verses below. The griffin carried off one sheep a day from a German village, till a man came with a "falchion" and split the griffin open. Goodness only knew what a falchion was, but there was the Griffin, nad his

history was an improvement upon the eternal Cat.

"This," said Punch, "means things, and now I will know all about everything in all the world." He read till the light failed, not understanding a tithe of the meaning, but tantalized by glimpses of new words hereafter to be revealed.

"What is a 'falchion'? What is a 'e-wee lamb'? What is a 'base *ussu*rper'? What is a 'verdant me-ad'?" he demanded, with flushed cheeks, at bedtime, of the astonished Aunt Rosa.

"Say your prayers and go to sleep," she replied, and that was all the help Punch then or afterward found at her hands in the new and delightful exercise of reading.

"Aunt Rosa only knows about God and things like that," argued Punch. "Uncle Harry will tell me."

The next walk proved that Uncle Harry could not help either; but he allowed Punch to talk, and even sat down on a bench to hear about the Griffin. Other walks brought other stories as Punch ranged further afield, for the house held large store of old books that no one ever opened—from Frank Fairlegh in serial numbers, and the earlier poems of Tennyson, contributed anonymously to Sharpe's Magazine, to '62 Exhibition Catalogues, gay with colors and delightfully incomprehensible, and odd leaves of Gulliver's Travels.

As soon as Punch could string a few pot-hooks together, he wrote to Bombay, demanding by return of post "all the books in all the world." Papa could not comply with this modest indent, but sent Grimm's Fairy Tales and a

Hans Andersen. That was enough. If he were only alone Punch could pass, at any hour he chose, into a land of his own, beyond the reach of Aunty Rosa and her God, Harry and his teasements, and Judy's claims to be played with.

"Don't disturve me, I'm reading. Go and play in the kitchen," grunted Punch. "Aunty Rosa lets *you* go there." Judy was cutting her second teeth and was fretful. She appealed to Aunty Rosa, who descended on Punch.

"I was reading," he explained, "reading a book. I *want* to read."

"You're only doing that to show off," said Aunty Rosa. "But we'll see. Play with Judy now, and don't open a book for a week."

Judy did not pass a very enjoyable playtime with Punch, who was consumed with indignation. There was a pettiness at the bottom of the prohibition which puzzled him.

"It's what I like to do," he said, "and she's found out that and stopped me. Don't cry, Ju— it wasn't your fault—*please* don't cry, or she'll say I made you."

Ju loyally mopped up her tears, and the two played in their nursery, a room in the basement and half underground, to which they were regularly sent after the midday dinner while Aunty Rosa slept. She drank wine—that is to say, something from a bottle in the cellaret —for her stomach's sake, but if she did not fall asleep she would sometimes come into the nursery to see that the children were really playing. Now bricks, wooden hoops, ninepins, and chinaware cannot amuse forever, especially when all Fairyland is to be won by the mere opening of a book, and, as often as not,

Punch would be discovered reading to Judy or telling her interminable tales. That was an offence in the eyes of the law, and Judy would be whisked off by Aunty Rosa, while Punch was left to play alone, "and be sure that I hear you doing it."

It was not a cheering employ, for he had to make a playful noise. At last, with infinite craft, he devised an arrangement whereby the table could be supported as to three legs on toy bricks, leaving the fourth clear to bring down on the floor. He could work the table with one hand and hold a book with the other. This he did till an evil day when Aunty Rosa pounced upon him unawares and told him that he was "acting a lie."

"If you're old enough to do that," she said—her temper was always worse after dinner—"you're old enough to be beaten."

"But—I'm—I'm not a animal!" said Punch, aghast. He remembered Uncle Harry and the stick, and turned white. Aunty Rosa had hidden a light cane behind her, and Punch was beaten then and there over the shoulders. It was a revelation to him. The room-door was shut, and he was left to weep himself into repentance and work out his own Gospel of Life.

Aunty Rosa, he argued, had the power to beat him with many stripes. It was unjust and cruel, and Mamma and Papa would never have allowed it. Unless perhaps, as Aunty Rosa seemed to imply, they had sent secret orders. In which case he was abandoned indeed. It would be discreet in the future to propitiate Aunty Rosa, but, then, again, even in matters in which he was innocent, he had been accused of wishing to "show off." He had "shown off" before visitors when he had attacked a strange gentleman—Harry's uncle, not his own —with requests for information about the Griffin and the falchion, and the precise nature of the Tilbury in which Frank Fairlegh rode—all points of paramount interest which he was bursting to understand. Clearly it would not do to pretend to care for Aunty Rosa.

At this point Harry entered and stood afar off, eyeing Punch, a disheveled heap in the corner of the room, with disgust.

"You're a liar—a young liar," said Harry, with great unction, "and you're to have tea down here because you're not fit to speak to us. And you're not to speak to Judy again till Mother gives you leave. You'll corrupt her. You're only fit to associate with the servant. Mother says so."

Having reduced Punch to a second agony of tears, Harry departed upstairs with the news that Punch was still rebellious.

Uncle Harry sat uneasily in the dining-room. "Damn it all, Rosa," said he, at last, "can't you leave the child alone? He's a good enough little chap when I meet him."

"He puts on his best manners with you, Henry," said Aunty Rosa, "but I'm afraid, I'm very much afraid, that he is the Black Sheep of the family."

Harry heard and stored up the name for future use. Judy cried till she was bidden to stop, her brother not being worth tears; and the evening concluded with the return of Punch to the upper regions and a private sitting at which all the blinding horrors of Hell were revealed to Punch with such store of imagery as Aunty Rosa's narrow mind possessed.

Most grievous of all was Judy's round-eyed reproach, and Punch went to bed in the depths of the Valley of Humiliation. He shared his room with Harry and knew the torture in store. For an hour and a half he had to answer that young gentleman's questions as to his motives for telling a lie, and a grievous lie, the precise quantity of punishment inflicted by Aunty Rosa, and had also to profess his deep gratitude for such religious instruction as Harry thought fit to impart.

From that day began the downfall of Punch, now Black Sheep.

"Untrustworthy in one thing, untrustworthy in all," said Aunty Rosa, and Harry felt that Black Sheep was delivered into his hands. He would wake him up in the night to ask him why he was such a liar."

"I don't know," Punch would reply.

"Then don't you think you ought to get up and pray to God for a new heart?"

"Y-yess."

"Get out and pray, then!" And Punch would get out of bed with raging hate in his heart against all the world, seen and unseen. He was always tumbling into trouble. Harry had a knack of cross-examining him as to his day's doings, which seldom failed to lead him, sleepy and savage, into half a dozen contradictions—all duly reported to Aunty Rosa next morning.

"But it *wasn't* a lie," Punch would begin, charging into a labored explanation that landed him more hopelessly in the mire. "I said that I didn't say my prayers *twice* over in the day, and *that* was on Tuesday. *Once* I did. I *know* I did, but Harry said I didn't," and so forth, till the tension brought tears, and he was dismissed from the table in disgrace.

"You usen't to be as bad as this?" said Judy, awe-stricken at the catalogue of Black Sheep's crimes. "Why are you so bad now?"

"I don't know," Black Sheep would reply. "I'm not, if I only wasn't bothered upside down. I knew what I *did*, and I want to say so; but Harry always makes it out different somehow, and Aunty Rosa doesn't believe a word I say. Oh, Ju! don't *you* say I'm bad too."

"Aunty Rosa says you are," said Judy. "She told the Vicar so when he came yesterday."

"Why does she tell all the people outside the house about me? It isn't fair," said Black Sheep. "When I was in Bombay, and was bad—*doing* bad, not made-up bad like this—Mamma told Papa, and Papa told me he knew, and that was all. *Outside* people didn't know too—even Meeta didn't know."

"I don't remember," said Judy, wistfully. "I was all little then. Mamma was just as fond of you as she was of me, wasn't she?"

" 'Course she was. So was Papa. So was everybody."

"Aunty Rosa likes me more than she does you. She says that you are a Trial and a Black Sheep, and I'm not to speak to you more than I can help."

"Always? Not outside of the times when you mustn't speak to me at all?"

Judy nodded her head mournfully.

Black Sheep turned away in despair, but Judy's arms were round his neck.

"Never mind, Punch," she whispered. "I *will* speak to you just the same as ever and ever. You're my own own brother though you are—though Aunty Rosa says you're Bad, and Harry says you're a little coward. He says that if I pulled your hair hard, you'd cry."

"Pull then," said Punch.

Judy pulled gingerly.

"Pull harder—as hard as you can! There! I don't mind how much you pull it *now*. If you'll speak to me same as ever I'll let you pull it as much as you like—pull it out if you like. But I know if Harry came and stood by and made you do it I'd cry."

So the two children sealed the compact with a kiss, and Black Sheep's heart was cheered within him, and by extreme caution and careful avoidance of Harry he acquired virtue, and was allowed to read undisturbed for a week. Uncle Harry took him for walks and consoled him with rough tenderness, never calling him Black Sheep. "It's good for you, I suppose, Punch," he used to say. "Let us sit down. I'm getting tired." His steps led him now not to the beach, but to the Cemetery of Rocklington, amid the potato-fields. For hours the grey man would sit on a tombstone, while Black Sheep read epitaphs, and then with a sigh would stump home again.

"I shall lie there soon," said he to Black Sheep, one winter evening, when his face showed white as a worn silver coin under the lights of the chapel-lodge. "You needn't tell Aunty Rosa."

A month later, he turned sharp round, ere half a morning walk was completed, and stumped back to the house. "Put me to bed, Rosa," he muttered. "I've walked my last. The wadding has found me out."

They put him to bed, and for a fortnight the shadow of his sickness lay upon the house, and Black Sheep went to and fro unobserved. Papa had sent him some new books, and he was told to keep quiet. He retired into his own world, and was perfectly happy. Even at night his felicity was unbroken. He could lie in bed and string himself tales of travel and adventure while Harry was downstairs.

"Uncle Harry's going to die," said Judy, who now lived almost entirely with Aunty Rosa.

"I'm very sorry," said Black Sheep, soberly. "He told me that a long time ago."

Aunty Rosa heard the conversation. "Will nothing check your wicked tongue?" she said, angrily. There were blue circles round her eyes.

Black Sheep retreated to the nursery and read "Cometh up as a flower" with deep and uncomprehending interest. He had been forbidden to read it on account of its "sinfulness," but the bonds of the Universe were crumbling, and Aunty Rosa was in great grief.

"I'm glad," said Black Sheep. "She's unhappy now. It wasn't a lie, though. I knew. He told me not to tell."

That night Black Sheep woke with a start. Harry was not in the room, and there was a sound of sobbing on the next floor. Then the voice of Uncle Harry, singing the song of the Battle of Navarino, cut through the darkness:

"Our vanship was the Asia—
The Albion and Genoa!"

"He's getting well," thought Black Sheep, who knew the song through all its seventeen verses. But the blood froze at his little heart as he thought. The voice leaped an octave and rang shrill as a boatswain's pipe:

"And next came on the lovely Rose,
The Philomel, her fire-ship, closed,
And the little Brisk was sore exposed
That day at Navarino."

"That day at Navarino, Uncle Harry!" shouted Black Sheep, half wild with excitement and fear of he knew not what.

A door opened and Aunty Rosa screamed up the staircase:—"Hush! For God's sake hush, you little devil. Uncle Harry is *dead!*"

THE THIRD BAG

Journeys end in lovers' meeting,
Every wise man's son doth know.

"I WONDER what will happen to me now," thought Black Sheep, when the semi-pagan rites peculiar to the burial of the Dead in middle-class houses had been accomplished, and Aunty Rosa, awful in black crepe, had returned to this life. "I don't think I've done anything bad that she knows of. I suppose I will soon. She will be very cross after Uncle Harry's dying, and Harry will be cross too. I'll keep in the nursery."

Unfortunately for Punch's plans, it was decided that he should be sent to a day-school which Harry attended. This meant a morning walk with Harry, and perhaps an evening one; but the prospect of freedom in the interval was refreshing. "Harry'll tell everything I do, but I won't do anything," said Black Sheep. Fortified with this virtuous resolution, he went to school only to find that Harry's version of his character had preceded him, and that life was a burden in consequence. He took stock of his associates. Some of them were unclean, some of them talked in dialect, many dropped their h's, and there were two Jews and a negro, or some one quite as dark, in the assembly. "That's a *hubshi*," said Black Sheep to himself. "Even Meeta used to laugh at a *hubshi*. I don't think this is a proper place." He was indignant for at least an hour, till he reflected that any expostulation on his part would be by Aunty Rosa construed into "showing off," and that Harry would tell the boys.

"How do you like school?" said Aunty Rosa, at the end of the day.

"I think it is a very nice place," said Punch, quietly.

"I suppose you warned the boys of Black Sheep's character?" said Aunty Rosa to Harry.

"Oh, yes," said the censor of Black Sheep's morals. "They know all about him."

"If I was with my father," said Black Sheep, stung to the quick, "I shouldn't *speak* to those boys. He wouldn't let me. They live in shops. I saw them go into shops—where their fathers live and sell things."

"You're too good for that school, are you?" said Aunty Rosa, with a bitter smile. "You ought to be grateful, Black Sheep, that those boys speak to you at all. It isn't every school that takes little liars."

Harry did not fail to make much capital out of Black Sheep's ill-considered remark; with the result that several boys, including the *hubshi*, demonstrated to Black Sheep the eternal equality of the human race by smacking his head, and his consolation from Aunty Rosa was that it "served him right for being vain." He learned, however, to keep his opinions to himself, and by propitiating Harry in carrying books and the like to secure a little peace. His existence was not too joyful. From nine till twelve he was at school, and from two to four, except on Saturdays. In the evenings he was sent down into the nursery to prepare his lessons for the next day, and every night came the dreaded cross-questionings at Harry's hand. Of Judy he saw but little. She was deeply religious—at six years of age Religion is easy to come by—and sorely divided between her natural love for Black Sheep and her love for Aunty Rosa, who could do wrong.

The lean woman returned that love with interest, and Judy, when she dared, took advantage of this for the remission of Black Sheep's penalties. Failures in lessons at school were punished at home by a week without reading other than school-books, and Harry brought the news of such a failure with glee. Further, Black Sheep was then bound to repeat his lessons at bedtime to Harry, who generally succeeded in making him break down, and consoled him by gloomiest forebodings for the morrow. Harry was at once spy, practical joker, inquisitor, and Aunty Rosa's deputy executioner. He filled his many posts to admiration. From his actions, now that Uncle Harry was dead, there was no appeal. Black Sheep had not been permitted to keep any self-respect at school: at home he was of course utterly discredited, and grateful for any pity that the servant girls—they changed frequently at Downe Lodge because they, too, were liars—might show. "You're just fit to row in the same boat with Black Sheep," was a sentiment that each new Jane or Eliza might expect to hear, before a month was over, from Aunty Rosa's lips; and Black Sheep was used to ask new girls whether they had yet been compared to him. Harry was "Master Harry" in their mouths; Judy was officially "Miss Judy"; but Black Sheep was never anything more than Black Sheep *tout court*.

As time went on and the memory of Papa and Mamma became wholly overlaid by the unpleasant task of writing them letters, under Aunty Rosa's eye, each Sunday, Black Sheep forgot what manner of life he had led in the beginning of things. Even Judy's appeals to "try and remember about Bombay" failed to quicken him.

"I can't remember," he said. "I know I used to give orders and Mamma kissed me."

"Aunty Rosa will kiss you if you are good," pleaded Judy.

"Ugh! I don't want to be kissed by Aunty Rosa. She'd say I was doing it to get something more to eat."

The weeks lengthened into months, and the holidays came; but just before the holidays Black Sheep fell into deadly sin.

Among the many boys whom Harry had incited to "punch Black Sheep's head because he daren't hit back," was one more aggravating than the rest, who, in an unlucky moment, fell upon Black Sheep when Harry was not near. The blows stung, and Black Sheep struck back at random with all the power at his command. The boy dropped and whimpered. Black Sheep was astounded at his own act, but, feeling the unresisting body under him shook it with both his hands in blind fury and then began to throttle his enemy; meaning honestly to slay him. There was a scuffle, and Black Sheep was torn off the body by Harry and some colleagues, and cuffed home tingling but exultant. Aunty Rosa was out: pending her arrival, Harry sent himself to lecture Black Sheep on the sin of murder—which he described as the offence of Cain.

"Why didn't you fight him fair? What did you hit him when he was down for, you little cur?"

Black Sheep looked up at Harry's throat and then at a knife on the dinner-table.

"I don't understand," he said, wearily. "You always set him on me and told me I was a coward when I blubbed. Will you leave me alone until Aunty Rosa comes in? She'll beat me if you tell her I ought to be beaten; so it's all right."

"It's all wrong," said Harry, magisterially. "You nearly killed him, and I shouldn't wonder if he dies."

"Will he die?" said Black Sheep.

"I dare say," said Harry, "and then you'll be hanged."

"All right," said Black Sheep, possessing himself of the table-knife. "Then I'll kill you now. You say things and do things and . . . and *I* don't know how things happen, and you never leave me alone—and I don't care *what* happens!"

He ran at the boy with the knife, and

Harry fled upstairs to his room, promising Black Sheep the finest thrashing in the world when Aunty Rosa returned. Black Sheep sat at the bottom of the stairs, the table-knife in his hand, and wept for that he had not killed Harry. The servant-girl came up from the kitchen, took the knife away, and consoled him. But Black Sheep was beyond consolation. He would be badly beaten by Aunty Rosa; then there would be another beating at Harry's hands; then Judy would not be allowed to speak to him; then the tale would be told at school and then . . .

There was no one to help and no one to care, and the best way out of the business was by death. A knife would hurt, but Aunty Rosa had told him, a year ago, that if he sucked paint he would die. He went into the nursery, unearthed the now disused Noah's Ark, and sucked the paint off as many animals as remained. It tasted abominable, but he had licked Noah's Dove clean by the time Aunty Rosa and Judy returned. He went upstairs and greeted them with "Please, Aunty Rosa, I believe I've nearly killed a boy at school, and I've tried to kill Harry, and when you've done all about God and Hell, will you beat me and get it over?"

The tale of the assault as told by Harry could only be explained on the ground of possession by the Devil. Wherefore Black Sheep was not only most excellently beaten, once by Aunty Rosa and once, when thoroughly cowed down, by Harry, but he was further prayed for at family prayers, together with Jane who had stolen a cold rissole from the pantry and snuffled audibly as her enormity was brought before the

Throne of Grace. Black Sheep was sore and stiff but triumphant. He would die that very night and be rid of them all. No, he would ask for no forgiveness from Harry, and at bedtime would stand no questioning at Harry's hands, even though addressed as "Young Cain."

"I've been beaten," said he, "and I've done other things. I don't care what I do. If you speak to me to-night, Harry, I'll get out and try to kill you. Now you can kill me if you like."

Harry took his bed into the spareroom, and Black Sheep lay down to die.

It may be that the makers of Noah's Arks know that their animals are likely to find their way into young mouths, and paint them accordingly. Certain it is that the common, weary next morning broke through the windows and found Black Sheep quite well and a good deal ashamed of himself, but richer by the knowledge that he could in extremity, secure himself against Harry for the future.

When he descended to breakfast on the first day of the holidays, he was greeted with the news that Harry, Aunty Rosa, and Judy were going away to Brighton, while Black Sheep was to stay in the house with the servant. His latest outbreak suited Aunty Rosa's plans admirably. It gave her good excuse for leaving the extra boy behind. Papa in Bombay, who really seemed to know a young sinner's wants to the hour, sent, that week, a package of new books. And with these, and the society of Jane on board-wages, Black Sheep was left alone for a month.

The books lasted for ten days. They

were eaten too quickly, in long gulps of four and twenty hours at a time. Then came days of doing absolutely nothing, of dreaming dreams and marching imaginary armies up and downstairs, of counting the number of banisters, and of measuring the length and breadth of every room in handspans—fifty down the side, thirty across, and fifty back again. Jane made many friends, and, after receiving Black Sheep's assurance that he would not tell of her absences, went out daily for long hours. Black Sheep would follow the rays of the sinking sun from the kitchen to the dining-room and thence upward to his own bed-room until all was grey dark, and he ran down to the kitchen fire and read by its light. He was happy in that he was left alone and could read as much as he pleased. But, later, he grew afraid of the shadows of window-curtains and the flapping of doors and the creaking of shutters. He went out into the garden, and the rustling of the laurel-bushes frightened him.

He was glad when they all returned —Aunty Rosa, Harry, and Judy—full of news, and Judy laden with gifts. Who could help loving loyal little Judy? In return for all her merry babblement, Black Sheep confided to her that the distance from the hall-door to the top of the first landing was exactly one hundred and eighty-four handspans. He had found it out himself.

Then the old life recommenced; but with a difference, and a new sin. To his other iniquities Black Sheep had now added a phenomenal clumsiness— was as unfit to trust in action as he was in word. He himself could not account for spilling everything he touched, up-

setting glasses as he put his hand out, and bumping his head against doors that were manifestly shut. There was a grey haze upon all his world, and it narrowed month by month, until at last it left Black Sheep almost alone with the flapping curtains that were so like ghosts, and the nameless terrors of broad daylight that were only coats on pegs after all.

Holidays came and holidays went and Black Sheep was taken to see many people whose faces were all exactly alike; was beaten when occasion demanded, and tortured by Harry on all possible occasions; but defended by Judy through good and evil report, though she hereby drew upon herself the wrath of Aunty Rosa.

The weeks were interminable and Papa and Mamma were clean forgotten. Harry had left school and was a clerk in a Banking-Office. Freed from his presence, Black Sheep resolved that he should no longer be deprived of his allowance of pleasure-reading. Consequently when he failed at school he reported that all was well, and conceived a large contempt for Aunty Rosa as he saw how easy it was to deceive her. "She says I'm a little liar when I don't tell lies, and now I do, she doesn't know," thought Black Sheep. Aunty Rosa had credited him in the past with petty cunning and stratagem that had never entered into his head. By the light of the sordid knowledge that she had revealed to him he paid her back full tale. In a household where the most innocent of his motives, his natural yearning for a little affection, had been interpreted into a desire for more bread and jam or to ingratiate himself with strangers and so put Harry into the background, his work was easy. Aunty Rosa could penetrate certain kinds of hypocrisy, but not all. He set his child's wits against hers and was no more beaten. It grew monthly more and more of a trouble to read the school-books, and even the pages of the open-print story-books danced and were dim. So Black Sheep brooded in the shadows that fell about him and cut him off from the world, inventing horrible punishments for "dear Harry," or plotting another line of the tangled web of deception that he wrapped round Aunty Rosa.

Then the crash came and the cobwebs were broken. It was impossible to foresee everything. Aunty Rosa made personal inquiries as to Black Sheep's progress and received information that startled her. Step by step, with a delight as keen as when she convicted an underfed housemaid of the theft of cold meats, she followed the trail of Black Sheep's delinquencies. For weeks and weeks, in order to escape banishment from the book-shelves, he had made a fool of Aunty Rosa, of Harry, of God, of all the world! Horrible, most horrible, and evidence of an utterly depraved mind.

Black Sheep counted the cost. "It will only be one big beating and then she'll put a card with 'Liar' on my back, same as she did before. Harry will whack me and pray for me, and she will pray for me at prayers and tell me I'm a Child of the Devil and give me hymns to learn. But I've done all my reading and she never knew. She'll say she knew all along. She's an old liar too," said he.

For three days Black Sheep was shut in his own bedroom—to prepare his heart. "That means two beatings. One at school and one here. *That* one will hurt most." And it fell even as he thought. He was thrashed at school before the Jews and the *hubshi*, for the heinous crime of bringing home false reports of progress. He was thrashed at home by Aunty Rosa on the same count, and then the placard was produced. Aunty Rosa stitched it between his shoulders and bade him go for a walk with it upon him.

"If you make me do that," said Black Sheep, very quietly, "I shall burn this house down, and perhaps I'll kill you. I don't know whether I *can* kill you—you're so bony—but I'll try."

No punishment followed this blasphemy, though Black Sheep held himself ready to work his way to Aunty Rosa's withered throat, and grip there till he was beaten off. Perhaps Aunty Rosa was afraid, for Black Sheep, having reached the Nadir of Sin, bore himself with a new recklessness.

In the midst of all the trouble there came a visitor from over the seas to Downe Lodge, who knew Papa and Mamma, and was commissioned to see Punch and Judy. Black Sheep was sent to the drawing-room and charged into a solid tea-table laden with china.

"Gently, gently, little man," said the visitor, turning Black Sheep's face to the light, slowly. "What's that big bird on the palings?"

"What bird?" asked Black Sheep.

The visitor looked deep down into Black Sheep's eyes for half a minute, and then said, suddenly:—"Good God, the little chap's nearly blind!"

It was a most business-like visitor. He gave orders, on his own responsibility, that Black Sheep was not to go to school or open a book until Mamma came home. "She'll be here in three weeks, as you know of course," said he, "and I'm Inverarity Sahib. I ushered you into this wicked world, young man, and a nice use you seem to have made of your time. You must do nothing whatever. Can you do that?"

"Yes," said Punch, in a dazed way. He had known that Mamma was coming. There was a chance, then, of another beating. Thank Heaven, Papa wasn't coming too. Aunty Rosa had said of late that he ought to be beaten by a man.

For the next three weeks Black Sheep was strictly allowed to do nothing. He spent his time in the old nursery looking at the broken toys, for all of which account must be rendered to Mamma. Aunty Rosa hit him over the hands if even a wooden boat were broken. But that sin was of small importance compared to the other revelations, so darkly hinted at by Aunty Rosa. "When your Mother comes, and hears what I have to tell her, she may appreciate you properly," she said, grimly, and mounted guard over Judy lest that small maiden should attempt to comfort her brother, to the peril of her own soul.

And Mamma came—in a four-wheeler and a flutter of tender excitement. Such a Mamma! She was young, frivolously young, and beautiful, with delicately flushed cheeks, eyes that shone like stars, and a voice that needed no additional appeal of outstretched arms to draw little ones to her heart. Judy ran straight to her, but Black Sheep hesitated. Could this wonder be "showing off"? She would not put out her arms when she knew of his crimes. Meantime was it possible that by fondling she wanted to get anything out of Black Sheep? Only all his love and all his confidence; but that Black Sheep did not know. Aunty Rosa withdrew and left Mamma, kneeling between her children, half laughing, half crying, in the very hall where Punch and Judy had wept five years before.

"Well, chicks, do you remember me?"

"No," said Judy, frankly, "but I said 'God bless Papa and Mamma,' ev'vy night."

"A little" said Black Sheep. "Remember I wrote to you every week, anyhow. That isn't to show off, but 'cause of what comes afterward."

"What comes after! What should come after, my darling boy?" And she drew him to her again. He came awkwardly, with many angles. "Not used to petting," said the quick Mother-soul. "The girl is."

"She's too little to hurt any one," thought Black Sheep, "and if I said I'd kill her, she'd be afraid. I wonder what Aunty Rosa will tell."

There was a constrained late dinner, at the end of which Mamma picked up Judy and put her to bed with endearments manifold. Faithless little Judy had shown her defection from Aunty Rosa already. And that lady resented it bitterly. Black Sheep rose to leave the room.

"Come and say good-night," said Aunty Rosa, offering a withered cheek.

"Huh!" said Black Sheep. "I never kiss you, and I'm not going to show off.

Tell that woman what I've done, and see what she says."

Black Sheep climbed into bed feeling that he had lost Heaven after a glimpse through the gates. In half an hour "that woman" was bending over him. Black Sheep flung up his right arm. It wasn't fair to come and hit him in the dark. Even Aunty Rosa never tried that. But no blow followed.

"Are you showing off? I won't tell you anything more than Aunty Rosa has, and *she* doesn't know everything," said Black Sheep as clearly as he could for the arms round his neck.

"Oh my son—my little, little son! It was my fault—*my* fault, darling—and yet how could we help it? Forgive me, Punch." The voice died out in a broken whisper, and two hot tears fell on Black Sheep's forehead.

"Has she been making you cry too?" he asked. "You should see Jane cry. But you're nice, and Jane is a Born Liar—Aunty Rosa says so."

"Hush, Punch, hush! My boy, don't talk like that. Try to love me a little bit—a little bit. You don't know how I want it. Punch-*baba*, come back to me! I am your Mother—your own Mother—and never mind the rest. I know—yes, I know, dear. It doesn't matter now. Punch, won't you care for me a little?"

It is astonishing how much petting a big boy of ten can endure when he is quite sure that there is no one to laugh at him. Black Sheep had never been made much of before, and here was this beautiful woman treating him—Black Sheep, the Child of the Devil and the Inheritor of Undying Flame—as though he were a small God.

"I care for you a great deal, Mother dear," he whispered at last, "and I'm glad you've come back; but are you sure Aunty Rosa told you everything?"

"Everything. What *does* it matter? But"—the voice broke with a sob that was also laughter—"Punch, my poor, dear, half blind darling, don't you think it was a little foolish of you?"

"*No.* It saved a lickin'."

Mamma shuddered and slipped away in the darkness to write a long letter to Papa. Here is an extract:

. . . Judy is a dear, plump little prig who adores the woman, and wears with as much gravity as her religious opinions—only eight. Jack—a venerable horse hair-atrocity which she calls her Bustle! I have just burned it, and the child is asleep in my bed as I write. She will come to me at once. Punch I cannot quite understand. He is well nourished, but seems to have been worried into a system of small deceptions which the woman magnifies into deadly sins. Don't you recollect our own upbringing, dear, when the Fear of the Lord was so often the beginning of falsehood? I shall win Punch to me before long. I am taking the children away into the country to get them to know me, and, on the whole, I am content, or shall be when you come home, dear boy, and then, thank God, we shall be all under one roof again at last!

Three months later, Punch, no longer Black Sheep, has discovered that he is the veritable owner of a real, live, lovely Mamma, who is also a sister, comforter, and friend, and that he must protect her till the Father comes home. Deception does not suit the part of a

protector and, when one can do anything without question, where is the use
of deception?

"Mother would be awfully cross if
you walked through that ditch," says
Judy, continuing a conversation.

"Mother's never angry," says Punch.
"She'd just say, 'You're a little *pagal*';
and that's not nice, but I'll show."

Punch walks through the ditch and
mires himself to the knees. "Mother,
dear," he shouts, "I'm just as dirty as
I can pos-*sib*-ly be!"

"Then change your clothes as quickly as you pos-*sib*-ly can!" rings out

Mother's clear voice from the house.
"And don't be a little *pagal!*"

"There! Told you so," says Punch.
"It's all different now, and we are just
as much Mother's as if she had never
gone."

Not altogether, O Punch, for when
young lips have drunk deep of the bitter
waters of Hate, Suspicion, and Despair,
all the Love in the world will not wholly
take away that knowledge; though it
may turn darkened eyes for a while to
the light, and teach Faith where no
Faith was.

His Majesty the King

"Where the word of a King is, there
is power: And who may say unto him—
What doest thou?"

"YETH! And Chimo to sleep at ve
foot of ve bed, and ve pink pikky-book,
and ve bwead—'cause I will be hungwy
in ve night—and vat's all, Miss Biddums. And now give me one kiss and
I'll go to sleep.—So! Kite quiet. Ow!
Ve pink pikky-book has slidded under
ve pillow and ve bwead is cwumbling!
Miss Biddums! Miss *Bid*dums! I'm *so*
uncomfy! Come and tuck me up, Miss
Biddums."

His Majesty the King was going to
bed; and poor, patient Miss Biddums,
who had advertised herself humbly as a
"young person, European, accustomed
to the care of little children," was forced
to wait upon his royal caprices. The
going to bed was always a lengthy
process, because His Majesty had a convenient knack of forgetting which of his
many friends, from the *mehter's* son to
the Commissioner's daughter, he had
prayed for, and, lest the Deity should
take offence, was used to toil through
his little prayers, in all reverence, five
times in one evening. His Majesty the
King believed in the efficacy of prayer
as devoutly as he believed in Chimo
the patient spaniel, or Miss Biddums,
who could reach him down his gun—
"with cursuffun caps—*reel* ones"—from
the upper shelves of the big nursery
cupboard.

At the door of the nursery his authority stopped. Beyond lay the empire of his father and mother—two very
terrible people who had no time to
waste upon His Majesty the King. His
voice was lowered when he passed the
frontier of his own dominions, his actions were fettered, and his soul was

filled with awe because of the grim man who lived among a wilderness of pigeon-holes and the most fascinating pieces of red tape, and the wonderful woman who was always getting into or stepping out of the big carriage.

To the one belonged the mysteries of the *"duftar*-room"; to the other the great, reflected wilderness of the "Mem-sahib's room" where the shiny, scented dresses hung on pegs, miles and miles up in the air, and the just-seen plateau of the toilet-table revealed an acreaage of speckly combs, broidered "hanafitch bags," and "white-headed" brushes.

There was no room for His Majesty the King either in official reserve or mundane gorgeousness. He had discovered that, ages and ages ago—before even Chimo came to the house, or Miss Biddums had ceased grizzling over a packet of greasy letters which appeared to be her chief treasure on earth. His Majesty the King, therefore, wisely confined himself to his own territories, where only Miss Biddums, and she feebly, disputed his sway.

From Miss Biddums he had picked up his simple theology and welded it to the legends of gods and devils that he had learned in the servants' quarters.

To Miss Biddums he confined with equal trust his tattered garments and his more serious griefs. She would make everything whole. She knew exactly how the Earth had been born, and had reassured the trembling soul of His Majesty the King that terrible time in July when it rained continuously for seven days and seven nights, and—there was no Ark ready and all the ravens had flown away! She was the most powerful person with whom he was brought

into contact—always excepting the two remote and silent people beyond the nursery door.

How was His Majesty the King to know that, six years ago, in the summer of his birth, Mrs. Austell, turning over her husband's papers, had come upon the intemperate letter of a foolish woman who had been carried away by the silent man's strength and personal beauty? How could he tell what evil the overlooked slip of note-paper had wrought in the mind of a desperately jealous wife? How could he, despite his wisdom, guess that his mother had chosen to make of it excuse for a bar and a division between herself and her husband, that strengthened and grew harder to break with each year; that she, having unearthed this skeleton in the cupboard, had trained it into a household God which should be about their path and about their bed, and poison all their ways?

These things were beyond the province of His Majesty the King. He only knew that his father was daily absorbed in some mysterious work for a thing called the *Sirkar* and that his mother was the victim alternately of the *Nautch* and the *Burrakhana*. To these entertainments she was escorted by a Captain-Man for whom His Majesty the King had no regard.

"He *doesn't* laugh," he argued with Miss Biddums, who would fain have taught him charity. "He only makes faces wiv his mouf, and when he wants to o-muse me I am *not* o-mused." And His Majesty the King shook his head as one who knew the deceitfulness of this world.

Morning and evening it was his duty

to salute his father and mother—the former with a grave shake of the hand, and the latter with an equally grave kiss. Once, indeed, he had put his arms round his mother's neck, in the fashion he used toward Miss Biddums. The openwork of his sleeve-edge caught in an earring, and the last stage of His Majesty's little overture was a sup-pressed scream and summary dismissal to the nursery.

"It's w'ong," thought His Majesty the King, "to hug Memsahibs wiv fings in veir ears. I will amember." He never repeated the experiment.

Miss Biddums, it must be confessed, spoiled him as much as his nature ad-mitted, in some sort of recompense for what she called "the hard ways of his Papa and Mamma." She, like her charge, knew nothing of the trouble be-tween man and wife—the savage con-tempt for a woman's stupidity on the one side, or the dull, rankling anger on the other. Miss Biddums had looked after many little children in her time, and served in many establishments. Be-ing a discreet woman, she observed little and said less, and, when her pupils went over the sea to the Great Unknown which she, with touching confidence in her hearers, called "Home," packed up her slender belongings and sought for employment afresh, lavishing all her love on each successive batch of in-grates. Only His Majesty the King had repaid her affection with interest; and in his uncomprehending ears she had told the tale of nearly all her hopes, her aspirations, the hopes that were dead, and the dazzling glories of her an-cestral home in "*Cal*cutta, close to Wellington Square."

Everything above the average was in the eyes of His Majesty the King "Cal-cutta good." When Miss Biddums had crossed his royal will, he reversed the epithet to vex that estimable lady, and all things evil were, until the tears of repentence swept away spite, "Calcutta bad."

Now and again Miss Biddums begged for him the rare pleasure of a day in the society of the Commissioner's child—the wilful four-year-old Patsie, who, to the intense amazement of His Majesty the King, was idolized by her parents. On thinking the question out at length, by roads unknown to those who have left childhood behind, he came to the conclusion that Patsie was petted be-cause she wore a big blue sash and yellow hair.

This precious discovery he kept to himself. The yellow hair was absolutely beyond his power, his own tousled wig being potato-brown; but something might be done toward the blue sash. He tied a large knot in his mosquito-curtains in order to remember to con-sult Patsie· on their next meeting. She was the· only child he had ever spoken to, and almost the only one that he had ever seen. The little memory and the very large and ragged knot held good.

"Patsie, lend me your blue wiband," said His Majesty the King.

"You'll bewy it," said Patsie, doubt-fully, mindful of certain fearful atro-cities committed on her doll.

"No, I won't—twoofanhonor. It's for me to wear."

"Pooh!" said Patsie. "Boys don't wear sa-ashes. Zey's only for dirls."

"I didn't know." The face of His Majesty the King fell.

"Who wants ribands? Are you playing horses, chickabiddies?' said the Commissioner's wife, stepping into the veranda.

"Toby wanted my sash," explained Patsie.

"I don't now," said His Majesty the King, hastily, feeling that with one of these terrible "grown-ups" his poor little secret would be shamelessly wrenched from him, and perhaps—most burning desecration of all—laughed at.

"I'll give you a cracker-cap," said the Commissioner's wife. "Come along with me, Toby, and we'll choose it."

The cracker-cap was a stiff, three-pointed vermillion-and-tinsel splendor. His Majesty the King fitted it on his royal brow. The Commissioner's wife had a face that children instinctively trusted, and her action, as she adjusted the toppling middle spike, was tender.

"Will it do as well?" stammered His Majesty the King.

"As what, little one?"

"As ve wiban?"

"Oh, quite. Go and look at yourself in the glass."

The words were spoken in all sincerity and to help forward any absurd "dressing-up" amusement that the children might take into their minds. But the young savage has a keen sense of the ludicrous. His Majesty the King swung the great cheval-glass down, and saw his head crowned with the staring horror of a fool's cap—a thing which his father would rend to pieces if it ever came into his office. He plucked it off, and burst into tears.

"Toby," said the Commissioner's wife, gravely, "you shouldn't give way

to temper. I am very sorry to see it. It's wrong."

His Majesty the King sobbed inconsolably, and the heart of Patsie's mother was touched. She drew the child on to her knee. Clearly it was not temper alone.

"What is it, Toby? Won't you tell me? Aren't you well?"

The torrent of sobs and speech met, and fought for a time, with chokings and gulpings and gasps. Then, in a sudden rush, His Majesty the King was delivered of a few inarticulate sounds, followed by the words:—"Go a—way you —dirty—little debbil!"

"Toby! What do you mean?"

"It's what he'd say. I *know* it is! He said vat when vere was only a little, little eggy mess, on my t-t-unic; and he'd say it again, and laugh, if I went in wif vat on my head."

"Who would say that?"

"M-m-my Papa! And I fought if I had ve blue wiban, he'd let me play in ve waste-paper basket under ve table."

"*What* blue riband, childie?"

"Ve same vat Patsie had—ve big blue wiban w-w-wound my t-ttummy!"

"What is it, Toby? There's something on your mind. Tell me all about it, and perhaps I can help."

"Isn't anyfing," sniffed His Majesty, mindful of his manhood, and raising his head from the motherly bosom upon which it was resting. "I only fought vat you—you petted Patsie 'cause she had ve blue wiban, and—and if I'd had ve blue wiban too, m-my Papa w-would pet me."

The secret was out, and His Majesty the King sobbed bitterly in spite of the arms round him, and the murmur of comfort on his heated little forehead.

Enter Patsie tumultuously, embarrassed by several lengths of the Commissioner's pet *mahseer*-rod. "Tum along, Toby! Zere's a *chu-chu* lizard in ze *chick*, and I've told Chimo to watch him till we tum. If we poke him wiz zis his tail will go *wiggle-wiggle* and fall off. Tum along! I can't weach."

"I'm· comin'," said His Majesty the King, climbing down from the Commissioner's wife's knee after a hasty kiss.

Two minutes later, the *chu-chu* lizard's tail was wriggling on the matting of the veranda, and the children were gravely poking it with splinters from the *chick*, to urge its exhausted vitality into "just one wiggle more, 'cause it doesn't hurt *chu-chu*."

The Commissioner's wife stood in the doorway and watched:—"Poor little mite! A blue sash . . . and my own precious Patsie! I wonder if the best of us, or we who love them best, ever understand what goes on in their topsy-turvy little heads."

A big tear splashed on the Commissioner's wife's wedding-ring, and she went indoors to devise a tea for the benefit of His Majesty the King.

"Their souls aren't in their tummies at that age in this climate," said the Commissioner's wife, "but they are not far off. I wonder if I could make Mrs. Austell understand. Poor little fellow!"

With simple craft, the Commissioner's wife called on Mrs. Austell and spoke long and lovingly about children; inquiring specially for His Majesty the King.

"He's with his governess," said Mrs. Austell, and the tone intimated that she was not interested.

The Commissioner's wife, unskilled in the art of war, continued her questionings. "I don't know," said Mrs. Austell. "These things are left to Miss Biddums, and, of course, she does not ill-treat the child."

The Commissioner's wife left hastily. The last sentence jarred upon her nerves. "Doesn't *ill-treat* the child! As if that were all! I wonder what Tom would say if I only 'didn't ill-treat' Patsie."

Thenceforward, His Majesty the King was an honored guest at the Commissioner's house, and the chosen friend of Patsie,· with whom he blundered into as many scrapes as the compound and the servants' quarters afforded. Patsie's Mamma was always ready to give counsel, help, and sympathy, and, if need were and callers few, to enter into their games with an *abandon* that would have shocked the sleek-haired subalterns who squirmed painfully in their chairs when they came to call on her whom they profanely nicknamed "Mother Bunch."

Yet, in spite of Patsie and Patsie's Mamma, and the love that these two lavished upon him, His Majesty the King fell grievously from grace, and committed no less a sin than that of theft—unknown, it is true, but burdensome.

There came a man to the door one day, when His Majesty was playing in the hall and the bearer had gone to dinner, with a packet for his Majesty's Mamma. And he put it upon the hall-table, and that there was no answer, and departed.

Presently, the pattern of the dado ceased to interest His Majesty, while the packet, a white, neatly wrapped one of fascinating shape, interested him very much indeed. His Mamma was out, so was Miss Biddums, and there was pink string round the packet. He greatly desired pink string. It would help him in many of his little businesses —the haulage across the floor of his small cane-chair, the torturing of Chimo, who could never understand harness— and so forth. If he took the string it would be his own, and nobody would be any the wiser. He certainly could not pluck up sufficient courage to ask Mamma for it. Wherefore, mounting upon a chair, he carefully untied the string and, behold, the stiff white paper spread out in four directions, and revealed a beautiful little leather box with gold lines upon it! He tried to replace the string, but that was a failure. So he opened the box to get full satisfaction for his iniquity, and saw a most beautiful Star that shone and winked, and was altogether lovely and desirable.

"Vat," said His Majesty, meditatively, "is a 'parkle cwown, like what I will wear when I go to heaven. I will wear it on my head—Miss Biddums says so. I would like to wear it now. I would like to play wiv it. I will take it away and play wiv it, very careful, until Mamma asks for it. I fink it was bought for me to play wiv—same as my cart."

His Majesty the King was arguing against his conscience, and he know it, for he thought immediately after: "Never mind. I will keep it to play wiv until Mamma says where is it, and then I will say:—'I tookt it and I am sorry.' I will not hurt it because it is a 'parkle cwown. But Miss Biddums will tell me to put it back. I will not show it to Miss Biddums."

If Mamma had come in at that moment all would have gone well. She did not, and His Majesty the King stuffed paper, case, and jewel into the breast of his blouse and marched to the nursery.

"When Mamma asks I will tell," was the salve that he laid upon his conscience. But Mamma never asked, and for three whole days His Majesty the King gloated over his treasure. It was of no earthly use to him, but it was splendid, and, for aught he knew, something dropped from the heavens themselves. Still Mamma made no inquiries, and it seemed to him, in his furtive peeps, as though the shiny stones grew dim. What was the use of a 'parkle cwown if it made a little boy feel all bad in his inside? He had the pink string as well as the other treasure, but greatly he wished that he had not gone beyond the string. It was his first experience of iniquity, and it pained him after the flush of possession and secret delight in the " 'parkle cwown" had died away.

Each day that he delayed rendered confession to the people beyond the nursery doors more impossible. Now and again he determined to put himself in the path of the beautifully attired lady as she was going out, and explain that he and no one else was the possessor of a " 'parkle cwown," most beautiful and quite uninquired for. But she passed hurriedly to her carriage, and the opportunity was gone before His Majesty the King could draw the deep breath which clinches noble resolve. The dread secret cut him off from Miss Biddums, Patsie, and the Commissioner's wife, and—doubly hard fate—when he brooded over it Patsie said, and told her mother, that he was cross.

The days were very long to His Majesty the King, and the inghts longer still. Miss Biddums had informed him, more than once, what was the ultimate destiny of "fieves," and when he passed the interminable mud flanks of the Central Jail, he shook in his little strapped shoes.

But release came after an afternoon spent in playing boats by the edge of the tank at the bottom of the garden. His Majesty the King went to tea, and, for the first time in his memory, the meal revolted him. His nose was very cold, and his cheeks were burning hot. There was a weight about his feet, and he pressed his head several times to make sure that it was not swelling as he sat.

"I feel vevy funny," said His Majesty the King, rubbing his nose. "Vere's a buzz-buzz in my head."

He want to bed quietly. Miss Biddums was out and the bearer undressed him.

The sin of the " 'parkle cwown" was forgotten in the acuteness of the discomfort to which he roused after a leaden slep of some hours. He was thirsty, and the bearer had forgotten to leave the drinking-water. "Miss Biddums! Miss Biddums! I'm so kirsty!"

No answer. Miss Biddums had leave to attend the wedding of a Calcutta schoolmate. His Majesty the King had forgotten that.

"I want a dwink of water!" he cried, but his voice was dried up in his throat. "I want a dwink! Vere is ve glass?"

He sat up in bed and looked round. There was a murmur of voices from the other side of the nursery door. It was better to face the terrible unknown than to choke in the dark. He slipped out of bed, but his feet were strangely wilful, and he reeled once or twice. Then he pushed the door open and staggered—a puffed and purple-faced little figure—into the brilliant light of the dining-room full of pretty ladies.

"I'm vevy hot! I'm vevy uncomfitivle," moaned His Majesty the King, clinging to the portière, "and vere's no water in ve glass, and I'm so kirsty. Give me a dwink of water."

An apparition in black and white—His Majesty the King could hardly see distinctly—lifted him up to the level of the table, and felt his wrists and forehead. The water came, and he drank deeply, his teeth chattering against the edge of the tumbler. Then every one seemed to go away—every one except the huge man in black and white, who carried him back to his bed; the mother and father following. And the sin of the " 'parkle cwown" rushed back and took possession of the terrified soul.

"I'm a fief!" he gasped. "I want to tell Miss Biddums vat I'm a fief. Vere is Miss Biddums?"

Miss Biddums had come and was bending over him. "I'm a fief," he whispered. "A fief—like ve men in the pwison. But I'll tell now. I tookt . . . I tookt ve 'parkle cwown when the man that came left it in ve hall. I bwoke ve paper and ve little bwown box, and it looked shiny, and I tookt it to play wif, and I was afwaid. It's in ve dooly-box at ve bottom. No one *never* asked for it, but I was afwaid. Oh, go an' get ve dooly-box!"

Miss Biddums obediently stooped to the lowest shelf of the *almirah* and unearthed the big paper box in which His Majesty the King kept his dearest possessions. Under the tin soldiers, and a layer of mud pellets for a pellet-bow, winked and blazed a diamond star, wrapped roughly in a half-sheet of notepaper whereon were a few words.

Somebody was crying at the head of the bed, and a man's hand touched the forehead of His Majesty the King, who grasped the packet and spread it on the bed.

"Vat is ve 'parkle cwown," he said, and wept bitterly; for now that he had made restitution he would fain have kept the shining splendor with him.

"It concerns you too," said a voice at the head of the bed. "Read the note. This is not the time to keep back anything."

The note was curt, very much to the point, and signed by a single initial. *"If you wear this to-morrow night I shall know what to expect."* The date was three weeks old.

A whisper followed, and the deeper voice returned: "And you drifted as far apart as *that!* I think it makes us

quits now, doesn't it? Oh, can't we drop this folly once and for all? Is it worth it, darling?"

"Kiss me too," said His Majesty the King, dreamily. "You isn't *vevy* angwy, is you?"

The fever burned itself out, and His Majesty the King slept.

When he waked, it was in a new world—peopled by his father and mother as well as Miss Biddums: and there was much love in that world and no morsel of fear, and more petting than was good for several little boys. His Majesty the King was too young to moralize on the uncertainty of things human, or he would have been impressed with the singular advantages of crime —ay, black sin. Behold, he had stolen the "'parkle cwown," and his reward was Love, and the right to play in the waste-paper basket under the table "fo, always."

*   *   *   *   *   *

He trotted over to spend an afternoon with Patsie, and the Commissioner's wife would have kissed him. "Not, not vere," said His Majesty the King, with superb insolence, fencing one corner of his mouth with his hand. "Vat's my Mamma's place—vere *she* kisses me."

"Oh!" said the Commissioner's wife, briefly. Then to herself: "Well, I suppose I ought to be glad for his sake. Children are selfish little grubs and— I've got my Patsie."

The Drums of the Fore and Aft

"And a little child shall lead them."

In the Army List they still stand as "The Fore and Fit Princess Hohenzollern - Sigmaringen - Auspach's Merther-Tydfilshire Own Royal Loyal Light Infantry, Regimental District 329A," but the Army through all its barracks and canteens knows them now as the "Fore and Aft." They may in time do something that shall make their new title honorable, but at present they are bitterly ashamed, and the man who calls them "Fore and Aft" does so at the risk of the head which is on his shoulders.

Two words breathed into the stables of a certain Cavalry Regiment will bring the men out into the streets with belts and mops and bad language; but a whisper of "Fore and Aft" will bring out this regiment with rifles.

Their one excuse is that they came again and did their best to finish the job in style. But for a time all their world knows that they were openly beaten, whipped, dumb-cowed, shaking and afraid. The men know it; their officers know it; the Horse Guards know it, and when the next war comes the enemy will know it also. There are two or three regiments of the Line that have a black mark against their names which they will then wipe out, and it will be excessively inconvenient for the troops upon whom they do their wiping.

The courage of the British soldier is officially supposed to be above proof, and, as a general rule, it is so. The exceptions are decently shoveled out of sight, only to be referred to in the freshet of unguarded talk that occasionally swamps a Mess-table at midnight. Then one hears strange and horrible stories of men not following their officers, of orders being given by those who had no right to give them, and of disgrace that, but for the standing luck of the British Army, might have ended in brilliant disaster. These are unpleasant stories to listen to, and the Messes tell them under their breath, sitting by the big wood fires, and the young officer bows him head and thinks to himself, please God, his men shall never behave unhandily.

The British soldier is not altogether to be blamed for occasional lapses; but this verdict he should not know. A moderately intelligent General will waste six months in mastering the craft of the particular war that he may be waging; a Colonel may utterly misunderstand the capacity of his regiment for three months after it has taken the field; and even a Company Commander may err and be deceived as to the temper and temperament of his own handful: wherefore the soldier, and the soldier of to-day more particularly, should not be blamed for falling back. He should be shot or hanged afterward—*pour encourager les autres;* but he should not be vilified in newspapers, for that is want of tact and waste of space.

He has, let us say, been in the service of the Empress for, perhaps, four years. He will leave in another two years. He has no inherited morals, and

879

four years are not sufficient to drive toughness into his fibre, or to teach him how holy a thing is his Regiment. He wants to drink, he wants to enjoy himself—in India he wants to save money —and he does not in the least like getting hurt. He has received just sufficient education to make him understand half the purport of the orders he receives, and to speculate on the nature of clean, incised, and shattering wounds. Thus, if he is told to deploy under fire preparatory to an attack, he knows that he runs a very great risk of being killed while he is deploying, and suspects that he is being thrown away to gain ten minutes' time. He may either deploy with desperate swiftness, or he may shuffle, or bunch, or break, according to the discipline under which he has lain for four years.

Armed with imperfect knowledge, cursed with the rudiments of an imagination, hampered by the intense selfishness of the lower classes, and unsupported by any regimental associations, this young man is suddenly introduced to an enemy who in eastern lands is always ugly, generally tall and hairy, and frequently noisy. If he looks to the right and the left and sees old soldiers—men of twelve years' service, who, he knows, know what they are about—taking a charge, rush, or demonstration without embarrassment, he is consoled and applies his shoulder to the butt of his rifle with a stout heart. His peace is the greater if he hears a senior, who has taught him his soldiering and broken his head on occasion, whispering:—"They'll shout and carry on like this for five minutes. Then they'll rush in, and then we've go 'em by the short hairs!"

But, on the other hand, if he sees only men of his own term of service, turning white and playing with their triggers and saying:—"What the Hell's up now?" while the Company Commanders are sweating into their sword-hilts and shouting:—"Front-rank, fix bayonets. Steady there—steady! Sight for three hundred—no, for five! Lie down, all! Steady! Front-rank, kneel!" and so forth, he becomes unhappy; and grows acutely miserable when he hears a comrade turn over with the rattle of fire-irons falling into the fender, and the grunt of a pole-axed ox. If he can be moved about a little and allowed to watch the effect of his own fire on the enemy he feels merrier, and may be then worked up to the blind passion of fighting, which is, contrary to general belief, controlled by a chilly Devil and shakes men like ague. If he is not moved about, and begins to feel cold at the pit of the stomach, and in that crisis is badly mauled and hears orders that were never given, he will break, and he will break badly; and of all things under the sight of the Sun there is nothing more terrible than a broken British regiment. When the worst comes to the worst and the panic is really epidemic, the men must be e'en let go, and the Company Commanders had better escape to the enemy and stay there for safety's sake. If they can be made to come again they are not pleasant men to meet, because they will not break twice.

About thirty years from this date, when we have succeeded in half-educating everything that wears trousers, our

Army will be a beautifully unreliable machine. It will know too much and it will do too little. Later still, when all men are at the mental level of the officer of to-day it will sweep the earth. Speaking roughly, you must employ either blackguards or gentlemen, or best of all, blackguards commanded by gentlemen, to do butcher's work with efficiency and despatch. The ideal soldier should, of course, think for himself— the *Pocketbook* says so. Unfortunately, to attain this virtue, he has to pass through the phase of thinking of himself, and that is misdirected genius. A blackguard may be slow to think for himself, but he is genuinely anxious to kill, and a little punishment teaches him how to guard his own skin and perforate another's. A powerfully prayerful Highland Regiment, officered by rank Presbyterians, is, perhaps, one degree more terrible in action than a hard-bitten thousand of irresponsible Irish ruffians led by most improper young unbelievers. But these things prove the rule—which is that the midway men are not to be trusted alone. They have ideas about the value of life and an upbringing that has not taught them to go on and take the chances. They are carefully unprovided with a backing of comrades who have been shot over, and until that backing is re-introduced, as a great many Regimental Commanders intend it shall be, they are more liable to disgrace themselves than the size of the Empire or the dignity of the Army allows. Their officers are as good as good can be, because their training begins early, and God has arranged that a clean run youth of the British middle classes shall, in the matter of backbone,

brains, and bowels, surpass all other youths. For this reason a child of eighteen will stand up, doing nothing, with a tin sword in his hand and joy in his heart until he is dropped. If he dies, he dies like a gentleman. If he lives, he writes Home that he has been "potted," "sniped," "chipped" or "cut over," and sits down to besiege Government for a wound-gratuity until the next little war breaks out, when he perjures himself before a Medical Board, blarneys his Colonel, burns incense round his Adjutant, and is allowed to go to the Front once more.

Which homily brings me directly to a brace of the most finished little fiends that ever banged drum or tootled fife in the Band of a British Regiment. They ended their sinful career by open and flagrant mutiny and were shot for it. Their names were Jakin and Lew— Piggy Lew—and they were bold, bad drummer-boys, both of them frequently birched by the Drum-Major of the Fore and Aft.

Jakin was a stunted child of fourteen, and Lew was about the same age. When not looked after, they smoked and drank. They swore habitually after the manner of the Barrack-room, which is cold-swearing and comes from between clinched teeth; and they fought religiously once a week. Jakin had sprung from some London gutter and may or may not have passed through Dr. Barnado's hands ere he arrived at the dignity of drummer-boy. Lew could remember nothing except the regiment and the delight of listening to the Band from his earliest years. He hid somewhere in his grimy little soul a genuine love for music, and was most mistakenly furnished with the head of a cherub: insomuch that beautiful ladies who watched the Regiment in church were wont to speak of him as a "darling." They never heard his vitriolic comments on their manners and morals, as he walked back to barracks with the Band and matured fresh causes of offence against Jakin.

The other drummer-boys hated both lads on account of their illogical conduct. Jakin might be pounding Lew, or Lew might be rubbing Jakin's head in the dirt, but any attempt at aggression on the part of an outsider was met by the combined forces of Lew and Jakin; and the consequences were painful. The boys were the Ishmaels of the corps, but wealthy Ishmaels, for they sold battles in alternate weeks for the sport of the barracks when they were not pitted against other boys; and thus amassed money.

On this particular day there was dissension in the camp. They had just been convicted afresh of smoking, which is bad for little boys who use plug-tobacco, and Lew's contention was that Jakin had "stunk so 'orrid bad from keepin' the pipe in pocket," that he and he alone was responsible for the birching they were both tingling under.

"I tell you I 'id the pipe o' barricks," said Jakin, pacifically.

"You're a bloomin' liar," said Lew, without heat.

"You're a bloomin' little barstard," said Jakin, strong in the knowledge that his own ancestry was unknown.

Now there is one word in the extended vacabulary of barrack-room abuse that cannot pass without comment. You may call a man a thief and risk noth-

ing. You may even call him a coward without finding more than a boot whiz past your ear, but you must not call a man a bastard unless you are prepared to prove it on his front teeth.

"You might ha' kep' that till I wasn't so sore," said Lew, sorrowfully dodging round Jakin's guard.

"I'll make you sorer," said Jakin, genially, and got home on Lew's alabaster forehead. All would have gone well and this story, as the books say, would never have been written, had not his evil fate prompted the Bazar-Sergeant's son, a long, employless man of five and twenty, to put in an appearance after the first round. He was eternally in need of money, and knew that the boys had silver.

"Fighting again," said he. "I'll report you to my father, and he'll report you to the Color-Sergeant."

"What's that to you?" said Jakin, with an unpleasant dilation of the nostrils.

"O! nothing to *me*. You'll get into trouble, and you've been up too often to afford that."

"What the Hell do you know about what we've done?" asked Lew the Seraph. "*You* aren't in the Army, you lousy, cadging civilian."

He closed in on the man's left flank.

"Jes' 'cause you find two gentlemen settlin' their diff'rences with their fistes you stick in your ugly nose where you aren't wanted. Run 'ome to your 'arfcaste slut of a Ma—or we'll give you what-for," said Jakin.

The man attempted reprisals by knocking the boys' heads together. The scheme would have succeeded had not Jakin punched him vehemently in the stomach, or had Lew refrained from kicking his shins. They fought together, bleeding and breathless, for half an hour, and after heavy punishment, triumphantly pulled down their opponent as terriers pull down a jackal.

"Now," gasped Jakin, "I'll give you what-for." He proceeded to pound the man's features while Lew stamped on the outlying portions of his anatomy. Chivalry is not a strong point in the composition of the average drummer-boy. He fights, as do his betters, to make his mark.

Ghastly was the ruin that escaped, and awful was the wrath of the Bazar-Sergeant. Awful too was the scene in Orderly-room when the two reprobates appeared to answer the charge of half-murdering a "civilian." The Bazar-Sergeant thirsted for a criminal action, and his son lied. The boys stood to attention while the black clouds of evidence accumulated.

"You little devils are more trouble than the rest of the Regiment put together," said the Colonel, angrily. "One might as well admonish thistledown, and I can't well put you in cells or under stoppages. You must be flogged again."

"Beg y' pardon, Sir. Can't we say nothin' in our own defence, Sir?" shrilled Jakin.

"Hey! What? Are you going to argue with me?" said the Colonel.

"No, Sir," said Lew. "But if a man come to you, Sir, and said he was going to report you, Sir, for 'aving a bit of a turn-up with a friend, Sir, an' wanted to get money out o' *you*, Sir"—

The Orderly-room exploded in a roar of laughter. "Well?" said the Colonel.

"That was what that measly *jarnwar*

there did, Sir, and 'e'd 'a' *done* it, Sir, if we 'adn't prevented 'im. We didn't 'it 'im much, Sir. 'E 'adn't no manner o' right to interfere with us, Sir. I don't mind bein' flogged by the Drum-Major, Sir, nor yet reported by *any* Corp'ral, but I'm—but I don't think it's fair, Sir, for a civilian to come an' talk over a man in the Army."

A second shout of laughter shook the Orderly-room, but the Colonel was grave.

"What sort of characters have these boys?" he asked of the Regimental Sergeant-Major.

"Accordin' to the Bandmaster, Sir," returned that reverend official—the only soul in the regiment whom the boys feared—"they do everything *but* lie, Sir."

"Is it like we'd go for that man for fun, Sir?" said Lew, pointing to the plaintiff.

"Oh, admonished,—admonished" said the Colonel, testily, and when the boys had gone he read the Bazar-Sergeant's son a lecture on the sin of unprofitable meddling, and gave orders that the Bandmaster should keep the Drums in better discipline.

"If either of you come to practice again with so much as a scratch on your two ugly little faces," thundered the Bandmaster, "I'll tell the Drum-Major to take the skin off your backs. Understand that, you young devils."

Then he repented of his speech for just the length of time that Lew, looking like a Seraph in red worsted embellishments, took the place of one of the trumpets—in hospital—and rendered the echo of a battle-piece. Lew certainly was a musician, and had often in his more exalted moments expressed a yearning to master every instrument of the Band.

"There's nothing to prevent your becoming a Bandmaster, Lew," said the Bandmaster, who had composed waltzes of his own, and worked day and night in the interests of the Band.

"What did he say?" demanded Jakin, after practice.

" 'Said I might be a bloomin' Bandmaster, an' be asked in to 'ave a glass o' sherry-wine on Mess-nights."

"Ho! 'Said you might be a bloomin' non-combatant, did 'e! That's just about wot 'e would say. When I've put in my boy's service—it's a bloomin' shame that doesn't count for pension—I'll take on a privit. Then I'll be a Lance in a year—knowin' what I know about the ins an' outs o' things. In three years I'll be a bloomin' Sergeant. I won't marry then, not I! I'll 'old on and learn the orf'cers' ways an' apply for exchange into a reg'ment that doesn't know all about me. Then I'll be a bloomin' orf'cer. Then I'll ask you to 'ave a glass o' sherry-wine, *Mister* Lew, an' you'll bloomin' well 'ave to stay in the hanty-room while the Mess-Sergeant brings it to your dirty 'ands."

" 'S'pose *I'm* going to be a Bandmaster? Not I, quite. I'll be a orf'cer too. There's nothin' like taking to a thing an' stickin' to it, the Schoolmaster says. The reg'ment don't go 'ome for another seven years. I'll be a Lance then or near to."

Thus the boys discussed their futures, and conducted themselves with exemplary piety for a week. That is to say, Lew started a flirtation with the Color-Sergeant's daughter, aged thirteen,—

"not," as he explained to Jakin, "with any intention o' matrimony, but by way o' keepin' my 'and in." And the black-haired Cris Delighan enjoyed that flirtation more than previous ones, and the other drummer-boys raged furiously together, and Jakin preached sermons on the dangers of "bein' tangled along o' petticoats."

But neither love nor virtue would have held Lew long in the paths of propriety had not the rumor gone abroad that the Regiment was to be sent on active service, to take part in a war which, for the sake of brevity, we call "The War of the Lost Tribes."

The barracks had the rumor almost before the Mess-room, and of all the nine hundred men in barracks not ten had seen a shot fired in anger. The Colonel had, twenty years ago, assisted at a Frontier expedition; one of the Majors had seen service at the Cape; a confirmed deserter in E Company had helped to clear streets in Ireland; but that was all. The Regiment had been put by for many years. The overwhelming mass of its rank and file had from three to four years' service; the non-commissioned officers were under thirty years old; and men and sergeants alike had forgotten to speak of the stories written in brief upon the Colors —the New Colors that had been formally blessed by an Archbishop in England ere the Regiment came away.

They wanted to go to the Front— they were enthusiastically anxious to go —but they had no knowledge of what war meant, and there was none to tell them. They were an educated regiment, the percentage of school-certificates in their ranks was high, and most

⸱ₒf the men could do more than read and write. They had ben recruited in loyal observance of the territorial idea; but they themselves had no notion of that idea. They were made up of drafts from an over-populated manufacturing district. The system had put flesh and muscle upon their small bones, but it could not put heart into the sons of those who for generations had done overmuch work for overscanty pay, had sweated in drying-rooms stooped over looms, coughed among white-lead and shivered on lime-barges. The men had found food and rest in the Army, and men now they were going to fight "niggers"—people who ran away if you shook a stick at them. Wherefore they cheered lustily when the rumor ran, and the shrewd, clerkly non-commissioned officers speculated on the chances of batta and of saving their pay. At Headquarters, men said:—"The Fore and Fit have never been under fire within the last generation. Let us, therefore, break them in easily by setting them to guard lines of communication." And this would have been done but for the fact that British Regiments were wanted— badly wanted—at the Front, and there were doubtful Native Regiments that could fill the minor duties. "Brigade 'em with two strong Regiments," said Headquarters. "They may be knocked about a bit, but they'll learn their business before they come through. Nothing like a night-alarm and a little cutting up of stragglers to make a Regiment smart in the field. Wait till they've had half a dozen sentries' throats cut."

The Colonel wrote with delight that the temper of his men was excellent, that the Regiment was all that could be wished and as sound as a bell. The Majors smiled with a sober joy, and the subalterns waltzed in pairs down the Mess-room after dinner and nearly shot themselves at revolver practice. But there was consternation in the hearts of Jakin and Lew. What was to be done with the drums? Would the Band go to the Front? How many of the drums would accompany the Regiment?

They took council together, sitting in a tree and smoking.

"It's more than a bloomin' toss-up they'll leave us b'hind at the Depôt with the women. You'll like that," said Jakin, sarcastically.

"'Cause o' Cris, y' mean? Wot's a woman or a 'ole bloomin' depôt o' women, 'longside o' the chanst of field-service? You know I'm as keen on goin' as you," said Lew.

"'Wish I was a bloomin' bugler," said Jakin, sadly. "They'll take Tom Kidd along, that I can plaster a wall with, an' like as not they won't take us."

"Then let's go an' make Tom Kidd so bloomin' sick 'e can't bugle no more. You 'old 'is 'ands an' I'll kick him," said Lew, wriggling on the branch.

"That ain't no good neither. We ain't the sort o' characters to presoon on our rep'tations—they're bad. If they have the Band at the Depôt we don't go, and no error *there*. If they take the Band we may get cast for medical unfitness. Are you medical fit, Piggy?" said Jakin, digging Lew in the ribs with force.

"Yus," said Lew, with an oath. "The Doctor says your 'eart's weak through smokin' on an empty stummick. Throw a chest an' I'll try yer."

Jakin threw out his chest, which Lew

smote with all his might. Jakin turned very pale, gasped, crowed, screwed up his eyes and said,—"That's all right."

"You'll do," said Lew. "I've 'eard o' men dyin' when you 'it 'em fair on the breast-bone."

"'Don't bring us no nearer goin', though," said Jakin. "Do you know where we're ordered?"

"Gawd knows, an' 'e won't split on a pal. Somewheres up to the Front to kill Paythans—hairy big beggars that turn you inside out if they get 'old o' you. They say their women are good-looking, too."

"Any loot?" asked the abandoned Jakin.

"Not a bloomin' anna, they say, unless you dig up the ground an' see what the niggers 'ave 'id. They're a poor lot." Jakin stood upright on the branch and gazed across the plain.

"Lew," said he, "there's the Colonel coming. 'Colonel's a good old beggar. Let's go an' talk to 'im."

Lew nearly fell out of the tree at the audacity of the suggestion. Like Jakin he feared not God neither regarded he Man, but there are limits even to the audacity of drummer-boy, and to speak to a Colonel was . . .

But Jakin had slid down the trunk and doubled in the direction of the Colonel. That officer was walking wrapped in thought and visions of a C. B.—yes, even a K. C. B., for had he not at command one of the best Regiments of the Line—the Fore and Fit? And he was aware of two small boys charging down upon him. Once before it had been solemnly reported to him that "the Drums were in a state of mutiny"; Jakin and Lew being the ring-leaders. This looked like an organized conspiracy.

The boys halted at twenty yards, walked to the regulation four paces, and saluted together, each as well set-up as a ramrod and little taller.

The Colonel was in a genial mood; the boys appeared very forlorn and unprotected on the desolate plain, and one of them was handsome.

"Well" said the Colonel, recognizing them. "Are you going to pull me down in the open? I'm sure I never interfere with you, even though"—he sniffed suspiciously—"you have been smoking."

It was time to strike while the iron was hot. Their hearts beat tumultuously.

"Beg y' pardon, Sir," began Jakin. "The Reg'ment's ordered on active service, Sir?"

"So I believe," said the Colonel, courteously.

"Is the Band goin', Sir?" said both together. Then, without pause, "We're goin', Sir, ain't we?"

"You" said the Colonel, stepping back the more fully to take in the two small figures. You! You'd die in the first march."

"No, we wouldn't, Sir. We can march with the Regiment anywheres—p'rade an' anywhere else," said Jakin.

"If Tom Kidd goes 'e'll shut up like a clasp-knife," said Lew. "Tom 'as very close veins in both 'is legs, Sir."

"Very how much?"

"Very close veins, Sir. That's why they swells after long p'rade, Sir. If 'e can go, we can go, Sir."

Again the Colonel looked at them long and intently.

"Yes, the Band is going," he said, as

gravely as though he had been addressing a brother officer. "Have you any
parents, either of you two?"

"No, Sir," rejoicingly from Lew and
Jakin. "We're both orphans, Sir.
There's no one to be considered of on
our account, Sir."

"You poor little sprats, and you want
to go up to the Front with the Regiment, do you? Why?"

"I've wore the Queen's Uniform for
two years," said Jakin. "It's very 'ard,
Sir, that a man don't get no recompense
for doin' 'is dooty, Sir."

"An'—an' if I don't go, Sir," interrupted Lew "the Bandmaster 'e says
'e'll catch an' make a bloo—a blessed
musician o' me, Sir. Before I've seen
any service, Sir."

The Colonel made no answer for a
long time. Then he said quietly:—"If
you're passed by the Doctor I dare say
you can go. I shouldn't smoke if I
were you."

The boys saluted and disappeared.
The Colonel walked home and told the
story to his wife, who nearly cried over
it. The Colonel was well pleased. If
that was the temper of the children,
what would not the men do?

Jakin and Lew entered the boys' barrack-room with great stateliness, and
refused to hold any conversation with
their comrades for at least ten minutes.
Then, bursting with pride, Jakin
drawled:—"I've bin intervooin' the Colonel. Good old beggar is the Colonel.
Says I to 'im, 'Colonel,' says I, 'let me
go the Front, along o' the Reg'ment.'
'To the Front you shall go,' says 'e, 'an'
I only wish there was more like you
among the dirty little devils that bang
the bloomin' drums.' Kidd, if you

throw your 'coutrements at me for tellin'
you the truth to your own advantage,
your legs'll swell."

None the less there was a Battle-
Royal in the barrack-room, for the boys
were consumed with envy and hate, and
neither Jakin nor Lew behaved in con-
ciliatory wise.

"I'm goin' out to say adoo to my
girl," said Lew, to cap the climax.
"Don't none o' you touch my kit because it's wanted for active service, me
bein' specially invited to go by the
Colonel."

He strolled forth and whistled in the
clump of trees at the back of the Married Quarters till Cris came to him, and,
the preliminary kisses being given and
taken, Lew began to explain the situation.

"I'm goin' to the Front with the Reg'-
ment," he said, valiantly.

"Piggy, you're a little liar," said Cris,
but her heart misgave her, for Lew was
not in the habit of lying.

"Liar yourself, Cris," said Lew, slipping an arm around her. "I'm goin'.
When the Reg'ment marches out you'll
see me with 'em, all galliant and gay.
Give us another kiss, Cris, on the
strength of it."

"If you'd on'y a-stayed at the Depôt
—where you *ought* to ha' bin—you
could get as many of 'em as—as you
dam please," whimpered Cris, putting
up her mouth.

"It's 'ard, Cris. I grant you it's 'ard.
But what's a man to do? If I'd a-stayed
at the Depôt, you wouldn't think anything of me."

"Like as not, but I'd 'ave you with
me, Piggy. An' all the thinkin' in the
world isn't like kissin'."

"An' all the kissin' in the world isn't like 'avin' a medal to wear on the front o' your coat."

"*You* won't get no medal."

"Oh, yus, I shall though. Me an' Jakin are the only acting-drummers that'll be took along. All the rest is full men, an' we'll get our medals with them."

"They might ha' taken anybody but you, Piggy. You'll get killed—you're so venturesome. Stay with me, Piggy, darlin', down at the Depôt, an' I'll love you true forever."

"Ain't you goin' to do that *now*, Cris? You said you was."

"O' course I am, but th' other's more comfortable. Wait till you've growed a bit, Piggy. You aren't no taller than me now."

"I've bin in the army for two years an' I'm not goin' to get out of a chanst o' seein' service an' don't you try to make me do so. I'll come back, Cris, an' when I take on as a man I'll marry you—marry you when I'm a Lance."

"Promise, Piggy?"

Lew reflected on the future as arranged by Jakin a short time previously, but Cris's mouth was very near to his own.

"I promise, s'elp me Gawd!" said he. Cris slid an arm round his neck.

"I won't 'old you back no more, Piggy. Go away an' get your medal, an' I'll make you a new button-bag as nice as I know how," she whispered.

"Put some o' your 'air into it, Cris, an' I'll keep it in my pocket so long's I'm alive."

Then Cris wept anew, and the interview ended. Public feeling among the drummer-boys rose to fever pitch and the lives of Jakin and Lew became unenviable. Not only had they been permitted to enlist two years before the regulation boy's age—fourteen—but, by virtue, it seemed, of their extreme youth, they were allowed to go to the Front— which thing had not happened to acting-drummers within the knowledge of boy. The Band which was to accompany the Regiment had been cut down to the regulation twenty men, the surplus returning to the ranks. Jakin and Lew were attached to the Band as supernumeraries, though they would much have preferred being Company buglers.

" 'Don't matter much," said Jakin, after the medical inspection. "Be thankful that we're 'lowed to go at all. The Doctor 'e said that if we could stand what we took from the Bazar-Sergeant's son we'd stand pretty nigh anything."

"Which we will," said Lew, looking tenderly at the ragged and ill-made housewife that Cris had given him, with a lock of her hair worked into a sprawling "L" upon the cover.

"It was the best I could," she sobbed. "I wouldn't let mother nor the Sergeant's tailor 'elp me. Keep it always, Peggy, an' remember I love you true."

They marched to the railway station, nine hundred and sixty strong, and every soul in cantonments turned out to see them go. The drummers gnashed their teeth at Jakin and Lew marching with the Band, the married women wept upon the platform, and the Regiment cheered its noble self black in the face.

"A nice level lot," said the Colonel to the Second-in-Command, as they watched the first four companies entraining.

"Fit to do anything," said the Second-in-Command, enthusiastically. "But it seems to me they're a thought too young and tender for the work in hand. It's bitter cold up at the Front now."

"They're sound enough," said the Colonel. "We must take our chance of sick casualties."

So they went northward, ever northward, past droves and droves of camels, armies of camp followers, and legions of laden mules, the throng thickening day by day, till with a shriek the train pulled up at a hopelessly congested junction where six lines of temporary track accommodated six forty-wagon trains; where whistles blew, Babus sweated and Commissariat officers swore from dawn till far into the night amid the wind-driven chaff of the fodder-bales and the lowing of a thousand steers.

"Hurry up—you're badly wanted at the Front," was the message that greeted the Fore and Aft, and the occupants of the Red Cross carriages told the same tale.

" 'Tisn't so much the bloomin' fighting," gasped a headbound trooper of Hussars to a knot of admiring Fore and Afts. " 'Tisn't so much the bloomin' fightin', though there's enough o' that. It's the bloomin' food an' the bloomin' climate. Frost all night 'cept when it hails, and biling sun all day, and the water stinks fit to knock you down. I got my 'ead chipped like a egg; I've got pneumonia too, an' my guts is all out o' order. 'Tain't no bloomin' picnic in those parts, I can tell you."

"Wot are the niggers like?" demanded a private.

"There's some prisoners in that train yonder. Go an' look at 'em. They're the aristocracy o' the country. The common folk are a dashed sight uglier. If you want to know what they fight with, reach under my seat an' pull out the long knife that's there."

They dragged out and beheld for the first time the grim, bone-handled, triangular Afghan knife. It was almost as long as Lew.

"That's the thing to jint ye," said the trooper, feebly.

"It can take off a man's arm at the shoulder as easy as slicing butter. I halved the beggar that used that 'un, but there's more of his likes up above. They don't understand thrustin', but they're devils to slice."

The men strolled across the tracks to inspect the Afghan prisoners. They were unlike any "niggers" that the Fore and Aft had ever met—these huge, black-haired, scowling sons of the Beni-Israel. As the men stared the Afghans spat freely and muttered one to another with lowered eyes.

"My eyes! Wot awful swine!" said Jakin, who was in the rear of the procession. "Say, old man, how you got *puckrowed*, eh? *Kiswasti* you wasn't hanged for your ugly face, hey?"

The tallest of the company turned, his leg-irons clanking at the movement, and stared at the boy. "See!" he cried to his fellows in Pushto. "They send children against us. What a people, and what fools!"

"*Hya!*" said Jakin, nodding his head cheerily. 'You go down-country. *Khana* get, *peenikap-anee* get—live like a bloomin' Raja *ke marfik*. That's a better *bandobust* than baynit get it in your innards. Good-bye, ole man. Take care o' your beautiful figure-'ed, an' try to look *kushy*."

The men laughed and fell in for their first march when they began to realize that a soldier's life was not all beer and skittles. They were much impressed with the size and bestial ferocity of the niggers whom they had now learned to call "Paythans," and more with the exceeding discomfort of their own surroundings. Twenty old soldiers in the corps would have taught them how to make themselves moderately snug at night, but they had no old soldiers, and, as the troops on the line of march said, "they lived like pigs." They learned the heart-breaking cussedness of camp-kitchens and camels and the depravity of an E. P. tent and a wither-wrung mule. They studied animalculæ in water, and developed a few cases of dysentery in their study.

At the end of their third march they were disagreeably surprised by the arrival in their camp of a hammered iron slug which, fired from a steadyrest at seven hundred yards, flicked out the brains of a private seated by the fire. This robbed them of their peace for a night, and was the beginning of a long-range fire carefully calculated to that end. In the daytime they saw nothing except an occasional puff of smoke from a crag above the line of march. At night there were distant spurts of flame and occasional casualties, which set the whole camp blazing into the gloom, and, occasionally, into opposite tents. Then they swore vehemently and vowed that this was magnificent but not war.

Indeed it was not. The Regiment could not halt for reprisals against the *franctireurs* of the country side. Its

duty was to go forward and make connection with the Scotch and Gurkha troops with which it was brigaded. The Afghans knew this, and knew too, after their first tentative shots, that they were dealing with a raw regiment. Thereafter they devoted themselves to the task of keeping the Fore and Aft on the strain. Not for anything would they have taken equal liberties with a seasoned corps—with the wicked little Gurkhas, whose delight it was to lie out in the open on a dark night and stalk their stalkers—with the terrible, big men dressed in women's clothes, who could be heard praying to their God in the night-watches, and whose peace of mind no amount of "sniping" could shake—or with those vile Sikhs, who marched so ostentatiously unprepared, and who dealt out such grim reward to those who tried to profit by their unpreparedness. This white regiment was different—quite different. It slept like a hog, and, like a hog, charged in every direction when it was roused. Its sentries walked with a footfall that could be heard for a quarter of a mile; would fire at anything that moved—even a driven donkey—and when they had once fired, could be scientifically "rushed" and laid out a horror and an offence against the morning sun. Then there were camp-followers who straggled and could be cut up without fear. Their shrieks would disturb the white boys, and the loss of their services would inconvenience them sorely.

Thus, at every march, the hidden enemy became bolder and the regiment writhed and twisted under attacks it could not avenge. The crowning triumph was a sudden night-rush ending in the cutting of many tent-ropes, the collapse of the sodden canvas and a glorious knifing of the men who struggled and kicked below. It was a great deed, neatly carried out, and it shook the already shaken nerves of the Fore and Aft. All the courage that they had been required to exercise up to this point was the "two o'clock in the morning courage"; and they, so far, had only succeeded in shooting their comrades and losing their sleep.

Sullen, discontented, cold, savage, sick, with their uniforms dulled and unclean, the "Fore and Aft" joined their Brigade.

"I hear you had a tough time of it coming up" said the Brigadier. But when he saw the hospital-sheets his face fell.

"This is bad," said he to himself. "They're as rotten as sheep." And aloud to the Colonel,—"I'm afraid we can't spare you just yet. We want all we have, else I should have given you ten days to recruit in."

The Colonel winced. "On my honor, Sir," he returned, "there is not the least necessity to think of sparing us. My men have been rather mauled and upset without a fair return. They only want to go in somewhere where they can see what's before them."

" 'Can't say I think much of the Fore and Fit," said the Brigadier, in confidence, to his Brigade-Major. "They've lost all their soldiering, and, by the trim of them, might have marched through the country from the other side. A more fagged-out set of men I never put eyes on."

"Oh, they'll improve as the work goes on. The parade gloss has been rubbed off a little, but they'll put on field polish before long," said the Brigade-Major. "They've been mauled, and they quite don't understand it."

They did not. All the hitting was on one side, and it was cruelly hard hitting with accessories that made them sick. There was also the real sickness that laid hold of a strong man and dragged him howling to the grave. Worst of all, their officers knew just as little of the country as the men themselves, and looked as if they did. The Fore and Aft were in a thoroughly unsatisfactory condition, but they believed that all would be well if they could once get a fair go-in at the enemy. Potshots up and down the valleys were unsatisfactory, and the bayonet never seemed to get a chance. Perhaps it was as well, for a long-limbed Afghan with a knife had a reach of eight feet, and could carry away enough lead to disable three Englishmen. The Fore and Fit would like some rifle-practice at the enemy—all seven hundred rifles blazing together. That wish showed the mood of the men.

The Gurkhas walked into their camp, and in broken, barrack-room English strove to fraternize with them; offered them pipes of tobacco and stood them treat at the canteen. But the Fore and Aft, not knowing much of the nature of the Gurkhas, treated them as they would treat any other "niggers," and the little men in green trotted back to their firm friends the Highlanders, and with many grins confided to them:— "That dam white regiment no dam use. Sulky—ugh! Dirty—ugh! Hya, any tot for Johnny?" Whereat the Highlanders smote the Gurkhas as to the head, and told them not to villify a British Regiment, and the Gurkhas grinned cavernously, for the Highlanders were their elder brothers and entitled to the privileges of kinship. The common soldier who touches a Gurkha is more than likely to have his head sliced open.

Three days later the Brigadier arranged a battle according to the rules of war and the peculiarity of the Afghan temperament. The enemy were massing in inconvenient strength among the hills, and the moving or many green standards warned him that the tribes were "up" in aid of the Afghan regular troops. A Squadron and a half of Bengal Lancers represented the available Cavalry, and two screw-guns borrowed from a column thirty miles away, the Artillery at the General's disposal.

"If they stand, as I've a very strong notion that they will, I fancy we shall see an infantry fight that will be worth watching," said the Brigadier. "We'll do it in style. Each regiment shall be played into action by its Band, and we'll hold the Cavalry in reserve."

"For *all* the reserve?" somebody asked.

"For all the reserve; because we're going to crumple them up," said the Brigadier, who was an extraordinary Brigadier, and did not believe in the value of a reserve when dealing with Asiatics. And, indeed, when you come to think of it, had the British Army consistently waited for reserves in all its little affairs, the boundaries of Our Empire would have stopped at Brighton beach.

That battle was to be a glorious battle.

The three regiments debouching from three separate gorges, after duly crowning the heights above, were to converge from the centre, left, and right upon what we will call the Afghan army, then stationed toward the lower extremity of a flat-bottomed valley. Thus it will be seen that three sides of the valley practically belonged to the English, while the fourth was strictly Afghan property. In the event of defeat the Afghans had the rocky hills to fly to, where the fire from the guerilla tribes in aid would cover their retreat. In the event of victory these same tribes would rush down and lend their weight to the rout of the British.

The screw-guns were to shell the head of each Afghan rush that was made in close formation, and the Cavalry, held in reserve in the right valley, were to gently stimulate the break-up which would follow on the combined attack. The Brigadier, sitting upon a rock overlooking the valley, would watch the battle unrolled at his feet. The Fore and Aft would debouch from the central gorge, the Gurkhas from the left, and the Highlanders from the right, for the reason that the left flank of the enemy seemed as though it required the most hammering. It was not every day that an Afghan force would take ground in the open, and the Brigadier was resolved to make the most of it.

"If we only had a few more men," he said, plaintively, "we could surround the creatures and crumble 'em up thoroughly. As it is, I'm afraid we can only cut them up as they run. It's a great pity."

The Fore and Aft had enjoyed unbroken peace for five days, and were beginning, in spite of dysentery, to recover their nerve. But they were not happy, for they did not know the work in hand, and had they known, would not have known how to do it. Throughout those five days in which old soldiers might have taught them the craft of the game, they discussed together their misadventures in the past—how such an one was alive at dawn and dead ere the dusk, and with what shrieks and struggles such another had given up his soul under the Afghan knife. Death was a new and horrible thing to the sons of mechanics who were used to die decently of zymotic disease; and their careful conservation in barracks had done nothing to make them look upon it with less dread.

Very early in the dawn the bugles began to blow, and the Fore and Aft, filled with a misguided enthusiasm, turned out without waiting for a cup of coffee and a biscuit; and were rewarded by being kept under arms in the cold while the other regiments leisurely prepared for the fray. All the world knows that it is ill taking the breeks off a Highlander. It is much iller to try to make him stir unless he is convinced of the necessity for haste.

The Fore and Aft awaited, leaning upon their rifles and listening to the protests of their empty stomachs. The Colonel did his best to remedy the default of lining as soon as it was borne in upon him that the affair would not begin at once, and so will did he succeed that the coffee was just ready when—the men moved off, their Band leading. Even then there had been a mistake in time, and the Fore and Aft came out into the valley ten minutes before the proper hour. Their Band wheeled to the right after reaching the open, and retired behind a little rocky knoll still playing while the regiment went past.

It was not a pleasant sight that opened on the uninstructed view, for the lower end of the valley appeared to be filled by an army in position—real and actual regiments attired in red coats, and—of this there was no doubt—firing Martini-Henri bullets which cup up the ground a hundred yards in front of the leading company. Over that pock-marked ground the regiment had to pass, and it opened the ball with a general and profound courtesy to the piping pickets; ducking in perfect time, as though it had been brazed on a rod. Being half-capable of thinking for itself, it fired a volley by the simple process of pitching its rifle into its shoulder and pulling the trigger. The bullets may have accounted for some of the watchers on the hillside, but they certainly did not affect the mass of enemy in front, while the noise of the rifles drowned any orders that might have been given.

"Good God!" said the Brigadier, sitting on the rock high above all. "That regiment has spoiled the whole show. Hurry up the others, and let the screw-guns get off."

But the screw-guns, in working round the heights, had stumbled upon a wasp's nest of a small mud fort which they incontinently shelled at eight hundred yards, to the huge discomfort of the occupants, who were unaccustomed to weapons of such devilish precision.

The Fore and Aft continued to go forward but with shortened stride. Where were the other regiments, and why did these niggers use Martinis? They took open order instinctively, lying down and firing at random, rushing a few paces forward and lying down again, according to the regualtions. Once in this formation, each man felt himself desperately alone, and edged in toward his fellow for comfort's sake.

Then the crack of his neighbor's rifle at his ear led him to fire as rapidly as he could—again for the sake of the comfort of the noise. The reward was not long delayed. Five volleys plunged the files in banked smoke impenetratable to the eye, and the bullets began to take ground twenty or thirty yards in front of the firers, as the weight of the bayonet dragged down, and to the right arms wearied with holding the kick of the leaping Martini. The Company Commanders peered helplessly through the smoke, the more nervous mechanically trying to fan it away with their helmets.

"High and to the left!" bawled a Captain till he was hoarse. "No good! Cease firing, and let it drift away a bit."

Three and four times the bugles shrieked the order, and when it was obeyed the Fore and Aft looked that their foe should be lying before them in mown swaths of men. A light wind drove the smoke to leeward, and showed the enemy still in position and apparently unaffected. A quarter of a ton of lead had been buried a furlong in front of them, as the ragged earth attested.

That was not demoralizing. They were waiting for the mad riot to die down, and were firing quietly into the heart of the smoke. A private of the Fore and Aft spun up his company

shrieking with agony, another was kicking the earth and gasping, and a third, ripped through the lower intestines by a jagged bullet, was calling aloud on his comrades to put him out of his pain. These were the casualties, and they were not soothing to hear or see. The smoke cleared to a dull haze.

Then the foe began to shout with a great shouting and a mass—a black mass—detached itself from the main body, and rolled over the ground at horrid speed. It was composed of, perhaps, three hundred men, who would shout and fire and slash if the rush of their fifty comrades who were determined to die carried home. The fifty were Ghazis, half-maddened with drugs and wholly mad with religious fanaticism. When they rushed the British fire ceased, and in the lull the order was given to close ranks and meet them with the bayonet.

Any one who knew the business would have told the Fore and Aft that the only way of dealing with a Ghazi rush is by volleys at long ranges; because a man who means to die, who desires to die, who will gain heaven by dying, must, in nine cases out of ten, kill a man who has a lingering prejudice in favor of life if he can close with the latter. Where they should have closed and gone forward, the Fore and Aft opened out and skirmished, and where they should have opened out and fired, they closed and waited.

A man dragged from his blankets half awake and unfed is never in a pleasant frame of mind. Nor does his happiness increase when he watches the whites of the eyes of three hundred six-foot fiends upon whose beards the foam is lying, upon whose tongues is a roar of wrath, and in whose hands are three-foot knives.

The Fore and Aft heard the Gurkha bugles bringing that regiment forward at the double, while the neighing of the Highland pipes came from the left. They strove to stay where they were, though the bayonets wavered down the line like the oars of a ragged boat. Then they felt body to body the amazing physical strength of their foes; a shriek of pain ended the rush, and the knives fell amid scenes not to be told. The men clubbed together and smote blindly—as often as not at their own fellows. Their front crumpled like paper, and the fifty Ghazis passed on; their backers, now drunk with success, fighting as madly as they.

Then the rear-ranks were bidden to close up, and the subalterns dashed into the stew—alone. For the rear-rank had heard the clamor in front, the yells and the howls of pain, and had seen the dark stale blood that makes afraid. They were not going to stay. It was the rushing of the camps over again. Let their officers go to Hell, if they chose; they would get away from the knives.

"Come on!" shrieked the subalterns, and their men, cursing them, drew back, each closing into his neighbor and wheeling round.

Charteris and Devlin, subalterns of the last company, faced their death alone in the belief that their men would follow.

"You've killed me, you cowards," sobbed Devlin and dropped, cut from the shoulder-strap to the centre of the chest, and a fresh detachment of his men retreating, always retreating, trampled him under foot as they made for the pass whence they had emerged.

I kissed her in the kitchen and I kissed her in the hall.
Child'un, child'un, follow me!
O Golly, said the cook, is he gwine to kiss us all?
Halla—Halla—Halla Halleujah!

The Gurkhas were pouring through the left gorge and over the heights at the double to the invitation of their regimental Quickstep. The black rocks were crowned with dark green spiders as the bugles gave tongue jubilantly:

In the morning! In the morning by the bright light!
When Gabriel blows his trumpet in the morning!

The Gurkhas were pouring through and blundered over loose stones. The front-files halted for a moment to take stock of the valley and to settle stray boot-laces. Then a happy little sigh o` contentment soughed down the ranks, and it was as though the land smiled, for behold there below was the enemy, and it was to meet them that the Gurkhas had doubled so hastily. There was much enemy. There would be amusement. The little men hitched their *kukris* well to hand, and gaped expectantly at their officers as terriers grin ere the stone is cast for them to fetch. The Gurkhas' ground sloped downward to the valley, and they enjoyed a fair view of the proceedings. They sat upon the bowlders to watch, for their officers were not going to waste their wind in assisting to repulse a Ghazi rush more than half a mile away. Let the white men look to their own front.

"Hi! yi!" said the Subadar-Major, who was sweating profusely. "Dam fools yonder, stand close-order! This is no time for close order, it's the time for volleys. Ugh!"

Horrified, amused, and indignant, the Gurkhas beheld the retirement—let us be gentle—of the Fore and Aft with a running chorus of oaths and commentaries.

They run! The white men run! Colonel Sahib, may *we* also do a little running?" murmured Runbir Thappa, the Senior Jemadar.

But the Colonel would have none of it. "Let the beggars be cut up a little," said he wrathfully. " 'Serves 'em right. They'll be prodded into facing round in a minute." He looked through his field-glasses, and caught the glint of an officer's sword.

"Beating 'em with the flat—damned conscripts! How the Ghazis are walking into them!" said he.

The Fore and Aft, heading back, bore with them their officers. The narrowness of the pass forced the mob into solid formation, and the rear-rank delivered some sort of a wavering volley. The Ghazis drew off, for they did not know what reserves the gorge might hide. Moreover, it was never wise to chase white men too far. They returned as wolves return to cover, satisfied with the slaughter that they had done, and only stopping to slash at the wounded on the ground. A quarter of a mile had the Fore and Aft retreated, and now, jammed in the pass, was quivering with pain, shaken and demoralized with fear, while the officers, maddened beyond control, smote the men with the hilts and the flats of their swords.

"Get back! Get back, you cowards— you women! Right about face—column of companies, form—you hounds!" shouted the Colonel, and the subalterns swore aloud. But the Regiment wanted to go—to go anywhere out of the range of those merciless knives. It swayed to and fro irresolutely with shouts and outcries, while from the right the Gurkhas dropped volley after volley of cripple-stopper Snider bullets at long range into the mob of the Ghazis returning to their own troops.

The Fore and Aft Band, though protected from direct fire by the rocky knoll under which it had sat down, fled at the first rush. Jakin and Lew would have fled also, but their short legs left them fifty yards in the rear, and by the time the Band mixed with the regiment, they were painfully aware that they would have to close in alone and unsupported.

"Get back to that rock," gasped Jakin. "They won't see us there."

And they returned to the scattered instruments of the Band; their hearts nearly bursting their ribs.

"Here's a nice show for *us*," said Jakin, throwing himself full length on the ground. "A bloomin' fine show for British Infantry! Oh, the devils! They've gone an' left us alone here! Wot'll we do?"

Lew took possession of a cast-off water bottle, which naturally was full of canteen rum, and drank till he coughed again.

"Drink," said he, shortly. "They'll come back in a minute or two—you see."

Jakin drank, but there was no sign of the regiment's return. They could hear a dull clamor from the head of the valley of retreat, and saw the Ghazis slink back, quickening their pace as the Gurkhas fired at them.

"We're all that's left of the Band, an' we'll be cut up as sure as death," said Jakin.

"I'll die game, then," said Lew, thickly, fumbling with his tiny drummer's sword. The drink was working on his brain as it was on Jakin's.

"'Old on! I know something better than fightin'," said Jakin, "stung by the splendor of a sudden thought" due chiefly to rum. "Tip our bloomin' cowards yonder the word to come back. The Paythan beggars are well away. Come on, Lew! We won't get hurt. Take the fife an' give me the drum. The Old Step for all your bloomin' guts are worth! There's a few of our men coming back now. Stand up, ye drunken little defaulter. By your right—quick march!"

He slipped the drum-sling over his shoulder, thrust the fife into Lew's hand, and the two boys marched out of the cover of the rock into the open, making a hideous hash of the first bars of the "British Grenadiers."

As Lew had said, a few of the Fore and Aft were coming back sullenly and shamefacedly under the stimulus of blows and abuse; their red coats shone at the head of the valley, and behind them were wavering bayonets. But between this shattered line and the enemy, who with Afghan suspicion feared that the hasty retreat meant an ambush, and had not moved therefore, lay half a mile of level ground dotted only by the wounded.

The tune settled into full swing and the boys kept shoulder to shoulder, Jakin banging the drum as one possessed. The one fife made a thin and pitiful squeaking, but the tune carried far, even to the Gurkhas.

"Come on, you dogs!" muttered Jakin, to himself. "Are we to play forever?" Lew was staring straight in front of him and marching more stiffly than ever he had done on parade.

And in bitter mockery of the distant mob, the old tune of the Old Line shrilled and rattled:

> Some talk of Alexander,
>   And some of Hercules;
> Of Hector and Lysander,
>   And such great names as these!

There was a far-off clapping of hands from the Gurkhas, and a roar from the Highlanders in the distance, but never a shot was fired by British or Afghan. The two little red dots moved forward in the open parallel to the enemy's front.

> But of all the world's great heroes
>   There's none that can compare,
> With a tow-row-row-row-row-row,
>   To the British Grenadier!

The men of the Fore and Aft were gathering thick at the entrance into the plain. The Brigadier on the heights far above was speechless with rage. Still no movement from the enemy. The day stayed to watch the children.

Jakin halted and beat the long roll of the Assembly, while the fife squealed despairingly.

"Right about face! Hold up, Lew, you're drunk," said Jakin. They wheeled and marched back:

> Those heroes of antiquity
>   Ne'er saw a cannon-ball,
> Nor knew the force o' powder,

"Here they come!" said Jakin. "Go on, Lew:"

To scare their foes withal!

The Fore and Aft were pouring out of the valley. What officers had said to men in that time of shame and humiliation will never be known; for neither officers nor men speak of it now.

"They are coming anew!" shouted a priest among the Afghans. "Do not kill the boys! Take them alive, and they shall be of our faith."

But the first volley had been fired, and Lew dropped on his face. Jakin stood for a minute, spun round and collapsed, as the Fore and Aft came forward, the maledictions of their officers in their ears, and in their hearts the shame of open shame.

Half the men had seen the drummers die, and they made no sign. They did not even shout. They doubled out straight across the plain in open order, and they did not fire.

"This," said the Colonel of Gurkhas, softly, "is the real attack, as it ought to have been delivered. Come on, my children."

"Ulu-lu-lu-lu!" squealed the Gurkhas, and came down with a joyful clicking of *kukris*—those vicious Gurkha knives.

On the right there was no rush. The Highlanders, cannily commending their souls to God (for it matters as much to a dead man whether he has been shot in a Border scuffle or at Waterloo) opened out and fired according to their custom, that is to say without heat and without intervals, while the screw-guns, having disposed of the impertinent mud fort aforementioned, dropped shell after shell into the clusters round the flickering green standards on the heights.

"Charrging is an unfortunate necessity," murmured the Color-Sergeant of the right company of the Highlanders.

"It makes the men sweer so, but I am thinkin' that it will come to a charrge if these black devils stand much longer. Stewarrt, man, you're firing into the eye of the sun, and he'll not take any harm for Government ammuneetion. A foot lower and a great deal slower! What are the English doing? They're very quiet there in the centre. Running again?"

The English were not running. They were hacking and hewing and stabbing, for though one white man is seldom physically a match for an Afghan in a sheepskin or wadded coat, yet, through the pressure of many white men behind, and a certain thirst for revenge in his heart, he becomes capable of doing much with both ends of his rifle. The Fore and Aft held their fire till one bullet could drive through five or six men, and the front of the Afghan force gave on the volley. They then selected their men, and slew them with deep gasps and short hacking coughs, and groanings of leather belts against strained bodies, and realized for the first time that an Afghan attacked is far less formidable than an Afghan attacking; which fact old soldiers might have told them.

But they had no old soldiers in their ranks.

The Gurkhas' stall at the bazar was the noisiest, for the men were engaged —to a nasty noise as of beef being cut on the block—with the *kukri*, which they preferred to the bayonet; well knowing how the Afghan hates the half-moon blade.

As the Afghans wavered, the green standards on the mountain moved down to assist them in a last rally. Which was unwise. The Lancers chafing in the right gorge had thrice despatched their only subaltern as galloper to report on the progress of affairs. On the third occasion he returned, with a bullet-graze on his knee, swearing strange oaths in Hindoostani, and saying that all things were ready. So that Squadron swung round the right of the Highlanders with a wicked whistling of wind in the pennons of its lances, and fell upon the remnant just when, according to all the rules of war, it should have waited for the foe to show more signs of wavering.

But it was a dainty charge, deftly delivered, and it ended by the Cavalry finding itself at the head of the pass by which the Afghans intended to retreat; and down the track that the lances had made streamed two companies of the Highlanders, which was never intended by the Brigadier. The new development was successful. It detached the enemy from his base as a sponge is torn from a rock, and left him ringed about with fire in that pitiless plain. And as a sponge is chased round the bath-tub by the hand of the bather, so were the Afghans chased till they broke into little detachments much more difficult to dispose of than large masses.

"See!" quoth the Brigadier. "Everything has come as I arranged. We've cut their base, and now we'll bucket 'em to pieces."

A direct hammering was all that the Brigadier had dared to hope for, considering the size of the force at his disposal; but men who stand or fall by the errors of their opponents may be forgiven for turning Chance into Design. The bucketing went forward merrily. The Afghan forces were upon the run—the run of wearied wolves who snarl and bite over their shoulders. The red lances dipped by twos and threes, and, with a shriek, up rose the lance-butt, like a spar on a stormy sea, as the trooper cantering forward cleared his point. The Lancers kept between their prey and the steep hills, for all who could were trying to escape from the valley of death. The Highlanders gave the fugitives two hundred yards' law, and then brought them down, gasping and choking ere they could reach the protection of the bowlders above. The Gurkhas followed suit; but the Fore and Aft were killing on their own account, for they had penned a mass of men between their bayonets and a wall of rock, and the flash of the rifles was lighting the wadded coats.

"We cannot hold them, Captain Sahib!" panted a Ressaidar of Lancers. "Let us try the carbine. The lance is good, but it wastes time."

They tried the carbine, and still the enemy melted away—fled up the hills by hundreds when there were only twenty bullets to stop them. On the heights the screw-guns ceased firing—they had run out of ammunition—and the Brigadier groaned, for the musketry fire could not sufficiently smash the retreat. Long before the last volleys were fired, the litters were out in force looking for the wounded. The battle was over, and, but for want of fresh troops, the Afghans would have been wiped off the earth. As it was they counted their dead by hundreds, and nowhere were the dead thicker than in the track of the Fore and Aft.

But the Regiment did not cheer with the Highlanders, nor did they dance uncouth dances with the Gurkhas among the dead. They looked under their brows at the Colonel as they leaned upon their rifles and panted.

"Get back to camp, you. Haven't you disgraced yourself enough for one day! Go and look to the wounded. It's all you're fit for," said the Colonel. Yet for the past hour the Fore and Aft had been doing all that mortal commander could expect. They had lost heavily because they did not know how to set about their business with proper skill, but they had borne themselves gallantly, and this was their reward.

A young and sprightly Color-Sergeant, who had begun to imagine himself a hero, offered his water-bottle to a Highlander, whose tongue was black with thirst. "I drink with no cowards," answered the youngster, huskily, and, turning to a Gurkha, said, "Hya, Johnny! Drink water got it?" The Gurkha grinned and passed his bottle. The Fore and Aft said no word.

They went back to camp when the field of strife had been a little mopped up and made presentable and the Brigadier, who saw himself a Knight in three months, was the only soul who was complimentary to them. The Colonel was heart-broken and the officers were savage and sullen.

"Well," said the Brigadier, "they are young troops of course, and it was not unnatural that they should retire in disorder for a bit."

"Oh, my only Aunt Maria!" murmured a junior Staff Officer. "Retire in disorder! It was a bally run!"

"But they came again as we all know," cooed the Brigadier, the Colonel's ashy-white face before him, "and they behaved as well as could possibly be expected. Behaved beautifully, indeed. I was watching them. It's not a matter to take to heart, Colonel. As some German General said of his men, they wanted to be shooted over a little, that was all." To himself he said: "Now they're blooded I can give 'em responsible work. It's as well that they got what they did. 'Teach 'em more than half a dozen rifle flirtations, that will—later—run alone and bite. Poor old Colonel, though."

All that afternoon the heliograph winked and flickered on the hills, striving to tell the good news to a mountain forty miles away. And in the evening there arrived, dusty, sweating, and sore, a misguided Correspondent who had gone out to assist at a trumpery village-burning and had read off the message from afar, cursing his luck the while.

"Let's have the details somehow—as full as ever you can, please. It's the first time I've ever been left this compaign," said the Correspondent to the Brigadier; and the Brigadier, nothing loath, told him how an Army of Communication had been crumpled up, destroyed, and all but annihilated by the craft, strategy, wisdom, and foresight of the Brigadier.

But some say, and among these be the Gurkhas who watched on the hillside, that that battle was won by Jakin and Lew, whose little bodies were borne up just in time to fit two gaps at the head of the big ditch-grave for the dead under the heights of Jagai.

VOLUME XI

The Story of the Gadsbys

Preface

To the address of

CAPTAIN J. MAFFLIN,
Duke of Derry's (Pink) Hussars.

Dear Mafflin,—You will remember that I wrote this story as an Awful Warning. None the less you have seen fit to disregard it and have followed Gadsby's example—as I betted you would. I acknowledge that you paid the money at once, but you have prejudiced the mind of Mrs. Mafflin against myself, for though I am almost the only respectable friend of your bachelor days, she has been *darwaza band* to me throughout the season. Further, she caused you to invite me to dinner at the Club, where you called me "a wild ass of the desert," and went home at half-past ten, after discoursing for twenty minutes on the responsibilities of housekeeping. You now drive a mail-phaeton and sit under a Church of England clergyman. I am not angry, Jack. It is your *kismet,* as it was Gaddy's, and his *kismet* who can avoid? Do not think that I am moved by a spirit of revenge as I write, thus publicly, that you and you alone are responsible for this book. In other and more expansive days, when you could look at a magnum without flushing and at a cheroot without turning white, you supplied me with most of the material. Take it back again—would that I could have preserved your fetterless speech in the telling—take it back, and by your slippered hearth read it to the late Miss Deercourt. She will not be any the more willing to receive my cards, but she will admire you immensely, and you, I feel sure, will love me. You may even invite me to another very bad dinner—at the Club, which, as you and your wife know, is a safe neutral ground for the entertainment of wild asses. Then, my very dear hypocrite, we shall be quits.

Yours always,
RUDYARD KIPLING.

P. S.—On second thoughts I should recommend you to keep the book away from Mrs. Mafflin.

Poor Dear Mamma

The wild hawk to the wind-swept sky,
  The deer to the wholesome wold,
And the heart of a man to the heart of
    a maid,
As it was in the days of old.
                        Gypsy Song.

SCENE. — *Interior of* MISS MINNIE THREEGAN'S *Bedroom at Simla.* MISS THREEGAN, *in window-seat, turning over a drawerful of things.* MISS EMMA DEERCOURT, *bosom - friend, who has come to spend the day, sitting on the bed, manipulating the bodice of a ballroom frock, and a bunch of artificial lilies of the valley. Time, 5:30 P. M. on a hot May afternoon.*

MISS DEERCOURT. And *he* said: "I shall *never* forget this dance," and, of course, I said: "Oh! how *can* you be so silly!" Do you think he meant anything, dear?

MISS THREEGAN. (*Extracting long lavender silk stocking from the rubbish.*) You know him better than *I* do.

MISS D. Oh, *do* be sympathetic, Minnie! I'm *sure* he does. At least I *would* be sure if he wasn't always riding with that odious Mrs. Hagan.

MISS T. I suppose so. How *does* one manage to dance through one's heels first? Look at this—isn't it shameful? (*Spreads stocking-heel on open hand for inspection.*)

MISS D. Never mind that! You can't mend it. Help me with this hateful bodice. I've run the string *so*, and I've run the string *so*, and I *can't* make the fulness come right. Where would

you put this? (*Waves lilies of the valley.*)

MISS T. As high up on the shoulder as possible.

MISS D. Am I quite tall enough? I know it makes May Olger look lopsided.

MISS T. Yes, but May hasn't your shoulders. Hers are like a hock-bottle.

BEARER. (*Rapping at door.*) Captain Sahib *aya.*

MISS D. (*Jumping up wildly, and hunting for body, which she has discarded owing to the heat of the day.*) Captain Sahib! What Captain Sahib? Oh, good gracious, and I'm only half dressed! Well, I sha'n't bother.

MISS T. (*Calmly.*) You needn't. It isn't for us. That's Captain Gadsby. He is going for a ride with Mamma. He generally comes five days out of the seven.

AGONIZED VOICE. (*From an inner apartment.*) Minnie, run out and give Captain Gadsby some tea, and tell him I shall be ready in ten minutes; and, O Minnie, come to me an instant, there's a dear girl!

MISS T. Oh, bother! (*Aloud.*) Very well, Mamma.

  Exit, and reappears, after five minutes, flushed, and rubbing her fingers.

MISS D. You look pink. What has happened?

MISS T. (*In a stage whisper.*) A twenty-four-inch waist, and she won't let it out. Where *are* my bangles? (*Rummages on the toilet-table, and*

902

dabs at her hair with a brush in the interval.)

MISS D. Who is this Captain Gadsby? I don't think I've met him.

MISS T. You *must* have. He belongs to the Harrar set. I've danced with him, but I've never talked to him. He's a big yellow man, just like a newly-hatched chicken, with an e-normous moustache. He walks like this (*imitates Cavalry swagger*), and he goes "Ha—Hmmm!" deep down in his throat when he can't think of anything to say. Mamma likes him. I don't.

MISS D. (*Abstractedly.*) Does he wax that moustache?

MISS T. (*Busy with powder-puff.*) Yes, I think so. Why?

MISS D. (*Bending over the bodice and sewing furiously.*) Oh, nothing—only—

MISS T. (*Sternly.*) Only what? Out with it, Emma.

MISS D. Well, May Olger—she's engaged to Mr. Charteris, you know—said—Promise you won't repeat this?

MISS T. Yes, I promise. What did she say?

MISS D. That—that being kissed (*with a rush*) by a man who *didn't* wax his moustache was—like eating an egg without salt.

MISS T. (*At her full height, with crushing scorn.*) May Olger is a horrid, nasty *Thing,* and you can tell her I said so. I'm glad she doesn't belong to my set—I must go and feed this *man!* Do I look presentable?

MISS D. Yes, perfectly. Be quick and hand him over to your Mother, and then we can talk. *I* shall listen at the door to hear what you say to him.

MISS T. 'Sure I don't care. *I'm* not afraid of Captain Gadsby.

In proof of this swings into the drawing-room with a mannish stride followed by two short steps, which produces the effect of a restive horse entering. Misses CAPTAIN GADSBY, *who is sitting in the shadow of the window-curtain, and gazes round helplessly.*

CAPTAIN GADSBY. (*Aside.*) The filly, by Jove! 'Must ha' picked up that action from the sire. (*Aloud, rising.*) Good evening, Miss Threegan.

MISS T. (*Conscious that she is flushing.*) Good evening, Captain Gadsby. Mamma told me to say that she will be ready in a few minutes. Won't you have some tea? (*Aside.*) I hope Mamma will be quick. What *am* I to say to the creature? (*Aloud and abruptly.*) Milk and sugar?

CAPT. G. No sugar, tha-anks, and very little milk. Ha-Hmmm.

MISS T. (*Aside.*) If he's going to do that, I'm lost. I shall laugh. I *know* I shall!

CAPT. G. (*Pulling at his moustache and watching it sideways down his nose.*) Ha-Hmmm. (*Aside.*) 'Wonder what the little beast can talk about. 'Must make a shot at it.

MISS T. (*Aside.*) Oh, this is agonizing. I *must* say something.

BOTH TOGETHER. Have you been—
CAPT. G. I beg your pardon. You were going to say—

MISS T. (*Who has been watching the moustache with awed fascination.*) Won't you have some eggs?

CAPT. G. (*Looking bewilderedly at the tea-table.*) Eggs! (*Aside.*) O

Hades! She must have a nursery-tea at this hour. S'pose they've wiped her mouth and sent her to me while the Mother is getting on her duds. (*Aloud.*) No, thanks.

MISS T. (*Crimson with confusion.*) Oh! I didn't mean that. I wasn't thinking of mou—eggs for an instant. I mean *salt.* Won't you have some sa—sweets? (*Aside.*) He'll think me a raving lunatic. I wish Mamma would come.

CAPT. G. (*Aside.*) It *was* a nursery-tea and she's ashamed of it. By Jove! She doesn't look half bad when she colors up like that. (*Aloud, helping himself from the dish.*) Have you seen those new chocolates at Peliti's?

MISS T. No, I made these myself. What are they like?

CAPT. G. These! *De*-licious. (*Aside.*) And that's a fact.

MISS T. (*Aside.*) Oh, bother! he'll think I'm fishing for compliments. (*Aloud.*) No, Peliti's of course.

CAPT. G. (*Enthusiastically.*) Not to compare with these. How d'you make them? I can't get my *khansamah* to understand the simplest thing beyond mutton and fowl.

MISS T. Yes? I'm not a *khansamah,* you know. Perhaps you frighten him. You should never frighten a servant. He loses his head. It's a very bad policy.

CAPT. G. He's so awf'ly stupid.

MISS T. (*Folding her hands in her lap.*) You should call him quietly and say: "O *khansamah jee!*"

CAPT. G. (*Getting interested.*) Yes? (*Aside.*) Fancy that little featherweight saying, "O *khansamah jee*" to my bloodthirsty Mir Khan!

MISS T. Then you should explain the dinner, dish by dish.

CAPT. G. But I can't speak the vernacular.

MISS T. (*Patronizingly.*) You should pass the Higher Standard and try.

CAPT. G. I have, but I don't seem to be any the wiser. Are you?

MISS T. I never passed the Higher Standard. But the *khansamah* is very patient with me. He doesn't get angry when I talk about sheep's *topees,* or order *maunds* of grain when I mean *seers.*

CAPT. G. (*Aside with intense indignation.*) I'd like to see Mir Khan being rude to that girl! Hullo! Steady the Buffs! (*Aloud.*) And do you understand about horses, too?

MISS T. A little—not very much. I can't doctor them, but I know what they ought to eat, and I am in charge of our stable.

CAPT. G. Indeed! You might help me then. What ought a man to give his *sais* in the Hills? My ruffian says eight rupees, because everything is so dear.

MISS T. Six rupees a month, and one rupee Simla allowance—neither more nor less. And a grass-cut gets six rupees. That's better than buying grass in the bazar.

CAPT. G. (*Admiringly.*) How do you know?

MISS T. I have tried both ways.

CAPT. G. Do you ride much, then? I've never seen you on the Mall.

MISS T. (*Aside.*) I haven't passed him *more* than fifty times. (*Aloud.*) Nearly every day.

CAPT. G. By Jove! I didn't know that. Ha-Hmmm! (*Pulls at his mous-*

!ache and is silént for forty seconds.)
MISS T. (*Desperately, and wondering what will happen next.*) It looks beautiful. I shouldn't touch it if I were you. (*Aside.*) It's all Mamma's fault for not coming before. I *will* be rude!

CAPT. G. (*Bronzing under the tan and bringing down his hand very quickly.*) Eh! Wha-at! Oh, yes! Ha! Ha! (*Laughs uneasily.*) (*Aside.*) Well, of *all* the dashed cheek! I never had a woman say that to me yet. She must be a cool hand or else—Ah! that nursery-tea!

VOICE FROM THE UNKNOWN. Tchk! Tchk! Tchk!

CAPT. G. Good gracious! What's that?

MISS T. The dog, I think. (*Aside.*) Emma *has* been listening, and I'll never forgive her!

CAPT. G. (*Aside.*) They don't keep dogs here. (*Aloud.*) 'Didn't sound like a dog, did it?

MISS T. Then it must have been the cat. Let's go into the veranda. What a lovely evening it is!

Steps into veranda and looks out across the hills into sunset. The Captain follows.

CAPT. G. (*Aside.*) Superb eyes! I wonder that I never noticed them before! (*Aloud.*) There's going to be a dance at Viceregal Lodge on Wednesday. Can you spare me one?

MISS T. (*Shortly.*) No! I don't want any of your charity-dances. You only ask me because Mamma told you to. I hop and I bump. You *know* I do!

CAPT. G. (*Aside.*) That's true, but little girls shouldn't understand these things. (*Aloud.*) No, on my word, I don't. You dance beautifully.

MISS T. Then why do you always stand out after half a dozen turns? I thought officers in the Army didn't tell fibs.

CAPT. G. It wasn't a fib, believe me. I really *do* want the pleasure of a dance with you.

MISS T. (*Wickedly.*) Why? Won't Mamma dance with you any more?

CAPT. G. (*More earnestly than the necessity demands.*) I wasn't thinking of your Mother. (*Aside.*) You little vixen!

MISS T. (*Still looking out of the window.*) Eh? Oh, I beg your pardon. I was thinking of something else.

CAPT. G. (*Aside.*) Well! I wonder what she'll say next. I've never known a woman treat *me* like this before. I might be—Dash it, I might be an Infantry subaltern! (*Aloud.*) Oh, *please* don't trouble. I'm not worth thinking about. Isn't your Mother ready yet?

MISS T. I should think so; but promise me, Captain Gadsby, you won't take poor dear Mamma twice round Jakko any more. It tires her so.

CAPT. G. She says that no exercise tires her.

MISS T. Yes, but she suffers afterward. *You* don't know what rheumatism is, and you oughtn't to keep her out so late, when it gets chill in the evenings.

CAPT. G. (*Aside.*) Rheumatism. I *thought* she came off her horse rather in a bunch. Whew! One lives and learns. (*Aloud.*) I'm sorry to hear that. She hasn't mentioned it to me.

MISS T. (*Flurried.*) Of course not! Poor dear Mamma never would. And you mustn't say that I told you either. Promise me that you won't. Oh, Captain Gadsby, *promise* me you won't!

CAPT. G. I am dumb, or—I shall be as soon as you've given me that dance, and another—if you can trouble yourself to think about me for a minute.

MISS T. But you won't like it one little bit. You'll be awfully sorry afterward.

CAPT. G. I shall like it above all things, and I shall only be sorry that I didn't get more. (*Aside.*) Now what in the world am I saying?

MISS T. Very well. You will have only yourself to thank if your toes are trodden on. Shall we say Seven?

CAPT. G. And Eleven. (*Aside.*) She can't be more than eight stone, but, even then, it's an absurdly small foot. (*Looks at his own riding boots.*)

MISS T. They're beautifully shiny. I can almost see my face in them.

CAPT. G. I was thinking whether I should have to go on crutches for the rest of my life if you trod on my toes.

MISS T. Very likely. Why not change Eleven for a square?

CAPT. G. No, *please!* I want them both waltzes. Won't you write them down?

MISS T. *I* don't get so many dances that I shall confuse them. *You* will be the offender.

CAPT. G. Wait and see! (*Aside.*) She doesn't dance perfectly, perhaps, but—

MISS T. Your tea must have got cold by this time. Won't you have another cup?

CAPT. G. No, thanks. Don't you think it's pleasanter out in the veranda? (*Aside.*) I never saw hair take that

color in the sunshine before. (*Aloud.*) It's like one of Dicksee's pictures.

MISS T. Yes! It's a wonderful sunset, isn't it? (*Bluntly.*) But what do *you* know about Dicksee's pictures?

CAPT. G. I go Home occasionally. And I used to know the Galleries. (*Nervously.*) You mustn't think me only a Philistine with—a moustache.

MISS T. Don't! *Please* don't! I'm *so* sorry for what I said then. I was *horribly* rude. It slipped out before I thought. Don't you know the temptation to say frightful and shocking things just for the mere sake of saying them? I'm afraid I gave way to it.

CAPT. G. (*Watching the girl as she flushes.*) I *think* I know the feeling. It would be terrible if we all yielded to it, wouldn't it? For instance, I might say—

POOR DEAR MAMMA. (*Entering, habited, hatted, and booted.*) Ah, Captain Gadsby? 'Sorry to keep you waiting. 'Hope you haven't been bored. 'My little girl been talking to you?

MISS T. (*Aside.*) I'm not sorry I spoke about the rheumatism. I'm not! I'm NOT! I only wish I'd mentioned the corns too.

CAPT. G. (*Aside.*) What a shame! I wonder how old she is. It never occurred to me before. (*Aloud.*) We've been discussing "Shakespeare and the musical glasses" in the veranda.

MISS T. (*Aside.*) Nice man! He knows that quotation. He *isn't* a Philistine with a moustache. (*Aloud.*) Good-bye, Captain Gadsby. (*Aside.*) What a huge hand and *what* a squeeze! I don't suppose he meant it, but he has driven the rings into my fingers.

POOR DEAR MAMMA. Has Vermillion

come round yet? Oh, yes! Captain Gadsby, don't you thing that the saddle is too far forward? (*They pass into the front veranda.*)

CAPT. G. (*Aside.*) How the dickens should I know what she prefers? She told me that she doted on horses. (*Aloud.*) I think it is.

MISS T. (*Coming out into front veranda.*) Oh! Bad Buldoo! I must speak to him for this. He has taken up the curb two links, and Vermillion hates that. (*Passes out and to horse's head.*)

CAPT. G. Let me do it!

MISS T. No, Vermillion understands me. Don't you, ald man? (*Looses curbchain skilfully, and pats horse on nose and throttle.*) Poor Vermillion! *Did* they want to cut his chin off? There!

CAPTAIN GADSBY *watches the interlude with undisguised admiration.*

POOR DEAR MAMMA. (*Tartly to MISS T.*) You've forgotten your guest, I think, dear.

MISS T. Good gracious! So I have! Good-bye. (*Retreats indoors hastily.*)

POOR DEAR MAMMA. (*Bunching reins in fingers hampered by too tight gauntlets.*) Captain Gadsby!

CAPTAIN GADSBY *stoops and makes the foot-rest.* POOR DEAR MAMMA *blunders, halts too long, and breaks through it.*

CAPT. G. (*Aside.*) Can't hold up eleven stone forever. It's all your rheumatism. (*Aloud.*) Can't imagine why I was so clumsy. (*Aside.*) Now Little Featherweight would have gone up like a bird.

They ride out of the garden. The Captain falls back.

CAPT. G. (*Aside.*) How that habit catches her under the arms! Ugh!

POOR DEAR MAMMA. (*With the worn smile of sixteen seasons, the worse for exchange.*) You're dull this afternoon, Captain Gadsby.

CAPT. G. (*Spurring up wearily.*) Why did you keep me waiting so long? *Et cætera, et cætera, et cætera.*

(AN INTERVAL OF THREE WEEKS.)

GILDED YOUTH. (*Sitting on railings opposite Town Hall.*) Hullo, Gaddy! 'Been trotting out the Gorgonzola! We all thought it was the Gorgon you're mashing.

CAPT. G. (*With withering emphasis.*) You young cub! What the——does it matter to you?

Proceeds to read GILDED YOUTH a lecture on discretion and deportment, which crumbles latter like a Chinese Lantern. Departs fuming.

(FURTHER INTERVAL OF FIVE WEEKS.)

SCENE.—*Exterior of New Simla Library on a foggy evening.* MISS THREEGAN *and* MISS DEERCOURT *meet among the 'rickshaws.* MISS T. *is carrying a bundle of books under her left arm.*

MISS D. (*Level intonation.*) Well?

MISS T. (*Ascending intonation.*) Well?

MISS D. (*Capturing her friend's left arm, taking away all the books, placing books in 'rickshaw, returning to arm, securing hand by third finger and investigating.*) Well! You *bad* girl! And you *never* told me.

MISS T. (*Demurely.*) He—he—he only spoke yesterday afternoon.

MISS D. Bless you, dear! And I'm

to be bridesmaid, aren't I? You *know* you promised *ever* so long ago.

Miss T. Of course. I'll tell you all about it to-morrow. (*Gets into 'rickshaw.*) O Emma!

Miss D. (*With intense interest.*) Yes, dear?

Miss T. (*Piano.*) It's quite true—about—the—egg.

Miss D. What egg?

Miss T. (*Pianissimo prestissimo.*) The egg without the salt. (*Forte.*) *Chalo ghar ko jaldi, jhampani!* (*Go home, jhampani.*)

The World Without

Certain people of importance.

SCENE.—*Smoking-room of the Degchi Club. Time, 10:30 P. M. of a stuffy night in the Rains. Four men dispersed in picturesque attitudes and easy-chairs. To these enter* BLAYNE *of the Irregular Moguls, in evening dress.*

BLAYNE. Phew! The Judge ought to be hanged in his own store-godown. Hi, *khitmatgar! Poora* whiskey-peg, to take the taste out of my mouth.

CURTISS. (*Royal Artillery.*) That's it, is it? What the deuce made you dine at the Judge's? You know his *bandobust.*

BLAYNE. 'Thought it couldn't be worse than the Club, but I'll swear he buys ullaged liquor and doctors it with gin and ink (*looking round the room.*) Is this all of you to-night?

DOONE. (*P.W.D.*) Anthony was called out at dinner. Mingle had a pain in his tummy.

CURTISS. Miggy dies of cholera once a week in the Rains, and gets drunk on chlorodyne in between. 'Good little chap, though. Any one at the Judge's, Blayne?

BLAYNE. Cockley and his *mensahib* looking awfully white and fagged. 'Female girl—couldn't catch the name—on her way to the Hills, under the Cockleys' charge—the Judge, and Markyn fresh from Simla—disgustingly fit.

CURTISS. Good Lord, how truly magnificent! Was there enough ice? When I mangled garbage there I got one whole lump—nearly as big as a walnut. What had Markyn to say for himself?

BLAYNE. 'Seems that every one is having a fairly good time up there in spite of the rain. By Jove, that reminds me! I know I hadn't come across just for the pleasure of your society. News! Great news! Markyn told me.

DOONE. Who's dead now?

BLAYNE. No one that I know of; but Gaddy's hooked at last!

DROPPING CHORUS. How much? The Devil! Markyn was pulling your leg. Not GADDY!

BLAYNE. (*Humming.*) "Yea, verily, verily, verily! Verily, verily, I say unto thee." Theodore, the gift o' God! Our Phillup! It's been given out up above.

MACKESY. (*Barrister-at-Law.*) Huh!

Women will give out anything. What does accused say?

BLAYNE. Markyn told me that he congratulated him warily—one hand held out, t'other ready to guard. Gaddy turned pink and said it was so.

CURTISS. Poor old Gaddy! They all do it. Who's *she?* Let's hear the details.

BLAYNE. She's a girl—daughter of a Colonel Somebody.

DOONE. Simla's stiff with Colonels' daughters. Be more explicit.

BLAYNE. Wait a shake. What *was* her name? Three—something. Three—

CURTISS. Stars, perhaps. Gaddy knows *that* brand.

BLAYNE. Threegan—Minnie Threegan.

MACKESY. Threegan! Isn't she a little bit of a girl with red hair?

BLAYNE. 'Bout that—from what from what Markyn said.

MACKESY. Then I've met her. She was at Lucknow last season. 'Owned a permanently juvenile Mamma, and danced damnably. I say, Jervoise, you knew the Threegans, didn't you?

JERVOISE. (*Civilian of twenty-five years' service, waking up from his doze.*) Eh? What's that? Knew who? How? I thought I was at Home, confound you!

MACKESY. The Threegan girl's engaged, so Blayne says.

JERVOISE. (*Slowly.*) Engaged—engaged! Bless my soul! I'm getting an old man! Little Minnie Threegan engaged. It was only the other day I went home with them in the *Surat*—no, the *Massilia*—and she was crawling about on her hands and knees among the *ayahs.* 'Used to call me the *"Tick Tack*

Sahib" because I showed her my watch. And that was in Sixty-Seven—no, Seventy. Good God, how time flies! I'm an old man. I remember when Threegan married Miss Derwent—daughter of old Hooky Derwent—but that was before your time. And so the little baby's engaged to have a little baby of her own! Who's the other fool?

MACKESY. Gadsby of the Pink Hussars.

JERVOISE. 'Never met him. Threegan lived in debt, married in debt, and'll die in debt. "Must be glad to get the girl off his hands.

BLAYNE. Gaddy has money—lucky devil. Place at Home, too.

DOONE. He comes of first-class stock. 'Can't quite understand his being caught by a Colonel's daughter, and (*looking cautiously round room.*) Black Infantry at that! No offence to you, Blayne.

BLAYNE. (*Stiffly.*) Not much, thanks.

CURTISS. (*Quoting motto of Irregular Moguls.*) "We are what we are," eh, old man? But Gaddy was such a superior animal as a rule. Why didn't he go Home and pick his wife there?

MACKESY. They are all alike when they come to the turn into the straight. About thirty a man begins to get sick of living alone—

CURTISS. And of the eternal muttony-chap in the morning.

DOONE. It's a dead goat as a rule, but go on, Mackesy.

MACKESY. If a man's once taken that way nothing will hold him. Do you remember Benoit of your service, Doone? They transferred him to Tharanda when his time came, and he married a platelayer's daughter, or something of that kind. She was the only female about the place.

DOONE. Yes, poor brute. That smashed Benoit's chances of promotion altogether. Mrs. Benoit used to ask: "Was you goin' to the dance this evenin'?"

CURTISS. Hang it all! Gaddy hasn't married beneath him. There's no tar-brush in the family, I suppose.

JERVOISE. Tar-brush! Not an anna. You young fellows talk as though the man was doing the girl an honor in marrying her. You're all too conceited—nothing's good enough for you.

BLAYNE. Not even an empty Club, a dam' bad dinner at the Judge's, and a Station as sickly as a hospital. You're quite right. We're a set of Sybarites.

DOONE. Luxurious dogs, wallowing in—

CURTISS. Prickly heat between the shoulders. I'm covered with it. Let's hope Beora will be cooler.

BLAYNE. Whew! Are *you* ordered into camp, too? I thought the Gunners had a clean sheet.

CURTISS. No, worse luck. Two cases yesterday—one died—and if we have a third, out we go. Is there any shooting at Beora, Doone?

DOONE. The country's under water, except the patch by the Grand Trunk Road. I was there yesterday, looking at a *bund,* and came across four poor devils in their last stage. It's rather bad from here to Kuchara.

CURTISS. Then we're pretty certain to have a heavy go of it. Heigho! I shouldn't mind changing places with Gaddy for a while. 'Sport with Amaryllis in the shade of the Town Hall, and

all that. Oh, why doesn't somebody come and marry me, instead of letting me go into cholera-camp?

MACKESY. Ask the Committee.

CURTISS. You ruffian! You'll stand me another peg for that. Blayne, what will you take? Mackesy is fine on moral grounds. Doone, have you any preference?

DOONE. Small glass Kümmel, please. Excellent carminative, these days. Anthony told me so.

MACKESY. (*Signing voucher for four drinks.*) Most unfair punishment. I only thought of Curtiss as Actæon being chivied round the billiard tables by the nymphs of Diana.

BLAYNE. Curtiss would have to import his nymphs by train. Mrs. Cockley's the only woman in the Station. She won't leave Cockley, and he's doing his best to get her to go.

CURTISS. Good, indeed! Here's Mrs. Cockley's health. To the only wife in the Station and a damned brave woman!

OMNES. (*Drinking.*) A damned brave woman!

BLAYNE. I suppose Gaddy will bring his wife here at the end of the cold weather. They are going to be married almost immediately, I believe.

CURTISS. Gaddy may thank his luck that the Pink Hussars are all detachment and no headquarters this hot weather, or he'd be torn from the arms of his love as sure as death. Have you ever noticed the thorough-minded way British Cavalry take to cholera? It's because they are so expensive. If the Pinks had stood fast here, they would have been out in camp a month ago. Yes, I should decidedly like to be Gaddy.

MACKESY. He'll go Home after he's married, and send in his papers—see if he doesn't.

BLAYNE. Why shouldn't he? Hasn't he money? Would any one of us be here if we weren't paupers?

DOONE. Poor old pauper! What has become of the six hundred you rooked from our table last month?

BLAYNE. It took unto itself wings. I think an enterprising tradesman got some of it, and a *shroff* gobbled the rest —or else I spent it.

CURTISS. Gaddy never had dealings with a *shroff* in his life.

DOONE. Virtuous Gaddy! If *I* had three thousand a month, paid from England, I don't think I'd deal with a *Shroff* either.

MACKESY. (*Yawning.*) Oh, it's a sweet life! I wonder whether matrimony would make it sweeter.

CURTISS. Ask Cockley—with his wife dying by inches!

BLAYNE. Go home and get a fool of a girl to come out to—what is it Thackeray says?—"the splendid palace of an Indian pro-consul."

DOONE. Which reminds me. My quarters leak like a sieve. I had fever last night from sleeping in a swamp. And the worst of it is, one can't do anything to a roof till the Rains are over.

CURTISS. What's wrong with you? *You* haven't eighty rotting Tommies to take into a running stream.

DOONE. No: but I'm mixed boils and bad language. I'm a regular Job all over my body. It's sheer poverty of blood, and I don't see any chance of getting richer—either way.

BLAYNE. Can't you take leave?

DOONE. That's the pull you Army men have over us. Ten days are nothing in your sight. *I'm* so important that Government can't find a substitute if I go away. Ye-es, I'd like to be Gaddy, whoever his wife may be.

CURTISS. You've passed the turn of life that Mackesy was speaking of.

DOONE. Indeed I have, but I never yet had the brutality to ask a woman to share my life out here.

BLAYNE. On my soul I believe you're right. I'm thinking of Mrs. Cockley. The woman's an absolute wreck.

DOONE. Exactly. Because she stays down here. The only way to keep her fit would be to send her to the Hills for eight months—and the same with any woman. I fancy I see myself taking a wife on those terms.

MACKESY. With the rupee at one and sixpence. The little Doones would be little Dehra Doones, with a fine Mussoorie *chi-chi* anent to bring home for the holidays.

CURTISS. And a pair of be-ewtiful *sambhur*-horns for Doone to wear, free of expense, presented by—

DOONE. Yes, it's an enchanting prospect. By the way, the rupee hasn't done falling yet. The time will come when we shall think ourselves lucky if we only lose half our pay.

CURTISS. Surely a third's loss enough. Who gains by the arrangement? That's what I want to know.

BLAYNE. The Silver Question! I'm going to bed if you begin squabbling. Thank Goodness, here's Anthony— looking like a ghost.

Enter ANTHONY, *Indian Medical Staff, very white and tired.*

ANTHONY. 'Evening, Blayne. It's raining in sheets. *Whiskey peg lao, khitmatgar.* The roads are something ghastly.

CURTISS. How's Mingle?

ANTHONY. Very bad, and more frightened. I handed him over to Fewton. Mingle might just as well have called him in the first place, instead of bothering me.

BLAYNE. He's a nervous little chap. What has he got, this time?

ANTHONY. 'Can't quite say. A very bad tummy and a blue funk so far. He asked me at once if it was cholera, and I told him not to be a fool. That soothed him.

CURTISS. Poor devil! The funk does half the business in a man of that build.

ANTHONY. (*Lighting a cheroot.*) I firmly believe the funk will kill him if he stays down. You know the amount of trouble he's been giving Fewton for the last three weeks. He's doing his very best to frighten himself into the grave.

GENERAL CHORUS. Poor little devil! Why doesn't he get away?

ANTHONY. 'Can't. He has his leave all right, but he's so dipped he can't take it, and I don't think his name on paper would raise four annas. That's in confidence, though.

MACKESY. All the Station knows it.

ANTHONY. "I suppose I shall have to die here," he said, squirming all across the bed. He's quite made up his mind to Kingdom Come. And I *know* he has nothing more than a wet-weather tummy if he could only keep a hand on himself.

BLAYNE. That's bad. That's *very*

bad. Poor little Miggy. Good little chap, too. I say—

ANTHONY. What do you say?

BLAYNE. Well, look here—anyhow. If it's like that—as you say—I say fifty.

CURTISS. I say fifty.

MACKESY. I go twenty better.

DOONE. Bloated Crœsus of the Bar! I say fifty. Jervoise, what do you say? Hi! Wake up!

JERVOISE. Eh? What's that? What's that?

CURTISS. We want a hundred rupees from you. You're a bachelor drawing a gigantic income, and there's a man in a hole.

JERVOISE. What man? Any one dead?

BLAYNE. No, but he'll die if you don't give the hundred. Here! Here's a peg-voucher. You can see what we've signed for, and Anthony's man will come round to-morrow to collect it. So there will be no trouble.

JERVOISE. (*Signing.*) One hundred, E. M. J. There you are (*feebly*). It isn't one of your jokes, is it?

BLAYNE. No, it really *is* wanted. Anthony, you were the biggest poker-winner last week, and you've defrauded the tax-collector too long. Sign!

ANTHONY. Let's see. Three fifties and a seventy—two twenty—three twenty—say four hundred and twenty. That'll give him a month clear at the Hills. Many thanks, you men. I'll send round the *chaprassi* to-morrow.

CURTISS. You must engineer his taking the stuff, and of course you mustn't—

ANTHONY. *Of* course. It would never do. He'd weep with gratitude over his evening drink.

BLAYNE. That's just what he would do, damn him. Oh! I say, Anthony, you pretend to know everything. Have you heard about Gaddy?

ANTHONY. No. Divorce Court at last?

BLAYNE. Worse. He's engaged!

ANTHONY. How much? He *can't* be!

BLAYNE. He *is*. He's going to be married in a few weeks. Markyn told me at the Judge's this evening. It's *pukka*.

ANTHONY. You don't say so? Holy Moses! There'll be a shine in the tents of Kedar.

CURTISS. 'Regiment cut up rough, think you?

ANTHONY. 'Don't know anything about the Regiment.

MACKESY. It is bigamy, then?

ANTHONY. Maybe. Do you mean to say that you men have forgotten, or is there more charity in the world than I thought?

DOONE. You don't look pretty when you are trying to keep a secret. You bloat. Explain.

ANTHONY. Mrs. Herriott!

BLAYNE. (*After a long pause, to the room generally.*) It's my notion that we are a set of fools.

MACKESY. Nonsense. *That* business was knocked on the head last season. Why, young Mallard—

ANTHONY. Mallard was a candlestick, paraded as such. Think awhile. Recollect last season and the talk then. Mallard or no Mallard, did Gaddy ever talk to any other woman?

CURTISS. There's something in that. It *was* slightly noticeable now you come to mention it. But she's at Naini Tal and he's at Simla.

ANTHONY. He had to go to Simla to look after a globe-trotter relative of his—a person with a title. Uncle or aunt.

BLAYNE. And there he got engaged. No law prevents a man growing tired of a woman.

ANTHONY. Except that he mustn't do it till the woman is tired of him. And the Herriott woman was not that.

CURTISS. She may be now. Two months of Naini Tal works wonders.

DOONE. Curious thing how some women carry a Fate with them. There was a Mrs. Deegie in the Central Provinces whose men invariably fell away and got married. It became a regular proverb with us when I was down there. I remember three men desperately devoted to her, and they all, one after another, took wives.

CURTISS. That's odd. Now I should have thought that Mrs. Deegie's influence would have led them to take other men's wives. It ought to have made them afraid of the judgment of Providence.

ANTHONY. Mrs. Herriott will make Gaddy afraid of something more than the judgment of Providence, I fancy.

BLAYNE. Supposing things are as you say, he'll be a fool to face her. He'll sit tight at Simla.

ANTHONY. 'Shouldn't be a bit surprised if he went off to Naini to explain. He's an unaccountable sort of man, and she's likely to be a more than unaccountable woman.

DOONE. What makes you take her character away so confidently?

ANTHONY. *Primum tempus.* Gaddy was her first, and a woman doesn't allow her first man to drop away without expostulation. She justifies the first transfer of affection to herself by swearing that it is forever and ever. Consequently—

BLAYNE. Consequently, we are sitting here till past one o'clock, talking scandal like a set of Station cats. Anthony, it's all your fault. We were perfectly respectable till you came in. Go to bed. I'm off. Good-night all.

CURTISS. Past one! It's past two, by Jove, and here's the *khit* coming for the late charge. Just Heavens! One, two, three, four, *five* rupees to pay for the pleasure of saying that a poor little beast of a woman is no better than she should be. I'm ashamed of myself. Go to bed, you slanderous villains, and if I'm sent to Beora to-morrow, be prepared to hear I'm dead before paying my card account!

The Tents of Kedar

Only why should it be with pain at all
Why must I 'twix the leaves of coronal
Put any kiss of pardon on thy brow?
Why should the other women know so
        much,
And talk together :—Such the look and
        such
The smile he used to love with, then
        as now.
            Any Wife to any Husband.

SCENE:—*A Naini Tal dinner for thirty-four. Plate, wines, crockery, and khitmatgars carefully calculated to scale of Rs. 6000 per mensem, less Exchange. Table split lengthways by bank of flowers.*

MRS. HERRIOTT. (*After conversation has risen to proper pitch.*) Ah! 'Didn't see you in the crush in the drawing-room. (*Sotto voce.*) Where *have* you been all this while, Pip?

CAPTAIN GADSBY. (*Turning from regularly ordained dinner partner and settling hock glasses.*) Good evening. (*Sotto voce.*) Not quite so loud another time. You've no notion how your voice carries. (*Aside.*) So much

for shirking the written explanation. It'll have to be a verbal one now. Sweet prospect! How on earth am I to tell her that I am a respectable, engaged member of society and it's all over between us?

MRS. H. I've a heavy score against you. Where were you at the Monday Pop? Where were you on Tuesday? Where were you at the Lamonts' tennis? I was looking everywhere.

CAPT. G. For me! Oh, I was alive somewhere, I suppose. (*Aside.*) It's for Minnie's sake, but it's going to be dashed unpleasant.

MRS. H. Have I done anything to offend you? I never meant it if I have. I couldn't help going for a ride with the Vaynor man. It was promised a week before you came up.

CAPT. G. I didn't know—

MRS. H. It really *was*.

CAPT. G. Anything about it, I mean.

MRS. H. What has upset you to-day? All these days? You haven't been near me for four whole days—nearly one hundred hours. Was it *kind* of you, Pip? And I've been looking forward so much to your coming.

CAPT. G. Have you?

MRS. H. You *know* I have! I've been as foolish as a schoolgirl about it. I made a little calendar and put it in my card-case, and every time the twelve o'clock gun went off I scratched out a square and said: "That brings me nearer to Pip. My Pip!"

CAPT. G. (*With an uneasy laugh*). What will Mackler think if you neglect him so?

MRS. H. And it hasn't brought you nearer. You seem farther away than ever. Are you sulking about something? I know your temper.

CAPT. G. No.

MRS. H. Have I grown old in the last few months, then? (*Reaches forward to bank of flowers for menu-card.*)

PARTNER ON LEFT. Allow me. (*Hands menu-card. MRS. H. keeps her arm at full stretch for three seconds.*)

MRS. H. (*To partner.*) Oh, thanks. I didn't see. (*Turns right again.*) Is anything in me changed at all?

CAPT. G. For Goodness's sake go on with your dinner! You must eat something. Try one of those cutlet arrangements. (*Aside.*) And I fancied she had good shoulders, once upon a time! What an ass a man can make of himself!

MRS. H. (*Helping herself to a paper frill, seven peas, some stamped carrots and a spoonful of gravy.*) That isn't an answer. Tell me whether I have done anything.

CAPT. G. (*Aside.*) If it isn't ended here there will be a ghastly scene somewhere else. If only I'd written to her and stood the racket—at long range! (*To Khitmatgar.*) Han! Simpkin do. (*Aloud.*) I'll tell you later on.

MRS. H. Tell me *now*. It must be some foolish misunderstanding, and you know that there was to be nothing of that sort between us. *We,* of all people in the world, can't afford it. Is it the Vaynor man, and don't you like to say so? On my honor—

CAPT. G. I haven't given the Vaynor man a thought.

MRS. H. But how d'you know that *I* haven't?

CAPT. G. (*Aside.*) Here's my chance and may the Devil help me through with it. (*Aloud and measuredly.*) Believe me, I do not care how often or how tenderly you think of the Vaynor man.

MRS. H. I wonder if you mean that! Oh, what *is* the good of squabbling and pretending to misunderstand when you are only up for so short a time? Pip, don't be a stupid!

Follows a pause, during which he crosses his left leg over his right and continues his dinner.

CAPT. G. (*In answer to the thunderstorm in her eyes.*) Corns—my worst.

MRS. H. Upon my word, you are the very rudest man in the world! I'll *never* do it again.

CAPT. G. (*Aside.*) No, I don't think you will; but I wonder what you will do before it's all over. (*To Khitmatgar.*) Thorah ur Simpkin do.

MRS. H. Well! Haven't you the grace to apologize, bad man?

CAPT. G. (*Aside.*) I mustn't let it drift back *now*. Trust a woman for being as blind as a bat when she won't see.

Mrs. H. I'm waiting: or would you like me to dictate a form of apology?

Capt. G. (*Desperately.*) By all means dictate.

Mrs. H. (*Lightly.*) Very well. Rehearse your several Christian names after me and go on: "Profess my sincere repentence."

Capt. G. "Sincere repentence."

Mrs. H. "For having behaved"—

Capt. G. (*Aside.*) At last! I wish to Goodness she'd look away. "For having behaved"—as I have behaved, and declare that I am thoroughly and heartily sick of the whole business, and take this opportunity of making clear my intention of ending it, now, henceforward, and forever. (*Aside.*) If any one had told me I should be such a blackguard!— !

Mrs. H. (*Shaking a spoonful of potato chips into her plate.*) That's not a pretty joke.

Capt. G. No. It's a reality. (*Aside.*) I wonder if smashes of this kind are always so raw.

Mrs. H. Really, Pip, you're getting more absurd every day.

Capt. G. I don't think you quite understand me. Shall I repeat it?

Mrs. H. No! For pity's sake don't do that. It's too terrible, even in fun.

Capt. G. I'll let her think it over for a while. But I ought to be horsewhipped.

Mrs. H. I want to know what you meant by what you said just now.

Capt. G. Exactly what I said. No less.

Mrs. H. But what have I done to deserve it? What *have* I done?

Capt. G. (*Aside.*) If she only wouldn't look at me. (*Aloud and very slowly, his eyes on his plate.*) D'you remember that evening in July, before the Rains broke, when you said that the end would have to come sooner or later—and you wondered for which of us it would come first?

Mrs. H. Yes! I was only joking. And you swore that, as long as there was breath in your body, it should *never* come. And I believed you.

Capt. G. (*Finegring menu-card.*) Well, it has. That's all.

A long pause, during which Mrs. H. *bows her head and rolls the bread-twist into little pellets;* G. *stares at the oleanders.*

Mrs. H. (*Throwing back her head and laughing naturally.*) They train us women well, don't they, Pip?

Capt. G. (*Brutally, touching shirt-stud.*) So far as the expression goes. (*Aside.*) It isn't in her nature to take things quietly. There'll be an explosion yet.

Mrs. H. (*With a shudder.*) Thank you. B-but even Red Indians allow people to wriggle when they're being tortured, I believe. (*Slips fan from girdle and fans slowly: rim of fan level with chin.*)

Partner on Left. Very close tonight, isn't it? 'You find it too much for you?

Mrs. H. Oh, no, not in the least. But they really ought to have punkahs, even in your cool Naini Tal, oughtn't they? (*Turns, dropping fan and raising eyebrows.*)

Capt. G. It's all right. (*Aside.*) Here comes the storm!

Mrs. H. (*Her eyes on the table-*

cloth: fan ready in right hand.) It was very cleverly managed, Pip, and I congratulate you. You swore—you never contented yourself with merely saying a thing—you *swore* that, as far as lay in your power, you'd make my wretched life pleasant for me. And you've denied me the consolation of breaking down. I should have done it—indeed I should. A woman would hardly have thought of this refinement, my kind, considerate friend. (*Fan-guard as before.*) You have explained things so tenderly and truthfully, too! You haven't spoken or written a word of warning, and you have let me believe in you till the last minute. You haven't condescended to give me your *reason* yet. No! A woman could not have managed it half so well. Are there many *men* like you in the world?

CAPT. G. I'm sure I don't know. (*To Khitmatgar.*) Ohé! *Simpkin do.*

MRS. H. You call yourself a man of the world, don't you? Do men of the world behave like Devils when they do a woman the honor to get tired of her?

CAPT. G. I'm sure I don't know. Don't speak so loud!

MRS. H. Keep us respectable, O Lord, whatever happens! Don't be afraid of my compromising you. You've chosen your ground far too well, and I've been properly brought up. (*Lowering fan.*) Haven't you *any* pity, Pip, except for yourself?

CAPT. G. Wouldn't it be rather impertinent of me to say that I'm sorry for you?

MRS. H. I think you have said it once or twice before. You're growing very careful of my feelings. My God,

Pip, I was a good woman once! You *said* I was. You've made me what I am. What are you going to do with me? What are you going to do with me? Won't you *say* that you are sorry? (*Helps herself to iced asparagus.*)

CAPT. G. I am sorry for you, if you want the pity of such a brute as I am. I'm *awf'ly* sorry for you.

MRS. H. Rather tame for a man of the world. Do you think that that admission clears you?

CAPT. G. What can I do? I can only tell you what I think of myself. You can't think worse than that?

MRS. H. Oh, yes, I can! And now, will you tell me the reason of all this? Remorse? Has Bayard been suddenly conscience-stricken?

CAPT. G. (*Angrily, his eyes still lowered.*) No! The thing has come to an end on my side. That's all. *Mafisch!*

MRS. H. "That's all. *Mafisch!*" As though I were a Cairene Dragoman. You used to make prettier speeches. D'you remember when you said?—

CAPT. G. For Heaven's sake don't bring that back! Call me anything you like and I'll admit it—

MRS. H. But you don't care to be reminded of old lies? If I could hope to hurt you one-tenth as much as you have hurt me to-night— No, I wouldn't —I couldn't do it—liar though you are.

CAPT. G. I've spoken the truth.

MRS. H. My *dear* Sir, you flatter yourself. You have lied over the reason. Pip, remember that I know you as you don't know yourself. You have been everything to me, though you are— (*Fan-guard.*) Oh, what a contemptible *Thing* it is! And so you are merely tired of me?

Capt. G. Since you insist upon my repeating it—Yes.

Mrs. H. Lie the first. I wish I knew a coarser word. Lie seems so ineffectual in your case. The fire has just died out and there is no fresh one? Think for a minute, Pip, if you care whether I despise you more than I do. Simply *Mafisch*, is it?

Capt. G. Yes. (*Aside.*) I think I deserve this.

Mrs. H. Lie number two. Before the next glass chokes you, tell me her name.

Capt. G. (*Aside.*) I'll make her pay for dragging Minnie into the business! (*Aloud.*) Is it likely?

Mrs. H. *Very* likely if you thought that it would flatter your vanity. You'd cry my name on the house-tops to make people turn round.

Capt. G. I wish I had. There would have ben an end of this business.

Mrs. H. Oh, no, there would not— And so you were going to be virtuous and *blasé*, were you? To come to me and say: "I've done with you. The incident is clo-osed." I ought to be proud of having kept such a man so long.

Capt. G. (*Aside.*) It only remains to pray for the end of the dinner. (*Aloud.*) You know what I think of myself.

Mrs. H. As it's the only person in the world you ever *do* think of, and as I know your mind thoroughly, I do. You want to get it all over and— Oh, I can't keep you back! And you're going—think of it, Pip—to throw me over for another woman. And you

swore that all other women were— Pip, my Pip! She *can't* care for you as I do. Believe me, she can't! Is it any one that I know?

Capt. G. Thank Goodness it isn't. (*Aside.*) I expected a cyclone, but not an earthquake.

Mrs. H. She *can't!* Is there anything that I wouldn't do for you—or haven't done? And to think that I should take this trouble over you, knowing what you are! Do you despise me for it?

Capt. G. (*Wiping his mouth to hide a smile.*) *Again?* It's entirely a work of charity on your part.

Mrs. H. Ahhh! But I have no right to resent it.—Is she better-looking than I? Who was it said?—

Capt. G. No—not that!

Mrs. H. I'll be more merciful than you were. Don't you know that all women are alike?

Capt. G. (*Aside.*) Then this is the exception that proves the rule.

Mrs. H. *All* of them! I'll tell you anything you like. I will, upon my word! They only want the admiration—from anybody—no matter who—anybody! But there is always *one* man that they care for more than any one else in the world, and would sacrifice all the others to. Oh, *do* listen! I've kept the Vaynor man trotting after me like a poodle, and he believes that he is the only man I am interested in. I'll tell you what he said to me.

Capt. G. Spare him. (*Aside.*) I wonder what *his* version is.

Mrs. H. He's been waiting for me to look at him all through dinner. Shall I do it, and you can see what an idiot he looks?

CAPT. G. "But what imports the nomination of this gentleman?"

MRS. H. Watch! (*Sends a glance to the Vaynor man, who tries vainly to combine a mouthful of ice pudding, a smirk of self-satisfaction, a glare of intense devotion, and the stolidity of a British dining countenance.*)

CAPT. G. (*Critically.*) He doesn't look pretty. Why didn't you wait till the spoon was out of his mouth?

MRS. H. To amuse you. She'll make an exhibition of you as I've made of him; and people will laugh at you. Oh, Pip, can't you *see* that? It's as plain as the noonday sun. You'll be trotted about and told lies, and made a fool of like the others. *I* never made a fool of you, did I?

CAPT. G. (*Aside.*) What a clever little woman it is!

MRS. H. Well, what have you to say?

CAPT. G. I feel better.

MRS. H. Yes, I suppose so, after I have come down to your level. I couldn't have done it if I hadn't cared for you so much. I have spoken the truth.

CAPT. G. It doesn't alter the situation.

MRS. H. (*Passionately.*) Then she *has* said that she cares for you! Don't believe her, Pip. It's a lie—as bad as yours to me!

CAPT. G. Ssssteady! I've a notion that a friend of yours is looking at you.

MRS. H. He! I *hate* him. He introduced you to me.

CAPT. G. (*Aside.*) And some people would like women to assist in making the laws. Introduction to imply condonement. (*Aloud.*) Well, you see, if you can remember so far back as

that, I couldn't, in common politeness, refuse the offer.

MRS. H. In common politeness! We have got beyond *that!*

CAPT. G. (*Aside.*) Old ground means fresh trouble. (*Aloud.*) On my honor—

MRS. H. Your *what?* Ha, ha!

CAPT. G. Dishonor, then. She's not what you imagine. I meant to—

MRS. H. Don't tell me anything about her! She *won't* care for you, and when you come back, after having made an exhibition of yourself, you'll find me occupied with—

CAPT. G. (*Insolently.*) You couldn't while I am alive. (*Aside.*) If that doesn't bring her pride to her rescue, nothing will.

MRS. H. (*Drawing herself up.*) Couldn't do it? *I?* (*Softening.*) You're right. I don't believe I could—though you are what you are—a coward and a liar in grain.

CAPT. G. It doesn't hurt so much after your little lecture—with demonstrations.

MRS. H. One mass of vanity! Will nothing *ever* touch you in this life? There must be a Hereafter if it's only for the benefit of— But you will have it all to yourself.

CAPT. G. (*Under his eyebrows.*) Are you so certain of that?

MRS. H. I shall have had mine in this life; and it will serve me right.

CAPT. G. But the admiration that you insisted on so strongly a moment ago? (*Aside.*) Oh, I *am* a brute!

MRS. H. (*Fiercely.*) Will *that* console me for knowing that you will go to her with the same words, the same arguments, and the—the same pet names you used to me? And if she cares for you, you two will laugh over my story. Won't that be punishment heavy enough even for me—even for me?— And it's all useless. That's another punishment.

CAPT. G. (*Feebly.*) Oh, come! I'm not so low as you think.

MRS. H. Not now, perhaps, but you will be. Oh, Pip, if a woman flatters your vanity, there's nothing on earth that you would not tell her; and no meanness that you would not do. Have I known you so long without knowing that?

CAPT. G. If you can trust me in nothing else—and I don't see why I should be trusted—you can count upon my holding my tongue.

MRS. H. If you denied everything you've said this evening and declared it was all in fun (*a long pause*), I'd trust you. Not otherwise. All I ask is, don't tell her my name. *Please* don't. A man might forget: a woman never would. (*Looks up table and sees hostess beginning to collect eyes.*) So it's all ended, through no fault of mine— Haven't I behaved beautifully? I've accepted your dismissal, and you managed it as cruelly as you coud, and I

have made you respect my sex, haven't I? (*Arranging gloves and fan.*) I only pray that she'll know you some day as I know you now. I wouldn't be you then, for I think even your conceit will be hurt. I hope she'll pay you back the humiliation you've brought on me. I hope— No. I don't I *can't* give you up! I must have something to look forward to or I shall go crazy. When it's all over, come back to me, come back to me, and you'll find that you're my Pip still!

CAPT. G. (*Very clearly.*) False move, and you pay for it. It's a girl!

MRS. H. (*Rising.*) Then it *was* true! They said—but I wouldn't insult you by asking. A girl! *I* was a girl not very long ago. Be good to her, Pip. I daresay she believes in you.

Goes out with an uncertain smile. He watches her through the door. and settles into a chair as the men redistribute themselves.

CAPT. G. Now, if there is any Power who looks after this world, will He kindly tell me what I have done? (*Reaching out for the claret, and half aloud.*) What *have* I done?

With Any Amazement

And are not afraid with any amazement.
Marriage Service.

SCENE.—*A bachelor's bedroom—toilet-table arranged with unnatural neatness.* CAPTAIN GADSBY *asleep and snoring heavily. Time,* 10:30 A. M.—

a glorious autumn day at Simla. Enter delicately CAPTAIN MAFFLIN *of* GADSBY'S *regiment. Looks at sleeper, and shakes his head murmuring "Poor Gaddy." Performs violent fantasia with hair-brushes on chairback.*

CAPT. M. Wake up, my sleeping beauty! (*Roars.*)

"Uprouse ye, then, my merry merry men!
 It is our opening day!
 It is our opening da-ay!"

Gaddy, the little dicky-birds have been billing and cooing for ever so long; and *I'm* here!

CAPT. G. (*Sitting up and yawning.*) 'Mornin'. This is awf'ly good of you, old fellow. Most awf'ly good of you. 'Don't know what I should do without you. 'Pon my soul, I don't. 'Haven't slept a wink all night.

CAPT. M. I didn't get in till half-past eleven. 'Had a look at you then, and you seemed to be sleeping as soundly as a condemned criminal.

CAPT. G. Jack, if you want to make those disgustingly worn-out jokes, you'd better go away. (*With portentous gravity.*) It's the happiest day in my life.

CAPT. M. (*Chuckling grimly.*) Not by a very long chalk, my son. You're going through some of the most refined torture you've ever known. But be calm. *I* am with you. 'Shun! *Dress!*

CAPT. G. Eh! Wha-at?

CAPT. M. *Do* you suppose that you are your own master for the next twelve hours? If you *do,* of course— (*Makes for the door.*)

CAPT. G. No! For Goodness' sake, old man, don't do that! You'll see me through, won't you? I've been mugging up that beastly drill, and can't remember a line of it.

CAPT. M. (*Overhauling* G.'s *uniform.*) Go and tub. Don't bother me. I'll give you ten minutes to dress in.

Interval, filled by the noise as of one splashing in the bath-room.

CAPT. G. (*Emerging from dressing-room.*) What time is it?

CAPT. M. Nearly eleven.

CAPT. G. Five hours more. O Lord!

CAPT. M. (*Aside.*) 'First sign of funk, that. 'Wonder if it's going to spread. (*Aloud.*) Come along to breakfast.

CAPT. G. I can't eat anything. I don't want any breakfast.

CAPT. M. (*Aside.*) So early! (*Aloud.*) Captain Gadsby, I *order* you to eat breakfast, and a dashed good breakfast, too. None of your bridal airs and graces with me!

Leads G. *downstairs, and stands over him while he eats two chops.*

CAPT. G. (*Who has looked at his watch thrice in the last five minutes.*) What time is it?

CAPT. M. Time to come for a walk. Light up.

CAPT. G. I haven't smoked for ten days, and I won't *now.* (*Takes cheroot which* M. *has cut for him, and blows smoke through his nose luxuriously.*) We aren't going down the Mall, are we?

CAPT. M. (*Aside.*) They're all alike in these stages. (*Aloud.*) No, my Vestal. We're going along the quietest road we can find.

CAPT. G. Any chance of seeing Her?

CAPT. M. Innocent! No! Come along, and, if you want me for the final obsequies, don't cut my eye out with your stick.

CAPT. G. (*Spinning round.*) I say, isn't She the dearest creature that ever walked? What's the time? What comes after "wilt thou take this woman"?

CAPT. M. You go for the ring. R'clect it'll be on the top of my right-hand little finger, and just be careful how you draw it off, because I shall have the Verger's fees somewhere in my glove.

CAPT. G. (*Walking forward hastily.*) D—— the Verger! Come along! It's past twelve and I haven't seen Her since yesterday evening. (*Spinning round again.*) She's an absolute angel, Jack, and She's a dashed deal too good for me. Look here, does She come up the aisle on my arm, or how?

CAPT. M. If I thought that there was the least chance of your remembering anything for two consecutive minutes, I'd tell you. Stop passaging about like that!

CAPT. G. (*Halting in the middle of the road.*) I say, Jack.

CAPT. M. Keep quiet for another ten minutes if you can, you lunatic; and *walk!*

> The two tramp at five miles an hour for fifteen minutes.

CAPT. G. What's the time? How about that cursed wedding-cake and the slippers? They don't throw 'em about in church, do they?

CAPT. M. In-variably. The Padre leads off with his boots.

CAPT. G. Confound your silly soul! Don't make fun of me. I can't stand it, and I won't!

CAPT. M. (*Untroubled.*) So-ooo, old horse! You'll have to sleep for a couple of hours this afternoon.

CAPT. G. (*Spinning round.*) I'm *not* going to be treated like a dashed child. Understand that!

CAPT. M. (*Aside.*) Nerves gone to fiddle-strings. What a day we're having! (*Tenderly putting his hand on G.'s shoulder.*) My David, how long have you known this Jonathan? Would I come up here to make a fool of you —after all these years?

CAPT. G. (*Penitently.*) I know, I know, Jack—but I'm as upset as I can be. Don't mind what I say. Just hear me run through the drill and see if I've got it all right:—

"To have and to hold for better or worse, as it was in the beginning, is now, and ever shall be, world without end, so help me God. Amen."

CAPT. M. (*Suffocating with suppressed laughter.*) Yes. That's about the gist of it. I'll prompt if you get into a hat.

CAPT. G. (*Earnestly.*) Yes, you'll stick by me, Jack, won't you? I'm awf-ly happy, but I don't mind telling *you* that I'm in a blue funk!

CAPT. M. (*Gravely.*) Are you? I should never have noticed it. You don't *look* like it.

CAPT. G. Don't I? That's all right. (*Spinning round.*) On my soul and honor, Jack, She's the sweetest little angel that ever came down from the sky. There isn't a woman on earth fit to speak to Her.

CAPT. M. (*Aside.*) And this is old Gaddy! (*Aloud.*) Go on if it relieves you.

CAPT. G. You can laugh! That's all you wild asses of bachelors are fit for.

CAPT. M. (*Drawling.*) You never *would* wait for the troop to come up. You aren't quite married yet, y'know.

CAPT. G. Ugh! That reminds me. I don't believe I shall be able to get into my boots. Let's go home and try 'em on! (*Hurries forward.*)

Capt. M. 'Wouldn't be in *your* shoes for anything that Asia has to offer.

Capt. G. (*Spinning round.*) That just shows your hideous blackness of soul—your dense stupidity—your brutal narrow-mindedness. There's only one fault about you. You're the best of good fellows, and I don't know what I should have done without you, but— you aren't married. (*Wags his head gravely.*) Take a wife, Jack.

Capt. M. (*With a face like a wall.*) Ya-as. Whose for choice?

Capt. G. If you're going to be a blackguard, I'm going on— What's the time?

Capt. M. (*Hums.*)—

"An' since 'twas very clear we drank only ginger-beer,
Faith, there must ha' been some stingo in the ginger."

Come back, you maniac. I'm going to take you home, and you're going to lie down.

Capt. G. What on earth do I want to lie down for?

Capt. M. Give me a light from your cheroot and see.

Capt. G. (*Watching cheroot-butt quiver like a tuning-fork.*) Sweet state I'm in!

Capt. M. You are. I'll get you a peg and you'll go to sleep.

They return and M. *compounds a four-finger peg.*

Capt. G. O *bus! bus!* It'll make me as drunk as an owl.

Capt. M. 'Curious thing, 'twon't have the slightest effect on you. Drink it off, chuck yourself down there, and go to bye-bye.

Capt. G. It's absurd. I sha'n't sleep. I *know* I sha'n't!

Falls into heavy doze at end of seven minutes. Capt. M. *watches him tenderly.*

Capt. M. Poor old Gaddy! I've seen a few turned off before, but never one who went to the gallows in this condition. 'Can't tell how it affects 'em, though. It's the thoroughbreds that sweat when they're backed into double-harness.—And that's the man who went through the guns at Amdheran like a devil possessed of devils. (*Leans over* G.) But this is worse than the guns, old pal—worse than the guns, isn't it? (G. *turns in his sleep, and* M. *touches him clumsily on the forehead.*) Poor, dear old Gaddy! Going like the rest of 'em—going like the rest of 'em—Friend that sticketh closer than a brother— eight years. Dashed bit of a slip of a girl—eight weeks! And—where's your friend? (*Smokes disconsolately till church clock strikes three.*)

Capt. M. Up with you! Get into your kit.

Capt. G. Already? Isn't it too soon? Hadn't I better have a shave?

Capt. M. *No!* You're all right. (*Aside.*) He'd chip his chin to pieces.

Capt. G. What's the hurry?

Capt. M. You've got to be there first.

Capt. G. To be stared at?

Capt. M. Exactly. You're part of the show. Where's the burnisher? Your spurs are in a shameful state.

Capt. G. (*Gruffly.*) Jack, I be damned if you shall do that for me.

Capt. M. (*More gruffly.*) Dry up

and get dressed! If I choose to clean your spurs, you're under *my* orders.

CAPT. G. *dresses.* M. *follows suit.*

CAPT. M. (*Critically, walking round.*) M'yes, you'll do. Only don't look so like a criminal. Ring, gloves, fees—that's all right for me. Let your moustache alone. Now, if the ponies are ready, we'll go.

CAPT. G. (*Nervously.*) It's much too soon. Let's light up! Let's have a peg! Let's—

CAPT. M. Let's make bally asses of ourselves!

BELLS. (*Without.*)—

"Good—peo—ple—all
To prayers—we call."

CAPT. M. There go the bells! Come on—unless you'd rather not. (*They ride off.*)

BELLS.—

"We honor the King
And Brides joy do bring—
Good tidings we tell,
And ring the Dead's knell."

CAPT. G. (*Dismounting at the door of the Church.*) I say, aren't we much too soon? There are no end of people inside. I say, aren't we much too late? Stick by me, Jack! What the devil do I do?

CAPT. M. Strike an attitude at the head of the aisle and wait for Her. (G. *groans as* M. *wheels him into position before three hundred eyes.*)

CAPT. M. (*Imploringly.*) Gaddy, if you love me, for pity's sake, for the Honor of the Regiment, stand up! Chuck yourself into your uniform! Look like a man! I've got to speak to the Padre a minute. (G. *breaks into*

a gentle perspiration.) If you wipe your face I'll *never* be your best man again. Stand *up!* (G. *trembles visibly.*)

CAPT. M. (*Returning.*) She's coming now. Look out when the music starts. There's the organ beginning to clack.

Bride steps out of 'rickshaw at Church door. G. *catches a glimpse of her and takes heart.*

ORGAN.—

"The Voice that breathed o'er Eden,
That earliest marriage day,
The primal marriage-blessing,
It hath not passed away."

CAPT. M. (*Watching* G.) By Jove! He *is* looking well. 'Didn't think he had it in him.

CAPT. G. How long does this hymn go on for?

CAPT. M. It will be over directly. (*Anxiously.*) Beginning to bleach and gulp? Hold on, Gaddy, and think o' the Regiment.

CAPT. G. (*Measuredly.*) I say, there's a big brown lizard crawling up that wall.

CAPT. M. My Sainted Mother! The last stage of collapse!

Bride comes up to left of altar, lifts her eyes once to G., *who is suddenly smitten mad.*

CAPT. G. (*To himself again and again.*) Little Featherweight's a woman —a woman! And I thought she was a little girl.

CAPT. M. (*In a whisper.*) Form the halt—inward *wheel.*

CAPT. G. *obeys mechanically and the ceremony proceeds.*

PADRE. . . . only unto her as ye both shall live?

CAPT. G. (*His throat useless.*) Ha—hmmm!

CAPT. M. Say you will or you won't There's no second deal here.

Bride gives response with perfect coolness, and is given away by the father.

CAPT. G. (*Thinking to show his learning.*) Jack give me away now, *quick!*

CAPT. M. You're given yourself away quite enough. Her *right* hand, man! Repeat! Repeat! "Theodore Philip." Have you forgotten your own name?

CAPT. G. *stumbles through Affirmation, which Bride repeats without a tremor.*

CAPT. M. Now the ring! Follow the Padre! Don't pull off my glove! Here it is! Great Cupid, he's found his voice.

G. *repeats Troth in a voice to be heard to the end of the Church and turns on his heel.*

CAPT. M. (*Desperately.*) Rein back! Back to your troop! 'Tisn't half legal yet.

PADRE. . . . joined together let no man put asunder.

CAPT. G. *paralyzed with fear jibs after Blessing.*

CAPT. M. (*Quickly.*) On your own front—one length. Take her with you. I don't come. You've nothing to say. (CAPT. G. *jingles up to altar.*)

CAPT. M. (*In a piercing rattle meant to be a whisper.*) Kneel, you stiff-necked ruffian! Kneel!

PADRE. . . . whose daughters are ye so long as ye do well and are not afraid with any amazement.

CAPT. M. Dismiss! Break off! Left wheel!

All troop to vestry. They sign.

CAPT. M. Kiss Her, Gaddy.

CAPT. G. (*Rubbing the ink into his glove.*) Eh! Wha-at?

CAPT. M. (*Taking one pace to Bride.*) If you don't, I shall.

CAPT. G. (*Interposing an arm.*) Not this journey!

General kissing, in which CAPT. G. *is pursued by unknown female.*

CAPT. G. (*Faintly to M.*) This is Hades! Can I wipe my face now?

CAPT. M. My responsibility has ended. Better ask *Misses* GADSBY.

CAPT. G. *winces as though shot and procession is Mendelssohned out of Church to house, where usual tortures take place over the wedding-cake.*

CAPT. M. (*At table.*) Up with you, Gaddy. They expect a speech.

CAPT. G. (*After three minutes' agony.*) Ha—hmmm. (*Thunders of applause.*)

CAPT. M. Doocid good, for a first attempt. Now go and change your kit while Mamma is weeping over—"the Missus." (CAPT. G. *disappears.* CAPT. M. *starts up tearing his hair.*) It's not half legal. Where are the shoes? Get an *ayah.*

AYAH. Missie Captain Sahib done gone *band karo* all the *jutis.*

CAPT. M. (*Brandishing scabbarded sword.*) Woman, produce those shoes! Some one lend me a bread-knife. We mustn't crack Gaddy's head more than it is. (*Slices heel off white satin slipper and puts slipper up his sleeve.*)

Where is the Bride? (*To the company at large.*) Be tender with that rice. It's a heathen custom. Give me the big bag.

*   *   *   *   *   *

> *Bride slips out quietly into 'rickshaw and departs toward the sunset.*

CAPT. M. (*In the open.*) Stole away, by Jove! So much the worse·for Gaddy! Here he is. Now Gaddy, this'll be livelier than Amdheran! Where's your horse?

CAPT. G. (*Furiously, seeing that the women are out of earshot.*) Where the—is my *Wife?*

CAPT. M. Half-way to Mahasu by this time. You'll have to ride like Young Lochinvar.

> *Horse comes round on his hind legs; refuses to let G. handle him.*

CAPT. G. Oh you will, will you? Get 'round, you brute—you hog—you beast! Get *round!*

> *Wrenches horse's head over, nearly breaking lower jaw; swings him self into saddle, and sends home both spurs in the midst of a spattering gale of Best Patna.*

CAPT. M. For your life and your love—ride, Gaddy!—And God bless you!

> *Throws half a pound of rice at G. who disappears, bowed forward on the saddle, in a cloud of sunlit dust.*

CAPT. M. I've lost old Gaddy. (*Lights cigarette and strolls off, singing absently*):—

"You may carve it on his tombstone, you may cut it on his card,
That a young man married is a young man marred!"

MISS DEERCOURT. (*From her horse.*) Really, Captain Mafflin! You are more plain spoken than polite!

CAPT. M. (*Aside.*) They say marriage is like cholera. 'Wonder who'll be the next victim.

> *White satin slipper slides from his sleeve and falls at his feet. Left wondering.*

The Garden of Eden

And ye shall be as—Gods!

SCENE.—*Thymy grass-plot at back of the Mahasu dâk-bungalow, overlooking little wooded valley. On the left, glimpse of the Dead Forest of Fagoo; on the right, Simla Hills. In background, line of the Snows. CAPTAIN GADSBY, now three weeks a husband, is smoking the pipe of peace on a rug in the sunshine. Banjo and tobacco-pouch on rug. Overhead the Fagoo eagles. MRS. G. comes out of bungalow.*

MRS. G. My husband!

CAPT. G. (*Lazily, with intense enjoyment.*) Eh, wha-at? Say that again

Mrs. G. I've written to Mamma and told her that we shall be back on the 17th.

Capt. G. Did you give her my love?

Mrs. G. No, I kept all that for myself. (*Sitting down by his side.*) I thought you wouldn't mind.

Capt. G. (*With mock sternness.*) I object awf'ly. How did you know that it was yours to keep?

Mrs. G. I guessed, Phil.

Capt. G. (*Rapturously.*) *Lit-tle* Featherweight!

Mrs. G. I *won't* be called those sporting pet names, bad boy.

Capt. G. You'll be called anything I choose. Has it ever occurred to you, Madam, that you are my Wife?

Mrs. G. It has. I haven't ceased wondering at it yet.

Capt. G. Nor I. It seems so strange; and yet, somehow, it doesn't. (*Confidently.*) You see, it could have been no one else.

Mrs. G. (*Softly.*) No. No one else —for me or for you. It must have been *all* arranged from the beginning. Phil, tell me again what made you care for me.

Capt. G. How could I help it? You were *you,* you know.

Mrs. G. Did you ever want to help it? Speak the truth!

Capt. G. (*A twinkle in his eye.*) I did, darling, just at the first. But only at the very first. (*Chuckles.*) I called you—stoop low and I'll whisper—"a little beast." Ho! Ho! Ho!

Mrs. G. (*Taking him by the moustache and making him sit up.*) "A—little—beast!" Stop laughing over your crime! And yet you had the—the —awful cheek to propose to me!

Capt. G. I'd changed my mind then. And you weren't a little beast any more.

Mrs. G. Thank you, sir! And when was I ever?

Capt. G. *Never!* But that first day, when you gave me tea in that peach-colored muslin gown thing, you looked—you did indeed, dear—such an absurd little mite. And I didn't know what to say to you.

Mrs. G. (*Twisting moutache.*) So you said "little beast." Upon my word, Sir! *I* called *you* a "Crrrreature," but I wish now I had called you something worse.

Capt. G. (*Very meekly.*) I apologize, but you're hurting me awf'ly. (*Interlude.*) You're welcome to torture me again on those terms.

Mrs. G. Oh, *why* did you let me do it?

Capt. G. (*Looking across valley.*) No reason in particular, but—if it amused you or did you any good—you might—wipe those dear little boots of yours on me.

Mrs. G. (*Stretching out her hands.*) Don't! Oh, don't! Philip, my King, *please* don't talk like that. It's how *I* feel. You're so much too good for me. So much too good!

Capt. G. Me! I'm not fit to put my arm round you. (*Puts it round.*)

Mrs. G. Yes, you are. But I— what have I ever done?

Capt. G. Given me a wee bit of your heart, haven't you, my Queen!

Mrs. G. *That's* nothing. Any one would do *that.* They cou—couldn't help it.

Capt. G. Pussy, you'll make me horribly conceited. Just when I was beginning to feel so humble, too.

MRS. G. Humble! I don't believe it's in your character.

CAPT. G. What do you know of my character, Impertinence?

MRS. G. Ah, but I shall, sha'n't I, Phil? I shall have time in all the years and years to come, to know everything about you; and there will be no secrets between us.

CAPT. G. Little witch! I believe you know me thorouhgly already.

MRS. G. I think I can guess. You're selfish?

CAPT. G. Yes.

MRS. G. Foolish?

CAPT. G. *Very.*

MRS. G. And a dear?

CAPT. G. That is as my lady pleases.

MRS. G. Then your lady *is* pleased. (*A pause.*) D'you know that we're two solemn, serious, grown-up people—

CAPT. G. (*Tilting her straw hat over her eyes.*) You grown-up! Pooh! You're a baby.

MRS. G. And we're talking nonsense.

CAPT. G. Then let's go on talking nonsense. I rather like it. Pussy, I'll tell you a secret. Promise not to repeat?

MRS. G. Ye—es. Only to you.

CAPT. G. I love you.

MRS. G. Re-ally! For how long?

CAPT. G. Forever and ever.

MRS. G. That's a long time.

CAPT. G. 'Think so? It's the shortest *I* can do with.

MRS. G. You're getting quite clever.

CAPT. G. I'm talking to *you.*

MRS. G. Prettily turned. Hold up your stupid old head and I'll pay you for it.

CAPT. G. (*Affecting supreme con- tempt.*) Take it yourself if you wanf it.

MRS. G. I've a great mind to—and I will! (*Takes it and is repaid with interest.*)

CAPT. G. Little Featherweight, it's my opinion that we *are* a couple of idiots.

MRS. G. We're the only two sensible people in the world. Ask the eagle. He's coming by.

CAPT. G. Ah! I dare say he's seen a good many sensible people at Mahasu. They say that those birds live for ever so long.

MRS. G. How long?

CAPT. G. A hundred and twenty years.

MRS. G. A hundred and twenty years! O-oh! And in a hundred and twenty years where will these two sensible people be?

CAPT. G. What does it matter so long as we are together now?

MRS. G. (*Looking round the horizon.*) Yes. Only you and I—I and you—in the whole wide, wide world until the end. (*Sees the line of the Snows.*) How big and quiet the hills look! D'you think they care for us?

CAPT. G. 'Can't say I've consulted 'em particularly. *I* care, and that's enough for me.

MRS. G. (*Drawing nearer to him.*) Yes, now—but afterward. What's that little black blur on the Snows?

CAPT. G. A snowstorm, forty miles away. You'll see it move, as the wind caries it across the face of that spur and then it will be all gone.

MRS. G. And then it will be all gone. (*Shivers.*)

CAPT. G. (*Anxiously.*) 'Not chilled,

pet, are you? 'Better let me get your cloak.

MRS. G. No. Don't leave me, Phil. Stay here. I believe I am afraid. Oh, why are the hills so *horrid!* Phil, promise me that you'll *always* love me.

CAPT. G. What's the trouble, darling? I can't promise any more than I have; but I'll promise that again and again if you like.

MRS. G. (*Her head on his shoulder.*) *Say* it, then—say it! N-no—don't! The—the—eagles would laugh. (*Recovering.*) My husband, you've married a little goose.

CAPT. G. (*Very tenderly.*) Have I? I am content whatever she is, so long as she is mine.

MRS. G. (*Quickly.*) Because she is yours or because she is me mineself?

CAPT. G. Because she is both. (*Piteously.*) I'm not clever, dear, and I don't think I can make myself understood properly.

MRS. G. *I* understand. Pip, will you tell me something?

CAPT. G. Anything you like. (*Aside.*) I wonder what's coming now.

MRS. G. (*Haltingly, her eyes lowered.*) You told me once in the old days—centuries and centuries ago— that you had been engaged before. I didn't say anything—*then.*

CAPT. G. (*Innocently.*) Why not?

MRS. G. (*Raising her eyes to his.*) Because—because I was afraid of losing you, my heart. But now—tell about it—*please.*

CAPT. G. There's nothing to tell. I was awf'ly old then—nearly two and twenty—and she was *quite* that.

MRS. G. That means she was older than you. I shouldn't like her to have been younger. Well?

CAPT. G. Well, I fancied myself in love and raved about a bit, and—oh, yes, by Jove! I made up poetry. Ha! Ha!

MRS. G. You never wrote any for *me!* What happened?

CAPT. G. I came out here, and the whole thing went *phut.* She wrote to say that there had been·a mistake, and then she married.

MRS. G. Did she care for you much?

CAPT. G. No. At least she didn't show it as far as I remember.

MRS. G. As far as you remember! Do you remember her name? (*Hears it and bows her head.*) Thank you, my husband.

CAPT. G. Who but you·had the right? Now, Little Featherweight, have you ever been mixed up in any dark and dismal tragedy?

MRS. G. If you call me Mrs. Gadsby, p'raps I'll tell.

CAPT. G. (*Throwing Parade rasp into his voice.*) Mrs. Gadsby, confess!

MRS. G. Good Heavens, Phil! I never knew that you could speak in that terrible voice.

CAPT. G. You don't know half my accomplishments yet. Wait till we are settled in the Plains, and I'll show you how I bark at my troop. You were going to say, darling?

MRS. G. I—I don't like to, after that voice. (*Tremulously.*) Phil, never you *dare* to speak to me in that tone, whatever I may do!

CAPT. G. My poor little love! Why, you're shaking all over. I *am* so sorry. Of course I never meant to upset you. Don't tell me anything. I'm a brute.

MRS. G. No, you aren't, and I *will* tell— There was a man.

CAPT. G. (*Lightly.*) Was there? Lucky man!

MRS. G. (*In a whisper.*) And I thought I cared for him.

CAPT. G. Still luckier man! Well?

MRS. G. And I thought I cared for him—and I didn't—and then you came —and I cared for you very, *very* much indeed. That's all. (*Face hidden.*) You aren't angry, are you?

CAPT. G. Angry? Not in the least. (*Aside.*) Good Lord, what have I done to deserve this angel?

MRS. G. (*Aside.*) And he never asked for the name! How funny men are! But perhaps it's as well.

CAPT. G. That man will go to heaven because you once thought you cared for him. 'Wonder if you'll ever drag me up there?

MRS. G. (*Firmly.*) 'Sha'n't go if you don't.

CAPT. G. Thanks. I say, Pussy, I don't know much about your religious beliefs. You were brought up to believe in a heaven and all that, weren't you?

MRS. G. Yes. But it was a pin-cushion heaven, with hymn-books in all the pews.

CAPT. G. (*Wagging his head with intense conviction.*) Never mind. There is a *pukka* heaven.

MRS. G. Where do you bring that message from, my prophet?

CAPT. G. Here! Because we care for each other. So it's all right.

MRS. G. (*As a troop of langurs crash through the branches.*) So it's all right. But Darwin says that we came from *those!*

CAPT. G. (*Placidly.*) Ah! Darwin was never in love with an angel. That settles it. Sstt, you brutes! Monkeys, indeed! You shouldn't read those books.

MRS. G. (*Folding her hands.*) If it pleases my Lord the King to issue proclamation.

CAPT. G. Don't, dear one. There are no orders between us. Only I'd *rather* you didn't. They lead to nothing, and bother people's heads.

MRS. G. Like your first engagement.

CAPT. G. (*With an immense calm.*) That was a necessary evil and led to you. Are *you* nothing?

MRS. G. Not so very much, am I?

CAPT. G. All this world and the next to me.

MRS. G. (*Very softly.*) My boy of boys! Shall I tell *you* something?

CAPT. G. Yes, if it's not dreadful— about other men.

MRS. G. It's about my own bad little self.

CAPT. G. Then it must be good. Go on, dear.

MRS. G. (*Slowly.*) I don't know why I'm telling you, Pip; but if ever you marry again—(*Interlude.*) Take your hand from my mouth or I'll *bite!* In the future, then remember—I don't know quite how to put it!

CAPT. G. (*Snorting indignantly.*) Don't try. "Marry again," indeed!

MRS. G. I must. Listen, my husband. Never, never, *never* tell your wife anything that you do not wish her to remember and think over all her life. Because a woman—yes, I *am* a woman —*can't* forget.

CAPT. G. By Jove, how do *you* know that?

Mrs. G. (*Confusedly.*) I don't. I'm only guessing. I am—I was—a silly little girl; but I feel that I know so much, oh, so very much more than you, dearest. To begin with, I'm your wife.

Capt. G. So I have been led to believe.

Mrs. G. And I shall want to know every one of your secrets—to share everything you know with you. (*Stares round desperately.*)

Capt. G. So you shall, dear, so you shall—but don't look like that.

Mrs. G. For your own sake don't stop me, Phil. I shall never talk to you in this way again. You must *not* tell me! At least, not now. Later on, when I'm an old matron it won't matter, but if you love me, be very good to me now; for this part of my life I shall *never* forget! Have I made you understand?

Capt. G. I think so, child. Have I said anything yet that you disapprove of?

Mrs. G. Will you be *very* angry? That—that voice, and what you said about the engagement—

Capt. G. But you *asked* to be told that, darling.

Mrs. G. And *that's* why you shouldn't have told me! You must be the Judge, and, oh, Pip, dearly as I love you, I sha'n't be able to help you! I shall hinder you, and you must judge in spite of me!

Capt. G. (*Meditatively.*) We have a great many things to find out together, God help us both—say so, Pussy—but we shall understand each other better every day; and I think I'm beginning to see now. How in the world did you come to know just the importance of giving me just that lead?

Mrs. G. I've told you that I *don't* know. Only somehow it seemed that, in all this new life, I was being guided for your sake as well as my own.

Capt. G. (*Aside.*) Then Mafflin was right! They know, and we—we're blind —all of us. (*Lightly.*) 'Getting a little beyond our depth, dear, aren't we? I'll remember, and, if I fail, let me be punished as I deserve.

Mrs. G. There shall be no punishment. We'll start into life together from here—you and I—and no one else.

Capt. G. And no one else. (*A pause.*) Your eyelashes are all wet, Sweet? Was there ever such a quaint little Absurdity?

Mrs. G. Was there ever such nonsense talked before?

Capt. G. (*Knocking the ashes out of his pipe.*) 'Tisn't what we say, it's what we don't say, that helps. And it's all the profoundest philosophy. But no one would understand—even if it were put into a book.

Mrs. G. The idea! No—only we ourselves, or people like ourselves—if there are any people like us.

Capt. G. (*Magisterially.*) All people, not like ourselves, are blind idiots.

Mrs. G. (*Wiping her eyes.*) Do you think, then, that there are any people as happy as we are?

Capt. G. 'Must be—unless we've appropriated all the happiness in the world.

Mrs. G. (*Looking toward Simla*). Poor dears! Just fancy if we have!

Capt. G. Then we'll hang on to the

whole show, for it's a great deal too jolly to lose—eh, wife o' mine?

MRS. G. O Pip! Pip! How much of you is a solemn, married man and how much a horrid slangy schoolboy?

CAPT. G. When you tell me how much of you was eighteen last birthday and how much is as old as the Sphinx and twice as mysterious, perhaps I'll attend to you. Lend me that banjo. The spirit moveth me to jowl at the sunset.

MRS. G. Mind! It's not tuned. Ah! How that jars!

CAPT. G. (*Turning pegs.*) It's amazingly different to keep a banjo to proper pitch.

MRS. G. It's the same with all musical instruments. What shall it be?

CAPT. G. "Vanity," and let the hills hear. (*Sings through the first and half of the second verse. Turning to MRS. G.*) Now, chorus! Sing, Pussy!

BOTH TOGETHER. (*Con brio, to the horror of the monkeys who are settling for the night.*)—

"Vanity, all is Vanity," said Wisdom,
    scorning me—
I clasped my true Love's tender hand
    and answered frank and free—
    ee :—
"If this be Vanity who'd be wise?
If this be Vanity who'd be wise?
If this be Vanity who'd be wi—ise
(*Crescendo.*) Vanity let it be!"

MRS. G. (*Defiantly to the grey of the evening sky.*) "Vanity let it be!"

ECHO. (*From the Fagoo spur.*) Let it be!

Fatima

And you may go in every room of the house and see everything that is there, but into the Blue Room you must *not* go.—*The Story of Blue Beard.*

SCENE.—*The* GADSBY'S *bungalow in the Plains. Time,* 11 A. M. *on a Sunday morning.* CAPTAIN GADSBY, *in his shirt-sleeves, is bending over a complete set of Hussar's equipment, from saddle to picketing-rope, which is neatly spread over the floor of his study. He is smoking an unclean briar, and his forehead is puckered with thought.*

CAPT. G. (*To himself, fingering a headstall.*) Jack's an ass. There's enough brass on this to load a mule—

and, if the Americans know anything about anything, it can be cut down to a bit only. 'Don't want the watering-bridle, either. Humbug!—Half a dozen sets of chains and pulleys for one horse! Rot! (*Scratching his head.*) Now, let's consider it all over from the beginning. By Jove, I've forgotten the scale of weights! Ne'er mind. 'Keep the bit only, and eliminate every boss from the crupper to breastplate. No breastplate at all. Simple leather strap across the breast—like the Russians. Hi! Jack never thought of *that!*

MRS. G. (*Entering hastily, her hand bound in a cloth.*) Oh, Pip, I've scalded my hand over that horrid, horrid Ti-paree jam!

CAPT. G. (*Absently.*) Eh! Wha-at?

MRS. G. (*With round-eyed reproach.*) I've scalded it *aw*-fully! Aren't you sorry? And I *did* so want that jam to jam properly.

CAPT. G. Poor little woman! Let me kiss the place and make it well. (*Unrolling bandage.*) You small sinner! Where's that scald? I can't see it.

MRS. G. On the top of the little finger. There!—It's a most 'normous big burn!

CAPT. G. (*Kissing little finger.*) Baby! Let Hyder look after the jam. You know I don't care for sweets.

MRS. G. In-deed?—Pip!

CAPT. G. Not of that kind, anyhow. And now run along, Minnie, and leave me to my own base devices. I'm busy.

MRS. G. (*Calmly settling herself in long chair.*) So I see. What a mess you're making! Why have you brought all that smelly leather stuff into the house?

CAPT. G. To play with. Do you mind, dear?

MRS. G. Let *me* play too. I'd like it.

CAPT. G. I'm afraid you wouldn't, Pussy— Don't you think that jam will burn, or whatever it is that jam does when it's not looked after by a clever little housekeeper?

MRS. G. I thought you said Hyder could attend to it. I left him in the veranda, stirring—when I hurt myself so.

CAPT. G. (*His eye returning to the equipment.*) Po-oor little woman!— Three pounds for and seven is three

eleven, and that can be cut down to two eight, with just a *lee*-tle care, without weakening anything. Farriery is all rot in incompetent hands. What's the use of a shoe-case when a man's scouting? He can't stick it on with a lick—like a stamp—the shoe! Skittles!

MRS. G. What's skittles? Pah! What *is* this leather cleaned with?

CAPT. G. Cream and champagne and— Look here, dear, do you really want to talk to me about anything important?

MRS. G. No. I've done my accounts, and I thought I'd like to see what you're doing.

CAPT. G. Well, love, now you've seen and— Would you mind?— That is to say—Minnie, I really *am* busy.

MRS. G. You want me to go?

CAPT. G. Yes, dear, for a little while. This tobacco will hang in your dress, and saddlery doesn't interest you.

MRS. G. Everything you do interests me, Pip.

CAPT. G. Yes, I know, I know, dear. I'll tell you all about it some day when I've put a head on this thing. In the meantime—

MRS. G. I'm to be turned out of the room like a troublesome child?

CAPT. G. No-o. I don't mean that exactly. But, you see, I shall be tramping up and down, shifting these things to and fro, and I shall be in your way. Don't you think so?

MRS. G. Can't I lift them about? Let me try. (*Reaches forward to trooper's saddle.*)

CAPT. G. Good gracious, child, don't touch it. You'll hurt yourself. (*Picking up saddle.*) Little girls aren't expected to handle *numdahs*. Now, where would you like it put? (*Holds saddle above his head.*)

MRS. G. (*A break in her voice.*) Nowhere. Pip, how good you are—and how strong! Oh, what's that ugly red streak inside your arm?

CAPT. G. (*Lowering saddle quickly.*) Nothing. It's a mark of sorts. (*Aside.*) And Jack's coming to tiffin with *his* notions all cut and dried!

MRS. G. I know it's a mark, but I've never seen it before. It runs all up the arm. What is it?

CAPT. G. A cut—if you want to know.

MRS. G. Want to know! Of course I do! I can't have my husband cut to pieces in this way. How did it come? Was it an accident? Tell me, Pip.

CAPT. G. (*Grimly.*) No. 'Twasn't an accident. I got it—from a man—in Afghanistan.

MRS. G. In action? Oh, Pip, and you *never* told me!

CAPT. G. I'd forgotten all about it.

MRS. G. Hold up your arm! What a horrid, ugly scar! Are you sure it doesn't hurt now! How did the man give it you!

CAPT. G. (*Desperately looking at his watch.*) With a knife. I came down—old Van Loo did, that's to say—and fell on my leg, so I couldn't run. And then this man came up and began chopping at me as I sprawled.

MRS. G. Oh, don't, don't! That's enough!— Well, what happened?

CAPT. G. I couldn't get to my holster, and Mafflin came round the corner and stopped the performance.

MRS. G. How? He's such a lazy man, I don't believe he did.

CAPT. G. Don't you? I don't think

the man had much doubt about it. Jack cut his head off.

MRS. G. Cut—his—head—off! "With one blow," as they say in the books?

CAPT. G. I'm not sure. I was too interested in myself to know much about it. Anyhow, the head was off, and Jack was punching old Van Loo in the ribs to make him get up. Now you know all about it, dear, and now—

MRS. G. You want me to go, of course. You never told me about this, though I've been married to you for *ever* so long; and you never *would* have told me if I hadn't found out; and you never *do* tell me anything about yourself, or what you do, or what you take an interest in.

CAPT. G. Darling, I'm always with you, aren't I?

MRS. G. Always in my pocket, you were going to say. I know you are; but you are always *thinking* away from me.

CAPT. G. (*Trying to hide a smile.*) Am I? I wasn't aware of it. I'm awf'ly sorry.

MRS. G. (*Piteously.*) Oh, don't make fun of me! Pip, you know what I mean. When you are reading one of those things about Cavalry, by that idiotic Prince—why doesn't he *be* a Prince instead of a stable-boy?

CAPT. G. Prince Kraft a stable-boy— Oh, my Aunt! Never mind, dear. You were going to say?

MRS. G. It doesn't matter; you don't care for what I say. Only—only you get up and walk about the room, staring in front of you, and then Mafflin comes in to dinner, and after I'm in the drawing-room I can hear you and him talking, and talking, and talking, about

Departmental Ditties and Other Verses

I have eaten your bread and salt,
  I have drunk your water and wine,
The deaths ye died I have watched be-
    side,
  And the lives that ye led were mine.

Was there aught that I did not share
  In vigil or toil or ease,—
One joy or woe that I did not know,
  Dear hearts across the seas?

    I have written the tale of our life
      For a sheltered people's mirth,
    In jesting guise—but ye are wise,
      And ye know what the jest is worth.

———————•———————

General Summary

WE are very slightly changed
From the semi-apes who ranged
  India's prehistoric clay;
Whoso drew the longest bow,
Ran his brother down, you know,
  As we run men down to-day.

"Dowb," the first of all his race,
Met the Mammoth face to face
  On the lake or in the cave,
Stole the steadiest canoe,
Ate the quarry others slew,
  Died—and took the finest grave.

When they scratched the reindeer-bone.
Some one made the sketch his own,
  Filched it from the artist—then,
Even in those early days,
Won a simple Viceroy's praise
  Through the toil of other men.

Ere they hewed the Sphinx's visage
Favoritism governed kissage,
Even as it does in this age.
Who shall doubt the secret hid
Under Cheops' pyramid
Was that the contractor did
  Cheops out of several millions?
Or that Joseph's sudden rise
To Comptroller of Supplies
Was a fraud of monstrous size
  On King Pharoah's swart Civilians?

Thus, the artless songs I sing
Do not deal with anything
  New or never said before.
As it was in the beginning,
Is to-day official sinning,
  And shall be forevermore.

953

Army Headquarters

Old is the song that I sing—
Old as my unpaid bills—
Old as the chicken that *kitmutgars*
  bring
Men at dâk-bungalows—old as the
  Hills.

AHASUERUS JENKINS of the "Operatic
Was dowered with a tenor voice of
  super-Santley tone.
His views on equitation were, perhaps,
  a trifle queer;
He had no seat worth mentioning, but
  oh! he had an ear.

He clubbed his wretched company a
  dozen times a day,
He used to quit his charger in a para-
  bolic way,
His method of saluting was the joy of
  all beholders,
But Ahasuerus Jenkins had a head upon
  his shoulders.

He took two months to Simla when the
  year was at the spring,
And underneath the deodars eternally
  did sing.
He warbled like a *bulbul*, but particularly at
Cornelia Agrippina who was musical and
  fat.

She controlled a humble husband, who,
  in turn, controlled a Dept.,
Where Cornelia Agrippina's human sing-
  ing-birds were kept

From April to October on a plump re-
  taining fee,
Supplied, of course, *per mensem*, by the
  Indian Treasury.

Cornelia used to sing with him, and
  Jenkins used to play;
He praised unblushingly her notes, for
  he was false as they:
So when the winds of April turned the
  budding roses brown,
Cornelia told her husband: "Tom, you
  mustn't send him down."

They haled him from his regiment
  which didn't much regret him;
They found for him an office-stool, and
  on that stool they set him,
To play with maps and catalogues three
  idle hours a day,
And draw his plump retaining fee—
  which means his double pay.

Now, ever after dinner, when the coffee-
  cups are brought,
Ahasuerus waileth o'er the grand pianoforte;
And, thanks to fair Cornelia, his fame
  hath waxen great,
And Ahasuerus Jenkins is a power in
  the State.

Study of an Elevation, in Indian Ink

This ditty is a string of lies.
But—how the deuce did Gubbins rise?

POTIPHAR GUBBINS, C. E.,
Stands at the top of the tree;
And I muse in my bed on the reasons
that led
To the hoisting of Potiphar G.

Potiphar Gubbins, C. E.,
Is seven years junior to Me;
Each bridge that he makes he either
buckles or breaks,
And his work is as rough as he.

Potiphar Gubbins, C. E.,
Is coarse as a chimpanzee;
And I can't understand why you gave
him your hand,
Lovely Mehitabel Lee.

Potiphar Gubbins, C. E.,
Is dear to the Powers that Be;
For They bow and They smile in an
affable style
Which is seldom accorded to Me.

Potiphar Gubbins, C. E.,
Is certain as certain can be
Of a highly-paid post which is claimed
by a host
Of seniors—including Me.

Careless and lazy is he,
Greatly inferior to Me.
What is the spell that you manage so
well,
Commonplace Potiphar G.?

Lovely Mehitabel Lee,
Let me inquire of thee,
Should I have riz to what Potiphar is,
Hadst thou been mated to me?

A Legend of the Foreign Office

This is the reason why Rustum Beg,
Rajah of Kolazai,
Drinketh the "simpkin" and brandy peg,
Maketh the money to fly,
Vexeth a Government, tender and kind,
Also—but this is a detail—blind.

RUSTUM BEG of Kolazai—slightly back-
ward native state—
Lusted for a C. S. I.,—so began to
sanitate.
Built a Jail and Hospital—nearly built a
City drain—
Till his faithful subjects all thought
their ruler was insane.

Strange departures made he then—yea,
Departments stranger still,
Half a dozen Englishmen helped the
Rajah with a will,
Talked of noble aims and high, hinted
of a future fine
For the state of Kolazai, on a strictly
Western line.

Rajah Rustum held his peace; lowered
octroi dues a half;
Organized a State Police; purified the
Civil Staff;

Settled cess and tax afresh in a very
  liberal way;
Cut temptations of the flesh—also cut
  the Bukhshi's pay;

Roused his Secretariat to a fine Mahratta fury,
By a Hookum hinting at supervision of
  dasturi;
Turned the State of Kolazai very nearly
  upside-down;
When the end of May was nigh, waited
  his achievement crown.

Then the Birthday Honors came. Sad
  to state and sad to see,
Stood against the Rajah's name nothing
  more than *C. I. E.!*

*   *   *   *   *   *

Things were lively for a week in the
  State of Kolazai.
Even now the people speak of that time
  regretfully.

How he disendowed the Jail—stopped at
  once the City drain;
Turned to beauty fair and frail—got his
  senses back again;
Doubled taxes, cesses, all; cleared away
  each new-built *thana;*
Turned the two-lakh Hospital into a
  superb *Zenana;*

Heaped upon the Bukhshi Sahib wealth
  and honors manifold;
Clad himself in Eastern garb—squeezed
  his people as of old.
Happy, happy Kolazai! Never more
  will Rustum Beg
Play to catch the Viceroy's eye. He
  prefers the "simpkin" peg.

———•———

The Story of Uriah

"Now there were two men in one city;
the one rich and the other poor."

JACK BARRETT went to Quetta
  Because they told him to.
He left his wife at Simla
  On three-fourths his monthly screw:
Jack Barrett died at Quetta
  Ere the next month's pay he drew.

Jack Barrett went to Quetta.
  He didn't understand
The reason of his transfer
  From the pleasant mountain-land:
The season was September,
  And it killed him out of hand.

Jack Barrett went to Quetta,
  And there gave up the ghost,
Attempting two men's duty
  In that very healthy post;
And Mrs. Barrett mourned for him
  Five lively months at most.

Jack Barrett's bones at Quetta
  Enjoy profound repose;
But I shouldn't be astonished
  If *now* his spirit knows
The reason of his transfer
  From the Himalayan snows.

And, when the Last Great Bugle Call
  Adown the Hurnai throbs,
When the last grim joke is entered
  In the big black Book of Jobs,

And Quetta graveyards give again
  Their victims to the air,
I shouldn't like to be the man
  Who sent Jack Barrett there.

The Post That Fitted

Though tangled and twisted the course
  of true love,
This ditty explains
No tangle's so tangled it cannot improve
If the Lover has brains.

ERE the steamer bore him Eastward,
  Sleary was engaged to marry
An attractive girl at Tunbridge, whom
  he called "my little Carrie."
Sleary's pay was very modest; Sleary
  was the other way.
Who can cook a two-plate dinner on
  eight paltry dibs a day?

Long he pondered o'er the question in
  his scantly furnished quarters—
Then proposed to Minnie Boffkin, eldest
  of Judge Boffkin's daughters.
Certainly an impecunious Subaltern was
  not a catch,
But the Boffkins knew that Minnie
  mightn't make another match.

So they recognized the business, and,
  to feed and clothe the bride,
Got him made a Something Something
  somewhere on the Bombay side.
Anyhow, the billet carried pay enough
  for him to marry—
As the artless Sleary put it: "Just the
  thing for me and Carrie."

Did he, therefore, jilt Miss Boffkin—
  impulse of a baser mind?
No! He started epileptic fits of an
  appalling kind.
(Of his *modum operandi* only this much
  I could gather:
"Pears' shaving sticks give you little
  taste and lots of lather.")

Frequently in public places his affliction
  used to smite
Sleary with distressing vigor—always in
  the Boffkins' sight.
Ere a week was over Minnie weepingly
  returned his ring,
Told him his "unhappy weakness"
  stopped all thought of marrying.

Sleary bore the information with a
  chastened holy joy,—
Epileptic fits don't matter in Political
  employ,—
Wired three short words to Carrie—
  took his ticket, packed his kit—
Bade farewell to Minnie Boffkin in one
  last, long, lingering fit.

Four weeks later, Carrie Sleary read—
  and laughed until she wept—
Mrs. Boffkin's warning letter on the
  "wretched epilept."
Year by year, in pious patience, vengeful
  Mrs. Boffkin sits
Waiting for the Sleary babies to develop
  Sleary's fits.

Public Waste

Walpole talks of "a man and his price."
List to a ditty queer—
The sale of a Deputy-Acting-Vice-Resi-
dent-Engineer,
Bought like a bullock, hoof and hide,
By the Little Tin Gods on the Mountain
Side.

By the Laws of the Family Circle 'tis
written in letters of brass
That only a Colonel from Chatham can
manage the Railways of State,
Because of the gold on his breeks, and
the subjects wherein he must pass:
Because in all matters that deal not with
Railways his knowledge is great.

Now Exeter Battleby Tring had labored
from boyhood to eld
On the Lines of the East and the West,
and eke of the North and South;
Many Lines had he built and surveyed—
important the posts which he held;
And the Lords of the Iron Horse were
dumb when he opened his mouth.

Black as the raven his garb, and his
heresies jettier still—
Hinting that Railways required lifetimes
of study and knowledge;
Never clanked sword by his side—Vau-
ban he knew not, nor drill—
Nor was his name on the list of the
men who had passed through the
"College."

Wherefore the Little Tin Gods harried
their little tin souls.
Seeing he came not from Chatham,
jingled no spurs at his heels,
Knowing that, nevertheless, was he first
on the Government rolls
For the billet of "Railway Instructor to
Little Tin Gods on Wheels."

Letters not seldom they wrote him,
"having the honor to state,"
It would be better for all men if he
were laid on the shelf:
Much would accrue to his bank-book,
and he consented to wait
Until the Little Tin Gods, built him a
berth for himself.

"Special, well paid, and exempt from
the Law of the Fifty and Five,
Even to Ninety and Nine"—these were
the terms of the pact:
Thus did the Little Tin Gods (long may
Their Highnesses thrive!)
Silence his mouth with rupees, keeping
their Circle intact;

Appointing a Colonel from Chatham
who managed the Bhamo State Line,
(The which was one mile and one furlong—a guaranteed twenty-inch
gauge).
So Exeter Battleby Tring consented his
claims to resign,
And died, on four thousand a month, in
the ninetieth year of his age.

Delilah

We have another Viceroy now, those
  days are dead and done,
Of Delilah Aberyswith and depraved
  Ulysses Gunne.

DELILAH Aberyswith was a lady—not
  too young—
With a perfect taste in dresses, and a
  badly-bitted tongue,
With a thirst for information, and a
  greater thirst for praise,
And a little house in Simla, in the Prehistoric Days.

By reason of her marriage to a gentleman in power,
Delilah was acquainted with the gossip
  of the hour;
And many little secrets, of a half-official
  kind,
Were whispered to Delilah, and she bore
  them all in mind.

She patronized extensively a man,
  Ulysses Gunne,
Whose mode of earning money was a
  low and shameful one.
He wrote for divers papers, which, as
  everybody knows,
Is worse than serving in a shop or scar-
  ing off the crows.

He praised her "queenly beauty" first;
  and, later on, he hinted
At the "vastness of her intellect" with
  compliment unstinted.
He went with her a-riding, and his love
  for her was such
That he loaned her all his horses, and—
  she galled them very much.

One day, THEY brewed a secret of a
  fine financial sort;
It related to Appointments, to a Man
  and a Report.
'Twas almost worth the keeping (only
  seven people knew it),
And Gunne rose up to seek the truth
  and patiently ensue it.

It was a Viceroy's Secret, but—perhaps
  the wine was red—
Perhaps an Aged Councillor had lost his
  aged head—
Perhaps Delilah's eyes were bright—
  Delilah's whispers sweet—
The Aged Member told her what 'twere
  treason to repeat.

Ulysses went a-riding, and they talked
  of love and flowers;
Ulysses went a-calling, and he called for
  several hours;
Ulysses went a-waltzing, and Delilah
  helped him dance—
Ulysses let the waltzes go, and waited
  for his chance.

The summer sun was setting, and the
  summer air was still,
The couple went a-walking in the shade
  of Summer Hill.
The wasteful sunset faded out in turkis-
  green and gold,
Ulysses pleaded softly, and . . . that
  bad Delilah told!

Next morn, a startled Empire learned
  the all-important news;
Next week, the Aged Councillor was
  shaking in his shoes;

Next month, I met Delilah, and she did
not show the least
Hesitation in affirming that Ulysses was
a "beast."

We have another Viceroy now, those
days are dead and done,
Of Delilah Aberyswith and most mean
Ulysses Gunne!

*   *   *   *   *   *

What Happened

HURREE CHUNDER MOOKERJEE, pride of
Bow Bazar,
Owner of a native press, "Barrishter-at-
Lar,"
Waited on the Government with a claim
to wear
Sabres by the bucketful, rifles by the
pair.

Then the Indian Government winked a
wicked wink,
Said to Chunder Moorkerjee: "Stick to
pen and ink,
They are safer implements; but, if you
insist,
We will let you carry arms wheresoe'er
you list."

Hurree Chunder Mookerjee sought the
gunsmith and
Bought the tuber of Lancaster, ballard,
Dean and Bland,
Bought a shiny bowie-knife, bought a
town-made sword,
Jingled like a carriage-horse when he
went abroad.

But the Indian Government, always
keen to please,
Also gave permission to horrid men like
these—

Yar Mahommed Yusufzai, down to kill
or steal,
Chimbu Singh from Bikaneer, Tantia
the Bhil.

Killar Khan the Marri chief, Jowar
Singh the Sikh,
Nubbee Baksh Punjabi Jat, Abdul Huq
Rafiq—
He was a Wahabi; last, little Boh Hla-oo
Took advantage of the act—took a
Snider too.

They were unenlightened men, Ballard
knew them not,
They procured their swords and guns
chiefly on the spot,
And the lore of centuries, plus a hundred fights,
Made them slow to disregard one another's rights.

With a unanimity dear to patriotic hearts
All those hairy gentlemen out of foreign
parts
Said: "The good old days are back—
let us go to war!"
Swaggered down the Grand Trunk Road
into Bow Bazar.

Nubbee Baksh Punjabi Jat found a hide-
hound flail,
Chimbu Singh from Bikaneer oiled his
Tonk jezail,
Yar Mahommed Yusufzai spat and
grinned with glee
As he ground the butcher-knife of the
Khyberee.

Jowar Singh the Sikh procured sabre,
quoit, and mace,
Abdul Huq, Wahabi, took the dagger
from its place,
While amid the jungle-grass danced and
grinned and jabbered
Little Boh Hla-oo and cleared the dah-
blade from the scabbard.

What became of Mookerjee? Soothly,
who can say?
Yar Mahommed only grins in a nasty
way,

Jowar Singh is reticent, Chimbu Singh
is mute,
But the belts of them all simply bulge
with loot.

What became of Ballard's guns?
Afghans black and grubby
Sell them for their silver weight to the
men of Pubbi;
And the shiny bowie-knife and the town-
made sword are
Hanging in a Marri camp just across
the Border.

What became of Mookerjee? Ask
Mahommed Yar
Prodding Siva's sacred bull down the
Bow Bazar.
Speak to placid Nubbee Baksh—ques-
tion land and sea—
Ask the India Congress men—only don't
ask me!

Pink Dominoes

"They are fools who kiss and tell"
  Wisely has the poet sung.
Man may hold all sorts of posts
  If he'll only hold his tongue.

JENNY and Me were engaged, you see,
  On the eve of the Fancy Ball;
So a kiss or two was nothing to you
  Or any one else at all.

Jenny would go in a domino—
  Pretty and pink but warm;
While I attended, clad in a splendid
  Austrian uniform.

Now we had arranged, through notes
  exchanged
  Early that afternoon,
At Number Four to waltz no more,
  But to sit in the dusk and spoon.

(I wish you to see that Jenny and Me
  Had barely exchanged our troth;
So a kiss or two was strictly due
  By, from, and between us both.)

When Three was over, an eager lover,
  I fled to the gloom outside;
And a Domino came out also
  Whom I took for my future bride.

That is to say, in a casual way,
  I slipped my arm around her;
With a kiss or two (which is nothing to
    you),
  And ready to kiss I found her.

She turned her head, and the name she
    said
  Was certainly not my own;
But ere I could speak, with a smothered
    shriek
  She fled and left me alone.

Then Jenny came, and I saw with shame
  She'd doffed her domino;
And I had embraced an alien waist—
  But I did not tell her so.

Next morn I knew that there were two
  Dominoes pink, and one
Had cloaked the spouse of Sir Julian
    Vouse,
  Our big political gun.

Sir J. was old, and her hair was gold,
  And her eye was a blue cerulean;
And the name she said when she turned
    her head
  Was not in the least like "Julian."

Now wasn't it nice, when want of *pice*
  Forbade us twain to marry,
That old Sir J., in the kindest way,
  Made me his *Secretarry?*

The Man Who Could Write

Shun—shun the Bowl! That fatal, facile
    drink
  Has ruined many geese who dipped
    their quills in't,
Bribe, murder, marry, but steer clear of
    Ink
  Save when you write receipts for paid-
    up bills in't.
There may be silver in the "blue-back"—
    all
I know of is the iron and the gall.

BOANERGES BLITZEN, servant of the
    Queen,
Is a dismal failure—is a Might-have-
    been.
In a luckless moment he discovered
    men
Rise to high position through a ready
    pen.

Boanerges Blitzen argued, therefore: "I
With the selfsame weapon can attain as
    high."
Only he did not possess, when he made
    the trial,
Wicked wit of C-lv-n, irony of L——l.

(Men who spar with Government need,
    to back their blows,
Something more than ordinary journal-
    istic prose.)

Never young Civilian's prospects were
    so bright,
Till an Indian paper found that he could
    write:
Never young Civilian's prospects were
    so dark,
When the wretched Blitzen wrote to
    make his mark.

Certainly he scored it, bold and black
and firm,
In that Indian paper—made his seniors
squirm,
Quoted office scandals, wrote the tact-
less truth—
Was there ever known a more misguided youth?

When the Rag he wrote for praised his
plucky game,
Boanerges Blitzen felt that this was
Fame:
When the men he wrote of shook their
heads and swore,
Boanerges Blitzen only wrote the more.

Posed as Young Ithuriel, resolute and
grim,
Till he found promotion didn't come to
him;

Till he found that reprimands weekly
were his lot,
And his many Districts curiously hot.

Till he found his furlough strangely
hard to win,
Boanerges Blitzen didn't care a pin:
Then it seemed to dawn on him something wasn't right—
Boanerges Blitzen put it down to
"spite."

Languished in a District desolate and
dry;
Watched the Local Government yearly
pass him by;
Wondered where the hitch was; called
it most unfair.

   *   *   *   *   *

That was seven years ago—and he still
is there.

———•———

Municipal

"Why is my District death-rate low?"
  Said Binks of Hezabad.
"Wells, drains, and sewage-outfalls are
  My own peculiar fad.
  I learned a lesson once." It ran
"Thus," quoth that most veracious man:

It was an August evening, and, in
snowy garments clad,
I paid a round of visits in the lines of
Hezabad;
When, presently, my Waler saw, and did
not like at all,
A Commissariat elephant careering down
the Mall.

I couldn't see the driver, and across my
mind it rushed
That that Commissariat elephant had
suddenly gone *musth*.
I didn't care to meet him, and I
couldn't well get down,
So I let the Waler have it, and we
headed for the town.

The buggy was a new one, and, praise
Dykes, it stood the strain,
Till the Waler jumped a bullock just
above the City Drain;

And the next that I remember was a
hurricane of squeals,
And the creature making toothpicks of
my five-foot patent wheels.

He seemed to want the owner, so I
fled, distraught with fear,
To the Main Drain sewage-outfall while
he snorted in my ear—
Reached the four-foot drain-head safely,
and, in darkness and despair,
Felt the brute's proboscis fingering my
terror-stiffened hair.

Heard it trumpet on my shoulder—tried
to crawl a little higher—
Found the Main Drain sewage-outfall
blocked, some eight feet up, with
mire;

And, for twenty reeking minutes, Sir,
my very marrow froze,
While the trunk was feeling blindly for
a purchase on my toes!

It missed me by a fraction, but my hair
was turning grey
Before they called the drivers up and
dragged the brute away.
Then I sought the City Elders, and my
words were very plain.
They flushed that four-foot drain-head,
and—it never choked again.

You may hold with surface-drainage,
and the sun-for-garbage cure,
Till you've been a periwinkle shrinking
coyly up a sewer.
I believe in well-flushed culverts . . .
This is why the death-rate's small;
And, if you don't believe me, get
shikarred yourself. That's all.

A Code of Morals

Lest you should think this story true,
I merely mention that I
Evolved it lately. 'Tis a most
Unmitigated misstatement.

Now Jones had left his new-wed bride
to keep his house in order,
And hied away to the Hurrum Hills
above the Afghan border,
To sit on a rock with a heliograph; but
ere he left he taught
His wife the working of the Code that
sets the miles at naught.

And Love had made him very sage, as
Nature made her fair;
So Cupid and Apollo linked, *per* helio-
graph, the pair.
At dawn, across the Hurrum Hills, he
flashed her counsel wise—
At e'en, the dying sunset bore her hus-
band's homilies.

He warned her 'gainst seductive youths
in scarlet clad and gold,
As much as 'gainst the blandishments
paternal of the old;

But kept his gravest warnings for
(hereby the ditty hangs)
That snowy-haired Lothario, Lieutenant-
General Bangs.

'Twas General Bangs, with Aide and
Staff, that tittupped on the way,
When they beheld a heliograph tem-
pestuously at play;
They thought of Border risings, and of
stations sacked and burned—
So stopped to take the message down—
and this is what they learned:

"Dash dot dot, dot, dot dash, dot dash
dot" twice. The General swore.
"Was ever General Officer addressed as
'dear' before?
" 'My Love,' i' faith! 'My Duck,'
Gadzooks! 'My darling popsy-
wop!'
Spirit of great Lord Wolseley, *who* is
on that mountain top?"

The artless Aide-de-camp was mute; the
gilded Staff were still,
As, dumb with pent-up mirth, they
booked that message from the hill;

For, clear as summer's lightning flare,
the husband's warning ran:
"Don't dance or ride with General
Bangs—a most immoral man."

(At dawn, across the Hurrum Hills, he
flashed her counsel wise—
But, howsoever Love be blind, the
world at large hath eyes.)
With damnatory dot and dash he helio-
graphed his wife
Some interesting details of the General's
private life.

The artless Aide-de-camp was mute; the
shining Staff were still,
And red and ever redder grew the Gen-
eral's shaven gill.
And this is what he said at last (his
feelings matter not):
"I think we've tapped a private line.
Hi! Threes about there! Trot!"

All honor unto Bangs, for ne'er did
Jones thereafter know
By word or act official who read off that
helio.;
But the tale is on the Frontier, and
from Michni to Mool*tan*
They know the worthy General as "that
most immoral man."

The Last Department

Twelve hundred million men are spread
  About this Earth and I and You
Wonder, when You and I are dead,
  What will those luckless millions do?

"NONE whole or clean," we cry, "or
    free from stain
Of favor." Wait awhile, till we attain
  The Last Department, where nor
      fraud nor fools,
Nor grade nor greed, shall trouble us
    again.

Fear, Favor, or Affection—what are
    these
To the grim Head who claims our
    services?
  I never knew a wife or interest yet
Delay that *pukka* step, miscalled "de-
    cease";

When leave, long overdue, none can
    deny;
When idleness of all Eternity
  Becomes our furlough, and the mari-
      gold
Our thriftless, bullion-minting Treasury.

Transferred to the Eternal Settlement,
Each in his strait, wood-scantled office
    pent,
  No longer Brown reverses Smith's
      appeals,
Or Jones records his Minute of Dissent.

And One, long since a pillar of the
    Court,
As mud between the beams thereof is
    wrought;
  And One who wrote on phosphates for
      the crops
Is subject-matter of his own Report.

(These be the glorious ends whereto we
    pass—
Let Him Who Is, go call on Him who
    Was;
  And He shall see the *mallie* steals the
      slab
For currie-grinder, and for goats the
    grass.)

A breath of wind, a Border bullet's flight
A draught of water, or a horse's fright—
  The droning of the fat *Sheristadar*
Ceases, the punkah stops, and falls the
    night

For you or Me. Do those who live
    decline
The step that offers, or their work re-
    sign?
  Trust me, To-day's Most Indispen-
      sables,
Five hundred men can take your place
    or mine.

Recessional

(A VICTORIAN ODE)

God of our fathers, known of old—
Lord of our far-flung battle line—
Beneath whose awful hand we hold
Dominion over palm and pine—
Lord God of Hosts, be with us yet,
Lest we forget—lest we forget!

The tumult and the shouting dies—
The Captains and the Kings depart—
Still stands Thine ancient sacrifice,
An humble and a contrite heart.
Lord God of Hosts, be with us yet,
Lest we forget—lest we forget!

Far-called our navies melt away—
On dune and headland sinks the fire—
Lo, all our pomp of yesterday
Is one with Nineveh and Tyre!

Judge of the Nations, spare us yet,
Lest we forget—lest we forget!

If, drunk with sight of power, we loose
Wild tongues that have not Thee in
awe—
Such boastings as the Gentiles use,
Or lesser breeds without the Law—
Lord God of Hosts, be with us yet,
Lest we forget—lest we forget!

For heathen heart that puts her trust
In reeking tube and iron shard—
All valiant dust that builds on dust,
And guarding calls not Thee to guard.
For frantic boast and foolish word,
Thy Mercy on Thy People, Lord!
Amen.

The Vampire

The verses—as suggested by the painting by Philip Burne Jones, first exhibited at the new gallery in London in 1897.

A FOOL there was and he made his
prayer
(Even as you and I!)
To a rag and a bone and a hank of hair
(We called her the woman who did not
care),
But the fool he called her his lady fair
(Even as you and I!)

Oh the years we waste and the tears we
waste
And the work of our head and hand,
Belong to the woman who did not know
(And now we know that she never could
know)
And did not understand.

A fool there was and his goods he spent
(Even as you and I!)
Honor and faith and a sure intent

But a fool must follow his natural bent
(And it wasn't the least what the lady
　　meant),
　　(Even as you and I!)

Oh the toil we lost and the spoil we lost
　And the excellent things we planned,
Belong to the woman who didn't know
　why
(And now we know she never knew
　why)
　And did not understand.

The fool was stripped to his foolish hide
　(Even as you and I!)

Which she might have seen when she
　threw him aside—
(But it isn't on record the lady tried)
So some of him lived but the most of
　him died—
　(Even as you and I!)

And it isn't the shame and it isn't the
　blame
　That stings like a white hot brand.
It's coming to know that she never
　knew why
(Seeing at last she could never know
　why)
　And never could understand.

To the Unknown Goddess

WILL you conquer my heart with your
　beauty; my soul going out from
　afar?
Shall I fall to your hand as a victim of
　crafty and cautious *shikar?*

Have I met you and passed you al-
　ready, unknowing, unthinking and
　blind?
Shall I meet you next session at Simla,
　O sweetest and best of your kind?

Does the P. and O. bear you to me-
　ward, or, clad in short frocks in the
　West,
Are you growing the charms that shall
　capture and torture the heart in my
　breast?

Will you stay in the Plains till Sep-
　tember—my passion as warm as the
　day?

Will you bring me to book on the
　Mountains, or where the thermanti-
　dotes play?

When the light of your eyes shall make
　pallid the mean lesser lights I
　pursue,
And the charm of your presence shall
　lure me from love of the gay
　"thirteen-two";

When the peg and the pig-skin shall
　please not; when I buy me Cal-
　cutta-built clothes;
When I quit the Delight of Wild Asses;
　forswearing the swearing of oaths;

As a deer to the hand of the hunter
　when I turn 'mid the gibes of my
　friends;
When the days of my freedom are num-
　bered, and the life of the bachelor
　ends.

Ah Goddess! child, spinster, or widow
—as of old on Mars Hill when they
    raised
To the God that they knew not an altar
—so I, a young Pagan, have praised

The Goddess I know not nor worship;
    yet, if half that men tell me be true,
You will come in the future, and there-
    fore these verses are written to you.

The Rupaiyat of Omar Kal'vin

[Allowing for the difference 'twixt
prose and rhymed exaggeration, this
ought to reproduce the sense of what Sir
A—— told the nation some time ago,
when the Government struck from our
incomes two per cent.]

Now the New Year, reviving last Year's
    Debt,
The Thoughtful Fisher casteth wide his
    Net;
    So I with begging Dish and ready
    Tongue
Assail all Men for all that I can get.

Imports indeed are gone with all their
    Dues—
Lo! Salt a Lever that I dare not use,
    Nor may I ask the Tillers in Bengal—
Surely my Kith and Kin will not refuse!

Pay—and I promise by the Dust of
    Spring,
Retrenchment. If my promises can
    bring
    Comfort, Ye have Them now a thou-
    sandfold—
By Allah! I will promise *Anything!*

Indeed, indeed, Retrenchment oft before
I swore—but did I mean it when I
    swore?

And then, and then, We wandered to
    the Hills,
And so the Little Less became Much
    More.

Whether at Boileaugunge or Babylon,
I know not how the wretched Thing is
    done,
    The Items of Receipt grow surely
    small;
The Items of Expense mount one by
    one.

I cannot help it. What have I to do
With One and Five, or Four, or Three,
    or Two?
    Let Scribes spit Blood and Sulphur as
    they please,
Or Statemen call me foolish—Heed not
    you.

Behold, I promise—Anything You will.
Behold, I greet you with an empty
    Till—
    Ah! Fellow-Sinners, of your Charity
Seek not the Reason of the Dearth, but
    fill.

For if I sinned and fell, where lies the
    Gain
Of Knowledge? Would it ease you of
    your Pain

To know the tangled Threads of
Revenue,
I ravel deeper in a hopeless Skein?

"Who hath not Prudence"—what was it
I said,
Of Her who paints her Eyes and tires
Her Head,
And gibes and mocks the People in
the Street,

And fawns upon them for Her thriftless Bread?

Accursed is She of Eve's daughters—She
Hath cast off Prudence, and Her End
shall be
Destruction . . . Brethren, of
your Bounty
Some portion of your daily Bread to *Me*.

La Nuit Blanche

A much-discerning Public hold
  The Singer generally sings
  Of personal and private things,
And prints and sells his past for gold.

Whatever I may here disclaim,
  The very clever folk I sing to
  Will most indubitably cling to
Their pet delusion, just the same.

I HAD seen, as dawn was breaking
  And I staggered to my rest,
Tari Devi softly shaking
  From the Cart Road to the crest.
I had seen the spurs of Jakko
  Heave and quiver, swell and sink.
Was it Earthquake or tobacco,
  Day of Doom or Night of Drink?

In the full, fresh fragrant morning
  I observed a camel crawl,
Laws of gravitation scorning,
  On the ceiling and the wall;
Then I watched a fender walking,
  And I heard grey leeches sing,
And a red-hot monkey talking
  Did not seem the proper thing.

Then a Creature, skinned and crimson,
  Ran about the floor and cried,
And they said I had the "jims" on,
  And they dosed me with bromide,
And they locked me in my bedroom—
  Me and one wee Blood Red Mouse—
Though I said: "To give my head room
  "You had best unroof the house."

But my words were all unheeded,
  Though I told the grave M.D.
That the treatment really needed
  Was a dip in open sea
That was lapping just below me,
  Smooth as silver, white as snow,
And it took three men to throw me
  When I found I could not go.

Half the night I watched the Heavens
  Fizz like '81 champagne—
Fly to sixes and to sevens,
  Wheel and thunder back again;
And when all was peace and order
  Save one planet nailed askew,
Much I wept because my warder
  Would not let me set it true.

After frenzied hours of waiting,
  When the Earth and Skies were dumb,
Pealed an awful voice dictating
  An interminable sum,
Changing to a tangle story—
  "What she said you said I said"—
Till the Moon arose in glory,
  And I found her . . . in my head;

Then a Face came, blind and weeping,
  And It couldn't wipe its eyes,
And It muttered I was keeping
  Back the moonlight from the skies;
So I patted it for pity,
  But It whistled shrill with wrath,
And a huge black Devil City
  Poured its peoples on my path.

So I fled with steps uncertain
  On a thousand-year long race,
But the bellying of the curtain
  Kept me always in one place;

While the tumult rose and maddened
  To the roar of Earth on fire,
Ere it ebbed and sank and saddened
  To a whisper tense as wire.

In tolerable stillness
  Rose one little, little star,
And it chuckled at my illness,
  And it mocked me from afar;
And its brethren came and eyed me,
  Called the Universe to aid,
Till I lay, with naught to hide me,
  'Neath the Scorn of All Things Made.

Dun and saffron, robed and splendid,
  Broke the solemn, pitying Day,
And I knew my pains were ended,
  And I turned and tried to pray;
But my speech was shattered wholly,
  And I wept as children weep,
Till the dawn-wind, softly, slowly,
  Brought to burning eyelids sleep.

My Rival

I go to concert, party, ball—
  What profit is in these?
I sit alone against the wall
  And strive to look at ease.
The incense that is mine by right
  They burn before Her shrine;
And that's because I'm seventeen
  And She is forty-nine.

I cannot check my girlish blush,
  My color comes and goes;
I redden to my finger-tips,
  And sometimes to my nose.
But She is white where white should be,
  And red where red should shine.
The blush that flies at seventeen
  Is fixed at forty-nine.

I wish I had Her constant cheek:
  I wish that I could sing
All sorts of funny little songs,
  Not quite the proper thing.
I'm very *gauche* and very shy,
  Her jokes aren't in my line;
And, worst of all, I'm seventeen
  While She is forty-nine.

The young men come, the young men go
  Each pink and white and neat,
She's older than their mothers, but
  They grovel at Her feet.
They walk beside Her *'rickshaw* wheels—
  None ever walk by mine;
And that's because I'm seventeen
  And She is forty-nine.

She rides with half a dozen men,
  (She calls them "boys" and "mashers")
I trot along the Mall alone;
  My prettiest frocks and sashes
Don't help to fill my programme-card,
  And vainly I repine
From ten to two A. M. Ah me!
  Would I were forty-nine!

She calls me "darling," "pet," and "dear,"
  And "sweet retiring maid."
I'm always at the back, I know,
  She puts me in the shade.

She introduces me to men,
  "Cast" lovers, I opine,
For sixty takes to seventeen,
  Nineteen to forty-nine.

But even She must older grow
  And end Her dancing days,
She can't go on forever so
  At concerts, balls, and plays.
One ray of priceless hope I see
  Before my footsteps shine;
Just think, that She'll be eighty-one
  When I am forty-nine.

The Lovers' Litany

Eyes of grey—a sodden quay,
Driving rain and falling tears,
As the steamer wears to sea
In a parting storm of cheers.
  Sing, for Faith and Hope are high—
  None so true as you and I—
  Sing the Lovers' Litany:
  "Love like ours can never die!"

Eyes of black—a throbbing keel,
Milky foam to left and right;
Whispered converse near the wheel
In the brilliant tropic night.
  Cross that rules the Southern Sky!
  Stars that sweep and wheel and fly,
  Hear the Lovers' Litany:
  "Love like ours can never die!"

Eyes of brown—a dusty plain
Split and parched with heat of June,
Flying hoof and tightened rein,
Hearts that beat the old, old tune.

Side by side the horses fly,
Frame we now the old reply
Of the Lovers' Litany:
"Love like ours can never die!"

Eyes of blue—the Simla Hills
Silvered with the moonlight hoar;
Pleading of the waltz that thrills,
Dies and echoes round Benmore.
  "Mabel," "Officers," "Good-bye,"
  Glamour, wine, and witchery—
  On my soul's sincerity,
  "Love like ours can never die!"

Maidens of your charity,
Pity my most luckless state.
Four times Cupid's debtor I—
Bankrupt in quadruplicate.
  Yet, despite this evil case,
  And a maiden showed me grace,
  Four-and-forty times would I
  Sing the Lovers' Litany:
  "Love like ours can never die!"

A Ballad of Burial

("Saint Praxed's ever was the Church for peace")

IF down here I chance to die,
　Solemnly I beg you take
All that is left of "I"
　To the Hills for old sake's sake.
Pack me very thoroughly
　In the ice that used to slake
Pegs I drank when I was dry—
　This observe for old sake's sake.

To the railway station hie,
　There a single ticket take
For Umballa—goods-train—I
　Shall not mind delay or shake.
I shall rest contentedly
　Spite of clamor coolies make;
Thus in state and dignity
　Send me up for old sake's sake.

Next the sleepy Babu wake,
　Book a Kalka van "for four."
Few, I think, will care to make
　Journeys with me any more
As they used to do of yore.
　I shall need a "special" break—
Thing I never took before—
　Get me one for old sake's sake.

After that—arrangements make.
　No hotel will take me in,
And a bullock's back would break
　'Neath the teak and leaden skin.
Tonga ropes are frail and thin,
　Or, did I a back-seat take,
In a tonga I might spin,—
　Do your best for old sake's sake.

After that—your work is done.
　Recollect a Padre must
Mourn the dear departed one—
　Throw the ashes and the dust.
Don't go down at once. I trust
　You will find excuse to "snake
Three days' casual on the bust."
　Get your fun for old sake's sake.

I could never stand the Plains.
　Think of blazing June and May
Think of those September rains
　Yearly till the Judgment Day!
I should never rest oin peace,
　I should sweat and lie awake.
Rail me then, on my decrease,
　To the Hills for old sake's sake.

———•———

Divided Destinies

IT was an artless *Bandar*, and he danced
　upon a pine,
And much I wondered how he lived, and
　where the beast might dine,

And many, many other things, till, o'er
　my morning smoke,
I slept the sleep of idleness and dreamt
　that *Bandar* spoke.

He said: "O man of many clothes!
  Sad crawler on the Hills!
Observe, I know not Ranken's shop, nor
  Ranken's monthly bills;
I take no heed to trousers or the coats
  that you call dress;
Nor am I plagued with little cards for
  little drinks at Mess.

"I steal the bunnia's grain at morn, at
  noon and eventide,
(For he is fat and I am spare), I roam
  the mountain side,
I follow no man's carriage, and no,
  never in my life
Have I flirted at Peliti's with another
  Bandar's wife.

"O man of futile fopperies—unnecessary wraps;
I own no ponies in the hills, I drive no
  tall-wheeled traps;
I buy me not twelve-button gloves,
  'short-sixes' eke, or rings,
Nor do I waste at Hamilton's my wealth
  on 'pretty things.'

"I quarrel with my wife at home, we
  never fight abroad;
But Mrs. B. has grasped the fact I am
  her only lord.
I never heard of fever—dumps nor
  debts depress my soul;
And I pity and despise you!" Here he
  pouched my breakfast-roll.

His hide was very mangy, and his face
  was very red,
And ever and anon he scratched with
  energy his head.
His manners were not always nice, but
  how my spirit cried
To be an artless *Bandar* loose upon the
  mountain side!

So I answered: "Gentle *Bandar*, an inscrutable Decree
Makes thee a gleesome fleasome Thou,
  and me a wretched Me.
Go! Depart in peace, my brother, to
  thy home amid the pine
Yet forget not once a mortal wished to
  change his lot with thine."

The Masque of Plenty

ARGUMENT.—The Indian Government, being minded to discover the economic condition of their lands, sent a Committee to inquire into it; and saw that it was good.

SCENE.—*The wooded heights of Simla. The Incarnation of the Government of India in the raiment of the Angel of Plenty sings, to pianoforte accompaniment:*

"How sweet is the shepherd's sweet life!
  From the dawn to the even he strays—
He shall follow his sheep all the day,

And his tongue shall be fillèd with
  praise.

  (*Adagio dim.*) Fillèd with praise!"

(*Largendo con sp.*) Now this is the
                       position,
                     Go make an in-
                       quisition
                     Into their real con-
                       dition
                     As swiftly as ye
                       may.

(*p.*) Ay, paint our swarthy billions
 The richest of vermilions
 Ere two well-led cotillions
  Have danced themselves away.

TURKISH PATROL, *as able and intelligent
Investigators wind down the
Himalayas*:

What is the state of the Nation?
 What is its occupation?
Hi! get along, get along, get along—
 lend us the information!

(*Dim.*) Census the *byle* and the *yabu*
 —capture a first-class Babu,
Set him to cut Gazetteers—Gazetteers . . .
  (*ff.*) What is the state of the Nation, etc., etc.

INTERLUDE, *from Nowhere in Particular,
to stringed and Oriental instruments.*

Our cattle reel beneath the yoke they
 bear—
The earth is iron, and the skies are
 brass—
And faint with fervor of the flaming air
 The languid hours pass.

The well is dry beneath the village tree—
 The young wheat withers ere it reach
 a span,
And belts of blinding sand show cruelly
 Where once the river ran.

Pray, brothers, pray, but to no earthly
 King—
 Lift up your hands above the blighted
 grain,
Look westward—if they please, the
 Gods shall bring
 Their mercy with the rain.

Look westward—bears the blue no
 brown cloud-bank?
Nay, it is written—wherefore should
 we fly?
On our own field and by our cattle's
 flank
 Lie down, lie down to die!

SEMI-CHORUS.

By the plumed heads of Kings
  Waving high,
Where the tall corn springs
  O'er the dead.

If they rust or rot we die,
If they ripen we are fed.
Very mighty is the power of our
 Kings!

*Triumphal return to Simla of the In-
vestigators, attired after the manner
of Dionysus, leading a pet tiger-cub
in wreaths of rhubarb leaves, sym-
bolical of India under medical treatment. They sing:*

We have seen, we have written—behold
 it, the proof of our manifold toil!
In their hosts they assembled and told
 it—the tale of the sons of the soil.
We have said of the Sickness, "Where
 is it?"—and of Death, "It is far
 from our ken;"
We have paid a particular visit to the
 affluent children of men.
We have trodden the mart and the well-
 curb— we have trooped to the
 bield and the byre;
And the King may the forces of Hell
 curb, for the People have all they
 desire!

Castanets and step-dance:

Oh, the *dom* and the *mag* and the
 thakur and the *thag,*
  And the *nat* and the *brinjaree,*
And the *bunnia* and the *ryot* are as
 happy and as quiet
  And as plump as they can be!
Yes, the *jain* and the *jat* in his stucco-
 fronted hut,
  And the bounding *bazugar,*
By the favor of the King are as fat as
 anything,
  They are—they are—they are!

Recitative, *Government of India, with
 white satin wings and electroplated
 harp:*

How beautiful upon the mountains—in
 peace reclining,
Thus to be assured that our people are
 unanimously dining.
And though there are places not so
 blessed as others in natural advantages, which, after all, was only to
 be expected,
Proud and glad are we to congratulate
 you upon the work you have thus
 ably effected.
(*Cres.*) How be-ewtful upon the
 mountains!

Hired Band, *brasses only, full chorus:*

God bless the Squire,
And all his rich relations
Who teach us poor people
We eat our proper rations—
  We eat our proper rations,
  In spite of inundations,
  Malarial exhalations,
  And casual starvations,
We have, we have, they say we have—
We *have* our proper rations!

(*Cornet.*)

Which nobody can deny!
If he does he tells a lie—
  We are all as willing as Barkis—
  We all of us loves the Markiss—
  We all of us stuffs our ca-ar-kis—
With food until we die! (*Da capo.*)

Chorus of the Crystallized Facts.

Before the beginning of years
There came to the rule of the State
Men with a pair of shears,
Men with an Estimate—
Strachey with Muir for leaven,
Lytton with locks that fell,
Ripon fooling with Heaven,
And Temple riding like H-ll!!
And the bigots took in hand
Cess and the falling rain,
And the measure of sifted sand
The dealer puts in the grain—
Imports by land and sea,
To uttermost decimal worth,
And registration—free—
In the houses of death and of birth:
And fashioned with pens and paper,
And fashioned in black and white,
With Life for a flickering taper
And Death for a blazing light—
With the Armed and the Civil Power,
That his strength might endure for a
 span,
From Adam's Bridge to Peshawur,
The Much Administered man.

In the towns of the North and the East,
They gathered as unto rule,
They bade him starve the priest
And send his children to school.
Railways and roads they wrought,
For the needs of the soil within;
A time to squabble in court,
A time to bear and to grin.

And gave him peace in his ways,
Jails—and Police to fight,
Justice at length of days,
And Right—and Might in the Right.
His speech is of mortgaged bedding,
On his kine he borrows yet,

At his heart is his daughter's wedding,
In his eye foreknowledge of debt.
He eats and hath indigestion,
He toils and he may not stop;
His life is a long-drawn question
Between a crop and a crop.

———————•———————

The Mare's Nest

JANE Austen Beecher Stowe de Rouse
  Was good beyond all earthly need;
But, on the other hand, her spouse
  Was very, very bad indeed.
He smoked cigars, called churches slow,
And raced—but this she did not know.

For Belial Machiavelli kept
  The little fact a secret, and,
Though o'er his minor sins she wept,
  Jane Austen did not understand
That Lilly—thirteen-two and bay—
Absorbed one-half her husband's pay.

She was so good, she made him worse;
  (Some women are like this, I think;)
He taught her parrot how to curse,
  Her Assam monkey how to drink.
He vexed her righteous soul until
She went up, and he went down hill.

Then came the crisis, strange to say,
  Which turned a good wife to a better.
A telegraphic peon, one day,
  Brought her—now, had it been a letter
For Belial Machiavelli, I
Know Jane would just have let it lie.

But 'twas a telegram instead,
  Marked "urgent," and her duty plain
To open it. Jane Austen read:
  "Your Lilly's got a cough again.
Can't understand why she is kept
At your expense." Jane Austen wept.

It was a misdirected wire.
  Her husband was at Shaitanpore.
She spread her anger, hot as fire,
  Through six thin foreign sheets or
      more.
Sent off that letter, wrote another
To her solicitor—and mother.

Then Belial Machiavelli saw
  Her error and, I trust, his own,
Wired to the minion of the Law,
  And traveled •wifeward—not alone.
For Lilly—thirteen-two and bay—
Came in a horse-box all the way.

There was a scene—a weep or two—
  With many kisses. Austen Jane
Rode Lilly all the season through,
  And never opened wires again.
She races now with Belial. This
Is very sad, but so it is.

Possibilities

Ay, lay him 'neath the Simla pine—
  A fortnight fully to be missed,
  Behold, we lose our fourth at whist,
A chair is vacant where we dine.

His place forgets him; other men
  Have bought his ponies, guns, and
    traps.
  His fortune is the Great Perhaps
And that cool rest-house down the glen,

Whence he shall hear, as spirits may,
  Our mundane revel on the height,
  Shall watch each flashing 'rickshaw-
    light
Sweep on to dinner, dance, and play.

Benmore shall woo him to the ball
  With lighted rooms and braying band,
  And he shall hear and understand
"Dream Faces" better than us all.

For, think you, as the vapors flee
  Across Sanjaolie after rain,
  His soul may climb the hill again
To each old field of victory.

Unseen, who women held so dear,
  The strong man's yearning to his kind
  Shall shake at most the window-
    blind,
Or dull awhile the card-room's cheer.

In his own place of power unknown,
  His Light o' Love another's flame,
  His dearest pony galloped lame,
And he an alien and alone.

Yet may he meet with many a friend—
  Shrewd shadows, lingering long un-
    seen
  Among us when "God save the
    Queen"
Shows even "extras" have an end.

And, when we leave the heated room,
  And, when at four the lights expire,
  The crew shall gather round the fire
And mock our laughter in the gloom.

Talk as we talked, and they ere death—
  First wanly, dance in ghostly wise,
  With ghosts of tunes for melodies,
And vanish at the morning's breath.

———•———

Christmas in India

Dim dawn behind the tamarisks—the
    sky is saffron-yellow—
  As the women in the village grind the
    corn,

And the parrots seek the riverside, each
    calling to his fellow
  That the Day, the staring Eastern
    Day is born.

Oh the white dust on the highway!
   Oh the stenches in the by-
      way!
  Oh the clammy fog that hovers
    over earth!
And at Home they're making merry
   'neath the white and scarlet
   berry—
  What part have India's exiles
    in their mirth?

Full day behind the tamarisks—the sky
  is blue and staring—
  As the cattle crawl afield beneath the
    yoke,
And they bear One o'er the field-path,
   who is past all hope or car-
   ing,
  To the ghât below the curling wreaths
    of smoke.
  Call on Rama, going slowly, as ye
    bear a brother lowly—
  Call on Rama—he may hear, per-
    haps, your voice!
With our hymn-books and our psalters
   we appeal to other altars,
  And to-day we bid "good Christian
    men rejoice!"

High noon behind the tamarisks—the
  sun is hot above us—
  As at Home the Christmas Day is
    breaking wan.
They will drink our healths at dinner—
   those who tell us how they
   love us,
And forget us till another year be
   gone!
  Oh the toil that knows no breaking!
    Oh the *Heimweh*, ceaseless,
    aching!
  Oh the black dividing Sea and alien
    Plain!

Youth was cheap—wherefore we
  sold it.
  Gold was good—we hoped to
   hold it,
  And to-day we know the fulness of
   our gain.

Grey dusk behind the tamarisks—the
  parrots fly together—
  As the sun is sinking slowly over
   Home;
And his last ray seems to mock us shack-
  led in a lifelong tether
  That drags us back howe'er so far we
   roam.
  Hard her service, poor her payment
   —she in ancient, tattered rai-
   ment—
    India, she the grim Stepmother
    of our kind.
  If a year of life be lent her, if her
    temple's shrine we enter,
    The door is shut—we may not
    look behind.

Black night behind the tamarisks—the
  owls begin their chorus—
  As the conches from the temple
   scream and bray.
With the fruitless years behind us, and
   the hopeless years before us,
  Let us honor, O my brothers, Christmas Day!
    Call a truce, then, to our labors—
    let us feast with friends and
    neighbors,
    And be merry as the custom of
    our caste;
  For if "faint and forced the laugh-
    ter," and if sadness follow
    after,
    We are riched by one mocking
    Christmas past.

Pagett, M.P.

The toad beneath the harrow knows
Exactly where each tooth-point goes.
The butterfly upon the road
Preaches contentment to that toad.

PAGETT, M. P., was a liar, and a fluent
liar therewith,—
He spoke of the heat of India as the
"Asian Solar Myth";
Came on a four months' visit, to "study
the East," in November,
And I got him to sign an agreement
vowing to stay till September.

March came in with the *köil*. Pagett
was cool and gay,
Called me a "bloated Brahmin," talked
of my "princely pay."
March went out with the roses. "Where
is your heat?" said he.
"Coming," said I to Pagett. "Skittles!"
said Pagett, M. P.

April began with the punkah, coolies,
and prickly-heat,—
Pagett was dear to mosquitoes, sand-
flies found him a treat.
He grew speckled and lumpy—hammered, I grieve to say,
Aryan brothers who fanned him, in an
illiberal way.

May set in with a dust-storm,—Pagett
went down with the sun.
All the delights of the season tickled
him one by one.
Imprimis—ten days' "liver"—due to his
drinking beer;
Later, a dose of fever—slight, but he
called it severe.

Dysent'ry touched him in June, after
the *Chota Bursat*—
Lowered his portly person—made him
yearn to depart.
He didn't call me a "Brahmin," or
"bloated," or "overpaid,"
But seemed to think it a wonder that
any one stayed.

July was a trifle unhealthy,—Pagett was
ill with fear,
'Called it the "Cholera Morbus," hinted
that life was dear.
He babbled of "Eastern exile," and
mentioned his home with tears;
But I haven't seen *my* children for
close upon seven years.

We reached a hundred and twenty once
in the Court at noon,
(I've mentioned Pagett was portly)
Pagett went off in a swoon.
That was an end to the business; Pa-
gett, the perjured, fled
With a practical, working knowledge of
"Solar Myths" in his head.

And I laughed as I drove from the station, but the mirth died out on my
lips
As I thought of the fools like Pagett
who write of their "Eastern trips,"
And the sneers of the traveled idiots
who duly misgovern the land,
And I prayed to the Lord to deliver another one into my hand.

The Song of the Women

(Lady Dufferin's Fund for medical aid to the Women of India)

How shall she know the worship we
would do her?
The walls are high, and she is very
far.
How shall the woman's message reach
unto her
Above the tumult of the packed bazaar?
Free wind of March, against the
lattice blowing,
Bear thou our thanks, lest she depart unknowing.

Go forth across the fields we may not
roam in,
Go forth beyond the trees that rim
the city,
To whatsoe'er fair place she hath her
home in,
Who dowered us with wealth of love
and pity.
Out of our shadow pass, and seek
her singing—
"I have no gifts but Love alone for
bringing."

Say that we be a feeble folk who greet
her,
But old in grief, and very wise in
tears;
Say that we, being desolate, entreat her
That she forget us not in after years;
For we have seen the light, and it
were grevious
To dim that dawning if our lady
leave us.

By life that ebbed with none to stanch
the failing
By Love's sad harvest garnered in the
spring,
When Love in ignorance wept unavailing
O'er young buds dead before their
blossoming;
By all the greyowl watched, the
pale moon viewed,
In past grim years, declare our
gratitude!

By hands uplifted to the Gods that
heard not,
By gifts that found no favor in their
sight,
By faces bent above the babe that
stirred not,
By nameless horrors of the stifling
night;
By ills foredone, by peace her toils
discover,
Bid Earth be good beneath and
Heaven above her!

If she have sent her servants in our
pain
If she have fought with Death and
dulled his sword;
If she have given back our sick again,
And to the breast the weakling lips
restored,
Is it a little thing that she has
wrought?
Then Life and Death and Motherhood be nought.

Go forth, O wind, our message on thy
wings,
And they shall hear thee pass and bid
thee speed,
In reed-roofed hut, or white-walled
home of kings,
Who have been helpen by her in their
need.
All spring shall give thee fragrance,
and the wheat
Shall be a tasselled floorcloth to
thy feet.

Haste, for our hearts are with thee, take
no rest!
Loud-voiced ambassador, from sea to
sea
Proclaim the blessing, manifold, confessed,
Of those in darkness by her hand set
free,
Then very softly to her presence
move,
And whisper: "Lady, lo, they know
and love!"

A Ballad of Jakko Hill

ONE moment bid the horses wait,
  Since tiffin is not laid till three,
Below the upward path and straight
  You climbed a year ago with me.
Love came upon us suddenly
  And loosed—an idle hour to kill—
A headless, armless armory
  That smote us both on Jakko Hill.

Ah Heaven! we would wait and wait
  Through Time and to Eternity!
Ah Heaven! we could conquer Fate
  With more than Godlike constancy
I cut the date upon a tree—
  Here stand the clumsy figures still:
"10-7-85, A.D."
  Damp with the mist on Jakko Hill.

What came of high resolve and great,
  And until Death fidelity!
Whose horse is waiting at your gate?
  Whose 'rickshaw-wheels ride over me?
No Saint's, I swear; and—let me see
  To-night what names your programme
  fill—
We drift asunder merrily,
  As drifts the mist on Jakko Hill!

L'ENVOI.

Princess, behold our ancient state
  Has clean departed; and we see
'Twas Idleness we took for Fate
  That bound light bonds on you and
  me.
Amen! Here ends the comedy
  Where it began in all good will;
Since Love and Leave together flee
  As driven mist on Jakko Hill!

The Plea of the Simla Dancers

Too late, alas! the song
To remedy the wrong;—
The rooms are taken from us, swept and
garnished for their fate.
But these tear-besprinkled pages
Shall attest to future ages
That we cried against the crime of it—
too late, alas! too late!

"WHAT have *we* ever done to bear this
grudge?"
Was there no room save only in Ben-
more
For docket, *duftar,* and for office drudge,
That you usurp our smoothest danc-
ing floor?
Must babus do their work on polished
teak?
Are ball-rooms fittest for the ink you
spill?
Was there no other cheaper house to
seek?
You might have left them all at
Strawberry Hill.

We never harmed you! Innocent our
guise,
Dainty our shining feet, our voices
low;
And we revolved to divers melodies,
And we were happy but a year ago.
To-night, the moon that watched our
lightsome wiles—
That beamed upon us through the
deodars—
Is wan with gazing on official files,
And desecrating desks disgust the
stars.

Nay! by the memory of tuneful nights—
Nay! by the witchery of flying feet—
Nay! by the glamour of foredone de-
lights—
By all things merry, musical, and
meet—
By wine that sparkled, and by spark-
ling eyes—
By wailing waltz—by reckless gallop's
strain—
By dim verandas and by soft replies,
Give us our ravished ball-room back
again!

Or—hearken to the curse we lay on
you!
The ghosts of waltzes shall perplex
your brain,
And murmurs of past merriment pursue
Your 'wildered clerks that they indite
in vain;
And when you count your poor Provincial millions,
The only figures that your pen shall
frame
Shall be the figures of dear, dear cotillions
Danced out in tumult long before you
came.

Yea! *"See Saw"* shall upset your estimates,
"Dream Faces" shall your heavy
heads bemuse,
Because your hand, unheeding, dese-
crates
Our temple; fit for higher, worthier
use.

And all the long verandas, eloquent
  With echoes of a score of Simla years,
Shall plague you with unbidden senti-
    ment—
  Babbling of kisses, laughter, love, and
    tears.

So shall you mazed amid old memories
    stand,
  So shall you toil, and shall accom-
    plish nought,

And ever in your ears a phantom Band
  Shall blare away the staid official
    thought.
Wherefore—and ere this awful curse be
    spoken,
  Cast out your swarthy sacrilegious
    train,
And give—ere dancing cease and hearts
    be broken—
  Give us our ravished ball-room back
    again!

———————•———————

Ballad of Fisher's Boarding-House

That night, when through the mooring-
    chains
  The wide-eyed corpse rolled free,
To blunder down by Garden Reach
  And rot at Kedgeree,
The tale the Hughli told the shoal
  The lean shoal told to me.

'Twas Fultah Fisher's boarding-house
  Where sailor-men reside,
And there were men of all the ports
  From Mississip to Clyde,
And regally they spat and smoked,
  And fearsomely they lied.

They lied about the purple Sea
  That gave them scanty bread,
They lied about the Earth beneath,
  The Heavens overhead,
For they had looked too often on
  Black rum when that was red.

They told their tales of wreck and
    wrong,
  Of shame and lust and fraud,

They backed their toughest statements
    with
  The Brimstone of the Lord,
And crackling oaths went to and fro
  Across the fist-banged board.

And there was Hans the blue-eyed Dane,
  Bull-throated, bare of arm,
Who carried on his hairy chest
  The maid Ultruda's charm—
The little silver crucifix
  That keeps a man from harm.

And there was Jake Without-the-Ears,
  And Pamba the Malay,
And Carboy Gin the Guinea cook,
  And Luz from Vigo Bay,
And Honest Jack who sold them slops
  And harvested their pay.

And there was Salem Hardieker,
  A lean Bostonian he—
Russ, German, English, Halfbreed, Finn,
  Yank, Dane, and Portugee,
At Fultah Fisher's boarding-house
  They rested from the sea.

Now Anne of Austria shared their
    drinks,
  Collinga knew her fame,
From Tarnau in Galicia
  To Juan Bazar she came,
To eat the bread of infamy
  And take the wage of shame.

She held a dozen men to heel—
  Rich spoil of war was hers,
In hose and gown and ring and chain,
  From twenty mariners,
And, by Port Law, that week, men called
  Her Salem Hardieker's.

But seamen learned—what landsmen
    know—
  That neither gifts nor gain
Can hold a winking Light o' Love
  Or Fancy's flight restrain,
When Anne of Austria rolled her eyes
  On Hans the blue-eyed Dane.

Since Life is strife, and strife means
    knife,
  From Howrah to the Bay,
And he may die before the dawn
  Who liquored out the day,
In Fultah Fisher's boarding-house
  We woo while yet we may.

But cold was Hans the blue-eyed Dane,
  Bull-throated, bare of arm,
And laughter shook the chest beneath
  The maid Ultruda's charm—
The little silver crucifix
  That keeps a man from harm.

"You speak to Salem Hardieker,
  You was his girl, I know.
I ship mineselfs to-morrow, see,
  Und round the Skaw we go,
South, down the Cattegat by Hjelm,
  To Besser in Saro."
When love rejected turns to hate,
  All ill betide the man.
"You speak to Salem Hardieker"—
  She spoke as woman can.
A scream—a sob—"He called me—
    names!"
  And then the fray began.

An oath from Salem Hadieker,
  A shriek upon the stairs,
A dance of shadows on the wall,
  A knife-thrust unawares—
And Hans came down, as cattle drop,
  Across the broken chairs.

*   *   *   *   *   *

In Anne of Austria's trembling hands
  The weary head fell low:
"I ship mineselfs to-morrow, straight
  For Besser in Saro:
Und there Ultruda comes to me
  At Easter, und I go

"South, down the Cattegat— What's
    here?
  There—are—no—lights—to—guide!"
The mutter ceased, the spirit passed,
  And Anne of Austria cried
In Fultah Fisher's boarding-house
  When Hans the mighty died.

Thus slew they Hans the blue-eyed
    Dane,
  Bull-throated, bare of arm,
But Anne of Austria looted first
  The maid Ultruda's charm—
The little silver crucifix
  That keeps a man from harm.

"As the Bell Clinks"

As I left the Halls at Lumley, rose the
    vision of a comely
Maid last season worshipped dumbly,
    watched with fervor from afar;
And I wondered idly, blindly, if the
    maid would greet me kindly.
That was all—the rest was settled by
    the clinking tonga-bar.
Yea, my life and hers were coupled
    by the tonga coupling-bar.

For my misty meditation, at the second
    changing-station,
Suffered sudden dislocation, fled before
    the tuneless jar
Of a Wagner *obbligato, scherzo*, double-
    hand *staccato*,
Played on either pony's saddle by the
    clacking tonga-bar—
Played with human speech, I fancied,
    by the jigging, jolting bar.

"She was sweet," thought I, "last sea-
    son, but 'twere surely wild unreason
Such tiny hope to freeze on as was
    offered by my Star,
When she whispered, something sadly:
    'I—we feel your going badly!' "
"And you let the chance escape you?"
    rapped the rattling tonga-bar.
"What a chance and what an idiot!"
    clicked the vicious tonga-bar.

Heart of man—oh, heart of putty! Had
    I gone by Kakahutti,
On the old Hill-road and rutty, I had
    'scaped that fatal car.

But his fortune each must bide by, so
    I watched the milestones slide by,
To *"You call on Her to-morrow!"*—
    fugue with cymbals by the bar—
"You must call on Her to-morrow!"—
    post-horn gallop by the bar.

Yet a further stage my goal on—we
    were whirling down to Solon,
With a double lurch and roll on, best
    foot foremost, *ganz und gar*—
"She was *very* sweet," I hinted. "If a
    kiss had been imprinted?"—
" 'Would ha' saved a world of trouble!"
    clashed the busy tonga-bar.
" 'Been accepted or rejected!" banged
    and clanged the tonga-bar.

Then a notion wild and daring, 'spite
    the income tax's paring,
And a hasty thought of sharing—less
    than many incomes are,
Made me put a question private, you
    can guess what I would drive at.
"You must work the sum to prove it,"
    clanked the careless tonga-bar.
"Simple Rule of Two will prove it,"
    lilted back the tonga-bar.

It was under Khyraghaut I muse. "Sup-
    pose the maid be haughty—
(There are lovers rich—and forty)—
    wait some wealthy Avatar?
Answer monitor untiring, 'twixt the
    ponies twain perspiring!"
"Faint heart never won fair lady,"
    creaked the straining tonga-bar.
"Can I tell you ere you ask Her?"
    pounded slow the tonga-bar.

Last, the Tara Devi turning showed the
　　lights of Simla burning,
Lit my little lazy yearning to a fiercer
　　flame by far.
As below the Mail we jingled, through
　　my very heart it tingled—

Did the iterated order of the threshing
　　tonga-bar—
"Try your luck—you can't do better!"
　　twanged the loosened tonga-bar.

An Old Song

So long as 'neath the Kalka hills
　　The tonga-horn shall ring,
So long as down the Solon dip
　　The hard-held ponies swing,
So long as Tara Devi sees
　　The lights o' Simla town,
So long as Pleasure calls us up,
　　And duty drives us down,
　　　If you love me as I love you,
　　　What pair so happy as we two?

So long as Aces take the King,
　　Or backers take the bet,
So long as debt leads men to wed,
　　Or marriage leads to debt,
So long as little luncheons, Love,
　　And scandal hold their vogue,
While there is sport at Annandale
　　Or whiskey at Jutogh,
　　　If you love me as I love you,
　　　What knife can cut our love in two?

So long as down the rocking floor
　　The raving polka spins,
So long as Kitchen Lancers spur
　　The maddened violins,
So long as through the whirling smoke
　　We hear the oft-told tale:
"Twelve hundred in the Lotteries,"
　　And *Whatshername* for sale?
　　　If you love me as I love you,
　　　We'll play the game and win it too.

So long as Lust or Lucre tempt
　　Straight riders from the course,
So long as with each drink we pour
　　Black brewage of Remorse,
So long as those unloaded guns
　　We keep beside the bed
Blow off, by obvious accident,
　　The lucky owner's head,
　　　If you love me as I love you,
　　　What can Life kill or Death undo?

So long as Death 'twixt dance and dance
　　Chills best and bravest blood,
And drops the reckless rider down
　　The rotten, rain-soaked *khud*,
So long as rumors from the North
　　Make loving wives afraid,
So long as Burma takes the boy
　　And typhoid kills the maid,
　　　If you love me as I love you,
　　　What knife can cut our love in two?

By all that lights our daily life
　　Or works our lifelong woe,
From Boileaugunge to Simla Downs
　　And those grim glades below,
Where, heedless of the flying hoof
　　And clamor overhead,
Sleep, with the grey langur for guard,
　　Our very scornful Dead,
　　　If you love me as I love you,
　　　All Earth is servant to us two?

By Docket, Billetdoux, and File,
  By Mountain, Cliff, and Fir,
By Fan and Sword and Office-box
  By Corset Plume, and Spur,
By Riot, Revel, Waltz, and War,
  By Women Work and Bills,

By all the life that fizzes in
  The everlasting Hills,
    If you love me as I love you,
    What pair so happy as we two?

———•———

Certain Maxims of Hafiz

I.

If It be pleasant to look on, stalled in
  the packed *serai,*
Does not the Young Man try Its tem-
  per and pace ere he buy?
If She be pleasant to look on, what
  does the Young Man say?
"Lo! She is pleasant to look on, give
  Her to me to-day!"

II.

Yea, though a Kafir die, to him is remitted Jehannum
If he borrowed in life from a native at
  sixty per cent. per annum.

III.

Blister we not for *bursati?* So when
  the heart is vexed,
The pain of one maiden's refusal is
  drowned in the pain of the next.

IV.

The temper of chums, the love of your
  wife, and a new piano's tune—
Which of the three will you trust at the
  end of an Indian June?

V.

Who are the rulers of Ind—to whom
  shall we bow the knee?
Make your peace with the women, and
  men will make you L. G.

VI.

Does the woodpecker flit round the
  young *ferash?*
Does grass clothe a new-built wall?
Is she under thirty, the woman who
  holds a boy in her thrall?

VII.

If She grow suddenly gracious—reflect.
  Is it all for thee?
The black-buck is stalked through the
  bullock, and Man through jealousy.

VIII.

Seek not for favor of women. So shall
  you find it indeed.
Does not the boar break cover just when
  you're lighting a weed?

IX.

If He play, being young and unskilful,
  for shekels of silver and gold,
Take His money, my son, praising Allah.
  The kid was ordained to be sold.

X.

With a "weed" among men or horses
  verily this is the best,
That you work him in office or dog-cart
  lightly—but give him no rest.

XI.

Pleasant the snaffle of Courtship, improving the manners and carriage;
But the colt who is wise will abstain
from the terrible thorn-bit of Marriage.

XII.

As the thriftless gold of the *babul,* so
is the gold that we spend
On a Derby Sweep, or our neighbor's
wife, or the horse that we buy from
a friend.

XIII.

The ways of man with a maid be
strange, yet simple and tame
To the ways of a man with a horse,
when selling or racing that same.

. XIV.

In public Her face turneth to thee, and
pleasant Her smile when ye meet.
It is ill. The cold rocks of El-Gidar
smile thus on the waves at their
feet.
In public Her face is averted, with anger
She nameth thy name.
It is well. Was there ever a loser content with the loss of the game?

XV.

If She have spoken a word, remember
thy lips are sealed,
And the Brand of the Dog is upon him
by whom is the secret revealed.
If She have written a letter, delay not
an instant, but burn it.

Tear it in pieces, O Fool, and the wind
to her mate shall return it!
If there be trouble to Herward, and a
lie of the blackest can clear,
Lie, while thy lips can move or a man
is alive to hear.

XVI.

My Son, if a maiden deny thee and scuf-
flingly bid thee give o'er,
Yet lip meets with lip at the lastword—
get out!
She has been there before.
They are pecked on the ear and the
chin and the nose who are lacking
in lore.

XVII.

If we fall in the race, though we win,
the hoof-slide is scarred on the
course.
Though Allah and Earth pardon Sin, re-
maineth forever Remorse.

XVIII.

"By all I am misunderstood!" if the
Matron shall say, or the Maid:
"Alas! I do not understand," my son,
be thou nowise afraid.
In vain in the sight of the Bird is the
net of the Fowler displayed.

XIX.

My son, if I, Hafiz, thy father, take
hold of thy knees in my pain,
Demanding thy name on stamped paper,
one day or one hour—refrain.
Are the links of thy fetters so light that
thou cravest another man's chain?

The Grave of the Hundred Head

There's a widow in sleepy Chester
* Who weeps for her only son;*
There's a grave on the Pabeng River,
* A grave that the Burmans shun,*
And there's Subadar Prag Tewarri
* Who tells how the work was done.*

A SNIDER spuibbed in the jungle,
  Somebody laughed and fled,
And the men of the First Shikaris
  Picked up their Subaltern dead,
With a big blue mark in his forehead
  And the back blown out of his head.

Subadar Prag Tewarri,
  Jemadar Hira Lal,
Took command of the party,
  Twenty rifles in all,
Marched them down to the river
  As the day was beginning to fall.

They buried the boy by the river,
  A blanket over his face —
They wept for their dead Lieutenant,
  The men of an alien race—
They made a *samádh* in his honor,
  A mark for his resting-place.

For they swore by the Holy Water,
  They swore by the salt they ate,
That the soul of Lieutenant Eshmitt
    Sahib
  Should go to his God in state;
With fifty file of Burman
  To open him Heaven's gate.

The men of the First Shikaris
  Marched till the break of day,
Till they came to the rebel village,
  The village of Pabengmay—
A *jingal* covered the clearing,
  Calthrops hampered the way.

Subadar Prag Tewarri,
  Bidding them load with ball,
Halted a dozen rifles
  Under the village wall;
Sent out a flanking-party
  With Jemadar Hira Lal.

The men of the First Shikaris
  Shouted and smote and slew,
Turning the grinning *jingal*
  On to the howling crew.
The Jemadar's flanking-party
  Butchered the folk who flew.

Long was the morn of slaughter,
  Long was the list of slain,
Five score heads were taken,
  Five score heads and twain;
And the men of the First Shikaris
  Went back to their grave again,

Each man bearing a basket
  Red as his palms that day,
Red as the blazing village—
  The village of Pabengmay.
And the *"drip-drip-drip"* from the bas-
    kets
  Reddened the grass by the way.

They made a pile of their trophies
  High as a tall man's chin,
Head upon head distorted,
  Set in a sightless grin,
Anger and pain and terror
  Stamped on the smoke-scorched skin.

Subadar Prag Tewarri
  Put the head of the Boh
On the top of the mound of triumph,
  The head of his son below,
With the sword and the peacock-ban-
    ner
  That the world might behold and
    know.

Thus the *samâdh* was perfect,
  Thus was the lesson plain

Of the wrath of the First Shikaris—
  The price of a white man slain;
And the men of the First Shikaris
  Went back into camp again.

Then a silence came to the river,
  A hush fell over the shore,
And Bohs that were brave departed,
  And Sniders squibbed no more;
    For the Burmans said
    That a *kullah's* head
Must be paid for with heads five score.

There's a widow in sleepy Chester
  Who weeps for her only son;
There's a grave on the Pabeng River,
  A grave that the Burmans shun,
And there's Subadar Prag Tewarri
  Who tells how the work was done.

The Moon of Other Days

BENEATH the deep veranda's shade,
  When bats begin to fly,
I sit me down and watch—alas!—
  Another evening die.
Blood-red behind the sere *ferash*
  She rises through the haze.
Sainted Diana! can that be
  The Moon of Other Days?

Ah! shade of little Kitty Smith,
  Sweet Saint of Kensington!
Say, was it ever thus at Home
  The Moon of August shone,
When arm in arm we wandered long
  Through Putney's evening haze,
And Hammersmith was Heaven beneath
  The Moon of Other Days?

But Wandle's stream is Sutlej now,
  And Putney's evening haze
The dust that half a hundred kine
  Before my window raise.
Unkempt, unclean, althwart the mist
  The seething city looms,
In place of Putney's golden gorse
  The sickly *babul* blooms.

Glare down, old Hecate, through the
    dust,
  And bid the pie-dog yell,
Draw from the drain its typhoid-germ,
  From each bazaar its smell;
Yea, suck the fever from the tank
  And sap my strength therewith:
Thank Heaven, you show a smiling face
  To little Kitty Smith!

The Overland Mail

(*Foot-Service to the Hills*)

IN the name of the Empress of India,
make way,
  O Lords of the Jungle, wherever you
roam.
The woods are astir at the close of the
day—
  We exiles are waiting for letters from
Home.
Let the robber retreat—let the tiger turn
tail—
In the Name of the Empress, the Over-
land Mail!

With a jingle of bells as the dusk gath-
ers in,
  He turns to the foot-path that heads
up the hill—
The bags on his back and a cloth round
his chin,
  And, tucked in his waist-belt, the
Post Office bill:
"Despatched on this date, as received
by the rail,
Per runner, two bags of the Overland
Mail."

Is the torrent in spate? He must ford
it or swim.
  Has the rain wrecked the road? He
must climb by the cliff.
Does the tempest cry "Halt"? What
are tempests to him?
  The Service admits not a "but" or
an "if."
While the breath's in his mouth, he
must bear without fail,
In the Name of the Empress, the Overland Mail.

From aloe to rose-oak, from rose-oak
to fir,
  From level to upland, from upland to
crest,
From rice-field to rock-ridge, from rock-
ridge to spur,
  Fly the soft sandalled feet, strains the
brawny brown chest.
From rail to ravine—to the peak from
the vale—
Up, up through the night goes the Overland Mail.

There's a speck on the hillside, a dot
on the road—
  A jingle of bells on the foot-path below—
There's a scuffle above in the monkey's
abode—
  The world is awake, and the clouds
are aglow.
For the great Sun himself must attend
to the hail:
"In the name of the Empress the Overland Mail!"

What the People Said

(June 21st, 1887)

By the well, where the bullocks go
Silent and blind and slow—
By the field where the young corn dies
In the face of the sultry skies,
They have heard, as the dull Earth hears
The voice of the wind of an hour,
The sound of the Great Queen's voice:
"My God hath given me years,
Hath granted dominion and power:
And I bid you, O Land, rejoice."

And the ploughman settles the share
More deep in the grudging clod;
For he saith: "The wheat is my care,
And the rest is the will of God.
He sent the Mahratta spear
As He sendeth the rain,
And the *Mlech,* in the fated year,
Broke the spear in twain.
And was broken in turn. Who knows
How our Lords make strife?
It is good that the young wheat grows,
For the bread is Life."

Then, far and near, as the twilight
    drew,
  Hissed up to the scornful dark
Great serpents, blazing, of red and blue,
That rose and faded, and rose anew,
  That the Land might wonder and
    mark

"To-day is a day of days," they said,
"Make merry, O People, all!"
And the Ploughman listened and bowed
    his head:
"To-day and to-morrow God's will," he
    said,
As he trimmed the lamps on the wall.

"He sendeth us years that are good,
As He sendeth the dearth.
He giveth to each man his food,
Or Her food to the Earth.
Our Kings and our Queens are afar—
On their peoples be peace—
God bringeth the rain to the Bar,
That our cattle increase."

And the Ploughman settled the share
More deep in the sun-dried clod:
"Mogul Mahratta, and *Mlech* from the
    North,
And White Queen over the Seas—
God raiseth them up and driveth them
    forth
As the dust of the ploughshare flies in
    the breeze;
But the wheat and the cattle are all my
    care,
And the rest is the will of God."

The Undertaker's Horse

"To-TSCHIN-SHU is condemned to death. How can he drink tea with the Executioner?"—*Japanese Proverb*.

THE eldest son bestrides him,
And the pretty daughter rides him,
And I meet him oft o' mornings on the Course;
And there wakens in my bosom
An emotion chill and gruesome
As I canter past the Undertaker's Horse.

Neither shies he nor is restive,
But a hideously suggestive
Trot, professional and placid, he affects;
And the cadence of his hoof-beats
To my mind, this grim reproof beats:
"Mend your pace, my friend, I'm coming.
    Who's the next?"

Ah! stud-bred of ill-omen,
I have watched the strongest go—men
Of pith and might and muscle—at your heels,
Down the plantain-bordered highway,
(Heaven send it ne'er be my way!)
In a lacquered box and jetty upon wheels.

Answer, sombre beast and dreary,
Where is Brown, the young, the cheery,
Smith, the pride of all his friends and half the Force?
You were at that last dread *dak*
We must cover at a walk
Bring them back to me, O Undertaker's Horse!

With your name unhogged and flowing,
And your curious way of going,
And that business-like black crimping of your tail,
E'en with Beauty on your back, sir,
Pacing as a lady's hack, Sir,
What wonder when I meet you I turn pale?

It may be you wait your time, Beast,
Till I write my last bad rhyme, Beast,
Quit the sunlight, cut the rhyming, drop the glass,
Follow after with the others,
Where some dusky heathen smothers
Us with marigolds in lieu of English grass.

Or, perchance, in years to follow,
I shall watch your plump sides hollow,
See Carnifex (gone lame) become a corse,
See old age at last o'erpower you,
And the Station Pack devour you,
I shall chuckle then, O Undertaker's Horse!

But to insult, gibe, and quest I've
Still the hideously suggestive
Trot that hammers out the grim and warning text,
And I hear it hard behind me,
In what place soe'er I find me:
"Sure to catch you sooner or later.
    Who's the next?"

The Fall of Jock Gillespie

THIS fell when dinner-time was done—
'Twixt the first an' the second rub—
That oor mon Jock cam' hame again
To his rooms abint the Club.

An' syne he laughed, an' syne he sang,
An' syne we thocht him fou,
An' syne he trumped his partner's trick,
An' garred his partner rue.

Then up and spake an elder mon,
That held the Spade its Ace—
"God save the lad! Whence comes the
lick,
That wimples on his face?"

An' Jock he sniggered, an' Jock he
smiled,
An' ower the card-brim wunk:
"I'm a' too fresh fra' the stirrup-peg,
May be that I am drunk."

"There's whusky brewed in Galashiels,
An' L. L. L. forbye;
But never liquor lit the low
That keeks fra' oot your eye.

"There's a thrid o' hair on your dress-
coat breast,
Aboon the heart a' wee?"
"Oh! that is fra' the lang-haired Skye
That slobbers ower me."

"Oh! lang-haired Skyes are lovin'
beasts,
An' terrier dogs are fair,
But never yet was terrier born
Wi' ell-lang gowden hair!

"There's a smirch o' pouther on your
breast,
Below the left lappel?"
"Oh! that is fra' my auld cigar,
Whenas the stump-end fell."

"Mon Jock, ye smoke the Trichi coarse
For ye are short o' cash,
An' best Havanas couldna leave
Sae white an' pure an ash.

Last nicht ye told that tale yoursel,
An' stopped it wi' a curse—
Last nicht ye told that tale yoursel,
An' capped it wi' a worse!

"Oh! we're no fou! Oh! we're no fou!
But plainly we can ken
Ye're fallin', fallin', fra' the band
O' cantie single men!"

An' it fell when *sirris*-shaws were sere,
An' the nichts were lang and mirk,
In braw new breeks, wi' a gowden ring,
Oor Jockie gaed to the Kirk.

Arithmetic on the Frontier

A GREAT and glorious thing it is
  To learn, for seven years or so,
The Lord knows what of that and this,
  Ere reckoned fit to face the foe—
The flying bullet down the Pass,
That whistles clear: "All flesh is grass."

Three hundred pounds per annum spent
  On making brain and body meeter
For all the murderous intent
  Comprised in "villanous saltpetre!"
And after—ask the Yusufzaies
What comes of all our 'ologies.

A scrimmage in a Border Station—
  A canter down some dark defile—
Two thousand pounds of education
  Drops to a ten-rupee *jezail*—
The Crammer's boast, the Squadron's
    pride,
Shot like a rabbit in a ride!

No proposition Euclid wrote,
  No formulæ the text-books know,
Will turn the bullet from your coat,
  Or ward the tulwar's downward blow.
Strike hard who cares—shoot straight
    who can—
The odds are on the cheaper man.

One sword-knot stolen from the camp
  Will pay for all the school expenses
Of any Kurrum Valley scamp
  Who knows no word or moods and
    tenses,
But, being blessed with perfect sight,
Picks off our messmates left and right.

With home-bred hordes the hillsides
    teem,
  The troop-ships bring us one by one,
At vast expense of time and steam,
  To slay Afridis where they run.
The "captives of our bow and spear"
Are cheap—alas! as we are dear.

———— • ————

One Viceroy Resigns

(*Lord Dufferin to Lord Lansdowne*)

So here's your Empire. No more wine,
    then?
Good.
We'll clear the Aides and *khitmatgars*
    away.
(You'll know that fat old fellow with
    the knife—
He keeps the Name Book, talks in Eng-
    lish too,

And almost thinks himself the Govern-
    ment.)
O Youth, Youth, Youth! Forgive me,
    you're so young.
Forty from sixty—twenty years of
    work
And power to back the working. *Ay de
    mi!*

You want to know, you want to see, to
touch,
And, by your lights, to act. It's natural.
I wonder can I help you. Let me try.
You saw—what did you see from Bom-
bay east?
Enough to frighten any one but me?
Neat that! It frightened Me in Eighty-
Four!
You shouldn't take a man from Canada
And bid him smoke in powder-maga-
zines;
Nor with a Reputation such as—Bah!
That ghost has haunted me for twenty
years,
My Reputation now full blown—Your
fault—
Yours, with your stories of the strife at
Home,
Who's up, who's down, who leads and
who is led—
One reads so much, one hears so little
here.
Well now's your turn of exile. I go back
To Rome and leisure. All roads lead to
Rome,

Or books—the refuge of the destitute.
When you . . . that brings me back to
India. See!
   Start clear. I couldn't. Egypt served
my turn.
You'll never plumb the Oriental mind,
And if you did it isn't worth the toil.
Think of a sleek French priest in Can-
ada;
Divide by twenty half-breeds. Multiply
By twice the Sphinx's silence. There's
your East,
And you're as wise as ever. So am I.
   Accept on trust and work in darkness,
strike

At venture, stumble forward, make your
mark,
(It's chalk on granite), then thank God
no flame
Leaps from the rock to shrivel mark and
man.
I'm clear—my mark is made. Three
months of drought
Had ruined much. It rained and washed
away
The specks that might have gathered on
my Name.
I took a country twice the size of
France,
And shuttered up one doorway in the
North.
I stand by those. You'll find that both
will pay,
I pledged my Name on both—they're
yours to-night.
Hold to them—they hold fame enough
for two.
I'm old, but I shall live till Burma pays.
Men there—*not* German traders—Cr-
sthw-te knows—
You'll find it in my papers. For the
North
Guns always—quietly—but always guns.
You've seen your Council? Yes, they'll
try to rule,
And prize their Reputations. Have you
met
A grim lay-reader with a taste for coins,
And faith in Sin most men withhold
from God?
He's gone to England. R-p-n knew his
grip
And kicked. A Council always has its
H-pes.
They look for nothing from the West
but Death
Or Bath or Bournemouth. Here's their
ground.

They fight
Until the middle classes take them
    back,
One of ten millions plus a C. S. I.
Or drop in harness. Legion of the Lost?
Not altogether—earnest, narrow men,
But chiefly earnest, and they'll do your
    work,
And end by writing letters to the *Times*.
(Shall *I* write letters, answering H-nt-r
    —fawn
With R-p-n on the Yorkshire grocers?
    Ugh!)
They have their Reputations. Look to
    one—
I work with him—the smallest of them
    all,
White-haired, red-faced, who sat the
    plunging horse
Out in the garden. He's your right-hand
    man,
And dreams of tilting W-ls-y from the
    throne,
But while he dreams gives work we
    cannot buy;
He has his Reputation—wants the Lords
By way of Frontier Roads. Meantime,
    I think,
He values very much the hand that
    falls
Upon his shoulder at the Council table—
Hates cats and knows his business:
    which is yours.
  Your business! Twice a hundred mil-
    lion souls.
Your business! I could tell you what
    I did
Some nights of Eighty-Five, at Simla,
    worth
A Kingdom's ransom. When a big ship
    drives,
God knows to what new reef the man
    at the wheel

Prays with the passengers. They lose
    their lives,
Or rescued go their way; but he's no
    man
To take his trick at the wheel again—
    that's worse
Than drowning. Well, a galled Masho-
    bra mule
(You'll see Mashobra) passed me on the
    Mall,
And I was—some fool's wife had ducked
    and bowed
To show the others I would stop and
    speak.
Then the mule fell—three galls, a hand-
    breadth each,
Behind the withers. Mrs. Whatsisname
Leers at the mule and me by turns,
    thweet thoul!
"How could they make him carry such
    a load!"
I saw—it isn't often I dream dreams—
More than the mule that minute—smoke
    and flame
From Simla to the haze below. That's
    weak.
You're younger. You'll dream dreams
    before you've done.
You've youth, that's one—good work-
    men—that means two
Fair chances in your favor. Fate's the
    third.
I know what *I* did. Do you ask me,
    "Preach"?
I answer by my past or else go back
To platitudes of rule—or take you thus
In confidence and say: "You know the
    trick:
You've governed Canada. You know.
    You know!"
And all the while commend you to Fate's
    hand
(Here at the top one loses sight o' God),

Commend you, then, to something more
    than you—
The Other People's blunders and
    . . . that's all.
I'd agonize to serve you if I could.
It's incommunicable, like the cast
That drops the tackle with the gut adry.
Too much—too little—there's your sal-
    mon lost!
And so I tell you nothing—wish you
    luck,
And wonder—how I wonder!—for your
    sake
And triumph for my own. You're young,
    you're young,
You hold to half a hundred Shibboleths.
I'm old. I followed Power to the last,
Gave her my best, and Power followed
    Me.
It's worth it—on my soul I'm speaking
    plain,
Here by the claret glasses!—worth it all.
I gave—no matter what I gave—I win.
I *know* I win. Mine's work, good work
    that live!
A country twice the size of France—the
    North
Safeguarded. That's my record: sink
    the rest
And better if you can. The Rains may
    serve,
Rupees may rise—three pence will give
    you Fame—
It's rash to hope for sixpence—If they
    rise
Get guns, more guns, and lift the salt-
    tax.
                      Oh!
I told you what the Congress meant or
    thought?
I'll answer nothing. Half a year will
    prove

The full extent of time and thought
    you'll spare
To Congress. Ask a Lady Doctor
    once
How little Begums see the light—de-
    duce
Thence how the True Reformer's child
    is born.
It's interesting, curious . . . and
    vile.
I told the Turk he was a gentleman.
I told the Russian that his Tartar veins
Bled pure Parisian ichor; and he purred.
The Congress doesn't purr. I think it
    swears.
You're young—you'll swear too ere
    you've reached the end.
The End! God help you, if there be a
    God.
(There must be one to startle Gl-dst-ne's
    soul
In that new land where all the wires
    are cut.
And Cr-ss snores anthems on the aspho-
    del.)
God help you! And I'd help you if I
    could,
But that's beyond me. Yes, your speech
    was crude.
Sound claret after olives—yours and
    mine;
But Medoc slips into vin ordinaire.
(I'll drink my first at Genoa to your
    health.)
Raise it to Hock. You'll never catch
    my style.
And, after all, the middle-classes grip
The middle-class—for Brompton talk
    Earl's Court.
Perhaps you're right. I'll see you in
    the *Times*—
A quarter-column of eye-searing print,
A leader once a quarter—then a war;

The Strand abellow through the fog:
"Defeat!"
" 'Orrible slaughter!" While you lie
awake
And wonder. Oh, you'll wonder ere
you're free!
I wonder now. The four years slide
away
So fast, so fast, and leave me here
alone.
R—y, C-lv-n, L—l, R-b-rts, B-ck, the
rest,
Princes and Powers of Darkness troops
and trains,
  (I *cannot* sleep in trains, land piled
on land,
Whitewash and weariness, red rockets,
dust,
White snows that mocked me, palaces—
with draughts,
And W-stl-nd with the drafts he couldn't
pay,
Poor W-ls-n reading his obituary.
Before he died, and H-pe, the man with
bones,
And A-tch-s-n a dripping mackintosh
At Council in the Rains, his grating
"Sirrr"
Half drowned by H-nt-r's silky: "Bát
my lanhd."
Hunterian always: M-rsh-l spinning
plates

Or standing on his head; the Rent Bill's
roar,
A hundred thousand speeches, much red
cloth,
And Smiths thrice happy if I call them
Jones,
(I can't remember half their names) or
reined
My pony on the Mall to greet their
wives.
More trains, more troops, more dust,
and then all's done.
Four years, and I forget. If I forget
How will *they* bear me in their minds?
The North
Safeguarded—nearly (R-b-rts knows the
rest),
A country twice the size of France an-
nexed.
That stays at least. The rest may pass
—may pass—
Your heritage—and I can teach you
nought.
"High trust," "vast honor," "interests
twice as vast,"
"Due reverence to your Council"—keep
to those.
I envy you the twenty years you've
gained,
But not the five to follow. What's that?
One?
Two!—Surely not so late. Good-night.
Don't dream.

The Betrothed

"You must choose between me and your
cigar."

Open the old cigar-box, get me a Cuba
stout,
For things are running crossways, and
Maggie and I are out.

We quarreled about Havanas—we fought
o'er a good cheroot,
And I know she is exacting, and she
says I am a brute.

Open the old cigar-box—let me consider
a space;
In the soft blue veil of the vapor, mu-
sing on Maggie's face.

Maggie is pretty to look at—Maggie's a
loving lass,
But the prettiest cheeks must wrinkle,
the truest of loves must pass.

There's peace in a Laraaga, there's calm
in a Henry Clay,
But the best cigar in an hour is finished
and thrown away—

Thrown away for another as perfect
and ripe and brown—
But I could not throw away Maggie for
fear o' the talk o' the town!

Maggie, my wife at fifty—grey and
dour and old—
With never another Maggie to purchase
for love or gold!

And the light of Days that have Been
the dark of the Days that Are,
And Love's torch stinking and stale,
like the butt of a dead cigar—

The butt of a dead cigar you are bound
to keep in your pocket—
With never a new one to light tho' it's
charred and black to the socket.

Open the old cigar-box—let me consider
a while—
Here is a mild Manilla—there is a wifely smile.

Which is the better portion—bondage
bought with a ring,
Or a harem of dusky beauties fifty tied
in a string?

Counsellors cunning and silent—com-
forters true and tried,
And never a one of the fifty to sneer
at a rival bride.

Thought in the early morning, solace
in time of woes,
Peace in the hush of the twilight, balm
ere my eyelids close.

This will the fifty give me, asking nought
in return,
With only a *Suttee's* passion—to do their
duty and burn.

This will the fifty give me. When they
are spent and dead,
Five times other fifties shall be my servants instead.

The furrows of far-off Java, the isles
of the Spanish Main,
When they hear my harem is empty,
will send me my brides again.

I will take no heed to their raiment, nor
food for their mouths withal,
So long as the gulls are nesting, so long
as the showers fall.

I will scent 'em with best vanilla, with
tea will I temper their hides,
And the Moor and the Mormon shall
envy who read of the tale of my
brides.

For Maggie has written a letter to give
me my choice between
The wee little whimpering Love and the
great god Nick o' Teen.

And I have been servant of Love for
barely a twelvemonth clear,
But I have been Priest of Partagas a
matter of seven year;

And the gloom of my bachelor days is
    flecked with the cheery light
Of stumps that I burned to Friendship
    and Pleasure and Work and Fight.

And I turn my eyes to the future that
    Maggie and I must prove,
But the only light on the marshes is the
    Will-o'-the-Wisp of Love.

Will it see me -safe through my journey,
    or leave me bogged in the mire?
Since a puff of tobacco can cloud it,
    shall I follow the fitful fire?

Open the old cigar-box—let me consider
    anew—
Old friends, and who is Maggie that I
    should abandon *you?*

A million surplus Maggies are willing to
    bear the yoke;
And a woman is only a woman, but a
    good cigar is a Smoke.

Light me another Cuba; I hold to my
    first-sworn vows,
If Maggie will have no rival, I'll have
    no Maggie for spouse!

A Tale of Two Cities

WHERE the sober-colored cultivator
        smiles
        On his *byles;*
Where the cholera, the cyclone, and the
        crow
        Come and go;
Where the merchant deals in indigo and
        tea,
        Hides and *ghi;*
Where the Babu drops inflammatory
        hints
        In his prints;
Stands a City—Charnock chose it—
        packed away
        Near a Bay—
By the sewage rendered fetid, by the
        sewer
        Made impure,
By the Sunderbunds unwholesome, by
        the swamp
        Moist and damp;
And the City and the Viceroy, as we
        see,
        Don't agree.

Once, two hundred years ago, the trader
        came
        Meek and tame.
Where his timid foot first halted, there
        he stayed,
        Till mere trade
Grew to Empire, and he sent his armies
        forth
        South and North
Till the country from Peshawur to Cey-
        lon
        Was his own.
Thus the midday halt of Charnock—
        more's the pity!
        Grew a City.
As the fungus sprouts chaotic from its
        bed,
        So it spread—
Chance-directed, chance-erected, laid
        and built
        On the silt—
Palace, byre, hovel—poverty and
        pride—
        Side by side;

And, above tne packed and pestilential
town,
　　　Death looked down.
But the Rulers in that City by the Sea
　　　Turned to flee—
Fled, with each returning spring-tide
from its ills
　　　To the Hills.
From the clammy fogs of morning,
from the blaze
　　　Of the days,
From the sickness of the noontide, from
the heat,
　　　Beat retreat;
For the country from Peshawur to Cey-
lon
　　　Was their own.
But the Merchant risked the perils of
the Plain
　　　For his gain.
Now the resting-place of Charnock,
'neath the palms,
　　　Asks an alms,
And the burden of its lamentation is,
　　　Briefly, this:
"Because for certain months, we boil
and stew,
　　　So should you.
Cast the Viceroy and his Council, to
perspire
　　　In our fire!"
And for answer to the argument, in vain
　　　We explain

That an amateur Saint Lawrence cannot
fry:
　　　"*All* must fry!"
That the Merchant risks the perils of
the Plain
　　　For his gain.
Nor can Rulers rule a house that men
grow rich in,
　　　From its kitchen.
Let the Babu drop inflammatory hints
　　　In his prints;
And mature—consistent soul—his plan
for stealing
　　　To Darjeeling:
Let the Merchant seek, who makes his
silver pile,
　　　England's isle;
Let the City Charnock pitched on—evil
day!
　　　Go Her way.
Though the argosies of Asia at Her
doors
　　　Heap their stores,
Though Her enterprise and enegry se-
cure
　　　Income sure,
Though "out-station orders punctually
obeyed"
　　　Swell Her trade—
Still, for rule, administration, and the
rest,
　　　Simla's best.

Hitherto Uncollected

The Lamentable Comedy of Willow Wood

O ye, all ye that walk in Willow Wood,
   That walk with hollow faces burning white;
What fathom-depth of soul-struck widow-
   hood,
   What long, what longers hours, one life-
   long night,
Ere ye again, who so in vain have wooed
   Your last hope lost, who so in vain invite
Your lips to that their unforgotten food,
   Ere ye, ere ye again shall see the light!

PERSONS CHIEFLY CONCERNED

HE (*a man*).
SHE (*a woman*).

SCENE.—*Grey Down, late in the afternoon;
a sea-fog coming over the cliffs.*

HE. (*Roan horse, second-best saddlery,
double-mouthed snaffle, nose-band, no
spurs, crop.*) It feels as though it were
going to rain. Suppose we . . .

SHE. (*Bay horse, third-best habit,
cloth cap, double bridle, martingale, and
worn gauntlets.*) I've nothing on that
can spoil, and there's nothing to go back
for before dinner. I *must* say the Deeleys
are the dearest hosts in the world. Fancy
them letting me take out Mickey. I
always thought he was specially reserved
for Mrs. Deeley.

HE. (*Aside.*) Exactly! Gets the pick
of the stable—hauls a man out of the
smoking-room, and *he* gets—Hold up,
you brute!—a yorking hog of a hack with
the mouth of a turnstile and the manners
of a steam-engine, and so must wait her
pleasure. (*Aloud.*) Yes, it's one of the
nicest country houses I know, but look
at this beast. The head-groom doesn't
love me.

SHE. (*Aside.*) Hands of a butcher,
if you only knew it. (*Aloud.*) I'm
afraid you have been unlucky. But
misfortunes never come singly. It was
your fault for loafing so aggressively in
the smoking-room.

HE. As how?

SHE. I saw you from the garden, and
it seemed that you might just as well
take me out as loll on a sofa. So I suggested to Mrs. Deeley—and there really
was no one else available. (*Aside.*)
Mustn't sulk for half an hour and not
expect to be paid out.

HE. Thank you. I had supposed there wasn't. They all went out after lunch. Er—er! have you noticed the deep interest that the young take in Norman ruins when two can look at them at the same time? It's natural, I suppose. (*Aside.*) I know she saw young Oulthorp go out with Miss Massing.

SHE. (*Aside.*) To my address, but clumsy. (*Aloud.*) Yes, I suggested their going.

HE. (*Aside.*) What an atrocious fib. I believe she sleeps regularly after lunch, and I know she never lets Oulthorp look at Miss Massing. (*Aloud.*) Well, shall we canter on and pick up our archeologists?

SHE. (*Sweetly.*) Can't you hold him in, then? He is dancing a little bit; but perhaps you are irritating his poor dear mouth?

HE. Poor dear mouth! He never had such a thing in his life.

SHE. But he must have some feelings, and it is hardly worth while harrowing them because your own are upset.

HE. You are saddling me with all sorts of sins that never came into my head. Of course I'm delighted to be your escort.

SHE. Of course. What else could you say?

HE. This only. If it has seemed good to you to drag out an almost entire stranger for a ride in this particularly sloppy country, I don't see that it is worth while squabbling with him. (*Aside.*) It's a strong face and I like it, but I hate having my riding scoffed at.

SHE. You are a remarkably plain-spoken person.

HE. I'm afraid I was led into it. Also I'll confess I did sulk.

SHE. I know you did, and I don't

wonder. After all, it must be a bore to entertain a woman who—how was it?— "goes to sleep over her soup and looks as though she fed on bolsters." Eh?

HE. (*Aside.*) Oh, damn!

SHE. You should never become confidential in the smoking-room with Mr. Dollin. He tells his wife everything, and she, not being too wise, tells me.

HE. (*Aside.*) I wonder if this is her method of being engaging. It is monotonous. (*Aloud.*) I deny every word of it. Dollin misunderstood.—Did Mrs. Dollin tell you everything that was said in the smoking-room?

SHE. (*Aside.*) Curiously alike men are when you make them uncomfortable. (*Aloud.*) Thank you. I know what you mean. Yes, she did; and I must say that you men might find some better amusement than making fun of poor Mr. Oulthorp.

HE. (*Aside.*) I thought so. (*Aloud, stiffly.*) Pardon me, but was it for this I was brought out?

SHE. No. But since you are here I may as well speak. Is it fair?

HE. There's a certain amount of frivolity in a smoking-room, and I suppose Oulthorp gets his share like everyone else.

SHE. But he doesn't like it.

HE. I'm afraid that makes no difference. (*Aside.*) This is a revelation. I object to being called to account like a schoolboy. (*Aloud.*) And you know Oulthorp is not very wise.

SHE. In that he is specially devoted to me?

HE. I never said that.

SHE. But what do you think?

HE. Nothing. Why should I? Am I his keeper—or yours? Indeed, I was no worse than the others.

SHE. No worse than the others! There speaks the man! Will you listen to me for a minute?

HE. It seems that I was invited to that end. (*Aside.*) If I sent my heel into the beast I know he'd bolt. Question is, could I pull him up this side the sunset. (*Aloud.*) Frankly, you know, I never understood what you saw in young Oulthorp—I mean what your object was in taking him up. As I said just now, he is not over wise, nor, for matter of that, very amusing.

SHE. (*After a pause.*) Have you ever been put on a pedestal and worshiped?

HE. No.

SHE. Have you ever known what it was to feel everything you said or did of more importance to one person than anything else in the world—to find yourself treated as absolutely perfect?

HE. Poor beggar! So bad as that, was he? (*Aside.*) I wonder if the beast would bolt. I don't like this talk.

SHE. But have you?

HE. N-no. Why should I?

SHE. How can I tell? And have you ever found all that trust, all that belief, and all that adoration bore you beyond words?

HE. (*As his heel goes home.*) Come round, you brute! Come round!

SHE. And yet have you felt thát you wouldn't give it up for anybody—that it was, somehow, a refuge from yourself, when you were afraid to think or remember? Can't you see? He believes in me absolutely.

HE. (*Looking between his horse's ears.*) Um!

SHE. (*Quickly.*) Has he said anything . . . in the smoking-room?

HE. Certainly not. (*Aside.*) Dollin

is a fool, but he has evidently sense enough not to tell everything.

SHE. Then what do you mean?

HE. Let us look this thing in the face since you will insist on scolding me. Will you do young Oulthorp any good?

SHE. I shall make a man of him, at least.

HE. I fancied Miss Massing was more than equal to that little business.

SHE. She is at perfect liberty—when I have finished.

HE. Which will be——?

SHE. When he goes of his own accord.

HE. Have you courage to wait for the end, then?

SHE. I don't think you quite understand. He bores me—horribly.

HE. So I am willing to believe.

SHE. Too good of you, I'm sure, to take the trouble. . . . It is only because he thinks me sweet and perfect. It is not (*in a low voice and slowly*) it is not—that I care; I don't. But I shall do him no harm—indeed I shan't.

HE. I have nothing to do with the affair.

SHE. Yes; you have. They'll listen to you for ever in the smoking-room. You have influence over them. Why can't you keep them amused, instead of helping to make fun of him? You tell them things—I know you do—for I hear of them from Mrs. Dollin.

HE. (*Aside.*) Seems to me that Dollin is making a burial service to be said over his own grave. (*Aloud.*) I never understood it was my mission to amuse a country house for the sake of young Oulthorp. And, really, do you think that a—a—regard that cannot stand a little chaff now and then——?

SHE. Oh, it will go fast enough under

any circumstances. Only—only I don't want to lose it before I must.

HE. (*Softly, looking at her.*) Forgive me. I'm *so* sorry.

SHE. Do I look like a woman who needs pity? Why should you give it to me?—I don't want it.

HE. Because of what must have gone before.

SHE. I don't know what you mean.

HE. Don't you? Would you like me to explain?

SHE. No. But what do you mean?

HE. Nothing. I ask no questions. Only, as a general rule, I imagine a woman does not take a deep interest in the blind adoration that a boy like Oulthorp gives—a boy for whom she does not care either—unless she has lost something much—much—more important.... But perhaps you are the exception?

SHE. (*Bowing her head.*) That's enough. I am the rule. . . . And now do you understand me?

HE. Less than ever, to tell you the truth.

SHE. Shall *I* tell you the truth for a change?

HE. At your own risk. Remember I can guess at the outlines, and you may hate me because you have told me. (*Aside.*) I wonder if she tells everybody. Couldn't be, 'r else I should have heard something about her in the smoking-room. What a chin it is!

SHE. Would you care if I hated you?

HE. Not a bit. It might worry you a little. Well, tell me.

SHE. (*After a pause.*) It's—it's difficult. There was—and I couldn't help it—and I had my warnings—lots of women told me about him, and I knew that he wasn't to be trusted, and I knew

that I was the only one who knew that. So I was sure of myself—and I was, you know. But I did care—everything, in every way. That was why, perhaps, it ended as it did. After seven years. My God, after seven years!

HE. And what did you do?

SHE. (*Simply.*) Said "Fank'oo," and went away smiling.

HE. You!

SHE. Yes, me! Why shouldn't I? It was everything in the world to me. And when it finished I hadn't the heart to complain.

HE. You don't look like a person who would be grateful for being treated in that way. And after?

SHE. I continued to exist beautifully —with variations.

HE. Of what kind?

SHE. Oh, pictures and the poor. Specially the poor. You can think sometimes if you sit alone painting. If you slumgullion you can't think. Many others have found out that trick, and the poor owe much to it. Then the boy —young Oulthorp came in, he was some sort of a rest. But I have found that I have a double brain that does its own thinking whatever I do. Did you ever find that?

HE. (*Incautiously.*) Yes, worse luck.

SHE. (*Aside.*) I knew the fire had gone over his face. (*Aloud and very slowly.*) Pleasant, isn't it—to find all the sorrow, and all the sacrifice——

HE. (*Hoarsely, looking into the fog.*) There's no sacrifice. I'll swear there isn't.

SHE. —*all* the sacrifice, the care and the tenderness, the forethought, the comprehension, and—and all the rest of it go for nothing just because one person has grown tired.

He. (*With a shiver.*) For goodness' sake, let's talk of something else.

She. (*Bitterly.*) What shall we talk about? Nice things—pretty things? Books and pictures and plays? I'm quite ready. You begin.

He. (*After a pause.*) Don't think the conversation led up to nice things, exactly.

She. How strange! Well?

He. Er—does the—does the pain last forever?

She. I don't know. I've only had four years of it—every day and all day long.

He. (*Feebly.*) Not really?

She. If—if the other thing was real, this is. It begins when I wake and it ends when I sleep—and it begins again when I wake again.

He. How you must hate that man!

She. Worse than that. I only hated a little in the beginning. Now I am beginning not to care. It's all over—all except the pain, and so, you see, it's doubly worthless. Believe me, if he were to cross the road now under my feet, I shouldn't even turn my head to—— Good God, what's that!

A shepherd jumps into the road from a bank. Mickey shies.

He. Drop your hands; he's going to bolt! Gone, by Jove! Do I follow?

She. (*Over her shoulder.*) Yes. I can just hold him. Come along! Where does this road end?

He. London, if you go far enough. Can you take a pull at your brute?

She. I'll try. (*Leans over.*) No! Wait till a hill tires him. I'm not afraid. Who'd have thought it in a quiet steady . . . I believe I *shall* be afraid in a minute. Ow! There goes my hair loose.

He. Shall I lean over and take a pull at him?

She. (*Gasping and pulling.*) No! Bring him down if you did. He's coming in—a—little—bit. Ouch! That's better. Steady, Mickey darling. There's nothing to be afraid of. Softly, old man. (*Pulls horse into a canter.*) I didn't like that.

He. Which? The man that appeared?

She. No. Trying to ride away from myself. We might have ended in a quarry.

He. It was the other beast behind him that drove Mickey mad. The best of horses get excited sometimes. By the way, have I to go back and pick up hairpins?

She. Poor thing—no. I'll bundle it up under my cap somehow with the few that remain to me. (*Aside.*) This man is a man. (*Aloud.*) I wish people wouldn't pop up so suddenly.

He. He came just in time to show how little you cared.

She. No, that was Mickey's fault.

He. Even if you caught Mickey short by the head and drove your spur into him.

She. I deny the spur. The other thing may be. (*Watching his face.*) It seems to please you, somehow.

He. No—I don't think so. But you *do* care for that man even now?

She. Yes.

He. In spite of everything?

She. In spite of everything—yes.

He. Good Lord!

She. I don't think He has anything to do with it. He doesn't even help one to forget. He leaves that to the Bambino.

He. That reminds me. Since we've gone so far, I shouldn't build too much on young Oulthorp's absolute devotion.

SHE. What do you mean? Julia Massing?

HE. Yes, I think so.

SHE. (*Absently*.) Little liar! He's like you, though.

HE. Why? *I* never adored you.

SHE. No, but you have lied to some-one else. I am certain of it.

HE. And if I did, what have you gained by keeping faith?

SHE. Seven years of life at least. I am only paying for them now.

HE. Is the price too high—are you sorry?

SHE. Yes, I am sorry—bitterly sorry —that I ever knew him. There's no dignity of tragedy to console me. I am sorry, and I laugh at myself for being sorry.

HE. But if you had the chance over again, what would you do?

SHE. Why do you ask—why do you want to find you? So that you may measure another woman's pain by mine; because you have treated some woman as . . . Is that it?

HE. I—I don't know.

SHE. But I do. (*Edging in towards him*.) Look at me. Even I—even I am Beatrice! That line at the corner of the eyes comes from crying—doctors will tell you so—crying till there are no more tears to cry. That little horseshoe in the forehead—now considered fascinating —comes from lying staring wide awake without shutting your eyes, night after night, thinking, thinking, thinking every-thing over again from the beginning. You can get that mark for life after three nights' pain. I have it. Those are the outward and visible signs—some of them. The mouth, too . . . (*Leaning to the off side*.)

HE. (*Dully*.) Yes, I see.

SHE. You don't. All you are think-ing of is——

HE. God forbid!

SHE. (*Leaning further*.) My dear sir, it would be quite enough if I (softening) gave permission.

HE. No, thank you. Not this dance.

SHE. (*Resettling herself in her saddle*.) Then I believe you do care for her.

HE. (*Aside*.) A chance missed. (*Aloud*.) Pooh! that's no proof. But you needn't continue your explanation.

SHE. I could say a lot if I chose.

HE. (*Leading toward the cliff's edge*.) Go on, then. You were talking about mental symptoms.

SHE. I was, but I won't go on. (*Aside, to herself*.) It seems to me that the fog or something is seriously affecting your brain, dear. Never mind. Dinner at eight, two gongs, and a fat man to take me in. Let us be thankful, O Civilization, for all thy mercies.

HE. I want you to, though.

SHE. Then I will. (*Aside*.) You will have it, and I would have let you off because you understood—a little. (*Aloud*.) There are one thousand differ-ent ways of going to perdition. She will probably choose the nine hundred and ninety-nine that I have not taken. And it will be your fault. She may even bless you later for setting her on one of those roads. Does that hurt sufficiently?

HE. I have known pleasanter things. Well?

SHE. There's no more to say. You can hurt yourself better than I can hurt you. How long was your affair for?

HE. Five years.

SHE. Who ended it?

HE. It ended itself.

SHE. Sweet child of nature! That

wrought *my* only woe. In other words, it was *your* vanity—as it was his.

HE. (*Aside.*) My turn now. (*Aloud.*) Perhaps your friend got tired.

SHE. It is very possible. I was everything and more than everything. Now I am nothing and less than nothing. But *I* never cheated in word or deed.

HE. Did he, then?

SHE. I was thinking of *her*.

HE. (*Wincing.*) I can do my own thinking there, thank you.

SHE. I fancied from your invitation you wanted an assistant.

HE. Good heavens! What is the use of two rats in a burning bucket biting at each other? Let's swear eternal peace.

SHE. Because you are getting hurt—eh? I am hurt day after day, hour after hour, minute after minute—but you only while you are talking to me—because you're a man and therefore a coward.

HE. And therefore a coward. It's a consoling knowledge. (*He edges horse toward cliff's edge.*)

SHE. Doesn't it make you want to swear at me?

HE. (*Reining up and looking at the beach below.*) No. Anything but that just now. Can you see down there, through the fog?

SHE. Yes! It's a remarkably pretty view. (*Sees* OULTHORP *and* MISS MASSING, *side by side.*) Aah!

HE. So much for Norman ruins.

SHE. Thank you. So one of them thinks. But what a finished liar Oulthorp must be. If he had only spoken the truth. (*To herself.*) Why, only to-day . . .

HE. I dare say he had a natural hesitation about approaching you on the subject.

SHE. He didn't understand. (*Critically peering down.*) He is kissing Julia Massing.

HE. Why not?

SHE. Why not, indeed? At this very moment, by the light of the knowledge you taught her, *she* may be—— (*His horse plunges away from the cliff.*)

HE (*Administering correction with the crop.*) That engagement will be given out to-night, in their faces, and announced at breakfast to-morrow. You'll have to congratulate him.

SHE. If you had only kept the smoking-room amused, I might have had three days more of Oulthorp's "eternal devotion." That's all.

HE. Remember, I only came into your councils this afternoon—late.

SHE. And we have done each other an immense amount of good since?

HE. We have sympathized, at least.

SHE. (*Throat-note in voice.*) There's nothing like sympathy—holy sympathy, is there?

HE. Nothing. Especially when one is in real trouble.

SHE. So sweet, when a man lays his hand on yours—quite by accident—and says he is prepared to sympathize with you to any extent.

HE. Ho! Ho! They do that, too.

SHE. You know. And the next minute you find that the hand has become an arm, and you are standing with your back to the mantelpiece spitting "Sir-r!" like an angry pussy-cat, and asking what in the world he means. For comprehension and disinterestedness, give me the sympathy of a man

HE. (*Tenderly.*) All the same, I am sorry for you—dear.

SHE. I didn't catch the last word. I'll believe the others.

HE. That's enough, then. I *am* sorry.

SHE. Because you see in me the best possible result of what you may have done to *her;* and you don't like it? Sorrow? What use is sorrow to me? If all the hosts of Heaven came down and said they were sorry for me, I could only give them tea, and tell them that they bored me. They should have set things right in the beginning.

HE. Blame the poor little cherubs, of course! I thought you were more honest than that!

SHE. I am only talking nonsense— you know what I mean. We have no right to complain. But we do.

HE. It takes a great deal to make people understand that if they break the Tables of Stone the pieces cut their feet.

SHE. And then they find out that they mustn't show the pain. It isn't pretty, and it doesn't amuse drawing-rooms. If it did, I should be happy to scream for hours like a steam-engine.

HE. Which reminds me—by way of stoking—I wonder what there'll be for dinner to-night.

SHE. The first and the last dish is Mr. Warbstow, who explains to us that we attach too much importance to the Deity. I yawn.

HE. Mrs. Deeley has a gift for collecting queer people at her troughs.

SHE. And none queerer than our two sweet selves. Fancy her face if she could listen now!

HE. She would be truly grieved. Don't you think we might try to change the conversation?

SHE. I forgot. I have my punishment here now, and yours comes later. Very well. What shall we talk about? The fog?

HE. (*After a pause.*) I don't see why you should be so certain of your own luck. I am punished too.

SHE. Only a little—for just as long as you are talking to me. Wait the hereafter.

HE. (*Wiping his forehead.*) But surely I am punished now. If I had killed anyone it couldn't be worse.

SHE. Killing's nothing. You may have done exactly the opposite. In which case, your torment will be heavier. Think of it for a minute. I was killed: and I am not grateful to the man who killed me. *She* may thank you yet for waking her to life. Does that hurt enough?

HE. Enough to pay for all.

SHE. Not unless you keep on thinking. One spasm of agony does not pay. You must think.

HE. I—I dare not.

SHE. Exactly. I dare because I must. You don't because you have other things to do. Therefore you will be dealt with later. As my murderer will be.

HE. How do you know?

SHE. I don't—and to tell the truth I don't care—as far as you're concerned.

HE. I know you don't, but you needn't have said so.

SHE. What mercy do you deserve? If you suffer as you say you do, so much the better for you. Oh, dear God! if I could believe that *he* felt for one little minute only a tithe of what I feel every hour I'd die contented.

HE. Have you never tried to go through the door, then?

SHE. Once. A year ago.

HE. How?

SHE. The silver cigarette-case and the graduated tubes, of course. Is there any other way? And—and when I had sat down—I was in that old black frock you spilt some coffee over the other night—I —I thought, when it would be all over, of a hand keeping me down in the chair, and saying— "Think. Go on thinking, dear. There's all eternity to think in." So it seemed to me I should gain nothing.

HE. An eternity of sitting still in a comfortable chair and thinking.

SHE. That was only my notion. We're told that God's mercies are infinite. There may be more horrible tortures.

HE. Which be they?

SHE. For you? Oh, watching her— perhaps. I don't think anything could make me do more than giggle. My punishment is now—now—now! Here, at the Deeleys' and anywhere else, and the only pauses allowed are like vinegar to give me fresh strength to feel. It's cruel.

HE. (*Laughing.*) Wages o' sin, mum, wages o' sin.

SHE. It's not fair. If the wages were death I'd have claimed them long ago— long ago.

HE. On the strict understanding that you went to sleep immediately afterward. Isn't that a little cowardly?

SHE. Oh, help me! Am I to endure forever?

HE. As long as the Law endures. You have given me the same comfort, and—it's very cold. (*A long pause, during which he watches her face.*)

SHE. (*Dropping right hand on the pommel-head.*) Let's protest. Let's rebel!

HE. Against what, and which, and how?

SHE. Everything that makes us what we are. Lost faith—lost hope—lost belief—and—and all the rest.

HE. Then isn't there anything to pick out of the wreck?

SHE. If you give everything nothing remains.

HE. Are you sure?

SHE. As sure as you are.

HE. Every moment tells me that—I am not sure.

SHE. (*Aside.*) How like a man. (*Aloud.*) That is the last five moments —only a little feeling born of pique and longing for the impossible.

HE. It is more. I am certain of it. All things have their first five minutes though they go on for centuries.

SHE. (*Aside.*) It grows amusing. He is almost interesting.

HE. . . . We both stand at the same starting-point; we have gone through the same fire. Doesn't it draw us together?

SHE. (*With a little laugh.*) How; in what? In that we have both come out on the other side with the life burnt out. The sympathy of cinders? Too late, it is all too late.

HE. I don't believe it's possible to suffer for—— (*Mickey shies violently and disappears into the fog.*) What's that— where have you gone to?

SHE. (*From the fog.*) A gypsy fire, I think. Burned out. What a stupid horse; he must have seen that a dozen times.

HE. The fog made it look large. Come back. (*Voice rising.*) Oh, come back to me, little woman!

SHE. I never came. How can I come back?

HE. Then come now.

SHE. Mickey's 'fraid.

HE. Cut his soul out!

SHE. And make him happier than myself. No. (*To horse.*) Come along,

Mickey. There's nothing to be scared at. Only ashes, little white ashes. (*Cantering through the fog; leaning off side and holding out her hand.*) I am tired, so tired—and I am here. We-ell?

HE. (*Taking her hand and dropping it.*) No use. It doesn't bite.

SHE. I thought it wouldn't, and now I know. All things are finished, there is no more fire, no more life, only the pretending, and the pain, that is all. This is part of the punishment. God help us both.

HE. He can't. But I hoped somehow that we might pick up some pieces sometime.

SHE. We could, if you could tell me one oath that I have not heard from *his* lips, or I could give you one promise that you had not heard from *hers*. And yet you were prepared to risk it?

HE. I am still—because you understand.

SHE. I think I understand too well. But you shall enlighten me. Suppose, for a minute, that you really love me.

HE. I have supposed that for some minutes already.

SHE. Then say it in a loud and cheerful voice. Can you?

HE. Yes. I love you.

SHE. (*Quietly.*) Do you know anything of the state of Mickey's hocks? (*Aside.*) I know if you put your hand behind the cantle he rears on end.

HE. Damn Mickey's hocks!

SHE. No, something quite different. (*Puts hand behind cantle. Mickey rears.*) Now recant quickly. Swear by the holiest thing you know—swear by *her* life—up, Mickey!—that you'd let me and this dear beast—doesn't he stand up beautifully and snort?—drown or die if you could get her back for half a minute.

Quick! recant, or I'll pull Mickey over backward.

HE. (*Wearily.*) Let him down. You needn't have thrown in the circus. It's true.

SHE. By Her life, is it true?

HE. By Her life.

SHE. (*As Mickey drops on his forelegs.*) Then you are——

HE. I am what I am. For pity's sake, let me be. Let's go back. (OUL-THORP *and* MISS MASSING *trot past in the fog.*)

SHE. Very good. Keep behind these two and contemplate the rewards of virtue. We'll go slowly in order that we may appreciate the things we have lost.

HE. Indeed we won't. We're going to ride as fast as we can.

SHE. You have no spur?

HE. He'll answer to the whip, and you can rowel enough for both. Take him up and we'll go.

(*They go.*)

SHE. We mustn't turn into the Deeleys' grounds at this rate. Pull up, and I promise not to say another word till we get in.

HE. On your honor?

SHE. You swear by strange gods—yes, if it will please you.

(*She keeps the promise till they are coming up the carriage-drive.*)

SHE. Oh, the girls have been singing all the afternoon. I wish I'd stayed in to assist. Listen!

(*They draw up by the shrubbery. Contralto* VOICE *from the music-room; piano and violin accompaniment.*)

"I am lost to faith, I am lost to hope,
I am lost to all that should make me fain—
I have lost my way in the light of day,
God send that I find it soon again!"

He. (*Taking her hand.*) Then there is one chance after all?

She. No; (*aside*) you threw it away by the fire. (*Aloud.*) Listen for the next verse. I know the song. It's a new setting.

Voice:

"The sun went down an hour ago,
I wonder if I face toward home.
If I lost my way in the light of day
How shall I find it now night is come—
    Now night is come!"

She. (*Dropping from her horse.*) Think! And—go on thinking.

The Legs of Sister Ursula

The one man of all men who could have told this tale and lived has long since gone to his place; and there is no apology for those that would follow in the footsteps of Laurence Sterne.

In a nameless city of a land that shall be nameless, a rich man lived alone. His wealth had bought him a luxurious flat on the fifth floor of a red-brick mansion, whose grilles were of hammered iron, and whose halls were of inlaid marble. When he needed attendance, coals, his letters, a meal, a messenger or a carriage, he pressed an electric button and his wants were satisfied almost as swiftly as even perpetual wealth could expect. An exceedingly swift lift bore him to and from his rooms, and in his rooms he had gathered about him all that his eyes desired—books in rich cases with felted hinges, ivories from all the world, rugs, lamps, cushions, couches, engravings and rings with engravings upon them, miniatures of pretty women, scientific toys and china from Persia. He had friends and acquaintances as many as he could befriend or know; and some said that more than one woman had given him her whole love. Therefore, he could have lacked nothing whatever.

One day, a hot sickness touched him with its finger, and he became no more than a sick man alone among his possessions, the sport of dreams and devils and shadows; sometimes a log and sometimes a lunatic crying in delirium. Before his friends forsook him altogether, as healthy brutes will forsake the wounded, they saw that he was efficiently doctored, and the expensive physician who called upon him at first three times a day, and later only once, caused him to be nursed by a nun. "Science is good," said the physician, "but for steady, continuous nursing, with no science in it, Religion is better—and I know Sister Ursula."

So this sick man was nursed by a nun, young and fairly pretty, but, above all, skilful. When he got better he would give the convent, and not Sister Ursula, a thank offering which would be spent among the poor whom Sister Ursula chiefly attended. At first the man knew nothing of the nun's existence—he was in the country beyond all creeds—but later a white coifed face came and went across his visions, and at last, spent and broken, he woke to see a very quiet young woman in black moving about his room. He was too weak to speak: too weak almost to cling to life any more. In despair he thought that it was not worth clinging to; but the woman was at least a woman and alive. The touch of her fingers in his as she gave him the medicine was warm. She testified to the existence of a world full of women also alive—the world he was beginning to disbelieve in. He watched her sitting in the sunshine by the window, and counted the light creeping down from bead to bead of the rosary at her waist. They then moved his bed to the window that he might look down upon the stately avenue that ran by the flat-house, and watch the people going to and fro about their business. But the change, instead of cheering, cast him into a deeper melancholy. It was nearly a hundred feet, sheer drop, to those healthy people walking so fast, and the mere distance depressed him unutterably.

One morning, he turned his face away from the sunlight and took no interest in anything, while the shadow swung back upon the dial so swiftly that it almost alarmed the doctor. He said to himself: "Bored, eh? Yes. You're just the kind of over-educated, over-refined man that would drop his hold on life through sheer boredom. You've been a most interesting case so far, and I won't lose you." He told Sister Ursula that he would send an entirely new prescription by his boy and that Sister Ursula must give it to the invalid every twenty minutes without fail. Also, if the man responded to the medicine, it might be well to talk to him a little. "He needs cheering up. There is nothing the matter with him now, but he won't pick up."

There can be few points of sympathy between a man born, bred, trained, and sold for and to the world and a good nun made for the service of other things. Sister Ursula's voice was very sweet, but the matter of her speech did not interest. The invalid lay still, looking out of the window upon the street all dressed in its Sunday afternoon emptiness. Then he shut his eyes. The doctor's boy rang at the door. Sister Ursula stepped out into the hall, not to disturb the sleeper, and took the medicine from the boy's hand. Then the lift shot down again, and even as she turned the wind of its descent puffed up and blew to the spring-lock door of the invalid's rooms with a click only a little more loud than the leap of her terrified heart.

Sister Ursula tried the door softly, but rich men with many hundred pounds' worth of *bric-à-brac* buy themselves very well made doors that fasten with singularly cunning locks. Then the lift returned with the boy in charge, and, so soon as his Sunday and rather distracted attention was drawn to the state of affairs, he suggested that Sister Ursula should go down to the basement and speak to the caretaker, who doubtless had a duplicate key. To the basement, therefore, Sister Ursula went with the medicine bottle clasped to her breast, and there, among mops and brooms and sinks and heating-pipes, and the termini of all the electric communications of that many storied warren, she found, not the caretaker, but his wife, reading a paper, with her feet on a box of soap. The caretaker's wife was Irish, and a Catholic, reverencing the Church in all its manifestations. She was not only sympathetic, but polite. Her husband had gone out, and, being a prudent guardian of the interests confided to him, had locked up all the duplicate keys.

"An' the saints only know whin Mike'll

be back av a Sunday," she concluded cheerfully, after a history of Mike's peculiarities. "He'll be afther havin' his supper wid friends."

"The medicine!" said Sister Ursula, looking at the inscription on the bottle. "It must begin at twenty minutes past five. There are only ten minutes now. There must—oh! there *must* be a way!"

"Give him a double dose next time. The docther won't know the differ." The convent of Sister Ursula is not modeled on Irish ideals, and the present duty before its nun was to return to the locked room with the medicine. Meantime the minutes flew bridleless, and Sister Ursula's eyes were full of tears.

"I must get to the room," she insisted. "Oh, surely, there is a way, any way!"

"There's wan way," said the caretaker's wife, stung to profitable thought by the other's distress. "And that's the way the tenants would go in case av fire. To be sure now I might send the lift boy."

"It would frighten him to death. He must not see strangers. What is the way?"

"If we wint into the cellar an' out into the area, we'll find the ground-ends av the fire-eshcapes that take to all the rooms. Go aisy, dear."

Sister Ursula had gone down the basement steps through the cellar into the area, and with clenched teeth was looking up the monstrous sheer of red-brick wall cut into long strips by the lessening perspective of perpendicular iron ladders. Under each window each ladder opened out into a little, a very little, balcony. The rest was straighter than a ship's mast.

The caretaker's wife followed, panting; came out into the sunshine, and, shading her eyes, took stock of the ground.

"He'll be Number 42 on the Fifth. Thin this ladder goes up to it. They've the eshcapes front an' back. Glory be to God, the avenue's empty!"

Two children were playing in the gutter. But for these the avenue was deserted, and the hush of a Sabbath afternoon hung over it all. Sister Ursula put the medicine bottle carefully into the pocket of her gown. Her face was as white as her coif.

" 'Tis not for me," said the caretaker's wife, shaking her head sadly. "I'm so's to be round, or I'd go wid ye. Those ladders do be runnin' powerful straight up an' down. 'Tis scandalous to think— but in a fire, an' runnin' in their nighties, they'd not stop to think. Go away, ye two little imps, there! The bottle's in your pocket? You'll not lose good hold av the irons. What is ut?—Oh!"

Sister Ursula retreated into the cellar, dropped on her knees, and was prayng— praying as Lady Godiva prayed before she mounted her palfrey. The caretaker's wife had barely time to cross herself and follow her example when she was on her feet again, and her feet were on the lowest rungs of the ladder.

"Hould tight," said the caretaker's wife. "Oh, darlint, wait till Mike comes! Come down, now!—the good angels be wid yo. There should have been a way at the back. Walk tinderly and hould tight. Heaven above sind there'll be no wind! Oh, why wasn't his ugly rooms at the back, where 'tis only yards and bedroom windows!"

The voice grew fainter and stopped. Sister Ursula was at the level of the first-floor windows when the two children caught sight of her, raising together a shrill shout. The devil that delights in torturing good nuns inspired them next to separate and run the one up and the other down the avenue, yelling, "O-oh! There's a nun on the fire-escape! A nun on the fire-escape!" and, since one word at least was familiar, a score of heads came to windows in the avenue, and were much interested.

In spite of her prayers, Sister Ursula was not happy. The medicine-bottle banged and bumped in her pocket as she gripped the iron bars hand over hand and toiled aloft. "It is for the sake of a life," she panted to herself. "It is a good work. He might die if I did not come. Ah! it is terrible." A flake of rust from the long disused irons had fallen on her nose. The rungs were chafing her hands, and the minutes were flying. The round, red face of the caretaker's wife grew smaller and smaller below her, and there was a rumbling of wheels in the avenue. An idle coachman, drawn by the shouts of the children, had turned the corner to see what was to be seen. And Sister Ursula climbed in agony of spirit, the heelless black cloth shoes that nuns wear slipping on the rungs of the ladder, and all earth reeling a hundred thousand feet below.

She passed one set of apartments, and they were empty of people, but the fire, the books on the table, and the child's toy cast on the hearth-rug showed it was deserted only for a minute. Sister Ursula drew breath on the balcony, and then hurried upward. There was iron rust red on both her hands, the front of her gown was speckled with it, and a reflection in the stately double window showed a stainless stiff fold of her head-gear battered down over her eye. Her shoe, yes, the mended one, had burst at the side near the toe in a generous bulge of white stockings. She climbed on wear-

ily, for the bottle was swinging again, and in her ears there came unbidden the nursery refrain that she used to sing to the little sick children in the hospital at Quebec:

"This is the cow with the crumpled horn."

Between earth and heaven, it is said, the soul on its upward journey must pass the buffeting of many evil spirits. There flashed into Sister Ursula's mind the remembrance of a picture of a man gazing from the leads down the side of a house—a wonderful piece of foreshortening that made one dizzy to see. Where had she seen that picture? Memory, that works indifferently on earth or in vacuo, told her of a book read by stealth in her novitiate, such a book as perils body and soul, and Sister Ursula blushed redder than the brickwork a foot before her nose. Everything that she had read in or thought about that book raced through her mind as all his past life does not race through the soul of a drowning man. It was horrible, most horrible. Then rose a fierce wave of rage and indignation that she, a sister of irreproachable life and demeanor (the book had been an indiscretion, long since bitterly repented of), should be singled out for these humiliating exercises. There were other nuns of her acquaintance, proud, haughty, and overbearing (her foot slipped here as a reminder against the sin of hasty judgments, and she felt that it was a small and niggling Justice that counted offences at such a crisis), and—and thinking too much of their holiness, to whom this mortification, with all the rust flakes in bosom and kerchief, would have been salutary and wholesome. But that she, Sister Ursula, who only desired a quiet life, should climb fire-escapes in the face of the shameless sun and a watching population! It was too terrible. None the less she did not come down.

Praying to be delivered from evil thoughts, praying that the swinging bottle would not smash itself against the iron ladders, she toiled on. The second and third flats were empty, and she heard a murmur in the street; a hum of encouraging tumult, cheerful outcries bidding her go up higher, and crisp inquiries as to whether this were the end of the performance. Her Saint—she that had not prevailed against the Huns—would not help Sister Ursula, and it came over her, as cold water slides down the spine, that at her journey's end she would have to—go—through—the window. There is no vestibule, portico, or robing-room at the upper end of a fire-escape. It is designed for such as move in a hurry, being for the most part not over-dressed, and yet seeking publicity—that publicity that came to Sister Ursula unsought. She must go through that window in order to give her invalid his medicine. Her head must go first, and her foot, with the bursten shoe, must go last. It was the very breaking point in the strain, and here her Saint, mistaking the needs of the case, sent her a companion. Her head was level with the window of the fourth story, and she was rejoicing to find that that also was empty when the door opened, and there entered a man something elderly, of prominent figure, and dressed according to the most rigid canons laid down for afternoon visits. He was millions of leagues removed from Sister Ursula's world—this person with the tall silk hat, the long frock-coat, the light gray trousers, and tiny yellow buttonhole rose, and the marvelous puffed cravat anchored about with black pearl-headed pins. But an imperative need for justification was upon her. Her own mission, the absolute rightness of her own mission, were so clear to herself that she never doubted anyone might misunderstand when she pointed upward to the skies, and the flat above.

The man, who was in the act of laying his tall hat absently upon the table, looked up as the shadow took the light, saw the gesture, and stared. Then his jaw dropped, and his face became ashy gray. Sister Ursula had never seen Terror in the flesh, well-dressed and fresh from a round of calls. She gathered herself up to climb on, but the man within uttered a cry that even the double windows could not altogether stifle, and ran round the room in circles as a dog runs seeking a lost glove.

"He is mad," thought Sister Ursula. "Oh, heavens, and *that* is what has driven him mad."

He was stooping fondly over something that seemed like the coffin of a little child. Then he rushed directly at the window open-mouthed. Sister Ursula went upward and onward, none the less swiftly because she had heard a muffled oath, the crash of broken glass, and the tinkling of the broken splinters on the pavestones below. For the second time only in her career, she looked down—down between the ladder and the wall. A silk hat was bobbing wildly, as a fishing-float on a troubled stream, not a dozen rungs beneath, and a voice—the voice of fear—cried hoarsely: "Where is it? Where is it?" Then went up to the roofs the roaring and the laughter of a great crowd; yells, cat-calls, ki-yis, and hootings many times multiplied. Her Saint had heard her at last, and caused Sister Ursula to disregard the pains of going through the window. Her one desire now was to reach that haven, to jump, dive, leap-frog through it if necessary, and shut out the unfortunate maniac. It was a short race, but swift, and Saint Ursula took care of the bottle. A long course of afternoon calls, with refreshments at clubs, in the intervals, is not such good training as the care of the sick in all weathers for sprinting over a course laid at ninety degrees. Nor again can the best of athletes go swiftly up a ladder if he carries a priceless violin in one hand and its equally priceless bow in his teeth, and handicaps himself with varnished leather buttoned boots.

They climbed, the one below the other. The window at the foot of the invalid's bed was open. At the next window was the white face of the invalid. Sister Ursula reached the sash, threw it up, went through—let no man ask how— shut it gently but with amazing quickness, and sank panting at the foot of the bed, one hand on the bottle.

"There was no other way," she panted. "The door was locked. I could not help. Oh! He is here!"

The face of Terror in the top hat rose to the window-level inch by inch. The violin-bow was between his teeth, and his hat hung over one eye in the fashion of early dawn.

"It's Cott van Cott," said the invalid, slowly and critically. "He looks quite an old man. Cott and his Strad. How very bad for the Strad!"

"Open the window. Where is it? Is there a way? Open the window!" roared Cott, without removing the violin-bow.

Sister Ursula held up one hand warningly as she stooped over the invalid.

For the second time did Cott misinterpret the gesture and heaved himself upward, the violin and bow clicking and rattling at every stride. He was fleeing to the leads to save his life and his violin from death by fire—fire in the basement —and the crowd in the street roared below him with the roar of a full-fed conflagration.

The invalid fell back on the pillows and wiped his eyes. The hands of the clock were on the hour appointed for the medicine, lacking only the thirty seconds necessary for pouring it into a wineglass. He took it from Sister Ursula's hand, still shaking with helpless laughter.

"God bless you, Sister Ursula," he said. "You've saved my life."

"The medicine was to be given," she answered simply. "I—I could not help coming that way."

"If you only knew, ' said the invalid. "If you only knew! I saw it from out of the windows. Good heavens! the dear old world is just the same as ever. I must get back to it. I must positively get well and get back. And, Sister Ursula, do you mind telling me when you're quite composed everything that happened between the time the door shut and—and you came in that way?"

After a little Sister Ursula told, and the invalid laughed himself faint once more. When Sister Ursula resettled the pillows, her hand fell on the butt of a revolver that had come from the desk by the head of the bed. She did not understand what it was, but the sight pained her.

"Wait a minute," said the invalid, and he took one cartridge from its inside. "I—I wanted to use it for something before you went out, but I saw you come up, and I don't want it any more. I must certainly get back to the world again. Dear old world! Nice old world! And Mrs. Cassidy prayed with you in the cellar, did she? And Van Cott thought it was a fire? Do you know, Sister Ursula, that all those things would have been impossible on any other planet? I'm going to get well, Sister Ursula."

In the long night, Sister Ursula, blushing all over under the eyes of the night-light, heard him laughing softly in his sleep.

For One Night Only

AND Mrs. Skittleworth told the tale at a place called the Arts and Crafts, which, when you think of it, was unnecessary; Mrs. Skittleworth herself being all the arts and most of the crafts known to civilization.

She was then practising a few of them on the center divan opposite the entrance, where the fountain plays and the unhappy little pot-palms live. In the first place it was her sworn duty to keep an evasive eye upon a Miss Dormil, who was to be most strictly deprived of the comfort and society of a gentleman called Evans —Richard Evans—who had specially come to the Arts and Crafts to meet the young lady, who was under the chaperonage of Mrs. Skittleworth, according to the manners and customs of the British, who are barbarians. Now since Mrs. Skittleworth had conveyed Miss Dormil wholly and solely to meet Mr. Evans, and since she had to pretend that she saw neither him nor the girl, nor both together, or something equally logical, and since she uneasily suspected that Mrs. Dormil might at any moment arrive and drive the daughter home, and particularly since neither man nor maid seemed to have any idea of the lapse of time, you will understand that Mrs. Skittleworth's attention was distracted from the door whereat she expected Skittleworth every minute to appear in the company of a man whom she most urgently desired to avoid.

I believe that I had the honor to supply the Missing Link, for on my wandering appearance her face brightened as a general's when reinforcements pour past to battle.

"There is a man," she said, "an Unutterable Man. He will arrive with Tom in ten minutes. I shall immediately introduce you to him with smirks and grins. You will more immediately talk. Talk about anything you understand least, but overwhelm him with your conversation as you value my friendship. Then I shall escape with Tom, catch Miss Dormil, drive the Evans boy into the stained-glass alcove—Good gracious! I hope he hasn't taken the girl there already!—and return to meet, under Providence, the very respectable Mrs. Dormil, who will ask the Unutterable Man to dinner. He is always hungry and . . . he has dined there before. Then you must transfer yourself to the Evans boy, and while we are all eating our artful afternoon tea and the craftful crumpet in the lunch-place you must escape with him secretly. There ought to be two ways out of every place of appointment." She poised for breath.

She was used to delivering orders with much clearness, and I gathered from the pucker between her eyebrows that she was in anxiety. Her theory that men do not marry their mothers-in-law, though many mothers-in-law think otherwise, was perpetually leading her into second-hand Comédie-Française embarrassments. All earth and Skittleworth—who at heart is just as bad—could not restrain her from helping forward the most undesirable match ever lighted among her circle of acquaintance. On the Other Side of the World, where I first had the honor of meeting her, this weakness did not alarm; in England—which, it must always be remembered, is the habitation of heathen the worse for being imperfectly converted—she was misunderstood. But all young maidens loved her.

And I said: "I hear and obey—on one condition."

"On no conditions. You want me to tell you something. I refuse beforehand."

"Very well, I shall begin to walk. I shall walk down Regent Street for hours and hours, and into the Mile End Road and when Mrs. Dormil comes to thank you for giving her dear Clara, who is so artistic, such a delightful afternoon, the Evans boy will hang in the background pulling pieces out of his gloves and Mrs. Dormil will not love you any more. Seriously, you went to the Theater of the Patent Deviltries——"

"No! Inner Sepulcher. Inner Sepulcher!" said Mrs. Skittleworth, with a shudder. "So glad we didn't invite you."

"So am I," I said icily. "You made a box party, and by all accounts you all behaved abominably. You dropped opera-glasses on the heads of the bald, you conducted yourselves in such a manner that the entire house stopped to look at you, and you, overcome by shame, left at the end of the first act—weeping."

"This," said Mrs. Skittleworth pensively, "is the hand of Mrs. Bletchley. She told you that at tea. What else did you learn?"

"The trouble is that I could learn no more. Not one of your guests would speak. Geissler, who can babble about founders' shares by the hour, was dumb. Skittleworth told me that I had better refer to you. I haven't seen Miss Dormil to speak to, and the Evans boy declares that it was a most enjoyable evening, but that you all left because the play was dull. The *Professor's Zoetrope* is not dull. It's the best play in London. What was the catastrophe? Everybody is wanting to talk about it, and no one knows anything. Six people have kept a secret for ten days—surely that's long enough. Tell, and I'll carry the Evans boy off through the roof if I can't smuggle him out any other way."

"Did anyone tell you it was Tom's fault?" began Mrs. Skittleworth cautiously, one eye on the door and another on the ironwork exhibits.

"They said Singleton gave the party—and so——"

"He did *not*. It was that man Geissler—the Chicago Jew. Ugh! Tom and he cluck like new laid hens over their offensive founders' shares, whatever those may be. Things that grow up in a night out of nothing and are sold by telegraph. I hate Geissler. I could never send him anything at dinner without hoping that the fat, or the drumstick, or the stuffing would choke him, and then I would *never* send for the doctor. Geissler found a box in the Inner Sepulchre. I know the shameful story now, but it almost reconciled me to the man for the moment. The very best box in the Inner Sepulcher —a five-guinea box that could have seated hordes—positive hordes. Do you know that he got it for twenty-five shillings? That was his ineffable meanness."

"But a Chicago Jew is not always mean," I adventured.

"Then he was a Levantine dragoman. I thank you for that. His father hauled Cook's tourists up and down the Pyramids for pence. And the worst of it is that he doesn't look like a Jew, and he ought to. We provided the dinner—he the box."

"Who came?"

"Mrs. Eva van Agnew and Geissler, both in one cab—two; Tom and I—four; and Miss Dormil and the Evans boy— six. That was all. I never allow a fortuitous concourse of atoms at my table; and, besides, we have no extra leaf in it. I had immense trouble in cajoling Mrs. Dormil to let her daughter go alone. She wished to assist. Heaven knows, I despise her as honorably as I despise most women; but when she strips for festivities, I always think that she should be 'hidden from the wise and prudent and'—how does it go? She makes *me* feel very undressed with draughts blowing all over me. And, you know, you can't say: 'Won't you put a counterpane over your shoulders, you dear fat thing?' So they dined, and I was glad, because I knew neither of the young people would remember

what they ate—they were in that stage; and Geissler was talking founders' shares to Tom, and Eva van Agnew was trying to talk to me and watch Geissler at the same time. Geissler wouldn't throw a word to her. There must have been a quarrel in the cab."

"But why were you so concerned about Miss Dormil and the Evans boy?"

"Because he had inflicted himself upon me four twilights out of the seven. He would arrive at half-past four and stay till half-past six, telling me that Miss Dormil was an angel and he was a ruffian, and did I think Mrs. Dormil could be brought to overlook his unworthiness? I liked it—I own I liked it immensely, even when he repeated himself for the twentieth time, and used to smash my drawing-room ornaments trying to make clear the intensity of his feelings. Oh, it's a relief to catch a young man devoid of nerves, and the less honorable emotions, who does not talk cheap French novels, and knows exactly what he wants, and is humble about it. He confessed all his little sins in the past to me, and I know exactly how his future is going to be arranged, and therefore I assist him in the present. And so we dined, and then we bundled off—Tom and I and the children in the brougham, and Eva and the Israelite, whom I will *never* forgive, in a hansom; and we saw the play and came away early. Isn't that enough for you?"

"You went in the brougham and the hansom—yes. And what happened after that?" I continued, unregarding.

"You won't believe what I tell you."

"*You* are speaking."

"But even I—consider dear Mother Dormil, and *do* watch the entrance, please—may tell a fib."

"Never without a motive."

"Yes—that was the horror of it. It was so—without motive. So purposeless —so cruel; and yet there was a brassy vulgarity about it all that I can't explain. Try to understand that I am telling you what happened as accurately as I can. We were late for the farce, of course, and the overture was beginning. Of all horrors, it was the *Bronze Horse* overture."

"That's only tinny—not terrifying, surely."

"Wait! I had arranged things beautifully. Tom and I and Eva and Geissler were to sit in front, and the children at the back, because they were tall and wanted to talk. You know when you are absolutely certain of seeing a thing, you carry the outline of it in your mind's eye so that it looks real, don't you? When we trooped in, I was quite certain that I saw the stage, and so on, because a stage is naturally what you expect to see from the best box in the theatre. We banged the chairs about—they were horribly dusty—and then I heard the Evans boy saying 'Good God!' under his breath. Tom put his hand on my wrist, and drove my pet bracelet into the bone. 'Don't jump or scream,' he said. 'Look!'"

"A headless woman in a vacant chair, or a red dog, or something nice and magaziny. Mrs. Skittleworth, *please* don't," I whimpered, because Mrs. Skittleworth is much above that sort of entertainment.

"I knew you would," she answered. "And now I'm sorry that I didn't invite you. We looked out of the box at the stage, and at the house, and there was nothing whatever to be seen! Do you understand that?—Nothing whatever to be seen."

"And what was it like?" I said with intense interest.

"It was awful. It was unspeakable. It was Chaos—raving, mad, howling Chaos! Have you ever been under chloroform, and do you know that die-away-and-away darkness when a train goes into a tunnel, through your head, and all the doors are being slammed, just before you lose consciousness? It was most like that feeling. But it wasn't. The darkness—the absolute blankness was in your head and your eyes, and yet you were staring into it—staring with your soul as well as your eyes. And then, through it all, we heard the rustle of the house, and the music of the *Bronze Horse*. That tune is the most diabolical one in the world."

"Then you could hear?"

"We could hear everything. That was a further horror. We could hear the people getting into their places below, and the crickle of the fans. You know what a hot house the Inner Sepulcher is. We could hear the rumble of traffic outside sometimes, but we could not see any single thing except ourselves in heaven above, or the earth beneath, or the waters under the earth."

"And what happened?"

"I don't quite remember. I think we must have all waited—I know I did— for the darkness to clear away. I felt as though I had been hit on the head, but would be all right presently if people took no notice and stood off from me, and, above all things, gave me air—plenty of air. Tom's hand on mine prevented me from making an absolute exhibition of myself. You know how Ashdown frizzes my hair for functions—I was frizzed all over my head very prettily, and I friz through my frizzes; and while I was staring and feeling, oh! so deathly sick, I was distinctly conscious that my hair was tightening—Ashdown had frizzed it too well for it to stand on end—tightening and dragging my eyebrows up and up, so that I must have looked like an Aunt Sally at a fair."

Mrs. Skittleworth laughed hysterically, and fluttered her very small hands.

A lean, unshorn, toadstool-colored young gentleman in a blue cloak which would have been useless on horseback or in a high wind, a dead-leaf silk throat-wrap, and a sort of football jersey that was doing duty as a shirt, threw himself down on the divan and curled his legs into esoteric attitudes. Mrs. Skittleworth shook the quaver out of her voice, jumped three notes on the piano, and began as one in the middle of things generally.

"And so, you know, they invented a sort of combination garment for the lower classes—to save washing. It's very effective if it isn't worn too long, especially at the wristbands and round the neck, but then they provide a clout called a belcher to wear there, and you can get them for one and sevenpence halfpenny in Westbourne Grove. And they come here and do a lot of good, and they are called Socialists. Of course the uniform confuses the sexes. If it's a he, for instance, it's wearing its petticoats where it shouldn't, you know, and if it's a she it wouldn't wear a silk hat. But perhaps it's an exhibit, and if we ask it . . ."

The young gentleman rose and regarded us with unholy eyes from the lunch balcony.

"A woman who cannot be vulgar on occasions does not know the meaning of True Deportment," said Mrs. Skittleworth. "You should hear Mrs. Dormil bullying her governess. And where were we? Oh, yes, in that darkness of terror. I think we must have been there for years and years before we heard the rustle of the curtain and the servants' opening

dialogue in the *Zoetrope*. I wanted to scream at the top of my voice, but it occurred to me that I had been standing up for untold ages in the face of the house. So I sat down and Tom began patting my hand in an absent-minded way and saying: 'Poor little woman!' I remembered then that when I was fearfully ill and delirious on the Other Side of the World—no, I won't say how many years ago—Tom used to sit by my bed for days and weeks doing exactly the same thing; and whenever I would half come to life I was conscious of one hand being patted and 'poored.' I knew endearment of that sort was not in place on the box-edge; but I couldn't take my hand away for all the world. I wanted Tom as I have never wanted him in my life—not even when they all thought I was dying. And the dear boy patted my hand—bless him! He was as white as a sheet. Then I began to think of mother, exactly as a Frenchwoman would. I wondered where she was, and if this hideous darkness was her portion in the other world, and I wanted to step into it and find out and drag her in across the edge of the box. I reflected that I should fall on somebody's head in the attempt, and I laughed aloud horribly in the one pathetic scene in the *Zoetrope*, where the Professor tells the little lodging-house servant the story of his life and his broken love-tale, and she cries and mops her face with the duster. And then I jumped, for I knew all the house was looking at me, and that upset the opera-glass, and I heard it fall and hit somebody below, and there was a scuffle, and every eye in everybody's head, I knew, was fixed on our unhappy, unhappy box. That was the incident of laughing and throwing glasses about that Mrs. Bletchley makes so much of.

The thing dropped into the dark as a stone into water."

"But why in the world didn't you all get up and run out, or complain or—or do something?"

"After the affair of the opera-glass? Mrs. Skittleworth's party romping in a box, dropping glasses, laughing, and then running out like children in a country church when they've tipped hymn-books from the gallery? *Never!* I may be introduced to the other world against my will, but I know my duty to this, as long as I am in it. I was praying for the first act to end, for I was afraid I could not stand the tension!"

"And the others?"

"You may well ask. I looked round when my own feelings were a little under control. What a blessed thing is a British education! All the Jew that ever cheated in Israel came out in Geissler's face. He was on the right of the box, half standing up in his chair and gripping the edge with both hands till the plush plumped up in red gores between his fingers. He was not looking at the stage, but into the darkness, and I was more than conscious that he must be staring fiendishly at the opposite box. Staring like a maniac. I felt that those stares were returned. Oh, I felt pins and needles all over, so sure I was that we were being watched while we were smitten with blindness! Complain? How could we complain? Can you go to an attendant at a theater and say, 'We can't see out of this box'—a five-guinea box on the grand tier—the best in the house? If there is one place whence you ought to see all that is to be seen"— Mrs. Skittleworth nearly broke down at this point—"it's a box. I'll never take a box again. Give me stalls, or the gallery, where you are in touch with your neighbor and all see ghosts together."

"Was there a ghost, then?"

"No, no, no—only their country: the room they had just left. Geissler may have seen some. He looked hideous—as though he were being burned alive. His shoulders were cramped up to the back of his head; but I don't think he was afraid. He seemed to be in pain. Thinking of founders' shares possibly. Eva made the most painful exhibition of us all. Promise you won't tell, of course. Her place was empty, and she was down on the floor of the box—mercifully out of sight—her face hidden in a coat thrown over a chair. She had pressed herself into one corner like a frightened rabbit, and was praying. A box isn't a place to pray in. At least, not when the house is full. You know Eva's High Church—extremely so; and even in her agony she was intoning. I stooped down and tried to take one of her hands, and said: 'Hush, dear, hush! think of your dress!' but she only went on bleating, 'Almighty and most merciful Father, we have erred and strayed from they ways l-l-like lost sheep,' over and over again. She was kneeling on that little cheap silk of hers, and nothing in the wide world will ever get the dust out of it again; and she had bundled my heavy white 'cloud' over her head to shut out the dark, and she looked just like a lost sheep. I might as well have spoken to one. I am very sorry for Eva."

"And the others?"

"They had arrived at a most complete understanding, and that nearly made me scream. I felt that I was responsible for everything—Chaos included. Clara was in the Evans boy's arms, totally and completely, at the back of the box to the left; and to this day I cannot tell why ll the house didn't see them. They must have fancied it was the Day of Judgment. They were murmuring things that you very seldom hear from dress coats and evening frocks, and I honestly believe they never saw the darkness after they had explained themselves."

"Poor Mrs. Dormil!"

"It wasn't my fault. I only wished them to improve their acquaintance with each other. Am I responsible if the Powers of darkness are leagued against me to precipitate matters? Yes, they were in each other's arms expecting immediate translation. What I saw and said passed in a flash, though I have been so long telling it. The rest was interminable waiting for the first act to end, Eva praying on the floor, and the house rocking with laughter at the jokes, Geissler glaring into Tophet, Tom patting my hand, the children in another world— bless them!—and I playing propriety for them all. Taking an interest in the play in order to prove that I saw it all, and was as much amused as anybody, clapping when the unseen hosts clapped, and smirking when I felt it was time to smirk. I was almost obsequiously attentive to the *Zoetrope*, and I flatter myself that even the Bletchley woman will admit that I behaved perfectly."

"Mrs. Skittleworth," I said, in a voice broken with emotion, "I have long admired and respected you beyond any human being alive. I now worship you with fear and trembling. Men have won the Victoria Cross for less than that."

Mrs. Skittleworth was graciously pleased to bow her head, always with one eye on the door. She continued:

"Then the curtain went down, and we fled. I have a dim recollection of flying into the cloak-room screaming like a pea-cock:'My things! My things! My things!' Eva was close behind me. We fell together into the tire-woman's arms. Luckily she was big, and ready with her blandishments at once. She said: 'There! there! there! Never mind. 'Ere's your cloak, mum'; and I answered, thickly: 'Yes, yes, yes. Of course—of course. Too hot, too cold; very fine weather indeed.' She gave us both the best thing available and on the spot. It proved the existence of a conspiracy. It was brandy-and-soda—strong! You should have seen Eva and me gulping it down like washerwomen, while that dear tall Clara drifted about like a saint in a holy dream, conscious that there might have been something wrong somewhere, but more conscious that things were right.

"We skipped down the passages. We dared not run, but we skipped; and Geissler and Eva went off in separate cabs. I know he volunteered to see her home, for I caught one gesture of hers that would have made the fortune of a tragedy actress. Villain as I am convinced he is, I admire that man for his nerve. Now comes the proof of the conspiracy. Our brougham was on hand when we came out. Generally Jobbins retires to a public-house, and Tom has to prance through the puddles and drag him out personally. But he was waiting, which was a greater miracle than anything else. I spoke to him about it the next day, complimenting him on his virtue.

"'Well, mum,' he said, 'I wouldn't ha' kep' the pore 'orses 'cept that every man of 'em in the theatre, an' the policemen, an' all the lot sez to me that you'd be out at the end of the fust act. And so you was, mum, an' it was a good job I waited 'stead o' savin' the pore 'orses.'

"That is the only approach to an explanation that I have been able to arrive at—that, and the fact that Geissler got the box for twenty-five shillings. The entire theater staff of the Inner Sepulcher must know all about it, and yet . . . Can you believe? Do you believe? Try to speak the truth. Geissler has never given any sign of his existence to me since that night. Eva has gone out of town, and Clara and the Evans boy . . . you see. Somehow I feel as though I were responsible for everything. You do believe, don't you?"

"Implicitly," I replied. "If *you* cannot see a thing which is in front of you, who am I to dissent? Of course I believe. You intend to take no further steps?"

"None whatever. I'll never set foot in that theater again. That's all; and Tom doesn't like me to talk about it. Clara won't speak either, I'm certain. She imagines it was sent from heaven to assist the Evans boy to propose ι her."

"Poor Mrs. Dormil!"

"Yes, and here, for my many sins, she comes, without Tom or the other man. Fly! Catch Miss Dormil and walk ostentatiously with her while I lure the old lady to the food-troughs. The Evans boy can escape unseen if he has any sense."

But at that crisis he had not, and they both glowered at me when I found them in the stained-glass alcove; and I had to explain matters apart to the Evans boy, and he left with the air of a baffled conspirator; and though I was dying to ask Miss Dormil twenty thousand questions, she being wrapped up in her own vain imaginings, I could never get any further than:

"What do you think of the Arts and Crafts?"

THE END